5·8·98

Foundations for Programming Languages

Foundations of Computing
Michael Garey and Albert Meyer, editors

Complexity Issues in VLSI: Optimal Layouts for the Shuffle-Exchange Graph and Other Networks, Frank Thomson Leighton, 1983

Equational Logic as a Programming Language, Michael J. O'Donnell, 1985

General Theory of Deductive Systems and Its Applications, S. Yu Maslov, 1987

Resource Allocation Problems: Algorithmic Approaches, Toshihide Ibaraki and Naoki Katoh, 1988

Algebraic Theory of Processes, Matthew Hennessy, 1988

PX: A Computational Logic, Susumu Hayashi and Hiroshi Nakano, 1989

The Stable Marriage Problem: Structure and Algorithms, Dan Gusfield and Robert Irving, 1989

Realistic Compiler Generation, Peter Lee, 1989

Single-Layer Wire Routing and Compaction, F. Miller Maley, 1990

Basic Category Theory for Computer Scientists, Benjamin C. Pierce, 1991

Categories, Types, and Structures: An Introduction to Category Theory for the Working Computer Scientist, Andrea Asperti and Giuseppe Longo, 1991

Semantics of Programming Languages: Structures and Techniques, Carl A. Gunter, 1992

The Formal Semantics of Programming Languages: An Introduction, Glynn Winskel, 1993

Hilbert's Tenth Problem, Yuri V. Matiyasevich, 1993

Exploring Interior-Point Linear Programming: Algorithms and Software, Ami Arbel, 1993

Theoretical Aspects of Object-Oriented Programming: Types, Semantics, and Language Design, edited by Carl A. Gunter and John C. Mitchell, 1994

From Logic to Logic Programming, Kees Doets, 1994

The Structure of Typed Programming Languages, David A. Schmidt, 1994

Logic and Information Flow, edited by Jan van Eijck and Albert Visser, 1994

Circuit Complexity and Neural Networks, Ian Parberry, 1994

Control Flow Semantics, Jaco de Bakker and Erik de Vink, 1996

Algebraic Semantics of Imperative Programs, Joseph A. Goguen and Grant Malcolm, 1996

Algorithmic Number Theory, Volume I: Efficient Algorithms, Eric Bach and Jeffrey Shallit, 1996

Foundations for Programming Languages, John C. Mitchell, 1996

Foundations for Programming Languages

John C. Mitchell

The MIT Press
Cambridge, Massachusetts
London, England

Second printing, 1998

This book was set in Times Roman by Windfall Software using ZzTEX and was printed and bound in the United States of America.

Library of Congress Cataloging-in-Publication Data

Mitchell, John C.
Foundations for programming languages / John C. Mitchell.
p. cm. — (Foundations of computing)
Includes bibliographical references and index.
ISBN 0-262-13321-0 (hc : alk. paper)
1. Programming languages (Electronic computers). I. Title.
II. Series.
QA76.7.M57 1996
005.13′1—dc20 95-45243
CIP

Contents

	Series Foreword	xiii
	Preface	xv
1	**Introduction**	1
1.1	Model Programming Languages	1
1.2	Lambda Notation	3
1.3	Equations, Reduction, and Semantics	5
	1.3.1 Axiomatic Semantics	6
	1.3.2 Operational Semantics	7
	1.3.3 Denotational Semantics	8
1.4	Types and Type Systems	9
1.5	Notation and Mathematical Conventions	11
1.6	Set-theoretic Background	13
	1.6.1 Fundamentals	13
	1.6.2 Relations and Functions	17
1.7	Syntax and Semantics	21
	1.7.1 Object Language and Meta-language	21
	1.7.2 Grammars	21
	1.7.3 Lexical Analysis and Parsing	23
	1.7.4 Example Mathematical Interpretation	25
1.8	Induction	27
	1.8.1 Induction on the Natural Numbers	27
	1.8.2 Induction on Expressions and Proofs	32
	1.8.3 Well-founded Induction	38
2	**The Language PCF**	45
2.1	Introduction	45
2.2	Syntax of PCF	46
	2.2.1 Overview	46
	2.2.2 Booleans and Natural Numbers	47
	2.2.3 Pairing and Functions	51
	2.2.4 Declarations and Syntactic Sugar	57
	2.2.5 Recursion and Fixed-point Operators	60
	2.2.6 PCF Syntax Summary and Collected Examples	65

2.3 PCF Programs and Their Semantics 67
2.3.1 Programs and Results 67
2.3.2 Axiomatic Semantics 69
2.3.3 Denotational Semantics 73
2.3.4 Operational Semantics 75
2.3.5 Equivalence Relations Defined by Each Form of Semantics 76
2.4 PCF Reduction and Symbolic Interpreters 79
2.4.1 Nondeterministic Reduction 79
2.4.2 Reduction Strategies 84
2.4.3 The Left-most and Lazy Reduction Strategies 86
2.4.4 Parallel Reduction 91
2.4.5 Eager PCF 92
2.5 PCF Programming Examples, Expressive Power and Limitations 96
2.5.1 Records and n-tuples 96
2.5.2 Searching the Natural Numbers 98
2.5.3 Iteration and Tail Recursion 101
2.5.4 Total Recursive Functions 105
2.5.5 Partial Recursive Functions 109
2.5.6 Nondefinability of Parallel Operations 113
2.6 Variations and Extensions of PCF 122
2.6.1 Summary of Extensions 122
2.6.2 Unit and Sum Types 122
2.6.3 Recursive Types 126
2.6.4 Lifted Types 132

3 Universal Algebra and Algebraic Data Types 145
3.1 Introduction 145
3.2 Preview of Algebraic Specification 146
3.3 Algebras, Signatures and Terms 148
3.3.1 Algebras 148
3.3.2 Syntax of Algebraic Terms 149
3.3.3 Algebras and the Interpretation of Terms 151
3.3.4 The Substitution Lemma 156
3.4 Equations, Soundness and Completeness 157
3.4.1 Equations 157
3.4.2 Term Algebras and Substitution 159

	3.4.3 Semantic Implication and an Equational Proof System	161
	3.4.4 Forms of Completeness	171
	3.4.5 Congruence, Quotients and Deductive Completeness	173
	3.4.6 Nonempty Sorts and the Least Model Property	177
3.5	Homomorphisms and Initiality	179
	3.5.1 Homomorphisms and Isomorphisms	179
	3.5.2 Initial Algebras	181
3.6	Algebraic Data Types	188
	3.6.1 Specification and Data Abstraction	188
	3.6.2 Initial Algebra Semantics and Datatype Induction	191
	3.6.3 Examples and Error Values	196
	3.6.4 Alternative Approaches to Error Values	202
3.7	Rewrite Systems	203
	3.7.1 Basic Definitions	203
	3.7.2 Confluence and Provable Equality	207
	3.7.3 Termination	210
	3.7.4 Critical Pairs	216
	3.7.5 Left-linear Non-overlapping Rewrite Systems	222
	3.7.6 Local Confluence, Termination and Completion	227
	3.7.7 Applications to Algebraic Datatypes	230
4	**Simply-typed Lambda Calculus**	235
4.1	Introduction	235
4.2	Types	237
	4.2.1 Syntax	237
	4.2.2 Interpretation of Types	237
4.3	Terms	239
	4.3.1 Context-sensitive Syntax	239
	4.3.2 Syntax of $\lambda^{\rightarrow}$ Terms	241
	4.3.3 Terms with Product, Sum and Related Types	248
	4.3.4 Formulas-as-types Correspondence	250
	4.3.5 Typing Algorithm	255
4.4	Proof Systems	257
	4.4.1 Equations and Theories	257
	4.4.2 Reduction Rules	267
	4.4.3 Reduction with Additional Rules	271
	4.4.4 Proof-theoretic Methods for Consistency and Conservativity	273

4.5 Henkin Models, Soundness and Completeness 279
4.5.1 General Models and the Meanings of Terms 279
4.5.2 Applicative Structures, Extensionality and Frames 280
4.5.3 Environment Model Condition 283
4.5.4 Type and Equational Soundness 288
4.5.5 Completeness for Henkin Models Without Empty Types 293
4.5.6 Completeness with Empty Types 295
4.5.7 Combinators and the Combinatory Model Condition 297
4.5.8 Combinatory and Lambda Algebras 300
4.5.9 Henkin Models for Other Types 301

5 Models of Typed Lambda Calculus 305
5.1 Introduction 305
5.2 Domain-theoretic Models and Fixed Points 306
5.2.1 Recursive Definitions and Fixed Point Operators 306
5.2.2 Complete Partial Orders, Lifting and Cartesian Products 308
5.2.3 Continuous Functions 312
5.2.4 Fixed Points and the Full Continuous Hierarchy 318
5.2.5 CPO Model for PCF 327
5.3 Fixed-point Induction 333
5.4 Computational Adequacy and Full Abstraction 339
5.4.1 Approximation Theorem and Computational Adequacy 339
5.4.2 Full Abstraction for PCF with Parallel Operations 345
5.5 Recursion-theoretic Models 354
5.5.1 Introduction 354
5.5.2 Modest Sets 357
5.5.3 Full Recursive Hierarchy 360
5.6 Partial Equivalence Relations and Recursion 364
5.6.1 Partial Equivalence Relation Interpretation of Types 364
5.6.2 Generalization to Partial Combinatory Algebras 368
5.6.3 Lifting, Partial Functions and Recursion 373
5.6.4 Recursion and the Intrinsic Order 375
5.6.5 Lifting, Products and Function Spaces of Effective CPOs 382

6 Imperative Programs 387
6.1 Introduction 387

6.2 While Programs 389
6.2.1 L–values and R–values 389
6.2.2 Syntax of While Programs 390
6.3 Operational Semantics 392
6.3.1 Basic Symbols in Expressions 392
6.3.2 Locations and Stores 392
6.3.3 Evaluation of Expressions 394
6.3.4 Execution of Commands 395
6.4 Denotational Semantics 401
6.4.1 Typed Lambda Calculus with Stores 401
6.4.2 Semantic Functions 405
6.4.3 Equivalence of Operational and Denotational Semantics 410
6.5 Before–after Assertions about While Programs 412
6.5.1 First-order and Partial Correctness Assertions 412
6.5.2 Proof Rules 415
6.5.3 Soundness 421
6.5.4 Relative Completeness 423
6.6 Semantics of Additional Program Constructs 429
6.6.1 Overview 429
6.6.2 Blocks with Local Variables 429
6.6.3 Procedures 438
6.6.4 Combining Blocks and Procedure Declarations 440
7 Categories and Recursive Types 445
7.1 Introduction 445
7.2 Cartesian Closed Categories 446
7.2.1 Category Theory and Typed Languages 446
7.2.2 Categories, Functors and Natural Transformations 446
7.2.3 Definition of Cartesian Closed Category 458
7.2.4 Soundness and the Interpretation of Terms 468
7.2.5 Henkin Models as CCCs 484
7.2.6 Categorical Characterization of Meaning Function 487
7.3 Kripke Lambda Models and Functor Categories 490
7.3.1 Overview 490
7.3.2 Possible Worlds 491
7.3.3 Applicative Structures 491

7.3.4 Extensionality, Combinators and Functor Categories 493
7.3.5 Environments and Meanings of Terms 497
7.3.6 Soundness and Completeness 499
7.3.7 Kripke Lambda Models as Cartesian Closed Categories 501
7.4 Domain Models of Recursive Types 505
7.4.1 A Motivating Example 505
7.4.2 Diagrams, Cones and Limits 509
7.4.3 F-algebras 512
7.4.4 ω-Chains and Initial F-algebras 514
7.4.5 O-categories and Embeddings 518
7.4.6 Colimits and O-colimits 521
7.4.7 Locally Continuous Functors 526
7.4.8 Examples of the General Method 528

8 Logical Relations 535
8.1 Introduction to Logical Relations 535
8.2 Logical Relations over Applicative Structures 536
8.2.1 Definition of Logical Relation 536
8.2.2 The Basic Lemma 538
8.2.3 Partial Functions and Theories of Models 544
8.2.4 Logical Partial Equivalence Relations 545
8.2.5 Quotients and Extensionality 546
8.3 Proof-Theoretic Results 550
8.3.1 Completeness for Henkin Models 550
8.3.2 Normalization 553
8.3.3 Confluence and Other Reduction Properties 556
8.3.4 Reduction with *Fix* and Additional Operations 562
8.4 Partial Surjections and Specific Models 573
8.4.1 Partial Surjections and the Full Classical Hierarchy 574
8.4.2 Full Recursive Hierarchy 576
8.4.3 Full Continuous Hierarchy 578
8.5 Representation Independence 580
8.5.1 Motivation 580
8.5.2 Example Language 581
8.5.3 General Representation Independence 585

8.6 Generalizations of Logical Relations 586
8.6.1 Introduction 586
8.6.2 Motivating Examples: Complete Partial Orders and Kripke Models 588
8.6.3 Sconing and Relations 595
8.6.4 Comparison with Logical Relations 600
8.6.5 General Case and Applications to Specific Categories 603
9 Polymorphism and Modularity 607
9.1 Introduction 607
9.1.1 Overview 607
9.1.2 Types as Function Arguments 608
9.1.3 General Products and Sums 613
9.1.4 Types as Specifications 614
9.2 Predicative Polymorphic Calculus 617
9.2.1 Syntax of Types and Terms 617
9.2.2 Comparison with Other Forms of Polymorphism 624
9.2.3 Equational Proof System and Reduction 628
9.2.4 Models of Predicative Polymorphism 630
9.2.5 ML-style Polymorphic Declarations 635
9.3 Impredicative Polymorphism 639
9.3.1 Introduction 639
9.3.2 Expressiveness and Properties of Theories 640
9.3.3 Termination of Reduction 657
9.3.4 Summary of Semantic Models 663
9.3.5 Models Based on Universal Domains 665
9.3.6 Partial Equivalence Relation Models 670
9.4 Data Abstraction and Existential Types 679
9.5 General Products, Sums and Program Modules 685
9.5.1 The ML Module Language 685
9.5.2 Predicative Calculus with Products and Sums 692
9.5.3 Representing Modules with Products and Sums 697
9.5.4 Predicativity and the Relationship between Universes 698
10 Subtyping and Related Concepts 703
10.1 Introduction 703
10.2 Simply Typed Lambda Calculus with Subtyping 706

10.3 Records 713
10.3.1 General Properties of Record Subtyping 713
10.3.2 Typed Calculus with Records and Subtyping 714
10.4 Semantic Models of Subtyping 718
10.4.1 Overview 718
10.4.2 Conversion Interpretation of Subtyping 718
10.4.3 Subset Interpretation of Types 727
10.4.4 Partial Equivalence Relations as Types 734
10.5 Recursive Types and a Record Model of Objects 739
10.6 Polymorphism with Subtype Constraints 750

11 Type Inference 765
11.1 Introduction to Type Inference 765
11.2 Type Inference for $\lambda^{\rightarrow}$ with Type Variables 769
11.2.1 The Language $\lambda_t^{\rightarrow}$ 769
11.2.2 Substitution, Instances and Unification 771
11.2.3 An Algorithm for Principal Curry Typings 777
11.2.4 Implicit Typing 782
11.2.5 Equivalence of Typing and Unification 784
11.3 Type Inference with Polymorphic Declarations 790
11.3.1 ML Type Inference and Polymorphic Variables 790
11.3.2 Two Sets of Implicit Typing Rules 791
11.3.3 Type Inference Algorithms 795
11.3.4 Equivalence of ML_1 and ML_2 802
11.3.5 Complexity of ML Type Inference 805

Bibliography 817
Index 837

Series Foreword

Theoretical computer science has now undergone several decades of development. The "classical" topics of automata theory, formal languages, and computational complexity have become firmly established, and their importance to other theoretical work and to practice is widely recongnized. Stimulated by technology advances, theoreticians have been rapidly expanding the areas under study, and the time delay between theoretical progress and its practical impact has been decreasing dramatically. Much publicity has been given recently to breakthroughs in cryptography and linear programming, and steady progress is being made on programming language semantics, computational geometry, and efficient data structures. Newer, more speculative, areas of study include relational databases, VLSI theory, and parallel and distributed computation. As this list of topics continues expanding, it is becoming more and more difficult to stay abreast of the progress that is being made and increasingly important that the most significant work be distilled and communicated in a manner that will facilitate further research and application of this work. By publishing comprehensive books and specialized monographs on the theoretical aspects of computer science, the series on Foundations of Computing provides a forum in which important research topics can be presented in their entirety and placed in perspective for researchers, students, and practitioners alike.

Michael R. Garey
Albert R. Meyer

Preface

This book presents a framework for the analysis of syntactic, operational and semantic properties of programming languages. The framework is based on a mathematical system called typed lambda calculus. The main features of lambda calculus are a notation for functions and other computable values, together with an equational logic and rules for evaluating expressions. The book is organized around a sequence of lambda calculi with progressively more complicated type systems. These are used to analyze and discuss relevant programming language concepts. The emphasis is on sequential languages, although many of the techniques and concepts also apply to concurrent programming languages.

The simplest system in the book is an equational system sometimes called universal algebra. This logic without function variables may be used to axiomatize and analyze many of the data types commonly used in programming. The next system is a lambda calculus with function types and, optionally, cartesian products and disjoint unions. When enriched with recursive definitions, this language provides a useful framework for studying operational and semantic properties of functional programs. When combined with algebraic data types, this system is adequate to define many conventional programming languages. In particular, with types for memory locations and stores, we may study traditional axiomatic, operational and denotational semantics of imperative programs. More advanced technical machinery, such as the method of logical relations, category theory, and the semantics of recursively defined types are covered in the middle chapters. The last three chapters of the book study polymorphic types, along with declaration forms for abstract data types and program modules, systems of subtyping, and type inference.

Prerequisites and Relation to Other Topics

The book is written for upper-level undergraduates or beginning graduate students specializing in theoretical computer science, software systems, or mathematics. It is also suitable for advanced study or technical reference. While the only true prerequisite is the proverbial "appropriate level of mathematical maturity," most students will find some prior experience with formal logic, computability or complexity theory, and programming languages helpful. In general, students familiar with these topics at the level of a general introductory course such as [AU92] or above should proceed with confidence and with their sleeves rolled up. To give the prospective reader or instructor more information, the primary connections with related topics are summarized below.

Mathematical Logic

The systems of lambda calculus used in this book share many features with traditional mathematical logic. Each has a syntax, a proof system, and a model theory. For this reason, general ideas from logic such as the definition of well-formed formulas, soundness and completeness of proof systems, and interpretation of expressions in mathematical structures are used. These are introduced briefly as needed. First-order logic itself is used only in the sections on proving properties of programs; here an intuitive understanding of the meaning of formulas is assumed.

Computability and Complexity Theory
The basic distinction between computable and non-computable functions is used in the study of PCF (Chapter 2). The text defines and uses the class of partial recursive functions and refers to Turing machines in the exercises of two sections. A few additional concepts from recursion theory are assumed in constructing semantic models using Gödel numbering of recursive functions (Chapter 4). All of these would be familiar from any course that covers universal Turing machines or undecidable properties of computable functions. A certain amount of basic recursion theory is developed in the text using PCF, including a simple exercise showing that the halting problem for PCF programs is not programmable in PCF.

Programming
Although no specific programming experience is required, students with some exposure to a programming language with higher-order functions, such as Lisp, Scheme or ML, will find it easier to relate this theory to practice. To give a general feel for the expressiveness of typed lambda calculus, Chapter 2 contains a series of programming examples and techniques. This provides a self-contained overview of some relevant programming issues.

Category Theory
Category theory appears only in more advanced sections of the book. While all the necessary definitions are presented and illustrated by example, a non-mathematical reader with no prior exposure to category theory may wish to consult additional sources. If a more leisurely or comprehensive introduction is needed, the reader is referred to an elementary introduction tailored to computer scientists, e.g., [BW90, Pie91].

Sample Course Outlines

Three sample course outlines are given in Tables 1 through 3. The first is an introductory course that has been taught several times as Stanford CS 258. The listed prerequisites for this course, which covers the core topics in Chapters 2–6, are a one-quarter course in automata and computability theory and a one-quarter course that includes mathematical logic but does not cover soundness, completeness or model-theoretic constructions in depth. CS 258 has been completed successfully by undergraduates, M.S. students specializing in systems or theory, and beginning Ph.D. students. While the Stanford course is taught in 10

Table 1
Introductory Course Outline

Sample Introductory Course

1. *Functional programming and typed lambda calculus* (Chapter 2)
   (a) Boolean, natural number, pairing and function expressions; definition of recursive functions using fixed-point operator (Section 2.2)
   (b) Comparison of axiomatic, operational and denotational semantics (Section 2.3)
   (c) Properties of reduction; deterministic symbolic interpreters (Section 2.4)
   (d) Programming techniques, expressive power, limitations (Section 2.5)
2. *Universal algebra and algebraic data types* (Chapter 3)
   (a) Algebraic terms, equations and algebras (Sections 3.1–3)
   (b) Equational proof system, soundness and completeness (Section 3.4)
   (c) Homomorphisms and initiality (Section 3.5)
   (d) Aspects of algebraic theory of data types (Section 3.6)
3. *Semantics of typed lambda calculus and recursion* (Parts of Chapters 4 and 5)
   (a) Presentation of context-sensitive syntax by typing rules (Sections 4.3.1, 4.3.2, 4.3.5)
   (b) General models, summary of soundness and completeness (Sections 4.5.1–4)
   (c) Domain-theoretic models of typed lambda calculus with fixed-point operators (Sections 5.1 and 5.2; Sections 5.3 and 5.4 time permitting)
4. *Imperative programs* (Chapter 6)
   (a) Syntax of `while` programs; L-values and R-values (Section 6.2)
   (b) Structured operational semantics (Section 6.3)
   (c) Denotational semantics using typed lambda calculus with *location* and *store* types, fixed-point operator (Section 6.4)
   (d) Partial correctness assertions. Soundness, relative completeness and example proofs (Section 6.5)

weeks, it is easy to expand the course to a 15-week semester. Some options for expansion are: (i) cover the topics listed at a more leisurely pace, (ii) include the section on algebraic rewrite systems, (iii) prove soundness, completeness and other properties of typed lambda calculus, or (iv) survey selected topics from Chapters 9–11. It is also possible to drop imperative programs (Chapter 6) in favor of one or more of these options. While the chapter on algebra (Chapter 3) is not strictly required for later topics, universal algebra provides a useful opportunity to introduce or review logical concepts in a relatively simple mathematical setting. This aspect of the chapter may be redundant if students have taken a more rigorous undergraduate course on mathematical logic.

The second course, in Table 2, is a more mathematical course on typed lambda calculus and semantic techniques, with more technical detail and less programming motivation. The third course, in Table 3, covers type systems, beginning with typed lambda calculus and proceeding with polymorphism, subtyping and type inference. These three overlapping courses cover most of the book.

Table 2
Mathematical course on typed lambda calculus

Course on semantics and typed lambda calculus

1. *Syntax and proof systems of typed lambda calculus*
   (a) Context-sensitive syntax and typing algorithm (Sections 4.1—3)
   (b) Equational proof system and reduction (Section 4.4)
   (c) Recursion using fixed-point operators (Skim 2.2.2–4, cover 2.2.5)
   (d) Recursive types and explicit lifting (Section 2.6)
2. *Model theory of typed lambda calculus*
   (a) General definitions, soundness and completeness (Sections 4.4.1, 4.5.1–6)
   (b) Domains (Sections 5.1, 5.2)
   (c) Modest sets (Sections 5.5, 5.6)
3. *Logical relations*
   (a) Definition and basic lemmas (Sections 8.1, 8.2)
   (b) Proof-theoretic results: completeness, normalization and confluence (Section 8.3)
   (c) Completeness theorems for set-theoretic hierarchy, modest sets and domains (Section 8.4)
4. *Category theory and recursive types*
   (a) Categories, functors and natural transformations (Sections 7.1, 7.2.1–2)
   (b) Cartesian closed categories and typed lambda calculus (Section 7.2.3–6)
   (c) An example of a category that is not well-pointed: Kripke lambda models (Section 7.3)
   (d) Domain models of recursive types (Section 7.4)

Acknowledgments and Disclaimers

Many people have read drafts and provided useful comments and suggestions. I would like to thank M. Abadi, S. Abramsky, V. Breazu-Tannen, K. Bruce, L. Cardelli, R. Casley, P.-L. Curien, P. Gardner, D. Gifford, D. Gries, C. Gunter, R. Harper, S. Hayashi, F. Henglein, B. Howard, P. Kanellakis, A. Kfoury, P. Lescanne, H. Mairson, I. Mason, A. Meyer, E. Moggi, N. Marti-Oliet, A. Pitts, J. Riecke, K. Ross, D. Sanella, P. Scott, D. Tranah, T. Uribe and the students of Stanford CS 258 and CS 358. Special thanks to teaching assistants My Hoang, Brian Howard and Ramesh Viswanathan for their help with homework exercises and sample solutions, a few of which made their way into examples in the text.

Almost all of this book is based on previously published research, some by the author. When specific results are taken from the literature, an effort has been made to cite original sources as well as relevant survey articles and books. However, as with any project of this size, there are likely to be some errors and omissions. In addition, while an effort has been

Table 3
Course on type theory

Course on type theory

1. *Simply-typed lambda calculus*
   (a) Context-sensitive syntax and typing algorithm (Sections 4.1–3)
   (b) Equational proof system and reduction (Section 4.4.1, 4.4.2)
2. *Polymorphism*
   (a) Introduction to polymorphic types (Section 9.1)
   (b) Predicative polymorphism (Section 9.2)
   (c) Properties of impredicative polymorphism (Section 9.3.1–4)
   (d) Data abstraction and existential types (Section 9.4)
   (e) General products, sums and program modules (Section 9.5)
3. *Subtyping*
   (a) Basic syntactic issues, equational reasoning, containment and conversion interpretations of subtyping (Sections 10.1–10.4)
   (b) Records, recursive types, records-as-objects (Section 10.5)
   (c) Polymorphism with subtype constraints (Section 10.6)
4. *Type inference*
   (a) Type inference and erasure functions (Section 11.1)
   (b) Type inference for simply-type lambda calculus using unification (Section 11.2)
   (c) ML-style polymorphic declarations (Section 11.3)

made to circulate and teach any original material or alternate proofs developed for this book, there are undoubtably some remaining errors.

John C. Mitchell
Stanford, CA

Foundations for Programming Languages

1 Introduction

1.1 Model Programming Languages

The mathematical analysis of programming languages begins with the formulation of "model" programming languages. For example, if we want to analyze procedure call mechanisms, we might begin by identifying a simple programming language whose main constructs are procedure declarations and calls. We may then analyze this simplified programming language without worrying about irrelevant details of a larger programming language. This process is not only useful in analyzing an existing programming language, but also in designing a new one. Since practical programming languages are typically large and very complex, programming language design involves careful and separate consideration of various sublanguages. Of course, it is important to keep in mind that a small language with only a few constructs may give false impressions. We might conclude that a programming language is much simpler than it really is, or we might rely on properties that are immediately destroyed when important features are added. Therefore, good taste and careful judgment are required. In developing a programming language theory, or applying theoretical analysis to practical situations, we must always keep in mind the nature of our simplifying assumptions and how they may affect the conclusions we reach.

In this book, we will will study programming language concepts using the framework of typed lambda calculus. The idea that lambda calculus is the basic mechanism underlying function definition and naming conventions in programming languages is an old one. It is described in an early paper of Landin [Lan66], for example, which suggests that whatever the next 700 programming languages turn out to be, they will surely be variants and extensions of lambda calculus. By adding to basic typed lambda calculus in various ways, we may devise model languages with a variety of historical, contemporary, or forward-looking features. An advantage of sticking to typed lambda calculus is that there is a certain degree of "modularity" to our theory. Although there are exceptions, many of the extensions to typed lambda calculus may be combined without unexpected synergistic effects. For example, after exploring polymorphism and records separately, we can easily formulate a language with polymorphism and records and identify many of its properties.

The main goal in our investigation of programming language concepts and features is to see beyond the surface syntax and understand the meanings of program phrases (expressions, commands, declarations, etc.) at an appropriate level of detail. Since it is impossible to select a single "appropriate level of detail" that is appropriate for all forms of programming and program analysis, we concentrate on general techniques that may be used in a variety of ways to abstract away from some properties of programs and focus on others.

The first chapter beyond this introduction is concerned with the syntax, operational semantics and programming capabilities of a simple, illustrative language for *Programming Computable Functions,* called PCF. This language is based on typed lambda calculus, with natural numbers and booleans (truth values) as basic types. PCF allows us to form pairs of values, and define recursive functions. Later in the book, we study the pure typed lambda calculus separately, as well as additional data types for PCF such as stacks and trees. Since the type system of PCF is not as flexible as we might want, we will consider systems with polymorphic functions and data type declarations. This brings us to languages that resemble and extend ML [GMW79, Mil85a] and Miranda [Tur85]. In a later chapter, we consider more flexible type systems based on subtyping, concluding with a chapter on type inference. Throughout, we rely on the basic mechanisms of lambda abstraction (for defining functions) and function application.

Organization of This Book

Each chapter of this book begins with a brief introductory section. Each introductory section contains a list of the main topics of that chapter. To give an example, and to warn the reader of what is ahead, here is a list of the main topics covered in this chapter:

- Overview of lambda notation and the system of lambda calculus.
- Brief discussion of types and type systems.
- List of standard mathematical notation used in this book.
- Background discussion on set theory.
- Background discussion on syntax and semantics, including a brief overview of grammars and parsing.
- Background discussion on induction, covering induction on the natural numbers, structural induction on expressions, structural induction on proofs, and well-founded induction. In discussing induction on proofs, we also review basic terminology and properties of formal proof systems.

Each of the background sections is intended to be used as reference for later chapters of the book.

Like most lists in later chapters, the topics listed here correspond closely to the subsections of the chapter that are listed in the Contents. Therefore, if you wish to find the reference section on standard mathematical notation, for example, you may turn to the Contents and look for the subsection entitled, "Notation and Mathematical Conventions." (You will find that this is Section 1.5.)

1.2 Lambda Notation

Lambda calculus has proven useful in describing, analyzing and implementing programming languages. With a little practice, the reader may become familiar enough with the notation to see C, Pascal or Ada program phrases as syntactic variants of lambda expressions. This will make the theory described in this book more useful, and also make it much easier to understand a variety of programming languages. The language PCF will use lambda notation directly, as do the programming languages Lisp [Ste84] and Scheme [AS85, SS75]. However, the reader familiar with Lisp should be warned that PCF does not have the complete "look and feel" of a Lisp-like language. There are no lists or atoms, there is a relatively rigid compile-time typing discipline, and the order of evaluation is different.

The primary features of lambda notation are *lambda abstraction,* which we use to write function expressions, and *application,* which allows us to make use of the functions we define. Expressions written in lambda notation are called *lambda expressions* or *lambda terms.* Lambda notation is used in both typed and untyped systems of lambda calculus. A comprehensive treatment of untyped lambda calculus may be found in [Bar84]. Some comments on the relationship between typed and untyped languages appear in Section 1.4.

In *typed* lambda calculus, the domain of a function is specified by giving a type to the formal parameter. If M is some expression that is well formed under the assumption that the variable x has type σ, then $\lambda x\colon \sigma.\, M$ defines the function mapping any x in σ to the value given by M. A simple example is the lambda expression

$$\lambda x\colon nat.\, x$$

for the identity function on natural numbers. The notation "$x\colon nat$" specifies that the domain of this function is *nat*, the type of natural numbers. Since the function value at $x\colon nat$ is x, the range is also *nat*. For each form of typed lambda calculus, there are precise rules saying which expressions are well formed under assumptions about the types of variables. These rules also tell us how to determine the range of $\lambda x\colon \sigma.\, M$ from the form of the function body M. Intuitively, in writing $\lambda x\colon \sigma.\, M$, we cannot apply any operations to x inside M that do not make sense for all values of type σ. For example, the expression $\lambda x\colon nat.\, x + true$ is not well formed, since it does not make sense to add *true* to a natural number.

One way to understand lambda terms is by comparison with alternative notations. Another way to describe the function taking any $x\colon nat$ to itself is by writing $x\colon nat \mapsto x$. Perhaps a more familiar way of defining the identity function in programming languages is by writing something like

$Id(x{:}\, nat) = x.$

However, this notation forces us to make up a name for every function we write, while lambda notation gives us a succinct way of defining functions directly. Some other examples of lambda expressions are

$\lambda x{:}\, nat.\, x + 1$

which defines the successor function on natural numbers, and the constant function

$\lambda x{:}\, nat.\, 5$

which returns the natural number 5, regardless of the value of its argument.

An important aspect of lambda abstraction is that λ is a binding operator. This means that in a lambda term $\lambda x{:}\, \sigma.\, M$, the variable x serves only as a "placeholder," like the variable x in the integral

$$\int f(x)\, dx.$$

Just as $\int f(x)\, dx$ and $\int f(y)\, dy$ are different ways of writing the same integral, $\lambda x{:}\, \sigma.\, x$ and $\lambda y{:}\, \sigma.\, y$ are different ways of writing the same function. Therefore, we can rename λ-bound variables without changing the meaning of any expression, as long as any new name we choose does not conflict with other variables already in use (see Exercise 1.2.3). Terms that differ only in the names of bound variables are called α-equivalent; we sometimes write $M =_\alpha N$ if M and N are α-equivalent. When a variable x occurs in an expression M, we say an occurrence of x is *bound* if it is inside a subexpression of the form $\lambda x{:}\, \sigma.\, N$, and *free* otherwise. We write $FV(M)$ for the set of free variables of M. An expression is *closed* if it has no free variables.

In lambda notation, we write function application just by putting a function expression next to one or more arguments. This lets us use parentheses to specify association of operations. For example, we apply the natural-number identity function to the number 3 by writing

$(\lambda x{:}\, nat.\, x)\, 3.$

The value of this application is the identity function applied to the number 3, which is just 3, of course. This gives us the equation

$(\lambda x{:}\, nat.\, x)\, 3 = 3.$

There are several methods for calculating the values of lambda expressions, or proving equations between lambda expressions, as we shall see in the next section.

Some notational conventions make it easier to write and read lambda expressions. Unfortunately, the conventions of lambda calculus seem slightly awkward at first, and take a little practice to get used to. The first convention is that application associates to the left, so that MNP should be read as $(MN)P$. In words, we can read MNP as the expression, "apply the function M to argument N, and then apply the resulting function to argument P." For this to make sense, M must be a function which, given one argument, returns a function. The second notational convention is that the scope of each lambda is interpreted as being as large as possible. In other words, an expression $\lambda x\colon\sigma.\ldots$ may be parenthesized by inserting a left parenthesis after the type σ, and the matching right parenthesis as far to the right as will produce a syntactically well-formed expression. For example, we read $\lambda x\colon\sigma.\, MN$ as $\lambda x\colon\sigma.(MN)$, rather than $(\lambda x\colon\sigma.\, M)N$. Similarly, $\lambda x\colon\sigma.\,\lambda y\colon\tau.\, MN$ is short-hand for the parenthesized expression $\lambda x\colon\sigma.(\lambda y\colon\tau.(MN))$. The two conventions work well together. For example, a multi-argument function application may be written

$$(\lambda x\colon\sigma.\,\lambda y\colon\tau.\,\lambda z\colon\rho.\, M)\ N\ P\ Q.$$

According to the two conventions, this expression is fully parenthesized as

$$(((\lambda x\colon\sigma.(\lambda y\colon\tau.(\lambda z\colon\rho.\, M)))\ N)\ P)\ Q$$

so that the i-th argument corresponds to the i-th formal parameter.

Exercise 1.2.1 Using the symbol $*$ for natural-number multiplication, write a lambda expression for the function mapping $x\colon nat \mapsto x^2$.

Exercise 1.2.2 Insert parentheses into the expression $(\lambda x\colon nat.\,\lambda y\colon nat.\, x + y)\ 3\ 2$ so that it is fully parenthesized. What would you expect the value of this expression to be? Given the type information about x and y, could you meaningfully insert parentheses in some other way?

Exercise 1.2.3 We may rename the bound variable x in $\lambda x\colon nat.\,\lambda y\colon nat.\, x + y$ to z without changing the function defined by this term. Explain why renaming x to y changes the meaning of the term and is therefore not a legal renaming of a bound variable. Can we rename x to y in $\lambda x\colon nat.\, x + y$?

1.3 Equations, Reduction, and Semantics

Historically, lambda notation developed as part of what is called *lambda calculus,* a system for reasoning about lambda expressions. In addition to syntax, there are three main parts of the formal system. In contemporary programming language terminology, these are called *axiomatic semantics, operational semantics,* and *denotational semantics.* A logician might call the first two "proof systems" and the third a "model theory." The axiomatic semantics is a formal system for deriving equations between expressions. The operational semantics is based on a directed form of equational reasoning called *reduction.* In computer science terminology, reduction may be regarded as a form of symbolic evaluation. The denotational semantics, or model theory, is similar in spirit to the model theories of other logical systems, such as equational logic or first-order logic: a model consists of a family of sets, one for each type, with the property that each well-typed expression may be interpreted as a specific element of the appropriate set.

1.3.1 Axiomatic Semantics

In the equational axiom system, we have an axiom for renaming bound variables, and an axiom relating function application to *substitution.* To write these axioms, we will use the notation $[N/x]M$ for the result of substituting expression N for variable x in M. One subtle aspect of substitution is that free variables should not become bound. The simplest way to substitute N for x in M systematically is to first rename all bound variables in M so that they are different from all free variables in N. Then we can replace all occurrences of x with N. (A more detailed definition is given in Section 2.2.3.) Using substitution, the axiom for renaming bound variables is written

$$\lambda x{:}\sigma.\, M = \lambda y{:}\sigma.[y/x]M, \quad y \text{ not free in } M \qquad (\alpha)$$

For example, we have $\lambda x{:}\sigma.\, x = \lambda y{:}\sigma.\, y$.

Since the lambda term $\lambda x{:}\sigma.\, M$ defines the function with value M on argument x, we can compute the value at argument N by substituting N for x. For example, the result of applying function $\lambda x{:}\, nat.\, x + 5$ to argument 3 is

$$(\lambda x{:}\, nat.\, x + 5)\, 3 = [3/x](x + 5) = 3 + 5.$$

More generally, we have the equational axiom

$$(\lambda x{:}\sigma.\, M)\, N = [N/x]M, \qquad (\beta)_{eq}$$

called β-equivalence. Essentially, β-equivalence says that we can evaluate a function application by substituting the actual argument for the formal parameter within the function body. In addition to these axioms, and a few others, the equational proof system includes rules like symmetry, transitivity, and a congruence rule that says, "equal functions applied to equal arguments yield equal results." The latter rule may be written out formally as

$$\frac{M_1 = M_2,\ \ N_1 = N_2}{M_1 N_1 = M_2 N_2},$$

although to be completely precise, we must also specify types to make sure everything makes sense. As with other logical proof systems, the equational proof rules of typed lambda calculus allow us to derive logical consequences of any set of equational hypotheses.

1.3.2 Operational Semantics

The reduction rules for lambda expressions give us a directed form of equational reasoning. Intuitively, the basic reduction rules describe single computation steps that can be repeated to evaluate an expression symbolically (or compute indefinitely if the expression does not have a simplest form). This symbolic "evaluation procedure," or "interpreter," is what gives lambda calculus its computational character. Although β-equivalence is an equation, we often tend to read it as a simplification rule, from left to right. For example, the equation $(\lambda x\colon nat.\, x + 5)\, 3 = 3 + 5$ suggests that we can simplify the function application to $3 + 5$. Using properties of addition, we may then simplify this to 8. Since reduction is asymmetric, an arrow $\rightarrow$ is commonly used for one-step reduction, and a double-headed arrow $\twoheadrightarrow$ for zero or more reduction steps.

The central reduction rule is a directed version of $(\beta)_{eq}$ called *β-reduction,* written

$$(\lambda x\colon \sigma.\, M)\, N \xrightarrow{\beta} [N/x]M. \qquad (\beta)_{red}$$

Since we may need to rename bound variables when performing a substitution, reduction is only defined up to α-equivalence. More precisely, the definition of substitution, $[N/x]M$, allows bound variables to be renamed, in order to avoid conflicts. As a result, the term obtained by β-reduction may depend on arbitrary choices of new bound variables; it is not uniquely determined. However, any two terms we might produce will differ only in the names of bound variables, and therefore be α-equivalent. An important point is that β-reduction often produces an expression that is much longer than the one we begin with, even though it might seem "simpler" in some intuitive sense. The reason is that when x occurs several times within M, the expression $[N/x]M$ may be much longer than $(\lambda x\colon \sigma.\, M)\, N$. Both α-conversion and renaming bound variables in substitution are part of providing *static scope,* as illustrated in Exercise 2.2.13.

The entire reduction system combines $(\beta)_{red}$ and other basic one-step reductions with rules that allow us to evaluate parts of a term, and repeat reduction steps. More precisely, we write $M \twoheadrightarrow N$ if we can produce N from M by repeatedly applying single-step reductions to subexpressions. For example,

$$(\lambda x\colon \sigma.\, M)((\lambda y\colon \tau.\, N)\, P) \twoheadrightarrow (\lambda x\colon \sigma.\, M)([P/y]N) \twoheadrightarrow [([P/y]N)/x]M.$$

Since there may be several ways to begin reducing an expression, $\twoheadrightarrow$ might be viewed as a "nondeterministic" model of execution. Another way to reduce the term above is to begin with the left-most lambda:

$$(\lambda x\colon \sigma.\, M)((\lambda y\colon \tau.\, N)\ P) \twoheadrightarrow [((\lambda y\colon \tau.\, N)\ P)/x]M \twoheadrightarrow [([P/y]N)/x]M.$$

However, choosing a different place to begin does not keep us from reaching the same final result. As we shall see, this is true in general about many forms of lambda calculus.

Two notable properties of reduction on pure typed lambda terms are the *Church-Rosser property,* and the *strong normalization property.* These are also called *confluence* and *termination,* respectively. The Church-Rosser property is that if $M \twoheadrightarrow N$ and $M \twoheadrightarrow N'$, then there exists an expression P such that $N \twoheadrightarrow P$ and $N' \twoheadrightarrow P$. It follows from confluence that an equation between lambda expressions is provable (using the equational proof system) iff both expressions may be reduced to a common form. Confluence may also be used to show that certain terms cannot be proved equal, establishing the consistency of the equational proof system. The strong normalization property states that no matter how we try to reduce a typed lambda expression, we cannot go on applying single-step reductions indefinitely. We eventually produce a *normal form,* an expression that cannot be simplified further. In PCF, we will add recursion to typed lambda calculus. This makes it possible to write nonterminating algorithms, and destroys strong normalization. However, PCF reduction remains confluent.

1.3.3 Denotational Semantics

In the denotational semantics of typed lambda calculus, each type expression is associated with a set, called the set of values of this type. A term of type σ is interpreted as an element of the set of values of type σ, according to a definition by induction on the structure of terms. The set of values of type $\sigma \to \tau$ is a set of functions (or isomorphic to this), so that a typed lambda term $\lambda x\colon \sigma.\, M$ is interpreted as a mathematical function. While the semantics of pure typed lambda calculus is relatively simple, the semantics of its extensions may be considerably more complex. Some features that provide a challenge are recursive function definitions, which are computationally important but difficult to accommodate in classical set theory, recursive definition of types, and polymorphic functions, which are functions that may be applied to arguments of many types.

For the reader familiar with untyped lambda calculus, it is worth mentioning that untyped lambda calculus may be derived from typed lambda calculus in a meaningful way. In fact, one of the most natural ways to think about the semantics of untyped lambda calculus begins with the semantics of typed lambda calculus. For this reason, we consider typed lambda calculus the more basic system, and a more appropriate place to begin our study.

Exercise 1.3.1 Use $(\beta)_{red}$ twice to simplify the lambda expression $(\lambda f\colon nat \to nat.\, f5)$ $(\lambda x\colon nat.\, x + x)$ to the sum of two natural numbers.

Exercise 1.3.2 For the purpose of this exercise and the next, the *length* of a typed lambda term is the number of symbols we use to write the term down, counting parentheses but not counting ":" or the type expressions inside the term. For example, the length of $\lambda x\colon a.\, \lambda y\colon b.\, y$ is 7. Find a pure typed lambda expression (without extra functions such as $+$) of the form

$$(\lambda f\colon (a \to a) \to (a \to a).\, \lambda x\colon a \to a.\, M)(\lambda f\colon a \to a.\, \lambda x\colon a.\, f(fx))$$

whose length at least doubles as the result of one or more β-reductions.

Exercise 1.3.3 Generalize the construction of Exercise 1.3.2 to show that as a result of performing one or more β-reductions, a pure typed lambda term of length $O(n)$ may produce a term whose length is greater than $f(n) = 2^{2^{\cdots 2^n}}$, where $f(n)$ is computed by exponentiating n times.

1.4 Types and Type Systems

In the general literature on computer science and mathematical logic, the word "type" is used in a variety of contexts and with a variety of meanings. In this book, *type* is a basic term whose meaning is determined by the precise definition of a *type system.* In any type system, types provide a division or classification of some universe of possible values: a type is a collection of values that share some property. Therefore, it always makes sense to ask what the elements of a type are. However, the kind of values that may have types, and the kinds of distinctions we make in typing, may vary from system to system.

Throughout this book, we will distinguish between *types,* which are collections, and *values,* which are members of types. In some systems, there may be types with types as members. Types with types as members are usually called something else, such as *universes, orders* or *kinds,* to avoid the impression of circularity. An exception is a language with a "type of all types," which is circular in the sense that the type of all types is a member of itself. However, since a type of all types introduces several anomalies (discussed in Chapter 9), none of the systems we consider in depth will have a type of all types.

In most programming languages, types are "checked" in some way, either during program compilation, or during execution. In compile-time type checking, we attempt to guarantee that each program phrase (expressions, declarations, etc.) defines an element of

In this brief section, we list some of the notational conventions associated with mathematical topics that are not covered explicitly in the book. Other symbols are defined as they are introduced. The point of definition of each symbol may be found in the index.

Equality Relations

Several forms of equality and equality-like relations are used. We use the standard equality symbol $=$ to assert that two expressions have equal value. This is consistent with standard mathematical usage, such as $3 + 4 = 5 + 2$. An exception is that we also use $=$ in the declaration form $\texttt{let}\ x = M\ \texttt{in}\ N$, which is an expression of some of the languages studied in the book. However, it should be easy to distinguish these two uses by context. When symbols such as M and N stand for expressions of some language, we use $M \equiv N$ to mean that they are syntactically identical. In other words, the symbols "M" and "N" stand for the same expression. The notions of free and bound variables are discussed in Section 1.2. We consider two expressions that differ only in the names of bound variables syntactically equal, *e.g.*, $\lambda x\colon int.\ \lambda y\colon int.\ x \equiv \lambda y\colon int.\ \lambda x\colon int.\ y$. However, the names of free variables do matter, so $\lambda x\colon int.\ fx \not\equiv \lambda x\colon int.\ gx$.

The main equality symbols and their meaning are listed below.

$=$	Two expressions have the same value.
$\equiv$	Two expressions are syntactically equal, except possibly for the names of bound variables, as discussed above.
$\stackrel{\text{def}}{=}$	We write $M \stackrel{\text{def}}{=} N$ to indicate that a symbol or expression M is defined to be equal to N.
$::=$	Symbol used in grammars to indicate possible forms of expressions.
$\cong$	Isomorphism of structures (sets, algebras, etc.).

Logical Symbols

$\forall$	Universal quantifier. The formula $\forall x.\ \phi$ may be read, " for all x, ϕ is true."
$\exists$	Existential quantifier. The formula $\exists x.\ \phi$ may be read, " there exists x such that ϕ is true."
$\wedge$	Conjunction. The formula $\phi \wedge \psi$ may be read, "ϕ and ψ."
$\vee$	Disjunction. The formula $\phi \vee \psi$ may be read, "ϕ or ψ."
$\neg$	Negation. The formula $\neg\phi$ may be read, "not ϕ."
$\supset$	Implication. The formula $\phi \supset \psi$ may be read, "ϕ implies ψ." (We do not use $\rightarrow$ for implication since $\rightarrow$ is used in type expressions and for reduction (evaluation) of expressions.)
iff	If and only if.

Like λ, discussed in Section 1.2, the quantifiers $\forall$ and $\exists$ are binding operators. Since a bound variable is just a place-holder, formulas $\forall x.\,\phi$ and $\forall y.\,[y/x]\phi$ are considered syntactically equal, provided y does not already occur free in ϕ and the substitution $[y/x]\phi$ is carried out with renaming of bound variables in ϕ to avoid capture, as summarized in Section 1.3 and explained in more detail in Section 2.2.3. Similarly, we have $\exists x.\,\phi \equiv \exists y.\,[y/x]\phi$.

Set Operations

Although some aspects of set theory are summarized in Section 1.6, the primary symbols are listed here for reference.

$\in$ Element of.

$\cup$ Union.

$\cap$ Intersection.

$\subseteq$ Subset.

$\times$ Cartesian product.

1.6 Set-theoretic Background

1.6.1 Fundamentals

In some ways, set theory is the "machine language" of mathematics. Most of the time, we work with higher-level notions that are definable in set theory, without worrying about exactly how these concepts would be expressed in pure set theory. This subsection illustrates some of the main ideas of "elementary" set theory, without going into the foundational issues in depth. The main emphasis is on the spirit of the system and how it is used; this is not a comprehensive presentation of any particular axiomatic set theory. A good general reference on set theory, at an accessible level of detail but covering far more than is needed for this book, is [Hal60].

Intuitively, a *set* is a collection of elements, possibly empty. This is formalized in set theory by giving specific methods for defining and reasoning about sets. The main ideas are largely straightforward, except that we must be careful about the way we define sets. For example, we might think that for any property P, there is a set S with

$$x \in S \quad \text{iff} \quad P(x).$$

However, this cannot be true for "$x \notin S$," since this would give us a set S with

$$x \in S \quad \text{iff} \quad x \notin S.$$

This "definition" implies that any x is in S iff x is not in S, which cannot be satisfied by any reasonable collection. This example, which is called *Russell's paradox* after the philosopher and mathematician Bertrand Russell [Rus03], shows that we cannot make arbitrary set definitions and hope to have a reasonable mathematical theory. (There are other paradoxes, but Russell's paradox is the easiest to describe.) After the discovery of this paradox in the early 1900's, several satisfactory set theories were developed. The main idea in modern set theory is to begin with some simple, non-problematic sets and give operations for constructing additional ones.

The most basic principle about sets is that two sets are equal iff they have the same elements. This may be written more precisely as

$$A = B \quad \text{iff} \quad \forall x\ (x \in A \text{ iff } x \in B),$$

which may be read, "sets A and B are equal iff, for all x, x is in A iff x is in B." This statement is called the axiom of *extension.* Since this is an obvious property of collections, the point of this axiom about sets is just to make explicit that sets are collections, determined by their elements.

A useful operation on sets is to form their *cartesian product.* If A and B are sets, then $A \times B$ is the set of *ordered pairs*

$$\langle a, b\rangle \in A \times B \quad \text{iff} \quad a \in A \text{ and } b \in B.$$

More precisely, $x \in A \times B$ iff x has the form of an ordered pair, $x = \langle a, b\rangle$, with $a \in A$ and $b \in B$. In the remainder of this book, we will consider forming a pair $\langle a, b\rangle$ from elements a and b a basic operation. However, to give some feel for the way many operations are defined in set theory, we will show how cartesian products may be defined using other set constructions.

A basic axiom of set theory is that there exists an *empty set,* $\emptyset$, with no elements. This may be stated formally by writing

$$\forall x.\ x \notin \emptyset.$$

In words, "for every x, x is not an element of $\emptyset$." In most versions of set theory, we build all other sets out of the empty set. This results in a set-theoretic universe where everything is a set. However, it is also possible to develop set theory with what are traditionally called *urelements.* These are basic values that may be elements of sets, but are not sets themselves. The difference between set theory with urelements, and set theory without, will have no bearing on the topics covered in this book.

A simple operation is to form, for any mathematical object x, the *singleton set* $\{x\}$ with

$$y \in \{x\} \quad \text{iff} \quad y = x.$$

In other words, x is the only element of $\{x\}$. Another basic operation is *set union,* $A \cup B$, with

$$x \in A \cup B \quad \text{iff} \quad x \in A \text{ or } x \in B$$

for any sets A and B. Using singletons and union, we can form a set with any two elements by writing

$$\{a, b\} \stackrel{\text{def}}{=} \{a\} \cup \{b\}.$$

It is not hard to see, using the properties of singleton and union given above, that this definition has the property

$$x \in \{a, b\} \quad \text{iff} \quad x = a \text{ or } x = b.$$

Although the general definition form $\{x \mid P(x)\}$ can be problematic, as we saw above with Russell's paradox, we can always write

$$\{x \in A \mid P(x)\}$$

for the set of all elements of A that satisfy the property P. A special case is the *intersection* of two sets,

$$A \cap B \stackrel{\text{def}}{=} \{x \in A \mid x \in B\}$$

Returning to ordered pairs, we can define the ordered pair $\langle a, b\rangle$ by

$$\langle a, b\rangle \stackrel{\text{def}}{=} \{\{a\}, \{a, b\}\}.$$

Before proceeding, it is worthwhile to pause and consider the sense of making this definition. If we were to define pairing as a basic notion, without reducing it to some construction on sets, two operations would be important. The first is that we need a way of forming the ordered pair $\langle a, b\rangle$ from a and b, and the other is that we need to be able to extract the components a and b from the pair $\langle a, b\rangle$. We show that our representation of ordered pairs is reasonable by showing that these essential operations are definable as set operations. If we define $\langle a, b\rangle$ as above, then we can form the ordered pair from a and b by taking the unions of singleton sets:

$$\{\{a\}, \{a, b\}\} = \{\{a\}\} \cup \{\{a\} \cup \{b\}\}.$$

Conversely, we can determine the first and second components of the pair uniquely. Specifically, if we write *fst* p for the first component, we can characterize *fst* by

$$\mathit{fst}\ p = a \quad \text{iff} \quad \{a\} \in p.$$

Similarly, we can characterize the second component, *snd p*, by

$$snd\ p = b \quad \text{iff} \quad \{(fst\ p), b\} \in p.$$

Now that we have seen that our representation of ordered pairs by sets is reasonable, we may try to define cartesian product by

$$A \times B \stackrel{?}{=} \{\langle a, b\rangle \mid a \in A \text{ and } b \in B\}.$$

However, this uses the set definition form that led to Russell's paradox. For this reason, we still do not have a correct set-theoretic definition. To use the definition form $\{x \in C \mid P(x)\}$, we must find a set C that contains $A \times B$ as a subset. For this, we need the "powerset" constructor.

An important construction of set theory is called the *powerset.* The powerset, $\mathcal{P}(A)$, of a set A is the set of all sets drawn from the elements of A. Another way of saying this is to define the *subset* relation by

$$A \subseteq B \quad \text{iff} \quad \forall x.\ (x \in A \text{ implies } x \in B)$$

and write

$$A \in \mathcal{P}(B) \quad \text{iff} \quad A \subseteq B.$$

The powerset operation may be used to build bigger and bigger sets. For example, beginning with only the empty set, we may define the sequence of sets

$$\emptyset,\ \mathcal{P}(\emptyset),\ \mathcal{P}(\mathcal{P}(\emptyset)),\ \mathcal{P}(\mathcal{P}(\mathcal{P}(\emptyset))),\ \ldots$$

The powerset $\mathcal{P}(\emptyset)$ of the empty set is the singleton $\{\emptyset\}$ whose only element is the empty set. The kth element in this sequence may be written $\mathcal{P}^k(\emptyset)$, where the superscript k indicates that $\mathcal{P}$ is applied a total of k times. If $k > 0$, then $\mathcal{P}^k(\emptyset)$ has 2^{k-1} elements (see Exercise 1.6.1).

Returning to cartesian products, let A and B be sets with $a \in A$ and $b \in B$. The singleton $\{a\}$ and the set $\{a, b\}$ with two elements are both in the powerset $\mathcal{P}(A \cup B)$. Therefore, the ordered pair $\{\{a\}, \{a, b\}\}$ is in $\mathcal{P}(\mathcal{P}(A \cup B))$, the powerset of the powerset. This finally gives us a way of defining the cartesian product using only set-theoretic operations that do not lead to paradoxes:

$$A \times B \stackrel{\text{def}}{=} \{\langle a, b\rangle \in \mathcal{P}(\mathcal{P}(A \cup B)) \mid a \in A \text{ and } b \in B\}.$$

In addition to ordered pairs, it is also possible to define ordered triples, or k-tuples for any positive integer k. If $A_1, \ldots, A_k$ are sets, then the cartesian product $A_1 \times \ldots \times A_k$ is the collection of all *k-tuples* $\langle a_1, \ldots, a_k\rangle$, with $a_i \in A_i$ for $1 \le i \le k$. The k-tuple $\langle a_1, \ldots, a_k\rangle$ may be defined as the set

$$\langle a_1, \ldots, a_k \rangle \stackrel{\text{def}}{=} \{\langle 1, a_1 \rangle, \langle 2, a_2 \rangle, \ldots, \langle k, a_k \rangle\}$$

with basic operations on tuples as defined for ordered pairs. Exercise 1.6.2 shows that k-tuples can also be represented by nested pairs.

The final axiom of set theory that we will consider here is that there exists an infinite set. Without this assumption (*i.e.*, using only the empty set and the operations described so far), we would only be able to define and reason about finite sets. The "infinity" axiom allows us to define the set of natural numbers (non-negative integers), for example. In defining the natural numbers in pure set theory, we represent natural numbers by sets in much the same way as we represented ordered pairs by sets. Specifically the natural number 0 is represented by the empty set and the natural number $n + 1$ by the set of all natural numbers $\leq n$. However, it will not be necessary to go into this construction in any detail.

Exercise 1.6.1 This exercise asks about the size of the powerset of a finite set.

(a) Show that if a set A has n elements, we can associate a sequence of n bits with each subset of A. Use this to show that if A has n elements, then $\mathcal{P}(A)$ has 2^n elements.

(b) Consider the sequence of sets $\mathcal{P}^0(\emptyset)$, $\mathcal{P}^1(\emptyset)$, $\mathcal{P}^2(\emptyset)$, ..., where the superscript k in $\mathcal{P}^k(\emptyset)$ indicates that $\mathcal{P}$ is applied a total of k times. Show by induction on k that if $k > 0$, then $\mathcal{P}^k(\emptyset)$ has 2^{k-1} elements.

Exercise 1.6.2 In addition to defining k-ary cartesian products directly, as above, we can also represent k-ary cartesian products as repeated binary products. Specifically, if $A_1, \ldots, A_k$ are sets, then we can use $A_1 \times (A_2 \times \ldots \times (A_{k-1} \times A_k) \ldots)$ as the representation of the k-ary cartesian product. Show how this works by showing that $A_1 \times (A_2 \times \ldots \times (A_{k-1} \times A_k) \ldots)$ is *isomorphic* to $A_1 \times A_2 \times \ldots \times A_{k-1} \times A_k$. More specifically, show that there are functions

$$f \;:\; A_1 \times (A_2 \times \ldots \times (A_{k-1} \times A_k) \ldots) \to A_1 \times A_2 \times \ldots \times A_{k-1} \times A_k$$

$$g \;:\; A_1 \times A_2 \times \ldots \times A_{k-1} \times A_k \to A_1 \times (A_2 \times \ldots \times (A_{k-1} \times A_k) \ldots)$$

so that both function compositions $f \circ g$ and $g \circ f$ are the identity. (The *composition* $f \circ g$ is the function h with $h(x) = f(g(x))$. This is discussed more generally for relations on Section 1.6.2 and in Exercise 1.6.6.)

1.6.2 Relations and Functions

Intuitively, a relation between elements of some set A and elements of a set B is a "binary property" R such that $R(a, b)$ is either true or false for each $a \in A$ and $b \in B$. The common representation of relations as sets uses subsets of the cartesian product. Formally, a *relation* R between sets A and B is a subset $R \subseteq A \times B$ of their cartesian product. If an ordered pair $\langle a, b\rangle$ is in the subset R, then we consider the relation true of a and b. If $\langle a, b\rangle$ is not in the subset R, then we consider the relation false of a and b. It is common to write $R(a, b)$ instead of $\langle a, b\rangle \in R$.

In addition to binary relations, it is possible to define k-ary relations, for any positive integer k. If $A_1, \ldots, A_k$ are sets, then a relation over $A_1, \ldots, A_k$ is a subset of the cartesian product $A_1 \times \ldots \times A_k$. In the special case $k = 1$, we have unary relations, or subsets, which are also called *predicates.*

Some important kinds of relations are equivalence relations and various kinds of orderings. A relation $R \subseteq A \times A$ is

Reflexive if $R(a, a)$, for all $a \in A$,

Symmetric if $R(a, b)$ implies $R(b, a)$, for all $a, b \in A$,

Transitive if $R(a, b)$ and $R(b, c)$ imply $R(a, c)$, for all $a, b, c \in A$.

An *equivalence relation* is a relation that is reflexive, symmetric and transitive. One example of an equivalence relation is equality, *i.e.*, the relation R with $R(a, b)$ iff $a = b$. Another example, on the natural numbers, is the relation $R \subseteq \mathcal{N} \times \mathcal{N}$ with $R(a, b)$ iff a and b are both odd or both even. A relation $R \subseteq A \times A$ is

Antisymmetric if $R(a, b)$ and $R(b, a)$ then $a = b$, for all $a, b \in A$.

A *partial order* is a relation $R \subseteq A \times A$ that is reflexive, antisymmetric and transitive. An example on the natural numbers is the usual ordering relation $R \subseteq \mathcal{N} \times \mathcal{N}$ with $R(a, b)$ iff $a \leq b$. Some other partial orders are discussed in Section 5.2.2. The usual $\leq$ relation on numbers is called a *total order* since it also satisfies the property

Total order: For all $a, b \in A$, either $R(a, b)$ or $R(b, a)$.

This is not generally true for partial orders. For example, the prefix order on strings described in Exercise 5.2.4 is not a total order.

The set-theoretic representation of a function uses a special kind of relation. Before defining this, let us recall the intuitive notion of function. Informally, a function from set A to B is some way of associating an element b of B with each element a of A. This could take the form of an algorithm for computing b from a, or the function might be given by some condition that could not be carried out by a computer.

In set theory, a function is identified with its *graph,* the set of pairs $\langle a, b\rangle$ such that the value of the function on a is b. The graph of a function from A to B is a relation that associates exactly one element of B with each element of A. More precisely, a *function* $f : A \to B$ from set A to B is a relation $f \subseteq A \times B$ satisfying the following properties:

(i) $\quad \forall a \in A.\, \exists b \in B.\, \langle a, b\rangle \in f$

(ii) $\quad \forall a \in A.\, \forall b, b' \in B.$ if $\langle a, b\rangle \in f$ and $\langle a, b'\rangle \in f$ then $b = b'$

Condition (i) says that the function is *defined* on every $a \in A$: for every a in A, there exists some b in B that is the value of f on a. Condition (ii) says that the function value is unique for each $a \in A$. The standard notation is to write $f(a)$ for the unique $b \in B$ with $\langle a, b\rangle \in f$. If $f : A \to B$, then we say A is the *domain* of f and B is the *range* or *codomain.*

Partial functions are important in computation since an algorithm for computing an element of set B, for each $a \in A$, might turn out not to halt for some $a \in A$. We think of such a rule as defining a *partial function,* which is like a function, but not necessarily defined on all $a \in A$. More precisely, a *partial function* $f : A \rightharpoonup B$ from set A to B is a relation $f \subseteq A \times B$ satisfying the property (ii) above, but not necessarily (i). Trivially, every total function from A to B is also a partial one. Exercises 1.6.4 and 1.6.5 show how to regard partial functions as total functions by changing either the domain or range. Note that we use an arrow $\rightharpoonup$ with a "partial" arrowhead to indicate that a function may be partial. If $f : A \rightharpoonup B$ is a partial function and $a \in A$, we write $f(a)$ for the unique element of b with $\langle a, b\rangle \in f$, if there is one. If not, then we consider $f(a)$ *undefined,* and say that the partial function f is undefined on a, or that a is outside the *domain of definition* of f.

Example 1.6.3 The recursive function expression

$$f(x\colon int) \;=\; \texttt{if}\ x = 0\ \texttt{then}\ 0\ \texttt{else}\ x + f(x-2)$$

defines a *partial* function on the integers. If we think of executing a function defined in this way on any number n, the result will be the sum of the even numbers up to n if n is even and not negative. Otherwise, the computation should continue indefinitely in principle, although most computers will terminate when the run-time stack is full or the smallest representable negative integer is reached. If we ignore this problem with "overflow," then the partial function defined by this expression is the following set of ordered pairs

$$f \;=\; \{\langle x, y\rangle \in int \times int \mid x = 2n \geq 0 \text{ and } y = \sum_{0 \leq i \leq n} 2i\}$$

It is easy to check that this relation satisfies condition (ii) above, but not condition (i) for odd numbers. ■

Although we represent functions as sets of ordered pairs, we generally do not apply set-theoretic operations like union or intersection to functions. An exception is the use of the subset ordering on partial functions in Section 5.2.1.

A useful operation on relations and functions is *composition.* Since functions and partial functions are special cases of relations, it is simplest to define this operation on relations first, and then see that the composition of two functions is always a function, and similarly for partial functions. If we have two relations $R \subseteq A \times B$ and $S \subseteq B \times C$, then we define their composition $S \circ R \subseteq A \times C$ by

$$S \circ R \stackrel{\text{def}}{=} \{\langle a, c\rangle \in A \times C \mid \exists b \in B.\, \langle a, b\rangle \in R \text{ and } \langle b, c\rangle \in S\}$$

In the case that these relations are functions $f\colon A \to B$ and $S\colon B \to C$, this definition gives us

$$g \circ f = \{\langle a, c\rangle \in A \times C \mid c = g(f(a))\}$$

and similarly for partial functions as verified in Exercise 1.6.6.

Some standard properties of functions are that a partial or total function $f\colon A \rightharpoonup B$ is *one-to-one,* sometimes written *1-1,* if

$$f(x) = f(y) \text{ implies } x = y$$

and *onto* if

$$\forall b \in B.\, \exists a \in A.\, f(a) = b$$

In words, a function is one-to-one if it maps distinct elements of its domain to distinct elements of its codomain and onto if every element in its codomain is the value of the function on some argument. These concepts generalize to relations in the obvious way, as noted in Exercise 1.6.6. Sometimes *injective* is used as a synonym for one-to-one and *surjective* as a synonym for onto. A function that is both injective and surjective is called *bijective.*

Exercise 1.6.4 Show that a relation $f \subseteq A \times B$ is a partial function $f : A \rightharpoonup B$ iff f is a total function $f : A' \to B$ on some subset of $A' \subseteq A$.

Exercise 1.6.5 Let A and B be sets and assume ∞ is not an element of B. Show that there is a one-to-one correspondence between partial functions $A \rightharpoonup B$ and total functions $A \to (B \cup \{\infty\})$.

Exercise 1.6.6 Prove the following facts about composition of relations $R \subseteq A \times B$ and $S \subseteq B \times C$:

(a) If R and S are partial functions, then $S \circ R$ is a partial function. Similarly for total functions.

(b) If R and S are one-to-one relations, then $S \circ R$ is one-to-one. Similarly for onto. (Begin by generalizing the definitions of one-to-one and onto from functions to relations.

The idea remains that a relation is one-to-one if it relates distinct elements of its "domain" to distinct elements of its "codomain" and onto if every element in its "codomain" is related to some element of the "domain.")

(c) For any additional relation $T \subseteq C \times D$, we have $T \circ (S \circ R) = (T \circ S) \circ R$. This is called *associativity of composition* for relations (or functions).

1.7 Syntax and Semantics

1.7.1 Object Language and Meta-language

One fundamental idea in this book is the mathematical interpretation of syntactic expressions. This is actually a familiar concept, from all of our basic math courses. When we write an expression $3 + 5 - 7$, we use symbols 3,5,7,+ and $-$ to denote a mathematical entity, the number 1. What makes it confusing to talk (or write!) about the interpretation of syntax is that everything we write is actually syntactic. When we study a programming language, we need to distinguish the language we study from the language we use to describe this language and its meaning. The language we study is traditionally called the *object language,* since this is the object of our attention, while the second language is called the *meta-language,* because it transcends the object language in some way. With this distinction in mind, we can describe the relation between the expression $3 + 5 - 7$ and the number it identifies more precisely. Specifically, in our meta-language for discussing arithmetic expressions, let us use an underlined number, such as $\underline{1}$, to mean "the mathematical entity called the natural number 1". Then we can say that the meaning of the object language expression $3 + 5 - 7$ is the natural number $\underline{1}$. In this sentence, the symbol $\underline{1}$ is a symbol of the meta-language, while the expression $3 + 5 - 7$ is written using symbols of the object language.

1.7.2 Grammars

Grammars provide a convenient method for defining infinite sets of expressions. In addition, the structure imposed by a grammar gives us a systematic way of defining properties of expressions, such as their semantic interpretation. This section summarizes basic properties of grammars, with parsing discussed briefly in the next section. In simple terms, the main point of these sections is to show how we can use ambiguous grammars, without getting bogged down in lots of details about parsing and ambiguity. The method we use, often referred to by the phrase *abstract syntax,* takes parse trees, rather than strings, as the true expressions of a language. We illustrate this use of grammars in Section 1.7.4 by giving the semantics of a simple expression language.

Consider the simple language of numeric expressions given by the grammar

$$e ::= n \mid e + e \mid e - e$$

$$n ::= d \mid nd$$

$$d ::= 0 \mid 1 \mid 2 \mid \ldots \mid 9$$

where e is what is called the *start symbol,* the symbol we begin with if we want to derive a well-formed expression from the rules of a grammar. The way a start symbol is used is that we begin with e, and continue to replace a symbol that occurs on the left of a $::=$ with one of the strings between vertical bars on the right until none of the *nonterminals* e, n or d are left. (The symbols that appear in expressions are called *terminals.*) For example, here are two derivations of well-formed expressions:

$$e \to n \to nd \to dd \to 2d \to 25$$
$$e \to e+e \to e+e-e \to \ldots \to n+n-n \to \ldots \to 10+15-12$$

It is often convenient to represent a derivation by a tree. This tree, called the *parse tree* of a derivation, or *derivation tree,* is constructed using the start symbol as the root of the tree. If a step in the derivation is to replace s by $x_1 \ldots x_n$, then the children of s in the tree will be nodes labeled $x_1, \ldots, x_n$. The parse tree for $10 + 15 - 12$ has some useful structure. Specifically, since the first step yields $e + e$, the parse tree has the form

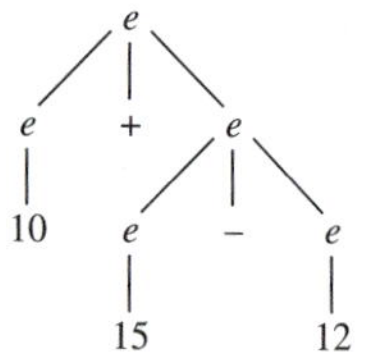

where we have contracted the subtrees for each two-digit number to a single node. What is useful to note about this tree is that it is different from

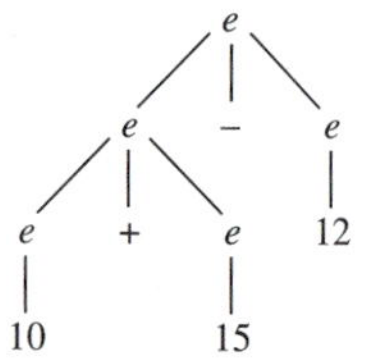

which is another parse tree for the same expression. An important fact about parse trees is that each corresponds to a unique parenthesization of the expression. Specifically, the first tree above corresponds to $10+(15-12)$ while the second corresponds to $(10+15)-12$. It is an accident that these expressions have the same numeric value. In general, the value of an expression may depend on how it is parsed or parenthesized, as illustrated by $1-1-1$.

A grammar is said to be *ambiguous* if there is some expression with more than one parse tree. If every expression has exactly one parse tree, the grammar is *unambiguous.*

Exercise 1.7.1 Draw the parse tree for the derivation of 25 given in this section. Is there another derivation for 25? Is there another parse tree?

1.7.3 Lexical Analysis and Parsing

Most compilers are structured into a series of distinct phases. In a standard compiler, the first two phases are lexical analysis and parsing:

⟨program text⟩ ⟶ [lexical analyzer] ⟶ [parser] ⟶ . . . rest of compiler . . .

Lexical analysis typically separates input characters into tokens and identifies the keywords of the language (also called "reserved words"). Parsing determines whether the program satisfies the conditions imposed by the context-free grammar of the language. In the process, a syntactically correct program is converted from a linear sequence of symbols to a tree representation. Although it is possible for the resulting tree to be the actual parse tree of the input program, this is not necessary. What we generally want is a parse tree for some related program, in a grammar that may be simpler. For example, if the input program contains parentheses, these need not occur in the parser output, since parenthesization is determined by the tree structure. Therefore, for the purposes of this book, we will consider a parser to be an algorithm that takes a string generated by one grammar as input and produces, as output, a parse tree for a possibly different grammar.

In programming language theory, we prefer to work with parsed expressions, instead of text strings. The reason is that parsing resolves ambiguities that are routine and syntactic and have nothing to do with more fundamental properties of programs. Just as compilers are structured so that program analysis and code generation phases take parsed programs as input, our mathematical treatment of programs works best if we assume programs are already parsed.

The traditional terminology of the field is that programs are written according to a *concrete syntax,* which specifies how expressions may (or must) be parenthesized, the spelling of keywords, and so on. The output of parsing may be a parse tree for an *abstract syntax,* which may be a grammar that does not include such things as parenthesization, since this has been resolved by the parser. The parse tree for an expression, written in the abstract syntax, is called an *abstract syntax tree.* In programming language theory, we write expressions in the usual way, but read these strings of symbols as if they are shorthand for some abstract syntax tree.

Example 1.7.2 There are several reasonable ways to write arithmetic expressions. One common variation is the position of the operand in an expression. In prefix expressions, the operand comes first, while postfix expressions have the operand last, and infix in the middle. These three choices are illustrated in the following three grammars.

$p \ ::= \ 0 \mid 1 \mid +pp \mid -pp$ (prefix expressions)

$s \ ::= \ 0 \mid 1 \mid ss+ \mid ss-$ (postfix expressions)

$i \ ::= \ 0 \mid 1 \mid (i+i) \mid (i-i)$ (infix expressions)

Regardless of which we choose as concrete syntax, we can parse expressions to the abstract syntax

$e \ ::= \ 0 \mid 1 \mid e+e \mid e-e$

More precisely, given any prefix, postfix or infix expression, we can write a unique parse tree in the fourth grammar that faithfully captures the syntactic structure and meaning of the expression. For example, the expressions $+-111$, $111-+$ and $(1-1)+1$ are all faithfully represented by the parse tree

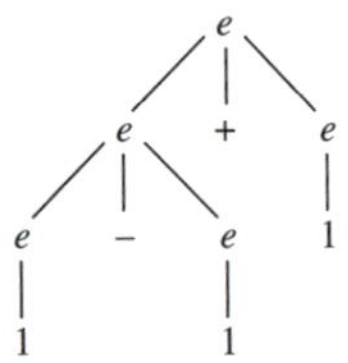

This would be the abstract syntax tree for each of these expressions.

Note that in prefix and postfix notation, parentheses are unnecessary. For example, the prefix expression $+-+0111$ can only be parenthesized as $+(-(+01)1)1$ and the postfix expression $010++$ can only be parenthesized as $0(10+)+$. However, parentheses are needed in the concrete syntax of infix expressions, since $1-1+1$ can be parenthesized as $(1-1)+1$ or $1-(1+1)$. ■

The useful syntactic conventions of *precedence* and *right-* or *left-associativity* are illustrated briefly by example in the following exercise. For more information, the reader may consult a compiler text such as [ASU86].

Exercise 1.7.3 A programming language designer might decide that expressions should include addition, subtraction, and multiplication and write the following *abstract syntax:*

$$e \ ::= \ 0 \mid 1 \mid e + e \mid e - e \mid e * e$$

(a) Explain why this is a perfectly reasonable abstract syntax for an expression language but not (by itself) a good concrete syntax.

We can make parsing "unambiguous" by adopting parsing conventions. Specifically, a plausible concrete syntax might be

$$e \ ::= \ 0 \mid 1 \mid (e + e) \mid (e - e) \mid (e * e) \mid e + e \mid e - e \mid e * e$$

combined with two parsing conventions that take effect when an expression is not fully parenthesized. The first convention is that $*$ has a higher *precedence* than $+$ and $-$, which have equal precedence. An unparenthesized expression $e\ op_1\ e\ op_2\ e$ is parsed as if parentheses are inserted around the operator of higher precedence. The second convention is that when identical operators, or operators of equal precedence, appear contiguously, the operations are associated to the left. This parses $e\ op\ e\ op\ e$ as if it were $(e\ op\ e)\ op\ e$. Write abstract syntax trees for the following expressions.

(b) $1 - 1 * 1$.

(c) $1 - 1 + 1$.

(d) $1 - 1 + 1 - 1 + 1$ if we give $+$ higher precedence than $-$.

1.7.4 Example Mathematical Interpretation

We may interpret the expressions given in Section 1.7.2 as natural numbers using induction on the structure of parse trees. More specifically, we define a function $\mathcal{E}$ from parse trees to natural numbers, defining the function on a compound expression by referring to its value on simpler expressions. An historical convention is to write $[\![e]\!]$ for any parse tree of the expression e. When we write $[\![e_1 + e_2]\!]$, for example, we mean a parse tree of the form

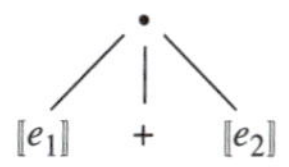

with $[\![e_1]\!]$ and $[\![e_2]\!]$ as immediate subtrees.

Using this notation, we may define the meaning $\mathcal{E}[\![e]\!]$ of an expression e, according to its parse tree $[\![e]\!]$, as follows:

$$\begin{aligned}
\mathcal{E}[\![0]\!] &= \underline{0}\\
\mathcal{E}[\![1]\!] &= \underline{1}\\
&\vdots\\
\mathcal{E}[\![9]\!] &= \underline{9}\\
\mathcal{E}[\![nd]\!] &= \mathcal{E}[\![n]\!] * \underline{10} + \mathcal{E}[\![d]\!]\\
\mathcal{E}[\![e_1 + e_2]\!] &= \mathcal{E}[\![e_1]\!] + \mathcal{E}[\![e_2]\!]\\
\mathcal{E}[\![e_1 - e_2]\!] &= \mathcal{E}[\![e_1]\!] - \mathcal{E}[\![e_2]\!]
\end{aligned}$$

In words, the value associated with a parse tree of the form $[\![e_1 + e_2]\!]$, for example, is the sum of the values given to the subtrees $[\![e_1]\!]$ and $[\![e_2]\!]$. Since these parse trees are shorter than the parse tree $[\![e_1 + e_2]\!]$ we may assume inductively that the function $\mathcal{E}$ is already defined on $[\![e_1]\!]$ and $[\![e_2]\!]$. This is the sense in which the definition of $\mathcal{E}$ is "by induction on the structure of (parse trees of) expressions." For those uncomfortable or unfamiliar with this form of induction, a summary of various forms of induction is given in Section 1.8. On the right of the equal signs, numbers and arithmetic operations $*$, $+$ and $-$ are meant to mean the actual natural numbers $\underline{0}, \ldots, \underline{10}$ and the standard integer operations of multiplication, addition and subtraction. In contrast, the symbols $+$ and $-$ in double square brackets on the left of the equal signs are symbols of the object language, the language of arithmetic expressions.

The main property to observe about this definition is that the meaning of a term depends on how it is parsed. If we take the example $6 - 3 - 2$, then we have two possibilities for $[\![6 - 3 - 2]\!]$. Both have the form $[\![e_1 - e_2]\!]$, but in one we have $e_1 \equiv 6$ and in the other $e_1 \equiv 6 - 3$. Using the first tree, we may work out the meaning of the term as

$$\begin{aligned}
\mathcal{E}[\![6 - 3 - 2]\!] &= \mathcal{E}[\![6]\!] - \mathcal{E}[\![3 - 2]\!]\\
&= \underline{6} - (\mathcal{E}[\![3]\!] - \mathcal{E}[\![2]\!])\\
&= \underline{6} - \underline{1}\\
&= \underline{5}
\end{aligned}$$

In general, we will define the syntax of terms using ambiguous grammars, but use parentheses or syntactic conventions such as precedence or association to the left to identify the intended parsing of each expression we write. In this view, using our example grammar without parentheses, the parentheses in $(1 - 1) + 1$ are not symbols of the object language, but additional symbols that indicate a specific abstract syntax tree. This abstract syntax tree represents the parenthesization of this expression by its tree structure.

1.8 Induction

This book contains many proofs by induction. The most common forms are induction on the structure of expressions and induction on the length or structure of proofs. This section explains these forms of induction and puts them in perspective by presenting some other forms of induction, beginning with induction on the natural numbers. In the process of covering induction on proofs, we also review some basic terminology and properties of formal proof systems. While some readers may choose to review induction on natural numbers and expressions immediately, the later topics in this section are more likely to be useful as reference for later parts of the book.

There are many books with additional discussion of induction at approximately this level, such as [AU92, Win93, MW90]. More thorough mathematical treatments of inductive proofs and inductive definitions may be found in [Acz77, Mos74].

1.8.1 Induction on the Natural Numbers

A simple and intuitive way to think of induction on the natural numbers is that it is a method for writing down an infinite proof in a finite way. Suppose we have a property P that we would like to prove for every natural number. For example, $P(n)$ might be the simple property "n is either odd or even." One way to prove $P(n)$ for every n, if we had an infinite amount of time and an infinite sheet of paper to write on, would be to write out the proof of $P(0)$, then write out the proof of $P(1)$, then write out the proof of $P(2)$, and so on. This is not really feasible, but if it were, the result should certainly be considered a proof. The value of induction is that it provides a simple way of demonstrating that if we had infinite time and space, we could write down a proof of $P(n)$ for every natural number n.

The most common form of induction on the natural numbers is this:

Natural Number Induction, Form 1: To prove that $P(n)$ is true for every natural number n, it is sufficient to prove $P(0)$ and to prove that for any natural number m, if $P(m)$ is true then $P(m+1)$ must also be true.

The proof of $P(0)$ is called the *base case* and the proof that $P(m)$ implies $P(m+1)$ is called the *induction step.* When we assume $P(m)$ in order to prove $P(m+1)$ in the induction step, this assumption is called the *induction hypothesis.* Sometimes natural-number induction is presented using a template like this:

Goal: Prove $P(n)$ for every natural number n.

Base case: Prove $P(0)$.

Induction step: Prove that for any natural number m, if $P(m)$ then $P(m+1)$.

It is easy to argue that if we can prove the base case and the induction step, then we could in principle write out the proof of $P(n)$ for every natural number n. We would begin by writing the base case at the top of our infinite sheet of paper. Then, since $P(0)$ implies $P(1)$, we can use the fact that we have already proved $P(0)$ to prove $P(1)$. Now we have a proof of $P(0)$ and a proof of $P(1)$. Repeating this idea, we can use the proof of $P(1)$ to write out a proof of $P(2)$, then the proof of $P(2)$ to write out a proof of $P(3)$, and so on indefinitely, eventually proving $P(n)$ for each n. Since the base case and the induction step are all that we needed to construct this "infinite proof," the base case and induction step for P certainly must imply $P(n)$ for every natural number n. In other words, induction is an intuitively sound (correct) proof method for establishing facts about the natural numbers. It is not clear that every "infinite proof" can be captured by an inductive argument, but the reader should be ready to believe that when we have a proof by induction, the conclusion must be true. We give a very simple example to illustrate the method.

Example 1.8.1 There is a story claiming that as a young child, the mathematician Gauss derived the formula

$$\sum_{i=1}^{n} i = \frac{n(n+1)}{2}$$

for the sum of the first n integers greater than 0. Gauss apparently figured this out when his teacher gave him the tedious chore of adding up the first hundred numbers, presumably in an attempt to keep him quiet. If we let $sum(n) = \sum_{i=1}^{n} i$ be the sum of the first n numbers, then we can easily prove by induction that for every natural number n, $sum(n) = n(n+1)/2$. For clarity, we use the template above.

Goal: Prove $sum(n) = n(n+1)/2$ for every natural number n.

Base case: We must prove $sum(0) = 0(0+1)/2$. This is an easy calculation.

Induction step: We must show that for any natural number n, if $sum(n) = n(n+1)/2$ then $sum(n+1) = (n+1)(n+2)/2$. We therefore assume that $sum(n) = n(n+1)/2$ for some (arbitrary) natural number, n, and show that this holds for the next natural number, $n+1$. Since the sum of the first $n+1$ numbers is just the sum of the first n, plus $n+1$, we have $sum(n+1) = sum(n) + (n+1)$. We may now apply the induction hypothesis, namely, $sum(n) = n(n+1)/2$. This gives us

$$sum(n+1) = sum(n) + (n+1) = n(n+1)/2 + (n+1),$$

which completes the proof since it is an easy calculation to show that $n(n+1)/2 + (n+1) = (n+1)(n+2)/2$. ■

There is an equivalent form of natural number induction that has a stronger-looking induction hypothesis. This may also be understood by thinking about infinite proofs. If we have written proofs of $P(0), P(1), \ldots, P(n)$ and our next task is to write out the proof for $n + 1$, then we should be able to use all of the facts $P(0), P(1), \ldots, P(n)$, not just $P(n)$. This leads to a second form that may be easier to use in some cases.

Natural Number Induction, Form 2: To prove that $P(n)$ is true for every natural number n, it is sufficient to prove that for any natural number m, if $P(i)$ is true for all $i < m$, then $P(m)$ must also be true.

In this form of induction, there is no base case, only an induction step. In the induction step, we assume that $P(i)$ is true for all $i < m$, which is again called the *induction hypothesis,* and show that $P(m)$ is true. In practice, we often treat the special case $m = 0$ separately since there are no natural numbers less than 0. The second form of natural-number induction is sometimes called *strong induction* or *complete induction,* but from a logical point of view there is nothing stronger or more complete about it than the first form.

Example 1.8.2 The second form of natural-number induction is more convenient for proving that every natural number greater than 1 is the product of primes. The reason is that when we factor a number $n > 1$ that is not prime, we generally get numbers that are less than $n - 1$. Therefore, it is useful to have an induction hypothesis that covers all numbers less than n. (We say a natural number is *composite* if it is the product of two natural numbers greater than 1, and *prime* otherwise.)

Let P be the property

$$P(n) \stackrel{\text{def}}{=} \text{if } n > 1 \text{ then there exist prime numbers } p_1, \ldots, p_k \text{ with } n = p_1 \ldots p_k.$$

Using the second form of induction, it suffices to show, for arbitrary m, if $P(i)$ for all $i < m$ then $P(m)$. Let m be any natural number. If $m \leq 1$, or m is prime, then it is easy to conclude $P(m)$. In the remaining case, m must be the product of two numbers, $m = m_1 m_2$, with both m_1 and m_2 greater than 1. The induction hypothesis is that $P(i)$ is true for all $i < m$. Since $m_1, m_2 < m$, it follows immediately from the induction hypothesis that m_1 and m_2 are both products of primes. Therefore m must also be a product of primes. Thus, by the second form of induction, we may conclude that every number greater than 1 is the product of primes. The reader may enjoy trying to prove this using the first form of induction. ∎

It is worth taking the time to show that even though the second form of induction may look more powerful, the first form of natural number induction implies the second. Let us assume that the first form of induction holds for every property of the natural numbers and that, for some property P, we can prove that if $P(i)$ is true for all $i < m$ then $P(m)$. We will show $\forall n.\, P(n)$ using only the first form of induction. The trick is to let Q be the property

$$Q(m) \stackrel{\text{def}}{=} \text{for all } i < m,\ P(i).$$

By the first form of induction, we can show $\forall n.\, Q(n)$ by showing the base case, $Q(0)$, and the induction step, $\forall m.\, (Q(m) \supset Q(m+1))$. Since there are no natural numbers less than 0, the base case is true, regardless of the property P. Therefore, we need only show the induction step, $Q(m) \supset Q(m+1)$ for every m. By definition of Q, $Q(m)$ means for all $i < m$, $P(i)$ and $Q(m+1)$ means for all $i < m+1$, $P(i)$. However, the only number covered by $Q(m+1)$ that is not already covered by $Q(m)$ is $P(m)$. Consequently, all we need to show is that if $P(i)$ for all $i < m$, then $P(m)$. But this was our original assumption about the property P. Therefore, the first form of induction implies the second. It is left to the reader, as Exercise 1.8.4, to show the converse.

Natural-number induction can also be used to prove properties of elements of other sets, using functions into the natural numbers. For example, we may establish some property of trees using natural-number induction on the size or height of trees. This is illustrated in Example 1.8.3 below. In more general terms, we can apply natural-number induction to a set A using any function $f\colon A \to \mathcal{N}$. (Of course, one function from A to $\mathcal{N}$ might make it possible to prove the property we are interested in while another function might not.) Using a function $f\colon A \to \mathcal{N}$, we can convert a property P of elements of A into a property on the natural numbers by defining

$$Q(n) \stackrel{\text{def}}{=} \forall a \in A.\, \text{if } f(a) = n \text{ then } P(a)$$

If we want to prove $P(a)$ for every $a \in A$, then since f maps every element of A to some natural number, it suffices to prove $Q(n)$ for every natural number n. If we use the first form of natural-number induction, then in the base case we must prove $P(a)$ for all a with $f(a) = 0$. In the induction step, we assume $P(a)$ for all a with $f(a) = n$ and prove $P(a)$ for all a with $f(a) = n + 1$. This general idea is used in Exercise 1.8.5.

Example 1.8.3 We illustrate natural-number induction on the height of trees. For the purposes of this example, a *binary tree* is either empty, a leaf or an "internal node" with two subtrees. Some examples are shown in Figure 1.1. The first, (a), is a single leaf, the second, (b), an internal node with two subtrees and the third, (c), consists of an internal node with two subtrees, one of them empty. The *height of a tree* is the length of the longest path from an internal node downward to a leaf. The tree (a) in Figure 1.1 has height 0, tree (b) height 1, and tree (c) height 2. Note that this definition gives both an empty tree and a single leaf height 0.

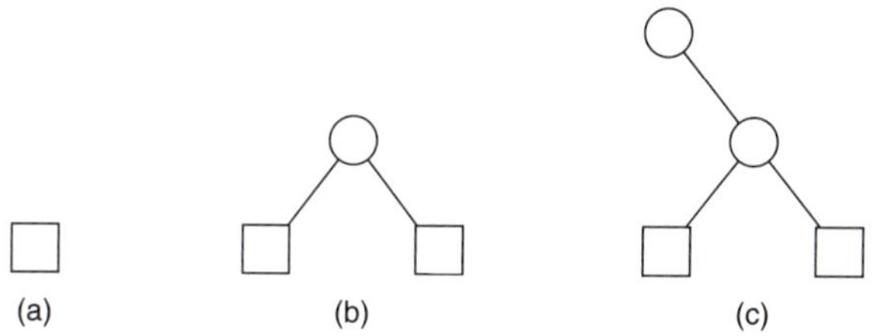

Figure 1.1
Binary trees.

We will prove that the number of leaves of any binary tree is at most one plus the number of internal nodes, using natural-number induction on the height of trees. More specifically, we define the property P of binary trees by

$P(t) \stackrel{\text{def}}{=}$ tree t has at most one more leaf than internal nodes.

Using the function $height : Trees \to \mathcal{N}$, we formulate the following property Q of natural numbers:

$Q(n) \stackrel{\text{def}}{=} \forall$ trees t, if $height(t) = n$ then $P(t)$.

We will prove $\forall n.\ Q(n)$ using the second form of natural-number induction since the two subtrees of an internal node may have different heights.

Let n be any natural number. We assume that for any $i < n$ and any tree t, if $height(t) = i$ then $P(t)$. We must show that for all trees t, if $height(t) = n$ then $P(t)$.

We first consider the special case $n = 0$. Since there is no natural number $i < 0$, we must prove directly that if $height(t) = 0$ then $P(t)$. However, this is easy to do. There are two trees with height 0, the empty tree and a single leaf. In each case, the number of leaves is clearly no greater than 1. This completes the proof for the special case $n = 0$.

If $n > 0$, then any tree t of height n must consist of an internal node with two subtrees, t_1 and t_2. Since the heights of t_1 and t_2 are both less than n, we may assume $P(t_1)$ and $P(t_2)$. The number of leaves of t is the sum of the leaves of the two subtrees, while the number of internal nodes is one greater than the sum of the internal nodes. Writing $leaves(s)$ for the number of leaves of tree s and $nodes(s)$ for the number of internal nodes, we therefore have

$$leaves(t) = leaves(t_1) + leaves(t_2) \leq nodes(t_1) + 1 + nodes(t_2) + 1 = nodes(t) + 1.$$

This completes the proof that the number of leaves of any binary tree is at most one plus the number of internal nodes. ■

Exercise 1.8.4 Prove that the second form of natural-number induction implies the first. More specifically, assume that for some property P, we know that for all m, if $P(m)$ then $P(m+1)$. Use the second form of natural-number induction to prove that $P(n)$ is true for every natural number n.

Exercise 1.8.5 We can prove $P(n)$ for all of the positive and negative integers (including 0) using a form of "integer" induction. Specifically, we show $P(0)$ as the base case and, as the induction step, show that $P(n)$ implies both $P(n-1)$ and $P(n+1)$. Explain intuitively why this makes sense and prove that this principle follows from either the first or the second form of natural-number induction given in this section.

1.8.2 Induction on Expressions and Proofs

As illustrated in Example 1.8.3, we can use natural-number induction to prove properties of trees (or other objects), as long as we have a way of associating a natural number with each tree. We can also formulate independent induction principles for trees and certain other mathematical objects. The important property, as characterized mathematically in Section 1.8.3, is that we must be able to arrange the objects in some order such that each object occurs at most a finite number of steps above some minimal object. Intuitively, this kind of ordering would allow us to write out a form of infinite proof, eventually covering each object we are interested in. For the examples we consider, our direct induction principles can be derived from natural-number induction. Or, conversely, we can consider natural-number induction a special case of the more general principle.

Induction on Expressions

As illustrated in Section 1.7, we often define sets of expressions using grammars. Let us use the grammar

$$e \ ::= \ 0 \mid 1 \mid v \mid e+e \mid e*e$$

as an example, where we assume that there is an infinite set $\mathcal{V}$ of variable symbols, and v in this grammar means that any element of $\mathcal{V}$ is an expression. The expressions generated by this grammar are precisely the strings that have a derivation or, equivalently, a parse tree, as explained in Section 1.7.2. Some examples are $0+1*x+y$ and $x+x+x+y$, assuming $x, y \in \mathcal{V}$. Since every expression has a parse tree, we can prove facts about expressions using induction on the height of parse trees, following the pattern illustrated in Example 1.8.3. More specifically, if P is a property of expressions, we can define a property Q of natural numbers by

$$Q(n) \stackrel{\text{def}}{=} \forall \text{ trees } t.\ \text{if } \mathit{height}(t) = n \text{ and } t \text{ is a parse tree of } e \text{ then } P(e)$$

Notice that this is a sensible property of natural numbers even when some expressions may have more than one parse tree. An alternative that often leads to cleaner proofs is to use a separate form of induction for expressions. We will explain this form of induction by considering the essential steps of an inductive proof using the natural numbers.

Suppose we begin with a property P on trees and define an associated property Q on the natural numbers as above. If we use natural-number induction to prove $\forall n.\ Q(n)$, then we will have to prove P directly for parse trees of height zero. For parse trees of height at least one, we can assume P for any expression with a shorter parse tree. For our example grammar, this means that for 0, 1 or a variable v, we must prove P directly. For a compound expression of the form $(e_1 + e_2)$ or $(e_1 * e_2)$, we could assume that P holds for subexpressions e_1 and e_2. Stating this generally for any grammar, we have the following form of induction on the structure of expressions:

Structural Induction, Form 1: To prove that $P(e)$ is true for every expression e generated by some grammar, it is sufficient to prove $P(e)$ for every atomic expression and, for any compound expression e with immediate subexpressions $e_1, \ldots, e_k$, prove that if $P(e_i)$ for $i = 1, \ldots, k$, then $P(e)$.

For the example grammar above, this gives us the following template:

Goal: Prove $P(e)$ for every expression e.

Base cases: Prove $P(0)$, $P(1)$ and $P(v)$ for any variable v.

Induction steps: Prove that for any expressions e_1 and e_2, if $P(e_1)$ and $P(e_2)$ then $P(e_1 + e_2)$ and $P(e_1 * e_2)$.

We have three base cases since there are three forms of atomic expressions without subexpressions, and two induction steps since there are two compound expression forms.

Example 1.8.6 We illustrate structural induction on expressions by proving that every expression given by the grammar above defines a multi-variate function bounded by a certain form of polynomial. More specifically, let P be the property of expressions

$P(e) \stackrel{\text{def}}{=}$ "for any list $v_0, \ldots, v_n$ of variables containing all the variables in e, there is a polynomial $cv_0^k v_1^k \ldots v_n^k$, such that for all natural number values of $v_0, \ldots, v_n$ greater than 0, the value of e is less than the value of the polynomial."

We show that for every expression e, we have $P(e)$, by induction on the structure of expressions. For clarity, we present this using the template above.

Goal: Prove $P(e)$ for every expression e.

Base cases: Prove $P(0)$, $P(1)$ and $P(v_i)$ for any variable v_i. These are immediate since $0 < v_0 v_1 \dots v_n$, $1 < 2v_0 v_1 \dots v_n$ and $v_i < 2v_0 v_1 \dots v_n$ for any values of $v_0, \dots, v_n$ greater than 0.

Induction steps: Prove that for any expressions e and e', if $P(e)$ and $P(e')$ then $P(e + e')$ and $P(e * e')$. Let $v_0, \dots, v_n$ be a list containing all the variables in e and e'. Our induction hypothesis implies that there exist polynomials $cv_0^k \dots v_n^k$ and $c'v_0^{k'} \dots v_n^{k'}$ that are greater than or equal to the values of e and e', respectively, for all natural number values of $v_0, \dots, v_n$ greater than 0. For the compound expression $e + e'$, we can establish $P(e + e')$ using the polynomial

$$(c + c')v_0^{\max(k,k')} \dots v_n^{\max(k,k')}$$

and for $e * e'$ the polynomial

$$cc'v_0^{(k+k')} \dots v_n^{(k+k')}$$

This completes the inductive proof. ■

Although the difference is not usually emphasized as much as for natural-number induction, there is a second form of structural induction that includes all subexpressions in the induction hypothesis.

Structural Induction, Form 2: To prove that $P(e)$ is true for every expression e generated by some grammar, it is sufficient to prove that for any expression e, if $P(e')$ for every subexpression e' of e, then $P(e)$.

The difference between Form 1 and Form 2 is that in the second form, the induction hypothesis includes all subexpressions, not just the immediate subexpressions. (For the expression $x + (y + z)$, the immediate subexpressions are x and $y + z$; the variable y is a subexpression but not an immediate subexpression.)

We can regard each form of natural-number induction as a special case of the corresponding form of structural induction. Specifically, consider the grammar

$$n \ ::= \ 0 \mid succ\, n$$

where intuitively the successor $succ\, n$ of n is $n + 1$. Every natural number can be written down using this grammar, and the two forms of induction on expressions give us exactly the two forms of natural-number induction.

Induction on Proofs

The main ideas behind induction on the structure of proofs are essentially the same as for induction on the structure of expressions. In many respects, both are really forms of induction on trees. Before stating induction on the structure of proofs, we review some basic concepts common to the most common form of proof systems.

A Hilbert-style *proof system* consists of axioms and proof rules. An *axiom* of a proof system is a formula that is provable by definition. An *inference rule* asserts that if some list of formulas is provable, then so is another formula. A *proof,* therefore, is a structured object built from formulas according to constraints established by a set of axioms and inference rules. Proofs are described more fully below.

Axioms and inference rules are generally written as schemes, representing all formulas or proof steps of a given form. For example, the reflexivity axiom for equality

$$e = e \qquad (ref)$$

is called a "scheme with metavariable e". This axiom scheme asserts that every equation of the form $e = e$ is an axiom. In particular, $x = x$, $y = y$ and $3 = 3$ are axioms, provided that x, y and 3 are all well-formed expressions of the language we have in mind. An inference rule scheme generally has the form

$$\frac{A_1 \ \ldots \ A_n}{B}$$

meaning that if we have proofs of formulas of the form $A_1, \ldots, A_n$, then we can combine these to obtain a proof of the corresponding formula B. For example, the inference rule for transitivity of equality is written

$$\frac{e_1 = e_2 \quad e_2 = e_3}{e_1 = e_3} \qquad (trans)$$

This means that if we have a proof of $3 + 5 = 8$ and a proof that $8 = 2^3$, for example, then we can combine these two proofs to form a proof of the equation $3 + 5 = 2^3$. Technically, the formulas above the horizontal line are called the *antecedents* of the proof rule, and the formula below the line the *consequent.*

Formally, a proof can be defined as a sequence of formulas, with each formula either an axiom or following from previous formulas by a single inference rule. This formal definition of proof is often useful; it lends itself to arguments by natural-number induction on the length of the proof (*i.e.*, the length of the sequence). An alternate view is often more insightful, however. Since an inference rule generally has a list of antecedents and one consequent, it is easy to visualize a proof as a form of tree with leaves and internal nodes labeled by formulas. More specifically, we think of each axiom as a possible leaf and each inference rule

$$\frac{A_1 \ \ldots \ A_n}{B}$$

as a possible internal tree node whose subtrees must be proofs of $A_1, \ldots, A_n$. Since this preserves the ordinary orientation of inference rules, it is common to draw proof trees with the trunk or root at the bottom. Thus if we construct a proof of B from proofs of $A_1, \ldots, A_n$, we would draw the resulting tree in the form

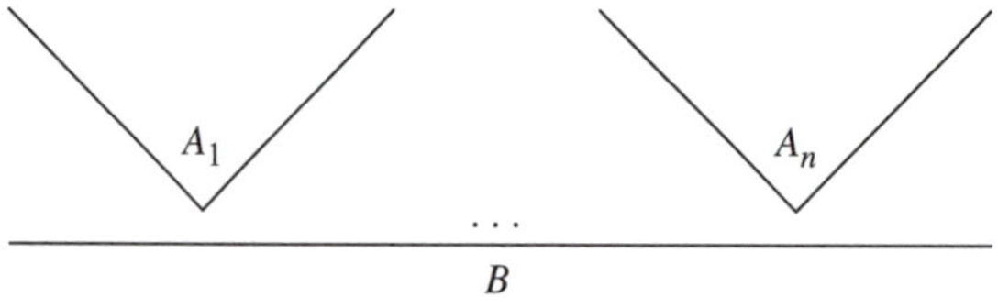

where each of the triangular shapes above the line represents a proof tree whose conclusion is one of the antecedents of the proof rule. One useful consequence of thinking of proofs as trees is that it suggests a form of induction that is essentially the same as induction on the structure of trees.

If we use induction on the height of trees as in Example 1.8.3, the base case establishes the property for each axiom. The induction step will be to assume that the property holds for any shorter proof, and establish the property for a proof ending in an inference rule. This leads to the following form of structural induction on proofs:

Structural Induction on Proofs: To prove that $P(\pi)$ is true for every proof π in some proof system, it is sufficient to show that P holds for every axiom of the proof system and then, assuming that P holds for proofs $\pi_1, \ldots, \pi_k$, prove that $P(\pi)$ for any proof that ends by extending one or more of the proofs $\pi_1, \ldots, \pi_k$ with one inference rule.

Example 1.8.7 We will illustrate induction on the structure of proofs using a simple proof system for inequalities $e \leq e'$, where e and e' are generated by the example grammar

$$e \ ::= \ 0 \mid 1 \mid v \mid e + e \mid e * e$$

also used above. The proof system has two axioms, one stating that $\leq$ is reflexive

$$e \leq e \qquad (refl)$$

and the other that 0 is less than any other expression.

$$0 \leq e \qquad (0 \leq)$$

There is a transitivity inference rule and two additional inference rules giving monotonicity of addition and multiplication.

$$\frac{e \le e' \quad e' \le e''}{e \le e''} \qquad (trans)$$

$$\frac{e_1 \le e_2 \quad e_3 \le e_4}{e_1 + e_3 \le e_2 + e_4} \qquad (+mon)$$

$$\frac{e_1 \le e_2 \quad e_3 \le e_4}{e_1 * e_3 \le e_2 * e_4} \qquad (*mon)$$

This is a relatively weak proof system for the ordinary ordering on natural numbers. However, it is sufficient to illustrate some basic ideas.

A very common property to establish for a proof system is that every provable formula is true (under some specific interpretation of formulas). This is called *soundness* of the proof system. We illustrate induction on the structure of proofs by proving soundness of our example proof system for $\le$, interpreting arithmetic expressions over the natural numbers in the usual way. More precisely, we show that the property

$P(\pi) \stackrel{\text{def}}{=}$ if π is a proof of $e \le e'$ then for all values of variables,

the value of e is $\le$ the value of e'

holds for every proof π in our system. In other words, if we can prove a formula, then the formula is true, for all possible values of the variables that occur in the formula.

The base cases are to establish the property P for each of the axioms. This is easy. Whatever values we give to the variables occurring in an expression e, the value of e is some specific natural number. Therefore, we always have $e \le e$ and $0 \le e$.

There are three induction steps. We show the cases for $(+mon)$ and $(*mon)$ and leave the case for $(trans)$ to the reader. Suppose that we may prove inequalities $e_1 \le e_2$ and $e_3 \le e_4$. Let us pick values for the variables that occur in $e_1, \ldots, e_4$ and call the resulting values of the expressions $n_1, \ldots, n_4$. By the inductive hypothesis, we have $n_1 \le n_2$ and $n_3 \le n_4$. It is easy to see that therefore $n_1 + n_3 \le n_2 + n_4$ and similarly $n_1 * n_3 \le n_2 * n_4$. Since this reasoning applies for all possible values of the variables, the property holds for proofs ending in $(+mon)$ and $(*mon)$. Since the $(trans)$ case is given as Exercise 1.8.10, this concludes the inductive proof. ■

The proof system in Example 1.8.7 is not only useful for proving inequalities that are true for all values of the variables, but also for proving inequalities that follow from additional assumptions. Such additional assumptions are sometimes called *nonlogical axioms*. Intuitively, these are assumptions that are true about a certain situation, but not always true. For example, if we assume that $1 \le x$ and $x \le 5$, we could prove that (under these assumptions) $1 + x \leq x + 5$ using $(+mon)$. This idea also applies to other proof systems, of course. In general, a *proof from assumptions* or *proof from nonlogical axioms* is a proof tree as described above, with each leaf either a (logical) axiom of the proof system or a nonlogical axiom (one of the given assumptions) and each internal node an inference rule of the proof system.

Exercise 1.8.8 Consider the set of variable-free expressions given by the following grammar:

$$e \; ::= \; 0 \mid 2 \mid e + e \mid e * e$$

where $+$ is interpreted as addition and $*$ multiplication, as usual. Use induction on the structure of expressions to show that the value of every expression produced by this grammar is an even number.

Exercise 1.8.9 We can apply structural induction to trees if we think of them as generated by the grammar

$$t \; ::= \; nil \mid leaf \mid node(t, t)$$

Use structural induction on trees (with two base cases and one induction step) to prove that the size of a binary tree is at most 2^h, where h is the height of the tree.

Exercise 1.8.10 Prove the (*trans*) case of the induction on proofs given in Example 1.8.7.

Exercise 1.8.11 Use induction on the structure of proofs to show that if $e \leq e'$ is provable (using the axioms and rules given in this section), then e' is at least as long an expression (counting symbols) as e. Use the form of inductive proof illustrated in Example 1.8.7.

1.8.3 Well-founded Induction

All of the forms of induction we have discussed so far are instances of a general form of induction on what are called "well-founded relations." Although it is seldom necessary to appeal to the general form of well-founded induction, this is occasionally the best way to carry out a proof. Well-founded relations are also important in computer science for their connection with termination of programs (see Section 3.7.3).

A *well-founded relation* on a set A is a binary relation $\prec$ on A with the property that there is no infinite descending sequence $a_0 \succ a_1 \succ a_2 \succ \cdots$. An example is the relation $i \prec j$ if $j = i + 1$ on the natural numbers. As this example illustrates, a well-founded relation does not have to be transitive. It is easy to see that every well-founded relation is irreflexive, *i.e.*, we do not have $a \prec a$ for any $a \in A$. The reason is that if $a \prec a$, then there is an infinite descending sequence $a \succ a \succ a \succ \cdots$.

An equivalent definition is that a binary relation $\prec$ on A is well-founded iff every nonempty subset B of A has a minimal element, where $a \in B$ is *minimal* if there is no $a' \in B$ with $a' \prec a$. This is proved in the following lemma.

Lemma 1.8.12 Let $\prec$ be a binary relation on set A. Then $\prec$ is well-founded iff every nonempty subset of A has a minimal element.

Proof Suppose that $\prec$ is a well-founded relation on A and let $B \subseteq A$ be any nonempty subset. We will show that B has a minimal element. The easiest way to do this is to argue by contradiction. If B does not have a minimal element, then for every $a \in B$ we can find some $a' \in B$ with $a' \prec a$. But in this case, we can construct an infinite decreasing sequence $a_0 \succ a_1 \succ a_2 \succ \ldots$ starting with any $a_0 \in B$ and using the fact that no a_i can be minimal since B has no minimal element. This proves the first half of the lemma.

For the converse, suppose that every subset has a minimal element. Then there can be no infinite decreasing sequence $a_0 \succ a_1 \succ a_2 \succ \ldots$ since such a sequence would give us a set $\{a_0, a_1, a_2, \ldots\}$ without a minimal element. This completes the proof. ∎

Proposition 1.8.13 (Well-founded Induction) Let $\prec$ be a well-founded binary relation on set A and let P be some property on A. If $P(a)$ holds whenever we have $P(b)$ for all $b \prec a$, then $P(a)$ is true for all $a \in A$.

Proof Suppose that for every $a \in A$, we have $P(a)$ if $P(b)$ for all $b \prec a$. (In symbols, we are assuming $\forall a.\ (\forall b.\ (b \prec a \supset P(b)) \supset P(a))$.) We will show that $P(a)$ holds for all $a \in A$ by contradiction. If there is some $x \in A$ with $\neg P(x)$, then the set

$$B = \{a \in A \mid \neg P(a)\}$$

is nonempty. Therefore, by Lemma 1.8.12, the set B must have a minimal element $a \in B$. But since we therefore have $P(b)$ for all $b \prec a$, this contradicts the assumption $\forall b.\ (b \prec a \supset P(b)) \supset P(a)$. This proves the proposition. ∎

Table 1.1 lists the well-founded relation associated with each form of induction we have already considered. A property of well-founded relations that is easy to establish is that the transitive closure of any well-founded relation is also well-founded. This is helpful in understanding the parallel between the two forms of natural-number induction and the two forms of structural induction. In both cases, the well-founded relation giving rise to the second form is just the transitive closure of the relation associated with the first form of induction.

Table 1.1
Well-founded relations for common forms of induction.

Form of Induction	Well-founded Relation
Natural number induction, Form 1	$m \prec n$ if $m + 1 = n$
Natural number induction, Form 2	$m \prec n$ if $m < n$
Structural induction, Form 1	$e \prec e'$ if e is an immediate subexpression of e'
Structural induction, Form 2	$e \prec e'$ if e is a subexpression of e'
Induction on proofs	$\pi \prec \pi'$ if π is the subproof for some antecedent of the last inference rule in proof π'

In each of the examples in Table 1.1, it is easy to see that the listed relation is in fact well-founded. For example, since each subexpression is shorter than the expression that contains it, there can be no infinite sequence of successively smaller subexpressions.

A useful class of well-founded relations that are more complicated than the ones in Table 1.1 are the *lexicographical orderings.* These are essentially dictionary-like orderings on sequences drawn from some ordered set. For simplicity, we just consider orderings on sequences of natural numbers.

A natural ordering on pairs of natural numbers is

$$\langle n, m\rangle \prec \langle n', m'\rangle \quad \text{iff} \quad n < n' \text{ or } (n = n' \text{ and } m < m')$$

In words, we say one pair is less than another if either the first (or "most significant") numbers are ordered, or, if the first numbers are the same, the second numbers are ordered. If we only consider the single-digit numbers $0, \ldots, 9$ and think of a pair $\langle n, m\rangle$ as the two-digit numeral nm, then this is the ordinary numeric ordering.

It is a little tricky to see that the relation $\prec$ on pairs of natural numbers is well-founded. We will argue that there is no infinite decreasing sequence. The trick is to arrange any decreasing sequence of pairs in a two-dimensional array, moving down when the first element decreases and across when the second decreases. Illustrated with specific numbers, the idea is to arrange any decreasing sequence like this:

$$\begin{array}{llllllll}
\langle 5,6\rangle & \succ \langle 5,5\rangle & & & & & & \\
& \succ \langle 4,50\rangle & \succ \langle 4,40\rangle & \succ \langle 4,30\rangle & & & & \\
& & & \succ \langle 3,300\rangle & \succ \langle 3,250\rangle & & & \\
& & & & \succ \langle 2,500\rangle & \succ \langle 2,450\rangle & \succ \langle 2,449\rangle & \succ \langle 2,448\rangle \\
& & & & & & & \vdots
\end{array}$$

For any decreasing sequence, we can see that no row can be infinite, since there is no infinite decreasing sequence of natural numbers. Therefore, if the table is going to be infinite, there must be infinitely many rows. But this is impossible since the first number must decrease each time we go down to another row.

We can generalize this ordering on pairs, which is technically called ω^2, to orderings on triples, sequences of length 4, and so on. We can also extend this ordering to sequences of differing lengths. Writing sequences of natural numbers in the form $\langle n_1, n_2, \ldots, n_k \rangle$, we define the more general ordering by

$$\langle n_1, n_2, \ldots, n_k \rangle \prec \langle m_1, m_2, \ldots, m_\ell \rangle \quad \text{iff} \quad \left[\begin{array}{l} k < \ell \text{ or} \\ k = \ell \text{ and } \exists i \leq k \text{ with} \\ \qquad n_j = m_j \text{ for } j < i \text{ and } n_i < m_i \end{array} \right]$$

In words, we first order sequences by length. Then, for sequences of the same length, we use the natural generalization of the ordering on pairs above, comparing numbers from left to right until two differ. It is a bit harder to draw an "infinite dimensional matrix" showing that this order is well-founded, but the idea is essentially similar to the argument given for the pair ordering above.

Example 1.8.14 We illustrate well-founded induction by proving a "normalization property" of proofs in the system of Example 1.8.7. This example may seem contrived, but it actually corresponds quite closely to the kinds of reasoning about typing derivations and subtyping derivations that appear occasionally in later chapters of the book. The property we will prove is that if there is a proof of an inequality, possibly from some set of assumptions (as described at the end of Section 1.8.2), then there is a proof of the same inequality that does not use (*trans*) after two uses of (+*mon*). (The same property also holds for (∗*mon*) but we will not take the time to show this.) This is best illustrated by example. If we assume $x \leq y \leq z$ and $x' \leq y' \leq z'$, then we can prove $x + x' \leq z + z'$ in two ways. The first,

$$\frac{\dfrac{x \leq y \quad x' \leq y'}{x + x' \leq y + y'} \qquad \dfrac{y \leq z \quad y' \leq z'}{y + y' \leq z + z'}}{x + x' \leq z + z'}$$

has two uses of monotonicity of +, before transitivity while the second

$$\frac{\dfrac{x \leq y \quad y \leq z}{x \leq z'} \qquad \dfrac{x' \leq y' \quad y' \leq z'}{x' \leq z'}}{x + x' \leq z + z'}$$

has two uses of (*trans*) first, followed by (+*mon*). We will show that we can eliminate all occurrences of the first pattern of proof steps from any proof. The reason we might want to do this is that it makes it easier to search for proofs of an inequality. The general principle is that if we know that any provable formula has a proof of a certain form, then we can decide whether a formula is provable by looking for proofs of this certain form.

In outline, our inductive argument will proceed by showing that if a proof has two uses of (+*mon*) before (*trans*), then we can eliminate this pattern of three steps in favor of two uses of (*trans*) followed by (+*mon*). However, in order for this argument to be correct, we must have an inductive hypothesis that applies to the proof produced by this transformation. Since the result of the proof transformation has the same number of proof rules, we cannot use induction on the structure, length or number of proof steps in the proof. In addition, we cannot use induction on the number of patterns that we are trying to eliminate, since our proof transformation moves transitivity toward the leaves, and may introduce new patterns of the form we are trying to eliminate. We could try to do some form of induction on the number of uses of (+*mon*) in the proof, which seems to involve some case analysis on the way in which these rules occur. However, the problem may be solved very simply by defining an appropriate well-founded relation on proofs.

We will order proofs by assigning a sequence of numbers to each proof and ordering these sequences lexicographically. For any proof π, we calculate the degree $deg(\pi)$ of π as follows. First, for each pattern of two uses of (+*mon*) before (*trans*), we count the number of +'s occurring in each of the expressions in the conclusion of (*trans*). If the two expressions differ in the number of +'s, we can just take the maximum of the two numbers. Call this number the *measure* of this pattern of steps. Now, for each measure up to the maximum measure occurring, count up the number of patterns with this measure and sort this sequence of counts (some possibly zero) in order of decreasing associated measure. This sequence of numbers will be our "degree" of the proof. With this form of induction, we can easily carry out the proof. The reason why this works is that whenever we replace two uses of (+*mon*) before (*trans*) in favor of two uses of (*trans*) followed by (+*mon*), we reduce the measure of any new pattern of two uses of (+*mon*) before (*trans*) that is created. ■

Exercise 1.8.15 A *string* s over alphabet Σ is a finite sequence of elements of Σ. In this problem, we use capitals of the ordinary (Roman) alphabet, so that any string s can be written $s = a_1 a_2 \dots a_k$ where each a_i is one of the twenty-six letters A, B, C, ..., Z. A special case is the empty string, written ϵ. Three relations on strings are given below, two well-founded and the other not. For each well-founded relation, give a short explanation of why it is well-founded. For the relation that is not well-founded, give an infinite decreasing sequence.

(a) Relation $\prec_1$ is the ordinary alphabetic order on strings (the "dictionary" ordering).

This is characterized by the following two axioms.

$$\epsilon \prec_1 s \quad \text{iff} \quad s \neq \epsilon$$

$$a_1 s \prec_1 a_2 t \quad \text{iff} \quad a_1 \text{ comes before } a_2 \text{ in the alphabet, or}$$
$$[a_1 = a_2 \text{ and } s \prec_1 t]$$

(b) The second relation orders strings by length:

$$a_1 \ldots a_k \prec_2 b_1 \ldots b_\ell \quad \text{iff} \quad k < \ell.$$

(c) The third relation, $\prec_3$, combines the previous two by using $\prec_2$ on strings of different length, and $\prec_1$ on strings of the same length.

$$a_1 \ldots a_k \prec_3 b_1 \ldots b_\ell \quad \text{iff} \quad k < \ell \text{ or } [k = \ell \text{ and } a_1 \ldots a_k \prec_1 b_1 \ldots b_\ell]$$

2 The Language PCF

2.1 Introduction

This chapter presents a language for *Programming Computable Functions* called PCF, originally formulated by Dana Scott in an influential unpublished manuscript [Sco69]. It is a typed functional language based on lambda calculus. The language is designed to be easily analyzed, rather than as a practical language for writing large programs. However, with certain extensions to the surface syntax, it is possible to write many functional programs in a comfortable style. The presentation of PCF here is informal in the sense that we will discuss the constructs of the language, and the axiomatic, operational and denotational semantics, without going into the proofs of basic theorems. The main topics of the chapter are:

- Introduction to syntax and semantics of typed lambda calculus and related languages by example.
- Treatment of recursive definitions by fixed-point operators.
- Discussion of axiomatic, operational and denotational semantics, with a summary of the relationships between them.
- Demonstration that basic programming methods may be carried out in a simplified functional language.
- Study of expressive power and limitations of the language using operational semantics.

The main goals are to develop a feel for the programming capabilities of lambda-calculus-based languages and summarize general properties and techniques that apply to a variety of languages. Operational semantics are considered in more depth than denotational semantics, since later chapters focus on the denotational and axiomatic semantics. We discuss "programming techniques" at some length, to give some intuition for the way that familiar programming constructs may be represented in lambda calculus and prove both positive and negative results about the expressiveness of PCF. The chapter concludes with a brief overview of extensions and variations of PCF that have either practical or theoretical significance. The technical theorems about PCF that are not proved in this chapter are proved in Chapters 5 and 8, as special cases of more general results.

For those familiar with denotational semantics, we point out several differences between the use of lambda calculus in this book and the traditional use of lambda calculus in denotational semantics. One is typing. The meta-language in standard texts on denotational semantics, such as [Gor79, MS76, Sch86, Sto77], is not explicitly typed. In contrast, we use only typed lambda calculus. This clarifies the kind of value each expression defines, and simplifies the technical analysis in several ways. Another difference is that we regard PCF itself as a language for writing programs, rather than solely as a meta-language for giving semantics to other languages. One reason for this approach is to develop some intuition for the expressive power of typed lambda calculus. Another is to suggest that lambda calculus may be used not only for denotational semantics, but for studying operational and pragmatic issues in programming language analysis and design.

The evaluation order used in PCF is *lazy* or *left-most*. This is the evaluation order used in the pure functional programming languages Haskell [HF92, $H^{+}92$] and Miranda [Tur85]. (See [Pey87] for information on the implementation of lazy functional languages.) In contrast, the languages Lisp [McC60, McC78, Ste84] and ML (Mil85a), MTH90, MT91, Ull94] use an *eager* form of evaluation. While most practical languages use eager evaluation, there are some advantages (as well as disadvantages) to developing a basic theory using lazy evaluation. To a first approximation, the choice between evaluation orders is a matter of taste. Since we can simulate eager reduction in a lazy language, and conversely [Plo75], the reduction systems are theoretically equivalent. The denotational semantics are also interdefinable, although there are some simplifications in the eager case. On the other hand, the axiomatic semantics of eager languages seem more complicated. The main reasons we prefer to study lazy PCF in this book are that this gives the simplest correspondence between axiomatic, operational, and denotational semantics, and also the most flexibility in operational semantics since we have equivalent deterministic, nondeterministic and parallel forms of program execution. The theory is also older and more fully developed. Since similar techniques apply in both cases, the ideas described in this book are useful for analyzing both forms of evaluation. A general setting for considering both evaluation orders is the extension of PCF with lifted types, described in Section 2.6.4.

2.2 Syntax of PCF

2.2.1 Overview

Every expression of PCF has a unique type. Therefore, we may summarize the constructs of PCF by listing the types of the language. The basic values are natural numbers and booleans (truth values *true* and *false*), which have types *nat* and *bool*, respectively. PCF also has pairs, which belong to cartesian product types, and functions, belonging to function types. The PCF notation for the cartesian product of types σ and τ is $\sigma \times \tau$. For example, the type of natural number pairs is written $nat \times nat$. The type of a function with domain σ and range τ is written $\sigma \to \tau$. Some notational conventions regarding type expressions are that $\to$ associates to the right, and $\times$ has higher precedence than $\to$. Thus $\sigma \to \tau \to \rho$ is parenthesized as $\sigma \to (\tau \to \rho)$, and $\sigma \times \tau \to \rho$ as $(\sigma \times \tau) \to \rho$.

One property of PCF is that only expressions that satisfy certain typing constraints are actually considered part of the language. For example, although PCF has addition, the expression *true* + 1 is not considered well formed. (It does not make sense to add a truth value to a natural number.) With variables, the typing conditions depend on the context in which an expression is used. For example, $x + 5$ only makes sense if the variable x is declared to have type *nat*. A precise description of PCF, using typing rules and assumptions about the types of variables, is given in Chapter 4. In the following informal presentation, we assume we have infinitely many variables of each type and that we can tell what type each variable has. When we write $\lambda x\colon\sigma$, it is implicitly assumed that x is a variable of type σ. When we need to refer to the types of variables that are not lambda bound, we will simply write typing assumptions $x_1\colon\sigma_1, \ldots, x_k\colon\sigma_k$ in parentheses or in the text.

A general syntactic issue, discussed in Section 1.7.1, is the distinction between object notation and meta-notation. The syntax of PCF, like other languages we will consider, is defined using some set *Var* of variables, some set *Cst* of constant symbols, and other classes of symbols. We do not need to be concerned with what the elements of the set *Var* actually are, as long as we have infinitely many of them (so we don't run out) and we can tell whether two are distinct or the same. We say that the symbols and expressions of PCF belong to the *object language* since PCF is the object of study. In studying PCF, it is convenient to use additional symbols to stand for arbitrary symbols and expressions of the object language. These are said to be symbols of the *meta-language,* the language we use in our study of the object language.

We use letters $x, y, z, \ldots$, possibly with subscripts, primes or superscripts, as meta-variables for arbitrary variables of PCF (elements of *Var*) and letters $M, N, P, \ldots$, again possibly with subscripts, primes or superscripts, as meta-variables for expressions of PCF. It is possible for two metavariables, x and y, to stand for the same object variable. We use the symbol $\equiv$ for syntactic equality of object expressions, writing $x \equiv y$ if x and y stand for the same variable of PCF and $x \not\equiv y$ to indicate that they are distinct variables. If we say, "let x and y be variables" or "let M and N be terms," then these could be distinct variables or expressions, or syntactically identical.

2.2.2 Booleans and Natural Numbers

The basic boolean expressions are the constants *true* and *false*, and the boolean-valued conditional expressions

$\texttt{if}\ \langle boolean\rangle\ \texttt{then}\ \langle boolean\rangle\ \texttt{else}\ \langle boolean\rangle.$

The basic natural number expressions include *numerals*

$0, 1, 2, 3, \ldots,$

ordinary interpreter fairly closely. We will discuss connections between nondeterministic and deterministic reduction in Section 2.3.4.

The reader may have noticed that we do *not* have the equational axiom $Eq?\,M\,M = true$, for arbitrary natural-number expression M. One reason is that the reduction axiom $Eq?\,M\,M \rightarrow true$ would lead to a non-confluent reduction system for PCF (see Section 2.3.4). In reducing an expression $Eq?\,M\,N$, we must first simplify M and N to numerals. This corresponds to actual implementations, where a test for natural number equality involves evaluating both expressions.

The denotational semantics of the basic natural number and boolean expressions falls under the general pattern of algebraic terms and their interpretation in a multi-sorted algebra, which is covered in detail in Chapter 3. To give a hint of things to come, we will summarize some of the main ideas here. We assign a "mathematical meaning," or *denotation* to every natural number and boolean expression by first choosing a set N of natural-number values and a set B of boolean values. In the standard semantics of natural-number and boolean expressions alone, these would be the usual set of natural numbers and the usual set of booleans. However, in the context of PCF, we will also include an extra element in each set to account for the fact that PCF has partial recursive functions on natural numbers, in addition to total functions, and similarly for booleans. The extra element arises from the fact that we may treat a partial function from N to N as a total function from N to $N \cup \{\infty\}$, as is sometimes done in recursive function theory.

Once we have chosen a set of values for each type, we can give meaning to expressions by choosing a value for each free variable. Then, using induction on expressions, we specify a unique mathematical value (element of the appropriate set) for each expression. In the standard interpretation of natural numbers and boolean expressions, $2 + 3$ has its usual value, 5, and so on, so there is nothing very surprising in this case. Since the denotational semantics of basic data types are a special case of first-order semantics (or model theory), the basic idea is probably familiar from logic. The main reason for mentioning the denotational semantics at this point is to contrast this with the axiomatic semantics (equational proof system) and operational semantics (reduction rules), which are entirely syntactic.

Definable Functions

Even without lambda abstraction, we can think of basic PCF natural-number expressions as defining numeric functions. To describe this precisely, we need to distinguish between the natural numbers and the symbols (called *numerals)* used in PCF. If $n \in \mathcal{N}$ is a natural number, then one of the symbols $0, 1, 2, \ldots$ of PCF is the numeral for n, *i.e.*, the symbol we usually use to write n on a piece of paper. For any $n \in \mathcal{N}$, let us write $\lceil n \rceil$ for this numeral. Using this notation, we say an expression $M\colon nat$ with natural number variable x *defines a numeric function* $f\colon \mathcal{N} \rightarrow \mathcal{N}$ *implicitly* if, for every natural number $n \in \mathcal{N}$, we have $[\ulcorner n\urcorner/x]M \twoheadrightarrow \ulcorner f(n)\urcorner$. In words, we can simplify the expression $[\ulcorner n\urcorner/x]M$, with the numeral for n in place of x, to the numeral for the function value $f(n)$.

Example 2.2.1 The numeric function $f(n) = n + 5$ is defined implicitly by the expression $x + 5$, where x ranges over natural numbers. ■

The notion of implicit definition may be extended to other types. A boolean expression M: *bool* with boolean variable x *defines a boolean function* f *implicitly* if $[true/x]M \twoheadrightarrow \ulcorner f(true)\urcorner$ and $[false/x]M \twoheadrightarrow \ulcorner f(false)\urcorner$. It is easy to see that negation is defined implicitly by the expression `if` x `then` *false* `else` *true*. Binary functions may also be defined implicitly, as in Exercises 2.2.2 and 2.2.3.

With recursion, we will be able to define all computable numeric functions in PCF. However, using only the basic natural-number and boolean expressions given in this section, there are many functions that cannot be defined. One example is given in Exercise 2.2.3.

Exercise 2.2.2 Write expressions with boolean variables x and y which implicitly define the conjunction $(x \wedge y)$ and disjunction $(x \vee y)$ of x and y.

Exercise 2.2.3 Show that the exponentiation function is not implicitly definable using PCF natural number and boolean expressions. In other words, prove that there is no basic natural number expression M with numeric variables x and y such that $[\ulcorner n\urcorner/x]([\ulcorner m\urcorner/y]M)$ has value $\ulcorner n^m\urcorner$.

2.2.3 Pairing and Functions

In PCF, we can form ordered pairs and functions of any type. If M and N are any PCF expressions, then $\langle M, N\rangle$ is the ordered pair whose first component has the same value as M and second component has the same value as N. Every PCF pair has a cartesian product type which is determined by the following simple rule: if M has type σ and N has type τ, then the pair $\langle M, N\rangle$ has type $\sigma \times \tau$. For example, $\langle 3, 5\rangle$ is an ordered pair of natural numbers, with $\langle 3, 5\rangle : nat \times nat$, and the "nested pair" $\langle 3, \langle 5, 7\rangle\rangle$ has type $nat \times (nat \times nat)$.

In addition to forming pairs, we can also "take pairs apart" using projection operations. The projection operations $\mathbf{Proj}_1$ and $\mathbf{Proj}_2$ return the first and second components of a pair. This is formalized in the two equational axioms

$$\mathbf{Proj}_1\langle M, N\rangle = M, \quad \mathbf{Proj}_2\langle M, N\rangle = N. \qquad (proj)$$

The final axiom for pairing is based on the idea that two pairs with the same first and second components must be equal (*i.e.*, the same pair). Since any $P\colon\sigma \times \tau$ is a pair, we can form a pair $\langle(\mathbf{Proj}_1 P), (\mathbf{Proj}_2 P)\rangle$ from the first and second components of P. This must be the same as P, since it has the same components. This gives us the equational axiom

$$\langle(\mathbf{Proj}_1 P), (\mathbf{Proj}_2 P)\rangle = P. \qquad (sp)$$

One point about the (*sp*) axiom, called *surjective pairing,* is that this is redundant for explicit pair terms of the form $\langle M, N\rangle$. This is easily demonstrated by substituting $\langle M, N\rangle$ for P and applying equational axioms to subterms:

$$\begin{aligned}&\langle(\mathbf{Proj}_1\langle M, N\rangle), (\mathbf{Proj}_2\langle M, N\rangle)\rangle\\ &= \langle M, (\mathbf{Proj}_2\langle M, N\rangle)\rangle\\ &= \langle M, N\rangle\end{aligned}$$

However, if $x\colon\sigma \times \tau$ is a variable of product type, then we cannot prove $\langle(\mathbf{Proj}_1 x), (\mathbf{Proj}_2 x)\rangle = x$ without the axiom that gives us this equation directly. This is demonstrated in Example 2.4.3, which appears in a later section since it depends on properties of confluent reduction systems. The reason the axiom is called surjective pairing is that it implies that the pairing function is surjective onto the set of elements of product type. A consequence of (*sp*) is given in part (a) of Exercise 2.2.7.

As for natural number and boolean expressions, the reduction rules for pairs are derived by reading the equational axioms from left to right. However, we only include reduction rules corresponding to the (*proj*) axioms. There is no (*sp*) reduction rule in the operational semantics of PCF for two reasons. The first is that it is not necessary, as demonstrated by the adequacy of the operational semantics without (*sp*), discussed in Sections 2.3 and 5.4.1. The second is that the rule causes confluence to fail, when combined with recursive definitions of functions (see Section 4.4.3).

Functions

PCF functions are written using lambda abstraction, and most of the examples given in Section 1.2 are PCF expressions. For example, since we have numerals and addition in PCF, both $\lambda x\colon nat.\, x + 1$ and $\lambda x\colon nat.\, 5$ are acceptable PCF, with type $nat \to nat$. In general, a PCF function may have any PCF type as domain or range. Since we can have functions that take functions as arguments and return functions as results, PCF is more flexible (in this direction) than many programming languages. A simple higher-order function is composition of numeric functions

$$comp \stackrel{\text{def}}{=} \lambda f\colon nat \to nat.\, \lambda g\colon nat \to nat.\, \lambda x\colon nat.\, f(gx).$$

To see how this works, suppose f and g are numeric functions. Then *comp* f g is the function $\lambda x\colon nat.\ f(gx)$; the function which, on argument x, returns $f(gx)$. Thus *comp* f g defines $f \circ g$.

As mentioned in Section 1.3, we have the equational axiom

$$\lambda x\colon \sigma.M = \lambda y\colon \sigma.[y/x]M, \quad y \text{ not free in } M \tag{α}$$

for renaming bound variables. This axiom is related only to the fact that λ is a binding operator, and does not have anything to do with the way that lambda abstraction defines a function. Since renaming of bound variables is so basic, it is useful to have a special name for it: we may write $M =_\alpha N$ if terms M and N differ only in the names of bound variables. It is often convenient to write $FV(M)$ for the free variables of M, *i.e.*, the variables appearing in M that are not bound by λ.

The second axiom,

$$(\lambda x\colon \sigma.M)N = [N/x]M, \tag{β}$$

gives us a way of computing the result of function application by substitution. To avoid any confusion about substitution and bound variables, we define substitution on typed lambda expressions precisely, by the following induction, with three subcases for different forms of lambda abstractions:

$$[N/x]x = N$$

$$[N/x]a = a, \text{ for constant or variable } a \neq x$$

$$[N/x](PQ) = ([N/x]P)([N/x]Q)$$

$$[N/x]\lambda x\colon \sigma.M = \lambda x\colon \sigma.M$$

$$[N/x]\lambda y\colon \sigma.M = \lambda y\colon \sigma.[N/x]M, \text{ provided } x \neq y \text{ and } y \notin FV(N)$$

$$[N/x]\lambda y\colon \sigma.M = (\lambda z\colon \sigma.[N/x][z/y]M), \text{ where } z \notin FV(MN) \text{ and } y, z \neq x$$

While most of these clauses are easily understood, it may be worth saying a few more words about the last three lines. The fourth line makes sense when we remember that a substitution $[N/x]$ only replaces *free* occurrences of x by N. Since x is bound in $\lambda x\colon \sigma.M$, the substitution $[N/x]$ has no effect on this term. The last two clauses tell how to substitute for a free variable inside the binding operator λ. If y is not free in the term N we are inserting into M, then we may go ahead and perform the substitution. This is the intent of the fifth line of the definition. However, if y is free in N, then we have a conflict and we must rename y to some other variable z to avoid capturing the free y in N. The option is provided by the last line of the definition. Since substitution may involve arbitrary renaming, substitution is only defined up to α-equivalence. In other words, if we compute $[N/x]M$ by this definition, we may end up with any one of an infinite number of possible terms. However, all of the possibilities are $=_\alpha$ to each other. Since we consider α-equivalent terms as essentially the same, and they are provably equal in the simplest possible way, this "nondeterminism" in the definition of substitution is completely harmless. It is easy to see that substitution respects α-equivalence, in the sense that $[N/x]M =_\alpha [N/x]P$ whenever $M =_\alpha P$.

Substitution is extended to PCF by adding cases for addition, conditional, etc. These are all straightforward, and follow the pattern of the application case above: we substitute $[N/x]$ in a compound expression by applying this substitution to each of its parts, *e.g.*, $[N/x](P + Q) = ([N/x]P) + ([N/x]Q)$. Exercise 2.2.6, which may be useful to remember, asks you to prove the following identities involving substitution.

$$[M/x]([N/x]P) = [([M/x]N)/x]P,$$

$$[M/x]([N/y]P) = [([M/x]N)/y]([M/x]P) \text{ if } y \not\equiv x \text{ and } y \notin FV(M)$$

The combination of α-conversion and renaming bound variables in substitution provide *static scope* in PCF, as illustrated in Exercise 2.2.13.

The final equational axiom for functions is based on the idea that two functions are equal if they produce equal values on all arguments. To see how this arises, suppose $M : \sigma \to \tau$ is a function expression, and $x : \sigma$ is some variable not appearing in M. The condition on x is to make sure that we do not use x in two different ways. Then since $(Mx) : \tau$, the expression $\lambda x : \sigma.(Mx)$ also defines a function from σ to τ. For any argument $N : \sigma$, we can apply either function to N. However, we get the same result in either case, since

$$(\lambda x : \sigma.Mx)N = MN$$

by (β). (Notice that we get $([N/x]M)N$, which is different, if we drop the assumption that x is not free in M.) Since the two functions return the same result on all arguments, we have the equational axiom

$$\lambda x : \sigma.Mx = M, \quad x \text{ not free in } M \tag{η}$$

Just as the final axiom for pairing is redundant for explicit pairs, the (η) axiom for functions is redundant for explicit function expressions. Specifically, if M has the form $\lambda y : \sigma.\ P$, and x is not free in M, then we can prove $\lambda x : \sigma.Mx = M$ using (β). However, we cannot prove $\lambda x : \sigma.Mx = M$ if M is a variable of function type without using (η). A consequence of (η) is given in part (b) of Exercise 2.2.7.

Both (β) and (η) could be used as reduction rules, read left to right. When it is important to distinguish between the equational axioms, we use $(\beta)_{eq}$ and $(\eta)_{eq}$ for the equational axioms and $(\beta)_{red}$ and $(\eta)_{red}$ for the reduction rules. While η-reduction is used in many versions of lambda calculus, we will *not* use $(\eta)_{red}$ in PCF reduction since it is not needed. As discussed in Section 1.3, we keep (α) as the single equational axiom of the reduction system for PCF. In other words, PCF reduction is a relation on α-equivalence classes of expressions.

For easy reference, the syntax of PCF is summarized in Section 2.2.6. The equational proof system appears in Table 2.1 and the reduction system in Table 2.2.

Currying

A traditional topic in lambda calculus is the relationship between multi-argument and higher-order functions. If we have a mathematical function of two arguments, such as the addition function $add(x, y\colon nat) = x + y$, then we generally think of this as a function on ordered pairs $add\colon (nat \times nat) \rightarrow nat$. This type of addition function may be written as the PCF expression

$$add = \lambda p\colon nat \times nat.\, (\mathbf{Proj}_1\, p) + (\mathbf{Proj}_2\, p)$$

In words, this *add* is the function which takes a pair of natural numbers, and returns the sum of its two components.

A related function is called the "curried" addition function

$$Curry(add) = \lambda x\colon nat.\, \lambda y\colon nat.\, x + y$$

after lambda calculus pioneer Haskell Curry. The curried addition function yields $x + y$ when applied to x and y, but the form of parameterization is different. Like many other lambda expressions, it is easiest to read *Curry*(*add*) from right to left. The final result of applying the function is the expression to the right of all of the λ's, which is $x + y$. The next smallest expression is $\lambda y.\, x + y$. This function adds x, whose value is not determined within this expression, to the function argument. So we might call this the "add x" function. Since this function takes a single natural-number argument and returns a natural number result, we have

$$\lambda y.\, x + y : nat \rightarrow nat.$$

Now let us look again at the whole function *Curry*(*add*). On argument x, the function *Curry*(*add*) returns the "add x" function. So *Curry*(*add*) is a function of a single natural-number argument, returning a numeric function. This is reflected in the type of the function

$$Curry(add) : nat \rightarrow (nat \rightarrow nat).$$

Thus the curried addition function yields $x + y$ when applied to two natural numbers x

and y, but as the type indicates, *Curry*(*add*) takes two natural number arguments one at a time, rather than all at once.

As suggested by the notation *Curry*(*add*), there is a higher-order transformation *Curry* which maps any binary natural- number function f to its curried form $Curry(f)$. This map can actually be written in PCF, as the lambda expression

$$Curry = \lambda f\colon (nat \times nat) \to nat.\ \lambda x\colon nat.\ \lambda y\colon nat.\ f\,\langle x, y\rangle.$$

Using the axiom of β-equivalence, it is easy to see that when applied to *add*, the function *Curry* produces the lambda expression written above.

$$\begin{aligned}
Curry(add) &= (\lambda f\colon (nat \times nat) \to nat.\lambda x\colon nat.\lambda y\colon nat.\ f\,\langle x, y\rangle)\ add \\
&= \lambda x\colon nat.\lambda y\colon nat.\ add\ \langle x, y\rangle \\
&= \lambda x\colon nat.\lambda y\colon nat.\ (\lambda p\colon nat \times nat.\ (\mathbf{Proj}_1\, p) + (\mathbf{Proj}_2 p))\ \langle x, y\rangle \\
&= \lambda x\colon nat.\lambda y\colon nat.\ \mathbf{Proj}_1\langle x, y\rangle + \mathbf{Proj}_2\langle x, y\rangle \\
&= \lambda x\colon nat.\lambda y\colon nat.\ x + y
\end{aligned}$$

Some properties of currying are given in Exercise 2.2.8.

Exercise 2.2.4 Write a PCF expression to take any numeric function f and return a numeric function g such that for any n, the value of $g(n)$ is twice $f(n)$.

Exercise 2.2.5 Perform the following substitution. (Do not reduce the expression.)

$$[(y + 3)/x]\ ((\lambda f\colon nat \to nat.\ \lambda y\colon nat.\ f(x + y))(\lambda x\colon nat.\ x + y))$$

Exercise 2.2.6 Prove the following substitution identities.

$$[M/x]([N/x]P) = [([M/x]N)/x]P, \qquad (a)$$

$$[M/x]([N/y]P) = [([M/x]N)/y]([M/x]P) \text{ if } y \not\equiv x \text{ and } y \notin FV(M). \qquad (b)$$

Exercise 2.2.7 Show that the following two inference rules are derivable, *i.e.*, the equation below the line is provable from the equation(s) above the line. For (a), you may assume that from $x = u$ and $y = v$ it is possible to prove $\langle x, y\rangle = \langle u, v\rangle$.

$$\frac{\mathbf{Proj}_1 p = \mathbf{Proj}_1 q,\ \ \mathbf{Proj}_2 p = \mathbf{Proj}_2 q}{p = q} \qquad (a)$$

$$\frac{Mx = Nx}{M = N}\ x \notin FV(M, N) \qquad (b)$$

Exercise 2.2.8 Write a PCF expression *Uncurry* which "uncurries" natural number functions. More specifically, if f is a curried function $f\colon nat \to (nat \to nat)$, then $Uncurry(f)$ should be an ordinary binary function $Uncurry(f)\colon (nat \times nat) \to nat$ taking a pair of numbers and producing a natural number result. Use the axioms for functions and pairing to prove the equations $Uncurry(Curry\, g) = g$ and $Curry(Uncurry\, f) = f$, for any ordinary binary $g\colon (nat \times nat) \to nat$ and any curried $f\colon nat \to (nat \to nat)$.

2.2.4 Declarations and Syntactic Sugar

One of the appeals of lambda calculus, as a model programming language, is the way that lambda abstraction corresponds to variable binding in common programming languages. This is immediately clear for Lisp and its dialects, which are based on lambda notation. It is also true for Algol-like languages, such as Pascal. For example, consider the following Algol-like program fragment

begin function $f(x\colon nat)\ nat$;
  return x;
  end;
$\langle body\rangle$
end

with a function declaration at the beginning of a block. We can easily write the function f as the lambda expression $\lambda x\colon nat.x$. We will also see that the entire block may be translated into lambda notation. The translation may be simplified by adopting a general notational convention.

A reasonable typed syntax for declarations is

$$\texttt{let } x\colon\sigma = M \texttt{ in } N,$$

which binds x to M within the declaration body N. In other words, the value of `let` $x\colon\sigma = M$ `in` N is the value of N with x set to M. We consider this well-typed only if M has type σ. Using `let`, we can now write the Algol-like block above as

$$\texttt{let } f\colon nat \to nat = \lambda x\colon nat.x \texttt{ in } \langle body\rangle.$$

Instead of adding `let` declarations to PCF directly, we will treat `let` as an abbreviation, or what is often called "syntactic sugar" in computer science. This means that we will feel free to use `let` in writing PCF expressions, but we do not consider `let` part of the actual syntax of PCF. Instead, we will think of `let` as an abbreviation for a lambda expression, according to the rule

$$\texttt{let } x\colon\sigma = M \texttt{ in } N \stackrel{\text{def}}{=} (\lambda x\colon\sigma.N)M$$

This treatment of `let` allows us to keep the size of PCF relatively small, which will pay off when we come to proving things about the language. In addition, we need not specify any additional equational axioms or reduction rules, as these are inherited directly from λ. To distinguish abbreviations from actual PCF syntax, we will use the symbol $\stackrel{\text{def}}{=}$, as above, when defining meta-notational conventions. In general, $M \stackrel{\text{def}}{=} N$ means that whenever we write a term of the form M, this is shorthand for a term of form N.

Example 2.2.9 We will translate the following "sugared" PCF expression into pure PCF (without syntactic sugar)

$$\begin{array}{l}\texttt{let}\ compose = \lambda f\colon nat \to nat.\lambda g\colon nat \to nat.\lambda x\colon nat.f(g\,x)\ \texttt{in}\\ \quad\texttt{let}\ h = \lambda x\colon nat.x + x\ \texttt{in}\\ \quad\quad compose\,h\,h\,3\end{array}$$

and simplify by applying the appropriate reduction rules. The "de-sugared," pure PCF expression, written using the same names for bound variables, is:

$$\begin{array}{l}(\lambda compose\colon (nat \to nat) \to (nat \to nat) \to nat \to nat.\\ \quad(\lambda h\colon nat \to nat.\ compose\ h\ h\ 3)\quad \lambda x\colon nat.x + x)\\ \quad\lambda f\colon nat \to nat.\lambda g\colon nat \to nat.\lambda x\colon nat.\ f(g\ x).\end{array}$$

This reduces as follows:

$$\begin{array}{l}\to (\lambda h\colon nat \to nat.\,(\lambda f\colon nat \to nat.\,\lambda g\colon nat \to nat.\,\lambda x\colon nat.\ f(g\ x))\ h\ h\ 3)(\lambda x\colon nat.x + x)\\ \to (\lambda f\colon nat \to nat.\,\lambda g\colon nat \to nat.\,\lambda x\colon nat.\ f(g\ x))\ (\lambda x\colon nat.x + x)\ (\lambda x\colon nat.x + x)\ 3\\ \twoheadrightarrow (\lambda x\colon nat.x + x)((\lambda x\colon nat.x + x)\ 3)\\ \to ((\lambda x\colon nat.x + x)\ 3) + ((\lambda x\colon nat.x + x)\ 3)\\ \twoheadrightarrow (3 + 3) + (3 + 3)\\ \twoheadrightarrow 12.\end{array}$$

■

The notion of "syntactic sugar" is very useful in programming language analysis. By considering certain constructs as syntactic sugar for others, we can write program examples in a familiar notation, and analyze these programs as if they are written using simpler or less troubling primitives. However, this technique must be used with care. Since computation may be modeled by substitution, as in the reduction rules for PCF, we do not want to make too many transformations under the umbrella of syntactic sugar. Three indications that the definition of `let` does not add any computational power to PCF are:

(i) $\texttt{let}\ x{:}\sigma = M\ \texttt{in}\ N$ and the lambda expression $(\lambda x{:}\,\sigma.N)M$ have approximately the same size (counting symbols);

(ii) both have the same typing constraints;

(iii) the two expressions have the same immediate subexpressions (syntactic constituents).

While these conditions are not absolute rules about syntactic sugar, they are a useful guide towards good use of syntactic sugar.

Another syntactic extension allows us to write function declarations in a more familiar form, as follows

$$\texttt{let}\ f(x{:}\,\tau){:}\,\sigma = M\ \texttt{in}\ N \stackrel{\text{def}}{=} \texttt{let}\ f{:}\,\tau \to \sigma = \lambda x{:}\,\tau.M\ \texttt{in}\ N$$

We can also add multi-argument function definitions, as in Exercise 2.2.12 below.

Example 2.2.10 The language ISWIM, described in [Lan66], has an expression form $M\ \texttt{where}\ x{:}\sigma = N$. Intuitively, the value of this expression is the value of M when the variable x is set to N. We can easily add `where` to PCF by the abbreviation

$$M\ \texttt{where}\ x{:}\sigma = N \stackrel{\text{def}}{=} \texttt{let}\ x{:}\sigma = N\ \texttt{in}\ M. \qquad \blacksquare$$

Exercise 2.2.11 Which PCF reduction rule is applicable to any term of the form $\texttt{let}\ x{:}\sigma = M\ \texttt{in}\ N$, and what is the result of a single application of this rule?

Exercise 2.2.12

(a) Show how to add two-argument functions to PCF by defining

$$\lambda\langle x{:}\,\sigma,\ y{:}\,\tau\rangle.\,M$$

as syntactic sugar. If $\lambda x{:}\,\sigma.\,\lambda y{:}\,\tau.\,M$ has type $\sigma \to \tau \to \rho$, then $\lambda\langle x{:}\,\sigma,\ y{:}\,\tau\rangle.\,M$ has type $\sigma \times \tau \to \rho$. You may want to use the results of Exercise 2.2.8.

(b) Introduce a two-argument function form of `let`

$$\texttt{let}\ f\langle x{:}\,\sigma,\ y{:}\,\tau\rangle{:}\,\rho = M\ \texttt{in}\ N$$

as syntactic sugar, using the result of part (a). Illustrate the induced reduction rule for this definition form by expanding $\texttt{let}\ f\langle x{:}\,\sigma,\ y{:}\,\rho\rangle{:}\,\tau = M\ \texttt{in}\ N$ into pure PCF and reducing.

Exercise 2.2.13 This exercise is concerned with *static scope* and renaming of bound variables. Intuitively, static scoping of variables means that the binding of a variable is always determined by finding the closest enclosing binding operator for that variable. Moreover, the binding of a variable does not change during evaluation of expressions. With *dynamic* *scoping,* the way a variable is bound may change during evaluation. This distinction will be intuitively familiar to computer scientists who have studied programming languages.

(a) Under static scope, the free x in the declaration of f is bound by the outer declaration. As a result, the function f always adds 3 to its argument, no matter where it is called.

$$\begin{array}{l} \texttt{let } x\colon nat = 3 \texttt{ in} \\ \quad \texttt{let } f(y\colon nat)\colon nat = x + y \texttt{ in} \\ \quad\quad \texttt{let } x\colon nat = 4 \texttt{ in} \\ \quad\quad\quad f\,5 \end{array}$$

Use reduction to simplify this PCF expression to 8. You may save yourself the trouble of rewriting `let`'s to λ's by using the derived rule $\texttt{let } x\colon \sigma = M \texttt{ in } N \rightarrow [M/x]N$.

(b) Suppose that in reducing the expression in part (a), you begin by substituting $\lambda y\colon nat.\ x + y$ for f in the inner expression, $\texttt{let } x\colon nat = 4 \texttt{ in } f\,5$. (This actually corresponds to the usual implementations, since we begin evaluation of $f\,5$ by passing 5 to the body of f.) Explain how renaming bound variables provides static scope. In particular, say which variable above (x, f or y) must be renamed, and how a specific occurrence of this variable is therefore resolved statically.

(c) Under dynamic scope, the binding for x in the body of f changes when f is called in the scope of the inner binding of x. Therefore, under dynamic scope, the value of this expression will be $4 + 5 = 9$. Show how you can reduce the expression to 9 by *not* renaming bound variables when you perform substitution.

(d) In the usual statically scoped lambda calculus, α-conversion (renaming bound variables) does not change the value of an expression. Use the example expression from part (a) to explain why α-conversion may change the value of an expression if variables are dynamically scoped.

(e) Show that confluence fails for dynamically-scoped PCF.

2.2.5 Recursion and Fixed-point Operators

The final construct of PCF provides definition by recursion. Rather than add a new declaration form, we will treat recursive declarations as a combination of `let` and one new basic function, a fixed-point operator fix_σ for each type σ. The reader should be warned that this construct raises more subtle issues than the parts of the language we have already discussed. To begin with, recursion makes it possible to write expressions with no normal form. This changes our basic intuition about the way that an expression defines a mathematical value. In addition, when there are several possible reductions that could be applied to a term, the choice between these becomes important.

We will see how fixed-point operators provide recursion by beginning with the declaration form

$\texttt{letrec}\ f\colon\sigma = M\ \texttt{in}\ N.$

This has the intended meaning that within N, the variable f denotes a solution to the equation $f = M$. In general, f may occur in M. The main typing constraint for this declaration is that M must have type σ, since otherwise the equation $f = M$ does not make sense. We will see that `letrec` may be treated as syntactic sugar for a combination of ordinary `let` and a fixed-point operator.

We can see how `letrec` works by writing the factorial function. To simplify the notation, let us write $x - 1$ for the predecessor of x, and $x * y$ for the product of x and y. (To stay within the natural-numbers, we consider $0 - 1 = 0$.) We will see later how to define predecessor and natural number multiplication in PCF using recursion. With these extra operations, we can define the factorial function and compute 5! by writing

$\texttt{letrec}\ f\colon nat \to nat = \lambda y\colon nat.\ (\texttt{if}\ Eq?\,y\,0\ \texttt{then}\ 1\ \texttt{else}\ y * f(y-1))\ \texttt{in}\ f\,5$

Since the variable f occurs free in the expression on the right-hand side of the equals sign, we cannot simply take f to refer to the expression on the right. Instead, we want f in the function body to refer "recursively" to the function being defined. We may summarize this by saying that f must be a solution to the equation

$f = \lambda y\colon nat.\ \texttt{if}\ Eq?\,y\,0\ \texttt{then}\ 1\ \texttt{else}\ y * f(y-1)$

with two occurrences of the function variable f. From a mathematical point of view, it is not clear that every equation $f\colon\sigma = M$ involving an arbitrary PCF expression M should have a solution, or which solution to choose if several exist. We will consider these questions more carefully when we investigate the denotational semantics of PCF in Chapter 5. However, recursive function declarations have a clear computational interpretation. Therefore, we will assume that every defining equation has *some* solution and add syntax to PCF for expressing this. The associated equational axiom and rewrite rule will allow us to think operationally about recursive definitions and provide a useful guide in discussing denotational semantics in Chapter 5.

Using lambda abstraction, we can represent any recursive definition $f\colon\sigma = M$ by a function $\lambda f\colon\sigma.\ M$. Rather than looking for a solution to a recursive defining equation, we will produce a fixed point of the associated function. In general, if $F\colon\sigma \to \sigma$ is a function from some type to itself, a *fixed point of* F is a value $x\colon\sigma$ such that $F(x) = x$. For example, returning to the factorial function, we can see that factorial is a fixed point of the operator

$$F \stackrel{\text{def}}{=} \lambda f\colon nat \to nat.\,\lambda y\colon nat.\ \texttt{if}\ Eq?\,y\,0\ \texttt{then}\ 1\ \texttt{else}\ y * f(y-1)$$

on natural-number functions. We show how factorial is defined and computed in PCF by applying a fixed-point operator to this function.

The last basic construct of PCF is a family of functions

$$\mathit{fix}_\sigma : (\sigma \to \sigma) \to \sigma,$$

one for each type σ. The function fix_σ produces a fixed point of any function from σ to σ. Using lambda abstraction and fix_σ, we can regard the recursive `letrec` declaration form as an abbreviation:

$$\texttt{letrec}\ f\colon\sigma = M\ \texttt{in}\ N \stackrel{\text{def}}{=} \texttt{let}\ f\colon\sigma = (\mathit{fix}_\sigma\ \lambda f\colon\sigma.M)\ \texttt{in}\ N.$$

Since we often use `letrec` to define functions, we also adopt the syntactic sugar

$$\texttt{letrec}\ f(x\colon\tau)\colon\sigma = M\ \texttt{in}\ N \stackrel{\text{def}}{=} \texttt{letrec}\ f\colon\tau \to \sigma = \lambda x\colon\tau.M\ \texttt{in}\ N.$$

The equational axiom for $\mathit{fix}_\sigma\colon (\sigma \to \sigma) \to \sigma$ is that it produces a fixed point

$$\mathit{fix}_\sigma = \lambda f\colon\sigma \to \sigma.f\ (\mathit{fix}_\sigma\ f). \tag{\textit{fix}}$$

Using (β), it is easy to derive the more intuitive equation

$$\mathit{fix}_\sigma\ M = M\ (\mathit{fix}_\sigma\ M)$$

for any $M\colon\sigma \to \sigma$. The (*fix*) reduction rule is obtained by reading the equational axiom from left to right. Some reasonable, non-equational properties of fix_σ are more subtle, and will be discussed in Sections 5.2 and 5.3.

To see how (*fix*) reduction works, we will continue the factorial example. Using $\mathit{fix}_{nat\to nat}$, the factorial function may be written $\mathit{fact} \stackrel{\text{def}}{=} \mathit{fix}_{nat\to nat}F$, where F is written out above. As a typographical simplification, we will drop the subscript of *fix* in the calculation below. To compute *fact n*, we may expand the definition, and use reduction to obtain the following.

$$\begin{aligned}
\mathit{fact}\ n &\equiv (\mathit{fix}\ F)n \\
&\twoheadrightarrow F(\mathit{fix}\ F)n \\
&\equiv (\lambda f\colon nat \to nat.\,\lambda y\colon nat.\ \texttt{if}\ Eq?\,y\,0\ \texttt{then}\ 1\ \texttt{else}\ y * f(y-1))\ (\mathit{fix}\ F)\ n \\
&\twoheadrightarrow \texttt{if}\ Eq?\,n\,0\ \texttt{then}\ 1\ \texttt{else}\ n * (\mathit{fix}\ F)(n-1)
\end{aligned}$$

Note that apart from (*fix*) reduction, we have used only ordinary β-reduction. When $n = 0$, we can use the axiom for conditional to simplify *fact* 0 to 1. For $n > 0$, we can simplify the test to obtain $n * (\mathit{fix}\ F)(n - 1)$ and continue as above. For any natural number n, it is clear that we will eventually compute $\mathit{fact}\ n = n!$. Put more formally, we may use ordinary natural-number induction to prove the theorem about PCF that for every natural number n the application of *fact* to the PCF numeral for n may be reduced to the numeral for $n!$.

As mentioned above, fixed-point operators raise mathematical problems. If we think of the functions from $nat \to nat$ to $nat \to nat$ as ordinary set-theoretic functions, then it does not make sense to postulate that every $f\colon (nat \to nat) \to (nat \to nat)$ has a fixed point x with the property $x = f(x)$. However, as shown in Exercise 2.2.16, we have fixed points of this type iff we allow numeric functions to be defined by recursion. Since recursion is fundamental to computation, it is important to have fixed-point operators in PCF. The way to make mathematical sense of *fix* is to realize that when we have recursion, we may write algorithms that define partial functions. If $f\colon (nat \to nat) \to (nat \to nat)$, then its fixed point may be a *partial* function, such as the function which is undefined on all integer arguments. Thus, when we add recursion to PCF, we must understand that an expression of type σ defines an algorithm for computing an element of type σ. In the case that this algorithm does not terminate, the expression may not define one of the standard values of that type. (A note for recursion theorists is that if we replace *fix* by some other construct that does not allow us to write nonterminating functions, there would be total recursive functions we could not write in PCF. This follows from the fact that the set of all total recursive functions is not *r.e.*)

Although *fix* takes the fixed point of a single function, we can actually use *fix* to define any number of mutually recursive functions. This is most easily illustrated for the case of two recursive functions. Suppose we want to define recursive functions f and g satisfying the equations

$$f = F\ f\ g$$

$$g = G\ f\ g$$

where we assume that neither f nor g appears free in F or G. Let us assume that $F\colon \sigma \to \tau \to \sigma$ and $G\colon \sigma \to \tau \to \tau$ so that both equations are type correct. We may then apply $\mathit{fix}_{\sigma \times \tau}$ to the function on pairs

$$\lambda\langle f\colon \sigma, g\colon \tau\rangle.\ \langle F\ f\ g,\ \ G\ f\ g\rangle.$$

This gives us a recursively-defined pair whose first and second components satisfy the original defining equations. The details are left as Exercise 2.2.15. An alternative approach which does not use pairing is given in Exercise 5.3.5.

Exercise 2.2.14 Assuming we have subtraction in PCF, write a `letrec` expression of the form

`letrec` $\mathit{fib}(x\colon nat)\colon nat = \ldots$ `in` $\mathit{fib}(4)$

which defines the Fibonacci function and applies it to 4 to compute the fourth Fibonacci number. (Recall that the zero-th Fibonacci number is 1, the first Fibonacci number is 1, and after that each Fibonacci number is the sum of the preceding two.) Show how your `letrec` expression reduces to the 4th Fibonacci number. You should give approximately the same amount of detail as in the factorial example of this section.

Exercise 2.2.15 Consider the pair of equations

$f = F\ f\ g$

$g = G\ f\ g$

where $F\colon \sigma \to \tau \to \sigma$, $G\colon \sigma \to \tau \to \tau$ and neither f nor g appears free in F or G. Show that the first and second components of

$\mathit{fix}_{\sigma\times\tau}\ (\lambda\langle f\colon\sigma, g\colon\tau\rangle.\ \langle F\ f\ g,\ \ G\ f\ g\rangle)$

satisfy these equations. (An alternative approach to mutually-recursive definitions is given in Exercise 5.3.5.)

Exercise 2.2.16 In this section, we defined `letrec` as syntactic sugar using *fix*. The point of this exercise is to demonstrate that *fix* is also definable from `letrec`.

(a) Write an expression *FIX* using `letrec` with the property that if we expand `letrec` $f\colon\sigma = M \mathtt{in} N$ to $(\lambda f\colon\sigma.N)(\mathit{fix}_\sigma\ (\lambda f\colon\sigma.M))$, we can reduce *FIX* to *fix* using only β-reduction and η-reduction.

(b) Write a reduction rule for `letrec` of the form

`letrec` $f\colon\sigma = M$ `in` $N \to P$,

where P is an expression containing M, N and `letrec`, but not *fix*. As a check that this is plausible, show that P is provably equal to

$[\,[(\mathit{FIX}\ (\lambda f\colon\sigma.M))/f]M]\,/\,f]N$,

which corresponds to the result of doing one *fix* reduction and one β-reduction to the term $(\lambda f\colon\sigma.N)(\mathit{fix}_\sigma\ (\lambda f\colon\sigma.M))$ mentioned in part *(a)*.

(c) Show that if we take `letrec` as basic, and use the reduction rule given in part *(b)*, the term *FIX* you gave in answer to part *(a)* is a fixed-point operator. That is, show that for any term M of the correct type, $FIX\ M \twoheadrightarrow M\,F$, where F is the result of applying one β-reduction to $(FIX\ M)$.

2.2.6 PCF Syntax Summary and Collected Examples

Pure PCF

The syntax of pure PCF, without extension by syntactic sugar, is summarized below by a BNF-like grammar. The first set of productions describe the expressions of an arbitrary type σ. These include variables, conditional expressions, and the results of function application, projection functions, and fixed-point application.

$$\langle \sigma\_exp \rangle \quad ::= \quad \langle \sigma\_var \rangle \mid \texttt{if}\ \langle bool\_exp \rangle\ \texttt{then}\ \langle \sigma\_exp \rangle\ \texttt{else}\ \langle \sigma\_exp \rangle \mid$$

$$\langle \sigma\_application \rangle \mid \langle \sigma\_projection \rangle \mid \langle \sigma\_fixed\_point \rangle$$

$$\langle \sigma\_application \rangle \ ::= \ \langle \tau \to \sigma\_exp \rangle \langle \tau\_exp \rangle$$

$$\langle \sigma\_projection \rangle \ ::= \ \mathbf{Proj}_1 \langle \sigma \times \tau\_exp \rangle \mid \mathbf{Proj}_2 \langle \tau \times \sigma\_exp \rangle$$

$$\langle \sigma\_fixed\_point \rangle \ ::= \ \mathit{fix}_\sigma\ \langle \sigma \to \sigma\_exp \rangle$$

For function and product types, we also have lambda abstraction and explicit pairing.

$$\langle \sigma \to \tau\_exp \rangle \ ::= \ \lambda x\!:\!\sigma.\langle \tau\_exp \rangle$$

$$\langle \sigma \times \tau\_exp \rangle \ ::= \ \langle\, \langle \sigma\_exp \rangle,\ \langle \tau\_exp \rangle\, \rangle$$

The constants and functions for natural numbers and booleans are covered by the following productions.

$$\langle bool\_exp \rangle \ ::= \ true \mid false \mid Eq?\ \langle nat\_exp \rangle\ \langle nat\_exp \rangle$$

$$\langle nat\_exp \rangle \ ::= \ 0 \mid 1 \mid 2 \mid \ldots \mid \langle nat\_exp \rangle + \langle nat\_exp \rangle$$

This concludes the definition of PCF. An alternate definition of the syntax of PCF may be given using the typing rule style of Chapter 4.

Syntactic Extensions

The most commonly used extensions of PCF by syntactic sugar are listed below, along with their definitions. To distinguish abbreviations from actual PCF syntax, we use the symbol $\stackrel{\text{def}}{=}$ to define meta-notational conventions. The definition $M \stackrel{\text{def}}{=} N$ means that whenever we write a term of the form M, this is short-hand for the corresponding term of the form N.

$$\texttt{let } x{:}\sigma = M \texttt{ in } N \quad \stackrel{\text{def}}{=} \quad (\lambda x{:}\sigma.\, N)M$$

$$\texttt{let } f(x{:}\sigma){:}\tau = M \texttt{ in } N \quad \stackrel{\text{def}}{=} \quad \texttt{let } f{:}\sigma \to \tau = \lambda x{:}\sigma.\, M \texttt{ in } N$$

$$\stackrel{\text{def}}{=} \quad (\lambda f{:}\sigma \to \tau.\, N)(\lambda x{:}\sigma.\, M)$$

$$\texttt{letrec } f{:}\sigma = M \texttt{ in } N \quad \stackrel{\text{def}}{=} \quad \texttt{let } f{:}\sigma = (\mathit{fix}_\sigma\ (\lambda f{:}\sigma.\, M)) \texttt{ in } N$$

$$\stackrel{\text{def}}{=} \quad (\lambda f{:}\sigma.\, N)(\mathit{fix}_\sigma\ (\lambda f{:}\sigma.\, M))$$

$$\texttt{letrec } f(x{:}\tau){:}\sigma = M \texttt{ in } N \quad \stackrel{\text{def}}{=} \quad \texttt{letrec } f{:}\tau \to \sigma = \lambda x{:}\tau.\, M \texttt{ in } N$$

$$\stackrel{\text{def}}{=} \quad \texttt{let } f{:}\tau \to \sigma = (\mathit{fix}_{\tau\to\sigma}\ (\lambda f{:}\tau \to \sigma.\, \lambda x{:}\tau.\, M)) \texttt{ in } N$$

$$\stackrel{\text{def}}{=} \quad (\lambda f{:}\tau \to \sigma.\, N)(\mathit{fix}_{\tau\to\sigma}\ (\lambda f{:}\tau \to \sigma.\, \lambda x{:}\tau.\, M))$$

$$\lambda\langle x{:}\sigma,\, y{:}\tau\rangle.\, M \quad \stackrel{\text{def}}{=} \quad \lambda p{:}\sigma \times \tau.(\lambda x{:}\sigma.\, \lambda y{:}\tau.\, M)(\mathbf{Proj}_1\, p)(\mathbf{Proj}_2\, p)$$

$$\texttt{let } \langle x{:}\sigma,\, y{:}\tau\rangle = M \texttt{ in } N \quad \stackrel{\text{def}}{=} \quad (\lambda\langle x{:}\sigma,\, y{:}\tau\rangle.\, N)M$$

A useful convention is to write $M^n N$ for the term $M\,(M\,\ldots(M\,N)\ldots)$ constructed by applying M to N a total of n times. A more precise definition is that $M^0 N \stackrel{\text{def}}{=} N$ and $M^{n+1} N \stackrel{\text{def}}{=} M(M^n N)$.

Examples

Boolean and natural-number expressions.

$$\texttt{if } \mathit{Eq?}\,(4+5)\,9 \texttt{ then } 27 \texttt{ else } 42$$

$$\texttt{if } (\texttt{if } \mathit{Eq?}\,(4+5)\,9 \texttt{ then } \mathit{false} \texttt{ else } \mathit{true}) \texttt{ then } 42 \texttt{ else } 27$$

$$(\texttt{if } \mathit{Eq?}\,(x+y)\,z \texttt{ then } \lambda x{:}\mathit{nat}.\, x+5 \texttt{ else } \lambda y{:}\mathit{nat}.\, y+7)$$
$$(\texttt{if } \mathit{Eq?}\,(x+y)\,z \texttt{ then } 7 \texttt{ else } 5)$$

Lambda abstraction and application.

$$\lambda x{:}\mathit{nat}.\, x$$

$$\lambda x{:}\mathit{nat}.\, x+1$$

$$(\lambda x{:}\mathit{nat}.\, x+1)((\lambda y{:}\mathit{nat}.\, 5+y)\,3)$$

$$(\lambda f{:}\mathit{nat} \to \mathit{nat}.\, \lambda x{:}\mathit{nat}.\, f(f(f\,x)))\,(\lambda y{:}\mathit{nat}.\, 5+y)\,3$$

Pairing and functions.

$$\lambda x{:}\mathit{nat} \times \mathit{nat}.\langle \mathbf{Proj}_1\, x+1,\, \mathbf{Proj}_2\, x+1\rangle \quad : \quad (\mathit{nat} \times \mathit{nat}) \to (\mathit{nat} \times \mathit{nat})$$

$$\lambda x{:}\sigma \times \tau.\langle \mathbf{Proj}_2\, x,\, \mathbf{Proj}_1\, x\rangle \quad : \quad (\sigma \times \tau) \to (\tau \times \sigma)$$

$\lambda x\colon nat \times nat.$

$\quad$ `if` $Eq?\,(\mathbf{Proj}_1\, x)\, 0$ `then` $\mathbf{Proj}_2\, x$ `else` 0	:	$nat \times nat \to nat$
$\lambda f\colon nat \to nat.\, \lambda g\colon nat \to nat.\, \lambda x\colon nat.\, f\,(g\, x)$	is	composition of numeric functions
$\lambda f\colon nat \to nat.\, \lambda g\colon nat \to nat.\, \lambda x\colon nat.$		
$\quad$ `if` $Eq?\,(f\, x)\, 0$ `then` $g\, x$ `else` 0	:	$(nat \to nat) \to (nat \to nat) \to (nat \to nat)$
$\lambda f\colon (nat \times nat) \to nat.\, \lambda x\colon nat.\, \lambda y\colon nat.\, f\,\langle x, y\rangle$	is	Curry for numeric functions

Declarations and recursion.

`let` $comp\colon (\tau \to \rho) \to (\sigma \to \tau) \to (\sigma \to \rho)$
$\quad = \lambda f\colon \tau \to \rho.\, \lambda g\colon \sigma \to \tau.\, \lambda x\colon \sigma.\, f\,(g\, x)$
$\quad$ `in` $comp\; f\; g$
`let` $add\colon (nat \times nat) \to nat$
$\quad = \lambda x\colon nat \times nat.(\mathbf{Proj}_1\, x) + (\mathbf{Proj}_2\, x)$
$\quad$ `in let` $curry\colon ((nat \times nat) \to nat) \to nat \to nat \to nat$
$\qquad = \lambda f\colon (nat \times nat) \to nat.\, \lambda x\colon nat.\, \lambda y\colon nat.\, f\,\langle x, y\rangle$
$\qquad$ `in` $curry\, add\, 5\, 7$

Assuming we have a predecessor function *pred* which maps each $n > 0$ to $n - 1$ and zero to zero, we can write multiplication as follows. A definition of *pred* is given in Section 2.5.2, using a general method described there.

`letrec` $mult\colon (nat \times nat) \to nat$
$\quad = \lambda p\colon nat \times nat.$
$\qquad$ `if` $Eq?\,(\mathbf{Proj}_1\, p)\, 0$ `then` 0 `else` $(\mathbf{Proj}_2\, p) + mult\langle pred\,(\mathbf{Proj}_1\, p), \mathbf{Proj}_2\, p\rangle$
$\quad$ `in` $mult\langle 6, 7\rangle$

We may rewrite this last example using more syntactic sugar to make it clearer:

`letrec` $mult\langle x\colon nat, y\colon nat\rangle\colon nat =$ `if` $Eq?\, x\, 0$ `then` 0 `else` $y + mult\langle pred\, x, y\rangle$
$\quad$ `in` $mult\langle 6, 7\rangle$

For further examples, see Section 2.5 and the exercises.

2.3 PCF Programs and Their Semantics

2.3.1 Programs and Results

Now that we have seen all of the constructs of PCF, we will take a step back and discuss the meaning, or *semantics*, of PCF in a general way that is intended to apply to a variety of programming languages. This should put the equational axioms and reduction rules that were presented along with the syntax of PCF in perspective. The three forms of semantics we will consider are axiomatic semantics, given by a proof system, operational semantics arising from a set of reduction rules, and denotational semantics (with details put off to Chapter 4). Each form of semantics has advantages and disadvantages for understanding properties of programs. In addition, there are standard connections between the three forms of semantics that should hold for any programming language. We discuss a few syntactic distinctions in this brief subsection before stating the connections precisely in the next three subsections.

Most programming languages have several different syntactic categories, or "kinds of expressions." These may include expressions as used in assignments or function calls, imperative statements, declarations or modules. However, not all well-formed syntactic entities can be executed or evaluated by themselves. Therefore, in any programming language, we distinguish *programs* from other syntactic forms that may be used only as parts of programs. The two characteristics that distinguish a program from an arbitrary syntactic form are that a program should not refer to any undeclared or unbound variables and a program should have the appropriate type or form to yield a printable value or observable effect.

In PCF, the two syntactic categories are types and terms (expressions that have types). If we think of giving a closed natural number or boolean term to an interpreter, then we could expect the interpreter to print its value. Therefore, we consider closed boolean and numeric expressions programs. But if we give an open natural number term such as $x + 5$ to an interpreter, there is no correct value since the value of x is not given. In addition, we cannot expect the value of a function expression to be printed with the same degree of accuracy as a natural number or boolean. Although an interpreter could certainly print back the function expression we give it, or perhaps print some kind of "optimized" code, no interpreter can print function expressions in a way that would tell us exactly which mathematical function is defined by the function expression typed in. This is because equality for partial recursive functions is undecidable and, as proved in Section 2.5.5, every partial recursive function is definable in PCF. For this reason, we say that natural number and boolean values are *observable,* but $nat \to nat$ values are not.

We give a precise definition of PCF *program* by defining the types of observable values. Although a pair of observable values could be considered observable, since an interpreter can easily print a pair of printable values, we will simplify several technical arguments by choosing a simpler set of observable types. This will not have any significant effect on our theory, as shown in Exercise 2.3.5. We say τ is an *observable type* if τ is either *nat* or *bool*. A PCF *program* is a well-formed, closed term of observable type. One potentially confusing aspect of this definition is that it does not consider input or output; it might be more accurate to call these "programs that require no additional input and produce one output." The reason we focus on programs which already have whatever input they require is that we use these programs to compare axiomatic, operational and denotational semantics. For this purpose, it is sufficient for each program to yield a single "data point" about the semantics.

Another general term we use in comparing semantics is *result*. Intuitively, a result is an observable effect of evaluating or executing a program. In a functional setting, this generally means a term giving an expected final result of program evaluation. For PCF, we make this precise by saying that a *result* is a closed normal form of observable type. In other words, the PCF results are the numerals, $0, 1, 2, \ldots$ and boolean constants *true* and *false*.

With this terminology, we can give a general definition of semantics, at least for programming languages: a *semantics of programs* is a relation between programs and results. This is a minimal condition; all of the semantics we consider give more information than the result of evaluating each program. Typically, axiomatic and denotational semantics give more useful information than operational semantics when it comes to expressions that may occur in programs but are not full programs themselves.

2.3.2 Axiomatic Semantics

In general, an axiomatic semantics consists of a proof system for deducing properties of programs and their parts. These properties may be equations, as in the PCF proof system (reviewed below), assertions about the output of programs, given certain inputs, or other properties. Since it is difficult to discuss all forms of axiomatic semantics in general, we will focus on equational axiomatic semantics. We may apply this discussion to axiomatic semantics that address other properties of programs by saying that two programs are equivalent in an axiomatic semantics whenever exactly the same assertions are derivable about each of them.

There are three general properties of axiomatic semantics that hold for PCF. The first is that the axiomatic semantics defines program behavior in some way. The other two are relations between the axiomatic and operational or denotational semantics.

- The axiomatic semantics determine the result (or output or observable effect, in general) of any program that has one.
- When two expressions are equivalent, according to the axiomatic semantics, we may safely substitute one for the other in any program without changing the operational semantics of that program. This could be called "soundness of the axiomatic semantics with respect to the operational semantics."

• The axiomatic semantics are sound with respect to the denotational semantics. Specifically, if we can prove any pair of PCF terms equal, then these terms must have the same denotation, regardless of which values we give to their free variables.

The PCF axiomatic semantics satisfies the first requirement since, for any full program that terminates according to the operational semantics, we may prove that this expression is equal to the appropriate numeral ($0, 1, 2, \ldots$) or boolean constant (*true* or *false*). This is a simple consequence of the fact that the PCF reduction axioms are a subset of the equational axioms. It follows from either of the last two conditions that, unless the operational or denotational semantics is degenerate, the axiomatic semantics does not equate all expressions of each type.

The axiomatic semantics of PCF is given by the proof system whose axioms are described in Sections 2.2.2 through 2.2.5 and listed again in Table 2.1. These axioms are combined with inference rules that make provable equality a congruence, also included in Table 2.1. *Congruence* means that provable equality is an equivalence relation (reflexive, symmetric and transitive), and that equality is preserved if we replace any subexpression by an equivalent one. We do not need a proof system for types, since two types are equal iff they are syntactically identical.

All of the congruence rules in Table 2.1, except the two concerned with lambda abstraction and application (the two at the bottom of the table) are in fact redundant. The reason is that we can use lambda abstraction and application to achieve the same effect. For example, suppose we can prove $M = N$ and $P = Q$, for four natural-number expressions M, N, P, and Q. We can derive $M + P = N + Q$ as follows. By the reflexivity axiom, we have the equation

$$\lambda x\colon nat.\lambda y\colon nat.\, x + y = \lambda x\colon nat.\lambda y\colon nat.\, x + y.$$

Therefore, by the congruence rule for application, we can prove

$$(\lambda x\colon nat.\lambda y\colon nat.\, x + y)\, M = (\lambda x\colon nat.\lambda y\colon nat.\, x + y)\, N.$$

Then, by axiom scheme (β) and transitivity,

$$\lambda y\colon nat.\, M + y = \lambda y\colon nat.\, N + y.$$

Repeating application, (β) and transitivity we may complete the proof of $M + P = N + Q$. The reason that the congruence rules are listed is that these are important properties of equality. In addition, if we were to develop a first-order theory of natural numbers and booleans, in the absence of lambda abstraction, we would need axioms expressing these properties.

Table 2.1
Equational Proof System for PCF.

Axioms	
Equality	
(*ref*)	$M = M$
Types *nat* and *bool*	
(*add*)	$0+0=0, 0+1=1, \ldots, 3+5=8, \ldots$
(*Eq?*)	$Eq?\,n\,n = true$, $Eq?\,n\,m = false$ (n, m distinct numerals)
(*cond*)	$\texttt{if } true \texttt{ then } M \texttt{ else } N = M$, $\texttt{if } false \texttt{ then } M \texttt{ else } N = N$
Pairs	
(*proj*)	$\mathbf{Proj}_1\langle M, N\rangle = M \quad \mathbf{Proj}_2\langle M, N\rangle = N$
(*sp*)	$\langle \mathbf{Proj}_1 P, \mathbf{Proj}_2 P\rangle = P$
Binding	
(α)	$\lambda x{:}\sigma.M = \lambda y{:}\sigma.[y/x]M$, provided y not free in M.
Functions	
(β)	$(\lambda x{:}\sigma.M)N = [N/x]M$
(η)	$\lambda x{:}\sigma.Mx = M$, provided x not free in M
Recursion	
(*fix*)	$fix_\sigma = \lambda f{:}\sigma \to \sigma.f(fix_\sigma\, f)$
Inference Rules	
Equivalence	
(*sym*), (*trans*)	$\dfrac{M = N}{N = M} \qquad \dfrac{M = N, N = P}{M = P}$
Congruence	
Types *nat* and *bool*	$\dfrac{M = N, P = Q}{M + P = N + Q} \qquad \dfrac{M = N, P = Q}{Eq?\,M\,P = Eq?\,N\,Q}$
	$\dfrac{M_1 = M_2, N_1 = N_2, P_1 = P_2}{\texttt{if } M_1 \texttt{ then } N_1 \texttt{ else } P_1 = \texttt{if } M_2 \texttt{ then } N_2 \texttt{ else } P_2}$
Pairs	$\dfrac{M = N}{\mathbf{Proj}_i M = \mathbf{Proj}_i N} \qquad \dfrac{M = N, P = Q}{\langle M, P\rangle = \langle N, Q\rangle}$
Functions	$\dfrac{M = N}{\lambda x{:}\sigma.\,M = \lambda x{:}\sigma.\,N} \qquad \dfrac{M = N, P = Q}{MP = NQ}$

It is worth mentioning that although the axiomatic semantics is powerful enough to determine the meaning of programs, this proof system is not as powerful as one might initially expect. For example, we cannot even prove that addition is commutative. Nor can we prove many interesting equivalences between recursive functions. For these kinds of properties, the most natural approach would be to add induction rules. Induction on natural numbers would let us prove commutativity quite easily, and a form of induction called "fixed-point induction" would allow us to prove a great many more equations between recursively-defined functions. For further information on natural-number induction, the reader may consult Section 1.8 or almost any book on mathematical logic, such as [End72]. Since fixed-point induction is specifically related to programs, and not a traditional topic in mathematical logic, we consider this in Section 5.3. A rudimentary form of fixed-point induction is discussed in Exercise 2.3.3 below.

Exercise 2.3.1 Use the equational proof system to prove that the following two terms are equal, for any M. You do not need any axioms about subtraction to carry out the proof.

$\mathtt{letrec}\ f(x{:}\,nat){:}\,nat = \mathtt{if}\ Eq?\,x\,0\ \mathtt{then}\ 1\ \mathtt{else}\ f(x-1)\ \mathtt{in}\ M$

$\mathtt{let}\ f(x{:}\,nat){:}\,nat = \mathtt{if}\ Eq?\,x\,0\ \mathtt{then}\ 1$
$\quad\mathtt{else}\ \mathtt{letrec}\ g(x{:}\,nat){:}\,nat = \mathtt{if}\ Eq?\,x\,0\ \mathtt{then}\ 1\ \mathtt{else}\ g(x-1)\ \mathtt{in}\ g(x-1)$
$\mathtt{in}\ M$

Exercise 2.3.2 A system for proving equations is *inconsistent* if every equation $M = N$ between well-formed expressions M and N of the same type is provable. Show that if $true = false$ is provable from the axioms and inference rules of PCF, then the proof system is inconsistent. Use the same idea to show that if we can prove $m = n$ for distinct numerals m and n, the proof system is also inconsistent.

Exercise 2.3.3 While we can prove some simple equations involving recursion, such as the one given in Exercise 2.3.1, many similar-looking equations cannot be proved in the equational proof system given here. The reason is subtle but important. Consider two recursive definitions of factorial, for example, $f_1 = fix\ F_1$ and $f_2 = fix\ F_2$. The two functions f_1 and f_2 may give the same result for any natural number argument, even though the functions F_1 and F_2 are quite different. However, the proof system does not seem to provide any way to deduce $f_1 = f_2$ without essentially showing that F_1 and F_2 are closely related.

A proof rule that helps prove equations involving fixed points is the following.

$$\frac{M \twoheadrightarrow N M}{M = fix\ N}. \qquad (rec\ ind)$$

The intuitive explanation of this rule, which is loosely based on McCarthy's rule of *recursion induction* [McC61, McC63], is that when M behaves computationally like a fixed point of N, then we conclude that M and *fix* N have the same value. The computational nature of reduction is important here, since the rule becomes unsound if the hypothesis is replaced by the equation $M = NM$, as may be seen by taking N to be the identity. For further discussion of this rule, see Exercise 5.4.9.

Prove the following equations using (*fix ind*) in combination with the other equational proof rules.

(a) $\mathit{fix}(f \circ g) = f(\mathit{fix}(g \circ f))$.

(b) $\mathit{fix}_\sigma = \mathit{fix}_{(\sigma\to\sigma)\to\sigma}\lambda f\colon(\sigma \to \sigma) \to \sigma.\lambda g\colon\sigma \to \sigma.g(fg)$ where $\sigma \equiv \sigma_1 \to \sigma_2$.

2.3.3 Denotational Semantics

The PCF denotational semantics assigns a natural number value (or a special additional value corresponding to nontermination) to each expression of type *nat*, a boolean value (or special value for nontermination) to each expression of type *bool*, and a mathematical function or pair of values to any function expression or expression of cartesian product type. The mathematical value of an expression is called its *denotation.* If a term has free variables, its denotation will generally depend on the values assumed for the free variables. While we will not go into details in this chapter, we will give a brief overview of the denotational semantics of PCF so that we can compare the three forms of semantics.

We give denotations to terms by first choosing a set of values for each type. In the standard semantics, the set of mathematical vales for type *nat* will include all of the natural numbers, plus a special element $\bot_{nat}$ representing nontermination. This extra value is needed since we have PCF expressions of type *nat* such as `letrec` $f(x\colon nat)\colon nat = f(x+1)$ `in` $f(0)$ which do not terminate under the standard interpreter, and do not denote any standard natural number. For similar reasons, the set of denotations of type *bool* includes *true*, *false* and an extra value $\bot_{bool}$. The mathematical values of a product type $\sigma \times \tau$ are ordered pairs, as you would expect. The mathematical values of type $\sigma \to \tau$ are functions from σ to τ with the property that if $\tau = \sigma$, then each function has a fixed point. The precise way of obtaining such a set of functions is discussed in Chapter 5. We interpret addition and other PCF functions in the usual way, for arguments that are ordinary natural numbers, and as the special value $\bot_{nat}$ when one of the arguments is $\bot_{nat}$. This is because we cannot compute an ordinary natural number by adding a number to an expression that does not define a terminating computation.

Once we have chosen a set of values for each type, we assign meanings to terms by choosing an *environment,* which is a mapping from variables to values. If x is a variable of type σ, and η is an environment, then $\eta(x)$ must be a mathematical value from type

σ. We then define the meaning $[\![M]\!]\eta$ of term M in environment η by induction, in the manner that may be familiar from first-order logic. Specifically, the meaning $[\![x]\!]\eta$ is the value given to variable x by the environment, namely $\eta(x)$. The meaning of an application $[\![MN]\!]\eta$ is obtained by applying the function $[\![M]\!]\eta$ denoted by M to the argument $[\![N]\!]\eta$ denoted by N. Other cases are handled in a similar way. An important property is that the meaning of a term of type σ will always be one of the mathematical values associated with this type. Therefore, in the case of an application MN, for example, the typing rules of PCF guarantee that the denotation of M will be a function and the denotation of N will be a value in its domain. In this way, the syntactic typing rules of PCF avoid possible complications in the denotational semantics of the language.

There are several properties of denotational semantics that generally hold. The first is an intrinsic property of denotational semantics that distinguishes it from other forms of semantics.

• The denotational semantics is *compositional,* which means that the meaning of any expression is determined from the meanings of its subexpressions. For example,

$$[\![\texttt{if } B \texttt{ then } M \texttt{ else } N]\!]\eta = \begin{cases} [\![M]\!]\eta & \text{if } [\![B]\!]\eta \text{ is true,} \\ [\![N]\!]\eta & \text{if } [\![B]\!]\eta \text{ is false,} \\ \bot & \text{otherwise.} \end{cases}$$

where $\bot$ is used as the meaning of the expression in the case that evaluation of the test B does not terminate. An immediate consequence of the compositional form of this definition is that if B', M' and N' have the same denotations as B, M and N, respectively, then

$$[\![\texttt{if } B \texttt{ then } M \texttt{ else } N]\!]\eta = [\![\texttt{if } B' \texttt{ then } M' \texttt{ else } N']\!]\eta.$$

The reason these two must be equivalent is that the meaning of the conditional expression `if` B `then` M `else` N cannot depend on factors such as the syntactic form of B, M and N, only their semantic meaning.

• If we can prove the same assertions about M and N in the axiomatic semantics, then M and N must have the same meaning in the denotational semantics. This is called *soundness,* for an equational proof system. This is a minimal property in the sense that if soundness fails, we would conclude that something was wrong with either the axiomatic or denotational semantics. It follows from soundness, by connections between the axiomatic and operational semantics of PCF, that if $M \twoheadrightarrow N$, then M and N must have the same meaning in the denotational semantics.

Both of these properties hold for the standard denotational semantics of PCF. Further connections between operational, denotational and axiomatic semantics are summarized in Section 2.3.5.

Table 2.2
Reduction axioms for PCF.

Types *nat* and *bool*	
(*add*)	$0+0 \to 0, 0+1 \to 1, \ldots, 3+5 \to 8, \ldots$
(*Eq?*)	$Eq?\, n\, n \to true$, $Eq?\, n\, m \to false$ (n, m distinct numerals)
(*cond*)	`if` $true$ `then` M `else` $N \to M$, `if` $false$ `then` M `else` $N \to M$
Pairs ($\sigma \times \tau$)	
(*proj*)	$\mathbf{Proj}_1 \langle M, N \rangle \to M \quad \mathbf{Proj}_2 \langle M, N \rangle \to N$
Rename bound variables	
(α)	$\lambda x\colon \sigma.M = \lambda y\colon \sigma.[y/x]M$, provided y not free in M.
Functions ($\sigma \to \tau$)	
(β)	$(\lambda x\colon \sigma.M)N \to [N/x]M$
Recursion	
(*fix*)	$fix_\sigma \to \lambda f\colon \sigma \to \sigma.f\,(fix_\sigma\, f)$

2.3.4 Operational Semantics

An operational semantics may be given in several ways. The most common mathematical presentations are proof systems for either deducing the final result of evaluation or for transforming an expression through a sequence of steps. An alternative that may provide more insight into practical implementation is to define an abstract machine, which is a theoretical computing machine that evaluates programs by progressing through a series of machine states. The most common practical presentations of operational semantics are interpreters and compilers. In this book, we concentrate on the first forms of operational semantics, proof systems defining either complete or step-by-step evaluation.

The operational semantics of PCF are given by the reduction axioms mentioned in Sections 2.2.2 through 2.2.5, which are summarized in Table 2.2. The reduction axioms are written with the symbol $\to$ instead of $=$, to emphasize the direction of reduction. Intuitively, $M \to N$ means that with one evaluation step, the expression M may be transformed to the expression N. While N may not be shorter than M, most of the rules have the "feel" of program execution; it seems that we are making progress towards a simpler expression in some way. We may define an *evaluation partial function* from the reduction system by $eval(M) = N$ iff M may be reduced to normal form N in zero or more steps.

This relatively abstract operational semantics, which lacks any specific evaluation order, may be refined in several ways. We will discuss three forms of "symbolic interpreters" in

Section 2.4, one deterministic, one nondeterministic, and the third a form of parallel interpreter. While all of the interpreters are defined from reduction axioms, each applies reduction axioms to subexpressions of programs in a different way. The deterministic interpreter is defined by choosing a specific "next reduction step" at each point in program evaluation, while the nondeterministic interpreter may choose to reduce any subexpression, or choose to halt. The parallel interpreter may apply several reductions simultaneously to disjoint subexpressions. All determine the same partial evaluation function.

With three exceptions, the PCF reduction axioms are exactly the left-to-right readings of the equational axioms. The first exception is that we allow renaming of bound variables at any point during reduction, without considering this as a reduction step. From a technical standpoint, the reason is that we cannot always do substitution without renaming. The other exceptions are that we do not have reductions corresponding to the *surjective pairing* axioms (sp) for pairs or the *extensionality* axiom (η) for functions. The reason for these two omissions is largely technical and discussed briefly in Section 2.4.1.

• In general, if M is a program (closed expression of observable type) and $eval(M) = N$, then N should be something that cannot be further evaluated. In PCF in particular, if $eval(M) = N$, then N is either a numeral $0, 1, 2, \ldots$ or a boolean constant, depending on the type of M.

• If $eval(M) = N$, then M and N are equivalent according to both the axiomatic and denotational semantics. This is true for PCF, since each term is provably equal to its normal form, and the proof rules are sound for the denotational semantics.

• If M is a program and M has the same denotation as a result N, then the result of executing program M in the operational semantics is N. This is commonly referred to as *computational adequacy* since, if we take the denotational semantics as our guide, it says that we have enough reduction rules to properly determine the value of any program. If computational adequacy fails, we generally look to see if we are missing some reduction rules, or consider whether the denotational semantics gives too many expressions equal meaning. It generally follows from connections between the axiomatic and denotational semantics that if the operational semantics are adequate with respect to the denotational semantics, they are also adequate with respect to the axiomatic semantics.

2.3.5 Equivalence Relations Defined by Each Form of Semantics

We may summarize the basic connections between axiomatic, operational and denotational semantics by comparing the equivalence relations defined by each one. Since the axiomatic semantics of PCF is a logical system for deriving equations, the obvious equivalence relation is provable equality. The denotational semantics gives us the relation of *denotational equivalence:* two terms are denotationally equivalent if they have the same denotation (for any association of values to free variables). The natural equivalence relation associated with the operational semantics involves substitution of terms into full programs, described below.

We say that two programs of PCF, or any similar language, are operationally equivalent if they have the same value under the operational semantics. In symbolic form, programs M and N are operationally equivalent if $eval(M) \simeq eval(N)$. The "Kleene equation" $eval(M) \simeq eval(N)$ means that either M and N both evaluate to the same term, or neither evaluation is defined. However, this is only an equivalence relation on programs, not arbitrary terms. We extend this relation to terms that may have free variables or non-observable types using an important syntactic notion called a context.

A *context* $\mathcal{C}[\ ]$ is a term with a "hole" in it, written as a pair of empty square brackets. An example is the context

$$\mathcal{C}_0[\ ] \stackrel{\text{def}}{=} \lambda x\colon nat.\, x + [\ ]$$

If we insert a term into a context, then this is done *without* renaming bound variables. For example, $\mathcal{C}_0[x]$ is $\lambda x\colon nat.\, x + x$. We can think of a context as an incomplete program, sitting in the buffer of a text editor. Inserting a program into a context corresponds to using the text editor to fill in the rest of the program. A special case is the empty context $[\ ]$, which corresponds to a text editor containing no program at all. In Exercise 2.3.4 below, the empty context is used to show that evaluation respects operational equivalence for programs.

Using contexts, we define *operational equivalence* on arbitrary terms, as follows. Terms M and N of the same type are operationally equivalent if, for every context $\mathcal{C}[\ ]$ such that both $\mathcal{C}[M]$ and $\mathcal{C}[N]$ are programs, we have $eval(\mathcal{C}[M]) \simeq eval(\mathcal{C}[N])$. In the literature, operational equivalence is sometimes called "observational equivalence" or "observational congruence."

If we write $M =_{ax} N$ for provable equality in the axiomatic semantics, $M =_{den} N$ for denotational equivalence, and $M =_{op} N$ for operational equivalence, then the minimal requirement on the three semantics, called *adequacy* or *computational adequacy,* is

$$(\forall\ programs\ M)\ (\forall\ results\ N) \quad M =_{ax} N \text{ iff } M =_{den} N \text{ iff } M =_{op} N.$$

We also expect that for arbitrary terms, the axiomatic semantics are sound for the denotational semantics, and that denotationally equivalent terms are operationally equivalent. These may be written as the following inclusions between relations on terms:

$$=_{ax} \subseteq =_{den} \subseteq =_{op}.$$

In general, operational equivalence is the coarsest of the three, *i.e.*, more terms are operationally equivalent than denotationally equivalent or provably equivalent. This is not an accidental fact about operational semantics, but a consequence of the way that operational equivalence is defined. For example, if two terms M and N are not operationally equivalent in PCF, then there is some context $\mathcal{C}[\ ]$ with $\mathcal{C}[M]$ and $\mathcal{C}[N]$ different numerals or boolean constants. Consequently, if we equate M and N in the axiomatic semantics, we would have an inconsistent proof system; see Exercise 2.3.2. Similar reasoning applies to the denotational semantics, so in general $=_{ax}$ and $=_{den}$ cannot be any coarser than $=_{op}$. The reason why we usually have $=_{ax} \subseteq =_{den}$ is that we usually justify our axiom system by showing it is sound for denotational semantics (which is just what $=_{ax} \subseteq =_{den}$ means). Since denotational equivalence is usually not recursively enumerable, we do not typically have complete axiom systems (systems where $=_{ax}$ and $=_{den}$ are the same) for languages with recursion (fixed-point operators). A related fact for PCF is given as Corollary 2.5.16 in Section 2.5.5. The relationship between $=_{den}$ and $=_{op}$ is discussed in the next paragraph.

A denotational semantics with $M =_{den} N$ iff $M =_{op} N$, for arbitrary terms, is called *fully abstract*. A fully abstract denotational semantics may be very useful, since reasoning about the denotational semantics therefore allows us to reason about $=_{op}$. This is important since $=_{op}$ is generally difficult to reason about directly, yet it is the most useful form of equivalence for program optimization or transformation. However, it is generally a difficult mathematical problem to construct fully-abstract denotational semantics. The CPO semantics of PCF in Chapter 5, for example, is shown *not* to be fully abstract in Section 5.4.2. On the other hand, it is also shown in Section 5.4.2 that this semantics is fully abstract for an extension of PCF. Some general and historical references on full abstraction are [Cur86, Mil77, Plo77, Sto88].

Exercise 2.3.4 This exercise demonstrates general properties of evaluation and operational equivalence that hold for a variety of languages. For concreteness, however, the problem is stated for PCF. You may assume that the PCF reduction rules are confluent and that *eval* is the partial function from PCF terms to PCF terms such that $eval(M) = N$ iff N is the unique normal form of M. Show that if programs M and N are operationally equivalent, then $eval(M) \simeq eval(N)$. Assuming that all programs with no normal form are operationally equivalent, which is justified for PCF in Exercise 2.5.27, show that if M and N are programs with $eval(M) \simeq eval(N)$, then M and N are operationally equivalent.

Exercise 2.3.5 In Section 2.3.1, we defined programs as closed terms of observable type, and chose *nat* and *bool* as observable. Show that the relation $=_{op}$ remains the same if we change the set of observable types in the following ways.

(a) Only *nat* is considered observable.

(b) We say τ is an observable type if τ is either *nat*, *bool*, or the product $\tau_1 \times \tau_2$ of two observable types τ_1 and τ_2.

Exercise 2.3.6 Show that if *eval* is a partial recursive function on a recursively enumerable language, then operational equivalence is Π^0_2. (This assumes some familiarity with recursive function theory.)

2.4 PCF Reduction and Symbolic Interpreters

2.4.1 Nondeterministic Reduction

The operational semantics given by reduction may be regarded as a "nondeterministic symbolic interpreter." However, only the order in which subterms are reduced is nondeterministic, not the final result of reducing all possible subterms. Section 2.4.3 presents a deterministic form of reduction that gives the same final results for terminating PCF programs, and Section 2.4.4 gives a related "parallel" form of reduction. An inequivalent but often used deterministic reduction is considered in Section 2.4.5.

In general, given any set of reduction rules, we say M *reduces to* N *in one step,* and write $M \rightarrow N$, if N may be obtained from M by applying one reduction rule to one *subexpression.* For any notion $\rightarrow$ of reduction, the corresponding multi-step reduction relation $\twoheadrightarrow$ is defined inductively by

$M \twoheadrightarrow N$ if $M =_\alpha N$, or

$$M \rightarrow M' \text{ and } M' \twoheadrightarrow N.$$

In other words, $\twoheadrightarrow$ is the least reflexive and transitive relation on α-equivalence classes of expressions that contains one-step reduction.

Example 2.4.1 Some differences between one-step reduction ($\rightarrow$), equality ($=$), and multi-step reduction ($\twoheadrightarrow$) are illustrated using PCF below.

(a) $(\texttt{if } M \texttt{ then } 3+4 \texttt{ else } 7) = (\texttt{if } M \texttt{ then } 7 \texttt{ else } 3+4)$
since we have $3+4=7$ and equations can be used in either direction

(b) $(\texttt{if } M \texttt{ then } 3+4 \texttt{ else } 7) \not\twoheadrightarrow (\texttt{if } M \texttt{ then } 7 \texttt{ else } 3+4)$
since $7 \not\twoheadrightarrow 3+4$

(c) $5+2 \twoheadrightarrow 5+2$ but $5+2 \not\rightarrow 5+2$
since one-step reduction is not reflexive

(d) `if` $(Eq?\,3\,4)$ `then` $5+2$ `else` $9 \twoheadrightarrow 9$
by first reducing $(Eq?\,3\,4)$

It is easy to see from the definition of reduction that if $M \twoheadrightarrow N$, then we can prove the equation $M = N$. It follows that if $M \twoheadrightarrow N$ and $P \twoheadrightarrow N$, we can also prove $M = P$.

For most notions of reduction, a term may be reduced in several ways. The reason is that a term may have many different subterms, each matching the left-hand side of a different reduction rule. We may think of reduction as defining a nondeterministic symbolic interpreter that evaluates an expression M by repeatedly choosing a reduction to apply or choosing to halt. At each step, the "state" of the interpreter is characterized by the expression that is produced. We have a reduction sequence $M \twoheadrightarrow N$ iff this nondeterministic interpreter, executing M, may choose to halt in state N. A necessarily halting state, which is a term N with $N \not\twoheadrightarrow P$ for any P, is called a *normal form.* Some example PCF normal forms are the truth values *true* and *false*, the numerals 0, 1, 2, ..., a tuple $\langle M_1, \ldots, M_k \rangle$ of distinct normal forms, and any function expression $\lambda x\colon \sigma.M$ with M in normal form. We consider the result of nondeterministic evaluation to be the set of normal forms produced. As we shall see below, there is at most one normal form of any PCF term, in spite of the nondeterministic choices involved.

A useful property of many sets of reduction rules, and PCF reduction in particular, is called *confluence,* or the *Church-Rosser property,* also mentioned in Section 1.3. This property may be sketched graphically as follows.

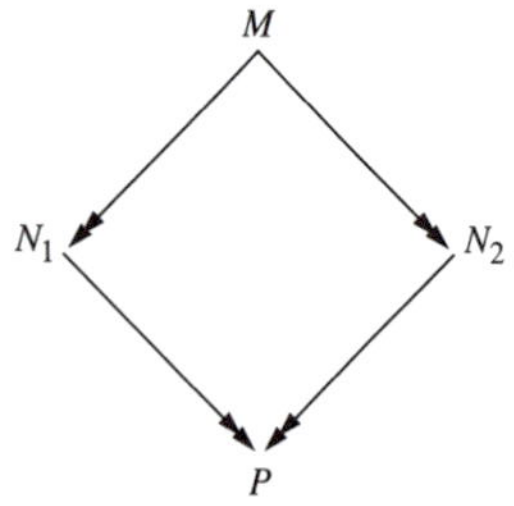

In this picture, the top two arrows are universally quantified, and the bottom two are existentially quantified. So the picture "says" that whenever $M \twoheadrightarrow N_1$ and $M \twoheadrightarrow N_2$, there exists a term P with $N_1 \twoheadrightarrow P$ and $N_2 \twoheadrightarrow P$. From Theorem 8.3.24 in Section 8.3.4, we have the following fact about PCF.

Proposition 2.4.2 PCF reduction is confluent.

If $\rightarrow$ is determined by directing a set of equational axioms, then confluence implies that an equation is provable iff both terms reduce to a common form. A corollary is that if two distinct terms cannot be reduced at all, they cannot be proved equal. This provides a useful syntactic technique for showing that an equational proof system does not prove all equations. Another simple corollary of confluence is that no term has more than one normal form. These and other general consequences of confluence are proved in Section 3.7.2.

To illustrate the value of confluence in analyzing a proof system, we justify the statement in Section 2.2.3 that (*sp*) is not derivable from (*proj*).

Example 2.4.3 Consider the reduction system with only two reduction axioms, $\mathbf{Proj}_1\ \langle M, N\rangle \rightarrow M$ and $\mathbf{Proj}_2\langle M, N\rangle \rightarrow N$. This system may be proved confluent and therefore an equation is provable from the two equational axioms $\mathbf{Proj}_1\ \langle M, N\rangle = M$ and $\mathbf{Proj}_2\langle M, N\rangle = N$ using reflexivity and the PCF equational inference rules iff the two terms reduce to a common term. It follows that the equation $x = \langle \mathbf{Proj}_1 x, \mathbf{Proj}_2 x\rangle$ cannot be proved from $\mathbf{Proj}_1\langle M, N\rangle = M$ and $\mathbf{Proj}_2\langle M, N\rangle = N$, since x and $\langle \mathbf{Proj}_1 x, \mathbf{Proj}_2 x\rangle$ are distinct normal forms. ■

While most of us are used to deterministic execution, there are some reasons to consider nondeterministic evaluation. A common reason for the designers of a programming language not to specify the order of evaluation completely is that this allows greater flexibility in optimization. An example of optimization is common subexpression elimination, which effectively reorders the evaluation of parts of an expression. A related issue is parallelism. If we are allowed to evaluate parts of an expression in any order, then it would be possible to evaluate parts of the expression in parallel, without concern for the relative speeds of the processors involved. However, in many languages where the design does not fully determine the order of evaluation, the output of some programs accepted by the compiler may depend on evaluation order. In contrast, confluence of PCF guarantees that the final result does not depend on the order in which subexpressions are evaluated.

The reason we do not use reduction axioms corresponding to equational axioms (η) and (sp) is that these would destroy confluence. It is acceptable to omit these two reductions since these are not necessary for reducing programs; reduction based on (η) and (sp) only affects the normal forms of terms that either have free variables or are not of observable type. This is an easy consequence of computational adequacy (Corollary 5.4.7). Intuitively, the reason that (η) is unnecessary is that if we have a reduction of the form

$$M \twoheadrightarrow (\ldots\ (\lambda x\colon\sigma.\, Mx)\ \ldots) \rightarrow (\ldots\ (M)\ \ldots) \twoheadrightarrow 5$$

for example, then since the result 5 does not contain any function expressions, the function expression M must eventually be applied to an argument or discarded in the reduction $(\ldots\ (M)\ \ldots) \twoheadrightarrow 5$. If M is applied, say in a subterm MN, then we would get the same result if we had not used (η) and had stuck with $\lambda x\colon\sigma.\, Mx$ in place of M, since

$(\lambda x\colon\sigma.\, Mx)N$ reduces to MN by (β) alone. The situation for surjective pairing is essentially similar.

Example 2.4.4 Consider the expression

$$\texttt{letrec}\ \ f(x\colon nat)\colon nat = \texttt{if}\ \ Eq?\,x\,0\ \ \texttt{then}\ \ 0\ \ \texttt{else}\ \ x + f(x-1)\ \ \texttt{in}\ \ f\,n$$

which we would expect to produce the natural number $n(n+1)/2$, under any ordinary interpreter. We can see how the nondeterministic PCF interpreter works by eliminating syntactic sugar and reducing. Letting

$$F \stackrel{\text{def}}{=} \lambda f\colon nat \to nat.\lambda x\colon nat.\texttt{if}\ \ Eq?\,x\,0\ \ \texttt{then}\ \ 0\ \ \texttt{else}\ \ x + f(x-1)$$

and taking $n = 2$, we have the following reduction sequence.

$$\begin{aligned}
(\mathit{fix}\ F)\,2 &\twoheadrightarrow (\lambda f\colon nat \to nat.\lambda x\colon nat.\texttt{if}\ \ Eq?\,x\,0\ \ \texttt{then}\ \ 0\ \ \texttt{else}\ \ x + f(x-1))\,(\mathit{fix}\ F)\,2\\
&\twoheadrightarrow \texttt{if}\ \ Eq?\,2\,0\ \ \texttt{then}\ \ 0\ \ \texttt{else}\ \ 2 + (\mathit{fix}\ F)(1)\\
&\twoheadrightarrow 2 + \texttt{if}\ \ Eq?\,1\,0\ \ \texttt{then}\ \ 0\ \ \texttt{else}\ \ 1 + (\mathit{fix}\ F)(0)\\
&\twoheadrightarrow 2 + 1 + (\mathit{fix}\ F)(0)\\
&\twoheadrightarrow 2 + 1 + 0 \twoheadrightarrow 3
\end{aligned}$$

Of course, other reduction sequences may be obtained by choosing *fix*-reduction in place of any of the reduction steps used here. However, by the confluence of PCF reduction, any finite interleaving of *fix*-reductions would still yield an expression that reduces to 3. ■

Example 2.4.5 Consider the expression `letrec` $f(x\colon nat)\colon nat = f(x+1)$ `in` $f\,1$. If we write a similar function declaration in another language like Lisp or Pascal, we would expect $f(n)$ not to terminate (except with stack overflow), regardless of the value of n. This is reflected in the fact that the PCF expression has no normal form. Letting

$$F \stackrel{\text{def}}{=} \lambda f\colon nat \to nat.\lambda x\colon nat.f(x+1),$$

we can de–sugar the `letrec` expression to $(\lambda f\colon nat \to nat.\ f\ 1)(\mathit{fix}\ F)$. Then we can reduce to $(\mathit{fix}\ F)1 \to F(\mathit{fix}\ F)1$. At this point, there are two possibilities

$$F(\mathit{fix}\ F)1 \to \begin{cases} F\,(F(\mathit{fix}\ F))\,1\\ (\lambda x\colon nat.(\mathit{fix}\ F)(x+1))\,1\end{cases}$$

one using *fix*-reduction, and the other β-reduction. By confluence, these two must reduce to some common form. This common form may be found by taking each term and applying the reduction used to produce the other. Applying β-reduction to the first and *fix*-reduction to the second, we obtain

$(\lambda x\colon nat.(F(\mathit{fix}\ F))(x+1))\ 1$

From here, we could either apply *fix*-reduction or (β). In either case, we obtain a term that reduces to

$(F^2(\mathit{fix}\ F))2$

Continuing in this way, we can see that regardless of our choice of reduction, we cannot ever produce an expression that does not contain $(\mathit{fix}\ F)$ as a subterm. Thus `letrec` $f(x\colon nat)\colon nat = f(x+1)$ `in` $f\,1$ has no normal form and the nondeterministic PCF interpreter need not halt. Although this brief argument is not a complete proof that the term has no normal form, a rigorous proof can be developed along these lines. A simpler proof method is to use the deterministic evaluator described in Section 2.4.3 (see Exercise 2.4.18). ■

Example 2.4.6 While PCF reduction agrees with the axiomatic semantics of PCF, this form of program execution may be slightly different from what most readers are familiar with. The difference may be illustrated by considering the following program.

`let` $f(x\colon nat)\colon nat = 3$ `in`
  `letrec` $g(x\colon nat)\colon nat = g(x+1)$ `in` $f(g\,5)$

In most familiar programming languages, this program would not halt, since the call $f(g\,5)$ is compiled or interpreted as code that computes $g\,5$ before calling f. Since the call to g runs forever, the program does not halt. However, in PCF, we can reduce the function call to f without reducing $g\,5$. Since f disregards its argument, we obtain the value 3. Although this explanation of termination uses the ability to reduce any subexpression, this is not essential. In particular, the deterministic evaluator defined in Section 2.4.3 will also reduce the term above to the numeral 3. (See Exercise 2.4.17.) Further comparison of evaluation orders appears in the next section. ■

As mentioned earlier in Section 2.3.4, it is important that the axiomatic semantics respect the operational semantics. Specifically, if we can prove $M = N$, then these two terms should produce the same result when placed inside any PCF program. The reader may wonder about the extensionality axiom (η), which is $\lambda x\colon\sigma.Mx = M$ for x not free in M. This equation seems very reasonable when viewed as a statement about mathematical functions, but it is not completely obvious that $\lambda x\colon\sigma.Mx$ and M are interchangeable with respect to the nondeterministic PCF interpreter. Since PCF reduction does not include η-reduction, the nondeterministic interpreter is forced to halt on $\lambda x\colon\sigma.yx$, for example, which is different from y; clearly $\lambda x\colon\sigma.yx$ and y do not have the same normal form if we omit (η). However, when placed inside a context $\mathcal{C}[\ ]$ such that both $\mathcal{C}[\lambda x\colon\sigma.yx]$ and $\mathcal{C}[y]$

are programs, we have already observed that $\mathcal{C}[\lambda x{:}\sigma.yx]$ and $\mathcal{C}[y]$ will have the same normal form, if any. (The situation for (*sp*), surjective pairing, is similar.) Thus, the equational proof system of PCF is sound for reasoning about program modification, or interchangeability of program "parts."

Exercise 2.4.7 Show that (*fix*) reduction may be applied indefinitely to any expression of the form $\texttt{letrec}\ f{:}\sigma = M\ \texttt{in}\ N$. Does this mean that recursive functions never "terminate" in PCF?

Exercise 2.4.8 Compute normal forms for the following terms.

(a) $\mathit{comp}\,(\lambda x{:}\mathit{nat}.\,x+1)\,(\lambda x{:}\mathit{nat}.\,x+1)\,5$, where the definition of natural number function composition is given in Section 2.2.3.

(b) $\texttt{let}\ \mathit{not} = \lambda x{:}\mathit{bool}.\,\texttt{if}\ x\ \texttt{then}\ \mathit{false}\ \texttt{else}\ \mathit{true}\ \texttt{in}$
$\texttt{letrec}\ f = \lambda x{:}\mathit{bool}.\,\texttt{if}\ x\ \texttt{then}\ \mathit{true}\ \texttt{else}\ f(\mathit{not}\,x)\ \texttt{in}$
$f\,\mathit{false}$

Exercise 2.4.9 Show that taken together the following three reduction rules for typed lambda calculus with fixed points are not confluent.

$$(\lambda x{:}\sigma.M)N \rightarrow [N/x]M \tag{β}$$

$$\lambda x{:}\sigma.Mx \rightarrow M, \quad x \text{ not free in } M \tag{η}$$

$$\mathit{fix}_\sigma M \rightarrow M(\mathit{fix}_\sigma M) \tag{fix_{alt}}$$

More specifically, find a term M that may be reduced in one step to N or P, where N and P cannot be reduced to a common term. *Hint:* It is possible to find such an M which has no (β) redexes. Your counterexample will not work if we use (*fix*) reduction, $\mathit{fix}_\sigma \rightarrow \lambda f{:}\sigma \rightarrow \sigma.\, f(\mathit{fix}_\sigma f)$, as in the text.

2.4.2 Reduction Strategies

We will discuss various deterministic interpreters using the notion of reduction strategy. A *reduction strategy* is a partial function F from terms to terms with the property that if $F(M) = N$, then $M \rightarrow N$. This is called a "strategy" since the function may be used to choose one out of many possible reductions. For any reduction strategy F, we may define a *partial evaluation function* $\mathit{eval}_F{:}\, \mathit{PCF} \rightarrow \mathit{PCF}$ on PCF expressions by

$$\mathit{eval}_F(M) = \begin{cases} M & \text{if } F(M) \text{ is not defined} \\ N & \text{if } F(M) = M' \text{ and } \mathit{eval}_F(M') = N \end{cases}$$

The evaluation function eval_F is the mathematical equivalent of a deterministic interpreter that repeats single reduction steps, following the strategy F, until this strategy cannot be followed any further (*i.e.*, we reach a term where the partial function F is undefined). If the strategy can be followed indefinitely from M, then the function $eval_F$ will be undefined on M, and an actual interpreter following F would run forever. (See Exercise 2.4.10 below for further discussion of the way $eval_F$ is defined from F.) As a notational convenience, we will omit the subscript F if the reduction strategy is clear from context or irrelevant.

In general, we will be interested in reduction strategies that choose a reduction whenever possible, at least if the term is a program. For such reduction strategies, the evaluation $eval(M)$ of a program M will either be the normal form of M, or undefined. In the terminology of [Bar84], the reduction strategies we consider are *one-step* reduction strategies, since they choose a single reduction step based on the form of the term alone. For discussion of multi-step reduction strategies, the reader may consult [Bar84].

It is possible to define a "brute force" reduction strategy F with the property that for any term M, $eval(M)$ is either the normal form of M or undefined. Given M, we can compute $F(M)$ by enumerating (in parallel) all reduction paths from M and seeing if any produces a normal form. If we find one reduction path, say $M \to M_1 \to M_2 \to \ldots \to N$, leading to a normal form, we let $F(M) = M_1$ be the first term along this reduction path. This is not a very satisfying reduction strategy, however, since it may take a long time to compute $F(M)$; it is not even decidable whether $F(M)$ is defined. However, we will see below that there is an efficiently computable reduction strategy which will always find the normal form of a term.

An important property of PCF is that the idealized nondeterministic interpreter may be implemented deterministically in an efficient manner. More specifically, there is an efficiently computable reduction strategy F such that whenever M reduces to a normal form N, we have $eval_F(M) = N$. This reduction strategy is called *left-most outer-most* or, more simply, *left-most reduction*. It is defined precisely in the next section. Another name that is sometimes used is *call-by-name* reduction, but this is sometimes confusing since call-by-name is also used to refer to a parameter-passing mechanism implemented by "thunks" (see [ASU86], for example). The difference between left-most reduction and other alternatives may be illustrated by considering an expression $(\lambda x\colon \sigma.M)N$, where $M \to M'$ and $N \to N'$. There are three possible ways to reduce this expression:

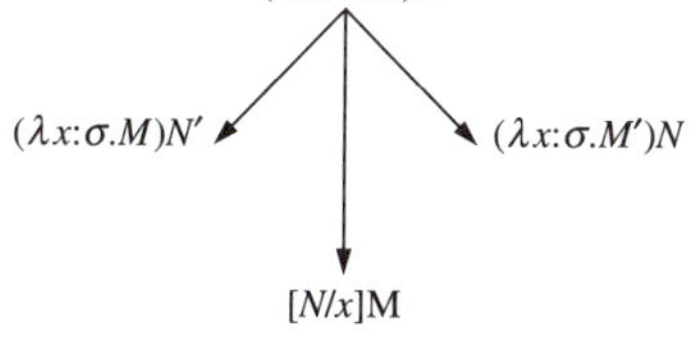

Table 2.3
Left-most Reduction for PCF.

Axioms

$$\frac{M \to N}{M \stackrel{\text{left}}{\to} N} \qquad M \to N \textit{ is a reduction axiom}$$

Subterm Rules

nat and *bool*

$$\frac{M \stackrel{\text{left}}{\to} M'}{M + N \stackrel{\text{left}}{\to} M' + N} \qquad \frac{M \stackrel{\text{left}}{\to} M'}{N + M \stackrel{\text{left}}{\to} N + M'} \qquad N \textit{ a normal form}$$

$$\frac{M \stackrel{\text{left}}{\to} M'}{Eq?MN \stackrel{\text{left}}{\to} Eq?M'N} \qquad \frac{M \stackrel{\text{left}}{\to} M'}{Eq?NM \stackrel{\text{left}}{\to} Eq?NM'} \qquad N \textit{ a normal form}$$

$$\frac{M \stackrel{\text{left}}{\to} M'}{\texttt{if } M \texttt{ then } N \texttt{ else } P \stackrel{\text{left}}{\to} \texttt{if } M' \texttt{ then } N \texttt{ else } P}$$

$$\frac{N \stackrel{\text{left}}{\to} N'}{\texttt{if } M \texttt{ then } N \texttt{ else } P \stackrel{\text{left}}{\to} \texttt{if } M \texttt{ then } N' \texttt{ else } P} \qquad M \textit{ a normal form}$$

$$\frac{P \stackrel{\text{left}}{\to} P'}{\texttt{if } M \texttt{ then } N \texttt{ else } P \stackrel{\text{left}}{\to} \texttt{if } M \texttt{ then } N \texttt{ else } P'} \qquad M, N \textit{ normal forms}$$

Pairs

$$\frac{M \stackrel{\text{left}}{\to} M'}{\langle M, N\rangle \stackrel{\text{left}}{\to} \langle M', N\rangle} \qquad \frac{N \stackrel{\text{left}}{\to} N'}{\langle M, N\rangle \stackrel{\text{left}}{\to} \langle M, N\rangle} \qquad M \textit{ a normal form}$$

$$\frac{M \stackrel{\text{left}}{\to} M'}{\mathbf{Proj}_i M \stackrel{\text{left}}{\to} \mathbf{Proj}_i M'}$$

Functions

$$\frac{M \stackrel{\text{left}}{\to} M'}{MN \stackrel{\text{left}}{\to} M'N} \qquad \frac{N \stackrel{\text{left}}{\to} N'}{MN \stackrel{\text{left}}{\to} MN'} \qquad M \textit{ a normal form}$$

$$\frac{M \stackrel{\text{left}}{\to} M'}{\lambda x\colon \sigma.\, M \stackrel{\text{left}}{\to} \lambda x\colon \sigma.\, M'}$$

Subterm rules apply only when no axiom applies to the entire term. For example, $\mathbf{Proj}_i M \stackrel{\text{left}}{\to} \mathbf{Proj}_i M'$ only when M is not of the form $\langle M_1, M_2\rangle$ and MN reduces to $M'N$ only when M is not of the form $\lambda x\colon \sigma.\, M_1$.

$$\begin{aligned}
& ((\underline{\lambda x\colon nat.\, \lambda y\colon nat.\, x + y)\, 7})\, 5 + (\lambda x\colon nat.\, x)\, 3 \\
\stackrel{\text{left}}{\to}\quad & \underline{(\lambda y\colon nat.\, 7 + y)\, 5} + (\lambda x\colon nat.\, x)\, 3 \\
\stackrel{\text{left}}{\to}\quad & (\underline{7 + 5}) + (\lambda x\colon nat.\, x)\, 3 \\
\stackrel{\text{left}}{\to}\quad & 12 + \underline{(\lambda x\colon nat.\, x)\, 3} \\
\stackrel{\text{left}}{\to}\quad & \underline{12 + 3} \\
\stackrel{\text{left}}{\to}\quad & 15
\end{aligned}$$

A second example, not producing a numeral, follows.

$$\underline{(\lambda x\colon nat.\, \lambda y\colon nat.\, x + (x + y))\,((\lambda z\colon nat.\, z)\, 12)}$$

$$\stackrel{\text{left}}{\rightarrow} \quad \lambda y\colon nat.(\underline{(\lambda z\colon nat.\, z)\, 12}) + (((\lambda z\colon nat.\, z)\, 12) + y)$$

$$\stackrel{\text{left}}{\rightarrow} \quad \lambda y\colon nat.\, 12 + ((\underline{(\lambda z\colon nat.\, z)\, 12}) + y)$$

$$\stackrel{\text{left}}{\rightarrow} \quad \lambda y\colon nat.\, 12 + (12 + y)$$

The last term is a normal form with respect to left-most reduction. Neither sum can be reduced since the parentheses associate the sums to the right. If we had $(12 + 12) + y$ instead, the body of this lambda term could be reduced to $24 + y$. ∎

As stated in the following proposition, left-most reduction will find the normal form of any term that has one.

Proposition 2.4.12 Let M be a PCF term of any type. Then for any normal form N, we have $M \stackrel{\text{left}}{\twoheadrightarrow} N$ iff $M \twoheadrightarrow N$.

This follows from Theorem 8.3.26 in Section 8.3.4, which gives a general condition guaranteeing completeness of left-most reduction for PCF-like languages.

Since $\stackrel{\text{left}}{\rightarrow}$ is a reduction strategy, we may apply the general definition of evaluation function from Section 2.4.2 to obtain an evaluation (partial) function $eval_{\stackrel{\text{left}}{\rightarrow}}$. For typographical reasons, we will write $eval_{left}$ instead of $eval_{\stackrel{\text{left}}{\rightarrow}}$. A corollary of Proposition 2.4.12 is that this evaluator finds the normal form of any term that has one.

Proposition 2.4.13 Let M be a PCF term of any type. Then $eval_{left}(M) = N$ iff $M \twoheadrightarrow N$ and N is a normal form.

If we only want Propositions 2.4.12 and 2.4.13 to hold for PCF programs (closed terms of observable type), then we may omit many of the reductions on subterms. The result is *lazy reduction,* which is far more commonly implemented in practice than left-most reduction. This is given by axioms and inference rules in Table 2.4. As usual, we write $\stackrel{\text{lazy}}{\twoheadrightarrow}$ for the reflexive and transitive closure of $\stackrel{\text{lazy}}{\rightarrow}$. We say a term M is in *lazy normal form* if there is no N with $M \stackrel{\text{lazy}}{\rightarrow} N$. Note that the lazy normal forms of types *nat* and *bool* are exactly the normal forms of these types. However, the lazy normal forms of function or product types may have subterms that are not in normal form (lazy or otherwise), as illustrated in the following example.

Example 2.4.14 The lazy reduction of the term $((\lambda x\colon nat.\, \lambda y\colon nat.\, x + y)\, 7)\, 5 + (\lambda x\colon nat.\, x)\, 3$ is exactly the left-most reduction given in Example 2.4.11. For the second

Table 2.4
Lazy reduction for PCF.

Axioms

$$\frac{M \to N}{M \stackrel{\text{lazy}}{\to} N} \qquad M \to N \text{ is a reduction axiom}$$

Subterm Rules

nat and *bool*

$$\frac{M \stackrel{\text{lazy}}{\to} M'}{M + N \stackrel{\text{lazy}}{\to} M' + N} \qquad \frac{M \stackrel{\text{lazy}}{\to} M'}{n + M \stackrel{\text{lazy}}{\to} n + M'} \qquad n \text{ a numeral}$$

$$\frac{M \stackrel{\text{lazy}}{\to} M'}{Eq?MN \stackrel{\text{lazy}}{\to} Eq?M'N} \qquad \frac{M \stackrel{\text{lazy}}{\to} M'}{Eq?nM \stackrel{\text{lazy}}{\to} Eq?nM'} \qquad n \text{ a numeral}$$

$$\frac{M \stackrel{\text{lazy}}{\to} M'}{\texttt{if } M \texttt{ then } N \texttt{ else } P \stackrel{\text{lazy}}{\to} \texttt{if } M' \texttt{ then } N \texttt{ else } P}$$

Pairs

$$\frac{M \stackrel{\text{lazy}}{\to} M'}{\mathbf{Proj}_i M \stackrel{\text{lazy}}{\to} \mathbf{Proj}_i M'}$$

Functions

$$\frac{M \stackrel{\text{lazy}}{\to} M'}{MN \stackrel{\text{lazy}}{\to} M'N}$$

---

term given in Example 2.4.11, lazy reduction terminates sooner, since lazy reduction does not change any subexpression inside the scope of a λ or inside a pair of the form $\langle\cdot, \cdot\rangle$.

$$\underline{(\lambda x\colon nat.\, \lambda y\colon nat.\, x + (x + y))\,((\lambda z\colon nat.\, z)\, 12)}$$
$$\stackrel{\text{lazy}}{\to} \quad \lambda y\colon nat.((\lambda z\colon nat.\, z)\, 12) + (((\lambda z\colon nat.\, z)\, 12) + y)$$

The last term is a lazy normal form, since there is no lazy reduction of this term. ∎

The main property of lazy reduction, in comparison with left-most reduction, follows from the following proposition.

Proposition 2.4.15 If M is a closed PCF term that does not have the form $\lambda x\colon \sigma.\, M_1$ or $\langle M_1, M_2\rangle$, then for any term N, we have $M \stackrel{\text{lazy}}{\to} N$ iff $M \stackrel{\text{left}}{\to} N$.

Proof It is easy to see that if $M \stackrel{\text{lazy}}{\to} N$ then $M \stackrel{\text{left}}{\to} N$. We prove the converse by induction on the proof (using the rules that appear in Table 2.3) that $M \stackrel{\text{left}}{\to} N$. The base case is that $M \to N$ is a reduction axiom, in which case $M \stackrel{\text{lazy}}{\to} N$.

The induction step for each inference rule that appears in both in Table 2.3 and Table 2.4 is straightforward. The only observation that is required, in the case $N + M \stackrel{\text{left}}{\to} N + M'$ with N a normal form, is that since N is closed, it must be a numeral. Therefore, $N + M \stackrel{\text{lazy}}{\to} N + M'$, and similarly for $Eq?\,N\,M \stackrel{\text{left}}{\to} Eq?\,N\,M'$.

If the left-most reduction is by

$\texttt{if } M \texttt{ then } N \texttt{ else } P \stackrel{\text{left}}{\rightarrow} \texttt{if } M \texttt{ then } N' \texttt{ else } P$

with M a normal form, then the assumption that the entire term is closed means that M must be *true* or *false*. Therefore, the left-most reduction should have been to eliminate the conditional and proceed with N or P.

The hypothesis that M is neither a λ-abstraction or pair rules out the cases for left-most reduction inside a λ-abstraction or pair.

The final case is the reduction of a closed term $MN \stackrel{\text{left}}{\rightarrow} MN'$ where M is a normal form. But since M must be closed, it must have the form $M \equiv \lambda x{:}\,\sigma.\, M_1$ or $M \equiv \mathit{fix}\, M_1$. In either case, this contradicts the assumption that $MN \stackrel{\text{left}}{\rightarrow} MN'$, concluding the proof. ■

Corollary 2.4.16 If P is a PCF program and R a result (closed normal form of the same type), then $P \stackrel{\text{lazy}}{\twoheadrightarrow} R$ iff $P \stackrel{\text{left}}{\twoheadrightarrow} R$.

Exercise 2.4.17 Show, by performing left-most reduction, that the deterministic evaluator halts with value 3 on the program given in Example 2.4.6.

Exercise 2.4.18 Show that the PCF expression $\texttt{letrec}\, f(x{:}\,\mathit{nat}){:}\,\mathit{nat} = f(x+1)$ in $f1$, described in Example 2.4.5, has no normal form.

2.4.4 Parallel Reduction

The general idea behind parallel evaluation of PCF is that whenever we can reduce either of two subterms independently, we may reduce both simultaneously. We might reach a normal form faster this way, although of course this is not guaranteed. However, there is no harm in doing so: since PCF reduction is confluent, we will not reach a different normal form by doing extra reduction in parallel.

We will define a parallel reduction relation $\Rightarrow$ from nondeterministic reduction using two inference rules. The first rule below says that a single reduction may be considered a special case of parallel reduction.

$$\frac{M \rightarrow N}{M \Rightarrow N}$$

where we intend $M \rightarrow N$ to indicate that N results from a single reduction to M itself or one of its subterms. If $\mathcal{C}[\ldots]$ is a context with places for k terms to be inserted, then a term of the form $\mathcal{C}[M_1, \ldots, M_k]$ will have nonoverlapping subterms $M_1, \ldots, M_k$. In this case, it makes sense to reduce these subterms simultaneously, possibly in parallel. This is expressed by the following rule.

$$\frac{M_1 \Rightarrow N_1, \ldots, M_k \Rightarrow N_k}{\mathcal{C}[M_1, \ldots, M_k] \Rightarrow \mathcal{C}[N_1, \ldots, N_k]}$$

As usual, multi-step parallel reduction $\Rightarrow\!\!\!\!\Rightarrow$ is the reflexive and transitive closure of single-step parallel reduction.

This parallel reduction relation gives us a nondeterministic form of reduction with the property that $M \twoheadrightarrow N$ by ordinary PCF reduction iff $M \Rightarrow\!\!\!\!\Rightarrow N$ by parallel reduction steps. It is also possible to define parallel reduction strategies which give the same normal form as sequential reduction. This may be done in a way that maximizes parallelism, optionally up to some bound which we may think of as the maximum feasible number of parallel processes for some parallel architecture. However, we will not go into the details.

Exercise 2.4.19 This exercise asks you to compare parallel and sequential reduction.

(a) Prove that $M \Rightarrow\!\!\!\!\Rightarrow N$ iff $M \twoheadrightarrow N$. You may use the fact that for any context $\mathcal{C}[\ ]$, the term $\mathcal{C}[M_1, \ldots, M_k]$ has independent subterms $M_1, \ldots, M_k$ which may be replaced separately by $N_1, \ldots, N_k$ to yield $\mathcal{C}[N_1, \ldots, N_k]$.

(b) Suppose $M \twoheadrightarrow N$ and N is a normal form. Use confluence of $\twoheadrightarrow$ and part (a) to show that if $M \Rightarrow\!\!\!\!\Rightarrow P$, then $P \Rightarrow\!\!\!\!\Rightarrow N$.

(c) Show by counterexample that part (b) fails if $\twoheadrightarrow$ is not confluent. In other words, give a single-step reduction relation $\rightarrow$ on some set of terms such that there exist M, N and P with $M \twoheadrightarrow N$, term N not reducible, and $M \Rightarrow\!\!\!\!\Rightarrow P$ with P not reducible to N by either parallel or sequential reduction.

2.4.5 Eager PCF

Left-most reduction matches the axiomatic semantics of PCF and allows nondeterministic or parallel implementations. However, most implementations of existing programming languages do not follow this evaluation order. (An exception is Algol 60, whose "copy rule" procedure-call semantics match PCF reduction; more modern examples are Haskell and Miranda, as noted in Section 2.1.) The more common order is eager evaluation, which does *not* match the PCF axiomatic semantics, as illustrated in Example 2.4.6 (see also Example 2.4.21 below). In this section, we give a precise definition of eager evaluation for PCF and consider a few properties. Eager PCF is also discussed in Section 2.6.4 in connection with "explicit lifting."

An important idea in eager reduction is the notion of *value,* which is a term that is not further reduced by eager reduction. The terms that are not values are function applications and pairs of non-values. The main difference between eager reduction and other reduction strategies considered in this chapter is that under eager reduction, we only apply β-reduction and $\mathbf{Proj}_i$-reduction when a function argument is a value. There is also a change in *fix* reduction to halt reduction of the argument to *fix*, as explained below. The name "value" comes from the fact that values are considered "fully evaluated." One-step

Table 2.5
Eager PCF reduction.

Values

V is a *value* if V is a constant, variable, lambda abstraction or pair of values.

$$delay_{\sigma\to\tau}[M] \stackrel{\text{def}}{=} \lambda x\colon\sigma.\, Mx \qquad x \text{ not free in } M\colon\sigma\to\tau$$

Axioms

$$(\lambda x\colon\sigma.M)V \stackrel{\text{eager}}{\rightarrow} [V/x]M \qquad V \text{ a value}$$

$$\mathbf{Proj}_i\langle V_1, V_2\rangle \stackrel{\text{eager}}{\rightarrow} V_i \qquad V_1, V_2 \text{ values}$$

$$\mathit{fix}_{\sigma\to\tau}\, V \stackrel{\text{eager}}{\rightarrow} V(delay_{\sigma\to\tau}[\mathit{fix}_{\sigma\to\tau}\, V]) \qquad V \text{ a value}$$

$$0+0 \stackrel{\text{eager}}{\rightarrow} 0,\ 0+1 \stackrel{\text{eager}}{\rightarrow} 1, \ldots, 3+5 \stackrel{\text{eager}}{\rightarrow} 8, \ldots$$

$$Eq?\, n\, n \stackrel{\text{eager}}{\rightarrow} true,\ Eq?\, n\, m \stackrel{\text{eager}}{\rightarrow} false \qquad n,m \text{ distinct numerals}$$

$$\texttt{if } true \texttt{ then } M \texttt{ else } N \stackrel{\text{eager}}{\rightarrow} M, \texttt{if } false \texttt{ then } M \texttt{ else } N \stackrel{\text{eager}}{\rightarrow} N$$

Subterm Rules

nat

$$\frac{M \stackrel{\text{eager}}{\rightarrow} M'}{M+N \stackrel{\text{eager}}{\rightarrow} M'+N} \qquad \frac{M \stackrel{\text{eager}}{\rightarrow} M'}{n+M \stackrel{\text{eager}}{\rightarrow} n+M'} \qquad n \text{ a numeral}$$

bool

$$\frac{M \stackrel{\text{eager}}{\rightarrow} M'}{Eq?MN \stackrel{\text{eager}}{\rightarrow} Eq?M'N} \qquad \frac{M \stackrel{\text{eager}}{\rightarrow} M'}{Eq?nM \stackrel{\text{eager}}{\rightarrow} Eq?nM'} \qquad n \text{ a numeral}$$

$$\frac{M \stackrel{\text{eager}}{\rightarrow} M'}{\texttt{if } M \texttt{ then } N \texttt{ else } P \stackrel{\text{eager}}{\rightarrow} \texttt{if } M' \texttt{ then } N \texttt{ else } P}$$

Pairs

$$\frac{M \stackrel{\text{eager}}{\rightarrow} M'}{\langle M, N\rangle \stackrel{\text{eager}}{\rightarrow} \langle M', N\rangle} \qquad \frac{N \stackrel{\text{eager}}{\rightarrow} N'}{\langle V, N\rangle \stackrel{\text{eager}}{\rightarrow} \langle V, N'\rangle} \qquad V \text{ a value}$$

$$\frac{M \stackrel{\text{eager}}{\rightarrow} M'}{\mathbf{Proj}_i M \stackrel{\text{eager}}{\rightarrow} \mathbf{Proj}_i M'}$$

Functions

$$\frac{M \stackrel{\text{eager}}{\rightarrow} M'}{MN \stackrel{\text{eager}}{\rightarrow} M'N} \qquad \frac{N \stackrel{\text{eager}}{\rightarrow} N'}{VN \stackrel{\text{eager}}{\rightarrow} VN'} \qquad V \text{ a value}$$

eager or *call-by-value reduction* is defined in Table 2.5. Like lazy reduction, eager reduction is only intended to produce a numeral or boolean constant from a full (closed) program; it is not intended to produce normal forms or fully reduce open terms that may have free variables. This can be seen in the rules for addition: there is no eager reduction from a term of the form $x + M$, even though M could be further reduced.

A significant restriction on eager PCF is that *we only have fixed-point operator fix_σ for function types $\sigma = \sigma_1 \to \sigma_2$*. The intuitive reason is that since a recursively-defined natural number, boolean or pair would be fully evaluated before any function could be applied to it, any such expression would cause the program containing it to diverge. In more detail, reduction of closed terms only halts on lambda abstractions, pairs of values and constants.

While lambda abstractions and pairs of values could contain occurrences of *fix*, analysis of a pair $\langle V_1, V_2\rangle$ with V_1 and V_2 values shows that any occurrence of *fix* must occur inside a lambda abstraction. Therefore, the only values that could involve recursion are functions. If we changed the system so that a pair $\langle M, N\rangle$ were a value, for any terms M and N, then it would make sense to have a fixed-point operator fix_σ for each product type $\sigma = \sigma_1 \times \sigma_2$.

It is easy to verify, by examination of Table 2.5, that for any M, there is at most one N with $M \stackrel{\text{eager}}{\to} N$. Since no values are reduced, $\stackrel{\text{eager}}{\to}$ is a partial function on terms whose domain contains only non-values.

The use of *delay* and *fix* reduction requires some explanation. Since eager reduction does not reduce under a lambda abstraction, a term of the form $\mathit{delay}_{\sigma\to\tau}[M] \equiv \lambda x\colon \sigma.\, Mx$ will not be reduced. This explains why we call the mapping $M \mapsto \lambda x\colon \sigma.\, Mx$ "delay." The reason that *delay* is used in *fix* reduction is to halt reduction of a recursive function definition until an argument is supplied. An example is given in Exercise 2.4.24; see also Exercise 2.4.25.

Example 2.4.20 Some of the characteristics of eager reduction are illustrated by reducing the term

$$(\mathit{fix}\,(\lambda x\colon \mathit{nat} \to \mathit{nat}.\, \lambda y\colon \mathit{nat}.\, y))\ ((\lambda z\colon \mathit{nat}.\, z + 1)\, 2)$$

to a value. This is only a trivial fixed point, but the term does give us a chance to see the order of evaluation. The first step in determining which reduction to apply is to check the entire term. This has the form of an application MN, but neither the function M nor the argument N is a value. According to the rule at the bottom left of Table 2.5, we must eager-reduce the function $M \equiv \mathit{fix}\,(\lambda x\colon \mathit{nat} \to \mathit{nat}.\, \lambda y\colon \mathit{nat}.\, y)$. Since the argument to *fix* is a value, we apply the reduction axiom for *fix*. Followed by β-reduction, since *delay*[...] is a value, this gives us a function value (lambda abstraction) as follows:

$$\begin{array}{ll} \multicolumn{2}{l}{\mathit{fix}\,(\lambda x\colon \mathit{nat} \to \mathit{nat}.\, \lambda y\colon \mathit{nat}.\, y)} \\ \stackrel{\text{eager}}{\to} & (\lambda x\colon \mathit{nat} \to \mathit{nat}.\, \lambda y\colon \mathit{nat}.\, y)\ (\mathit{delay}[\mathit{fix}\,(\lambda x\colon \mathit{nat} \to \mathit{nat}.\, \lambda y\colon \mathit{nat}.\, y)]) \\ \stackrel{\text{eager}}{\to} & \lambda y\colon \mathit{nat}.\, y \end{array}$$

Note that without *delay*[ ], the eager strategy would have continued *fix* reduction indefinitely.

We have now reduced the original term MN to a term VN with function $V \equiv \lambda y\colon \mathit{nat}.\, y$ a value but argument $N \equiv (\lambda z\colon \mathit{nat}.\, z + 1)\, 2$ not a value. According to the rule at the bottom right of Table 2.5, we must eager-reduce the function argument. Since $\lambda z\colon \mathit{nat}.\, z + 1$ and 2 are both values, we can apply β-reduction, followed by reduction of the sum of two numerals:

$$(\lambda z\colon \mathit{nat}.\, z + 1)\, 2 \stackrel{\text{eager}}{\to} 2 + 1 \stackrel{\text{eager}}{\to} 3$$

This now gives us the application $(\lambda y\colon nat.\, y)\,3$ of one value to another, which can be reduced to 3. ∎

Example 2.4.21 Divergence of eager evaluation can be seen in the term

$$\texttt{let}\ f(x\colon nat)\colon nat = 3\ \ \texttt{in}$$
$$\quad \texttt{letrec}\ \ g(x\colon nat)\colon nat = g(x+1)\ \ \texttt{in}\ \ f(g\,5)$$

from Example 2.4.6. Exercise 2.4.22 asks you to reduce this term. Since we can easily prove that this term is equal to 3, this term shows that the equational proof system of PCF is not sound for proving equivalence under eager evaluation. It is possible to develop an alternative proof system for eager equivalence, restricting β-conversion to the case where the function argument is a value, for example. However, due to restrictions on replacing subexpressions, the resulting system is more complicated than the equational system for PCF. ∎

The deterministic call-by-value evaluator $eval_V$ is defined from $\stackrel{\text{eager}}{\rightarrow}$ in the usual way. Since the partial function $\stackrel{\text{eager}}{\rightarrow}$ selects a reduction step iff the term is not a value, $eval_V$ may also be defined as follows.

$$eval_V(M) = \begin{cases} M & \text{if } M \text{ is a value} \\ N & \text{if } M \stackrel{\text{eager}}{\rightarrow} M' \text{ and } eval_V(M') = N \end{cases}$$

There seem to be two main reasons for implementing eager rather than left-most (or lazy) evaluation in practice. The first is that even for a purely functional language such as PCF (*i.e.*, a language without assignment or other operations with side effects), the usual implementation of left-most reduction is less efficient. The reason for the inefficiency appears to be that when an argument such as $f\,x$ is passed to a function g, it is necessary to pass a pointer to the code for f and to keep a record of the appropriate lexical environment. As a result, there is significantly more overhead to implementing function calls. It would be simpler just to call f with argument x immediately and then pass the resulting integer, for example, to g. The second reason that left-most reduction is not usually implemented has to do with side effects. As illustrated by the many tricks used in Algol 60, the combination of left-most evaluation and assignment is often confusing. In addition, in the presence of side effects, left-most evaluation does not coincide with nondeterministic or parallel evaluation. The reason is that the order in which assignments are made to a variable will generally affect the program output. We cannot expect different orders of evaluation to produce the same result. Since most languages in common use include assignment, many of the advantages of left-most or lazy evaluation are lost.

Exercise 2.4.22 Show, by performing eager reduction, that the eager interpreter does not halt on the program given in Example 2.4.21.

Exercise 2.4.23 Assuming appropriate reduction rules for the function symbols used in the factorial function *fact* of Section 2.2.5, show that $fact\ 3 \overset{eager}{\twoheadrightarrow} 6$.

Exercise 2.4.24 An alternate eager reduction for *fix* might be

$$fix_\sigma\ (\lambda x\colon \sigma.\, M) \overset{eager}{\rightarrow} [fix_\sigma\ (\lambda x\colon \sigma.\, M)/x]M$$

Find a term $\lambda x\colon \sigma.\, M$ where eager reduction as defined in Table 2.5 would terminate, but the alternate form given by this rule would not. Explain why, for programs of the form $\mathtt{letrec}\ \ f(x\colon\sigma) = M\ \ \mathtt{in}\ \ N$ with *fix* not occurring in M or N, it does not seem possible to distinguish between the two possible eager reductions for *fix*.

Exercise 2.4.25 Eager or call-by-value reduction may also be applied to untyped lambda calculus. With ordinary (left-most) reduction, an untyped fixed-point operator, Y, may be written $Y \overset{def}{=} \lambda f.(\lambda x.\, f(xx))(\lambda x.\, f(xx))$. Under eager, or call-by-value reduction, the standard untyped fixed-point operator is written $Z \overset{def}{=} \lambda f.(\lambda x.\, f(delay[xx]))(\lambda x.\, f(delay[xx]))$ where $delay[U] \overset{def}{=} \lambda z.\, Ux$ for x not free in untyped term U. Show that for $M \overset{def}{=} \lambda x.\lambda y.\, y$, the application YM lazy or left-most reduces to a term beginning with a lambda, and similarly for ZM using untyped eager reduction. What happens when we apply eager reduction to YM?

2.5 PCF Programming Examples, Expressive Power and Limitations

2.5.1 Records and n-tuples

Records are a useful data type in Pascal and many other languages. We will see that record expressions may be translated into PCF using pairing and projection. Essentially, a record is an aggregate of one or more *components,* each with a different label. We can combine any expressions $M_1\colon\sigma_1, \ldots, M_k\colon\sigma_k$ and form a record $\{\ell_1 = M_1, \ldots, \ell_k = M_k\}$ whose ℓ_i component has the value of M_i. The type of this record may be written $\{\ell_1\colon\sigma_1, \ldots, \ell_k\colon\sigma_k\}$. We select the ℓ_i component of any record r of this type $(0 \le i \le k)$ using the "dot" notation $r.\ell_i$. For example, the record $\{A = 3,\ B = true\}$ with components labeled A and B has type $\{A\colon nat,\ B\colon bool\}$. The A component is selected by writing $\{A = 3,\ B = true\}.A$. In general, we have the equational axiom

$$\{\ell_1 = M_1, \ldots, \ell_k = M_k\}.\ell_i = M_i \qquad (record\ selection)$$

for component selection, which may be used as a reduction rule from left to right.

One convenient aspect of records is that component order does not matter (in the syntax just introduced and in most languages). We can access the A component of a record r without having to remember which component we listed first in defining r. In addition, we may choose mnemonic names for labels, as in

$$\texttt{let}\ person = \{name\colon string,\ age\colon nat,\ married\colon bool, \ldots\}$$

However, these are the only substantive differences between records and cartesian products; by choosing an ordering of components, we can translate records and record types into pairs and product types of PCF. For records with two components, such as $\{A\colon nat,\ B\colon bool\}$, we can translate directly into pairs by choosing one component to be first. However, for records with more than two components, we must translate into "nested" pairs.

To simplify the translation of n-component records into PCF, we will define n-tuples as syntactic sugar. For any sequence of types $\sigma_1, \ldots, \sigma_n$, we introduce the n-ary product notation

$$\sigma_1 \times \ldots \times \sigma_n \stackrel{\text{def}}{=} \sigma_1 \times (\sigma_2 \times \ldots (\sigma_{n-1} \times \sigma_n) \ldots)$$

by associating to the right. (This is an arbitrary decision. We could just as easily associate n-ary products to the left.) To define elements of an n-ary product, we use the tupling notation

$$\langle M_1, \ldots, M_n \rangle \stackrel{\text{def}}{=} \langle M_1, \langle M_2, \ldots \langle M_{n-1}, M_n \rangle \ldots \rangle\rangle$$

as syntactic sugar for a nested pair. It is easy to check that if $M_i\colon \sigma_i$, then

$$\langle M_1, \ldots, M_n \rangle\colon \sigma_1 \times \ldots \times \sigma_n$$

To retrieve the components of an n-tuple, we use the following notation for combinations of binary projection functions.

$$\mathbf{Proj}_i^{\sigma_1 \times \ldots \times \sigma_n} \stackrel{\text{def}}{=} \lambda x\colon \sigma_1 \times \ldots \times \sigma_n.\mathbf{Proj}_1(\mathbf{Proj}_2^{i-1} x) \qquad (i < n)$$

$$\mathbf{Proj}_n^{\sigma_1 \times \ldots \times \sigma_n} \stackrel{\text{def}}{=} \lambda x\colon \sigma_1 \times \ldots \times \sigma_n.(\mathbf{Proj}_2^{n-1} x)$$

We leave it as an exercise to check that

$$\mathbf{Proj}_i^{\sigma_1 \times \ldots \times \sigma_n} \langle M_1, \ldots, M_n \rangle \twoheadrightarrow M_i,$$

justifying the use of this notation. A useful piece of meta-notation is to write σ^k for the product $\sigma \times \ldots \times \sigma$ of k σ's.

Using n-tuples, we can now translate records with more than two components into PCF quite easily. If we want to eliminate records of some type $\{\ell_1: \sigma_1, \ldots, \ell_k: \sigma_k\}$, we choose some ordering of the labels $\ell_1, \ldots, \ell_k$ and write each type expression and record expression using this order. (Any ordering will do, as long as we are consistent. For concreteness, we could use alpha-numeric lexicographical order.) We then translate expressions with records into PCF as follows.

$$\{\ell_1: \sigma_1, \ldots, \ell_k: \sigma_k\} \stackrel{\text{def}}{=} \sigma_1 \times \ldots \times \sigma_k$$

$$\{\ell_1 = M_1, \ldots, \ell_k = M_k\} \stackrel{\text{def}}{=} \langle M_1, \ldots, M_k \rangle$$

$$M.\ell_i \stackrel{\text{def}}{=} \mathbf{Proj}_i^{\sigma_1 \times \ldots \times \sigma_k} M$$

If an expression contains more than one type of records, we apply the same process to each type independently.

Example 2.5.1 We will translate the expression

$\texttt{let } r: \{A: int,\ B: bool\} = \{A = 3,\ B = true\} \texttt{ in if } r.B \texttt{ then } r.A \texttt{ else } r.A + 1$

into PCF. The first step is to number the record labels. Using the number 1 for A and 2 for B, the type $\{A: int,\ B: bool\}$ becomes $int \times bool$ and a record $\{A = x,\ B = y\} : \{A: int,\ B: bool\}$ becomes a pair $\langle x,\ y\rangle : int \times bool$. Following the general procedure outlined above, we desugar the expression with records to the following expression with product types and pairing:

$\texttt{let } r: int \times bool = \langle 3,\ true\rangle \texttt{ in if } \mathbf{Proj}_2 r \texttt{ then } \mathbf{Proj}_1 r \texttt{ else } (\mathbf{Proj}_1 r) + 1$

Some slightly more complicated examples are given in the exercise. ■

Exercise 2.5.2 Desugar the following expressions with records to expressions with product types and pairing.

(a) $\texttt{let } r: \{A: int, B: bool, C: int \to int\} = \{A = 5, B = false, C = \lambda x: int.\, x\}$
$\texttt{in if } r.B \texttt{ then } r.A \texttt{ else } (r.C)(r.A)$

(b) $\texttt{let } f(r: \{A: int, C: bool\}): \{A: int, B: bool\} = \{A = r.A, B = r.C\}$
$\texttt{in } f\{A = 3, C = true\}$

You may wish to eliminate one type of records first and then the other. If you do this, the intermediate term should be a well-typed expression with only one type of records.

2.5.2 Searching the Natural Numbers

One useful programming technique in PCF is to "search" the natural numbers, starting from 0. In recursive function theory, this method is called *minimization,* and written using the operator μ. Specifically, if p is a computable predicate on the natural numbers (which means a computable function from *nat* to *bool*), then $\mu x[p\,x]$ is the least natural number n such that $p\,n = true$ and $p\,n' = false$ for all $n' < n$. If there is no such n, then $\mu x[p\,x]$ is "undefined," which means that there is no natural number n with $\mu x[p\,x] = n$.

In PCF, given a natural number predicate $p\colon nat \to bool$, we can compute $\mu x[p\,x]$ using the expression

$$\texttt{letrec}\ f(x\colon nat)\colon nat = \texttt{if}\ \ p\,x\ \ \texttt{then}\ x\ \texttt{else}\ \ f(x+1)\ \ \texttt{in}\ \ f\,0$$

Intuitively, the recursive function f tests to see if its argument x is has the property p. If so, then this is the result of the function call. Otherwise, the function f is called recursively on $x + 1$. Since the first call is to $f\,0$, we start with 0 and test all natural numbers in succession. However, if $p\,n$ may be reduced indefinitely without producing either *true* or *false*, then it is possible to reduce this expression indefinitely without testing $p(n + 1)$.

Since we will use minimization several times, we will adopt the abbreviation

$$search \stackrel{\text{def}}{=} \lambda p\colon nat \to bool.\ \texttt{letrec}\, f(x\colon nat)\colon nat =$$
$$\texttt{if}\ (p\,x)\ \texttt{then}\ x\ \texttt{else}\ f(x+1)\ f\,0$$

The main property of *search* is described by the following proposition, which relies on the fact that no expression reduces to both *true* and *false*.

Proposition 2.5.3 Let $M\colon nat \to bool$ be any PCF predicate on the natural numbers. If $M\,n \twoheadrightarrow true$ and $M\,n' \twoheadrightarrow false$ for all $n' < n$, then $search\ M \twoheadrightarrow n$.

The astute reader may notice a convenient pun in the statement of this proposition. The statement includes a condition $n' < n$ on n and n' of PCF, not natural numbers. To be precise, we should distinguish between numerals, symbols used in expressions of PCF, and the "mathematical objects" we usually refer to by these symbols. However, it is convenient to order the numerals by the usual ordering on natural numbers, use induction on numerals, and transfer other properties of the natural numbers to numerals. This makes many statements about PCF, such as the inductive argument in the proof below, much easier to phrase.

Proof We will prove the following statement by induction on n:

If $M\,n' \twoheadrightarrow false$ for all $n' < n$, then

$$search\ M \twoheadrightarrow \texttt{if}\ (Mn)\ \texttt{then}\ n\ \texttt{else}\ (\mathit{fix}\ F)(n+1), \qquad (*)$$

where F is $\lambda f\colon nat \to nat.\lambda x\colon nat.\,\texttt{if}\ (Mx)\ \texttt{then}\ x\ \texttt{else}\ f(x+1)$.

The proposition follows from $(*)$ by noticing that if $Mn \twoheadrightarrow true$, the conditional expression reduces to n.

The inductive proof begins with the base case $n = 0$. By expanding definitions and reducing, we have

$$\begin{aligned} search\ M &\twoheadrightarrow (\lambda f\colon nat \to nat.\, f\ 0)(fix\ F) \\ &\twoheadrightarrow (fix\ F)\ 0 \\ &\twoheadrightarrow F\ (fix\ F)\ 0 \\ &\twoheadrightarrow \texttt{if}\ \ (M0)\ \ \texttt{then}\ \ 0\ \ \texttt{else}\ \ (fix\ F)(1) \end{aligned}$$

To prove the inductive step, suppose the claim holds for n, and that $M\,n' \twoheadrightarrow false$ for all $n' < n+1$. Starting with the inductive hypothesis and continuing with the assumption that $M\,n \twoheadrightarrow false$, we have

$$\begin{aligned} search\ M &\twoheadrightarrow \texttt{if}\ \ (Mn)\ \ \texttt{then}\ \ n\ \ \texttt{else}\ \ (fix\ F)(n+1) \\ &\twoheadrightarrow (fix\ F)(n+1) \\ &\twoheadrightarrow F\ (fix\ F)(n+1) \\ &\twoheadrightarrow \texttt{if}\ \ (M\,(n+1))\ \ \texttt{then}\ \ n+1\ \ \texttt{else}\ \ (fix\ F)((n+1)+1). \end{aligned}$$

Since n is a meta-variable for some numeral $0, 1, 2, \ldots$ of PCF, we can simplify $n+1$ to a numeral, obtaining an expression of the desired form. This proves $(*)$, and hence the proposition. ■

Example 2.5.4 The definition of factorial uses a *predecessor* function $\lambda x\colon nat.\, x - 1$, which is not a basic operation of PCF. However, using *search,* it is easy to compute the predecessor of any natural number x. We simply search for the first y satisfying $y + 1 = x$. Accounting for the special case $x = 0$, whose "predecessor" is 0 by convention, we define the predecessor function on the natural numbers by the PCF expression

$$pred \stackrel{\text{def}}{=} \lambda x\colon nat.\,\texttt{if}\ \ Eq?\,x\,0\ \ \texttt{then}\ \ 0\ \ \texttt{else}\ \ (search\ \lambda y\colon nat.\, Eq?\,(y+1)\,x)$$

Using Proposition 2.5.3 and properties of *Eq*?, it is straightforward to show that *pred* computes the predecessor function. ■

Exercise 2.5.5 Write a PCF function $half\colon nat \to nat$ mapping any numeral n to the numeral for $\lfloor n/2 \rfloor$, the greatest natural number not exceeding $n/2$.

Exercise 2.5.6 Write a function *comp* that maps any natural number n to the n-fold composition function $\lambda f\colon nat \to nat.\lambda x\colon nat.\, f^n x$, where $f^n x$ is an abbreviation for the application $f(f(\ldots(fx)\ldots))$ of f to x a total of n times. Use this to define multiplication $mult\colon nat \times nat \to nat$ in PCF. (Hint: multiply $m \cdot n$ by repeatedly adding n to itself.)

Exercise 2.5.7 This question is about a restricted form of recursion called *primitive recursion.* One property of primitive recursion is that if f is defined from g and h by primitive recursion, and g and h are both total functions (*i.e.*, yield natural-number results for all natural number arguments), then f is also total.

(a) A function $f\colon nat \to \sigma$ is *defined from* $g\colon \sigma$ *and* $h\colon (\sigma \times nat) \to \sigma$ *by primitive recursion* if

$$f\,0 \quad = \quad g$$

$$f(n+1) = \quad h\langle (f\,n), n\rangle$$

Write a PCF function $prim_\sigma\colon \sigma \to (\sigma \times nat \to \sigma) \to (nat \to \sigma)$ such that for any g and h of the appropriate types, the function $(prim_\sigma\; g\; h)$ satisfies the equations for f above. You will need to use the fact that PCF allows conditional expressions of any type.

(b) In PCF, both addition and equality test are basic operations. However, if we add primitive recursion to PCF, we may remove $+$ and $Eq?$ from PCF and replace them with the simpler functions of successor and zero test, without changing the set of definable functions. This may be proved by showing that addition and equality test are definable in a version of PCF with addition and equality replaced by primitive recursion, successor and zero test. This problem asks you to prove slightly more. Using functions $succ\colon nat \to nat$, $zero?\colon nat \to bool$, and $prim?\colon \sigma \to (\sigma \times nat \to \sigma) \to nat \to \sigma$, satisfying the infinite collection of equations

$$succ\,0 = 1$$
$$succ\,1 = 2$$
$$\vdots$$
$$zero?\,0 = true$$
$$zero?\,1 = false$$
$$\vdots$$
$$prim?\; g\; h\; 0 = g$$
$$prim?\; g\; h\; (succ\; n) = h\;\langle prim?\; g\; h\; n, n\rangle,$$

along with the other basic operations of PCF (except $+$, $Eq?$ and *fix*), show how to define predecessor, addition and equality test. Since `letrec` is defined using *fix*, do not use `letrec`. (*Hint:* Try predecessor first.)

2.5.3 Iteration and Tail Recursion

Many algorithms, when written in an imperative language like Pascal, use the following pattern of initialization and iteration.

Initialize;
while $\neg$*Done* **do** *Stmt* **end**

If the sections *Initialize* and *Stmt* only change the values of a fixed, finite set of variables, and *Done* is a side-effect-free test depending on the values of these variables, then we may easily transform a program segment of this form into a functional program. Let us assume for simplicity that there is only one variable involved; there is no loss of generality in this since we can replace a finite set of variables by a record or n-tuple containing their values. To put this in the context of PCF, suppose we have PCF expressions

$init : \sigma$
$next : \sigma \to \sigma$
$done : \sigma \to bool$

so that the iteration could be written

$x := init;$
while $\neg(done\, x)$ **do** $x := (next\, x)$ **end**

using an assignable variable x of type σ. We may compute the final value of x produced by this loop, using essentially the same sequence of operations, with the expression *loop init next done* defined by.

$$loop\ init\ next\ done \stackrel{\text{def}}{=} \texttt{letrec}\ f(x{:}\sigma) = \texttt{if}\ (done\, x)\ \texttt{then}\ x\ \texttt{else}\ f\,(next\, x)\ \texttt{in}\ (f\ init)$$

Since *loop* is a straightforward generalization of the function *search,* the analysis given in Proposition 2.5.3 applies. To be more specific, writing $next^n\, x$ for the result $next(next(\ldots (next\, x)\ldots))$ of applying *next* to x a total of n times, we we have the following proposition.

Proposition 2.5.8 If $done\,(next^i\ init) \twoheadrightarrow false$ for all $i < n$ and $done\,(next^n\ init) \twoheadrightarrow true$, then

$$loop\ init\ next\ done \twoheadrightarrow next^n\ init$$

The translation of iterative loops into recursive functions always produces a recursive function with a particular form. A recursive function with a definition of the form

$$f(x) = \texttt{if}\ B\ \texttt{then}\ M\ \texttt{else}\ f(N),$$

where neither B, M nor N contains f, is called a *tail-recursive function.* In languages such as Lisp and Scheme, where recursive functions are used extensively, tail-recursive functions are often recognized by the compiler. The reason for treating tail-recursive functions separately is that these may be compiled into efficient iterative code that does not require a new activation record (stack frame) for each recursive call in the source program.

Example 2.5.9 Using pairing, we may translate the following iterative algorithm into PCF.

$x := 100;$
$y := 0;$
while $\neg(Eq?\, x\, y)$ **do** $x := x - 1;\ y := y + 1$ **end**

The initial value of the pair $\langle x, y\rangle$ is $\langle 100, 0\rangle$. Using the syntactic sugar introduced in Exercise 2.2.12, we may write the body of the **while** loop as the following "next" function

$$next \stackrel{\text{def}}{=} \lambda\langle x\colon nat, y\colon nat\rangle.\, \langle x - 1,\ x + 1\rangle.$$

The test for loop termination may be written similarly as $done \stackrel{\text{def}}{=} \lambda\langle x\colon nat, y\colon nat\rangle.$ $(Eq?\, x\, y)$. Putting these together, the **while** loop may be written as

$$L \stackrel{\text{def}}{=} loop\, \langle 100, 0\rangle\, next\, done$$

If we let F be the term

$$F \stackrel{\text{def}}{=} \lambda f\colon nat \times nat \to nat \times nat.\, \lambda p\colon nat \times nat.\, \mathtt{if}\ \ (done\, p)\ \ \mathtt{then}\ \ p\ \ \mathtt{else}\ \ f(next\, p).$$

then we may reduce the PCF expression representing the `while` loop as follows:

$$\begin{aligned}
L &\equiv (\lambda f\colon nat \times nat \to nat \times nat.\ f\langle 100, 0\rangle)(fix\ F)\\
&\to (fix\ F)\langle 100, 0\rangle\\
&\to (fix\ F)\langle 100, 0\rangle\\
&\to (\lambda p\colon nat \times nat.\, \mathtt{if}\ \ Eq?(Proj_1 p)(Proj_2 p)\ \ \mathtt{then}\ \ p\\
&\qquad \mathtt{else}\ \ (fix\ F)\langle (Proj_1 p) - 1,\ (Proj_2 p) + 1\rangle)\langle 100, 0\rangle\\
&\qquad \to\ \ \mathtt{if}\ \ Eq?(Proj_1\langle 100, 0\rangle)(Proj_2\langle 100, 0\rangle)\ \ \mathtt{then}\ \ \langle 100, 0\rangle\\
&\qquad\qquad \mathtt{else}\ \ (fix\ F)\langle (Proj_1\langle 100, 0\rangle) - 1,\ (Proj_2\langle 100, 0\rangle) + 1\rangle
\end{aligned}$$

At this point, we depart from left-most reduction order and evaluate all the projections, additions and subtractions before continuing.

$$\begin{aligned}
&\twoheadrightarrow \mathtt{if}\ \ Eq?\, 100\, 0\ \ \mathtt{then}\ \ \langle 100, 0\rangle\ \ \mathtt{else}\ \ (fix\ F)\langle 99, 1\rangle\\
&\to \mathtt{if}\ \ false\ \ \mathtt{then}\ \ \langle 100, 0\rangle\ \ \mathtt{else}\ \ (fix\ F)\langle 99, 1\rangle\\
&\to (fix\ F)\langle 99, 1\rangle
\end{aligned}$$

At this point, we have completed "execution" of one iteration of the `while` loop. Continuing in this manner, we can see that the functional expression computes the final values of x and y by approximately the same sequence of additions, subtractions and tests as the iterative **while** loop. ∎

We may compare the sequence of operations involved in a **while** loop and its PCF translation by giving a reduction rule for **while** loops. A natural rule which corresponds to the way that iteration is actually implemented is

while $\neg B$ **do** S **end** $\rightarrow$ **if** B **then** *skip* **else**(S; **while** $\neg B$ **do** S **end**)

where *skip* is a statement that does nothing. We may use this reduction rule to argue informally that an iterative algorithm

$x := init$;
while $\neg(done\, x)$ **do** $x := (next\, x)$ **end**

and its translation into PCF perform the same sequence of evaluations of *init,next* and *done*. The reader is encouraged to work this out in Exercise 2.5.10.

Exercise 2.5.10 Translate the imperative algorithm

$q := 0$;
$r := m$;
while $r \geq n$ do
  $q := q + 1$;
  $r := r - n$;
  od

into PCF by defining functions *init next done*. (You will have to use recursion to implement the test $r \geq n$.) Use the reduction rule for **while** loops to argue informally that the loop and its PCF translation involve essentially the same arithmetic operations. You may assume left-most order of PCF evaluation.

Exercise 2.5.11 Translate the following imperative algorithm to compute the greatest common divisor into PCF by defining functions *init next done*.

while $n \neq 0$ do
  $r := m$;
  while $r \geq n$ do
    $r := r - n$;
    od
  $m := n$;
  $n := r$;
  od

Think of this program as using m and n as input, and producing a new value of m as output.

2.5.4 Total Recursive Functions

In this section and the next, we compare the natural-number functions definable in PCF with the classes of total and partial recursive functions (defined below and in the next section). The main results are that all recursive total and partial functions on the natural numbers are definable in PCF. Similar proofs using Turing machines are given in the exercises.

A commonly accepted belief, called *Church's thesis,* is that every numeric function that is computable by any practical computer is recursive. This thesis was formulated in the 1930's, before electronic computers, during a period when mathematicians were actively investigating the possibility and impossibility of solving problems by systematic algorithms. One reason for believing Church's thesis is that all of the formalisms for defining computable functions that were proposed in the 1930's, and since, give rise to the same set of functions on the natural numbers. The early formalisms include the recursive functions, Turing machines, and lambda calculus. It follows from Church's thesis (although this is no way to prove something rigorously), that every partial or total function definable in PCF is recursive. The reason is that we have an algorithm for computing any definable function, namely reduction. It is not hard to give a rigorous proof that every PCF-definable function is recursive, although we will not do so since this involves tricks with recursive functions and does not shed much light on PCF itself. One reason for proving that every recursive total or partial function is definable in PCF is that, via Church's thesis, this gives evidence that every computable function on the natural numbers is definable in PCF. In other words, this is as close as we can get to showing that, at least for natural-number functions, PCF is a "universal" programming language. The second reason is that, by appealing to undecidable properties of recursive functions, we obtain interesting undecidability properties of PCF.

A subtle issue that is not often discussed in basic courses on computability or complexity theory is the limitation of Church's thesis for functions on types other than the natural numbers. For basic data such as booleans, strings or arrays of such data, it makes sense to think of the computable functions as precisely those functions we can compute when we code each boolean, string or array by a natural number. By this reasoning, we can see that any programming language that lets us associate natural numbers with its basic data types, and compute all recursive functions on the natural numbers, is "universal" for defining computable functions on all the basic data types. However, for "infinite" values, such as functions, the issue is not as clear cut. In particular, mathematical logicians have identified several distinct classes of "computable functions on the natural-number functions" and have not been able to prove that these are identical. A related phenomenon is discussed in Section 2.5.6, where we show that certain "parallel" operations are not definable in PCF, in spite of the ability to define all recursive functions on the natural numbers.

Since there are some subtle points about termination and function composition for partial functions, we begin with the simple case of total functions. Since we have pairing in PCF, we will consider total recursive functions of more than one argument. A function f is *numeric* if $f\colon \mathcal{N}^k \to \mathcal{N}$ for some $k > 0$. If $\mathcal{C}$ is a class of numeric functions, we say $\mathcal{C}$ is

- *Closed under composition* if, for every $f_1, \ldots, f_\ell\colon \mathcal{N}^k \to \mathcal{N}$ and $g\colon \mathcal{N}^\ell \to \mathcal{N}$ from $\mathcal{C}$, the class $\mathcal{C}$ also contains the function h defined by

$$h(n_1, \ldots, n_k) = g(f_1(n_1, \ldots, n_k), \ldots, f_\ell(n_1, \ldots, n_k)),$$

- *Closed under primitive recursion* if, for every $f\colon \mathcal{N}^k \rightharpoonup \mathcal{N}$ and $g\colon \mathcal{N}^{k+2} \rightharpoonup \mathcal{N}$ from $\mathcal{C}$, the class $\mathcal{C}$ contains the function h defined by

$$\begin{aligned} h(0, n_1, \ldots, n_k) &= f(n_1, \ldots, n_k) \\ h(m+1, n_1, \ldots, n_k) &= g(h(m, n_1, \ldots, n_k), m, n_1, \ldots, n_k), \end{aligned}$$

- *Closed under minimization* if, for every $f\colon \mathcal{N}^{k+1} \to \mathcal{N}$ from $\mathcal{C}$ such that $\forall n_1, \ldots, n_k.\ \exists m.\ f(m, n_1, \ldots, n_k) = 0$, the class $\mathcal{C}$ contains the function g defined by

$$g(n_1, \ldots, n_k) = \text{the least } m \text{ such that } f(m, n_1, \ldots, n_k) = 0.$$

The class $\mathcal{R}$ of *total recursive functions* is the least class of numeric functions that contains the projection functions $\mathbf{Proj}_i^k(n_1, \ldots, n_k) = n_i$, the successor function $\lambda x\colon nat.\, x + 1$, the constant zero function $\lambda x\colon nat.\, 0$, and that is closed under composition, primitive recursion, and minimization.

We can show that every total recursive function is definable in PCF, in the following precise sense. For any natural number $n \in \mathcal{N}$, let us write $\lceil n \rceil$ for the corresponding numeral of PCF. We say a numeric function $f\colon \mathcal{N}^k \to \mathcal{N}$ is *PCF-definable,* or simply *definable,* if there is a closed PCF expression $M\colon nat^k \to nat$, where nat^k is the k-ary product type $nat \times \ldots \times nat$, such that

$$\forall n_1, \ldots, n_k \in \mathcal{N}.\ M\langle \lceil n_1 \rceil, \ldots, \lceil n_k \rceil \rangle = \lceil f(n_1, \ldots, n_k) \rceil.$$

Theorem 2.5.12 Every total recursive function is definable in PCF.

Proof To show that every total recursive function is definable in PCF, we must give the projection functions $\mathbf{Proj}_i^k$, the successor function, and the constant zero function, and show closure under composition, primitive recursion, and minimization. Some of the work has already been done in Exercise 2.5.7 and Proposition 2.5.3. Following the definitions in Section 2.5.1, we let

$$\mathbf{Proj}_1^1 \stackrel{\text{def}}{=} \lambda x\colon nat.\, x$$

$$\mathbf{Proj}_1^k \stackrel{\text{def}}{=} \lambda x\colon nat^k.\, \mathbf{Proj}_1 x \qquad (1 < k)$$

$$\mathbf{Proj}_i^k \stackrel{\text{def}}{=} \lambda x\colon nat^k.\, \mathbf{Proj}_{i-1}^{k-1}(\mathbf{Proj}_2 x) \quad (1 < i \le k)$$

As in the definition of the class of total recursive functions, we may define successor and the constant function returning zero by

$$succ \stackrel{\text{def}}{=} \lambda x\colon nat.\, x + 1,$$

$$zero \stackrel{\text{def}}{=} \lambda x\colon nat.\, 0.$$

If $f_1 \dots f_\ell\colon \mathcal{N}^k \to \mathcal{N}$ and $g\colon \mathcal{N}^\ell \to \mathcal{N}$ are represented by the PCF terms $M_1 \dots M_\ell$ and N, respectively, then the function h defined by composition is represented by the term

$$\lambda x\colon nat^k.\, N\langle M_1 x,\ \dots\ , M_\ell x\rangle.$$

If $f\colon \mathcal{N}^k \to \mathcal{N}$ and $g\colon \mathcal{N}^{k+2} \to \mathcal{N}$ are represented by M and N, then the function h defined by primitive recursion is represented by

$$\lambda\langle x\colon nat, y\colon nat^k\rangle.\, prim\,(M\,y)\,(\lambda\langle m\colon nat, n\colon nat\rangle.\, N\,\langle m, \langle n, y\rangle\rangle)\, x,$$

where *prim* is as in Exercise 2.5.7. Finally, to establish closure under minimization, suppose $f\colon \mathcal{N}^{k+1} \to \mathcal{N}$ is represented by M, and for every $n_1 \dots n_k$ there exists an m such that $f(m, n_1 \dots n_k) = 0$. By Proposition 2.5.3, the function g defined by minimization is represented by

$$\lambda x\colon nat^k.\, search(\lambda n\colon nat.\, M\,\langle n, x\rangle). \qquad \blacksquare$$

Exercise 2.5.13 Although a Turing machine may compute a partial function, there is a natural total function associated with every Turing machine, namely, the function giving the contents of the tape after n steps. This exercise asks you to show directly that this function is definable in PCF and conclude that every function computed by a Turing machine that halts on all input is definable in PCF.

There are a number of equivalent definitions of Turing machines. As a reminder, and to set notation, we briefly review one standard definition (from [HU79]) before stating the problem. A *Turing machine* is given by a tuple

$\langle Q, \Sigma, \Gamma, \delta, q_1, \not b, F\rangle$

where $Q = \{q_1, ..., q_n\}$ is a finite set of *states;* Σ is the (finite) input alphabet, not including $\not b$, the "blank" symbol; Γ is the (finite) tape alphabet with $\Gamma \supseteq \Sigma$;

$\delta : Q \times \Gamma \rightharpoonup Q \times \Gamma \times \{L, R\}$

is a partial function telling the next state, symbol to write on the tape, and direction to move the tape head; q_1 is the start state; $\not b$ is the "blank" symbol; and $F \subseteq Q$ is the set of final *accepting states.* Since δ may be a partial function, $\delta(q, g)$ may be undefined for some state $q \in Q$ and tape symbol $g \in \Gamma$. In this case, the machine halts and does not move. (The machine also halts if it moves off the left end of the tape.) The machine accepts its input if it halts in a final state $q \in F$. Since Q, Γ and $\{L, R\}$ are all finite, the transition function δ is a finite set. There is no loss of generality in assuming that there is exactly one final state $q_f \in F$ and that $\delta(q, g)$ is defined iff $q \neq q_f$. This makes δ a total function from $(Q - \{q_f\}) \times \Gamma$ to $Q \times \Gamma \times \{L, R\}$. We may assume that $\Sigma = \{0, 1\}$ and $\Gamma = \Sigma \cup \{\not b\}$, since any symbol may be coded by a sequence of bits (using ASCII, for example). In this problem, you may represent $\not b$ by the number 2.

(a) We will code a Turing machine tape using a coding of pairs as natural numbers. Specifically, a pair of natural numbers $\langle n, m\rangle$ may be coded by the natural number

$pr(n, m) = (n + m)(n + m + 1)/2 + m.$

This may be understood by arranging all the pairs of natural numbers in an infinite table, with $\langle 0, 0\rangle$ in the upper left corner and first and second coordinates increasing as we move down and right in the table (respectively). If we "walk" through this table along the northeast diagonals, moving to the next diagonal when we reach the top border, then the pair $\langle n, m\rangle$ is reached after $pr(n, m)$ steps. Show that the pairing function pr and the corresponding projection functions p_1 and p_2 mapping $pr(n, m)$ to n and m are definable in PCF.

(b) We may code a finite sequence of natural numbers as follows:

$seq() \quad = pr(0, 0)$

$seq(ns) = pr((k + 1),\ pr(n,\ seq(s)))$

where in the $seq(ns)$ case we may follow the convention that k is the length of sequence s. Show that if $m = seq(ns)$, we may compute n from m in PCF. Show that if $m = seq(s)$, we may compute $seq(ns)$ from m and n in PCF.

(c) Let $\mathcal{M}$ be a Turing machine, as described above, with states numbered 1 through q_M.

Suppose $q \leq q_M$ is a natural number representing a state of $\mathcal{M}$, natural number n_ℓ codes the sequence of tape symbols to the left of the tape head, as in (b) above, and n_r codes the sequence of tape symbols under and to the right of the tape head. Show that the next state and two numbers representing the contents of the Turing machine tape are computable from the q, n_ℓ and n_r in PCF.

(d) Show that for any Turing machine $\mathcal{M}$, the function

$$f_{\mathcal{M}}(j, s, n) = \text{ the } j\text{th tape symbol after } n \text{ computation steps of } \mathcal{M} \text{ on initial tape } s$$

is representable in PCF, where the initial tape contents are coded as a natural number.

(e) A Turing machine $\mathcal{M}$ computes a total numeric function $f : \mathcal{N} \to \mathcal{N}$ if, when started with the binary representation of n on the tape, the machine halts with the binary representation of $f(n)$ on the tape. Show that every total function computed by a Turing machine is definable in PCF.

2.5.5 Partial Recursive Functions

In this section, we show that every partial recursive function is definable in PCF. Since it is generally believed that all mechanically computable functions are partial recursive functions, as discussed in Section 2.5.4, the main theorem of this section suggests that every function on the natural numbers that could be computed by any ordinary computer is definable in PCF. Two corollaries are that there is no algorithm to determine whether a PCF expression has a normal form and no algorithm to determine whether two PCF expressions are provably equal.

Although we may prove the main theorem of this section without repeating the inductive argument of Theorem 2.5.12, there are two reasons for giving a direct inductive proof. The first is to emphasize the difference between representing a total function and representing a partial one. The second is to gain further intuition for the evaluation mechanism of PCF and its relation to standard mathematical conventions about partial functions. This intuition may be useful in considering "parallel" functions in the next section.

We discuss the representation of partial functions before defining the class of partial recursive functions.

Suppose we have some partial function $f : \mathcal{N} \rightharpoonup \mathcal{N}$ which we would like to represent by a PCF expression. We clearly want a closed term $M : nat \to nat$ such that $M\lceil n \rceil$ gives the value of $f(n)$ when $f(n)$ is defined. However, it is not as clear what property M should have if $f(n)$ is *not* defined. One possibility, of course, is to not to require any property of $M\lceil n \rceil$. However, an accurate representation of a partial function is a term M with $M\lceil n \rceil$ "defined" iff $f(n)$ is defined. This requires some notion of "undefined term." A convenient representation of undefinedness, or nontermination, is that $M\lceil n \rceil$ should have no normal form when $f(n)$ is undefined. We will adopt this below for terms that represent numeric functions.

We say a partial function $f: \mathcal{N}^k \rightharpoonup \mathcal{N}$ is *PCF-definable,* or simply *definable,* if there is a closed PCF expression $M: nat^k \to nat$ such that for all $n_1, \ldots, n_k \in \mathcal{N}$, we have

$$M\langle \ulcorner n_1 \urcorner, \ldots, \ulcorner n_k \urcorner \rangle = \begin{cases} \ulcorner f(n_1, \ldots, n_k) \urcorner & \text{if } f(n_1, \ldots, n_k) \text{ is defined,} \\ \text{has no normal form} & \text{otherwise} \end{cases}$$

The reader familiar with untyped lambda calculus may know that the convention for partial functions is to represent undefinedness by lack of a head normal form. For PCF, a *head normal form,* is either a numeral, a boolean constant (*true* or *false*), or term of the form $\lambda x\colon \sigma.M$ or $\langle M, N \rangle$, according to its type. Since a term of type *nat* or *bool* has a normal form iff it has a head normal form, the type constraints of PCF make the two possible definitions equivalent. Those interested in untyped lambda calculus may wish to consult [Bar84, Section 8.4] for a discussion of partial recursive functions in the pure, untyped lambda calculus.

To show that every partial recursive function is definable in PCF, we give a precise definition of the class of all partial recursive functions. A partial function f is *numeric* if $f: \mathcal{N}^k \rightharpoonup \mathcal{N}$ for some $k > 0$. If $\mathcal{C}$ is a class of partial numeric functions, we say $\mathcal{C}$ is

- *Closed under composition* if, for all partial functions $f_1, \ldots, f_\ell: \mathcal{N}^k \rightharpoonup \mathcal{N}$ and $g: \mathcal{N}^\ell \rightharpoonup \mathcal{N}$ from $\mathcal{C}$, the class $\mathcal{C}$ also contains the partial function h defined by

$$h(n_1, \ldots, n_k) = \begin{cases} g(m_1, \ldots, m_\ell) & \text{if } m_i = f_i(n_1, \ldots, n_k) \text{ defined } 1 \le i \le \ell \\ & \text{and } g(m_1, \ldots, m_\ell) \text{ is defined,} \\ \text{undefined} & \text{otherwise.} \end{cases}$$

- *Closed under primitive recursion* if, for every $f: \mathcal{N}^k \rightharpoonup \mathcal{N}$ and $g: \mathcal{N}^{k+2} \rightharpoonup \mathcal{N}$ from $\mathcal{C}$, the class $\mathcal{C}$ contains the partial function h defined by

$$h(0, n_1, \ldots, n_k) = \begin{cases} f(n_1, \ldots, n_k) & \text{if } f(n_1, \ldots, n_k) \text{ defined} \\ \text{undefined} & \text{otherwise.} \end{cases}$$

$$h(m+1, n_1, \ldots, n_k) = \begin{cases} g(p, m, n_1, \ldots, n_k), & \text{if } p = h(m, n_1, \ldots, n_k) \text{ and} \\ & g(p, m, n_1, \ldots, n_k) \text{ are defined,} \\ \text{undefined} & \text{otherwise.} \end{cases}$$

- *Closed under minimization* if, for every partial $f: \mathcal{N}^{k+1} \rightharpoonup \mathcal{N}$ from $\mathcal{C}$, the class $\mathcal{C}$ contains the partial function g defined by

$$g(n_1, \ldots, n_k) = \begin{cases} \text{the least } m \text{ with } f(m, n_1, \ldots, n_k) = 0, \\ \text{when such an } m \text{ exists,} \\ \\ \text{undefined otherwise.} \end{cases}$$

The class $\mathcal{PR}$ of *partial recursive functions* is the least class of partial numeric functions containing the projection functions $\mathbf{Proj}_i^k(n_1, \ldots, n_k) = n_i$, the successor function $\lambda x\colon nat.\, x + 1$, the constant zero function $\lambda x\colon nat.\, 0$, and closed under composition, primitive recursion, and minimization.

Theorem 2.5.14 Every partial recursive function is definable in PCF

Proof The proof is similar to the proof of Theorem 2.5.12, except that the term representing a partial recursive function must not have a normal form when the partial recursive function is undefined. We can see that this requires some changes by considering the composition case. If $f, g\colon \mathcal{N} \rightharpoonup \mathcal{N}$ are unary partial recursive functions, represented by PCF terms M and N, then in the proof of Theorem 2.5.12, we represent the composition $h(n) = g(f(n))$ by the term $\lambda x\colon nat.\, N\,(Mx)$. However, this does not have the correct termination behavior when f may be partial. For example, let g be the constant function $g(x) = 3$ and f a partial function with $f(5)$ undefined. The ordinary mathematical convention is to consider $h(5) = g(f(5))$ undefined since $f(5)$ is undefined. However, the application $(\lambda x\colon nat.\, N\,(Mx))\ 5$ reduces to 3 in PCF.

A simple trick is to define a function *cnvg* that may be used to force nontermination in PCF when required. Due to typing restrictions, we will define a separate function $cnvg_k$ for each natural number $k > 0$. If f and g are numeric functions of k arguments, then $cnvg_k\ f\ g$ will behave like g, except that an application to k arguments will only have a normal form (or "halt") when the application of f has a normal form. For any $k > 0$, the function $cnvg_k$ may be written as follows:

$$cnvg_k\ f\ g \stackrel{\text{def}}{=} \lambda x\colon nat^k.\, \texttt{if}\ Eq?\,(fx)\,0\ \texttt{then}\ gx\ \texttt{else}\ gx.$$

For any x, if fx can be reduced to normal form then (whether this is equal to zero or not) the result is gx. However, if fx cannot be reduced to a normal form, then the conditional can never be eliminated and $cnvg_k\ f\ g$ will not have a normal form. The main reason why this works is that we cannot reduce $Eq?\,(fx)\,0$ to *true* or *false* without reducing fx to normal form.

Using *cnvg,* we can define a composition f and g that is defined only when f is defined. For example, if $f, g\colon \mathcal{N} \rightharpoonup \mathcal{N}$ are unary partial recursive functions represented by PCF terms M and N, we represent their composition by the term $cnvg\ M\ (\lambda x\colon nat.(N(Mx)))$.

The generalization to the composition of partial functions $f_1, \ldots, f_\ell : \mathcal{N}^k \rightharpoonup \mathcal{N}$ and $g: \mathcal{N}^\ell \rightharpoonup \mathcal{N}$ is straightforward and left to the reader.

The remaining cases of the proof are treated similarly, using $cnvg_k$ for appropriate k. The reader is encouraged to write out the argument for primitive recursion, and convince him- or herself that no modification is needed for minimization. ∎

This theorem has some important corollaries. Both of the corollaries below follow from a well-known undecidability property of recursive functions. Specifically, there is no recursive, or algorithmic, method for deciding whether a recursive partial function is defined on some argument. This fact is often referred to as the recursive unsolvability of the *Halting Problem.* Exercise 2.5.18 describes a direct proof that the PCF halting problem is not solvable in PCF.

Corollary 2.5.15 There is no algorithm for deciding whether a given PCF expression has a normal form.

Proof If there were such an algorithm, then by Theorem 2.5.14, we could decide whether a given partial recursive function was defined on some argument, simply by writing the function applied to its argument in PCF. ∎

Corollary 2.5.16 There is no algorithm for deciding equality between PCF expressions.

Proof If there were such an algorithm, then by Theorem 2.5.14, we could decide whether a given partial recursive function was defined on some argument. Specifically, given a description of a partial function f, we may produce PCF term M representing the application $f(n)$ by the straightforward algorithm outlined in the proof of Theorem 2.5.14, for any n. Then, using the supposed algorithm to determine whether $\texttt{if } Eq?\, M\, M \texttt{ then } 0 \texttt{ else } 0 = 0$, we could decide whether $f(n)$ is defined. ∎

Exercise 2.5.17 A *primitive recursive function* is a total recursive function that is defined without using minimization. The Kleene normal form theorem states that every partial recursive function $f: \mathcal{N}^k \rightharpoonup \mathcal{N}$ may be written in the form

$$f(n_1, \ldots, n_k) = p(\text{the least } n \text{ with } t_k(i, n_1, \ldots, n_k, n) = 1)$$

where p and t_k are primitive recursive functions that are independent of f, and i depends on f. This is called the *Kleene normal form of* f, after Stephen C. Kleene, and the number i is called the *index* of partial recursive function f. The Kleene normal form theorem may be found in standard books on computability or recursion theory, such as [Rog67].

(a) Use the Kleene normal form theorem and Theorem 2.5.12 to show that every partial recursive function is definable in PCF.

(b) Using the results of Exercise 2.5.13, show that every partial function computed by a Turing machine is definable in PCF.

Exercise 2.5.18 It is easy to show the halting problem for PCF is not solvable in PCF. Specifically, the *halting function on type* σ, H_σ, is a function which, when applied to any PCF term M_σ, returns *true* if M has a normal form ("halts"), and *false* otherwise. In this exercise, you are asked to show that there is no PCF term H_{bool} defining the halting function on type *bool*, using a variant of the diagonalization argument from recursive function theory. Since the proof proceeds by contradiction, assume there is a PCF term $H_{bool}\colon bool \to bool$ defining the halting function.

(a) Show that using H_{bool}, we may write a PCF term $G\colon bool \to bool$ with the property that for any PCF term $M\colon bool$, the application GM has a normal form iff M does not.

(b) Derive a contradiction by considering whether or not *fix* G has a normal form.

2.5.6 Nondefinability of Parallel Operations

We have seen in Sections 2.5.4 and 2.5.5 that the PCF-definable functions on numerals correspond exactly to the recursive functions and (in the exercises) the numeric functions computable by Turing machines. By Church's thesis, as discussed in Section 2.5.4, this suggests that all mechanically computable functions on the natural numbers are definable in PCF. However, as we shall see in this section, there *are* operations that are computable in a reasonable way, but *not* definable in PCF. The main theorem and the basic idea of Lemma 2.5.24 are due to Plotkin [Plo77]. A semantic proof of Theorem 2.5.19 appears as Example 8.6.3, using logical relations and the denotational semantics of PCF.

The main example we consider in this section is called *parallel-or.* Before discussing this function, it is worth remembering that for a PCF term to represent a k-ary function on the natural numbers, we only consider the result of applying the PCF term to a tuple of numerals. It is not important how the PCF term behaves when applied to expressions that are not in normal form. The difference between the positive results on representing numeric functions in Sections 2.5.4 and 2.5.5 and the negative result in this section is that we now take into account the way a function evaluates its arguments.

It is easiest to describe the parallel-or function algorithmically. Suppose we are given closed terms $M, N\colon bool$ and wish to compute the logical disjunction, $M \vee N$. We know that either $M \twoheadrightarrow true$, $M \twoheadrightarrow false$, or M has no normal form, and similarly for N. One way to compute $M \vee N$ is to first reduce both M and N to normal form, then return *true* if either is *true* and *false* otherwise. This algorithm computes what is called the *sequential-or* of M and N; it will only terminate if both M and N have a normal form. For *parallel-or,* we wish to return *true* if either M or N reduces to *true,* regardless of

Table 2.6
Evaluation contexts for lazy PCF reduction.

$\text{EV}[\,]$	$::=$	$[\,] \mid \text{EV}[\,] + M \mid n + \text{EV}[\,]$ for numeral n
		$\mid Eq?\,\text{EV}[\,]\,M \mid Eq?\,n\,\text{EV}[\,]$ for numeral n
		$\mid$ `if` $\text{EV}[\,]$ `then` N `else` P
		$\mid \mathbf{Proj}_i\,\text{EV}[\,] \mid \text{EV}[\,]\,M$

whether the other term has a normal form. It is easy to see how to compute parallel-or in a computational setting with explicit parallelism. We begin reducing M and N in parallel. If either terminates with value *true*, we abort the other computation and return *true*. Otherwise we continue to reduce both, hoping to produce two normal forms. If both reduce to *false*, then we return *false*. To summarize, the parallel-or of M and N is *true* if either M or N reduces to *true*, *false* if both reduce to *false*, and nonterminating otherwise.

The rest of this section will be devoted to proving that parallel-or is not definable in PCF, as stated in the following theorem.

Theorem 2.5.19 There is no PCF expression *POR* with the following behavior

$$POR\ M\ N \twoheadrightarrow \begin{cases} true & \text{if } M \twoheadrightarrow true \text{ or } N \twoheadrightarrow true \\ false & \text{if } M \twoheadrightarrow false \text{ and } N \twoheadrightarrow false \\ \text{no normal form} & \text{otherwise} \end{cases}$$

for all closed boolean expressions M and N.

We will prove Theorem 2.5.19 by analyzing the operational semantics of PCF. This gives us an opportunity to develop some general tools for operational reasoning. The first important decision is to choose a deterministic reduction strategy instead of reasoning about arbitrary reduction order. Since we will only be interested in reduction on terms of type *nat* or *bool*, we can use lazy reduction, defined in Section 2.4.3, instead of the more complicated left-most reduction strategy. A convenient way to analyze the reduction of subterms is to work with contexts. To identify a critical subterm, we define a special form of context called an *evaluation context*. While the analysis of parallel-or only requires evaluation contexts for boolean terms, we give the general definition for use in the exercises and in Section 5.4.2. The evaluation contexts of PCF are defined in Table 2.6.

An example appears below, after two basic lemmas. To make the outline of the proof of Theorem 2.5.19 as clear as possible, we postpone the proofs of the lemmas to the end of the section.

There are two main properties of evaluation contexts. The first is that if $M \xrightarrow{lazy} N$, then M matches the form of some evaluation context and N is obtained by reducing the indicated term.

Lemma 2.5.20 If $M \stackrel{lazy}{\to} N$, then there is a unique evaluation context $\text{EV}[\ ]$ such that $M \equiv \text{EV}[M']$, the reduction $M' \to N'$ is an instance of one of the PCF reduction axioms, and $N \equiv \text{EV}[N']$.

Since we can determine the unique evaluation context mentioned in the lemma by pattern matching, evaluation contexts provide a complete characterization of lazy reduction.

The second basic property of evaluation contexts is that the lazy reduction of $\text{EV}[M]$ is the lazy reduction of M, when M has one. This is stated more precisely in the following lemma.

Lemma 2.5.21 If $M \stackrel{lazy}{\to} M'$ then, for any evaluation context $\text{EV}[\ ]$, we have $\text{EV}[M] \stackrel{lazy}{\to} \text{EV}[M']$.

A subtle point is that when M is a lazy normal form, the lazy reduction of $\text{EV}[M]$ may be a reduction that does not involve M.

Example 2.5.22 The left-most reduction of the term $((\lambda x\colon nat.\, \lambda y\colon nat.\, x + y)\, 7)\, 5 + (\lambda x\colon nat.\, x)\, 3$ is given in Example 2.4.11. As observed in Example 2.4.14 this is also the lazy reduction of this term. We illustrate the use of evaluation contexts by writing the evaluation context for each term in the reduction sequence. Since we underline the active redex, the evaluation context is exactly the part of the term that is not underlined.

$(\underline{(\lambda x\colon nat.\, \lambda y\colon nat.\, x + y)\, 7})\, 5 + (\lambda x\colon nat.\, x)\, 3$	$\text{EV}[\ ] \equiv ([\ ]\, 5) + (\lambda x\colon nat.\, x)\, 3$
$\stackrel{left}{\to}$ $\underline{(\lambda y\colon nat.\, 7 + y)\, 5} + (\lambda x\colon nat.\, x)\, 3$	$\text{EV}[\ ] \equiv [\ ] + (\lambda x\colon nat.\, x)\, 3$
$\stackrel{left}{\to}$ $\underline{(7 + 5)} + (\lambda x\colon nat.\, x)\, 3$	$\text{EV}[\ ] \equiv [\ ] + (\lambda x\colon nat.\, x)\, 3$
$\stackrel{left}{\to}$ $12 + \underline{(\lambda x\colon nat.\, x)\, 3}$	$\text{EV}[\ ] \equiv 12 + [\ ]$
$\stackrel{left}{\to}$ $\underline{12 + 3}$	$\text{EV}[\ ] \equiv [\ ]$
$\stackrel{left}{\to}$ 15	

If we look at the second evaluation context, $\text{EV}[\ ] \equiv [\ ] + (\lambda x\colon nat.\, x)\, 3$, then it is easy to see that when $M \stackrel{lazy}{\to} M'$ the lazy reduction of $\text{EV}[M]$ will be $\text{EV}[M] \stackrel{lazy}{\to} \text{EV}[M']$, as guaranteed by Lemma 2.5.21. However, if we insert a lazy normal form such as 2 into the context, then the resulting term, $\text{EV}[2] \equiv 2 + (\lambda x\colon nat.\, x)\, 3$, will have its lazy reduction completely to the right of the position marked by the placeholder [ ] in the context. Another case arises with the first context, $\text{EV}[\ ] \equiv ([\ ]\, 5) + (\lambda x\colon nat.\, x)\, 3$. If we insert the lazy normal form $M \equiv \lambda y\colon nat.\, 7 + y$, we obtain a term $\text{EV}[M]$ whose lazy reduction involves a larger subterm than M. ■

We note here that left-most reduction can also be characterized using evaluation contexts. To do so, we add six more forms to the definition of evaluation context, corresponding to the six rules that appear in Table 2.3 but not in Table 2.4. Lemma 2.5.20 extends easily to left-most reduction, but Lemma 2.5.21 requires the additional hypothesis that M does not have the form $\lambda x{:}\,\sigma.\, M_1$ or $\langle M_1, M_2\rangle$.

We use Lemma 2.5.21 in the analysis of parallel-or by showing that if the normal form of a compound term depends on the subterms $M_1, \ldots, M_k$, as we expect the parallel-or of M_1 and M_2 to depend on M_1 and M_2, then we may reduce the term to the form $\textsc{ev}[M_i]$, for some i independent of the form of $M_1, \ldots, M_k$. The intuition behind this is that some number of reduction steps may be independent of the chosen subterms. But if any of these subterms has any effect on the result, then eventually we must come to some term $\textsc{ev}[M_i]$ where the next reduction depends on the form of M_i. The "sequential" nature of PCF is that when we reach a term of the form $\textsc{ev}[M_i]$, it follows from Lemma 2.5.21 that if M_i is not a lazy normal form, we continue to reduce M_i until this subterm term does not lazy-reduce further.

Since we are interested in analyzing the reduction steps applied to a function of several arguments, we will use contexts with more than one "hole" (place for inserting a term). A *context* $\mathcal{C}[\cdot, \ldots, \cdot]$ *with k holes* is a syntactic expression with exactly the same form as a term, but containing zero or more occurrences of the placeholders $[\ ]_1, \ldots, [\ ]_k$, each assumed to have a fixed type within this expression. As for contexts with a single hole, we write $\mathcal{C}[M_1, \ldots, M_k]$ for the result of replacing the ith placeholder $[\ ]_i$ by M_i, without renaming bound variables.

Our first lemma about reduction in arbitrary contexts is that the lazy reduction of a term of the form $\mathcal{C}[M_1, \ldots, M_k]$ is either a reduction on $\mathcal{C}$, independent of the terms $M_1, \ldots, M_k$ placed in the context, or a reduction that depends on the form of one of the terms $M_1, \ldots, M_k$.

Lemma 2.5.23 Let $\mathcal{C}[\cdot, \ldots, \cdot]$ be a context with k holes. Suppose that there exist closed terms $N_1, \ldots, N_k$ of the appropriate types such that $\mathcal{C}[N_1, \ldots, N_k]$ is not in lazy normal form. Then $\mathcal{C}$ must have one of the following two properties:

(i) There is a context $\mathcal{C}'[\cdot, \ldots, \cdot]$ such that for all closed terms $M_1, \ldots, M_k$ of the appropriate types $\mathcal{C}[M_1, \ldots, M_k] \stackrel{lazy}{\to} \mathcal{C}'[M_1, \ldots, M_k]$.

(ii) There is some i such that for all closed terms $M_1, \ldots, M_k$ of the appropriate types there is an evaluation context $\textsc{ev}[\ ]$ with $\mathcal{C}[M_1, \ldots, M_k] \equiv \textsc{ev}[M_i]$.

We use Lemma 2.5.23 to prove the following statement about sequences of lazy reductions.

Lemma 2.5.24 Let $\mathcal{C}[\cdot, \ldots, \cdot]$ be a context with k holes, let $M_1, \ldots, M_k$ be closed terms of the appropriate types for $\mathcal{C}$ and suppose $\mathcal{C}[M_1, \ldots, M_k]$ is a program with normal form N. Then either $\mathcal{C}[M_1', \ldots, M_k']$ reduces to N for all closed $M_1', \ldots, M_k'$ of the appropriate types or there is some integer i such that for all closed $M'_1, \ldots, M'_k$ of the appropriate types there is an evaluation context EV[ ] with $\mathcal{C}[M'_1, \ldots, M'_k] \xrightarrow{\text{lazy}}\!\!\!\!\!\rightarrow \text{EV}[M'_i]$.

An intuitive reading of this lemma is that some number of reduction steps of a term $\mathcal{C}[M_1, \ldots, M_k]$ may be independent of all the M_i. If this does not produce a normal form, then eventually the reduction of $\mathcal{C}[M_1, \ldots, M_k]$ will reach a step that depends on the form of some M_i, with the number i depending only on $\mathcal{C}$.

If we replace lazy reduction with left-most reduction, then we may change lazy normal form to normal form in Lemma 2.5.23 and drop the assumption that $\mathcal{C}[M_1, \ldots, M_k]$ is a program in Lemma 2.5.24.

Using Lemmas 2.5.21 and 2.5.24, we now prove Theorem 2.5.19.

Proof of Theorem 2.5.19 Suppose we have a PCF expression *POR* defining parallel-or and consider the context $\mathcal{C}[\cdot, \cdot] \stackrel{\text{def}}{=} POR[\ ]_1[\ ]_2$. Since *POR* defines parallel-or, $\mathcal{C}[true, true] \twoheadrightarrow true$ and $\mathcal{C}[false, false] \twoheadrightarrow false$. By Lemma 2.5.24, there are two possibilities for the lazy reduction of $\mathcal{C}[true, true]$ to *true*. The first implies that $\mathcal{C}[M_1, M_2] \twoheadrightarrow true$ for all closed boolean terms M_1 and M_2. But this contradicts $\mathcal{C}[false, false] \twoheadrightarrow false$. Therefore, there is an integer $i \in \{1, 2\}$ such that for all closed boolean terms M_1, M_2, there is an evaluation context EV[ ] with $\mathcal{C}[M_1, M_2] \xrightarrow{\text{lazy}}\!\!\!\!\!\rightarrow \text{EV}[M_i]$. But, by Lemma 2.5.21, this implies that if we apply *POR* to *true* and the term $fix_{bool}\,(\lambda x\colon bool.\, x)$ with no normal form, making $fix_{bool}\,(\lambda x\colon bool.\, x)$ the ith argument, we cannot reduce the resulting term to *true*. This contradicts the assumption that *POR* defines parallel-or. ∎

The reader may reasonably ask whether the non-definability of parallel-or is a peculiarity of PCF or a basic property shared by sequential programming languages such as Pascal and Lisp. The main complicating factor in comparing PCF to these languages is the order of evaluation. Since a Pascal function call `P(M,N)` is compiled so that expressions `M` and `N` are evaluated *before* `P` is called, it is clear that no boolean function `P` could compute parallel-or. However, we can ask whether parallel-or is definable by a Pascal (or Lisp) context with two boolean positions. More precisely, consider a Pascal program context `P[·, ·]` with two "holes" for boolean expressions (or bodies of functions that return boolean values). An important part of the execution of `P[M, N]` is what happens when `M` or `N` may run forever. Therefore, it is sensible and nontrivial to ask whether parallel-or is definable by a Pascal or Lisp context. If we were to go to the effort of formalizing the execution of Pascal programs in the way that we have formalized PCF evaluation, it seems very likely that we could prove that parallel-or is not definable by any context. The reader may enjoy trying to demonstrate otherwise by constructing a Pascal context that defines parallel-or and seeing what obstacles are involved. In Lisp, it is possible to define parallel-or by defining your own `eval` function. However, the apparent need to define a non-standard `eval` illustrates the sequentiality of standard Lisp evaluation.

Proof of Lemma 2.5.20 We use induction on the proof, in the system of Table 2.4, that $M \stackrel{lazy}{\to} N$. The base case is that $M \to N$ is one of the reduction axioms (these are listed in Table 2.2). If this is so, then the lemma holds with $\text{EV}[\,] \equiv [\,]$. The induction steps for the inference rules in Table 2.4 are all similar and essentially straightforward. For example, if we have $P + R \stackrel{lazy}{\to} Q + R$ by the rule

$$\frac{P \stackrel{lazy}{\to} Q}{P + R \stackrel{lazy}{\to} Q + R},$$

then by the induction hypothesis there is a unique evaluation context $\text{EV}'[\,]$ such that $P \equiv \text{EV}'[P']$, $P' \to Q'$ is a reduction axioms, and $Q \equiv \text{EV}'[Q']$. The lemma follows by taking $\text{EV}[\,] \equiv \text{EV}'[\,] + R$. ∎

Proof of Lemma 2.5.21 We prove the lemma by induction on the structure of evaluation contexts. In the base case, we have an evaluation context $\text{EV}[\,] \equiv [\,]$. Since $\text{EV}[M] \equiv M$ and $\text{EV}[M'] \equiv M'$, it is easy to see that under the hypotheses of the lemma, $\text{EV}[M] \stackrel{lazy}{\to} \text{EV}[M']$.

There are a number of induction cases, corresponding to the possible syntactic forms of $\text{EV}[\,]$. Since the analysis of each of these is similar, we consider three representative cases.

The case $\text{EV}[\,] \equiv \text{EV}'[\,] + M_1$ is similar to most of the compound evaluation contexts. In this case, $\text{EV}[M] \equiv \text{EV}'[M] + M_1$ and, by the induction hypothesis, $\text{EV}'[M] \stackrel{lazy}{\to} \text{EV}'[M']$. Since $\text{EV}'[M]$ is not syntactically a numeral, no axiom can apply to the entire term $\text{EV}'[M] + M_1$. Therefore the only rule in Table 2.4 that applies is

$$\frac{\text{EV}'[M] \stackrel{lazy}{\to} \text{EV}'[M']}{\text{EV}'[M] + M_1 \stackrel{lazy}{\to} \text{EV}'[M'] + M_1}.$$

This gives us $\text{EV}[M] \stackrel{lazy}{\to} \text{EV}[M']$.

The two other cases we will consider are projection and function application. A context $\text{EV}[\,] \equiv \mathbf{Proj}_i \text{EV}'[\,]$ is an evaluation context only if $\text{EV}'[\,]$ does not have the syntactic form of a pair. Since $M \stackrel{lazy}{\to} M'$ implies that M is not a pair, we know that $\text{EV}[M]$ and $\text{EV}'[M]$ do not have the syntactic form of a pair. It follows that no reduction axiom applies to the entire term $\mathbf{Proj}_i \text{EV}'[M]$. Therefore, by the induction hypothesis that $\text{EV}'[M] \stackrel{lazy}{\to} \text{EV}'[M']$, we conclude that $\text{EV}[M] \equiv \mathbf{Proj}_i \text{EV}'[M] \stackrel{lazy}{\to} \mathbf{Proj}_i \text{EV}'[M'] \equiv \text{EV}[M']$.

The last case we consider is $\text{EV}[\,] \equiv \text{EV}'[\,]\,N$. This is similar to the projection case. The context $\text{EV}'[\,]$ cannot be a lambda abstraction, by the definition of evaluation contexts, and M is not a lambda abstraction since $M \stackrel{lazy}{\to} M'$. It follows that $\text{EV}'[M]$ does not have the syntactic form of a lambda abstraction. Since the reduction axiom (β) does not apply to the entire term $\text{EV}'[M]\,N$, we use the induction hypothesis $\text{EV}'[M] \stackrel{lazy}{\rightarrow} \text{EV}'[M']$ and the definition of lazy reduction in Table 2.4 to conclude that $\text{EV}[M] \stackrel{lazy}{\rightarrow} \text{EV}[M']$. ■

Proof of Lemma 2.5.23 We prove the lemma by induction on the structure of contexts. If $\mathcal{C}$ is a single symbol, then it is either one of the placeholders, $[\;]_i$, a variable or a constant. It is easy to see that $\mathcal{C}$ has property *(ii)* if it is a placeholder and property *(i)* if it is some other symbol.

For a context $\mathcal{C}_1[\cdot, \ldots, \cdot] + \mathcal{C}_2[\cdot, \ldots, \cdot]$, we consider two cases, each dividing into two subcases when we apply the induction hypothesis. If there exist terms $M_1, \ldots, M_k$ with $\mathcal{C}_1[M_1, \ldots, M_k]$ not in lazy normal form, then we apply the induction hypothesis to $\mathcal{C}_1$. If $\mathcal{C}_1[M_1, \ldots, M_k] \stackrel{lazy}{\rightarrow} \mathcal{C}_1'[M_1, \ldots, M_k]$ for all $M_1, \ldots, M_k$, then it is easy to see from the definition of lazy reduction that

$$\mathcal{C}_1[M_1, \ldots, M_k] + \mathcal{C}_2[M_1, \ldots, M_k] \stackrel{lazy}{\rightarrow} \mathcal{C}_1'[M_1, \ldots, M_k] + \mathcal{C}_2[M_1, \ldots, M_k]$$

for all $M_1, \ldots, M_k$. On the other hand, if for every $M_1, \ldots, M_k$ we can write $\mathcal{C}_1[M_1, \ldots, M_k] \equiv \text{EV}[M_i]$, then

$$\mathcal{C}_1[M_1, \ldots, M_k] + \mathcal{C}_2[M_1, \ldots, M_k] \equiv \text{EV}[M_i] + \mathcal{C}_2[M_1, \ldots, M_k]$$

and we have an evaluation context for M_i. The second case is that $\mathcal{C}_1[M_1, \ldots, M_k]$ is a numeral and therefore $M_1, \ldots, M_k$ do not occur in $\mathcal{C}_1[M_1, \ldots, M_k]$. In this case, we apply the induction hypothesis to $\mathcal{C}_2$ and reason as above.

The induction steps for *Eq*? and `if ... then ... else ...` are similar to the addition case. The induction steps for pairing and lambda abstraction are trivial, since these are lazy normal forms.

For a context $\mathbf{Proj}_i\mathcal{C}[\cdot, \ldots, \cdot]$, we must consider the form of $\mathcal{C}$. If $\mathcal{C}[\cdot, \ldots, \cdot] \equiv [\;]_j$, then $\mathbf{Proj}_i\mathcal{C}[\cdot, \ldots, \cdot]$ satisfies condition *(ii)* of the lemma since this is an evaluation context. If $\mathcal{C}[\cdot, \ldots, \cdot] \equiv \langle \mathcal{C}_1[\cdot, \ldots, \cdot], \mathcal{C}_2[\cdot, \ldots, \cdot]\rangle$, then $\mathbf{Proj}_i\mathcal{C}[\cdot, \ldots, \cdot]$ satisfies condition *(i)*. If $\mathcal{C}[\cdot, \ldots, \cdot]$ has some other form, then $\mathbf{Proj}_i\mathcal{C}[M_1, \ldots, M_k]$ cannot be a *(proj)* redex. Therefore, we apply the induction hypothesis to $\mathcal{C}$ and reason as in the earlier cases.

The induction step for a context $\mathcal{C}_1[\cdot, \ldots, \cdot]\,\mathcal{C}_2[\cdot, \ldots, \cdot]$ is similar to the $\mathbf{Proj}_i$ case, except that we will need to use the assumption that all the terms we place in contexts are closed. Specifically, if $\mathcal{C}_1[\cdot, \ldots, \cdot] \equiv \lambda x\!:\!\sigma.\,\mathcal{C}_3[\cdot, \ldots, \cdot]$, then let $\mathcal{C}'$ be the context $\mathcal{C}'[\cdot, \ldots, \cdot] \equiv [\mathcal{C}_2[\cdot, \ldots, \cdot]/x]\mathcal{C}_1[\cdot, \ldots, \cdot]$. For all *closed* $M_1, \ldots, M_k$ we have

$$(\lambda x\!:\!\sigma.\,\mathcal{C}_3[M_1, \ldots, M_k])\mathcal{C}_2[M_1, \ldots, M_k] \stackrel{lazy}{\rightarrow} \mathcal{C}'[M_1, \ldots, M_k]$$

and the context satisfies condition *(i)* of the lemma. If $\mathcal{C}_1[\cdot, \ldots, \cdot] \equiv [\;]_i$, then as in the projection case, the application context satisfies condition *(ii)* of the lemma. Finally, if

$\mathcal{C}_1[\cdot, \ldots, \cdot]$ is some context that is not of one of these two forms, we reason as in the addition case, applying the induction hypothesis to either $\mathcal{C}_1$ or, if $\mathcal{C}_1[M_1, \ldots, M_k]$ is a lazy a normal form for all $M_1, \ldots, M_k$, the context $\mathcal{C}_2$. This completes the proof. ∎

Proof of Lemma 2.5.24 Let $\mathcal{C}[\cdot, \ldots, \cdot]$ be a context with k holes and let $M_1, \ldots, M_k$ be closed terms of the appropriate types such that $\mathcal{C}[M_1, \ldots, M_k]$ has normal form N of observable type. Then $\mathcal{C}[M_1, \ldots, M_k] \stackrel{lazy}{\twoheadrightarrow}_n N$, where n indicates the number of reduction steps. We prove the lemma by induction on n.

In the base case, $\mathcal{C}[M_1, \ldots, M_k] \equiv N$ is in normal form. There are two cases to consider. The degenerate one is that $\mathcal{C}[M_1', \ldots, M_k']$ is in normal form for all closed terms $M_1', \ldots, M_k'$ of the appropriate types. But since the only results are numerals and boolean constants, $M_1', \ldots, M_k'$ must not appear in N and the lemma easily follows. The second case is that $\mathcal{C}[M_1', \ldots, M_k']$ is not in normal form for some $M_1', \ldots, M_k'$. Since $\mathcal{C}[M_1, \ldots, M_k]$ is in normal form, condition (i) of Lemma 2.5.23 cannot hold. Therefore $\mathcal{C}[M_1', \ldots, M_k'] \equiv \text{EV}[M_i']$.

In the induction step, with $\mathcal{C}[M_1, \ldots, M_k] \stackrel{lazy}{\twoheadrightarrow}_{m+1} N$, Lemma 2.5.23 gives us two cases. The simpler is that there is some i such that for all closed terms $M_1', \ldots, M_k'$ of the appropriate types $\mathcal{C}[M_1', \ldots, M_k']$ has the form $\text{EV}[M_i']$. But then clearly $\mathcal{C}[M_1', \ldots, M_k'] \stackrel{lazy}{\twoheadrightarrow} \text{EV}[M_i']$ and the lemma holds. The remaining case is that there is some context $\mathcal{C}'[\cdot, \ldots, \cdot]$ such that for all $M_1', \ldots, M_k'$ of appropriate types, we have a reduction of the form

$$\mathcal{C}[M_1, \ldots, M_k] \stackrel{lazy}{\rightarrow} \mathcal{C}'[M_1, \ldots, M_k] \stackrel{lazy}{\twoheadrightarrow}_m N.$$

The lemma follows by the induction hypothesis for $\mathcal{C}'[\cdot \ldots, \cdot]$. This concludes the proof.
∎

Exercise 2.5.25 Show that Lemma 2.5.24 fails if we drop the assumption that $\mathcal{C}[M_1, \ldots, M_k]$ is a program.

Exercise 2.5.26 This exercise asks you to prove that parallel-conditional is not definable in PCF. Use Lemmas 2.5.21 and 2.5.24 to show that there is no PCF expression $PIF_{nat} : bool \to nat \to nat \to nat$ such that for all closed boolean expressions $M : bool$ and $N, P, Q : nat$ with Q in normal form,

$$PIF_{nat}\, M\, N\, P \twoheadrightarrow Q \text{ iff } \begin{bmatrix} M \twoheadrightarrow true \text{ and } N \text{ has normal form } Q \text{ or,} \\ M \twoheadrightarrow false \text{ and } P \text{ has normal form } Q \text{ or,} \\ N, P \text{ both have normal form } Q. \end{bmatrix}$$

(If we extend Lemmas 2.5.21 and 2.5.24 to left-most reduction, the same proof shows that PIF_σ is not definable for any type σ.)

Exercise 2.5.27 The operational equivalence relation $=_{op}$ on terms is defined in Section 2.3.5. Show that if M and N are either closed terms of type *nat* or closed terms of type *bool*, neither having a normal form, then $M =_{op} N$.

Exercise 2.5.28 A plausible statement that is stronger than Lemma 2.5.24 is this:

Let $\mathcal{C}[\cdot, \ldots, \cdot]$ be a context with k holes, let $M_1, \ldots, M_k$ be closed terms of the appropriate types for $\mathcal{C}$ and suppose $\mathcal{C}[M_1, \ldots, M_k] \xrightarrow{\text{lazy}}\!\!\!\!\!\rightarrow N$, where N does not further reduce by lazy reduction. Then either $\mathcal{C}[M'_1, \ldots, M'_k]$ reduces to N for all closed $M'_1, \ldots, M'_k$ of the appropriate types or there is some integer i such that for all closed $M'_1, \ldots, M'_k$ of the appropriate types there is an evaluation context $\text{EV}[\;]$ with $\mathcal{C}[M'_1, \ldots, M'_k] \xrightarrow{\text{lazy}}\!\!\!\!\!\rightarrow \text{EV}[M'_i]$.

The only difference is that we do not require N to be in normal form. Show that this statement is *false* by giving a counterexample. This may be done using a context $\mathcal{C}[\;]$ with only one placeholder.

Exercise 2.5.29 [Sto91a] This problem asks you to show that parallel-or, boolean parallel-conditional and natural-number parallel-conditional are all interdefinable. Parallel-or is defined in the statement of Theorem 2.5.19 and parallel-conditional is defined in Exercise 2.5.26. An intermediate step involves parallel-and, defined below.

(a) Show how to define POR from PIF_{bool} by writing a PCF expression containing PIF_{bool}.

(b) Show how to define PIF_{bool} from PIF_{nat} using an expression of the form

$\lambda x\colon bool.\, \lambda y\colon bool.\, \lambda z\colon bool.\, Eq?\ 1\ (PIF_{nat}\ x\ M\ N).$

(c) Parallel-and, *PAND*, has the following behavior:

$$PAND\ M\ N \twoheadrightarrow \begin{cases} true & \text{if } M \twoheadrightarrow true \text{ and } N \twoheadrightarrow true, \\ false & \text{if } M \twoheadrightarrow false \text{ or } N \twoheadrightarrow false, \\ \text{no normal form} & \text{otherwise.} \end{cases}$$

Show how to define *PAND* from *POR* by writing a PCF expression containing *POR*.

(d) Show how to define PIF_{nat} from *POR* using an expression of the form

$\lambda x\colon bool.\, \lambda y\colon nat.\, \lambda z\colon nat.\, search\ P$

where $P\colon nat \to bool$ has x, y, z free and contains *POR, PAND,* and *Eq?*. The essential properties of *search* are summarized in Proposition 2.5.3 on page 99.

2.6 Variations and Extensions of PCF

2.6.1 Summary of Extensions

This section briefly summarizes several important extensions of PCF. All are obtained by adding new types. The first extension is a very simple one, a type *unit* with only one element. The second extension is *sum,* or disjoint union, types. With unit and disjoint unions, we can define *bool* as the disjoint union of *unit* and *unit*. This makes the primitive type *bool* unnecessary. The next extension is recursive type definitions. With recursive type definitions, *unit* and sum types, we can define *nat* and its operations, making the primitive type *nat* also unnecessary. Other commonly-used types that have straightforward recursive definitions are stacks, lists and trees. Another use of recursive types is that we can define the fixed-point operator *fix* on any type. Thus with *unit*, sums and recursive types, we may define all of the type and term constants of PCF.

The final language is a variant of PCF with lifted types, which give us a different view of nontermination. With lifted types, written in the form $\sigma_\perp$, we can distinguish between natural-number expressions that necessarily have a normal form and those that may not. Specifically, natural-number terms that do not involve *fix* may have type *nat*, while terms that involve *fix*, and therefore may not have a normal form, have the lifted type $nat_\perp$. Thus the type *nat* of PCF corresponds to type $nat_\perp$ in this language. The syntax of many common programs becomes more complicated, since the distinction between lifted and unlifted types forces us to include additional lifting operations in terms. However, the refinement achieved with lifted types has some theoretical advantages. One is that many more equational or reduction axioms become consistent with recursion. Another is that we may study different evaluation orders within a single framework. For this reason, explicit lifting seems useful in meta-languages for studying other programming languages.

All of the extensions summarized here may be combined with polymorphism, treated in Chapter 9 and other typing ideas in Chapters 10 and 11.

2.6.2 Unit and Sum Types

We add the one-element type *unit* to PCF, or any language based on typed lambda calculus, by adding *unit* to the type expressions and adding the constant $*: unit$ to the syntax of terms. The equational axiom for $*$ is

$$M = *: unit \qquad (unit)$$

for any term $M: unit$. Intuitively, this axiom says that every element of type *unit* is equal to $*$. This may be used as a reduction rule, read left to right. While *unit* may not seem very interesting, it is surprisingly useful in combination with sums and other forms of types.

It should be mentioned that the reduction rule for *unit* terms causes confluence to fail, when combined with η-reduction [CD91, LS86]. This does not have an immediate consequence for PCF, since we do not use η-reduction.

Intuitively, the *sum type* $\sigma + \tau$ is the disjoint union of types σ and τ. The difference between a disjoint union and an ordinary set union is that with a disjoint union, we can tell which type any element comes from. This is particularly noticeable when the two types overlap or are identical. For example, if we take the set union of *int* and *int*, we just get *int*. In contrast, the disjoint union of *int* and *int* has two "copies" of *int*. Informally, we think of the sum type *int* + *int* as the collection of "tagged" integers, with each tag indicating whether the integer comes from the left or right *int* in the sum.

The term forms associated with sums are injection and case functions. For any types σ and τ, the injection functions $\mathbf{Inleft}^{\sigma,\tau}$ and $\mathbf{Inright}^{\sigma,\tau}$ have types

$$\mathbf{Inleft}^{\sigma,\tau} \;:\; \sigma \to \sigma + \tau$$

$$\mathbf{Inright}^{\sigma,\tau} \;:\; \tau \to \sigma + \tau$$

Intuitively, the injection functions map σ or τ to $\sigma + \tau$ by "tagging" elements. However, since the operations on tags are encapsulated in the injection and case functions, we never say exactly what the tags actually are.

The **Case** function applies one of two functions to an element of a sum type. The choice between functions depends on which type of the sum the element comes from. For all types σ, τ and ρ, the case function $\mathbf{Case}^{\sigma,\tau,\rho}$ has type

$$\mathbf{Case}^{\sigma,\tau,\rho} \;:\; (\sigma + \tau) \to (\sigma \to \rho) \to (\tau \to \rho) \to \rho$$

Intuitively, $\mathbf{Case}^{\sigma,\tau,\rho}\, x\, f\, g$ inspects the tag on x and applies f if x is from σ and g if x is from τ. The main equational axioms are

$$\mathbf{Case}^{\sigma,\tau,\rho}\, (\mathbf{Inleft}^{\sigma,\tau}\, x)\, f\, g \;= f x \qquad (case)_1$$

$$\mathbf{Case}^{\sigma,\tau,\rho}\, (\mathbf{Inright}^{\sigma,\tau}\, x)\, f\, g = g x \qquad (case)_2$$

Both of these give us reduction axioms, read left to right. There is also an extensionality axiom for sum types,

$$\mathbf{Case}^{\sigma,\tau,\rho}\, x\, (f \circ \mathbf{Inleft}^{\sigma,\tau})\, (f \circ \mathbf{Inright}^{\sigma,\tau}) = f\, x, \qquad (case)_3$$

where $f\colon (\sigma + \tau) \to (\sigma + \tau)$. Some consequences of this axiom are given in Exercise 2.6.3. Since the extensionality axiom leads to inconsistency, when combined with *fix*, we do not include this equational axiom in the extension of PCF with sum types (see Exercise 2.6.4). We will drop the type superscripts from injection and case functions when the type is either irrelevant or determined by context.

As an illustration of *unit* and sum types, we will show how *bool* may be eliminated if *unit* and sum types are added to PCF. We define *bool* by

$$bool \stackrel{\text{def}}{=} unit + unit$$

and boolean values *true* and *false* by

$$true \stackrel{\text{def}}{=} \mathbf{Inleft}\ *$$

$$false \stackrel{\text{def}}{=} \mathbf{Inright}\ *$$

The remaining basic boolean expression is conditional, `if ... then ... else ...`. We may consider this sugar for **Case**, as follows:

$$\texttt{if}\ M\ \texttt{then}\ N\ \texttt{else}\ P \stackrel{\text{def}}{=} \mathbf{Case}^{,,\rho}\ M\ (K_{\rho,unit}N)\ (K_{\rho,unit}P),$$

where $N, P\colon \rho$ and $K_{\rho,unit}$ is the lambda term $\lambda x\colon \rho.\, \lambda y\colon unit.\, x$ that produces a constant function. To show that this works, we must check the two equational axioms for conditional:

$$\texttt{if}\ true\ \texttt{then}\ M\ \texttt{else}\ N = M,$$

$$\texttt{if}\ false\ \texttt{then}\ M\ \texttt{else}\ N = N.$$

The reader may easily verify that when we eliminate syntactic sugar, the first equational axiom for **Case** yields $\texttt{if}\ true\ \texttt{then}\ M\ \texttt{else}\ N = K_{\rho,unit}M * = M$, and similarly for the second equation.

Other uses of sum types include *variants* and *enumeration types,* considered in Exercises 2.6.1 and 2.6.2.

Exercise 2.6.1 A *variant type* is a form of labeled sum, bearing the same relationship to sum types as records do to product types. A variant type defining a sum of types $\sigma_1, \ldots, \sigma_k$ is written $[\ell_1\colon \sigma_1, \ldots, \ell_k\colon \sigma_k]$, where $\ell_1, \ldots, \ell_k$ are distinct syntactic labels. As for records, the order in which we write the label/type pairs does not matter. For example, $[A\colon int,\ B\colon bool]$ is the same type as $[B\colon bool,\ A\colon int]$.

Intuitively, an element of the variant type $[\ell_1\colon \sigma_1, \ldots, \ell_k\colon \sigma_k]$ is an element of one of the types σ_i, for $1 \le i \le k$, tagged with label ℓ_i. More precisely, if $M\colon \sigma_i$, then the expression $\ell_i^{[\ell_1:\sigma_1,\ldots,\ell_k:\sigma_k]}(M_i)$ is an expression of type $[\ell_1\colon \sigma_1, \ldots, \ell_k\colon \sigma_k]$. The case function for $[\ell_1\colon \sigma_1, \ldots, \ell_k\colon \sigma_k]$ has type

$$\mathbf{Case}^{[\ell_1:\sigma_1,\ldots,\ell_k:\sigma_k],\,\rho}\colon [\ell_1\colon \sigma_1, \ldots, \ell_k\colon \sigma_k] \to (\sigma_1 \to \rho) \to \ldots \to (\sigma_k \to \rho) \to \rho$$

and satisfies the equation

$$\mathbf{Case}^{[\ell_1:\sigma_1,\ldots,\ell_k:\sigma_k],\,\rho}\ \ell_i(M_i)\ f_1\ \ldots\ f_k = f_i\ M_i.$$

(Although the label/type pairs are unordered in $[\ell_1\colon \sigma_1, \ldots, \ell_k\colon \sigma_k]$, the order of arguments clearly matters for $\mathbf{Case}^{[\ell_1:\sigma_1,\ldots,\ell_k:\sigma_k],\,\rho}$.) Following the pattern we use to treat records as sugar for products (see Section 2.5.1), show how to treat variants as syntactic sugar for sums. Illustrate this by translating an expression containing occurrences of two different variant types into PCF with sums.

Exercise 2.6.2 *Enumeration types* appear in Pascal and some subsequent programming languages. The elements of an enumeration type $(\ell_1, \ldots, \ell_n)$ are the literals $\ell_1, \ldots, \ell_n$, which are considered distinct values not equal to any values of any other type. (We do not consider subranges or subtypes of enumeration types here.) Show how to regard the enumeration type $(\ell_1, \ldots, \ell_n)$ as syntactic sugar for the variant $[\ell_1\colon unit, \ldots, \ell_k\colon unit]$ and illustrate your technique by showing how to translate an expression containing enumeration types and literals into a PCF expression with *unit* and variants.

Exercise 2.6.3 Prove the following consequences of the extensionality axiom for sum types, using the equational axioms and inference rules of PCF as needed.

(a) $\mathbf{Case}\, x\ \mathbf{Inleft}\ \mathbf{Inright} = x$.

(b) $f(\mathbf{Case}\, x\ (g \circ \mathbf{Inleft})\ (g \circ \mathbf{Inright})) = \mathbf{Case}\, x\ (f \circ g \circ \mathbf{Inleft})\ (f \circ g \circ \mathbf{Inright})$.

(c) $f(\texttt{if}\ M\ \texttt{then}\ N\ \texttt{else}\ P) = \texttt{if}\ M\ \texttt{then}\ fN\ \texttt{else}\ fP$, when desugared into sum operations as described in this section.

(d) $M = \lambda z\colon \sigma + \tau.\, \mathbf{Case}\, z\ N\ P : (\sigma + \tau) \to (\sigma + \tau)$ is provable whenever $\lambda x\colon \sigma.\, M\, (\mathbf{Inleft}\, x) = N : \sigma \to (\sigma + \tau)$ and $\lambda y\colon \tau.\, M(\mathbf{Inright}\, y) = P : \tau \to (\sigma + \tau)$ are both provable and z is not free in N or P.

Exercise 2.6.4 This exercise asks you to show that the extensionality axiom for sums is inconsistent with the equational axiom for *fix,* when combined with the rest of the equational proof system of PCF. The first observation of this phenomenon is generally credited to Lawvere [Law69].

(a) Define functions $not\colon bool \to bool$ and $eq?\colon bool \to bool \to bool$ and show that when we regard *bool* as sugar for $unit + unit$, we can prove the following three equations with boolean variable x:

$$not\ (not\ x) \quad = x$$

$$eq?\, x\ (not\ x) = false$$

$$eq?\, x\, x \qquad = true$$

You may use the results of Exercise 2.6.3.

(b) Recall from Exercise 2.3.2 that every equation between well-formed terms of the same type is provable from $true = false$ by the axioms and inference rules of PCF. Use the three equations proved in part (a) to prove $true = false$. You can do this by substituting a boolean expression of the form $fix\ B$ for x in two of the equations.

2.6.3 Recursive Types

In some programming languages, it is possible to define types recursively. An example is ML, which has recursive `datatype` declarations (see Exercise 2.6.8). We may add recursively-defined types to PCF, or any related language based on lambda calculus, by adding type variables $r, s, t, \ldots$ to the syntax of type expressions and a new form of type expression, $\mu t.\sigma$. Intuitively, $\mu t.\sigma$ is the smallest type (collection of values) satisfying the equation

$$t = \sigma,$$

where t will generally occur in σ. As with recursive definitions in PCF, we could introduce a fixed-point operator and write $fix\ (\lambda t.\, \sigma)$ for a solution to the equation $t = \sigma$. The syntax $\mu t.\sigma$ could be considered sugar for $fix\ (\lambda t.\, \sigma)$. However, we will avoid lambda abstraction in types by taking μ as primitive. We consider the denotational semantics of recursive type declarations in Section 7.4.

The operator μ binds t in $\mu t.\sigma$, so we have both free and bound type variables in type expressions. However, since no term constructs bind type variables, we only use closed types in terms. More specifically, the type expressions of PCF with *nat* and *bool* eliminated but *unit*, sum and recursive types added are the *closed* type expressions generated by the following grammar:

$$\sigma \ ::= \ t \mid unit \mid \sigma + \sigma \mid \sigma \times \sigma \mid \sigma \to \sigma \mid \mu t.\sigma$$

Since terms that contain types with free type variables lead to polymorphism, these are discussed in Chapter 9. We consider type expressions that differ in the names of bound variables equivalent.

With recursive types, we must consider the issue of type equality with some care. Although intuitively $\mu t.\sigma$ introduces a solution to the equation $t = \sigma$, there are two possible interpretations. One is that these are truly indistinguishable types. In this view, type equality becomes relatively complicated, since $t = \sigma$ implies that $t = [\sigma/t]\sigma$. Written using the μ syntax, this gives us the equation

$$\mu t.\sigma = [\mu t.\sigma/t]\sigma \qquad (unfold)$$

Many other equations follow, including some that are not directly derivable from an axiom of this form [AC91]. While the type equality view has some appeal, this makes it more difficult to determine whether terms are well typed. Specifically, we must consider type equality in terms, allowing a term of one type to be used wherever a term of equal but syntactically different type is required. We may avoid this by taking the second view of type recursion.

The alternate view is to solve an equation $t = \sigma$ by finding a type t that is *isomorphic* to σ. Isomorphic, in this context, means that there is a function from $\mu t.\sigma$ to $[\mu t.\sigma \,/\, t]\sigma$, and one in the opposite direction, each the inverse of the other. We express this by writing

$$\mu t.\sigma \cong [\mu t.\sigma/t]\sigma$$

where $\cong$ indicates an isomorphism. In the isomorphism view, $\mu t.\sigma$ is not *equal* to $[\mu t.\sigma/t]\sigma$, but there are functions that allow us to "convert" a value of type $\mu t.\sigma$ to $[\mu t.\sigma/t]\sigma$, and vice versa. With recursive types satisfying isomorphisms instead of equations, we may continue to use syntactic equality for type equality (except for renaming of bound type variables). The price is that we must write the conversion functions between $\mu t.\sigma$ and $[\mu t.\sigma/t]\sigma$ in terms so that we know the syntactic type of each term exactly.

The term forms associated with recursive types allow us to convert a term of type $\mu t.\sigma$ to type $[\mu t.\sigma/t]\sigma$, and vice versa.

If $M\colon [\mu t.\sigma/t]\sigma$ then $\text{up}\, M\colon \mu t.\sigma$. ($\mu$ *Intro*)
If $M\colon \mu t.\sigma$ then $\text{dn}\, M\colon [\mu t.\sigma/t]\sigma$. ($\mu$ *Elim*)

These two functions are inverses, as stated by the following equational axioms.

$$\text{dn}(\text{up}\, M) = M, \quad \text{up}(\text{dn}\, M) = M. \qquad (up/dn)$$

Only the first axiom is traditionally used as a reduction rule (read left to right). While the operations up and dn disambiguate the types of terms, these are often cumbersome to write. In later chapters, we will occasionally omit up and dn from examples to improve readability.

We will show that with recursive type definitions, *unit* and sum types, we can define *nat*, numerals for 0, 1, 2, ..., and the successor, predecessor and zero-test functions. As shown in Exercise 2.5.7, we may replace addition and equality test (*Eq*?) of PCF by successor, predecessor and zero-test without changing the set of definable functions. Therefore, we can translate any expression of PCF into the language with recursive type definitions, *unit* and sum types.

A distinguishing feature of the natural numbers is that if we add one more element to the set of natural numbers, we obtain a set that is in one-to-one correspondence, or isomorphic, to the set of natural numbers. Since the sum $unit + \tau$ has one more element than τ, we therefore expect *nat* to satisfy the isomorphism

$nat \cong unit + nat$

This leads us to the following definition of *nat* as a recursive type

$nat \stackrel{\text{def}}{=} \mu t.\, unit + t$

Intuitively, this may be understood by considering the isomorphisms

$$\begin{aligned} nat &\cong unit + nat \\ &\cong unit + (unit + nat) \\ &\cong unit + (unit + (unit + nat)) \\ &\cong \ldots \\ &\cong unit + (unit + (unit + (unit + (unit + \ldots + nat \ldots)))) \end{aligned}$$

Since we can continue this expansion as long as we like, we can think intuitively of *nat* as the disjoint union of infinitely many one-element types. We can think of the natural number 0 as coming from the first *unit* in this sum, 1 from the second *unit*, and so on for each natural number.

To avoid confusion between natural numbers and the terms that we use to represent natural numbers, we will write $\ulcorner n \urcorner$ for the numeral (term) for n. Following the intuitive picture above, we let the numeral $\ulcorner 0 \urcorner$ for natural number 0 be the term

$\ulcorner 0 \urcorner \stackrel{\text{def}}{=} \text{up}\,(\textbf{Inleft}\,*).$

For any natural number $n > 0$, we may similarly define the numeral $\ulcorner n \urcorner$ by

$\ulcorner n \urcorner \stackrel{\text{def}}{=} \text{up}\,(\textbf{Inright}\ \text{up}\,(\textbf{Inright}\ \ldots \text{up}\,(\textbf{Inleft}\,*) \ldots))$

with n occurrences of **Inright** and $n + 1$ applications of up. The successor function just applies up and **Inright**:

$succ \stackrel{\text{def}}{=} \lambda x\colon nat.\, \text{up}(\textbf{Inright}\ x)$

We can check that this has the right type by noting that if $x\colon nat$, then $\textbf{Inright}\ x$ belongs to $unit + nat$. Therefore, $\text{up}(\textbf{Inright}\ x)\colon nat$. The reader may verify that $S\ulcorner n \urcorner = \ulcorner n + 1 \urcorner$ for any natural number n.

The zero-test operation works by taking $x\colon nat$ and applying dn to obtain an element of $unit + nat$, then using **Case** to see whether the result is an element of *unit* (*i.e.*, equal to 0) or not.

$zero? \stackrel{\text{def}}{=} \lambda x\colon nat.\, \textbf{Case}^{unit,nat,bool}\,(\text{dn}\ x)\,(\lambda y\colon unit.\, true)\,(\lambda z\colon nat.\, false)$

The reader may easily check that $zero?\ \ulcorner 0 \urcorner = true$ and $zero?\ \ulcorner n \urcorner = false$ for $n > 0$.

The final operation we need is predecessor. Recall that although there is no predecessor of 0, it is conventional to take $pred\, 0 = 0$. The predecessor function is similar to *zero?* since it works by taking $x\colon nat$ and applying dn, then using **Case** to see whether the result is an element of *unit* (*i.e.*, equal to 0) or not. If so, then the predecessor is 0; otherwise, the element of *nat* already obtained by applying dn is the predecessor.

$$pred \stackrel{\text{def}}{=} \lambda x\colon nat.\, \mathbf{Case}^{unit,nat,bool}\, (\text{dn}\ x)\, (\lambda y\colon unit.\, 0)\, (\lambda z\colon nat.\, z)$$

The reader may verify that for any $x\colon nat$ we have $pred(succ\, x) = x$. (This is part of Exercise 2.6.5 below.)

A second illustration of the use of recursive types has a very different flavor. While most common uses of recursive types involve data structures, we may also write recursive definitions over any type using recursive types. More specifically, we may define a function fix_σ with the reduction property $fix_\sigma \twoheadrightarrow \lambda f\colon \sigma \to \sigma.\, f(fix_\sigma\, f)$ using only typed lambda calculus with recursive types. The main idea is to use "self-application," which is not possible without recursive types. More specifically, if M is any PCF term, the application MM cannot be well-typed. The reason is simply that if $M\colon \tau$, then τ does not have enough symbols to have the form $\tau \to \tau'$. However, with recursive types, $(\text{dn}\ M)M$ may be well-typed, since the type of M could have the form $\mu t.t \to \tau$.

We will define fix_σ using a term of the form $\text{dn}\, MM$. The main property we want for $\text{dn}\, MM$ is that

$$\text{dn}\, MM \twoheadrightarrow \lambda f\colon \sigma \to \sigma.\, f(\text{dn}\, MM\ f).$$

This reduction gives us a good clue about the form of M. Specifically, we can let M have the form

$$M \stackrel{\text{def}}{=} \text{up}(\ \lambda x\colon \tau.\, \lambda f\colon \sigma \to \sigma.\, f(\text{dn}\, x\, x\ f)\ )$$

if we can find an appropriate type τ. Since we want $\text{dn}\, MM : (\sigma \to \sigma) \to \sigma$, the expression $\text{dn}\, x\, x\ f$ in the body of M must have type σ. Therefore, τ must satisfy the isomorphism

$$\tau \cong \tau \to (\sigma \to \sigma) \to \sigma.$$

We can easily achieve this by letting

$$\tau \stackrel{\text{def}}{=} \mu t.\, t \to (\sigma \to \sigma) \to \sigma.$$

We leave it to the reader to verify that if we define $fix_\sigma \stackrel{\text{def}}{=} \text{dn}\, MM$, or more simply

$$fix_\sigma \stackrel{\text{def}}{=} (\lambda x\colon \tau.\, \lambda f\colon \sigma \to \sigma.\, f(\text{dn}\, x\, x\ f))\ (\text{up}(\lambda x\colon \tau.\, \lambda f\colon \sigma \to \sigma.\, f(\text{dn}\, x\, x\ f)))$$

we have a well-typed expression with $fix_\sigma \twoheadrightarrow \lambda f\colon \sigma \to \sigma.\ f\,(fix_\sigma\ f)$.

The fixed-point operator we have just derived is a typed version of the fixed-point operator Θ from untyped lambda calculus [Bar84]. As outlined in Exercise 2.6.7 below, any untyped lambda term may be written in a typed way using recursive types.

Exercise 2.6.5 Using the definitions given in this section, show that we have the following reductions on natural number terms.

(a) For every natural number n, we have $S\lceil n\rceil \twoheadrightarrow \lceil n+1\rceil$.

(b) $zero?\ \lceil 0\rceil \twoheadrightarrow true$ and $zero?\ \lceil n\rceil \twoheadrightarrow false$ for $n > 0$.

(c) If x is a natural number variable, then $pred(succ\ x) \twoheadrightarrow x$.

Exercise 2.6.6 We may define the type of lists of natural numbers using the following recursive type:

$$list \stackrel{\text{def}}{=} \mu t.\, unit + (nat \times t)$$

The intuition behind this definition is that a list is either empty, which we represent using the element $*\colon unit$, or may be regarded as a pair consisting of a natural number and a list.

(a) Define the empty list $nil\colon list$ and the function $cons\colon nat \times list \to list$ that adds a natural number to a list.

(b) The function *car* returns the first element of a list and the function *cdr* returns the list following the first element. We can define versions of these functions that make sense when applied to the empty list by giving them types

$$car : list \to unit + nat$$

$$cdr : list \to unit + list$$

and establishing the convention that when applied to the empty list, each returns **Inleft** $*$. Write terms defining *car* and *cdr* functions so that the following equations are provable:

$$car\ nil = \mathbf{Inleft}\ *$$

$$car\ (cons\ x\ \ell) = x$$

$$cdr\ nil = \mathbf{Inleft}\ *$$

$$cdr\ (cons\ x\ \ell) = \ell$$

for $x\colon nat$ and $\ell\colon list$.

(c) Using recursion, it is possible to define "infinite" lists of type *list*. Show how to use *fix* to define a list L_n, for any numeral n, such that $car\ L_n = n$ and $cdr\ L_n = L_n$.

Exercise 2.6.7 The terms of pure untyped lambda calculus (without constant symbols) are given by the grammar

$$U \ ::= \ x \mid UU \mid \lambda x.\, U$$

The main equational properties of untyped lambda terms are untyped versions of (α), (β) and (η). We may define untyped lambda terms in typed lambda calculus with recursive types using the type $\mu t.\, t \to t$. Intuitively, the reason this type works is that terms of type $\mu t.\, t \to t$ may be used as functions on this type, and conversely. This is exactly what we need to make sense of the untyped lambda calculus.

(a) Show that if we give every free or bound variable type $\mu t.\, t \to t$, we may translate any untyped term into a typed lambda term of type $\mu t.\, t \to t$ by inserting up, dn, and type designations on lambda abstractions. Verify that untyped (α) follows from typed (α), untyped (β) follows from $\mathrm{dn}(\mathrm{up}\, M) = M$ and untyped (β) and, finally, untyped (η) follows from typed (η) and $\mathrm{up}(\mathrm{dn}\, M) = M$.

(b) Without recursive types, every typed lambda term without constants has a unique normal form. Show that by translating $(\lambda x.\, xx)\, \lambda x.\, xx$ into typed lambda calculus, we can use recursive types to write terms with no normal form.

(c) A well-known term in untyped lambda calculus is the fixed-point operator

$$Y \stackrel{\text{def}}{=} \lambda f.(\lambda x.\, f(xx))(\lambda x.\, f(xx)).$$

Unlike Θ, this term is only an equational fixed-point operator, *i.e.*, $Yf = f(Yf)$ but Yf does not reduce to $f(Yf)$. Use a variant of the translation given in part (a) to obtain a typed equational fixed point operator from Y. Your typed term should have type $(\sigma \to \sigma) \to \sigma$. Show that although Yf does not reduce to $f(Yf)$, Yf reduces to a term M_f such that $M_f \twoheadrightarrow f\, M_f$.

Exercise 2.6.8 The programming language ML has a form of recursive type declaration, called `datatype`, that combines sums and type recursion. In general, a datatype declaration has the form

$$\texttt{datatype}\ t = \ell_1\ \texttt{of}\ \sigma_1 \mid \ \ldots \ \mid \ell_k\ \texttt{of}\ \sigma_k$$

where the syntactic labels $\ell_1, \ldots, \ell_k$ are used in the same way as in variant types (labeled sums). Intuitively, this declaration defines a type t that is the sum of $\sigma_1, \ldots, \sigma_k$, with labels $\ell_1, \ldots, \ell_k$ used as injection functions as in Exercise 2.6.1. If the declared type t occurs in $\sigma_1, \ldots, \sigma_k$, then this is a recursive declaration of type t. Note that the vertical bar | is part of the syntax of ML, not the meta-language we are using to describe ML. A similar exercise on ML datatype declarations, using algebraic specifications instead of recursive types and sums, appears in Chapter 3 (Exercise 3.6.4).

The type of binary trees, with natural numbers at the leaves, may be declared using `datatype` by

$\texttt{datatype}\ \mathit{tree} = \mathit{leaf}\ \texttt{of}\ \mathit{nat}\ |\ \mathit{node}\ \texttt{of}\ \mathit{tree} \times \mathit{tree}.$

Using the notation for variants given in Exercise 2.6.1, this declares a type *tree* satisfying

$$\mathit{tree} \cong [\mathit{leaf}\colon \mathit{nat},\ \mathit{node}\colon \mathit{tree} \times \mathit{tree}]$$

(a) Explain how to regard a `datatype` declaration as a recursive type expression of the form $\mu t.[\ldots]$ using variants as in Exercise 2.6.1. Illustrate your general method on the type of trees above.

(b) A convenient feature of ML is the way that pattern matching may be used to define functions over declared datatypes. A function over trees may be declared using two "clauses," one for each form of tree. In our variant of ML syntax, a function over *tree*'s defined by pattern matching will have the form

$$\begin{array}{lll} \texttt{letrec fun} & f(\mathit{leaf}(x\colon \mathit{nat})) & = M \\ \quad\quad\ | & f(\mathit{node}(t_1\colon \mathit{tree}, t_2\colon \mathit{tree})) & = N \\ & \texttt{in}\ P & \end{array}$$

where variables $x\colon \mathit{nat}$ and $f\colon \mathit{tree} \to \sigma$ are bound in M, $t_1, t_2\colon \mathit{tree}$ and f are bound in N and f is bound in the the declaration body P. The compiler checks to make sure there is one clause for each constructor of the datatype. For example, we may declare a function f that sums up the values of all the leaves as follows.

$$\begin{array}{lll} \texttt{letrec fun} & f(\mathit{leaf}(x\colon \mathit{nat})) & = x \\ \quad\quad\ | & f(\mathit{node}(t_1\colon \mathit{tree}, t_2\colon \mathit{tree})) & = f(t_1) + f(t_2) \end{array}$$

Explain how to regard a function definition with pattern matching as a function with **Case** and illustrate your general method on the function that sums up the values of all the leaves of a tree.

2.6.4 Lifted Types

Lifted types may be used to distinguish possibly nonterminating computations from ones that are guaranteed to terminate. We can see how lifted types could have been used in PCF by recalling that every term that does not contain *fix* has a normal form. If we combine basic boolean and natural number expressions, pairs and functions, we therefore have a language in which every term has a normal form. Let us call this language PCF_0. In Section 2.2.5, we completed the definition of PCF by adding *fix* to PCF_0. In the process, we extended the set of terms of each type in a nontrivial way. For example, while every PCF_0 term of type *nat* reduces to one of the numerals $0, 1, 2, \ldots$, PCF contains terms such as *fix* $(\lambda x\colon nat.\, x)$ of type *nat* that do not have any normal form and are not provably equal to any numeral. This means that if we want to associate a mathematical value with every PCF term, we cannot think of the values of type *nat* as simply the natural numbers. We must consider some superset of the natural numbers that contains values for all the terms without normal form. (Since it is very reasonable to give all *nat* terms without normal form the same value, we only need one new value, representing nontermination, in addition to the usual natural numbers.) An alternative way of extending PCF_0 with a fixed-point operator is to use lifted types. Although lifted types are sometimes syntactically cumbersome, when it comes to writing common functions or programs, lifted types have some theoretical advantages since they let us clearly identify the sources of nontermination, or "undefinedness," in expressions.

One reason to use lifted types is that many equational axioms that are inconsistent with *fix* may be safely combined with lifted types. One example, which is related to the inconsistency of sum types and *fix* outlined in Exercise 2.6.4, is the pair of equations

$$Eq?\ x\ x = true,$$

$$Eq?\ x\ (n + x) = false \quad \text{numeral } n \text{ different from } 0.$$

While these equations make good sense for the ordinary natural numbers, it is inconsistent to add them to PCF. To see this, the reader may substitute *fix* $(\lambda x\colon nat.\, 1 + x)$ for x in both equations and derive $true = false$. In contrast, it follows from the semantic construction in Section 5.2 that we may consistently add these two equations to the variant of PCF with lifted types (see Example 2.6.10).

Another important reason to consider lifted types is that this provides an interesting and insightful way to incorporate alternative reduction orders into a single system. In particular, as we shall see below, both ordinary (nondeterministic or leftmost) PCF and Eager PCF (defined in Section 2.4.5) can be expressed in PCF with lifted types. This has an interesting consequence for equational reasoning about eager reduction. The equational theory of Eager PCF is not given in Section 2.4.5 since it is relatively subtle and has a different form from the equational theory of PCF. An advantage of lifted types is that we may essentially express eager reduction, and at the same time allow ordinary equational reasoning. In particular, equational axioms may be used to "optimize" a term without changing its normal form. This follows from confluence of PCF with lifted types [How92]. These advantages notwithstanding, the use of lifted types in programming language analysis is a relatively recent development and some syntactic and semantic issues remain unresolved. Consequently, this section will be a high-level and somewhat informal overview.

The types of the language $PCF_\perp$, called "PCF with lifted types," are given by the grammar

$$\sigma \ ::= \ bool \mid nat \mid \sigma \times \sigma \mid \sigma \to \sigma \mid \sigma_\perp$$

These are the types of PCF, plus the form $\sigma_\perp$ which is read "σ lifted." Intuitively, the elements of $\sigma_\perp$ are the same as the elements of σ, plus the possibility of "nontermination" or "divergence". Mathematically, we can interpret $\sigma_\perp$ as the union of σ and one extra element, written $\perp_\sigma$, which serves as the value of any "divergent" term that is not equal to an element of type σ.

The terms of $PCF_\perp$ include all of the general forms of PCF, extended to $PCF_\perp$ types. Specifically, we have pairing, projection, lambda abstraction and application for all product and function types. Since we can use `if ... then ... else ...` on all types in PCF, we extend this to all $PCF_\perp$ types. More specifically, `if` M `then` N `else` P is well-formed whenever $M\colon bool$ and $N, P\colon \sigma$, for any σ. However, the basic natural number and boolean functions of PCF (numerals, boolean constants, addition and equality test) keep the same types as in PCF. For example, $5 + x$ is a *nat* expression of $PCF_\perp$ if $x\colon nat$; it is not an expression of type $nat_\perp$. The equational and reduction axioms for all of these operations are the same as for PCF. The language $PCF_\perp$ also has two operations associated with lifted types and a restricted fixed-point operator. Since both involve a class of types called the "pointed" types, we discuss these before giving the remaining basic operations of the language.

Intuitively, the pointed types of $PCF_\perp$ are the types that contain terms which do not yield any meaningful computational value. More precisely, we can say that a closed term $M\colon \sigma$ is *noninformative* if, for every context $\mathcal{C}[\ ]$ of observable type, if $\mathcal{C}[M]$ has a normal form, then $\mathcal{C}[N]$ has the same normal form for every closed $N\colon \sigma$. (An example noninformative term is $fix(\lambda x\colon \sigma.\, x)$; see Lemma 2.5.24.) Formally, we say a type σ *is pointed* if either $\sigma \equiv \tau_\perp$, $\sigma \equiv \sigma_1 \times \sigma_2$ and both σ_1, σ_2 are pointed, or $\sigma \equiv \sigma_1 \to \sigma_2$ and σ_2 is pointed. The reason $\tau_\perp$ has noninformative terms will become apparent from the type of the fixed-point operator. For a product $\sigma_1 \times \sigma_2$, we can write a noninformative term by combining noninformative terms of types σ_1 and σ_2. If $M\colon \sigma_2$ is noninformative, and $x\colon \sigma_1$ is not free in M, then $\lambda x\colon \sigma_1.\, M$ is a noninformative term of type $\sigma_1 \to \sigma_2$. The name "pointed," which is not very descriptive, comes from the fact that a pointed type has a distinguished element (or "point") representing the value of any noninformative term.

The language $PCF_\perp$ has a fixed-point constant for each pointed type:

$$fix_\sigma\colon (\sigma \to \sigma) \to \sigma \qquad \sigma \text{ pointed}$$

The equational axiom and reduction axiom for *fix* are as in PCF.

The first term form associated with lifted types is that if $M\colon\sigma$, then

$$\lfloor M \rfloor\colon \sigma_\perp. \qquad (\lfloor\ \rfloor \text{ Intro})$$

Intuitively, since the elements of σ are included in $\sigma_\perp$, the term $\lfloor M \rfloor$ defines an element of σ, considered as an element of $\sigma_\perp$. The second term form associated with lifting allows us to evaluate expressions of $\sigma_\perp$ to obtain expressions of type σ. Since some terms of type $\sigma_\perp$ do not define elements of σ, this is formalized in a careful way. If $M\colon\sigma_\perp$ and $N\colon\tau$, with τ pointed and N possibly containing a variable x of type σ, then

$$\texttt{let}\ \lfloor x\colon\sigma \rfloor = M\ \texttt{in}\ N \qquad (\lfloor\ \rfloor \text{ Elim})$$

is a term of type τ. The reader familiar with ML may recognize this syntax as a form of "pattern-matching" `let`. Intuitively, the intent of $\texttt{let}\ \lfloor x\colon\sigma \rfloor = M\ \texttt{in}\ N$ is that we "hope" that M is equal to $\lfloor M' \rfloor$ for some M'. If so, then the value of this expression is the value of N when x has the value of M'.

The main equational axiom for $\lfloor\ \rfloor$ and `let` is

$$\texttt{let}\ \lfloor x\colon\sigma \rfloor = \lfloor M \rfloor\ \texttt{in}\ N = [M/x]N \qquad (\texttt{let}\ \lfloor\ \rfloor)$$

This is also used as a reduction axiom, read left to right. Intuitively, the value of $M\colon\sigma_\perp$ is either $\perp$ or an element of σ. If $M = \perp$, then $\texttt{let}\ \lfloor x\colon\sigma \rfloor = M\ \texttt{in}\ N$ will have value $\perp_\tau$. In operational terms, if M cannot be reduced to the form $\lfloor M' \rfloor$, then $\texttt{let}\ \lfloor x\colon\sigma \rfloor = M\ \texttt{in}\ N$ not be reducible to a useful form of type τ. If M is equal to some $\lfloor M' \rfloor$, then the value of $\texttt{let}\ \lfloor x\colon\sigma \rfloor = M\ \texttt{in}\ N$ is equal to $[M'/x]N$.

If we add a constant $\perp_\tau\colon\tau$ representing "undefinedness" or nontermination at each pointed type τ, we can also state some other equational properties.

$$(\texttt{let}\ \lfloor x \rfloor = \perp_{\sigma_\perp}\ \texttt{in}\ M) = \perp_\tau$$

$$\frac{M\ \perp_{\sigma_\perp} = N\ \perp_{\sigma_\perp} \qquad M \lfloor x \rfloor = N \lfloor x \rfloor}{M = N}\ x \text{ not free in } M, N\colon \sigma_\perp \to \tau$$

Intuitively, the first equation reflects the fact that if we cannot reduce M to the form $\lfloor M' \rfloor$, then $\texttt{let}\ \lfloor x \rfloor = M\ \texttt{in}\ N$ is "undefined." The inference rule is a form of reasoning by cases, based on the intuitive idea that any element of a lifted type $\sigma_\perp$ is either the result of lifting an element of type σ or the value $\perp_{\sigma\perp}$ representing "undefinedness" or nontermination at type σ. However, we will not use constants of the form $\perp_\tau$ or either of these properties in the remainder of this section. In general, they are not especially useful for proving equations between expressions unless we have a more powerful proof system (such as the one using fixed-point induction in Section 5.3) for proving that terms are equal to $\perp$.

We will illustrate the use of lifted types by translating both PCF and Eager PCF into $\mathrm{PCF}_\bot$. A number of interesting relationships between lifted types and sums and recursive types are beyond the scope of this section but may be found in [How92], for example. Before proceeding, we consider some simple examples.

Example 2.6.9 While there is only one natural way to write factorial in PCF, there are some choices with explicit lifting. This example shows two essentially equivalent ways of writing factorial. For simplicity, we assume we have natural number subtraction and multiplication operations so that if $M, N\colon nat$, then $M - N\colon nat$ and $M * N\colon nat$. Using these, we can write a factorial function as $fact_1 \stackrel{\text{def}}{=} fix_{nat \to nat_\bot} F_1$, where

$$F_1 \stackrel{\text{def}}{=} \lambda f\colon nat \to nat_\bot .\, \lambda x\colon nat.$$
$$\mathtt{if}\ Eq?\, x\, 0\ \mathtt{then}\ \lfloor 1 \rfloor\ \mathtt{else\ let}\ \lfloor y \rfloor = f(x-1)\ \mathtt{in}\ \lfloor x * y \rfloor$$

In the definition here, the type of *fact* is $nat \to nat_\bot$. This is a pointed type, which is important since we only have fixed points at pointed types. This type for $fact_1$ is also the type of the lambda-bound variable f in F_1. Since $f\colon nat \to nat_\bot$, we can apply f to arguments of type *nat*. However, the result $f(x-1)$ of calling f will be an element of $nat_\bot$, and therefore we must use `let` to extract the natural number value from the recursive call before multiplying by x. If we wish to apply $fact_1$ to an argument M of type $nat_\bot$, we do so by writing

$$\mathtt{let}\ \lfloor x \rfloor = M\ \mathtt{in}\ fact_1\, x$$

An alternative definition of factorial is $fact_2 \stackrel{\text{def}}{=} fix_{nat_\bot \to nat_\bot} F_2$, where

$$F_2 \stackrel{\text{def}}{=} \lambda f\colon nat_\bot \to nat_\bot .\, \lambda x\colon nat_\bot .\, \mathtt{let}\ \lfloor z \rfloor = x\ \mathtt{in}$$
$$\mathtt{if}\ Eq?\, z\, 0\ \mathtt{then}\ \lfloor 1 \rfloor\ \mathtt{else\ let}\ \lfloor y \rfloor = f \lfloor z-1 \rfloor\ \mathtt{in}\ \lfloor z * y \rfloor$$

Here, the type of factorial is different since the domain of the function is $nat_\bot$ instead of *nat*. The consequence is that we could apply $fact_2$ to a possibly nonterminating expression. However, since the first thing $fact_2$ does with an argument $x\colon nat_\bot$ is force it to some value $z\colon nat$, there is not much flexibility gained in this definition of factorial. In particular, as illustrated below, both functions calculate 3! in essentially the same way. The reason $fact_2$ immediately forces $x\colon nat_\bot$ to some natural number $z\colon nat$ is that equality test *Eq*? requires a *nat* argument, instead of a $nat_\bot$.

For the first definition of factorial, we can compute 3! by expanding out three recursive calls and simplifying as follows:

$$(fix\, F_1)\, 3$$

$$
\begin{array}{ll}
\twoheadrightarrow & \texttt{if}\ Eq?\,3\,0\ \texttt{then}\ \lfloor 1 \rfloor\ \texttt{else}\ \texttt{let}\ \lfloor y \rfloor = (\mathit{fix}\ F_1)(3-1)\ \texttt{in}\ \lfloor 3 * y \rfloor \\
\twoheadrightarrow & \texttt{let}\ \lfloor y \rfloor = \\
& \quad \texttt{let}\ \lfloor y' \rfloor = (\mathit{fix}\ F_1)(1)\ \texttt{in}\ \lfloor 2 * y' \rfloor \\
& \texttt{in}\ \lfloor 3 * y \rfloor \\
\twoheadrightarrow & \texttt{let}\ \lfloor y \rfloor = \\
& \texttt{let}\ \lfloor y' \rfloor = \\
& \qquad \texttt{let}\ \lfloor y'' \rfloor = (\mathit{fix}\ F_1)0\ \texttt{in}\ \lfloor 1 * y'' \rfloor \\
& \quad \texttt{in}\ \lfloor 2 * y' \rfloor \\
& \texttt{in}\ \lfloor 3 * y \rfloor
\end{array}
$$

Then, once we have reduced $(\mathit{fix}\ F_1)0 \twoheadrightarrow \lfloor 1 \rfloor$, we can set y'' to 1, then y' to 1, then y to 2, then perform the final multiplication and produce the final value 6.

For the alternative definition, we have essentially the same expansion, beginning with $\lfloor 3 \rfloor$ instead of 3 for typing reasons:

$$
\begin{array}{ll}
\multicolumn{2}{l}{(\mathit{fix}\ F_2)\ \lfloor 3 \rfloor} \\
\twoheadrightarrow & \texttt{let}\ \lfloor z \rfloor = \lfloor 3 \rfloor\ \texttt{in} \\
& \texttt{if}\ Eq?\,z\,0\ \texttt{then}\ \lfloor 1 \rfloor\ \texttt{else}\ \texttt{let}\ \lfloor y \rfloor = (\mathit{fix}\ F_2)\lfloor z-1 \rfloor\ \texttt{in}\ \lfloor z * y \rfloor \\
\twoheadrightarrow & \ldots \\
\twoheadrightarrow & \texttt{let}\ \lfloor y \rfloor = \\
& \quad \texttt{let}\ \lfloor y' \rfloor = \\
& \qquad \texttt{let}\ \lfloor y'' \rfloor = \mathit{fix}\ F_2)\lfloor 0 \rfloor\ \texttt{in}\ \lfloor 1 * y'' \rfloor \\
& \quad \texttt{in}\ \lfloor 2 * y' \rfloor \\
& \texttt{in}\ \lfloor 3 * y \rfloor
\end{array}
$$

The only difference here is that in each recursive call, the argument is lifted to match the type of the function. However, the body F_2 immediately uses `let` to "unlift" the argument, so the net effect is the same as for fact_1. ∎

Example 2.6.10 As mentioned above, the equations

$Eq?\ x\ x = \mathit{true}$,

$Eq?\ x\ (n + x) = \mathit{false}$ numeral n different from 0.

are consistent with $\text{PCF}_\bot$, when $x\colon nat$ is a natural number variable, but inconsistent when added to PCF. We will see how these equations could be used in $\text{PCF}_\bot$ by considering the PCF expression

$$
\begin{array}{l}
\texttt{letrec}\ f(x\colon nat)\colon nat = \texttt{if}\ Eq?\,x\,0\,\texttt{then}\ 1\ \texttt{else} \\
\qquad\qquad\qquad\qquad\qquad \texttt{if}\ Eq?\,f(x-1)\ f(x-1)\ \texttt{then}\ 2\ \texttt{else}\ 3 \\
\ \texttt{in}\ f3
\end{array}
$$

If we apply left-most reduction to this expression, we end up with an expression of the form

$$\texttt{if } Eq?\,((\mathit{fix}\,F)(3-1))\,((\mathit{fix}\,F)(3-1)) \texttt{ then } 2 \texttt{ else } 3$$

which requires us to simplify two applications of the recursive function in order to determine that $f(2) = f(2)$. We might like to apply some "optimization" which says that whenever we have a subexpression of the form $Eq?\,M\,M$ we can simplify this to *true*. However, the inconsistency of the two equations above shows that this optimization cannot be combined with other reasonable optimizations of this form.

We cannot eliminate the need to compute at least one recursive call, but we can eliminate the equality test using lifted types. A natural and routine translation of this expression into $\mathrm{PCF}_\perp$ is

$$\begin{array}{l} \texttt{letrec } f(x\colon nat)\colon nat_\perp = \texttt{if } Eq?\,x\,0 \texttt{ then } \lfloor 1 \rfloor \texttt{ else} \\ \qquad\qquad\qquad\qquad \texttt{let } \lfloor y \rfloor = f(x-1) \texttt{ in if } Eq?\,y\,y \texttt{ then } \lfloor 2 \rfloor \texttt{ else } \lfloor 3 \rfloor \\ \texttt{in } f3 \end{array}$$

In this form, we have a subexpression of the form $Eq?\,y\,y$ where $y\colon nat$. With the equations above, we can replace this $\mathrm{PCF}_\perp$ expression by an equivalent one, obtaining the provably equivalent expression

$$\begin{array}{l} \texttt{letrec } f(x\colon nat)\colon nat_\perp = \texttt{if } Eq?\,x\,0 \texttt{ then } \lfloor 1 \rfloor \texttt{ else} \\ \qquad\qquad\qquad\qquad\quad \texttt{let } \lfloor y \rfloor = f(x-1) \texttt{ in } \lfloor 2 \rfloor \\ \texttt{in } f3 \end{array}$$

The reason we cannot expect to simplify $\texttt{let } \lfloor y \rfloor = f(x-1) \texttt{ in } \lfloor 2 \rfloor$ to $\lfloor 2 \rfloor$ by any local optimization that does not analyze the entire declaration of f is that when $f(x-1)$ does not terminate (*i.e.*, cannot be reduced to the form $\lfloor M \rfloor$), the two are not equivalent. ■

Translation of PCF into $\mathrm{PCF}_\perp$

The translation of PCF into $\mathrm{PCF}_\perp$ has two parts. The first is a translation of types. We will map expressions of type σ from PCF to expressions of type $\overline{\sigma}$ in $\mathrm{PCF}_\perp$, where $\overline{\sigma}$ is the result of replacing *nat* by $nat_\perp$ and *bool* by $bool_\perp$. More specifically, we may define $\overline{\sigma}$ by induction on types:

$$\begin{array}{ll} \overline{bool} & = bool_\perp \\ \overline{nat} & = nat_\perp \\ \overline{\sigma_1 \times \sigma_2} & = \overline{\sigma_1} \times \overline{\sigma_2} \\ \overline{\sigma_1 \to \sigma_2} & = \overline{\sigma_1} \to \overline{\sigma_2} \end{array}$$

It is easy to check that for any PCF type σ, the type $\overline{\sigma}$ is pointed. This gives us a fixed-point operator of each type $\overline{\sigma}$.

The translation of compound PCF terms into PCF$_\perp$ is essentially straightforward. The most interesting part of the translation lies in the basic natural number and boolean operations. If $M\colon\sigma$ in PCF, we must find some suitable term $\overline{M}$ of type $\overline{\sigma}$ in PCF$_\perp$. The translation $\overline{n}$ of a numeral n is $\lfloor n \rfloor$ and the translations of *true* and *false* are similarly $\lfloor true \rfloor$ and $\lfloor false \rfloor$. It is easy to see these have the right types. For each of the operations *Eq*?, $+$ and conditional, we will write a lambda term of the appropriate PCF$_\perp$ type. Since *Eq*? compares two natural number terms and produces a boolean, we will write a PCF$_\perp$ term $\overline{Eq?}$ of type $nat_\perp \to nat_\perp \to bool_\perp$. The term for equality test is

$$\overline{Eq?} = \lambda x\colon nat_\perp.\,\lambda y\colon nat_\perp.\,\mathtt{let}\ \lfloor x' \rfloor = x\ \mathtt{in}\ \mathtt{let}\ \lfloor y' \rfloor = y\ \mathtt{in}\ \lfloor Eq?\,x'\,y' \rfloor$$

An intuitive explanation of this function is that $\overline{Eq?}$ takes two arguments of type $nat_\perp$, evaluates them to obtain elements of type *nat* (if possible), and then compares the results for equality. If either argument does not reduce to the form $\lfloor M \rfloor$ for $M\colon nat$, then the corresponding `let` cannot be reduced. But if both arguments do reduce to the form $\lfloor M \rfloor$, then we are certain to be able to reduce both to numerals, and hence we will be able to obtain $\lfloor true \rfloor$ or $\lfloor false \rfloor$ by the reduction axiom for *Eq*?. The reader is encouraged to try a few examples in Exercise 2.6.14.

The terms $\overline{+}$ for addition and $\overline{cond}$ for `if ... then ... else ...` are similar in spirit to $\overline{Eq?}$.

$$\overline{+} \quad = \lambda x\colon nat_\perp.\,\lambda y\colon nat_\perp.\,\mathtt{let}\ \lfloor x' \rfloor = x\ \mathtt{in}\ \mathtt{let}\ \lfloor y' \rfloor = y\ \mathtt{in}\ \lfloor x' + y' \rfloor$$

$$\overline{cond_\sigma} = \lambda x\colon bool_\perp.\,\lambda y\colon \overline{\sigma}.\,\lambda z\colon \overline{\sigma}.\,\mathtt{let}\ \lfloor x' \rfloor = x\ \mathtt{in}\ \mathtt{if}\ x'\ \mathtt{then}\ y\ \mathtt{else}\ z$$

In the translation of conditional, it is important to notice that $\overline{\sigma}$ is pointed. As a result, the function body $\mathtt{let}\ \lfloor x' \rfloor = x\ \mathtt{in}\ \mathtt{if}\ x'\ \mathtt{then}\ y\ \mathtt{else}\ z$ is well-typed.

For pairing and lambda abstraction, we let

$$\overline{\langle M, N \rangle} \quad = \langle \overline{M}, \overline{N} \rangle$$

$$\overline{\lambda x\colon \sigma.\, M} = \lambda x\colon \overline{\sigma}.\, \overline{M}$$

and similarly for application, projections and fixed points. Some examples appear in Exercises 2.6.14 and 2.6.16.

The main properties of this translation are

(i) If $M\colon\sigma$ in PCF, then $\overline{M}\colon\overline{\sigma}$ in PCF$_\perp$.

(ii) If M, N are syntactically distinct terms of PCF, then $\overline{M}, \overline{N}$ are syntactically distinct terms of PCF$_\bot$.

(iii) If $M \to N$ in PCF, then $\overline{M} \to \overline{N}$ in PCF$_\bot$. Conversely, if M is a normal form in PCF, then $\overline{M}$ is a normal form in PCF$_\bot$.

(iv) If $M = N$ is provable in PCF, then $\overline{M} = \overline{N}$ is provable in PCF$_\bot$.

While there are a number of cases, it is essentially straightforward to verify these properties. It follows from properties (ii) and (iii) that if M, N are distinct normal forms of PCF, then $\overline{M}, \overline{N}$ are distinct normal forms of PCF$_\bot$.

Translation of Eager PCF into PCF$_\bot$

Like the translation of PCF into PCF$_\bot$, the translation of Eager PCF into PCF$_\bot$ has two parts. We begin with the translation of types.

For any type σ of Eager PCF, we define the associated type $\underline{\sigma}$. Intuitively, $\underline{\sigma}$ is the type of Eager PCF values (in the technical sense of Section 2.4.5) of type σ. Since any Eager PCF term will either reduce to a value, or diverge under eager reduction, an Eager PCF term of type σ will be translated to a PCF$_\bot$ term of type $\underline{\sigma}_\bot$. After defining $\underline{\sigma}$ by induction on the structure of type expressions, we give an informal explanation.

$$\underline{nat} = nat$$

$$\underline{bool} = bool$$

$$\underline{\sigma \to \tau} = \underline{\sigma} \to \underline{\tau}_\bot$$

$$\underline{\sigma \times \tau} = \underline{\sigma} \times \underline{\tau}$$

The Eager PCF values of type *nat* or *bool* correspond to PCF$_\bot$ terms of type *nat* or *bool*. An Eager PCF function value of type $\sigma \to \tau$ has the form $\lambda x{:}\,\sigma.\, M$, where for any argument V, the body $[V/x]M$ may either reduce to a value of type τ or diverge under eager reduction. Therefore, in PCF$_\bot$, the values of type $\sigma \to \tau$ are functions from $\underline{\sigma}$ to $\underline{\tau}_\bot$. Finally, the Eager PCF values of type $\sigma \times \tau$ are pairs of values, and therefore have type $\underline{\sigma} \times \underline{\tau}$ in PCF$_\bot$.

We translate a term $M{:}\,\sigma$ of Eager PCF with free variables $x_1{:}\,\sigma_1, \ldots, x_k{:}\,\sigma_k$ to a term $\underline{M}{:}\,\underline{\sigma}_\bot$ of PCF$_\bot$ with free variables $x_1{:}\,\underline{\sigma}_1, \ldots, x_k{:}\,\underline{\sigma}_k$, as follows:

$$\underline{x} = \lfloor x \rfloor$$

$$\underline{n} = \lfloor n \rfloor$$

$$\underline{true} = \lfloor true \rfloor$$

$$\underline{false} = \lfloor false \rfloor$$

$$\underline{M+N} = \texttt{let } \lfloor x \rfloor = \underline{M} \texttt{ in let } \lfloor y \rfloor = \underline{N} \texttt{ in } \lfloor x+y \rfloor$$

$$\underline{Eq?MN} = \texttt{let } \lfloor x \rfloor = \underline{M} \texttt{ in let } \lfloor y \rfloor = \underline{N} \texttt{ in } \lfloor Eq?\,x\,y \rfloor$$

$$\underline{\texttt{if } M \texttt{ then } N \texttt{ else } P} = \texttt{let } \lfloor x \rfloor = \underline{M} \texttt{ in if } x \texttt{ then } \underline{N} \texttt{ else } \underline{P}$$

$$\underline{MN} = \texttt{let } \lfloor f \rfloor = \underline{M} \texttt{ in let } \lfloor x \rfloor = \underline{N} \texttt{ in } f x$$

$$\underline{\lambda x\colon\sigma.\,M} = \lfloor \lambda x\colon\underline{\sigma}.\,\underline{M} \rfloor$$

$$\underline{fix_{\sigma\to\tau}} = \lfloor fix(\lambda f\colon \underline{((\sigma\to\tau)\to(\sigma\to\tau))\to(\sigma\to\tau)}.$$
$$\lambda g\colon \underline{(\sigma\to\tau)\to(\sigma\to\tau)}.\,g(\lambda x\colon\underline{\sigma}.\,\texttt{let } \lfloor h \rfloor = f g \texttt{ in } h x)) \rfloor$$

The translation of the fixed-point operator needs some explanation. As discussed in Section 2.4.5, Eager PCF only has fixed-point operators on function types. The translation of the fixed-point operator on type $\sigma \to \tau$ is recursively defined to satisfy

$$\underline{fix_{\sigma\to\tau}} = \lambda g\colon \underline{(\sigma\to\tau)\to(\sigma\to\tau)}.\,g(\lambda x\colon\underline{\sigma}.\,\texttt{let } \lfloor h \rfloor = \underline{fix_{\sigma\to\tau}}\ g \texttt{ in } h x)$$

This is essentially the Eager PCF property "$fix = \lambda g\colon(\ldots).\,g(delay[fix\ g])$" from Section 2.4.5, where with $delay[M] \equiv \lambda x\colon(\ldots).\,Mx$, using the fact that

$$\begin{aligned} \underline{Mx} &\equiv \texttt{let } \lfloor f \rfloor = \underline{M} \texttt{ in let } \lfloor y \rfloor = \lfloor x \rfloor \texttt{ in } f y \\ &= \texttt{let } \lfloor f \rfloor = \underline{M} \texttt{ in } f x \end{aligned}$$

by axiom (let $\lfloor\ \rfloor$).

In the next two examples, we discuss the way that eager reduction is preserved by this translation. A general difference between the eager reduction strategy given in Section 2.4.5 and reduction in PCF$_\bot$ is that eager reduction is deterministic. In particular, eager reduction of an application MN specifies reduction of M to a value (*e.g.*, $\lambda x\colon(\ldots).\,M'$) before reducing N to a value. However, from the point of view of accurately representing the termination behavior and values of any expression, the order of evaluation between M and N is not significant. When an application MN of Eager PCF is translated into PCF$_\bot$, it will be necessary to reduce both to the form $\lfloor\ldots\rfloor$, intuitively corresponding to the translation of an Eager PCF value, before performing β-reduction. However, PCF$_\bot$ allows either the function M or the argument N to be reduced first.

Example 2.6.11 We may apply this translation to the term considered in Example 2.4.20. Since this will help preserve the structure of the expression, we use the syntactic sugar

$$M \cdot N \stackrel{\text{def}}{=} \texttt{let } \lfloor f \rfloor = M \texttt{ in let } \lfloor x \rfloor = N \texttt{ in } f x$$

for eager application. For readability, we will also use the simplification

$\underline{u+v} = \texttt{let}\ \lfloor x \rfloor = \lfloor u \rfloor\ \texttt{in}\ (\texttt{let}\ \lfloor y \rfloor = \lfloor v \rfloor\ \texttt{in}\ \lfloor x+y \rfloor) = \lfloor u+v \rfloor$

for any variables or constants u and v, since this consequence of our equational axioms does not change the behavior of the resulting term. Applying the translation to the term

$(\mathit{fix}\ (\lambda x{:}\,nat \to nat.\,\lambda y{:}\,nat.\,y))\ ((\lambda z{:}\,nat.\,z+1)\ 2)$

gives us

$(\underline{\mathit{fix}} \cdot \lfloor\ \lambda x{:}\,nat \to nat_\bot.\lfloor \lambda y{:}\,nat.\lfloor y \rfloor \rfloor\ \rfloor) \cdot (\lfloor\ \lambda z{:}\,nat.\lfloor z+1 \rfloor\ \rfloor \cdot \lfloor 2 \rfloor)$

A useful general observation is that

$\lfloor\ M\ \rfloor \cdot \lfloor N \rfloor \twoheadrightarrow M N$

but that we cannot simplify a form $M' \cdot N'$ unless M' has the form $\lfloor M \rfloor$ and N' has the form $\lfloor N \rfloor$. The need to produce "lifted values" (or, more precisely, the lifting of terms that reduce to values) is important in expressing eager reduction with lifted types. We can see that there are two possible reductions of the term above, one involving $\underline{\mathit{fix}}$ and the other $(\lfloor \lambda z{:}\,nat.\lfloor z+1 \rfloor \rfloor \cdot \lfloor 2 \rfloor) \twoheadrightarrow \lfloor 2+1 \rfloor$. The reader may enjoy leftmost reducing the entire expression and seeing how the steps correspond to the eager reduction steps carried out in Example 2.4.20. ■

Example 2.6.12 We can see how divergence is preserved by considering the term

```
let f(x:nat):nat = 3 in
  letrec g(x:nat):nat = g(x+1) in f(g 5)
```

from Example 2.4.21. After replacing `let`'s by lambda abstraction and application, the translation of this term is

$\lfloor\ \lambda f{:}\,nat \to nat_\bot.\lfloor \lambda g{:}\,nat \to nat_\bot.\lfloor f \rfloor \cdot (g\,5)\ \rfloor \rfloor$
$\cdot \lfloor\ \lambda x{:}\,nat.\lfloor 3 \rfloor\ \rfloor$
$\cdot(\ \underline{\mathit{fix}} \cdot \lfloor \lambda g{:}\,nat \to nat_\bot.\lfloor \lambda x{:}\,nat.\,g(x+1) \rfloor \rfloor\ )$

where for simplicity we have used $\lfloor g \rfloor \cdot \lfloor 5 \rfloor = g\,5$ and $\lfloor g \rfloor \cdot (\underline{x+1}) = \lfloor g \rfloor \cdot \lfloor x+1 \rfloor = g(x+1)$. Recall from Examples 2.4.6 and 2.4.21 that if we apply leftmost reduction to the original term, we obtain 3, while eager reduction does not produce a normal form. We can see how the translation of Eager PCF into $\mathrm{PCF}_\bot$ preserves the absence of normal forms by leftmost-reducing the result of this translation.

Since the first argument and the main function have the form $\lfloor \ldots \rfloor$, we can apply β-reduction as described in Example 2.6.11. This gives us

$$\lfloor \lambda g\colon nat \to nat_\perp . \lfloor \lambda x\colon nat . \lfloor 3 \rfloor \rfloor \cdot (g\,5)\ \rfloor \cdot (\ \underline{fix} \cdot \lfloor G \rfloor\ )$$

where $G \stackrel{\text{def}}{=} \lambda g\colon nat \to nat_\perp . \lfloor \lambda x\colon nat.\ g(x+1) \rfloor$. Our task is to reduce the argument $(\ \underline{fix} \cdot \lfloor G \rfloor\ )$ to the form $\lfloor \ldots \rfloor$ before performing the leftmost β-reduction. We do this using the that

$\underline{fix_{nat \to nat}} = \lfloor\ fix_{nat \to nat_\perp}\ F\ \rfloor \twoheadrightarrow$
$\lfloor\ \lambda g\colon (nat \to nat_\perp) \to (nat \to nat_\perp).\ g(\lambda x\colon nat.\,\texttt{let}\ \lfloor h \rfloor = fix\ F\ g\ \texttt{in}\ hx)\ \rfloor$

where

$$F \stackrel{\text{def}}{=} (\lambda f\colon ((nat \to nat_\perp) \to (nat \to nat_\perp)) \to (nat \to nat_\perp).$$
$$\lambda g\colon (nat \to nat_\perp) \to (nat \to nat_\perp).\ g(\lambda x\colon nat.\,\texttt{let}\ \lfloor h \rfloor = fg\ \texttt{in}\ hx))$$

However, we will see in the process that the application to 5 resulting from β-reduction cannot be reduced to the form $\lfloor \ldots \rfloor$, keeping us from every reaching the normal form $\lfloor 3 \rfloor$ for the entire term.

The expansion of $\underline{fix}$ above gives us

$$\begin{array}{ll} \multicolumn{2}{l}{\underline{fix} \cdot \lfloor G \rfloor \twoheadrightarrow fix\ F\ G} \\ \twoheadrightarrow & G\ (\lambda x\colon nat.\,\texttt{let}\ \lfloor h \rfloor = fix\ F\ G\ \texttt{in}\ hx) \\ \twoheadrightarrow & \lfloor \lambda x\colon nat.((\lambda x\colon nat.\,\texttt{let}\ \lfloor h \rfloor = fix\ F\ G\ \texttt{in}\ hx)\ (x+1)) \rfloor \\ \twoheadrightarrow & \lfloor \lambda x\colon nat.\,\texttt{let}\ \lfloor h \rfloor = fix\ F\ G\ \texttt{in}\ h(x+1) \rfloor \end{array}$$

When the function inside the $\lfloor\ \rfloor$ is applied to 5, the result must be reduced to a form $\lfloor \ldots \rfloor$ to complete the reduction of the entire term. However, this leads us to again reduce $fix\ F\ G$ to this form and apply the result to 6. Since this process may be continued indefinitely, the entire term does not have a normal form. ∎

The main properties of the translation from Eager PCF into PCF$_\perp$ are:

(i) If $M\colon \sigma$ in Eager PCF, with free variables $x_1\colon \sigma_1, \ldots, x_k\colon \sigma_k$, then $\underline{M}\colon \underline{\sigma}_\perp$ in PCF$_\perp$ with free variables $x_1\colon \underline{\sigma}_1, \ldots, x_k\colon \underline{\sigma}_k$.

(ii) If $M \stackrel{\text{eager}}{\to} N$ in Eager PCF, then $\underline{M} \twoheadrightarrow \underline{N}$ in PCF$_\perp$.

(iii) If M is a closed term of Eager PCF of type *nat* or *bool* and c is a numeral or *true* or *false*, then $M \stackrel{\text{eager}}{\twoheadrightarrow} c$ in Eager PCF iff $\underline{M} \twoheadrightarrow \lfloor c \rfloor$ in PCF$_\perp$.

(iv) If we let $=_{eager}$ be operational equivalence of Eager PCF term, defined in the same was as $=_{op}$ in Section 2.3.5 but using eager evaluation, and let $=_{PCF\perp}$ be operational equivalence in PCF$_\perp$, then for closed terms M, N we have $M =_{eager} N$ iff $\underline{M} =_{PCF\perp} \underline{N}$.

It is largely straightforward to verify properties (i)–(iii). Property (iv), however, involves construction of fully abstract models satisfying the properties described in Section 5.4.2. A proof has been developed by R. Viswanathan.

Exercise 2.6.13 Suppose that instead of having fix_σ for every pointed σ, we only have fixed-point operators for types of the form $\tau_\bot$. Show that it is still possible to write a term with no normal form of each pointed type.

Exercise 2.6.14 Reduce the application of $\overline{Eq?}$ to the following pairs of terms. You should continue until you obtain $\lfloor true \rfloor$ or $\lfloor false \rfloor$ or it is apparent that one of the `let`'s can never be reduced.

(a) $\lfloor 3+2 \rfloor$ and $\lfloor 5 \rfloor$.

(b) $(\lambda x\colon nat_\bot.\, x)\lfloor 3+2 \rfloor$ and $\lfloor (\lambda x\colon nat.\, x+1)\, 3 \rfloor$.

(c) $\mathit{fix}(\lambda x\colon nat_\bot.\, x)$ and $\lfloor 19 \rfloor$.

Exercise 2.6.15 Carry out the reduction of the term $\underline{\mathit{fix}} \cdot \lfloor \lambda x\colon nat \to nat_\bot.\lfloor \lambda y\colon nat.\lfloor y \rfloor \rfloor \rfloor$ from Example 2.6.11.

Exercise 2.6.16 The fibonacci function may be written in PCF as $\mathit{fib} \stackrel{\text{def}}{=} \mathit{fix}_{nat \to nat} F$, where

$$F \stackrel{\text{def}}{=} \lambda f\colon nat \to nat.\, \lambda x\colon nat.$$

$$\texttt{if } (Eq?\, x\, 0)\ or\ (Eq?\, x\, 1) \texttt{ then } 1 \texttt{ else } f(x-1) + f(x-2)$$

We assume for simplicity that we have natural number subtraction and a boolean *or* function.

(a) Translate the definition from (ordinary) PCF into PCF$_\bot$ and describe the reduction of *fib* 3 in approximately the same detail as Example 2.6.9. (Subtraction and *or* should be translated into PCF$_\bot$ following the pattern given for $+$ and $Eq?$. You may simplify $\lfloor M \rfloor - \lfloor N \rfloor$ to $\lfloor M - N \rfloor$, or perform other simplifications that are similar to the ones used in Example 2.6.11.)

(b) Same as part (a), but use the translation from Eager PCF into PCF$_\bot$.

3 Universal Algebra and Algebraic Data Types

3.1 Introduction

The language PCF may be viewed as the sum of three parts: pure typed lambda calculus with function and product types; the natural numbers and booleans; and fixed-point operators. If we replace the natural numbers and booleans by some other basic types, such as characters and strings, we obtain a language with a similar type structure (functions and pairs), but oriented towards computation on different kinds of data. If we wish to make this change to PCF, we must decide on a way to name basic characters and strings in terms, the way we have named natural numbers by $0, 1, 2, \ldots$, and choose basic functions for manipulating characters and strings, in place of $+$, *Eq*? and `if ... then ... else ...`. Then, we must write a set of equational axioms that characterize these functions. This would define the terms of the language and give us an axiomatic semantics. Once we have the syntax of expressions and axiomatic semantics, we can proceed to select reduction axioms, write programs, and/or investigate denotational semantics.

An *algebraic datatype* consists of one or more sets of values, such as natural numbers, booleans, characters or strings, together with a collection of functions on these sets. A fundamental restriction on algebraic datatypes is that none of the functions may have function parameters; this is what "algebraic" means. A expository issue is that in this chapter, we use the standard terminology of universal algebra for the sets associated with an algebra. Apart from maintaining consistency with the literature on algebra, the main reason for doing so is to distinguish algebraic datatypes, which consist of sets and functions, from the sets alone. Therefore, basic "type" symbols such as *nat*, *bool*, *char* and *string* are called *sorts* when they are used in algebraic expressions. In algebraic datatype theory, the distinction between type and sort is that a type comes equipped with specific operations, while a sort does not. This distinction is actually consistent with the terminology of Chapter 2, since function types and product types come equipped with specific operations, namely, lambda abstraction, application, pairing and projection.

Universal algebra, also called *equational logic,* is a general mathematical framework that may be used to define and study algebraic datatypes. In universal algebra, the axiomatic semantics of an algebraic datatype is given by a set of equations between terms. The denotational semantics of an algebraic datatype involves structures called *algebras,* which consist of a collection of sets, one for each sort, and a collection of functions, one for each function symbol used in terms. The operational semantics of algebraic terms are given by directing algebraic equations. Traditionally, reduction axioms for algebraic terms are called *rewrite rules.* Some examples of datatypes that may be defined and studied using universal algebra are natural numbers, booleans, lists, finite sets, multisets, stacks, queues, and trees, each with various possible functions.

In this chapter, we will study universal algebra and its use in defining the kind of datatypes that commonly occur in programming. While the presentation of PCF in Chapter 2 centered on axiomatic and operational semantics, this chapter will be primarily concerned with the connection between axiomatic semantics (equations) and denotational semantics (algebras), with a separate section on operational semantics at the end of the chapter. In studying algebra, we will cover several topics that are common to most logical systems. The main topics of the chapter are:

- Algebraic terms and their interpretation in multi-sorted algebras,
- Equational (algebraic) specifications and the equational proof system,
- Soundness and completeness of the equational proof system (equivalence of axiomatic and denotational semantics),
- Homomorphisms and initiality,
- Introduction to the algebraic theory of datatypes,
- Rewrite rules (operational semantics) derived from algebraic specifications.

The first four topics provide a brief introduction to the mathematical system of universal algebra. The subsequent discussion of the algebraic theory of datatypes points out some of the differences between traditional concerns in mathematics and the use of algebraic datatypes in programming. In the final section of this chapter, we consider reduction on algebraic terms. This has two applications. The first is to analyze properties of equational specifications and the second is to model computation on algebraic terms. A pedagogical reason to study universal algebra before proceeding with the denotational semantics of typed lambda calculus is that many technical concepts appear here in a simpler and more accessible form.

There are many additional topics in the algebraic theory of datatypes. The most important omitted topics are: hierarchical specifications, parameterized specifications, refinement of one specification into another, and correctness of implementations. While we discuss problems that arise when a function application produces an error, we do not consider some of the more sophisticated approaches to errors such as algebras with partial functions or order-sorted algebras. The reader interested in more detailed investigation may consult [EM85, Wir90].

3.2 Preview of Algebraic Specification

The algebraic approach to data abstraction involves specifying the behavior of each datatype by writing a set of equational axioms. A signature, which is a way of defining the syntax of terms, combined with a set of equational axioms, is called an *algebraic specification.* If a program using a set of specified datatypes is designed so that the correctness of the program depends only on the algebraic specification, then the primary concern of the datatype implementor is to satisfy the specification. In this way, the specification serves as a contract between the user and the implementor of a datatype; neither needs to worry about additional details of the other's program. This methodology is not specific to equational specifications, but equations are the simplest specification language that is expressive enough to be used for this purpose. The reader interested in specification and software development may wish to consult [BJ82, GHM78, LG86, Mor90, Spi88], for example.

When we view a set of equations as a specification, we may regard an algebra, which consists of a set of values for each sort and a function for each function symbol, as the mathematical abstraction of an implementation. In general, a specification may be satisfied by many different algebras.

In program development, it is often useful to identify a "standard" implementation of a specification. One advantage is that it is easier to think about an equational specification if we choose a concrete, "typical" implementation. We can also use a standard implementation to be more specific about which implementations we consider acceptable. In datatype theory and in practical tools using algebraic datatypes, the so-called *initial* algebra (defined in this chapter) is often taken as the standard implementation. The main reasons to consider initiality are that it gives us a specific implementation that can be realized automatically and the initial algebra has some useful properties that cannot be expressed by equational axioms. In particular, there is a useful form of induction associated with initial algebras.

Initial algebras are defined in Section 3.5.2, while their use in datatype theory is discussed in Section 3.6. In addition to initial algebras, so-called *final algebras* have also been proposed as standard implementations of an algebraic specification [Wan79]. Other computer scientists prefer to consider any "generated" algebra without extra elements. A short discussion of these alternatives appears in Section 3.6.2 and its exercises. For further information, the reader may consult [Wir90] and the references cited there.

One limitation of the algebraic approach to datatypes is that some of the operations we use in programming languages are type specific in some arguments, and type-independent in others. For example, the PCF conditional `if ... then ... else ...` requires a boolean as its first argument, but the next two arguments may have any type (as long as both have the same type). For this reason, a discussion of the algebra of PCF *nat* and *bool* values does not tell the whole story of PCF conditional expressions. Another limitation of the algebraic approach is that certain types (such as function types) have properties that are not expressible by equations alone. (Specifically, we need a quantifier to axiomatize extensional equality of functions.) For this reason, it does not seem accurate to view *all* types algebraically. However, it does seem profitable to separate languages like PCF into an algebraic part, comprising basic datatypes such as *nat*, *bool*, *string*, and so on, and a "higher-order" or lambda calculus part, comprising ways of building more complex types from basic ones.

Some general references for further reading are [Grä68], a reference book on universal algebra, and [EM85, Wir90], which cover algebraic datatypes and specifications. Some historically important research articles are [Hoa72, Par72], on the relationships between datatypes and programming style, and [LZ74, GHM78, GTW78] on algebraic datatypes and specifications.

3.3 Algebras, Signatures and Terms

3.3.1 Algebras

An algebra consists of one or more sets, called *carriers,* together with a collection of distinguished elements and *first-order* (or *algebraic*) *functions*

$$f : A_1 \times \ldots \times A_k \to A$$

over the carriers of the algebra. An example is the algebra

$$\mathcal{N} = \langle \mathcal{N}, 0, 1, +, *\rangle,$$

with carrier $\mathcal{N}$ the set of natural numbers, distinguished elements $0, 1 \in \mathcal{N}$, and functions $+, * : \mathcal{N} \times \mathcal{N} \to \mathcal{N}$. The difference between a "distinguished" element of a carrier and any other element is that we have a name for each distinguished element in the language of algebraic terms. As an economy measure, we will consider distinguished elements like $0, 1 \in \mathcal{N}$ as "zero-ary" functions, or "functions of zero arguments." This is not a deep idea at all, just a convenient way to treat distinguished elements and functions uniformly.

An example with more than one carrier is the algebra

$$\mathcal{A}_{pcf} = \langle \mathcal{N}, \mathcal{B}, 0, 1, \ldots, +, \mathit{true}, \mathit{false}, Eq?, \ldots\rangle$$

where $\mathcal{N}$ is the set of natural numbers, $\mathcal{B}$ the set of booleans, $0, 1, \ldots$ are the natural numbers, $+$ is the addition function, and so on. These are the mathematical values that we usually think of when we write basic numeric and boolean expressions of PCF. In studying algebras, we will make the correspondence between the syntactic expressions of PCF and the semantic values of this algebra precise.

3.3.2 Syntax of Algebraic Terms

The syntax of algebraic terms depends on the basic symbols and their types. This information is collected together in what is called a signature. In algebra, as mentioned earlier, it is traditional to call the basic type symbols *sorts*.

A *signature* $\Sigma = \langle S, F \rangle$ consists of

- A set S whose elements are called *sorts*,
- A collection F of pairs $\langle f, s_1 \times \ldots \times s_k \to s \rangle$, with $s_1, \ldots, s_k, s \in S$ and no f occurring in two distinct pairs.

In the definition of signature, a symbol f occurring in F is called a *typed function symbol* (or *function symbol* for short), and an expression $s_1 \times \ldots \times s_k \to s$ a *first-order* (or *algebraic*) *function type over* S. We usually write $f\colon \tau$ instead of $\langle f, \tau \rangle \in F$.

A sort is a name for a carrier of an algebra, and a function symbol $f\colon s_1 \times \ldots \times s_k \to s$ is a name for a k-ary function. We allow $k = 0$, so that a "function symbol" $f\colon s$ may be a name for an element of the carrier for sort s. A symbol $f\colon s$ is called a *constant symbol,* and $f\colon s_1 \times \ldots \times s_k \to s$ with $k \geq 1$ is called a *proper function symbol*. The restriction that we cannot have $f\colon \tau$ and $f\colon \tau'$ means that each constant or function symbol has a unique sort or type.

Example 3.3.1 A simple signature for writing natural number expressions is $\Sigma_{\mathcal{N}} = \langle S, F \rangle$, where $S = \{nat\}$ contains only one sort and F provides function symbols $0\colon nat$, $1\colon nat$, $+\colon nat \times nat \to nat$ and $*\colon nat \times nat \to nat$. A convenient syntax for describing signatures is the following tabular format.

sorts:*nat*

fctns:$0, 1 : nat$

$+, * : nat \times nat \to nat$

In this notation, we often write several function symbols of the same type on one line. This saves space and usually makes the list easier to read. ■

The purpose of a signature is to allow us to write algebraic terms. We assume we have some infinite set $\mathcal{V}$ of symbols we call *variables,* and assume that these are different from all the symbols we will ever consider using as constants, function symbols or sort symbols. Since it is not meaningful to write a variable without specifying its sort, we will always list the sorts of variables. A *sort assignment* is a finite set

$$\Gamma = \{x_1\colon s_1, \ldots, x_k\colon s_k\}$$

of ordered *variable*: *sort* pairs, with no variable given more than one sort. Given a signature $\Sigma = \langle S, F \rangle$ and sort assignment Γ using sorts from S, we define the set $Terms^s(\Sigma, \Gamma)$ of *algebraic terms of sort s over signature* Σ *and variables* Γ as follows

$$x \in Terms^s(\Sigma, \Gamma) \text{if } x{:}\, s \in \Gamma,$$

$$f M_1 \ldots M_k \in Terms^s(\Sigma, \Gamma) \text{if } f : s_1 \times \ldots \times s_k \to s \text{ and}$$

$$M_i \in Terms^{s_i}(\Sigma, \Gamma) \text{ for } i = 1, \ldots, n.$$

In the special case $k = 0$, the second clause should be interpreted as

$f \in Terms^s(\Sigma, \Gamma)$ if $f : s$.

For example, $0 \in Terms^{nat}(\Sigma_{\mathcal{N}}, \emptyset)$ and $+01$ is a term in $Terms^{nat}(\Sigma_{\mathcal{N}}, \emptyset)$, since $+$ is a binary numeric function symbol of $\Sigma_{\mathcal{N}}$. It is also easy to see that $+01 \in Terms^{nat}(\Sigma_{\mathcal{N}}, \Gamma)$ for any sort assignment Γ. To match the syntax of PCF, we may treat $0 + 1$ as syntactic sugar for $+01$. When there is only one sort, it is common to assume that all variables have that sort. In this case, we can simplify sort assignments to lists of variables. We write $Var(M)$ for the set of variables that appear in M.

In algebra, the *substitution* $[N/x]M$ of N for all occurrences of x in M is accomplished by straightforward replacement of each occurrence of x by N, since there are no bound variables in algebraic terms. It is easy to see that if we replace a variable by a term of the right sort, we obtain a well-formed term of the same sort we started with. This is stated more precisely below. In the following lemma, we use the notation $\Gamma, x{:}\, s'$ for the sort assignment

$\Gamma, x{:}\, s' = \Gamma \cup \{x{:}\, s'\}$

where x does not occur in Γ.

Lemma 3.3.2 If $M \in Terms^s(\Sigma, \Gamma, x{:}\, s')$ and $N \in Terms^{s'}(\Sigma, \Gamma)$, then $[N/x]M \in Terms^s(\Sigma, \Gamma)$.

A related property is given in Exercise 3.3.4.

Proof The proof is by induction on the structure of terms in $Terms^s(\Sigma, \Gamma, x{:}\, s')$. Since this is the first inductive proof in the chapter, we will give most of the details. Subsequent inductive proofs will give only the main points. Since every term is either a variable or the application of a function symbol to one or more arguments, induction on algebraic terms has one base case (variables) and one induction step (function symbols). In the base case, we must prove the lemma directly. In the induction step, we assume that the lemma holds for all of the subterms. This assumption is called the *inductive hypothesis*.

For the base case we consider a variable $y \in Terms^s(\Sigma, \Gamma, x\colon s')$. If y is different from x, then $[N/x]y$ is just y. In this case, we must have $y\colon s \in \Gamma$, and hence $y \in Terms^s(\Sigma, \Gamma)$. If our term is the variable x itself, then the result $[N/x]x$ of substitution is the term N, which belongs to $Terms^s(\Sigma, \Gamma)$ by similar assumption. This proves the base case of the induction.

For the induction step, we assume that $[N/x]M_i \in Terms^{s_i}(\Sigma, \Gamma)$, for $1 \leq i \leq k$, and consider a term of the form $f M_1 \ldots M_k$. The result of substituting N for x in this term may be written $f[N/x]M_1 \ldots [N/x]M_k$. Since we assume $f M_1 \ldots M_k \in Terms^s(\Sigma, \Gamma, x\colon s')$, the function symbol must have type $s_1 \times \ldots \times s_k \to s$. It follows that $f[N/x]M_1 \ldots [N/x]M_k \in Terms^s(\Sigma, \Gamma)$, which finishes the induction step and proves the lemma. ∎

Example 3.3.3 We may write natural number and stack expressions using the signature $\Sigma_{stk} = \langle S, F\rangle$ with $S = \{nat, stack\}$ and F containing the function symbols listed below.

sorts:*nat*, *stack*

fctns:$0, 1, 2, \ldots : nat$

$+, * : nat \times nat \to nat$

$empty : stack$

$push : nat \times stack \to stack$

$pop : stack \to stack$

$top : stack \to nat$

The terms of this signature include the expression *push*2(*push*1(*push*0*empty*)), which would name a stack with elements 0,1 and 2 in the standard interpretation of this signature. Using a stack variable, we can also write an expression *push*1(*push*0*s*) $\in Terms(\Sigma_{stk}, \{s\colon stack\})$ which defines the stack obtained by pushing 0 and 1 onto s. ∎

Exercise 3.3.4 Use induction on terms to show that if $M \in Terms^s(\Sigma, \Gamma)$ and Γ' is a sort assignment containing Γ, then $M \in Terms^s(\Sigma, \Gamma')$.

3.3.3 Algebras and the Interpretation of Terms

Algebras are mathematical structures that provide meaning, or denotational semantics, for algebraic terms. To make the mapping from symbols to algebras explicit, we will use a form of algebra that gives a value to every sort and function symbol of some signature. If Σ is a signature, then a Σ-*algebra* $\mathcal{A}$ consists of

- Exactly one carrier A^s for each sort symbol $s \in S$,

- An interpretation map $\mathcal{I}$ assigning a function

$$\mathcal{I}(f): A^{s_1} \times \ldots \times A^{s_k} \to A^s$$

to each proper function symbol $f: s_1 \times \ldots \times s_k \to s \in F$ and an element $\mathcal{I}(f) \in A^s$ to each constant symbol $f: s \in F$.

If Σ has only one sort, then we say that a Σ-algebra is *single-sorted;* otherwise, we say an algebra is *many-sorted* or *multi-sorted.*

If $\mathcal{A} = \langle \{A^s\}_{s \in S}, \mathcal{I} \rangle$ is a Σ-algebra, and f is a function symbol of Σ, it is often convenient to write $f^{\mathcal{A}}$ for $\mathcal{I}(f)$. In the case that there are finitely many or countably many function symbols, it is also common to list the functions, as in the example algebras $\mathcal{N}$ and $\mathcal{A}_{pcf}$ given earlier. Combining these two conventions, we may write out the $\Sigma_{\mathcal{N}}$-algebra $\mathcal{N}$ as

$$\mathcal{N} = \langle \mathcal{N}, 0^{\mathcal{N}}, 1^{\mathcal{N}}, +^{\mathcal{N}}, *^{\mathcal{N}} \rangle.$$

This gives us all the information we need to interpret terms over $\Sigma_{\mathcal{N}}$, since the interpretation map $\mathcal{I}$ is given by the way the functions of the algebra are named.

It is a relatively simple matter to say what the meaning of a term $M \in Terms(\Sigma, \Gamma)$ is in any Σ-algebra. The only technical machinery that might not be familiar is the use of variable assignments, or environments. An *environment* η for $\mathcal{A}$ is a mapping $\eta: \mathcal{V} \to \cup_s A^s$ from variables to elements of the carriers of $\mathcal{A}$. The reason that we need an environment is that a term M may have a variable x in it, and we need to give x a value before we can say what M means. If someone asks you, "What is the value of $x + 1$?" it is difficult to answer without choosing a value for x. Of course, an environment must map each variable to a value of the appropriate carrier. We say an environment η *satisfies* Γ if $\eta(x) \in A^s$ for each $x: s \in \Gamma$.

Given an environment η for $\mathcal{A}$ that satisfies Γ, we define the meaning $\mathcal{A}[\![M]\!]\eta$ of any $M \in Terms(\Sigma, \Gamma)$ in η as follows

$$\begin{aligned} \mathcal{A}[\![x]\!]\eta &= \eta(x) \\ \mathcal{A}[\![f M_1 \ldots M_k]\!]\eta &= f^{\mathcal{A}}(\mathcal{A}[\![M_1]\!]\eta, \ldots, \mathcal{A}[\![M_k]\!]\eta). \end{aligned}$$

In the special case that $f: s$ is a constant symbol, we have $[\![f]\!]\eta = f^{\mathcal{A}}$, since there are no function arguments. It is common to omit $\mathcal{A}$ and write $[\![M]\!]\eta$ if the algebra $\mathcal{A}$ is clear from context. If M has no variables, then $\mathcal{A}[\![M]\!]\eta$ does not depend on η. In this case, we may omit the environment and write $\mathcal{A}[\![M]\!]$ for the meaning of M in algebra $\mathcal{A}$.

Example 3.3.5 The signature $\Sigma_{\mathcal{N}}$ of Example 3.3.1 has a single sort, *nat*, and function symbols 0, 1, +, $*$. We may interpret terms over this signature in the $\Sigma_{\mathcal{N}}$-algebra $\mathcal{N}$ given in Section 3.3.1. Let η be an environment for $\mathcal{N}$ with $\eta(x) = 0$. The meaning of $x + 1$ in η is determined as follows. (Remember that $x + 1$ is syntactic sugar for $+x1$.)

$$\begin{aligned}
[\![x + 1]\!]\eta &= +^{\mathcal{N}}([\![x]\!]\eta, [\![1]\!]\eta) \\
&= +^{\mathcal{N}}(\eta(x), 1^{\mathcal{N}}) \\
&= +^{\mathcal{N}}(0^{\mathcal{N}}, 1^{\mathcal{N}}) \\
&= 1 \qquad \blacksquare
\end{aligned}$$

Example 3.3.6 The signature $\Sigma_{stk} = \langle S, F\rangle$ of Example 3.3.3 has sorts *nat* and *stack*, and function symbols $0, 1, 2, \ldots, +, *$, *empty*, *push*, *pop* and *top*. One algebra $\mathcal{A}_{stk}$ for this signature interprets the natural numbers in the standard way and interprets stacks as sequences of numbers. To describe the functions on stacks, let us write $n{::}s$ for the result of adding natural number n onto the front of sequence $s \in \mathcal{N}^*$. Using this notation, we have

$$\mathcal{A}_{stk} = \langle \mathcal{N}, \mathcal{N}^*, 0^{\mathcal{A}}, 1^{\mathcal{A}}, 2^{\mathcal{A}}, \ldots, +^{\mathcal{A}}, *^{\mathcal{A}}, empty^{\mathcal{A}}, push^{\mathcal{A}}, pop^{\mathcal{A}}, top^{\mathcal{A}}\rangle$$

with stack functions determined as follows

$$\begin{aligned}
empty^{\mathcal{A}} &= \epsilon, \text{ the empty sequence} \\
push^{\mathcal{A}}(n, s) &= n{::}s \\
pop^{\mathcal{A}}(n{::}s) &= s \\
pop^{\mathcal{A}}(\epsilon) &= \epsilon \\
top^{\mathcal{A}}(n{::}s) &= n \\
top^{\mathcal{A}}(\epsilon) &= 0
\end{aligned}$$

In words, the constant symbol *empty* is interpreted as $empty^{\mathcal{A}}$, the empty sequence of natural numbers, and the function symbol *push* is interpreted as $push^{\mathcal{A}}$, the function that adds a natural number onto the front of a sequence. The function $pop^{\mathcal{A}}$ removes the first element of a sequence if the sequence is nonempty, as described by the first equation for $pop^{\mathcal{A}}$. Since *pop(empty)* is a well-formed algebraic term, this must be given some interpretation in the algebra. Since we do not have "error" elements in this algebra, we let $pop^{\mathcal{A}}(\epsilon)$ be the empty sequence. A similar situation occurs with *top,* which is intended to return the top element of a stack. When the stack is empty, we simply return 0, which is an arbitrary decision.

We can work out the meanings of terms using the environment η mapping variable $x\colon nat$ to 3 and variable $s\colon stack$ to the sequence $\langle 2, 1\rangle$ whose first element is 2 and second element is 1.

$$\begin{aligned}[\![pop(push\,x\,s)]\!]\eta &= pop^{\mathcal{A}}(push^{\mathcal{A}}([\![x]\!]\eta, [\![s]\!]\eta))\\ &= pop^{\mathcal{A}}(push^{\mathcal{A}}(3, \langle 2, 1\rangle))\\ &= pop^{\mathcal{A}}(\langle 3, 2, 1\rangle)\\ &= \langle 2, 1\rangle\end{aligned}$$

$$\begin{aligned}[\![top(push\,x\,s)]\!]\eta &= top^{\mathcal{A}}(push^{\mathcal{A}}([\![x]\!]\eta, [\![s]\!]\eta))\\ &= top^{\mathcal{A}}(push^{\mathcal{A}}(3, \langle 2, 1\rangle))\\ &= top^{\mathcal{A}}(\langle 3, 2, 1\rangle)\\ &= 3\end{aligned}$$

It is easy to see from these examples that for any environment η mapping x to a natural number and s to a stack, we have

$$[\![pop(push\,x\,s)]\!]\eta = [\![s]\!]\eta$$

$$[\![top(push\,x\,s)]\!]\eta = [\![x]\!]\eta \quad \blacksquare$$

One important property of the meaning function is that the meaning of a term $M \in Terms^s(\Sigma, \Gamma)$ is an element of the appropriate carrier A^s, as stated in the lemma below. This lemma should be regarded as a justification of our definitions, since if it failed, we would change the definitions to make it correct.

Lemma 3.3.7 Let $\mathcal{A}$ be a Σ-algebra, $M \in Terms^s(\Sigma, \Gamma)$, and η be an environment satisfying Γ. Then $[\![M]\!]\eta \in A^s$

Proof The proof is by induction on the structure of terms in $Terms^s(\Sigma, \Gamma)$.

The base case is to show that for any variable $x \in Terms^s(\Sigma, \Gamma)$ and environment η satisfying Γ, we have $[\![x]\!]\eta \in A^s$. From the definition of $Terms^s(\Sigma, \Gamma)$, we can see that $x\colon s \in \Gamma$. By the definition of meaning, we know that $[\![x]\!]\eta = \eta(x)$. But since η satisfies Γ, it follows that $\eta(x) \in A^s$. This proves the base case of the induction.

For the induction step, we assume that $[\![M_i]\!]\eta \in A^{s_i}$, for $1 \le i \le k$, and consider a term of the form $f\,M_1 \ldots M_k$. The meaning of this term is

$$[\![f\,M_i \ldots M_k]\!]\eta = f^{\mathcal{A}}([\![M_1]\!]\eta, \ldots, [\![M_k]\!]\eta)$$

From the definition of Σ-algebra, and the fact that $f M_1 \ldots M_k \in Terms^s(\Sigma, \Gamma)$, we know that $f^{\mathcal{A}}$ is a function mapping a k-tuple in $A^{s_1} \times \ldots \times A^{s_k}$, to the carrier A^s. Therefore,

$$f^{\mathcal{A}}([\![M_1]\!]\eta, \ldots, [\![M_k]\!]\eta) \in A^s.$$

This proves the lemma. The reader should verify that the argument given in the inductive step applies to the special case $k = 0$. ∎

Another straightforward property is that the meaning of a term depends only on the values of variables that appear in it.

Lemma 3.3.8 Let $x_1, \ldots, x_k$ be a list containing all the variables which occur in $M \in Terms^s(\Sigma, \Gamma)$, and let η_1, η_2 be environments satisfying Γ with $\eta_1(x_i) = \eta_2(x_i)$ for $i = 1, \ldots, k$. Then $[\![M]\!]\eta_1 = [\![M]\!]\eta_2$.

It follows from this lemma that if η_1 and η_2 agree on every variable in Γ, then for every $M \in Terms^s(\Sigma, \Gamma)$, we have $[\![M]\!]\eta_1 = [\![M]\!]\eta_2$. The reason is that every variable in M must appear in Γ.

Proof The proof is by induction on terms whose variables are among $x_1, \ldots, x_k$. For any variable x_i, it is clear that

$$[\![x_i]\!]\eta_1 = \eta_1(x_i) = \eta_2(x_i) = [\![x_i]\!]\eta_2.$$

For any term $f M_1 \ldots M_k$, we assume that the lemma holds for each M_i and prove that $[\![f M_1 \ldots M_k]\!]\eta_1 = [\![f M_1 \ldots M_k]\!]\eta_2$. By the inductive hypothesis, we have $[\![M_i]\!]\eta_1 = [\![M_i]\!]\eta_2$. Therefore

$$\begin{aligned}[\![f M_1 \ldots M_k]\!]\eta_1 &= f^{\mathcal{A}}([\![M_1]\!]\eta_1, \ldots, [\![M_k]\!]\eta_1)\\ &= f^{\mathcal{A}}([\![M_1]\!]\eta_2, \ldots, [\![M_k]\!]\eta_2)\\ &= [\![f M_1 \ldots M_k]\!]\eta_2.\end{aligned}$$

This proves the lemma. ∎

Exercise 3.3.9 This exercise asks about the signature $\Sigma_{\mathcal{N}}$ of Example 3.3.1 and the algebra $\mathcal{N}$ of Section 3.3.1. Let us write $M * N$ as syntactic sugar for $*MN$.

(a) Assuming $\eta(x) = 1$ and $\eta(y) = 2$, calculate the meaning $[\![(x + 1) * 2]\!]\eta$ in the same level of detail as Example 3.3.5.

(b) Show that for any environment η, we have $[\![(x + y) * z]\!]\eta = [\![(x * z) + (y * z)]\!]\eta$.

Exercise 3.3.10 This exercise asks about the signature Σ_{stk} of Example 3.3.3 and the algebra $\mathcal{A}_{stk}$ of Example 3.3.6.

(a) Assuming η maps $x\colon nat$ to 3 and $s\colon stack$ to $\langle 2, 1\rangle$, calculate the meaning $[\![push\ x(pop\ s)]\!]\eta$ in the same level of detail as Example 3.3.6.

(b) Show that for any environment η mapping $s\colon stack$ to a nonempty sequence, we have $[\![push(top\ s)(pop\ s)]\!]\eta = [\![s]\!]\eta$. What changes when $\eta(s) = \epsilon$?

3.3.4 The Substitution Lemma

A very important property of algebra, shared by first-order logic and typed lambda calculus, is the substitution lemma. Intuitively, this lemma says that substituting a term N for a variable x in M has the same effect on the meaning of M as changing the environment so that the value of x is the value of N. In other words, when we substitute a term for a variable, what matters is the meaning of the term being substituted, not its syntactic form. A consequence of this is that we may replace any subterm by an equivalent one. This is a very useful property which we use often in reasoning informally and which will be central to the equational proof system for algebraic terms.

In stating this lemma, we use the notation $\eta[x \mapsto a]$ for the environment that is identical to η on every variable except x, and maps x to a. We also assume Lemma 3.3.2, since without this the statement of the following lemma would not make sense.

Lemma 3.3.11 (Substitution) Let $M \in Terms^{s}(\Sigma, \Gamma, x\colon s')$ and $N \in Terms^{s'}(\Sigma, \Gamma)$, so that $[N/x]M \in Terms^{s}(\Sigma, \Gamma)$. Then for any environment respecting η, we have

$$[\![[N/x]M]\!]\eta = [\![M]\!](\eta[x \mapsto a])$$

where $a = [\![N]\!]\eta$ is the meaning of N at η.

Proof The proof is by induction on the structure of M. If M is a variable, then there are two cases, depending on whether M is the variable x or some other variable different from x. The reader may verify that in each case, the proof is straightforward.

For the induction step, we consider a term of the form $f M_1 \ldots M_k$. The relevant substitution instance of this term is $f [N/x]M_1 \ldots [N/x]M_k$. From the definition of meaning, we have

$$[\![f [N/x]M_1 \ldots [N/x]M_k]\!]\eta = f^{\mathcal{A}}([\![[N/x]M_1]\!]\eta, \ldots, [\![[N/x]M_k]\!]\eta)$$

By the inductive hypothesis, we have $[\![[N/x]M_i]\!]\eta = [\![M_i]\!](\eta[x \mapsto a])$ for $1 \le i \le k$. Using the definition of meaning again, we have

$$f^{\mathcal{A}}([\![M_1]\!](\eta[x \mapsto a]), \ldots, [\![M_k]\!](\eta[x \mapsto a])) = [\![f M_1 \ldots M_k]\!](\eta[x \mapsto a]),$$

and the lemma follows. ∎

Exercise 3.3.12 Show that the substitution rule

$$\frac{M = N[\Gamma, x\colon s]}{[P/x]M = [P/x]N[\Gamma]} \quad P \in \mathit{Terms}^s(\Sigma, \Gamma),$$

is semantically sound. In other words, assume that $M, N \in \mathit{Terms}^{s'}(\Sigma, \Gamma, x\colon s)$, $P \in \mathit{Terms}^s(\Sigma, \Gamma)$ and $[\![M]\!]\eta' = [\![N]\!]\eta'$ for every environment η' satisfying $\Gamma, x\colon s$. Use the Substitution Lemma to prove that for every environment η satisfying Γ, we have $[\![[P/x]M]\!]\eta = [\![[P/x]N]\!]\eta$.

3.4 Equations, Soundness and Completeness

3.4.1 Equations

The axiomatic semantics of an algebraic datatype is given by a set of equations between terms over a signature. Together, a signature and set of equations (between terms over this signature) is called an algebraic specification. From an algebraic specification, we may either use the equational proof system to derive additional equations between terms, or ask which algebras satisfy the requirements imposed by these equations. These two are closely related: the equations we derive from a specification should hold in any algebra that satisfies the specification. This property is called *soundness* of the algebraic proof system. The converse is that that every equation that holds in all algebras satisfying the specification is provable from the specification. This is called *completeness*. The algebraic proof system is presented in Section 3.4.3 and proved complete in Section 3.4.5. The intervening sections develop the technical machinery needed for the proofs.

A minor generalization, from most treatments of algebra or first-order logic, is that we allow empty carriers. The reasons we consider empty carriers are so that every specification will have an initial algebra and because of the parallel with empty types in typed lambda calculus. (In comparison with single-sorted first-order logic, it is worth mentioning that if there is only one sort, it makes sense to assume that the single sort is nonempty. Otherwise, every formula of logic is true in the model.)

To see why empty carriers present a technical problem, recall that the meaning of a term $M \in \mathit{Terms}^s(\Sigma, \Gamma)$ is defined only with respect to an environment η satisfying Γ. But if $x\colon s \in \Gamma$ and $A^s = \emptyset$ is empty, there cannot be any environment satisfying Γ. As a consequence, it is not clear whether we should say that every pair of terms in $\mathit{Terms}^s(\Sigma, \Gamma)$ are equal (since none has a meaning), or that such an equation simply does not make sense. The choice that gives us the simplest theory is to say that if A^s is empty, then any pair of terms involving $x\colon s$ are equal. Since emptiness affects the truth of equations, and variables can only be given values if their sorts are nonempty, the proof system will involve keeping track of variables and their sorts explicitly. We will see how keeping track of variables affects the proof system in Proposition 3.4.14.

An *equation* is a formula $M = N[\Gamma]$ with $M, N \in \mathit{Terms}^s(\Sigma, \Gamma)$ for some s. Note that an equation has *three* parts: two terms and a set of typed variables. If η satisfies Γ, then we say that an algebra $\mathcal{A}$ *satisfies* $M = N[\Gamma]$ *at environment* η, written

$$\mathcal{A}, \eta \models M = N[\Gamma],$$

whenever $[\![M]\!]\eta = [\![N]\!]\eta$. If $\mathcal{A}$ satisfies an equation at η, we also say the equation *holds* at η. For terms containing variables, we are usually more interested in whether an equation holds for all values of the variables than at a specific environment. We say $\mathcal{A}$ satisfies $M = N[\Gamma]$, and write

$$\mathcal{A} \models M = N[\Gamma],$$

if $\mathcal{A}, \eta \models M = N[\Gamma]$ for every η satisfying Γ. Satisfaction may also be extended to sets of equations or algebras. If $\mathcal{E}$ is a set of Σ-equations, then $\mathcal{A}$ *satisfies* $\mathcal{E}$ if $\mathcal{A}$ satisfies every equation in $\mathcal{E}$. Similarly, if $\mathcal{C}$ is a class of algebras, then $\mathcal{C} \models M = N[\Gamma]$ if we have $\mathcal{A} \models M = N[\Gamma]$ for every $\mathcal{A} \in \mathcal{C}$.

Example 3.4.1 Let Σ be a signature with two sorts, a and b, and let $\mathcal{A}$ be a Σ-algebra with $A^a = \{0, 1\}$ and $A^b = \emptyset$. Since A^a has two elements, we have

$$\mathcal{A} \not\models x = y[x\colon a, y\colon a].$$

More specifically, the equation $x = y[x\colon a, y\colon a]$ fails at an environment mapping $x \mapsto 0$ and $y \mapsto 1$. However, if we add an additional variable condition, we have an equation

$$\mathcal{A} \models x = y[x\colon a, y\colon a, z\colon b]$$

that holds *vacuously* since no assignment can give the variable z a value in A^b. ■

A standard concept in logic is validity. We say an equation $M = N[\Gamma]$ between Σ-terms is *valid,* and write

$$\models M = N[\Gamma]$$

if this equation is satisfied by every Σ-algebra. An example is the equation $x = x[x\colon s]$, which is valid since it holds in every algebra for any signature including sort s. The reader is encouraged to understand why this equation is valid, even when s may be empty (see Exercise 3.4.2). As we shall see, the valid equations are not very interesting, so we will be primarily concerned with the equations that hold in specific algebras or classes of algebras.

We say a Σ-algebra $\mathcal{A}$ is *trivial* if $\mathcal{A}$ satisfies all equations over Σ. A characterization of trivial algebras is given in Exercise 3.4.3.

Exercise 3.4.2 Show that the equation $x = x[x\colon s]$ is valid. More precisely, let $\Sigma = \langle S, F\rangle$ be any signature with $s \in S$ and let $\mathcal{A}$ be any Σ algebra. Show that for every environment η respecting the sort assignment $\{x\colon s\}$, we have

$$\mathcal{A}, \eta \models x = x[x\colon s].$$

Be sure to consider the possibility that $A^s = \emptyset$.

Exercise 3.4.3 Show that an algebra $\mathcal{A}$ is trivial iff each carrier A^s is either empty or has exactly one element.

Exercise 3.4.4 Let $\mathcal{A} = \langle A, \cdot^{\mathcal{A}}, K^{\mathcal{A}}\rangle$ be a single-sorted algebra for the signature with one binary operation $\cdot$, which we will write in infix notation, and one constant symbol K. Suppose $\mathcal{A} \models (K \cdot x) \cdot y = x$, where the sorts of the variables need not be specified since there is only one sort.

(a) Show that if A has more than one element, then A must be infinite. (*Hint:* Show that if A is finite, then there is some $a \in A$ with $K^{\mathcal{A}} \cdot^{\mathcal{A}} a = K^{\mathcal{A}}$.)

(b) Show that if A has more than one element, then $\cdot$ is not associative.

3.4.2 Term Algebras and Substitution

A useful fact about algebraic terms is that the collection $Terms(\Sigma, \Gamma)$ of terms over any signature and sort assignment gives us a Σ-algebra, called a *term algebra.* In the definition of algebraic terms, we defined a set $Terms^s(\Sigma, \Gamma)$ of terms for each sort s, which we may take as the carrier for s in the algebra of terms. It remains to give an interpretation to each function symbol $f\colon s_1 \times \ldots \times s_k \to s$. To be precise about it, if $\Sigma = \langle S, F\rangle$, we define the Σ-algebra

$$Terms(\Sigma, \Gamma) = \langle \{Terms^s(\Sigma, \Gamma)\}, \mathcal{I}\rangle$$

of terms over Σ and sort assignment Γ by taking

$$\mathcal{I}(f)(M_1, \ldots, M_k) = f M_1 \ldots M_k.$$

Since the definition is so simple, it is easy to see that $Terms(\Sigma, \Gamma)$ is a Σ-algebra; see Exercise 3.4.7.

The meaning of a term in a term algebra is easy to describe using substitution. If η is an environment for $Terms(\Sigma, \Gamma)$, then η is a mapping from variables to terms, which is also called a *substitution*. In general, if S is any substitution, then we write SM for the result of simultaneously replacing each variable x in M by the term Sx. Since an environment η for $Terms(\Sigma, \Gamma)$ is a substitution, we may write ηM for the result of applying the substitution η to M.

Example 3.4.5 Let Σ be the signature with sort u and function symbols $f\colon u \to u$ and $g\colon u \times u \to u$. In the term algebra $\mathcal{T} = Terms(\Sigma, \Gamma)$, with $\Gamma = \{a\colon u, b\colon u, c\colon u\}$, the carrier of u will be the set of all terms of sort u over a, b, c and functions f and g, specifically,

$$T^u = \{a, b, c, fa, fb, fc, gaa, gab, gac, gbb, \ldots g(f(fa))(f(gbc)), \ldots\}$$

The interpretation $f^{\mathcal{T}}$ of function symbol f in the term algebra is the function mapping any term M to fM and similarly for $g^{\mathcal{T}}$. If we let η be the environment mapping variable x to a and y to fb, then we have

$$\mathcal{T}[\![g(fx)(fy)]\!]\eta = g(fa)(f(fb))$$

■

We have the following lemma relating meaning and substitution.

Lemma 3.4.6 Let $M \in Terms(\Sigma, \Gamma)$ and let η be an environment for $Terms(\Sigma, \Gamma)$ which satisfies Γ. Then $[\![M]\!]\eta = \eta M$.

Proof We use induction on terms. For a variable x, we have $[\![x]\!]\eta = \eta x$ by definition. For a compound term $fM_1 \ldots M_k$, we have

$$[\![fM_1 \ldots M_k]\!]\eta = f^{Terms}([\![M_1]\!]\eta, \ldots, [\![M_k]\!]\eta)$$

by the definition of meaning in any algebra. By the induction hypothesis, we know $[\![M_i]\!]\eta = \eta M_i$ and since $Terms(\Sigma, \Gamma)$ is a term algebra, we have

$$[\![fM_1 \ldots M_k]\!]\eta = f(\eta M_1) \ldots (\eta M_k),$$

which is just the substitution η applied to M. ■

Term algebras give us an easy way of seeing that an equation $M = N[\Gamma]$ is valid only if M and N are actually the same term. This is the intent of Exercise 3.4.8.

Exercise 3.4.7 Explain the definition of $Terms(\Sigma, \Gamma)$ as an algebra, and check that it really satisfies the conditions for being an algebra.

Exercise 3.4.8 Use Lemma 3.4.6 to show that for the term algebra $Terms(\Sigma, \Gamma)$, we have $Terms(\Sigma, \Gamma) \models M = N[\Gamma]$ iff M and N are syntactically identical.

Exercise 3.4.9 In applying a substitution S of many variables to a term P, we *simultaneously* replace each x in P by Sx. If P has variables $x_1, \ldots, x_k$, then this is not necessarily equivalent to substituting Sx_1 for x_1, followed by Sx_2 for x_2, and so on. The simultaneous substitution mapping $x_i \mapsto M_i$ is commonly written $[M_1, \ldots, M_k/x_1, \ldots x_k]$.

(a) Find expressions M, N, P such that $[M, N/x, y]P \not\equiv [M/x]([N/y]P)$.

(b) Let V be an infinite set of variables. Show that for any simultaneous substitution $[M_1, \ldots, M_k/x_1, \ldots x_k]$, there is a sequence of single-variable substitutions $[N_1/y_1]$, $[N_2/y_2], \ldots, [N_\ell/y_\ell]$ that has the same effect when applied to any term not containing variables in V. In symbols, show

$$[M_1, \ldots, M_k/x_1, \ldots x_k]P = [N_1/y_1]([N_2/y_2](\ldots, ([N_\ell/y_\ell]P)\ldots))$$

for any P not containing variables in V.

3.4.3 Semantic Implication and an Equational Proof System

A pair $Spec = \langle \Sigma, \mathcal{E} \rangle$ consisting of a signature Σ and a set $\mathcal{E}$ of Σ-equations is called an *algebraic specification.* We generally think of an algebraic specification $Spec = \langle \Sigma, \mathcal{E} \rangle$ as specifying a set of algebras, namely, the set of Σ-algebras that satisfy $\mathcal{E}$. This leads us to the notion of semantic implication.

A set $\mathcal{E}$ of equations over signature Σ *semantically implies* another Σ-equation $M = N[\Gamma]$, written

$$\mathcal{E} \models M = N[\Gamma]$$

if every Σ-algebra $\mathcal{A}$ satisfying $\mathcal{E}$ also satisfies the equation $M = N[\Gamma]$. It is easy to see that the equations that hold in all algebras satisfying a specification $Spec = \langle \Sigma, \mathcal{E} \rangle$ are the Σ-equations semantically implied by $\mathcal{E}$.

A set of equations closed under semantic implication is called a theory. More precisely, a set $\mathcal{E}$ of equations is called a *semantic theory* if $\mathcal{E} \models M = N[\Gamma]$ implies $M = N[\Gamma] \in \mathcal{E}$. The *theory Th*($\mathcal{A}$) *of an algebra* $\mathcal{A}$ is the set of all equations which hold in $\mathcal{A}$. As the reader may easily verify, the theory of an algebra is a semantic theory. The proof is Exercise 3.4.16.

The rest of this section is devoted to an algebraic proof system for semantic implication. As mentioned earlier, two important properties of a proof system are *soundness* and *completeness.* Soundness means that if an equation is provable from a set $\mathcal{E}$ of hypotheses, then $\mathcal{E}$ semantically implies the equation. Completeness is the converse, namely, that if $\mathcal{E}$ semantically implies an equation, then this equation is provable from $\mathcal{E}$. We will show soundness of the proof system for algebra in this section and completeness in Section 3.4.5.

Some properties of equality are "universal" and do not depend on particular properties of algebras. Specifically, semantic equality is always an *equivalence relation.* This means that every instance of the reflexivity axiom

$$M = M[\Gamma], \qquad (\mathit{ref})$$

is valid and that equality is symmetric and transitive. The latter two properties are formalized by the inference rules

$$\frac{M = N[\Gamma]}{N = M[\Gamma]} \qquad (\mathit{sym})$$

$$\frac{M = N[\Gamma],\ N = P[\Gamma]}{M = P[\Gamma]} \qquad (\mathit{trans})$$

The next inference rule allows us to extend sort assignments in equations. This rule is not very interesting, but it is necessary. The reason for the rule is that we can consider extra variables as occurring "vacuously" in terms. Therefore, we need a way to derive $M = N[\Gamma, x\colon s]$ from $M = N[\Gamma]$. The rule

$$\frac{M = N[\Gamma]}{M = N[\Gamma, x\colon s]} \quad x \text{ not in } \Gamma \qquad (\mathit{add\ var})$$

allows us to add a variable to any sort assignment. By repeated application, we can add any finite number of variables. It is easy to verify that if an algebra $\mathcal{A}$ satisfies the hypothesis of this rule, $\mathcal{A}$ must also satisfy the conclusion.

The final rule is called *substitutivity of equivalents* and, intuitively, it says that we can substitute equals for equals. Without mentioning sort assignments, the substitution rule is simply that if $M = N$ and $P = Q$, then the result of substituting P for x in M is the same as substituting Q for x in N. Written out more formally, the rule is

$$\frac{M = N[\Gamma, x\colon s],\ P = Q[\Gamma]}{[P/x]M = [Q/x]N[\Gamma]} \quad P, Q \in \mathit{Terms}^s(\Sigma, \Gamma), \qquad (\mathit{subst})$$

where $\Gamma, x\colon s = \Gamma \cup \{x\colon s\}$. In writing $\Gamma, x\colon s$, as mentioned earlier, we assume that x does not occur in Γ. An apparent limitation of this rule is that we cannot substitute P and Q containing x into an equation $M = N[\Gamma, x\colon s]$, since the sort assignment for P and Q is assumed not to contain x. However, this is not really a problem, as shown in Exercise 3.4.18.

We say $M = N[\Gamma]$ is *provable* from a set $\mathcal{E}$ of equations, and write

$$\mathcal{E} \vdash M = N[\Gamma]$$

if we can derive $M = N[\Gamma]$ from the equations in $\mathcal{E}$ and instances of the axiom (*ref*) using the inference rules (*sym*), (*trans*), (*subst*) and (*add var*). More formally, a *proof* of E from

$\mathcal{E}$ is a sequence of equations such that each equation is either an axiom, an equation from $\mathcal{E}$, or follows from one or more equations that occur earlier in the sequence by a single inference rule. A useful form of reasoning about proofs is by induction on the length of the proof of E from $\mathcal{E}$.

If $\mathcal{E}$ is closed under provability, then we say $\mathcal{E}$ is a *syntactic theory*. Put another way, $\mathcal{E}$ is a syntactic theory if $\mathcal{E} \vdash M = N[\Gamma]$ implies $M = N[\Gamma] \in \mathcal{E}$. If $\mathcal{E}$ is any set of equations, the syntactic theory of $\mathcal{E}$, written $Th(\mathcal{E})$, is the set of all equations provable from $\mathcal{E}$. By proving completeness, we will show that syntactic and semantic algebraic theories are the same. But until then it is useful to have both definitions. A set $\mathcal{E}$ of equations is *semantically consistent* if there is some equation $M = N[\Gamma]$ that is not semantically implied by $\mathcal{E}$ and *syntactically consistent* if there is some equation $M = N[\Gamma]$ that is not provable from $\mathcal{E}$.

Example 3.4.10 (Continuation of Examples 3.3.3 and 3.3.6.) The signature $\Sigma_{stk} = \langle S, F\rangle$ of Example 3.3.3 has sorts *nat* and *stack*, and function symbols $0, 1, 2, \ldots, +, *$, *empty*, *push*, *pop* and *top*. The algebra $\mathcal{A}_{stk}$ for this signature, given in Example 3.3.6, interprets the natural numbers in the usual way and interprets stacks as sequences of numbers. Two equations that hold in $\mathcal{A}_{stk}$ are

$$top(push\, x\, s) = x[s\colon stack, x\colon nat]$$

$$pop(push\, x\, s) = s[s\colon stack, x\colon nat]$$

We can use these to prove the equation

$$top(push\, 3\, empty) = 3$$

between Σ_{stk} terms, as follows:

$$\dfrac{\dfrac{top(push\, x\, s) = x[s\colon stack, x\colon nat], \quad empty = empty[x\colon nat]}{top(push\, x\, empty) = x[x\colon nat]} \qquad 3 = 3[\,]}{top(push\, 3\, empty) = 3[\,]}$$

This proof uses two instances of axiom (*ref*), one of the stack axioms, and two applications of the (*subst*) rule. Another stack proof is given in Example 3.4.11, using a derived proof rule discussed below. ∎

A *derived rule* of a proof system is an inference rule

$$\dfrac{antecedent}{consequent}$$

such that for any instance of the antecedent, we can derive the corresponding instance of the consequent using the axioms and other proof rules of the system. For example,

$$\frac{M = N[\Gamma],\ N = P[\Gamma],\ P = Q[\Gamma]}{M = Q[\Gamma]}$$

is a derived rule of the algebraic proof system since, from any three equations of the form $M = N$, $N = P$, $P = Q$, we can derive $M = Q$ by two uses of the transitivity rule. If we show that a rule is derivable, then we may use it as if it were a proof rule of the system. Therefore, if we were to do a large number of proofs, it would make sense to build up a library of derived proof rules.

An example of a derived rule is the following "congruence" rule. Intuitively, congruence means that "equals applied to equals produce equals."

$$\frac{M_1 = N_1[\Gamma], \ldots, M_k = N_k[\Gamma]}{f M_1 \ldots M_k = f N_1 \ldots N_k[\Gamma]} \quad \begin{array}{l} f\colon s_1 \times \ldots \times s_k \to s \text{ and} \\ M_i, N_i \in Terms^{s_i}(\Sigma,\Gamma) \end{array} \qquad (cong)$$

We show that (*cong*) is a derived rule using (*add var*), (*ref*), and (*subst*) as follows. From the hypotheses, we may use (*add var*) to derive equations

$$M_i = N_i[\Gamma, x_1\colon s_1, \ldots, x_k\colon s_k]$$

where $x_1, \ldots, x_k$ are fresh variables not occurring in Γ. By (*ref*), we also have the equation

$$f x_1 \ldots x_k = f x_1 \ldots x_k[\Gamma, x_1\colon s_1, \ldots, x_k\colon s_k].$$

Using (*subst*) repeatedly, we may replace the left-hand occurrence of x_i by M_i and the right-hand occurrence by N_i. This gives us the consequent of (*cong*),

$$f M_1 \ldots M_k = f N_1 \ldots N_k[\Gamma]$$

Although (*cong*) is subsumed by the other proof rules, it is a handy derived rule.

Example 3.4.11 (Continuation of Example 3.4.10.) We can use the derived congruence rule to prove the equation

$$top(pop(push\, x\,(push\, 3\, empty))) = 3[x\colon nat],$$

from the stack axioms given in Example 3.4.10. To prove this equation, we begin with a stack axiom and an instance of (*ref*), apply (*subst*) and then the derived (*cong*) rule:

$$\frac{\dfrac{pop(push\, x\, s) = s[s\colon stack, x\colon nat], \quad push\, 3\, empty = push\, 3\, empty[x\colon nat]}{pop(push\, x\, (push\, 3\, empty)) = push\, 3\, empty[x\colon nat]}}{top(pop(push\, x\,(push\, 3\, empty))) = top(push\, 3\, empty)[x\colon nat]},$$

From the equation proved in Example 3.4.10, we can use (*add var*) to obtain

$$\frac{top(push\,3\,empty) = 3[\,]}{top(push\,3\,empty) = 3[x\colon nat]}.$$

Putting these together with (*trans*) yields

$$top(pop(push\,x\,(push\,3\,empty))) = 3[x\colon nat].$$ ■

Example 3.4.12 The following rule allows us to eliminate redundant variables from the sort assignment of any equation. Essentially, a sort assignment Γ in an equation $M = N[\Gamma]$ serves two purposes. First, it says what the sorts of the variables in M and N are, so that we can see that these terms are well-formed. The second role is to keep track of which carriers we assume are nonempty. If a variable x does not occur in M or N, and we know (by some other means) that s is not empty, then $x\colon s$ serves no purpose in an equation $M = N[\Gamma, x\colon s]$. Since the carrier for s must be nonempty if we can name an element of s by writing a term $P \in Terms^s(\Sigma, \Gamma)$, the following inference rule makes semantic sense.

$$\frac{M = N[\Gamma, x\colon s]}{M = N[\Gamma]} \quad x \text{ not in } M, N;\ Terms^s(\Sigma, \Gamma) \text{ not empty}$$

We can show that this is a derived rule using (*ref*) and (*subst*). Since $Terms^s(\Sigma, \Gamma)$ is not empty, we have the reflexivity axiom $P = P[\Gamma]$ for some $P \in Terms^s(\Sigma, \Gamma)$. Combining this with our hypothesis $M = N[\Gamma, x\colon s]$, we may use (*subst*) to prove the equation $[P/x]M = [P/x]N[\Gamma]$. But since x does not occur in M or N, the substitution has no effect, and we have $M = N[\Gamma]$. ■

The main theorem of this section is that the proof system for equations is sound, which means that if we can prove an equation E from a set $\mathcal{E}$ of equational hypotheses, then $\mathcal{E}$ semantically implies E.

Theorem 3.4.13 (Soundness) If $\mathcal{E} \vdash M = N[\Gamma]$, then $\mathcal{E} \models M = N[\Gamma]$.

Proof We prove soundness by induction on the length of the proof. More specifically, suppose there is a proof of E from $\mathcal{E}$. We show then $\mathcal{E} \models E$ by induction on the length of the proof of E from $\mathcal{E}$.

The base case of the induction is a proof of length 1, which is either an axiom or an equation from $\mathcal{E}$. In either case, it is easy to see that any algebra satisfying $\mathcal{A}$ must satisfy this equation as well.

For the induction step, we assume that E follows from equations $E_1, \ldots, E_n$ by a single proof rule, and $E_1, \ldots, E_n$ are provable by shorter proofs. By the inductive hypothesis, we may assume that if $\mathcal{A} \models \mathcal{E}$, then $\mathcal{A}$ satisfies $E_1, \ldots, E_n$. It therefore suffices to show that if $\mathcal{A}$ satisfies the antecedents of the last rule used, then $\mathcal{A}$ satisfies E. This leads us to a case analysis on the set of proof rules. Rather than show each case, we will give the proof for the substitution rule and leave the others to the reader.

We assume $\mathcal{A} \models M = N[\Gamma, x{:}s]$ and $\mathcal{A} \models P = Q[\Gamma]$. We must show that $\mathcal{A} \models [P/x]M = [Q/x]N[\Gamma]$. To do this, we let η be any environment satisfying Γ. We must show that $[\![[P/x]M]\!]\eta = [\![[Q/x]N]\!]\eta$.

Let $a = [\![P]\!]\eta = [\![Q]\!]\eta$, and note that $\eta[x \mapsto a]$ satisfies $\Gamma, x{:}s$. By the Substitution Lemma (Lemma 3.3.11), we have

$$[\![[P/x]M]\!]\eta = [\![M]\!](\eta[x \mapsto a])$$

and similarly

$$[\![[Q/x]N]\!]\eta = [\![N]\!](\eta[x \mapsto a]).$$

But since $\mathcal{A} \models M = N[\Gamma]$, we also have

$$[\![M]\!](\eta[x \mapsto a]) = [\![N]\!](\eta[x \mapsto a]).$$

It follows that $[\![[P/x]M]\!]\eta$ and $[\![[Q/x]N]\!]\eta$ are equal, which proves the lemma. ∎

We can use this theorem to show why it is essential to keep track of variables in equations.

Proposition 3.4.14 There is an algebraic theory $\mathcal{E}$ and terms M and N without x free such that $\mathcal{E} \vdash M = N[\Gamma, x{:}s]$ but $\mathcal{E} \nvdash M = N[\Gamma]$

Proof Let Σ be the signature with sorts a and b and function symbols $f{:}a \to b$ and $c, d{:}b$. Let $\mathcal{E}$ be the theory consisting of all equations provable from $fx = c[x{:}a]$ and $fx = d[x{:}a]$ and consider the equation $c = d[x{:}a]$. This clearly follows from the equations in $\mathcal{E}$ by transitivity. However, we can see that the equation $c = d[\emptyset]$ is not provable, by the following semantic argument.

Consider a Σ-algebra with the carrier for a empty but c and d denoting two distinct elements of the nonempty carrier for b. The equations $fx = c[x{:}a]$ and $fx = d[x{:}a]$ are true in this model, since there is no possible value for $x{:}a$. However, the equation $c = d[\emptyset]$ does not hold in this model. Therefore, by soundness of the equational proof system, $c = d[\emptyset]$ is not provable from $\mathcal{E}$. ∎

The soundness theorem not only shows that the proof system is semantically correct, but also, as in the proof of Proposition 3.4.14, may be used to show that an equation is *not* provable from some set of equations. Specifically, if we can find an algebra satisfying $\mathcal{E}$ but not satisfying an equation E, then $\mathcal{E}$ does not semantically imply E. It follows by soundness there cannot be a proof of E from $\mathcal{E}$. In cases where we do not know if an

Table 3.1
Algebraic specification of stacks.

sorts:	$nat, stack$
fctns:	$0, 1, 2, \ldots : nat$
	$+, * : nat \times nat \to nat$
	$empty : stack$
	$push : nat \times stack \to stack$
	$pop : stack \to stack$
	$top : stack \to nat$
eqns:	$[s\colon stack, x\colon nat]$
	$0+0=0,\ 0+1=1,\ \ldots$
	$0*0=0,\ 0*1=0,\ \ldots$
	$top\,(push\,x\,s) = x$
	$pop\,(push\,x\,s) = s$

equation E follows from a set of equations $\mathcal{E}$, we generally try both to prove E from $\mathcal{E}$ and find an algebra satisfying $\mathcal{E}$ but not E. It follows from the completeness theorem that, in principle, one of these is possible. However, it is important to realize that there is a significant difference between searching for a proof and searching for an algebra that demonstrates that there is no proof. The difference is that there is an effective and routine method for enumerating all proofs. Therefore, if there is a proof of E from $\mathcal{E}$, a routine method will eventually find it. However, there is no routine method for finding an algebra to show that there is no proof.

Example 3.4.15 This example presents some equations, written using the stack signature of Example 3.3.3, that are not provable from the equational axioms of Example 3.4.10. For easy reference, the signatures and equational axioms from these examples are collected in a tabular form of specification in Table 3.1. In the notation used in this figure, the sort of each variable is given at the beginning of the list of equations. This may be regarded as a shorthand for writing the same sort assignment as part of each equation.

An algebra $\mathcal{A}_{stk}$ satisfying this specification is given in Example 3.3.6. We can see that the equation

$$push(top\,s)(pop\,s) = s[s\colon stack]$$

is not provable from the stack specification by observing that this equation does not hold in the algebra $\mathcal{A}_{stk}$. Specifically, this equation fails at an environment mapping s to the empty sequence.

A related but more complicated fact is that we cannot prove any equation of the form *top empty* $= M[\Gamma]$,

assuming the term M of sort *nat* does not contain *empty*. This may be demonstrated using algebras that are almost the same as $\mathcal{A}_{stk}$, but differ in the interpretation of the function symbol *top*. For any $n \in \mathcal{N}$, let $\mathcal{A}_n$ be the algebra that is the same as $\mathcal{A}_{stk}$, but with $top^{\mathcal{A}_n}(\epsilon) = n$. (This gives us $\mathcal{A}_{stk} = \mathcal{A}_0$.) Note that if η is an environment for $\mathcal{A}_{stk}$ that satisfies Γ, then η is also an environment for any $\mathcal{A}_n$, again satisfying Γ. We will show that for any M of sort *nat* that does not contain *empty*, we can find an environment η so that $\mathcal{A}_i[\![M]\!]\eta = \mathcal{A}_j[\![M]\!]\eta$ for all i and j. The main idea is that as long η maps all the variables of sort *stack* that appear in M to large enough stacks (long enough sequences), the meaning of M will be independent of the value given to *top empty*.

We begin by showing that if P is a term of sort *stack* containing only stack variables $x_1, \ldots, x_j$, natural number variables $y_1, \ldots, y_k$ and not containing *empty*, then for any number ℓ, there is a minimum number m such that as long as environment η sends each stack variable x_i to a stack with at least m elements, $\mathcal{A}_n[\![P]\!]\eta$ has at least ℓ elements (for every n). We use induction on the structure of P. If P is a stack variable x_i, then clearly we can choose η so that $\eta(x_i)$ will have as many elements as we like. If P is *push* P_1 P_2, then the meaning of P will have at least ℓ elements as long as the meaning of P_2 has at least $\ell - 1$ elements. By the inductive hypothesis, this is achievable. Finally, if we want *pop* P_1 to have at least ℓ elements, it similarly suffices to find an environment giving P_1 at least $\ell + 1$ elements.

The second step is to show that if M is a term of sort *nat* that does not contain *empty*, then there is an environment (for $\mathcal{A}_{stk}$ and therefore for each $\mathcal{A}_n$) such that $\mathcal{A}_n[\![M]\!]\eta = \mathcal{A}_{stk}[\![M]\!]\eta$ for all n. This is proved by a straightforward induction on the structure of M, using the fact that for a term of the form *top* N, we can choose η so that neither $\mathcal{A}_n[\![N]\!]\eta$ nor $\mathcal{A}_{stk}[\![N]\!]\eta$ is the empty stack.

We conclude the argument by observing that if M is a term of sort *nat* that does not contain *empty*, the equation *top empty* $= M[\Gamma]$ fails in some $\mathcal{A}_n$ at some environment. Specifically, let η be an environment such that $\mathcal{A}_n[\![M]\!]\eta = \mathcal{A}_{stk}[\![M]\!]\eta$ for all n. Then since $\mathcal{A}_n[\![top\ empty]\!]\eta$ depends on n, we must have $\mathcal{A}_n[\![top\ empty]\!]\eta \neq \mathcal{A}_n[\![M]\!]\eta$ for some n. Therefore, the equation *top empty* $= M[\Gamma]$ cannot be proved from the axioms for stacks.

■

Exercise 3.4.16 Show that for any algebra $\mathcal{A}$, the set $Th(\mathcal{A})$ of all equations that hold in $\mathcal{A}$ is a semantic theory.

Exercise 3.4.17 Show that a set $\mathcal{E}$ of equations is semantically consistent iff there is a nontrivial algebra $\mathcal{A} \models \mathcal{E}$.

Exercise 3.4.18 Show that

$$\frac{M = N[\Gamma, x\colon s],\ P = Q[\Gamma']}{[P/x]M = [Q/x]N[\Gamma \cup \Gamma']} \quad P, Q \in \mathit{Terms}^s(\Sigma, \Gamma'),$$

is a derived rule. Be sure to consider the case where x occurs in Γ', P and Q. Note that in writing $[P/x]M = [Q/x]N[\Gamma \cup \Gamma']$, we assume that $\Gamma \cup \Gamma'$ is a well-formed sort assignment, so that no variable is given two different sorts.

Exercise 3.4.19 Let us call a substitution S a (Γ, Γ')-*substitution* if S maps every x with $x\colon s \in \Gamma$, to some term $Sx \in \mathit{Terms}^s(\Sigma, \Gamma')$. Show that the rule

$$\frac{M = N[\Gamma]}{SM = SN[\Gamma']} \quad \text{any } (\Gamma, \Gamma')\text{-substitution } S$$

is a derived rule. In other words, show that from $M = N[\Gamma]$, we may prove every equation of the form $SM = SN[\Gamma']$. (*Hint:* see Exercise 3.4.9.)

Exercise 3.4.20 Consider the specification of multisets, natural numbers and booleans in Table 3.2. (In this specification, `if` u `then` x `else` y is used as syntactic sugar for $\mathit{cond}\, u\, x\, y$.) In case you are not familiar with multisets, a multiset is similar to a set except that an element may occur more than once. Therefore, the membership test (called *count*) returns a natural number instead of a boolean. Parts (b) and (c) use variables $x, y\colon \mathit{nat}$ and $m\colon \mathit{mset}$.

(a) Prove the equation

$\mathit{count}\, 3 (\mathit{insert}\, 5\, (\mathit{insert}\, 3\, \mathit{empty})) = 1$

from this specification.

(b) Show that for any numerals a,b and c the equation

$\mathit{count}\, a\, (\mathit{insert}\, b\, (\mathit{insert}\, c\, m)) = \mathit{count}\, a\, (\mathit{insert}\, c\, (\mathit{insert}\, b\, m))$

is provable from this specification

(c) Show that the equation

$\mathit{insert}\, x (\mathit{insert}\, y\, m) = \mathit{insert}\, y (\mathit{insert}\, x\, m)$

is *not* provable from this specification by finding an algebra that satisfies all of the equations in the specification but does not satisfy this one.

is when every valid formula is provable. For algebra, this kind of completeness is too weak to be interesting: all valid equations are instances of axiom (*ref*). The next form, called *deductive completeness,* holds when every semantic implication is derivable in the proof system. More specifically, for equations, deductive completeness is the property that whenever $\mathcal{E} \models M = N[\Gamma]$, we have $\mathcal{E} \vdash M = N[\Gamma]$. A stronger form of completeness may be called *least model completeness.* This holds when every syntactic theory (set of formulas closed under provability) is the semantic theory of some "least" model. For algebras, least model completeness would imply that every syntactic theory is $Th(\mathcal{A})$ for some algebra $\mathcal{A}$. What may be slightly confusing about the name is that "least models" are least when we order models by containment of their theories, not the size of their carriers.

Least model completeness is related to a semantic condition we might call the *least model property:* every *semantic* theory is the theory of a single model (algebra). If we have soundness and least model completeness, then every semantic theory is a syntactic theory, and so the least model property holds. The contrapositive is that when the least model property fails, we cannot have least model completeness for any sound proof system.

We will prove deductive completeness for algebra in the next section. In the remainder of this section, we show that the least model property fails for algebras that may have empty carriers. It follows that we cannot have least model completeness with empty carriers. In Section 3.4.6, we show that if empty carriers are ruled out either by fiat or by restricting signatures, we can prove least model completeness for multi-sorted algebras.

In general, the least model property fails when logical formulas can express "disjunctive" information. While we do not ordinarily think of equations as disjunctive, the possibility of empty carriers introduces a form of disjunction. To see why, consider the equation

$$E \stackrel{\text{def}}{=} x = y[x\colon a,\ y\colon a,\ z\colon b]$$

discussed in Example 3.4.1. We will see that any algebra satisfying E must satisfy one of the following equations

$$E_1 \stackrel{\text{def}}{=} x = y[x\colon a,\ y\colon a], \quad E_2 \stackrel{\text{def}}{=} z = w[z\colon b,\ w\colon b].$$

However, E does not semantically imply either E_1 or E_2.

There are two ways that E might be satisfied. One is that the carrier for a does not have two distinct elements, forcing x and y to have the same value. The other case is that the carrier for b is empty, which makes the equation hold vacuously. Using the notation $|s|$ for the cardinality of the carrier for s, we can see that E "says"

$$E \approx (|a| \leq 1 \text{ or } |b| = 0)$$

When $|a| \leq 1$, the equation E_1 without the variable $z\colon b$ must hold, while E_2 must hold when $|b| = 0$. Thus any algebra for the signature with sorts a, b which satisfies E must satisfy one of these other equations. However, it is easy to see that neither equation is semantically implied by E. Thus the semantic theory consisting of all equational consequences of E cannot be the theory of a single algebra. This causes the least model property to fail.

3.4.5 Congruence, Quotients and Deductive Completeness

The main result of this section is the deductive completeness theorem for multi-sorted algebras that may have empty carriers. The proof of this theorem uses congruence relations and quotient algebras, which we develop first.

Many readers will be familiar with the general notion of an *equivalence relation,* a reflexive, symmetric and transitive binary relation. It is easy to see from the proof rules that provable equality is an equivalence relation. In addition, the derived rule (*cong*) demonstrates that every function preserves provable equality. An equivalence relation with this additional property is called a congruence relation.

For a single-sorted algebra $\mathcal{A} = \langle A, f_1^{\mathcal{A}}, f_2^{\mathcal{A}}, \ldots, \rangle$ a *congruence relation* is an equivalence relation on the carrier A such that, for every k-ary function $f^{\mathcal{A}}$ from $\mathcal{A}$, if $a_i \sim b_i$ for $i = 1, \ldots, k$ then $f^{\mathcal{A}}(a_1, \ldots, a_k) \sim f^{\mathcal{A}}(b_1, \ldots, b_k)$. In words, a congruence relation is an equivalence relation with the added property that every function of the algebra maps related arguments to related results. An example is the relation "equivalence modulo k" on the single-sorted algebra $\langle \mathcal{N}, 0, 1, + \rangle$. It is easy to see that this is an equivalence relation. The additional requirements for a congruence are that $0 = 0 \bmod k$, $1 = 1 \bmod k$ and whenever $n = n' \bmod k$ and $m = m' \bmod k$, we have $n + m = n' + m' \bmod k$. These are easily verified, as many may remember from secondary school.

For a multi-sorted Σ-algebra $\mathcal{A} = \langle \{A^s\}, \mathcal{I} \rangle$, a *congruence relation* is a family $\sim = \{\sim_s\}$ of equivalence relations $\sim_s \subseteq A^s \times A^s$, one for each sort, such that for every $f : s_1 \times \ldots \times s_k \to s$ and sequences of arguments $a_1, \ldots, a_k$ and $b_1, \ldots, b_k$ with $a_i \sim_{s_i} b_i \in A^{s_i}$, we have $f^{\mathcal{A}}(a_1, \ldots, a_k) \sim_s f^{\mathcal{A}}(b_1, \ldots, b_k)$. An example that we will use is the relation of provable equality (from any set of equations) on the term algebra. It is easy to see that this is a congruence relation since we have an axiom and proof rules to make provable equality an equivalence relation, and (*cong*) is a derived inference rule.

Given any congruence relation $\sim$ on $\mathcal{A}$, we may construct an algebra $\mathcal{A}/{\sim}$ called the *quotient of* $\mathcal{A}$ *modulo* $\sim$. The intuitive idea behind $\mathcal{A}/{\sim}$ is that we "collapse" related elements $a \sim a'$ from $\mathcal{A}$ into one element of $\mathcal{A}/{\sim}$.

If $\sim$ is a congruence relation on $\mathcal{A}$ and $a \in A^s$, then the *equivalence class* $[a]_\sim$ *of* a *with respect to* $\sim$ is defined by

$$[a]_\sim = \{a' \in A^s \mid a \sim a'\}.$$

Another common notation for the equivalence class of a is $a/\!\sim$. We often leave off the symbol $\sim$ and write $[a]$ when the congruence relation $\sim$ is clear from context. The quotient Σ-algebra $\mathcal{A}/\!\sim$ is defined by taking $(A/\!\sim)^s$ to be the set

$$A^s/\!\sim_s = \{[a]_{\sim_s} \mid a \in A\}.$$

of all equivalence classes from A^s. A function $f^{\mathcal{A}}$ from $\mathcal{A}$ determines a function $f^{\mathcal{A}/\sim}$ satisfying

$$f^{\mathcal{A}/\sim}([a_1], \ldots, [a_k]) = [f^{\mathcal{A}}(a_1, \ldots, a_k)]$$

for all $a_1, \ldots, a_k$ of the appropriate carriers. In other words, the function value $f^{\mathcal{A}/\sim}([a_1], \ldots, [a_k])$ on a sequence of equivalence classes is the equivalence class of $f^{\mathcal{A}}(a_1, \ldots, a_k)$. It is not completely obvious that this definition makes sense, since the value $f^{\mathcal{A}/\sim}([a_1], \ldots, [a_k])$ must depend only on the sets $[a_1], \ldots, [a_k]$ and not on the representatives $a_1, \ldots, a_k$ we have chosen in writing this down. This problem is addressed in Exercise 3.4.26.

For the congruence relation "equivalence modulo k" on the single-sorted algebra $\langle \mathcal{N}, 0, 1, + \rangle$, the reader may verify that the quotient algebra is the familiar structure of integer addition modulo k. For example, if $k = 5$, then the sum of equivalence classes $[3]$ and $[4]$ is the equivalence class $[3 + 4] = [7]$. Since $[7] = [2]$, this is the same as what is more commonly written $3 + 4 = 2 \bmod 5$. More details are given in Exercise 3.4.25.

The meaning of a term M in a quotient algebra $\mathcal{A}/\!\sim$ has an easy description, based on the meaning of M in $\mathcal{A}$. If M has no variables, then the meaning of M in $\mathcal{A}/\!\sim$ is the equivalence class of the meaning of M in $\mathcal{A}$. If M has variables, then we need to pick an environment η for $\mathcal{A}$ and relate this to some environment for $\mathcal{A}/\!\sim$.

If η is an environment for $\mathcal{A}$ and $\sim$ is a congruence relation, we define the environment $\eta_\sim$ for $\mathcal{A}/\!\sim$ by

$$\eta_\sim(x) = [\eta(x)]_\sim.$$

We can also choose an $\mathcal{A}$-environment corresponding to any $\mathcal{A}/\!\sim$-environment. If η' is a mapping from variables to elements of $A/\!\sim$, then we can define an environment η for $\mathcal{A}$ by choosing an arbitrary element $\eta(x) \in \eta'(x)$ for each variable x. This gives us an environment η with $\eta_\sim = \eta'$.

Using the correspondence between environments for $\mathcal{A}$ and $\mathcal{A}/\!\sim$, we have the following description of the meaning of a term in a quotient algebra.

Lemma 3.4.22 Let $\sim$ be a congruence relation on Σ-algebra $\mathcal{A}$, term $M \in \mathit{Terms}(\Sigma, \Gamma)$ and η an environment satisfying Γ. Then the meaning $(\mathcal{A}/\!\sim)[\![M]\!]\eta_\sim$ of M in environment $\eta_\sim$ for the quotient algebra $\mathcal{A}/\!\sim$ is given by

$(\mathcal{A}/\!\sim)[\![M]\!]\eta_\sim = [\mathcal{A}[\![M]\!]\eta]_\sim.$

Proof We use induction on the structure of M. The base case follows easily from the definition of $\eta_\sim$. For the induction step, we have

$$\begin{aligned}(\mathcal{A}/\!\sim)[\![f M_1 \dots M_k]\!]\eta_\sim &= f^{\mathcal{A}/\sim}((\mathcal{A}/\!\sim)[\![M_1]\!]\eta_\sim, \dots, (\mathcal{A}/\!\sim)[\![M_k]\!]\eta_\sim)\\ &= f^{\mathcal{A}/\sim}([\mathcal{A}[\![M_1]\!]\eta], \dots, [\mathcal{A}[\![M_k]\!]\eta])\\ &= [f^{\mathcal{A}}(\mathcal{A}[\![M_1]\!]\eta, \dots, \mathcal{A}[\![M_k]\!]\eta)]\\ &= [\mathcal{A}[\![f M_1 \dots M_k]\!]\eta].\end{aligned}$$

The first equation is just the definition of meaning in $\mathcal{A}/\!\sim$. After that, we use the inductive hypothesis and the interpretation of a function symbol in a quotient algebra. ■

As the final step toward proving the completeness theorem, we will show that any set of equational hypotheses determines a congruence relation on the algebra of terms. For any set $\mathcal{E}$ of Σ-equations, and any sort assignment Γ, we define the relation $\sim_{\mathcal{E},\Gamma}$ on the algebra $\mathit{Terms}(\Sigma, \Gamma)$ by taking

$M \sim_{\mathcal{E},\Gamma} N$ iff $\mathcal{E} \vdash M = N[\Gamma]$.

This is a congruence relation, as shown by the following lemma.

Lemma 3.4.23 Let $\mathcal{E}$ be a set of Σ-equations and let $\mathit{Terms}(\Sigma, \Gamma)$ be a term algebra over signature Σ. The relation $\sim_{\mathcal{E},\Gamma}$ determined by provability from $\mathcal{E}$ is a congruence relation on $\mathit{Terms}(\Sigma, \Gamma)$.

Proof It is easy to see that $\sim_{\mathcal{E},\Gamma}$ is an equivalence relation on each sort, since we have axiom (*ref*) and inference rules (*sym*) and (*trans*). To simplify notation, let us write $\mathcal{T}$ for the algebra $\mathit{Terms}(\Sigma, \Gamma)$. It follows easily from the derived rule (*cong*) that

$f^{\mathcal{T}}(M_1, \dots, M_k) \sim_{\mathcal{E},\Gamma} f^{\mathcal{T}}(N_1, \dots, N_k)$

whenever $M_i \sim_{\mathcal{E},\Gamma} N_i$. ■

Theorem 3.4.24 (Completeness) Let $\mathcal{E}$ be any set of Σ-equations, and E be a single Σ-equation. If $\mathcal{E} \models E$, then $\mathcal{E} \vdash E$.

Proof Suppose the equation $M_0 = N_0[\Gamma_0]$ is not provable from $\mathcal{E}$. We will prove the deductive completeness theorem by showing that there is an algebra satisfying $\mathcal{E}$ but not satisfying this equation. We will use the quotient algebra $\mathcal{A} = \mathit{Terms}(\Sigma, \Gamma_0)/\!\sim_{\mathcal{E},\Gamma_0}$. To simplify notation, let us write $\sim$ for the congruence relation $\sim_{\mathcal{E},\Gamma_0}$ and $\mathcal{T}$ for the term algebra $Terms(\Sigma, \Gamma_0)$. We must show that $\mathcal{A}$ satisfies every equation in $\mathcal{E}$, but not the equation $M_0 = N_0[\Gamma_0]$.

It is easier to see that $\mathcal{A}$ does not satisfy $M_0 = N_0[\Gamma_0]$ since this requires only one environment. Let η be the environment for the term algebra $\mathcal{T}$ mapping each variable x to itself. Then by Lemma 3.4.6, we know the meaning $\mathcal{T}[\![M_0]\!]\eta$ of M_0 at this environment is simply M_0. Consequently, by Lemma 3.4.22, we have

$$\mathcal{A}[\![M_0]\!]\eta_\sim = [M_0]$$

and similarly for N_0. But by hypothesis, we know $[M_0] \neq [N_0]$, so the equation $M_0 = N_0[\Gamma_0]$ does not hold at environment $\eta_\sim$.

It remains to show that $\mathcal{A} \models \mathcal{E}$. Suppose $M = N[\Gamma] \in \mathcal{E}$. As noted in the discussion just above Lemma 3.4.22, every environment for $\mathcal{A}$ may be written $\eta_\sim$ for some environment η for the term algebra $\mathcal{T}$. Specifically, suppose we are given some $\hat{\eta}$ for $\mathcal{A}$. For each variable x, we choose some $P \in \hat{\eta}(x)$ and let $\eta(x) = P$. Then we have $\eta_\sim = \hat{\eta}$. Therefore, it suffices to show that $\mathcal{A}[\![M]\!]\eta_\sim = \mathcal{A}[\![N]\!]\eta_\sim$ for every such $\mathcal{T}$ environment η satisfying Γ.

For any $\mathcal{T}$ environment η satisfying Γ, we have $\mathcal{A}[\![M]\!]\eta_\sim = [\mathcal{T}[\![M]\!]\eta]_\sim$ by Lemma 3.4.22, and so by Lemma 3.4.6 it follows that

$$\mathcal{A}[\![M]\!]\eta_\sim = [\mathcal{T}[\![M]\!]\eta]_\sim = [\eta M]_\sim.$$

Since the same reasoning applies to N, we have $\mathcal{A}[\![N]\!]\eta_\sim = [\eta N]_\sim$. Now, using rules (*ref*) and (*subst*), we can show that $\mathcal{E} \vdash \eta M = \eta N[\Gamma]$ (see Exercise 3.4.19). But this means that $[\eta M]_\sim = [\eta N]_\sim$, and so we conclude that M and N have the same meaning in $\mathcal{A}$. This proves the theorem. ■

The completeness theorem shows that syntactic and semantic theories are identical.

Exercise 3.4.25 Let Σ be the single-sorted algebraic signature

sorts:*nat*

fctns:0, 1 : *nat*

$+ : nat \times nat \to nat$

and let $\mathcal{A}$ be the Σ algebra whose carrier $A^{nat} = \mathcal{N}$ is the set of natural numbers and with function symbols 0, 1, + interpreted as the usual natural numbers and addition function.

(a) Show that ordinary "congruence modulo n," for any natural number $n > 0$, is a congruence relation on $\mathcal{A}$. In other words, let $\equiv_n$ be the relation $i \equiv_n j$ *iff* n divides $|i - j|$ and show that $\equiv_n$ is a congruence relation on $\mathcal{A}$.

(b) Describe the quotient structure $\mathcal{A}/\equiv_n$. How many elements does the carrier $A^{nat}/\equiv_n$ have?

(c) If we extend the signature with a multiplication symbol, and extend the algebra $\mathcal{A}$ to interpret this symbol in the usual way, is $\equiv_n$ still a congruence relation on $\mathcal{A}$? What if we add a unary function symbol p, interpreted so that $p(i)$ is the least prime greater than i?

Exercise 3.4.26 Show that the equation defining $f^{\mathcal{A}/\sim}$ actually determines a function from equivalence classes to equivalence classes. This means that you should show that if $[a_i] = [b_i]$ for $i = 1, \ldots, k$, then $[f(a_1, \ldots, a_k)] = [f(b_1, \ldots, b_k)]$. What would go wrong if $\sim$ were an equivalence relation but not a congruence? What if $\sim$ were not transitive?

Exercise 3.4.27 If signature $\Sigma = \langle S, F \rangle$, a *partial congruence relation* over Σ-algebra $\mathcal{A}$ is a family $\sim = \{\sim_s | s \in S\}$ of symmetric and transitive relations $\sim_s \subseteq A^s \times A^s$ such that for every $f : s_1 \times \ldots \times s_k \to s$ in F and sequences of arguments $a_1, \ldots, a_k$ and $b_1, \ldots, b_k$ with $a_i \sim_{s_i} b_i \in A^{s_i}$, we have $f^{\mathcal{A}}(a_1, \ldots, a_k) \sim_s f^{\mathcal{A}}(b_1, \ldots, b_k)$. The difference between this and an ordinary congruence relation is that a partial congruence relation does not have to be reflexive. If $x \sim x$, then we define the "equivalence class" of x as for a total congruence relation, and define the *partial quotient* structure $\mathcal{A}/\sim$ by letting the carrier $A^s/\sim_s$ be the set of all nonempty equivalence classes. Show that $\mathcal{A}/\sim$ is an algebra with the property that if η is an environment for $\mathcal{A}$ with $\eta(x) \sim \eta(x)$ for each x in M, then

$(\mathcal{A}/\sim)[\![M]\!]\eta_\sim = [\mathcal{A}[\![M]\!]\eta]_\sim$.

3.4.6 Nonempty Sorts and the Least Model Property

For algebras without empty carriers, we have least model completeness. There are two ways of eliminating empty carriers:

(i) Assume that no algebra has any empty carriers, and add a corresponding inference rule to the proof system;

(ii) Consider signatures which yield variable-free terms of each sort. Since these terms must have values, this eliminates empty carriers.

In either of these cases, essentially the same construction used in the proof of Theorem 3.4.24 may be used to prove least model completeness.

A completeness theorem covering both cases of nonemptiness may be stated using the inference rule

$$\frac{M = N[\Gamma, x : s]}{M = N[\Gamma]} \quad \text{not in } M, N \qquad (\textit{nonempty})$$

which allows us to eliminate assumptions about any variables which do not occur in the equation. We will see below how this rule is derivable for certain signatures. If we know that the carrier for s is not empty, then it is easy to see that this rule is sound. Specifically, if the top equation is satisfied in some algebra $\mathcal{A}$, and η is an environment satisfying Γ we can find some environment η' satisfying $\Gamma, x\colon s$ which is identical to η on all variables in Γ. By Lemma 3.3.8, terms M and N have the same meaning in η' as in η, and so the rule is sound. The following theorem shows that the rule gives us least model completeness.

Theorem 3.4.28 Let $\mathcal{E}$ be any syntactic theory closed under rule (*nonempty*). There is an algebra $\mathcal{A}$ with all carriers nonempty such that $\mathcal{E} = Th(\mathcal{A})$.

The proof is outlined at the end of this section.

We may use this theorem to show completeness of the ordinary proof system without (*nonempty*) in the case that our signature forces every carrier nonempty. To put this precisely, we use the following definition. A sort s is Σ-*nonvoid* if signature Σ contains a constant symbol of sort s, or Σ has a function symbol $f\colon s_1 \times \ldots \times s_k \to s$ and sorts $s_1, \ldots, s_k$ are Σ-nonvoid. It is easy to see that if s is Σ-nonvoid, then there is a term $M \in Terms^s(\Sigma, \emptyset)$ without variables, and so the carrier for s cannot be empty in any Σ algebra. As described in Example 3.4.12, we may eliminate extraneous variables by substitution when all sorts are nonvoid, and so (*nonempty*) becomes a derived rule.

Corollary 3.4.29 If Σ is a signature with every sort Σ-nonvoid, then for every syntactic Σ-theory $\mathcal{E}$, there is an algebra $\mathcal{A}$ with $\mathcal{E} = Th(\mathcal{A})$.

Proof of Theorem 3.4.28 Suppose $\mathcal{E}$ is a syntactic Σ-theory closed under inference rule (*nonempty*). To avoid some technical details about the names of variables, let us assume we have an infinite set Γ_∞ of pairs of the form $x\colon s$, providing infinitely many variables for each sort of Σ, and suppose that all the terms we are interested in belong to some $Terms(\Sigma, \Gamma)$ for $\Gamma \subseteq \Gamma_\infty$. There is no loss of generality in this, since Γ_∞ has plenty of variables, and renaming variables has no effect on whether an algebra satisfies a given equation. It is easy to see that the definition of a term algebra $Terms(\Sigma, \Gamma)$ does not depend on Γ being finite, and so we may let $\mathcal{T}$ be the term algebra $\mathcal{T} = Terms(\Sigma, \Gamma_\infty)$. We let $\sim$ be the binary relation on $\mathcal{T}$ given by $M \sim N$ iff $\mathcal{E} \vdash M = N[\Gamma]$ for some finite $\Gamma \subseteq \Gamma_\infty$. It is easy to check that $\sim$ is a congruence relation on $\mathcal{T}$. It remains to show that for the quotient algebra $\mathcal{A} = \mathcal{T}/{\sim}$, we have $\mathcal{E} = Th(\mathcal{A})$. The steps of the argument are essentially the same as in the proof of Theorem 3.4.24. ■

Exercise 3.4.30 Show that least model completeness implies deductive completeness. Conclude that with rule (*nonempty*), we have soundness and deductive completeness for multi-sorted algebras without empty carriers.

Exercise 3.4.31 Finish the proof of Theorem 3.4.28 by completing the argument that $\mathcal{E} = Th(\mathcal{A})$.

3.5 Homomorphisms and Initiality

3.5.1 Homomorphisms and Isomorphisms

A homomorphism is a structure-preserving map from one algebra to another. We will use homomorphisms primarily as a way of defining initial algebras, developing some additional properties in the exercises.

For multi-sorted algebras, a *homomorphism* $h\colon \mathcal{A} \to \mathcal{B}$ *from* Σ*-algebra* $\mathcal{A}$ *to* Σ*-algebra* $\mathcal{B}$ is a family of maps $h = \{h^s \mid s \in S\}$ indexed by sorts such that

$$h^s(f^{\mathcal{A}}(a_1, \ldots, a_k)) = f^{\mathcal{B}}(h^{s_1}a_1, \ldots, h^{s_k}a_k)$$

for every function symbol $f\colon s_1 \times \ldots \times s_k \to s$ of Σ. Intuitively, we may think of a homomorphism h from $\mathcal{A}$ to $\mathcal{B}$ as a way of "translating" from values of $\mathcal{A}$ to values of $\mathcal{B}$. This intuition is supported by the way homomorphisms preserve meanings of terms, discussed below.

A trivial example of a homomorphism is the identity map from $\mathcal{A}$ to $\mathcal{A}$. For an algebra with more than one sort, the identity homomorphism $Id_{\mathcal{A}}$ from $\mathcal{A}$ to $\mathcal{A}$ is a family of functions $Id_{\mathcal{A}} = \{id^s\}$ with $id^s\colon A^s \to A^s$ the identity function on the carrier for sort s. Two more examples are the homomorphism from natural numbers to natural numbers modulo k, and the meaning function for the term algebra to any algebra, discussed in Examples 3.5.1 and 3.5.2.

Example 3.5.1 The function from natural numbers to natural numbers modulo k that sends each $n \in \mathcal{N}$ to the integer $n \bmod k$ is a homomorphism. More specifically, let $\mathcal{N} = \langle \mathcal{N}, 0, 1, + \rangle$ be the usual natural numbers with $0, 1, +$ and let $\sim$ be equivalence modulo k. Then the map h sending $n \in \mathcal{N}$ to its equivalence class $[n]_\sim$ is a homomorphism from $\mathcal{N}$ to $\mathcal{N}/\sim$ since we have

$$h(0) = 0^{\mathcal{N}/\sim} = [0]$$

$$h(n+m) = h(n) +^{\mathcal{N}/\sim} h(m) = [n+m]$$

In general, there is a homomorphism from any algebra $\mathcal{A}$ to any of its quotients $\mathcal{A}/\sim$, defined in exactly this way. For a general statement, see Exercise 3.5.7. ■

Example 3.5.2 The meaning function is a homomorphism from the term algebra to any algebra. More specifically, let $\mathcal{A}$ be any Σ algebra and let $\mathcal{T} = Terms(\Sigma, \Gamma)$ be any term algebra over Σ. If η is an $\mathcal{A}$ environment satisfying Γ, then we can define a homomorphism $h: \mathcal{T} \rightarrow \mathcal{A}$ by

$$h(M) = \mathcal{A}[\![M]\!]\eta$$

It is easy to see that this is a homomorphism since the definition of the meaning of a term in an algebra gives us

$$\begin{aligned} h(f M_1 \ldots M_k) &= \mathcal{A}[\![f M_1 \ldots M_k]\!]\eta = f^{\mathcal{A}}(\mathcal{A}[\![M_1]\!]\eta, \ldots, \mathcal{A}[\![M_k]\!]\eta) \\ &= f^{\mathcal{A}}(h(M_1), \ldots, h(M_k)) \end{aligned}$$

by definition. More generally, we can define a homomorphism from the quotient *Terms* $(\Sigma, \Gamma)/\sim_{\mathcal{E},\Gamma}$ to an algebra $\mathcal{A}$ satisfying $\mathcal{E}$ by similar means. This will be used in the proof of Proposition 3.5.11.

To state the connection between homomorphisms and meaning precisely, we need a "translation" of environments. If $h: \mathcal{A} \rightarrow \mathcal{B}$ and η is an environment for $\mathcal{A}$, then we define the $\mathcal{B}$-environment η^h by

$$\eta^h(x) = h(\eta(x))$$

for any variable x. It is easy to see that if η satisfies some sort assignment Γ, so does η^h.

Lemma 3.5.3 Let $h: \mathcal{A} \rightarrow \mathcal{B}$ be any homomorphism and η any environment for $\mathcal{A}$ satisfying sort assignment Γ. Then for any term $M \in Terms^s(\Sigma, \Gamma)$, we have

$$h(\mathcal{A}[\![M]\!]\eta) = \mathcal{B}[\![M]\!]\eta^h$$

A special case is that if M does not contain any variables, then $\mathcal{B}[\![M]\!]\eta^h$ does not depend on the environment η^h and $h(\mathcal{A}[\![M]\!]) = \mathcal{B}[\![M]\!]$ is uniquely determined.

Proof The proof is a straightforward induction on terms. The variable case follows from the definition of η^h. For a compound term $f M_1 \ldots M_k$, we assume inductively that $h(\mathcal{A}[\![M_i]\!]\eta) = \mathcal{B}[\![M]\!]\eta^h$. By the definition of homomorphism, we must have

$$\begin{aligned} h(\mathcal{A}[\![f M_1 \ldots M_k]\!]\eta) &= f^{\mathcal{B}}(h(\mathcal{A}[\![M_1]\!]\eta), \ldots, h(\mathcal{A}[\![M_k]\!]\eta)) \\ &= f^{\mathcal{B}}(\mathcal{B}[\![M_1]\!]\eta^h, \ldots, \mathcal{B}[\![M_k]\!]\eta^h). \end{aligned}$$

This proves the lemma. ∎

If $h: \mathcal{A} \rightarrow \mathcal{B}$ and $k: \mathcal{B} \rightarrow \mathcal{C}$ are homomorphisms of Σ-algebras, then the composition $k \circ h: \mathcal{A} \rightarrow \mathcal{C}$ is the family of maps $(k \circ h)^s = k^s \circ h^s$ obtained by composing maps for each sort. A useful fact is that the composition of two homomorphisms is always a homomorphism.

Lemma 3.5.4 If $h\colon \mathcal{A} \to \mathcal{B}$ and $k\colon \mathcal{B} \to \mathcal{C}$ are homomorphisms of Σ-algebras, then the composition $k \circ h\colon \mathcal{A} \to \mathcal{C}$ is a homomorphism.

The proof is Exercise 3.5.5 below.

A bijective (one-to-one and onto) homomorphism is called an *isomorphism;* when there is an isomorphism from $\mathcal{A}$ to $\mathcal{B}$, we say $\mathcal{A}$ and $\mathcal{B}$ are *isomorphic* and write $\mathcal{A} \cong \mathcal{B}$. Intuitively, an isomorphism just "renames" elements without changing the algebraic structure. Consequently, we think of isomorphic algebras as "essentially the same." Using Lemma 3.5.3, it is easy to show that isomorphic algebras satisfy the same equations, as outlined in Exercise 3.5.6 below.

Exercise 3.5.5 Show that the composition of two homomorphisms is a homomorphism.

Exercise 3.5.6 Use Lemma 3.5.3 to prove the following connections between homomorphisms and equations.

(a) If h is a surjective homomorphism from $\mathcal{A}$ to $\mathcal{B}$, *i.e.*, for every $b \in B^s$ there is some $a \in A^s$ with $h^s(a) = b$, then $Th(\mathcal{A}) \subseteq Th(\mathcal{B})$.

(b) If $\mathcal{A}$ and $\mathcal{B}$ are isomorphic, then $Th(\mathcal{A}) = Th(\mathcal{B})$.

(c) Show that "surjective" is essential in part *(a)* by finding algebras $\mathcal{A}$ and $\mathcal{B}$ for the same signature with homomorphism h from $\mathcal{A}$ to $\mathcal{B}$, but such that $Th(\mathcal{A})$ is not a subset of $Th(\mathcal{B})$.

Exercise 3.5.7 Prove that there is a surjective homomorphism from $\mathcal{A}$ to $\mathcal{B}$ (see Exercise 3.5.6 above) iff $\mathcal{B}$ is isomorphic to $\mathcal{A}/{\sim}$ for some congruence relation $\sim$. Use the result of Exercise 3.5.6 to conclude that $Th(\mathcal{A}) \subseteq Th(\mathcal{A}/{\sim})$ for any congruence $\sim$ on $\mathcal{A}$.

3.5.2 Initial Algebras

Initial algebras are important in the study of algebraic data types because they often coincide with the "intended" or "standard" implementation of an algebraic specification. If $\mathcal{C}$ is a class of Σ-algebras and $\mathcal{A} \in \mathcal{C}$, then $\mathcal{A}$ *is initial for* $\mathcal{C}$ if, for every $\mathcal{B} \in \mathcal{C}$, there is a *unique* homomorphism $h\colon \mathcal{A} \to \mathcal{B}$. If we regard a homomorphism $h\colon \mathcal{A} \to \mathcal{B}$ as a "translation" from $\mathcal{A}$ to $\mathcal{B}$, then an initial algebra is "typical" in that we may translate from the initial algebra to all other algebras in the class. An initial algebra has as few nonempty sorts as possible, since every element of an initial algebra must correspond (via some homomorphism) to an element of every other algebra. Subject to this condition, an initial algebra satisfies as few equations as possible, by Lemma 3.5.3. The main results of this section are Proposition 3.5.11, which states that quotients of term algebras are initial, and Proposition 3.5.14 describing the equational theory of an initial algebra.

Example 3.5.8 Consider the signature Σ_0 with single sort *nat*, for natural numbers, and function symbols $0\colon nat$ and $S\colon nat \to nat$, for successor. Let $\mathcal{C}$ be the class of all Σ_0 algebras. An initial algebra for $\mathcal{C}$ is the term algebra $\mathcal{T} = Terms(\Sigma_0, \emptyset)$ whose carrier is the collection of variable-free terms 0, $S0$, $S(S0)$, ..., S^k0, ... The single proper function of this algebra, S, maps $S^k0 \mapsto S^{k+1}0$. This algebra has only as many elements as are minimally required to interpret all function symbols, and satisfies as few equations as possible between these elements.

The first step in showing that $\mathcal{T}$ is initial in $\mathcal{C}$ is to show that there is a homomorphism from the term algebra to any other algebra in $\mathcal{C}$. However, as shown in Example 3.5.2, the meaning function $\mathcal{A}[\![\cdot]\!]$ is a homomorphism from $\mathcal{T}$ to any other Σ-algebra $\mathcal{A}$. The remaining step in proving that $\mathcal{T}$ is initial is to show that this is the only homomorphism. But if h is any homomorphism from $\mathcal{T}$ to Σ-algebra $\mathcal{A}$, then by Lemma 3.5.3, h is identical to the meaning function. Note that this argument fails for a term algebra containing terms with variables.

Before proceeding, we show that all initial algebras of any class are isomorphic. Since isomorphic algebras are essentially the same, this means that the initial algebra of any class, if it exists, is unique.

Lemma 3.5.9 Suppose $h\colon \mathcal{A} \to \mathcal{B}$ and $k\colon \mathcal{B} \to \mathcal{A}$ are homomorphisms with $h \circ k = Id_{\mathcal{B}}$ and $k \circ h = Id_{\mathcal{A}}$. Then $\mathcal{A}$ and $\mathcal{B}$ are isomorphic.

Proof The proof only uses the fact that h and k are sort-indexed families of functions, and does not really depend on h and k being homomorphisms. We simply show that for each sort s, the function h^s is bijective. Clearly h must be onto, since k^s maps every $x \in B^s$ back to some $y \in A^s$ with $h^s(y) = x$. By similar reasoning, we can see that h^s must be one-to-one. ∎

Proposition 3.5.10 If $\mathcal{A}$ and $\mathcal{B}$ are initial algebras for some class $\mathcal{C}$, then $\mathcal{A}$ and $\mathcal{B}$ are isomorphic.

Proof Suppose $\mathcal{A}$ and $\mathcal{B}$ are initial algebras in class $\mathcal{C}$. This means that there exist homomorphisms $h\colon \mathcal{A} \to \mathcal{B}$ and $k\colon \mathcal{B} \to \mathcal{A}$. By Lemma 3.5.9, it suffices to show that $h \circ k = Id_{\mathcal{B}}$ and $k \circ h = Id_{\mathcal{A}}$.

By Lemma 3.5.4, $h \circ k$ and $k \circ h$ are both homomorphisms. In addition, by initiality, these are the only homomorphisms from $\mathcal{A}$ to $\mathcal{A}$ and $\mathcal{B}$ to $\mathcal{B}$. But the identity maps are also homomorphisms from $\mathcal{A}$ to $\mathcal{A}$ and $\mathcal{B}$ to $\mathcal{B}$, so both compositions must produce identity homomorphisms. ∎

In writing the symbols *nat*, $0{:}\,nat$ and $S{:}\,nat \to nat$, as in Example 3.5.8, we usually think of the natural numbers, the number 0, and the successor function. This is the "intended model" of the signature. Although the phrase "intended model" is often used in logic, it has no technical meaning. Rather, it is a description of how we think about some formal syntax. From Example 3.5.8, we see that the initial algebra for signature Σ_0 is isomorphic to the intended model of this signature. This is a coincidence we will often observe for initial algebras. Although it is difficult to say precisely why initial algebras often turn out to be our intended models, we will see that they are generated inductively from the symbols of the signature. Since many familiar structures, such as the integers, are defined inductively, these structures are initial algebras. The reader familiar with mathematical logic will recognize that since the natural numbers cannot be characterized by any set of first-order formulas, initiality is not a first-order property. The natural translation of initiality into formal logic is second-order, since the initial algebra is defined by quantifying over all algebras, and hence all possible carriers and functions.

If $\mathcal{E}$ is a set of Σ-equations, we say $\mathcal{A}$ is *initial for* $\mathcal{E}$ if $\mathcal{A}$ is initial in the class of all Σ-algebras satisfying $\mathcal{E}$. We may show that for any set $\mathcal{E}$ of Σ-equations, the algebra $\mathit{Terms}(\Sigma, \emptyset)/\sim_{\mathcal{E},\emptyset}$ of variable-free terms modulo provable equality is initial. It follows that every algebraic specification has an initial algebra.

Proposition 3.5.11 Let $\mathcal{E}$ be any set of Σ-equations and let $\mathcal{A} = \mathit{Terms}(\Sigma, \emptyset)/\sim_{\mathcal{E},\emptyset}$ be the algebra of variable-free terms, modulo provable equality. Then $\mathcal{A}$ is an initial algebra for $\mathcal{E}$.

In the special case that $\mathcal{E}$ is the empty set of equations, it is easy to see that $\mathit{Terms}\,(\Sigma, \emptyset)/\sim_{\mathcal{E},\emptyset}$ is isomorphic to $\mathit{Terms}\,(\Sigma, \emptyset)$. It follows that the term algebra is initial in the class of all Σ algebras.

Proof It is easy to see, by properties of term algebras and quotients, that every equation provable from $\mathcal{E}$ holds in $\mathcal{A}$. It remains to show that there is a unique homomorphism from $\mathcal{A}$ to any other algebra satisfying $\mathcal{E}$.

Let $\mathcal{B}$ be any algebra satisfying $\mathcal{E}$. For any equivalence class $[M]$ in $\mathcal{A}$, let $h(M)$ be the meaning $\mathcal{B}[\![M]\!]$ of variable-free term M in $\mathcal{B}$. Since $\mathcal{B}$ satisfies $\mathcal{E}$, this map is well defined. It also easy to check that h is a homomorphism. By Lemma 3.5.3, any other homomorphism $h'{:}\,\mathcal{A} \to \mathcal{B}$ must have the same value as h, and so h is the unique homomorphism from $\mathcal{A}$ to $\mathcal{B}$. ∎

The following example contains an extended discussion of natural numbers as an initial algebra. Additional examples may be found in Section 3.6.

Example 3.5.12 Consider the signature Σ_1 with single sort *nat*, for natural numbers, and function symbols $0: nat$, $S: nat \rightarrow nat$ and $+: nat \times nat \rightarrow nat$. (This is an extension of the signature Σ_0 of Example 3.5.8.) Let $\mathcal{E}$ be the set of equations

$$x + 0 \quad = x$$

$$x + (Sy) = S(x + y),$$

where we omit sort assignments since there is only one sort. Let $\mathcal{C}$ be the class of all Σ_1 algebras satisfying $\mathcal{E}$.

The initial algebra of $\mathcal{C}$ may be described using some facts about $\mathcal{E}$. It is easy to show that for any terms of the form S^k0 and $S^\ell 0$, we can prove $S^k0 + S^\ell 0 = S^{k+\ell}$ from $\mathcal{E}$. This may be established by induction on the natural number ℓ. It follows that for any variable-free term M over this signature, we can prove $M = S^k0$ for some natural number k. Since $\mathcal{E}$ is satisfied by the standard model of the natural numbers with 0, S, $+$, we can also see that no equation $S^k0 = S^\ell 0$ is provable from $\mathcal{E}$, unless $k = \ell$. Therefore, each equivalence class of variable-free terms contains exactly one term of the form S^k0.

Since we have a bijective correspondence between equivalence classes and terms of the form S^k0, we can think of the carrier of the initial term algebra as the collection of variable-free terms $0, S0, S(S0), \ldots, S^k0, \ldots$. This is the same as the initial algebra in Example 3.5.8. It is easy to see that in this algebra, the function S maps $S^k0 \mapsto S^{k+1}0$, and $+$ maps $(S^k0, S^\ell 0) \mapsto S^{k+\ell}0$. Thus the initial algebra is isomorphic to the standard model for this signature, the usual natural numbers with successor and addition.

The initial algebra for this specification may be contrasted with algebras that have more or fewer elements. Generally speaking, we would expect algebras with more elements to have what is sometimes called "junk," since the additional elements would not be definable by terms, and therefore would not arise in computation over the algebra. An algebra with fewer elements would have what is sometimes called "confusion" since distinct elements that are not provably equal would be identified. We illustrate both of these possibilities by specific algebras. The proof that the algebras below are not initial is left as Exercise 3.5.15.

An example of an algebra with more elements than the initial algebra is the algebra, $\mathcal{Z}$, of positive and negative integers. Another example may be constructed by adding "infinite" integers to $\mathcal{N}$. This second example is a little more general, since we can also construct non-initial algebras for list, set, tree and other specifications by including infinite lists, sets or trees. For Σ_1, the non-initial algebra $\mathcal{A} = \langle A^{nat}, 0^{\mathcal{A}}, S^{\mathcal{A}}, +^{\mathcal{A}} \rangle$ has

$$A^{nat} = (\{0\} \times \mathcal{N}) \cup (\{1\} \times \mathcal{Z})$$

where $\mathcal{N}$ is the set of natural numbers and $\mathcal{Z}$ is the set of positive and negative integers. Intuitively, A^{nat} contains one "copy" of the natural numbers, each in the form of a pair $\langle 0, n\rangle$, and one "copy" of the positive and negative integers, each in the form of a pair $\langle 1, n\rangle$. We can visualize this set by arranging all of the natural numbers in an infinite line to the left of the integers.

$$0, 1, 2, 3, \ldots \quad \ldots, -3, -2, -1, 0, 1, 2, 3, \ldots$$

We think of the natural numbers on the left as "small" or "finite" numbers, and the integers on the right as "large" or "infinite" numbers since they are considered larger than all of the finite natural numbers. We interpret $0^{\mathcal{A}}$ as the zero at the far left. The successor of any number is the number to its right in this picture. If we add two numbers from the same part, then we get the standard result (either finite or infinite). If we add a finite number to an infinite one, the result is infinite. This is given formally by the following definitions:

$$0^{\mathcal{A}} = \langle 0, 0\rangle$$

$$S^{\mathcal{A}}\langle i, n\rangle = \langle i, n+1\rangle$$

$$\langle i, n\rangle +^{\mathcal{A}} \langle j, m\rangle = \langle \max(i, j), n+m\rangle$$

We leave it to the reader to check that the axioms hold for this algebra. The reason why we might consider the subset $(\{1\} \times \mathcal{Z})$ of A^{nat} "junk" is that this set of "infinite" numbers is not needed to satisfy the axioms, and none are definable by variable-free terms. Since the initial algebra only contains elements definable by variable-free terms, such elements do not appear in the initial algebra.

An example of an algebra with fewer elements than the initial algebra is the natural numbers modulo k for any natural number k. This algebra was discussed in Exercise 3.4.25 and Example 3.5.1. The reader may easily check that the axioms of our specification hold in this algebra. The reason we might consider the integers modulo k to have some "confusion" is that distinct numerals that are not provably equal in the specification are given the same value. In contrast, we will see that two variable-free terms have the same value in the initial algebra only if they are provably equal. ∎

It is important to realize that the initial algebra for a set $\mathcal{E}$ of equations may satisfy additional equations not provable from $\mathcal{E}$. Intuitively, the reason is that adding elements to an algebra may cause an equation with variables to become false, since a new element may conflict with a property shared by all the other elements. Since the carrier of an initial algebra is as small as possible (given the signature), the initial algebra for $\mathcal{E}$ is likely to satisfy some equations that do not hold in other algebras satisfying $\mathcal{E}$ that have more elements. A trivial example occurs with a signature having only one sort and two constants

a and b. The initial algebra satisfying $a = b$ will have only one element. Consequently, the initial algebra satisfies the equation $x = y$. However, the equation $x = y$ with variables is not semantically implied by the equation $a = b$ between constants since there are larger algebras satisfying $a = b$ but not $x = y$. A more natural example is given below.

Example 3.5.13 The equation saying that $+$ is commutative holds in the initial algebra described in Example 3.5.12, even though commutativity is not provable from the set of equations given there. It is easy to see that addition is commutative in the initial algebra, since for any variable-free terms M and N, we have $\mathcal{E} \vdash M = S^k 0$ and $\mathcal{E} \vdash N = S^\ell 0$ for some k, ℓ, and so $\mathcal{E} \vdash M + N = S^{k+l} 0 = N + M$. However, the equation $x + y = y + x$ is *not* provable from $\mathcal{E}$. This may be demonstrated by giving an algebra that satisfies $\mathcal{E}$, but has a non-commutative interpretation of $+$. Rather than give a term algebra, we will use an algebra whose elements are functions. This gives some illustration of the range of algebras satisfying the axioms for successor and addition.

Let X be any set with at least two elements, and let A^{nat} be the collection of all functions $f: X \to X$. Let $0^\mathcal{A}$ be the identity function on X, let $S^\mathcal{A}$ be the identity map on functions in A^{nat}, and let $+^\mathcal{A}$ be function composition. It is easy to check that the algebra $\mathcal{A} = \langle A^{nat}, 0^\mathcal{A}, S^\mathcal{A}, +^\mathcal{A} \rangle$ satisfies $\mathcal{E}$. In particular, we have

$$S^\mathcal{A}(f +^\mathcal{A} g) = f \circ g = f \circ S^\mathcal{A}(g) = f +^\mathcal{A} S^\mathcal{A}(g)$$

since $S^\mathcal{A}$ is the identity map on functions. However, the commutativity axioms for $+$ fails in this algebra since function composition is not commutative. More specifically, since X has at least two elements, we can find two functions $f, g: X \to X$ such that $f \circ g \neq g \circ f$.

■

A variable-free term is often called a *ground term.* If S is a substitution mapping every variable in Γ to a ground term over Σ, we say S *is a* Σ, Γ*-ground substitution.* If $M \in Terms^s(\Sigma, \Gamma)$ and S is a Σ, Γ-ground substitution, we say SM is a *ground instance* of M. Similarly, if $M = N[\Gamma]$ is an equation between terms of $Terms^s(\Sigma, \Gamma)$, and S is a Σ, Γ-ground substitution, we say $SM = SN[\emptyset]$ is a *ground instance* of $M = N[\Gamma]$. The following proposition characterizes the equations that hold in an initial algebra.

Proposition 3.5.14 Let $\mathcal{E}$ be a set of Σ-equations and $\mathcal{A}$ be the initial algebra for $\mathcal{E}$. For any Σ-equation $M = N[\Gamma]$, the following three conditions are equivalent:

(i) $\mathcal{A}$ satisfies $M = N[\Gamma]$,

(ii) $\mathcal{A}$ satisfies every ground instance of $M = N[\Gamma]$,

(iii) Every ground instance of $M = N[\Gamma]$ is provable from $\mathcal{E}$. ■

Proof We assume, without loss of generality, that the initial algebra $\mathcal{A}$ is *Terms* $(\Sigma, \emptyset)/\sim_{\mathcal{E},\emptyset}$. We will use the fact that a Σ, Γ-ground substitution is exactly the same as a $\mathcal{T} = \mathit{Terms}(\Sigma, \emptyset)$ environment η satisfying Γ.

Consider any equation $M = N[\Gamma]$. This equation is satisfied in $\mathcal{A}$ iff, for every $\mathcal{T}$ environment η satisfying Γ, we have $\mathcal{A}[\![M]\!]\eta_\sim = \mathcal{A}[\![N]\!]\eta_\sim$. But by Lemmas 3.4.6 and 3.4.22, this is equivalent to

$$[\eta M]_\sim = [\mathcal{T}[\![M]\!]\eta]_\sim = [\mathcal{T}[\![N]\!]\eta]_\sim = [\eta N]_\sim.$$

Since these equivalence classes of terms are determined by provability from $\mathcal{E}$, we have $\mathcal{A}, \eta_\sim \models M = N[\Gamma]$ iff $\mathcal{E} \vdash \eta M = \eta N$. This shows that *(i)* and *(iii)* are equivalent.

We can see that *(ii)* and *(iii)* are equivalent by noting that if S is any Σ, Γ-ground substitution, then $\mathcal{A}[\![SM]\!]$ does not depend on any environment. Therefore $\mathcal{A}[\![SM]\!] = [SM]_\sim$, and similarly for N. Reasoning as above, it follows that $\mathcal{A}$ satisfies every ground instance of $M = N[\Gamma]$ iff every ground $SM = SN$ is provable from $\mathcal{E}$.

Exercise 3.5.15 Let $\mathcal{A}_1$ be the standard, initial algebra of natural numbers for signature Σ_1 of Example 3.5.12, let $\mathcal{A}_2$ be the algebra (described in Example 3.5.12) with infinite integers added and let $\mathcal{A}_3$ be the algebra of natural numbers modulo k, for some k (also discussed in Example 3.5.12). Show that neither $\mathcal{A}_2$ nor $\mathcal{A}_3$ is initial by showing there is more than one homomorphism $\mathcal{A}_2 \to \mathcal{A}_1$ and no homomorphism $\mathcal{A}_3 \to \mathcal{A}_1$.

Exercise 3.5.16 Consider the signature Σ_2 with single sort *nat*, for natural numbers, and function symbols $0\colon nat$, $S\colon nat \to nat$ and $+, *\colon nat \times nat \to nat$. (This is an extension of the signature Σ_1 of Example 3.5.12.) Let $\mathcal{E}$ be the set of equations

$$\begin{aligned}
x + 0 &= x, \\
x + (Sy) &= S(x + y), \\
x * 0 &= 0, \\
x * (Sy) &= x * y + x,
\end{aligned}$$

where we omit sort assignments since there is only one sort. Let $\mathcal{C}$ be the class of all Σ_2 algebras satisfying $\mathcal{E}$.

(a) Show that for any variable-free term M over this signature, we can prove $M = S^k 0$ from $\mathcal{E}$, for some natural number k.

(b) Use Soundness (Theorem 3.4.13) and part *(a)* to show that if we equate terms provably equal from $\mathcal{E}$, each equivalence class of variable-free terms contains exactly one term of the form $S^k 0$.

(c) Give a description of the initial algebra for class $\mathcal{C}$, along the lines of the description given in Example 3.5.12. Do not make any unsupported assertions.

(d) Show that given an equation E over signature Σ_2, it is co-r.e. to determine whether E holds in the initial algebra satisfying $\mathcal{E}$. (In other words, show that there is a procedure which halts with output "no" whenever E does *not* hold in the initial algebra. This procedure does not have to halt if E is satisfied by the initial algebra.)

3.6 Algebraic Data Types

3.6.1 Specification and Data Abstraction

In discussing natural numbers and boolean expressions in PCF, we generally have the standard mathematical structures of the natural numbers and booleans in mind. For most of us, it is hard to regard a set of axioms as "defining" the natural numbers; we know too much about natural numbers already. However, this is not the case for many other datatypes in programming. For priority queues and symbol tables, for example, there is no standard mathematical construction, and no single standard computer implementation. Many different implementations are used in practice. Since we commonly describe these datatypes by listing the operations and describing their behavior, these structures are defined axiomatically, rather than by mathematical construction. The advantage of an axiomatic approach in practice, whether or not we write our axioms in a formal language, is that we may specify precisely what we want from every implementation, without biasing our thinking towards one implementation or another. Moreover, as mentioned in Section 3.2, a specification provides useful guidelines when we implement a datatype. A well-written specification tells an implementor exactly what is assumed in the rest of the program, without otherwise constraining implementation decisions.

Recall that a pair $Spec = \langle \Sigma, \mathcal{E} \rangle$ consisting of a signature Σ and a set $\mathcal{E}$ of Σ-equations is called an *algebraic specification.* Some general properties of algebraic specifications may be illustrated using the example of natural numbers and booleans in PCF. Without saying how PCF is actually implemented, the algebraic specification in Section 2.2.2 tells us which numeric and boolean expressions must have equal values. From these equational axioms, we may prove equations between other PCF expressions, such as functions. The equational axioms also determine a set of reduction rules, which let us simulate an interpreter using only substitution and symbol manipulation. Although it is difficult to say when we have "enough" axioms about an arbitrary datatype, there is some comfort in the case of natural numbers and booleans. The reader familiar with mathematical logic will know that no first-order (let alone equational) axioms characterize the natural numbers exactly. How-

Table 3.4
A Specification for *set, nat* and *bool*.

sorts:	*set, nat, bool*
fctns:	$0, 1, 2, \ldots : nat$
	$+ : nat \times nat \to nat$
	$Eq?: nat \times nat \to bool$
	$true, false : bool$
	$empty : set$
	$insert : nat \times set \to set$
	$union : set \times set \to set$
	$ismem? : nat \times set \to bool$
	$cond_n : bool \times nat \times nat \to nat$
	$cond_b : bool \times bool \times bool \to bool$
	$cond_s : bool \times set \times set \to set$
eqns:	$[x, y: nat,\ s, s' : set,\ u, v : bool]$
	$0 + 0 = 0,\ 0 + 1 = 1, 1 + 1 = 2, \ldots$
	$Eq?\, x\, x = true$
	$Eq?\, 0\, 1 = false,\ Eq?\, 0\, 2 = false, \ldots$
	$ismem?\, x\ empty = false$
	$ismem?\, x\ (insert\ y\ s) = \texttt{if}\ Eq?\, x\, y\ \texttt{then}\ true\ \texttt{else}\ ismem?\, x\, s$
	$union\ empty\ s = s$
	$union\ (insert\ y\ s)\ s' = insert\ y\ (union\ s\ s')$
	$cond_n\ true\ x\ y = x$
	$cond_n\ false\ x\ y = y$
	$cond_b\ true\ u\ v = u$
	$cond_b\ false\ u\ v = v$
	$cond_s\ true\ s\ s' = s$
	$cond_s\ false\ s\ s' = s'$

ever, the initial algebra for the PCF specification is the standard algebra of natural numbers and booleans. This may be interpreted as meaning that we have "enough" axioms. A related way of seeing that we have enough axioms is to examine the reduction rules and show that every algebraic term for a natural number that does not contain variables may be simplified to one of the numerals $0, 1, 2, 3, \ldots$. Further discussion of this property appears in the section on algebraic rewrite rules. In the remainder of this section we will discuss some general aspects of the axiomatic approach to datatypes.

A convenient example is the datatype of finite sets with membership test, union and an insert operation. We may extend PCF with sets by adding a *set* sort to the multi-sorted algebra of *nat* and *bool*. A specification is given in Table 3.4.

Intuitively, a set is either *empty,* or obtained by *insert*ing a natural number into a set. We test whether a natural number x is an element of a set s using *ismem?*xs. In keeping with the syntax of PCF, we regard $x + y$ as syntactic sugar for $+xy$, the expression `if` M `then` N `else` P as syntactic sugar for $cond_n MNP$ if N and P are natural number expressions, and similarly for boolean and set conditionals. In the context of PCF, it is natural to think of the set part of this specification as defining sets from natural numbers and booleans. Almost any programming language would allow us to read and write natural numbers and booleans, referring to them by their standard names. However, finite sets do not have a standard print representation, and are not as likely to be used as input or output values. Since our only access to elements of this datatype is through the functions *empty, insert* and *ismem?,* we do not really care how sets are represented internally. Except for efficiency, it does not matter whether sets are implemented using bit vectors, arrays, linked lists, or any of a number of other data structures (*c.f.* [AHU83]). All we really care about is the behavior of sequences of operations that give natural number or boolean results. This suggests that our *set* datatype is *abstract,* in the sense of "defined axiomatically." Some general principles of data abstraction are listed below.

• An abstract datatype is *defined* by its specification. A program using a datatype should only depend on properties guaranteed by the specification, and not on properties of any particular implementation.

• Only the functions that are given as part of the datatype definition may be applied to elements of the datatype. (This principle can be violated only by writing programs that are not well-typed.) Consequently, all that matters about a datatype are the properties we may observe by applying combinations of functions to produce "observable" values like booleans or natural numbers.

• For many common examples, the functions of a data type may be partitioned into constructors, operators and observers. Intuitively, a *constructor* is a function that builds a new element of a datatype, an *operator* is a function on the datatype that produces no new elements, and an *observer* returns elements of some other datatype. We may reason about the datatype using induction on the constructors.

• There are criteria for determining whether an implementation correctly satisfies a specification. However, there are several approaches, and we will not go into this topic in any detail.

In the set example of Table 3.4, the set constructors are *empty* and *insert,* since every set may be produced by adding elements to the empty set. However, *union* is an operator, since the result of any set union could have been produced by inserting elements into the empty set; *union* does not produce any "new" sets. The function *ismem?* is an observer, since this function produces boolean values from sets. The classification of functions into constructors, operators and observers may seem a little fuzzy, but may be made precise using initial algebras. We will discuss this in the next section and give a precise argument in Example 3.6.1.

3.6.2 Initial Algebra Semantics and Datatype Induction

Several forms of "semantics" appear in the literature on algebraic specification. Put formally, each "semantics" consists of a condition saying when an algebra models a specification. The most general semantics, often called *loose semantics,* is the standard mathematical view considered so far in this chapter: the algebras that model a specification are exactly the algebras that satisfy the set of equations given in the specification. The most commonly used alternative is called *initial algebra semantics.* In the initial algebra semantics, the algebras that model a specification are all of its initial algebras. Since these are all isomorphic, initial algebra semantics essentially gives a unique "standard" model for each specification. While there are good reasons to consider more than the initial algebra, it is often insightful to examine the initial algebras for a specification. In particular, initial algebras give us a direct way of understanding a useful form of induction. Some alternative semantics are given in Exercises 3.6.5 and 3.6.6.

Intuitively, the initial algebra for an algebraic specification is an algebra that contains only as many elements as are minimally required. For example, the initial algebra for natural number and boolean expressions of PCF contains only elements that are named by the numerals, $0, 1, 2, \ldots,$ and the boolean constants *true* and *false*. In contrast, an arbitrary algebra for this specification might have "extra" elements such as integers that behave as if they are "infinite." The second important property of an initial algebra is that it satisfies all of the logical consequences of the equational axioms, and no other "accidental" equations between the elements of the algebra. The initial algebra cannot be axiomatized equationally, since we cannot derive *in*equations as logical consequences of equations. This is an advantage of the initial algebra approach since we want any implementation of integer arithmetic to satisfy the inequation $0 \neq 1$, for example. The two main properties of initial algebras are summarized by the slogans

- *No junk,* meaning that there are no extra elements which cannot be named by algebraic terms.
- *No confusion,* meaning no elements are identified unless this is required by the specification.

Since we have proved that the term algebra $Terms(\Sigma, \emptyset)/\sim_{\mathcal{E},\emptyset}$ is initial for specification $\langle \Sigma, \mathcal{E} \rangle$, we can explain the intuitive slogans above in more precise terms.

- *No junk:* the initial algebra contains only elements definable by ground terms.
- *No confusion:* the initial algebra satisfies only the provable equations between ground terms.

An important consequence is that the initial algebra supports a form of induction on the constructors of the datatype. This is called *datatype induction.* In the remainder of this section we illustrate datatype induction by example.

Before proceeding, we should make the distinction between constructors and other functions more precise. Formally, a set F_0 of function symbols from $Spec = \langle \Sigma, \mathcal{E} \rangle$ is a *set of constructors* if F_0 is a set of function symbols such that every equivalence class of $Terms(\Sigma, \emptyset)/\sim_{\mathcal{E},\emptyset}$ is the equivalence class of some variable-free term over only the function symbols in F_0. It is easy to see that we may prove properties of an initial algebra by induction on constructors, since every element of the algebra is covered in this way. Although our induction will be simpler if we choose the smallest set of constructors possible, there is no harm in considering more constructors than necessary. This means that in the absence of any insight, we can use induction on all terms to prove properties of the initial algebra for some specification.

Example 3.6.1 This example discusses the set specification in Table 3.4, which appears in Section 3.6.1. In discussing this specification, we claimed informally that the functions *empty* and *insert* are constructors, *union* is an operator, and *ismem?* is an observer. With a precise definition of constructor, we are now in a position to prove that *empty* and *insert* form a set of constructors.

We must show that every equivalence class of terms of sort *set* in the initial algebra has an element (term) written using only *insert, empty*, and constants of sort *nat*. We prove this by induction on the structure of terms. To be strictly correct we should simultaneously prove that every equivalence class of terms of sort *bool* or *nat* in the initial algebra contains *true*, *false* or one of the *nat* constants $0, 1, 2, \ldots$. However, since the argument for these other sorts does not involve any additional ideas, we will do the induction for terms of sort *set* only. The base case is the term *empty* which is one of the constructors. For the induction step, assume that M and N are terms of sort *set* expressible with constructors, and that A and B are terms of sort *nat* and *bool*. Then we can create more complex *set* terms in three ways. The term $insert A M$ is expressible using constructors and constants since M is, and A is expressible by one of the *nat* constants. The term $cond_s B M N$ is provably equivalent to either M or N, depending on whether B is equivalent to *true* or *false*, and hence expressible by the inductive hypothesis. The *union* case is the most difficult. Let P be the term $union M N$. Since M is expressible with constructors, M is either provably equivalent to *empty* or $insert a Q$, where a is a *nat* constant and Q is a *set*. In the former case, P is equivalent to N, which is expressible. In the latter case, P is equivalent to $inserta(union Q N)$. Now, $union Q N$ is a simpler term, so by the induction hypothesis this term, and hence P, must be expressible by constructors. This establishes that *empty* and *insert* are constructors for *set*.

To give an example of datatype induction, we can prove the simple property that every set in the initial algebra has only finitely many elements. To be precise, we say that a set s is *finite* if $ismem?\,x\,s = true$ for only finitely many atoms x.

Since every *set* element of the initial algebra is representable by a term constructed from *empty* and *insert*, we use induction over the structure of such terms to show that for any set s the expression $ismem?\,x\,s$ will evaluate to *true* for only finitely many atoms x. In the base case, $ismem\,x empty$ is false for all x. For the induction step, assume that $ismem?\,x\,s$ is *true* for at most n atoms x; then $ismem?\,x(insert\;a\;s)$ will be true for at most $n+1$ atoms x. This concludes the proof. ■

Exercise 3.6.2 This question is about the *set* datatype specified in Table 3.4 and discussed in Example 3.6.1. Show that the equation

$$union\,s\,s' = union\,s'\,s[s\colon set, s'\colon set]$$

does *not* hold in the initial algebra. You may assume that the rewrite rules obtained by directing each of the equational axioms from left to right are confluent. Confluence implies that two terms are provably equal iff they reduce to a common term.

Exercise 3.6.3 This exercise analyzes the algebraic specification of multisets given in Table 3.2, extended with an intersection operation defined by the axioms

$$intersect\;empty\,m = empty$$

$$intersect\;(insert\;x\;m)\,m' = \texttt{if}\;\; mem?\,x\,m'\;\;\texttt{then}\;\; insert\,x\;(intersect\,m\,m')\;\;\texttt{else}\;\; intersect\,m\,m'$$

(a) Show that *empty* and *insert* are constructors for multisets.

(b) Show that the equation

$$insert\,x(insert\;y\;m) = insert\;y\;(insert\;x\;m)$$

does not hold in the initial algebra. You may assume, as in Exercise 3.6.2, that the rewrite rules obtained by directing each of the equational axioms from left to right are confluent.

(c) Show, by constructing an algebra, that if we add the equation

$$insert\;x\;(insert\;y\;m) = insert\;y\;(insert\;x\;m)$$

as an axiom, the specification remains consistent.

Exercise 3.6.4 The *ML* programming language has a `datatype` declaration which is used to define datatypes generated by typed constructors. For example, the ML declaration for binary trees with integers at the leaves looks something like this:

`datatype` $tree = leaf$ `of` $nat \mid node$ `of` $tree \times tree$

This declaration "says" that a *tree* is either the result of applying *leaf* to a natural number, or *node* to a pair of trees. The functions *leaf* and *node* are called "constructors" in the ML documentation, since every tree is either a leaf or constructed from a pair of trees using the function *node.* For typographical reasons, Standard ML actually uses the ASCII character $*$ for cartesian product, instead of $\times$. Another exercise on ML datatype declarations, using recursive types instead of algebraic specifications, appears in Chapter 2 (Exercise 2.6.8).

A convenient feature of ML is the way that pattern matching may be used to define functions over declared datatypes. A function over trees may be declared using two "clauses," one for each constructor. Using a slight modification of the ML syntax, we may declare a function f which sums up the values of all the leaves as follows.

$$\begin{array}{lll} \texttt{letrec fun} & f(leaf(x\colon nat)) & = x \\ \quad\mid & f(node(t_1\colon tree, t_2\colon tree)) & = f(t_1) + f(t_2) \end{array}$$

In general a function over *trees* defined by pattern matching will have the form

$$\begin{array}{lll} \texttt{letrec fun} & f(leaf(x\colon nat)) & = M \\ \quad\mid & f(node(t_1\colon tree, t_2\colon tree)) & = N \\ & \quad\texttt{in } P & \end{array}$$

where variables $x\colon nat$ and $f\colon tree \to \sigma$ are bound in M, $t_1, t_2\colon tree$ and f are bound in N and f is bound in the the declaration body P. The compiler checks to make sure there is one clause for each constructor of the datatype.

(a) We may consider the ML datatype definition for trees to be a declaration of an initial algebra generated by *leaf* and *node,* with additional functions *isleaf?, label, lsub* and *rsub.* An algebraic specification for this signature is given in Table 3.3. Show that in the initial algebra for this specification, every tree is named by an expression of the form $leaf(n)$, for some natural number n, or $node(t_1, t_2)$, where t_1 and t_2 are tree expressions of this form.

(b) Show how to translate a function declaration of the form

$$\begin{array}{lll} \texttt{letrec fun} & f(leaf(x\colon nat)) & = M \\ \quad\mid & f(node(t_1\colon tree, t_2\colon tree)) & = N \\ & \quad\texttt{in } P & \end{array}$$

into an expression of the form

$$\texttt{letrec } f(t\colon tree)\colon \sigma = M' \texttt{ in } P$$

in the language PCF_{tree} of PCF over *nat*, *bool* and *tree*, assuming that M, N and P have the correct types and are already expressions of this language.

(c) One obvious advantage of the ML syntax is that it is succinct and easy to read. There is also a technical advantage. Specifically, suppose that in writing axioms in part (a) above, you considered two possible axioms of the form $lsub(leaf\ n) = T_i$, for two tree expressions T_1 and T_2. Show that in general (for some choice of T_1 and T_2), it is possible to write a PCF_{tree} expression $M: bool$ with value *true* if $lsub(leaf\ n) = T_1$ and value *false* if $lsub(leaf\ n) = T_2$. Therefore, the behavior of programs using this datatype will depend on properties of trees that do not follow from the specification.

Now consider expressions written using the pattern matching syntax of ML, and without using functions *isleaf?, label, lsub* and *rsub* directly. Is it possible to write a function which translates into a PCF_{tree} function applying *lsub* to a leaf? Give an example or explain why not. This finesses a problem with specifications and error elements discussed in the next section.

Exercise 3.6.5 An alternative to loose and initial algebra semantics is the *generated* or *reachable* semantics. (Some authors call this the loose semantics.) In this approach, the models of a specification are all the generated algebras that satisfy the specification, where a Σ-algebra $\mathcal{A}$ is *generated* (also called *reachable* or *term-generated*) if, for every element $a \in A^s$, there is a variable-free term M over Σ with $a = \mathcal{A}[\![M]\!]$. This exercise asks you to demonstrate some connections between generated algebras and the initial algebra.

(a) Show that if generated Σ-algebra $\mathcal{A}$ satisfies $\mathcal{E}$, then there is a surjective homomorphism from the initial algebra $\mathcal{T} = Terms(\Sigma, \emptyset)/ \sim_{\mathcal{E},\emptyset}$ onto $\mathcal{A}$.

(b) Use Exercise 3.5.6 to show that if generated Σ-algebra $\mathcal{A}$ satisfies $\mathcal{E}$, then $Th(\mathcal{A})$ contains the theory of the initial algebra for specification $\langle \Sigma, \mathcal{E} \rangle$.

(c) Show that an equation $M = N[\Gamma]$ holds in all generated Σ-algebras satisfying $\mathcal{E}$ iff $M = N[\Gamma]$ holds in the initial algebra for specification $\langle \Sigma, \mathcal{E} \rangle$.

Exercise 3.6.6 An alternative called *final algebra semantics*, motivated by a problem with initial algebras described in [GHM78], are developed in [Wan79]; some other references are [BT83, Kam83]. The final algebra in a class is the "opposite" of the initial one: an algebra $\mathcal{A} \in \mathcal{C}$ is final in $\mathcal{C}$ if there is a unique homomorphism from every $\mathcal{B} \in \mathcal{C}$ to $\mathcal{A}$. This degenerates (as shown in (b) below) if $\mathcal{C}$ is the class of all algebras satisfying some specification, but it is a useful concept in cases where the interpretations of some sorts are fixed and others might vary. This situation arises when, for example, we have "already defined" natural numbers and booleans and want to use these to specify sets (of natural numbers). We will use the specification of sets in Table 3.4 as an illustrative example in this exercise.

(a) Show that if algebras $\mathcal{A}$ and $\mathcal{B}$ are both final in any class $\mathcal{C}$ of algebras, then $\mathcal{A} \cong \mathcal{B}$.

(b) Let $\mathcal{C}$ be the class of all algebras satisfying the specification in Table 3.4. Show that the algebra with one element in each carrier is final in $\mathcal{C}$. (Your argument should not depend on any particular properties of this specification.)

(c) Let $\mathcal{C}$ be the class of all algebras $\mathcal{A}$ satisfying the specification in Table 3.4 with the additional property that the "restriction"

$$\mathcal{A}_{nat,bool} = \langle A^{nat}, A^{bool}, 0^{\mathcal{A}}, 1^{\mathcal{A}}, \ldots, +^{\mathcal{A}}, Eq?^{\mathcal{A}}, true^{\mathcal{A}}, false^{\mathcal{A}}, cond_n^{\mathcal{A}}, cond_b^{\mathcal{A}} \rangle$$

of $\mathcal{A}$ to natural numbers and booleans is isomorphic to the standard algebra of natural numbers and booleans with these operations. Show that every algebra $\mathcal{B}$ in this class must have more than one element in B^{set}.

(d) Exercise 3.6.2 shows that the initial algebra for the set specification does not satisfy the equation

$$union\ s\ s' = union\ s'\ s[s\colon set,\ s'\colon set]$$

Let $\mathcal{C}'$ be the set of all generated algebras (see Exercise 3.6.5) that are in the class $\mathcal{C}$ of part (c). Show that an algebra $\mathcal{B}$ with B^{set} the collection of finite sets of natural numbers is final in the class $\mathcal{C}'$ and conclude that the (desirable) equation above holds in the final algebra for $\mathcal{C}'$. (*Hint:* for $s \in B^{set}$, consider $\{n \mid ismem?^{\mathcal{B}}\ n\ s = true\}$.)

3.6.3 Examples and Error Values

A problem that often arises in programming is that certain expressions are not meaningful. It is clear that a call to a nonterminating function does not return a value. However, this is not the only situation in which expression values are "undefined." For example, the typing rules of most programming languages specify that for every x, $y\colon real$, the quotient x/y is a real number. However, division is only a *partial* function on real numbers since the result of division by zero is undefined. This is different from nontermination, since we can test for division by zero before we attempt to compute a quotient, whereas testing a function for termination on a given argument is not algorithmically possible. If we want to specify that division by zero produces an error, for example, then we must add error terms to the signature.

Error-producing operations cause problems in algebraic specification, since the framework is constrained so that every well-formed term will have a value in every algebra for the signature. We will explore three possible approaches. Roughly speaking, these are: "don't say anything," "make an arbitrary decision," and "specify exactly what you want very carefully."

An illustrative example is the specification of lists in Table 3.5. Intuitively, a list is either empty, or obtained by adding an element to a list. Following Lisp nomenclature,

Table 3.5
A specification for *list*, *atom* and *bool*.

sorts:	*list, atom, bool*
fctns:	$a, b, c, d, \ldots : atom$
	$true, false : bool$
	$nil : list$
	$cons : atom \times list \to list$
	$car : list \to atom$
	$cdr : list \to list$
	$isempty? : list \to bool$
	$cond_a : bool \times atom \times atom \to atom$
	$cond_b : bool \times bool \times bool \to bool$
	$cond_l : bool \times list \times list \to list$
eqns:	$[x, y : atom,\ l, l' : list,\ u, v : bool]$
	$car\ (cons\ x\ l) = x$
	$cdr\ (cons\ x\ l) = l$
	$isempty?\ nil = true$
	$isempty?\ (cons\ x\ l) = false$
	$cond_a\ true\ x\ y = x$
	$cond_a\ false\ x\ y = y$
	$cond_b\ true\ u\ v = u$
	$cond_b\ false\ u\ v = v$
	$cond_l\ true\ l\ l' = l$
	$cond_l\ false\ l\ l' = l'$

the empty list is called *nil* in Table 3.5, and the operation for adding an atom to a list is called *cons*. A nonempty list may be separated into an atom (the first atom in the list), and a list of remaining atoms. The function returning the first element is called *car,* and the function returning the list of remaining elements is called *cdr.* (These names come from the machine instructions on an early computer used in the development of Lisp.) The straightforward equations describing the results of various operations are listed in Table 3.5.

The problem is that it does not make sense to ask for the first element of the empty list; there simply isn't one. Therefore, *carnil* has no "natural" value. While we could say the list *cdr nil* of "remaining" elements is empty, this does not make much sense either. In the equational specification given in Table 3.5, the problem has been addressed by leaving out equations for *car nil* and *cdr nil*. This choice may be justified by saying that since these expressions do not make sense, we do not want to say they are equal to any meaningful value. If we use the equational axioms as reduction rules, the net effect is to halt execution at *car nil* or *cdr nil*, since no reduction rule applies. However, if we consider the "standard meaning" of a specification to be the initial algebra, then we see some drawbacks of leaving function values unspecified. This could be taken as a problem with errors in algebraic specifications, or a reason to deemphasize initial algebras. In the initial algebra $\mathcal{A}$, we will have elements $car\ nil \in A^{atom}$ and $cdr\ nil \in A^{list}$, since *car nil* cannot be proved equal to any of the atom constants $a, b, c, \ldots$ and *cdr nil* cannot be proved equal to any list constructed using only *cons* and *nil*. However, the "extra" elements do not stop here. Once we have the atom *car nil*, we may add this element to lists, as in *cons* (*car nil*) *nil*. Similarly, we may test whether the extra list *cdr nil* is empty by applying *isempty*?(*cdr nil*). This produces an extra boolean value not provably equal to either *true* or *false*. By applying functions to *car nil* and *cdr nil*, we generate infinitely many elements of the initial algebra. These invalidate reasoning by induction on the intended list constructors *nil* and *cons,* and create similar problems for *atom* and *bool*.

There are two other alternatives within the framework of algebraic specifications. A convenient but questionable one is simply to make arbitrary decisions. For example, we could specify that $car\ nil = a$, for some arbitrary atom a, and let $cdr\ nil = nil$. This restores datatype induction over the expected constructors. However, the decision that $car\ nil = a$ seems a bit arbitrary. It also destroys the property that if two lists have the same *car* and *cdr,* then they must be the same list, for $car\ nil = car(cons\ a\ nil)$, and similarly for *cdr.* While arbitrary decisions may work well in certain contexts, it does not always seem reasonable to define errors away by giving "meaningful" values to erroneous expressions. In the case of real arithmetic, for example, postulating $1/0 = 3$ seems ridiculous.

A more direct treatment of errors involves explicit error values and equational axioms for them. This leads to more reasonable initial algebras and allows us to include "error-handling" functions that test for error conditions and attempt to repair them. However, we shall see that the axioms are more complicated than one might expect. The rest of this section is devoted to the axiomatic treatment of error values.

A naive attempt to add error elements to the list datatype would add constant symbols $error_a\colon atom$ and $error_l\colon list$ and equations $car\ nil = error_a$ and $cdr\ nil = error_l$. However, once we add two error elements, we are led to add a third, since asking whether the error list is empty seems to be an error. In other words, we are led to introduce an error element $error_b$ of sort boolean and let $isempty?\ error_l = error_b$. Having added constants to each sort, we must say how each function behaves on the new arguments. For most of the functions of this example, we will simply say that a function applied to an error value returns *error* of the appropriate sort. An exception is conditional, which we will allow to return a meaningful value if the error branch is not taken. This is a bit arbitrary, since it also seems plausible to say that any $cond_a\ true\ a\ error_a = error_a$, for example. The additional function symbols and equational axioms in our first attempt to add error values are given in Table 3.6.

Table 3.6
Naive treatment of error values for *list*, *atom* and *bool*.

fctns:	$error_l : list$
	$error_a : atom$
	$error_b : bool$
eqns:	$[x, y{:}\, atom, l, l'{:}\, list, u, v{:}\, bool]$
	$car\ nil = error_a$
	$cdr\ nil = error_l$
	$cons\ error_a\ l = error_l$
	$cons\ x, error_l = error_l$
	$car\ error_l = error_a$
	$cdr\ error_l = error_l$
	$isempty?\ error_l = error_b$
	$cond_a\ error_b\ x\ y = error_a$
	$cond_b\ error_b\ u\ v = error_b$
	$cond_l\ error_b\ l\ l' = error_l$

While the combined signature and equational axioms of Tables 3.5 and 3.6 may seem reasonable at first glance, there is a serious problem with them. In writing the original axioms for *car* and *cdr* on nonempty lists, we did not consider the possibility of error values. In other words, the equational axiom

$$car(cons\ x\ l) = x\ [x{:}\, atom, l{:}\, list]$$

assumes implicitly that any list equal to $cons\, x\, l$ for some atom x and list l will be a sensible list with first element x. However, the axiom

$$cons\ x\ error_l = error_l\ [x{:}\, atom]$$

violates this assumption. In fact, putting these two equational axioms together gives us

$$x = car(cons\ x\ error_l) = car\ error_l = error_a \qquad [x{:}\, atom]$$

Semantically, this equation says that every algebra satisfying the combined specification of Tables 3.5 and 3.6 may have only one atom. Similar reasoning shows that there can only be one list and only one boolean. Thus, the naive treatment of errors leads to inconsistent specifications.

This problem may be repaired by making explicit assumptions about function arguments. If we were to extend the language of algebra to include negation and other logical connectives, we could write an axiom

$$x \neq error_a \wedge l \neq error_l \supset car(cons\, x\, l) = x \qquad [x{:}\, atom, l{:}\, list]$$

that explicitly assumes the function arguments are not error values. By adding a few more functions to our signature, we may achieve the same result within the framework of algebraic specifications. The general approach is taken from [GTW78].

For each sort s, we add a function $OK_s{:}\, s \rightarrow bool$ which tells whether its argument is $error_s$ or not. We write axioms to say which elements are OK, and use conditional to test for error values in equations. For the signature of Table 3.5, we add function symbols OK_a, OK_b, OK_l and axioms such as

$$OK_a\, a = true,\ OK_a\, b = true, \ldots,\ OK_a\, error_a = false$$

to make every non-error value "*OK*" and every error value not. We then use *OK* and conditional to revise the axiom for *car* of a nonempty list as follows. (As usual, we write `if ... then ... else ...` as syntactic sugar for *cond*.)

$$car(cons\, x\, l) = \texttt{if } OK_a\, x \texttt{ then (if } OK_l\, l \texttt{ then } x \texttt{ else } error_a\texttt{) else } error_a$$

$$[x{:}\, atom, l{:}\, list]$$

Intuitively, this axiom says that if we have a list constructed by adding a non-error atom x to a non-error list l, then the first element of this list is x. Otherwise, the result is $error_a$. Since we will keep the axiom $cons\, x\, error_l = error_l$, we may derive the equation $car\, error_l = error_a$ from the revised axiom with conditional. A full specification of lists using explicit error values and "*OK*" predicates is given in Table 3.7. The initial algebra for this specification is analyzed using rewrite-rule techniques in Section 3.7.7. The main results of the analysis are that the specification is consistent and that each carrier of the initial algebra has one error element and distinct non-error elements as intended.

Exercise 3.6.7 In an important early paper, Guttag [Gut77] gave the following specification for queues,

sorts:*queue*, *item*, *bool*

fctns:*new*: *queue*

$add{:}\, queue \times item \rightarrow queue$

$front{:}\, queue \rightarrow item$

$remove{:}\, queue \rightarrow queue$

$is\_empty?{:}\, queue \rightarrow bool$

Table 3.7
A specification for *list*, *atom* and *bool* with error values.

sorts: *list*, *atom*, *bool*

fctns:
$a, b, c, d, \ldots : atom$
$true, false : bool$
$nil : list$
$cons : atom \times list \to list$
$car : list \to atom$
$cdr : list \to list$
$isempty? : list \to bool$
$cond_a : bool \times atom \times atom \to atom$
$cond_b : bool \times bool \times bool \to bool$
$cond_l : bool \times list \times list \to list$
$error_a : atom,\ error_b : bool,\ error_l : list$
$OK_a : atom \to bool,\ OK_b : bool \to bool,\ OK_l : list \to bool$

eqns:
$[x, y : atom,\ l, l' : list,\ u, v : bool]$
$car\ error_l = error_a$
$car\ nil = error_a$
$car\ (cons\ x\ l) = \texttt{if}\ OK_a\ x\ \texttt{then}\ (\texttt{if}\ OK_l\ l\ \texttt{then}\ x\ \texttt{else}\ error_a)\ \texttt{else}\ error_a$
$cdr\ error_l = error_l$
$cdr\ nil = error_l$
$cdr\ (cons\ x\ l) = \texttt{if}\ OK_a\ x\ \texttt{then}\ (\texttt{if}\ OK_l\ l\ \texttt{then}\ l\ \texttt{else}\ error_l)\ \texttt{else}\ error_l$
$isempty?\ error_l = error_b$
$isempty?\ nil = true$
$isempty?\ (cons\ x\ l) = \texttt{if}\ OK_a\ x\ \texttt{then}\ (\texttt{if}\ OK_l\ l\ \texttt{then}\ false\ \texttt{else}\ error_b)\ \texttt{else}\ error_b$
$cons\ x\ error_l = error_l$
$cons\ error_a\ l = error_l$
$cond_a\ true\ x\ y = x$
$cond_a\ false\ x\ y = y$
$cond_a\ error_b\ x\ y = error_a$
(similarly for $cond_b$ and $cond_l$)
$OK_a\ a = true,\ OK_a\ b = true\ OK_a\ c = true,\ \ldots$
$OK_a error_a = false$
$OK_b\ true = true,\ OK_b false = true$
$OK_b\ error_b = false$
$OK_l\ nil = true$
$OK_l\ (cons\ x\ l) = \texttt{if}\ OK_a\ x\ \texttt{then}\ (\texttt{if}\ OK_l\ l\ \texttt{then}\ true\ \texttt{else}\ false)\ \texttt{else}\ false$

eqns:$[q\colon queue, i\colon item]$

$$is\_empty?\ new = true$$

$$is\_empty?\ (add\ q\ i) = false$$

$$front\ new = error$$

$$front(add\ q\ i) = i$$

$$remove\ new = error$$

$$remove\ (add\ q\ i) = q$$

with the informal comment that "*error* is a distinguished value with the property that the value of any operation applied to an argument list containing *error* is *error*." Assume that boolean constants are *true* and *false*, with conditional on each sort, as usual. Also assume that there are constants $a, b, c, \ldots$ of sort *item*.

(a) Write additional equations reflecting the informal description of the result of applying any function to *error*. Use error constants $error_q$, $error_i$ and $error_b$ of each sort. Show that if combined with the equations above, the result will be an inconsistent specification.

(b) Rewrite the axioms for *is_empty?*, *front* and *remove* applied to queues of the form $add\ q\ i$ in the manner described in this section. Show that the resulting specification (including the equations you wrote for part (a) and the original equations that you did not change) is consistent by constructing an algebra.

Exercise 3.6.8 Devise a specification of trees with an explicit treatment of errors using *OK* functions as outlined in this section. A specification without error elements is given in Table 3.3.

3.6.4 Alternative Approaches to Error Values

One completely different approach to errors allows functions to be partial, rather than total. Instead of treating *car nil* as an expression of sort *atom* which must be given a value in any algebra, we may simply say that this expression is "undefined," and give it no value whatsoever. (This is *not* the same as calling an extra element $\perp$ "undefined," as is done in Scott semantics. The use of $\perp$ in Scott domains resembles the introduction of explicit error elements.) With partial functions, and *car nil* undefined, we may have lists generated only by *nil* and *cons*. This is the primary advantage. A disadvantage of partial functions is that we cannot discuss error-handling functions, since an undefined expression does not produce any value that could be passed to another function. In addition, we cannot have "lazy" functions that do not depend on whether their arguments are defined. This is because an expression with an undefined subexpression cannot be given a value in any reasonable (*i.e.*, compositional) way. Finally, algebra with partial functions is somewhat more complicated than ordinary algebra with only total functions. For these reasons, it is not clear whether partial functions are worth the effort. Since programming language semantics using partial functions is a current research area, the trade-offs may be better understood in the future.

Another method that has several advantages is the system of order-sorted algebra, proposed by Goguen [Gog78]. For information on order-sorted algebra, the reader may consult [SNGM89, Wir90].

3.7 Rewrite Systems

3.7.1 Basic Definitions

There are two main uses for rewrite systems, which are reduction systems for algebraic terms. The first is that a rewrite system may provide a useful model of computation (or evaluation) for algebraic terms. This is emphasized in the discussion of the rewrite rules for PCF natural number and boolean expressions in Section 2.2.2. The second common application is in automated theorem proving. If we begin with a set of equational hypotheses, then these may be used to formulate a set of rewrite rules. If the resulting rewrite rules are confluent, as discussed in Section 3.7.2, then the consequences of the equational hypotheses may be characterized using the rewrite system. One advantage of this characterization is that it provides a simple algorithm (namely, reduction) for seeing if an equation is provable. Although this algorithm may not always terminate, it does for terminating rewrite systems. In addition, it may terminate in failure, showing that an equation does not follow from the hypotheses. This is useful, since the only other straightforward way of showing that an equation does not follow from some hypotheses is to construct an algebra (as in Example 3.4.15), and this is not easily automated. More specifically, the only way to automate search for algebras contradicting an implication seems to be brute enumeration of finite algebras, and this seldom produces useful results. In addition to studying properties of rewrite systems, this section illustrates general problems with reduction systems for non-algebraic terms using algebraic examples.

A rewrite system is a reduction system for algebraic terms given by a set of directed equations called rewrite rules. More formally, a *rewrite system* $\mathcal{R}$ *over* Σ is a set of *rewrite rules* $L \to R$, where $L, R \in \mathit{Terms}^s(\Sigma, \Gamma)$ are terms of the same sort, L is not a variable, and $\mathit{Var}(R) \subseteq \mathit{Var}(L)$. A rule $L \to R$ lets us simplify any substitution instance SL to SR, anywhere inside a term. The two main uses of rewrite systems are to analyze equational axioms and to model computation on algebraic terms.

The careful reader may wonder about the restriction $Var(R) \subseteq Var(L)$ on variables. One intuitive justification is that rewrite rules are intended to simplify expressions. Since $L \to R$ lets us replace a substitution instance SL by the corresponding instance SR, a variable occurring only in R could be replaced by any term. For example, the rule $a \to x$ lets us rewrite a to any term. This does not seem like much of a simplification. (See Exercise 3.7.4 for the effect of such a rule on termination). A more technical reason has to do with sorts. With $Var(R) \subseteq Var(L)$, we will see that rewriting preserves the sort of a term. However, this fails without the restriction on variables.

The *one-step reduction relation* $\to_{\mathcal{R}}$ *determined by* $\mathcal{R}$ is the least relation on terms such that

$$[SL/x]M \to_{\mathcal{R}} [SR/x]M$$

for every rule $(L \to R) \in \mathcal{R}$, term M with single occurrence of x, and substitution S such that $[SL/x]M \in Terms(\Sigma, \Gamma)$. The relation $\twoheadrightarrow_{\mathcal{R}}$ is the reflexive and transitive closure of $\to_{\mathcal{R}}$. We will omit subscripts when this does not seem likely to be confusing. It is easy to see that systematically renaming variables in any rule $(L \to R) \in \mathcal{R}$ does not change the relation $\to_{\mathcal{R}}$. Consequently, we may assume whenever convenient that no variable appears in more than one rewrite rule. This is useful when comparing pairs of rules.

Example 3.7.1 [KB70, Example 3] The signature

sorts:*nat*

fctns:$0 : nat$

$- : nat \to nat$

$+ : nat \times nat \to nat$

for writing natural number expressions includes only 0, unary minus, and addition. Some reasonable rewrite rules over this signature are

$$x + 0 \to x$$

$$x + (-x) \to 0$$

$$(x + y) + z \to x + (y + z)$$

Using these rules, we can carry out the following rewrite (reduction) steps, where the underlined subterm is the one rewritten to obtain the subsequent term:

$$\underline{(x + y) + (-y)} \to x + \underline{(y + (-y))} \to \underline{x + 0} \to x.$$

Notice that a reduction step may be done by matching the entire term against the left-hand-side of one of the rewrite rules, or by matching any subterm. Although there is only one possible rewrite at each step, in this example, there are terms where several subterms may match the left-hand-side of a rule. For example, the term $(x + 0) + y$ may be reduced to either $x + y$, by the first rule, or $x + (0 + y)$ by the second. Note that neither of these terms can be reduced further. ■

A straightforward fact is that reduction preserves sort.

Lemma 3.7.2 Let $\mathcal{R}$ be a rewrite system over Σ. If $M \in \mathit{Terms}^s(\Sigma, \Gamma)$ and $M \twoheadrightarrow_{\mathcal{R}} N$, then $N \in \mathit{Terms}^s(\Sigma, \Gamma)$.

The proof is Exercise 3.7.6.

Two important properties are confluence and termination. Let us write $N \twoheadleftarrow M$ if $M \twoheadrightarrow N$ and $M \twoheadrightarrow \circ \twoheadleftarrow N$ if there exists a term P with $M \twoheadrightarrow P \twoheadleftarrow N$. We say $\twoheadrightarrow$ is *confluent* if $N \twoheadleftarrow M \twoheadrightarrow P$ implies $N \twoheadrightarrow \circ \twoheadleftarrow P$. A relation $\rightarrow$ is *terminating* if there is no infinite sequence $M_0 \rightarrow M_1 \rightarrow M_2 \ldots$ of one-step reductions. A rewrite system $\mathcal{R}$ is *confluent* if $\twoheadrightarrow_{\mathcal{R}}$ is confluent and *terminating* if $\rightarrow_{\mathcal{R}}$ is terminating. As in lambda calculus, a *normal form* is a term that cannot be reduced.

Rewrite systems that are confluent and terminating are often referred to as *canonical*. While canonical rewrite systems are often desirable, non-canonical systems are also useful, particularly if the rules are at least confluent on some subset of terms. As we shall see in Section 3.7.6, termination may make it easier to determine whether a rewrite system is confluent.

A useful relation is an undirected version of reduction called conversion. Terms $M, N \in \mathit{Terms}^s(\Sigma, \Gamma)$ are *convertible,* written $M \leftrightarrow_{\mathcal{R}} N\ [\Gamma]$, if M and N are identical, or there is some $M' \in \mathit{Terms}^s(\Sigma, \Gamma)$ with $M' \leftrightarrow_{\mathcal{R}} N\ [\Gamma]$ and either $M \twoheadrightarrow_{\mathcal{R}} M'$ or $M' \twoheadrightarrow_{\mathcal{R}} M$. In other words, $M \leftrightarrow N\ [\Gamma]$ iff there is a sequence of terms $M_1, \ldots, M_k \in \mathit{Terms}^s(\Sigma, \Gamma)$ with

$$M \twoheadrightarrow M_1 \twoheadleftarrow M_2 \twoheadrightarrow M_3 \ldots M_k \twoheadleftarrow N,$$

where the directions of arrows need not be regarded as significant. (In fact, by the reflexivity and transitivity of $\twoheadrightarrow$, this picture is completely general.) In the next section, we will see that for *any* rewrite system, conversion coincides with equational provability. If a system is confluent, then we will see that $M \leftrightarrow_{\mathcal{R}} N\ [\Gamma]$ iff $M \twoheadrightarrow \circ \twoheadleftarrow N$.

A few definitions will be useful when we analyze reductions more closely. Since two subterms may be syntactically identical, we will need some way to refer to a specific occurrence of a subterm. Intuitively, a *position* in a term is the location of a particular subterm. We will identify a position by a finite sequence of natural numbers that tells us how to "walk" down the parse tree of a term. To illustrate this method by example, the parse tree of $f(gx(hab))(gba)x$ is drawn below.

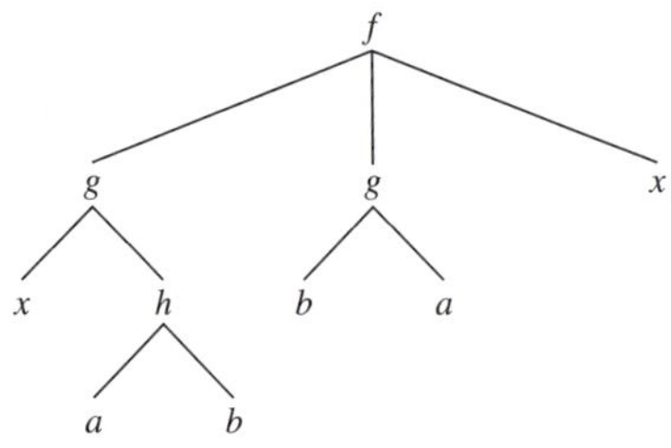

To find the position named by sequence $1, 2$ for example, we start at the top of the tree. The number 1 means we look for our subterm by taking the first (*i.e.*, the leftmost) branch down from the root. This places us at the top of the tree for $gx(hab)$. The number 2 now points to the second subterm, so position $1, 2$ is occupied by the subterm hab. To be more precise, we define the *subterm of M at position $\vec{n}$* by induction on the length of a sequence $\vec{n} = n_1, \ldots, n_k$. If ϵ is the empty sequence, then the subterm M at position ϵ is the entire term M. If M has the form $f(M_1, \ldots, M_k)$ and $\vec{n} = i, n_2, \ldots, n_\ell$ with $1 \le i \le k$, then the subterm at position $\vec{n}$ is the subterm of M_i named by $n_2, \ldots, n_\ell$. For example, the subterm of $f(gx(hab))(gba)x$ at position $1, 2, 1$ is the first occurrence of the symbol a, read from left to right. The subterm at position 2 is gba, while there is no subterm at position $3, 2$.

If $\vec{n}$ is a position in M, we write $M|_{\vec{n}}$ for the subterm of M at position $\vec{n}$ and $[N/\vec{n}]M$ for the term obtained by substituting N for the subterm at position $\vec{n}$. Using this notation, we may characterize one-step reduction by $M \to_{\mathcal{R}} N$ iff there is some position $\vec{n}$ in M with $M|_{\vec{n}} \equiv SL$ and $N \equiv [SR/\vec{n}]M$. One straightforward property of positions is that $M|_{\vec{n}}$ is a subterm of $M|_{\vec{p}}$ iff $\vec{n}$ is a subsequence of the sequence $\vec{p}$ of natural numbers. It is sometimes useful to refer to the first function symbol of a term as its *principal function symbol*. For example, f is the principal function symbol of $f(M_1, \ldots, M_k)$.

Exercise 3.7.3 Consider the algebraic term $f(gxy)(f(gu(huv)))(f(g(gxy)z))$

(a) Write out the subterm at position 2, 1, 2.

(b) Describe the positions of gxy by sequences of natural numbers.

Exercise 3.7.4 Show that if $\mathcal{R}$ contains a rule $L \to R$, where either L is a variable or R contains one variable not in L, then the system $\mathcal{R}$ is not terminating.

Exercise 3.7.5 Let $\mathcal{R}$ be any rewrite system and let $\mathcal{R}^{op}$ be the set of "opposite" rules $R \to L$ with $(L \to R) \in \mathcal{R}$. Show that the rewrite system $\mathcal{R} \cup \mathcal{R}^{op}$ is confluent but not terminating.

Exercise 3.7.6 Prove Lemma 3.7.2.

3.7.2 Confluence and Provable Equality

Confluent rewrite systems are very useful for analyzing provable equality. The main reason is that for confluent systems, an equation is provable precisely when both terms reduce to a single term. In proving this theorem, we will also show that equational provability coincides with conversion, even if confluence fails. While the results are stated for algebra, essentially the same proofs apply to reduction and provable equality in many other equational systems, including typed and untyped lambda calculus.

If $\mathcal{R}$ is a set of rewrite rules, we let $\mathcal{E}_{\mathcal{R}}$ be the set of corresponding undirected equations. Using this notation, the main result of this section may be written

$\mathcal{E}_{\mathcal{R}} \vdash M = N[\Gamma]$ iff $M \twoheadrightarrow_{\mathcal{R}} \circ \twoheadleftarrow_{\mathcal{R}} N$,

for confluent $\mathcal{R}$. As a corollary, confluence allows us to demonstrate consistency by finding two distinct normal forms. If $\twoheadrightarrow$ is both confluent and terminating, then reduction also provides a decision procedure for $\mathcal{E}_{\mathcal{R}}$: we may decide whether $\mathcal{E}_{\mathcal{R}} \vdash M = N[\Gamma]$ simply by reducing both terms to normal form and comparing for syntactic equality. In reading the remainder of this section, the reader may wish to think of the rewrite system $\mathcal{R}$ consisting of all the algebraic rewrite rules of PCF (*i.e.*, the rules for natural numbers and booleans), with $\mathcal{E}_{\mathcal{R}}$ the corresponding set of equational axioms for PCF.

We begin by showing that provable equality is closed under reduction.

Lemma 3.7.7 Let $M \in \mathit{Terms}^s(\Sigma, \Gamma)$. If $M \twoheadrightarrow_{\mathcal{R}} N$, then $\mathcal{E}_{\mathcal{R}} \vdash M = N[\Gamma]$.

Proof If $M \to_{\mathcal{R}} N$, then we have $M \equiv [SL/x]P$ and $N \equiv [SR/x]P$ for some term $P \in \mathit{Terms}(\Sigma, (\Gamma, x\colon s))$, and rewrite rule $L \to R \in \mathcal{R}$. We may assume without loss of generality that x does not occur in SL or SR. By rule (*subst*), we have $\mathcal{E}_{\mathcal{R}} \vdash SL = SR[\Gamma]$. Since $P = P[\Gamma, x\colon s]$ by reflexivity, we have $\mathcal{E}_{\mathcal{R}} \vdash M = N[\Gamma]$ by (*subst*). For multi-step reduction $M \twoheadrightarrow_{\mathcal{R}} N$, the lemma follows by induction on the number of reduction steps. ■

The next goal is to show that reduction is closed under substitution. More precisely, we will establish that if $M \twoheadrightarrow M'$ and $P \twoheadrightarrow P'$, then $[M/x]P \twoheadrightarrow [M'/x]P'$. Rather than prove this directly, we will break it into simpler lemmas.

Lemma 3.7.8 If $P \to P'$, then for any term M we have $[M/x]P \to [M/x]P'$.

Proof The basic idea is that if $P \to P'$ by rewrite rule $L \to R$, we may use $L \to R$ to reduce $[M/x]P \to [M/x]P'$. If x does not occur in the subterm of P that is rewritten, then this is straightforward. Otherwise, we must use a substitution instance of L with x replaced by M. This is worked out in the next paragraph.

Since $P \to P'$, there is some term Q with $P \equiv [SL/y]Q$ and $P' \equiv [SR/y]Q$. We are free to choose Q so that y does not occur in M, P or P'. Consequently, $[M/x]P \equiv [M/x]([SL/y]Q) \equiv ([([M/x]SL)/y]([M/x]Q)$ by Exercise 2.2.6. If we let S' be the substitution $[M/x] \circ S$ and Q' be the term $Q' \equiv [M/x]Q$, then we see that $[M/x]P$ has the form $[M/x]P \equiv [S'L/y]Q'$. By similar reasoning, we have $[M/x]P' \equiv [S'R/y]Q'$. Therefore, $[M/x]P \to [M/x]P'$. ■

Lemma 3.7.9 If $M \to M'$, then for any term P we have $[M/x]P \twoheadrightarrow [M'/x]P$.

Proof The proof uses induction on the number of occurrences of x in P. The lemma clearly holds when x does not occur in P, so we move on to the induction step. If there are $n+1$ occurrences of x, then let Q be a term obtained from P by substituting a fresh variable y for all but one occurrence. Then $[M/x]P \equiv [M/y]([M/x]Q)$ and $[M'/x]P = [M'/y]([M'/x]Q)$. We will show that $[M/x]Q \to [M'/x]Q$.

Since $M \to M'$, there is an position $\vec{n}$ in M of the form SL, and $M' \equiv [SR/\vec{n}]M$. Since x occurs exactly once in Q, we have $Q|_{\vec{m}} \equiv x$ for some $\vec{m}$. Therefore, the position $\vec{m}\vec{n}$ of $[M/x]Q$ has the form SL and $[M'/x]Q \equiv [SR/\vec{m}\vec{n}]([M/x]Q)$. Thus $[M/x]Q \to [M'/x]Q$.

We now have $[M/y]([M/x]Q) \to [M/y]([M'/x]Q)$ by Lemma 3.7.8, and $[M/y]([M'/x]Q) \twoheadrightarrow [M'/y]([M'/x]Q)$ by the inductive hypothesis. Thus

$$[M/x]P \equiv [M/y]([M/x]Q) \to$$
$$[M/y]([M'/x]Q) \twoheadrightarrow [M'/y]([M'/x]Q) \equiv [M'/x]P.$$

This proves the lemma. ■

Lemma 3.7.10 If $M \twoheadrightarrow M'$ and $P \twoheadrightarrow P'$, then $[M/x]P \twoheadrightarrow [M'/x]P'$.

Proof By induction on the length of the reduction sequence $P \twoheadrightarrow P'$, we have $[M/x]P \twoheadrightarrow [M/x]P'$ by Lemma 3.7.8. It remains to show that $[M/x]P' \twoheadrightarrow [M'/x]P'$. For this we use induction on the length of the reduction $M \twoheadrightarrow M'$ and Lemma 3.7.9. ■

These lemmas allow us to show that conversion is equivalent to provable equality.

Lemma 3.7.11 For any rewrite system, we have $M \leftrightarrow_{\mathcal{R}} N\ [\Gamma]$ iff $\mathcal{E}_{\mathcal{R}} \vdash M = N[\Gamma]$.

Proof Suppose $M \leftrightarrow N\ [\Gamma]$. Then there is a sequence of terms $M_0, \ldots, M_k \in Terms^s(\Sigma, \Gamma)$ with $M \equiv M_0$, $N \equiv M_k$ and either $M_i \twoheadrightarrow M_{i+1}$ or $M_{i+1} \twoheadrightarrow M_i$ for $0 \le i < k$. By

Lemma 3.7.7, we have $\mathcal{E}_{\mathcal{R}} \vdash M_i = M_{i+1}[\Gamma]$ for each i. So straightforward induction on k shows that $\mathcal{E}_{\mathcal{R}} \vdash M = N[\Gamma]$.

To prove the converse, we show that the convertibility relation contains all the axioms and is closed under the proof rules. Reflexivity is straightforward. If $M = N[\Gamma] \in \mathcal{E}_{\mathcal{R}}$ is a nonlogical axiom, then either $M \to N$ or $N \to M$ is a rewrite rule of $\mathcal{R}$. So clearly $M \leftrightarrow_{\mathcal{R}} N\ [\Gamma]$.

It is easy to see that convertibility is closed under symmetry, transitivity and (*add var*). The only difficult case is (*subst*), but most of the work was already done proving Lemma 3.7.10. We will show that if $M \leftrightarrow N\ [\Gamma, x{:}\, s]$ and $P \leftrightarrow Q\ [\Gamma]$ for terms P, Q of sort s, then $[P/x]M \leftrightarrow [P/x]N\ [\Gamma]$ and $[P/x]N \leftrightarrow [Q/x]N\ [\Gamma]$. By definition of conversion, we have

$$M \equiv M_0 \twoheadrightarrow M_1 \twoheadleftarrow M_2 \twoheadrightarrow M_3 \ldots \twoheadleftarrow M_k \equiv N$$

and similarly

$$P \equiv P_0 \twoheadrightarrow P_1 \twoheadleftarrow P_2 \twoheadrightarrow P_3 \ldots \twoheadleftarrow P_\ell \equiv Q.$$

Since $\twoheadrightarrow$ is reflexive, we may assume without loss of generality that $k = \ell$. Therefore, by Lemma 3.7.10, we have

$$[P/x]M \equiv [P_0/x]M_0 \twoheadrightarrow [P_1/x]M_1 \twoheadleftarrow [P_2/x]M_2 \twoheadrightarrow [P_3/x]M_3 \ldots$$
$$\twoheadleftarrow [P_k/x]M_k \equiv [Q/x]N.$$

This proves the lemma. ∎

Lemma 3.7.12 If $\twoheadrightarrow$ is confluent, then $M \leftrightarrow N\ [\Gamma]$ iff $M \twoheadrightarrow \circ \twoheadleftarrow N$.

Proof Suppose $M \leftrightarrow N\ [\Gamma]$. Consider any sequence of terms $M_1, \ldots M_k$ such that

$$M \twoheadrightarrow M_1 \twoheadleftarrow M_2 \twoheadrightarrow M_3 \twoheadleftarrow \ldots \twoheadleftarrow M_k \equiv N.$$

By reflexivity and transitivity of $\twoheadrightarrow$ we may always express $M \leftrightarrow N\ [\Gamma]$ in this form, with the first sequence of reductions proceeding from $M \twoheadrightarrow M_1$, and the next in the opposite direction. If $k = 2$, then the lemma holds. Otherwise, we will show how to shorten the sequence of alternations. By confluence, there is some term P with $M_1 \twoheadrightarrow P \twoheadleftarrow M_3$. By transitivity of $\twoheadrightarrow$, this gives us a shorter conversion sequence

$$M \twoheadrightarrow P \twoheadleftarrow M_4 \twoheadrightarrow \ldots \twoheadleftarrow M_k \equiv N.$$

By induction on k, we conclude that $M \twoheadrightarrow \circ \twoheadleftarrow N$. ∎

Theorem 3.7.13 For any confluent rewrite system $\mathcal{R}$, we have $\mathcal{E}_{\mathcal{R}} \vdash M = N[\Gamma]$ iff $M \twoheadrightarrow_{\mathcal{R}} \circ \twoheadleftarrow_{\mathcal{R}} N$.

Proof By Lemma 3.7.11, we know $\mathcal{E}_{\mathcal{R}} \vdash M = N[\Gamma]$ iff $M \leftrightarrow_{\mathcal{R}} N\ [\Gamma]$. By Lemma 3.7.12, confluence implies $M \leftrightarrow_{\mathcal{R}} N\ [\Gamma]$ iff $M \twoheadrightarrow_{\mathcal{R}} \circ \twoheadleftarrow_{\mathcal{R}} N$. ∎

Corollary 3.7.14 If $\twoheadrightarrow_{\mathcal{R}}$ is confluent and there exist two distinct normal forms of sort s, then $\mathcal{E}_{\mathcal{R}}$ is consistent.

3.7.3 Termination

There are many approaches to proving termination of rewrite systems. Several methods involve assigning some kind of "weights" to terms. For example, suppose we assign a natural number weight w_M to each term M and show that whenever $M \to N$, we have $w_M > w_N$. It follows that there is no infinite sequence $M_0 \to M_1 \to M_2 \to \ldots$ of one-step reductions, since there is no infinite decreasing sequence of natural numbers.

While this approach may seem straightforward, it is often very difficult to devise a weighting function that does the job. In fact, there is no algorithmic test to determine whether a rewrite system is terminating. Nonetheless, there are reasonable methods that work in many simple cases. Rather than survey the extensive literature on termination proofs, we will just take a quick look at a simple method based on algebras with ordered carriers. More information may be found in the survey articles [DJ90, HO80, Klo87] and references cited there.

The method we will consider in this section uses binary relations that prohibit infinite sequences. Before considering well-founded relations, also used in Section 1.8.3, we review some notational conventions. If $\prec$ is a binary relation on a set A, we will write $\preceq$ for the union of $\prec$ and equality, and $\succ$ for the complement of $\preceq$. In other words, $x \preceq y$ iff $x \prec y$ or $x = y$ and $x \succ y$ iff $\neg(y \preceq x)$. Note that in using the symbol $\prec$ as the name of a relation, we do not necessarily assume that $\prec$ is transitive or has any other properties of an ordering. However, since most of the examples we will consider involve ordering, the choice of symbol provides helpful intuition. A binary relation $\prec$ on a set A is *well-founded* if there is no infinite decreasing sequence, $a_0 \succ a_1 \succ a_2 \succ \ldots$, of elements of A. The importance of well-founded relations is that if we can establish a correspondence between terms and elements of a set A with well-founded binary relation $\prec$, we can use this to show there is no infinite sequence of reductions $M_0 \to M_1 \to M_2 \to \ldots$ An example well-founded relation is the standard ordering of natural numbers. Another example is pairs of natural numbers ordered *lexicographically, i.e.*, $\langle m_1, m_2\rangle \prec \langle n_1, n_2\rangle$ iff either $m_1 \prec n_1$ or both $m_1 = n_1$ and $m_2 \prec n_2$. Some other examples are given in Exercise 1.8.15.

There are several ways to map terms to sets with well-founded relations. Since we have already studied the interpretation of terms in algebras, we will take advantage of the semantic structure of algebra. An algebra $\mathcal{A} = \langle A^{s_1}, A^{s_2}, \ldots, f_1^{\mathcal{A}}, f_s^{\mathcal{A}}, \ldots \rangle$ is *well-founded* if

(i) There is a well-founded relation $\prec_s$ on each carrier $\mathcal{A}^s$.

(ii) For each n-ary function symbol f, if $x_1 \preceq y_1, \ldots, x_n \preceq y_n$ and $x_i \prec y_i$ for some i with $1 \leq i \leq n$, then

$$f^{\mathcal{A}}(x_1, \ldots, x_n) \prec f^{\mathcal{A}}(y_1, \ldots, y_n).$$

A simple example is to let each carrier be the set of natural numbers $\mathcal{N}$, with the usual ordering, and define each function $f^{\mathcal{A}}$ by a nonconstant polynomial with positive coefficients.

If $\mathcal{A}$ is a well-founded algebra and M and N are terms of sort s, the we write

$$\mathcal{A}, \eta \models M \prec N$$

if $[\![M]\!]\eta \prec_s [\![N]\!]\eta$ and, similarly, $\mathcal{A} \models M \prec N$ if $\mathcal{A}, \eta \models M \prec N$ for every environment η giving variables values of the appropriate sorts.

The reason for defining well-founded algebras is given by the following lemma.

Lemma 3.7.15 Let $\mathcal{R}$ be a rewrite system on Σ terms and let $\mathcal{A}$ be a well-founded Σ-algebra. If $\mathcal{A} \models L \succ R$ for each rule $L \to R$ in $\mathcal{R}$, then $\mathcal{R}$ is terminating.

Proof The proof uses the substitution lemma and other facts about the interpretation of terms. The only basic fact we must prove directly is that for any term $M \in Terms(\Sigma, \Gamma, x\colon s)$ containing the variable x, and any environment η, if $a \succ b \in A^s$, then

$$[\![M]\!]\eta[x \mapsto a] \succ [\![M]\!]\eta[x \mapsto b].$$

This is an easy induction on M that is left to the reader.

To prove the lemma, it suffices to show that if $M \to N$, then for any environment η, we have $[\![M]\!]\eta \succ [\![N]\!]\eta$, since no well-founded carrier has any infinite sequence of "decreasing" elements. In general, a single reduction step has the form $[SL/x]M \to [SR/x]M$, where x occurs exactly once in M. Therefore, we must show that for any environment η satisfying the appropriate sort assignment,

$$[\![[SL/x]M]\!]\eta \succ [\![[SR/x]M]\!]\eta.$$

Let η be any environment and let $a = [\![SL]\!]\eta$ and $b = [\![SR]\!]\eta$. By the substitution lemma, we have $a = [\![L]\!]\eta'$ and $b = [\![R]\!]\eta'$, for some environment η' determined by η and the substitution S. Therefore, by the hypothesis of the lemma, $a \succ b$. It follows (by the easy induction mentioned in the first paragraph of the proof) that

$[\![M]\!]\eta[x \mapsto a] \succ [\![M]\!]\eta[x \mapsto b]$.

The lemma follows by the substitution lemma. ∎

It is important to realize that when we prove termination of a rewrite system by interpreting terms in a well-founded algebra, the algebra we use does *not* satisfy the equations associated with the rewrite system. The reason is that reducing a term must "decrease" its value in the well-founded algebra. However, rewriting does not change the interpretation of a term in any algebra satisfying the equations associated with the rewrite system.

An essentially trivial termination example is the rewrite system for stacks, obtained by orienting the two equations in Table 3.1 from left to right. We can easily see that this system terminates since each rewrite rule reduces the number of symbols in the term. This argument may be carried out using a well-founded algebra whose carriers are the natural numbers. To do so, we interpret each function symbol as a numeric function that adds one to the sum of its arguments. Since the meaning of a term is then found by adding up the number of function symbols, it is easy to check that each rewrite rule reduces the value of a term.

It is easy to see that when the conditions of Lemma 3.7.15 are satisfied, and each carrier is the natural numbers, the numeric meaning of a term is an upper-bound on the longest sequence of reduction steps from the term. Therefore, if the number of rewrite steps is a fast-growing function of the length of a term, it will be necessary to interpret at least one function symbol as a numeric function that grows faster than a polynomial. The following example uses an exponential function to show that rewriting to disjunctive normal form always terminates.

Example 3.7.16 (Attributed to Filman [DJ90].) Consider the following rewrite system on formulas of propositional logic. As usual, we write the unary function $\neg : bool \to bool$ as a prefix operator, and binary functions $\wedge, \vee : bool \times bool \to bool$ as infix operations.

$$\begin{aligned}
\neg\neg x &\to x \\
\neg(x \vee y) &\to (\neg x \wedge \neg y) \\
\neg(x \wedge y) &\to (\neg x \vee \neg y) \\
x \wedge (y \vee z) &\to (x \wedge y) \vee (x \wedge z) \\
(y \vee z) \wedge x &\to (y \wedge x) \vee (z \wedge x).
\end{aligned}$$

This system transforms a formula into disjunctive normal form.

We can prove that this rewrite system is terminating using a well-founded algebra of natural numbers. More specifically, let $\mathcal{A} = \langle A^{bool}, or^{\mathcal{A}}, and^{\mathcal{A}}, not^{\mathcal{A}} \rangle$ be the algebra with carrier the $A^{bool} = \mathcal{N} - \{0, 1\}$, the natural numbers greater than 1, and

$$or^{\mathcal{A}}(x, y) = x + y + 1$$

$$and^{\mathcal{A}}(x, y) = x * y$$

$$not^{\mathcal{A}}(x) = 2^x$$

It is easy to see that each of these functions is strictly monotonic on the natural numbers (using the usual ordering). Therefore, $\mathcal{A}$ is a well-founded algebra.

To show that the rewrite rules are terminating, we must check that for natural number values of the free variables, the left-hand side defines a larger number than the right. For the first rule, this is obvious since for any natural number $x > 1$, we have $2^{2^x} > x$. For the second rule, we have $2^{(x+y+1)} = 2^x 2^y 2 > 2^x 2^y$ for any $x, y > 1$. The remaining rules rely on similar routine calculations. ∎

Example 3.7.17 In this example, we will show termination of a rewrite system derived from the integer multiset axioms given in Table 3.2. For simplicity, we will omit the rules for conditionals on multisets and booleans, since these do not interact with any of the other rules. Specifically, let us consider the signature with sorts *mset*, *nat*, *bool*, constants for natural numbers, the empty multiset and *true*, *false*, and functions + and *Eq*? on natural numbers, *insert* and *mem*? on multisets, and $cond_n$, conditional for natural numbers. The rewrite rules are

$$0 + 0 \rightarrow 0, 0 + 1 \rightarrow 1, \ldots$$

$$Eq?\, x\, x \rightarrow true$$

$$Eq?\, 0\, 1 \rightarrow false, Eq?\, 0\, 2 \rightarrow false, \ldots$$

$$mem?\, x\, empty \rightarrow 0$$

$$mem?\, x\, (insert\, y\, m) \rightarrow \texttt{if}\ Eq?\, x\, y\ \texttt{then}\ (mem?\, x\, m) + 1\ \texttt{else}\ mem?\, x\, m$$

$$cond_n\, true\, x\, y \rightarrow x$$

$$cond_n\, false\, x\, y \rightarrow y$$

We will interpret this signature in an algebra $\mathcal{A}$ with $A^{nat} = A^{mset} = A^{bool} \subseteq \mathcal{N}$. We must choose strictly monotonic functions for each function symbol so that the meaning of the left-hand side of each rule is guaranteed to be a larger natural number than the meaning of the right-hand side. For most of the functions, this may be done in a straightforward manner. However, since the second membership rule does not decrease the number of symbols in a term, we will have to give more consideration to the numeric interpretation of *mem*?.

An intuitive way to assign integers to terms is to give an upper bound on the longest possible sequence of reductions. For example, the longest sequence from a term of the form $cond_n M_1 M_2 M_3$ reduces all three subterms as much as possible, then (assuming M_1 reduces to *true* or *false*) reduces the conditional. Therefore, a reasonable numeric interpretation for $cond_n$ is

$$cond_n^{\mathcal{A}}\, x\, y\, z = 1 + x + y + z.$$

Following the same line of reasoning, we are led to the straightforward interpretations of all the other functions, except *mem?*.

$$+^{\mathcal{A}}\, x\, y \quad = 1 + x + y$$

$$Eq?^{\mathcal{A}}\, x\, y \quad = 1 + x + y$$

$$insert^{\mathcal{A}}\, x\, m = 1 + x + m$$

For technical reasons that will become apparent, we will interpret

$$A^{nat} = A^{mset} = A^{bool} = \mathcal{N} - \{0, 1\}$$

rather than using all natural numbers. Therefore, we interpret each constant symbol as 2.

For *mem*?, we must choose a function so that the left-hand side of each *mem*? rule will give a larger number than the right-hand side. The first *mem*? rule only requires that the function always have a value greater than 2. From the second rule, we obtain the condition

$$mem?^{\mathcal{A}}\, x\, (y + m) > 5 + x + y + 2 * (mem?^{\mathcal{A}}\, x\, m).$$

We can surmise by inspection that value of $mem?^{\mathcal{A}}\, x\, m$ should depend exponentially on its second argument, since $mem?^{\mathcal{A}}\, x\, (y + m)$ must be more than twice $mem?^{\mathcal{A}}\, x\, m$, for any $y \geq 2$. We can satisfy the numeric condition by taking

$$mem?^{\mathcal{A}}\, x\, m = x * 2^m.$$

With this interpretation, it is straightforward to verify the conditions of Lemma 3.7.15 and conclude that the rewrite rules for multisets are terminating. The only nontrivial case is *mem*?. A simple way to see that

$$x * 2^{(y+m)} - (5 + x + y + x * 2^{m+1}) > 0$$

is to verify the inequality for $x = y = m = 2$ and then check the derivative with respect to each variable. ∎

Exercise 3.7.18 Consider the following rewrite system on formulas of propositional logic.

$$\neg\neg x \to x$$
$$\neg(x \vee y) \to (\neg x \wedge \neg y)$$
$$\neg(x \wedge y) \to (\neg x \vee \neg y)$$
$$x \vee (y \wedge z) \to (x \vee y) \wedge (x \vee z)$$
$$(y \wedge z) \vee x \to (y \vee x) \wedge (z \vee x).$$

This is similar to the system in Example 3.7.16, except that these rules transform a formula into conjunctive normal form instead of disjunctive normal form. Show that this rewrite system is terminating by defining and using a well-founded algebra whose carrier is some subset of the natural numbers. (This is easy if you understand Example 3.7.16.)

Exercise 3.7.19 Show that the following rewrite rules are terminating, using a well-founded algebra.

(a)

$0 + x \quad\to x$

$(Sx) + y \to S(x + y)$

(b) The rules of part (a) in combination with

$0 * x \quad\to 0$

$(Sx) * y \to (x * y) + y$

(c) The rules of parts (a) and (b) in combination with

$\mathit{fact}\, 0 \quad\to 1$

$\mathit{fact}\, (Sx) \to (Sx) * (\mathit{fact}\, x)$

Termination for a more complicated version of this example is proved in [Les92] using a lexicographic order.

Exercise 3.7.20 An algebraic specification for *set, nat* and *bool* is given in Table 3.4. We may derive a rewrite system from the the equational axioms by orienting them from left to right.

(a) Show that this rewrite system is terminating by interpreting each of the function symbols as a function over a subset of the natural numbers.

(b) We may extend the set datatype with a cardinality function defined by the following axioms.

$card\ empty \quad = 0$

$card(insert\ x\ s) = cond\ (ismem?\ x\ s)(card\ s)((card\ s) + 1)$

Show that this rewrite system is terminating by interpreting each of the function symbols as a function over a subset of the natural numbers.

3.7.4 Critical Pairs

We will consider two classes of confluent rewrite systems, one necessarily terminating and the other not. In the first class, discussed in Section 3.7.5, the rules do not interact in any significant way. Consequently, we have confluence regardless of termination. In the second class, discussed in Section 3.7.6, we use termination to analyze the interaction between rules. An important idea in both cases is the definition of *critical pair,* which is a pair of terms representing an interaction between rewrite rules. Another general notion is *local confluence,* which is a weak version of confluence. Since local confluence may be used to motivate the definition of critical pair, we begin by defining local confluence.

A relation $\rightarrow$ is *locally confluent* if $N \leftarrow M \rightarrow P$ implies $N \twoheadrightarrow \circ \twoheadleftarrow P$. This is strictly weaker than confluence since we only assume $N \twoheadrightarrow \circ \twoheadleftarrow P$ when M rewrites to N or P by a single step. However, as shown in Section 3.7.6, local confluence is equivalent to ordinary confluence for terminating rewrite systems.

Example 3.7.21 A simple example of a rewrite system that is locally confluent but not confluent is

$a \rightarrow b, b \rightarrow a$

$a \rightarrow a_0, b \rightarrow b_0$

Both a and b can be reduced to a_0 and b_0. But since neither a_0 nor b_0 can be reduced to the other, confluence fails. However, a straightforward case analysis shows that $\mathcal{R}$ is locally confluent. A pictorial representation of this system appears in Figure 3.1. Another rewrite system that is locally confluent but not confluent, and which has no loops, appears in Example 3.7.26. ■

In the rest of this section, we will consider the problem of determining whether a rewrite system $\mathcal{R}$ is locally confluent. For rewrite systems with a finite number of rules, we may demonstrate local confluence by examining a finite number of cases called "critical pairs." Pictorial representations of terms and reductions, illustrating the three important cases, are given in Figures 3.2, 3.3 and 3.4. (Similar pictures appear in [DJ90, Hue80, Klo87].)

Suppose we have some finite set $\mathcal{R}$ of rewrite rules and a term M that can be reduced in two different ways. This means that there are rewrite rules $L \rightarrow R$ and $L' \rightarrow R'$ and

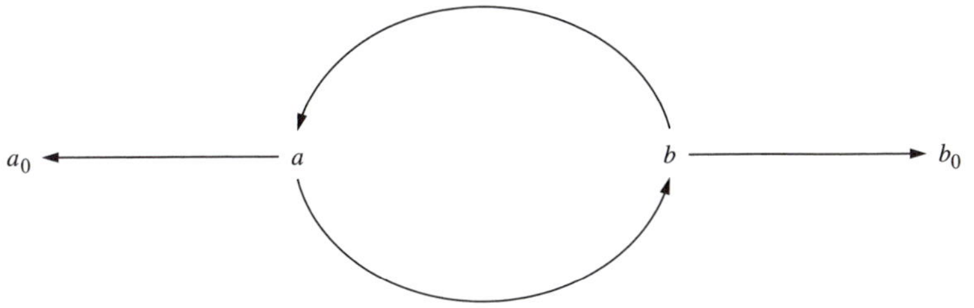

Figure 3.1
A locally confluent but non-confluent reduction.

substitutions S and S' such that the subterm of M at one position, $\vec{n}$, has the form SL and the subterm at another position, $\vec{m}$, has the form $S'L'$. It is not necessary that $L \to R$ and $L' \to R'$ be different rules. However, if we may rename variables so that L and L' have no variables in common, then we may assume that S and S' are the same substitution. There are several possible relationships between $\vec{n}$ and $\vec{m}$. In some cases, we can see that there is essentially no interaction between the rules. But in one case, the "critical pair" case, there is no *a priori* guarantee of local confluence.

The simplest case, illustrated in Figure 3.2, is if neither SL nor SL' is a subterm of the other. This happens when neither $\vec{n}$ nor $\vec{m}$ is a subsequence of the other. In this case, it does not matter which reduction we do first. We may always perform the second reduction immediately thereafter, producing the same result by either pair of reductions. For example, if M has the form $f SL\ SL'$, the two reductions produce $f SR\ SL'$ and $f SL\ SR'$, respectively. But then each reduces to $f SR\ SR'$ by a single reduction.

The second possibility is that one subterm may contain the other. In this case, both reductions only effect the larger subterm. For the sake of notational simplicity, we will assume that the larger subterm is all of M. Therefore, we assume $\vec{n}$ is the empty sequence, so $M \equiv SL$, and SL' is a subterm of SL and position $\vec{m}$. There are two subcases.

A "trivial" way for SL' to be a subterm of SL is when S substitutes a term containing SL' for some variable in L. In other words, if we divide SL into symbol occurrences that come from L and symbol occurrences that are introduced by S, the subterm at position $\vec{m}$ only contains symbols introduced by S. This is pictured in Figure 3.3. In this case, reducing SL to SR either eliminates the subterm SL', if R does not contain x, or gives us a term containing one or more occurrences of SL'. Since we can reduce each occurrence of SL' to SR', we have local confluence in this case.

The remaining case is the one we must consider in more detail: SL' is at position $\vec{m}$ of SL and $L|_{\vec{m}}$ is not a variable. Clearly, this may only happen if the principal (first) function symbol of L' occurs in L, as the principal function symbol of $L|_{\vec{m}}$. If we apply the first

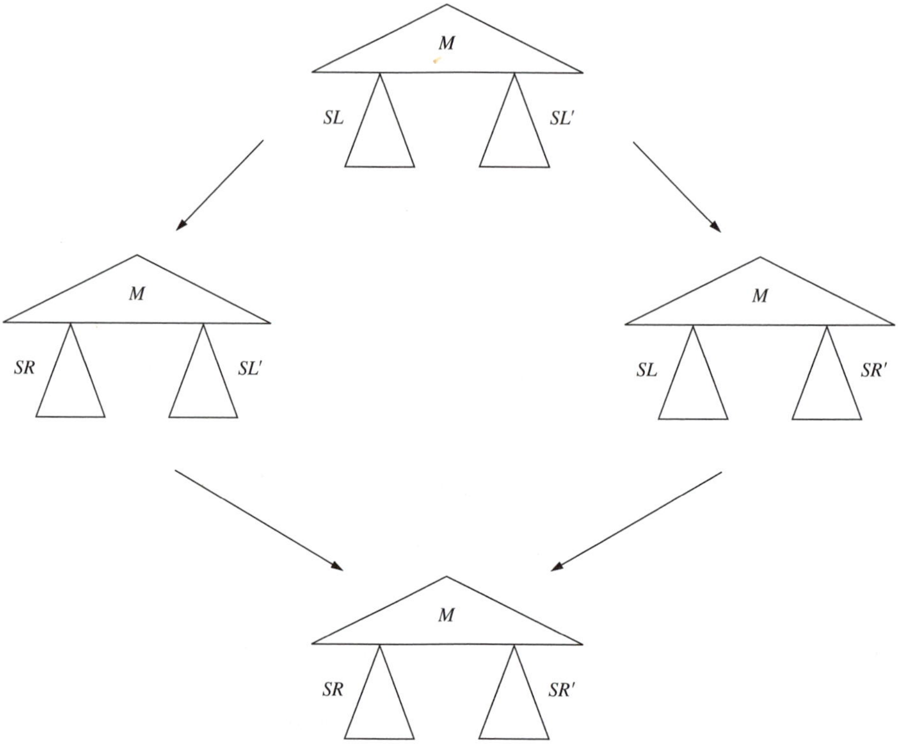

Figure 3.2
Disjoint reductions

rewrite rule, we obtain SR. The second rewrite rule gives us the term $[SR'/\vec{m}]SL$ with our chosen occurrence of SL' replaced by SR'. This is pictured in Figure 3.4. Although we may have $SR \twoheadrightarrow \circ \twoheadleftarrow [SR'/\vec{m}]SL$ "accidentally," there is no reason to expect this in general.

Example 3.7.22 Disjoint (Figure 3.2) and trivially overlapping (Figure 3.3) reductions are possible in every rewrite system. The following two rewrite rules for lists also allow conflicting reductions (Figure 3.4):

$$cdr(cons\,x\,\ell) \rightarrow \ell$$

$$cons(car\,\ell')(cdr\,\ell') \rightarrow \ell'$$

We obtain a disjoint reduction by writing a term that contains the left-hand sides of both rules. For example,

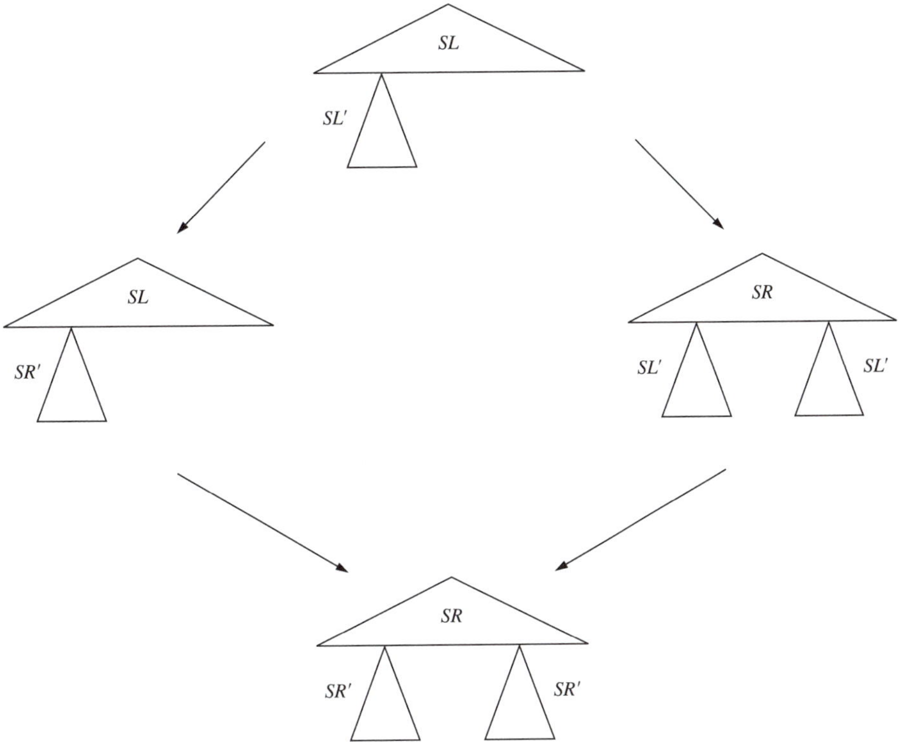

Figure 3.3
Trivial overlap

$cond\, B(\underline{cdr(cons\, x\, \ell)})(\underline{cons(car\, \ell')(cdr\, \ell')})$

may be reduced using either rewrite rule. The two subterms that may be reduced independently are underlined. A term with overlap only at a substitution instance of a variable (Figure 3.3) is

$\underline{cdr(cons\, x\, (\underline{cons(car\, \ell')(cdr\, \ell')}))}$

which is obtained by substituting the left hand side of the second rule for the variable ℓ in the first. Notice that if we reduce the larger subterm, the underlined smaller subterm remains intact. Finally, we obtain a nontrivial overlap by replacing x and ℓ in the first rule by $car\, \ell'$ and $cdr\, \ell'$.

$\underline{cdr(\underline{cons(car\, \ell')(cdr\, \ell')})}$

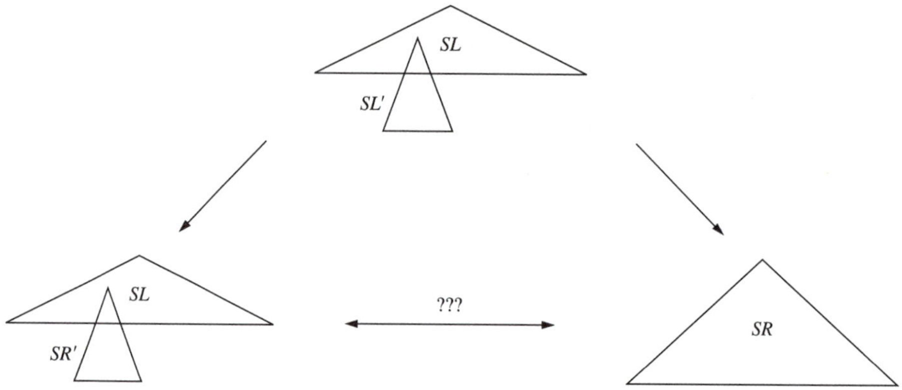

Figure 3.4
Critical pair

If we apply the first rule to the entire term, the *cons* in the smaller subterm is removed by the rule. If we apply the second rule to the smaller subterm, *cons* is removed and the first rule may no longer be applied. However, it is easy to see that the rules are locally confluent, since in both cases we obtain the same term, ℓ.

A system where local confluence fails due to overlapping rules appears in Example 3.7.1. Specifically, the term $(x + 0) + y$ may be reduced to either $x + y$ or $x + (0 + y)$, but neither of these terms can be reduced further. Associativity (as in the third rule of Example 3.7.1) and commutativity are difficult to treat by rewrite rules. Techniques for rewriting with an associative and commutative equivalence relation are surveyed in [DJ90], for example. ■

It might appear that for two (not necessarily distinct) rules $L \to R$ and $L' \to R'$, we must consider infinitely many substitutions S in looking for nontrivial overlaps. However, for each term L, position $\vec{m}$ in L, and term L', if any substitution S gives $SL' \equiv SL|_{\vec{m}}$, there is a simplest such substitution. More specifically, we may choose the *minimal* (most general) substitution S under the ordering $S \leq S'$ if there exist S'' with $S' = S'' \circ S$. Using unification, we may compute a most general substitution for each L' and non-variable subterm $L|_{\vec{m}}$, or determine that none exists. For many pairs of rewrite rules, this is a straightforward hand calculation.

Intuitively, a critical pair is the result of reducing a term with overlapping redexes, obtained with a substitution that is as simple as possible. An *overlap* is a triple $\langle SL, SL', \vec{m}\rangle$ such that SL' occurs at position $\vec{m}$ of SL and $L|_{\vec{m}}$ is not a variable. If S is the simplest substitution such that $\langle SL, SL', \vec{m}\rangle$ is an overlap, then the pair $\langle SR, [SR'/\vec{m}]SL\rangle$ is called a *critical pair*. In Example 3.7.22 the two nontrivial overlaps give us critical pairs $\langle \ell, \ell\rangle$ and $\langle Sx + (y + z), S(x + y) + z\rangle$, since the simplest possible substitutions were used.

A useful fact to remember is that a critical pair may occur only between rules $L \to R$ and $L' \to R'$ when the principal function symbol f of L' occurs in L. Moreover, if f is applied to non-variable terms in both L' and the relevant occurrence in L, then the principal function symbols of corresponding arguments must be identical. For example, if we have a rule $f(gxy) \to R'$, then this may lead to a critical pair only if there is a rule $L \to R$ such that either fz or a term of the form $f(gPQ)$ occurs in L. A subterm of the form $f(h\ldots)$ does not give us a critical pair, since there is no substitution making $(h\ldots)$ syntactically identical to any term with principal function symbol g.

In general, it is important to consider overlaps involving two uses of the same rule. For example, the rewrite system with the single rule $f(fx) \to a$ is not locally confluent since we have an overlap $\langle f(f(fx)), f(fx), 1\rangle$ leading to a critical pair $\langle fa, a\rangle$. (The term $f(f(fx))$ can be reduced to both fa and a.) It is also important to consider the case where two left-hand sides are identical, since a rewrite system may have two rules, $L \to R$ and $L \to R'$, that have the same left-hand side. (In this case, $\langle R, R'\rangle$ is a critical pair.) Since any rule $L \to R$ results in overlap $\langle L, L, \epsilon\rangle$, where ϵ is the empty sequence, any rule results in a critical pair $\langle R, R\rangle$ of identical terms. We call a critical pair of identical terms, resulting from two applications of the a single rule $L \to R$ to L, a *trivial critical pair.*

Proposition 3.7.23 [KB70] A rewrite system $\mathcal{R}$ is locally confluent iff $M \twoheadrightarrow_{\mathcal{R}} \circ \twoheadleftarrow_{\mathcal{R}} N$ for every critical pair $\langle M, N\rangle$.

If a finite rewrite system $\mathcal{R}$ is terminating, then this lemma gives us an algorithmic procedure for deciding whether $\mathcal{R}$ is locally confluent. We will consider this in Section 3.7.6.

Proof The implication from left to right is straightforward. The proof in the other direction follows the line of reasoning used to motivate the definition of critical pair. More specifically, suppose M may be reduced to two subterms, N and P, using $L \to R$ and $L' \to R'$. Then there are three possible relationships between the relevant subterms SL and SR of M. If these subterms are disjoint or overlap trivially, then as argued in this section, we have $N \twoheadrightarrow \circ \twoheadleftarrow P$. The remaining case is that N and P contain substitution instances of a critical pair. Since the symbols not involved in the reductions $M \to N$ and $M \to P$ will not play any role in determining whether $N \twoheadrightarrow \circ \twoheadleftarrow P$, we may simplify notation by assuming that there is some critical pair $\langle SR, [SR'/\vec{m}]SL\rangle$ of $\mathcal{R}$ with

$N \equiv S'(SR)$ and $P \equiv S'([SR'/\vec{m}]SL)$. However, by the hypothesis of the lemma, we have $SR \twoheadrightarrow \circ \twoheadleftarrow [SR'/\vec{m}]SL$. Therefore, since each reduction step applies to any substitution instance of the term involved (see Lemmas 3.7.10 and 3.7.11), we have $N \twoheadrightarrow \circ \twoheadleftarrow P$. ∎

Exercise 3.7.24 Using the signature of Example 3.7.1, we may also consider the rewrite system

$$0 + x \to x$$

$$(-x) + x \to 0$$

$$(x + y) + z \to x + (y + z)$$

You may replace infix addition by a standard algebraic (prefix) function symbol if this makes it easier for you.

(a) Find all critical pairs of this system.

(b) For each critical pair $\langle SR, [SR'/\vec{m}]SL\rangle$, determine whether $SR \twoheadrightarrow \circ \twoheadleftarrow [SR'/\vec{m}]SL$.

Exercise 3.7.25 A rewrite system for formulas of propositional logic is given in Example 3.7.16. You may translate into standard algebraic terms if this makes it easier for you.

(a) Find all critical pairs of this system.

(b) For each critical pair $\langle SR, [SR'/\vec{m}]SL\rangle$, determine whether $SR \twoheadrightarrow \circ \twoheadleftarrow [SR'/\vec{m}]SL$.

3.7.5 Left-linear Non-overlapping Rewrite Systems

A rewrite system is *non-overlapping* if it has no nontrivial critical pairs. In other words, the only way to form a critical pair is by using a rule $L \to R$ to reduce L to R twice, obtaining the pair $\langle R, R\rangle$. Since trivial critical pairs do not effect confluence, we might expect every non-overlapping rewrite system to be confluent. However, this is not true; a counterexample is given in Example 3.7.26 below. Intuitively, the problem is that since rewrite rules allow us to replace terms of one form with terms of another, we may have rules that only overlap after some initial rewriting. However, if we restrict the left-hand sides of rules, then the absence of critical pairs ensures confluence. The standard terminology is that a rule $L \to R$ is *left-linear* if no variable occurs twice in L. A set of rules is *left-linear* if every rule in the set is left-linear.

The main result in this section is that left-linear, non-overlapping rewrite systems are confluent. The earliest proofs of this fact are probably proofs for combinatory logic (see Example 3.7.31) that generalize to arbitrary left-linear and non-overlapping systems [Klo87]. The general approach using parallel reduction is due to Huet [Hue80].

Example 3.7.26 The following rewrite system for finite and "infinite" numbers has no critical pairs (and is therefore locally confluent) but is not confluent.

$$\infty \to S\,\infty$$

$$Eq?\,x\,x \to true$$

$$Eq?\,x\,(Sx) \to false$$

Intuitively, the two $Eq?$ rules would be fine, except that the "infinite number" ∞ is its own successor. With ∞, we have

$$Eq?\,\infty\,\infty \to true$$

$$Eq?\,\infty\,\infty \to Eq?\,\infty\,(S\infty) \to false$$

so one term has two distinct normal forms, *true* and *false*.

The intuitive reason why confluence fails in this situation is fairly subtle. The only possible critical pair in this system would arise from a substitution R such that $R(Eq?\,x\,x) \equiv R(Eq?\,x\,(Sx))$. Any such substitution R would have to be of the form $R = [M/x]$, where $M \equiv SM$. But since no term M is syntactically equal to its successor, SM, this is impossible. However, the term ∞ is reducible to its own successor. Therefore, the rules have the same effect as an overlap at substitution instances $Eq?\,\infty\,\infty$ and $Eq?\,\infty\,(S\infty)$. Another, way of saying this is that since $\infty \to S\infty$, we have $[\infty/x](Eq?\,x\,x) \to [\infty/x](Eq?\,x\,(Sx))$, and the "overlap after reduction" causes confluence to fail. ∎

We will analyze left-linear, non-overlapping rewrite systems using parallel reduction, which was considered in Section 2.4.4 for PCF. We define the *parallel reduction* relation, $\Rightarrow_{\mathcal{R}}$ for a set $\mathcal{R}$ of algebraic rewrite rules by

$$[SL_1, \ldots, SL_k/\vec{n}_1, \ldots \vec{n}_k]M \Rightarrow_{\mathcal{R}} [SR_1, \ldots, SR_k/\vec{n}_1, \ldots \vec{n}_k]M$$

where $\vec{n}_1, \ldots \vec{n}_k$ are disjoint positions in M (*i.e.*, none of these sequences of natural numbers is a subsequence of any other) and $L_1 \to R_1, \ldots, L_k \to R_k$ are rewrite rules in $\mathcal{R}$ that need not be distinct (and which have variables renamed if necessary). An alternate characterization of $\Rightarrow_{\mathcal{R}}$ is that this is the least relation on terms that contains $\to_{\mathcal{R}}$ and is closed under the rule

$$\frac{M_1 \Rightarrow_{\mathcal{R}} N_1, \ldots, M_k \Rightarrow_{\mathcal{R}} N_k}{\mathcal{C}[M_1, \ldots, M_k] \Rightarrow_{\mathcal{R}} \mathcal{C}[N_1, \ldots, N_k]}$$

for any context $\mathcal{C}[\ldots]$ with places for k terms to be inserted. This was the definition used for parallel PCF reduction in Section 2.4.4.

Some useful notation is to write $M \twoheadrightarrow_n N$ if $M \twoheadrightarrow N$ by a reduction sequence of length n, and $M \twoheadrightarrow_{<n} N$ if there is a reduction sequence of length less than n.

The reason we use parallel reduction to analyze linear, non-overlapping rewrite systems is that parallel reduction has a stronger confluence property that is both easier to prove directly than confluence of sequential reduction and interesting in its own right. A relation $\rightarrow$ on terms is *strongly confluent* if, whenever $M \rightarrow N$ and $M \rightarrow P$, there is a term Q with $N \twoheadrightarrow_{<2} Q$ and $P \twoheadrightarrow_{<2} Q$. The reader who checks other sources should know that an alternate, slightly weaker definition of strong confluence is sometimes used.

We now show that $\Rightarrow$ is strongly confluent. This is called the "parallel moves lemma." After proving this lemma, we will show that strong confluence of $\Rightarrow_{\mathcal{R}}$ implies confluence of $\twoheadrightarrow_{\mathcal{R}}$.

Lemma 3.7.27 [Hue80] If $\mathcal{R}$ is left-linear and non-overlapping, then $\Rightarrow_{\mathcal{R}}$ is strongly confluent.

The lemma proved in [Hue80] is actually stronger, since it applies to systems with the property that for every critical pair $\langle M, N\rangle$, we have $M \Rightarrow_{\mathcal{R}} N$ or $N \Rightarrow_{\mathcal{R}} M$. However, the left-linear and non-overlapping case is easier to prove and will be sufficient for our purposes.

Proof Suppose that $M \Rightarrow_{\mathcal{R}} N$ and $M \Rightarrow_{\mathcal{R}} P$. We must show that $N \Rightarrow_{\mathcal{R}} \circ \Leftarrow_{\mathcal{R}} P$. For notational simplicity, we will drop the subscript $\mathcal{R}$ in the rest of the proof.

The reduction $M \Rightarrow N$ results from the replacement of subterms $SL_1, \ldots, SL_k$ at positions $\vec{n}_1, \ldots, \vec{n}_k$ by $SR_1, \ldots, SR_k$ and, similarly, the reduction $M \Rightarrow P$ involves replacement of terms at positions $\vec{p}_1, \ldots, \vec{p}_\ell$. By hypothesis, the positions $\vec{n}_1, \ldots, \vec{n}_k$ must be disjoint and similarly for $\vec{p}_1, \ldots, \vec{p}_\ell$. There may be some overlap between some of the $\vec{n}_i$'s and $\vec{p}_j$'s, but the kinds of overlaps are restricted by the disjointness of the two sets of positions. Specifically, if some $\vec{n}_i$ is a subsequence of one or more $\vec{p}_j$'s, say $\vec{p}_1, \ldots, \vec{p}_j$, then none of $\vec{p}_1, \ldots, \vec{p}_j$ can be a subsequence of any $\vec{n}_m$. Therefore, the only kind of overlap we must consider is a subterm SL of M that is reduced by a single rule $L \rightarrow R$ in one reduction, but has one or more disjoint subterms reduced in the other. Since there are no critical pairs, we have only the trivial case that $\vec{n}_i = \vec{p}_j$, with the same rule applied in both cases, and the nontrivial case with all of the effected subterms of SL arising from substitution for variables in L.

For notational simplicity, we assume in the rest of this proof that we do not have $\vec{n}_i = \vec{p}_j$ for any i and j. The modifications required to treat $\vec{n}_i = \vec{p}_j$ are completely straightforward, since N and P must be identical at this position.

To analyze this situation systematically, we reorder the sequences of disjoint positions so that for some $r \leq k$ and $s \leq \ell$, the initial subsequences $\vec{n}_1, \ldots, \vec{n}_r$ and $\vec{p}_1, \ldots, \vec{p}_s$

have two properties. First, none has any proper subsequences among the complete lists $\vec{n}_1, \ldots, \vec{n}_k$ and $\vec{p}_1, \ldots, \vec{p}_\ell$. Second, every sequence in either complete list must have some proper subsequence among the initial subsequences $\vec{n}_1, \ldots, \vec{n}_r$ and $\vec{p}_1, \ldots, \vec{p}_s$.

If we let $t = r + s$ and let $M_1, \ldots, M_t$ be the subterms $M|_{\vec{n}_1}, \ldots, M|_{\vec{n}_k}, M|_{\vec{p}_1}, \ldots, M|_{\vec{p}_s}$ then every $M_1, \ldots, M_t$ is reduced in producing N or P, and all of the reductions occur in $M_1, \ldots, M_t$. Therefore, we may write M, N and P in the form

$$M \equiv \mathcal{C}[M_1, \ldots, M_t]$$

$$N \equiv \mathcal{C}[N_1, \ldots, N_t]$$

$$P \equiv \mathcal{C}[P_1, \ldots, P_t]$$

where, for $1 \le i \le t$, we have $M_i \equiv SL \to N_i \equiv SR$, for some rule $L \to R$, and $M_i \Rightarrow P_i$ by zero or more disjoint reductions that occur within subterms that arise by substitution into L, or similarly with the roles of N_i and P_i reversed. We will complete the proof by showing that in each case, $N_i \Rightarrow \circ \Leftarrow P_i$.

Suppose that M_i occurs at position $\vec{n}_i$ in M and $M_i \equiv SL \to N_i \equiv SR$, for some rule $L \to R$. If $\vec{n}_i$ is not a subsequence of any $\vec{p}_j$ then we have $N_i \Rightarrow \circ \Leftarrow P_i$ by the rule $L \to R$. Otherwise, there exist positions $\vec{m}_1, \ldots, \vec{m}_q$ in M_i such that for $u \le q$,

$$(M_i)|_{\vec{m}_u} \equiv SL_u \quad \text{and} \quad (P_i)|_{\vec{m}_u} \equiv SR_u$$

for some rules $L_1 \to R_1, \ldots, L_q \to R_q$, and, since the rewrite system $\mathcal{R}$ is non-overlapping, each position $\vec{m}_u$ in $M_i \equiv SL$ is at or below a variable in L. Since positions $\vec{m}_1, \ldots, \vec{m}_k$ are at or below variables in L, there is some substitution S' of terms for variables such that $P_i \equiv S'L$. Since the rule $L \to R$ is left-linear, we have $P_i \to S'R$. It remains to show that $N_i \equiv SR \Rightarrow S'R$. Reasoning as in the variable overlap case in Section 3.7.4 (Figure 3.3), we can see that for each variable x in R, we must have $Sx \Rightarrow S'x$. Therefore $SR \Rightarrow S'R$. The case $N_i \to P_i$ is completely analogous. This concludes the proof. ∎

Lemma 3.7.28 If $\Rightarrow_\mathcal{R}$ is strongly confluent then both $\Rightarrow\!\!\!\!\!\Rightarrow_\mathcal{R}$ and $\twoheadrightarrow_\mathcal{R}$ are confluent.

Proof It is not hard to see that $\Rightarrow\!\!\!\!\!\Rightarrow_\mathcal{R}$ and $\twoheadrightarrow_\mathcal{R}$ are the same relation on terms. (This is part (a) of Exercise 2.4.19 in Section 2.4.4.) Therefore, it suffices to show that if $\Rightarrow_\mathcal{R}$ is strongly confluent then $\Rightarrow\!\!\!\!\!\Rightarrow_\mathcal{R}$ is confluent. For notational simplicity, we will drop the subscript $\mathcal{R}$ in the rest of the proof. Recall that we write $M \Rightarrow\!\!\!\!\!\Rightarrow_n N$ if there is a reduction sequence from M to N of length n, and $M \Rightarrow\!\!\!\!\!\Rightarrow_{<n} N$ if the length is less than n.

Suppose $\Rightarrow$ is strongly confluent. We first show by induction on n that if $M \Rightarrow\!\!\!\!\!\Rightarrow_n N$ and $M \Rightarrow P$ then there is some term Q with $N \Rightarrow\!\!\!\!\!\Rightarrow_{<2} Q$ and $P \Rightarrow\!\!\!\!\!\Rightarrow_{<n} Q$. For the base case, $M \Rightarrow\!\!\!\!\!\Rightarrow_0 N$, this is trivial. For the induction step, suppose $M \Rightarrow\!\!\!\!\!\Rightarrow_n N_1 \Rightarrow\!\!\!\!\!\Rightarrow N$ and

$M \Rightarrow P$. By the induction hypothesis, there is some Q with $N_1 \Rrightarrow_{<2} Q$ and $P \Rrightarrow_{<n} Q$. If $N_1 \equiv Q$, then we are done. Otherwise, since $N_1 \Rightarrow Q$ and $N_1 \Rightarrow N$, we may use strong confluence of $\Rightarrow$ to prove the claim.

It remains to consider the general case $M \Rrightarrow_n N$ and $M \Rrightarrow_p P$. However, it is easy to show by induction on p that there is some term Q with $N \Rrightarrow_{<p} Q$ and $P \Rrightarrow_{<n} Q$, by the same form of reasoning used in the special case $p = 1$ above. This proves the lemma. ∎

It follows immediately from Lemmas 3.7.27 and 3.7.28 that every left-linear and non-overlapping rewrite system is confluent.

Proposition 3.7.29 If $\mathcal{R}$ is left-linear and non-overlapping, then $\Rrightarrow_{\mathcal{R}}$ and $\twoheadrightarrow_{\mathcal{R}}$ are confluent.

Example 3.7.30 The following rewrite system for list expressions is left-linear and non-overlapping, and therefore confluent.

$$car(cons\, x\, \ell) \to x$$

$$cdr(cons\, x\, \ell) \to \ell$$

$$isempty?\, nil \to true$$

$$isempty?(cons\, x\, \ell) \to false$$

However, left-linearity is destroyed if we add the non-linear rule

$$cons(car\, \ell)(cdr\, \ell) \to \ell.$$

We have already seen, in Example 3.7.22, that the non-linear rule does not interact badly with the *cdr* rule; the overlap with *car* is similarly benign. However, the interaction with the second *isempty?* causes local confluence to fail. Specifically, since $isempty?(cons(car\, \ell)(cdr\, \ell))$ reduces to *false* and $isempty?(\ell)$, we have a critical pair consisting of distinct normal forms. ∎

Example 3.7.31 Untyped combinatory logic has the following algebraic specification.

sorts:ι

fctns:$S,\, K,\, I\colon \iota$

$$ap\colon \iota \to \iota \to \iota$$

eqns:$ap(ap(ap\, S\, x)y)z = ap(ap\, x\, z)(ap\, y\, z)$

$$ap(ap\, K\, x)y = x$$

$$ap\, I\, x = x$$

It is easy to see that if we orient the three equational axioms from left to right, we have a left-linear and non-overlapping rewrite system. Therefore, combinatory logic is confluent. It is conventional to write *ap* as an infix operator, and even to omit *ap*. In the rest of this example, we will write $x \cdot y$ for $ap\, x\, y$. When parentheses are omitted, we associate $\cdot$ to the left.

It is not very hard to show that this rewrite system is not terminating. For example, consider the term $S \cdot I \cdot I$. It is easy to see that

$$(S \cdot I \cdot I) \cdot x \twoheadrightarrow x \cdot x.$$

Therefore, we have

$$(S \cdot I \cdot I) \cdot (S \cdot I \cdot I) \twoheadrightarrow (S \cdot I \cdot I) \cdot (S \cdot I \cdot I).$$

An important motivation for combinatory logic is that every untyped lambda term can be translated into combinatory logic. The untyped translation is the same as the translation of typed lambda terms into typed combinators given in Section 4.5.7. An algebra satisfying the axioms of (untyped) combinatory logic is called an (untyped) *combinatory algebra.* ■

3.7.6 Local Confluence, Termination and Completion

In the last section, we saw that every left-linear, non-overlapping rewrite system is confluent, regardless of termination. In this section, we consider a sufficient condition for confluence that allows rules which are not left-linear, but requires termination. Specifically, every terminating and locally confluent relation is confluent. This fact, which is often called "Newman's Lemma," after [New42], does not depend on the structure of algebraic terms at all. For this reason, it applies to a variety of other systems, including lambda calculus reduction and various graph manipulation rules. It has been discovered by many different researchers.

Proposition 3.7.32 Let $\mathcal{R}$ be a terminating rewrite system. Then $\mathcal{R}$ is confluent iff $\mathcal{R}$ is locally confluent.

Proof We say $\mathcal{R}$ is *confluent from M* if, whenever $N \twoheadleftarrow_{\mathcal{R}} M \twoheadrightarrow_{\mathcal{R}} P$, we have $N \twoheadrightarrow_{\mathcal{R}} \circ \twoheadleftarrow_{\mathcal{R}} P$. Since $\mathcal{R}$ is terminating, we may let the norm, $|M|$, of term M be the length of the longest sequence of reductions from M. We will show by induction on the norm that $\mathcal{R}$ is confluent from every term. Let us write $\twoheadrightarrow$ instead of $\twoheadrightarrow_{\mathcal{R}}$. The base case, $|M| = 0$, is trivial.

Suppose that $M \twoheadrightarrow N$, $M \twoheadrightarrow P$ and for every Q with $|Q| < |M|$, $\mathcal{R}$ is confluent from Q. If either reduction, $M \twoheadrightarrow N$ or $M \twoheadrightarrow P$, has length 0, then clearly $N \twoheadrightarrow \circ \twoheadleftarrow P$. Therefore, we assume $M \rightarrow N_1 \twoheadrightarrow N$ and $M \rightarrow P_1 \twoheadrightarrow P$. By local confluence, there is some term Q with $N_1 \twoheadrightarrow Q$ and $P_1 \twoheadrightarrow Q$. By the induction hypothesis, there is some term R with $N_1 \twoheadrightarrow R$ and $Q \twoheadrightarrow R$. Since $P_1 \twoheadrightarrow Q \twoheadrightarrow R$ and $P_1 \twoheadrightarrow P$, we may apply the induction hypothesis again to obtain a term S with $R \twoheadrightarrow S$ and $P \twoheadrightarrow S$. By combining reductions already listed, we can see that both N and P reduce to S. This proves the lemma. ∎

Example 3.7.33 The following rewrite rules for conditional are locally confluent and terminating but not left-linear.

$$\texttt{if}\ \textit{true}\ \texttt{then}\ x\ \texttt{else}\ y \rightarrow x$$

$$\texttt{if}\ \textit{false}\ \texttt{then}\ x\ \texttt{else}\ y \rightarrow y$$

$$\texttt{if}\ u\ \texttt{then}\ x\ \texttt{else}\ x \rightarrow x$$

Termination is straightforward since all rules reduce the length of terms. There are two critical pairs, both involving the third, non-linear rule. The first results from reducing

$$\texttt{if}\ \textit{true}\ \texttt{then}\ x\ \texttt{else}\ x,$$

by the first and third rules. This gives us the critical pair $\langle x, x\rangle$, which clearly does not present a problem. The second critical pair is also $\langle x, x\rangle$. ∎

Proposition 3.7.23, often called the *Knuth-Bendix test,* was originally presented in [KB70] as part of an algorithm that not only tests a set of terminating rewrite rules for local confluence, but adds additional rules if the test fails. This algorithm is called the *Knuth-Bendix completion procedure,* or *completion* for short. The rules added by the procedure are conservative over the original ones, in the sense that if the Knuth-Bendix algorithm produces $\mathcal{R}' \supseteq \mathcal{R}$, then $\mathcal{E}_{\mathcal{R}'}$ and $\mathcal{E}_{\mathcal{R}}$ determine the same algebraic theory. The completion procedure requires an algorithm for determining whether any inequality of the form $M > N$ holds, in some well-founded algebra.

The completion procedure begins by testing whether $L > R$, for each rewrite rule $L \rightarrow R$. If so, then the rewrite system is terminating and we may proceed to test for local confluence. This may be done algorithmically by computing critical pairs $\langle M, N\rangle$ and searching the possible reductions from M and N to see whether $M \twoheadrightarrow \circ \twoheadleftarrow N$. Since the rewrite system is terminating, there are only finitely many possible reductions to consider. If all critical pairs converge, then the algorithm terminates with the result that the rewrite system is confluent and terminating.

If we do not have $M \twoheadrightarrow \circ \twoheadleftarrow N$ for some critical pair $\langle M, N\rangle$ then by definition of critical pair, there is some term that reduces to both M and N. Therefore, M and N may be proved equal by equational reasoning and it makes logical sense to add $M \rightarrow N$ or $N \rightarrow M$ as a rewrite rule. If $M > N$ or $N > M$, then the completion procedure adds the appropriate rule and continues the test for local confluence. However, if M and N

are incomparable (neither $M > N$ nor $N > M$), there is no guarantee that either rule preserves termination, and so the procedure terminates inconclusively. This procedure may not terminate, as illustrated in the following example, based on [Bel86].

Example 3.7.34 In this example, we show that the completion procedure may continue indefinitely, neither producing a confluent system after adding any finite number of rules, nor reaching a state where there is no rule to add. Let us consider two rewrite rules, called H for *homomorphism* and A for *associativity.*

$$fx + fy \quad \to f(x + y) \qquad (H)$$

$$(x + y) + z \to x + (y + z) \qquad (A)$$

We can see that these are terminating by constructing a well-founded algebra, $\mathcal{A}$. As the single carrier, we may use the natural numbers greater than 2. To make (A) decreasing, we must choose some non-associative interpretation for $+$. The simplest familiar arithmetic operation is exponentiation. We may use

$$+^{\mathcal{A}}(x, y) = y^x,$$

$$f^{\mathcal{A}}(x) = x^2.$$

An easy calculation shows that each rule is decreasing in this algebra.

The only critical pair is the result of unifying $fx + fy$ with the subterm $(x + y)$ of the left-hand side of (A). Reducing the term $(fx + fy) + z$ in two ways gives us the critical pair

$$\langle f(x + y) + z, fx + (fy + z)\rangle,$$

with weights

$$f^{\mathcal{A}}(x +^{\mathcal{A}} y) +^{\mathcal{A}} z = z^{(y^x)^2} = z^{(y^{2x})}$$

$$f^{\mathcal{A}}x +^{\mathcal{A}} (f^{\mathcal{A}}y +^{\mathcal{A}} z) = (z^{y^2})^{x^2} = z^{(y^2)(x^2)}$$

Comparing the numeric values of these expressions for $x, y, z \geq 3$, we can see that termination is preserved if we add the rule rewriting the first term to the second. This gives us a rewrite rule that we may recognize as an instance of the general pattern

$$f^n(x + y) + z \to f^n x + (f^n y + z), \qquad (A)_n$$

with $(A) \equiv (A)_0$.

The general pattern, if we continue the completion procedure, is that by reducing the term $f^{n-1}(fx + fy) + z$ by (H) and $(A)_{n-1}$, for $n > 1$, we obtain a critical pair of the form

$\langle f^n(x+y)+z,\ f^nx+(f^ny+z)\rangle$

with weights

$$(f^A)^n(x +^A y) +^A z = z^{((y^x)^{2n})} = z^{(y^{2nx})}$$

$$(f^A)^n x +^A ((f^A)^n y +^A z) = (z^{(y^{2n})})^{(x^{2n})} = z^{(y^{2n})(x^{2n})}$$

This leads us to add the rewrite rule $(A)_n$. For this reason, the completion procedure will continue indefinitely. ■

There are a number of issues involved in mechanizing the completion procedure that we will not go into. A successful example of completion, carried out by hand, is given in the next section.

Exercise 3.7.35 Consider the infinite rewrite system consisting of rule (H) of Example 3.7.34, along with each rule of the form $(A)_n$ given in that example. Prove that this infinite system is confluent and terminating, or give a counterexample.

Exercise 3.7.36 The rewrite system with the single rule

$f(g(fx)) \to g(fx)$

is terminating, since this rule reduces the number of function symbols in a term. Carry out several steps of the completion procedure. For each critical pair, add the rewrite rule that reduces the number of function symbols. What is the general form of rewrite rule that is added?

3.7.7 Applications to Algebraic Datatypes

There are several ways that rewrite rules may be used in the design, analysis and application of algebraic specifications. If equational axioms may be oriented (or completed) to form a confluent rewrite system, then this gives us a useful way to determine whether two terms are provably equal. In particular, a confluent rewrite system allows us to show that two terms are *not* provably equal by showing that they have distinct normal forms. A potential use of rewrite rules in practice is that rewriting may be used as a prototype implementation of a specified datatype. While this may be useful for simple debugging of specifications, reduction is seldom efficient enough for realistic programming. Finally, since our understanding of initial algebras is largely syntactic (based on provability), rewrite systems are very useful in the analysis and understanding of initial algebras.

We will illustrate two uses of rewrite systems using the algebraic specifications of lists with error elements. The first is that we may discover the inconsistency of our first specification by testing for local confluence. The second is that we may characterize the initial algebra for the revised specification by completing directed equations to a confluent rewrite system.

In Tables 3.5 and 3.6 of Section 3.6.3, we considered a naive treatment of error values that turned out to be inconsistent. Let us consider the rewrite system obtained by reading the equations from left to right. It is easy to see that these rules are terminating, since every rule reduces the length of an expression. Before checking the entire system for confluence, let us check Table 3.5 and Table 3.6 individually for critical pairs. The only pair of rules that give us a critical pair are the rules

$$cons\ error_a\ l = error_l$$

$$cons\ x\ error_l = error_l$$

of Table 3.6. Since the left-hand sides are unified by replacing x and l by error values, we have the critical pair $\langle error_l, error_l\rangle$. However, this critical pair obviously does not cause local confluence to fail. It follows that, taken separately, the rules determined from Tables 3.5 or Table 3.6 are confluent and terminating. Hence by Corollary 3.7.14, the equations in each figure are consistent.

Now let us examine rules from Table 3.6 that might overlap with a rule from Table 3.5. The first candidate is $cons\ error_a\ l \to error_l$, since a rule $car(cons\ x\ l) \to x$ containing $cons$ appears in Table 3.5. We have a nontrivial overlap since the term $car(cons\ error_a\ l)$ is a substitution instance of one left-hand side and also has a subterm matching the left-hand side of another rule. Applying one reduction, we obtain $error_a$, while the other gives us $car\ error_l$. Thus our first non-trivial critical pair is $\langle error_a, car\ error_l\rangle$. However, this critical pair is benign, since $car\ error_l \to error_a$.

The next critical pair is obtained by unifying the left-hand side of $cons\ error_a\ l \to error_l$ with a subterm of the next rule, $cdr(cons\ x\ l) \to l$. Substituting $error_a$ for x produces a term $cdr(cons\ error_a\ l)$, which reduces either to the list variable l or $cdr\ error_l$. Since the latter only reduces to $error_l$, we see that confluence fails. In addition, we have found a single expression that reduces both to a list variable l, and a list constant $error_l$. Therefore, $error_l \leftrightarrow l\ [l\colon list]$ and so by Lemma 3.7.11 the equational specification given in Tables 3.5 and 3.6 proves the equation $error_l = l[l\colon list]$. This shows that all lists must be equal in any algebra satisfying the specification. From this point, it is not hard to see that similar equations are provable for the other sorts. Thus we conclude that the specification is inconsistent.

The revised specification of lists with error elements is given in Table 3.7. We obtain a rewrite system by reading each equation from left to right. Before checking the critical pairs, let us establish termination. This will give us a basis for orienting additional rules that arise during the completion procedure.

We can show termination of this rewrite system using a well-founded algebra $\mathcal{A}$ with each carrier the set of positive natural numbers (the numbers greater than 0). We interpret each of the constants as 1 and the functions as follows. This interpretation was developed by estimating the maximum number of reduction steps that could be applied to a term of each form, as described in Example 3.7.17.

$$cons^{\mathcal{A}}\, x\, \ell \quad = x + \ell$$

$$car^{\mathcal{A}}\, \ell \quad = 2 * \ell + 5$$

$$cdr^{\mathcal{A}}\, \ell \quad = 2 * \ell + 5$$

$$isempty?^{\mathcal{A}}\, \ell = \ell + 8$$

$$cond^{\mathcal{A}}\, u\, x\, y = u + x + y + 1$$

$$OK^{\mathcal{A}}\, x \quad = x + 8$$

It is straightforward to check that $L > R$ for each of the rewrite rules derived from the specification.

There are several critical pairs, all involving the rules for $cons\,x\,error$ and $cons\,error\,\ell$. The first overlap we will check is

$\underline{car\,(\underline{cons\; error\; \ell})}$

If we reduce the outer term, we get

$cond\;(OK\; error)\;(cond\,(OK\;\ell)\,error\; error)\; error$

while the inner reduction gives us $car\,error$. This is a nontrivial critical pair. However, both terms reduce to $error$, so there is no problem here.

The next overlap is

$\underline{car\,(\underline{cons\; x\; error})}$

which gives us the similar-looking critical pair

$\langle cond\;(OK\; x)\;(cond\,(OK\; error)\; x\; error)\; error, \quad car\; error\rangle$

The second term clearly reduces to $error$, but the closest we can come with the first term (by reducing the inner conditional) is

$cond\;(OK\; x)\,error\; error.$

This gives us a candidate for completion. In the well-founded algebra $\mathcal{A}$, it is easy to see that

$cond\ (OK\ x) error\ error > error$

so we will preserve termination by adding the rewrite rule

$cond\ (OK\ x) error\ error \rightarrow error.$

Since the left-hand and right-hand sides of this rule are already provably equal from this specification, adding this rule does not change the conversion relation between terms.

The critical pairs for *cdr* and *isempty*? are similar. For both functions, the first critical pair converges easily and the second converges using the new rule added for the *car* case.

The final critical pairs are for *OK* applied to a *cons*. For $car(\underline{cons\ error\ \ell})$, we get *false* in both cases. However, for

$car(\underline{cons\ x\ error})$

we must add the rewrite rule

$cond\ (OK\ x) false\ false \rightarrow false.$

Thus two new rules give us a confluent rewrite system.

The initial algebra for a specification consists of the equivalence classes of ground (variable-free) terms, modulo provable equality. Since the confluent and terminating rewrite system for the list specification allows us to test provable equality by reduction, we may use the rewrite system to understand the initial algebra. Specifically, since every equivalence class has exactly one normal form, the initial algebra is isomorphic to the algebra whose carriers are the ground normal forms of each sort. Therefore, the atoms in the initial algebra are $a, b, c, d, \ldots, error_a$, the booleans in the initial algebra are $true, false, error_b$, and the lists all have the form *nil*, *error* or $cons\ A\ L$ where neither A nor L contains *error*. Thus this specification correctly adds exactly one error element to each carrier and eliminates undesirable lists that contain error elements. The reader interested in a general theorem about initial algebras with error elements may consult [GTW78, Wir90].

Exercise 3.7.37 Exercise 3.6.7 asks you to write an algebraic specification of queues with error elements, in the same style as the specification of lists in Table 3.7. Complete this specification to a confluent set of rewrite rules and use these rules to characterize the initial algebra.

Exercise 3.7.38 Exercise 3.6.8 asks you to write an algebraic specification of trees with error elements, in the same style as the specification of lists in Table 3.7. Complete this specification to a confluent set of rewrite rules and use these rules to characterize the initial algebra.

4 Simply-typed Lambda Calculus

4.1 Introduction

This chapter presents the pure simply-typed lambda calculus. This system, which is extended with natural numbers, booleans and fixed-point operators to produce PCF, is the core of all of the calculi studied in this book, except for the simpler system of universal algebra used in Chapter 3. The main topics of this chapter are:

- Presentation of context-sensitive syntax using typing axioms and inference rules.
- The equational proof system (axiomatic semantics) and reduction system (operational semantics), alone and in combination with additional equational axioms or rewrite rules.
- Henkin models (denotational semantics) of typed lambda calculus and discussion of general soundness and completeness theorems.

Since Chapter 2 describes the connections between typed lambda calculus and programming in some detail, this chapter is more concerned with mathematical properties of the system. We discuss three examples of models, set-theoretic models, domain-theoretic models using partial orders, and models based on traditional recursive function theory, but leave full development of domain-theoretic and recursion-theoretic models to Chapter 5. The proofs of some of the theorems stated or used in this chapter are postponed to Chapter 8. Although versions of typed lambda calculus with product, sum, and other types described in Section 2.6 are useful for programming, the pure typed lambda calculus with only function types is often used in this chapter to illustrate the main concepts.

Church developed lambda calculus in the 1930's as part of a formal logic [Chu32] and as a formalism for defining computable functions [Chu36, Chu41]. The original logic, which was untyped, was intended to serve a foundational role in the formalization of mathematics. The reason that lambda calculus is relevant to logic is that logical quantifiers (such as universal, $\forall$, and existential, $\exists$, quantifiers) are binding operators and their usual proof rules involve substitution. Using lambda abstraction, logical quantifiers may be treated as constants, in much the same way that recursive function definitions may be treated using fixed-point constants (see Example 4.4.7 and associated exercises). However, a paradox was discovered in logic based on untyped lambda calculus [KJ35]. This led to the development of typed lambda calculus, as part of a consistent, typed higher-order logic [Chu40, Hen50].

In 1936, Kleene proved that the natural number functions definable in untyped lambda calculus are exactly the recursive functions [Kle36]. Turing, in 1937, then proved that the λ-definable numeric functions are exactly as the functions computable by Turing machines

[Tur37]. Together, these results, which are analogous to properties of PCF considered in Sections 2.5.4 and 2.5.5, establish connections between lambda calculus and other models of computation. After the development of electronic computers, untyped lambda calculus clearly influenced the development of Lisp in the late 1950's [McC60]. (See [McC78, Sto91b] for many interesting historical comments.) General connections between lambda notation and other programming languages were elaborated throughout the 1960's by various researchers [BG66, Lan63, Lan65, Lan66], leading to the view that the semantics of programming languages could be given using extensions of lambda calculus [Str66, MS76, Sto77].

Although untyped lambda calculus provides a simpler execution model, a modern view is that typed lambda calculus leads to a more insightful analysis of programming languages. Using typed lambda calculi with type structures that correspond to types in programming languages, we may faithfully model the power and limitations of typed programming languages.

Like many-sorted algebra and first-order logic, typed lambda calculus may be defined using any collection of type constants (corresponding to sorts in algebra) and term constants (corresponding to function symbols). Typical type constants in programming languages are numeric types and booleans, as in PCF, as well as characters, strings, and other sorts that appear in the algebraic datatypes of Chapter 3. In typed lambda calculus, the term constants may have any type. Typical constants in programming languages include 3, $+$ and `if ... then ... else ...`, as in PCF. As in algebra, the set of type constants and term constants are given by a signature. The axiom system (axiomatic semantics), reduction rules (operational semantics) and model theory (denotational semantics) are all formulated in a way that is applicable to any signature.

Exercise 4.1.1 In the untyped logical system Church proposed in 1932, *Russell's paradox* (see Section 1.6) results in the untyped lambda term

$(\lambda x.\, not(xx))(\lambda x.\, not(xx))$

This may be explained as follows. If we identify sets with predicates, and assume that x is a set, then the formula xx is true if x is an element of x, and $not(xx)$ is true if x is not an element of x. Therefore the predicate $(\lambda x.\, not(xx))$ defines the set of all sets that are not members of themselves. Russell's paradox asks whether this set is a member of itself, resulting in the application above. Show that if this term is equal to *false*, then it is also equal to *true*, and conversely. You may assume that $not\ true = false$ and $not\ false = true$. (Church did not overlook this problem. He attempted to avoid inconsistency by not giving either truth value to this paradoxical term.)

4.2 Types

4.2.1 Syntax

We will use the phrase "simply-typed lambda calculus" to refer to any version of typed lambda calculus whose types do not contain type variables. The standard type forms that occur in simply-typed lambda calculus are function types, cartesian products, sums (disjoint unions) and initial ("null" or "empty") and terminal ("trivial" or "one-element") types. We do not consider recursive types, which were introduced in Section 2.6.3 and are considered again in Section 7.4, a form of simple type. (Recursive types contain type variables but a type variable alone is not a type, so this could be considered a borderline case.) Since lambda calculus would not be lambda calculus without lambda, all versions of simply-typed lambda calculus include function types.

The type expressions of full simply-typed lambda calculus are given by the grammar

$$\sigma \ ::= \ b \mid null \mid unit \mid \sigma + \sigma \mid \sigma \times \sigma \mid \sigma \rightarrow \sigma$$

where b may be any type constant, *null* is the initial (empty) type and, otherwise, terminal (one-element), sum, product and function types are as in Chapter 2. (Type connectives $\times$ and $\rightarrow$ are used throughout Chapter 2; *unit* and $+$ appear in Section 2.6.) Recall that when parentheses are omitted, we follow the convention that $\rightarrow$ associates to the right. In addition, we give $\times$ higher precedence than $\rightarrow$, and $\rightarrow$ higher precedence than $+$, so that $a + b \times c \rightarrow d$ is read as $a + ((b \times c) \rightarrow d)$.

To keep all the possibilities straight, we will name versions of typed lambda calculus by their types. The simplest language, called *simply-typed lambda calculus with function types,* will be indicated by the symbol $\lambda^{\rightarrow}$. With sums, products and functions, we have $\lambda^{+,\times,\rightarrow}$, and so on. A $\lambda^{\rightarrow}$ *type expression* is a type expression containing only $\rightarrow$ and type constants. A $\lambda^{\times,\rightarrow}$ *type expression* is a type expression containing only $\times$, $\rightarrow$ and type constants, and similarly for other fragments of simply-typed lambda calculus.

4.2.2 Interpretation of Types

There are two general frameworks for describing the denotational semantics of typed lambda calculus, Henkin models and cartesian closed categories. While cartesian closed categories are more general, they are also more abstract and therefore more difficult to understand at first. Therefore, we will concentrate on Henkin models in this chapter and postpone category theory to Chapter 7.

In a Henkin model, each type expression is interpreted as a set, the set of values of that type. The most important aspect of a Henkin model is the interpretation of function types, since the interpretation of other types is generally determined by the function types.

Intuitively, $\sigma \to \tau$ is the type, or collection, of all functions from σ to τ. However, there are important reasons *not* to interpret $\sigma \to \tau$ as *all* set-theoretic functions from σ to τ. The easiest to state is that not all set-theoretic functions have fixed points. In the denotational semantics of any typed lambda calculus with a fixed-point constant, fix_σ, the type $\sigma \to \sigma$ must contain all functions definable in the language, but must not contain any functions that do not have fixed points.

There are many reasonable interpretations of function types. A general intuitive guide is to think of $\sigma \to \tau$ as containing all functions from σ to τ that have some general and desirable property, such as computability or continuity. To emphasize from the outset that many views are possible, we will briefly summarize three representative interpretations: classical set-theoretic functions, recursive functions coded by Gödel numbers, and continuous functions on complete partial orders (domains). Each will be explained fully later.

In the *full set-theoretic interpretation,*

a type constant b may denote any set A^b, and

the function type $\sigma \to \tau$ denotes the set $A^{\sigma\to\tau}$ of all functions from A^σ to A^τ.

Note that $A^{\sigma\to\tau}$ is determined by the sets A^σ and A^τ.

There are several forms of recursion-theoretic interpretation for $\lambda^\to$, each involving sets with some kind of enumeration function or relation. We will consider a representative framework based on partial enumeration functions. A *modest set* $\langle A, e_A\rangle$ is a set A together with a surjective partial function $e_A : \mathcal{N} \rightharpoonup A$ from the natural numbers to A. Intuitively, the natural number n is the "code" for $e_A(n) \in A$. Since e_A is partial, $e_A(n)$ may not be defined, in which case n is not a code for any element of A. The importance of having codes for every element of A is that we use coding to define the recursive functions on A. Specifically, $f : A \to B$ is *recursive* if there is a recursive map on natural numbers taking any code for $a \in A$ to some code for $f(a) \in B$. In the *recursive interpretation,*

a type constant b may denote any modest set $\langle A^b, e_b\rangle$, and

the function type $\sigma \to \tau$ denotes the modest set $\langle A^{\sigma\to\tau}, e_{\sigma\to\tau}\rangle$ of all total *recursive* functions from A^σ to A^τ.

Since every total recursive function from A^σ to A^τ has a Gödel number, we can use any standard numbering of recursive functions to enumerate the elements of the function type $A^{\sigma\to\tau}$. Thus, if we begin with modest sets for each type constant, we can associate a modest set with every functional type.

The *continuous* or *domain-theoretic interpretation* uses complete partial orders. The primary motivations for this interpretation are to give semantics to recursively defined functions and recursive type definitions. A *complete partial order,* or *CPO,* $\langle D, \leq \rangle$ is a set D partially ordered by $\leq$ in such a way that every directed subset $E \subseteq D$ has a least upper bound, or "limit," $\bigvee E$. (A subset E of a CPO is *directed* if every finite subset $S \subseteq E$ has an upper bound in E.) A function $f \colon A^\sigma \to A^\tau$ is *continuous* if it is monotonic and preserves limits of directed sets. In the domain-theoretic interpretation,

a type constant b may denote any CPO $\langle A^b, \leq_b \rangle$, and

the function type $\sigma \to \tau$ denotes the CPO $\langle A^{\sigma \to \tau}, \leq_{\sigma \to \tau} \rangle$ of all *continuous* functions from A^σ to A^τ

Note that in order to make sense of higher types like $(b \to b) \to (b \to b)$, we need to make sure that every function type denotes a CPO. This may be accomplished by considering $f \leq_{\sigma \to \tau} g$ whenever we have $f(x) \leq_\tau g(x)$ for every $x \in A^\sigma$.

In general, the interpretation of initial and terminal types is determined by the function spaces. Specifically, there must be exactly one function from *null* to σ and exactly one function from σ to *unit* in every model. This often means that *null* is interpreted as the empty set and *unit* as any one-element set. (It does not matter which one, since we have no operations to distinguish one such interpretation of *unit* from another.) A sum type $\sigma + \tau$ is generally interpreted as the disjoint union of σ and τ. The standard *disjoint union* of two sets A and B is the union of $A \times \{0\}$ and $B \times \{1\}$, with "tags" 0 and 1 serving to distinguish elements of A from elements of B in the union. A cartesian product type $\sigma \times \tau$ is generally interpreted as the set of all ordered pairs with first component from σ and second component from τ.

4.3 Terms

4.3.1 Context-sensitive Syntax

Programming languages are often defined using a context-free grammar, as in the definition of type expressions above. However, a context-free description of a statically-typed language tells only half the story, since typing constraints are context sensitive. For example, the expression $x + 3$ is well-typed only if the declaration of this x specifies that x is a numeric variable. In most languages, the declaration of x may precede the expression $x + 3$ by an arbitrary number of other declarations. Using Ogden's lemma, it is straightforward to prove that there is no context-free grammar generating precisely the well-typed terms of $\lambda^\to$ (see, *e.g.*, [HU79]).

We will define typed languages using a formalism based on logic. Specifically, we will define expressions and their types simultaneously using axioms and inference rules. The atomic expressions of a language are given by *typing axioms.* Informally, a typing axiom $c\colon \tau$ means that the symbol c has type τ. Put another way, $c\colon \tau$ is an axiom about the type membership relation, which we write as ":". The axiom says that the type membership relation holds between c and τ. An example axiom for a language with natural numbers is $3\colon nat$, which specifies that 3 is a natural number.

The compound expressions and their types are defined using inference rules. These are rules that let us derive more complicated facts about the ":" relation. One form of inference rule is

$$\frac{M_1\colon \sigma_1, \ldots, M_k\colon \sigma_k}{N\colon \tau}.$$

Intuitively, this rule says that if $M_1, \ldots, M_k$ are well-formed terms of types $\sigma_1, \ldots, \sigma_k$, respectively, then N is a well-formed term of type τ. Typically, $M_1, \ldots, M_k$ are the subterms of N, since the type of a term will depend on the types of its subterms. This rule tells us how to produce a well-formed term N of type τ from well-formed terms $M_1, \ldots, M_k$.

The inference rule above is not powerful enough to capture the context-sensitive syntax of expressions that declare the types of variables. To take the types of variables into account, we will work with typing assertions

$$\Gamma \rhd M\colon \tau,$$

where Γ is a *type assignment* of the form

$$\Gamma = \{x_1\colon \sigma_1, \ldots, x_k\colon \sigma_k\},$$

with no x_i occurring twice. Intuitively, the assertion $\Gamma \rhd M\colon \tau$ says that if variables $x_1, \ldots, x_k$ have types $\sigma_1, \ldots, \sigma_k$ (respectively), then M is a well-formed term of type τ. A type assignment is also called a *typing context* so that $\Gamma \rhd M\colon \tau$ may be read, "in context Γ, the term M has type τ." In some presentations of typed languages and calculi, typing contexts are ordered sequences. In this book, type assignments will be unordered sets, except in Section 7.2.4, where we consider the categorical interpretation of terms, and parts of Chapter 9 on polymorphism.

The general form of a typing rule with contexts is

$$\frac{\Gamma_1 \rhd M_1\colon \sigma_1, \ldots, \Gamma_k \rhd M_k\colon \sigma_k}{\Gamma \rhd N\colon \tau},$$

which says that if each M_i has type σ_i in typing context Γ_i, then N has type τ in context Γ. In all the typing rules we will use, the terms $M_1, \ldots, M_k$ will be the subterms of N.

If Γ is any type assignment, we will write $\Gamma, x\colon \sigma$ for the type assignment

$\Gamma, x{:}\sigma = \Gamma \cup \{x{:}\sigma\}$.

In doing so, we always assume that x does not appear in Γ.

Technically speaking, our proof system for typing assertions is a simple form of sequent calculus. Logicians may realize that we could also formalize the same basic ideas using what is called natural deduction. In some of the literature on type systems, natural deduction proof systems are used. In these sources, it is common to use $\Gamma \vdash M{:}\sigma$ to indicate that the typing assertion $M{:}\sigma$ is provable from the set Γ of typing assumptions. Other references also use sequent calculus, but often use the notation $\Gamma \vdash M{:}\sigma$ for typing assertions. The main reason we use $\rhd$ instead of $\vdash$ is to reserve $\vdash$ for provability in the equational proof system. Typing assertions are sometimes called *typing judgements* in the literature.

4.3.2 Syntax of $\lambda^{\to}$ Terms

The syntax of terms depends on the choice of type and term constants. A $\lambda^{\to}$ *signature* $\Sigma = \langle B, C\rangle$ consists of

- A set B whose elements are called *base types* or *type constants*.
- A collection C of pairs of the form $\langle c, \sigma\rangle$, where σ is a $\lambda^{\to}$ type expression over B and no c occurs in two distinct pairs.

A symbol c occurring in some pair $\langle c, \sigma\rangle \in C$ is called a *term constant of type* σ. We generally write $c{:}\sigma$ if $\langle c, \sigma\rangle \in C$. Note that the type and term constants must be consistent, in that the type of each term constant may only contain the given type constants. For example, it only makes sense to have a natural number constant $3{:}\,nat$ when we have nat as a type constant.

If Σ is a signature for multi-sorted algebra, there is a standard way to regard Σ as a $\lambda^{\to}$ signature. The $\lambda^{\to}$ signature $\Sigma_{\to} = \langle B, C\rangle$ corresponding to the algebraic signature $\Sigma = \langle S, F\rangle$ is defined by letting B be S and, for each $f{:}\,s_1 \times \ldots \times s_k \to s$ from F, including constant $f{:}\,s_1 \to \ldots \to s_k \to s$ in C. In other words, we let the type constants be the sorts and the term constants be curried function symbols. The reason for converting constants to curried form is just to avoid using cartesian products (see Section 2.2.3 for discussion of curried functions). If we use $\lambda^{\times,\to}$ instead of $\lambda^{\to}$, then we can give the lambda calculus constants their algebraic types.

Example 4.3.1 The algebraic signature Σ for the natural number and boolean expressions of PCF may be written as

sorts: *nat*, *bool*

fctns: $0, 1, 2, 3, 4, \ldots : nat$

$true, false: bool$

$plus: nat \times nat \to nat$

$Eq?: nat \times nat \to bool$

$cond_n: bool \times nat \times nat \to nat$

$cond_b: bool \times bool \times bool \to bool$

This may be considered a signature for $\lambda^{\times,\to}$, without change. We may also derive a $\lambda^{\to}$ signature, $\Sigma_{\to}$, from this algebraic signature by currying all of the function constants. To obtain the full $\lambda^{\to}$ signature Σ_{PCF} for PCF without products, we will add a few other constants. Since we would also like to have conditional on other types, we include $cond_\sigma$ for each type σ. We also include fixed-point operators at all types.

type constants: *nat*, *bool*

term constants: $0, 1, 2, 3, 4, \ldots : nat$

$true, false: bool$

$plus: nat \to nat \to nat$

$Eq?: nat \to nat \to bool$

$cond_\sigma: bool \to \sigma \to \sigma \to \sigma$ each type σ

$fix_\sigma: (\sigma \to \sigma) \to \sigma$ each type σ

We may write terms over this signature in the familiar form of PCF described in Chapter 2 using the syntactic sugar

$M + N \quad \stackrel{\text{def}}{=} \quad plus\ M\ N$

$\texttt{if}\ M\ \texttt{then}\ N\ \texttt{else}\ P \stackrel{\text{def}}{=} cond_\sigma\ M\ N\ P$

where the type subscript on *cond* is determined by the types of N and P. ■

The $\lambda^{\to}$ terms over Σ and their types are defined simultaneously using axioms and inference rules. For each constant c of type σ, we have the axiom

$$\emptyset \rhd c: \sigma \qquad (cst)$$

The typing context here is empty, since the type of a constant is fixed, and therefore independent of the context in which it occurs.

We assume some countably infinite set *Var* of variables $\{v_0, v_1, \ldots\}$. Variables are given types by the axiom

$$x\colon\sigma \rhd x\colon\sigma \qquad (var)$$

where σ must be a $\lambda^{\rightarrow}$ type over Σ. This axiom simply says that a variable x has whatever type it is declared to have. Some authors assume each variable $v \in Var$ has a fixed type, and therefore do not mention typing contexts explicitly. However, this seemingly simpler presentation does not generalize to lambda calculi with polymorphic functions or abstract data type declarations. In addition, when we wish to reason about types that may be empty, it is essential to keep track of the free variables used in proofs. This is easily taken care of in the formalism we use.

Compound expressions and their types are specified using inference rules. A straightforward one is the following "add var" rule that applies to terms of any form. The rule

$$\frac{\Gamma \rhd M\colon\sigma}{\Gamma, x\colon\tau \rhd M\colon\sigma} \qquad (add\ var)$$

allows us to add an additional hypothesis to the typing context. In words, rule (*add var*) says that if M has type σ in context Γ, then M has type σ in the context $\Gamma, x\colon\tau$ which also gives a type to x. Recall that in writing $\Gamma, x\colon\tau$ we assume x does not appear in Γ. Consequently, the type of M could not have depended on the type of x. In fact, after we have seen all of the rules, it will be easy to prove that if $\Gamma \rhd M\colon\sigma$ is derivable, then every free variable of M must appear in Γ. Therefore, in rule (*add var*), we can be sure that x does not occur free in M.

In lambda calculus, lambda abstraction is used to identify the variable that is used as the function argument. This is made precise by the following term-formation rule.

$$\frac{\Gamma, x\colon\sigma \rhd M\colon\tau}{\Gamma \rhd (\lambda x\colon\sigma.\, M)\colon\sigma \to \tau} \qquad (\to \text{Intro})$$

Intuitively, the rule says that if M specifies a result of type τ for every $x\colon\sigma$, then the expression $\lambda x\colon\sigma.\, M$ defines a function of type $\sigma \to \tau$. (Other free variables of M are unaffected by lambda abstraction, and must be given types in Γ.) Note that while the type of M may depend on the type of variable x, the type of $\lambda x\colon\sigma.\, M$ does not, since the type of x is explicitly declared in $\lambda x\colon\sigma$. This rule is called ($\to$ Intro), since it "introduces" a term of functional type. As mentioned in Chapter 1 and discussed in detail in Chapter 2, the variable x is *bound* in $\lambda x\colon\sigma.\, M$.

An alternative reading of the ($\rightarrow$ Intro) rule may make it seem more familiar to computer scientists. Suppose we want to type-check a function expression $\lambda x : \sigma . M$, and we have a "symbol table" Γ associating types with variables that might occur free in M. Then reading from bottom to top, the ($\rightarrow$ Intro) rule says that in order to check that $\Gamma \triangleright \lambda x : \sigma . M : \sigma \rightarrow \tau$, we add the specification $x : \sigma$ to the symbol table Γ, and then check that the function body M has type τ. This should be familiar to anyone who has considered how to type check a function declaration

function f(x: σ);
  begin
    ⟨*function_body*⟩
  end;

in any Algol-like programming language. A $\lambda^{\rightarrow}$ typing algorithm that works in precisely this way is given in Section 4.3.5.

Function applications are written according to the rule

$$\frac{\Gamma \triangleright M : \sigma \rightarrow \tau, \ \ \Gamma \triangleright N : \sigma}{\Gamma \triangleright MN : \tau} \qquad (\rightarrow \text{Elim})$$

which says that we may apply any function with type $\sigma \rightarrow \tau$ to an argument of type σ to produce a result of type τ. Note that while $\rightarrow$ appears in the antecedent, this symbol has been "eliminated" in the consequent, hence the name ($\rightarrow$ Elim).

We say *M is a $\lambda^{\rightarrow}$ term over signature Σ with type τ in context Γ* if $\Gamma \triangleright M : \tau$ is either a typing axiom for Σ, or follows from axioms by rules (*add var*), ($\rightarrow$ Intro) and ($\rightarrow$ Elim). As an expository convenience, we will often write $\Gamma \triangleright M : \tau$ to mean that "$\Gamma \triangleright M : \tau$ is derivable," in much the same way as one often writes a formula $\forall x . P(x)$, in logic, as a way of saying "$\forall x . P(x)$ is true." A proof of a typing assertion is called a *typing derivation.*

Example 4.3.2 A term that requires all of the typing rules is $y : \sigma \triangleright (\lambda x : \sigma . x)\, y : \sigma$. A first step is to derive the typing assertion $\emptyset \triangleright \lambda x : \sigma . x : \sigma \rightarrow \sigma$. If we start with the typing axiom $x : \sigma \triangleright x : \sigma$, then $\emptyset \triangleright \lambda x : \sigma . x : \sigma \rightarrow \sigma$ follows by rule ($\rightarrow$ Intro). We would now like to apply this term to the variable y, typed by the axiom $y : \sigma \triangleright y : \sigma$, and show that the result is well-typed by rule ($\rightarrow$ Elim). However, we can only use rule ($\rightarrow$ Elim) when both terms have the same typing context. Therefore, we use (*add var*) to derive $y : \sigma \triangleright \lambda x : \sigma . x : \sigma \rightarrow \sigma$ from the earlier typing assertion about $\lambda x : \sigma . x$, and then combine this with $y : \sigma \triangleright y : \sigma$ by rule ($\rightarrow$ Elim) to obtain $y : \sigma \triangleright (\lambda x : \sigma . x)\, y : \sigma$. ■

In Exercise 4.3.9, you are asked to show that every well-formed algebraic term is a well-typed $\lambda^{\rightarrow}$ term over the appropriate signature. Another typing example appears in Example 4.3.7, using some of the following lemmas.

The next four lemmas are each proved by a straightforward induction on typing derivations. Since all of the arguments are similar, we give only the proof of Lemma 4.3.6.

Lemma 4.3.3 If $\Gamma \triangleright M : \sigma$, then every free variable of M appears in Γ.

Lemma 4.3.4 If $\Gamma \triangleright M : \sigma$ and $\Gamma \cap \Gamma'$ contains all free variables of M, then $\Gamma' \triangleright M : \sigma$.

If we let $\Gamma_M = \Gamma|_{FV(M)}$ be the set of typing assumptions $x : \tau$ with $x \in FV(M)$, then Lemma 4.3.4 shows that $\Gamma \triangleright M : \sigma$ is provable iff $\Gamma_M \triangleright M : \sigma$ is provable. In Section 4.3.5 we will use Lemma 4.3.4 to show how to determine efficiently whether a typing assertion $\Gamma \triangleright M : \sigma$ is provable.

We have two useful lemmas about typing and substitution. Since substitution $[N/x]M$ of N for free occurrences of x in M is discussed in detail in Chapter 2, we will not discuss substitution and renaming of bound variables here. We write $[y/x]\Gamma$ for the result of substituting y for any occurrence of x in Γ. In doing so, we must assume that y does not occur in Γ. Otherwise, $[y/x]\Gamma$ would not be a well-formed type assignment.

Lemma 4.3.5 If $\Gamma \triangleright M : \sigma$ and y does not occur in Γ, then $[y/x]\Gamma \triangleright [y/x]M : \sigma$.

Lemma 4.3.6 If $\Gamma_1, x : \sigma \triangleright M : \tau$ and $\Gamma_2 \triangleright N : \sigma$ are terms of $\lambda^{\rightarrow}$, with $\Gamma_1 \cup \Gamma_2$ a well-formed type assignment, then the substitution instance $\Gamma_1 \cup \Gamma_2 \triangleright [N/x]M : \tau$ is a well-formed term.

These lemmas generalize to most type systems, including all of the systems covered in this book.

Proof The proof of the lemma is by induction on the proof of typing assertion $\Gamma_1, x : \sigma \triangleright M : \tau$. This is almost the same as induction on the structure of M, except that we have a stronger induction hypothesis for lambda abstractions, as noted below.

There are two base cases, one for the typing axiom for constants and one for the typing axiom for variables. However, the only axiom of the form $\Gamma_1, x : \sigma \triangleright M : \tau$ is the variable axiom $\Gamma_1, x : \tau \triangleright x : \tau$, with Γ_1 empty. (See Exercise 4.3.11 for a discussion of term constants.) We assume that $\Gamma_2 \triangleright N : \tau$ is derivable. Since $[N/x]x$ is just N, the typing assertion $\Gamma_1 \cup \Gamma_2 \triangleright [N/x]x : \tau$ is just $\Gamma_2 \triangleright N : \tau$ and therefore derivable. This proves the base case of the induction.

There are three induction steps, corresponding to typing rules ($\rightarrow$ Intro), ($\rightarrow$ Elim) and (*add var*). A proof ending with ($\rightarrow$ Intro) concludes by deriving

$$\Gamma_1, x : \sigma \triangleright \lambda y : \tau' . M : \tau' \rightarrow \tau$$

from

$\Gamma_1, x\colon\sigma,\ y\colon\tau' \rhd M\colon\tau.$

Since $\Gamma_1, x\colon\sigma,\ y\colon\tau'$ is a well-formed type assignment, we know that y does not appear in $\Gamma_1, x\colon\sigma$. In particular, y is different from x. (This would not be guaranteed if we tried to prove the lemma by induction on the structure of terms.) By the inductive hypothesis,

$\Gamma_1 \cup \Gamma_2,\ y\colon\tau' \rhd [N/x]M\colon\tau$

is provable, and the lemma follows by rule ($\rightarrow$ Intro).

The induction step for a proof of $\Gamma_1, x\colon\sigma \rhd PQ\colon\tau$ from $\Gamma_1, x\colon\sigma \rhd P\colon\tau' \rightarrow \tau$ and $\Gamma_1, x\colon\sigma \rhd Q\colon\tau'$ by rule ($\rightarrow$ Elim) is similar. By the induction hypothesis, both $\Gamma_1 \cup \Gamma_2 \rhd [N/x]P\colon\tau' \rightarrow \tau$ and $\Gamma_1 \cup \Gamma_2 \rhd [N/x]Q\colon\tau'$ are derivable and the lemma follows by rule ($\rightarrow$ Elim).

If the derivation of $\Gamma_1, x\colon\sigma \rhd M\colon\tau$ ends with (*add var*), there are two cases to consider. The degenerate case is when (*add var*) is used to add the hypothesis $x\colon\sigma$. In this case, x does not appear in M and so $[N/x]M \equiv M$. It follows from Lemma 4.3.4 that $\Gamma_1 \cup \Gamma_2 \rhd M\colon\tau$ is derivable. The final case is where (*add var*) is used to add a hypothesis $y\colon\rho$, and $\Gamma_1 \equiv \Gamma_1', y\colon\rho$. By the induction hypothesis, we know that since $\Gamma_1', x\colon\sigma \rhd M\colon\tau$ and $\Gamma_2 \rhd N\colon\sigma$ are derivable, so is $\Gamma_1' \cup \Gamma_2 \rhd [N/x]M\colon\tau$ The typing assertion $\Gamma_1 \cup \Gamma_2 \rhd [N/x]M\colon\tau$ follows by (*add var*). This finishes the proof. ∎

Example 4.3.7 A $\lambda^{\rightarrow}$ signature Σ_{PCF} with term constants corresponding to PCF is given in Example 4.3.1. Recall that the factorial function may be written as *fix* F, where

$F \stackrel{\text{def}}{=} \lambda f\colon nat \rightarrow nat.\ \lambda y\colon nat.\ \texttt{if}\ Eq?\, y\, 0\ \texttt{then}\ 1\ \texttt{else}\ y * f(y-1)$

We will show that the typing assertion $\emptyset \rhd fix\ F\colon nat \rightarrow nat$ is provable over signature Σ_{PCF}. Recall that `if ... then ... else ...` is syntactic sugar for *cond*.

Since $y\colon nat \rhd y\colon nat$ is an axiom and typing assertions $y\colon nat \rhd Eq?\colon nat \rightarrow nat \rightarrow bool$ and $y\colon nat \rhd 0\colon nat$ are easily derived using (*add var*), we have

$y\colon nat \rhd Eq?\ y\ 0\colon bool$

using ($\rightarrow$ Elim) twice. Proceeding similarly, we can prove

$y\colon nat \rhd cond_{nat}\ (Eq?\ y\ 0)\ 0\colon nat \rightarrow bool$

by ($\rightarrow$ Elim).

Let us assume that $y - 1$ is syntactic sugar for *pred* y, for some term *pred*. We assume that the typing assertion $y\colon nat \rhd y - 1\colon nat$ provable, and similarly $x * y \stackrel{\text{def}}{=} mult\ x\ y$ with $u\colon nat,\ v\colon nat \rhd u * v\colon nat$ provable. From this assumption about subtraction, we can derive

$f: nat \to nat,\ y: nat \rhd f(y-1): nat$

Applying Lemma 4.3.6 twice, to substitute terms for variables u and v in $u: nat, v: nat \rhd u * v: nat$, it follows that

$f: nat \to nat,\ y: nat \rhd y * f(y-1): nat$

is provable. Combining this with the typing assertion above, we obtain

$f: nat \to nat,\ y: nat \rhd \texttt{if } Eq?\, y\, 0 \texttt{ then } 0 \texttt{ else } y * f(y-1): nat$

The desired typing of factorial now follows using ($\to$ Intro) twice and ($\to$ Elim) to apply $\mathit{fix}_{nat \to nat}$ to F. ■

Exercise 4.3.8 Draw a proof tree for the typing derivation described in Example 4.3.2. This tree should have a leaf for each axiom used, and an internal node for each inference rule ($\to$ Intro), ($\to$ Elim) or (*add var*). You may draw the tree with the leaves at the bottom if you like, but it is traditional to draw proof trees with the leaves at the top. Now draw the proof tree for another derivation of the same typing. The second tree will have the same rules, but they will be used in a different order.

Exercise 4.3.9 As described at the beginning of this section, there is a straightforward way of forming a $\lambda^{\to}$ signature $\Sigma_{\to}$ from an algebraic signature Σ.

(a) Show that for any Σ, if $M \in \mathit{Terms}^s(\Sigma, \Gamma)$ is a well-formed algebraic term of sort s, then the typing assertion $\Gamma \rhd M: s$ is provable over $\Sigma_{\to}$. This is straightforward since algebraic terms are formed by application and $\lambda^{\to}$ application has precisely the same type restrictions as the sort restrictions on algebraic terms.

(b) Find an algebraic signature Σ with function symbols f, a and b such that $f\, a\, b$ is a well-formed algebraic term and $f\, a$ is a well-formed lambda term over $\Sigma_{\to}$ but not a well-formed algebraic term over Σ.

Exercise 4.3.10 Prove the following typing assertions using the typing axioms and inference rules.

(a) $x: \sigma, y: \sigma \to \tau \rhd yx: \tau$

(b) $x: \sigma, y: \sigma \rhd \lambda y: \sigma \to \tau.\, yx: (\sigma \to \tau) \to \tau$

(c) $\emptyset \rhd (\lambda x: \sigma \to \sigma.\, \lambda y: \tau.\, x)(\lambda x: \sigma.\, x): \tau \to \sigma \to \sigma$

Exercise 4.3.11 In the proof of Lemma 4.3.6, the base case for term constants is trivial because no typing assertion of the form $\Gamma_1, x: \sigma \rhd c: \tau$ is an instance of the typing axiom for term constants. Explain how the proof shows that if $\Gamma_1, x{:}\,\sigma \rhd c{:}\,\tau$ and $\Gamma_2 \rhd N{:}\,\sigma$ are derivable then $\Gamma_1 \cup \Gamma_2 \rhd c{:}\,\tau$ is also derivable.

Exercise 4.3.12 Prove the following lemmas by induction on typing derivations or induction on the structure of terms.

(a) Lemma 4.3.3

(b) Lemma 4.3.4

(c) Lemma 4.3.5

4.3.3 Terms with Product, Sum and Related Types

The typing rules for the standard simply-typed extensions of $\lambda^{\rightarrow}$ are listed below. For each version of simply-typed lambda calculus, the definition of signature and well-formed terms with respect to a given signature are analogous to the definitions for $\lambda^{\rightarrow}$. The definition of well-formed terms of $\lambda^{\times,\rightarrow}$ is stated below, to give an example, but the straightforward definitions for other variants are omitted.

Cartesian Products

Intuitively, as explained in Chapter 2, a pair belongs to $\sigma \times \tau$ iff the first component belongs to σ, and the second component to τ. One part of this "iff" is that if $M{:}\,\sigma$ and $N{:}\,\tau$, then the pair $\langle M, N\rangle$ has type $\sigma \times \tau$. This is written symbolically in the rule

$$\frac{\Gamma \rhd M{:}\,\sigma,\ \ \Gamma \rhd N{:}\,\tau}{\Gamma \rhd \langle M, N\rangle{:}\,\sigma \times \tau} \qquad (\times\ \text{Intro})$$

which is called an introduction rule since it lets us "introduce" an element of product type. This rule implies that if $1{:}\,nat$ and $2{:}\,nat$, for example, then the pair $\langle 1, 2\rangle$ has type $nat \times nat$.

If M is an element of type $\sigma \times \tau$, then M consists of an element of σ and an element of τ. The rules

$$\frac{\Gamma \rhd M{:}\,\sigma \times \tau}{\Gamma \rhd \mathbf{Proj}_1^{\sigma,\tau} M{:}\,\sigma} \qquad (\times\ \text{Elim})_1$$

$$\frac{\Gamma \rhd M{:}\,\sigma \times \tau}{\Gamma \rhd \mathbf{Proj}_2^{\sigma,\tau} M{:}\,\tau} \qquad (\times\ \text{Elim})_2$$

describe the syntactic forms $\mathbf{Proj}_1^{\sigma,\tau} M$ and $\mathbf{Proj}_2^{\sigma,\tau} M$ which we use to obtain the first and second components of a pair $M{:}\,\sigma \times \tau$. These are called elimination rules since the $\times$ in the type of M is "eliminated." We often omit the type superscripts from $\mathbf{Proj}_1^{\sigma,\tau}$ and $\mathbf{Proj}_2^{\sigma,\tau}$.

We say $\Gamma \triangleright M{:}\,\sigma$ is a *term of* $\lambda^{\to,\times}$ if $\Gamma \triangleright M{:}\,\sigma$ is a typing axiom, or follows by rules (*add var*), ($\times$ Intro), ($\times$ Elim), ($\to$ Intro) and ($\to$ Elim). All of the syntactic properties of $\lambda^{\to}$ terms mentioned in the last section extend easily to $\lambda^{\times,\to}$.

An alternate presentation of products is that for all types σ and τ, there are term constants

$$\mathbf{Pair}^{\sigma,\tau}{:}\,\sigma \to \tau \to (\sigma \times \tau)$$

$$\mathbf{Proj}_1^{\sigma,\tau}{:}\,(\sigma \times \tau) \to \sigma$$

$$\mathbf{Proj}_2^{\sigma,\tau}{:}\,(\sigma \times \tau) \to \tau$$

with $\langle M, N\rangle^{\sigma,\tau}$ treated as syntactic sugar for $\mathbf{Pair}^{\sigma,\tau}\, M\, N$ and type superscripts omitted when clear from context. The main difference between the two presentations is that **Pair**, $\mathbf{Proj}_1$ and $\mathbf{Proj}_2$ are terms themselves in the second presentation, while only $\lambda x{:}\,\sigma.\,\lambda y{:}\,\tau.\,\mathbf{Pair}\, x\, y$, $\lambda x{:}\,\sigma \times \tau.\,\mathbf{Proj}_1 x$ and $\lambda x{:}\,\sigma \times \tau.\,\mathbf{Proj}_2 x$ are well-formed terms in the first. This does not effect the set of expressible functions or any other pragmatic use of the language. However, it has some significance in proofs by induction. In the first presentation, we have an induction step for ($\times$ Intro) and an induction step for ($\times$ Elim). With term constants, we must consider the constants **Pair**, $\mathbf{Proj}_1$ and $\mathbf{Proj}_2$ in the base case of the induction. Generally speaking, the formulation with inference rules ($\times$ Intro) and ($\times$ Elim) is more useful.

Sums

Sum types are discussed in Section 2.6.2. The term forms associated with sums are injection and case expressions. Terms of sum type are formed according to the following rules:

$$\frac{\Gamma \triangleright M{:}\,\sigma}{\Gamma \triangleright \mathbf{Inleft}^{\sigma,\tau} M{:}\,\sigma + \tau} \qquad (+\ \text{Intro})_1$$

$$\frac{\Gamma \triangleright M{:}\,\tau}{\Gamma \triangleright \mathbf{Inright}^{\sigma,\tau} M{:}\,\sigma + \tau} \qquad (+\ \text{Intro})_2$$

These are called introduction rules since they introduce terms of sum type into the language. Intuitively, the injection functions map σ or τ to $\sigma + \tau$ by "tagging" elements with **Inleft** or **Inright**.

The elimination rule characterizes the type-correct use of **case** expressions.

$$\frac{\Gamma \triangleright M{:}\,\sigma + \tau,\ \Gamma \triangleright N{:}\,\sigma \to \rho,\ \Gamma \triangleright P{:}\,\tau \to \rho}{\Gamma \triangleright \mathbf{Case}^{\sigma,\tau,\rho} M\, N\, P{:}\,\rho} \qquad (+\ \text{Elim})$$

Intuitively, $\mathbf{Case}^{\sigma,\tau,\rho}\ M\ N\ P$ inspects the tag on M and applies N if M is from σ and P if M is from τ.

As with products, sums may be defined using term constants instead of formation rules. The constants, for any types ρ, σ and τ, are:

$\mathbf{Inleft}^{\sigma,\tau} \quad : \sigma \to \sigma + \tau$

$\mathbf{Inright}^{\sigma,\tau} : \tau \to \sigma + \tau$

$\mathbf{Case}^{\sigma,\tau,\rho} \ : (\sigma + \tau) \to (\sigma \to \rho) \to (\tau \to \rho) \to \rho$

Initial and Terminal Types

It is sometimes useful to have an initial ("empty") type, *null*, or a terminal ("one-element") type, *unit*. The only term form associated with *unit* is the term constant

$*: unit$ (*unit* Intro)

The term form associated with *null* is that for each type σ, there is a term constant

$\mathbf{Zero}^{\sigma} : null \to \sigma$ (*null* Elim)

Intuitively, $\mathbf{Zero}^{\sigma}$ is the empty function, "the function mapping nothing nowhere." In the set-theoretic representation of functions as ordered pairs, $\mathbf{Zero}^{\sigma}$ is the empty set. The constant $*$ is called an "Intro" form since it gives us a way of naming an element of type *unit*. The constant $\mathbf{Zero}^{\sigma}$ is called an "Elim" form since it gives us a way of using an element of type *null* if we had one (which we generally do not).

4.3.4 Formulas-as-types Correspondence

There is a correspondence between between formulas of constructive logic and types in typed lambda calculus that is useful in proof theory [CF58, DB80, GLT89, How80, Lam80, Lau65, Lau70, Mar82, Sta79, Ste72]. The programming significance of the correspondence has been stressed by Martin-Löf [Mar82, Mar84] and used as the basis for the Nuprl proof development system [C+86]. The main idea may be illustrated using implicational logic.

Implicational propositional logic uses formulas that contain only propositional variables and implication, which we will write as $\to$. The formulas of implicational propositional logic are defined by the grammar

$$\sigma \ ::= \ b \mid \sigma \to \sigma$$

where b may be any propositional variable. We will be concerned with an *intuitionistic* interpretation of formulas, so it is best not to think of formulas as simply being true or false whenever we assign truth values to each variable. While various forms of intuitionistic semantics have been developed [Kri65, Kle71, Fit69, Tro73], we will not go into this topic. Instead, we will concentrate on a proof system for intuitionistic implicational logic.

Natural deduction is a style of proof system that is intended to mimic the common blackboard-style argument

Assume σ.

By . . . we conclude τ.

From this argument, we can see that $\sigma \to \tau$.

This argument begins by assuming some proposition σ, which is used to derive τ. At this point, we have proved τ but the proof depends on the assumption of σ. In the third step of the argument, we observe that since σ leads to a proof of τ, the implication $\sigma \to \tau$ follows. Since the proof of $\sigma \to \tau$ is sound without proviso, we have "discharged" the assumption of σ in proceeding from τ to $\sigma \to \tau$. In a natural deduction proof, each proposition may depend on one or more assumptions and a proposition is considered *proved* only when all assumptions have been discharged.

The natural deduction proof system for implicational propositional logic may be characterized using an axiom and three inference rules, given below. For technical reasons, we use labeled assumptions. This is useful from a proof-theoretic point of view, as a means of distinguishing between different assumptions of the same formula. Let $\mathcal{V}$ be a set, intended to be the set of labels, and let Γ be a finite set of labeled assumptions. If x is a label and σ a formula, then we write $x\colon\sigma$ for the assumption of σ with label x. We will use the notation $\Gamma \vdash_M \sigma$ to mean that M is a proof with consequence σ, relying on the set Γ of labeled assumptions. For example, we may write $x\colon\sigma,\ y\colon\sigma \vdash_x \sigma$ to indicate that if x and y are assumptions of the formula σ, then x is a proof of σ that relies on assumptions x and y.

The natural deduction proofs and their consequences are defined as follows:

$$x\colon\sigma \vdash_x \sigma$$

$$\frac{\Gamma \vdash_M \sigma}{\Gamma, x\colon\tau \vdash_M \sigma}\ x \text{ not in } \Gamma$$

$$\frac{\Gamma \vdash_M \sigma \to \tau,\quad \Gamma \vdash_N \sigma}{\Gamma \vdash_{MN} \tau}$$

$$\frac{\Gamma, x\colon\sigma \vdash_M \tau}{\Gamma \vdash_{\lambda x:\sigma.\, M} \sigma \to \tau}$$

A formula σ is *provable* if there is a proof M with $\emptyset \vdash_M \sigma$. In English, we may summarize the proof forms as follows.

If x is an assumption of σ, then x is a proof of σ.

If M is a proof of σ with assumptions Γ, then we may also consider M a proof of σ with assumptions $\Gamma, x\colon\tau$.

If M is a proof of $\sigma \to \tau$ and N is a proof of σ, both with assumptions Γ, then MN is a proof of τ with assumptions Γ.

If M is a proof of τ with assumption x of σ, possibly among others, then $\lambda x\colon\sigma. M$ is a proof of $\sigma \to \tau$ with the assumption x discharged.

Even when $\to$ is the only propositional connective, there are classical tautologies that are not intuitionistically provable. For example, it is easy to check that the formula $((a \to b) \to a) \to a$ is a classical tautology just by trying all possible assignments of *true* and *false* to a and b. However, this formula is not intuitionistically provable (see Exercise 4.3.16).

It is easy to see that we have just defined the typed lambda calculus: the terms of typed lambda calculus are precisely the proofs defined above and their types are exactly the formulas proved. Symbolically, $\Gamma \vdash_M \sigma$ iff $\Gamma \rhd M\colon\sigma$. The correspondence is more than just a connection between terms and proofs. There are standard methods for simplifying proofs to normal form that may be used to prove the consistency of various logics. This is one of the basic techniques of proof theory, discussed in [GLT89], for example. For implicational logic, the proof simplifications are exactly the reduction rules on typed lambda terms. Thus, the *formulas-as-types correspondence* has three parts:

formula	$\approx$ type
proof	$\approx$ lambda term
proof normalization	$\approx$ reduction

This correspondence is also called the *Curry-Howard isomorphism* after [CF58, How80]. The correspondence extends to the other propositional connectives and quantifiers. The standard natural deduction proof rules for $\wedge$ and $\vee$ are precisely the formation rules given for product and sum types, respectively [Pra65]. The type constants *null* and *unit* correspond exactly to logical constants for *false* and *true*. The quantifiers, which give us polymorphism and data abstraction, are discussed in Section 9.1.4.

Since our only presentation of intuitionistic logic is via typed lambda calculus, we state the following proposition without proof.

Proposition 4.3.13 [CF58, How80] There is a closed $\lambda^{\rightarrow}$ term of type τ iff τ is a valid formula of intuitionistic propositional logic, with $\rightarrow$ read as implication.

This is a well-known fact about typed lambda calculus that was probably first observed by Curry. We give some intuition for the connection between a formula and its proof in the proof of Lemma 4.3.14 below.

An interesting feature of the proof rule for $\vee$, given in [Pra65], for example, is that it took some time for computer scientists to arrive at the proper formulation of sums. For example, the variant record types of Pascal are a form of sum type, but have a type insecurity discussed in [WSH77]. A related issue arises in "Classic" ML [GMW79]. Although the original formulation of sums in Classic ML was not incorrect, it did rely on exceptions to prevent type insecurity. Specifically, ML had functions **outleft**: $\sigma + \tau \rightarrow \sigma$ and **outright**: $\sigma + \tau \rightarrow \tau$. If $x\colon\tau$ in ML, then (**inright**x): $\sigma + \tau$ and **outleft**(**inright**x): σ. However, since we cannot actually compute a value of type σ from $x\colon\tau$, this is not semantically sensible. The ML solution to this problem is to raise a run-time exception when **outleft**(**inright**x) is evaluated, which introduces a form of run-time type checking. In contrast, the discriminating case statement of CLU [L^{+}81] is a correct form of sum (or disjoint union) type without the insecurities of Pascal variant records (see [LSAS77, page 569]) or reliance on exceptions. It is exactly the same as the $\vee$ rule from intuitionistic logic, known to proof theorists for many years. Since the $\vee$ rule leads us directly to a case statement that requires no run-time type checking, it seems that the formulas-as-types correspondence can be a useful source of inspiration in programming language design.

An interesting fact about intuitionistic implicational logic, easily proved using lambda calculus, is that when only one propositional symbol is used, the logic becomes classical. A consequence for lambda calculus is that, in general, the special case with only one type constant may differ from lambda calculus with two or more type constants.

Lemma 4.3.14 Let Σ be a $\lambda^{\rightarrow}$ signature with one type constant, b, and no term constants. Then for every type σ over this signature, there is a closed term $M\colon\sigma$ iff σ is a true formula of classical propositional logic, reading $\rightarrow$ as implication and b as *false*.

Note that every type σ over the kind of signature described in the lemma may be written in the form $\sigma \equiv \sigma_1 \rightarrow \ldots \rightarrow \sigma_k \rightarrow b$, for some sequence of types $\sigma_1, \ldots, \sigma_k$. We will use this in the proof of the lemma below. It is useful to observe that a propositional implication $\sigma \equiv \sigma_1 \rightarrow \ldots \rightarrow \sigma_k \rightarrow b$ is classically valid iff it is true when b is interpreted as *false*. The reason is that the implication is clearly true with b is interpreted as *true*.

Proof We use induction on types to show that there exists a closed term $M\colon\sigma$ iff σ is true, reading $\rightarrow$ as implication and b as *false*. (As noted above, this is equivalent to σ

being a classical tautology.) The base case is $\sigma \equiv b$. Since we consider b false, and there is no closed term $M\colon b$, the claim holds.

For the inductive step, we show that there is a closed term $M\colon \sigma \to \tau$ iff either σ is false or τ is true. If there is a closed term $M\colon \sigma \to \tau$ and σ is true, then by the inductive hypothesis there is a closed term $N\colon \sigma$ and therefore a closed term $MN\colon \tau$. This shows that if there is a closed term $M\colon \sigma \to \tau$ then either σ is false or τ is true. It remains to establish the reverse implication.

There are two cases to consider. If τ is true, then by the inductive hypothesis there is some closed $P\colon \tau$ and therefore we may write a closed term $\lambda x\colon \sigma.\, P$ of type $\sigma \to \tau$.

The remaining case is when σ is false. We write σ in the form $\sigma \equiv \sigma_1 \to \ldots \to \sigma_k \to b$ and observe that since the implication σ is false, all of the propositional formulas $\sigma_1, \ldots, \sigma_k$ must be true. Therefore, by the inductive hypothesis, there exist closed terms $M_1\colon \sigma_1, \ldots, M_k\colon \sigma_k$. If we write τ in the form $\tau \equiv \tau_1 \to \ldots \to \tau_\ell \to b$, then we may write the closed term

$$\lambda x\colon \sigma.\, \lambda y_1\colon \tau_1. \ldots \lambda y_\ell\colon \tau_\ell.\, x M_1 \ldots M_k.$$

with type

$$\sigma \to \tau \equiv (\sigma_1 \to \ldots \to \sigma_k \to b) \to \tau_1 \to \ldots \to \tau_\ell \to b.$$

This completes the proof.

Exercise 4.3.15 Prove the following implicational formulas by finding closed $\lambda^{\to}$ terms (with type constants but without term constants) of each type.

(a) $a \to a$.

(b) $(a \to b) \to c \to a \to b$.

(c) $(a \to b) \to (b \to c) \to (a \to c)$.

Exercise 4.3.16 This exercise assumes familiarity with normal form lambda terms, discussed in Chapter 2 and Section 4.4.2. In the discussion above, the implicational formula $((a \to b) \to a) \to a$ is given as an example of a formula that is valid classically but not intuitionistically.

(a) Explain why the formula is classically valid.

(b) It is difficult to show directly that this formula is not intuitionistically provable. However, it is not very hard if we use the fact that each proof may be written out as a closed $\lambda^{\to}$ term with type constants a and b and no term constants. The reason why lambda terms are helpful is that if there is a closed lambda term $M\colon ((a \to b) \to a) \to a$ then there is a closed normal form (the normal form of M) of this type. Show that this implicational formula is not provable by showing that there is no closed normal form term of this type.

4.3.5 Typing Algorithm

There are several algorithmic problems associated with the syntax of simply-typed lambda calculus. For example, given Γ, M and σ, we would like to determine efficiently whether $\Gamma \triangleright M : \sigma$ is a provable typing assertion. A variant that does not appear to be any harder is to determine, given only M and Γ, whether there is some σ with $\Gamma \triangleright M : \sigma$ provable. If so, we would like to determine σ. We will see that this problem is solvable by a straightforward algorithm. A completely different problem is to determine, given Γ and σ, whether there is some M with $\Gamma \triangleright M : \sigma$ provable. We will see that this is significantly more difficult. Some related problems are considered in Chapter 11.

Before discussing the type-checking algorithm, it is useful to identify the context-free syntax of the underlying expressions of $\lambda^{\rightarrow}$. We shall call these *pre-terms*. The $\lambda^{\rightarrow}$ pre-terms over signature Σ are given by the grammar

$$M \ ::= \ c \mid x \mid MM \mid \lambda x : \sigma . M$$

where c may be any constant from Σ and σ may be any $\lambda^{\rightarrow}$ type over Σ. This grammar may be derived from the typing axioms and inference rules in an obvious and routine way. In particular, there is one clause on the right of the $::=$ for each typing axiom or inference rule. The input to the type-checking algorithm will be a pre-term, since there are standard algorithms for determining whether a string is generated by a context-free grammar. This is consistent with standard compiler design, where context-free parsing precedes type analysis [ASU86].

A type-checking algorithm is given in Table 4.1. Given a type assignment Γ and pre-term M as input, the algorithm either returns a type σ with $\Gamma \triangleright M : \sigma$ derivable or halts with failure. The correctness of the algorithm is stated in the following proposition.

Proposition 4.3.17 Let Σ be a $\lambda^{\rightarrow}$ signature, Γ a type assignment using types over Σ, and M a $\lambda^{\rightarrow}$ pre-term over Σ. Then algorithm $TC(\Gamma, M)$ terminates with type σ iff the typing assertion $\Gamma \triangleright M : \sigma$ is derivable. If there is no derivable typing assertion for Γ and M, then the algorithm halts with failure.

In practice, a type checker is usually designed to check complete programs, which are closed terms. However, if we call $TC(\emptyset, M)$ for closed M, then recursive calls for subterms of M will involve open terms and nonempty type assignments. Some examples are given in Exercise 4.3.18.

Table 4.1
Type-checking algorithm.

$TC(\Gamma, c)$	$=$	σ if $c\colon\sigma$ is a constant of the signature else *fail*
$TC(\Gamma, x)$	$=$	σ if $x\colon\sigma \in \Gamma$ else *fail*
$TC(\Gamma, MN)$	$=$	τ if $TC(\Gamma, M) = \sigma \to \tau$ and $TC(\Gamma, N) = \sigma$ else *fail*
$TC(\Gamma, \lambda x\colon\sigma.\, M)$	$=$	$\sigma \to \tau$ if $TC((\Gamma_{\lambda x:\sigma.\,M}, x\colon\sigma), M) = \tau$ else *fail*

Proof The proof proceeds by induction on the structure of pre-terms. For a constant, we know by Lemma 4.3.4 that $\Gamma \triangleright c\colon\sigma$ is derivable iff c is given type σ by the signature. The variable case is similar.

For the application case, we know by Lemma 4.3.4 that for each σ, the assertion $\Gamma \triangleright MN\colon\sigma$ is derivable iff $\Gamma_{MN} \triangleright MN\colon\sigma$ is derivable. By Lemma 4.3.3 and inspection of the typing rules, we can see that if $\Gamma_{MN} \triangleright MN\colon\sigma$ is derivable, there must be a derivation ending with rule ($\to$ Elim). Using Lemma 4.3.4 again, we can see that

$\Gamma \triangleright MN\colon\sigma$ is derivable iff

$\Gamma_{MN} \triangleright MN\colon\sigma$ is derivable iff

$\Gamma_{MN} \triangleright M\colon\tau \to \sigma$ and $\Gamma_{MN} \triangleright N\colon\tau$ are derivable for some τ iff

$\Gamma \triangleright M\colon\tau \to \sigma$ and $\Gamma \triangleright N\colon\tau$ are derivable for some τ.

Using the inductive hypothesis for $TC(\Gamma, M)$ and $TC(\Gamma, N)$, this proves the lemma in the application case.

For the lambda abstraction case, we again use Lemma 4.3.4 to see that $\Gamma \triangleright \lambda x\colon\sigma.\, M\colon\rho$ is derivable iff $\Gamma_{\lambda x:\sigma.\,M} \triangleright \lambda x\colon\sigma.\, M\colon\rho$ is derivable and note that the latter typing assertion must be proved using rule ($\to$ Intro). It follows that ρ must have the form $\rho \equiv \sigma \to \tau$ and $\Gamma_{\lambda x:\sigma.\,M}, x\colon\sigma \triangleright M\colon\tau$ must be derivable. The lemma follows by the inductive hypothesis. ■

The other algorithmic problem mentioned at the beginning of this section is, given Γ and σ, to find M such that $\Gamma \triangleright M\colon\sigma$ is derivable. This may seem like an artificial problem, from a programming point of view, unless you think of Γ and σ as a simple specification and an algorithm for this problem as an algorithm for "program derivation." For $\lambda^{\to}$, such specifications are sufficiently vague that this form of program derivation does not seem likely to be useful in practice. Using the formulas-as-types correspondence described in the last section, we can see that this problem is quite difficult.

From the formulas-as-types correspondence, we can see that there is a term M with

$$x_1\colon\sigma_1, \ldots, x_k\colon\sigma_k \triangleright M\colon\sigma$$

derivable iff the implicational formula

$$\sigma_1 \to \ldots \to \sigma_k \to \sigma$$

is intuitionistically provable. In other words, the problem of constructing a term with a given typing is the problem of constructing a proof of a given formula. The problem of determining whether an intuitionistic implicational formula is provable is PSPACE-complete [Sta79]. Therefore, given Γ and σ, it is PSPACE-complete to determine whether there exists an M with $\Gamma \triangleright M\colon\sigma$ derivable. Since there is no chance of finding a more efficient algorithm, we will not consider the problem of constructing the actual proof/term.

Exercise 4.3.18 Use algorithm *TC* to compute types for the following closed lambda terms. Assume numerals $0, 1, 2, \ldots$ of type *nat* are given by the signature and use the empty type assignment.

(a) $\lambda x\colon nat \to nat.\,\lambda y\colon nat.\,xy$

(b) $\lambda x\colon nat \to nat.\,\lambda y\colon nat.((\lambda x\colon nat.\,3)(xy))$

(c) $\lambda x\colon nat \to nat.\,\lambda y\colon nat.((\lambda x\colon nat.\,3)(xz))$

4.4 Proof Systems

4.4.1 Equations and Theories

The equational proof system of typed lambda calculus may be used to derive equations that hold in all models, and to derive equations that follow from equational hypotheses. Unlike algebra, the valid equations between typed lambda terms are nontrivial. However, in the absence of recursive types, which allow us to express recursion and many interesting datatypes (as shown in Section 2.6.3), we must generally add type and term constants to simply typed lambda calculus and adopt appropriate axioms in order to obtain a language with interesting computational properties. As illustrated by the programming capabilities of PCF, typed lambda theories for many interesting computational systems consist of algebraic axioms for datatypes, together with non-algebraic axioms for fixed-point operators or other forms of recursion. For this reason, we devote some attention to the relationship between typed lambda calculus and algebra. In addition, to illustrate the expressiveness of typed lambda calculus, we also describe the lambda theory corresponding to a fixed set of recursive types and a theory for higher-order logic.

As in algebra, we write equations between typed lambda terms in a form that includes the assignment of types to variables. Since the types of terms will be used in the equational proof system, we also include the types of terms. Specifically, a typed equation has the form

$$\Gamma \triangleright M = N : \tau$$

where we assume that M and N have type τ in context Γ. Intuitively, the equation $\{x_1 : \sigma_1, \ldots, x_k : \sigma_k\} \triangleright M = N : \tau$ means that for all type-correct values of the variables $x_1 : \sigma_1, \ldots, x_k : \sigma_k$, expressions M and N denote the same element of type τ. Another way of writing this equation might be

$$\forall x_1 : \sigma_1 \ldots \forall x_k : \sigma_k . \, M = N : \tau.$$

Because the variables listed in the type assignment are universally quantified, an equation may hold vacuously if some type is empty. Specifically, if σ is empty, then the equation $\forall x : \sigma . \, M = N : \tau$ is true simply because there is no possible value for x.

Since we include type assignments in equations, we have an equational version of the typing rule that adds variables to type assignments,

$$\frac{\Gamma \triangleright M = N : \sigma}{\Gamma, x : \tau \triangleright M = N : \sigma} \qquad (add\ var)$$

The next group of axioms and inference rules make provable equality an equivalence relation, and a congruence with respect to the term-formation operations (see Section 2.3.2). To make equality an equivalence relation, we have the axiom and rules

$$\Gamma \triangleright M = M : \sigma \qquad (ref)$$

$$\frac{\Gamma \triangleright M = N : \sigma}{\Gamma \triangleright N = M : \sigma} \qquad (sym)$$

$$\frac{\Gamma \triangleright M = N : \sigma, \ \Gamma \triangleright N = P : \sigma}{\Gamma \triangleright M = P : \sigma} \qquad (trans)$$

The two term-formation operations of $\lambda^{\rightarrow}$ are abstraction and application, both of which preserve equality. The rule

$$\frac{\Gamma, x : \sigma \triangleright M = N : \tau}{\Gamma \triangleright \lambda x : \sigma . \, M = \lambda x : \sigma . \, N : \sigma \rightarrow \tau} \qquad (\xi)$$

says that if M and N are equal for all values of x, then the two functions $\lambda x : \sigma . \, M$ and

$\lambda x\colon\sigma.\, N$ are equal. For application, we have the rule

$$\frac{\Gamma \rhd M_1 = M_2\colon \sigma \to \tau,\ \ \Gamma \rhd N_1 = N_2\colon \sigma}{\Gamma \rhd M_1 N_1 = M_2 N_2\colon \tau} \qquad (\nu)$$

saying that equals applied to equals yield equals. Rules (ξ) and (ν) may be explained using the equality principle associated with function types: two functions are equal iff they map equal arguments to equal results. One direction of this "iff" gives rule (ν), and the other (ξ). It is interesting to note that the two congruence rules have the same form as the introduction and elimination rules for $\to$.

For $\lambda^{\to}$, three axioms remain. The first describes renaming of bound variables, while the other two specify that the introduction and elimination rules are "inverses" of each other. Since these axioms are described and illustrated by example in Chapter 2, we will not discuss them in detail here. The first, (α), allows us to rename bound variables.

$$\Gamma \rhd \lambda x\colon \sigma.\, M = \lambda y\colon \sigma.[y/x]M\colon \sigma \to \tau, \text{ provided } y \notin FV(M) \qquad (\alpha)$$

The second, (β) shows how to evaluate a function application using substitution.

$$\Gamma \rhd (\lambda x\colon \sigma.\, M)N = [N/x]M\colon \tau \qquad (\beta)$$

In the special case that the argument N is a variable, this axiom says that introduction (lambda abstraction) composed with elimination (application) is the identity operation. The other composition of elimination and introduction is also the identity.

$$\Gamma \rhd \lambda x\colon \sigma.(Mx) = M\colon \sigma \to \tau, \text{ provided } x \notin FV(M) \qquad (\eta)$$

Recall from Chapter 2 that if $x \notin FV(M)$, then by (β) we have $(\lambda x\colon \sigma.\, Mx)y = My$ for any argument $y\colon \sigma$. Therefore M and $\lambda x\colon \sigma.\, Mx$ define the same function.

The following lemma is easily proved by induction on equational proofs.

Lemma 4.4.1 If $\vdash \Gamma \rhd M = N\colon \sigma$ and $\Gamma \cap \Gamma'$ contains all free variables of M and N, then $\vdash \Gamma' \rhd M = N\colon \sigma$

This shows that if we only consider proofs from the axioms, it is not necessary to including type assignments in equations. However, it follows from Proposition 4.4.5, below, that type assignments are needed for deductions from equational hypotheses.

A *typed lambda theory* (or $\lambda^{\to}$ *theory*) over signature Σ is a set of well-typed equations between Σ-terms that includes all instances of the axioms and is closed under the inference rules. If $\mathcal{E}$ is any set of well-typed equations, we write $\mathcal{E} \vdash \Gamma \rhd M = N\colon \sigma$ to mean that the equation $\Gamma \rhd M = N\colon \sigma$ is provable from the axioms and equations of $\mathcal{E}$. The *theory of* $\mathcal{E}$, written $Th(\mathcal{E})$, is the set of equations provable from the axioms and equations of $\mathcal{E}$.

Given any algebraic signature Σ, there is a corresponding $\lambda^{\rightarrow}$ signature $\Sigma_{\rightarrow}$ (defined in Section 4.3.2; see Exercise 4.3.9) such that every algebraic term over Σ is a $\lambda^{\rightarrow}$ term over $\Sigma_{\rightarrow}$. This allows us to regard any algebraic equations as $\lambda^{\rightarrow}$ equations. An example involving the algebraic specification of trees is given in Exercise 4.4.8.

An important relationship between algebra and simply-typed lambda calculus is that every algebraic proof can be carried out in $\lambda^{\rightarrow}$. Since the only algebraic proof rule that is not a $\lambda^{\rightarrow}$ rule is (*subst*), we show that this is a derived rule of $\lambda^{\rightarrow}$.

Lemma 4.4.2 The algebraic rule

$$\frac{\Gamma, x\!:\!\sigma \triangleright M = N\!:\!\tau,\ \ \Gamma \triangleright P = Q\!:\!\sigma}{\Gamma \triangleright [P/x]M = [Q/x]N\!:\!\tau} \qquad (subst)$$

is a derivable proof rule of $\lambda^{\rightarrow}$.

Proof From $\Gamma, x\!:\!\sigma \triangleright M = N\!:\!\tau$, we can prove

$\Gamma \triangleright \lambda x\!:\!\sigma.\, M = \lambda x\!:\!\sigma.\, N\!:\!\sigma \rightarrow \tau$

by rule (ξ). Then by rule (ν), we have

$\Gamma \triangleright (\lambda x\!:\!\sigma.\, M)P = (\lambda x\!:\!\sigma.\, N)Q\!:\!\tau$

The lemma follows by (β) and transitivity. ∎

Using this lemma, it is easy to prove the following proposition by induction on proofs in the algebraic proof system.

Proposition 4.4.3 Let $\mathcal{E}$ be a set of equations between algebraic terms over algebraic signature Σ, and let E be a single such equation. If $\mathcal{E} \vdash E$ in the algebraic proof system, then $\mathcal{E} \vdash E$ in the $\lambda^{\rightarrow}$ proof system, regarding E and the elements of $\mathcal{E}$ as equations between $\lambda^{\rightarrow}$ terms over signature $\Sigma_{\rightarrow}$.

The converse of this proposition is that simply-typed lambda calculus is *conservative* over algebra. (The general notion of conservativity is discussed at the end of this section.)

Proposition 4.4.4 (Conservativity) Let $\mathcal{E}$ be as set of equations between algebraic terms over algebraic signature Σ, and let E be a single such equations. If $\mathcal{E} \vdash E$, when we regard E and the equations in $\mathcal{E}$ as equations between $\lambda^{\rightarrow}$ terms over signature $\Sigma^{\rightarrow}$, then $\mathcal{E} \vdash E$ using the algebraic proof system.

This is proved in Exercise 4.5.19 using a semantic construction. The main idea is that if $\mathcal{E} \vdash E$ in $\lambda^{\rightarrow}$ then by soundness, E must hold in every Henkin model satisfying $\mathcal{E}$.

By showing that every algebra can be extended to a Henkin model, the result follows by completeness of the algebraic proof system.

Using conservativity, we can show that keeping track of variables in equations affects provability.

Proposition 4.4.5 There is a typed lambda theory $\mathcal{E}$ and terms M and N without x free such that $\mathcal{E} \vdash \Gamma, x\colon\sigma \triangleright M = N\colon\tau$ but $\mathcal{E} \nvdash \Gamma \triangleright M = N\colon\tau$

This follows from the corresponding fact for algebra, Proposition 3.4.14, by conservativity and Proposition 4.4.3. While it is not conservative to add fixed-point operators at all types, fixed-point operators may be added conservatively using lifted types, as discussed in Section 2.6.4. We consider some important non-algebraic theories in the next two examples.

Example 4.4.6 Although we do not consider lambda calculus with recursive types a form of "simply-typed lambda calculus," there is a sense in which any particular use of recursive types can be expressed as a simply-typed lambda theory. For example, suppose we are only interested in the type *nat*, which may be defined recursively as

$$nat = unit + nat,$$

as shown in Section 2.6.3. Instead of adding constants for the numerals and basic functions such as successor, addition, and so on, we can add *nat* to simply-typed lambda calculus using a general method that applies to any recursive type.

Recall from Section 2.6.3 that the basic operations associated with a recursive type are functions up and dn. If we want to add *nat* to $\lambda^{unit,+,\rightarrow}$, we can do so by adding a type constant *nat* and term constants for the particular up and dn functions associated with the recursive definition above. Specifically, we define the single recursive type *nat* using term constants with the following types and equational axioms:

$$\mathrm{up}_{nat}\colon (unit + nat) \rightarrow nat$$
$$\mathrm{dn}_{nat}\colon nat \rightarrow (unit + nat)$$
$$\lambda x\colon (unit + nat).\, \mathrm{dn}_{nat}(\mathrm{up}_{nat}\, x) = \lambda x\colon (unit + nat).\, x$$
$$\lambda x\colon nat.\, \mathrm{up}_{nat}(\mathrm{dn}_{nat}\, x) = \lambda x\colon nat.\, x.$$

Note that these two equations yield $\mathrm{dn}(\mathrm{up}\, M) = M$ and $\mathrm{up}(\mathrm{dn}\, M) = M$, for any term M of the appropriate type, by application. Without adding any other constants or equational axioms, we may write terms that define the numerals and basic functions as illustrated in Section 2.6.3. A related treatment of untyped lambda calculus, as a $\lambda^{\rightarrow}$ theory, is given in Exercise 4.4.12. ■

Example 4.4.7 As mentioned in the introductory remarks of Section 4.1, lambda calculus was originally developed with logic in mind. One way to obtain logic from typed lambda calculus is to add a type for "truth values", which we write *tv* instead of *bool* to avoid confusion, together with constants

$$or\colon tv \to tv \to tv$$

$$not\colon tv \to tv$$

$$\forall_\sigma\colon (\sigma \to tv) \to tv$$

for each type σ. These constants should be familiar, except possibly for the constant $\forall_\sigma$. The intended use of $\forall_\sigma$ is that instead of writing a universally quantified formula in the form $\forall x\colon\sigma.\,\phi$, using $\forall$ as a binding operator, we will write $\forall_\sigma\,(\lambda x\colon\sigma.\,\phi)$. In the logic obtained from typed lambda calculus, a logical formula is a term of type *tv*, and a predicate variable (for example) is a variable of type $\sigma \to tv$.

To simplify the axioms of higher-order logic, we adopt the following abbreviations.

$$\neg M \stackrel{\text{def}}{=} not\ M$$

$$M \vee N \stackrel{\text{def}}{=} or\ M\ N$$

$$M \wedge N \stackrel{\text{def}}{=} \neg((\neg M) \vee (\neg N))$$

$$M \supset N \stackrel{\text{def}}{=} (\neg M) \vee N$$

$$\forall x\colon\sigma.\,M \stackrel{\text{def}}{=} \forall_\sigma\,(\lambda x\colon\sigma.\,M)$$

$$\exists x\colon\sigma.\,M \stackrel{\text{def}}{=} \neg(\forall x\colon\sigma.\,\neg M)$$

$$eq_\sigma \stackrel{\text{def}}{=} \lambda x\colon\sigma.\,\lambda y\colon\sigma.\,\forall f\colon\sigma \to tv.\,(f\,M \supset f\,N)$$

$$M \approx N \stackrel{\text{def}}{=} eq_\sigma\ M\ N$$

This allows us to write any of the standard formulas of higher-order logic as a lambda term of type *tv*. This definition of equality, written here as $\approx$ to avoid confusion with $=$, is often called *Leibniz equality,* after the philosopher and mathematician. Intuitively, we may read $\forall f\colon\sigma \to tv.\,(f\,M \supset f\,N)$ as saying that any property of M is also a property of N. Some properties of $\approx$ are given in Exercise 4.4.14.

Classical higher-order logic, sometimes called *type theory* or *Church's theory of simple types*, may be axiomatized using the following formulas, taken from [Hen50].

$$(x \vee x) \supset x$$

$$x \supset (x \vee y)$$

$(x \vee y) \supset (y \vee x)$

$(x \supset y) \supset ((z \vee x) \supset (z \vee y))$

$\forall_\sigma f \supset fx$

$\forall x{:}\sigma.\,(y \vee fx) \supset (x \vee \forall_\sigma f)$

$((x \supset y) \wedge (y \supset x)) \supset x \approx y$

$\forall x{:}\sigma.\,(fx \approx gx) \supset f \approx g$

If we read each axiom M as an abbreviation for the equation $M = \mathit{true}$, where $\mathit{true} \stackrel{\text{def}}{=} \forall x{:}\mathit{tv}.\,(x \supset x)$, then we may read each of the standard axioms as a $\lambda^{\rightarrow}$ equation. To show that we can present higher-order logic as a $\lambda^{\rightarrow}$ theory, we show that for each inference rule of higher-order logic, we may carry out the required deduction in lambda calculus. For this, we will need one additional equational axiom,

$x = (\mathit{true} \supset x).$

There are six inference rules of higher-order logic, as presented in [Hen50].

(I) Rename bound variables in any formula.

(II) Replace $(\lambda x{:}\sigma.\,M)N$ by $[N/x]M$ in any formula.

(III) Replace $[N/x]M$ by $(\lambda x{:}\sigma.\,M)N$ in any formula (the converse of II).

(IV) From Mx infer MN, provided $x \notin FV(M)$.

(V) From $M \supset N$ and M infer N.

(VI) From Mx infer $\forall_\sigma M$, provided $x \notin FV(M)$.

It is easy to see that inference rules I–III are derivable in $\lambda^{\rightarrow}$, as direct consequences of (α) and (β) and the congruence rules. Derivations of rules IV–VI are left as Exercise 4.4.13, which completes the proof that if M is a provable formula of classical higher-order logic, then the equation $M = \mathit{true}$ is provable from the equational axioms given above. The converse is given as Exercise 4.4.15. Since the models and interpretations of formulas are virtually identical for higher-order logic and typed lambda calculus, it is also easy to see directly that the axioms and proof rules here are sound for general models of higher-order logic. Semantic connections between higher-order logic and typed lambda calculus are given in Exercises 4.5.20 and 4.5.27. For more information on classical higher-order logic, the reader may consult [And86, Gor93, Hen50, Hen63, Mon76]. For information on intuitionistic higher-order logic and its relationship to typed lambda calculus with a type of truth values, see [LS86]. ∎

It is tempting to combine theories of the form described in Example 4.4.6, providing instances of recursive types, with the theory in Example 4.4.7 giving us higher-order logic. The reason is that with enough recursive types, or, alternatively, with fixed-point operators, we would obtain a higher-order logic for reasoning about programs. However, this must be done with great care. For example, it is possible to prove in classical higher-order logic, for each type σ, that $\sigma \to \sigma$ is *not* isomorphic to σ. Therefore, if we add axioms solving the recursive type equation $t = t \to t$ to the equational theory giving us higher order logic, we obtain an inconsistent theory. Similar problems arise with fixed points, since, for example, it is inconsistent to have a fixed-point of negation. While there appear to be solutions to these problems using intuitionistic logic and explicit lifting (Section 2.6.4), this issue remains a research topic.

Product Types

The equational axioms for product types are explained in Chapter 2.

$$\Gamma \rhd \mathbf{Proj}_1 \langle M, N\rangle = M\colon \sigma \qquad (proj_1)$$

$$\Gamma \rhd \mathbf{Proj}_2 \langle M, N\rangle = N\colon \sigma \qquad (proj_2)$$

$$\Gamma \rhd \langle \mathbf{Proj}_1\, M, \mathbf{Proj}_2\, M\rangle = M\colon \sigma \qquad (sp)$$

Sum Types

The equational axioms for sums are presented in Section 2.6.2, where several examples and exercises are also given.

$$\Gamma \rhd \mathbf{Case}^{\sigma,\tau,\rho}\, (\mathbf{Inleft}^{\sigma,\tau}\, M)\, N\, P = N M\colon \rho \qquad (case)_1$$

$$\Gamma \rhd \mathbf{Case}^{\sigma,\tau,\rho}\, (\mathbf{Inright}^{\sigma,\tau}\, M)\, N\, P = P M\colon \rho \qquad (case)_2$$

$$\Gamma \rhd \mathbf{Case}^{\sigma,\tau,\rho}\, M\, (N \circ \mathbf{Inleft}^{\sigma,\tau})\, (N \circ \mathbf{Inright}^{\sigma,\tau}) = N M\colon \sigma + \tau \qquad (case)_3$$

It is easy to check that axiom $(\mathbf{Case})_3$ is well-formed only if $\Gamma \rhd N\colon (\sigma + \tau) \to (\sigma + \tau)$.

Terminal Type

The axiom for the terminal type, *unit*, is explained in Section 2.6.2.

$$\Gamma \rhd M = *\colon unit \qquad (unit)$$

The category-theoretic characterization of *unit* is as a *terminal object*. The definition of terminal object is that for every type σ, there is a unique function $\mathbf{One}^{\sigma}\colon \sigma \to unit$. In any lambda calculus with *unit*, we can write $\mathbf{One}^{\sigma}$ as $\lambda x\colon \sigma.\, *$. This gives us one function from σ to *unit*. The equational axiom above lets us show that any other function from σ to *unit* is equal to $\mathbf{One}^{\sigma}$. Specifically, if $\Gamma \rhd M\colon \sigma \to unit$, then for some fresh x we have $\Gamma, x\colon \sigma \rhd Mx\colon unit$ and therefore

$\Gamma, x\colon\sigma \triangleright Mx = *\colon unit$

by the axiom above. Using rule (ξ) and (η), we may conclude $\Gamma \triangleright M = \lambda x\colon\sigma.\, *\colon \sigma \rightarrow unit$.

Another description of *unit* is as the "zero-ary product," or cartesian product of zero types. This sounds a little cryptic, but may be made precise in a meaningful way using category theory. A simple consequence is that for any type σ, there is an isomorphism $\sigma \cong \sigma \times unit$. This is shown in Exercise 4.4.9.

Initial Type

The category-theoretic characterization of *null* is as an *initial object.* The definition of initial object is that for every type σ, there is a unique function $\mathbf{Zero}^{\sigma}\colon null \rightarrow \sigma$. In any lambda calculus with *null*, we assume we have the term form $\mathbf{Zero}^{\sigma}$. The following equational axiom lets us show immediately that any other function from *null* to σ is equal to $\mathbf{Zero}^{\sigma}$.

$$\Gamma \triangleright M = \mathbf{Zero}^{\sigma}\colon null \rightarrow \sigma \qquad (null)$$

Another description of *null* is as the "zero-ary sum," or sum of zero types. A consequence is that for any type σ, there is an isomorphism $\sigma \cong \sigma + null$. This is shown in Exercise 4.4.10.

Relationship Between Versions of Simply-typed Lambda Calculus

In general, if one logical system or language, $\mathcal{L}_2$, contains another, $\mathcal{L}_1$, it is useful to compare the two using the formulas of the smaller language. The main technical definition is that if $\mathcal{L}_2$ contains $\mathcal{L}_1$, then we say $\mathcal{L}_2$ is *conservative over* $\mathcal{L}_1$ if, whenever $\mathcal{F}$ is a set of formulas in the language of $\mathcal{L}_1$ and F is a single such formula, we have $\mathcal{F} \vdash F$ in the proof system of $\mathcal{L}_1$ whenever $\mathcal{F} \vdash F$ in the proof system of $\mathcal{L}_2$. A common situation is that the proof rules of $\mathcal{L}_2$ include those of $\mathcal{L}_1$. In this case, conservativity implies that $\mathcal{F} \vdash F$ in $\mathcal{L}_1$ iff $\mathcal{F} \vdash F$ in $\mathcal{L}_2$. An example is that the proof system and language of $\lambda^{\times,\rightarrow}$ contain the proof system and language of $\lambda^{\rightarrow}$. Therefore, if $\mathcal{E}$ is a set of $\lambda^{\rightarrow}$ equations and E is a single $\lambda^{\rightarrow}$ equation, it is natural to ask whether we can prove E from $\mathcal{E}$ in one proof system but not the other. As shown in Section 4.4.4, $\lambda^{\times,\rightarrow}$ is conservative over $\lambda^{\rightarrow}$, which means that the two proof systems are equivalent for reasoning about $\lambda^{\rightarrow}$ equations.

There are two methods for proving conservativity, one by analyzing proof systems and the other by semantic construction. For versions of simply-typed lambda calculus, we can use confluence of reduction to prove conservativity. The general method, which is also applicable to other typed or untyped calculi, is illustrated in Section 4.4.4. A related general technique for analyzing theories is given in Section 9.3.2. A semantic proof of conservativity is described in connection with Proposition 4.4.4.

Exercise 4.4.8 An algebraic specification of trees is given in Table 3.3. Let Σ be the $\lambda^{\rightarrow}$ signature obtained by currying all function types in this specification and adding the constants

$$Eq? \quad : atom \rightarrow atom \rightarrow bool$$

$$fix_{tree \rightarrow atom}: ((tree \rightarrow atom) \rightarrow (tree \rightarrow atom)) \rightarrow (tree \rightarrow atom)$$

with their usual axioms

$$Eq?\, a\, a \quad = true \quad \text{any atom constant } a$$

$$Eq?\, a\, b \quad = false \quad \text{distinct atom constants } a, b$$

$$fix_{tree \rightarrow atom} = \lambda f\colon (tree \rightarrow atom) \rightarrow (tree \rightarrow atom).\ f\,(fix_{tree \rightarrow atom}\ f)$$

Write a function *find_a*: $tree \rightarrow atom$ over this signature and prove that if $M\colon tree$ is a closed expression then one of the equations *find_a* $M = true$ or *find_a* $M = false$ is provable, depending on whether one of the leaves of the tree defined by M is the atom a.

Exercise 4.4.9 Show that in any lambda calculus with function types, cartesian products and *unit*, there is an isomorphism $\sigma \cong \sigma \times unit$, for every type σ. More specifically, give closed terms

$$M\colon \sigma \rightarrow \sigma \times unit$$

$$N\colon \sigma \times unit \rightarrow \sigma$$

and show that both compositions, $M \circ N$ and $N \circ M$, are provably equal to the identity function of the appropriate type.

Exercise 4.4.10 Show that in any lambda calculus with function types, sums and *null*, there is an isomorphism $\sigma \cong \sigma + null$, for every type σ. More specifically, give closed terms

$$M\colon \sigma \rightarrow \sigma + null$$

$$N\colon \sigma + null \rightarrow \sigma$$

and show that both compositions, $M \circ N$ and $N \circ M$, are provably equal to the identity function of the appropriate type. This is slightly harder than Exercise 4.4.9. You may wish to use the results of Exercise 2.6.3.

Exercise 4.4.11 A simpler definition of *conservative* is that if $\mathcal{L}_2$ contains $\mathcal{L}_1$ and F is a formula in the language of $\mathcal{L}_1$, then $\mathcal{L}_2$ is *conservative* over $\mathcal{L}_1$ if $\vdash F$ in the logic of $\mathcal{L}_2$ implies $\vdash F$ in the logic of $\mathcal{L}_1$. The difference is that this simpler definition does not involve deduction from arbitrary sets of hypotheses. Show that for any logic with conjunction, implication, and deductive soundness and completeness theorems, the two definitions are equivalent.

Exercise 4.4.12 Following the method illustrated in Example 4.4.6, show how to define pure untyped lambda calculus, as presented in Exercise 2.6.7, as a $\lambda^{\rightarrow}$ theory. You will need one type constant, *untyped*, two term constants, and two equations. Related semantic connections between typed and untyped lambda calculus are described in Exercise 4.5.21.

Exercise 4.4.13 This exercise asks you to show that inference rules IV–VI of higher-order logic are derivable in $\lambda^{\rightarrow}$, given the equational axioms listed in Example 4.4.7.

(IV) Show that from $Mx = \mathit{true}$, we can prove $MN = \mathit{true}$, provided $x \notin FV(M)$.

(VI) Show that from $Mx = \mathit{true}$, we can prove $\forall_\sigma M = \mathit{true}$, provided $x \notin FV(M)$.

(V) Show that from $(M \supset N) = \mathit{true}$ and $M = \mathit{true}$, we can prove infer $N = \mathit{true}$. (*Hint:* Remember the equation $x = \mathit{true} \supset x$; this is the trickiest of the inference rules.)

Exercise 4.4.14 Show that for each formula R that follows, the equation $R = \mathit{true}$ is provable from the $\lambda^{\rightarrow}$ equations given in Example 4.4.7.

(a) $M \approx N \supset N \approx M$

(b) $(M \approx N) \wedge (N \approx P) \supset M \approx P$

(c) $(M \approx N) \wedge (P \approx Q) \supset MP \approx NQ$

Exercise 4.4.15 Show that if the equation $M = N$ is provable from the equational axioms of Example 4.4.7, then the formula $M \approx N$ is provable in higher-order logic (as formulated in Example 4.4.7). Use this to conclude that if $M = \mathit{true}$ is provable in the equational system, the formula M is provable in higher-order logic.

4.4.2 Reduction Rules

Reduction is a "directed" form of equational reasoning that corresponds to symbolic evaluation of programs. As in the examples of Chapters 2 and 3, most reduction systems are obtained by orienting the equational axioms. In simply-typed lambda calculus, we orient each of the equational axioms except (α). We begin by discussing properties of "pure" β, η-reduction on $\lambda^{\rightarrow}$ terms over any signature, or any superset of $\lambda^{\rightarrow}$. Reductions for term forms associated with products, sums and other simple types are given at the end of the section.

While we are only interested in reducing typed terms, we define reduction without mentioning types. Since reduction models program execution, this is a way of emphasizing that $\lambda^{\rightarrow}$ execution may be done without examining the types of terms. We will also see that the type of a term does not change as it is reduced. Together, these two facts imply that type-independent execution of $\lambda^{\rightarrow}$-terms is type-correct, or "$\lambda^{\rightarrow}$ does not require run time type checking."

Since the reduction rules are described and illustrated by example in Chapter 2, we simply list them here.

$$(\lambda x\colon\sigma.\,M)N \rightarrow [N/x]M, \qquad (\beta)_{red}$$

$$\lambda x\colon\sigma.\,Mx \rightarrow M, \text{ provided } x \notin FV(M). \qquad (\eta)_{red}$$

A term of the form $(\lambda x\colon\sigma.\,M)N$ is called a *β-redex* and $\lambda x\colon\sigma.\,Mx$ an *η-redex*. We say *M β,η-reduces to N in one step,* written $M \rightarrow_{\beta,\eta} N$, if N can be obtained by applying (β) or (η) to some subterm of M. The reduction relation $\twoheadrightarrow_{\beta,\eta}$ is the reflexive and transitive closure of one-step β,η-reduction.

Using Lemma 4.3.6 and inspection of an *η-redex,* it is easy to show that one step reduction preserves type.

Lemma 4.4.16 If $\Gamma \rhd M\colon\sigma$, and $M \rightarrow_{\beta,\eta} N$, then $\Gamma \rhd N\colon\sigma$.

It follows by an easy induction that $\twoheadrightarrow_{\beta,\eta}$ also preserves type. This is often called the *subject reduction property,* based on terminology that calls $M\colon\sigma$ as a "sentence" whose subject is M and predicate is σ.

Since we are only interested in reduction on well-typed terms, it is useful to write $\Gamma \rhd M \twoheadrightarrow N\colon\sigma$ when $\Gamma \rhd M\colon\sigma$ is well-typed and $M \twoheadrightarrow N$. We know by the Lemma above that in this case, we also have $\Gamma \rhd N\colon\sigma$. A term M is in *β,η-normal form* if there is no N with $M \rightarrow_{\beta,\eta} N$.

The main theorems about β,η-reduction are confluence and strong normalization. These are proved in Sections 8.3.2 and 8.3.3, using the technique of logical relations.

- **Confluence** (Theorem 8.3.10): β,η-Reduction is confluent on $\lambda^{\rightarrow}$ terms.
- **Strong Normalization** (Theorem 8.3.6): There is no infinite sequence $M_0 \rightarrow_{\beta,\eta} M_1 \rightarrow_{\beta,\eta} M_2 \rightarrow_{\beta,\eta} \ldots$ of β,η-reductions on $\lambda^{\rightarrow}$ terms.

Theorem 8.3.6 is called "normalization" since it shows that every term may be reduced to a normal form (a term that cannot be reduced further). The "strong" part of the theorem is that a normal form is reached by *any* sequence of reductions. In contrast, weak normalization is the property that every term may be reduced to a normal form by some sequence of reductions, but not necessarily all.

Since reduction is effectively computable, strong normalization implies that, for any reasonable encoding of the natural numbers, we cannot encode all partial recursive functions in pure $\lambda^{\rightarrow}$. This is because any function we can encode in pure $\lambda^{\rightarrow}$ must terminate on all input. However, as shown in Section 2.5.5, we can define all partial recursive functions if we add constants for basic numeric functions and fixed-point operators.

It is worth emphasizing that reduction is not confluent on *pre-terms,* strings that look like terms but are not necessarily well-typed. To see this, consider the pre-term

$$\lambda x\colon \sigma.(\lambda y\colon \tau.\, y)\, x$$

Using β-reduction, we may simplify this to $\lambda x\colon \sigma.\, x$, while η-reduction gives us $\lambda y\colon \tau.\, y$. Since these normal forms differ by more than names of bound variables when $\sigma \not\equiv \tau$, confluence fails for pre-terms.

One consequence of this example, which is taken from [vD80, Ned73], is that confluence for typed lambda calculus does not follow immediately from the confluence of untyped lambda calculus, even though the typed terms could be considered as a subset of the untyped terms (*c.f.* [Bar84, Appendix A]). The reason is that the simple "proof" of confluence for typed lambda calculus by appeal to the Church-Rosser theorem for untyped lambda calculus applies to pre-terms as well as typed terms. Since this leads to an incorrect conclusion for pre-terms, it is not a correct proof for typed terms. The reader familiar with other presentations of typed lambda calculus may wonder whether this is still the case if we do not write type expressions in typed terms, but use variables that are each given a fixed type. In the alternate presentation of $\lambda^{\rightarrow}$, α-conversion must be restricted so that we only replace one bound variable by another with the same type. With this restriction on α-conversion, the example demonstrating failure of confluence still applies. Thus confluence for $\lambda^{\rightarrow}$ does not seem to follow from the Church-Rosser theorem for untyped β, η-reduction directly. It is worth noting, however, that if we drop η-reduction, then we *do* have confluence for β-reduction on $\lambda^{\rightarrow}$ pre-terms.

The convertibility relation $\leftrightarrow_{\beta,\eta}$ on typed terms is the least type-respecting equivalence relation containing reduction $\twoheadrightarrow_{\beta,\eta}$. For typographical simplicity, we will drop the β, η subscripts for the rest of this section. Conversion can be visualized by saying that $\Gamma \rhd M \leftrightarrow N\colon \sigma$ iff there is a sequence of terms $M_0, \ldots, M_k$ with $\Gamma \rhd M_i\colon \sigma$ such that

$$M \equiv M_0 \twoheadrightarrow M_1 \twoheadleftarrow \ldots \twoheadrightarrow M_k \equiv N.$$

In this picture, the directions of $\twoheadrightarrow$ and $\twoheadleftarrow$ need not be regarded as significant. However, by reflexivity and transitivity of $\twoheadrightarrow$, this order of reduction and "backward reduction" is completely general.

A few words are in order regarding the assumption that $\Gamma \rhd M_i\colon \sigma$ for each i. For pure β, η-conversion, this assumption is not necessary. The reason is that if $\Gamma \rhd M \leftrightarrow N\colon \sigma$ and $\Gamma \cap \Gamma'$ mentions all free variables of M and N, then $\Gamma' \rhd M \leftrightarrow N\colon \sigma$. However, for extensions of pure typed lambda calculus obtained by adding algebraic rewrite rules for basic types, this fails. This may be illustrated using the same theory that is used in the proof of Proposition 4.4.5. Specifically, suppose we have a function symbol f and constants c and d with equational axioms $\{x: a\} \triangleright fx = c: b$ and $\{x: a\} \triangleright fx = d: b$, and corresponding rewrite rules $fx \to c$ and $fx \to d$. Then without the constraint mentioned above, we would have $\emptyset \triangleright c \leftrightarrow d: b$. However, the equation $c = d$ would not be provable without assuming a variable $x: a$. Thus we can derive unprovable equations by conversion. Since the main applications of typed lambda calculus to the study of programming languages involve extensions of the pure calculus, we have chosen notation and basic definitions which accommodate extensions of the pure theory.

A consequence of confluence is the following connection between reduction and provable equality.

Corollary 4.4.17 An equation $\Gamma \triangleright M = N: \tau$ is provable from the axioms of $\lambda^{\to}$ iff $\Gamma \triangleright M \leftrightarrow N: \tau$ iff there is some term P with $M \twoheadrightarrow_{\beta,\eta} P$ and $N \twoheadrightarrow_{\beta,\eta} P$.

The proof for simply typed lambda calculus is essentially the same as the the proof for algebra given in Section 3.7.2.

Reduction for Products, Sums and Other Simple Types

Reduction axioms for typed lambda calculus with product, sum, *unit* and *null* types are obtained by directing the equational axioms given in Section 4.4.1 from left to right. We list them here for completeness and for reference.

$$\mathbf{Proj}_1 \langle M, N \rangle \to M \qquad (proj_1)_{red}$$

$$\mathbf{Proj}_2 \langle M, N \rangle \to N \qquad (proj_2)_{red}$$

$$\langle \mathbf{Proj}_1\, M, \mathbf{Proj}_2\, M \rangle \to M \qquad (sp)_{red}$$

$$\mathbf{Case}^{\sigma,\tau,\rho}\, (\mathbf{Inleft}^{\sigma,\tau}\, M)\, N\, P \to N M \qquad (case)_{1\ red}$$

$$\mathbf{Case}^{\sigma,\tau,\rho}\, (\mathbf{Inright}^{\sigma,\tau}\, M)\, N\, P \to P M \qquad (case)_{2\ red}$$

$$\mathbf{Case}^{\sigma,\tau,\rho}\, M\, (N \circ \mathbf{Inleft}^{\sigma,\tau})\, (N \circ \mathbf{Inright}^{\sigma,\tau}) \to N M \qquad (case)_{3\ red}$$

$$M \to * \qquad (unit)_{red}$$

$$M \to \mathbf{Zero}^{\sigma} \qquad (null)_{red}$$

In defining reduction with $(unit)_{red}$ and $(null)_{red}$, we must restrict these to terms of the appropriate type. For example, we can only use $(unit)_{red}$ to reduce an arbitrary term M to $*$ when $M: unit$. This is done by defining reduction $\Gamma \triangleright M \twoheadrightarrow N: \sigma$ on typed terms, in a manner similar to the definition of conversion, $\Gamma \triangleright M \leftrightarrow N: \sigma$, earlier in this section.

Strong normalization holds for all of the versions of simply-typed lambda calculus (without additional reductions such as algebraic rules), but confluence is more subtle. With products and sums, we have confluence, but the *unit* reduction problematic; some repairs for the failure of confluence are suggested in [LS86, CD91]. Confluence does not appear to have been studied for typed lambda calculus with *null*. We discuss confluence with additional rules, such as algebraic rules or *fix* reduction, in the next section.

4.4.3 Reduction with Additional Rules

As pointed out in Section 4.3.2, every algebraic signature may be regarded as a $\lambda^{\rightarrow}$ signature. This allows us to consider algebraic terms as a subset of $\lambda^{\rightarrow}$ terms, and apply algebraic rewrite rules to lambda terms. More specifically, if Σ is an algebraic signature, and $\mathcal{R}$ is an algebraic rewrite system over Σ, then we may consider the rules $L \rightarrow R$ of $\mathcal{R}$ as rewrite rules for lambda terms over any $\lambda^{\rightarrow}$ signature Σ' containing Σ. One-step reduction $\rightarrow_{\mathcal{R}}$ on lambda terms over Σ' is the least relation such that

$$[SL/x]M \rightarrow_{\mathcal{R}} [SR/x]M$$

whenever $[SL/x]M$ is a well-typed term over Σ', S is any substitution of lambda terms for variables and M has exactly one occurrence of variable x. This is exactly the same as reduction on algebraic terms, except the rule $L \rightarrow R$ may be applied inside a lambda term, and the variables in L and R may be replaced by lambda terms in any way that produces a well-typed term.

Example 4.4.18 Consider the algebraic signature Σ with the following type constants and term constants.

type constants: *nat*

term constants: $0\colon nat$

$S\colon nat \rightarrow nat$

$plus\colon nat \rightarrow nat \rightarrow nat$

and let Σ' be Σ with term constant $fix\colon (nat \rightarrow nat) \rightarrow nat$ added. While Σ is an algebraic signature, Σ' is not since the domain of *fix* is a function type.

Let $\mathcal{R}$ be the algebraic rewrite system over Σ with the rewrite rules

$$plus\, 0\, y \rightarrow y$$

$$plus\, (Sx)\, y \rightarrow S\, (plus\, x\, y)$$

Then we have the following algebraic reduction on lambda terms:

$$\lambda x\colon nat.\, plus\, (Sx)\, (fix\, S) \rightarrow \lambda x\colon nat.\, S\, (plus\, x\, (fix\, S))$$

Note that the usual reduction rule for *fix* is not an algebraic rule since *fix* is not an algebraic constant. ■

If Σ is an algebraic signature, $\mathcal{R}$ a rewrite system over Σ, and Σ' is a $\lambda^{\rightarrow}$ signature containing Σ, then for terms M and N over Σ', we say M $\mathcal{R}, \beta, \eta$-reduces to N if we can reduce M to N using rewrite rules from $\mathcal{R}$, together with β, η-reduction, and similarly for $\mathcal{R}, \beta$-reduction. We may also combine algebraic reduction with *fix*-reduction on signatures that contain fixed-point constants fix_σ for one or more types, resulting in $\mathcal{R}, \beta, \eta, fix$-reduction and $\mathcal{R}, \beta, fix$-reduction. It is easy to show that all of these combined forms of reduction preserve type, using Lemmas 3.7.2 and 4.4.16.

The main theorems about combined algebraic and lambda calculus reduction are proved in Section 8.3.4, for typed lambda calculus with functions, products and fixed-point operators. It follows that these properties hold for any subset of such a language. For clarity, we summarize some consequences of the theorems of Section 8.3.4 below. In each case, we assume Σ is an algebraic signature, $\mathcal{R}$ an algebraic rewrite system over Σ, and Σ' a $\lambda^{\rightarrow}$ (or $\lambda^{\times,\rightarrow}$) signature containing Σ.

- If $\mathcal{R}$ is confluent and terminating, then $\mathcal{R}, \beta$-reduction is confluent and terminating on $\lambda^{\rightarrow}$ terms over Σ'.
- If $\mathcal{R}$ is confluent and left-linear, then $\mathcal{R}, \beta, fix$-reduction is confluent on $\lambda^{\rightarrow}$ terms and $\mathcal{R}, \beta, proj, fix$-reduction is confluent on $\lambda^{\times,\rightarrow}$ terms over Σ'.
- If $\lambda^{\times,\rightarrow}$ term M over Σ' $\mathcal{R}, \beta, fix$-reduces to normal form N, and $\mathcal{R}$ is confluent, terminating, left-linear, and left-normal, then there is a reduction from M to N that reduces the leftmost redex at each step.

The definition of left-normal appears in Section 8.3.4.

As mentioned in Section 2.2.3, we do not use $(sp)_{red}$, often called *surjective pairing,* in PCF. The reason, apart from the fact that it is unnecessary for programs (closed terms of observable type) and not generally implemented, is that the rule causes confluence to fail when combined with *fix* reduction. This is a classical theorem from untyped lambda calculus. The original proof in [Klo80] can be carried out in a typed calculus, while an apparent simplification in [Bar84] does not appear typable. We sketch a simplified, typable proof from [CH94b].

Proposition 4.4.19 Reduction in simply-typed lambda calculus with $(\beta)_{red}$, $(proj_i)_{red}$, $(sp)_{red}$ and *fix* is not confluent.

Proof Sketch The proof uses the following terms, written using a free variable $f\colon \tau_1 \times \tau_2 \rightarrow \tau_1 \times \tau_2$ for any types τ_1 and τ_2:

$$B \stackrel{\text{def}}{=} \mathit{fix}\ C$$

$$C \stackrel{\text{def}}{=} \mathit{fix}\ V$$

$$V \stackrel{\text{def}}{=} \lambda x{:}\, \tau_1 \times \tau_2 \to \tau_1 \times \tau_2.\, \lambda y{:}\, \tau_1 \times \tau_2.\langle \mathbf{Proj}_1(fy), \mathbf{Proj}_2(f(xy))\rangle$$

The three steps of the proof are:

1. Show that for any term M of the right type, we have $CM \twoheadrightarrow VCM \twoheadrightarrow \langle \mathbf{Proj}_1(fM), \mathbf{Proj}_2(f(CM))\rangle$.
2. Use this to show that for $A \stackrel{\text{def}}{=} f(CB)$, we have $B \twoheadrightarrow A$ and $B \twoheadrightarrow CA$.
3. Prove that A and CA do not reduce to a common term and therefore confluence fails from B.

The reader may enjoy carrying out the first two steps. The difficult part of the proof is the third step. While Klop's original proof required more detailed analysis of reduction and reduction strategies, the argument required for these particular terms can be carried out using elementary reasoning about reduction. ∎

4.4.4 Proof-theoretic Methods for Consistency and Conservativity

For many systems and theories, the simplest way to prove consistency is by constructing a semantic model. This is also true for conservativity, as in the proof of Proposition 4.4.4. However, there are situations in which proof-theoretic methods may be useful. The most common are when it is difficult to construct a semantic model with the required properties, or when we are interested in the proof-theoretic analysis for other reasons. One historical example is the proof of consistency of untyped lambda calculus by confluence [CR36], which predated Dana Scott's construction of the first semantic model, in 1969, by 33 years. In this section, we review the use of confluence for proving consistency, then investigate a general method for proving conservativity and consistency that does not require the equational axioms to yield confluence, but nonetheless uses reduction on typed lambda terms. Another general technique for analyzing theories is given in Section 9.3.2.

If an equational proof system gives rise to a confluent reduction system, then this generally gives a proof of consistency. More specifically, if we know that an equation $M = N$ is provable only if M and N reduce to some common term P, and reduction is confluent, then we may prove consistency by finding two distinct normal forms. It therefore follows from Corollary 4.4.17 that $\lambda^{\to}$ is consistent. We can also apply this method to show that an algebraic theory is consistent, using the results given in Section 3.7.2 and the methods in other parts of Section 3.7 for showing confluence. By Proposition 4.4.4, we can show that the combination of an algebraic theory and a typed lambda calculus is consistent by showing that the algebraic theory is consistent.

The simplest form of conservativity only involves provability without equational hypotheses. This form follows immediately from confluence. For example, we can see that if E is an equation between $\lambda^{\rightarrow}$ terms, then $\vdash E$ using the proof system of $\lambda^{unit,\times,\rightarrow}$ iff $\vdash E$ using the proof system of $\lambda^{\rightarrow}$. The reason is that the equation if provable iff both terms reduce to a common term, and this reduction cannot involve any $\lambda^{unit,\times,\rightarrow}$ reductions if both terms are from $\lambda^{\rightarrow}$. However, the more interesting form of conservativity is to show that if $\mathcal{E}$ is a set of equations between $\lambda^{\rightarrow}$ terms, and E is a single such equation, then $\mathcal{E} \vdash E$ using the proof system of $\lambda^{\rightarrow}$ whenever $\mathcal{E} \vdash E$ using the proof system of $\lambda^{unit,\times,\rightarrow}$. We will use this as an illustrative example for the rest of this section.

One way to show conservativity of $\lambda^{unit,\times,\rightarrow}$ over $\lambda^{\rightarrow}$ is by semantic means. The standard method for doing this, described after the statement of Proposition 4.4.4, requires completeness of $\lambda^{\rightarrow}$. However, we do not have completeness of $\lambda^{\rightarrow}$, in general, for the simplest form of model (Henkin models). Therefore, we must use cartesian closed categories. An alternative is the general proof-theoretic method described below, based on [Jac75]. This method may also be used to prove conservativity of polymorphic typed lambda calculus over simply-typed lambda calculus. In this case, we are unable to embed every model of simply-typed lambda calculus into some model of polymorphic typed lambda calculus.

If $\mathcal{E}$ is a finite set of equations between closed $\lambda^{unit,\times,\rightarrow}$ terms, say

$$\mathcal{E} = \{U_1 = V_1, \ldots, U_n = V_n\},$$

then we write $\Gamma \rhd M \overset{\mathcal{E}}{\leftrightarrow} N\colon\sigma$ if there is a term P over the same signature and free variables as M and N such that

$$\vdash \Gamma \rhd P U_1 V_1 \ldots U_n V_n = M\colon\sigma \quad \text{and} \quad \vdash \Gamma \rhd P V_1 U_1 \ldots V_n U_n = N\colon\sigma.$$

It is easy to see that if $\Gamma \rhd M \overset{\mathcal{E}}{\leftrightarrow} N\colon\sigma$, then $\mathcal{E} \vdash \Gamma \rhd M = N\colon\sigma$. We will give a proof of a form of converse, showing that provable equality from a set of equational hypothesis may be characterized using $\overset{\mathcal{E}}{\leftrightarrow}$. Since provable equality without equational hypotheses can be characterized using reduction, this allows us to use reduction to study provability from equational hypotheses. While we state and prove the lemmas for $\lambda^{unit,\times,\rightarrow}$, these hold for a variety of lambda calculi, including untyped lambda calculus.

Lemma 4.4.20 For any finite set $\mathcal{E}$ of equations between $\lambda^{unit,\times,\rightarrow}$ terms, the relation $\overset{\mathcal{E}}{\leftrightarrow}$ has the following properties:

(a) If $\vdash \Gamma \rhd M = N\colon\sigma$, then $\Gamma \rhd M \overset{\mathcal{E}}{\leftrightarrow} N\colon\sigma$.

(b) If $(U = V) \in \mathcal{E}$, then $U \overset{\mathcal{E}}{\leftrightarrow} V$.

(c) If $\mathcal{E} \vdash \Gamma \triangleright M = N\colon \sigma$ by a single proof step other than transitivity, then $\Gamma \triangleright M \overset{\mathcal{E}}{\leftrightarrow} N\colon \sigma$.

Proof Properties (a) and (b) are immediate. To show property (c), we must consider each of the $\lambda^{unit,\times,\rightarrow}$ axioms and inference rules. If $\Gamma \triangleright M = N\colon \sigma$ is an axiom or equation in $\mathcal{E}$, then (c) follows from (a) or (b). Therefore, it remains to consider each of the inference rules. For notational simplicity, we will assume that $\mathcal{E}$ contains only one equation, $U = V$.

Since (*sym*) is immediate, we begin with (ν). Suppose $\Gamma \triangleright M_1 \overset{\mathcal{E}}{\leftrightarrow} N_1\colon \sigma \rightarrow \tau$ and $\Gamma \triangleright M_2 \overset{\mathcal{E}}{\leftrightarrow} N_2\colon \sigma$. By definition, there are terms P_1, P_2 with $\Gamma \triangleright P_i U V = M_i$ and $\Gamma \triangleright P_i V U = N_i$. We must show $\Gamma \triangleright M_1 M_2 \overset{\mathcal{E}}{\leftrightarrow} N_1 N_2\colon \tau$. This means we must find a term P such that $\Gamma \triangleright P U V = M_1 M2$ and $\Gamma \triangleright P V U = N_1 N_2$. This is accomplished by letting P be $\lambda u\colon \rho.\, \lambda v\colon \rho.(P_1 u v)(P_2 u v)$.

For rule (ξ), we suppose $\Gamma, x\colon \sigma \triangleright M \overset{\mathcal{E}}{\leftrightarrow} N\colon \tau$ and prove $\Gamma \triangleright \lambda x\colon \sigma.\, M \overset{\mathcal{E}}{\leftrightarrow} \lambda x\colon \sigma.\, N \tau$. Given term P with $\Gamma, x\colon \sigma \triangleright P U V = M\colon \tau$ $\Gamma, x\colon \sigma \triangleright P V U = N\colon \tau$, this is established using $\lambda u\colon \rho.\, \lambda v\colon \rho.\, \lambda x\colon \sigma.\, P u v$. Here it is important that both U and V are closed.

The remaining rule, (*add var*), is trivial. This proves the lemma. ■

Lemma 4.4.21 If $\mathcal{E} \vdash \Gamma \triangleright M = N\colon \sigma$, then there exist terms $M_0, \ldots, M_k$, with $M \equiv M_0$ and $M_k \equiv N$, such that $\mathcal{E} \vdash \Gamma \triangleright M_i = M_{i+1}\colon \sigma$ without using the transitivity proof rule.

Proof We use induction on proofs from $\mathcal{E}$. If the equation is an axiom or element of $\mathcal{E}$, then the lemma clearly holds. The symmetry rule is straightforward, since if

$$\mathcal{E} \vdash M_0 = M_1 = \ldots = M_k,$$

then clearly

$$\mathcal{E} \vdash M_k = M_{k-1} = \ldots = M_0.$$

The transitivity case is easy. This leaves (ν), (ξ) and (*add var*). Since (ν) is the most difficult, and most informative, we do that case and leave the other to the reader.

Suppose $\mathcal{E} \vdash M_0 = M_1 = \ldots = M_k$, $\mathcal{E} \vdash N_0 = N_1 = \ldots = N_\ell$ and we wish to prove $M_0 N_0 = M_k N_\ell$ by a proof of the appropriate form. If $k > \ell$, for example, then using reflexivity we may increase the length of the first sequence by repeating terms. We may prove the required equation by

$$\mathcal{E} \vdash M_0 N_0 = M_1 N_1 = \ldots = M_\ell N_\ell.$$

This completes the proof. ■

Theorem 4.4.22 Let $\hat{\mathcal{E}}$ be any set of equations between $\lambda^{unit,\times,\rightarrow}$ terms. Then $\hat{\mathcal{E}} \vdash \Gamma \triangleright M = N\colon \sigma$ iff there is some finite $\mathcal{E} \subseteq \hat{\mathcal{E}}$ and sequence of $\lambda^{unit,\times,\rightarrow}$ terms $M_0, \ldots, M_k$, with $M \equiv M_0$ and $M_k \equiv N$, such that $\Gamma \triangleright M_i \overset{\mathcal{E}}{\leftrightarrow} M_{i+1}\colon \sigma$

Proof One implication is straightforward, so we concentrate on the other. Suppose $\hat{\mathcal{E}} \vdash \Gamma \triangleright M = N{:}\,\sigma$ and let $\mathcal{E} \subseteq \hat{\mathcal{E}}$ be the set of equations from $\hat{\mathcal{E}}$ that are used in the proof. (Since a proof is finite, $\mathcal{E}$ must be finite.) By Lemma 4.4.21, there is are terms $M_0, \ldots, M_k$, with $M \equiv M_0$ and $M_k \equiv N$, such that $\mathcal{E} \vdash \Gamma \triangleright M_i = M_{i+1}{:}\,\sigma$ without using transitivity. By Lemma 4.4.20, we have $\Gamma \triangleright M_i \overset{\mathcal{E}}{\leftrightarrow} M_{i+1}{:}\,\sigma$, and the theorem follows. ■

It is easy to see, from the proofs, that Theorem 4.4.22 also holds for $\lambda^{\rightarrow}$, with $M_0, \ldots, M_k$ in the statement of the theorem $\lambda^{\rightarrow}$ terms, and similarly for other fragments of $\lambda^{null,unit,+,\times,\rightarrow}$. In fact, since all fragments of $\lambda^{null,unit,+,\times,\rightarrow}$ have the same inference rules, the proofs are essentially the same for all cases. In Exercise 4.4.26, Theorem 4.4.22 is used to show that it is consistent to add the equation $\mathit{fix}(\lambda x{:}\, nat.\, x) = 0$, for example, to a simplification of PCF.

We use Theorem 4.4.22 to prove conservativity of $\lambda^{unit,\times,\rightarrow}$ over $\lambda^{\rightarrow}$ by proving a form of "conservativity" of existence of normal form terms.

Lemma 4.4.23 If $\Gamma \triangleright M{:}\,\sigma$ is a $\lambda^{unit,\times,\rightarrow}$ term in normal form, over a $\lambda^{\rightarrow}$ signature Σ, with σ and every type in Γ a $\lambda^{\rightarrow}$ type, then $\Gamma \triangleright M{:}\,\sigma$ is a $\lambda^{\rightarrow}$ term.

In the proof of Lemma 4.4.23, we will write normal form terms in a particular way. This may be visualized using a representation called *Böhm trees,* after C. Böhm (see [Bar84]). The Böhm tree of a term $\lambda x_1{:}\,\sigma_1 \ldots \lambda x_j{:}\,\sigma_j.\, z M_1 \ldots M_k$ in normal form is written

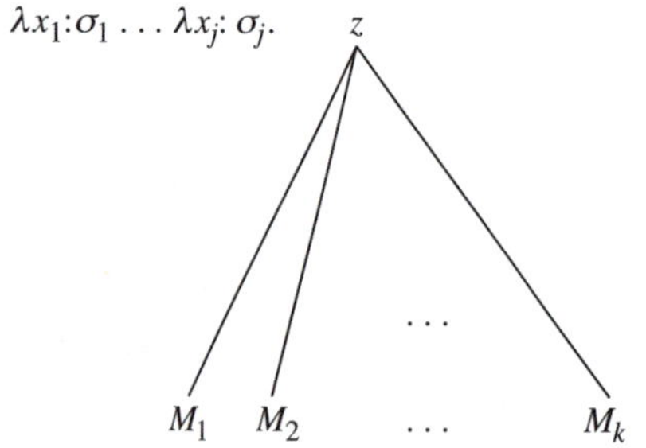

where z is a variable or constant and $M_1, \ldots, M_k$ are written out as Böhm trees. It is not hard to see that every normal form may be written as $\lambda x_1{:}\,\sigma_1 \ldots \lambda x_j{:}\,\sigma_j.\, z M_1 \ldots M_k$, for $j, k \geq 0$. Specifically, any term has the form $\lambda x_1{:}\,\sigma_1 \ldots \lambda x_j{:}\,\sigma_j.\, M$, where M does not begin with λ. We may write any such M as $M \equiv M_0 M_1 \ldots M_k$, where M_0 is not an application. If M_0 is a lambda abstraction, then this is not a normal form. Therefore, M_0 must be a variable or constant. We will adopt the alternative formulation of $\lambda^{unit,\times,\rightarrow}$

in which **Pair**, $\mathbf{Proj}_1$, $\mathbf{Proj}_2$ and $*$ are constants. For $\lambda x_1{:}\sigma_1 \ldots \lambda x_j{:}\sigma_j . zM_1 \ldots M_k$ to be a $\lambda^{unit,\times,\rightarrow}$ normal form, z may be $\mathbf{Proj}_1$ or $\mathbf{Proj}_2$ only if M_1 does not begin with **Pair**.

Proof Lemma 4.4.23 We use induction on the height of the Böhm tree of M. For a term $\lambda x_1{:}\sigma_1 \ldots \lambda x_j{:}\sigma_j . z$, the lemma clearly holds, since if z is **Pair**, $\mathbf{Proj}_1$, $\mathbf{Proj}_2$ or $*$, the term will not have a $\lambda^{\rightarrow}$ type.

For the induction step, we consider $\lambda x_1{:}\sigma_1 \ldots \lambda x_j{:}\sigma_j . zM_1 \ldots M_k$, with $k \geq 1$, assume the lemma holds for $M_1 \ldots M_k$ and all of their subterms. If z is a free or bound variable, or a constant from Σ, then it must have a $\lambda^{\rightarrow}$ type and therefore all of $M_1 \ldots M_k$ must have $\lambda^{\rightarrow}$ types. By the inductive hypothesis, we must have a $\lambda^{\rightarrow}$ term. Since $k \geq 1$, z cannot be $*$. It is easy to see that z cannot be **Pair**, so the remaining cases are $\mathbf{Proj}_1$ and $\mathbf{Proj}_2$.

If $z \equiv \mathbf{Proj}_1$, say, then $M_1{:}\,\tau_1 \times \tau_2$, where only τ_1 is necessarily a $\lambda^{\rightarrow}$ type. We prove the lemma by examining the form of M_1. Because of its type, M_1 cannot begin with a λ, and so we may write M_1 as $z'M'_1 \ldots M'_k$. The symbol z' cannot be a variable, since all variables have $\lambda^{\rightarrow}$ type, and cannot be **Pair** since then the term containing M_1 would not be in normal form. It is also easy to see that z' cannot be $*$, so the only possibility is that $z' \equiv \mathbf{Proj}_i$. However, repeating this argument for M'_1, we can see that the term must have infinitely many $\mathbf{Proj}_i$'s. Since this is contradictory, we must not have $z \equiv \mathbf{Proj}_1$ or, by similar reasoning, $\mathbf{Proj}_2$. This proves the lemma. ∎

Using normalization of $\lambda^{unit,\times,\rightarrow}$, we may now prove conservativity of $\lambda^{unit,\times,\rightarrow}$ over $\lambda^{\rightarrow}$.

Proposition 4.4.24 If $\mathcal{E}$ is a set of equations between $\lambda^{\rightarrow}$ terms, and E is a single such equation, then $\mathcal{E} \vdash E$ using the proof system of $\lambda^{unit,\times,\rightarrow}$ iff $\mathcal{E} \vdash E$ using the proof system of $\lambda^{\rightarrow}$.

Proof Since the axioms of $\lambda^{\rightarrow}$ are a subset of those for $\lambda^{unit,\times,\rightarrow}$, one implication is immediate. To prove the proposition, we therefore assume that $\hat{\mathcal{E}} \vdash \Gamma \triangleright M = N{:}\,\sigma$ using the proof system of $\lambda^{unit,\times,\rightarrow}$ and show that may be carried out using the proof system of $\lambda^{\rightarrow}$.

By Theorem 4.4.22, there is some finite $\mathcal{E} \subseteq \hat{\mathcal{E}}$ and sequence of $\lambda^{unit,\times,\rightarrow}$ terms $M_0, \ldots, M_k$, with $M \equiv M_0$ and $M_k \equiv N$, such that $\Gamma \triangleright M_i \overset{\mathcal{E}}{\leftrightarrow} M_{i+1}{:}\,\sigma$. By definition of $\overset{\mathcal{E}}{\leftrightarrow}$, there are terms $P_0, \ldots, P_{k-1}$ over the same signature and free variables as M and N such that

$$\vdash \Gamma \triangleright P_i U_1 V_1 \ldots U_n V_n = M_i{:}\,\sigma \quad \text{and} \quad \vdash \Gamma \triangleright P_i V_1 U_1 \ldots V_n U_n = M_{i+1}{:}\,\sigma.$$

However, since all $M_0, \ldots, M_k$, and all of the equations from $\mathcal{E}$ have $\lambda^{\rightarrow}$ types, so must $P_0, \ldots, P_{k-1}$. If we reduce each P_i to normal form, then by Lemma 4.4.23, we obtain a sequence of equivalent $\lambda^{\rightarrow}$ terms. It follows that we may prove each $\Gamma \triangleright M_i = M_{i+1} \colon \sigma$ from $\mathcal{E}$ using only the proof rules of $\lambda^{\rightarrow}$. This proves the proposition. ∎

It is interesting to notice that the proof of Proposition 4.4.24 does not require confluence of $\lambda^{unit,\times,\rightarrow}$, only weak normalization and a typing property of normal forms.

Exercise 4.4.25 Prove Lemma 4.4.23, with $\lambda^{+,\rightarrow}$ in place of $\lambda^{unit,\times,\rightarrow}$.

Exercise 4.4.26 This exercise asks you to show that it is consistent to add an equation to the variant of $\lambda^{\rightarrow}$ with *fix* constants and equational axioms (β) and (*fix*), but without the equational axiom (η). We assume the signature includes a type constant b and at least two constants, $true, false \colon b$ (This is a simplification of PCF that avoids some technical complications.) We adapt the definition of $\overset{\mathcal{E}}{\leftrightarrow}$ to this language by saying $\Gamma \triangleright M \overset{\mathcal{E}}{\leftrightarrow} N \colon \sigma$ if there is a term P over the same free variables such that $\Gamma \triangleright P U_1 V_1 \ldots U_n V_n = M \colon \sigma$ and $\Gamma \triangleright P V_1 U_1 \ldots V_n U_n = N \colon \sigma$ are both provable using (β) and (*fix*). It is easy to check that Theorem 4.4.22 holds. Show that for closed term $Z \colon \sigma$, it is consistent to add the equation $fix(\lambda x \colon \sigma.x.) = Z$, by the steps outlined below. You will need to use the fact that β, *fix*-reduction is confluent. For notational simplicity, we adopt the abbreviation $\Omega \overset{\text{def}}{=} fix(\lambda x \colon \sigma.x.)$.

(a) Use Lemma 2.5.24, in combination with Lemma 2.5.21, to show that if $P\,\Omega\,Z$ and $P\,Z\,\Omega$ are closed terms that both reduce to normal forms of type b, then they must reduce to the same normal form. (The use of programs and type constants in this exercise is needed only so that Lemmas 2.5.21 and 2.5.24, stated for lazy rather than left-most reduction, apply.)

(b) Let us write $M \overset{\Omega,Z}{\longrightarrow} N$ if there is some term P with the same free variables as M and N such that $P\,\Omega = M$ and $P\,Z = N$ are provable from (β) and (*fix*). Show that if $M \overset{\Omega,Z}{\longrightarrow} N$, and $M \colon b$ is a closed normal form, then the equation $M = N$ is provable from (β) and (*fix*).

(c) Show that if $\Gamma \triangleright M \overset{\Omega=Z}{\leftrightarrow} N : \sigma$, then there is some Q with $M \overset{\Omega,Z}{\longleftarrow} Q \overset{\Omega,Z}{\longrightarrow} N$.

(d) Show that if $M \overset{\Omega,Z}{\longrightarrow} Q \overset{\Omega,Z}{\longleftarrow} N$, where all terms are programs, then $\Gamma \triangleright M \overset{\Omega=Z}{\leftrightarrow} N : b$. (This is harder than (c).)

(e) Use Theorem 4.4.22, (c), (b) and then (d) to show, by contradiction, that the equation $true = false$ is not provable from $\Omega = Z$, (β) and (*fix*).

4.5 Henkin Models, Soundness and Completeness

4.5.1 General Models and the Meanings of Terms

For most logical systems, a *model* provides a mechanism for giving mathematical meaning to each well-formed expression, in sufficient detail to determine whether any formula of the logic is true. For logics with variables, it is common to separate the assignment of values to variables from the general notion of model. For example, an algebra provides a set of possible values for each variable and an interpretation for each function symbol. After choosing values for variables (by selecting an environment), we use the functions given by the algebra to determine the value of an algebraic term. Doing this for two terms, we may determine whether an equation between algebraic terms holds. Another example is first-order logic, which has predicate symbols and function symbols. A model for first-order logic includes a set of possible values for each variable, an interpretation for each function symbol, and an interpretation for each predicate symbol. The interpretation of each first-order term is determined as in algebra. Then, the interpretation of predicate symbols is used to see whether a formula is true or false in the model.

A model for typed lambda calculus is similar to an algebra, in that we require a set of possible values for each variable and an interpretation for each constant symbol that appears in the signature. This means that we need a set of values for each type, and a specific one of these chosen for each constant symbol. However, that is not all, since we have to make sense of application and lambda abstraction. More specifically, suppose $A^{\sigma\to\tau}$ is the set of values of type $\sigma \to \tau$, and A^σ is similarly the set of values of type σ. If $f \in A^{\sigma\to\tau}$ and $x \in A^\sigma$, then we need to be able to apply f to x. The simplest condition on models that would make this possible is to require that $A^{\sigma\to\tau}$ be a set of functions from A^σ to A^τ. Then ordinary function application would give us $f(x)$ in the set of values for type τ. A more subtle issue is that we also need to be able to interpret every lambda abstraction, which means that every lambda-definable function must lie in the appropriate set of values. If we impose the stronger requirement that $A^{\sigma\to\tau}$ must be the set of *all* functions from A^σ to A^τ, then certainly every lambda-definable function will exist in the model, and we can interpret every well-typed lambda term as a value in the correct set.

What makes the model theory of typed lambda calculus complicated is that we need to be relatively flexible about the interpretation of function types. We cannot simply say that in any model $\mathcal{A}$, $A^{\sigma\to\tau}$ must be the set of all functions from A^σ to A^τ. The main reason is that, as pointed out in Section 4.2.2, we need to be able to interpret constants such as *fix*, whose equational axiom forces every function to have a fixed point. If A^σ has more than one element, then there exists at least one function on A^σ without a fixed point. Therefore, if we force $A^{\sigma\to\tau}$ to contain all functions, we cannot have models for PCF, or any other typed lambda theory involving fixed points. But since fixed points are needed to interpreted recursive definitions, and recursion is central to computation, we need models where every element of at least some non-trivial function type can have a fixed point. This forces us to define models using a more flexible, and more abstract, condition on function spaces. This condition must be flexible enough so that the three examples described briefly in Section 4.2.2, classical set-theoretic functions, recursive functions on modest sets, and continuous functions on CPOs, all satisfy the technical definition of model.

There are several equivalent definitions of "general models," which we will call *Henkin models* after [Hen50]. The definition we will use has three parts. We first define typed applicative structures, and then specify two additional conditions that applicative structures must have to be models. A typed applicative structure consists of families of sets and mappings indexed by types, or pairs of types, of the form necessary to give meanings to terms. To be a model, an applicative structure must be extensional, and there must be enough elements so that every lambda-definable function is in the model. The extensionality condition is equivalent to saying that the interpretation of a function type must be some set of functions. We consider two ways of formalizing the condition that there must be "enough elements" and prove that these are equivalent. The first is the environment model condition, which is straightforward but syntactic in flavor, and the combinatory model condition, which is less intuitive but more algebraic.

A slightly more general form of model may be defined using category theory. Categorical models of $\lambda^{unit,\times,\rightarrow}$ are called *cartesian closed categories,* or *CCCs* for short. These are discussed in Section 7.2.

4.5.2 Applicative Structures, Extensionality and Frames

A *typed applicative structure* $\mathcal{A}$ for $\lambda^{\rightarrow}$ signature Σ is a tuple

$\langle \{A^{\sigma}\}, \{\mathbf{App}^{\sigma,\tau}\}, \mathit{Const}\rangle$

of families of sets and mappings indexed by type expressions over the type constants from Σ. For each σ and τ we assume the following conditions.

- A^{σ} is a set,
- $\mathbf{App}^{\sigma,\tau}$ is a map $\mathbf{App}^{\sigma,\tau} : A^{(\sigma\rightarrow\tau)} \rightarrow A^{\sigma} \rightarrow A^{\tau}$,
- *Const* is a map from term constants of Σ to elements of the union of all the A^{σ}'s such that if $c{:}\,\sigma$, then $\mathit{Const}(c) \in A^{\sigma}$.

The intuition behind this definition is that the terms of type σ will be interpreted as elements of A^{σ}. For any types σ and τ, the application map $\mathbf{App}^{\sigma,\tau}$ lets us use each $a \in A^{\sigma\rightarrow\tau}$ as a function from A^{σ} to A^{τ}. Finally, the map *Const* gives the meaning of each term constant.

Another way to view an applicative structure for Σ is as a multi-sorted algebra for a signature derived from Σ. Specifically, if $\Sigma = \langle B, C\rangle$ is a $\lambda^{\rightarrow}$ signature, we can define an algebraic signature $\Sigma_{alg} = \langle S, F\rangle$ by letting the set S of sorts be the set of types over Σ and letting the set F of function symbols be

$$F = C \cup \{\mathbf{App}^{\sigma,\tau} \mid \sigma, \tau \text{ types over } \Sigma\}$$

Note that since all of the type expressions are regarded as sorts, all of the term constants become algebraic constants. For example, if $c\colon b \to b \to b$ in the $\lambda^{\rightarrow}$ signature Σ, then $b \to b \to b$ becomes a sort in Σ_{alg} and c becomes an algebraic constant of this sort. With this construction, it is easy to see that an applicative structure for $\lambda^{\rightarrow}$ signature Σ is exactly a multi-sorted algebra for signature Σ_{alg}. Since applicative structures may be regarded as multi-sorted algebras, we can immediately apply the definitions of homomorphism, isomorphism, and other concepts in Chapter 3 to applicative structures.

An important part of the definition of Henkin model is that equality between elements of function types must be standard equality of functions. An applicative structure is *extensional* if it satisfies the condition

- For all $f, g \in A^{\sigma\to\tau}$, if $\mathbf{App}\, f\, d = \mathbf{App}\, g\, d$ for all $d \in A^{\sigma}$, then $f = g$

Extensionality means that $f, g \in A^{\sigma\to\tau}$ are equal iff $\mathbf{App}\, f$ and $\mathbf{App}\, g$ are the same function from A^{σ} to A^{τ}. Another way of saying this is that the function $\mathbf{App}$ must be one-to-one from $A^{\sigma\to\tau}$ into the set of functions from A^{σ} to A^{τ}. The set-theoretic, recursion-theoretic and continuous interpretations all yield extensional applicative structures in which $\mathbf{App}^{\sigma,\tau}\, f\, x = f(x)$ is simply function application. The set of terms over any signature Σ may also be viewed as an applicative structure that is not necessarily extensional, as described in the following example.

Example 4.5.1 Let Σ be any signature and let $\mathcal{H}$ be any finite or infinite type assignment $\mathcal{H} = \{x_1\colon \sigma_1, x_2\colon \sigma_2, \ldots\}$. An applicative structure

$$\mathcal{T} = \langle \{T^{\sigma}\}, \{\mathbf{App}^{\sigma,\tau}\}, \mathit{Const}\rangle$$

may be defined by letting

$$T^{\sigma} = \{M \mid \Gamma \triangleright M\colon \sigma \text{ some finite } \Gamma \subseteq \mathcal{H}\}$$

and defining $\mathbf{App}^{\sigma,\tau}\, M\, N = MN$ for every $M \in T^{\sigma\to\tau}$ and $N \in T^{\sigma}$. For each term constant from Σ, we take $\mathit{Const}(c) = c$. If $\mathcal{H}$ provides variables of each type, then $\mathcal{T}$ is extensional. However, if $\mathcal{H}$ does not then some T^{σ} may be empty. If T^{σ} is empty, then any two elements of $T^{\sigma\to\tau}$ will be extensionally equal (vacuously), so extensionality will fail if $T^{\sigma\to\tau}$ has more than one element. (See Exercise 4.5.4.) ■

Example 4.5.2 We may construct a "recursive" applicative structure using any enumeration $\phi_0, \phi_1, \phi_2, \ldots$ of the partial recursive functions on the natural numbers. In this structure, each type A^σ will be a subset of the natural numbers and application will be defined by $\mathbf{App}\ n\ m = \phi_n(m)$. For each base type b, we may choose A^b arbitrarily. However, since **App** must be a total function, we must select the elements of function types more carefully. Specifically, for any function type $\sigma \to \tau$, we let $A^{\sigma\to\tau}$ be the set of all natural numbers $n \in \mathcal{N}$ such that for all $m \in A^\sigma$, $\phi_n(m)$ is defined and an element of A^τ. If A^b is the set of all natural numbers, then $A^{b\to b}$ will be the set of all n such that ϕ_n is a total recursive function. Therefore, although application is computable in this structure, it may not be decidable whether n is an element of some A^σ. This applicative structure is not extensional, since there will generally be several natural numbers that all code (correspond to) the same recursive function. ■

In place of applicative structures, it is possible to use a definition of model that assumes extensionality. Instead of letting $A^{\sigma\to\tau}$ be any set, and requiring an application map to make elements of $A^{\sigma\to\tau}$ behave like functions, we could require that $A^{\sigma\to\tau}$ actually be some set of functions from A^σ to A^τ. To be precise, a *type frame* is an applicative structure $\langle\{A^\sigma\}, \{\mathbf{App}^{\sigma,\tau}\}, \mathit{Const}\rangle$ such that

$$A^{\sigma\to\tau} \subseteq A^{\tau(A^\sigma)}$$

and $\mathbf{App}^{\sigma,\tau}\ f\ d = f(d)$. In the formula above, exponentiation A^B denotes the usual set-theoretic collection of all functions from B to A. Since **App** is always function application in any type frame, it is common to omit **App**, writing $\mathcal{A} = \langle\{A^\sigma\}, \mathit{Const}\rangle$. If Σ has no constants, then we may also drop *Const,* and think of a type frame $\mathcal{A} = \{A^\sigma\}$ as simply an indexed family of sets. An example type frame is the *full set-theoretic function hierarchy* over any base types. This is a frame $\mathcal{A} = \langle\{A^\sigma\}, \mathit{Const}\rangle$ such that $A^{\sigma\to\tau}$ contains all set-theoretic functions from A^σ to A^τ.

Lemma 4.5.3 An applicative structure $\mathcal{A}$ is extensional iff there is an isomorphic type frame $\mathcal{B} \cong \mathcal{A}$.

The proof is by straightforward induction on types, given as Exercise 4.5.5 below. Although we will not pursue this direction, it is possible to generalize $\lambda^\to$ to allow certain types to be identified. In this case, the equivalence between type frames and extensional applicative structures fails. For example, it is possible to have an extensional applicative structure with $A^\sigma = A^{\sigma\to\sigma}$ the same set, but in this case $A^{\sigma\to\sigma}$ cannot be a set of functions from A^σ to A^σ.

Exercise 4.5.4 This exercise is about the applicative structure of terms described in Example 4.5.1.

(a) Verify the claim that if $\mathcal{H}$ provides variables of each type, then $\mathcal{T}$ is extensional.

(b) Find a set $\mathcal{H}$ of typing assumptions about variables such that the term applicative structure $\mathcal{T}$ is not extensional. Give two distinct elements of some $T^{\sigma\to\tau}$ that determine the same function from T^{σ} to T^{τ}.

Exercise 4.5.5 Prove Lemma 4.5.3. This is a straightforward induction on types, using the definitions of applicative structure, extensionality and frame given in this section.

4.5.3 Environment Model Condition

One characterization of Henkin model uses the environment model condition, relying on the subsidiary notion of environment. As in algebra, an *environment* η for applicative structure $\mathcal{A}$ is a mapping from variables to the union of all A^{σ}. If Γ is a type assignment, then we say η *satisfies* Γ, written $\eta \models \Gamma$, if $\eta(x) \in A^{\sigma}$ for every $x\colon\sigma \in \Gamma$. If η is any environment for $\mathcal{A}$, and $d \in A^{\sigma}$, then $\eta[x \mapsto d]$ is the environment mapping x to d, and y to $\eta(y)$ for y different from x.

An applicative structure $\mathcal{A}$ satisfies the *environment model condition* if the clauses below define a total meaning function $\mathcal{A}[\![\cdot]\!]\cdot$ on terms $\Gamma \triangleright M\colon\sigma$ and environments η such that $\eta \models \Gamma$. Recall that if $\Gamma \triangleright M\colon\sigma$ is well-typed, then there is proof of this using the typing rules. To make the definition of meaning as simple as possible, we will use induction on typing derivations, later showing that the meaning is independent of which derivation we choose. Specifically, we define the meaning $\mathcal{A}[\![M]\!]\eta$ of a well-typed term $\Gamma \triangleright M\colon\sigma$ in environment $\eta \models \Gamma$ by five inductive clauses, corresponding to typing axioms (*var*), (*cst*), and typing rules (*add var*), ($\to$ Elim) and ($\to$ Intro). In computer science jargon, we can think of the "abstract syntax" of lambda terms as typing derivations. This allows us to determine the type and free variables of a term and the typing rules used to establish that the term is well-typed.

$$\mathcal{A}[\![\emptyset \triangleright c\colon\sigma]\!]\eta = \mathit{Const}(c),$$

$$\mathcal{A}[\![x\colon\sigma \triangleright x\colon\sigma]\!]\eta = \eta(x)$$

$$\mathcal{A}[\![\Gamma, x\colon\sigma \triangleright M\colon\tau]\!]\eta = \mathcal{A}[\![\Gamma \triangleright M\colon\tau]\!]\eta$$

$$\mathcal{A}[\![\Gamma \triangleright MN\colon\tau]\!]\eta = \mathbf{App}^{\sigma,\tau}\mathcal{A}[\![\Gamma \triangleright M\colon\sigma \to \tau]\!]\eta\mathcal{A}[\![\Gamma \triangleright N\colon\sigma]\!]\eta$$

$$\mathcal{A}[\![\Gamma \triangleright \lambda x\colon\sigma.\, M\colon\sigma \to \tau]\!]\eta = \text{the unique } f \in A^{\sigma\to\tau} \text{ such that}$$

$$\forall d \in A^{\sigma}.\, \mathbf{App}\, f\, d = \mathcal{A}[\![\Gamma, x\colon\sigma \triangleright M\colon\tau]\!]\eta[x \mapsto d]$$

The main reason for using induction on typing derivations is that in defining the meaning of a lambda abstraction $\Gamma \rhd \lambda x{:}\sigma.\, M{:}\sigma \to \tau$, we need to refer to the meaning of M in typing context $\Gamma, x{:}\sigma$. If we know that $\Gamma \rhd \lambda x{:}\sigma.\, M{:}\sigma \to \tau$ is typed according to rule ($\to$ Intro), then we are guaranteed that $\Gamma, x{:}\sigma$ is well-formed, since this must have occurred in the hypothesis of the rule. If we used induction on the structure of terms, then we would have difficulty with a term such as $x{:}\sigma \rhd \lambda x{:}\tau.\, x$, where the lambda-bound variable appears in the type assignment. There are other ways to solve this minor technical problem, which may become more severe in extensions to simply-typed lambda calculus. Overall, induction on typing derivations is as simple as any of the alternatives, and also generalizes most easily to other type systems. When the model $\mathcal{A}$ is either irrelevant or clear from context, it is common to write $[\![\Gamma \rhd M{:}\sigma]\!]\eta$ for $\mathcal{A}[\![\Gamma \rhd M{:}\sigma]\!]\eta$. Similarly, the environment may be omitted if the term is closed.

An extensional applicative structure might fail to satisfy the environment model condition if $A^{\sigma\to\tau}$ does not contain any f satisfying the conditions given in the clause for $\mathcal{A}[\![\Gamma \rhd \lambda x{:}\sigma.\, M{:}\sigma \to \tau]\!]\eta$. This is the only possible problem, since extensionality guarantees that if any f exists, it is unique. It is easy to show that any full set-theoretic hierarchy satisfies the environment model condition (see Exercise 4.5.10). We will show later that frames of recursion-theoretic or continuous functions also satisfy the environment model condition and are therefore Henkin models.

Example 4.5.6 We may define a Henkin model $\mathcal{A}$ for the signature with single base type *nat* by letting A^{nat} be the usual set of natural numbers and $A^{\sigma\to\tau}$ the set of all functions from A^{σ} to A^{τ}, for all σ and τ. This is called the full set-theoretic function hierarchy over the natural numbers. We apply a function $f \in A^{\sigma\to\tau}$ to argument $x \in A^{\sigma}$ as usual by **App** $f\, x = f(x)$. We will work out the meaning of the term $\lambda x{:}nat \to nat.\, \lambda y{:}nat.\, xy$. Since this term is closed, it does not matter which environment we choose. Using the inductive definition of meaning, we can make the following calculation. For typographic simplicity, we omit the types of terms.

$$[\![\emptyset \rhd \lambda x{:}nat \to nat.\, \lambda y{:}nat.\, xy]\!]\eta$$

$$= \left(\begin{array}{c} \text{the unique } f \in A^{(nat\to nat)\to nat\to nat} \text{ such that} \\ \forall h \in A^{nat\to nat}.\, \mathbf{App}\, f\, h = [\![x{:}\,(nat \to nat) \rhd \lambda y{:}nat.\, xy]\!]\eta[x \mapsto h] \end{array} \right)$$

The meaning of the lambda term with one less λ is defined similarly, and simplified as follows.

$$
\begin{aligned}
&[\![x\colon nat \to nat \triangleright \lambda y\colon nat.\, xy]\!]\eta[x \mapsto h] \\
&= \left(\begin{array}{c}\text{the unique } g \in A^{nat\to nat} \text{ such that} \\ \forall n \in A^{nat}.\, \mathbf{App}\, g\, n = [\![x\colon nat \to nat,\, y\colon nat \triangleright xy]\!]\eta[x \mapsto h][y \mapsto n]\end{array}\right) \\
&= \left(\begin{array}{c}\text{the unique } g \in A^{nat\to nat} \text{ such that} \\ \forall n \in A^{nat}.\, \mathbf{App}\, g\, n = \mathbf{App}\, h\, n\end{array}\right) \\
&= h
\end{aligned}
$$

This allows us to complete our calculation of the meaning of the original term.

$$
\begin{aligned}
&[\![\emptyset \triangleright \lambda x\colon nat \to nat.\, \lambda y\colon nat.\, xy]\!]\eta \\
&= \left(\begin{array}{l}\text{the unique } f \in A^{(nat\to nat)\to nat\to nat} \text{ such that} \\ \qquad\qquad\qquad\qquad \forall h \in A^{nat\to nat}.\, \mathbf{App}\, f\, h = h\end{array}\right)
\end{aligned}
$$

Thus the meaning of this term is the unique element of $A^{(nat\to nat)\to nat\to nat}$ representing the identity function. We can check this calculation by seeing that, by (η),

$$x\colon nat \to nat \triangleright \lambda y\colon nat.\, xy = x\colon nat$$

and therefore we can prove the equation

$$\emptyset \triangleright \lambda x\colon nat \to nat.\, \lambda y\colon nat.\, xy = \lambda x\colon nat \to nat.\, x$$

■

We will now show that the meaning of a well-typed term does not depend on the typing derivation we use. This is the intent of the following two lemmas. The first requires some special notation for typing derivations. In general, a typing derivation is a tree, with each leaf an instance of a typing axiom, and each internal node (non-leaf) an instance of an inference rule. In the special case that an inference rule has only one premise, then uses of this rule result in a linear sequence of proof steps. If we have a derivation ending in a sequence of uses of (*add var*), this derivation has the form Δ,Δ', where Δ is generally a tree, and Δ' is a sequence of instances of (*add var*) concatenated onto the end of Δ. We use this notation to state that (*add var*) does not effect the meanings of terms.

Lemma 4.5.7 Suppose Δ is a derivation of $\Gamma \triangleright M\colon \sigma$ and Δ,Δ' is a derivation of $\Gamma' \triangleright M\colon \sigma$ such only rule (*add var*) appears in Δ'. Then for any $\eta \models \Gamma'$, we have

$$[\![\Gamma \triangleright M\colon \sigma]\!]\eta = [\![\Gamma' \triangleright M\colon \sigma]\!]\eta,$$

where the meanings are taken with respect to derivations Δ and Δ,Δ'.

The proof is an easy induction on typing derivations, left to the reader. We can now show that the meanings of "compatible" typings of a term are equal.

Lemma 4.5.8 Suppose Δ and Δ' are derivations of typings $\Gamma \rhd M\colon\sigma$ and $\Gamma' \rhd M\colon\sigma$, respectively, and that Γ and Γ' give the same type to every x free in M. Then

$$[\![\Gamma \rhd M\colon\sigma]\!]\eta = [\![\Gamma' \rhd M\colon\sigma]\!]\eta,$$

where the meanings are defined using Δ and Δ', respectively.

The proof, which we leave as an exercise, is by induction on the structure of terms. It follows that the meaning of any well-typed term is independent of the typing derivation. This lemma allows us to regard an equation $\Gamma \rhd M = N\colon\sigma$ as an equation between M and N, rather than derivations of typings $\Gamma \rhd M\colon\sigma$ and $\Gamma \rhd N\colon\sigma$.

Lemma 4.5.8 is a simple example of a *coherence theorem.* In general, a coherence problem arises when we interpret syntactic expressions using some extra information that is not uniquely determined by the expressions themselves. In the case at hand, we are giving meaning to terms, not typing derivations. However, we define the meaning function using extra information provided by typing derivations. Therefore, we must show that the meaning of a term depends only on the term itself, and not the typing derivation.

The final lemma about the environment model condition is that it does not depend on the set of term constants in the signature.

Lemma 4.5.9 Let $\mathcal{A}$ be an environment model for terms over signature Σ and let Σ' be a signature containing Σ (*i.e.*, containing all the type and term constants of Σ). If we expand $\mathcal{A}$ to Σ' by interpreting the additional term constants as any elements of the appropriate types, then we obtain an environment model for terms over Σ'.

Proof This lemma is easily proved using the fact that every constant is equal to some variable in some environment. More specifically, if we want to know that a term $\Gamma \rhd M\colon\sigma$ with constants from Σ' has a meaning in some environment, η, we begin by replacing the constants with fresh variables. Then, we choose some environment η_1 that is identical to η on the free variables of M, giving the new variables the values of the constants they replace. If $\mathcal{A}$ is an environment model, then the new term must have a meaning in environment η_1, and so it is easy to show that the original term must have a meaning in η.

■

Exercise 4.5.10 Recall that in a full set-theoretic function hierarchy, $A^{\sigma\to\tau}$ contains all set-theoretic functions from A^σ to A^τ. Show, by induction on typing derivations, that for any full set-theoretic hierarchy $\mathcal{A}$, typed term $\Gamma \rhd M\colon\sigma$ and any environment $\eta \models \Gamma$, the meaning $\mathcal{A}[\![\Gamma \rhd M\colon\sigma]\!]\eta$ is well-defined and an element of A^σ.

Exercise 4.5.11 Recall that in a full set-theoretic function hierarchy, $A^{\sigma\to\tau}$ contains all set-theoretic functions from A^σ to A^τ. If there are no term constants, then this frame is simply a family of sets $\mathcal{A} = \{A^\sigma\}$ indexed by types. This problem is concerned with the full set-theoretic hierarchy for the signature with one base type b and no term constants, determined by $A^b = \{0, 1\}$. It is easy to see that there are two elements of A^b, four elements of $A^{b\to b}$ and $4^4 = 256$ elements of type $A^{(b\to b)\to(b\to b)}$.

1. (a) Calculate the meaning of the term $\lambda f\colon b \to b.\, \lambda x\colon b.\, f(fx)$ in this model using the inductive definition of meaning.
2. (b) Express your answer to part (a) by naming the four elements of $A^{b\to b}$ and stating the result of applying the function defined by $\lambda f\colon b \to b.\, \lambda x\colon b.\, f(fx)$ to each element.
3. (c) Recall that every pure typed lambda term has a unique normal form. It follows from the soundness theorem for Henkin models that the meaning of any term in any model is the same as the meaning of its normal form. Use these facts about normal forms to determine how many elements of each of the types A^b, $A^{b\to b}$ and $A^{(b\to b)\to(b\to b)}$ are the meanings of closed typed lambda term without term constants.

Exercise 4.5.12 [Fri75] This exercise is also concerned with the full set-theoretic hierarchy, $\mathcal{A}$, for one type constant, b. We assume that A^b has at least two elements, so that the model is nontrivial. We define a form of higher-order logic with formulas

$$\phi \ ::= \ M = N \mid \neg\phi \mid \phi \wedge \phi \mid \forall x\colon \sigma.\phi$$

where in writing these formulas we assume that M and N have the same type (in some typing context) and that, in the final case, ϕ is well-formed under the assumption that x is a variable of type σ. Each formula may be interpreted in $\mathcal{A}$ in the obvious way. We will use the abbreviation $M \approx N \stackrel{\text{def}}{=} (M \supset N) \wedge (N \supset N)$, and assume abbreviations for other connectives and quantifier as in Example 4.4.7. We will also use the abbreviations $T \stackrel{\text{def}}{=} \lambda x\colon b.\, \lambda y\colon b.\, x$, $F \stackrel{\text{def}}{=} \lambda x\colon b.\, \lambda y\colon b.\, y$ and, for $M\colon \sigma$ and $N\colon \tau$, $\langle M, N\rangle \stackrel{\text{def}}{=} \lambda x\colon \sigma \to \tau \to b.\, xMN$. Show that for every ϕ, there exist terms M and N such that $\mathcal{A} \models \phi \approx \forall x\colon \sigma.\, M \neq N$, by the steps given below.

(a) Show $\mathcal{A} \models T \neq F$.

(b) For that any M, N, P, Q of appropriate types, $\mathcal{A} \models (\langle M, N\rangle = \langle P, Q\rangle) \approx (M = P \wedge N = Q)$.

(c) We say ϕ is *existential* if ϕ has the form $\exists x\colon \sigma (M = N)$. Show that if ϕ is existential, then there is an existential ψ with the same free variables such that $\mathcal{A} \models \phi \approx \neg\psi$.

(d) Show that if ϕ and ψ are existential, then there is an existential θ with $FV(\theta) = FV(\phi) \cup FV(\psi)$ such that $\mathcal{A} \models \theta \approx (\phi \wedge \psi)$.

(e) Show that if ϕ is existential, there is an existential ψ with the same free variables as $\exists x\colon\sigma.\,\phi$ such that $\mathcal{A} \models \phi \approx \exists x\colon\sigma.\,\psi$.

(f) Prove the main claim, using the argument that for any ϕ, there is an existential formula equivalent to $\neg\phi$.

4.5.4 Type and Equational Soundness

Since there are two proof systems, one for proving typing assertions and one for equations, there are two forms of soundness for $\lambda^{\rightarrow}$ and other typed lambda calculi. The first, *type soundness,* is stated precisely in the following lemma.

Lemma 4.5.13 (Type Soundness) Let $\mathcal{A}$ be any Henkin model for signature Σ, $\Gamma \triangleright M\colon\sigma$ a provable typing assertion, and $\eta \models \Gamma$ an environment for $\mathcal{A}$. Then $\mathcal{A}[\![\Gamma \triangleright M\colon\sigma]\!]\eta \in A^{\sigma}$.

This has the usual form for a soundness property: if a typing assertion is provable, then it holds semantically. The proof is a straightforward induction on typing derivations, which is omitted.

With a little thought, we may interpret Lemma 4.5.13 as saying that well-typed $\lambda^{\rightarrow}$ terms do not contain type errors. In a general framework for analyzing type errors, we would expect to identify certain function applications as erroneous. For example, in the signature for PCF, we would say that an application of $+$ to two arguments would produce a type error if either of the arguments is not a natural number. We will use this example error to show how Lemma 4.5.13 rules out errors.

Suppose we have a signature that gives addition the type $+\colon nat \rightarrow nat \rightarrow nat$ and a Henkin model $\mathcal{A}$ that interprets $+$ as a binary function on A^{nat}. We consider any application of $+$ to arguments that are not elements of A^{nat} an error. It is easy to see that the only way to derive a typing for an application $+\,M\,N$ is to give M and N type *nat*. By Lemma 4.5.13, if we can prove typing assertions $\Gamma \triangleright M\colon nat$ and $\Gamma \triangleright N\colon nat$, then in any Henkin model the semantic meaning of M and N will be an element of the set A^{nat} of semantic values for natural numbers. Therefore, the meaning of a syntactically well-typed application $+\,M\,N$ will be determined by applying the addition function to two elements of A^{nat}. It follows that no type error arises in the semantic interpretation of any well-typed term in this Henkin model. To conclude that no type errors arise in a specific operational semantics, we may prove an equivalence between the denotational and operational semantics, or give a separate operational proof. The standard statement of type soundness for an operational semantics given by reduction is Lemma 4.4.16.

Before proving equational soundness, we state some important facts about variables and the meanings of terms. The most important of these is the substitution lemma, which is analogous to the substitution lemma for algebra in Chapter 3.

A simple, preliminary fact is that the meaning of $\Gamma \triangleright M\colon\sigma$ in environment η can only depend on $\eta(y)$ if y is free in M.

Lemma 4.5.14 [Free Variables] Suppose $\eta_1, \eta_2 \models \Gamma$ are environments for $\mathcal{A}$ such that $\eta_1(x) = \eta_2(x)$ for every $x \in FV(M)$. Then

$$[\![\Gamma \triangleright M\colon\sigma]\!]\eta_1 = [\![\Gamma \triangleright M\colon\sigma]\!]\eta_2.$$

The proof is a straightforward inductive arguments, following the pattern of the proof of Lemma 4.3.6.

Since substitution involves renaming of bound variables, we will prove that the names of bound variables does not effect the meaning of a term. To make the inductive proof go through, we need a stronger inductive hypothesis that includes renaming free variables and setting the environment appropriately.

Lemma 4.5.15 Let $\Gamma = \{x_1\colon\sigma_1, \ldots, x_k\colon\sigma_k\}$ and suppose $\Gamma \triangleright M\colon\sigma$ is a well-typed term. Let $\Gamma' = \{y_1\colon\sigma_1, \ldots, y_k\colon\sigma_k\}$ and let N be any term that is α-equivalent to $[y_1, \ldots, y_k/x_1, \ldots, x_k]M$. If $\eta'(y_i) = \eta(x_i)$, for $1 \le i \le k$, then

$$[\![\Gamma \triangleright M\colon\sigma]\!]\eta = [\![\Gamma' \triangleright N\colon\sigma]\!]\eta'.$$

Proof The proof is by induction on the typing derivation of M. The only nontrivial case is lambda abstraction (by ($\rightarrow$ Intro)). Suppose that $\Gamma \triangleright \lambda z\colon\rho.\, M\colon\rho \rightarrow \tau$ is typed using $\Gamma, z\colon\rho \triangleright M\colon\tau$. The meaning of the lambda term is

$$\begin{aligned} &[\![\Gamma \triangleright \lambda z\colon\rho.\, M\colon\rho \rightarrow \tau]\!]\eta \\ = \quad &\text{the unique } f \in A^{\rho\rightarrow\tau} \text{ such that} \\ &\forall a \in A^{\rho}.\, \mathbf{App}\ f\ a = [\![\Gamma, z\colon\rho \triangleright M\colon\tau]\!]\eta[z \mapsto a] \end{aligned}$$

We must show that this is the same as the meaning of any term obtained by renaming free and bound variables, in an appropriate environment, such as

$$\begin{aligned} &[\![\Gamma' \triangleright \lambda w\colon\rho.\, N\colon\rho \rightarrow \tau]\!]\eta' \\ = \quad &\text{the unique } f \in A^{\rho\rightarrow\tau} \text{ such that} \\ &\forall a \in A^{\rho}.\, \mathbf{App}\ f\ a = [\![\Gamma', w\colon\rho \triangleright N\colon\tau]\!]\eta'[w \mapsto a] \end{aligned}$$

However, by the inductive hypothesis, we know that for any $a \in A^{\rho}$,

$$[\![\Gamma, z\colon\rho \triangleright M\colon\tau]\!]\eta[z \mapsto a] = [\![\Gamma', w\colon\rho \triangleright N\colon\tau]\!]\eta'[w \mapsto a]$$

This proves the lemma. ∎

This brings us to the substitution lemma for $\lambda^{\rightarrow}$.

Lemma 4.5.16 (Substitution) Let $\Gamma, x\colon\sigma \rhd M\colon\tau$ and $\Gamma \rhd N\colon\sigma$ be terms, $\eta \models \Gamma$, and $d = [\![\Gamma \rhd N\colon\sigma]\!]\eta$. Then

$$[\![\Gamma \rhd [N/x]M\colon\tau]\!]\eta = [\![\Gamma, x\colon\sigma \rhd M\colon\tau]\!]\eta[x \mapsto d].$$

Like the substitution lemma for algebra (Lemma 3.3.11), Lemma 4.5.16 says that the effect of syntactically substituting an expression N for x is the same as letting x denote the semantic meaning of N. The proof is left as a worthwhile exercise (Exercise 4.5.18).

The standard notions of satisfaction and validity for equations between typed lambda terms have routine definitions. As in our treatment of algebra, we only define satisfaction for environments that give variables values of the correct semantic type. A Henkin model $\mathcal{A}$ and environment $\eta \models \Gamma$ *satisfy* an equation $\Gamma \rhd M = N\colon\sigma$, written

$$\mathcal{A}, \eta \models \Gamma \rhd M = N\colon\sigma,$$

if

$$\mathcal{A}[\![\Gamma \rhd M\colon\sigma]\!]\eta = \mathcal{A}[\![\Gamma \rhd N\colon\sigma]\!]\eta.$$

We say a model $\mathcal{A}$ *satisfies* an equation $\Gamma \rhd M = N\colon\sigma$ if $\mathcal{A}$ and environment η satisfy this equation, for every η satisfying Γ. As discussed at some length in Section 3.4.1, an equation may hold vacuously in model $\mathcal{A}$ if some A^{σ} is empty.

Theorem 4.5.17 (Soundness) If $\mathcal{E} \vdash \Gamma \rhd M = N\colon\tau$, for any set $\mathcal{E}$ of typed equations, then every Henkin model satisfying $\mathcal{E}$ also satisfies $\Gamma \rhd M = N\colon\tau$.

Proof The proof is by induction on equational proofs from the set $\mathcal{E}$ of equational hypotheses. The base cases are that $E \in \mathcal{E}$ or E is one of the axioms (*ref*), (α), (β), or (η). The cases for $E \in \mathcal{E}$ and (*ref*) are trivial. The (α) case follows from Lemma 4.5.15.

For (β), we use the substitution lemma, as follows. The meaning of an application is

$$[\![\Gamma \rhd (\lambda x\colon\sigma.\, M)N\colon\tau]\!]\eta = \mathbf{App}\ f\ a$$

where a is the meaning of N and f is the unique element of $A^{\sigma\rightarrow\tau}$ satisfying

$$\mathbf{App}\ f\ a' = [\![\Gamma, x\colon\sigma \rhd M\colon\tau]\!]\eta[x \mapsto a']$$

for all $a' \in A^{\sigma}$. We must show that the meaning of the application is the same as the meaning of the substitution instance

$$[\![\Gamma \rhd [N/x]M\colon\tau]\!]\eta$$

However, by the substitution lemma we have

$$\mathbf{App}\ f\ a = [\![\Gamma, x\colon\sigma \triangleright M\colon\tau]\!]\eta[x \mapsto a'] = [\![\Gamma \triangleright [N/x]M\colon\tau]\!]\eta$$

which proves this case of the theorem.

The (η) case is a routine calculation, similar to Example 4.5.6.

There are inductive steps for inference rules (*sym*), (*trans*), (ξ) and (ν). The (*sym*) and (*trans*) cases are trivial. The most interesting case is (ξ), which is still essentially straightforward. For this rule, we assume that

$$\mathcal{A} \models \Gamma, x\colon\sigma \triangleright M = N\colon\tau.$$

We must show

$$\mathcal{A} \models \Gamma \triangleright \lambda x\colon\sigma.\, M = \lambda x\colon\sigma.\, N\colon\sigma \to \tau.$$

This may be calculated as follows, using the induction hypothesis in the second step.

$$\begin{aligned}[\![\Gamma \triangleright \lambda x\colon\sigma.\, M\colon\sigma \to \tau]\!]\eta &= \text{the unique } f \in A^{\sigma\to\tau} \text{ such that} \\ &\qquad \forall a \in A^{\sigma}.\, \mathbf{App}\ f\ a = [\![\Gamma, x\colon\sigma \triangleright M\colon\tau]\!]\eta[x \mapsto a] \\ &= \text{the unique } f \in A^{\sigma\to\tau} \text{ such that} \\ &\qquad \forall a \in A^{\sigma}.\, \mathbf{App}\ f\ a = [\![\Gamma, x\colon\sigma \triangleright N\colon\tau]\!]\eta[x \mapsto a] \\ &= [\![\Gamma \triangleright \lambda x\colon\sigma.\, N\colon\sigma \to \tau]\!]\eta\end{aligned}$$

The (ν) case is straightforward and omitted. This finishes the proof. ■

Exercise 4.5.18 Lemma 4.5.16 is proved by induction on typing derivations. This exercise asks you to prove some of the cases. If you get stuck, you may wish to look at the proofs of Lemmas 3.3.11 and 4.3.6. In each case, assume $\Gamma, x\colon\sigma \triangleright M\colon\tau$ and $\Gamma \triangleright N\colon\sigma$ are provable typing assertions, $\eta \models \Gamma$, and $d = [\![\Gamma \triangleright N\colon\sigma]\!]\eta$. Suppose that a typing derivation for $\Gamma, x\colon\sigma \triangleright M\colon\tau$ is given and assume that if $\Gamma, x\colon\sigma \triangleright M'\colon\tau'$ is proved by a shorter derivation, then

$$[\![\Gamma \triangleright [N/x]M'\colon\tau]\!]\eta = [\![\Gamma, x\colon\sigma \triangleright M'\colon\tau]\!]\eta[x \mapsto d].$$

Show that this holds for $\Gamma, x\colon\sigma \triangleright M\colon\tau$.

(a) Consider the case where M is a variable, not necessarily distinct from x, typed using the axiom (*var*).

(b) Consider the case where $\Gamma, x\colon\sigma \triangleright M\colon\tau$ follows by (*add var*), not necessarily adding the variable x to the type assignment.

(c) Consider the case where $\Gamma, x\colon\sigma \rhd M\colon\tau$ follows by ($\rightarrow$ Intro).

Exercise 4.5.19 Prove Proposition 4.4.4 by showing that every multi-sorted algebra may be extended to a Henkin model. You may want to read the brief proof outline following the statement of the proposition.

Exercise 4.5.20 If we write formulas of higher-order logic as described in Example 4.4.7, then formulas are terms over a $\lambda^{\rightarrow}$ signature that includes type constant *tv*, term constants *or*, *not* and $\forall_\sigma$, and possibly other type and term constants. A general, or Henkin, model for classical higher-order logic is a Henkin model $\mathcal{A}$ for the appropriate signature such that $A^{tv} = \{true, false\}$ and the logical constants *or*, *not* and $\forall_\sigma$ have their standard interpretation. The meaning of a logical formula in a general model is defined in exactly the same way as the meaning of a term in a Henkin model of typed lambda calculus, so it is easy to see that a formula M holds in $\mathcal{A}$ (*i.e.*, it has value *true*) iff the equation $M = true$ holds in $\mathcal{A}$ (regarding $\mathcal{A}$ as a typed lambda model).

(a) Show that the axioms for $\approx$ hold in all general models.

(b) Show that if $\mathcal{A}$ is a full classical hierarchy, then $\approx$ is semantic equality (at each type). This is not the case for all Henkin models.

Exercise 4.5.21 Untyped lambda calculus is defined in Exercise 2.6.7 and a corresponding typed equational theory in Exercise 4.4.12. A *model of untyped lambda calculus* $\mathcal{D} = \langle D, [D \rightarrow D], \Phi, \Psi\rangle$ consists of a set D, a set $[D \rightarrow D]$ of functions from D to D, and functions

$$\Phi\colon D \rightarrow [D \rightarrow D]$$

$$\Psi\colon [D \rightarrow D] \rightarrow D$$

such that both compositions $\Phi \circ \Psi$ and $\Psi \circ \Phi$ are identity functions and every lambda term has a meaning when interpreted as follows

$$\mathcal{D}[\![x]\!]\eta \quad = \eta(x)$$

$$\mathcal{D}[\![U\,V]\!]\eta \;= \Phi\ (\mathcal{D}[\![U]\!]\eta)\ (\mathcal{D}[\![V]\!]\eta)$$

$$\mathcal{D}[\![\lambda x U]\!]\eta = \Psi\ (\lambda d \in D.\, \mathcal{D}[\![U]\!]\eta[x \mapsto d])$$

Show that from any untyped lambda model $\mathcal{D}$ we can construct a Henkin model for the $\lambda^{\rightarrow}$ signature described in Exercise 4.4.12 so that each untyped term has has the same meaning as the typed lambda term determined as in Exercise 2.6.7. Use this to conclude that the equational axioms of untyped lambda calculus hold in all untyped lambda models.

4.5.5 Completeness for Henkin Models Without Empty Types

There are three completeness theorems for $\lambda^{\rightarrow}$. This is more complicated than the situation for multi-sorted algebra, where there are only two completeness theorems (deductive completeness in general, and least model completeness if empty sorts are eliminated). The case that is similar to algebra is that we have least model completeness if we rule out empty types: for every theory closed under an additional "nonempty" rule, there is a model satisfying precisely the equations in this theory. However, we do not have deductive completeness for Henkin models without extending the proof system. On the other hand, if we consider more general categorical models or Kripke models, described in Chapter 7, we do have straightforward least model completeness for the proof system as given. In this section, we state least model completeness without empty types and sketch a direct proof. A full proof, resembling the completeness proof for algebra, is given in Section 8.3.1, using logical relations as an analog for congruence relations over algebras. Deductive completeness for an extended proof system is described in Section 4.5.6, with completeness for cartesian closed categories and Kripke lambda models considered in Sections 7.2.6, 7.3.6 and 7.3.7.

The inference rule for reasoning about nonempty types,

$$\frac{\Gamma, x{:}\sigma \triangleright M = N{:}\tau}{\Gamma \triangleright M = N{:}\tau}\ x \text{ not free in } M, N. \qquad (nonempty)$$

is the same as the rule we used for algebra, except that here M and N may be lambda terms instead of algebraic terms. If we know σ is not empty, then the Free Variable Lemma may be used to show that (*nonempty*) is sound. However, if a type σ is empty (*i.e.*, $A^{\sigma} = \emptyset$), then $\Gamma, x{:}\sigma \triangleright M = N{:}\tau$ may hold solely because no environment can give x a value of type σ. Therefore, it is incorrect to apply rule (*nonempty*) if a type may be empty. As explained in the discussion of empty types in algebra (Section 3.4.6), this is a derived rule in any signature that allows us to write a term $\Gamma \triangleright P{:}\sigma$ with the same type as the variable x that we wish to eliminate by using this rule. In particular, a theory will be closed under this rule if the signature allows us to write a closed term of each type.

Theorem 4.5.22 Let $\mathcal{E}$ be any lambda theory closed under the rule *(nonempty)*. Then there is a Henkin model $\mathcal{A}$, with no $A^{\sigma} = \emptyset$, satisfying precisely the equations belonging to $\mathcal{E}$.

This theorem may be proved directly using a "term model" construction similar to the applicative structure $\mathcal{T}$ in Example 4.5.1. We will sketch the direct proof below, and give another construction of the same structure using logical relations in Section 8.3.1.

Proof Sketch Let $\mathcal{H}$ be any infinite set of variable typings $x\colon\sigma$ such that there are infinitely many variables of each type and no variable appears twice. Define the equivalence class $[M]_{\mathcal{E}}$ of M by

$$[M]_{\mathcal{E}} = \{N \mid \mathcal{E} \vdash \Gamma \triangleright M = N\colon\tau, \text{ some finite } \Gamma \subseteq \mathcal{H}\}$$

and let A^{τ} be the collection of all $[M]_{\mathcal{E}}$ with $\Gamma \triangleright M\colon\tau$ some $\Gamma \subseteq \mathcal{H}$. This gives us an applicative structure, with

$$\mathbf{App}\, [M]_{\mathcal{E}}\, [N]_{\mathcal{E}} = [MN]_{\mathcal{E}}$$

called the *term model* for the signature and theory. It is possible to show that the meaning of a term in the term model is a substitution instance (as for term algebras), and that the term model for $\mathcal{E}$ satisfies exactly the equations provable from $\mathcal{E}$. ∎

Some consequences of Theorem 4.5.22 are the completeness of the equational axioms of PCF for reasoning about all Henkin models of the axioms, completeness for untyped lambda calculus (see Exercise 4.5.26) and completeness of higher-order logic over general (Henkin) models, provided the signature does not allow empty types (see Exercise 4.5.27 below). Another special case of Theorem 4.5.22 is the pure theory $\mathcal{E}$ closed under the inference rules of Section 4.4.1, with no nonlogical axioms. It follows from Proposition 4.4.1 that although rule (*nonempty*) is not among the rules in Section 4.4.1, the pure theory is closed under (*nonempty*). Therefore, we have the following corollary.

Corollary 4.5.23 Let $\mathcal{E}$ be the pure theory of β, η-conversion. There is a Henkin model $\mathcal{A}$ without empty types satisfying precisely the equations of $\mathcal{E}$.

A model $\mathcal{A}$ is *nontrivial* if there is some equation that is not satisfied by $\mathcal{A}$. If a signature Σ has only one base type b, then a simple argument shows that any nontrivial Henkin model must satisfy (*nonempty*). If A^b is empty, then by induction on types no A^{σ} may have more than one element. Therefore, if $\mathcal{A}$ is nontrivial, A^b must not be empty. But then no type is empty, as is easily verified by induction on types. For this reason, when only one base type is used, it has been common practice to write equations without specifying the set of free variables explicitly.

Exercise 4.5.24 Let P_1 and P_2 be the lambda terms

$$P_1 \stackrel{\text{def}}{=} \lambda x\colon a.\, \lambda y\colon a.\, x, \quad P_2 \stackrel{\text{def}}{=} \lambda x\colon a.\, \lambda y\colon a.\, y.$$

Show that with rule (*nonempty*), we can prove the equation $f\colon (a \to a \to a) \to b \triangleright f\ P_1 = f\ P_2\colon b$ from the hypothesis $\lambda z\colon a.\ f\ P_1 = \lambda z\colon a.\ f\ P_2$. It is shown in Example 7.3.4 that this proof cannot be carried out without (*nonempty*) or some other addition to the proof system. (See also Exercise 4.5.29.)

Exercise 4.5.25 Show that if we add rule (*nonempty*) to $\lambda^{null,\rightarrow}$, we obtain an inconsistent proof system.

Exercise 4.5.26 Untyped lambda calculus and its syntactic and semantic connections with typed lambda calculus are discussed in Exercises 2.6.7, 4.4.12 and 4.5.21. Following the correspondence described in these exercises, use Theorem 4.5.22 to prove completeness of untyped lambda calculus.

Exercise 4.5.27 General models of higher-order logic are described in Exercise 4.5.20. Theorem 4.5.22 does not immediately imply completeness for general models, since the Henkin model $\mathcal{A}$ satisfying a theory $\mathcal{E}$ with *tv* might not have exactly two elements of A^{tv}, or one of the logical constants might be interpreted in a nonstandard way. Suppose $\mathcal{E}$ is a theory over a signature corresponding to higher-order logic, containing the axioms of higher-order logic and closed under the proof rules. Assume that the signature prevents any type from being empty. Show that there is some *maximal consistent theory* $\hat{\mathcal{E}} \supseteq \mathcal{E}$ such that model of $\hat{\mathcal{E}}$ described in the proof sketch of Theorem 4.5.22 has two elements of type *tv*, with the logical constants interpreted in the standard way.

4.5.6 Completeness with Empty Types

In general, we may be interested in typed lambda calculus over an arbitrary collection of type constants. Since some of these may not have any definable elements, or may naturally be considered empty (as may arise when types are given by specifications), it may be useful to reason about terms over possibly empty types. For Henkin models that may have empty types, we may achieve completeness using additional rules first presented in [MMMS87]. The main purpose of these additional rules is to capture reasoning of the form "if $M = N$ whenever σ is empty, and $M = N$ whenever σ is nonempty, then we must have $M = N$". To facilitate reasoning about empty types, it is convenient to add assumptions of the form *empty* σ to type assignments. An *extended equation* is a formula $\Gamma \triangleright M = N\colon\sigma$ with Γ the union of a type assignment Γ_1 and a set Γ_2 of formulas *empty* τ. We require that $\Gamma_1 \triangleright M\colon\sigma$ and $\Gamma_1 \triangleright N\colon\sigma$, so that emptiness assertions do not affect the syntactic types of terms.

Just as an ordinary equation $\Gamma \triangleright M = N\colon\sigma$ may be read as an implication, "if Γ is satisfied, then M and N denote the same value of type σ," we interpret extended equations as a simple form of implication. For example, $x\colon\sigma$, *empty* $\tau \triangleright M = N\colon\sigma$ holds if M and N are equal whenever x is given a value of type σ and the type τ is empty. More specifically, if Γ the union of a type assignment Γ_1 and a set Γ_2 of formulas of the form *empty* τ, we say $\mathcal{A}$ and η satisfy Γ, written $\mathcal{A}, \eta \models \Gamma$, if $\mathcal{A}, \eta \models \Gamma_1$ according to the usual definition and, for every *empty* $\tau \in \Gamma_2$, the set A^τ is empty. (In versions of lambda calculus with type variables, a type might be empty in some environments, and nonempty in others.) The remaining definitions of satisfaction by a model and validity are as given in Section 4.5.4.

The proof system for reasoning about empty types uses an axiom scheme for introducing equations with emptiness assertions and an inference rule that lets us use emptiness assertions to reason by cases. The axiom is

$$\Gamma, \mathit{empty}\, \sigma, x\colon \sigma \rhd M = N\colon \tau. \qquad (\mathit{empty}\ I)$$

Any equation of this form is valid, since it is impossible to give x a value of type σ if σ is empty. Therefore, since the extended type assignment $\Gamma, \mathit{empty}\, \sigma, x\colon \sigma$ is unsatisfiable, the implication $\Gamma, \mathit{empty}\, \sigma, x\colon \sigma \rhd M = N\colon \tau$ holds vacuously. The inference rule for empty types is

$$\frac{\Gamma, x\colon \sigma \rhd M = N\colon \tau,\ \Gamma, \mathit{empty}\, \sigma \rhd M = N\colon \tau}{\Gamma \rhd M = N\colon \tau}\ x \notin FV(M, N) \qquad (\mathit{empty}\ E)$$

This is the rule that formalizes the reasoning "if $M = N$ when σ is empty, and $M = N$ when σ is nonempty, then we must have $M = N$". Technically speaking, the side condition of this rule is redundant, since the second equation in the antecedent can be well-formed only if $x \notin FV(M, N)$. We write $\vdash^{(\mathit{empty} I, E)}$ for provability using the proof rules of Section 4.4.1 and the additional axiom and inference rule for empty types. A simple example of the kind of deduction that is possible in this proof system is given in Exercise 4.5.29.

The following theorem was announced in [MMMS87] for polymorphic lambda calculus with the axiom and inference rule above. We give a direct proof sketch below, and give a more complete proof using logical relations in Exercise 8.3.3.

Theorem 4.5.28 Let $\mathcal{E}$ be a set of extended equations, possibly containing emptiness assertions, and $\Gamma \rhd M = N\colon \sigma$ an extended equation. Then $\mathcal{E} \vdash^{(\mathit{empty} I, E)} \Gamma \rhd M = N\colon \sigma$ iff every Henkin model satisfying $\mathcal{E}$ also satisfies $\Gamma \rhd M = N\colon \sigma$.

Proof Sketch The completeness proof uses an infinite set $\mathcal{H}$ of typings $x\colon \sigma$ and emptiness assertions $\mathit{empty}\, \sigma$. If $\Gamma \rhd M_0 = N_0\colon \sigma_0$ is a chosen equation not provable from $\mathcal{E}$, then $\mathcal{H}$ is constructed so that (i) $\Gamma \subseteq \mathcal{H}$, (ii) for every σ, either $x\colon \sigma \in \mathcal{H}$ for infinitely many x, or $\mathit{empty}\, \sigma \in \mathcal{H}$, (iii) for every finite $\Gamma' \subset \mathcal{H}$, the equation $\Gamma' \rhd M_0 = N_0\colon \sigma_0$ is not provable from $\mathcal{E}$. The construction of $\mathcal{H}$ proceeds in stages, using an enumeration of all types. The remainder of the proof is similar to the proof of Theorem 4.5.22. ∎

Since (*empty E*) is not an equational inference, the rules for reasoning about empty types have a different flavor from the proof systems without (*empty E*). In particular, it is not clear if the consequences of this proof system may be captured by any natural form of reduction on terms.

A subtle issues is the difference between an *initial type null* and an empty type. As shown in Exercise 4.5.25, it is inconsistent to treat *null* as a nonempty type. However, there are Henkin models for $\lambda^{null,\rightarrow}$ in which *null* is not empty. A simple example is a term model where, as in the proof of Theorem 4.5.22, we include infinitely many variables of each type.

Exercise 4.5.29 Let P_1 and P_2 be the lambda terms

$$P_1 \stackrel{\text{def}}{=} \lambda x\colon a.\, \lambda y\colon a.\, x, \qquad P_2 \stackrel{\text{def}}{=} \lambda x\colon a.\, \lambda y\colon a.\, y,$$

as in Exercise 4.5.24. Show that with axiom (*empty I*) and rule (*empty E*), we can prove the equation $f\colon (a \rightarrow a \rightarrow a) \rightarrow b \triangleright f\, P_1 = f\, P_2\colon b$ from the hypothesis $\lambda z\colon a.\, f\, P_1 = \lambda z\colon a.\, f\, P_2$. Explain why this implication is sound for Henkin models in which a or b may be empty. It is shown in Example 7.3.4 that this proof cannot be carried out without some addtion to the proof system.

4.5.7 Combinators and the Combinatory Model Condition

The environment model condition is equivalent to the existence of certain elements called combinators, each characterized by an equational axiom. This is called the combinatory model condition. One advantage of the combinatory model condition is that it does not refer to syntax or the meaning function on typed lambda terms.

The simplest way to prove the equivalence of the combinatory and environment model conditions involves translations between lambda terms and combinatory terms. A combinatory term is an applicative term, or lambda term not containing λ, over a certain kind of signature. If Σ is a $\lambda^{\rightarrow}$ signature, then $CL(\Sigma)$ is a signature with exactly the same type constants as Σ but with additional term constants. Specifically, $CL(\Sigma)$ has all the term constants of Σ, together with constant symbols

$$K_{\sigma,\tau} \;\colon \sigma \rightarrow \tau \rightarrow \sigma$$

$$S_{\rho,\sigma,\tau}\colon (\rho \rightarrow \sigma \rightarrow \tau) \rightarrow (\rho \rightarrow \sigma) \rightarrow \rho \rightarrow \tau$$

for all types ρ, σ and τ over the type constants of Σ. A *combinatory term over signature* Σ is a term, not containing λ, over the signature $CL(\Sigma)$ with constants K and S added. It is important to realize that the main purpose of the environment model condition is to guarantee that every term containing λ has a meaning in the structure. However, since combinatory terms do not contain λ, every combinatory term over Σ has a meaning in any applicative structure for signature $CL(\Sigma)$. We use the letters "CL" in the signature with combinators since a historical term for the algebraic system with combinators is *combinatory logic*.

We say an applicative structure $\mathcal{A}$ *has combinators,* or *satisfies the combinatory model condition* if, for all ρ, σ, τ, there exist elements

$$K_{\sigma,\tau} \in A^{\sigma\to(\tau\to\sigma)}$$

$$S_{\rho,\sigma,\tau} \in A^{(\rho\to\sigma\to\tau)\to(\rho\to\sigma)\to\rho\to\tau}$$

satisfying the equational conditions

$$K_{\sigma,\tau}xy \quad = x$$

$$S_{\rho,\sigma,\tau}xyz = (xz)(yz)$$

for all x, y, z of the appropriate types. If applicative structure $\mathcal{A}$ for signature Σ has combinators, then we write $\mathcal{A}^{CL}$ for the applicative structure derived from $\mathcal{A}$ by interpreting the additional constants of $CL(\Sigma)$ as elements satisfying the equations above. If $\mathcal{A}$ is extensional, then $\mathcal{A}^{CL}$ is uniquely determined.

The main idea behind the equivalence of the combinatory and environment model conditions is that combinators K and S allow us to write all lambda-definable functions using only application. To show how this works, we define "pseudo-abstraction." For every combinatory term $\Gamma, x\colon\sigma \rhd M\colon\tau$, we define the combinatory term $\Gamma \rhd \langle x\colon\sigma\rangle\, M\colon\sigma \to \tau$ using induction on the structure of M as follows.

$$\langle x\colon\sigma\rangle\, x \qquad = S_{\sigma,\sigma\to\sigma,\sigma}\, K_{\sigma,\sigma\to\sigma} K_{\sigma,\sigma},$$

$$\langle x\colon\sigma\rangle\, y \qquad = K_{\tau,\sigma} y, \text{ where } \tau \text{ is the type of } y \text{ and } y \text{ is different from } x,$$

$$\langle x\colon\sigma\rangle\, c \qquad = K_{\tau,\sigma} c, \text{ where } \tau \text{ is the type of constant } c,$$

$$\langle x\colon\sigma\rangle\, (MN) = S_{\sigma,\rho,\tau}(\langle x\colon\sigma\rangle\, M)(\langle x\colon\sigma\rangle\, N), \text{ where } \Gamma, x\colon\sigma \rhd M\colon\rho \to \tau,$$

The definition of $\langle x\colon\sigma\rangle\, x$ is analogous to the usual untyped translation into combinators $\langle x\rangle x = SKK$. It is not hard to verify that $\Gamma \rhd \langle x\colon\sigma\rangle\, M\colon\sigma \to \tau$ is well-typed.

The essential properties of pseudo-abstraction are described by the following lemma.

Lemma 4.5.30 Let $\mathcal{A}$ be an applicative structure for $CL(\Sigma)$ satisfying the equational axioms for K and S. For any combinatory terms $\Gamma, x\colon\sigma \rhd M\colon\tau$ and $\Gamma \rhd N\colon\sigma$ over $CL(\Sigma)$, we have

$$\mathcal{A} \models \Gamma \rhd (\langle x\colon\sigma\rangle\, M)N = [N/x]M\colon\tau.$$

The Lemma is proved by an easy induction, left as Exercise 4.5.35.

Let $\Gamma \rhd M\colon\sigma$ be a lambda term over Σ. We define the combinatory term $\Gamma \rhd \mathrm{CL}(M)\colon\sigma$ by induction on the derivation of $\Gamma \rhd M\colon\sigma$. The (*add var*) case requires no translation and is omitted.

$$\begin{aligned}
\text{CL}(x) &= x\\
\text{CL}(c) &= c\\
\text{CL}(MN) &= \text{CL}(M)\text{CL}(N)\\
\text{CL}(\lambda x\!:\!\sigma.\, M) &= \langle x\!:\!\sigma\rangle\, \text{CL}(M)
\end{aligned}$$

We can use the translation of λ-terms into combinatory terms to interpret a λ-term in any applicative structure with combinators. If the applicative structure is extensional, then we may show this yields the standard meaning of the lambda term.

Lemma 4.5.31 Suppose $\mathcal{A}$ is an extensional applicative structure for $CL(\Sigma)$ satisfying the axioms for K and S and $\Gamma \rhd M\!:\!\sigma$ is a lambda term over Σ. If $\eta \models \Gamma$, then the meaning of $\Gamma \rhd M\!:\!\sigma$ exists in $\mathcal{A}$ and is given by

$$[\![\Gamma \rhd M\!:\!\sigma]\!]\eta = [\![\Gamma \rhd (M)\!:\!\sigma]\!]\eta.$$

Proof The lemma is proved by induction on the typing of terms. The only nontrivial case is ($\rightarrow$ Intro). Recall that the meaning of $\Gamma \rhd \lambda x\!:\!\sigma.\, M\!:\!\sigma \rightarrow \tau$ typed by ($\rightarrow$ Intro) is

$$[\![\Gamma \rhd \lambda x\!:\!\sigma.\, M\!:\!\sigma \rightarrow \tau]\!]\eta = \text{the unique } f \in A^{\sigma\rightarrow\tau} \text{ such that}$$
$$\forall a \in A^{\sigma}.\, \mathbf{App}\, f\, a = [\![\Gamma, x\!:\!\sigma \rhd M\!:\!\tau]\!]\eta[x \mapsto a]$$

By the inductive hypothesis,

$$\mathbf{App}\, f\, a = [\![\Gamma, x\!:\!\sigma \rhd (M)\!:\!\tau]\!]\eta[x \mapsto a]$$

for all $a \in A^{\sigma}$. By the substitution lemma and Lemma 4.5.30,

$$\mathbf{App}[\![\Gamma \rhd \langle x\!:\!\sigma\rangle\, (M)\!:\!\sigma \rightarrow \tau]\!]\eta\, a = [\![\Gamma, x\!:\!\sigma \rhd (M)\!:\!\tau]\!]\eta[x \mapsto a]$$

for all $a \in A^{\sigma}$. This proves the lemma. ∎

We may also translate combinatory terms into lambda terms, as follows.

$$\begin{aligned}
\text{LAM}(x) &= x\\
\text{LAM}(c) &= c \text{ for constant } c \text{ different from } K, S\\
\text{LAM}(K_{\sigma,\tau}) &= \lambda x\!:\!\sigma.\, \lambda y\!:\!\tau.\, x\\
\text{LAM}(S_{\rho,\sigma,\tau}) &= \lambda x\!:\!(\rho \rightarrow \sigma \rightarrow \tau).\, \lambda y\!:\!\rho \rightarrow \sigma.\, \lambda z\!:\!\rho.\, xz(yz)\\
\text{LAM}(MN)f &= \text{LAM}(M)\text{LAM}(N)
\end{aligned}$$

It is easy to prove the following lemma.

Lemma 4.5.32 Let $\mathcal{A}$ be an environment model for signature Σ. Then for every combinatory term $\Gamma \triangleright M\colon\sigma$ over $CL(\Sigma)$, we have $\mathcal{A}^{CL} \models \Gamma \triangleright M = (M)\colon\sigma$.

Using Lemmas 4.5.31 and 4.5.32, we can now prove the following combinatory model theorem. This theorem is analogous to the combinatory model theorem of [Mey82], but somewhat more simply stated since we have only considered extensional structures.

Theorem 4.5.33 An extensional applicative structure satisfies the environment model condition iff it satisfies the combinatory model condition.

Proof If applicative structure $\mathcal{A}$ satisfies the environment model condition, then $\mathcal{A}$ has combinators since, by Lemma 4.5.32, every combinator is definable by a closed lambda term. Conversely, if $\mathcal{A}$ satisfies the combinatory model condition, then by Lemma 4.5.31, each lambda term must have a meaning in $\mathcal{A}$. ∎

In logical terms, a typed applicative structure may be viewed as a first-order model of a many-sorted signature with one sort for each type, as discussed at the beginning of Section 4.5.2. Extensionality may be written as a first-order formula (over the same signature), while each combinator is defined by an equational axiom. Therefore, Henkin models may be characterized as models of a multi-sorted first-order theory comprising the extensionality and combinator axioms.

Exercise 4.5.34 Translate the following lambda terms into combinators.

(a) $\lambda x\colon\sigma.\, \lambda y\colon\tau.\, x$

(b) $\lambda x\colon(\rho \to \sigma \to \tau).\, \lambda y\colon\rho \to \sigma.\, \lambda z\colon\rho.\, xz(yz)$

Exercise 4.5.35 Prove Lemma 4.5.30.

4.5.8 Combinatory and Lambda Algebras

Two nonextensional structures are occasionally of interest. These are typed analogs of untyped structures discussed in [Bar84], for example. Since the main interest in these structures is technical, we sketch only the main ideas. The reader interested in further information is encouraged to consult [Bar84].

Combinatory algebras are typed applicative structures that have combinators (as described above), but are not necessarily extensional. In a sense, every term can be given a meaning in a combinatory algebra, since every term can be translated into combinators, and every applicative combination of combinators has a straightforward interpretation. However, many natural equations between lambda terms may fail. For example,

$SKK = SKS$ holds in every lambda model (when these combinators are each typed appropriately), since these functions are extensionally equal. However, both are in combinatory normal form, and so by the confluence of combinatory reduction (Example 3.7.31) these terms are not provably equal. It follows from completeness for algebra that they may have distinct interpretations in a combinatory algebra. In particular, they are not equal in the term combinatory algebra (the term algebra for combinatory logic). Consequently, combinatory algebras are not models of the equational theory of typed lambda calculus.

There exists an equationally axiomatized class of combinatory algebras satisfying the pure equational theory of typed lambda calculus (β, η-conversion). These structures are called *lambda algebras,* and the unmemorable axioms may be found in [Bar84, Mey82], for example. The main difference between lambda algebras and models is that lambda algebras do not satisfy (ξ) in the standard sense. As a consequence, the set of equations satisfied by an arbitrary lambda algebra is not necessarily closed under (ξ). We generally interpret

$$\frac{\Gamma, x\colon\sigma \rhd M = N\colon\tau}{\Gamma \rhd \lambda x\colon\sigma.\, M = \lambda x\colon\sigma.\, N\colon\sigma \to \tau}. \qquad (\xi)$$

as saying that whenever M and N have the same meaning for all values of x, we have $\lambda x\colon\sigma.\, M = \lambda x\colon\sigma.\, N$. This semantic interpretation of (ξ) is guaranteed by extensionality, but fails in arbitrary lambda algebras.

4.5.9 Henkin Models for Other Types

We extend the definition of Henkin model to other versions of simply-typed lambda calculus by extending the definitions of applicative structure, extensionality, and the environment and combinatory model conditions. In this section, we describe Henkin models for $\lambda^{null,unit,+,\times,\to}$ by reference to the definitions already given for $\lambda^{\to}$. Models for intermediate simply-typed lambda calculi may obtained by dropping the irrelevant conditions.

Applicative Structures

A $\lambda^{null,unit,+,\times,\to}$ applicative structure differs from a $\lambda^{\to}$ applicative structure in that we need additional operations associated with the additional types. While it is possible to reduce the definition of $\lambda^{null,unit,+,\times,\to}$ applicative structure to the definition of $\lambda^{\to}$ structure by adding constants to a $\lambda^{\to}$ signature, it is simpler to take a more direct approach.

A *typed applicative structure* $\mathcal{A}$ for signature Σ is a tuple

$$\langle \{A^\sigma\}, \{\mathbf{Inleft}^{\sigma,\tau}, \mathbf{Inright}^{\sigma,\tau}, \mathbf{Proj}_1^{\sigma,\tau}, \mathbf{Proj}_2^{\sigma,\tau}, \mathbf{App}^{\sigma,\tau}\}, \mathit{Const}\rangle$$

of families of sets and mappings indexed by types, with

- $\mathbf{Inleft}^{\sigma,\tau}\colon A^{\sigma} \longrightarrow A^{\sigma+\tau}$,
- $\mathbf{Inright}^{\sigma,\tau}\colon A^{\tau} \longrightarrow A^{\sigma+\tau}$,
- $\mathbf{Proj}_1^{\sigma,\tau}\colon A^{\sigma\times\tau} \longrightarrow A^{\sigma}$,
- $\mathbf{Proj}_2^{\sigma,\tau}\colon A^{\sigma\times\tau} \longrightarrow A^{\tau}$,

for all types σ and τ over Σ, and $\mathbf{App}^{\sigma,\tau}$ as described in Section 4.5.2.

It may appear strange that we assume injection and projection functions as part of the structure, but not case or pairing functions. However, this is consistent with our earlier treatment of function types. We assume application as part of the applicative structure, leaving it to the the extensionality and environment or combinatory condition to guarantee that we may interpret lambda abstraction in a Henkin model. Similarly, the extensionality and environment or combinatory conditions will guarantee that case, pairing, $*$ and **Zero** may be interpreted uniquely in every $\lambda^{null,unit,+,\times,\rightarrow}$ Henkin model.

Extensionality

We will use the term *extensionality* for the conjunction of several conditions, one for each type. Intuitively, each extensionality conditions says that equality on the type is "standard" in some way. For example, the extensionality condition for products says that two elements representing pairs are equal iff they have the same first and second components.

An applicative structure is *extensional* if it satisfies the following conditions.

- $A^{null\rightarrow\sigma}$ and $A^{\sigma\rightarrow unit}$ each have exactly one element,
- $\forall f, g \in A^{(\sigma+\tau)\rightarrow\rho}. (f \circ \mathbf{Inleft} = g \circ \mathbf{Inleft} \wedge f \circ \mathbf{Inright} = g \circ \mathbf{Inright}) \supset f = g$
- $\forall p, q \in A^{\sigma\times\tau}. (\mathbf{Proj}_1 p = \mathbf{Proj}_1 q \wedge \mathbf{Proj}_2 p = \mathbf{Proj}_2 q) \supset p = q$

The first condition should be self-explanatory. In the second condition, an equation $f \circ h = g \circ h$ should be read as an abbreviation for a formula of the form

$\forall x.\mathbf{App}\, f\, (\mathbf{App}\, h\, x) = \mathbf{App}\, g\, (\mathbf{App}\, h\, x)$

Intuitively, the second condition says that a function on a sum type is determined by the elements in the range of the injections (see Exercise 2.6.3). The last condition guarantees that for every pair of elements $a \in A^{\sigma}$ and $b \in A^{\tau}$, there is at most one "pair" $p \in A^{\sigma\times\tau}$ whose first and second projections yield a and b, respectively.

Frames

If we are only interested in extensional applicative structures, then, as for $\lambda^{\rightarrow}$, we may formulate a simpler, combined definition. For $\lambda^{null,unit,+,\times,\rightarrow}$, a frame satisfies the following conditions:

- $A^{null \to \sigma}$ and $A^{\sigma \to unit}$ each have exactly one element,
- $A^{\sigma+\tau} \supseteq A^{\sigma} \uplus A^{\tau}$ is a superset of the *disjoint union* $A^{\sigma} \uplus A^{\tau} = (\{0\} \times A^{\sigma}) \cup (\{1\} \times A^{\tau})$,
- $\mathbf{Inleft}^{\sigma,\tau} x = \langle 0, x \rangle$ and $\mathbf{Inright}^{\sigma,\tau} y = \langle 1, y \rangle$,
- $A^{\sigma \times \tau} \subseteq A^{\sigma} \times A^{\tau}$ is a set of ordered pairs
- $\mathbf{Proj}_1^{\sigma,\tau} \langle x, y \rangle = x$ and $\mathbf{Proj}_2^{\sigma,\tau} \langle x, y \rangle = y$

in addition to the conditions on $A^{\sigma \to \tau}$ and **App** stated in Section 4.5.2. It is possible to generalize Lemma 4.5.3 to the calculus $\lambda^{null,unit,\times,\to}$ without sums (see Exercise 4.5.36). Sums are problematic since $A^{(\sigma+\tau)\to\rho}$ could be empty in some applicative structure $\mathcal{A}$. However, any nontrivial Henkin model with sum types is isomorphic to some frame.

Meaning and the Environment Model Condition

The meaning of a $\lambda^{null,unit,+,\times,\to}$ term is given by extending the definition of the meaning function for $\lambda^{\to}$ terms with the following additional clauses.

$$[\![\emptyset \triangleright \mathbf{Zero}^{\sigma} : null \to \sigma]\!]\eta = \text{the unique element of } A^{null \to \sigma}$$

$$[\![\emptyset \triangleright * : unit]\!]\eta = \text{the unique element of } A^{unit}$$

$$[\![\Gamma \triangleright \mathbf{Inleft}^{\sigma,\tau} M : \sigma + \tau]\!]\eta = \mathbf{Inleft}^{\sigma,\tau}\ [\![\Gamma \triangleright M : \sigma]\!]\eta$$

$$[\![\Gamma \triangleright \mathbf{Inright}^{\sigma,\tau} M : \sigma + \tau]\!]\eta = \mathbf{Inright}^{\sigma,\tau}\ [\![\Gamma \triangleright M : \tau]\!]\eta$$

$$[\![\Gamma \triangleright \mathbf{Case}\, M N P : \rho]\!]\eta = \mathbf{App}\ f\ [\![\Gamma \triangleright M : \sigma + \tau]\!]\eta$$

where $f \in A^{\sigma+\tau\to\rho}$ is uniquely determined by

$f \circ \mathbf{Inleft}^{\sigma,\tau} = [\![\Gamma \triangleright N : \sigma \to \rho]\!]\eta$ and

$f \circ \mathbf{Inright}^{\sigma,\tau} = [\![\Gamma \triangleright P : \tau \to \rho]\!]\eta$

$$[\![\Gamma \triangleright \mathbf{Proj}_1^{\sigma,\tau} M : \sigma]\!]\eta = \mathbf{Proj}_1^{\sigma,\tau}\ [\![\Gamma \triangleright M : \sigma \times \tau]\!]\eta$$

$$[\![\Gamma \triangleright \mathbf{Proj}_2^{\sigma,\tau} M : \tau]\!]\eta = \mathbf{Proj}_2^{\sigma,\tau}\ [\![\Gamma \triangleright M : \sigma \times \tau]\!]\eta$$

$$[\![\Gamma \triangleright \langle M, N \rangle : \sigma \times \tau]\!]\eta = \text{the unique } p \in A^{\sigma \times \tau} \text{ such that}$$

$\mathbf{Proj}_1^{\sigma,\tau}\ p = [\![\Gamma \triangleright M : \sigma]\!]\eta$ and

$\mathbf{Proj}_2^{\sigma,\tau}\ p = [\![\Gamma \triangleright N : \tau]\!]\eta$

Recall that an applicative structure satisfies the *environment model condition* if the standard inductive clauses define a total meaning function $[\![\cdot]\!]\cdot$ on terms $\Gamma \triangleright M : \sigma$ and environments η such that $\eta \models \Gamma$. In other words, for every well-typed term $\Gamma \triangleright M : \sigma$, and every environment $\eta \models \Gamma$, the meaning $[\![\Gamma \triangleright M : \sigma]\!]\eta \in A^{\sigma}$ must exist as defined above.

Combinatory Model Condition
As for $\lambda^{\rightarrow}$, the condition that every term has a meaning is equivalent to the existence of combinators, where each combinator is characterized by an equational axiom. To avoid any confusion, the constants for combinators and their types are listed below.

$$\begin{array}{ll}
\mathbf{Zero}^{\sigma} & : null \rightarrow \sigma \\
* & : unit \\
\mathbf{Inleft}^{\sigma,\tau} & : \sigma \rightarrow (\sigma + \tau) \\
\mathbf{Inright}^{\sigma,\tau} & : \tau \rightarrow (\sigma + \tau) \\
\mathbf{Case}^{\sigma,\tau,\rho} & : (\sigma + \tau) \rightarrow (\sigma \rightarrow \rho) \rightarrow (\tau \rightarrow \rho) \rightarrow \rho \\
\mathbf{Pair}^{\sigma,\tau} & : \sigma \rightarrow \tau \rightarrow (\sigma \times \tau) \\
\mathbf{Proj}_1^{\sigma,\tau} & : (\sigma \times \tau) \rightarrow \sigma \\
\mathbf{Proj}_2^{\sigma,\tau} & : (\sigma \times \tau) \rightarrow \tau
\end{array}$$

The equational axioms for these constants are the equational axioms of $\lambda^{null,unit,+,\times,\rightarrow}$.

It is straightforward to extend Theorem 4.5.33 and the associated lemmas in Section 4.5.7 to $\lambda^{null,unit,+,\times,\rightarrow}$. Most of the work lies in defining pseudo-abstraction and verifying its properties. However, all of this has been done in Section 4.5.7.

Exercise 4.5.36 Prove Lemma 4.5.3 for $\lambda^{null,unit,\times,\rightarrow}$. Show that if $\mathcal{A}$ is a $\lambda^{null,unit,+,\times,\rightarrow}$ Henkin model, then $A^{\sigma+\tau}$ is isomorphic to a superset of $A^{\sigma} \uplus A^{\tau}$.

5 Models of Typed Lambda Calculus

5.1 Introduction

This chapter develops two classes of models for typed lambda calculus, one based on partially-ordered structures called *domains,* and the other based on traditional recursive function theory (or Turing machine computation). The second class of models is introduced using partial recursive functions on the natural numbers, with the main ideas later generalized to a class of structures called *partial combinatory algebras.*

The main topics of this chapter are:

- Domain-theoretic models of typed lambda calculus with fixed-point operators based on complete partial orders (CPOs).
- Fixed-point induction, a proof method for reasoning about recursive definitions.
- Computational adequacy and full abstraction theorems, relating the operational semantics of PCF (and variants) to denotational semantics over domains.
- Recursion-theoretic models of typed lambda calculus without fixed-point operators, using a class of structures called modest sets.
- Relationship between modest sets and partial equivalence relations over untyped computation structures called partial combinatory algebras.
- Fixed-point operators in recursive function models.

In the sections on domain-theoretic models, we are primarily concerned with the simplest class of domains, called *complete partial orders,* or *CPOs* for short. The main motivation for studying domains is that they provide a class of models with fixed-point operators and methods for interpreting recursive type expressions. Our focus in this chapter is on fixed points of functions, with recursive types considered in Section 7.4. Since fixed-point operators are essential for recursion, and recursion is central to computation, domains are widely studied in the literature on programming language mathematics.

A current trend in the semantics of computation is towards structures that are related to traditional recursive function theory. One reason for this trend is that recursive function models give a pleasant and straightforward interpretation of polymorphism and subtyping (studied in Chapters 9 and 10, respectively). Another reason for developing recursion-theoretic models is the close tie with constructive logic and other theories of computation. In particular, complexity theory and traditional studies of computability are based on recursive functions characterized by Turing machines or other computation models. It remains to be seen, from further research, how central the ideas from domain theory are for models based on recursive function theory. Some indication of the relationships are discussed in Section 5.6.4.

Both classes of structures are presented primarily as $\lambda^{\times,\rightarrow}$ models, leaving the interpretation of sums (disjoint union) and other types to the exercises. The proofs of some of the theorems stated or used in this chapter are postponed to Chapter 8.

5.2 Domain-theoretic Models and Fixed Points

5.2.1 Recursive Definitions and Fixed Point Operators

Before defining complete partial orders and investigating their properties, we motivate the central properties of domains using an intuitive discussion of recursive definitions. Recall from Section 2.2.5 that if we wish to add a recursive definition form

$$\texttt{letrec}\ f\colon\sigma = M\ \texttt{in}\ N$$

to typed lambda calculus, it suffices to add a fixed-point operator fix_σ that returns a fixed point of any function from σ to σ. Therefore, we study a class of models for $\lambda^{\times,\rightarrow}$, and extensions, in which functions of the appropriate type have fixed points. A specific example will be a model (denotational semantics) of PCF.

We will use properties of *fix* reduction to motivate the semantic interpretation of *fix*. To emphasize a few points about (*fix*) reduction, we will review the factorial example from Section 2.2.5. In this example, we assume reduction rules for conditional, equality test, subtraction and multiplication.

Using $\mathit{fix}_{nat\rightarrow nat}$, the factorial function may be written $\mathit{fact} \stackrel{\text{def}}{=} \mathit{fix}_{nat\rightarrow nat}\ F$, where F is the expression

$$F \stackrel{\text{def}}{=} \lambda f\colon nat\rightarrow nat.\,\lambda y\colon nat.\ \texttt{if}\ Eq?\ y\ 0\ \texttt{then}\ 1\ \texttt{else}\ y * f(y-1).$$

Since the type is clear from context, we will drop the subscript from *fix*. To compute *fact* n, we expand the definition, and use reduction to obtain the following.

$$\begin{aligned}
\mathit{fact}\ n &= (\lambda f\colon nat\rightarrow nat.\ f(\mathit{fix}\ f))\ F\ n \\
&= F\ (\mathit{fix}\ F)\ n \\
&= (\lambda f\colon nat\rightarrow nat.\,\lambda y\colon nat.\ \texttt{if}\ Eq?\ y\ 0\ \texttt{then}\ 1\ \texttt{else}\ y * f(y-1))\ (\mathit{fix}\ F)\ n \\
&= \texttt{if}\ Eq?\ n\ 0\ \texttt{then}\ 1\ \texttt{else}\ n * (\mathit{fix}\ F)(n-1)
\end{aligned}$$

When $n = 0$, we can use the reduction axiom for conditional to simplify *fact* 0 to 1. For $n > 0$, we can simplify the test to obtain $n * (\mathit{fix}\ F)(n-1)$, and continue as above. For any numeral n, we will eventually reduce *fact* n to the numeral for $n!$.

An alternative approach to understanding *fact* is to consider the finite expansions of *fix* F. To make this as intuitive as possible, let us temporarily think of $nat \to nat$ as a collection of partial functions on the natural numbers, represented by sets of ordered pairs. Using a constant *diverge* for the "nowhere defined" function (the empty set of ordered pairs), we let the "zero-th expansion" $\mathit{fix}^{[0]}\ F = \mathit{diverge}$ and define

$$\mathit{fix}^{[n+1]}\ F \ = \ F\ (\mathit{fix}^{[n]}\ F)$$

In computational terms, $\mathit{fix}^{[n]}\ F$ describes the recursive function computed using at most n evaluations of the body of F. Or, put another way, $\mathit{fix}^{[n]}\ F$ is the best we could do with a machine having such limited memory that allocating space for more than n function calls would overflow the run-time stack. For example, we can see that $(\mathit{fix}^{[2]}\ F)\,0 = 1$ and $(\mathit{fix}^{[2]}\ F)\,1 = 1$, but $(\mathit{fix}^{[2]}\ F)\,n$ is undefined for $n \geq 2$.

Viewed as sets of ordered pairs, the finite expansions of *fix* F are linearly ordered by set-theoretic containment. Specifically, $\mathit{fix}^{[0]}\ F = \emptyset$ is the least element in this ordering, and $\mathit{fix}^{[n+1]}\ F = (\mathit{fix}^{[n]}\ F) \cup \langle n, n! \rangle$ properly contains all $\mathit{fix}^{[i]}\ F$ for $i \leq n$. This reflects the fact that if we are allowed more recursive calls, we may compute factorial for larger natural numbers. In addition, since every terminating computation involving factorial uses only a finite number of recursive calls, it makes intuitive computational sense to let $\mathit{fact} = \bigcup_n (\mathit{fix}^{[n]}\ F)$; this gives us the standard factorial function. However, *a priori,* there is no reason to believe that for arbitrary F, $\bigcup_n \mathit{fix}^{[n]}\ F$ is a fixed point of F. This may be guaranteed by imposing relatively natural conditions on F (or the basic functions used to define F). Since any fixed point of F must contain the functions defined by finite expansions of F, $\bigcup_n \mathit{fix}^{[n]}\ F$ will be the least fixed point of F (when we order partial functions by set containment).

In domain-theoretic models of typed lambda calculus, types denote partially-ordered sets of values called domains. Although it is possible to develop domains using partial functions [Plo85], we will follow the more standard approach of total functions. However, we will alter the interpretation of *nat* so that $nat \to nat$ "contains" the partial functions on the ordinary natural numbers in a straightforward way. This will allow us to define an ordering on total functions that reflects the set-theoretic containment $\mathit{fix}^{[n]}\ F \subseteq \mathit{fix}^{[n+1]}\ F$ of partial functions. In addition, all functions in domain-theoretic models will be continuous, in a certain sense. This will imply that least fixed-points can be characterized as least upper bounds of countable sets like $\{\mathit{fix}^{[n]}\ F \mid n \geq 0\}$.

A specific problem related to recursion is the interpretation of terms that define nonterminating computations. Since recursion allows us to write expressions that have no normal form, we must give meaning to expressions that do not seem to define any standard value. For example, it is impossible to simplify the PCF expression

$$\texttt{letrec}\ f\colon nat \to nat = \lambda x\colon nat.\ f\,(x+1)\ \texttt{in}\ f\,3$$

to a numeral, even though the type of this expression is *nat*. It is sensible to give this term type *nat*, since it is clear from the typing rules that if any term of this form were to have a normal form, the result would be a natural number. Rather than say that the value of this expression is undefined, which would make the meaning function on models a partial function, we extend the domain of "natural numbers" to include an additional value $\bot_{nat}$ to represent nonterminating computations of type *nat*. This gives us a way to represent partial functions as total ones, since we may view any partial numeric function as a function into the domain of natural numbers with $\bot_{nat}$ added.

The ordering of a domain is intended to characterize what might be called "information content" or "degree of definedness." Since a nonterminating computation is less informative than any terminating computation, $\bot_{nat}$ will be the least element in the ordering on the domain of natural numbers. We order $nat \to nat$ point-wise, which gives rise to an ordering that strongly resembles the containment ordering on partial functions. For example, since the constant function $\lambda x\colon nat.\ \bot_{nat}$ produces the least element from any argument, it will be the least element of $nat \to nat$. Functions that are defined on some arguments, and intuitively "undefined" elsewhere, will be greater than the least element of the domain, but less than functions that are defined on more arguments. By requiring that every function be continuous with respect to the ordering, we may interpret *fix* as the least fixed-point functional. For continuous F, the least fixed point will be the least upper bound of all finite expansions $fix^{[k]}\ F$.

5.2.2 Complete Partial Orders, Lifting and Cartesian Products

Many families of ordered structures with the general properties described above are called *domains*. We will focus on the complete partial orders, since most families of domains are obtained from these by imposing additional conditions. In this section, we define complete partial orders and investigate two operations on complete partial orders, lifting and cartesian product. Lifting is useful for building domains with least elements, an important step in finding fixed points, and for relating total and partial functions. Cartesian products of CPOs are used to interpret product types.

The definition of complete partial order requires subsidiary definitions of partial order and directed set. A *partial order* $\langle D, \leq \rangle$ is a set D with a reflexive, anti-symmetric and transitive relation $\leq$. Reflexivity means that $d \leq d$ for every $d \in D$, and transitivity means that if $d \leq d'$ and $d' \leq d''$, then $d \leq d''$. A relation is anti-symmetric if $d \leq d'$ and $d' \leq d$ imply $d = d'$. Antisymmetry implies that there are no "loops" $d \leq d' \leq d$ with $d \neq d'$. (See Exercise 5.2.3.) Any set can be considered a partial order using the *discrete order* $x \leq y$ iff $x = y$. Another example of a partial order is the *prefix order* on sequences. More precisely, let S be any set and let S^* be the set of finite sequences of elements of S. We say $s \leq_{\text{prefix}} s'$ iff sequence s is an initial segment of sequence s'. This gives is a partial order $\langle S^*, \leq_{\text{prefix}} \rangle$. We can also partially order the finite and infinite sequences this way. (See Exercise 5.2.4.)

If $\langle D, \leq \rangle$ is a partial order, then an *upper bound* of a subset $S \subseteq D$ is an element $x \in D$ with $y \leq x$ for every $y \in S$. A *least upper bound* of S is an upper bound which is $\leq$ every upper bound of S. It is easy to see that if a subset S of a partial order D has a least upper bound, the least upper bound is unique (by antisymmetry).

If $\langle D, \leq \rangle$ is a partial order, then a subset $S \subseteq D$ is *directed* if every finite $S_0 \subseteq S$ has an upper bound in S. One property of directed sets is that every directed set is nonempty. The reason is that even the empty subset of a directed S must have an upper bound in S. It is easy to see that if $S \subseteq D$ is linearly ordered, which means that $x \leq y$ or $y \leq x$ for all $x, y \in S$, then S is directed. Another example of a directed set is the partial order $\{a_0, b_0, a_1, b_1, a_2, b_3, \ldots\}$ with $a_i \leq a_j, b_j$ for all $i < j$ and similarly $b_i \leq a_j, b_j$ for all $i < j$. This partial order consists of two linear orders, $a_0 \leq a_1 \leq a_2 \leq \ldots$ and $b_0 \leq b_1 \leq b_2 \leq \ldots$, connected together so that a_i and b_i have upper bounds a_{i+1} and b_{i+1}, but no least upper bound.

A *complete partial order,* or *CPO* for short, is a partial order $\langle D, \leq \rangle$ such that every directed $S \subseteq D$ has a least upper bound, written $\bigvee S$. Any set may be considered a complete partial order using the discrete order. It is also easy to show that any finite partial order is a CPO.

A non-example is that with respect to the ordinary arithmetic ordering, the natural numbers are not a CPO. The reason is that the set $\mathcal{N}$ itself is directed, but has no least upper bound. If we add an extra element ∞ greater than all the ordinary numbers, then we have a CPO. Any closed interval of the real line, under the standard order is easily seen to be a CPO. A nontrivial closed interval of the rational numbers fails to be a CPO, however, since there are increasing sequences without least upper bounds, namely, the sequences of rationals whose least upper bounds would be irrational.

A trivial but very useful fact is that if $S, T \subseteq D$ are directed, and every element of S is less than or equal to some element of T, then $\bigvee S \leq \bigvee T$. In particular $\bigvee S = \bigvee T$ if every element of either set is $\leq$ some element of the other. This is used in Exercise 5.2.6 at the end of this section.

In interpreting *fix,* we will be particularly interested in CPOs that have least elements. The reason is that every continuous function on a CPO with a least element has a fixed point, as we shall see. If $\mathcal{D} = \langle D, \leq \rangle$ is a partial order with least element, then we say $\mathcal{D}$ is *pointed.* In this case, we write $\perp_D$ for the least element of D. When the CPO is clear from context, we will omit the subscript from $\perp_D$.

A simple class of pointed CPOs are the so-called *lifted sets.* If A is any set, then we write

$A_\perp$ for the CPO whose elements are $A \cup \{\perp\}$, ordered so that $x \leq y$ iff $x = y$ or $x = \perp$. The CPO $A_\perp$ is commonly called "*A lifted.*" We may also lift any CPO $\mathcal{D} = \langle D, \leq_D \rangle$. The result, $\mathcal{D}_\perp$, has elements $D \cup \{\perp\}$, where $\perp$ is distinct from all elements of D. We order $\mathcal{D}_\perp$ so that $x \leq y$ iff $x = \perp$ or $x, y \in D$ with $x \leq_D y$. In the case that $\leq_D$ is the discrete order, this is the same as the lifted set $D_\perp$.

Lemma 5.2.1 If $\mathcal{D}$ is a CPO then $\mathcal{D}_\perp$ is a pointed CPO (CPO with a least element).

Proof The proof is easy. The directed subset $\{\perp\}$ of $D_\perp$ has least upper bound $\perp$. A directed subset S of $D_\perp$ that is not the singleton $\{\perp\}$ has the same least upper bound as the subset $S - \{\perp\}$ of D. Therefore every directed subset of $D_\perp$ has a least upper bound. The least element of $D_\perp$ is clearly $\perp$. ■

Two examples that are of particular interest in connection with PCF are $\mathcal{N}_\perp$, the lifted natural numbers, and $\mathcal{B}_\perp$, the lifted booleans. The CPO $\mathcal{N}_\perp$ looks like this

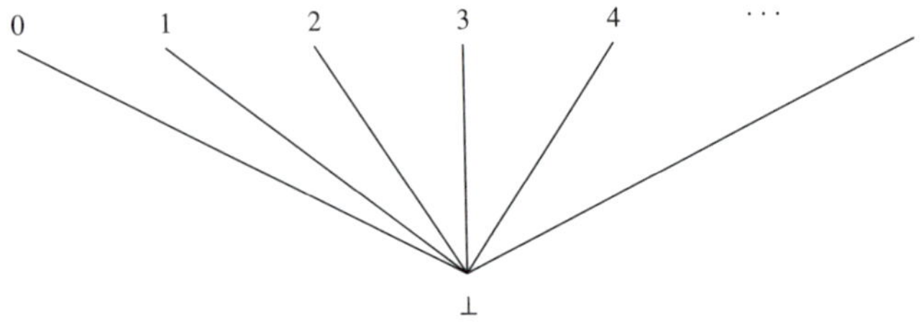

Since this picture is quite flat, a lifted set is sometimes referred to as a *flat CPO*.

If $\mathcal{D} = \langle D, \leq_D \rangle$ and $\mathcal{E} = \langle E, \leq_E \rangle$ are CPOs, then we may define a cartesian product CPO as follows. We let $\mathcal{D} \times \mathcal{E} = \langle D \times E, \leq_{D \times E} \rangle$, where $D \times E$ is the familiar set of ordered pairs, and the ordering $\leq_{D\times E}$ is defined as follows.

$\langle d, e \rangle \leq_{D\times E} \langle d', e' \rangle$ iff $d \leq_D d'$ and $e \leq_E e'$

If $S \subseteq D \times E$, it is useful to define sets $\mathbf{Proj}_1 S = \{d \mid \langle d, e \rangle \in S\}$ and $\mathbf{Proj}_2 S = \{e \mid \langle d, e \rangle \in S\}$.

Lemma 5.2.2 Suppose $\mathcal{D}$ and $\mathcal{E}$ are CPOs. Their product, $\mathcal{D} \times \mathcal{E}$, is a CPO which is pointed (has a least element) if both $\mathcal{D}$ and $\mathcal{E}$ are pointed. Moreover, if $S \subseteq D \times E$ is directed, then $\bigvee S = \langle \bigvee S_1, \bigvee S_2 \rangle$, where $S_i = \mathbf{Proj}_i S$.

Before reading the proof, you might find it useful to draw the partial order $\mathcal{B}_\perp \times \mathcal{B}_\perp$, which has nine elements. Find the least element and check that every directed set has a least upper bound.

Proof We first check that each directed set in $\mathcal{D} \times \mathcal{E}$ has a least upper bound. Let $S \subseteq D \times E$ be any directed set and define sets S_1 and S_2 by $S_i = \mathbf{Proj}_i S$. We prove the lemma by showing that if S is directed, then $S_1 \subseteq D$ is directed and $S_2 \subseteq E$ is directed. It is then easy to check that the least upper bound of S is the pair $\langle \bigvee S_1, \bigvee S_2 \rangle$. We leave this last step to the reader.

To show that S_1 is directed, consider any finite subset $T \subseteq S_1$. We must show that T has an upper bound in S_1. For every $d \in T$ there is an element $e \in E$ with $\langle d, e \rangle \in S$, by definition of S_1. This means that there is a finite subset $R \subseteq S$ with $\mathbf{Proj}_1 R = T$. But since the first component of an upper bound of R gives us an upper bound of T, it follows that T has an upper bound in S_1. Similar reasoning shows that S_2 is also directed.

It is easy to see that if $\mathcal{D}$ and $\mathcal{E}$ have least elements $\bot_D$ and $\bot_E$, then $\langle \bot_D, \bot_E \rangle$ is the least element of $\mathcal{D} \times \mathcal{E}$. ■

Exercise 5.2.3 Suppose $\leq$ is a reflexive and transitive order on D, and define the relation $<$ on D by $x < y$ iff $x \leq y$ and $x \neq y$. Show that $<$ is transitive iff $\leq$ is antisymmetric.

Exercise 5.2.4 Let S be a set with at least two elements and consider the following sets of sequences, partially ordered by the prefix ordering $s \leq_{\text{prefix}} s'$ iff sequence s is an initial segment of sequence s':

S^* finite sequences from S

S^+ finite, nonempty sequences from S

S^∞ finite and countably infinite sequences from S

A *countably infinite sequence* is given by a function from the natural numbers to S. (Specifically, a sequence may be regarded as a function $f : \mathcal{N} \to S$, with $f(n)$ giving the nth element of the sequence.)

(a) Say briefly why all three cases are partial orders. Since $S^+ \subset S^* \subset S^\infty$, it suffices to check that S^∞ is partially ordered.

(b) Which partial orders have a least element? What is it?

(c) What do directed sets in all three partial orders look like? In particular, if a set $\{s, s'\}$ with two elements is directed, what is the necessary relationship between s and s'?

(d) Which of these three partial orders are CPOs?

Exercise 5.2.5 Let $P = \mathcal{N} \rightharpoonup \mathcal{N}$ be the set of partial functions on the natural numbers, where a *partial function* $f : \mathcal{N} \rightharpoonup \mathcal{N}$ is a set of ordered pairs, $f \subseteq \mathcal{N} \times \mathcal{N}$, such that if $\langle x, y \rangle, \langle x', y' \rangle \in f$ with $x = x'$, then $y = y'$. We partially order P by set inclusion.

(a) Describe the directed subsets of P.

(b) Give an example of an infinite subset of P which is not directed.

(c) Show that every directed subset of P has a least upper bound.

Exercise 5.2.6 An alternate definition of CPO uses chains instead of directed sets. The general proof that these definitions are equivalent requires well-ordered chains, for ordinals larger than ω, and the axiom of choice. However, for countable CPOs the proof is much simpler. (A set A is countable if there is a function $f: \mathcal{N} \to A$ from the natural numbers *onto* A.) If D is a partial order, then an *ω-chain in D* is a non-decreasing, countable sequence $d_0 \leq d_1 \leq d_2 \leq \ldots$ of elements of D. A partial order D is an *ω-chain CPO* if every ω-chain in D has a least upper bound. Show that if D is a countable partial order, then D is an ω-chain CPO iff every directed subset of D has a least upper bound. (A related result for arbitrary CPOs is given in [Mar76]; see also [SP82, Page 775].)

Exercise 5.2.7 In the proof of Lemma 5.2.2, we define two sets $\mathbf{Proj}_1 S$ and $\mathbf{Proj}_2 S$ from S and show that if S is directed then so are both of these sets. Prove that the converse of this statement is false by finding a subset S of $\mathcal{B}_\bot \times \mathcal{B}_\bot$ that is not directed, but with both $\mathbf{Proj}_1 S$ and $\mathbf{Proj}_2 S$ directed.

5.2.3 Continuous Functions

The continuous functions on CPOs include all of the usual functions we use in programming, and give us a class of functions with fixed points. In this section, we show that the collection of all continuous functions from one CPO to another forms a CPO. This is an essential step towards constructing a model with each type a CPO, since in order to do so, function types must be interpreted as CPOs.

Suppose $\mathcal{D} = \langle D, \leq_D \rangle$ and $\mathcal{E} = \langle E, \leq_E \rangle$ are CPOs, and $f: D \to E$ is a function on the underlying sets. If $S \subseteq D$, we will write $f(S)$ for the subset of E given by

$$f(S) = \{f(d) \mid d \in S\}.$$

We say f is *monotonic* if $d \leq d'$ implies $f(d) \leq f(d')$. It is easy to see that if f is monotonic and S is directed, then $f(S)$ is directed. A monotonic function f is *continuous* if, for every directed $S \subseteq D$, we have $f(\bigvee S) = \bigvee f(S)$.

A degenerate but important example is that if $\mathcal{D}$ is discretely ordered, then *every* function on $\mathcal{D}$ is continuous. A constant function on any CPO is also trivially continuous. Another example is that any continuous function, in the ordinary sense of calculus, on a closed interval $[x, y]$ of the real line is also a continuous function when we regard $[x, y]$ as a CPO. However, the converse fails, since a continuous function, as defined for CPOs, need only be continuous "from the left." (See Exercise 5.2.12 below.)

It is easy to find examples of continuous functions on lifted sets, since any monotonic function from a lifted set $A_\perp$ to any CPO is continuous. The reason is that in $A_\perp$, all nontrivial directed sets have the form $\{\perp, a\}$ and every monotonic function f must map $\bigvee\{\perp, a\} = a$ to

$$\bigvee f(\{\perp, a\}) = \bigvee\{f(\perp), f(a)\} = f(a).$$

It is useful to work out a general construction for continuous functions from one lifted CPO to another. If $\mathcal{D}$ and $\mathcal{E}$ are CPOs, and $f: D \to E$ is continuous, we define the *lifted function* $f_\perp: (D \cup \{\perp\}) \to (E \cup \{\perp\})$ by

$$f_\perp(d) = \begin{cases} f(d) & \text{if } d \in D \\ \perp & \text{otherwise} \end{cases}$$

We summarize the main properties of lifting in the following lemma. If f is a function on pointed CPOs with $f(\perp) = \perp$, then we say f is *strict.*

Lemma 5.2.8 Let $\mathcal{D}$ and $\mathcal{E}$ be CPOs. If $f: \mathcal{D} \to \mathcal{E}$ is continuous, then $f_\perp: \mathcal{D}_\perp \to \mathcal{E}_\perp$ is strict and continuous.

An important special case is that if A and B are sets and $f: A \to B$, then $f_\perp: A_\perp \to B_\perp$ is a strict continuous function.

Proof A lifted function $f_\perp: \mathcal{D}_\perp \to \mathcal{E}_\perp$ is strict by definition. We assume that $f: \mathcal{D} \to \mathcal{E}$ is continuous and show that $f_\perp$ is continuous. To show this, let S be any directed set in $\mathcal{D}_\perp$. We must show that $f_\perp(\bigvee S) = \bigvee f_\perp(S)$. The main idea is that either $S = \{\perp\}$ or the difference between f and $f_\perp$ does not matter.

If $S = \{\perp\}$, then $f_\perp(\bigvee S) = f_\perp(\perp) = \perp = \bigvee f_\perp(S)$. If $S \neq \{\perp\}$, then let $S' \subseteq D$ be $S - \{\perp\}$. Since $S \subseteq D$ and every element of S' is greater than $\perp$ of $\mathcal{D}_\perp$, we have $\bigvee S = \bigvee S' \in D$ and $\bigvee f_\perp(S) = \bigvee f_\perp(S') = \bigvee f(S')$. Since f is continuous, we have $f_\perp(\bigvee S) = f(\bigvee S') = \bigvee f(S') = \bigvee f_\perp(S)$. This proves the lemma. ∎

It is worth noting that strict functions are not sufficient to model lambda calculus, and therefore PCF; we need non-strict functions. The reason is that we can define constant functions using lambda terms, and constant functions do not necessarily map $\perp$ to $\perp$. In particular, if we interpret *nat* as the flat CPO $\mathcal{N}_\perp$, the interpretation of $(\mathit{fix}\,\lambda x{:}\,\mathit{nat}.\,x)$ will be $\perp$. Therefore, the value of the term $(\lambda x{:}\,\mathit{nat}.\,3)(\mathit{fix}\,\lambda x{:}\,\mathit{nat}.\,x)$ will be the result of applying a constant function to $\perp$. To be faithful to PCF, the interpretation of this application must be 3, since we can prove $(\lambda x{:}\,\mathit{nat}.\,3)(\mathit{fix}\,\lambda x{:}\,\mathit{nat}.\,x) = 3$, not $\perp$. Therefore, we cannot model PCF, or typed lambda calculus, using only strict functions. On the other hand, there is a close connection between strict functions and eager PCF, described in Section 2.4.5.

To associate a CPO with each type, we must be able to view the collection of continuous functions from one CPO to another as a CPO. We will partially order functions point-wise, as follows. Suppose $\mathcal{D} = \langle D, \leq_D \rangle$ and $\mathcal{E} = \langle E, \leq_E \rangle$ are CPOs. For continuous $f, g \colon D \to E$, we say $f \leq_{D \to E} g$ if, for every $d \in D$, we have $f(d) \leq_E g(d)$. We will write $\mathcal{D} \to \mathcal{E} = \langle D \to E, \leq_{D \to E} \rangle$ for the collection of continuous functions from $\mathcal{D}$ to $\mathcal{E}$, ordered point-wise. Some useful notation is that if $S \subseteq D \to E$ is a set of functions, and $d \in D$, then $S(d) \subseteq E$ is the set given by

$$S(d) = \{f(d) \mid f \in S\}.$$

Example 5.2.9 There are eleven monotonic functions from $\mathcal{B}_\perp$ to itself, listed in the following table.

	$f(\perp)$	$f(\mathit{true})$	$f(\mathit{false})$
f_0	$\perp$	$\perp$	$\perp$
f_1	$\perp$	*true*	$\perp$
f_2	$\perp$	*false*	$\perp$
f_3	$\perp$	$\perp$	*true*
f_4	$\perp$	$\perp$	*false*
f_5	$\perp$	*true*	*true*
f_6	$\perp$	*false*	*true*
f_7	$\perp$	*true*	*false*
f_8	$\perp$	*false*	*false*
f_9	*true*	*true*	*true*
f_{10}	*false*	*false*	*false*

All are continuous since $\mathcal{B}_\perp$ is finite. These functions are ordered as shown in Figure 5.1. The extension $\mathit{not}_\perp \colon \mathcal{B}_\perp \to \mathcal{B}_\perp$ of negation is function f_6 in this table. Although $\mathit{not} \colon \mathcal{B} \to \mathcal{B}$ has no fixed point, it is easy to see that $\perp$ is a fixed point of $\mathit{not}_\perp$. ∎

Lemma 5.2.10 For any CPOs $\mathcal{D}$ and $\mathcal{E}$, the collection $\mathcal{D} \to \mathcal{E}$ of continuous functions, ordered point-wise, is a CPO. In particular, if $S \subseteq D \to E$ is directed, the least upper bound is the function f given by $f(d) = \bigvee S(d)$. The CPO $\mathcal{D} \to \mathcal{E}$ has a least element if $\mathcal{E}$ does.

Proof It is easy to check that $\mathcal{D} \to \mathcal{E}$ is a partial order and that if $\mathcal{E}$ has a least element then $\lambda x \colon \mathcal{D}.\, \perp_E$ is the least element of $\mathcal{D} \to \mathcal{E}$. It remains to show that every directed

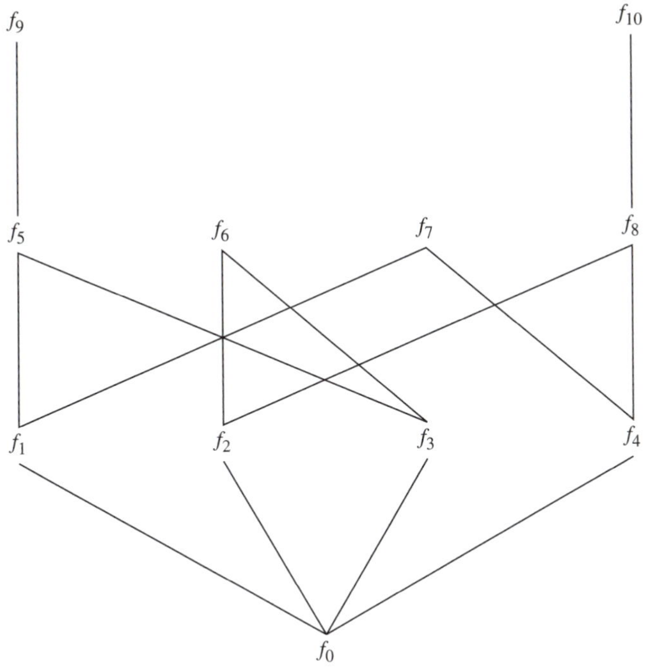

Figure 5.1
Ordering of continuous functions $\mathcal{B}_\perp \to \mathcal{B}_\perp$

set has a least upper bound. Suppose $S \subseteq D \to E$ is directed. We first show that for any $d \in D$, the subset $S(d) \subseteq E$ is directed. By definition of $S(d)$, any n elements of this set will have the form $g_1(d), \ldots, g_n(d)$ for some $g_1, \ldots, g_n \in S$. But since S is directed, these n functions must have some upper bound $g \in S$. By the point-wise ordering on S, it follows that $g(d) \in S(d)$ is an upper bound in $S(d)$. Therefore $S(d)$ is directed and it makes sense to define the function $f: D \to E$ by $f(d) = \bigvee S(d)$.

The next step is to verify that f is the least upper bound of S. It is easy to see from the definition of $S(d)$ and the definition of the ordering on functions that $g: D \to E$ is an upper bound of S iff $g(d)$ is an upper bound of $S(d)$ for every $d \in D$. Since f satisfies this condition, and is the least such function, f is the least upper bound of S.

The final step of the proof is to show that f is continuous. This is necessary, since otherwise we have not shown that the least upper bound of S belongs to the set of continuous functions $D \to E$. Suppose $T \subseteq D$ is directed. Then we have the following calculation.

$$
\begin{aligned}
f(\bigvee T) &= \bigvee\{g(\bigvee T) \mid g \in S\} \\
&= \bigvee\{\bigvee g(T) \mid g \in S\} \text{ by continuity of each } g \in S \\
&= \bigvee\{g(t) \mid g \in S,\ t \in T\} \\
&= \bigvee\{\bigvee\{g(t) \mid g \in S\}\, t \in T\} \\
&= \bigvee\{f(t) \mid t \in T\} \\
&= \bigvee f(T)
\end{aligned}
$$

The reader is advised to study this calculation and understand why each step makes sense. ■

If $\mathcal{D}$ and $\mathcal{E}$ are CPOs, we will write $f\colon \mathcal{D} \to \mathcal{E}$ to indicate that f is a *continuous* function from $\mathcal{D}$ to $\mathcal{E}$.

It is not hard to show that n-ary function $f\colon D_1 \times \ldots \times D_n \to E$ is continuous, as a function on the product CPO, iff it is continuous in each argument, varied separately. This is explained in more detail in Exercise 5.2.17. We also have the following general list of continuous operations.

Lemma 5.2.11 Pairing, projection, application and composition are continuous. In more detail,

(a) If $S \subseteq D$ and $T \subseteq E$ are directed, then $\langle \bigvee S, \bigvee T\rangle = \bigvee\{\langle s, t\rangle \mid s \in S, t \in T\}$,

(b) If $S \subseteq D \times E$ is directed, then $\mathbf{Proj}_i(\bigvee S) = \bigvee\{\mathbf{Proj}_i(x) \mid x \in S\}$,

(c) If $S \subseteq D \to E$ and $T \subseteq D$ are directed, then $\bigvee S(\bigvee T) = \bigvee\{f(x) \mid f \in S, x \in T\}$,

(d) If $S \subseteq D \to E$ and $T \subseteq E \to F$ are directed, then $(\bigvee S) \circ (\bigvee T) = \bigvee\{g \circ f \mid f \in S, g \in T\}$.

The proof of this lemma is Exercise 5.2.18 below. An interesting example, parallel-or, appears in Exercise 5.2.19.

Exercise 5.2.12 Let $[x, y]$ be a closed interval of the real line, and let $f\colon [x, y] \to [x, y]$. Recall that $[x, y]$ is a CPO, when ordered in the usual way. Show that if f is monotonic and continuous, in the usual ϵ, δ sense of calculus, then f is a continuous function on CPOs. Show that the converse fails by finding a CPO-continuous function g that is not ϵ, δ-continuous.

Exercise 5.2.13 A partial order $\langle P, \leq\rangle$ is *essentially flat* if every directed subset of P is finite.

(a) Show that if $\langle P, \leq \rangle$ is an essentially flat partial order, then $\langle P, \leq \rangle$ is a CPO.

(b) Suppose $\langle D, \leq_D \rangle$ and $\langle E, \leq_E \rangle$ are CPOs and $f : D \to E$ is monotonic. Show that if D is essentially flat, then f is continuous.

Exercise 5.2.14 Consider the following alternative ordering on functions:

$$f \leq_{D \to E} g \text{ iff } \forall d \leq_D d' \in D.\ f(d) \leq_E g(d').$$

Show that this is equivalent to the ordering defined in this section for continuous functions from CPO $\mathcal{D}$ to $\mathcal{E}$.

Exercise 5.2.15 Find CPOs $\mathcal{D}$ and $\mathcal{E}$ and a subset S of the continuous functions from $\mathcal{D}$ to $\mathcal{E}$ such that each $S(d)$ is directed but S itself is not.

Exercise 5.2.16 Let $f : \mathcal{D} \to \mathcal{D}$ be continuous. Show that for each $n \geq 0$, we have $f^{n+1}(\bot) \geq f^n(\bot)$.

Exercise 5.2.17 If $f : D_1 \times \ldots \times D_n \to E$, then there are two ways that we might think of f being continuous. The first is that we could fix $n - 1$ arguments, and ask whether the resulting unary function is continuous from D_i to E. The second is that since the product $D_1 \times \ldots \times D_n$ of CPOs is a CPO, we can apply the general definition of continuous function from one CPO to another. Show that these two coincide, *i.e.*, a function $f : D_1 \times \ldots \times D_n \to E$ is continuous from the product CPO $D_1 \times \ldots \times D_n$ to E iff each unary function obtained by holding $n - 1$ arguments fixed is continuous.

Exercise 5.2.18 Prove the four parts of Lemma 5.2.11 as parts *(a)*, *(b)*, *(c)* and *(d)* of this exercise.

Exercise 5.2.19 Show that the parallel-or function described in Section 2.5.6 is continuous. More specifically, show that there is a continuous function $por : \mathcal{B}_\bot \to \mathcal{B}_\bot \to \mathcal{B}_\bot$ satisfying

$$\begin{aligned} &\textit{por true } x &&= \textit{true} \\ &\textit{por } x \textit{ true} &&= \textit{true} \\ &\textit{por false false} &&= \textit{false} \end{aligned}$$

by defining the function completely and proving that it is continuous. You may use the names for functions in $\mathcal{B}_\bot \to \mathcal{B}_\bot$ given in Example 5.2.9.

5.2.4 Fixed Points and the Full Continuous Hierarchy

Our current motivation for studying domain-theoretic models is to construct Henkin models of typed lambda calculi with fixed-point operators. The type frame, $\mathcal{A}$, called the *full continuous* $\lambda^{\times,\rightarrow}$ *hierarchy over* CPOs $\langle A^{b_0}, \leq_0\rangle, \ldots, \langle A^{b_k}, \leq_k\rangle$ is defined by taking $A^{b_0}, \ldots, A^{b_k}$ as base types, and

$$A^{\sigma\times\tau} = A^\sigma \times A^\tau$$

$$A^{\sigma\rightarrow\tau} = \text{all continuous } f\colon \langle A^\sigma, \leq_\sigma\rangle \rightarrow \langle A^\tau, \leq_\tau\rangle$$

with $A^{\sigma\times\tau}$ ordered coordinate-wise by $\leq_{\sigma\times\tau}$ and $A^{\sigma\rightarrow\tau}$ ordered point-wise by $\leq_{\sigma\rightarrow\tau}$. By Lemmas 5.2.2 and 5.2.10, each $\langle A^\sigma, \leq_\sigma\rangle$ is a CPO. The main result of this section is that the full continuous type hierarchy over any CPOs forms a Henkin model, with least-fixed-point operators at all pointed types. Before proving that the full continuous hierarchy is a Henkin model, we consider the interpretation of *fix*.

We say a is the *least fixed point* of f if $a = f(a)$ and, whenever $b = f(b)$, we have $a \leq b$. As suggested in Section 5.2.1, the least fixed point of any function f is the least upper bound of the set obtained by repeatedly applying f to the least element of its domain.

Lemma 5.2.20 If $\mathcal{D}$ is a pointed CPO and $f\colon\mathcal{D}\rightarrow\mathcal{D}$ is continuous, then f has a least fixed point

$$\mathit{fix}_{\mathcal{D}}\, f = \bigvee\{f^n(\bot) \mid n \geq 0\}.$$

In addition, the map $\mathit{fix}_{\mathcal{D}}$ is continuous.

Proof Let $f\colon\mathcal{D}\rightarrow\mathcal{D}$ be continuous. Since f is monotonic, and $\bot \leq f(\bot)$, we can see that $f^n(\bot) \leq f^{n+1}(\bot)$. It follows that $\{f^n(\bot) \mid n \geq 0\}$ is linearly ordered and therefore directed. Let a be the least upper bound $a = \bigvee\{f^n(\bot) \mid n \geq 0\}$.

We must show that a is a fixed point of f. By continuity of f,

$$\begin{aligned} f(a) &= f(\bigvee\{f^n(\bot) \mid n \geq 0\}) \\ &= \bigvee\{f^{(n+1)}(\bot) \mid n \geq 0\} \end{aligned}$$

But since $\{f^n(\bot)\}$ and $\{f^{(n+1)}(\bot)\}$ have the same least upper bound, we have $f(a) = a$.

To see that a is the least fixed point of f, suppose $b = f(b)$ is any fixed point. Since $\bot \leq b$, we have $f(\bot) \leq f(b)$ and similarly $f^n(\bot) \leq f^n(b)$ for any $n \geq 0$. But since b is a fixed point of f, $f^n(b) = b$. Therefore b is an upper bound for the set $\{f^n(\bot) \mid n \geq 0\}$. Since the least upper bound of this set is a, it follows that $a \leq b$.

The final step is to show that the function fix_D mapping f to $\bigvee\{f^n(\bot)\}$ is itself continuous. Let us suppose that $S \subseteq D \to D$ is directed, with $\bigvee S = f$. We must show that $\mathit{fix}_D\, f = \bigvee\{\mathit{fix}_D\, g \mid g \in S\}$. By continuity of function application (Lemma 5.2.11c), each $f^n(\bot)$ is the least upper bound of the set of all $g^n(\bot)$ with $g \in S$. Therefore,

$$\mathit{fix}_D\, f = \bigvee\{f^n(\bot) \mid n \geq 0\}$$

$$[1.5ex] = \bigvee\{g^n(\bot) \mid n \geq 0,\, g \in S\}.$$

It is easy to see that $\{g^n(\bot) \mid n \geq 0,\, g \in S\}$ and $\{\mathit{fix}_D\, g \mid g \in S\}$ have the same least upper bound, since any upper bound for the $g^n(\bot)$'s must be an upper bound for the $(\mathit{fix}_D\, g)$'s. Therefore

$$\mathit{fix}_D\, f = \bigvee\{\mathit{fix}_D\, g \mid g \in S\}.$$

This proves the lemma. ■

A trivial example is $\mathit{fix}\ \mathit{id}$, where $\mathit{id}\colon \mathcal{D} \to \mathcal{D}$ is the identity function on the pointed CPO $\mathcal{D}$. We can calculate the least fixed point of id as follows.

$$\begin{aligned}\mathit{fix}\ \mathit{id} &= \bigvee\{\, \mathit{id}^n(\bot_D) \mid n \geq 0\,\}\\ &= \bigvee\{\,\bot_D\,\}\\ &= \bot_D\end{aligned}$$

This calculation clearly gives the right answer, since $\bot$ is a fixed point of the identity function, and no element of D is less than $\bot$.

Example 5.2.21 Let $\mathcal{PN}$ be the collection of all subsets of the natural numbers, $\mathcal{N}$, ordered by set containment. It is easy to check that this is a CPO since the union of a set of directed subsets is an element of $\mathcal{PN}$. (In fact, $\mathcal{PN}$ is a special kind of partial order called a lattice.) The least element of $\mathcal{PN}$ is the empty set, $\emptyset$. We will show that the function f with

$$f(A) = A \cup \{\text{ the least } i \in \mathcal{N} \text{ not in } A, \text{ if one exists }\}$$

is continuous and determine its least fixed point.

It is easy to see that f is monotonic, since if $A \subseteq B \subseteq \mathcal{N}$, and i is the least number not in A, then either $i \in B \subseteq f(B)$, or f adds i to B. To check continuity, suppose S is some directed set of subsets of $\mathcal{N}$. We must show that $f(\bigcup S) = \bigcup f(S)$. Let n be the least natural number not in $\bigcup S$ and let A be the set of all i that are the least natural number not in some set $B \in S$. Since $f(\bigcup S) = \bigcup S \cup \{n\}$ and $\bigcup f(S) = \bigcup S \cup A$, it suffices to show that every $i \in A$ that is different from n is in some $B \in S$. Since n is not in any $B \in S$, no element of A is greater than n. But if any $i \in A$ less than n was not in any $B \in S$, then f would add this i to $\bigcup S$. Therefore every $i \in A$ different from n must be in some $B \in S$.

Since f is continuous, its least fixed-point is the union of the sets in the sequence $\emptyset, f(\emptyset), f(f(\emptyset)), \ldots, f^k(\emptyset), \ldots$. But it is easy to see that $f^k(\emptyset) = \{0, \ldots, k-1\}$, and therefore *fix* $f = \mathcal{N}$. We can also see that $\mathcal{N}$ is a fixed point of f directly, and it must be the least fixed point since $f(A) \neq A$ for any $A \subseteq \mathcal{N}$ not containing all the natural numbers.

■

Example 5.2.22 Let Σ be an algebraic signature and let $\mathcal{E}$ be the set of all well-formed equations between Σ-terms. Let $\mathcal{C}$ be the set of all subsets of $\mathcal{E}$. We may regard $\mathcal{C}$ as a CPO, ordered by set containment. Let $F: \mathcal{C} \to \mathcal{C}$ be the function mapping any set $H \in \mathcal{C}$ to the set of all equations that are either axioms of the algebraic proof system, elements of H, or provable from equations in H using a single inference rule. In this example, we will demonstrate the following properties of provability.

(a) The function F is monotonic and continuous.

(b) The least fixed point of F is the set of all valid formulas.

(c) Let $H \in \mathcal{C}$ and let $T(H) = \bigvee\{F^n(H) \mid n \geq 0\}$. Then an equation E is in $T(H)$ iff E is provable from H.

It is useful to introduce some additional notation. Let A be the set of all equations that are instances of axioms of the algebraic proof system. For any set of equations H, let $P(H)$ denote the set of all equations that are provable from equations in $H \cup A$ using a single inference rule. These definitions allow us to write F as

$$F(H) = A \cup H \cup P(H).$$

(a) We show that F is monotonic as follows. Suppose $H_1 \subseteq H_2$. It suffices to demonstrate that $P(H_1) \subseteq P(H_2)$. If $E \in P(H_1)$, then let $S \subseteq H_1 \cup A$ be the equations used as hypotheses in the inference rule that yields E. Since $S \subseteq (H_1 \cup A) \subseteq (H_2 \cup A)$, we can see that E is also provable in a single step from equations in $H_2 \cup A$. Therefore $E \in P(H_2)$.

To demonstrate continuity, let C be a directed subset of $\mathcal{C}$. Recall that the least upper bound of C is the ordinary union $\bigcup C$. Since C is directed, any finite collection of subsets, $S_1, \ldots, S_k \in C$, are contained in some $S \supseteq S_1, \ldots, S_k$ also in C.

We must show that $F(\bigcup C) = \bigcup F(C)$. Since $F(\bigcup C) = A \cup \bigcup C \cup P(\bigcup C)$ and

$$\begin{aligned}\bigcup F(C) &= \bigcup\{A \cup S \cup P(S) \mid S \in C\}\\ &= A \cup \bigcup\{S \mid S \in C\} \cup \bigcup\{P(S) \mid S \in C\}\\ &= A \cup \bigcup C \cup \bigcup P(C)\end{aligned}$$

it suffices to show that $P(\bigcup C) = \bigcup P(C)$. By monotonicity, we have $P(S) \subseteq P(\bigcup C)$ for each $S \in C$, and therefore $\bigcup P(C) \subseteq P(\bigcup C)$. Therefore, we only need to show that $P(\bigcup C) \subseteq \bigcup P(C)$. For any equation $E \in P(\bigcup C)$, there is a finite set $S \subseteq \bigcup C$ of equations used to prove E in a single step. Since S is finite, there is a finite list of subsets, $S_1, \ldots, S_k \in C$, with $S \subseteq S_1 \cup \ldots \cup S_k$. Since C is directed, there must be a single $S' \in C$ with $(S_1 \cup \ldots \cup S_k) \subseteq S'$. From this, we can conclude that $E \in P(S')$ and therefore $E \in \bigcup P(C)$. This shows that $P(\bigcup C) \subseteq \bigcup P(C)$ and concludes the proof of continuity.

(b) By induction on n, we may prove that $F^n(\emptyset)$ is the set of all equations provable from axioms using proofs of depth less than n, where the depth of a proof is the depth of the tree we obtain by writing out the proof with each equation E the parent of all the equations $E_1, \ldots, E_k$ used as hypotheses in the inference rule yielding E. Since every proof is finite, $\mathit{fix}\ F = \bigcup\{F^n(\emptyset) \mid n \geq 0\}$ is the set of all equations provable from the axioms.

(c) Using an inductive argument similar to the one sketched in part (b), we may show that $F^n(H)$ is the set of all equations provable from axioms and equations in H using proofs of depth less than n. Since every proof has finite depth, $T(H) = \bigcup\{F^n(H) \mid n \geq 0\}$ is the set of all equations provable from axioms and elements of H. ∎

In the remainder of this section, we show that the full continuous hierarchy is a Henkin model. The following two lemmas are essential to the inductive proof of the environment model condition. The second is a continuous analogue to the *s-m-n* theorem for recursive functions.

Lemma 5.2.23 If $f : \mathcal{C} \to (\mathcal{D} \to \mathcal{E})$ and $g : \mathcal{C} \to \mathcal{D}$ are continuous, then so is the function $\mathit{App}\ f\ g$ given by

$(\mathit{App}\ f\ g)\, c = (f\, c)(g\, c)$

for all $c \in C$. In addition, the map *App* is continuous.

Lemma 5.2.24 If $f : \mathcal{C} \times \mathcal{D} \to \mathcal{E}$ is continuous, then there is a unique continuous function $(\mathit{Curry}\ f) : \mathcal{C} \to (\mathcal{D} \to \mathcal{E})$ such that for all $c \in C$ and $d \in D$, we have

$(\mathit{Curry}\ f)\, c\, d = f\langle c, d\rangle$.

In addition, the map *Curry* is continuous.

Proof of Lemma 5.2.23 The monotonicity of *App f g* and of *App* itself is left to the reader. We first show that *App f g* is continuous. If $S \subseteq C$ is directed, then we can make the following calculation:

$$\begin{aligned}\bigvee\{(App\ f\ g)\,c \mid c \in S\} &= \bigvee\{(f\ c)(g\ c) \mid c \in S\}\\ &= (\bigvee\{f\ c \mid c \in S\})\,(\bigvee\{g\ c \mid c \in S\}) \text{ by Lemma 5.2.11c}\\ &= f(\bigvee S)\,g(\bigvee S) \text{ by continuity of } f, g\\ &= (App\ f\ g)\,(\bigvee S)\end{aligned}$$

To show that *App* itself is continuous, suppose $S_1 \subseteq (C \to D \to E)$ and $S_2 \subseteq (C \to D)$ are directed. We can check continuity by this calculation:

$$\begin{aligned}\bigvee\{App\ f\ g \mid f \in S_1,\ g \in S_2\} &= \bigvee\{c \mapsto (f\ c)(g\ c) \mid f \in S_1,\ g \in S_2\}\\ &= c \mapsto \{(f\ c)(g\ c) \mid f \in S_1,\ g \in S_2\} \text{ by Lemma 5.2.10}\\ &= c \mapsto (\bigvee\{f\ c \mid f \in S_1\})\,(\bigvee\{g\ c \mid g \in S_2\}) \text{ by Lemma 5.2.11c}\\ &= c \mapsto ((\bigvee S_1)c)\,((\bigvee S_2)c) \text{ by Lemma 5.2.11c}\\ &= App\,(\bigvee S_1)\,(\bigvee S_2)\end{aligned}$$

■

Proof of Lemma 5.2.24 As in the proof of Lemma 5.2.23, we leave monotonicity to the reader. To show that *Curry f* is continuous, we assume that $S \subseteq C$ is directed. Using similar reasoning as in the proof of Lemma 5.2.23, we have the following continuity calculation.

$$\begin{aligned}\bigvee\{(Curry\ f)c \mid c \in S\} &= \bigvee\{d \mapsto f\langle c, d\rangle \mid c \in S\}\\ &= d \mapsto \bigvee\{f\langle c, d\rangle \mid c \in S\} \text{ by Lemma 5.2.10}\\ &= d \mapsto f\langle \bigvee S,\ d\rangle \text{ by Lemma 5.2.11}\\ &= (Curry\ f)\bigvee S\end{aligned}$$

To show that Curry itself is continuous, we assume that $S \subseteq (C \times D \to E)$ is directed and make a similar calculation:

$$\begin{aligned}\bigvee\{Curry\ f \mid f \in S\} &= \bigvee\{c \mapsto d \mapsto f\langle c, d\rangle \mid f \in S\}\\ &= c \mapsto \bigvee\{d \mapsto f\langle c, d\rangle \mid f \in S\} \text{ by Lemma 5.2.10}\\ &= c \mapsto (d \mapsto \bigvee\{f\langle c, d\rangle \mid f \in S\}) \text{ by Lemma 5.2.10}\end{aligned}$$

$$= c \mapsto (d \mapsto (\bigvee S) \langle c, d \rangle) \text{ by Lemma 5.2.11}$$

$$= Curry (\bigvee S)$$

This proves the lemma. ∎

We now show that the full continuous hierarchy is a Henkin model.

Lemma 5.2.25 The full continuous hierarchy over any collection of CPOs is a Henkin model.

In Chapter 8, using logical relations, we will prove that if all base types are infinite, then β, η-conversion is complete for equations that hold in the full continuous model.

Proof It is easy to see that the full continuous hierarchy for $\lambda^{\times,\rightarrow}$ is an extensional applicative structure. We prove that the environment model condition is satisfied using an induction hypothesis that is slightly stronger than the theorem. Specifically, in addition to showing that the meaning of every term exists, we show that the meaning is a continuous function of the values assigned to free variables by the environment. We use the assumption that meanings are continuous to show that a function defined by lambda abstraction is continuous.

We say $[\![\Gamma \triangleright M\colon \tau]\!]$ is *continuous* if, for every $x\colon \sigma \in \Gamma$ and $\eta \models \Gamma$, the map

$$a \in A^{\sigma} \mapsto [\![\Gamma \triangleright M\colon \tau]\!]\eta[x \mapsto a]$$

is a continuous function from A^{σ} to A^{τ}. By Exercise 5.2.17, this is the same as saying $[\![\Gamma \triangleright M\colon \tau]\!]$ is continuous as an n-ary function $A^{\sigma_1} \times \ldots \times A^{\sigma_n} \rightarrow A^{\tau}$, where $\Gamma = \{x_1\colon \sigma_1, \ldots, x_n\colon \sigma_n\}$.

Using Lemmas 5.2.24 and 5.2.23, the inductive proof is straightforward. It is easy to see that

$$[\![x_1\colon \sigma_1, \ldots, x_k\colon \sigma_k \triangleright x_i\colon \sigma_i]\!]\eta = \eta(x_i)$$

is continuous, since identity and constant functions are continuous, and similarly for the meaning of a constant symbol. For application, we use Lemma 5.2.23, and for lambda abstraction, Lemma 5.2.24. ∎

We have the following theorem, as a consequence of Lemmas 5.2.20 and 5.2.25.

Theorem 5.2.26 The full continuous $\lambda^{\times,\rightarrow}$ hierarchy $\mathcal{A}$ over any collection of CPOs is a Henkin model with the property that whenever A^{σ} is pointed there is a least fixed point operator $fix_{\sigma} \in A^{\sigma\rightarrow\sigma}$.

Recall that if A^τ is pointed, then $A^{\sigma\to\tau}$ is pointed and if both A^σ and A^τ are pointed, then $A^{\sigma\times\tau}$ is pointed. In particular, if we choose pointed CPOs for the type constants, then every A^σ will be pointed and we will have least-fixed-point operators at all types. We consider a specific case, a CPO model for PCF, in the next section. The extension of Theorem 5.2.26 to sums is described in Exercise 5.2.33.

Exercise 5.2.27 Find a CPO $\mathcal{D}$ without least element and a continuous function $f : \mathcal{D} \to \mathcal{D}$ such that f does not have a *least* fixed point (*i.e.*, the set of fixed points of f does not have a least element).

Exercise 5.2.28 Calculate the least fixed point of the following continuous function from $\mathcal{B}_\perp \to \mathcal{B}_\perp$ using the identity given in Lemma 5.2.20.

$$f = \lambda g : \mathcal{B}_\perp \to \mathcal{B}_\perp . \begin{cases} \perp & \mapsto & \bigwedge\{g(\mathit{true}),\ g(\mathit{false})\} \\ \mathit{true} & \mapsto & \mathit{true} \\ \mathit{false} & \mapsto & g(\mathit{true}) \end{cases}$$

where $\bigwedge\{g(\mathit{true}),\ g(\mathit{false})\}$ is the greatest lower bound of $g(\mathit{true})$ and $g(\mathit{false})$. You may want to look at Example 5.2.9 to get a concrete picture of the CPO $\mathcal{B}_\perp \to \mathcal{B}_\perp$.

Exercise 5.2.29 Let S be some set with at least two elements and let S^∞ be the set of finite and infinite sequences of elements of S, as in Exercise 5.2.4. This is a CPO with the prefix order. For each of the following functions on S^∞, show that the function is continuous and calculate its least fixed point using the identity given in Lemma 5.2.20. We assume $a, b \in S$ and write the concatenation of sequences s and s' as $s\,s'$.

(a) $f(s) = ab\,s$, the concatenation of ab and sequence s.

(b) $f(s) = abab\,s'$, where s' is derived from s by replacing every a by b.

(c) $f(s) = a\,s'$, where s' is derived from s by replacing every a by ab.

Exercise 5.2.30 Recall from Example 5.2.21 that the collection $\mathcal{PN}$ of all sets of natural numbers forms a CPO, ordered by set inclusion. This exercise asks you to show that various functions on $\mathcal{PN}$ are continuous or calculate their least fixed points using the identity given in Lemma 5.2.20.

(a) Show that if $f : \mathcal{N} \to \mathcal{N}$ is any function and $A_0 \subseteq \mathcal{N}$ any subset, then the function $F : \mathcal{PN} \to \mathcal{PN}$ defined by

$F(A) = A_0 \cup \{\, f(n) \mid n \in A \,\}$

is continuous.

(b) Find the least fixed points of the functions determined by the following data according to the pattern given in part *(a)*.

(i) $A_0 = \{2\}$, $f(n) = 2n$
(ii) $A_0 = \{1\}$, $f(n) =$ the least prime $p > n$

(c) Show that if $f : \mathcal{P}_{fin}\mathcal{N} \rightarrow \mathcal{N}$ is any function from finite subsets of $\mathcal{N}$ to $\mathcal{N}$ and $A_0 \subseteq \mathcal{N}$ is any subset, then the function $F : \mathcal{PN} \rightarrow \mathcal{PN}$ defined by

$$F(A) = A_0 \cup \{\, f(A') \mid A' \subseteq A \text{ finite} \,\}$$

is continuous.

(d) Find the least fixed points of the functions determined by the following data according to the pattern given in part *(c)*.

(i) $A_0 = \{2, 4, 6\}$, $f(A) = \sum_{n \in A} n$.
(ii) $A_0 = \{3, 5, 7\}$, $f(A) = \prod_{n \in A} n$.

Exercise 5.2.31 If $\mathcal{D}$ is a partial order and $f : \mathcal{D} \rightarrow \mathcal{D}$, then a *pre-fixed-point* of f is an element $x \in \mathcal{D}$ with $f(x) \leq x$.

(a) Show that if $\mathcal{D}$ is a CPO (not necessarily pointed) and $f : \mathcal{D} \rightarrow \mathcal{D}$ is continuous, then the set of pre-fixed-points of f is a CPO, under the same order as $\mathcal{D}$.

(b) Show that if $\mathcal{D}$ is a pointed CPO and $f : \mathcal{D} \rightarrow \mathcal{D}$ is continuous, then the set of pre-fixed-points of f is a pointed CPO (under the same order as $\mathcal{D}$) whose least element is the least fixed-point of f.

Exercise 5.2.32 Lemma 5.2.25, showing that the CPOs form a Henkin model, is proved using the environment model condition. An alternative is to use the combinatory model condition and show that the full continuous hierarchy has combinators. Prove that for all types ρ, σ, τ, the combinators $K_{\sigma,\tau}$ and $S_{\rho,\sigma,\tau}$ are continuous.

Exercise 5.2.33 This exercise is about adding sum types to the full continuous hierarchy.

(a) The disjoint union of two CPOs, $\mathcal{D} = \langle D, \leq_D \rangle$ and $\mathcal{E} = \langle E, \leq_E \rangle$, is $\mathcal{D} + \mathcal{E} = \langle D \uplus E, \leq_{D+E} \rangle$, with the disjoint union of the two sets ordered by the least relation satisfying

$$\langle 0, d \rangle \leq_{D+E} \langle 0, d' \rangle \quad \text{if} \quad d \leq_D d', \text{ and}$$

$$\langle 1, e \rangle \leq_{D+E} \langle 1, e' \rangle \quad \text{if} \quad e \leq_E e'.$$

(Recall that $D \uplus E = (\{0\} \times D) \cup (\{1\} \times E)$.) We say "least relation satisfying . . . " since we do not want any ordering between $\langle 0, d \rangle$ and $\langle 1, e \rangle$. Show that the disjoint union of two CPOs is a CPO that has no least element.

(b) Show that if we extend the $\lambda^{\times,\rightarrow}$ hierarchy to sum types by $A^{\sigma+\tau} = A^{\sigma} + A^{\tau}$, we obtain a $\lambda^{+,\times,\rightarrow}$ Henkin model. By the combinatory condition explained in Section 4.5.9, it suffices to provide continuous $\mathbf{Inleft}^{\sigma,\tau}$, $\mathbf{Inright}^{\sigma,\tau}$ and $\mathbf{Case}^{\sigma,\tau,\rho}$ satisfying the required equational axioms.

(c) If we want $A^{\sigma+\tau}$ to be pointed, so that we may define elements of this type recursively, then we must alter the construction given in part (a). Specifically, we define the *separated sum of CPOs* $\mathcal{D} = \langle D, \leq_D \rangle$ and $\mathcal{E} = \langle E, \leq_E \rangle$ by

$$\mathcal{D}\,\langle + \rangle\,\mathcal{E} = \langle (\{0\} \times D) \cup (\{1\} \times E) \cup \{\bot\}, \leq_{D\langle+\rangle E} \rangle$$

where $\leq_{D\langle+\rangle E}$ is identical to $\leq_{D+E}$ except that $\bot$ is less than every $\langle 0, d\rangle$ and $\langle 1, e\rangle$ and, of course, $\bot \leq \bot$. Show that the separated sum of any CPOs is a pointed CPO.

(d) By Exercise 2.6.4, we cannot expect to obtain a Henkin model if we interpret sum types as separated sums. The reason is that if we have a Henkin model, then all of the equational axioms associated with sums must hold (including the extensionality axiom $(\mathbf{Case})_3$). But since separated sum types are pointed, we have fixed-point operators on each sum type, and therefore an inconsistency by Exercise 2.6.4. Show, however, that if we modify the $\lambda^{+,\times,\rightarrow}$ applicative structure defined in part (b) by using separated sums instead of disjoint unions, we obtain a structure that satisfies all the conditions for a $\lambda^{+,\times,\rightarrow}$ Henkin model except the extensionality condition for sums.

(e) A third form of sums on CPOs, used in the semantics of eager, or call-by-value languages, is called the *coalesced sum.* This is defined only for pointed CPOs. If $\mathcal{D} = \langle D, \leq_D \rangle$ and $\mathcal{E} = \langle E, \leq_E \rangle$ are pointed CPOs, then we define the coalesced sum $\mathcal{D} \oplus \mathcal{E} = \langle D \oplus E, \leq_{D\oplus E} \rangle$ by

$$\begin{array}{ll} D \oplus E & = (\{0\} \times (D - \{\bot_D\})) \cup (\{1\} \times (E - \{\bot_E\})) \cup \bot \\ \langle 0, d\rangle \leq_{D\oplus E} \langle 0, d'\rangle \text{ if } d \leq_D d', & \\ \langle 1, e\rangle \leq_{D\oplus E} \langle 1, e'\rangle \text{ if } e \leq_E e' & \\ \bot \leq_{D\oplus E} x & \text{all } x \in D \oplus E \end{array}$$

and no ordering between $\langle 0, d\rangle$ and $\langle 1, e\rangle$. Show that the coalesced sum of any pointed CPOs is a CPO and, for not necessarily pointed $\mathcal{D}$ and $\mathcal{E}$, we have $\mathcal{D}\,\langle + \rangle\,\mathcal{E} = (\mathcal{D}_\bot) \oplus (\mathcal{E}_\bot)$.

Exercise 5.2.34 An alternate form of products on CPOs, used in the semantics of eager, or call-by-value languages, is called the *smash product.* This is defined only for pointed CPOs. If $\mathcal{D} = \langle D, \leq_D \rangle$ and $\mathcal{E} = \langle E, \leq_E \rangle$ are pointed CPOs, then we define the smash product $\mathcal{D} \otimes \mathcal{E} = \langle D \otimes E, \leq_{D\otimes E} \rangle$ by

$$\begin{array}{rcl} D \otimes E & = & (D - \{\bot_D\}) \times (E - \{\bot_E\}) \cup \bot \\ \langle d, e\rangle \leq_{D\otimes E} \langle d', e'\rangle & \text{if} & d \leq_D d', e \leq_E e' \\ \bot \leq_{D\otimes E} x & \text{all} & x \in D \otimes E \end{array}$$

Show that the smash product of any pointed CPOs is a CPO and, for any CPOs $\mathcal{D}$ and $\mathcal{E}$, we have $(\mathcal{D} \times \mathcal{E})_\bot = (\mathcal{D}_\bot) \otimes (\mathcal{E}_\bot)$.

5.2.5 CPO Model for PCF

In this section, we consider the domain-theoretic semantics for PCF. This provides some insight into properties of CPOs, and also provides the basis for semantic reasoning about PCF. We show soundness of the PCF equational axioms system, and therefore the reduction rules, for our CPO model, called $\mathcal{A}_{\text{PCF}}$. It is impossible for the PCF equational proof system to be complete for proving all equations between PCF terms that hold in PCF. The reason is that, as shown in Chapter 2, every partial recursive function is definable in PCF. By soundness, and the fact that all the numerals denote distinct elements of the model, two expressions of type $nat \to nat$ will be equal in PCF iff they operationally define the same partial recursive function. Since equality between partial recursive functions is not recursively enumerable, no recursive axiom system could be complete for $\mathcal{A}_{\text{PCF}}$. In Section 5.3, we consider an extension to the equational axiom system, based on the CPO model, that proves more properties of terms.

The model $\mathcal{A}_{\text{PCF}}$ is the full continuous hierarchy over $A^{nat}_{\text{PCF}} = \mathcal{N}_\bot$ and $A^{bool}_{\text{PCF}} = \mathcal{B}_\bot$, with constants of PCF interpreted as described below.

Since the type constants of PCF are interpreted as pointed CPOs, and cartesian product and continuous function space constructors preserve pointedness, all of the types of PCF are interpreted as pointed CPOs. This gives us least-fixed-point operators at all types, allowing us to interpret the fixed-point constants of PCF according to Lemma 5.2.20.

We interpret constants $0, 1, 2, \ldots$ and *true*, *false* as the standard natural number and boolean elements of the lifted sets $\mathcal{N}_\bot$ and $\mathcal{B}_\bot$. It follows from Theorem 5.2.26 that if we choose continuous functions for basic PCF operations $+$, *Eq*? and conditional, then every term of PCF will have a meaning in $\mathcal{A}_{\text{PCF}}$.

We interpret $+$ and *Eq*? in $\mathcal{A}_{\text{PCF}}$ as the lifted versions, $+_\bot$ and $Eq?_\bot$, of the standard functions. In other words, we interpret $+$ as the extension of addition that is strict in both arguments, so that for every $x \in A^{nat}_{\text{PCF}}$,

$$\bot_{nat} + x \;=\; x + \bot_{nat} = \bot_{nat}$$

We treat the PCF equality test similarly, so that the PCF expression $Eq?\, M\, N$ has value *true* if M and N denote the same element of $\mathcal{N}_\bot$ different from $\bot$, value *false* if M and N denote different non-$\bot$ elements of $\mathcal{N}_\bot$, and value $\bot$ if either M and N denotes the bottom element of $\mathcal{N}_\bot$. Since the equational axioms of PCF only mention sums and equality tests involving numerals 0, 1, 2, ... and each numeral denotes a non-$\bot$ element of $\mathcal{N}_\bot$, it is easy to see that the equational axioms are satisfied by this interpretation.

The interpretation of conditional in $\mathcal{A}_{\text{PCF}}$ is a little more subtle. The reader might first guess that we could also interpret conditional as a strict function, with value $\bot$ of the appropriate type whenever any of its arguments is $\bot$ of some type. However, this does not work, since in the case that M denotes $\bot$ but N does not, we would have

$$\texttt{if } \mathit{false} \texttt{ then } M \texttt{ else } N = \bot,$$

which contradicts an equational axiom of PCF. An interpretation of conditional that satisfies the equational axioms of PCF, and therefore coincides with the operational semantics, is the following.

$$\mathcal{A}_{\text{PCF}}[\![\texttt{ if } P \texttt{ then } M \texttt{ else } N]\!]\eta = \begin{cases} \mathcal{A}_{\text{PCF}}[\![M]\!]\eta & \text{if } \mathcal{A}_{\text{PCF}}[\![P]\!]\eta = \mathit{true} \\ \mathcal{A}_{\text{PCF}}[\![N]\!]\eta & \text{if } \mathcal{A}_{\text{PCF}}[\![P]\!]\eta = \mathit{false} \\ \bot & \text{otherwise} \end{cases}$$

Since the equational axioms of PCF only mention conditional expressions when the first argument is *true* or *false*, it is easy to see that the axioms are satisfied. This completes the definition of $\mathcal{A}_{\text{PCF}}$. Since we have checked all of the equational axioms for constants, we have the following immediate consequences of the general soundness theorem for Henkin models (Theorem 4.5.17) and the connections between PCF equational axioms and reduction discussed in Section 2.3.

Theorem 5.2.35 Let M and N be expressions of PCF over typed variables from Γ. If $\Gamma \triangleright M = N{:}\,\sigma$ is provable from the axioms for PCF, then the CPO model $\mathcal{A}_{\text{PCF}}$ satisfies the equation $\Gamma \triangleright M = N{:}\,\sigma$.

Corollary 5.2.36 If $\Gamma \triangleright M{:}\,\sigma$ is a well-typed term of PCF, and $M \twoheadrightarrow N$, then the CPO model $\mathcal{A}_{\text{PCF}}$ satisfies the equation $\Gamma \triangleright M = N{:}\,\sigma$.

These soundness results show that the denotational semantics given by $\mathcal{A}_{\text{PCF}}$ has the minimal properties required of any denotational semantics for PCF. Specifically, if we can prove $M = N$, or reduce one term to the other, then these two terms will have the same meaning in $\mathcal{A}_{\text{PCF}}$. It follows that if two terms have different meaning, then we cannot prove them equal or reduce one to the other. Therefore, we can use $\mathcal{A}_{\text{PCF}}$ to reason about unprovability or the non-existence of reductions. Some additional connections between $\mathcal{A}_{\text{PCF}}$ and the operational semantics of PCF are discussed in Sections 5.4.1 and 5.4.2. A weak form of completeness called computational adequacy, proved in Section 5.4.1, allows us to use $\mathcal{A}_{\text{PCF}}$ to reason about provability and the existence of reductions. As remarked at the beginning of this section, it is impossible to have full equational completeness for $\mathcal{A}_{\text{PCF}}$.

In the rest of this section and the exercises, we work out the meaning of some expressions in $\mathcal{A}_{\text{PCF}}$ and make some comments about the difference between the least fixed point of a function and other fixed points.

Example 5.2.37 Recall that the factorial function may be written $fact \stackrel{\text{def}}{=} fix_{nat \to nat}\ F$, where F is the expression

$$F \stackrel{\text{def}}{=} \lambda f\colon nat \to nat.\,\lambda y\colon nat.\ \texttt{if}\ Eq?\ y\ 0\ \texttt{then}\ 1\ \texttt{else}\ y * f(y-1).$$

We will work out the meaning of this closed term assuming that $*$ and $-$ denote multiplication and subtraction functions which are strict extensions of the standard ones. In other words, we assume that subtraction and multiplication have their standard meaning on non-bottom elements of $\mathcal{N}_{\perp}$, but have value $\perp$ if either of their arguments is $\perp$.

Following the definition of *fix* in a CPO, we can see that the meaning of factorial is the least upper bound of a directed set. Specifically, $\mathcal{A}_{\text{PCF}}[\![fact]\!]$ is the least upper bound $\bigvee\{\bar{F}^n(\perp) \mid n \geq 0\}$, where $\bar{F} = \mathcal{A}_{\text{PCF}}[\![F]\!]$. We will work out the first few cases of $\bar{F}^n(\perp)$ to understand what this means. Since all of the lambda terms involved are closed, we will dispense with the formality of writing $\mathcal{A}_{\text{PCF}}[\![\ ]\!]$ and use lambda terms as names for elements of the appropriate domains.

$$\bar{F}^0(\perp) = \perp_{nat \to nat}$$

$$\begin{aligned}
\bar{F}^1(\perp) &= \lambda y\colon nat.\ \texttt{if}\ Eq?\ y\ 0\ \texttt{then}\ 1\ \texttt{else}\ y * (\bar{F}^0(\perp))(y-1)\\
&= \lambda y\colon nat.\ \texttt{if}\ Eq?\ y\ 0\ \texttt{then}\ 1\ \texttt{else}\ y * (\perp_{nat \to nat})(y-1)\\
&= \lambda y\colon nat.\ \texttt{if}\ Eq?\ y\ 0\ \texttt{then}\ 1\ \texttt{else}\ \perp_{nat}
\end{aligned}$$

$$\begin{aligned}
\bar{F}^2(\perp) &= \lambda y\colon nat.\ \texttt{if}\ Eq?\ y\ 0\ \texttt{then}\ 1\ \texttt{else}\ y * (\bar{F}^1(\perp))(y-1)\\
&= \lambda y\colon nat.\ \texttt{if}\ Eq?\ y\ 0\ \texttt{then}\ 1\ \texttt{else}\ y *\\
&\qquad (\lambda x\colon nat.\ \texttt{if}\ Eq?\ x\ 0\ \texttt{then}\ 1\ \texttt{else}\ \perp_{nat})(y-1)\\
&= \lambda y\colon nat.\ \texttt{if}\ Eq?\ y\ 0\ \texttt{then}\ 1\ \texttt{else}\ y * (\texttt{if}\ Eq?\ (y-1)\ 0\ \texttt{then}\ 1\ \texttt{else}\ \perp_{nat})
\end{aligned}$$

Continuing in this way, we can see that $\bar{F}^n(\perp)$ is the function which computes $y!$ whenever $0 \leq y < n$ and has value $\perp_{nat}$ otherwise. Since $\perp_{nat}$ represents "undefined," this means that $\bar{F}^n(\perp)$ is defined for $0 \leq y < n$, and undefined otherwise. A property of this collection of functions is that for a particular argument $y \neq \perp$, there are two possible values for $\bar{F}^n(\perp)\ y$. If $n \leq y$, then the value is $\perp$, while if $n > y$, the value is $y!$.

As spelled out in the statement of Lemma 5.2.10, the least upper bound of $\{\bar{F}^n(\bot) \mid n \geq 0\}$ is the function mapping any $y \in \mathcal{N}_\bot$ to the least upper bound of the set $\{\bar{F}^n(\bot)\, y \mid n \geq 0\}$. This set contains only $\bot$, if $y = \bot$, and has the two elements $\bot$ and $y!$ otherwise. Therefore $\mathcal{A}_{\text{PCF}}[\![\mathit{fact}]\!]$ is the function from $\mathcal{N}_\bot$ to $\mathcal{N}_\bot$ which maps $\bot$ to $\bot$, and any other $y \in \mathcal{N}$ to $y!$. The strictness of factorial agrees with our computational intuition and experience, since we do not expect any computation of *fact* M to terminate if the expression M cannot be simplified to a numeral. But in the case that M reduces to a numeral for y, we can reduce *fact* M to the numeral for $y!$. ■

In general, the least fixed point of a function is the fixed point that is "computed in practice." We will prove a precise version of this statement in Section 5.4.1 by showing that for programs (closed terms of observable type), the PCF operational and denotational semantics coincide. An intuitive understanding of this correspondence comes from observing that the least fixed point of a function f has all the properties of *fix* f that we can determine by applying *fix*-reduction some number of times. For example, if f is a function from some function type to itself, then the function *fix* f will be least in the sense that it is defined only where a value could be determined by reduction (or the equational proof system), although functions which give non-$\bot$ results on more arguments could also be fixed points of f. The following example illustrates the difference between the least fixed point of a function and other fixed points.

Example 5.2.38 Consider the function $F\colon (nat \to nat) \to (nat \to nat)$ defined by

$$F \stackrel{\text{def}}{=} \lambda f\colon nat \to nat.\, \lambda x\colon nat.\, \texttt{if } Eq?\, x\, 1 \texttt{ then } 1 \texttt{ else } f(x-2)$$

where subtraction $x - y$ yields 0 if $y \geq x$. In contrast to the function used to define factorial, we will see that F has many fixed points. The reason is that F is a function mapping even arguments to $\bot$. This allows us to find greater fixed points (in the point-wise order) which map even arguments to natural numbers other than $\bot$. Before discussing alternate fixed points further, we will work out the meaning of *fix* F.

As with factorial, we let $\bar{F} = \mathcal{A}_{\text{PCF}}[\![F]\!]$. The least fixed point of $\bar{F}$ is the least upper bound of the set $\{\bar{F}^n(\bot) \mid n \geq 0\}$. The simplest way to understand this set is to begin by working out the first few functions.

$$\bar{F}^0(\bot) = \bot_{nat \to nat}$$

$$\bar{F}^1(\bot) = \lambda x\colon nat.\, \texttt{if } Eq?\; x\; 1 \texttt{ then } 1 \texttt{ else } (\bar{F}^0(\bot))(x-2)$$

$$= \lambda x\colon nat.\, \texttt{if } Eq?\; x\; 1 \texttt{ then } 1 \texttt{ else } \bot_{nat}$$

$$\bar{F}^2(\bot) = \lambda x\colon nat.\ \texttt{if}\ \ Eq?\ x\ 1\ \ \texttt{then}\ \ 1\ \ \texttt{else}\ \ (\bar{F}^1(\bot))(x-2)$$

$$= \lambda x\colon nat.\ \texttt{if}\ \ Eq?\ x\ 1\ \ \texttt{then}\ \ 1\ \ \texttt{else}$$

$$(\lambda y\colon nat.\ \texttt{if}\ \ Eq?\ y\ 1\ \ \texttt{then}\ \ 1\ \ \texttt{else}\ \ \bot_{nat})(x-2)$$

$$= \lambda x\colon nat.\ \texttt{if}\ \ Eq?\ x\ 1\ \ \texttt{then}\ \ 1\ \ \texttt{else}\ \ \texttt{if}\ \ Eq?\ (x-2)\ 1\ \ \texttt{then}\ \ 1\ \ \texttt{else}\ \ \bot_{nat}$$

Continuing in this way, we can see that $\bar{F}^n(\bot)$ is the function which maps any odd $x < 2n$ to 1 and has value $\bot_{nat}$ otherwise. The least upper bound f of all such functions is the function mapping all odd x to 1, and any other natural number to $\bot$. This corresponds to the fact that if we try to compute the value of $(\mathit{fix}\ F)x$ by reduction, we will succeed after a finite number of reduction steps iff x is odd. If x is even, we can reduce the expression indefinitely, but will never produce a numeral.

It is not hard to see that the fixed points of F above are precisely the functions $g\colon nat \to nat$ satisfying the two conditions

$$g(1) = 1$$

$$g(x+2) = g(x)$$

Since these two equations do not determine a value for even x, any function mapping all even x (and 0) to some number n will be a fixed point of F. All of these alternatives are greater than f since any natural number n is greater than $\bot$ in the ordering on the lifted CPO of natural numbers. However, none of these alternative fixed points is the function computed by reduction. ■

Exercise 5.2.39 Determine the value of each of the following expressions in the CPO model described in this section. In each case, determine the least fixed point *fix F* by identifying the directed set $\{F^n(\bot) \mid n \geq 0\}$ and working out enough expressions in the sequence $F^0(\bot)$, $F^1(\bot)$, $F^2(\bot)$, … to confidently (and correctly) state the general pattern.

(a) $\mathit{fix}\ (\lambda f\colon nat \to nat.\lambda x\colon nat.\ (f\ x) + 1)$

(b) $\mathit{fix}\ (\lambda f\colon nat \to nat.\lambda x\colon nat.\ \texttt{if}\ \ Eq?\, x\, 0\ \ \texttt{then}\ \ 1\ \ \texttt{else}\ \ f(x-1) + f(x-1))$

You may assume that subtraction has its standard meaning on non-bottom elements of $\mathcal{N}_\bot$, and has value $\bot$ if either of its arguments is $\bot$.

Exercise 5.2.40 Suppose that we interpret conditional as strict in all arguments. In particular, assume that $\texttt{if}\ \ x\ \ \texttt{then}\ \ y\ \ \texttt{else}\ \ z = \bot_{nat}$ if either $x = \bot_{bool}$, $y = \bot_{nat}$ or $z = \bot_{nat}$. What will be the interpretation of

$$\mathit{fix}\ (\lambda f\colon nat \to nat.\lambda x\colon nat.\ \texttt{if}\ \ Eq?\, x\, 0\ \ \texttt{then}\ \ 1\ \ \texttt{else}\ \ f\ x)?$$

Show that this does not agree with the result we may derive using either the reduction rules or equational axioms for PCF. Then show that we do get the computationally correct result with the non-strict interpretation of conditional described in this section.

Exercise 5.2.41 It is well-known that it is not possible to write a program that decides whether any other program halts. We may state this precisely for PCF using the model $\mathcal{A}_{PCF}$. A solution to the "halting problem" in PCF would be a definable function *total*?: (*nat* → *nat*) → *bool* with the property that for every $f\colon nat \to nat$,

$$total?\ f = \begin{cases} true & \text{if } \forall n \neq \bot_{nat} \,.\, f(n) \neq \bot_{nat}, \\ false & \text{otherwise.} \end{cases}$$

Show that there is no PCF expression defining *total?* by showing that this function is not continuous. (*Hint:* You might want to try the problem for *total*?: (*bool* → *bool*) → *bool* first, since there are fewer directed sets.)

Exercise 5.2.42 Consider an extension of PCF with a third type constant, *tree,* and the additional operations listed below:

fctns:$leaf : nat \to tree$

$$node : tree \times tree \to tree$$

$$is\_leaf? : tree \to bool$$

$$lsub : tree \to tree$$

$$rsub : tree \to tree$$

$$label : tree \to nat$$

eqns:$[x, y\colon nat,\ t, t' : tree]$

$$is\_leaf?(leaf\ \ x) = true$$

$$is\_leaf?(node\ t\ t') = false$$

$$label(leaf\ \ x) = x$$

$$lsub(node\ t\ t') = t$$

$$rsub(node\ t\ t') = t'$$

This is similar to the data type of trees given in Table 3.3, except that the data stored at the leaves are natural numbers instead of atoms. We construct a CPO model for this extension to PCF by adding a CPO A^{tree} to $\mathcal{A}_{\text{PCF}}$ and interpreting cartesian product and function types as in $\mathcal{A}_{\text{PCF}}$.

(a) Give a CPO A^{tree} for the interpretation of trees and describe continuous interpretations for each of the functions in this extension of PCF. *Hint:* You may have to choose A^{tree} carefully for part (b) to work out; $\mathcal{A}^{tree}$ need not be not pointed.

(b) Show that the equational axioms for the new functions are satisfied.

(c) Determine the meaning of the function *fix* F, where

$$F \stackrel{\text{def}}{=} \lambda f\colon tree \to nat.\, \lambda t\colon tree.\, \texttt{if}\ \ is\_leaf?\, t\ \ \texttt{then}\ \ label\, t\ \ \texttt{else}\ \ f(lsub\, t) + f(rsub\, t),$$

by identifying the directed set $\{F^n(\bot) \mid n \geq 0\}$ and working out enough elements in the sequence $F^0(\bot)$, $F^1(\bot)$, $F^2(\bot)$, ... to state the general pattern.

Exercise 5.2.43 PCF has two basic operations on natural numbers, addition and equality test. In parts (a) – (c) of this problem, you are asked to prove that if equality is eliminated from PCF, we cannot define equality using the other operations. More specifically, we say that closed term $EQ\colon nat \to nat \to bool$ *defines nat equality* if the equation $EQ\, n\, n = true$ is provable for any numeral n, and $EQ\, n\, m = false$ is provable for distinct numerals n and m. Parts (a) – (c) ask you to show that in the language PCF^{-eq} obtained by dropping *Eq*? from PCF, there is no closed term defining *nat* equality. Part (d) asks a related question about test for zero and predecessor.

(a) Show that if $\mathcal{A}$ is a CPO model of PCF^{-eq} with A^{nat} finite, then there exist distinct numerals n and m with $\mathcal{A} \models n = m$.

(b) Show that if $\mathcal{A}$ is a CPO model of PCF^{-eq} with A^{nat} finite, and there is a closed term $EQ\colon nat \to nat \to bool$ defining equality, then $\mathcal{A} \models true = false$.

(c) Show that there is no closed PCF^{-eq} term defining equality by finding a CPO model satisfying all of the equational axioms for PCF^{-eq} but with A^{nat} finite and A^{bool} the standard three-element CPO $\mathcal{B}_\bot$.

(d) Let PCF$^{-eq+zerop}$ be the variant of PCF with *Eq*? omitted, and a constant *Zero*?: $nat \to bool$ added. The equational axioms for this constant are $Zero?\, 0 = true$ and $Zero?\, n = false$ for each numeral n different from 0. (The reduction rules are obtained by reading these from left to right.) Show that predecessor is not definable in PCF$^{-eq+zerop}$.

5.3 Fixed-point Induction

The equational proof system for PCF is sound for the CPO model and other semantic models of PCF. It is also adequate to specify the result of any program, since it follows from computational adequacy (proved in Section 5.4.1) that if $P\colon nat$ is closed, and P denotes a number n in the CPO model $\mathcal{A}_{PCF}$, then we can prove $P = n$. However, the equational proof system is not very powerful when it comes to proving equations between parts of programs, such as terms defining functions. This is illustrated in Example 5.3.1 below. In this section, we study an extension to the equational proof system that has been found, in practice, to be sufficient for proving many equations between PCF terms. We also discuss fixed-point induction in predicate logic very briefly at the end of the section and in the exercises. The resulting logic, first proposed in [Sco69], is commonly called *LCF*, for *logic for computable functions.* A general presentation of an implementation of LCF, with examples, appears in [Pau87].

Example 5.3.1 If $f: D \to D$ and $g: D \to D$ are continuous functions on some CPO D, then it is not hard to see that $\mathit{fix}(f \circ g) = f(\mathit{fix}(g \circ f))$. (This equation is used in Exercises 2.3.3 and 5.3.3.) The reason is that

$$\begin{aligned}
\mathit{fix}(f \circ g) &= \bigvee\{(f \circ g)^i(\bot) \mid i \geq 0\} \\
&= \bigvee\{(f \circ g)(\bot),\ (f \circ g \circ f \circ g)(\bot),\ (f \circ g \circ f \circ g \circ f \circ g)(\bot),\ \ldots\} \\
&= \bigvee\{(f \circ (g \circ f)^i)(\bot) \mid i \geq 0\} \\
&= f(\mathit{fix}(g \circ f))
\end{aligned}$$

by monotonicity, general facts about least upper bounds, and the associativity of composition.

In the rest of this example, we show that there is no equational proof of $\mathit{fix}(f \circ g) = f(\mathit{fix}(g \circ f))$, treating f and g as variables of type $\sigma \to \sigma$, for any type σ, using only the equational proof system of PCF. Although a proof can be carried out for the entire PCF proof system, we will simplify the discussion and consider only the restricted proof system without (η) or (sp) (See Table 2.1). Intuitively, neither (η) nor (sp) should matter here, since there are no lambda abstractions or pairs in either expression.

By Theorem 8.3.24, the reduction rules of PCF are confluent. Since the reduction rules of PCF are exactly directed versions of the equational axioms, plus symmetry, transitivity and congruence rules, it follows from the general argument in Section 3.7.2 that the equation $\mathit{fix}(f \circ g) = f(\mathit{fix}(g \circ f))$ is provable iff both terms reduce to a common term. However, an easy induction shows that any term obtained by reducing $\mathit{fix}(f \circ g)$ will have an equal number of f's and g's, while terms obtained from $f(\mathit{fix}(g \circ f))$ will have one more f than g. Therefore, we cannot prove $\mathit{fix}(f \circ g) = f(\mathit{fix}(g \circ f))$ using the equational proof system. ■

The extended proof system is based on the CPO interpretation of terms. In addition to equations, we will use formulas which assert that the meaning of one term is an approximation of another. More specifically, we use assertions of the form $M \leq N$ or, written out with type assignments, $\Gamma \rhd M \leq N : \sigma$. To be precise, an approximation $\Gamma \rhd M \leq N : \sigma$ is satisfied at environment $\eta \models \Gamma$ for CPO model $\mathcal{A}$ if $\mathcal{A}[\![M]\!]\eta \leq \mathcal{A}[\![N]\!]\eta$. The proof system given in this section is sound for deriving assertions that hold in all CPO models. A common way of reading $M \leq N$ is, "M is an approximation of N."

One obvious inference rule is

$$\frac{\Gamma \rhd M = N : \sigma}{\Gamma \rhd M \leq N : \sigma} \qquad (eq)$$

which allows us to derive approximations from equations. This rule may be used to derive versions of the (β) and (η) axioms using approximation in place of equality. A "converse" to this rule is

$$\frac{\Gamma \rhd M \leq N : \sigma, \ \Gamma \rhd N \leq M : \sigma}{\Gamma \rhd M = N : \sigma} \qquad (asym)$$

which is sound since a partial order is anti-symmetric. This rules lets us derive equations from approximations. Since $\leq$ is transitive, we also have the rule

$$\frac{\Gamma \rhd M \leq N : \sigma, \ \Gamma \rhd N \leq P : \sigma}{\Gamma \rhd M \leq P : \sigma} \qquad (trans)$$

If we add a constant $\bot_\sigma$ to the language, for each type σ, then we have the axiom scheme

$$\Gamma \rhd \bot_\sigma \leq M : \sigma \qquad (bot)$$

since $\bot_\sigma$ is the least element of type σ. We also know that the least element of a function type is the function mapping each argument to $\bot$. This gives us the equational axiom scheme.

$$\Gamma \rhd \bot = \lambda x \colon \sigma.\ \bot : \sigma \to \tau \qquad (botf)$$

We also have a congruence rule for each syntactic form. For application, the rule

$$\frac{\Gamma \rhd M_1 \leq M_2 : \sigma \to \tau, \ \Gamma \rhd N_1 \leq N_2 : \sigma}{\Gamma \rhd M_1 N_1 \leq M_2 N_2 : \tau} \qquad (acong)$$

tells us that every continuous function is monotonic. The congruence rule for lambda abstraction

$$\frac{\Gamma, x \colon \sigma \rhd M \leq N : \tau}{\Gamma \rhd \lambda x \colon \sigma.M \leq \lambda x \colon \sigma.N : \sigma \to \tau} \qquad (fcong)$$

is sound since we order functions point-wise.

The final rule is an induction rule for fixed points. From the equational axiom for fixed points, we can prove that $f(\mathit{fix}\ f) \leq \mathit{fix}\ f$, and similar properties that follow from $\mathit{fix}\ f$ being a fixed point of f. However, in the standard equational proof system, there is no obvious way to make use of the fact that $\mathit{fix}\ f$ is the *least* fixed point of f. With approximations instead of equations, we could write a rule

$$\frac{\Gamma \triangleright MN = N\colon \sigma}{\Gamma \triangleright \mathit{fix}\ M \leq N : \sigma}$$

saying that $\mathit{fix}\ M$ is an approximation to any fixed point of M. This follows from the more powerful rule of "fixed point induction," also called *Scott induction* after Dana Scott.

In stating the rule of fixed point induction, we write $\Phi \vdash A$ to mean that the equation or approximation A is provable from the set Φ of equations and approximations using the axioms and inference rules given here, combined with the equational axioms and inference rules of typed lambda calculus with fixed points and any additional equational hypotheses (such as axioms for algebraic datatypes). If A has the form $\Gamma, x\colon \sigma \triangleright M \leq N : \tau$, then we write $[P/x]A$ for the result $\Gamma \triangleright [P/x]M \leq [P/x]N : \tau$ of removing variable x from the type assignment and substituting P for x in both terms, assuming $\Gamma \triangleright P\colon \sigma$. If A is an equation, we define $[P/x]A$ similarly. Using this notation, the rule is written as follows.

$$\frac{\Phi \vdash [\bot/x]A, \quad \Phi, [c/x]A \vdash [F(c)/x]A}{\Phi \vdash [\mathit{fix}\ F/x]A} \text{ constant } c \text{ not in } \Phi \qquad (\mathit{fpind})$$

If we think of A as a way of saying that the variable x has some property, then $[\bot/x]A$ says that this property holds for $\bot$. The second hypothesis, $\Phi, [c/x]A \vdash [F(c)/x]A$, is a way of saying that if this property holds for some arbitrary value c, then it holds for $F(c)$. It follows that this property holds for every element of the set $\{F^n(\bot) \mid n \geq 0\}$, by induction on n. Using the fact that the value of any term depends continuously on each of its free variables, we can easily verify that the property A holds for the least upper bound of this set, namely $\mathit{fix}\ F$. This gives us the conclusion of the fixed point induction rule.

A feature of fixed-point induction is that we reason implicitly about sets of the form $\{F^i \bot \mid i \geq 0\}$ without introducing natural numbers into the formal system. While the soundness proof for fixed-point induction uses induction on the integers, the proof system only uses formulas such as approximation or equality.

Example 5.3.2 To illustrate the use of fixed-point induction, we will show that if N is a fixed point of M, then $\mathit{fix}\ M \leq N$. We assume $\Gamma \triangleright MN = N\colon \sigma$, which gives us

$$\Gamma \triangleright MN \leq N : \sigma$$

since equality implies approximation. This will be useful at a later step of the proof.

Let us now think about how we can use the fixed point induction rule. The conclusion of the rule has the form $[\mathit{fix}\, F/x]A$, which matches the statement we wish to prove if we take

$$A \equiv \Gamma, x{:}\sigma \rhd x \leq N : \sigma,$$

with x not free in N, and let F be M. Reading the fixed point induction rule from the bottom up, we can see that it suffices to prove

$$[\bot/x]A \equiv \Gamma \rhd \bot \leq N : \sigma,$$

which is an axiom, and to show that we can prove

$$[Mc/x]A \equiv \Gamma \rhd Mc \leq N : \sigma$$

if we take $[c/x]A \equiv \Gamma \rhd c \leq N : \sigma$ as an additional hypothesis.

If we begin with $c \leq N$, then by monotonicity (the "congruence rule" for application), we have

$$\Gamma \rhd Mc \leq MN : \sigma$$

But since we have already proved $MN \leq N$ above, this gives us

$$\Gamma \rhd Mc \leq N : \sigma$$

which is exactly what we need in order to finish the proof by fixed point induction. ■

Although we have only used fixed-point induction to prove approximations and equations, it is also possible to use this proof rule in a predicate logic. However, in the more general setting, fixed-point induction is only sound if predicates are restricted in some way. This is illustrated in Exercise 5.3.6. We say a predicate P is *admissible* or *inclusive* if, for every directed S, if $P(d)$ for all $d \in S$, then $P(\bigvee S)$. It is easy to see that both $=$ and $\leq$ are inclusive predicates on any $\mathcal{D} \times \mathcal{D}$. Some closure conditions on inclusive predicates are given in Exercise 5.3.7.

Exercise 5.3.3 Use fixed point induction to prove the following equations. A common pattern, which you will probably want to use for parts (a) and (c), is to prove an equation $M = N$ by proving the pair of approximations $M \leq N$ and $N \leq M$ by separate fixed point inductions. You can solve part (b) using induction on equations instead of approximations (*i.e.*, take A in the fixed point induction rule to be an equation) but you do not have to.

(a) $\mathit{fix}(f \circ g) = f(\mathit{fix}\,(g \circ f))$

Hint: To show the first approximation, take $A \equiv \Gamma, x{:}\sigma \rhd x \leq f(\mathit{fix}\,(g \circ f)) : \sigma$ and $F \equiv$

$f \circ g$. You will need to use the equational axiom (*fix*) once. The reverse approximation is proved similarly.

(b) $\mathit{fix}(\lambda f\colon nat \to nat.\, \lambda x\colon nat.\, f(x+1)) = \mathit{fix}(\lambda f\colon nat \to nat.\, f)$
Hint: For fun, try proving this directly. Then try proving that each term is equal to $\bot_{nat \to nat}$.

(c) Prove $((\mathit{fix}\ F)\, x\ y) + 1 = (\mathit{fix}\ F)\, x\ (y+1)$, where
$F \stackrel{\text{def}}{=} \lambda f\colon nat \to nat \to nat.\, \lambda x\colon nat.\, \lambda y\colon nat.\, \texttt{if}\ Eq?\, x\, 0\ \texttt{then}\ y\ \texttt{else}\ f(x-1, y+1)$. You may use the proof rule

$$\frac{f\ \bot = \bot}{f(\texttt{if}\ B\ \texttt{then}\ M\ \texttt{else}\ N) = \texttt{if}\ B\ \texttt{then}\ fM\ \texttt{else}\ fN}$$

stating that any *strict* function f distributes over conditional.

Exercise 5.3.4 Show that the following rule is not sound.

$$\frac{\Phi \vdash [\bot/x]A, \quad \Phi, A \vdash [F(x)/x]A}{\Phi \vdash [\mathit{fix}\ F/x]A}\ x \text{ not free in } \Phi$$

Exercise 5.3.5 This exercise gives an alternative approach to Exercise 2.2.15 for the problem of finding a pair of functions satisfying the recursive equations

$f = F\ f\ g$

$g = G\ f\ g$

where $F\colon \sigma \to \tau \to \sigma$, $G\colon \sigma \to \tau \to \tau$ and neither f nor g appears free in F or G. The first step is to define a parameterized solution $F'\colon \tau \to \sigma$ to the first equation and a similar parameterized solution $G'\colon \sigma \to \tau$ to the second.

$F' \stackrel{\text{def}}{=} \lambda g\colon \tau.\, (\mathit{fix}_\sigma(\lambda f\colon \sigma. F\ f\ g))$

$G' \stackrel{\text{def}}{=} \lambda f\colon \sigma.\, (\mathit{fix}_\tau(\lambda g\colon \tau. G\ f\ g))$

These may now be substituted into the original defining equations to eliminate one variable from each. Use fixed point induction to show that the two terms $\mathit{fix}(\lambda f\colon \sigma.\, F\ f\ (G'\ f))$ and $\mathit{fix}(\lambda g\colon \tau.\, G\ (F'\ g)\ g)$, satisfy the original equations.

Exercise 5.3.6 Fixed-point induction is sound for equations and approximations because $=$ and $\leq$ are both inclusive predicates. However, $\neq$ is not inclusive, and fixed-point induction is unsound for proving that two terms are not equal. Demonstrate this by using fixed-point induction to prove $\mathit{fix}\ F \neq \mathit{fix}\ F$, where

$$F \stackrel{\text{def}}{=} \lambda f{:}\, nat \to nat.\, \lambda x{:}\, nat.\, \texttt{if}\ Eq?\, x\, 0\ \texttt{then}\ 0\ \texttt{else}\ f(x-1).$$

You may invent proof rules such as

$$\frac{M\,P \neq N\,P{:}\,\tau}{M \neq N{:}\,\sigma \to \tau}$$

as needed, or simply describe the correctness of assertions such as $\bot \neq (\mathit{fix}\ F)$ informally. The main point is to demonstrate the problem with fixed-point induction and non-inclusive predicates, not to develop a proof system for inequality.

Exercise 5.3.7 This exercise asks you to show that various operations yield inclusive predicates. Suppose $P, Q \subseteq \mathcal{D}$ and $\{P_i \subseteq \mathcal{D} \mid i \in I\}$ are inclusive predicates and show the following.

(a) $P \cap Q$ and $P \cup Q$ are inclusive.

(b) The complement, $D - P$, of P is not necessarily inclusive.

(c) If $f{:}\, \mathcal{E} \to \mathcal{D}$ is continuous, then $Q = \{e \in E \mid P(f\, e)\}$ is inclusive.

(d) Show that if $\{P_i \subseteq D \mid i \in I\}$ is a family of inclusive predicates, then the intersection $\bigcap_i P_i$ is inclusive but the union $\bigcup_i P_i$ need not be. Note that if R is a binary predicate we interpret universal quantification $\forall x{:}\, \sigma. R(x, y)$ as the intersection $\bigcap_{d \in D} R(d, y)$ and, similarly, existential quantification as union.

5.4 Computational Adequacy and Full Abstraction

5.4.1 Approximation Theorem and Computational Adequacy

As discussed in Section 2.3, there are several general connections between axiomatic, operational and denotational semantics that we might hope to establish for any language. In Section 2.3.5, these are characterized using equivalence relations as

$$=_{ax}\ \subseteq\ =_{den}\ \subseteq\ =_{op}$$

and

$$(\forall\ programs\ M)\ (\forall\ results\ N)\ \ M =_{ax} N\ \text{ iff }\ M =_{den} N\ \text{ iff }\ M =_{op} N.$$

Intuitively, the line of containments says that the axiomatic semantics are sound for the denotational semantics, and that any programs identified in the denotational semantics must be observationally equivalent in the operational semantics. The second line above says that the three relations should be identical as far as specifying the result of any program.

For PCF, taking $\mathcal{A}_{\text{PCF}}$ as the denotational semantics, we have

$$=_{ax} \;\subseteq\; =_{den},$$

by the soundness theorem of Section 5.2.5. It is also observed in Section 5.2.5 that the equational axiom system is not (and cannot be) complete for $\mathcal{A}_{\text{PCF}}$, so the relations $=_{ax}$ and $=_{den}$ are different. The main result of this section is that

$$=_{den} \;\subseteq\; =_{op},$$

with the two relations coinciding for programs. It therefore follows from the fact that the reduction axioms are a subset of the equational axioms that

$$(\forall\ programs\ M)\ (\forall\ results\ N)\ \ M =_{ax} N\ \text{ iff }\ M =_{den} N\ \text{ iff }\ M =_{op} N,$$

which completes the positive results for PCF. We show in the next section that $=_{den}$ and $=_{op}$ are different for PCF, but become identical when PCF is extended with parallel-or (from Section 2.5.6). For concreteness, we work specifically with PCF in this section; it is straightforward to extend the results to other versions of typed lambda calculus with *fix* and any algebraic data types that have a confluent and terminating left-linear rewrite system. (See Section 8.3.4.)

One way to establish connections between operational and denotational semantics is by a direct logical predicate or logical relation argument. (One version of this approach is documented in [Gun92].) An alternative that seems to provide more insight is through a more general result called the "approximation theorem." This theorem gives a correspondence between the meaning of a term and a set of "syntactic approximations" in normal form. We prove an approximation theorem for PCF in this section and derive computational adequacy as a corollary.

We may approximate the normal form of a term of PCF, or other versions of typed lambda calculus with *fix*, by applying some number of reduction steps, then replacing any subterm that is not in normal form by the constant $\bot_\sigma$, for the appropriate type σ. In general, if M is a typed lambda term over some signature, possibly containing *fix*, then we say N is an *approximate normal form* of M, and write $N \in \mathit{anf}(M)$, if N is a normal form that may be obtained from M in this way. Note that even if a PCF term does not have a normal form, this process may still produce a normal form in the extension of PCF with $\bot$ constants at all types.

Example 5.4.1 Every approximate normal form of fix_σ is equal to some term of the form $\lambda f\colon \sigma \to \sigma.\ f^n(\bot)$, $n \geq 0$. If we begin with *fix*, then the only way to replace a subterm by $\perp$ and obtain a normal form is to replace *fix* by $\perp$, yielding $\perp$. If we reduce fix_σ to $\lambda f\colon\sigma\to\sigma.\, f(fix_\sigma f)$, then we can obtain a normal form by replacing fix_σ by $\perp_{(\sigma\to\sigma)\to\sigma}$, for example. However, in the denotational model, we have

$$\lambda f\colon\sigma\to\sigma.\, f(\perp_{(\sigma\to\sigma)\to\sigma}\, f) \quad = \quad \lambda f\colon\sigma\to\sigma.\, f(\perp_\sigma)$$

We can also obtain the latter term as an approximate normal form by replacing $fix_\sigma f$ by $\perp_\sigma$. We can reduce *fix* twice, then use β-reduction to obtain $\lambda f\colon\sigma\to\sigma.\, f^2(fix_\sigma f)$. If we replace $fix_\sigma f$ by $\perp_\sigma$, this gives us the approximate normal form $\lambda f\colon\sigma\to\sigma.\, f^2(\perp)$. By case analysis and induction on the number of *fix*-reductions, we can show that every approximate normal form of *fix* is equal to a term of the form $\lambda f\colon\sigma\to\sigma.\, f^n(\perp)$. By introducing reduction rules for $\perp$, such as $\perp_{\sigma\to\tau} M = \perp_\tau$, we can in fact simplify each approximate normal form to this pattern. However, we will not need to simplify the set of approximate normal forms in this way. ■

Example 5.4.2 The only approximate normal form of $fix(\lambda x\colon\tau.\, x)$ is $\perp_\tau$. This is easy to verify directly. If we want to produce a normal form without using reduction, then the only possibility is to replace the entire term by $\perp_\tau$. The same applies if we reduce $fix(\lambda x\colon\tau.\, x)$ to $(\lambda f\colon\tau\to\tau.\, f(fix\, f))(\lambda x\colon\tau.\, x)$ or $(\lambda x\colon\tau.\, x)(fix(\lambda x\colon\tau.\, x))$ or $fix(\lambda x\colon\tau.\, x)$, which brings us back where we started. ■

If a term M has a normal form, then M will have finitely many approximate normal forms, all essentially resembling the normal form, but with some subterms possibly replaced by $\perp$. As illustrated in Examples 5.4.1 and 5.4.2 above, a term with no normal form may either have finitely or infinitely many approximate normal forms. If M has infinitely many approximate normal forms, then all of them may be regarded as finite approximations to an infinite structure called the *Böhm tree* of M. Due to the number of basic operations in PCF, the precise definition of Böhm tree for PCF is somewhat lengthy. Since we will not need Böhm trees for arbitrary PCF terms (only the finite Böhm trees of finite normal forms in Section 4.4.4), we will not consider them here. The reader interested in Böhm trees may read about the simpler but essentially similar trees of untyped lambda terms in [Bar84].

It is relatively easy to show that for any term $\Gamma \rhd M\colon\sigma$, the meaning of each term in $anf(M)$ is an approximation to the meaning of M. To simplify notation, we write $[\![anf(M)]\!]\eta$ for the set of elements

$$[\![anf(M)]\!]\eta = \{[\![\Gamma \rhd N\colon\sigma]\!]\eta \mid N \in anf(M)\}.$$

Lemma 5.4.3 Let $\Gamma \rhd M\colon\sigma$ be a PCF term and η any environment for $\mathcal{A}_{\text{PCF}}$ satisfying Γ. Then every element of the set $[\![anf(M)]\!]\eta$ is less than or equal to $[\![\Gamma \rhd M\colon\sigma]\!]\eta$

Proof Using the proof system for approximation given in the last section, it is easy to see that if $N \in anf(M)$, then $\mathcal{A} \models \Gamma \triangleright N \leq M : \sigma$. More specifically, we first reduce $M \twoheadrightarrow N'$, and then replace chosen subterms of N' by $\perp$ of the appropriate type. Clearly, $\mathcal{A}$ satisfies $M = N'$, and an easy induction on the structure of N shows that $N \leq N'$. ■

We use a particular class of approximate normal forms to show that $anf(M)$ is directed, with least upper bound M. These are obtained by choosing a bound on the number of times *fix* reduction may be applied to each subterm. For this purpose, we add a constant fix_σ^n to the language, for each type σ and natural number n. We refer to fix_σ^n as the *labeled fixed-point operator with label n*. The label gives an upper bound on the number of times we may apply *fix* reduction to any copy of this operator. More formally, the reduction rules for the labeled fixed-point operators are:

$$\mathit{fix}_\sigma^{n+1} \rightarrow \lambda f\colon \sigma \rightarrow \sigma.\, f\,(\mathit{fix}_\sigma^n\, f),$$

$$\mathit{fix}_\sigma^0 \quad \rightarrow \lambda f\colon \sigma \rightarrow \sigma.\, \perp_\sigma .$$

We say a term is *labeled* if it does not contain any *fix* without a superscript, and write $lab(M)$ for the set of labeled terms that become syntactically identical to M when we replace each fix_σ^n by fix_σ. Since each fix_σ^n may be reduced to a term $\lambda f\colon \sigma \rightarrow \sigma.\, f(f(\ldots f(\perp)\ldots))$ not containing any labeled fixed-point operator, the meaning of each labeled fixed-point operator is completely determined. Since fix_σ^n reduces to an approximate normal form of fix_σ, we have $\mathit{fix}_\sigma^n \leq \mathit{fix}_\sigma$ in any CPO model.

We say M reduces to N by PCF, *lab*-reduction if M reduces to N by applying any number of PCF reductions and the two reduction rules for labeled fixed-point operators given above. From Theorems 8.3.22 and 8.3.24, we have the following property of PCF, *lab*-reduction.

Fact: PCF, *lab*-reduction is confluent and terminating on labeled terms.

A simple correspondence between PCF, *lab*-normal forms and approximate normal forms is given in the following lemma.

Lemma 5.4.4 Let $\Gamma \triangleright M\colon \sigma$ be a PCF term. If $P \in lab(M)$ and N is the PCF, *lab*-normal form of P, then $N \in anf(M)$.

Proof Consider the reduction $P \equiv P_0 \rightarrow P_1 \rightarrow \ldots \rightarrow P_n \equiv N$ of the labeled term to normal form. For simplicity, we assume this reduction has a particular form. Specifically, we count two reduction steps of the form

$$\mathit{fix}_\sigma^0 R \quad \rightarrow \quad (\lambda f\colon \sigma \rightarrow \sigma.\, \perp_\sigma)R \quad \rightarrow \quad \perp_\sigma$$

as a single step and assume that every step of the form $\mathit{fix}^0_\sigma R \to (\lambda f\colon\sigma\to\sigma.\ \bot_\sigma)R$ is followed by a reduction of this subterm to $\bot_\sigma$. By confluence and termination of PCF, *lab*-reduction, there is no loss of generality in this assumption about the reduction of P to normal form. (If we construct $P_1 \to \ldots \to P_n$ by always contracting the leftmost redex, for example, then the sequence will satisfy our assumption.)

For each P_i, we can define a term Q_i with the property that $M \twoheadrightarrow Q_i$ and $P \in \mathit{lab}(Q_i')$ for some term Q_i' obtained from Q_i by replacing one or more subterms with $\bot$. The main idea, which can be made more rigorous by induction on i, is that we reduce $M \twoheadrightarrow Q_i$ by following the same reductions as $P \twoheadrightarrow P_i$, ignoring labels. The reason we may need to replace some subterms by $\bot$ is that the reduction rule for fix^0 may introduce $\bot$ into P_i. For $i = n$, it follows that N may be obtained from M by reduction, followed by replacement of one or more subterms by $\bot$. This completes the proof. ∎

The next step toward the approximation theorem is to show that the meaning of a term M is the least upper bound of the meanings of terms in $\mathit{lab}(M)$. This will let us prove the approximation theorem by showing that $\mathit{anf}(M)$ and $\mathit{lab}(M)$ have the same least upper bound. Using the notation

$$[\![\mathit{lab}(M)]\!]\eta = \{[\![\Gamma \triangleright N\colon\sigma]\!]\eta \mid N \in \mathit{lab}(M)\},$$

we have the following semantic connection between terms and their labelings.

Lemma 5.4.5 Let $\Gamma \triangleright M\colon\sigma$ be a PCF term and η any $\mathcal{A}_{\text{PCF}}$ environment satisfying Γ. Then the set $[\![\mathit{lab}(M)]\!]\eta$ is directed, with $[\![\Gamma \triangleright M\colon\sigma]\!]\eta = \bigvee [\![\mathit{lab}(M)]\!]\eta$.

Proof We show that $[\![\mathit{lab}(M)]\!]\eta$ is directed by observing a simple property of labels. Suppose that $N, P \in \mathit{lab}(M)$ are identical terms, except that the label on one occurrence of *fix* in P is greater than the corresponding label in N. An easy induction on terms shows that $N \leq P$. It follows that if $N, P \in \mathit{lab}(M)$ differ by several labels, with each label in P greater than the corresponding label in N, then $N \leq P$. Therefore, if $N, P \in \mathit{lab}(M)$, we can find a term $Q \in \mathit{lab}(M)$ with $N, P \leq Q$ by labeling each *fix* in Q with the maximum of the corresponding labels in N and P. This shows that $[\![\mathit{lab}(M)]\!]\eta$ is directed.

It remains to show that $[\![\Gamma \triangleright M\colon\sigma]\!]\eta = \bigvee [\![\mathit{lab}(M)]\!]\eta$. This is surprisingly easy, using induction on M. The base cases for variables or constants other than *fix* are trivial. The case for *fix* is straightforward, by Lemma 5.2.20. This leaves application, which follows from Lemma 5.2.11, and lambda abstraction. For lambda abstraction, using the induction hypothesis, we have

$$
\begin{aligned}
[\![\Gamma \rhd \lambda x\colon \sigma.\, M\colon \sigma \to \tau]\!]\eta &= \text{the unique } f \in A^{\sigma\to\tau} \text{ such that} \\
&\quad \forall d \in A^{\sigma}.\, \mathbf{App}\, f\, d = [\![\Gamma, x\colon \sigma \rhd M\colon \tau]\!]\eta[x \mapsto d] \\
&= \text{the unique } f \in A^{\sigma\to\tau} \text{ such that} \\
&\quad \forall d \in A^{\sigma}.\, \mathbf{App}\, f\, d = \bigvee [\![lab(M)]\!]\eta[x \mapsto d]
\end{aligned}
$$

By Lemma 5.2.10, this f is the least upper bound of the directed set of functions in $[\![lab(\lambda x\colon \sigma.\, M)]\!]\eta$. This completes the proof. ∎

Theorem 5.4.6 (Approximation Theorem) Let $\Gamma \rhd M\colon \sigma$ be a PCF term and η any $\mathcal{A}_{\text{PCF}}$ environment satisfying Γ. Then the sets $[\![anf(M)]\!]\eta$ and $[\![lab(M)]\!]\eta$ are directed, with

$$
\begin{aligned}
[\![\Gamma \rhd M\colon \sigma]\!]\eta &= \bigvee [\![lab(M)]\!]\eta \\
&= \bigvee [\![anf(M)]\!]\eta
\end{aligned}
$$

Proof It is already shown in Lemma 5.4.5 that $[\![\Gamma \rhd M\colon \sigma]\!]\eta = \bigvee [\![lab(M)]\!]\eta$. Therefore, it suffices to show that $[\![anf(M)]\!]\eta$ is directed with $\bigvee [\![lab(M)]\!]\eta = \bigvee [\![anf(M)]\!]\eta$.

It is useful to show that every approximate normal form is $\leq$ some labeling of M. If $N \in anf(M)$, then N is obtained by reducing $M \twoheadrightarrow P$ and replacing subterms of P by $\bot$ to obtain a normal form. By connections between labeled and unlabeled reduction discussed in Section 8.3.4, there is some labeling M^* of M such that M^* PCF, *lab*-reduces to a labeling of P^* of P. Since each *fix* that occurs in P must be eliminated in producing N, we may show by induction on N that $N \leq P^* = M^*$. This shows that for every $N \in anf(M)$ there is some labeling M^* of M with $N \leq M^*$.

We can now see that $[\![anf(M)]\!]\eta$ is directed using Lemma 5.4.4. If $N_1, N_2 \in anf(M)$, then there are terms $P_1, P_2 \in lab(M)$ with $N_i \leq P_i$. But since $lab(M)$ is directed by Lemma 5.4.5, there is some term $Q \in lab(M)$ with $P_1, P_2 \leq Q$. It follows from Lemma 5.4.4 that the normal form of Q is an upper bound of N_1 and N_2 in $anf(M)$. Similar reasoning using Lemma 5.4.4 shows that $\bigvee [\![lab(M)]\!]\eta = \bigvee [\![anf(M)]\!]\eta$. This proves the theorem. ∎

Computational adequacy of a model $\mathcal{A}$ is the property that if $\mathcal{A} \models P = N$, for program P and result N, then $eval(P) = N$. Computational adequacy for $\mathcal{A}_{\text{PCF}}$ is an easy corollary of the approximation theorem.

Corollary 5.4.7 The model $\mathcal{A}_{\text{PCF}}$ is computationally adequate for PCF.

Proof Suppose that P is a program and R is a result with $\mathcal{A}_{\text{PCF}} \models P = R$. By the approximation theorem, the meaning of P in $\mathcal{A}_{\text{PCF}}$ is the least upper bound of its approximate normal forms. But since the observable types *nat* and *bool* are interpreted as flat CPOs in

$\mathcal{A}_{\text{PCF}}$, there must be some $N \in \mathit{anf}(P)$ with $\mathcal{A}_{\text{PCF}} \models N = R$. An analysis of PCF normal forms, when the language contains added constants $\perp_\sigma$, shows that $N \equiv R$. Specifically, it is an easy induction on terms to show that if Q is a normal form of type *nat* or *bool* containing $\perp$, then $Q = \perp$ in the CPO model. Therefore, if $N \in \mathit{anf}(P)$ is equal to R in the model, and R is not $\perp$, then we must have $N \equiv R$ and therefore $P \twoheadrightarrow R$. ■

We can use adequacy to show that $=_{den} \subseteq =_{op}$ for PCF.

Corollary 5.4.8 For any PCF terms $\Gamma \triangleright M{:}\,\sigma$ and $\Gamma \triangleright N{:}\,\sigma$, if $\mathcal{A}_{\text{PCF}} \models \Gamma \triangleright M = N{:}\,\sigma$, then $M =_{op} N$.

A more general form of this property, with an essentially similar proof, is given in Exercise 5.4.20.

Proof If $\mathcal{A}_{\text{PCF}} \models \Gamma \triangleright M = N{:}\,\sigma$, then by the soundness of the equational proof system, we can see that for any context $\mathcal{C}[\ ]$ with both $\mathcal{C}[M]$ and $\mathcal{C}[N]$ programs, say of type *nat*, we have

$$\mathcal{A}_{\text{PCF}} \models \Gamma \triangleright \mathcal{C}[M] = \mathcal{C}[N]{:}\, \mathit{nat}.$$

If both denote some numeral, then by computational adequacy (Corollary 5.4.7) we have $\mathit{eval}(\mathcal{C}[M]) = \mathit{eval}(\mathcal{C}[N])$. If neither denotes a numeral, then by soundness both $\mathit{eval}(\mathcal{C}[M])$ and $\mathit{eval}(\mathcal{C}[N])$ must be undefined. Thus $\mathit{eval}(\mathcal{C}[M]) \simeq \mathit{eval}(\mathcal{C}[N])$ and $M =_{op} N$. ■

Exercise 5.4.9 Using the approximation theorem, prove that the inference rule used in Exercise 2.3.3 is sound for $\mathcal{A}_{\text{PCF}}$. More specifically, show that if $M \twoheadrightarrow NM$, then $\bigvee \mathit{anf}(M) = \bigvee \mathit{anf}(\mathit{fix}\ N)$.

5.4.2 Full Abstraction for PCF with Parallel Operations

As mentioned in Section 2.3.5, a denotational semantics is fully abstract if $=_{den}$ coincides with $=_{op}$. We have shown that for PCF, $=_{den} \subseteq =_{op}$, so we have one "half" of full abstraction. However, full abstraction fails for PCF and $\mathcal{A}_{\text{PCF}}$. This was first observed by Plotkin [Plo77], with related observations about the nondefinability of parallel-or made independently by Sazonov [Saz76]. After showing why full abstraction fails, we demonstrate full abstraction when parallel-or is added to PCF.

In general terms, the reason full abstraction fails for PCF is that parallel-or, described in Section 2.5.6, is continuous (by Exercise 5.2.19) but not definable in PCF. More specifically, as shown in Theorem 2.5.19 in Section 2.5.6, there is no PCF expression *POR* with the following behavior

$$POR\, M\, N \twoheadrightarrow \begin{cases} true & \text{if } M \twoheadrightarrow true \text{ or } N \twoheadrightarrow true \\ false & \text{if } M \twoheadrightarrow false \text{ and } N \twoheadrightarrow false \\ \text{no normal form} & \text{otherwise} \end{cases}$$

for all closed boolean expressions M and N. However, we can write a PCF term to test whether its argument has this behavior. Specifically, let us adopt the abbreviation

$$diverge_\sigma \stackrel{\text{def}}{=} fix_\sigma\,(\lambda x{:}\,\sigma.\,x),$$

omitting the type subscript when clear from context, and consider the term

$$\begin{aligned} Is\_POR? \stackrel{\text{def}}{=} \lambda P{:}\, bool \to bool \to bool.\ & \\ & \texttt{if}\ P\ true\ diverge\ \texttt{then} \\ & \quad \texttt{if}\ P\ diverge\ true\ \texttt{then} \\ & \quad\quad \texttt{if}\ \ P\ false\ false\ \texttt{then}\ diverge\ \texttt{else}\ true \\ & \quad \texttt{else}\ diverge \\ & \texttt{else}\ diverge \end{aligned}$$

If we could define POR in PCF, then we could reduce $Is\_POR?\, POR \twoheadrightarrow true$. However, by Theorem 2.5.19, the result of applying $Is\_POR?$ to any closed PCF term $M{:}\, bool \to bool \to bool$ will have no normal form and therefore have value $\bot_{nat}$ in the model $\mathcal{A}_{\text{PCF}}$.

We show below, using Lemma 2.5.24, that

$$Is\_POR? =_{op} \lambda P{:}\, bool \to bool \to bool.\, diverge.$$

However, clearly

$$Is\_POR? \neq_{den} \lambda P{:}\, bool \to bool \to bool.\, diverge$$

since the two differ when applied to the element of $A^{bool \to bool \to bool}$ corresponding to POR. We show that the two terms are operationally equivalent by contradiction. Suppose there is a context $\mathcal{C}[\ ]$ such that both $\mathcal{C}[Is\_POR?]$ and $\mathcal{C}[\lambda P{:}\, bool \to bool \to bool.\, diverge]$ are programs, one terminating and the other not. (If both terminate with different results, we can change the context $\mathcal{C}[\ ]$ to satisfy this assumption.) If $\mathcal{C}[Is\_POR?]$ reduces to a result N, then by Lemma 2.5.24 there is an evaluation context $\text{EV}[\ ]$ such that

$$\mathcal{C}[Is\_POR?] \stackrel{\text{lazy}}{\twoheadrightarrow} \text{EV}[Is\_POR?]$$

Since $\text{EV}[Is\_POR?]$ has type nat or $bool$, we can see that $\text{EV}[\ ]$ has the form $\text{EV}'[[\ ]M]$. If M is not closed, then any free x must be lambda-bound in $\text{EV}[\ ]$. But since $\text{EV}[Is\_POR?]$ has type nat or $bool$, this lambda abstraction in $\text{EV}[\ ]$ must be applied to an argument, contradicting the definition of evaluation context. Therefore,

$\mathcal{C}[Is\_POR?] \stackrel{lazy}{\twoheadrightarrow} \text{EV}'[Is\_POR?M]$

with M closed. But since parallel-or is not definable by any closed PCF term, by Theorem 2.5.19, we can see by Lemma 2.5.21 that $\mathcal{C}[Is\_POR?]$ does not have a normal form. Since we also have

$$\mathcal{C}[\lambda P\colon bool \to bool \to bool.\, diverge] \stackrel{lazy}{\twoheadrightarrow} \text{EV}'$$
$$[(\lambda P\colon bool \to bool \to bool.\, diverge)M]$$

we can see that neither program reduces to a normal form. The assumption that $\mathcal{C}[\lambda P\colon bool \to bool \to bool.diverge]$ has a normal form leads to a similar contradiction. Therefore, the two programs must be operationally equivalent.

In the rest of this section, we will show that if parallel-or is added to PCF, then $\mathcal{A}_{\text{PCF}}$ is fully abstract. This extension, PCF $+\, por$, is obtained by adding the constant $por\colon bool \to bool \to bool$, interpreted as the continuous parallel-or function, with the following reduction axioms.

$$por\ true\ M \quad \to true$$

$$por\ M\ true \quad \to true$$

$$por\ false\ false \to false$$

Since these axioms are all left-linear, the reduction system for PCF $+\, por$ may be proved confluent, and PCF, *lab*, *por*-reduction confluent and terminating, as in Theorems 8.3.22 and 8.3.24. It is therefore straightforward to extend the approximation theorem and computational adequacy results of the last section to PCF $+\, por$.

The main technical step in showing full abstraction for PCF $+\, por$ is to show that enough elements in $\mathcal{A}_{\text{PCF}}$ are definable in this language. This requires careful analysis of the CPOs that are used in $\mathcal{A}_{\text{PCF}}$. Specifically, we show that all CPOs in $\mathcal{A}_{\text{PCF}}$ are "algebraic," which involves the additional concept of pairwise consistent completeness. It follows from algebraicity that if two terms are denotationally different, they can be distinguished using only certain "compact" elements. Therefore, we prove full abstraction by proving that every compact element of $\mathcal{A}_{\text{PCF}}$ is definable in PCF $+\, por$. The full abstraction theorem in this section is originally due to Plotkin [Plo77]; the proof we use is a variant due to Meyer [Mey92a].

An important idea is the notion of "compact element" of a CPO. It is trivially true that every element of a CPO is the least upper bound of the elements $\leq$ to it. What distinguishes the compact elements is that they are not the least upper bound of any set of elements that are strictly less. More precisely, if d is an element of CPO $\mathcal{D}$, then d is *compact* if, for every directed $S \subseteq D$ with $d \leq \bigvee S$, we have $d \leq d'$ for some $d' \in S$. In the CPOs used in $\mathcal{A}_{\text{PCF}}$, every compact element is definable (possibly using parallel operations), so every compact element is "finitely computable" in some way. For this reason, compact elements are sometimes called *finite elements*. If $\mathcal{D}$ is a CPO, we write $K(\mathcal{D})$ for the set of compact elements of $\mathcal{D}$.

We will be interested in CPOs where each element is the least upper bound of the compact elements below it. We say a CPO $\mathcal{D}$ is *algebraic* if every $d \in D$ is the limit of its compact approximants, *i.e.*,

$$d = \bigvee\{a \leq d \mid a \in K(\mathcal{D})\}.$$

It is easy to see that every discrete or flat CPO is algebraic. In addition, the product $\mathcal{D} \times \mathcal{E}$ of two algebraic CPOs is algebraic, with compact elements $K(\mathcal{D}) \times K(\mathcal{E})$. However, there exist algebraic CPOs $\mathcal{D}$ and $\mathcal{E}$ such that $\mathcal{D} \to \mathcal{E}$ is not algebraic. For this reason, when working with algebraic CPOs, it is common to identify stronger conditions that are preserved by products and function space constructions.

There are several consistency conditions in the literature on domain theory. (See [Gun92, GS90], for example.) We will use a relatively strong condition, since this will simplify the proof that all compact elements are definable. If $\mathcal{D}$ is a CPO and $d, d' \in D$, we say *d and d' are consistent* if there is some $d'' \in D$ with $d, d' \leq d''$. In words, two elements are consistent if they have an upper bound. We write $d \uparrow d'$ if d and d' are consistent. A subset $S \subseteq D$ is *pairwise consistent* if every pair of elements from S is consistent and a CPO $\mathcal{D}$ is *pairwise-consistent complete* if every pairwise-consistent subset has a least upper bound. Since "pairwise-consistent complete CPO" is quite a mouthful (even if you are reading silently to yourself), we will abbreviate this phrase to *PCPO*. To repeat the definition, a PCPO is a partial order $\mathcal{D} = \langle D, \leq_D \rangle$ with the property that every $S \subseteq D$ that is either directed *or* pairwise consistent has a least upper bound, $\bigvee S$. A weaker condition that is more commonly used in the literature is described in Exercise 5.4.17. It is easy to see that every PCPO is pointed, since the empty subset is pairwise consistent.

An interesting, and perhaps unexpected, property of PCPOs is that every set has a greatest lower bound.

Lemma 5.4.10 If $\mathcal{D}$ is a PCPO (pairwise-consistent complete CPO) and $S \subseteq D$ is any subset, then S has a greatest lower bound $\bigwedge S$.

Proof The set $L_S = \{d \in D \mid d \leq d' \text{ for every } d' \in S\}$ of lower bounds of S is pairwise consistent, so it has a least upper bound $\bigvee L_S$. It is easy to check that this is the greatest lower bound of S. ∎

The next lemma about PCPOs is that any CPOs built from PCPOs by our usual constructors is a PCPO.

Lemma 5.4.11 Every flat CPO is a PCPO (pairwise-consistent complete CPO). If $\mathcal{D}$ and $\mathcal{E}$ are PCPOs, then so are $\mathcal{D}_\bot$, $\mathcal{D} \times \mathcal{E}$ and $\mathcal{D} \to \mathcal{E}$. Moreover, if $S \subseteq D \times E$ is pairwise consistent, then $\bigvee S = \langle \bigvee(\mathbf{Proj}_1 S), \bigvee(\mathbf{Proj}_2 S)\rangle$ and if $S \subseteq D \to E$ is pairwise consistent, the least upper bound of S is the function f given by $f(d) = \bigvee S(d)$.

Proof The cases for flat and lifted PCPOs are straightforward and left to the reader. For a product CPO, we note that if $\langle d, e\rangle \uparrow \langle d', e'\rangle$, then $d \uparrow d'$ and $e \uparrow e'$. Therefore, if $S \subseteq D \times E$ is pairwise consistent, then so are the sets $\mathbf{Proj}_1 S$ and $\mathbf{Proj}_2 S$. The proof that $\bigvee S = \langle \bigvee(\mathbf{Proj}_1 S), \bigvee(\mathbf{Proj}_2 S)\rangle$ is the same as for Lemma 5.2.2. The argument for $\mathcal{D} \to \mathcal{E}$ is similar, showing first that for each $d \in D$, the set $S(d)$ is pairwise consistent. The argument given in the proof of Lemma 5.2.10 shows that the function f given by $f(d) = \bigvee S(d)$ is continuous and the least upper bound of S. ■

Our next goal is to show that if $\mathcal{D}$ and $\mathcal{E}$ are algebraic PCPOs, then so is $\mathcal{D} \to \mathcal{E}$. This will allow us to conclude that every CPO in $\mathcal{A}_{\text{PCF}}$ is algebraic. Before we show that $\mathcal{D} \to \mathcal{E}$ is algebraic, however, we introduce notation for some simple compact elements of $\mathcal{D} \to \mathcal{E}$.

For $a \in D$ and $b \in E$, we define the *step function* $a \searrow b \colon D \to E$ by

$$(a \searrow b)(d) = \begin{cases} b & \text{if } d \geq a \\ \bot & \text{otherwise} \end{cases}$$

It is left as Exercise 5.4.16 to show that if $a \in D$ is compact, the step function $a \searrow b$ is continuous. In general, we will be interested in step functions $a \searrow b$ with both a and b compact, since these are used to define the compact elements of a function CPO.

It follows from the following lemma that every continuous function is the least upper bound of a set of compact step functions. However, the shortcoming of step functions alone is that there are functions that are not the least upper bound of any *directed* set of step functions. To form a directed set of functions less than some continuous function, we need to consider least upper bounds of finite sets of step functions.

Lemma 5.4.12 Let $\mathcal{D}$ and $\mathcal{E}$ be algebraic PCPOs. Then $\mathcal{D} \to \mathcal{E}$ is an algebraic PCPO whose compact elements are least upper bounds $\bigvee\{a_1 \searrow b_1, \ldots, a_n \searrow b_n\}$ of finite sets of step functions, with all $a_i \in D$ and $b_i \in E$ compact and such that if $a_i \uparrow a_j$, then $b_i \uparrow b_j$.

Proof We know, by Exercise 5.4.16, that if $a \in D$ and $b \in E$ are compact, $a \searrow b$ is continuous. To show that $a \searrow b$ is compact, suppose $S \subseteq \mathcal{D} \to \mathcal{E}$ is a directed set with $(a \searrow b) \leq \bigvee S$. By Lemma 5.2.10, $f = \bigvee S$ is given by $f(d) = \bigvee S(d)$. In particular, we have $(a \searrow b)(a) = b \leq \bigvee S(b)$. But since b is compact, it follows that there is some $g \in S$ with $b \in g(b)$. It is not hard to check that $a \searrow b \leq g$, since by monotonicity $(a \searrow b)(d) = b \leq g(d)$ for $d \geq b$, and otherwise $(a \searrow b)(d) = \bot \leq g(d)$. This proves that $a \searrow b$ is compact.

It is easy to see that two step functions, $a_1 \searrow b_1$ and $a_2 \searrow b_2$, are consistent precisely if $a_1 \uparrow a_2$ implies $b_1 \uparrow b_2$. By Exercise 5.4.15, the least upper bound of two consistent compact elements is compact. It follows that any finite least upper bound $\bigvee\{a_1 \searrow b_1, \ldots, a_n \searrow b_n\}$ is compact if all $a_i \in D$ and $b_i \in E$ are compact and, $a_i \uparrow a_j$ implies $b_i \uparrow b_j$.

The next step is to show that for every continuous $f\colon \mathcal{D} \to \mathcal{E}$, the set S_f of all compact elements below f is directed and has least upper bound f. We know from Exercise 5.4.15 that S_f is directed, since any pair of compact elements below f are necessarily consistent. We proceed by showing that $f = \bigvee S$, where $S = \{a \searrow b \mid a, b \text{ compact and } f(a) \geq b\}$. It follows easily from the final step of the proof that $\bigvee S = \bigvee S_f$. Since S is bounded by f, S is pairwise consistent and so, since $\mathcal{D} \to \mathcal{E}$ is a PCPO, $\bigvee S$ exists. It remains to show that $f \leq \bigvee S$.

Consider any $d \in D$. Since $\mathcal{D}$ is algebraic, we have

$$f(d) = f(\bigvee\{a \leq d \mid a \in K(\mathcal{D})\}) = \bigvee f(\{a \leq d \mid a \in K(\mathcal{D})\}).$$

Therefore, if compact $b \leq f(d)$, we have $b \leq f(a)$ for some compact $a \leq d$ and hence the step function $a \searrow b$ is in S. It follows that every compact $b \leq f(d)$ is $\leq \bigvee S$. Since this holds for all $d \in D$, we have $f \leq \bigvee S$, which completes the proof that $\mathcal{D} \to \mathcal{E}$ is algebraic.

The final step of the proof is to show that all compact elements of $\mathcal{D} \to \mathcal{E}$ have the form $\bigvee\{a_1 \searrow b_1, \ldots, a_n \searrow b_n\}$ with all $a_i \in D$ and $b_i \in E$ compact and, if $a_i \uparrow a_j$, then $b_i \uparrow b_j$. Suppose $g\colon \mathcal{D} \to \mathcal{E}$ is compact and let S be the set of all functions of this form that are $\leq g$. As we have shown above, $\bigvee S = g$. But then, since g is compact, we have $g \leq h$ for some $h \in S$. But by definition of S, $h \leq g$. Therefore, $g = h$ and g must have the required form. ■

The final lemma before proving the full abstraction theorem establishes the definability of all compact elements in PCF + *por*. As shown in Exercise 2.5.29, we can define parallel-conditionals PIF_{nat} on type *nat* and PIF_{bool} on type *bool* from parallel-or. From these, we may define a parallel-conditional of each type, by

$$PIF_{\sigma\to\tau} \stackrel{\text{def}}{=} \lambda x\colon bool.\, \lambda f\colon \sigma \to \tau.\, \lambda g\colon \sigma \to \tau.$$
$$\lambda y\colon \sigma.\, PIF_{\tau}\, x\, (f\, y)\, (g\, y)$$

$$PIF_{\sigma\times\tau} \stackrel{\text{def}}{=} \lambda x\colon bool.\, \lambda p\colon \sigma \times \tau.\, \lambda q\colon \sigma \times \tau.$$
$$\langle PIF_{\sigma}\, x\, (\mathbf{Proj}_1 f)\, (\mathbf{Proj}_1 g),\ PIF_{\tau}\, x\, (\mathbf{Proj}_2 f)\, (\mathbf{Proj}_2 g)\rangle$$

It is easy to see that semantically,

$$PIF_\sigma\ x\ y\ z = \begin{cases} y & \text{if } x = true \\ z & \text{if } x = false \\ y \wedge z & \text{if } x = \bot \end{cases}$$

It is also easy to define a "bounded least upper bound" function $BLUB_\sigma : \sigma \to \sigma \to \sigma \to \sigma$ on each type with the semantic property that

$$BLUB_\sigma\ x\ y\ z = (x \wedge y) \vee (x \wedge z).$$

This is left as Exercise 5.4.18, which contains a hint. The reason that $BLUB_\sigma$ is called a "bounded least upper bound" is that when $x \geq y, z$ we have $BLUB_\sigma\ x\ y\ z = y \vee z$. These functions will be used in the proof of the following lemma.

Lemma 5.4.13 If a is a compact element of $\mathcal{A}_{\mathrm{PCF}}$, then a is definable by a closed PCF + *por* term.

Proof We use induction on types to show that for all compact $a, a' \in A^\sigma_{\mathrm{PCF}}$,

1. The step function $a \searrow true$ is definable,
2. If a and a' are inconsistent, then $(a \searrow true) \vee (a' \searrow false)$ is definable,
3. The compact element a is definable.

The proof is by induction on types.

The base cases, conditions (1)–(3) for *nat* and *bool*, are all straightforward. The most difficult is (2), which we prove for *nat*. If $a, a' \in \mathcal{N}_\bot$ are inconsistent, then neither can be $\bot$. This allows us to write $(a \searrow true) \vee (a' \searrow false)$ as

$$\lambda x{:}\,nat.\,\texttt{if}\ Eq?\,x\ \lceil a \rceil \texttt{then}\ true$$
$$\texttt{else if}\ Eq?\,x\ \lceil a' \rceil\ \texttt{then}\ false\ \texttt{else}\ diverge$$

where $\lceil a \rceil$ is the PCF numeral for a.

Since PCF has product and function types, there are two induction steps. We prove the lemma for function types, and leave the simpler arguments for product types as Exercise 5.4.19. For a function type $\sigma \to \tau$, we know by Lemma 5.4.12 that a has the form

$$a = \bigvee \{a_1 \searrow b_1, \ldots, a_n \searrow b_n\},$$

where $a_1, \ldots, a_n, b_1, \ldots, b_n$ are compact and $a_i \uparrow a_j$ implies $b_i \uparrow b_j$.

1. We define the step function $a \searrow true$ by

$$\lambda f{:}\,\sigma \to \tau.((b_1 \searrow true)(f\,a_1))\ and\ \ldots\ and\ ((b_n \searrow true)(f\,a_n))$$

where all $(b_i \searrow true)$ and a_i are definable by the induction hypothesis. To see that this term is correct, recall that $a \leq f$ iff each $a_i \searrow b_i$ approximates f, which is equivalent to $f(a_i) \geq b_i$, for each i.

2. Suppose a and a' are inconsistent compact elements. Expressing each as the least upper bound of a finite set of step functions as in Lemma 5.4.12, it is easy to see that there must be some compact $b \in A^\sigma$ with ab and $a'b$ inconsistent and compact. This allows us to define $(a \searrow \mathit{true}) \vee (a' \searrow \mathit{false})$ by

$\lambda f\colon \sigma \to \tau.$

$$\texttt{if}\ ((ab \searrow \mathit{true}) \vee (a'b \searrow \mathit{false}))(fb)\ \texttt{then}\ (a \searrow \mathit{true})f\ \texttt{else}\ \mathit{not}\,((a' \searrow \mathit{true})f)$$

where $a \searrow \mathit{true}$ and $a' \searrow \mathit{false}$ are definable by (1), and b and $(ab \searrow \mathit{true}) \vee (a'b \searrow \mathit{false})$ are definable by the induction hypothesis.

3. This is the most complicated condition. We proceed by induction on n, the number of step functions used to construct a. If $n = 1$, then $a = a_1 \searrow b_1$ and we may define a by

$$\lambda x\colon \sigma.\, \texttt{if}\ (a_1 \searrow \mathit{true})\,x\ \texttt{then}\ b_1\ \texttt{else}\ \mathit{diverge}_\tau$$

where $a_1 \searrow \mathit{true}$ and b_1 are definable by the induction hypothesis.

For $n > 1$, there are two cases. The first is that the set $\{a_1, \ldots, a_n\}$ is pairwise consistent. Since $\{b_1, \ldots, b_n\}$ must also be pairwise consistent, we may let $b = \bigvee\{b_1, \ldots, b_n\}$. Since $a \leq \lambda x\colon \sigma.\, b$, we define a by

$$\mathit{BLUB}\,(\lambda x\colon \sigma.\, b)\ (a_1 \searrow b_1)\ (\bigvee\{a_2 \searrow b_2, \ldots, a_n \searrow b_n\})$$

where $(a_1 \searrow b_1)$ and $\bigvee\{a_2 \searrow b_2, \ldots, a_n \searrow b_n\}$ are definable by the hypothesis of the subinduction on number of step functions and b is definable by the main induction hypothesis.

The remaining case is to define a when the set $\{a_1, \ldots, a_n\}$ is not pairwise consistent. This is where we finally use a parallel operation. Without loss of generality we may assume a_1 and a_2 are inconsistent. Let

$$a^{(wo1)} = \bigvee\{a_2 \searrow b_2, \ldots, a_n \searrow b_n\}$$

$$a^{(wo2)} = \bigvee\{a_1 \searrow b_1, a_3 \searrow b_3, \ldots, a_n \searrow b_n\}$$

which are both definable by the hypothesis of the subinduction. Then we may define a by

$$\lambda x\colon \sigma.\, \mathit{PIF}_\tau\ (((a_1 \searrow \mathit{true}) \vee (a_2 \searrow \mathit{false}))\,x)\ (a^{(wo2)}x)\ (a^{(wo1)}x).$$

In words, this function checks its argument to see if it is approximated by either a_1 or a_2. In the first case, since a_1 and a_2 are inconsistent, the step function $a_2 \searrow b_2$ does not contribute to the value of ax and we obtain the correct result since $ax = a^{(wo2)}x$. In the second case, we similarly have $ax = a^{(wo1)}x$. The third possibility is that neither $a_1 \le x$ nor $a_2 \le z$. In this event, neither $a_1 \searrow b_1$ nor $a_2 \searrow b_2$ contributes to value of $a\,x$, and we have $a\,x = (a^{(wo1)}x) \wedge (a^{(wo2)}x)$. Since this is exactly the result given by *PIF*, this definition of a is correct for all $x \in A^\sigma$. This concludes the proof.

Theorem 5.4.14 (Full Abstraction) For PCF + *por*, the relations $=_{den}$, determined by $\mathcal{A}_{\text{PCF}}$ and $=_{op}$, determined by the reduction system, are identical.

A more general form of full abstraction, with a similar proof, is given in Exercise 5.4.20.

Proof Since we have $=_{den} \subseteq =_{op}$ by Corollary 5.4.8 of the approximation theorem, it remains to prove the reverse inclusion. We assume that $M \ne_{den} N$ and show $M \ne_{op} N$, for PCF terms $\Gamma \rhd M\colon\sigma$ and $\Gamma \rhd N\colon\sigma$. Since the CPOs in $\mathcal{A}_{\text{PCF}}$ are all algebraic, there is some environment η and compact $a \in A^\sigma_{\text{PCF}}$ with $a \le [\![\Gamma \rhd M\colon\sigma]\!]\eta$ but not $a \le [\![\Gamma \rhd N\colon\sigma]\!]\eta$ (or conversely, with the roles of M and N reversed). By Lemma 5.4.13, the step function $a \searrow \mathit{true}$ is definable in PCF + *por*. By computational adequacy (Corollary 5.4.7), $(a \searrow \mathit{true})M \twoheadrightarrow \mathit{true}$ while by soundness, $(a \searrow \mathit{true})N$ has no normal form. Therefore $M \ne_{op} N$. This proves the theorem. ∎

Exercise 5.4.15 Show that if $\mathcal{D}$ is a PCPO with $a, b \in D$ consistent compact elements, then $a \vee b = \bigvee\{a, b\}$ is compact.

Exercise 5.4.16 Show that if a is compact, the step function $a \searrow b$ is continuous. Give an example of a CPO $\mathcal{D}$ and elements $d, d' \in D$ such that $d \searrow d'$ is not a continuous function from $\mathcal{D}$ to $\mathcal{D}$.

Exercise 5.4.17 A CPO $\mathcal{D}$ is *bounded complete* if every subset $S \subseteq D$ that has an upper bound has a least upper bound. In other words, $\bigvee S$ exists whenever S is either directed or bounded. We will abbreviate bounded complete CPO to *BCPO*.

(a) Show that every PCPO is a BCPO.

(b) Find a BCPO that is not a PCPO.

(c) Show that Lemma 5.4.12 holds if we replace PCPO by BCPO.

(d) Find the step in the proof of Lemma 5.4.13 that requires pairwise-consistent completeness instead of bounded completeness.

Exercise 5.4.18 Show how to define a bounded least upper bound function for each type. For *nat*, the definition is

$$\mathit{BLUB}_{nat} \stackrel{\text{def}}{=} \lambda x\colon nat.\,\lambda y\colon nat.\,\lambda z\colon nat.$$

$$\texttt{if } \mathit{por}\,(\mathit{Eq?}\,x\,y)\,(\mathit{Eq?}\,x\,z) \texttt{ then } x \texttt{ else } \mathit{diverge}_{nat}.$$

The definition for *bool* is similar. The definitions for function or product types resemble the inductive definitions of *PIF*.

Exercise 5.4.19 Prove conditions (1)–(3), used in the proof of Lemma 5.4.13, for a product type $\sigma \times \tau$, assuming all three hold for types σ and τ.

Exercise 5.4.20 The form of full abstraction proved in this section is sometimes called *equational* full abstraction to distinguish it from an inequational (or approximation) form. To state inequational full abstraction, we define $M \leq_{den} N$ if the meaning of M is $\leq$ the meaning of N in every environment and $M \leq_{op} N$ if, for every context $\mathcal{C}[\,]$ such that $\mathcal{C}[M]$ and $\mathcal{C}[N]$ are programs and every result R, if $eval(\mathcal{C}[M]) = R$ then $eval(\mathcal{C}[N]) = R$.

(a) Using adequacy, prove $\leq_{den} \subseteq \leq_{op}$, which is the inequational form of Corollary 5.4.8.

(b) Using the lemmas given in this section, prove $\leq_{op} \subseteq \leq_{den}$, which, with (a) establishes the inequational form of Theorem 5.4.14 for PCF $+$ *por*.

Exercise 5.4.21 In the proof of Theorem 5.4.14, we show that if $M \neq_{den} N$ then $M \neq_{op} N$ using a context of the form $\mathcal{C}[\,] \equiv F[\,]$. We might also wish to show that if $M \neq_{den} N$ then these terms can be distinguished using a special form of context called an *elimination context,* a form also used in Section 8.3.4. Elimination contexts are defined inductively by

$$\mathcal{E}[\,] \;::=\; [\,] \mid \mathcal{E}[[\,]M] \mid \mathcal{E}[\mathbf{Proj}_i\,[\,]]$$

Without using Theorem 5.4.14, prove by induction on types that if $M \neq_{den} N$, then M and N are operationally distinguishable by an elimination context.

5.5 Recursion-theoretic Models

5.5.1 Introduction

While domain-theoretic models are commonly used in programming language semantics, the traditional study of computability and complexity uses Turing machines or equivalent machine models. These machine models all compute precisely the partial recursive functions on the natural numbers, as described in Sections 2.5.4 and 2.5.5. One way of establishing a connection between program semantics and traditional computability is through semantic models based on recursive function theory. An intuitive reason that we should be able to construct models with every function Turing computable is that every lambda-definable function is computable by reduction. We therefore expect that a hierarchy containing all the computable functions will contain all the lambda-definable functions and form a Henkin model. A difference between computability theory and models of lambda calculus is that models must satisfy equations between terms, whereas computability theory admits many possible algorithms computing the same function. In the jargon of the field, lambda calculus is an *extensional* theory of functions while computability theory is an *intensional* theory. This is clearly illustrated in the construction of partial equivalence relation models, which use equivalence classes of codes for computable functions.

Since models of $\lambda^{\times,\rightarrow}$ involve sets of functions and sets of pairs, we need a general notion of computability that applies to sets other than the natural numbers. The main idea used in this section is that we can extend computability to any set by associating one or more natural number "codes" with each element. This leads us to the definition of *modest sets*. While the most common modest set models are based on standard Turing-machine computation, it is also possible to use "codes" from any structure that allow us to represent functions and pairs. Since the codes themselves play a more fundamental role than the elements they code, we may also take a more abstract view of these models by representing elements of each type as equivalence classes of codes. This leads to a class of models in which every type is interpreted as a binary relation (partial equivalence relation, or per) over some set of codes. These models are particularly convenient for interpreting languages with polymorphism or subtyping, as we shall see in Chapters 9 and 10.

Modest sets are defined in Section 5.5.2, where we also define product and function space constructions on modest sets. These are used in Section 5.5.3 to construct a Henkin model called the full recursive function hierarchy over any collection of modest sets. In Section 5.6, an equivalent formulation using partial equivalence relations instead of modest sets is developed, followed by a generalization from the natural numbers (used as codes for partial recursive functions) to other structures with similar properties. Section 5.6 concludes with a section outlining the issues involved in interpreting fixed-point operators in recursive models.

The framework of modest sets was first formulated in [Hyl82], where sets with partial enumeration functions were characterized as the "effective objects" of a natural category. These were later dubbed the "modest sets" by Dana Scott (see [Hyl88]). A number of related ideas appear earlier in Kleene realizability [Kle45, Kle71], a study of first-order recursive functions [MS55], recursion in higher types [Kre59], the model HEO described in [Tro73], and the development of numbered sets carried out by Malcev and Ershov [Mal70, Ers71, Ers72, Ers76].

In the rest of this introductory section, we review well-known properties of recursive functions that are needed for the development of modest sets and related structures.

As discussed in Section 2.5.4, the standard notion of computability on the natural numbers may be characterized using Turing machines, the inductive definition of partial recursive functions, or definability in PCF. To simplify the presentation and some of the proofs, we will use the definition of the partial recursive functions, given in Sections 2.5.4 and 2.5.5, and the characterization of these functions using Turing machines, interchangeably.

Let $\mathcal{PR}$ be the set of all unary partial recursive (computable) functions on the natural numbers and let $\phi_0, \phi_1, \ldots$ be some enumeration that contains all functions in $\mathcal{PR}$. We only need one-argument functions since we may treat multi-argument functions using either a recursive pairing function or Currying. We say that i is an *index* of the partial recursive function ϕ_i. Since ϕ_i and ϕ_j may be the same function, for $i \neq j$, a partial recursive function may (and in fact always does) have more than one index. The reader familiar with recursive function theory will know that there are several ways that an enumeration of $\mathcal{PR}$ might be determined. Specifically, every recursive function has a description, as a "program" or definition in some language. We may take these descriptions and arrange them in some order, letting ϕ_0 be the function computed by the first program, ϕ_1 the function computed by the second, and so on. We assume this is done in such a way that we can compute the ith function on argument n (as a function of i and n), compute the number k such that ϕ_k is the composition of ϕ_i and ϕ_j, and similarly for other simple operations on functions. It is traditional in recursive function theory to call any enumeration with these properties an *acceptable enumeration* of the partial recursive functions and only to consider acceptable enumerations.

It is easy to define computable pairing and projection functions on the natural numbers, as outlined in Exercise 2.5.13. To fix notation, let us write pr for the function

$$pr(n, m) = (n + m)(n + m + 1)/2 + m$$

and $(n)_1$, $(n)_2$ for the numbers such that

$$(pr(n, m))_1 = n \quad \text{and} \quad (pr(n, m))_2 = m.$$

We can also represent any sequence of natural numbers by single natural number, using nested pairing, as in Lisp and as described in Exercise 2.5.13. We will use the *s-m-n* theorem from recursion theory, namely, given any recursive function $f(x_1, \ldots, x_m, y_1, \ldots, y_n)$ of $m + n$ arguments, and natural numbers $a_1, \ldots, a_m$, we may effectively find a recursive function g of n arguments such that $g(y_1, \ldots, y_n) = f(a_1, \ldots, a_m, y_1, \ldots, y_n)$. Since computation on recursive functions is carried out using indices, this really means that there is a computable function which, given an index i for f, and numbers $a_1, \ldots, a_m$, returns an index for g. A time-honored general reference on recursive function theory is [Rog67]. Some computer science students find [Cut80], which uses computability based on register machines, more accessible.

5.5.2 Modest Sets

We will define the computable functions on a set, A, by choosing a function e_A from the natural numbers to A and appealing to standard computability on the natural numbers. Specifically, a *modest set* is a pair $\langle A, e_A \rangle$, where A is a set and $e_A: \mathcal{N} \rightharpoonup A$ is a surjective partial function from the natural numbers to A. We refer to e_A as the *partial enumeration function for* A. Intuitively, if $e_A(n) = a$, we think of n as the "code" for the element a of A; this is elaborated below. The function e_A must be surjective, since in order to define computability on A, every element of A must have a numeric code. This forces A to be countable. However, e_A need not be a total function. In fact, if we wish to form a modest set of total recursive functions, it is necessary to have $e_A(n)$ be undefined for some natural number n, as illustrated in Exercise 5.5.9 below. Since e_A will be used simply to define a class of recursive functions on A, we will not require effective procedures for determining whether given $n, m \in \mathcal{N}$ code the same (or any) element of A.

Computer scientists may gain stronger intuition for modest sets by identifying natural numbers with bit strings, and considering computer representations for various data. In more detail, we may regard any natural number as the sequence of bits obtained by writing the number out base two. If we wish to compute with any kind of value, we must represent it by some sequence of bits, and therefore a natural number. It is quite common to have more than one representation for a single value, such as in representing functions by their compiled code. Since there are many possible programs computing a given function, there are many possible bit strings representing a single mathematical function. On the other hand, each sequence of bits obtained by compiling code represents only one function. Therefore, we have a partial function from natural numbers to the values we are representing; if a natural number codes a value, then it is the code for exactly one value.

A trivial example of a modest set is $\langle \mathcal{N}, \lambda n.\, n \rangle$, the natural numbers enumerated by the identity function. Several other examples are listed below.

Example 5.5.1 The pair $\langle \mathcal{PR}, \lambda n.\phi_n \rangle$ is a modest set whose elements are functions. The enumeration function $\lambda n.\phi_n$, mapping n to the nth partial recursive function, is total and surjective, but not one-to-one. ■

Example 5.5.2 If $\mathcal{T}ot$ is the set of total recursive functions, and e_{tot} is the map

$$e_{tot}(n) = \begin{cases} \phi_n & \text{if } \phi_n \text{ is total} \\ \text{undefined} & \text{otherwise} \end{cases}$$

then $\langle \mathcal{T}ot, e_{tot} \rangle$ is a modest set. In this example, there is no effective procedure for determining whether $e_{tot}(n)$ is defined, or whether $e_{tot}(n) = e_{tot}(m)$, given natural numbers n and m. ■

Example 5.5.3 The set of typed lambda terms forms a modest set, with enumeration e_{terms} mapping n to the term M with Gödel code $\ulcorner M \urcorner = n$. Just as we have not been overly specific about how recursive functions are enumerated (or "coded by natural numbers"), we will not generally be concerned with how a lambda term is assigned a number. All that matters, when we assign Gödel numbers to syntactic expressions, is that we can compute standard operations on syntax from the Gödel number of a term. For example, we assume there are computable functions on codes that determine whether a term is a variable, lambda abstraction, or application, and compute the codes of any subexpressions. This is illustrated in Exercise 5.5.14, which gives a specific coding of terms. General discussion of Gödel numbering may be found in standard texts on logic [End72], but it is unlikely that the reader will require additional information. An intuitive way of assigning natural numbers to terms, familiar to computer scientists, is to associate a bit string of some fixed length (*e.g.*, one or two bytes) with each symbol of the language, and use the binary number obtained by concatenating bit strings as the Gödel number of a term. ■

Example 5.5.4 In the proofs of Theorems 4.5.22 and 4.5.28, we construct a Henkin model whose elements are equivalence classes of terms. A type $A^\sigma = \{[M\!:\sigma] \mid \Gamma \rhd M\!:\sigma\}$ of this term model may be enumerated by the function e_σ with $e_\sigma(m) = [M\!:\sigma]$ iff m is a Gödel number (code) for some term in the equivalence class $[M\!:\sigma]$. (Gödel numbering of terms is described in Example 5.5.3.) In Exercise 5.5.13, it is shown that the β, η-term model is isomorphic to an applicative structure of modest sets and recursive functions. Exercise 5.5.14 shows that not all recursive functions appear in the term model. ■

An aspect of modest sets that is sometimes confusing is that the partial enumeration function is not forced to be the "natural" assignment of codes. For example, there is a modest set $\langle \mathcal{PR}, e\rangle$ where e is *not* an acceptable enumeration of the partial recursive functions (in the sense described in Section 5.5.1). For this modest set, the usual, computable operations on partial recursive functions may not be recursive functions from $\langle \mathcal{PR}, e\rangle \to \langle \mathcal{PR}, e\rangle$ and, conversely, the recursive functions on this modest set need not be computable in the standard sense. However, there is no easy way to sharpen the definition of modest set to exclude such structures. Perhaps the situation is best summarized by saying that if a modest set uses the "standard" partial enumeration function (or one that is recursively equivalent), as in $\langle \mathcal{PR}, \lambda n.\phi_n\rangle$ of Example 5.5.1, then computability on modest sets will coincide with the standard notion of computability on the underlying set. However, if we consider a modest set with a "nonstandard" enumeration function, then modest set computability will be a nonstandard form of computability.

We will often wish to refer to the set of codes of an element. For any modest set $\langle A, e_A\rangle$ and element $a \in A$, we will write $|a|_A$ for the set of natural numbers

$|a|_A = \{n \mid e_A(n) = a\}$.

We will omit the subscript when it is clear from context. Note that since e_A is a function, the sets $|a|$ and $|b|$ are disjoint whenever $a \neq b$. Furthermore, it is easy to see that if $|\cdot|: A \to \mathcal{P}(\mathcal{N})$ is some function assigning disjoint, nonempty sets to distinct elements of A, then $|\cdot|$ determines a unique partial surjection $e: \mathcal{N} \rightharpoonup A$. Thus a modest set may be defined by giving $|\cdot|$ instead of e.

It is relatively easy to make the cartesian product of two modest sets into a modest set, using recursive pairing operations on natural numbers. If $A = \langle A, e_A \rangle$ and $B = \langle B, e_B \rangle$ are modest sets, then we let $A \times B = \langle A \times B, e_{A \to B} \rangle$ be the collection of all ordered pairs, $A \times B$, enumerated by

$e_{A \times B}(n) = \langle a, b \rangle$ iff $e_A((n)_1) = a$ and $e_B((n)_2) = b$.

Lemma 5.5.5 If A and B are modest sets, then $A \times B$ is a modest set.

Proof We must check that $e_{A \times B}$ is a surjective partial function. It is a partial function since e_A and e_B are partial functions. The partial function $e_{A \times B}$ is surjective since e_A and e_B are surjective, and if $e_A(n) = a$ and $e_B(m) = b$, then $e_{A \times B}(pr(n, m)) = \langle a, b \rangle$. ■

Intuitively, the recursive functions on modest sets are the functions that may be computed by recursive functions on codes. To be more precise, let $f: A \to B$ be a total function on the underlying values of modest sets $\langle A, e_A \rangle$ and $\langle B, e_B \rangle$. A partial function $g: \mathcal{N} \rightharpoonup \mathcal{N}$ *tracks* f if

$n \in |a|$ implies $g(n)\downarrow$ and $g(n) \in |f(a)|$,

where $g(n)\downarrow$ means that the partial function g is defined on n. We say f is *recursive* (or *computable*) if there is a partial recursive g tracking f. Note that while f is total, g may be partial. More specifically, we assume that $f: A \to B$ is total on A, and require g to be defined on every number that codes an element of A. However, g may be undefined on natural numbers that are not codes for elements of A.

When f is recursive, we write $|f|$ for the set of codes of partial recursive functions tracking f, *i.e.*,

$|f| = \{n \mid \phi_n \text{ tracks } f\}$.

If $A = \langle A, e_A \rangle$ and $B = \langle B, e_B \rangle$ are modest sets, then we let $A \to B = \langle A \to B, e_{A \to B} \rangle$ be the collection of all total recursive functions from A to B, enumerated by $e_{A \to B}(n) = f$ iff $n \in |f|$.

Lemma 5.5.6 If A and B are modest sets, then $A \to B$ is a modest set.

Proof We must check that $e_{A \to B}$ is surjective and a partial function. It is surjective since every recursive function has a code. By the definition of tracking, we can see that if $n \in |f|$, then n determines the value of $f(a)$ for all $a \in A$. Therefore, if $n \in |f|$ and $n \in |g|$, then f and g must be the same function from A to B. It follows that $e_{A \to B}$ is a partial function. ■

Two modest sets $\langle A, e_A \rangle$ and $\langle B, e_B \rangle$ are *isomorphic* if there is a function $f: A \to B$ that is bijective (one-to-one and onto). These modest sets are *recursively isomorphic* if the bijective function $f: A \to B$ is recursive. When we say two modest sets are isomorphic, we will always mean that they are recursively isomorphic, unless specifically noted otherwise.

Exercise 5.5.7 If $A = \langle A, e_A \rangle$ and $B = \langle B, e_B \rangle$ are modest sets, then we let $A + B = \langle A \uplus B, e_{A+B} \rangle$ be the disjoint union, $A \uplus B = (\{0\} \times A) \cup (\{1\} \times B)$, enumerated by

$$e_{A+B}(n) = \begin{cases} \langle 0, a \rangle & \text{if } (n)_1 = 0 \text{ and } (n)_2 \in |a| \\ \langle 1, b \rangle & \text{if } (n)_1 = 1 \text{ and } (n)_2 \in |b| \\ \text{undefined} & \text{otherwise} \end{cases}$$

Show that if A and B are modest sets, then $A + B$ is a modest set.

Exercise 5.5.8 Let $N_1 = \langle \mathcal{N}, e_1 \rangle$ and $N_2 = \langle \mathcal{N}, e_2 \rangle$ be two modest sets whose underlying set is the natural numbers and let $f: \mathcal{N} \to \mathcal{N}$ be a total recursive function on the natural numbers. Show that $f: N_1 \to N_2$ is also a recursive function from modest set N_1 to N_2, or give a counterexample for some specific enumeration functions e_1 and e_2.

Exercise 5.5.9 Since application is lambda definable, and we want the meaning of every lambda-definable function to be computable, it is essential that given a code n for a function f and a code m for an element a in the domain of f, we can compute a code for $f(a)$. Given this, show that if $\mathcal{N}$ is the modest set of natural numbers, enumerated by the identity, there is no *total* function $e_{\mathcal{N} \to \mathcal{N}}$ for the modest set of total recursive functions from $\mathcal{N}$ to $\mathcal{N}$. (*Hint:* It may be helpful to know that some set is not recursively enumerable.)

5.5.3 Full Recursive Hierarchy

In this section, we show that any full hierarchy of recursive functions over modest sets forms a Henkin model. The interpretation of a variant of PCF, with primitive recursion in place of *fix,* is given in Exercise 5.5.12. We cannot interpret fixed-point operators using the modest set constructions given so far, since we only have total function spaces and not partial ones. As with domain models, the interpretation of fixed-point operators requires either a partial form of function space, or some convention (such as least elements of pointed CPOs) for encoding partial functions as total ones. We investigate a special class of modest sets allowing recursion in Sections 5.6.3 through 5.6.5.

Let $\Sigma = \langle B, C \rangle$ be a $\lambda^{\times,\to}$ signature, with $B = \{b_0, b_1, \ldots\}$, and let $\langle A^{b_i}, e_i \rangle$ be a modest set, for each $b_i \in B$. A *full recursive hierarchy* $\mathcal{A}$ *for* Σ *over modest sets* $\langle A^{b_0}, e_0 \rangle, \ldots, \langle A^{b_k}, e_k \rangle$ is an applicative structure with

$$A^{\sigma\times\tau} = A^{\sigma} \times A^{\tau},$$

$$A^{\sigma\to\tau} = \text{all recursive } f\colon \langle A^{\sigma}, e_{\sigma} \rangle \to \langle A^{\tau}, e_{\tau} \rangle,$$

enumerated by $e_{A^{\sigma}\times A^{\tau}}$ and $e_{A^{\sigma}\to A^{\tau}}$, with

$$\mathbf{App}^{\sigma,\tau}\, f\, x = f(x),$$

$$\mathbf{Proj}_1^{\sigma,\tau}\, \langle x, y \rangle = x,$$

$$\mathbf{Proj}_2^{\sigma,\tau}\, \langle x, y \rangle = y.$$

The function *Const*, choosing $Const(c) \in A^{\sigma}$ for each $c\colon \sigma \in C$, may be chosen arbitrarily.

Note that technically speaking, an applicative structure is given by a collection of sets, rather than a collection of modest sets. In other words, while partial enumerations are used to define function types, they are not part of the resulting structure. This technical point emphasizes that the meaning of a pure lambda term does not depend on the way any modest set is enumerated. However, when we consider a specific recursive hierarchy, we will assume that a partial enumeration function is given for each type.

Theorem 5.5.10 Every full recursive hierarchy is a Henkin model.

Proof It is easy to see that the full recursive hierarchy for $\lambda^{\times,\to}$ is an extensional applicative structure. We will prove that the environment model condition is satisfied, using a slightly stronger induction hypothesis than the theorem. Specifically, we will show that the meaning of every term exists and is computable from a finite portion of the environment. We use the assumption that meanings are computable to show that every function defined by lambda abstraction is computable.

To state the induction hypothesis precisely, we assume that all variables are numbered in some standard way. To simplify the notation a bit, we will assume that the variables used in any type assignment are numbered consecutively. We say that a sequence $\langle n_1, \ldots, n_k \rangle$ of natural numbers *codes environment* η *on* $\Gamma = \{x_1\colon \sigma_1, \ldots, x_k\colon \sigma_k\}$ if $n_i \in |\eta(x_i)|$ for $1 \le i \le k$. Again assuming $\Gamma = \{x_1\colon \sigma_1, \ldots, x_k\colon \sigma_k\}$, we say $[\![\Gamma \triangleright M\colon \sigma]\!]$ is *computable* if there is a partial recursive function $f\colon \mathcal{N}^k \rightharpoonup \mathcal{N}$ such whenever$\langle n_1, \ldots, n_k \rangle$ codes η on Γ, the application $f(n_1, \ldots, n_k)$ is defined and $f(n_1, \ldots, n_k) \in |[\![\Gamma \triangleright M\colon \sigma]\!]\eta|$. In other words, $[\![\Gamma \triangleright M\colon \sigma]\!]$ is computable if we can compute a code for $[\![\Gamma \triangleright M\colon \sigma]\!]\eta$ from codes for $\eta(x_1), \ldots, \eta(x_n)$.

Like the definition of the meaning function for Henkin models, the proof proceeds by induction on typing derivations. The main steps of the inductive argument are given below.

$[\![x\colon\sigma \triangleright x\colon\sigma]\!]\eta \qquad = \eta(x)$ is computed by the identity function

$[\![\Gamma \triangleright MN\colon\tau]\!]\eta \qquad = \mathbf{App}\,([\![\Gamma \triangleright M\colon\sigma \to \tau]\!]\eta)\,([\![\Gamma \triangleright N\colon\sigma]\!]\eta)$ is computed by $\phi_m(n)$,

where $m \in |[\![\Gamma \triangleright M\colon\sigma \to \tau]\!]\eta|$ and $n \in |[\![\Gamma \triangleright N\colon\sigma]\!]\eta|$,

$[\![\Gamma \triangleright \lambda x\colon\sigma.M\colon\sigma \to \tau]\!]\eta = f$ with $f(a) = [\![\Gamma, x\colon\sigma \triangleright M\colon\tau]\!]\eta[x \mapsto a]$ is computable since

$m \in |[\![\Gamma, x\colon\sigma \triangleright M\colon\tau]\!]\eta[x \mapsto a]|$ is computable from $n \in |a|$.

More specifically, in the lambda abstraction case, it follows from the *s-m-n* theorem that if

$m \in |[\![\Gamma, x\colon\sigma \triangleright M\colon\tau]\!]\eta[x \mapsto a]|$

is computable from a coding of $\eta[x \mapsto a]$ on $\Gamma, x\colon\sigma$, then the function mapping

$n \in |a| \;\mapsto m \in |[\![\Gamma, x\colon\sigma \triangleright M\colon\tau]\!]\eta[x \mapsto a]|$

is computable from a coding of η on Γ. The (*add var*) case is straightforward and the pairing and projection cases are left as Exercise 5.5.11. This completes the proof. ∎

In Chapter 8, using logical relations, we will prove that if all the base types are infinite, then β, η-conversion is complete for proving the equations between lambda terms without term constants that hold in a full recursive hierarchy.

Exercise 5.5.11 State and prove the inductive steps of Theorem 5.5.10 for terms with pairing and projection functions.

Exercise 5.5.12 This exercise is concerned with a variant of PCF with primitive recursion, described in Exercise 2.5.7. Let $\mathcal{A}$ be the full recursive hierarchy with products and functions types over *nat*, interpreted as $\langle \mathcal{N}, \lambda n.\, n\rangle$, and *bool*, interpreted as $\langle \{true, false\}, e_{bool}\rangle$, where $e_{bool}(n)$ is *true* if n is odd and *false* if n is even.

(a) Show that successor and zero test may be interpreted in $\mathcal{A}$ in a way that satisfies the equational axioms.

(b) Show that for any type σ, the primitive recursion constant $prim_\sigma$ may be interpreted in $\mathcal{A}$ in a way that satisfies the equational axioms.

(c) Show that we cannot interpret every fixed-point constant fix_σ in $\mathcal{A}$ in a way that satisfies the equational axiom.

An approach to interpreting *fix* in recursion-theoretic models is described in Sections 5.6.3 through 5.6.5.

Exercise 5.5.13 Let $\mathcal{H}$ be a set of assumptions of the form $x\colon\sigma$, giving types to variables, such that every type has infinitely many variables and no variable is given more than one type. Let $\mathcal{A}$ be the applicative structure with

$$A^\sigma = \{[M] \mid \Gamma \triangleright M\colon\sigma \text{ some finite } \Gamma \subseteq \mathcal{H}\}$$

where the equivalence class of term M is defined by

$$[M] = \{N \mid \vdash \Gamma \triangleright M = N\colon\sigma \text{ some finite } \Gamma \subseteq \mathcal{H}\},$$

or equivalently,

$$[M] = \{N \mid M, N \text{ have the same } \beta, \eta\text{-normal form}\}.$$

Application is given by $\mathbf{App}\,[M]\,[N] = [MN]$. This exercise asks you to show that $\mathcal{A}$ is isomorphic to a model in which every type is a modest set and all functions represented in the model are recursive. For simplicity, we consider $\lambda^{\rightarrow}$ only, although the argument extends easily to product types.

(a) Show that for an enumeration of each A^σ as described in Example 5.5.4, each $\mathbf{App}^{\sigma,\tau}$ is a recursive function

$$\mathbf{App}^{\sigma,\tau} : \langle A^{\sigma\rightarrow\tau}, e_{A^{\sigma\rightarrow\tau}}\rangle \rightarrow (\langle A^\sigma, e_{A^\sigma}\rangle \rightarrow \langle A^\tau, e_{A^\tau}\rangle).$$

(b) Show by induction on types that $\mathcal{A}$ is isomorphic to a type frame $\mathcal{B}$ with each $B^{\sigma\rightarrow\tau}$ a set of recursive functions from $\langle B^\sigma, e_{B^\sigma}\rangle$ to $\langle B^\tau, e_{B^\tau}\rangle$ and such that each isomorphism $\langle A^\sigma, e_{A^\sigma}\rangle \cong \langle B^\sigma, e_{B^\sigma}\rangle$ is recursive.

It is shown in Section 8.3.1 that $\mathcal{A}$ is a model, and in Exercise 5.5.14 that it does not contain all recursive functions. In other words, although $\mathcal{B}$ is a hierarchy of modest sets of recursive functions, it is not a *full* hierarchy of all recursive functions.

Exercise 5.5.14 [N. Bjorner] This exercise asks you to prove that not all recursive functions appear in the model of β, η-equivalence classes of terms. More specifically, although we can see from Exercise 5.5.13 that the term model may be viewed as a model of modest sets and recursive functions, a function type $A^{\sigma\rightarrow\tau}$ in this model does not contain all total recursive functions from A^σ to A^τ. Before proceeding, we must be more specific than Example 5.5.3 about the numbering of terms. We assume that all variables are numbered, as $v_1, v_2, v_3, \ldots$, and type constants as $b_1, b_2, b_3, \ldots$. We code a type constant b_i by $\ulcorner b_i \urcorner = pr(0, i)$ and function type $\sigma \rightarrow \tau$ by $\ulcorner \sigma \rightarrow \tau \urcorner = pr(1, pr(\ulcorner\sigma\urcorner, \ulcorner\tau\urcorner))$. Using the recursive projection functions, we can compute any necessary syntactic operations on type expressions. We assume that the infinite type assignment $\mathcal{H}$ used to construct the term model has the form $\mathcal{H} = \{v_1 : \sigma_1, v_2 : \sigma_2, \ldots\}$ where the function mapping $i \mapsto \ulcorner \sigma_i \urcorner$ is recursive. We code terms by

$$\begin{aligned}
\ulcorner v_i \urcorner &= pr(2, i)\\
\ulcorner MN \urcorner &= pr(3, pr(\ulcorner M \urcorner, \ulcorner N \urcorner))\\
\ulcorner \lambda v_i : \sigma.\, M \urcorner &= pr(4, pr(pr(i, \ulcorner \sigma \urcorner), \ulcorner M \urcorner))
\end{aligned}$$

Some aspects of this coding are clearly arbitrary; any variant that allows reasonable syntactic operations on terms to be computed would do as well.

(a) Show that there exist recursive functions computing the free and bound variables of a term from its code. Given the code for a term, these functions should compute a finite sequence (coded as in Example 2.5.13) of codes for variables. You only need to give one function in detail.

(b) Give convincing high-level arguments that the normal form of a term is computable from its code and that, given codes for M and N, the normal form of MN is computable.

(c) Use the fact that every term has a finite number of free variables to prove that if $\langle A^\sigma, e_{A^\sigma} \rangle$ and $\langle A^\tau, e_{A^\tau} \rangle$ are types of a term model, regarded as modest sets as in Example 5.5.4, there is a recursive function from modest set $\langle A^\sigma, e_{A^\sigma} \rangle$ to $\langle A^\tau, e_{A^\tau} \rangle$ that is not the function defined by any term of type $\sigma \to \tau$.

5.6 Partial Equivalence Relations and Recursion

5.6.1 Partial Equivalence Relation Interpretation of Types

Modest sets embody an intuitive way of extending computability on natural numbers to arbitrary "numbered sets." However, from a technical point of view, all that turns out to be important about a modest set $\langle A, e_A \rangle$ is a relation on natural numbers obtained from e_A. As a consequence, modest sets may be "simplified" to relations on the natural numbers. This leads to an alternative formulation of recursive models using partial equivalence relations (*per*'s) instead of partial enumeration functions.

There are two equivalent definitions of partial equivalence relation. The more intuitive one is that a *partial equivalence relation on a set* A is an equivalence relation on some subset of A, *i.e.*, a pair $\langle A', R \rangle$ with $A' \subseteq A$ and $R \subseteq A' \times A'$ an equivalence relation. However, because R determines A' by $A' = \{a \mid a\ R\ a\}$, the subset A' is technically redundant. Moreover, R is an equivalence relation on the subset $A' = \{a \mid a\ R\ a\}$ iff R is symmetric and transitive on A. Therefore, we use a second and technically simpler definition: a *partial equivalence relation,* or *per,* is a symmetric and transitive relation. A straightforward, useful fact about partial equivalence relations is that if $a\ R\ b$, for any per R, then $a\ R\ a$.

Example 5.6.1 Partial equivalence relations over the natural numbers have an intuitive computer-related explanation, which we illustrate here using the examples of booleans and characters. If we want to explain the types of a language using the result of compilation, then we might choose to explain the values of each type using the sequences of bits that are stored in memory. Since any sequence of bits may be interpreted as a natural number (written out base two), we may therefore explain the result of compilation using natural numbers. In this context, it is very natural to think of a type as a membership predicate, or subset of $\mathcal{N}$, together with an equivalence relation on this subset. The membership predicate tells which bit sequences are valid representations of elements of the type, and the equivalence relation tells when two bit sequences represent the same abstract value. For example, we might choose to represent boolean values as single bytes. If we regard every byte with least significant bit 1 as a representing *true*, and every byte with least significant bit 0 as a representing *false*, then all bytes with the same final bit will be considered equivalent. If a byte consists of eight bits, then a byte is interpreted as a natural number less than $2^8 = 256$, with all odd numbers equivalent and all even numbers equivalent. This gives us the per

$$bool_{one\ byte} = \{\langle n, m\rangle \mid n, m < 256 \text{ and } n, m \text{ both odd or both even }\}.$$

If we also represent characters by a single byte, then the type of characters will have the same membership predicate, but a different equivalence relation. Put as a symmetric and transitive relation on the natural numbers, we have

$$char_{one\ byte} = \{\langle n, m\rangle \mid n, m < 256 \text{ and } n = m\},$$

assuming that each byte represents a different character. An alternate per interpretation of *bool* is described in Exercise 5.6.3. ∎

It is generally useful to think of a partial equivalence relation as representing a modest set. With a few definitions, we can make the connection between pers and modest sets precise. If $\langle A, e_A\rangle$ is a modest set, then we define the relation $\sim_A$ on natural numbers by

$$m \sim_A n \text{ iff } e_A(m) = e_A(n).$$

This is the same as saying that $m \sim_A n$ whenever $m, n \in |a|$ for some $a \in A$. It is easy to verify that for any modest set $\langle A, e_A \rangle$, the relation $\sim_A$ is a per on $\mathcal{N}$. An intuitive view of $\sim_A$ is that it tells us what the sets $|a|$ are, without mentioning any elements of A.

The converse mapping, from partial equivalence relations to modest sets, involves a form of quotient construction. If $\sim$ is a per on A, then we form the *subquotient* $A/\sim$ by taking the collection

$$A/\sim = \{[a] \mid a \sim a\}$$

of nonempty equivalence classes

$$[a] = \{a' \mid a' \sim a\}.$$

If $\sim$ is a per on $\mathcal{N}$, then the corresponding modest set is $A = \langle \mathcal{N}/\sim, \lambda n.[n]_\sim \rangle$ whose underlying set is a subquotient of $\mathcal{N}$ and partial enumeration function, $\lambda n.[n]_\sim$, maps each natural number to its $\sim$-equivalence class.

It is relatively easy to see that our maps between partial equivalence relations and modest sets are inverses of each other, provided we do not distinguish between isomorphic modest sets. To begin with, any a modest set $\langle A, e_A \rangle$ is isomorphic to the modest set $\mathcal{N}/A = \langle \mathcal{N}/\sim_A, \lambda n.[n]_{\sim_A} \rangle$. Since the identity on $\mathcal{N}$ tracks the isomorphism $a \mapsto |a|$, the correspondence between an arbitrary modest set and the corresponding modest set given by a per on $\mathcal{N}$ is a recursive isomorphism. We leave it to the reader to verify that if $\sim$ is any per on $\mathcal{N}$, and $A = \langle \mathcal{N}/\sim, \lambda n.[n]_\sim \rangle$ is the corresponding modest set, then $\sim = \sim_A$.

One reason for establishing the correspondence between pers and modest sets is to motivate the definition of isomorphism of pers. Since we consider pers as concise representations of modest sets, we say two pers, R and S, are *isomorphic* if the associated modest sets $\mathcal{N}/R = \langle \mathcal{N}/R, \lambda n.[n]_R \rangle$ and $\mathcal{N}/S = \langle \mathcal{N}/S, \lambda n.[n]_S \rangle$ are isomorphic. As with modest sets, when we say two pers are isomorphic, we will always mean that they are recursively isomorphic, unless specifically noted otherwise. An example isomorphism between pers appears in Exercise 5.6.3.

Since pers are technically simpler than modest sets, it is convenient to characterize cartesian product and function space constructions on modest sets as operations on pers. If $R, S \subseteq \mathcal{N} \times \mathcal{N}$ are partial equivalence relations on the natural numbers, then we define the partial equivalence relations $R \times S$ and $R \to S$ by

$$n\ R \times S\ m \quad \text{iff} \quad (n)_1\ R\ (m)_1 \text{ and } (n)_2\ R\ (m)_2,$$

$$m_1\ R \to S\ m_2 \quad \text{iff} \quad \forall n_1, n_2 \in \mathcal{N}.\, n_1\ R\ n_2 \supset \phi_{m_1}(n_1)\ S\ \phi_{m_2}(n_2).$$

These are explained below. In writing $\phi_{m_1}(n_1)\ S\ \phi_{m_2}(n_2)$, we assume $\phi_{m_1}(n_1)\downarrow$ and $\phi_{m_2}(n_2)\downarrow$.

The relations $R \times S$ and $R \to S$ may be explained directly, reading $m\ R\ n$ as, "m and n represent the same element of R." Specifically, the definition of $R \times S$ is that n and m represent the same pair in $R \times S$ if $(n)_1$ and $(m)_1$ represent the same element of R and $(n)_2$ and $(m)_2$ represent the same element of S. For a function per $R \to S$, m_1 and m_2 represent the same function from R to S if, whenever n_1 and n_2 represent the same element of R, both $\phi_{m_1}(n_1)$ and $\phi_{m_2}(n_2)$ are defined and represent the same element of S. A simplified way of understanding each definition is to separate membership from equality by focusing on when an element is related to itself. For a product per $R \times S$, we have $n\ R \times S\ n$ iff $(n)_1\ R\ (n)_1$ and $(n)_2\ S\ (n)_2$. In words, n codes an element of $R \times S$ iff $(n)_1$ codes an element of R and $(n)_2$ codes an element of S. For a function per $R \to S$, we may similarly see that m represents a function from R to S if, for each equivalence class of R, the result of application is a unique equivalence class of S.

If $R \subseteq \mathcal{N} \times \mathcal{N}$ is a per, it is useful to write $n\colon R$ as an abbreviation

$$n\colon R \stackrel{\text{def}}{=} n\ R\ n$$

For the pers given in Example 5.6.1, we have $n\colon bool_{one\ byte}$ and $n\colon char_{one\ byte}$ exactly if $n < 256$.

Lemma 5.6.2 Let $A = \langle A, e_A\rangle$ and $B = \langle B, e_B\rangle$ be modest sets and let $R = \sim_A$ and $S = \sim_B$ be the corresponding partial equivalence relations over $\mathcal{N}$. Then we have recursive isomorphisms

$$A \times B \cong \langle \mathcal{N}/(R \times S), \lambda n.[n]_{R\times S}\rangle$$

$$A \to B \cong \langle \mathcal{N}/(R \to S), \lambda n.[n]_{R\to S}\rangle$$

The proof is left as Exercise 5.6.4. It follows that if we begin with partial equivalence relations $\sim_{b_0}, \ldots, \sim_{b_k}$, for the type constants $b_0, \ldots b_k$ of some $\lambda^{\times,\to}$ signature, and inductively associate a per $\sim_\sigma$ with each type expression σ using the definitions of product and function space relations given above, then for each type σ, the type $\langle A^\sigma, e_\sigma\rangle$ of the full recursive hierarchy over $\langle \mathcal{N}/\sim_{b_0}, \lambda n.[n]_{\sim_{b_0}}\rangle, \ldots, \langle \mathcal{N}/\sim_{b_k}, \lambda n.[n]_{\sim_{b_k}}\rangle$ is isomorphic to the modest set $\langle \mathcal{N}/\sim_\sigma, \lambda n.[n]_{\sim_\sigma}\rangle$.

Exercise 5.6.3 We may regard any subset $A \subseteq \mathcal{N}$ as a per by $diag(A) = \{\langle a, a\rangle \mid a \in A\}$. Show that if we take $bool_{subs} = diag(\{0, 1\})$, then there is a recursive isomorphism between $bool_{subs}$ and $bool_{one\ byte}$ of Example 5.6.1.

Exercise 5.6.4 Prove the product and function space parts of Lemma 5.6.2 as parts (a) and (b) of this exercise.

5.6.2 Generalization to Partial Combinatory Algebras

The definition of modest set may be generalized to use partial enumeration functions from any set D, in place of the natural numbers, as long as we can code functions and pairs as elements of D. A general setting is to use structures called partial combinatory algebras, which are an untyped version of the combinatory algebras discussed in Section 4.5.7, with the added generalization that application may be partial. Some additional discussion of partial combinatory algebras may be found in [Bee85].

A *partial combinatory algebra,* or *pca,* is a structure $\mathcal{D} = \langle D, \cdot, K, S\rangle$ where D is a set, $\cdot$ is a partial binary operation (*i.e.*, a partial function of two arguments that we write as an infix operation), and $K, S \in D$ are elements with the following properties:

$$(K \cdot x) \cdot y = x \qquad \text{all } x, y \in D,$$

$$(S \cdot x) \cdot y \downarrow \qquad \text{all } x, y \in D,$$

$$((S \cdot x) \cdot y) \cdot z = \begin{cases} (x \cdot z) \cdot (y \cdot z) & \text{if } (x \cdot z) \cdot (y \cdot z) \downarrow, \\ \text{undefined} & \text{otherwise} \end{cases}$$

where $M \downarrow$ means the expression M is defined (has a value), and $M = N$ means both expressions are defined and equal. Another useful notation is to write $M \uparrow$ if M is undefined (has no value). It is common to omit $\cdot$ and associate unparenthesized expressions to the left. In working with expressions that may or may not be defined, depending on the values given to their free variables, it is useful to write $M \simeq N$ to mean that if either M or N is defined, then both are defined and have the same value.

Example 5.6.5 The natural numbers, with partial recursive function application, form a partial combinatory algebra. More specifically, the partial combinatory algebra used in the definition of modest sets is

$$\mathcal{N}_{pca} = \langle \mathcal{N}, \cdot, K, S\rangle$$

with $m \cdot n = \phi_m(n)$ and elements K and S determined as follows. For K, we need some natural number such that ϕ_K is a total function and, if $n = \phi_K(x)$, then for all y, $\phi_n(y) = n$. Therefore, we may let K be any index of the partial recursive function which, given argument x, returns an index of the constant function returning x.

The natural number S is slightly more complicated. There is a partial recursive function f of three arguments such that for all natural numbers x, y, z, we have

$$f(x, y, z) \simeq (x \cdot z) \cdot (y \cdot z) \simeq \phi_{\phi_x(z)}(\phi_y(z)).$$

This function is easiest to explain using Turing machines, or some other model of computation: given descriptions x and y of Turing machines, and string z, the function f is computed by the Turing machine that runs x on z and y on z, interpreting the first as the description of a Turing machine that is run on the result of computing y on z. By the *s-m-n* theorem of recursion theory (or a simple argument about Turing machine encodings), it follows that there is some natural number S with the required property. ■

Example 5.6.6 Total combinatory algebras, in which $\cdot$ is a total operation instead of a partial one, have an ordinary equational axiomatization. This is illustrated in Example 3.7.31, which includes I in addition to S and K. However, I is definable from S and K as $S \cdot K \cdot K$. Since every total combinatory algebra satisfies the axioms for partial combinatory algebras, an example partial combinatory algebra is the algebra of terms over S, K and $\cdot$, possibly containing variables, modulo provable equality from the algebraic axioms. Provable equality may be characterized by a confluent reduction system, as shown in Example 3.7.31. ■

Example 5.6.7 Untyped lambda terms, modulo provable equality, also form a total combinatory algebra. This is true for provability using (α) and (β), or (α), (β) and (η). We can construct a combinatory algebra of untyped lambda terms using any set of variables (allowed to occur free in terms), or using only closed terms. ■

A partial combinatory algebra $\mathcal{D} = \langle D, \cdot^{\mathcal{D}}, K^{\mathcal{D}}, S^{\mathcal{D}} \rangle$ is an algebra for the signature with carrier ι, function symbol $\cdot : \iota \to \iota \to \iota$, and constants $K, S : \iota$, except that $\cdot$ is interpreted as a partial instead of total function. However, we can still interpret any algebraic term over this signature in any partial combinatory algebra using the standard definition from algebra. More specifically, given an environment η for $\mathcal{D}$, the meaning $\mathcal{D}[\![M]\!]\eta$ of a term may be either defined or undefined, according to the following clauses:

$$\mathcal{D}[\![x]\!]\eta = \eta(x)$$

$$\mathcal{D}[\![K]\!]\eta = K^{\mathcal{D}}$$

$$\mathcal{D}[\![S]\!]\eta = S^{\mathcal{D}}$$

$$\mathcal{D}[\![M \cdot N]\!]\eta = \begin{cases} \mathcal{D}[\![M]\!]\eta \cdot^{\mathcal{D}} \mathcal{D}[\![N]\!]\eta & \text{if defined} \\ \text{undefined} & \text{otherwise} \end{cases}$$

In other words, for any partial combinatory algebra $\mathcal{D}$ and environment η, the meaning function $\mathcal{D}[\![\ \ ]\!]\eta$ is a partial function from combinatory terms to D.

For any partial combinatory algebra $\mathcal{D}$, a $\mathcal{D}$-modest set is a pair $\langle A, e_A \rangle$ with A any set, and $e_A : D \rightharpoonup A$ a partial surjective function from D onto A. To regard the cartesian product of two $\mathcal{D}$-modest sets as a $\mathcal{D}$-modest set, we must find pairing and projection functions that are represented in D. More specifically, we must find elements $pr, p_1, p_2 \in D$ such that for all $x, y \in D$,

$$p_1 \cdot (pr \cdot x \cdot y) = x$$

$$p_2 \cdot (pr \cdot x \cdot y) = y$$

and use these in place of the natural number functions pr, $(\_)_1$ and $(\_)_2$. The easiest way to understand $pr, p_1, p_2 \in D$ is via lambda abstraction and the translation of lambda terms into combinators described in Section 4.5.7, ignoring types since there is only one set D involved. More specifically, we may represent a pair $\langle x, y\rangle$ of elements of D by the function $\lambda f.\, fxy$ which applies its argument to both x and y. The reason why this works is that if *fst* is the functions that returns the first of two arguments, and *snd* similarly returns the second, then we may define p_1 and p_2 by

$$p_1 = \lambda q.\, q\, \mathit{fst},$$

$$p_2 = \lambda q.\, q\, \mathit{snd}.$$

This gives us $p_1\langle x, y\rangle = p_1(\lambda f.\, fxy) = (\lambda f.\, fxy)\mathit{fst} = x$, and similarly $p_2\langle x, y\rangle = y$. This can be carried out entirely within D by letting $pr, p_1, p_2 \in D$ be the result of translating the following untyped lambda terms into combinators

$$pr = \lambda x.\, \lambda y.\, \lambda f.\, fxy$$

$$p_1 = \lambda q.\, q\, (\lambda x.\, \lambda y.\, x)$$

$$p_2 = \lambda q.\, q\, (\lambda x.\, \lambda y.\, y)$$

using the algorithm given in Section 4.5.7, ignoring types. The reader may verify this in Exercise 5.6.10.

For any $\mathcal{D}$-modest sets A and B, the cartesian product $\mathcal{D}$-modest set $A \times B$ and function $\mathcal{D}$-modest set $A \to B$ are defined as for $\mathcal{N}$-modest sets in Section 5.5.2. Lemmas 5.5.5 and 5.5.5 are proved in the same way as for $\mathcal{N}$-modest sets. In addition, the correspondence given in Lemma 5.6.2 between modest sets and pers holds for any partial combinatory algebra.

It is possible to show that the hierarchy of $\mathcal{D}$-recursive functions over any $\mathcal{D}$-modest sets forms a Henkin model, by essentially the argument used to prove Theorem 5.5.10. Instead of carrying this out, we will show how to construct a typed combinatory algebra (of total functions) from any partial combinatory algebra. This will allow us to view any hierarchy of modest sets as the result of taking the quotient of a combinatory algebra by a logical partial equivalence relation. This is discussed in Section 8.2.5 (referring to Exercise 8.2.23), in connection with general properties of quotients using logical partial equivalence relations.

The main idea for constructing a typed applicative structure from a partial combinatory algebra is to define function types using the set of total functions represented in the pca, and similarly for cartesian products. The function types will depend on the pca, but the product types are essentially standard, since every pair is definable by the pairing function associated with the partial combinatory algebra.

Let Σ be a $\lambda^{\times,\rightarrow}$-signature, with type constants $b_0, \ldots, b_k$, and let $\mathcal{D} = \langle D, \cdot, K, S\rangle$ be a partial combinatory algebra. If $A^{b_0}, \ldots, A^{b_k}$ are any subsets of D, then we define the typed $\lambda^{\times,\rightarrow}$-applicative structure $\mathcal{A}_{\mathcal{D}}$ by letting

$$A^{\sigma\rightarrow\tau} = \{d \in D \mid \forall x \in A^{\sigma},\ d \cdot x \in A^{\tau}\},$$

$$A^{\sigma\times\tau} = \{d \in D \mid p_1 \cdot d \in A^{\sigma} \text{ and } p_2 \cdot d \in A^{\tau}\},$$

with

$$\mathbf{App}^{\sigma,\tau}\ f\, x = f \cdot x,$$

$$\mathbf{Proj}_1^{\sigma,\tau}\ x \quad = p_1 \cdot x,$$

$$\mathbf{Proj}_2^{\sigma,\tau}\ x \quad = p_2 \cdot x.$$

Note that for every type σ, we have $A^{\sigma} \subseteq D$.

If $\Gamma \triangleright M{:}\,\sigma$ is a typed $\lambda^{\times,\rightarrow}$ term, then we may translate M into combinators, as described in Section 4.5.7. The following lemma shows that since $\mathcal{A}_{\mathcal{D}}$ is a typed combinatory algebra, this gives us a way to interpret M as an element of $\mathcal{A}_{\mathcal{D}}$ and, therefore, as an element of $\mathcal{D}$. We will see in Section 8.2.5 that the meaning of $\Gamma \triangleright M{:}\,\sigma$ in the per model built from $\mathcal{A}_{\mathcal{D}}$ is the equivalence class of the interpretation of M in $\mathcal{D}$.

Lemma 5.6.8 For any partial combinatory algebra, and choice $A^{b_0}, \ldots, A^{b_k}$ of subsets of D for type constants, the typed applicative structure $\mathcal{A}_{\mathcal{D}}$ is a typed combinatory algebra.

Proof It is easy to see that $\mathcal{A}_{\mathcal{D}}$ is a typed applicative structure since, by construction, if $f \in A^{\sigma\rightarrow\tau}$ and $a \in A^{\sigma}$, then $f \cdot a \downarrow$ and $\mathbf{App}\ f\, a = f \cdot a \in A^{\tau}$. It remains to show that $\mathcal{A}_{\mathcal{D}}$ has combinators of each type.

We will show that for all ρ, σ, τ, there exist elements

$$K_{\sigma,\tau} \quad \in A^{\sigma\rightarrow(\tau\rightarrow\sigma)},$$

$$S_{\rho,\sigma,\tau} \quad \in A^{(\rho\rightarrow\sigma\rightarrow\tau)\rightarrow(\rho\rightarrow\sigma)\rightarrow\rho\rightarrow\tau},$$

$$Pair^{\sigma,\tau} \in A^{\sigma\rightarrow\tau\rightarrow(\tau\times\sigma)},$$

$$Proj_1^{\sigma,\tau} \in A^{(\sigma\times\tau)\rightarrow\sigma},$$

$$Proj_2^{\sigma,\tau} \in A^{(\sigma\times\tau)\rightarrow\sigma},$$

satisfying the equational conditions

$$K_{\sigma,\tau}xy = x,$$

$$S_{\rho,\sigma,\tau}xyz = (xz)(yz),$$

$$Proj_1^{\sigma,\tau}(Pair^{\sigma,\tau}xy) = x,$$

$$Proj_2^{\sigma,\tau}(Pair^{\sigma,\tau}xy) = y,$$

for all x, y, z of the appropriate types. Not surprisingly, each $K_{\sigma,\tau}$ and $S_{\rho,\sigma,\tau}$ will be the K or S (respectively) of the partial combinatory algebra $\mathcal{D}$, and $Pair^{\sigma,\tau}$, $Proj_1^{\sigma,\tau}$ and $Proj_2^{\sigma,\tau}$ are pr, p_1 and p_2.

Since $A^{\sigma\to\tau}$ contains all elements of D that represent total functions from A^σ to A^τ, all that is required to complete the proof is to show that S, K, pr, p_1 and p_2 define total functions of the appropriate types.

For $K = K_{\sigma,\tau}$, we must show that if $x \in A^\sigma$, then $K \cdot x \in A^{\tau\to\sigma}$. To do this, we let $y \in A^\tau$. By the definition of partial combinatory algebra, we have $(K \cdot x) \cdot y = x \in A^\tau$, and so by definition of $\mathcal{A}_{\mathcal{D}}$ we have $K \cdot x \in A^{\tau\to\sigma}$. Therefore $K \in A^{\sigma\to\tau\to\sigma}$.

For $S = S_{\rho,\sigma,\tau}$, we must show that if $x \in A^{\rho\to\sigma\to\tau}$, then $S \cdot x \in A^{(\rho\to\sigma)\to\rho\to\tau}$. As in the preceding case, we let $y \in A^{\rho\to\sigma}$ and $z \in A^\rho$. From the definition of partial combinatory algebra, we have $S \cdot x \cdot y \cdot z = (x \cdot z) \cdot (y \cdot z)$ whenever $(x \cdot z) \cdot (y \cdot z) \downarrow$. But since $x \in A^{\rho\to\sigma\to\tau}$ and $z \in A^\rho$, we have $x \cdot z \downarrow$ with $x \cdot z \in A^{\sigma\to\tau}$. Similarly, $(y \cdot z)$ and $(x \cdot z) \cdot (y \cdot z)$ are both defined, with $(x \cdot z) \cdot (y \cdot z) \in A^\tau$. This shows that $S \in A^{(\rho\to\sigma\to\tau)\to(\rho\to\sigma)\to\rho\to\tau}$.

The proofs for pr, p_1 and p_2 are similar, given the results of Exercise 5.6.10, and omitted. ■

Exercise 5.6.9 Suppose we replace the three axioms of partial combinatory algebras by the following two:

$$(K \cdot x) \cdot y \simeq x,$$

$$((S \cdot x) \cdot y) \cdot z \simeq (x \cdot z) \cdot (y \cdot z).$$

Is this equivalent to the definition given in the text? Explain.

Exercise 5.6.10 Write pr and p_1, as given by untyped lambda terms above, out as applicative combinations of K and S, and verify that the equation $p_1 \cdot (pr \cdot x \cdot y) = x$ holds in every partial combinatory algebra. (The equation $p_2 \cdot (pr \cdot x \cdot y) = y$ holds by similar reasoning.) You may want to write a short computer program to do some of the work.

5.6.3 Lifting, Partial Functions and Recursion

There are several ways to construct modest set, or per, models with fixed point operators at various types. Although modest sets are sometimes more intuitive, we will work with pers since the technical details are simpler.

One approach uses domain theory, constructing a per model over a partial combinatory algebra that is a CPO containing a total fixed-point function. An advantage of this setting is that the underlying CPO has a partial order that may be used to define a partial order on each per. With appropriate restrictions on pers, we can regard each per as a CPO and interpret fixed point operators in the usual way. The main challenge in developing this kind of model lies in identifying a natural class of pers that each determine a CPO. Some discussion of this form of model appears in [Ama91, Car89, AP90, BM92], for example.

Another approach may be illustrated using the partial combinatory algebra $\mathcal{N}_{pca}$ of natural numbers with recursive function application, $n \cdot m = \phi_n(m)$. We will develop these models using intuition from computability theory as much as possible. However, the failure of the recursion (fixed point) theorem on certain pers leads us to adapt a substantial number of ideas from domain theory. Using a form of computable test, we may identify an intrinsic partial order on each per. If we restrict our attention to pers where this order is complete (in a computable sense), then we obtain a model where types with least elements are guaranteed to have fixed-point operators. Although this construction appears applicable to other partial combinatory algebras, we will only consider the natural numbers with recursive function application.

A number of recent research papers present constructions that are similar to or extend the development of the "effective CPOs" below [AP90, CP92, FRMS92, Pho90b, Pho90a]. Thanks to R. Viswanathan for his assistance with this section.

There are several instances in which we need a one-element per *unit*. In general, it does not matter which per we use for *unit*, as long as there is exactly one equivalence class. The largest such relation is $unit = \mathcal{N} \times \mathcal{N}$. However, some arguments are simplified if we take a smaller relation. We will therefore use

$$unit \stackrel{\text{def}}{=} \{\langle 0, 0\rangle\}$$

The slight advantage of this definition is that in reasoning about functions from *unit* to another per, we only need to consider the function value at 0.

Partial Functions, Total Functions and Lifting

Since recursion generally involves partial functions, we begin by defining partial function pers. These may be related to total function pers using a form of lifting. Although we could define lifting initially, and take partial functions as a derived notion, there are several constructions that might, *a priori,* appear to be reasonable definitions of lifting. Therefore, we begin with the natural and intuitive definition of partial function and use the connection between partial functions, total functions and lifting to justify our definition of lifted pers.

Given two pers $R, S \subseteq \mathcal{N} \times \mathcal{N}$, the per $R \rightharpoonup S$ of computable partial functions from R to S is defined by

$$m_1\ R \rightharpoonup S\ m_2 \quad \text{iff} \quad \forall n_1, n_2 \in \mathcal{N}.\ \text{if}\ n_1\ A\ n_2\ \text{then}$$
$$\text{if}\ m_1 \cdot n_1 \downarrow\ \text{or}\ m_2 \cdot n_2 \downarrow\ \text{then}\ m_1 \cdot n_1\ S\ m_2 \cdot n_2.$$

This may be explained relatively simply in words, reading $m\ R\ n$ as, "m and n represent the same element of R." The definition of $R \rightharpoonup S$ says that m_1 and m_2 represent the same partial function from R to S if, whenever n_1 and n_2 represent the same element of R, if either $m_1 \cdot n_1$ or $m_2 \cdot n_2$ represent an element of S, then both must be defined and represent the same element of S. A second way of understanding this definition is to consider the weaker condition

$$m\colon R \rightharpoonup S \quad \text{implies} \quad \forall n \in \mathcal{N}.\ \text{if}\ n\colon A\ \text{then}$$
$$\text{if}\ m \cdot n \downarrow\ \text{then}\ m \cdot n : S$$

involving membership only. In this case, the definition says that for m to represent a partial function from R to S, the result of applying m to any $n\colon R$ must either be undefined or an element $m \cdot n$ of S . Once we have this understanding of a partial function, we can see that m_1 and m_2 define the same partial function if they are either both undefined on all elements of an equivalence class, or both defined and produce elements of the same S-equivalence class. The definition is reformulated for modest sets in Exercise 5.6.26.

Example 5.6.11 A simple example of a partial function per is $N \rightharpoonup N$, where $N \subseteq \mathcal{N} \times \mathcal{N}$ is the per $N \stackrel{\text{def}}{=} \{\langle n, n\rangle \mid n \in \mathcal{N}\}$. It is easy to see that $n\colon N \rightharpoonup N$, for every natural number n, since every n is the code of some partial function on the natural numbers. In addition, we have $n_1\ N \rightharpoonup N\ n_2$ exactly when $n_1 \cdot m \simeq n_2 \cdot m$ for all $m \in \mathcal{N}$. In other words, $n_1\ N \rightharpoonup N\ n_2$ precisely when n_1 and n_2 are indices for the same partial recursive function. ■

It is easy to check the following lemma, whose proof is left as Exercise 5.6.25.

Lemma 5.6.12 For all partial equivalence relations $R, S \subseteq \mathcal{N} \times \mathcal{N}$, the relation $R \rightharpoonup S$ is a per.

Using a form of lifting, we can also characterize partial function pers using total function pers. The main property we want is that for all pers $R, S \subseteq \mathcal{N} \times \mathcal{N}$, there should be an isomorphism

$$R \rightharpoonup S \;\cong\; R \to S_\perp$$

between the partial functions from R to S and the total functions from R into "S lifted," written here as $S_\perp$.

Lifting may be defined naturally using the partial functions from a one-element per. To put this in perspective, remember that if A is a set, and W is a one-element set, then the elements of A are in bijective correspondence with the total functions from W to A. If we consider the partial functions from W to A instead, there is one more possibility, the function that is not defined on the single element of W. This way of adding "one element" to a set allows us to "lift" pers over the natural numbers. Specifically, if $S \subseteq \mathcal{N} \times \mathcal{N}$ is a per, we define

$$S_\perp \stackrel{\text{def}}{=} \mathit{unit} \rightharpoonup S,$$

using the per *unit* with exactly one equivalence class. By Lemma 5.6.12, the relation $S_\perp$ is a per.

Lemma 5.6.13 For all pers $R, S \subseteq \mathcal{N} \times \mathcal{N}$ over the natural numbers, we have $R \rightharpoonup S \cong R \to S_\perp$. Moreover, the isomorphism is given by a pair of recursive functions.

Some other aspects of lifting are given in Exercises 5.6.27 and 5.6.28.

Proof Given $n\colon R \rightharpoonup S$, let $\hat{n}\colon R \to S_\perp$ be any index of the Turing machine which, on input x returns an index of the Turing machine that, on input y, computes $n \cdot x$. In other words $\hat{n} = K \cdot n$. It is clear that we can compute $\hat{n}$ from n.

The reverse isomorphism involves evaluation at 0 since $\mathit{unit} = \{\langle 0, 0\rangle\}$. More specifically, given $n\colon R \to S_\perp$, we let $\check{n}\colon R \rightharpoonup S$ be any index of the Turing machine that, on input x, computes $n \cdot x \cdot 0$. The reader is encouraged to check that these functions are well-defined on equivalence classes and that they are inverses of each other. ∎

5.6.4 Recursion and the Intrinsic Order

For the special case of total functions on $N \rightharpoonup N$, Kleene's recursion theorem shows that we have fixed points. More specifically, the recursion theorem that may be found in any book on computability theory states that for every $n : (N \rightharpoonup N) \to (N \rightharpoonup N)$, there is some $k \in \mathcal{N}$ with $n \cdot k \downarrow$ and $\phi_k = \phi_{n \cdot k}$. Since therefore $k\ N \rightharpoonup N\ n \cdot k$, the equivalence class $[k]_{N \rightharpoonup N} = [n \cdot k]_{N \rightharpoonup N}$ is a fixed point of the function given by n. However, this fixed-point property does not hold for arbitrary functions $(R \rightharpoonup S) \to (R \rightharpoonup S)$, as shown in Example 5.6.14 below.

Example 5.6.14 The recursion theorem shows that every total recursive function on partial recursive functions has a fixed point. Therefore, we might conjecture that for any pers R and S, every recursive function $(R \rightharpoonup S) \to (R \rightharpoonup S)$ has a fixed point. We will see that this is not the case, even when $R = unit$ and therefore $R \rightharpoonup S = S_\perp$.

Let S be the following per whose elements are functions with finite domains:

$$i\ S\ j \quad \text{iff} \quad \exists n \in \mathcal{N} \forall x < n\ (i \cdot x \downarrow \text{ and } j \cdot x \downarrow \text{ with } i \cdot x = j \cdot x) \text{ and}$$
$$\forall x \geq n\ (i \cdot x \uparrow \text{ and } j \cdot x \uparrow)$$

Note that if ϕ_i and ϕ_j are undefined on every argument, then $i\ S\ j$.

We will define a function $F : S_\perp \to S_\perp$ without a fixed point in $S_\perp$, using the the fact that S is not "complete." More precisely, if we order S as we would order a set of functions from one flat CPO to another, with $i \leq j$ if $\phi_i(n) \downarrow$ implies $\phi_i(n) = \phi_j(n)$ for all n, then S is not a CPO. The reason is that the least upper bound (limit) of a sequence of functions with increasingly larger finite domains will be a function with infinite domain. While S contains functions with arbitrarily large finite domains, S has no function with an infinite domain of definition.

To understand the following definition of F, recall that $S_\perp = unit \rightharpoonup S$ and $unit = \{\langle 0, 0\rangle\}$. Let F be an index of the function which, on input f, returns an index of the function which, on input 0, returns an index of the function given by the following algorithm:

$F \cdot f \cdot 0 \cdot n =$ compute $g = f \cdot 0$;
  if the computation of g halts
    then if $y = 0$ return 0 else return $g \cdot (y - 1)$
    else do not halt.

Note that for any $f\colon unit \rightharpoonup S$, $F \cdot f$ is the index of a function that, on argument 0 returns the index of a function. Therefore, F is a total function $S_\perp \to S_\perp$ which, on any $f\colon unit \rightharpoonup S = S_\perp$ returns a total function in $unit \rightharpoonup S = S_\perp$.

There are two cases to consider in analyzing the possible fixed points of F. The first is that if $f\colon unit \rightharpoonup S$ is undefined on 0, then $F \cdot f\colon unit \rightharpoonup S$ is a total function. Therefore, the undefined function $unit \rightharpoonup S$ is not a fixed point of F. Second, if $f\colon unit \rightharpoonup S$ is defined on 0, with $f \cdot 0 = g$, then by the assumption that $g\colon S$, we know that g is the index of a function with finite domain $\{0, \ldots, k\}$. In this case, $F \cdot f \cdot 0$ is the index of a function with larger domain $\{0, \ldots, k, k+1\}$. Therefore no $f\colon unit \rightharpoonup S$ with $f \cdot 0 \downarrow$ gives us a fixed point of F in $S_\perp$. ∎

Example 5.6.14 shows that we do not have fixed-points of total recursive functionals on all lifted pers. This suggests that if we want fixed points on lifted types, we should restrict our attention to some special class of pers. An important idea in Example 5.6.14 is that if we order the per S in the example as we would in domain theory, then S is not a CPO.

Therefore, it seems natural to circumvent the problem illustrated by the per S by selecting a class of CPO-like pers. The first step is to associate an order with each per.

One intuition associated with domain theory is that the order on a CPO represents the "observable behavior" of elements. In a CPO of functions, for example, we can observe the behavior of a function by applying it to some number of arguments. The functions are ordered so that if one function gives more results than the other, it is "greater" in the ordering. This can be generalized using the idea of a "test" on values of some domain. A natural form of "test" in domain theory might be a function into the two element CPO $\{\top, \bot\}$ with $\bot < \top$. We can say that an element a of CPO A "passes the test" given by a continuous function $f: A \to \{\top, \bot\}$ if $f(a) = \top$ and fails if $f(a) = \bot$. Using the continuity of certain step functions (see Exercise 5.4.16), it is not hard to show that if D is an algebraic CPO, then $a \leq_D b$ iff, for all continuous $f: D \to \{\top, \bot\}$, if $f(a) = \top$ then $f(b) = \top$. Note that $\{\top, \bot\}$ is the result of lifting a one-element CPO.

We may adopt the intuitive idea of ordering by tests by saying that a *computable test* on a per $A \subseteq \mathcal{N} \times \mathcal{N}$ is any recursive partial functions $A \rightharpoonup unit$. By Lemma 5.6.13, this is equivalent to taking total computable functions $A \to unit_\bot$. We say an element $n: A$ *passes the test* $f: A \rightharpoonup unit$ if $f \cdot n \downarrow$. Our analogy with CPOs suggests the following "intrinsic order" on pers.

If $A \subseteq \mathcal{N} \times \mathcal{N}$ is any per and $f: A \rightharpoonup unit$, then the *intrinsic preorder* on A is defined by

$$n \leq_A m \quad \text{iff} \quad \forall f: A \rightharpoonup unit.\ f \cdot n \downarrow \supset f \cdot m \downarrow$$

It is an easy consequence of standard properties of computable functions that this relation is a preorder, as verified in Exercise 5.6.29. However, the intrinsic order is not always antisymmetric, as shown in Exercise 5.6.31. The intrinsic orders on $N \to N$ and $N \rightharpoonup N$ are described in two examples below.

Once we have a preorder on each per, we can easily identify a class of CPO-like pers. Specifically, we take the pers where the intrinsic preorder is a complete partial order, with one qualification. The qualification is that we must take a restricted, computable form of completeness. The reason is that a per on the natural numbers can have only countably many elements. However, it is possible for a countable partial order to have uncountably many directed sets. For example, the per $N \rightharpoonup N$ contains all functions with finite domain, since every partial function with finite domain is computable. However, every total function on the natural numbers is the least upper bound of some directed set (or increasing sequence) of partial functions with finite domain. Since there are uncountably many total functions, no per can be the full CPO of all partial functions on the natural numbers.

Fortunately, we do not need least upper bounds of all directed sets. For the purpose of interpreting expressions of any reasonable (computable) language, we only need least upper bounds of computable increasing sequences. This leads us to the following definition of "effective" (in the sense of "computable") CPO.

If A is any per, then a *computable increasing sequence* in A is a computable function $s\colon N \to A$ with $s \cdot n \leq_A s \cdot (n+1)$ for all $n \in \mathcal{N}$. A *least upper bound* of a computable increasing sequence s is an element a whose equivalence class is the least upper bound of the equivalence classes of $s \cdot 0,\ s \cdot 1,\ s \cdot 2, \ldots$. In other words, $a \geq_A s \cdot i$ for all i, and if $b \geq_A s \cdot i$ for all i, then $b \geq_A a$. We say a per $A \subseteq \mathcal{N} \times \mathcal{N}$ is an *effective CPO* if

- The intrinsic preorder $\leq_A$ on A is antisymmetric, *i.e.*, if $x \leq_A y$ and $y \leq_A x$ then $x\ A\ y$,
- There is a computable supremum function with index sup_A such that if $s\colon N \to A$ a computable increasing sequence in A, then $sup_A \cdot s$ is a least upper bound of s in A.

Thus $A \subseteq \mathcal{N} \times \mathcal{N}$ is an effective CPO if the intrinsic preorder is a partial order and there is a computable function finding the least upper bound of every computable increasing sequence.

It is straightforward to see that any per A with $\leq_A$ antisymmetric and discrete is an effective CPO. The reason is that the least upper bound of any computable increasing sequence s is just $s \cdot 0$. In particular, *unit* is an effective CPO.

Example 5.6.15 We can show that the per $N \to N$ is a discrete effective CPO by showing that if $f \cdot x \downarrow$ implies $f \cdot y \downarrow$ for all $f\colon (N \to N) \rightharpoonup unit$, then $x\ (N \to N)\ y$.

For any pair of natural numbers n and m, we can define a test

$$t_{\langle n,m\rangle} \stackrel{\text{def}}{=} \lambda z \in \mathcal{N}.\,\texttt{if}\ z \cdot n = m\ \texttt{then}\ \downarrow\ \texttt{else}\ \uparrow$$

which terminates on argument $x\colon N \to N$ iff $x \cdot n = m$. It is easy to see that for any n and m, $t_{\langle n,m\rangle}\colon (N \to N) \rightharpoonup unit$. Moreover, if y passes every test $t_{\langle n,m\rangle}$ that x does, then we have $x \cdot n = y \cdot n$ for every n. This shows that if $x \leq_{N \to N} y$ then $x\ (N \to N)\ y$.

Since the intrinsic order is the discrete order, the only computable increasing sequences are constant sequences, modulo $N \to N$. (In other words, $s \cdot n(N \to N)s \cdot (n+1)$ for all n). Therefore the least upper bound of any computable increasing sequence s in $N \to N$ is easily computed from s. ∎

Example 5.6.16 The per $N \rightharpoonup N$ is an effective CPO with the expected pointwise order. We first investigate the intrinsic order and then show how to compute the least upper bound of any computable increasing sequence.

It is easy to see that $\leq_{N \rightharpoonup N}$ is antisymmetric by showing that if natural numbers x and y pass the same computable tests then $x\ (N \rightharpoonup N)\ y$. Returning to the tests $t_{\langle n,m\rangle}$ of

Example 5.6.15, we can see that $t_{\langle n,m\rangle}$ terminates on argument x iff $x \cdot n \downarrow$ with $x \cdot n = m$. Since $t_{\langle n,m\rangle}\colon (N \rightharpoonup N) \rightharpoonup unit$ for all n, m, it follows that $x \leq_{N \rightharpoonup N} y$ and $y \leq_{N \rightharpoonup N} x$ together imply $x\ (N \rightharpoonup N)\ y$.

We can get a better understanding of the intrinsic order by showing that $x \leq_{N \rightharpoonup N} y$ iff $\forall n.\ x \cdot n \downarrow \supset x \cdot n = y \cdot n$. In other words, the intrinsic order is determined by a particular form of computable test involving application to a single number. This property of $N \rightharpoonup N$ is a special case of Lemma 5.6.24 below. If $\forall n.\ x \cdot n \downarrow \supset x \cdot n = y \cdot n$ is false then there is some n with $x \cdot n \downarrow$ and either $y \cdot n \uparrow$ or $y \cdot n \neq x \cdot n$. This provides a computable test $t_{\langle n, x \cdot n\rangle}\colon (N \rightharpoonup N) \rightharpoonup unit$ passed by x but not by y.

For the converse implication, we assume $\forall n.\ x \cdot n \downarrow \supset x \cdot n = y \cdot n$ but there is some $f\colon (N \rightharpoonup N) \rightharpoonup unit$ with $f \cdot x \downarrow$ and $f \cdot y \uparrow$. We show that this leads to a contradiction. Let $\bar{K} = \{n \mid \phi_n(n) \uparrow\}$, which is not recursively enumerable. We derive a contradiction by showing that under our assumptions, $\bar{K}$ is r.e.

For any natural number z, let $g \cdot z$ be an index of the function determined by the following algorithm with input n:

$g \cdot z \cdot n =$ compute $z \cdot z$, $x \cdot n$ and $y \cdot n$ in parallel (by interleaving);
    if $x \cdot n \downarrow$ then return the value of $x \cdot n$;
    if $z \cdot z \downarrow$ and $y \cdot n \downarrow$ then return the value of $y \cdot n$;
    else do not halt.

Note that if $z \cdot z$, $x \cdot n$ and $y \cdot n$ all terminate, the result could be either $x \cdot n$ or $y \cdot n$. But in this case, we have $x \cdot n = y \cdot n$. It is easy to verify that $g \cdot z\ (N \rightharpoonup N)\ x$ if $z \in \bar{K}$ and $g \cdot z\ (N \rightharpoonup N)\ y$ if $z \notin \bar{K}$. We can therefore determine whether $z \in \bar{K}$ by determining whether $f \cdot (g \cdot z) \downarrow$. Since $f \cdot (g \cdot z) \downarrow$ is an r.e. property of z, this means that $\bar{K}$ is r.e. But since this is a contradiction, we have shown that if $\forall n.\ x \cdot n \downarrow \supset x \cdot n = y \cdot n$ then $x \leq_{N \rightharpoonup N} y$. This completes the proof that $\leq_{N \rightharpoonup N}$ is the expected pointwise order on partial functions.

Finally, we come to computing least upper bounds of computable increasing sequences. If s is a computable increasing sequence, then $s \cdot 0, s \cdot 1, s \cdot 2, \ldots$ is a sequence of indices of partial recursive functions, increasing in the point-wise order. This means that if $i > j$, then $s \cdot i$ is the index of a function that is defined everywhere that $s \cdot j$ is, and possibly on additional arguments. Where both are defined, the functions must be equal. Given s, we need to be able to compute the index of a function f with $f(n) = m$ if there is some i with $s \cdot i \cdot n = m$. Therefore, we may let *sup* s be the index of the function f computed by the following algorithm:

$f \cdot n =$ compute $s \cdot 0 \cdot n,\ \ s \cdot 1 \cdot n,\ \ s \cdot 2 \cdot n,\ \ \ldots$ in parallel (by interleaving);
    if $s \cdot i \cdot n \downarrow$ for some i then halt with result $s \cdot i \cdot n$

Since this produces the least upper bound of any computable increasing sequence, $N \rightharpoonup N$ is an effective CPO. ■

A useful lemma is that every computable function on effective CPOs is monotonic with respect to the intrinsic order. It follows that if $s\colon N \to A$ is an increasing sequence in A and $f\colon A \to B$ is computable, then their composition $f \circ s$ is an increasing sequence in B.

Lemma 5.6.17 Let $A, B \subseteq \mathcal{N} \times \mathcal{N}$ be any pers. Every computable $f\colon A \rightharpoonup B$ is monotonic, *i.e.*, for all $x, y\colon A$, if $x \leq_A y$ then $f \cdot x \downarrow$ implies $f \cdot y \downarrow$ with $f \cdot x \leq_B f \cdot y$. In particular, if $f\colon A \to B$ is a total function and $x \leq_A y$ then $f \cdot x \leq_B f \cdot y$.

Proof Suppose $x \leq_A y$ and $f\colon A \rightharpoonup B$. Let $g\colon B \rightharpoonup \mathit{unit}$. We must show that if $g \cdot (f \cdot x) \downarrow$ then $g \cdot (f \cdot y) \downarrow$. But $x \leq_A y$ means that for every $h\colon A \rightharpoonup \mathit{unit}$, if $h \cdot x \downarrow$ then $h \cdot y \downarrow$. In particular, since $g \circ f\colon A \rightharpoonup \mathit{unit}$, if $(g \circ f) \cdot x \downarrow$ then $(g \circ f) \cdot y \downarrow$, which is what we needed to prove. ■

Since every effective CPO is a per over the natural numbers, there are two natural classes of functions from one effective CPO to another: the computable functions on pers and the continuous functions on CPOs. An important property of effective CPOs is that all computable functions on the underlying pers are continuous. Therefore, we can apply order-theoretic arguments to functions on effective CPOs without changing our notion of function from one effective CPO to another. After establishing the connection between computability and continuity, we use this to show that every computable function on a pointed effective CPO has a least fixed point. The first lemma below establishes a property of computable tests that is useful in relating computability to continuity.

Lemma 5.6.18 Let A be a per with sup_A computing the least upper bound of every computable increasing sequence and let $f\colon A \rightharpoonup \mathit{unit}$ be a computable test on A. If s is a computable increasing sequence then $f \cdot (\mathit{sup}_A \cdot s) \downarrow$ iff there is some n with $f \cdot (s \cdot n) \downarrow$.

Proof For the implication to the left, suppose $f \cdot (s \cdot n) \downarrow$ for some n. We will show that $f \cdot (\mathit{sup}_A \cdot s) \downarrow$. Since sup_A finds the least upper bound, $s \cdot i \leq_A \mathit{sup}_A \cdot s$ for all i. Therefore, by Lemma 5.6.17, we have $f \cdot (\mathit{sup}_A \cdot s) \downarrow$.

For the implication to the right, suppose that $f \cdot (\mathit{sup}_A \cdot s) \downarrow$ and, for the purpose of deriving a contradiction, $f \cdot (s \cdot n) \uparrow$ for all n. We will derive a contradiction by defining an increasing sequence from s that lets us show that $\bar{K} = \{n \mid n \cdot n \uparrow\}$ is r.e. The idea is that for any $x \in \mathcal{N}$, the sequence t_x will be equivalent to s if $x \in \bar{K}$ and equivalent to an initial segment of s, repeating the nth element indefinitely for some $n > 0$, if $x \notin \bar{K}$. For any $x \in \mathcal{N}$, let t_x be any index of the function computed by the following algorithm:

$t_x \cdot y$ = compute $x \cdot x$ for y steps;
if $x \cdot x$ halts in $i \leq y$ steps, then return $s \cdot i$ else return $s \cdot y$.

If $x \in \bar{K}$, then $t_x \cdot n = s \cdot n$ for all $n \in \mathcal{N}$ and so by assumption $f \cdot (sup_A \cdot t_x) \downarrow$. On the other hand, if $x \notin \bar{K}$ then $(sup_A \cdot t_x)\ A\ (s \cdot n)$ for some n representing the number of steps required for the computation of $x \cdot x$ to halt. In this case, $f \cdot (sup_A \cdot t_x) \uparrow$ since we assume that $f \cdot (c \cdot n) \uparrow$ for all n. Therefore, we have $x \in \bar{K}$ iff $f \cdot (sup_A \cdot t_x) \downarrow$. Since it is r.e. to determine if $f \cdot (sup_A \cdot t_x) \downarrow$, this shows that $\bar{K}$ is r.e., which is our desired contradiction. This completes the proof. ■

Lemma 5.6.19 Let pers $A, B \subseteq \mathcal{N} \times \mathcal{N}$ be effective CPOs. Every computable $f: A \to B$ is continuous, *i.e.*, if $s: N \to A$ is an increasing sequence, then $f \cdot (sup_A \cdot s)\ B\ sup_B \cdot (f \circ s)$.

Proof Let $f: A \to B$ be computable and $s: N \to A$ an increasing sequence in A. By Lemma 5.6.17, $f \circ s$ is a computable increasing sequence in B.

We first show that $sup_B \cdot (f \circ s) \leq_B f \cdot (sup_A \cdot s)$. By monotonicity of f, from Lemma 5.6.17, and $s \cdot n \leq_A sup_A \cdot s$, we have

$$f \cdot (s \cdot n) \leq_B f \cdot (sup_A \cdot s)$$

for all n. Therefore $sup_B \cdot (f \circ s) \leq_B f \cdot (sup_A\, s)$.

For the reverse inequality, we consider any computable test $g: B \rightharpoonup unit$. Suppose $g \cdot (f \cdot (sup_A \cdot s)) \downarrow$, or, equivalently, $(g \circ f) \cdot (sup_A \cdot s) \downarrow$. By Lemma 5.6.18, there is some n with $(g \circ f) \cdot (s \cdot n) \downarrow$, which can also be written $g \cdot ((f \circ s) \cdot n) \downarrow$. Using Lemma 5.6.18 in the opposite direction, it follows that $g \cdot (sup_B \cdot (f \circ s)) \downarrow$. Since this holds for any computable test on B, we have $f \cdot (sup_A \cdot s) \leq_B sup_B \cdot (f \circ s)$ by definition of the intrinsic order on B. By antisymmetry of the intrinsic order, we have therefore shown that $f \cdot (sup_A \cdot s)\ B\ sup_B \cdot (f \circ s)$. ■

By analogy with ordinary CPOs, we say an effective CPO A is *pointed* if there is some $n: A$ with $n \leq_A m$ for all $m: A$. In other words, an effective CPO is pointed if there is some least equivalence class with respect to the intrinsic order. It follows from Lemma 5.6.24 below that every lifted effective CPO is a pointed effective CPO.

Lemma 5.6.20 Let per $A \subseteq \mathcal{N} \times \mathcal{N}$ be a pointed effective CPO. Every computable $f: A \to A$ has a least fixed point $\mathit{fix}_A\, f$. Moreover, the function $\mathit{fix}_A: (A \to A) \to A$ is computable.

Proof The proof is essentially similar to the proof of Lemma 5.2.20, which asserts the existence of least fixed points for "non-effective" CPOs. Given $f: A \to A$, we define the computable increasing sequence s by letting $s \cdot 0$ be a number in the least equivalence class of A and letting $s \cdot (n+1) = f(s \cdot n)$. Then we let $\mathit{fix}_A\, f = \mathit{sup}_A \cdot s$. It is easy to see that fix_A is computable, since sup_A is given for any effective CPO A. The proof that $\mathit{fix}_A\, f$ is in fact the least fixed point of f proceeds as in the proof of Lemma 5.2.20, using the preceding lemmas of this section for monotonicity and continuity of f. ■

5.6.5 Lifting, Products and Function Spaces of Effective CPOs

We have now established the main properties that distinguish effective CPOs from arbitrary pers, namely, every computable function is continuous and the least fixed point of any computable f on a pointed effective CPO is computable from f. In the remainder of this section, we show that the cartesian product of two effective CPOs is again an effective CPO, and similarly for total and partial function spaces. Since lifting is defined using partial functions, it follows that lifting an effective CPO always yields an effective CPO.

Lemma 5.6.21 If pers A and B are effective CPOs, then the cartesian product per $A \times B$ is an effective CPO with intrinsic order satisfying $x \leq_{A\times B} y$ iff $(x)_1 \leq_A (y)_1$ and $(x)_2 \leq_B (y)_2$.

Proof We first show that the intrinsic order satisfies $x \leq_{A\times B} y$ iff $(x)_1 \leq_A (y)_1$ and $(x)_2 \leq_B (y)_2$. From this, it is easy to see that $\leq_{A\times B}$ is antisymmetric and has computable least upper bounds. We have already seen that the projection functions $(\_)_1 \colon A \times B \to A$ and $(\_)_2 \colon A \times B \to B$ are computable functions on pers. Since both are therefore monotonic by Lemma 5.6.17, we can see that $x \leq_{A\times B} y$ implies $(x)_1 \leq_A (y)_1$ and $(x)_2 \leq_B (y)_2$. It remains to prove the reverse implication.

Suppose $(x)_1 \leq_A (y)_1$ and $(x)_2 \leq_B (y)_2$ and consider any computable test $f \colon A \times B \rightharpoonup \mathit{unit}$. If $f \cdot x \downarrow$, then $f \cdot (pr \cdot (x)_1 \cdot (x)_2) \downarrow$. If we let $f_1 = \lambda z \in \mathcal{N}.\, f(pr \cdot (x)_1 \cdot z)$ then by the assumption that $(x)_1 \leq_A (y)_1$, we have $f_1 \cdot (x)_1 \downarrow$ implies $f_1 \cdot (y)_1 \downarrow$, and similarly for an analogous computable test $f_2 \colon B \rightharpoonup \mathit{unit}$. Thus

$$
\begin{aligned}
f \cdot x \downarrow \quad & \text{implies} (f_1 \cdot (x)_1 \downarrow \text{ and } f_2 \cdot (x)_2 \downarrow) \\
& \text{implies} (f_1 \cdot (y)_1 \downarrow \text{ and } f_2 \cdot (y)_2 \downarrow) \\
& \text{implies} f \cdot y \downarrow
\end{aligned}
$$

This shows that $x \leq_{A\times B} y$ iff $(x)_1 \leq_A (y)_1$ and $(x)_2 \leq_B (y)_2$. It is an easy exercise for the reader to complete the proof that $\leq_{A\times B}$ is antisymmetric and that $\mathit{sup}_{A\times B}$ is definable from sup_A and sup_B. ■

Lemma 5.6.22 For any effective CPO A, there is a computable convergence test, cnvg_A, such that for all $x \colon \mathit{unit} \rightharpoonup \mathit{unit}$ and $a, b \colon A$ with $a \leq_A b$,

$$x \cdot 0 \uparrow \quad \text{implies} \quad cnvg_A \cdot x \cdot a \cdot b \;\; A \;\; a$$

$$x \cdot 0 \downarrow \quad \text{implies} \quad cnvg_A \cdot x \cdot a \cdot b \;\; A \;\; b$$

Proof Given x: *unit* $\rightharpoonup$ *unit* and a, b: A, let $s_{x,a,b}$ be the computable increasing sequence given by the following algorithm:

$s_{x,a,b} \cdot n =$ compute $x \cdot 0$ for n steps
if $x \cdot 0 \downarrow$ in $\leq n$ steps then return b else return a

On input x,a,b, the function $cnvg_A$ returns $sup_A \cdot s_{x,a,b}$. The reason we need $a \leq_A b$ is that $s_{x,a,b}$ may not be an increasing sequence otherwise. ■

Lemma 5.6.23 If pers A and B are effective CPOs, then $A \to B$ is an effective CPO with intrinsic order satisfying $f \leq_{A \to B} g$ iff $\forall x\colon A.\, f \cdot x \leq_B g \cdot x$.

Proof We first show that $f \leq_{A \to B} g$ iff $\forall x\colon A.\, f \cdot x \leq_B g \cdot x$ and then use this to verify that $A \to B$ is an effective CPO. If $f \leq_{A \to B} g$, then since application $\lambda h\colon A \to B.\, h \cdot x$ to any x: A is computable and therefore monotonic by Lemma 5.6.17, we have $f \cdot x \leq_B g \cdot x$ for any x: A.

For the reverse implication, suppose that $\forall x\colon A.\, f \cdot x \leq_B g \cdot x$ and, for the sake of deriving a contradiction, $f \not\leq_{A \to B} g$. By definition of the intrinsic order, there is some computable test h: $(A \to B) \rightharpoonup$ *unit* with $h \cdot f \downarrow$ and $h \cdot g \uparrow$. As in the proof of Lemma 5.6.21, we will derive a contradiction by showing that $\bar{K}$ is r.e. Using the convergence test $cnvg_B$ of Lemma 5.6.22, we define a function k_x: $A \to B$, for any $x \in \mathcal{N}$, by

$$k_x \cdot y \;=\; cnvg_B \cdot (\lambda z \in \mathcal{N}.\, x \cdot x) \cdot (f \cdot y) \cdot (g \cdot y)$$

Then for any $x \in \mathcal{N}$ we have $x \in \bar{K}$ iff $k_x \; (A \to B) \; f$ iff $h \cdot f \downarrow$. Since this implies that $\bar{K}$ is r.e., we have shown that $f \leq_{A \to B} g$ iff $\forall x\colon A.\, f \cdot x \leq_B g \cdot x$.

Using this characterization of the intrinsic order, we can easily see that antimonotonicity of $\leq_B$ implies antimonotonicity of $\leq_{A \to B}$. For any computable increasing sequences s in $A \to B$, we can compute $sup_{A \to B} \cdot s$ "pointwise" by returning an index of the function mapping x: A to the least upper bound in B of the computable increasing sequence $\lambda n \in \mathcal{N}.\, s \cdot n \cdot x$. ■

Lemma 5.6.24 If pers A and B are effective CPOs, then $A \rightharpoonup B$ is an effective CPO with intrinsic order satisfying $f \leq_{A \rightharpoonup B} g$ iff $\forall x\colon A.\; f \cdot x \downarrow \supset f \cdot x \leq_B g \cdot x$.

Proof The proof is similar to the proof of Lemma 5.6.23. The two differences lie in the pointwise characterization of the intrinsic order and computing the least upper bound of an increasing sequence.

In showing $\forall x\colon A.\, f \cdot x \downarrow \supset f \cdot x \leq_B g \cdot x$ implies $f \leq_{A \rightharpoonup B} g$ by contradiction, we define k_x by the algorithm

$k_x \cdot y =$ compute $x \cdot x$, $f \cdot y$ and $g \cdot y$ in parallel (by interleaving)
  if $f \cdot y \downarrow$ then return $cnvg_B \cdot (\lambda z \in \mathcal{N}.\, x \cdot x) \cdot (f \cdot y) \cdot (g \cdot y)$;
  if $x \cdot x \downarrow$ then return $g \cdot y$;
  else do not halt.

For any computable increasing sequence s in $A \rightharpoonup B$, we might attempt to follow the proof of Lemma 5.6.23 and compute $sup_{A \rightharpoonup B} \cdot s$ "pointwise" by returning an index of the function mapping $x\colon A$ to the least upper bound in B of the computable increasing sequence $\lambda n \in \mathcal{N}.\, s \cdot n \cdot x$. The problem with this is that when s is an increasing sequence of partial functions, we might have $s \cdot i \cdot x \uparrow$ for some i and $s \cdot j \cdot x \downarrow$ for some $j > i$. In this case, $\lambda n \in \mathcal{N}.\, s \cdot n \cdot x$ is not a total function, and therefore not a computable increasing sequence in B. We circumvent this problem with partiality by letting $sup_{A \rightharpoonup B} \cdot s$ be an index of the function computed by the following algorithm:

$sup_{A \rightharpoonup B} \cdot s \cdot x =$ compute $s \cdot 0 \cdot x,\ s \cdot 1 \cdot x,\ s \cdot 2 \cdot x,\ \ldots$ in parallel (by interleaving);
  if $s \cdot j \cdot x \downarrow$ for some j
    then return $sup_B \cdot (\lambda n \in \mathcal{N}.\, s \cdot (n + j) \cdot x)$
    else do not halt

The reader may wish to compare this computation with $sup_{N \rightharpoonup N}$ in Example 5.6.16, which is simpler since the intrinsic order on N is discrete, whereas the intrinsic order on B here may not be. ■

Exercise 5.6.25 Prove Lemma 5.6.12.

Exercise 5.6.26 Suppose $\langle A, e_A \rangle$ and $\langle B, e_B \rangle$ are modest sets. Define the modest set $\langle A \rightharpoonup B, e_{A \rightharpoonup B} \rangle$ of partial recursive functions from A to B, enumerated by the partial enumeration function $e_{A \rightharpoonup B}$. Check your definition by showing that if $R = \sim_A$ and $S = \sim_B$ are the pers given by $\langle A, e_A \rangle$ and $\langle B, e_B \rangle$, then $\langle A \rightharpoonup B, e_{A \rightharpoonup B} \rangle$ is isomorphic to $R \rightharpoonup S$ as defined above.

Exercise 5.6.27 The main property of lifting is $R \rightharpoonup S \cong R \to \mathit{lift}(S)$. Suppose *lift* is any function on pers such that this isomorphism holds for all pers R and S. Show that $\mathit{lift}(S) \cong \mathit{unit} \rightharpoonup S$ for all S.

Exercise 5.6.28 With CPOs, we lift a CPO by adding one new element. By analogy, we might expect to lift pers by taking the disjoint union with a one-element per. Specifically, suppose that we define $\mathit{lift}(S) = S + \mathit{unit}$, where the sum of pers is defined in

Exercise 5.5.7. Show that although we have a non-recursive isomorphism $R \rightharpoonup S \cong R \rightarrow \mathit{lift}(S)$, there exist pers R and S such that this isomorphism cannot be recursive.

Exercise 5.6.29 Show that the intrinsic preorder $\leq_A$ on any per A is reflexive and transitive.

Exercise 5.6.30 Show that under each of the following assumptions about a per A, the intrinsic preorder $\leq_A$ is the discrete order with $x \leq_A y$ iff $x\ A\ y$.

(a) The relation $A \subseteq \mathcal{N} \times \mathcal{N}$ is decidable, *i.e.*, there is an algorithm which decides whether $i\ A\ j$ for any given pair $\langle i, j\rangle \in \mathcal{N} \times \mathcal{N}$.

(b) The relation A is recursively enumerable.

(c) The complement of A is recursively enumerable.

Exercise 5.6.31 Let A be the per $A = \{\langle i, j\rangle \mid i, j \in \mathit{Tot}\} \cup \{\langle i, j\rangle \mid i, j \notin \mathit{Tot}\}$ where $\mathit{Tot} = \{n \mid \forall i.\, \phi_n(i)\downarrow\}$. Show that the intrinsic preorder on A is not antisymmetric, *i.e.*, we have $x \leq_A y$ if either $x \in \mathit{Tot}$ and $y \notin \mathit{Tot}$ or $x \notin \mathit{Tot}$ and $y \in \mathit{Tot}$.

Exercise 5.6.32 This problem asks you to show some connections between isomorphism of pers and their intrinsic preorder.

(a) Show that if $A \cong B$ is a recursive isomorphism of pers, then the isomorphism preserves the intrinsic preorders, *i.e.*, if $f\colon A \to B$ is a recursive function with recursive inverse, then $x \leq_A y$ iff $f \cdot x \leq_B f \cdot y$.

(b) There exist pers A and B with $B \subseteq A$ and with the same number of equivalence classes but such that the structure $\langle A, \leq_A\rangle$ is not isomorphic to $\langle B, \leq_B\rangle$. In particular, we may take

$A = \{\langle i, j\rangle \mid i, j \in K \text{ or } i, j \notin K\}$

$B = \{\langle i, j\rangle \mid i, j \in K \text{ both even}\} \cup \{\langle i, j\rangle \mid i, j \notin K \text{ both odd }\}$

where $K = \{n \mid \phi_n(n)\downarrow\}$. Show that $\leq_A$ is antisymmetric with one equivalence class of A strictly $<_A$ the other.

(c) Show that $\leq_B$ is the discrete order on the equivalence classes of B.

It follows from (a)–(c) that the isomorphism between A and B cannot be recursive.

6 Imperative Programs

6.1 Introduction

In the preceding chapters, we considered *functional* programs that do not contain assignment or other operations that change the values of identifiers. In computing practice, of course, it is more common to use *imperative* programs. A typical example of an imperative construct is the assignment statement $x := y$, which sets the value of x to the value y. Most of this chapter is concerned with the simple imperative language of so-called `while` programs, with semantics of additional program constructs considered in the last section of the chapter.

In outline, the main topics are:

- Operational semantics of imperative programs based on a form of rewrite rules, commonly called *structured operational semantics* after [Plo81].
- Denotational semantics of imperative programs using a typed lambda calculus and domains (CPOs). This typed lambda calculus will include explicit operations on *stores,* which may be viewed as an abstraction of machine states.
- Floyd-Hoare logic, which makes assertions relating initial and final values of variables that occur in programs.
- Denotational semantics of imperative procedures and local variable declarations.

The language of `while` programs may be defined over any class of value expressions and boolean expressions. Without specifying any particular basic expressions, we may summarize the structure of `while` programs by the grammar

$$P \ ::= \ x := M \mid P; P \mid \texttt{if} \ B \ \texttt{then} \ P \ \texttt{else} \ P \mid \texttt{while} \ B \ \texttt{do} \ P \ \texttt{od}$$

where we assume that x has the appropriate type to be assigned value M, and that the test B has type *bool*. Since this language does not have explicit input or output, or local variable declarations, the distinction between input, output and "temporary" or "scratch" variables will not be an explicit part of a program. However, we will usually separate variables into these three groups informally when describing programs. Using natural number operations and assignment, we may write the following simple program.

$$x := 1;\ y := 0;\ \texttt{while} \ x < z \ \texttt{do} \ x := x + x;\ y := y + 1 \ \texttt{od}$$

We may think of this program as having input z and output y. This program uses a "scratch" variable x to set y to an integer approximation of the logarithm of any $z > 0$.

The behavior of an imperative program depends on the values of assignable variables. We will keep track of the values of variables by associating a "location" with each assignable variable and maintaining a map from locations to values. Following tradition, this map will be called the *store*. Using stores, we can give a direct and readable form of operational semantics that resembles the reduction-rule operational semantics of lambda terms. For `while` programs, we define a three-place relation $\overset{exec}{\leadsto}$ between programs, stores and stores. Intuitively, if P is a `while` program and s, s' are stores, then $\langle P, s\rangle \overset{exec}{\leadsto} s'$ means that if we execute P from store s, the program will halt with final store s'. Since `while` programs are deterministic, $\overset{exec}{\leadsto}$ is a partial function, not an arbitrary relation. However, this is an artifact of the programming language we have chosen, and not inherent to the basic approach. We could easily extend the language to include some form of nondeterminism and define a nondeterministic execution relation by the same method.

In computer science, the phrase *denotational semantics* often refers to a specific style of mathematical semantics for imperative programs, although the phrase also has the more general usage of Chapter 2. Denotational semantics, in the specific sense, developed in the late 1960's and early 1970's, following the pioneering work of Christopher Strachey and Dana Scott at Oxford University [Str66, Str67, SS71, Sto77]. The term "denotational semantics" suggests that a meaning or *denotation* is associated with each program. The denotation of a program is a mathematical object, typically a function, as opposed to a process, algorithm or sequence of actions to perform. One of the main tenets of denotational semantics is that programs should be understood *compositionally,* which means that if we want to say what a compound program such as `if` B `then` P `else` Q means, then we should do so using only the denotations of B, P and Q. In particular, we should not refer to programs constructed from B, P and Q by syntactic operations such as substitution. The importance of compositionality, which may seem rather subtle at first, is that if two program pieces have the same denotation, then either may safely be substituted for the other in any program. More specifically, if B, P and Q have the same denotations as B', P' and Q' (respectively), then `if` B' `then` P' `else` Q' must have the same denotation as `if` B `then` P `else` Q. Thus compositionality guarantees that denotational program equivalence is a congruence relation. This makes denotational semantics useful for understanding and reasoning about such pragmatic issues as program transformation and optimization. Some books devoted to denotational semantics are [All86, Gor79, Sch86, Sto77].

There are several ways of viewing the standard techniques of denotational semantics. Typically, a denotational semantics is given by associating a function over domains (in the technical sense of Chapter 5) with each program. One reason why domains are used is that most programming languages allow functions to be defined using recursion, and domains provide a convenient space of mathematical functions with fixed points. In fact, the development of domains was largely motivated by denotational semantics. As many researchers in denotational semantics have observed, a mapping from programs to functions must be written in some language. This language is commonly called the *meta-language*, to distinguish it from the programming language. Since typed lambda calculus with fixed points provides a useful notation for functions over domains, it is common to use a typed lambda calculus as a meta-language. Thus most denotational semantics have two parts, a translation of programs into a lambda calculus with fixed points, and a semantic interpretation of the lambda calculus into domains, although older presentations do not emphasize the use of typed lambda calculus as much as we do here. We will give semantics to a language of `while` programs using a typed lambda calculus with locations and stores, and prove the equivalence of operational and denotational semantics.

Floyd-Hoare logic [Flo67, Hoa69] is a logic for making *before–after* assertions about imperative programs. The formulas of this logic are triples

$$F\{P\}G$$

where F and G are first order formulas. Intuitively, F describes the values of variables before executing P, and G the values afterwards. Thus we may read this triple as, "if F holds initially, then after executing P we will be in a store satisfying G." Since P might not halt, we must be more precise about what happens if we do not reach a final store by executing P. There are two natural choices, one leading to *partial correctness assertions* and the other to *termination assertions.* In Floyd-Hoare logic, we prove partial correctness assertions $F\,\{P\}\,G$ which mean that if F is true initially, then *if* P halts, the program halts in a store with G true. The corresponding termination assertion, sometimes written $F\,\langle P\rangle\,G$, means that if F is true initially, program P *will* halt in a store where G is true. We will explain the proof rules of Floyd–Hoare logic, and prove a certain form of completeness theorem, using denotational semantics.

6.2 While Programs

6.2.1 L–values and R–values

One basic property of Algol– and Pascal–like languages is that assignable variables have two kinds of "values." These have traditionally been called *L–values* and *R–values,* since they correspond to occurrences on the left and right hand side of an assignment statement. In elementary terms, the L–value of a variable is its location in memory and the R–value is the contents of this location. To see how this distinction arises, consider the assignment statement $x := y + 3$. A compiler for a register–based machine might compile this statement into the following instructions:

1. Put the contents of location y in register a.
2. Add 3 to register a.
3. Store the contents of register a in location x.

It is easy to see from this "compiled code" that the occurrence of y on the right hand of the assignment refers to the contents of a location, while the occurrence of x on the left refers to the location itself. Another way of saying this is that the assignment $x := y' + 3$ will have the same effect as $x := y + 3$ if the contents of y' is the same as y', but $x' := y + 3$ will have the same effect only if x' names the same location as x. In general, the type of the L–value of a variable is different from the type of its R–value. The L–value is a location, while the R–value may be an integer or other storable value.

In giving denotational semantics to programs, it is necessary to distinguish between L–values and R–values. This is not overly difficult, but it leads to slight technical complication since the distinction relies on context. As a simplifying assumption, we will use a version of `while` programs in which the distinction between L–values and R–values is explicit. Specifically, we will use variables of type *loc* for assignable variables, and apply a "contents" function *cont* to a location to extract its contents. This is similar to the way pointer variables are used in Pascal, for example, where we write $x \uparrow$ for the contents of x; the C equivalent is $*x$. This is also the way all assignable variables are treated in the programming language ML, which does not seem to suffer from this approach. In fact, explicit location expressions in ML provide some useful flexibility.

6.2.2 Syntax of While Programs

For simplicity, we assume we are only interested in values of two basic types, *val* and *bool*, and that only elements of type *val* may be stored. In writing examples, it is helpful to regard *val* as *nat*, and assume common numeric and boolean operations. However, when we analyze the logic for reasoning about `while` programs, it will be useful to consider different semantic interpretations of *val*, and arbitrary algebraic functions over *val* and *bool*.

Let Σ be an algebraic signature over basic types *val* and *bool*, and let us assume the function symbol

$$cont : loc \rightarrow val$$

is distinct from the function symbols of Σ. To simplify syntactic considerations, let us choose some infinite sets Γ_{loc}, Γ_{val} and Γ_{bool} of variables of types *loc*, *val* and *bool*, respectively, and use these throughout our discussion of `while` programs and Floyd–Hoare logic. Using algebraic terms of types *val* and *bool* over Σ and function symbol *cont*, we define the language of `while` programs by

$$P \ ::= \ x := M \mid P;\, P \mid \texttt{if}\ B\ \texttt{then}\ P\ \texttt{else}\ P \mid \texttt{while}\ B\ \texttt{do}\ P\ \texttt{od}$$

where we assume that variable x has type *loc*, expression M has type *val* and B has type *bool*. Since Σ is an arbitrary signature with sorts *val* and *bool*, we essentially allow arbitrary operations on these types. However, since Σ does not mention *loc*, we have restricted the operations on locations to those definable from *cont*.

Using *cont* to map L–values to R–values, we may write the logarithm program of Section 6.1 as follows.

$$x := 1;\ y := 0;\ \texttt{while}\ \ cont\, x < z\ \ \texttt{do}\ \ x := cont\, x + cont\, x;\ \ y := cont\ y + 1\ \ \texttt{od}$$

Exercise 6.2.1 Rewrite the following "informal" `while` program using *cont* to map locations to values.

```
q := 0;
r := m;
while r ≥ n do
        q := q + 1;
        r := r − n;
        od
```

Note that there are two choices for the types of m and n, but only one choice for q and r. This program computes values of q and r from m and n. What standard arithmetic function does it compute?

Exercise 6.2.2 Rewrite the following "informal" `while` program to compute the greatest common divisor using *cont* to map locations to values.

```
while n ≠ 0 do
        r := m;
        while r ≥ n do
                r := r − n;
                od
        m := n;
        n := r;
        od
```

Think of this program as taking m and n as input, and producing a new value of m as output. (This is probably the most famous algorithm of all time.)

Exercise 6.2.3 Write a `while`-program with two location variables, x, y: *loc*, that halts iff x and y share the same location. It is not necessary to preserve the initial contents of x or y.

6.3 Operational Semantics

6.3.1 Basic Symbols in Expressions

Expressions in `while` programs may contain variables from Γ_{loc}, Γ_{val} and Γ_{bool}, the special function symbol *cont,* and function symbols from any two-sorted algebraic signature Σ. Since we let Σ be arbitrary, our semantics will be developed with respect to an arbitrary interpretation of the symbols in Σ. To allow easy comparison between operational and denotational semantics, we will assume we are given a two-sorted algebra $\mathcal{A}_0 = \langle A^{val}, A^{bool}, f^{\mathcal{A}}, \ldots \rangle$ for signature Σ. Although our operational semantics will make sense for any interpretation of *val* and *bool*, many intuitive properties of programs depend on *bool* having its standard interpretation. Since this will be important in establishing the soundness and completeness of Floyd–Hoare logic, we will assume from the outset that A^{bool} is the familiar two–element set $\{true, false\}$ of booleans.

Since `while` programs contain variables, we need an environment η mapping variables from $\Gamma_{loc} \cup \Gamma_{val} \cup \Gamma_{bool}$ to elements of $\mathcal{A}$ of the appropriate type. If location variables x and y are given the same location by the environment, then an assignment to x will also change the contents of y. Since this effect, commonly called *aliasing,* is important in reasoning about programs, the logic we consider in Section 6.5 will allow hypotheses like $x \neq y$ to prevent distinct location variables from denoting the same location.

6.3.2 Locations and Stores

Both the operational and denotational semantics of `while` programs will involve data structures called *stores.* Intuitively, *stores* represent the "memory contents" of some simple machine. Since we have restricted `while` programs so that only elements of type *val* may be stored, a store is just a function from *loc* to *val*. However, the way that the store is affected by `while` programs is somewhat special. Although `while` programs do not mention the store explicitly, the current store may be referenced using the function *cont,* and updated via assignment.

We begin with an algebraic specification of the operations on stores, which will be useful for reasoning about programs. We extend our signature to a fourth sort *store* and function symbols *init*, *update* and *lookup* with the following types.

$$\begin{aligned} &init \quad : store \\ &update : store \times loc \times val \rightarrow store \\ &lookup : store \times loc \rightarrow val \end{aligned}$$

Intuitively, *init* is some distinguished store which might, for example, contain 0 in every location, *update* is a function that changes the value associated with some location, and *lookup* reads the value stored in some location. The behavior of these functions is characterized by the following algebraic axioms, written using equality test on locations, conditional, and variables $\ell\colon loc$, $\ell'\colon loc$, $s\colon store$, $v\colon val$.

$$lookup\,(update\,s\,\ell'\,v)\,\ell = \texttt{if}\ \ Eq?\,\ell\,\ell'\ \ \texttt{then}\ \ v\ \ \texttt{else}\ \ (lookup\,s\,\ell) \qquad (lookup)$$

$$update\,s\,\ell\,(lookup\,s\,\ell) = s \qquad (update)_1$$

$$\begin{aligned} update\ mvarupdate\,\ell\,u)\,\ell'\,v = \texttt{if}\ Eq?\,\ell\,\ell'\ \texttt{then}\ update\,s\,\ell\,v \\ \texttt{else}\ update\,(update\,s\,\ell'\,v)\,\ell\,u \end{aligned} \qquad (update)_2$$

To interpret these operations, we extend $\mathcal{A}_0$ to a four-sorted algebra $\mathcal{A}$ with locations and stores by letting A^{loc} be any countably infinite set, and letting A^{store} be the set of all functions from A^{loc} to A^{val}. We let $init^{\mathcal{A}}$ be any constant function, $lookup^{\mathcal{A}}(s, \ell) = s(\ell)$, and $update^{\mathcal{A}}(s, \ell, v)$ is the function s' that is identical to s except that $s'(\ell) = v$. Since $\mathcal{A}$ and $\mathcal{A}_0$ give the same interpretation to each symbol of Σ, we may write $f^{\mathcal{A}}$ without ambiguity. For notational convenience, we sometimes write *lookup* instead of $lookup^{\mathcal{A}}$, and similarly for *update* and *init*, when there is no danger of confusion.

A common question is why we have separated environments and stores, instead of using a single function mapping identifiers to values. For programs that do not contain declarations, it is technically possible to give both operational and denotational semantics using only a single mapping. In some cases, this is the best approach, since there is less machinery involved. However, there are both intuitive and technical reasons for separating environments from stores, as we do here. An intuitive reason is that environments and stores are conceptually different, and correspond to different mechanisms in actual language implementations. The environment corresponds, roughly, to the symbol table that is used during compilation to keep an association between program identifiers and memory locations. The store models the contents of memory locations during execution of the compiled program. For `while` programs, the entire program is understood with respect to a single environment while the store changes during program execution. From a technical standpoint, we give denotational semantics by translating `while` programs into lambda terms that manipulate the store explicitly. This translation is simplified by using the same form of environment for `while` programs as lambda terms with store operations. This would not be possible if we did not separate environments from stores in the semantics of `while` programs.

6.3.3 Evaluation of Expressions

The operational semantics for `while` programs has two parts. The first is a four–place relation $\stackrel{eval}{\leadsto}$ between algebraic expressions, environments, stores and semantic values of algebraic terms. We will write this as an infix relation $\langle M, s\rangle_\eta \stackrel{eval}{\leadsto} v$ to suggest that we "evaluate" expression M in store s with respect to environment η and obtain value v. The approach we use is suited to programming languages with nondeterministic or non–terminating expressions. However, the expressions we use in `while` programs are single-valued and terminating. Consequently, our evaluation relation is a total function. This function is type-respecting, in the sense that if M has type b, and $\langle M, s\rangle_\eta \stackrel{eval}{\leadsto} v$, then $v \in A^b$. To simplify the notation, we will omit the subscript for the environment and assume that we have chosen one fixed environment.

To illustrate a general method for defining evaluation relations, we will present $\stackrel{eval}{\leadsto}$ using a form of proof system. This is similar to the presentation of reduction strategies by proof systems in Chapter 2, except that we are now defining an evaluation function instead of a one-step evaluation relation. The method is developed for a variety of languages in [Plo81], where many examples and general properties are given; a good reference is the later book [Hen90b].

There are two axioms for $\stackrel{eval}{\leadsto}$, one for variables and one for constants. In words, the value of a variable is given by the environment, and the value of a constant is given by the algebraic structure $\mathcal{A}$. Note that since we use *cont* to access the store, *cont* x may depend on the store, but the value of a variable x does not.

$$\langle x, s\rangle \stackrel{eval}{\leadsto} \eta(x)$$

$$\langle c, s\rangle \stackrel{eval}{\leadsto} c^{\mathcal{A}}$$

There are two inference rules for compound terms, one for application of an algebraic function (interpreted by $\mathcal{A}$), and one for the special function *cont* which accesses the store. The rule for algebraic functions is essentially a formalization of the way we define the meaning of an algebraic term.

$$\frac{\langle M_1, s\rangle \stackrel{eval}{\leadsto} v_1, \ldots, \langle M_k, s\rangle \stackrel{eval}{\leadsto} v_k}{\langle f M_1 \ldots M_k,\ s\rangle \stackrel{eval}{\leadsto} v}\ f^{\mathcal{A}}(v_1, \ldots, v_k) = v$$

The value of *cont* x is determined by looking up location x in the store,

$$\frac{\langle x, s\rangle \overset{\text{eval}}{\leadsto} \ell}{\langle cont\, x, s\rangle \overset{\text{eval}}{\leadsto} v}\ lookup^{\mathcal{A}}(s, \ell) = v$$

as explained below. The side-conditions about the semantic interpretations of f and *lookup* are written off to the side of these rules since they are not assertions about the $\overset{\text{eval}}{\leadsto}$ relation, but facts about the algebra $\mathcal{A}$.

While the axioms for $\overset{\text{eval}}{\leadsto}$ are straightforward, it may help to give some hints on reading the inference rules. In general, it seems best to read the rules in "clockwise" order, starting from the lower left. Taking the rule for *cont* as an example, the main point of the rule is to describe the evaluation of an expression of the form $cont\ x$ in a store s. This is indicated by the fact that $\langle cont\, x,\ s\rangle$ appears in the lower line, to the left of $\overset{\text{eval}}{\leadsto}$. The result of evaluation appears on the lower right, but the expression there (in this case v) cannot be understood without reading the rest of the rule. The top line "says" we should evaluate x in s to get a value ℓ. In this rule, the type of *cont* guarantees that x is a location variable. Now we may proceed clockwise to the lower right, and see that the result of evaluating $cont\, x$ is obtained by looking up the value v of location ℓ in the store.

For a pure algebraic term not containing *cont,* it is easy to check that evaluation is independent of the store, and results in the ordinary meaning of the term in algebra $\mathcal{A}$.

It is worth mentioning that this style of operational semantics is also applicable to purely symbolic evaluation. Instead of using some algebra $\mathcal{A}$ to interpret the basic symbols of programs, we could evaluate expressions and execute programs symbolically using rewrite rules on terms involving *lookup*, *update*, and so on. However, there is no loss of generality in the approach we use here, since the algebra $\mathcal{A}$ may be an algebra of terms, modulo some theory given by rewrite rules.

6.3.4 Execution of Commands

Execution of commands is characterized using another relation, $\overset{\text{exec}}{\leadsto}$, axiomatized in a manner similar to $\overset{\text{eval}}{\leadsto}$. The first rule describes the execution of an assignment statement. In words, we execute $x := M$ in store s by evaluating M and then updating s so that location x now contains this value.

$$\frac{\langle M, s\rangle \overset{\text{eval}}{\leadsto} v}{\langle x := M,\ s\rangle \overset{\text{exec}}{\leadsto} s'}\ update^{\mathcal{A}}(s, \eta(x), v) = s'$$

The remaining rules explain the execution of compound programs using the results of executing their parts. It is worth mentioning that the execution relation defined here represents complete execution. If $\langle P, s\rangle \overset{\text{exec}}{\leadsto} s'$, then this is to be understood as meaning that if we start executing P with store s, we will eventually halt with store s'. An alternative to this "all at once" notion of execution is to axiomatize a single execution step. This is developed in the exercises.

Sequencing and conditional are not very complicated. To execute $P_1; P_2$, we "first" execute P_1, and then execute P_2 in the resulting store. For $\texttt{if}\ B\ \texttt{then}\ P_1\ \texttt{else}\ P_2$, we evaluate B and then execute P_1 or P_2 accordingly. It takes two inference rules to express this, one for the case when B evaluates to *true* and the other for *false*.

$$\frac{\langle P_1,\ s\rangle \overset{\text{exec}}{\rightsquigarrow} s',\ \langle P_2,\ s'\rangle \overset{\text{exec}}{\rightsquigarrow} s''}{\langle P_1;\ P_2,\ \ s\rangle \overset{\text{exec}}{\rightsquigarrow} s''}$$

$$\frac{\langle B, s\rangle \overset{\text{eval}}{\rightsquigarrow} \mathit{true},\ \langle P_1,\ s\rangle \overset{\text{exec}}{\rightsquigarrow} s'}{\langle \texttt{if}\ \ B\ \ \texttt{then}\ \ P_1\ \ \texttt{else}\ \ P_2,\ \ s\rangle \overset{\text{exec}}{\rightsquigarrow} s'}$$

$$\frac{\langle B, s\rangle \overset{\text{eval}}{\rightsquigarrow} \mathit{false},\ \langle P_2,\ s\rangle \overset{\text{exec}}{\rightsquigarrow} s'}{\langle \texttt{if}\ \ B\ \ \texttt{then}\ \ P_1\ \ \texttt{else}\ \ P_2,\ \ s\rangle \overset{\text{exec}}{\rightsquigarrow} s'}$$

There are two rules for $\texttt{while}\ \ B\ \ \texttt{do}\ \ P\ \ \texttt{od}$. The first takes care of the case when B evaluates to *false*. The second rule "says" that when B is true, we execute $\texttt{while}B\texttt{do}$ $P\texttt{od}$ by first executing P, and then executing $\texttt{while}\ \ B\ \ \texttt{do}\ \ P\ \ \texttt{od}$ in the resulting store.

$$\frac{\langle B, s\rangle \overset{\text{eval}}{\rightsquigarrow} \mathit{false}}{\langle \texttt{while}\ \ B\ \ \texttt{do}\ \ P\ \ \texttt{od},\ \ s\rangle \overset{\text{exec}}{\rightsquigarrow} s}$$

$$\frac{\langle B, s\rangle \overset{\text{eval}}{\rightsquigarrow} \mathit{true},\ \ \langle P,\ s\rangle \overset{\text{exec}}{\rightsquigarrow} s',\ \ \langle \texttt{while}\ \ B\ \ \texttt{do}\ \ P\ \ \texttt{od},\ \ s'\rangle \overset{\text{exec}}{\rightsquigarrow} s''}{\langle \texttt{while}\ \ B\ \ \texttt{do}\ \ P\ \ \texttt{od},\ \ s\rangle \overset{\text{exec}}{\rightsquigarrow} s''}$$

The second rule may be slightly unsettling, since it might appear that we are defining the execution of a $\texttt{while}$ loop in terms of itself. However, this set of rules is not intended to be a definition of $\overset{\text{exec}}{\rightsquigarrow}$ by induction on the structure of formulas. (That would be a denotational semantics.) Instead, this is an inference rule telling us some fact about execution. This fact has a computational interpretation, since we may read the rule as a list of instructions for executing $\texttt{while}\ \ B\ \ \texttt{do}\ \ P\ \ \texttt{od}$. From a mathematical point of view, we should think of the entire collection of rules as determining the *least* execution relation satisfying these conditions, in just the way that axioms and proof rules in logic determine the *least* provability relation $\vdash$ (see Example 5.2.22). More specifically, the rules define the relation $\overset{\text{exec}}{\rightsquigarrow}$ with the property that $\langle P, s\rangle \overset{\text{exec}}{\rightsquigarrow} s'$ iff there is a finite proof of $\langle P, s\rangle \overset{\text{exec}}{\rightsquigarrow} s'$ in the inference system.

To get some feel for how the rules work, it is best to work a few examples. In Example 6.3.1 below, an important general idea is illustrated. Namely, if we want to figure out what final store is produced by executing program P from initial store s, we look at the syntactic form of P and see which inference rule could be the last rule in a proof of $\langle P, s\rangle \overset{\text{exec}}{\rightsquigarrow} s'$. There will be only one possible rule, except in the case of a conditional statement or `while` loop. In these cases, we must evaluate a boolean expression to determine which rule would apply. Having done so, we repeat this process to see how we might deduce the hypotheses of the last inference rule in the proof. Therefore, the natural way to read these proof rules is bottom up. As illustrated in Example 6.3.1 below, this bottom-up reading of operational semantics inference rules leads us to "execute" a program in a way that closely resembles the way a simple-minded interpreter might actually execute the program. This is an important fact about structured operational semantics: although the formalism resembles logic, the general intuitive reading of the rules leads to a procedure for actually executing programs in a simple but illustrative manner.

Example 6.3.1 We will work out the execution of a simple predecessor program that sets p to $n - 1$, using a "scratch" variable m. Since p and m are updated, we let $m, p\colon loc$; since n is not, we let $n\colon val$. We assume that val is the type of natural numbers, that we have basic functions for addition and testing inequality, and that variables p and m denote different locations. Under these assumptions, we may write the following program to compute predecessor.

$p := 0;$
$m := 0;$
`while` $(cont\, m) \neq n$ `do`
  $p := cont\, m;$
  $m := (cont\, m) + 1;$
  `od`

For concreteness, let us assume that the value of n is 3, and write ℓ_p and ℓ_m for locations $\eta(p)$ and $\eta(m)$, respectively. Since we will use this fact repeatedly, we begin by noting that in any store s, we have $\langle m, s\rangle \overset{\text{eval}}{\rightsquigarrow} \ell_m$, and similarly for p.

If we use the symbol P for the entire program above, our goal is to construct a proof of an assertion $\langle P, s\rangle \overset{\text{exec}}{\rightsquigarrow} s'$ using the axioms and inference rules of the operational semantics. Since P initializes all of its assignable variables, it does not matter what the initial store s is. In attempting to find a proof, we will discover the unique store s' for which $\langle P, s\rangle \overset{\text{exec}}{\rightsquigarrow} s'$ is provable. As mentioned above, we proceed by selecting an inference rule whose conclusion matches the form of P, and continue by reading inference rules from the bottom up.

Since program P has the form $p := 0;\ Q$, we look at the sequence rule. If we execute $\langle p := 0,\ s\rangle$, the result is $s_1 = update\ s\ \ell_p\, 0$. We must now execute the remaining program with store s_1. Since the next statement is also an assignment, similar reasoning applies, and so it remains to execute the `while` loop from store s_2 with $lookup\, s_2\, \ell_m = lookup\, s_2\, \ell_p = 0$. We determine which `while` inference rule applies by evaluating the boolean test. Since

$\langle (cont\, m) \neq n, s_2 \rangle \overset{\text{eval}}{\rightsquigarrow} true,$

we must use the second inference rule for `while`. This rule requires us to determine both the store obtained by executing the loop body, and the result of executing the entire `while` statement in this store. It is not hard to see that

$\langle (p := cont\, m;\;\; m := (cont\, m) + 1), s_2 \rangle \overset{\text{exec}}{\rightsquigarrow} s_3$

where $lookup\, s_3\, \ell_p = 0$ and $lookup\, s_3\, \ell_m = 1$. We then test the boolean expression and find

$\langle (cont\, m) \neq n, s_3 \rangle \overset{\text{eval}}{\rightsquigarrow} true,$

which leads us to calculate

$\langle (p := cont\, m;\;\; m := (cont\, m) + 1), s_3 \rangle \overset{\text{exec}}{\rightsquigarrow} s_4$

where $lookup\, s_4\, \ell_p = 1$ and $lookup\, s_4\, \ell_m = 2$. Repeating the loop body again, we get

$\langle (cont\, m) \neq n, s_4 \rangle \overset{\text{eval}}{\rightsquigarrow} true,$

$\langle (p := cont\, m;\;\; m := (cont\, m) + 1), s_4 \rangle \overset{\text{exec}}{\rightsquigarrow} s_5$

where $lookup\, s_5\, \ell_p = 2$ and $lookup\, s_5\, \ell_m = 3$. It is easy to see that

$\langle (cont\, m) \neq n, s_5 \rangle \overset{\text{eval}}{\rightsquigarrow} false,$

so finally we have reached a store where the loop test fails. At this point, we can construct a proof that execution of the entire program P from store s terminates in store s_5. The way to write this proof down is simply to combine the assertions about evaluation and execution above using the inference rules for `while` loops. The reader may find it useful to write this proof out and see the correspondence between the bottom-up procedure we followed in identifying stores $s_1, \ldots, s_5$ and the direct proof of $\langle P, s \rangle \overset{\text{exec}}{\rightsquigarrow} s_5$ written out using axioms and inference rules in the usual manner. ■

Exercise 6.3.2 We may generalize assignment to allow more complex location expressions. For example, suppose we add a location conditional `if`⟨*boolean*⟩⟨*location*⟩ `else`⟨*location*⟩ to the syntax of expressions and allow assignment statements of the form $N := M$, where N: *loc* and M: *val*. Write evaluation rules for location conditional and an execution rule for an assignment $N := M$.

Exercise 6.3.3 The operational semantics given in this section only specifies the final result of executing a program. If we want to keep track of how many steps a program takes before it halts, for example, we might prefer to take a single evaluation step as the basic relation. Another advantage of single-step evaluation, illustrated in Exercise 6.3.4 below, is that it allows us to incorporate parallel execution, as interleaving. This does not seem possible with "final result" operational semantics. In this exercise, we will axiomatize a relation $\overset{exec}{\mapsto}$ which characterizes "step-by-step" evaluation of `while` programs.

In describing complete execution, we used a relation $\overset{exec}{\leadsto} \subseteq \textit{program} \times \textit{store} \times \textit{store}$, since the result of executing a `while` program is a final store. We will describe one-step execution using a relation

$$\overset{exec}{\mapsto} \subseteq (\textit{program} \times \textit{store}) \times ((\textit{program} \times \textit{store}) + \textit{store}),$$

where $+$ denotes disjoint union. Intuitively, $\langle P, s\rangle \overset{exec}{\mapsto} \langle P', s'\rangle$ means that if we execute a single step of program P, starting with store s, the result is store s', with P' representing the remaining work to be done. We write $\langle P, s\rangle \overset{exec}{\mapsto} s'$ if P from s halts in one step, with final store s'. In the case $\langle P, s\rangle \overset{exec}{\mapsto} \langle P', s'\rangle$ of unfinished computation, we may think of the difference between P and P' as representing a change in the "program counter," in a slightly abstract sense. For example, suppose we execute one step of a sequence $x := 1;\ y := 2$. The result will be some updated store, with the second assignment $y := 2$ still remaining. However, to handle loops, we will also have rules in which the length of the program increases as a result of executing one program step. This could be regarded as an artifact of the approach, but it is really not too far from the fixed-point semantics of `while` loops explained in Section 6.4. The rest of this exercise consists of six questions.

(a) Write a rule for assignment of the form

$$\frac{\ldots}{\langle x := M, s\rangle \overset{exec}{\mapsto} s'}$$

You may use the relation $\overset{eval}{\leadsto}$ given in Section 6.3.3 in your hypothesis. An implicit assumption is that evaluating M can be done as part of a single execution step.

(b) One rule for sequencing is

$$\frac{\langle P_1, s\rangle \overset{exec}{\mapsto} \langle P_1', s'\rangle}{\langle P_1;\ P_2, s\rangle \overset{exec}{\mapsto} \langle P_1';\ P_2, s'\rangle}$$

which allows us to execute one step of $P_1;\ P_2$ by executing a single step of P_1. Write a second rule of the form

$$\frac{\langle P_1, s\rangle \overset{exec}{\mapsto} s'}{\langle P_1;\ P_2, s\rangle \overset{exec}{\mapsto} \langle Q,\ s'\rangle}$$

(for some Q) to handle the last step of P_1 properly.

(c) Write one rule for conditional of the form

$$\frac{\langle B, s\rangle \overset{\text{eval}}{\rightsquigarrow} \mathit{true}}{\langle \texttt{if } B \texttt{ then } P_1 \texttt{ else } P_2, s\rangle \overset{\text{exec}}{\mapsto} \langle Q, s\rangle}$$

for some program Q. Describe a second rule for the case that B evaluates to *false*.

(d) There are two rules for `while` B `do` P `od`, one for each boolean value of B. In the case that $\langle B,\ s\rangle \overset{\text{eval}}{\rightsquigarrow} \mathit{false}$, this loop halts in one step. Write a rule to express this. For the second case, write a rule of the form

$$\frac{\langle B,\ s\rangle \overset{\text{eval}}{\rightsquigarrow} \mathit{true}}{\langle \texttt{while } B \texttt{ do } P \texttt{ od}, s\rangle \overset{\text{exec}}{\mapsto} \langle Q; \texttt{while } B \texttt{ do } P \texttt{ od}, s\rangle}$$

for some program Q.

(e) Write out the step-by-step execution of $x := 3;\ y := (\mathit{cont}\,x) + 3$.

(f) Assuming x is large, write out the first four or five execution steps of

$y := 0;$ `while` $\mathit{cont}\, y \neq x$ `do` $y := (\mathit{cont}\ y) + 1$ `od`.

How many steps does it take for this program to halt, if the initial value of x is k?

Exercise 6.3.4 In Exercise 6.3.3 above, you axiomatized a "one–step" execution relation $\overset{\text{exec}}{\mapsto}$ for `while` programs. This problem asks you to extend that operational semantics to `while` programs with nondeterminism and concurrency.

We begin by extending the syntax of `while` programs as follows:

$P\ ::=\ x := M \mid P;\, P \mid$ `if` B `then` P `else` $P \mid$ `while` B `do` P `od` $\mid$

$\qquad P \cup P \mid P \parallel P$

Intuitively, the program $P_1 \cup P_2$ proceeds by arbitrarily choosing to execute P_1 or P_2 (but not both), and the program $P_1 \parallel P_2$ executes P_1 and P_2 in parallel. For example, the program $(x := 1) \cup (x := 2)$ nondeterministically chooses either to set x to 1 or to 2. If we describe parallelism by interleaving (this will make the problem manageable), then the program

$(x := 1;\ x := (\mathit{cont}\,x) + 1) \parallel (x := 2;\ x := (\mathit{cont}\,x) + 2)$

may execute the four assignments in any order as long as x is set to 1 before being incremented by 1, and set to 2 before being incremented by 2. The possible final values of x are 2, 4 and 5.

The two parts of this question ask you to write rules for the execution of nondeterministic and parallel `while` programs. Since there may be more than one possible final store, it is necessary to think of

$$\stackrel{exec}{\mapsto} \subseteq (program \times store) \times ((program \times store) + store)$$

as a relation rather than a partial function from $(program \times store)$ to $((program \times store) + store)$. Intuitively, $\langle P, s\rangle \stackrel{exec}{\mapsto} \langle P', s'\rangle$ means that if we execute a single step of program P, starting with store s, then *one possible result* is the store s', with P' representing the remaining work to be done in this case.

(i) Write execution rules for executing a nondeterministic choice $P_1 \cup P_2$. You should have either two or four rules, depending on the way you approach the problem, with one set corresponding to executing P_1, and the other for executing P_2.

(ii) Write four execution rules for the interleaving semantics of $P_1 \parallel P_2$, one pair for the case where we begin by executing the first statement of P_1 and the second pair for beginning execution with P_2.

6.4 Denotational Semantics

6.4.1 Typed Lambda Calculus with Stores

We will give a denotational semantics for `while` programs using a typed lambda calculus with locations and stores, which we interpret over CPOs. The lambda calculus we use, which resembles PCF with locations and stores added, will be referred to as $\lambda^{store,fix,\to}$. This calculus has type constants *val*, *bool*, *loc*, *store*, and $store_\bot$, with the first four interpreted as in the algebra $\mathcal{A}$. The difference between *store* and $store_\bot$ is that the latter will have an added least element, $\bot_{store}$. The operations on $store_\bot$ will be a special case of the general operations on lifted types discussed in Section 2.6.4. (This chapter does not depend on Section 2.6.4, however.) In addition to function symbols from the signature Σ, giving functions on *val* and *bool*, the calculus $\lambda^{store,fix,\to}$ has an equality test

$$Eq? : loc \to loc \to bool$$

on locations, store operations *init, update* and *lookup,* a conditional `if ... then ... else ...` of each type, as in PCF, lifting operations (described below), lambda abstraction, application, and a fixed-point operator fix_{store} of type

$$fix_{store}: ((store \to store_\bot) \to (store \to store_\bot)) \to (store \to store_\bot).$$

This will be used to define functions from *store* to $store_\bot$ recursively.

The CPO model, $\mathcal{A}_\lambda$, for $\lambda^{store,fix,\to}$ will be an extension of the four-sorted algebra, $\mathcal{A}$, that was constructed by extending $\mathcal{A}_0$ with locations and stores. Since any set may be regarded as a discrete CPO, we may continue to interpret *val*, *bool*, *loc* and *store* as in

$\mathcal{A}$. We interpret $store_\perp$ as the lifted set $A^{store_\perp} = (A^{store})_\perp$, and extend to function types by letting $A^{\sigma\to\tau}$ be all continuous functions from A^σ to A^τ, ordered point-wise, as described in Section 5.2. Since $A^{store_\perp}$ is pointed, $A^{store\to store_\perp}$ is also pointed, by Lemma 5.2.10. By Theorem 5.2.26, this continuous hierarchy has a least fixed-point operator of the required type. We discuss the interpretation of lifting operations in $\mathcal{A}_\lambda$ after giving their syntactic forms and typing rules.

The operations associated with $store_\perp$ are a map from *store* to $store_\perp$, which we write $\lfloor \cdot \rfloor$, as in Section 2.6.4. If $M\colon store$, then $\lfloor M \rfloor\colon store_\perp$ denotes the same store as M, but regarded as an element of the lifted set of stores, $A_\perp^{store}$. The other operation is a strict form of function application , which we write as an infix operator, $\cdot$. To be precise, we give a typing rule for this operation.

$$\frac{\Gamma \rhd M\colon store \to store_\perp,\ \ \Gamma \rhd N\colon store_\perp}{\Gamma \rhd M \cdot N\colon store_\perp} \qquad (store_\perp \text{ Elim})$$

The semantic interpretation of $\cdot$ is that if N is $\perp$, then $M \cdot N$ is $\perp$, and otherwise $M \cdot N$ is the result of applying M to the denotation of N, which must belong to A^{store}. Two equational axioms associated with these operations are

$$\Gamma \rhd M \cdot \perp = \perp\colon store_\perp$$

$$\Gamma \rhd M \cdot \lfloor N \rfloor = MN\colon store_\perp$$

which are easily seen to be sound for the interpretation in $\mathcal{A}_\lambda$. It is also easy to check that strict application, $\cdot$, is continuous in both arguments. The relationship between strict application and the syntax used in Section 2.6.4 is considered in Exercise 6.4.2. It is useful to define a strict form of function composition as syntactic sugar, by

$$M \diamond N \stackrel{\text{def}}{=} \lambda s\colon store.\, M \cdot (N\, s).$$

To give some idea of how $\lambda^{store,fix,\to}$ will be used, recall that according to the operational semantics, executing an assignment statement $x := 3$ updates the store so that the contents of x becomes 3. If we ignore the difference between location variables and the locations they denote, then the operational semantics might be written

$$\langle x := 3,\ s\rangle \stackrel{\text{exec}}{\leadsto} update^{\mathcal{A}}(s, x, 3).$$

Put another way, executing $x := 3$ maps any store s to the store $update^{\mathcal{A}}(s, x, 3)$. In the lambda calculus of locations and stores, we may write this function on stores as

$$\lambda s\colon store.\, update\ s\ x\ 3.$$

Note that this lambda expression is well-typed, since the typing constraints on assignment requires $x{:}\,loc$. A technical detail is that this is a function from *store* to *store*, and A^{store} has no least element. Since a `while` program may not terminate, the type of lambda term giving the meaning of a program must be $store \to store_\perp$ instead of $store \to store$. Therefore, we write the meaning of the assignment as the lambda expression

$$\lambda s{:}\, store.\ \lfloor update\ s\ x\ 3 \rfloor.$$

For any `while` program S, we will be able to write a $\lambda^{store, fix, \to}$ expression for the mapping from *store* to $store_\perp$ given by the execution rules for S. We will use stores and associated operations for assignment and variable access, as illustrated here, strict composition for sequences of statements, and fixed points for iteration (`while` loops).

The use of strict composition may appear accidental, but it is actually essential. This may be understood by considering a sequence such as $P;\, x := 3$. The meaning of this program will be given by the strict composition, $g \diamond f$, of the function f from *store* to $store_\perp$ determined by P and the function g from *store* to $store_\perp$ determined by $x := 3$. If we use functions f and g from $store_\perp$ to $store_\perp$, and ordinary composition instead, then we have the following problem. Suppose that when we begin in store s, program P does not terminate. Since the least element $\perp$ of a CPO is used to give a mathematical value to a nonterminating computation, the meaning of P would be a function f with $f\, s = \perp_{store}$. Since $P;\ x := 3$ cannot terminate (operationally) if P does not, the meaning of $P;\ x := 3$ should map s to $\perp_{store}$. But if we treated stores as functions from locations to values and used a nonstrict update function

$$update_{non-strict}\ s\ x\ v \stackrel{\text{def}}{=} \lambda y{:}\, loc.\, \texttt{if}\ Eq?\, y\, x\ \texttt{then}\ v\ \texttt{else}\ lookup\, s'\, y$$

then $(g \circ f)(s)$ could be some store different from $\perp$ which in fact contained a value for x. This would cause both the equivalence between operational and denotational semantics and the soundness of the proof rules for the denotational semantics to fail. We therefore use strict composition to guarantee that the meaning of a sequence $P;\ Q$ yields $\perp$ whenever the meaning of P yields $\perp$.

While strictness, in our approach, arises naturally from the type of function used for the meaning of a program, other approaches to denotational semantics must enforce strictness of basic programs explicitly. This may be seen in the "direct semantics" of [Gor79, Sch86, Sto77], for example. The usual method uses only $store_\perp$, not *store*. In this case, it is common to use a function *strict* which, when applied to any function $f : store_\perp \to store_\perp$, returns a function $strict\ f : store_\perp \to store_\perp$ with

$$strict\ f\ s = \begin{cases} f\, s & s \neq \perp_{store}, \\ \perp_{store} & \text{otherwise.} \end{cases}$$

Another relatively recent presentation departing from the older tradition is [Ten91].

As the careful reader may have noticed, our assumption that there is only one type of storable values is helpful when it comes to writing functions to manipulate stores. If we had two types of storable values, say val_1 and val_2, then these would lead us to two types of stores, $store_1$ and $store_2$. This would lead us to define two *lookup* functions and two *update* functions. Since the two *lookup* functions, for example, behave in essentially the same way, this seems unnecessarily complicated. However, this seems the best we could do within the type system of $\lambda^{\rightarrow}$.

Exercise 6.4.1 We might try to simplify the language $\lambda^{store,fix,\rightarrow}$ by using only one type of stores, instead of two. Since we need a fixed point operator to give the semantics of `while` loops, we need a pointed type $store_\perp$. If we therefore try to eliminate *store*, we must alter functions *lookup* and *update* to have types $lookup\colon store_\perp \times loc \rightarrow val$ and $update\colon store_\perp \times loc \times val \rightarrow store_\perp$.

(a) Show that for the interpretation of *lookup* to be continuous, we must impose some nontrivial ordering on the elements of A^{val}.

(b) Show that if *update* is strict, the axiom (*lookup*) must fail.

Exercise 6.4.2 Here and in Section 2.6.4, if $M\colon\sigma$, we write $\lfloor M \rfloor$ for the corresponding element of the lifted type $\sigma_\perp$. However, the term form $\texttt{let}\ \lfloor x \rfloor = N\ \texttt{in}\ M$ is used in Section 2.6.4 instead of the strict application form $M \cdot N$ used here. (The reason for the change of notation is that $M \cdot N$ is more convenient for the special case of functions $store \rightarrow store_\perp$.) In general, the two forms have typing rules

$$\frac{\Gamma, x\colon\sigma \rhd M\colon\tau \quad \Gamma \rhd N\colon\sigma_\perp}{\Gamma \rhd \texttt{let}\ \lfloor x \rfloor = N\ \texttt{in}\ M\colon\tau} \qquad \frac{\Gamma \rhd M\colon\sigma \rightarrow \tau \quad \Gamma \rhd N\colon\sigma_\perp}{\Gamma \rhd MN\colon\tau}$$

where in both cases it is necessary for τ to be pointed. This exercise asks you to show that these are interdefinable.

(a) Given $M\colon\sigma \rightarrow \tau$ and $N\colon\sigma_\perp$, show how to use `let` to write an expression corresponding to $M \cdot N$. Show that $M \cdot \lfloor N \rfloor = MN$ follows from the equational axiom $\texttt{let}\ \lfloor x \rfloor = \lfloor N \rfloor\ \texttt{in}\ M = [N/x]M$.

(b) Given $M\colon\tau$ with free $x\colon\sigma$ and $N\colon\sigma_\perp$, show how to use $\cdot$ to write an expression corresponding to $\texttt{let}\ \lfloor x \rfloor = N\ \texttt{in}\ M$. Show that $\texttt{let}\ \lfloor x \rfloor = \lfloor N \rfloor\ \texttt{in}\ M = [N/x]M$ follows from the equational axiom $M \cdot \lfloor N \rfloor = MN$.

(c) Show that for your translations between `let` and $\cdot$, the axiom $(M \cdot \perp) = \perp$ is equivalent to $(\texttt{let}\ \lfloor x \rfloor = \perp\ \texttt{in}\ M) = \perp$.

6.4.2 Semantic Functions

There are two main parts of the denotational semantics of `while` programs. The first is a syntactic translation of expressions and commands into lambda terms of $\lambda^{store,fix,\to}$, and the second is the standard interpretation of this lambda calculus in the model $\mathcal{A}_\lambda$. While many texts define the interpretation of `while` program syntax into a lambda model such as $\mathcal{A}_\lambda$ directly, one advantage of an intermediate translation is that it lets us make effective use of the machinery we have already developed. Specifically, we may use ordinary reasoning about lambda terms to prove equations between `while` programs, and we may use facts about the semantic interpretation of typed lambda calculus from Chapters 4 and 5. Moreover, we may consider some extensions of `while` programs without changing the lambda calculus, and others with only minor additions to $\lambda^{store,fix,\to}$. The reasons for using a translation into lambda calculus may seem familiar to computer scientists, since these are also the reasons for using an intermediate language in compiler construction.

Since `while` programs have two syntactic classes, the syntactic translation comes in two parts. The function $\mathcal{V}[\![\cdot]\!]$ translates boolean and value expressions of `while` programs into lambda terms of type $store \to bool$ and $store \to val$, respectively. If $M\colon val$ is an expression that might occur on the right side of an assignment, the translation $\mathcal{V}[\![M]\!]$ will be a lambda term of type $store \to val$ with the same free variables. The function $\mathcal{C}[\![\cdot]\!]$ is a similar translation from commands to lambda terms of type $store \to store_\perp$. Combining these translations with the ordinary meaning function from $\lambda^{store,fix,\to}$ to the model $\mathcal{A}_\lambda$, we obtain two functions

$$\bar{\mathcal{V}} : expressions \to environments \to store \to values$$

$$\bar{\mathcal{C}} : commands \to environments \to store \to store_\perp$$

where "*values*" is used here to indicate that expressions may have type *val* or *bool*. In the jargon of denotational semantics, $\bar{\mathcal{V}}$ and $\bar{\mathcal{C}}$ are called *semantic functions.* As suggested in the previous section, an important property is that these functions make dependence on the store explicit: an algebraic expression of sort *val* becomes a function from stores to values, and commands become mappings from stores to stores.

We now define the syntactic translation and semantic function for expressions. Essentially, $\mathcal{V}[\![M]\!]$ is defined by replacing *cont* with *lookup* and treating the store explicitly.

$$\mathcal{V}[\![x]\!] = \lambda s\colon store.\, x$$

$$\mathcal{V}[\![cont\ x]\!] = \lambda s\colon store.\, lookup\ s\ x$$

$$\mathcal{V}[\![f\ M_1\ \dots\ M_k]\!] = \lambda s\colon store.\, f\ \mathcal{V}[\![M_1]\!]s\ \dots\ \mathcal{V}[\![M_k]\!]s$$

The *meaning of expression M in environment* η is the meaning of $\mathcal{V}[\![M]\!]$ in environment η. More precisely, in symbols, we have

$$\bar{\mathcal{V}}[\![M]\!]\,\eta = \mathcal{A}_\lambda[\![\ \mathcal{V}[\![M]\!]\ ]\!]\eta.$$

Since the meaning of a value expression $M{:}\,val$ in η is a function from stores to values, we may find the value $\bar{\mathcal{V}}[\![M]\!]\,\eta\, s$ of M in environment η and store $s \in A^{store}$ by function application

$$\bar{\mathcal{V}}[\![M]\!]\,\eta\, s = (\bar{\mathcal{V}}[\![M]\!]\,\eta)(s).$$

Note that since our language does not allow calls to recursive functions in expressions, we do not need lifted types of values in defining $\mathcal{V}$.

The syntactic translation of a command produces a lambda term mapping *store* to $store_\perp$. The effect of an assignment is to update the store. A sequence of commands denotes the strict composition of the corresponding maps on stores, and the semantics of conditional is essentially straightforward. The semantics of `while` is the fixed-point of a functional described in more detail below.

$$\begin{aligned}
\mathcal{C}[\![x := M]\!] &= \lambda s{:}\,store.\ \lfloor update\ s\ x\ (\mathcal{V}[\![M]\!]s)\rfloor \\
\mathcal{C}[\![P_1;\ P_2]\!] &= \mathcal{C}[\![P_2]\!] \diamond \mathcal{C}[\![P_1]\!] \\
\mathcal{C}[\![\texttt{if}\ B\ \texttt{then}\ P_1\ \texttt{else}\ P_2]\!] &= \lambda s{:}\,store.\,\texttt{if}\ \mathcal{V}[\![B]\!]s\ \texttt{then}\ \mathcal{C}[\![P_1]\!]s\ \texttt{else}\ \mathcal{C}[\![P_2]\!]s \\
\mathcal{C}[\![\texttt{while}\ B\ \texttt{do}\ P\ \texttt{od}]\!] &= fix(\lambda f{:}\,store \to store_\perp. \\
&\qquad \lambda s{:}\,store.\,\texttt{if}\ \mathcal{V}[\![B]\!]s\ \texttt{then}\ (f \diamond \mathcal{C}[\![P]\!])s\ \texttt{else}\ \lfloor s\rfloor)
\end{aligned}$$

The *meaning of program P in environment* η is defined by

$$\bar{\mathcal{C}}[\![P]\!]\,\eta = \mathcal{A}_\lambda[\![\ \mathcal{C}[\![P]\!]\ ]\!]\eta$$

and the meaning in environment η and store $s \in A^{store}$ by

$$\bar{\mathcal{C}}[\![P]\!]\,\eta\, s = (\bar{\mathcal{C}}[\![P]\!]\,\eta)(s).$$

Intuitively, there are two cases to consider in understanding the meaning of `while`B `do`P`od`. If B is false, then the command terminates in the same store as it started. If B is true, then P is executed, and the entire process is repeated. Consequently, the command `while` B `do` P `od` denotes the function f from stores to stores satisfying

$$f\ s = \texttt{if}\ \mathcal{V}[\![B]\!]s\ \texttt{then}\ (f \diamond \mathcal{C}[\![P]\!])s\ \texttt{else}\ \lfloor s\rfloor.$$

This equation may be understood by noting that if B is false in the initial store s, the function returns the same store (regarded as an element of $store_\perp$). If B is true, f is applied to the store obtained as a result of "executing" P. Another way of understanding the fixed-point interpretation of `while` is by *fix* reduction, which we consider below.

Example 6.4.3 One simple program is

$$skip \stackrel{\text{def}}{=} x := cont\ x$$

where x is some location variable. This program does nothing in our semantics, a fact that is proved in three steps.

$$\begin{aligned} \mathcal{C}[\![skip]\!] &= \lambda s\colon store.\ \lfloor update\ s\ x\ (\mathcal{V}[\![x]\!]s)\rfloor \\ &= \lambda s\colon store.\ \lfloor update\ s\ x\ (lookup\ s\ x)\rfloor \\ &= \lambda s\colon store.\ \lfloor s\rfloor \end{aligned}$$

In the second step, we use the algebraic axiom $(update)_1$ for *lookup* and *update*. The result of executing *skip* in environment η and store s is given by $\bar{\mathcal{C}}$ as follows.

$$\begin{aligned} \bar{\mathcal{C}}[\![skip]\!]\ \eta\ s &= (\mathcal{A}[\![\ \mathcal{C}[\![skip]\!]\ ]\!]\eta)(s) \\ &= (\mathcal{A}[\![\ \lambda s\colon store.\ \lfloor s\rfloor\ ]\!]\eta)(s) \\ &= \lfloor s\rfloor \end{aligned}$$

■

We should note that the assignment $x := cont\ x$ does not denote the identity map in every programming language. For example, in a language with variable declarations and storage allocation, $x := cont\ x$ might produce an error if x is undeclared. A surprising interpretation of $x := x$ also exists in Pascal, as pointed out by Yuri Gurevich. In Pascal, a function procedure may be called by writing its name in an expression, and the return value of a function procedure is specified by assigning to the name of a procedure. Thus if $x := x$ occurs in the body of a function procedure named x, this apparent assignment may actually be a recursive call.

Using *skip,* from Example 6.4.3, we can show that a `while` loop is equivalent to a test containing a `while`. This equivalence is commonly referred to as "loop unwinding." The equivalence

$$\texttt{while}\ B\ \texttt{do}\ P\ \texttt{od} = \texttt{if}\ B\ \texttt{then}\ (P; \texttt{while}\ B\ \texttt{do}\ P\ \texttt{od})\ \texttt{else}\ skip$$

is proved using *fix* reduction as follows:

$\mathcal{C}[\![\texttt{while } B \texttt{ do } P \texttt{ od}]\!]$

$= \mathit{fix}(\lambda f\colon \mathit{store} \to \mathit{store}_\perp .\, \lambda s\colon \mathit{store}.\, \texttt{if } \mathcal{V}[\![B]\!]s \texttt{ then } (f \diamond \mathcal{C}[\![P]\!])s \texttt{ else } \lfloor s \rfloor)$

$= \lambda s\colon \mathit{store}.\, \texttt{if } \mathcal{V}[\![B]\!]s \texttt{ then } (\mathcal{C}[\![\texttt{while } B \texttt{ do } P \texttt{ od}]\!] \diamond \mathcal{C}[\![P]\!])s \texttt{ else } \lfloor s \rfloor$

$= \mathcal{C}[\![\texttt{if } B \texttt{ then } (P; \texttt{while } B \texttt{ do } P \texttt{ od}) \texttt{ else } \mathit{skip}]\!].$

One commonly cited advantage of denotational semantics is the ease with which we may prove simple program equivalences. Using $\lambda^{\mathit{store},\mathit{fix},\to}$, we can carry out most proofs using lambda calculus.

Exercise 6.4.4 Write the denotational semantics (as $\lambda^{\mathit{store},\mathit{fix},\to}$ terms) for the two `while` programs

$x := (\mathit{cont}\, x) + 3$
$x := (\mathit{cont}\, x) + 1;\ x := (\mathit{cont}\, x) + 2$

and use standard reasoning about lambda terms, *lookup* and *update* to argue that these programs define the same function from *store* to $\mathit{store}_\perp$.

Exercise 6.4.5 Write the denotational semantics (as a $\lambda^{\mathit{store},\mathit{fix},\to}$ term) for the `while` program

$y := (\mathit{cont}\, x);$
$z := 1;$
`while` $(\mathit{cont}\, y) \neq 0$ `do`
    $z := (\mathit{cont}\, z) * (\mathit{cont}\, y);$
    $y := (\mathit{cont}\, y) - 1;$
    `od`

You may use arithmetic operations $*$ and $-$ and comparison $\neq$ in your lambda term and assume these are interpreted in the usual way. Use standard reasoning about lambda terms, *fix*, *lookup* and *update* to show that if we apply this function to a store s with contents of x equal to natural number n, then we obtain a final store s' with contents of z equal to natural number $n!$.

Exercise 6.4.6 In this section, we first defined the syntactic translations $\mathcal{V}[\![\cdot]\!]$ and $\mathcal{C}[\![\cdot]\!]$ by induction on the structure of algebraic terms and programs, and then defined $\bar{\mathcal{V}}[\![\cdot]\!]$ and $\bar{\mathcal{C}}[\![\cdot]\!]$ from $\mathcal{V}[\![\cdot]\!]$ and $\mathcal{C}[\![\cdot]\!]$. It is a useful exercise to work out independent inductive definitions of $\bar{\mathcal{V}}[\![\cdot]\!]$ and $\bar{\mathcal{C}}[\![\cdot]\!]$, since these are often useful in proving facts about the semantics of programs.

(a) Write out an inductive definition of $\bar{\mathcal{V}}[\![\cdot]\!]$ that refers only to $\bar{\mathcal{V}}[\![\cdot]\!]$ on simpler terms and does not mention the syntactic translation $\mathcal{V}[\![\cdot]\!]$. Show that this is equivalent to the "two-stage" definition of $\bar{\mathcal{V}}[\![\cdot]\!]$ given in this section.

(b) Repeat part (a) for $\bar{\mathcal{C}}[\![\cdot]\!]$.

Exercise 6.4.7 An alternate form of iterative loop is `repeat` P `until` B. Informally, this statement is executed by repeatedly executing P, until test B is true after some execution.

(i) Give a denotational semantics for `repeat` P `until` B. In other words, give a clause of the form

$$\mathcal{C}[\![\texttt{repeat } P \texttt{ until } B]\!] = \mathit{fix}(\lambda f\colon \mathit{store} \to \mathit{store}_\bot.\, \lambda s\colon \mathit{store}.\ldots \mathcal{V}[\![B]\!] \ldots \mathcal{C}[\![P]\!] \ldots)$$

of the form used for `while` programs.

(ii) Your semantics should make it easy to prove the identity

$$\texttt{repeat } P \texttt{ until } B = P;\ \texttt{if } B \texttt{ then } \mathit{skip} \texttt{ else repeat } P \texttt{ until } B.$$

If this is the case, outline the straightforward proof. If not, go back and change your semantics to make this possible.

(iii) An identity that does not seem provable by equational lambda calculus reasoning is

$$\texttt{repeat } P \texttt{ until } B = P;\ \texttt{while } \neg B \texttt{ do } P \texttt{ od}$$

However, this is not too hard to prove using a form of induction. If you write out the typed lambda terms corresponding to both program forms, you will see that you need to prove an equation of the form

$$\mathit{fix}\, M = (\mathit{fix}\, N) \diamond L$$

By the continuity of composition, and the interpretation of fixed-point operators over CPOs, it is possible to prove that an equation of this form holds over CPOs by proving that for every natural number k, we have

$$M^k(\lambda s\colon \mathit{store}.\, \bot_{\mathit{store}}) = (N^k(\lambda s\colon \mathit{store}.\, \bot_{\mathit{store}})) \diamond L \qquad (*)$$

where as usual $M^k N$ indicates the result of applying M to N a total of k times. You may take it as given that it suffices to prove $(*)$, for M, N and L determined from the denotational semantics of `while` and `repeat`. Prove the identity between `repeat` and `while` by using induction on k to prove that $(*)$ holds for every natural number k.

(iv) Do part (c) using fixed-point induction. More specifically, write out the equation between typed lambda terms of the form $\mathit{fix}\ M = (\mathit{fix}\ N) \diamond P$ that says that the two imperative programs have the same meaning and prove this using fixed point induction.

6.4.3 Equivalence of Operational and Denotational Semantics

In this section, we show that the operational and denotational semantics of `while` programs are equivalent. Before proving the main result, we state and prove two lemmas. The first gives an equivalence between operational and denotational semantics for expressions and the second an "unwinding" property of the fixed points of functions used in the semantics of `while` loops.

Lemma 6.4.8 Let η be an environment and $s \in A^{store}$ any "non-bottom" store. For any expression M of type *loc*, *val* or *bool*, and a in A^{loc}, A^{val} or A^{bool}, we have

$$\langle M, s\rangle_\eta \overset{\text{eval}}{\rightsquigarrow} a \text{ iff } \bar{\mathcal{V}}[\![M]\!]\,\eta\, s = a.$$

Proof We prove the lemma by induction on the structure of M. For a variable x, we have

$$\langle M, s\rangle_\eta \overset{\text{eval}}{\rightsquigarrow} \eta(x) = \bar{\mathcal{V}}[\![M]\!]\,\eta\, s.$$

For an application of the contents function *cont*, we have

$$\langle cont\ x, s\rangle_\eta \overset{\text{eval}}{\rightsquigarrow} lookup\ s\ x = \bar{\mathcal{V}}[\![cont\ x]\!]\,\eta\, s.$$

The final case is an application of an algebraic function,

$$\langle f\, M_1 \ldots M_k, s\rangle_\eta \overset{\text{eval}}{\rightsquigarrow} f^A(a_1, \ldots, a_k) = \bar{\mathcal{V}}[\![f\, M_1 \ldots M_k]\!]\,\eta\, s,$$

where by the inductive hypothesis we may assume $\langle M_i, s\rangle_\eta \overset{\text{eval}}{\rightsquigarrow} a_i = \bar{\mathcal{V}}[\![M_i]\!]\,\eta\, s$ for $1 \le i \le k$. ∎

In stating the following lemma, we will write $P^{\diamond k} s$, where $P\colon store \to store_\perp$, for the result of appling the k-fold strict composition of P to s, *i.e.*, $P^{\diamond k} s \overset{\text{def}}{=} P \cdot (P \cdot \ldots (P s) \ldots)$.

Lemma 6.4.9 Let F be a function

$$F \overset{\text{def}}{=} \lambda f\colon store \to store_\perp.\, \lambda s\colon store.\, \texttt{if}\ \ Bs\ \ \texttt{then}\ \ f \cdot (Ps)\ \ \texttt{else}\ \ \lfloor s \rfloor$$

of the form obtained when translating a `while` loop into $\lambda^{store, fix, \to}$, with $B\colon store \to bool$ and $P\colon store \to store_\perp$. Let $s \in A^{store}$ be a store different from $\perp_{store}$. For any natural number n, if $(F^n \perp s) = \lfloor s' \rfloor$ then there is some $m \le n$ such that $\lfloor s' \rfloor = P^{\diamond m} s$, $Bs' = \mathit{false}$ and for all $k < m$ we have $P^{\diamond k} s = \lfloor s_k \rfloor$ with $Bs_k = \mathit{true}$.

Proof This is difficult to prove directly by induction on n. The reason is that if we expand $F^{n+1} \perp s$ in the obvious way, as

$$F^{n+1} \perp s = \texttt{if}\ Bs\ \texttt{then}\ (F^n \perp) \cdot (Ps)\ \texttt{else}\ \lfloor s \rfloor,$$

then we need to reason about the function $F^n \perp$ on the store Ps different from s. The solution is to prove a more general assertion about stores of the form $(P^{\diamond k} s)$.

We prove by induction on n that for all k, if $(F^n \perp) \cdot (P^{\diamond k} s) = \lfloor s' \rfloor$ then there is some natural number $j < n$ satisfying the condition $C(k, j)$ defined as follows

$$\lfloor s' \rfloor = P^{\diamond(k+j)} s, \quad Bs' = \mathit{false} \text{ and for all} i < j, \qquad C(k, j)$$
$$P^{\diamond(k+i)} s = \lfloor s_i \rfloor \text{ with } Bs_i = \mathit{true}$$

The lemma follows as the special case $k = 0$.

The base case of the proof is vacuously true, since $F^0 \perp (P^{\diamond k} s) = \perp_{store}$.

For the induction step, we assume the implication for n and all k and suppose that $(F^{n+1} \perp) \cdot (P^{\diamond k} s) = \lfloor s' \rfloor$. An easy calculation shows that there is some store s'' with $P^{\diamond k} s = \lfloor s'' \rfloor$ such that either $Bs'' = \mathit{false}$ and $s' = s''$ or $Bs'' = \mathit{true}$ and $s' = (F^n \perp) \cdot (P^{\diamond(k+1)} s)$. It is not hard to check that if $Bs'' = \mathit{false}$ then $C(k, 0)$ holds. On the other hand, if $Bs'' = \mathit{true}$ then we may apply the induction hypothesis to obtain $C(k+1, j)$ for some $j < n$. But it is easy to check that $C(k, j+1)$ iff $Bs'' = \mathit{true}$ and $C(k+1, j)$. Therefore, we conclude $\exists j < n+1.\, C(k, j)$, which proves the lemma. ■

Recall that since $\overset{\text{exec}}{\rightsquigarrow}$ determines a partial function from stores to stores, while $\bar{\mathcal{C}}[\![\cdot]\!]$ defines a total function from A^{store} to $A_{\perp}^{store}$, the operational and denotational semantics handle nontermination in different ways. Taking this into account, we have the following statement of their equivalence.

Theorem 6.4.10 Let η be an environment and $s, s' \in A^{store}$ any "non-bottom" stores. For any program P we have

$$\langle P, s \rangle_\eta \overset{\text{exec}}{\rightsquigarrow} s' \text{ iff } \bar{\mathcal{C}}[\![P]\!]\,\eta\, s = \lfloor s' \rfloor.$$

Proof The proof proceeds by induction on the structure of programs. For an assignment $x := M$, we have $\langle M, s \rangle_\eta \overset{\text{eval}}{\rightsquigarrow} a = \bar{\mathcal{V}}[\![M]\!]\,\eta\, s$ by Lemma 6.4.8 and therefore

$$\langle x := M, s \rangle_\eta \overset{\text{exec}}{\rightsquigarrow} \mathit{update}\ s\ \eta(x)\ a \text{ and } \bar{\mathcal{C}}[\![x := M]\!]\,\eta\, s = \lfloor \mathit{update}\ s\ \eta(x)\ a \rfloor.$$

The inductive steps for a sequence $P_1; P_2$ or conditional statement $\texttt{if}B\texttt{then}P_1$ $\texttt{else}P_2$ are straightforward and left as Exercise 6.4.11. The main case is an iterative loop $\texttt{while}\ B\ \texttt{do}\ P\ \texttt{od}$.

To prove the theorem for `while` B `do` P `od`, let F be the function

$$F \stackrel{\text{def}}{=} \lambda f\colon store \to store_\perp.\, \lambda s\colon store.\, \texttt{if}\ \hat{B}s\ \texttt{then}\ f \cdot (\hat{P}s)\ \texttt{else}\ \lfloor s \rfloor$$

where $\bar{B}$ is $\bar{\mathcal{V}}[\![B]\!]\eta$ and $\bar{P}$ is $\bar{\mathcal{C}}[\![P]\!]\eta$, so that $\bar{\mathcal{C}}[\![\texttt{while}\ B\ \texttt{do}\ P\ \texttt{od}]\!]\eta = \mathit{fix}\, F$.

Suppose $\langle \texttt{while}\ B\ \texttt{do}\ P\ \texttt{od},\ s\rangle_\eta \overset{\text{exec}}{\leadsto} s'$. By examining the operational semantics, we can see that there must be a finite sequence $s_0, \ldots, s_n$ of stores with $s = s_0$ and $s' = s_n$ such that $\langle B,\ s_i\rangle_\eta \overset{\text{eval}}{\leadsto} \mathit{true}$ for $i < n$, $\langle B,\ s_n\rangle_\eta \overset{\text{eval}}{\leadsto} \mathit{false}$, and $\langle P,\ s_i\rangle_\eta \overset{\text{exec}}{\leadsto} s_{i+1}$ for $i < n$. We show by induction on n that $\bar{\mathcal{C}}[\![\texttt{while}\ B\ \texttt{do}\ P\ \texttt{od}]\!]\eta = \mathit{fix} F$ is a function mapping s_0 to $\lfloor s_n \rfloor$. The base case is $n = 0$, $s' = s$ and $\langle B,\ s\rangle_\eta \overset{\text{eval}}{\leadsto} \mathit{false}$. Since $\mathit{fix} F = \lambda s\colon store.\, \texttt{if}\ \bar{B}s\ \texttt{then}\ (\mathit{fix} F) \cdot (\bar{P}s)\ \texttt{else}\ \lfloor s \rfloor$, and $\bar{B}s = \mathit{false}$ by Lemma 6.4.8, we have $\mathit{fix} F s = \lfloor s \rfloor$. For the inductive step, we assume a sequence $s_0, \ldots, s_n$ of $n+1$ stores with $s = s_0$ and $s' = s_n$ such that $\langle B,\ s_i\rangle_\eta \overset{\text{eval}}{\leadsto} \mathit{true}$ for $i < n$, $\langle B,\ s_n\rangle_\eta \overset{\text{eval}}{\leadsto} \mathit{false}$, and $\langle P,\ s_i\rangle_\eta \overset{\text{exec}}{\leadsto} s_{i+1}$ for $i < n$. This gives us a sequence $s_1, \ldots, s_n$ of n stores with properties needed to apply the inductive hypothesis to obtain $\mathit{fix}\, F\, s_1 = \lfloor s_n \rfloor$. Reasoning as in the base case, we may conclude that $\mathit{fix} F s_0 = \lfloor s_n \rfloor$.

For the converse, suppose that $\bar{\mathcal{C}}[\![\texttt{while}\ B\ \texttt{do}\ P\ \texttt{od}]\!]\,\eta\, s = \lfloor s' \rfloor$. Recall that $\bar{\mathcal{C}}[\![\texttt{while}\ B\ \texttt{do}\ P\ \texttt{od}]\!]\,\eta\, s$ is the result of applying the fixed point $\mathit{fix}\, F$ to s. Since fix produces the least fixed point of F, and there are no infinite directed sets of stores in the CPO $A_\perp^{store}$, we know that $(\mathit{fix}\, F)s = \lfloor s' \rfloor$ iff $(F^n \perp)s = \lfloor s' \rfloor$ for some n. By Lemma 6.4.9, there is some $m \le n$ such that $\lfloor s' \rfloor = \bar{P}^{\diamond m} s$, $\bar{B}s' = \mathit{false}$ and for all $k < m$ we have $\bar{P}^{\diamond k} s = \lfloor s_k \rfloor$ with $\bar{B}s_k = \mathit{true}$. A straightforward induction on m shows that $\langle \texttt{while}\ B\ \texttt{do}\ P\ \texttt{od},\ s\rangle_\eta \overset{\text{exec}}{\leadsto} s'$. This proves the theorem. ∎

Notice that the proof depends on *fix* producing the least fixed point; Theorem 6.4.10 fails if $\mathit{fix}\, F$ is an arbitrary fixed point of F.

Exercise 6.4.11 Complete the inductive steps of the proof of Theorem 6.4.10, for sequence $P_1; P_2$ and conditional statement `if` B `then` P_1 `else` P_2, as parts (a) and (b) of this exercise.

6.5 Before–after Assertions about While Programs

6.5.1 First-order and Partial Correctness Assertions

Since the denotational semantics of `while` programs provides a translation into typed lambda calculus, one way of proving properties of `while` programs might be to use a general proof system for typed lambda terms. This is a very reasonable idea, and several automated theorem–proving environments suitable for this purpose have been developed (*e.g.*, [GMW79, Pau87]). An alternative is a logic more closely tailored to the syntax of while programs. Although this approach is less general, there are some advantages. To begin with, a programmer familiar with while programs could reason about programs without learning the vocabulary of typed lambda calculus and least fixed points. Second, if we have some intuitive justification for the correctness of a program, much of this justification is likely to be related to the structure of the program. Consequently, we might expect it to be easier to prove the correctness of our program using a logic whose structure follows the programming language. Finally, there may be some direct influence on programming style. If we get into the habit of proving properties of programs, our programming style might be influenced by the way we intend to prove properties of programs. This seems particularly beneficial if the proof system mirrors the structure of the programming language in a natural way. Some discussion of programs and proofs may be found in [Ben86, Dij76], for example.

As mentioned in Section 6.1, we will consider a logic whose basic formulas are partial correctness assertions

$$F\,\{P\}\,G$$

about while programs. Intuitively, this assertion means that if the first-order formula F is true of some initial store s, then if P halts from s, the final store satisfies the first-order formula G. The first-order formulas F and G will be written in a three–sorted language, with sorts *loc*, *val* and *bool*, using the same function symbols that occur in while programs. In particular, first-order formulas may refer to the store using *cont*, but will not contain lambda abstractions or store variables. A simple example of the kind of partial correctness assertion we might prove is

$$(x \neq y \wedge cont\, x = 3)\,\{y := 1\}\,(cont\, y = 1 \wedge cont\, x = 3)$$

where x and y are variables of type *loc*. Informally, this assertion says that if x and y are not aliases for the same location, and the value stored in x is 3, then after executing the assignment $y := 1$, the value stored in y is 1 and the value stored in x is still 3. It is worth noticing that this partial correctness assertion is not valid if we drop the hypothesis that $x \neq y$, since then an assignment to y might change the value of x.

Before giving the proof rules for while programs, we define the three-sorted first-order logic used to express preconditions and postconditions. The terms used in this logic will have sort *loc*, *val* or *bool*. For technical convenience, we will include equality test *Eq*? on locations and a value conditional, although these are not strictly necessary since they are first-order expressible. Given an algebraic signature Σ over sorts *val* and *bool*, as used in the syntax of while programs, we define the *first-order terms over* Σ by the grammar

$$M \;::=\; x \mid f M \ldots M \mid cont\ y \mid Eq?\ y\ z \mid \mathtt{if}\ B\ \mathtt{then}\ M\ \mathtt{else}\ M,$$

where f is a function symbol of Σ, in $f M_1 \ldots M_k$, the terms $M_1, \ldots, M_k$ must have the appropriate sorts for $f M_1 \ldots M_k$ to be well-formed, y and z must be location variables, B must be a boolean term, and the terms M_1 and M_2 in the conditional expression `if` B `then` M_1 `else` M_2 must have sort *val*. We define the meaning functions $\mathcal{V}$ and $\bar{\mathcal{V}}$ as in Section 6.4, using functions *Eq*? and `if ... then ... else ...` of $\lambda^{store,fix,bool}$ to interpret the corresponding functions in first-order terms.

The first-order formulas over signature Σ are defined by

$$F \ ::= \ M = N \mid F \wedge F \mid \neg F \mid \forall_{loc} x . F \mid \forall_{val} x . F \mid \forall_{bool} x . F$$

where M and N may be any first-order terms of the same sort. In writing $\forall_{loc} x . F$, we assume x is a variable of type *loc* (*i.e.*, $x \in \Gamma_{loc}$), and similarly for *val* and *bool*. As is common, we introduce inequality, additional connectives and quantifiers by abbreviation:

$$M \neq N \ \stackrel{\text{def}}{=} \ \neg(M = N)$$

$$F_1 \vee F_2 \ \stackrel{\text{def}}{=} \ \neg(\neg F_1 \wedge \neg F_2)$$

$$F_1 \supset F_2 \ \stackrel{\text{def}}{=} \ \neg F_1 \vee F_2$$

$$\exists_b x . F \ \stackrel{\text{def}}{=} \ \neg(\forall_b x . \neg F) \text{ for } b \in \{bool, val, loc\}$$

We define *satisfaction* of a first-order formula at a store $s \neq \perp_{store}$ and environment η inductively as follows:

$$\eta, s \models M = N \ \textit{ iff } \bar{\mathcal{V}}[\![M]\!]\,\eta\, s = \bar{\mathcal{V}}[\![N]\!]\,\eta\, s,$$

$$\eta, s \models F_1 \wedge F_2 \ \textit{ iff } \eta, s \models F_1 \textit{ and } \eta, s \models F_2,$$

$$\eta, s \models \neg F \qquad \textit{iff not } \eta, s \models F,$$

$$\eta, s \models \forall_b x . F \ \textit{ iff } \eta[x \mapsto a] \models F \text{ for all } a \in A^b.$$

A partial correctness assertion $F\,\{P\}\,G$ is *satisfied* at environment η and store $s \neq \perp_{store}$ if the following implication holds:

If $\eta, s \models F$ and $\bar{\mathcal{C}}[\![P]\!]\,\eta\, s = \lfloor s' \rfloor$ then $\eta, s' \models G$.

Note that if $\bar{\mathcal{C}}[\![P]\!]\,\eta\, s = \perp_{store}$, then $F\,\{P\}\,G$ is satisfied at s. It is sometimes convenient to write $\{P\}\ G$ as an abbreviation for *true* $\{P\}\ G$.

Exercise 6.5.1 For each of the following partial correctness assertions, use the denotational semantics of `while` programs to explain why the assertion is valid. Your explanation should refer to stores and the semantics of programs, but need not be more than a short paragraph in length for each assertion. When programs refer to operations on natural numbers, you may assume that these operations are interpreted in the standard way.

(a) $x \neq y\,\{x := cont\ y;\ \ x := cont\ x + 1\}\, cont\ x \neq cont\ y$

(b) $x \neq y \neq z\,\{$`if` $cont\ x \geq cont\ y$ `then` *skip* `else` *swap*$\}\, cont\ x \geq cont\ y$, where *swap* is the sequence of assignments $z := cont\ x;\ \ x := cont\ y;\ \ y := cont\ z$

(c) $true\,\{$`while` $cont\ x \neq 1$ `do` $x := (cont\ x) - 1$ `od`$\}\, cont\ x = 1$

(d) $F\,\{m := 0;\ \ n := 100;$ `while` $cont\ m < cont\ n$ `do` P `od`$\}\, f(cont\ n) = 0$, where F is the formula $(\exists x\colon nat)[0 \leq x \leq 100 \wedge f(x) = 0] \wedge m \neq n$ and P is the program

```
if Eq? f(cont m) 0
   then n := cont m
   else if Eq? f(cont n) 0
      then m := cont n
      else m := (cont m) + 1;  n := (cont n) − 1
```

6.5.2 Proof Rules

Each of the axioms and inference rules for proving partial correctness assertions applies to one form of `while` program. The one exception is the logical *rule of consequence*

$$\frac{F\,\{P\}\,G,\ F' \supset F,\ G \supset G'}{F'\,\{P\}\,G'} \qquad (conseq)$$

which is based on logical implication. In applying this rule, we will feel free to use any valid first-order implications; we will not be concerned with formal proofs of the first-order assertions we use. It is easy to see from the definition of satisfaction that the rule of consequence is sound, in the sense that if the hypotheses hold with respect to some environment, for all stores, then the conclusion holds in all stores (with respect to the same environment). We will give a complete inductive proof that the inference rules are sound in Section 6.5.3 and prove a form of completeness in Section 6.5.4.

The most complicated parts of the proof system are the assignment axiom and the `while` inference rule. Rather than tackle these right away, we will discuss the simpler conditional and sequencing inference rules first. A rough reading of the following sequencing rule is that if P_1 produces a store with G true, and executing P_2 from any store satisfying G is guaranteed to produce a store with H true, then executing $P_1;\ P_2$ must produce a store with H true.

$$\frac{F\,\{P_1\}\,G,\ G\,\{P_2\}\,H}{F\,\{P_1;\ P_2\}\,H} \qquad (seq)$$

In a conditional statement `if` B `then` P_1 `else` P_2, there are two statements that might be executed. If we want to end up with G true, it suffices for P_1 to do this when B is true, and P_2 to produce a store satisfying G when B is false. This informal thinking leads us to the following rule:

$$\frac{(F \wedge B)\,\{P_1\}\,G,\ (F \wedge \neg B)\,\{P_2\}\,G}{F\,\{\texttt{if}\ B\ \texttt{then}\ P_1\ \texttt{else}\ P_2\}\,G} \qquad (cond)$$

Before discussing the axiom for assignment statements, we will look at a few examples to gain some intuition for the problems that arise. As a historical note, it is worth mentioning that writing sound assignment axioms was one of the stumbling blocks when this field developed in the early 1970's. Although assignment seems trivial because it is so familiar, it is actually a bit tricky to give a correct logical treatment of assignment in languages with features such as assignable arrays. A valid assertion about assignment is

$$y \neq z\,\{x := y\}\,cont\,x \neq z$$

with $x\colon loc$ and $y, z\colon val$. It is quite easy to see that this is true, since the assignment to x cannot change the value of either value variable y or z. The variant,

$$cont\,w \neq z\,\{x := cont\,w\}\,cont\,x \neq z$$

of this assertion with location (assignable) variable w in place of y is still valid. However, there are two cases to consider when reasoning informally about it. If x and w name different locations, then this is just like the assertion with y in place of $cont\,w$. On the other hand, if x and w name the same location, then the assertion remains valid since the assignment does not change the value in any location and the preconditions and postconditions place the same constraints on stores. But the related assertion

$$y \neq cont\,v\,\{x := y\}\,cont\,x \neq cont\,v$$

with location (assignable) variable v in place of z is not valid since x and v could name the same location. This is a counterexample to the otherwise plausible looking axiom scheme

$$F\,\{x := y\}\,[(cont\,x)/y]F$$

which is *not valid.* The reason why this scheme looks valid is that it seems to say that if some property (described by F) holds for y, then after storing the value y in x, the same property holds of $cont\,x$. However, aliasing is one reason why the simple formulation above of this plausible intuitive statement fails. It is a worthwhile exercise to see that this axiom scheme also fails even without aliasing. This is described in Exercise 6.5.5.

An important property of Floyd-Hoare logic is that substitution does *not* preserve validity. This is explained in Exercise 6.5.6.

The assignment axiom we will use involves substituting a function in place of *cont,* which might seem a bit complicated at first. However, given the subtleties illustrated by the examples in the last paragraph, the reader should not be too surprised to find that the rule is at least slightly complex. One way to understand the axiom is to think "backwards," as follows. Suppose we have an assignment $x := M$ and a first-order formula F that we want to be true after doing the assignment. In other words, we would like to find a first-order formula F' so that $F'\,\{x := M\}F$ is valid. There is always some such F', since *false* $\{P\}\,F$ is trivially valid. However, we would like the "best" possible F'. The best formula we could hope for is a formula F' such that for any environment, store $s \neq \perp_{store}$ satisfies F' iff s satisfies $\{x := M\}F$. Such a formula is called the *weakest precondition of* $\{x := M\}F$. (Weakest preconditions are defined in general in Section 6.5.4.)

To find the weakest precondition of $\{x := M\}F$, let us consider the meaning of $x := M$. If we execute this assignment from store $s \neq \perp_{store}$, we end up with the store $\lfloor update\ s\ \eta(x)\ (\bar{\mathcal{V}}[\![M]\!]\eta s)\rfloor$. Thus we want a formula F' with

$$\eta, s \models F' \textit{ iff } \eta, (update\ s\ \eta(x)\ (\bar{\mathcal{V}}[\![M]\!]\eta s)) \models F.$$

How might we construct such a formula? The solution is to observe that the only way for F or F' to depend on the store is through the function *cont*. If we replace the function *cont* in F by some "updated" function *cont'* which gives location x value M, we will obtain a formula F' with the desired property. We may almost do this directly, using equality test and conditional. Specifically, let $cont_{x:=M}$ be the lambda expression

$$cont_{x:=M} \stackrel{\text{def}}{=} \lambda\ell\colon loc.\,\texttt{if}\ Eq?\,\ell\,x\ \texttt{then}\ M\ \texttt{else}\ (cont\,\ell).$$

It is not too difficult to check that the function *cont* in store $update\ s\ \eta(x)\ (\bar{\mathcal{V}}[\![M]\!]\eta s)$ defines the same function from locations to values as the lambda expression $cont_{x:=M}$ in store s. Thus, if we let $[cont_{x:=M}/cont]F$ be the formula obtained by replacing *cont* with $cont_{x:=M}$, we will have a formula with

$$\eta, s \models [cont_{x:=M}/cont]F \textit{ iff } \eta, (update\ s\ \eta(x)\ (\bar{\mathcal{V}}[\![M]\!]\eta s)) \models F.$$

The only problem is that since $cont_{x:=M}$ is a lambda abstraction, the substitution $[cont_{x:=M}/cont]F$ does not produce a first-order formula. However, the syntax of first-order terms guarantees that every occurrence of *cont* is applied to some argument. Therefore, after substituting $cont_{x:=M}$ for *cont*, straightforward β-reduction will give us an equivalent first-order formula. Thus we will consider $[cont_{x:=M}/cont]F$ as shorthand for the final result of function substitution followed by β-reduction. Using this notation, we may now state the partial correctness axiom for assignment.

$$[cont_{x:=M}/cont]F\ \ \{x := M\}\ \ F \qquad (asg)$$

To see how this works, it is best to work a few examples.

Example 6.5.2 We can prove $y \neq z\,\{x := y\}\,(cont\,x) \neq z$ using the assignment axiom and the rule of consequence. The first step is to find an instance of the axiom of the form $F'\,\{x := y\}\,(cont\,x) \neq z$. To match the form of the axiom, let F be the formula $(cont\,x) \neq z$ and M the value variable y. The assignment axiom gives us the partial correctness assertion $F'\,\{x := y\}\,(cont\,x) \neq z$, where F' is the formula

$$[cont_{x:=y}/cont]F \equiv (\texttt{if } Eq?\,x\,x \texttt{ then } y \texttt{ else } cont\,z) \neq z.$$

It is easy to see that this is logically equivalent to the formula $y \neq z$, which gives us the desired partial correctness assertion. ■

Additional examples are given in Exercise 6.5.4.

The `while` rule uses what is commonly called a *loop invariant.* Although we will eventually prove that this rule is "complete" for proving all valid partial correctness assertions about `while` loops, it is simpler to disregard this for now and only consider soundness on first reading. The inference rule is this:

$$\frac{(F \wedge B)\,\{P\}\,F}{F\,\{\texttt{while } B \texttt{ do } P \texttt{ od}\}\,(F \wedge \neg B)} \qquad (while)$$

In this rule, F is called the loop invariant since F remains true, no matter how many times the loop body is executed. To see that the rule is intuitively sound, suppose that the hypothesis $(F \wedge B)\,\{P\}\,F$ is valid, and that store s satisfies F. If B is false in s, then the `while` loop does nothing, and so we end up with a store satisfying F and $\neg B$. On the other hand, if B holds, then we begin to execute the loop body. If the loop never halts, then the conclusion of the rule is vacuously satisfied. If the loop eventually terminates, then we will have executed the body P n times, for some positive integer n. It is easy to see by induction on n that each time we start the loop, we begin in a store with B true and each time the loop body terminates, F is true. Since the loop only terminates when B fails, the loop may only halt in a store satisfying $F \wedge \neg B$. This is the conclusion of the `while` inference rule.

Although many pragmatic issues in proving properties of programs are beyond the scope of this short chapter, it seems appropriate to make a few general comments. The hardest part of proving a partial correctness assertion about a `while` program, almost invariably, is choosing appropriate loop invariants. From a theoretical point of view, as demonstrated by the relative completeness theorem in the Section 6.5.4, there will always be a loop invariant if the assertion language is sufficiently powerful. However, from a more practical point of view, it seems safe to say that the most effective way to obtain a program that provably has a certain behavior is to write the program and the proof simultaneously. This way, there is some hope of making the loop invariants easy to determine. Otherwise, it may be quite difficult to find a loop invariant that adequately summarizes the relevant properties of a loop body. Some basic strategy is illustrated in the following example.

Example 6.5.3 Consider the following simple `while` program for computing the difference $x - y$, under the assumption that $y \leq x$.

$d := 0;$
`while` $(cont\ d) + y < x$ `do`
  $d := (cont\ d) + 1;$
  `od`

Let us write P_0 for the statement $d := 0$, B for the test $(cont\ d) + y \neq x$ and P_1 for the loop body $d := (cont\ d) + 1$. We will show that this program is correct by proving the assertion

$y \leq x\ \{P_0;$ `while` B `do` P_1 `od`$\}\ (cont\ d) + y = x.$

The hardest part of the proof is to choose a postcondition for P_0 that will be an adequate invariant for the `while` loop. This will decompose the problem into two separate proofs about simpler programs. Since the program is a sequence of two statements, it is clear that we must choose some first-order formula G so that both

$y \leq x\ \{P_0\}\ G$ and $G\ \{$`while` B `do` P_1 `od`$\}\ (cont\ d) + y = x$

are provable. Since the tricky part of this proof is the `while` loop, let us concentrate on the loop first. We will work backwards from the postcondition for the program and try to determine a reasonable formula G.

Reading the `while` proof rule from bottom to top, we can see that $G\ \{$`while` B `do` P_1 `od`$\}\ G \wedge \neg B$ follows from $G \wedge B\ \{P_1\}\ G$, so we will choose some formula G that is an invariant of the loop body P_1. Since the program we are working with is so simple, it is not hard to see that executions of P_1, under the hypothesis that B is true, preserve the relationship $G \stackrel{\text{def}}{=} (cont\ d) + y \leq x$. Therefore, we consider the two partial correctness assertions

(i) $y \leq x\ \{d := 0\}\ (cont\ d) + y \leq x$
(ii) $((cont\ d) + y \leq x) \wedge B\ \{d := (cont\ d) + 1\}\ (cont\ d) + y \leq x$

It will suffice to prove these, since from the second assertion we have

$(cont\ d) + y \leq x\ \{$`while` B `do` P_1 `od`$\}\ ((cont\ d) + y \leq x) \wedge \neg B$

by the `while` rule, and it is easy to see that $((cont\ d) + y \leq x) \wedge \neg B$ implies $(cont\ d) +$

$y = x$. Thus the partial correctness assertion we are trying to prove follows easily from (*i*) and (*ii*) by the `while` rule, the sequencing rule, and the rule of consequence. Since (*i*) and (*ii*) are simple assertions about assignments, we leave these to the reader. ∎

Additional examples are given in the exercises.

Exercise 6.5.4 This exercise is concerned with the assignment axiom and partial correctness assertions derived from this axiom by the rule of consequence. Recall that in applying the rule of consequence, you may use any valid first-order implications; you do not need to worry about proving the first-order assertions you use in any formal proof system.

(a) Find a formula F' such that $F'\,\{x := 3\}\,(cont\, u) \neq (cont\, v)$ is an instance of the assignment axiom.

(b) Show for any first-order formula F not containing *cont* and possibly containing value variable y, the assertion

$$[M/y]F\ \{x := M\}\ [(cont\, x)/y]F$$

is provable from the assignment axiom and the rule of consequence.

(c) Suppose $x_1, \ldots, x_k$ are *loc* variables and $M_1, \ldots, M_k$ are *val* terms with x_i not occurring in M_j for any $j > i$. Let NE be the conjunction

$$\text{NE} \stackrel{\text{def}}{=} \bigwedge_{i \neq j} x_i \neq x_j$$

of all inequalities $x_i \neq x_j$ for $i \neq j$. Intuitively, NE says that all of the location variables are different. Show that for any first-order formula G not containing cont and possibly containing value variables $y_1, \ldots, y_k$, the formula

$$\text{NE} \wedge [M_1, \ldots, M_k/y_1, \ldots, y_k]G\ \{x_1 := M_1;\ \ldots\ ; x_k := M_k\}$$
$$[\text{cont}\, x_1, \ldots, \text{cont}\, x_k/y_1, \ldots, y_k]G$$

is provable using the assignment axioms, sequencing rule, and rule of consequence.

Exercise 6.5.5 Find first-order formula F, store s and environment η mapping each location variable to a distinct location with the property that the assertion $F\,\{x := y\}\,[(cont\, x)/y]F$ is not satisfied by s and η.

Exercise 6.5.6 In most logics, substitution is a sound inference rule. In algebra, we have the explicit substitution rule (*subst*) given in Chapter 3. In lambda calculus, we can achieve the same effect using lambda abstraction and application, as shown in Lemma 4.4.2. In first-order logic, if we can prove ϕ, then we can prove $\forall x.\phi$ by universal generalization and use this to prove $[M/x]\phi$ for any term M. However, Floyd-Hoare logic does *not* have a corresponding substitution property. Prove this by finding a valid partial correctness assertion $F\,\{P\}\,G$ and substitution $[M/x]$ such that $[M/x]F\,\{[M/x]P\}\,[M/x]G$ is not valid. (*Hint:* You may use a simple assertion, with P a single assignment, that is used as an example in this section.)

Exercise 6.5.7 This exercise uses the same partial correctness assertions as Exercise 6.5.1, which asks you to use the denotational semantics of `while` programs to explain why each assertion is valid. Now prove each assertion using the proof rules given in this section. When programs refer to operations on natural numbers, you may assume that these operations are interpreted in the standard way. You do not have to prove any first-order formulas, but be sure the ones you use are true in the intended interpretation.

(a) $x \neq y\,\{x := cont\,y;\;\; x := cont\,x + 1\}\,cont\,x \neq cont\,y$

(b) $x \neq y \neq z\,\{$`if` $cont\,x \geq cont\,y$ `then` $skip$ `else` $swap\}\,cont\,x \geq cont\,y$, where $swap$ is the sequence of assignments $z := cont\,x;\;\; x := cont\,y;\;\; y := cont\,z$

(c) $true\,\{$`while` $cont\,x \neq 1$ `do` $x := (cont\,x) - 1$ `od`$\}\,cont\,x = 1$

(d) $F\,\{m := 0;\;\; n := 100;$ `while` $cont\,m < cont\,n$ `do` P `od`$\}\,f(cont\,n) = 0$, where F is the formula $(\exists x\colon nat)[0 \leq x \leq 100 \wedge f(x) = 0] \wedge m \neq n$ and P is the program

```
if Eq? f(cont m) 0
   then n := cont m
   else if Eq? f(cont n) 0
      then m := cont n
      else m := (cont m) + 1;  n := (cont n) − 1
```

6.5.3 Soundness

In the last section, except for the assignment axiom, the proof system was justified only by intuitive operational arguments. Since this kind of reasoning is imprecise, and sometimes failed to detect unsound rules in the early development of Hoare logics for various languages, it is worthwhile to prove soundness more carefully. We will do this using the denotational semantics of programs. If $\mathcal{A}_0$ is an algebra for two-sorted signature Σ, then we say first-order formula F is $\mathcal{A}_0$-*valid* if F is true in every environment for every model $\mathcal{A}$ obtained by adding countably infinite carrier A^{loc} for sort loc, interpreting equality test and conditional in the standard way, and interpreting $cont$ as any function from A^{loc} to A^{val}.

Theorem 6.5.8 (Soundness) Let Σ be any algebraic signature over the two sorts val and $bool$ and let $\mathcal{A}_0$ be any Σ algebra. Suppose program P and first-order assertions F and G are written using symbols from Σ and $F\,\{P\}\,G$ is provable from $\mathcal{A}_0$-valid first-order assertions. Then $F\,\{P\}\,G$ holds in the model $\mathcal{A}_\lambda$ obtained by extending $\mathcal{A}_0$ with *loc* and *store*.

The rest of this subsection is devoted to the proof.

The hardest cases are the assignment axiom and the `while` rule. However, since the discussion of assignment in the last section gave all the essential steps for proving soundness, we will skip the assignment case here. We will prove soundness for sequencing, leave conditional as an exercise, and then concentrate on the `while` rule. We will not discuss the rule of consequence, since this is straightforward.

We will use properties of strict composition to show that the sequencing rule is sound. Suppose $F\,\{P_1\}\,G$ and $G\,\{P_2\}\,H$ are valid partial correctness assertions, and that $\eta, s \models F$. We must show that if $\bar{\mathcal{C}}[\![P_1;\ P_2]\!]\,\eta\,s = \lfloor s''\rfloor$, then $\eta, s'' \models H$. Since

$$\bar{\mathcal{C}}[\![P_1;\ P_2]\!]\,\eta = \bar{\mathcal{C}}[\![P_2]\!]\eta\ \diamond\ \bar{\mathcal{C}}[\![P_1]\!]\,\eta,$$

we must have $\lfloor s''\rfloor = \bar{\mathcal{C}}[\![P_2]\!]\,\eta\,s'$, where $\lfloor s'\rfloor = \bar{\mathcal{C}}[\![P_1]\!]\,\eta\,s$. In other words, it follows from the definition of strict composition that if $s'' \neq \bot_{store}$, then the store obtained by executing P_1 from s must be different from $\bot_{store}$. Therefore, $\eta, s' \models G$ by validity of $F\,\{P_1\}\,G$, Since $G\,\{P_2\}\,H$ is also valid, it follows that $\eta, s'' \models H$. This proves the soundness of the sequencing proof rule.

It remains for us to prove that the `while` rule is sound. In essence, we will show soundness by using properties of *fix* to carry out the informal argument given in the preceding section. We assume that $(F \wedge B)\,\{P\}\,F$ is valid and that $\eta, s \models F$. We must show that if $s' = \bar{\mathcal{C}}[\![\texttt{while}\ B\ \texttt{do}\ P\ \texttt{od}]\!]\,\eta\,s$ is different from $\bot_{store}$, then $\eta, s' \models F \wedge \neg B$.

Lemma 6.4.9, used in proving the equivalence of operational and denotational semantics, now provides the essential facts about the meaning of `while` B `do` P `od`. Let $\bar{B} \stackrel{\text{def}}{=} \bar{\mathcal{V}}[\![B]\!]\eta$ and $\bar{P} \stackrel{\text{def}}{=} \bar{\mathcal{C}}[\![P]\!]\eta$ so that the meaning of `while` B `do` P `od` in environment η is the least fixed point of the function

$$Q \stackrel{\text{def}}{=} \lambda f\colon store \to store_\bot.\ \lambda s\colon store.\ \texttt{if}\ \ \bar{B}s\ \ \texttt{then}\ \ f\cdot(\bar{P}s)\ \ \texttt{else}\ \ \lfloor s\rfloor.$$

If $\lfloor s'\rfloor = \mathit{fix}\ Q\ s$, then since the domain of stores is flat, $s' = Q^n\ s$ for some natural number n. By Lemma 6.4.9, there is some $m \le n$ such that $\lfloor s'\rfloor = \bar{P}^{\diamond m}s$, $\bar{B}s' = \mathit{false}$ and for all $k < m$ we have $\bar{P}^{\diamond k}s = \lfloor s_k\rfloor$ with $\bar{B}s_k = \mathit{true}$. In particular, $\eta, s' \models \neg B$. An easy induction, using the validity of $(F \wedge B)\,\{P\}\,F$, shows that $\eta, s_k \models F$ for all $k < m$ and therefore $\eta, s' \models F$. This completes the proof.

Exercise 6.5.9 Show that the conditional rule is sound by showing that if $\eta, s \models (F \wedge B)\,\{P_1\}\,G$ and $\eta, s \models (F \wedge \neg B)\,\{P_2\}\,G$ then $\eta, s \models F\,\{\texttt{if}\ \ B\ \ \texttt{then}\ \ P_1\ \ \texttt{else}\ \ P_2\}\,G$.

6.5.4 Relative Completeness

There are several forms of completeness that we might consider for Floyd-Hoare logic. To put these in perspective, we must look at the general form of the logic. The syntax of programs, syntax of first-order assertions, and therefore the syntax of partial correctness assertions are determined by choosing an algebraic signature Σ. The semantics are determined by choosing a Σ-algebra $\mathcal{A}_0$ and extending it with locations and stores. In carrying out proofs, we use the assignment axiom and four proof rules. Since the rule of consequence requires implications between first-order formulas, we should think of the proof system as a system for deriving partial correctness assertions from first-order assertions about the structure determined from $\mathcal{A}_0$. Since the proof system requires first-order formulas as "input," it makes sense to evaluate the proof system by asking if it does as well as possible, relative to the formulas we supply it. This leads us to consider a form of completeness called *relative completeness.*

Relative Completeness Property: Let Σ be any algebraic signature over the two sorts *val* and *bool* and let $\mathcal{A}_0$ be any Σ algebra. Suppose program P and first-order assertions F and G are written using symbols from Σ and $F\,\{P\}\,G$ holds in the semantics obtained by extending $\mathcal{A}_0$ to a CPO model $\mathcal{A}_\lambda$. Then $F\,\{P\}\,G$ is provable from $\mathcal{A}_0$-valid first-order assertions.

Although the proof system for partial correctness assertions is not relatively complete for *all* signatures and algebras, we will see that relative completeness does hold for a significant class of signatures and algebras. We also discuss an "absolute" form of completeness, which fails, at the end of this section.

We can see why some condition on Σ and $\mathcal{A}_0$ may be neeeded for relative completeness by considering how we might prove a partial correctness assertion that is true in some structure. If some assertion $F\,\{x := M\}\,G$ holds for some $\mathcal{A}_0$, then we might expect to prove this from the assignment axiom and the rule of consequence. Similarly, we should be able to prove any true $F\,\{\texttt{if}\ B\ \texttt{then}\ P_1\ \texttt{else}\ P_2\}\,G$ if every true assertion about P_1 and P_2 is provable. However, we get stuck when we come to a sequence of statements. How could we hope to prove $F\,\{P_1;\,P_2\}\,G$? Even if we replace F and G by some F' and G', using the rule of consequence, we still must eventually prove some assertion of the form $F\,\{P_1;\,P_2\}\,G$ using the rule for sequencing. Therefore, we need some first-order assertion H over signature Σ such that both $F\,\{P_1\}\,H$ and $H\,\{P_2\}\,G$ are provable. Intuitively, this formula H must describe properties common to all possible halting stores of P_1, accurately enough to guarantee $H\,\{P_2\}\,G$. If the ways that P_1 may halt are complicated enough, or the first-order signature is "poor" enough, then we might not be able to express the properties of stores resulting from the execution of P_1 accurately. Therefore, in general, there may not be a formula H that allows us to prove a valid partial correctness assertion $F\,\{P_1;\ P_2\}\,G$.

The way we will work around this problem is by defining it away. This solution was first proposed in [Coo78], and the approach has not been substantially improved upon since. We will see how to define the problem away by considering the requirements on the "intermediate assertion" H needed to prove $F\,\{P_1;\ P_2\}\,G$ by the sequencing proof rule. The first requirement on H is that it must imply that G will hold after executing P_2. Among all such formulas, we might try to let H be the "weakest" one, in the sense that if $H'\,\{P_2\}\,G$ holds, then H' implies H. The reason is that if H is the weakest possible, then $F\,\{P_1\}\,H$ should be true, since F implies that any store reached by P_1 has the property that G will hold after executing P_2. In short, if there is a "weakest" first-order formula H with $H\,\{P_2\}\,G$, then if any assertion will work, we should be able to use H to prove $F\,\{P_1;\ P_2\}\,G$. This leads us to the notion of *weakest liberal precondition,* originally formulated by Dijkstra [Dij75].

Formula F is the *weakest liberal precondition of P and G* if, for every environment η and store s,

$\eta, s \models F$ *iff* $\eta, s \models \{P\}\,G$.

In other words, the weakest liberal precondition of P and G is a formula which implies that if P halts, G will be true. It is the weakest such formula, since any other formula implying that if P halts then G will be true must imply the weakest liberal precondition. The word "liberal" refers to the fact that we are working with *partial* correctness assertions; the *weakest precondition* of P and G is the weakest formula implying that P *does* halt in a store satisfying G.

We say a signature Σ and Σ-algebra $\mathcal{A}_0$ are *expressive* if there is a weakest liberal precondition for every program and first-order assertion over Σ. In this case, we write $wlp(P, G)$ for the first-order formula that is the weakest liberal precondition of P and G.

Theorem 6.5.10 (Relative Completeness) Let Σ be an algebraic signature over sorts *val* and *bool*, and let $\mathcal{A}_0$ be a Σ-algebra. If Σ and $\mathcal{A}_0$ are expressive, then every partial correctness assertion $F\,\{P\}\,G$ over Σ that holds in $\mathcal{A}_\lambda$ is provable from $\mathcal{A}_0$-valid first-order assertions.

Proof We use induction on the structure of programs. If $F\,\{x := M\}\,G$ holds, then by the reasoning given in developing the assignment axiom, F must imply $[cont_{x:=M}/cont]G$. Therefore, we may prove $F\,\{x := M\}\,G$ from the assignment axiom $[cont_{x:=M}/cont]G$ $\{x := M\}\,G$ and the rule of consequence.

Suppose $F\,\{P_1;\ P_2\}\,G$ holds in $\mathcal{A}_\lambda$. As mentioned in the discussion motivating the definition of weakest liberal precondition, we need a first-order formula H such that both

$F\{P_1\}H$ and $H\{P_2\}G$ hold. We let H be $wlp(P_2, G)$. Recall that

$$\eta, s \models H \textit{ iff } \eta, s \models \{P_2\}G.$$

Therefore $H\{P_2\}G$ holds and, by the inductive hypothesis, must be provable. It remains to show that $F\{P_1\}H$ holds. We use the fact that $F\{P_1; P_2\}G$ holds in $\mathcal{A}_\lambda$. Let η be an environment and $s \in A^{store}$ a store with $\eta, s \models F$. If $\lfloor s' \rfloor = \mathcal{C}[\![P_1]\!]s$, then $\eta, s' \models \{P_2\}G$. Therefore $\eta, s' \models H$. This shows that $F\{P_1\}H$ holds in $\mathcal{A}_\lambda$.

The conditional case is straightforward. However, we will go through this case since the argument is needed for the `while` case. Suppose $F\{\texttt{if}\ B\ \texttt{then}\ P_1\ \texttt{else}\ P_2\}G$ holds and let η and s be an environment and store satisfying F. If $\eta, s \models B$, then any $s' = \mathcal{C}[\![P_1]\!]s$ with $s' \neq \perp_{store}$ must satisfy G, and similarly for $s' = \mathcal{C}[\![P_2]\!]s$ if $\eta, s \models \neg B$. Thus both $(F \wedge B)\{P_1\}G$ and $(F \wedge \neg B)\{P_2\}G$ hold. By the inductive hypothesis, both are provable. This allows us to prove $F\{\texttt{if}\ B\ \texttt{then}\ P_1\ \texttt{else}\ P_2\}G$.

The final case, an assertion of the form $F\{\texttt{while}\ B\ \texttt{do}\ P\ \texttt{od}\}G$, requires a little more work. We need to find some formula H such that $H \wedge B\{P\}H$ and both implications $F \supset H$ and $(H \wedge \neg B) \supset G$ hold in $\mathcal{A}_\lambda$. If we can show this, then we may conclude $H\{\texttt{while}\ B\ \texttt{do}\ P\ \texttt{od}\}(H \wedge \neg B)$ by the `while` rule and the desired partial correctness assertion by the rule of consequence.

We let H be the weakest liberal precondition of `while` B `do` P `od` and G. This gives us the implication $F \supset H$ immediately. It remains to show that the partial correctness assertion $(H \wedge B)\{P\}H$ and the first-order formula $(H \wedge \neg B) \supset G$ both hold.

Recall from Section 6.4.2 that

$$\texttt{while}\ B\ \texttt{do}\ P\ \texttt{od} = \texttt{if}\ B\ \texttt{then}\ (P; \texttt{while}\ B\ \texttt{do}\ P\ \texttt{od})\ \texttt{else}\ \textit{skip}.$$

Therefore, since $H\{\texttt{while}\ B\ \texttt{do}\ P\ \texttt{od}\}G$ is valid, the corresponding assertion

$$H\{\texttt{if}\ B\ \texttt{then}\ (P; \texttt{while}\ B\ \texttt{do}\ P\ \texttt{od})\ \texttt{else}\ \textit{skip}\}G.$$

about an equivalent program must hold. Reasoning as in the conditional case, it follows that both $(H \wedge B)\{P; \texttt{while}\ B\ \texttt{do}\ P\ \texttt{od}\}G$ and $(H \wedge \neg B)\{\textit{skip}\}G$ hold. Since *skip* does nothing, the implication $(H \wedge \neg B) \supset G$ must be $\mathcal{A}_0$-valid. Since H is the weakest precondition of `while` B `do` P `od` for G, it follows that $(H \wedge B)\{P\}H$ holds. This completes the proof. ■

Since relative completeness is proved using the rather technical assumption of expressiveness, we will try to understand this condition. It is important, first of all, to realize that expressiveness is a property of both the underlying algebraic structure and the signature. More specifically, if we do not have expressiveness for one choice of Σ and $\mathcal{A}_0$, it may be possible to add function symbols to Σ, interpret them naturally in $\mathcal{A}_0$, and obtain expressiveness. This is in fact the case for the signature providing only a constant for $0\colon nat$, the successor function $S\colon nat \to nat$, and an equality test $Eq?\colon nat \to nat \to bool$. If we interpret these symbols over the natural numbers and booleans in the standard way, then expressiveness fails (see Exercise 6.5.11). However, if we add function symbols for addition and multiplication, interpreted in the usual way, then expressiveness holds (see Exercise 6.5.13). Intuitively, this may be explained by saying that for some P and G containing only $0, S$ and $Eq?$, we cannot define the stores under which $\{P\}\,G$ holds without using addition and multiplication. The weakest liberal precondition, $wlp(P, G)$, can be written out as a first-order formula using function symbols for addition and multiplication, but not using the less expressive signature with only zero, successor and test for equality.

Another way to understand expressiveness is to consider the recursion-theoretic implications of the relative completeness theorem (Theorem 6.5.10). Specifically, if expressiveness holds between a signature and algebra, then the partial correctness theory is recursively enumerable from the first-order theory, using the complete proof system. However, a partial correctness assertion of the form $F\,\{P\}\mathit{false}$ expresses the *non-termination* of program P.

For most familiar structures, such as the natural numbers or characters and strings, the set of programs that terminate on some input is recursively enumerable, but not recursive (decidable). It follows that the set of programs that do not terminate on any input are neither recursively enumerable nor recursive. Therefore, on intuitive grounds, we would expect the partial correctness assertions of the form $F\,\{P\}\mathit{false}$ not to be recursively enumerable. This suggests that if expressiveness holds, then either the the termination behavior of programs must be unexpectedly simple, or the first-order theory of the interpretation is more complicated than recursively enumerable. As described in [Apt81, Lip77], it may be proved that either each program is degenerate, or the first-order theory is as complex as the first-order theory of the standard natural numbers. More specifically, if expressiveness holds for Σ and $\mathcal{A}_0$, then either

(i) a standard model of Peano arithmetic can be defined in $\mathcal{A}_0$ using first-order formulas over Σ, or

(ii) for every program P, there is some number n such that for any initial store, the computation of P involves at most n stores.

It follows that if computations are not bounded (*i.e.*, we are not in case (ii)), then the first-order theory must be as complicated as the first-order theory of the standard natural numbers, with addition and multiplication.

The reader familiar with recursion theory will know that the first-order theory of the natural numbers is not recursively enumerable, and in fact sits well above the familiar classes of recursive and recursively enumerable sets in the arithmetic hierarchy (see [Rog67], for example). As a consequence, this first-order theory does not have any complete axiomatization. We may therefore summarize the situation by saying that if we have expressiveness, and program behavior is not bounded, then we can prove all true partial correctness assertions, but the first-order theory we use must be *highly* intractable. This may seem rather discouraging, if we hope to prove programs correct in practice. (The situation for finite interpretations is considered in more detail in Exercise 6.5.12.)

The counter-argument that is made by proponents of program verification is that if we believe a program is correct, and formalize this with an assertion $F\,\{P\}\,G$, then part of our understanding that the program is correct is understanding why the first-order implications needed in the proof of $F\,\{P\}\,G$ are true about the values used in computation. Therefore, we should not expect arbitrarily complicated statements about natural numbers, for example, to be needed, but only statements that reflect our understanding of the program. These are likely to be provable from the axioms of Peano arithmetic. This argument notwithstanding, it seems fair to say that proving correctness using Floyd-Hoare, or any other, logic is a substantial task for practical programs.

A final question about completeness is whether a pure, "non-relative" form of completeness might hold. Specifically, if we choose some signature, Σ, then all valid first-order formulas over this signature are provable from a standard axiom system. (This is the standard completeness theorem of first-order logic [End72, Men64].) Can we therefore prove all partial correctness assertions that hold in all Σ-algebras, using a complete proof system of first-order logic to derive implications for use in the rule of consequence? Unfortunately, the answer is no. The simplest explanation is again based on recursion theory. The set of all partial correctness assertions derived from a proof system for first-order logic, together with the proof system described here for `while` programs, is recursively enumerable. However, the set of valid partial correctness assertions is not recursively enumerable. Intuitively, this is again because partial correctness assertions express nontermination, and the non-terminating programs are not recursively enumerable (see [Apt81], for example). Therefore, the provable partial correctness assertions cannot include all the valid ones.

Further information on the use of Hoare logic may be found in [AO91], for example. Mathematical properties of Hoare logic and related logics of programs are surveyed in [Apt81, Har84, KT90].

Exercise 6.5.11 Let Σ be the first-order signature with $0{:}\,nat$, the successor function $S{:}\,nat \rightarrow nat$, and an equality test $Eq?{:}\,nat \rightarrow nat \rightarrow bool$. Let $\mathcal{A}_0$ be the standard interpretation of these symbols, with $A_0^{nat} = \mathcal{N}$ the usual set of natural numbers. The decidability of the first-order theory of $\mathcal{A}_0$, when extended with locations and location equality test, follows from standard decidability results for fragments of number theory [End72]. Use this fact from logic to prove that expressiveness fails for Σ and $\mathcal{A}_0$ by the following steps.

(a) Show that there is a program *Plus* computing the sum of any two integers. More precisely, write a program *Plus* using the symbols of Σ such that if $n, m{:}\,nat$ are value variables, then for any store s, we have $\bar{\mathcal{C}}[\![Plus]\!]\eta s = \lfloor s' \rfloor$ with $lookup\, s'\, \eta(x) = \eta(n) + \eta(m)$.

(b) Show that there is a program *Mult* computing the product of any two integers, in the same sense as elaborated for *Plus* in (a).

(c) Sketch an argument showing that for any partial recursive function $f{:}\,\mathcal{N}^k \rightharpoonup \mathcal{N}$ on the natural numbers (see Section 2.5.5), there is a program over Σ that computes f, when the symbols of Σ are interpreted according to $\mathcal{A}_0$.

(d) Show that expressiveness fails for Σ and $\mathcal{A}_0$. Use the fact that the set of pairs $\langle f, n \rangle$, where $f{:}\,\mathcal{N} \rightharpoonup \mathcal{N}$ a partial recursive function that is *not* defined on n, is *not* recursively enumerable.

Exercise 6.5.12 This exercise asks you to show that expressiveness for a finite interpretation implies decidability of the halting problem for programs over this interpretation. As noted above, if expressiveness holds between a signature Σ and $\mathcal{A}_0$, then the partial correctness theory over Σ and $\mathcal{A}_\lambda$ is recursively enumerable from the first-order theory of $\mathcal{A}_0$ with locations added as a third sort. Let Σ be any two-sorted signature (with *val* and *bool*) for writing `while` programs and let $\mathcal{A}_0$ be a Σ algebra with A_0^{bool} standard and A_0^{val} finite. You may assume that decidability of the first-order theory of $\mathcal{A}_0$ implies decidability of the first-order theory of $\mathcal{A}_0$ with locations added.

(a) Sketch a brief argument showing that the first-order theory of $\mathcal{A}_0$ is decidable.

(b) Sketch a brief argument showing that we may recursively enumerate the programs over Σ that halt in every store. (*Hint:* this does not involve partial correctness assertions.)

(c) Show that if Σ and $\mathcal{A}_0$ are expressive, then we may recursively enumerate the programs over Σ that do not halt in any store. (*Hint:* this *does* involve partial correctness assertions.)

(d) Show that if Σ and $\mathcal{A}_0$ are expressive, there is a recursive (computable) procedure to determine whether a program P halts from every store.

It is interesting to note that this argument does not rely on any particular properties of `while` programs, other than an effective interpreter. Therefore, it is a general fact about

Hoare logics for various languages that if relative completeness holds, the halting problem must be decidable on finite interpretations.

Exercise 6.5.13 Let Σ be the signature with $0\colon nat$, successor $S\colon nat \to nat$, addition, $+$, multiplication, $*$, and an equality test $Eq?\colon nat \to nat \to bool$. Let $\mathcal{A}_0$ be the standard interpretation of these symbols, with $A_0^{nat} = \mathcal{N}$ the usual natural numbers. It is a standard fact from mathematical logic that for every partial recursive function $f\colon \mathcal{N} \rightharpoonup \mathcal{N}$, there is a first-order formula, $F(x, y)$, over the signature Σ, such that for any natural numbers n and m, we have $\mathcal{A} \models F(n, m)$ iff $f(n) = m$. Use this to show that expressiveness holds for Σ and $\mathcal{A}_0$, possibly appealing to Church's Thesis for properties of programs (see Sections 2.5.4 and 2.5.5).

6.6 Semantics of Additional Program Constructs

6.6.1 Overview

In the remainder of this chapter, we summarize the denotational semantics for some extensions of `while` programs. In Section 6.6.2, we consider declarations of local variables, and in Section 6.6.3, procedure declarations. The final subsection discusses interaction between procedures and variable declarations. While soundness and relative completeness theorems have been proved for appropriate extensions of Floyd-Hoare Logic, we refer the reader to other sources for these results [Apt81, AO91]. The main emphasis is on the translation of imperative constructs into typed lambda terms that may be interpreted in CPO models. Perhaps surprisingly, it is much harder to give a satisfactory account of variable declarations than procedures. In the interest of conveying the main ideas simply, we consider a relatively direct approach in Section 6.6.2, discussing deficiencies and improvements in Section 6.6.4.

6.6.2 Blocks with Local Variables

We may extend `while` programs with a simple form of variable declaration,

P ::= ... |`begin new` $x := M$; P `end`

with the intuitive meaning that program P is executed after x is given a new location, initialized to the value of M. To give denotational semantics to this program, we must have some mechanism for keeping track of the locations that have been allocated, so that x can be given a location that is different from all of these. This leads us to change the interpretation of type *store* (and therefore $store_\perp$) in our CPO model.

The store operations we will use in the denotational semantics are

$$newloc\colon store \rightarrow loc$$

$$alloc\ \ \colon store \rightarrow loc \rightarrow store$$

$$freeloc\colon store \rightarrow loc \rightarrow store$$

where, intuitively, *newloc* selects a new location from a store, *alloc* marks the store so that a given location is known to be allocated, and *freeloc* makes an allocated location available for reuse. An important property of these operations is given by the following axiom, written using variable $s\colon store$.

$$freeloc\ (alloc\, s\ (newloc\, s))\ (newloc\, s) = s$$

In words, if we allocate the "next" free location in a store, then free it, we obtain the store that we began with.

Additional properties of the storage allocation operations may be stated using a boolean-valued function

$$is\_free?\colon store \rightarrow loc \rightarrow bool$$

which tells whether a location is free to be allocated or not. Some reasonable axioms using this function are

$$is\_free?\, s\ (newloc\, s) \quad = true$$

$$is\_free?\ (alloc\, s\, \ell)\, \ell' \quad = \texttt{if}\ Eq?\, \ell\, \ell'\ \texttt{then}\ false\ \texttt{else}\ is\_free?\, s\, \ell'$$

$$is\_free?\ (freeloc\, s\, \ell)\, \ell = true$$

which say that a "new" location is free to be allocated, *alloc* marks a location as no longer free to be allocated, and freeing a location makes it free to be allocated.

The function *is_free?* may be used in the semantics of programs to test that all locations read or assigned to in a program have been allocated. For example, we may revise the semantics of an assignment $x := cont\ y$ to first test whether x and y are allocated in the store, and if not return the bottom store (or some error) since a program should only use the locations allocated to it. However, instead of checking each location used in a program, we will only consider the meaning of a program in a store that has all the accessible locations already allocated. In keeping with this decision, we adopt the axioms

$$lookup\ \ (alloc\, s\, x)\ \ y \qquad = lookup\ \ s\ \ y$$

$$lookup\ \ (freeloc\, s\, x)\ \ y \quad = lookup\ \ s\ \ y$$

$$update\ \ (alloc\, s\, x)\ \ y\ \ v \quad = alloc\ \ (update\, s\ y\ v)\ \ x$$

$$update\ \ (freeloc\, s\, x)\ \ y\ \ v = freeloc\ \ (update\, s\ y\ v)\ \ x$$

which say, intuitively, that allocation does not effect the contents of any location.

Since we now keep track of the locations that are available for allocation, the semantic interpretation of stores must change. Writing $(A^{loc} \to A^{val})$ for the set of functions from locations to values, we now interpret the type *store* of stores by

$$A^{store} = \mathcal{P}_{fin}(A^{loc}) \times (A^{loc} \to A^{val})$$

where $\mathcal{P}_{fin}(A^{loc})$ is the set of finite subsets of A^{loc}. Intuitively, in the store $\langle L, f \rangle$, where $L \subseteq A^{loc}$ and $f\colon A^{loc} \to A^{val}$, the finite set L contains all the used, or already allocated, locations and the function f gives the value stored in each location. The reason we assume that L is finite, apart from the fact that no program can allocate more than a finite number of locations, is that otherwise we might have a store with every location allocated, and therefore be unable to allocate a new location.

With this interpretation of stores, functions *lookup* and *update* use only the function $A^{loc} \to A^{val}$, as before, ignoring the set of allocated locations or, in the case of *update*, leaving this set unchanged. The new operations have the following effects on stores and locations.

$\mathit{newloc}\ \langle L, f \rangle$ returns some $\ell \notin L$

$\mathit{alloc}\langle L, f \rangle\ \ell$ returns store $\langle L \cup \{\ell\}, f \rangle$

$\mathit{freeloc}\ \langle L, f \rangle\ \ell$ returns store $\langle L - \{\ell\}, f \rangle$

$\mathit{is\_free?}\ \langle L, f \rangle\ \ell$ returns *true* iff $\ell \in L$

We show below, in Lemma 6.6.3, that the meaning of a program is independent of the way *newloc* chooses a new location, as long as this location is not already accessible to the program.

A first approximation to the semantics of variable declarations is

$$\mathcal{C}[\![\texttt{begin new } x := M;\ P\ \texttt{ end}]\!] = \lambda s\colon \mathit{store}.\,\texttt{let } x\colon \mathit{loc} = (\mathit{newloc}\ s)\ \texttt{in}$$
$$\mathcal{C}[\![P]\!]\ (\mathit{update}\ (\mathit{alloc}\, s\, x)\ x\ (\mathcal{V}[\![M]\!]\, s)),$$

which allocates a new location and initializes it before applying the function given by the meaning of the block-body P. Note that if x occurs, undeclared, in P then x will occur free in the lambda term $\mathcal{C}[\![P]\!]$. Any such free occurrence of x is bound by `let` in the clause above.

An immediate consequence of renaming bound variables in lambda terms is the following equation between programs,

$$\texttt{begin new } x := M;\ P\ \texttt{ end} = \texttt{begin new } y := M;\ [y/x]P\ \texttt{ end},$$

provided y does not occur free in P and substitution of y for free occurrences of x in P includes renaming of bound variables in P as usual. Our refinement of the semantic interpretation for `begin` above will similarly bind the local variable x in $\mathcal{C}[\![$`begin new` $x := M;\ P$ `end`$]\!]$, preserving the soundness of α-conversion for `while` programs.

Our approximate semantics will result in a store with the right final values of assignable global variables. However, some useful semantic equations between programs fail. More specifically, two programs are semantically equal if, for any possible initial store, they result in the same final store. However, since the store now includes a list of allocated locations, a program which allocate a location will be semantically different from one that does not, unless we modify the semantics to free locations that are no longer needed. For example, the equation

`begin new` $x := 7;\ \mathit{skip}$ `end` $= \mathit{skip}$

fails in the approximate semantics because the program on the left produces a store with one more location allocated than the program on the right. In addition, the value in this location, used only for a local variable, remains set to 7 after the program terminates, while the value in this location is not changed by the program on the right. This problem is repaired using the more accurate semantics

$$\begin{aligned}\mathcal{C}[\![\texttt{begin new } x := M;\ P \texttt{ end}]\!] = \lambda s\colon \mathit{store}.\ & \texttt{let } x\colon \mathit{loc} = (\mathit{newloc}\ s) \texttt{ in} \\ & \texttt{let } v\colon \mathit{val} = (\mathit{lookup}\ s\ x) \texttt{ in} \\ & (\lambda s'\colon \mathit{store}.\lfloor \mathit{freeloc}\ (\mathit{update}\ s'\ x\ v)\ x\rfloor)\cdot \\ & (\mathcal{C}[\![P]\!]\ (\mathit{update}\ (\mathit{alloc}\ s\ x)\ x\ (\mathcal{V}[\![M]\!]\ s)))\end{aligned}$$

where lambda abstraction and $\cdot$ are used to apply *freeloc* and *update* to any store that is different from $\perp$. Since this interpretation of `begin new` $x := M;\ P$ `end` restores the original value of x and returns this location to the free list, the "temporary" use of this location is not recorded in the store resulting from execution of this program. We will see, in the example below, that allocating and assigning to a new location has no effect on the final store.

Example 6.6.1 We will show that the equation

`begin new` $x := M;\ y := \mathit{cont}\ y$ `end` $= y := \mathit{cont}\ y$

holds in the denotational semantics. From Example 6.4.3, we know that

$$\mathcal{C}[\![y := \mathit{cont}\ y]\!] = \lambda s\colon \mathit{store}.\lfloor s\rfloor$$

Using the semantics of variable declarations above, we also have

$\mathcal{C}[\![\texttt{begin new } x := M;\ y := cont\ y \texttt{ end}]\!]\ s$

$= \texttt{let } x{:}\ loc = (newloc\ \ s) \texttt{ in}$

$\quad \texttt{let } v{:}\ val = (lookup\ \ s\ \ x) \texttt{ in}$

$\quad\quad (\lambda s'{:}\ store. \lfloor freeloc\ (update\ s'\ x\ v)\ x \rfloor) \cdot$

$\quad\quad (\mathcal{C}[\![y := cont\ y]\!]\ (update\ \ (alloc\ s\ x)\ \ x\ \ (\mathcal{V}[\![M]\!]\ s)))$

$= \texttt{let } x{:}\ loc = (newloc\ \ s) \texttt{ in}$

$\quad \texttt{let } v{:}\ val = (lookup\ \ s\ \ x) \texttt{ in}$

$\quad\quad (\lambda s'{:}\ store. \lfloor freeloc\ (update\ s'\ x\ v)\ x \rfloor) \cdot$

$\quad\quad \lfloor update\ \ (alloc\ s\ x)\ \ x\ \ (\mathcal{V}[\![M]\!]\ s)) \rfloor$

$= \texttt{let } x{:}\ loc = (newloc\ \ s) \texttt{ in}$

$\quad \texttt{let } v{:}\ val = (lookup\ \ s\ \ x) \texttt{ in}$

$\quad\quad \lfloor freeloc\ \ (update\ \ (update\ (alloc\ s\ x)\ x\ (\mathcal{V}[\![M]\!]\ s))\ \ x\ \ v)\ x \rfloor$

where the first equation is derived using the meaning of $y := cont\ y$ and the second using β-reduction and the fact that the store expression has the form $\lfloor s \rfloor$. We may now simplify this expression using the equational axiom for repeated updates to the same location,

$(update\ \ (update\ (alloc\ s\ x)\ x\ (\mathcal{V}[\![M]\!]\ s))\ \ x\ \ v) = update\ \ (alloc\ s\ x)\ \ x\ \ v.$

We complete the proof by replacing v by its definition, using the fact that $lookup\ \ s\ \ x = lookup\ \ (alloc\ s\ x)\ \ x$, and proceeding as follows:

$\mathcal{C}[\![\texttt{begin new } x := M;\ y := cont\ y \texttt{ end}]\!]\ s$

$= \texttt{let } x{:}\ loc = (newloc\ \ s) \texttt{ in}$

$\quad \lfloor freeloc\ \ (update\ \ (alloc\ s\ x)\ \ x\ \ (lookup\ \ (alloc\ s\ x)\ \ x))\ x \rfloor$

$= \texttt{let } x{:}\ loc = (newloc\ \ s) \texttt{ in}$

$\quad \lfloor freeloc\ \ (alloc\ s\ x)\ \ x \rfloor$

$= \texttt{let } x{:}\ loc = (newloc\ \ s) \texttt{ in} \lfloor s \rfloor$

$= \lfloor s \rfloor$

This proves the equivalence. Note that this entire proof is carried out in lambda calculus, using the algebraic axioms for store operations in combination with standard lambda calculus proof rules. ■

In addition to the syntactic translation, $\mathcal{C}[\![\ ]\!]$, of programs into lambda terms, we also have the semantic meaning $\bar{\mathcal{C}}[\![\ ]\!]$ of programs in the CPO model, given by $\bar{\mathcal{C}}[\![P]\!]\eta = \mathcal{A}[\![\,\mathcal{C}[\![P]\!]\,]\!]\eta$. For begin blocks, the semantic function may be simplified, using the property

$$\mathcal{A}[\![\texttt{let } x = M \texttt{ in } N]\!]\eta = \mathcal{A}[\![N]\!]\eta[x \mapsto \mathcal{A}[\![M]\!]\eta]$$

of the meaning of lambda terms. This gives us the following clause, written in lambda-calculus-like notation.

$$\bar{\mathcal{C}}[\![\texttt{begin new } x := M;\ P \texttt{ end}]\!]\eta =$$

$$\lambda s \in A^{store}.\,\texttt{let } \ell \in A^{loc} = (newloc\ s) \texttt{ in}$$

$$\texttt{let } v \in A^{val} = (lookup\ s\ \ell) \texttt{ in}$$

$$(\lambda s' \in A^{store}.\lfloor freeloc\,(update\,s'\,\ell\,v)\,\ell\rfloor)\cdot$$

$$(\bar{\mathcal{C}}[\![P]\!]\ \eta[x \mapsto \ell]\ (update\ (alloc\,s\,\ell)\ \ell\ (\bar{\mathcal{V}}[\![M]\!]\,\eta\,s)))$$

Note that the meaning of a begin block involves the meaning of a subprogram in a different environment. Intuitively, the environment associates locations with variables, while the store associates values with locations. Since begin new $x := M;\ P$ end involves a new location for x, the meaning of this program, in some environment η, depends on the meaning of P in an environment $\eta[x \mapsto \ell]$, where the location ℓ is chosen to be different from the locations allocated in the current store.

While the equivalence given in Example 6.6.1 holds in all stores, we generally wish to restrict our attention to stores that allocate all the locations used by a program. In order to make this precise, we define the set $access(P)$ of locations accessible in P by induction on programs. In this definition, we write $FV_{loc}(M)$ for the set of free location variables in algebraic term M.

$$access(x := M) = \{x\} \cup FV_{loc}(M)$$

$$access(P_1;\ P_2) = access(P_1) \cup access(P_2)$$

$$access(\texttt{if } B \texttt{ then } P_1 \texttt{ else } P_2) = FV_{loc}(B) \cup access(P_1) \cup access(P_2)$$

$$access(\texttt{while } B \texttt{ do } P \texttt{ od}) = FV_{loc}(B) \cup access(P)$$

$$access(\texttt{begin new } x := M;\ P \texttt{ end}) = FV_{loc}(M) \cup (access(P) - \{x\})$$

It is easy to check, by induction on programs, that $access(P)$ is exactly the set of free location variables in the lambda term $\mathcal{C}[\![P]\!]$. We say an environment η and store $s = \langle L, f \rangle$ are *appropriate to* P if, for every location variable $x \in access(P)$, we have $\eta(x) \in L$. We show below, in Lemma 6.6.2, that a program only changes accessible locations.

Intuitively, we are interested in *appropriate* environment-stores pairs since an inappropriate environment and store may violate the standard conventions of storage allocation. To give an example, the partial correctness assertion

$$cont\, x = 3 \wedge x \neq y \, \{\texttt{begin new } z := 5; \, y := 7 \texttt{ end}\} \, cont\, x = 3$$

holds in every appropriate environment and store. The reason is that locations x, y, and z are all distinct, $x \neq y$ by hypothesis and $z \neq x, y$ because z is a "new" location declared locally inside the program. However, this assertion fails in an inappropriate environment and store. More specifically, let $\eta(x) = \ell$ and suppose store $s = \langle L, f \rangle$ has $\ell \notin L$ with $newloc\, s = \ell$. Then the program above, in environment η and store s, sets the contents of x to 7. Generally, if we see the program fragment `begin new` $z := 5; \, y := 7$ `end` in the middle of some Pascal program, say, then we know from properties of the Pascal implementation that the location given to the local variable z will be different from the location of any variable global to the block. The definition of "appropriate environment and store" guarantees that locations have been allocated for all global variables, allowing new locations to be chosen for local variables.

Lemma 6.6.2 Let P be a `while` program, possibly containing variable declarations, and let η and s be an environment and store appropriate to P. Let L be the set of locations $L = \{\eta(x) \mid x \in access(P)\}$ accessible from P. If $\bar{\mathcal{C}}[\![P]\!]\eta s = \lfloor s' \rfloor$ then $lookup\, s\, \ell = lookup\, s'\, \ell$ for all $\ell \notin L$.

The proof is by induction on the structure of programs. Since this is similar to the proof of the more complicated Lemma 6.6.3 below, we leave this proof as Exercise 6.6.6 (see also Exercise 6.6.8). The following lemma shows that a program only depends on the values stored in accessible locations, and the equations that hold between location variables.

Lemma 6.6.3 Let P be a `while` program, possibly containing variable declarations, and let η_1 and η_2 be environments such that for all $x, y \in access(P)$, we have $\eta_1(x) = \eta_1(y)$ iff $\eta_2(x) = \eta_2(y)$. Let s_1 be a store appropriate to P with respect to η_1 and similarly s_2 appropriate to P with respect to η_2. Suppose that for all $x \in access(P)$, we have $lookup\, s_1\, \eta_1(x) = lookup\, s_2\, \eta_2(x)$. If $\bar{\mathcal{C}}[\![P]\!]\eta_1 s_1 = \lfloor s_1' \rfloor$, then $\bar{\mathcal{C}}[\![P]\!]\eta_2 s_2 = \lfloor s_2' \rfloor$ with $lookup\, s_1'\, \eta_1(x) = lookup\, s_2'\, \eta_2(x)$ for all $x \in access(P)$.

Proof We leave it to the reader to verify that for any algebraic term M, if η_1, s_1 and η_2,s_2 are as in the statement of the lemma, then $\bar{\mathcal{V}}[\![M]\!]\eta_1 s_1 = \bar{\mathcal{V}}[\![M]\!]\eta_2 s_2$. Note that this remains true if, in addition to *cont*: *loc* $\rightarrow$ *val*, we allow *Eq*?: *loc* $\rightarrow$ *loc* $\rightarrow$ *bool* in terms. Given this property of terms, the proof proceeds by induction on the structure of programs. To simplify notation, let us write $s_i \sim s_j$ if $lookup\, s_i\, \eta_1(x) = lookup\, s_j\, \eta_2(x)$ for all $x \in access(P)$. Note that $\sim$ is not a symmetric relation on stores.

For an assignment, we have

$$\bar{\mathcal{C}}[\![x := M]\!]\eta_i s_i = \lfloor update\, s_i\, \eta_i(x)\, (\bar{\mathcal{V}}[\![M]\!]\eta_i s_i)\rfloor = \lfloor s_i'\rfloor$$

for $i = 1, 2$. It is easy to check that if η_1, s_1 and η_2,s_2 are as in the statement of the lemma, then $s_1' \sim s_2'$.

For a sequence of programs, we have

$$\bar{\mathcal{C}}[\![P_1;\, P_2]\!]\eta_i s_i = (\bar{\mathcal{C}}[\![P_2]\!]\eta_i) \cdot (\bar{\mathcal{C}}[\![P_1]\!]\eta_i s_i)$$

for $i = 1, 2$. Assume η_1, s_1 and η_2,s_2 are as in the statement of the lemma. If $\bar{\mathcal{C}}[\![P_1]\!]\eta_1 s_1 = \lfloor s_1''\rfloor$, then by the induction hypothesis, and $access(P_1) \subseteq access(P_1;\, P_2)$, we have $\bar{\mathcal{C}}[\![P_1]\!]\eta_2 s_2 = \lfloor s_2''\rfloor$ with $s_1'' \sim s_2''$. Reasoning similarly about $\bar{\mathcal{C}}[\![P_2]\!]\eta_1 s_1''$, we can see that if $\bar{\mathcal{C}}[\![P_1;\, P_2]\!]\eta_1 s_1 = \lfloor s_1'\rfloor$, then $\bar{\mathcal{C}}[\![P_1;\, P_2]\!]\eta_2 s_2 = \lfloor s_2'\rfloor$ with $s_1' \sim s_2'$. The case for `if` B `then` P_1 `else` P_2 is similar.

For a `while` loop, we have

$$\bar{\mathcal{C}}[\![\texttt{while}\ B\ \texttt{do}\ P\ \texttt{od}]\!]\eta_i s_i = (\mathit{fix}\, (\lambda f\colon store \rightarrow store.\, \lambda s\colon store.$$

$$\texttt{if}\ \bar{\mathcal{V}}[\![B]\!]\eta_i s\ \texttt{then}\ f \cdot (\bar{\mathcal{C}}[\![P]\!]\eta_i s)\ \texttt{else}\ \lfloor s\rfloor\,)\, s_i$$

Assume η_1, s_1 and η_2,s_2 are as in the statement of the lemma. As observed in the proof of Theorem 6.4.10, we may apply Lemma 6.4.9 since there are no infinite directed sets of stores in the CPO $A_\perp^{store}$. To simplify notation, let us write $\bar{B}_i$ for $\bar{\mathcal{V}}[\![B]\!]\eta_i$ and similarly $\bar{P}_i$ for $\bar{\mathcal{C}}[\![P]\!]\eta_i$. By Lemma 6.4.9, if $\bar{\mathcal{C}}[\![\texttt{while}\ B\ \texttt{do}\ P\ \texttt{od}]\!]\eta_1 s_1 = \lfloor s_1'\rfloor$, there is some natural number m with $\lfloor s_1'\rfloor = \bar{P}_1^{\diamond m} s_1$, $\bar{B}_1 s_1' = \mathit{false}$ and for all $k < m$ we have $\bar{P}_1^{\diamond k} s_1 = \lfloor s_1^k\rfloor$ with $\bar{B} s_1^k = \mathit{true}$. The lemma follows by straightforward induction on m, reasoning as in the sequence and conditional cases.

The final case is a variable declaration, where we again assume η_1, s_1 and η_2,s_2 are as in the statement of the lemma. If we let location $\ell_i = (newloc\ s_i)$, value $v_i = (lookup\ s_i\ \ell_i)$, environment $\eta_i' = \eta_i[x \mapsto \ell_i]$ and store

$$s_i'' = update\ (alloc\, s_i\, \ell_i)\ \ell_i\ (\bar{\mathcal{V}}[\![M]\!]\, \eta_i\, s_i)),$$

then we have

$\bar{\mathcal{C}}[\![\texttt{begin new } x := M;\ P\ \texttt{ end}]\!]\eta_i s_i =$

$$(\lambda s'\colon store.\lfloor freeloc\,(update\,s'\,\ell_i\,v_i)\,\ell_i\rfloor)\ \cdot\ (\bar{\mathcal{C}}[\![P]\!]\ \eta_i'\ s_i'').$$

It follows from the definition of strict function application, $\cdot$, that if $\bar{\mathcal{C}}[\![\texttt{begin new } x := M;\ P\ \texttt{ end}]\!]\eta_1 s_1 = \lfloor s_1'\rfloor \neq \bot$, must have $\bar{\mathcal{C}}[\![P]\!]\ \eta_1'\ s_1'' \neq \bot$. Applying the induction hypothesis to P, for η_1', s_1'' and η_2', s_2'', we can see that if $\bar{\mathcal{C}}[\![P]\!]\ \eta_1'\ s_1'' = \lfloor s_1'''\rfloor$, then $\bar{\mathcal{C}}[\![P]\!]\ \eta_2'\ s_2'' = \lfloor s_2'''\rfloor$ with $s_1''' \sim s_2'''$. In this case,

$\bar{\mathcal{C}}[\![\texttt{begin new } x := M;\ P\ \texttt{ end}]\!]\eta_i s_i = \lfloor s_i'\rfloor = \lfloor freeloc\,(update\,s_i'''\,\ell_i\,v_i)\,\ell_i\rfloor.$

It is easy to check that since $s_1''' \sim s_2'''$, we have $s_1' \sim s_2'$. This proves the lemma. ■

Exercise 6.6.4 Use Lemma 6.6.3 to show that the two programs

$\texttt{begin new } x := M; \texttt{begin new } y := N;\ P\ \texttt{ end end}$

$\texttt{begin new } y := N; \texttt{begin new } x := M;\ P\ \texttt{ end end}$

have the same meaning in all appropriate environments and stores, provided neither x nor y occurs in M or N. Explain why this equivalence may fail in an environment and store that are not appropriate (in the technical sense) to either program.

Exercise 6.6.5 Show that if x does not occur in P, then P has the same meaning as

$\texttt{begin new } x := M; \texttt{if } Eq?\,x\,y \texttt{ then } Q \texttt{ else } P \texttt{ end}$

in any appropriate environment and store. Explain why this equivalence may fail in an environment and store that are not appropriate to P.

Exercise 6.6.6 Prove Lemma 6.6.2 by induction on the structure of programs. Your proof should be similar in outline to the proof of Lemma 6.6.3. Be sure you do not write down any statement that you do not understand.

Exercise 6.6.7 Show that the proof rule

$$\frac{F \wedge (cont\ y = M) \wedge y \neq x_1 \wedge \ldots y \neq x_k\ \{[y/x]P\}\ G}{F\ \{\texttt{begin new } x := M;\ P\ \texttt{ end}\}\ G}\quad \begin{array}{l} y\colon loc \text{ not free in } F, P, G \\ x_1, \ldots, x_k \in access(P)\end{array}$$

for proving partial correctness assertions about variable declarations is sound, in the sense that if the hypothesis holds in all appropriate environments and stores, so does the conclusion. (The reason we rename x to y in the hypothesis is to avoid possible conflicts with free occurrences of x in F or G, as in the assertion $cont\,x > 3\ \{\texttt{begin new } x := 5; x := 0 \texttt{ end}\}\ cont\,x > 3$.)

Exercise 6.6.8 The semantic proof of Lemma 6.6.2, given in Exercise 6.6.6, uses properties of the CPO interpretation of lambda terms to apply Lemma 6.4.9. Specifically, we use the fact that every directed set of A^{store} is finite to apply induction in the `while` case, as in the proof of Lemma 6.6.3 written out in this section. An alternate form of induction that could be used is fixed-point induction, described in Section 5.3, which may be applied directly to lambda terms containing *fix*, or the `while` partial correctness rule, which is a form of the fixed-point induction rule tailored to `while` programs. Show, by induction on programs, that if $access(P) = \{y_1, \ldots, y_k\}$, we can prove the partial correctness assertion

$$x \neq y_1 \wedge \ldots \wedge x \neq y_k \wedge cont\, x = v\ \{P\}\ cont\, x = v,$$

using the rules for `while` programs, together with the rule for variable declarations given in Exercise 6.6.7. Since this assertion says that the contents any location not in $access(P)$ does not change, it is equivalent to the statement of Lemma 6.6.2.

Exercise 6.6.9 Suppose we redefine A^{val} and A^{store} so that A^{val} is a pointed CPO and A^{store} is the CPO of all continuous functions from A^{loc} to A^{val}. This allows us to identify the available locations in store s with the set of locations ℓ such that $s\,\ell = \bot_{val}$. Show that in this plausible setting, any function *newloc* with the property that if $newloc\, s = \ell$, then $s\,\ell = \bot_{val}$, is not continuous.

6.6.3 Procedures

We may give straightforward denotational semantics to `while` programs that include procedure declarations and calls. This is simpler than the extension of `while` programs with variable declarations, since lambda calculus already gives us the appropriate form of function. For simplicity, we assume that procedures are added to pure `while` programs without variable declarations, considering the combination of variable and procedure declarations in the next section.

The first step is to add procedure names to the syntax of programs. For simplicity, let us assume procedures each have one location (pass-by-reference) and one value parameter. (Unlike what is often called "pass-by-value" in programming language texts, the value parameter will not be assignable in the procedure body; see Example 6.6.13 in the next section.) Assuming some infinite set of procedure names, $p, q, r, \ldots$, we extend the syntax of programs with the forms

$$P\ ::=\ \ldots \mid p(x, M) \mid \texttt{let}\ p(x\colon loc, y\colon val) = P\ \texttt{in}\ P$$

where $x\colon loc$ and $M\colon val$ in the procedure call $p(x, M)$, and $x\colon loc$ and $y\colon val$ in the procedure body P_1 of $\texttt{let}\ p(x\colon loc, y\colon val) = P_1\ \texttt{in}\ P_2$.

The denotational semantics of procedure declarations and calls is given by showing how to translate programs into lambda terms, as before, but now the lambda terms will involve procedure names. Since programs have type $store \to store_{\perp}$, we will use procedure names in lambda terms as variables of type $loc \to val \to store \to store_{\perp}$. With this typing convention, we can write the denotational semantics as

$$\mathcal{C}[\![p(x, M)]\!] = \lambda s\colon store.\ p\, x\, (\mathcal{V}[\![M]\!]s)\, s$$

$$\mathcal{C}[\![\texttt{let}\ p(x\colon loc,\ y\colon val) = P_1\ \texttt{in}\ P_2]\!] = \texttt{let}\ p = \lambda x\colon loc.\ \lambda y\colon val.\ \mathcal{C}[\![P_1]\!]\ \texttt{in}\ \mathcal{C}[\![P_2]\!]$$

where the `let` to the right of the equal sign in the second clause may be regarded as an abbreviation for lambda abstraction and application, as usual.

As for variable declarations (in the last section), we may work out the semantic meaning of a procedure declaration explicitly and see that this involves the meaning of the block body in an environment altered to reflect the declaration. Specifically, we have

$$\bar{\mathcal{C}}[\![\texttt{let}\ p(x\colon loc,\ y\colon val) = P_1\ \texttt{in}\ P_2]\!]\eta = \texttt{let}\ f = \mathcal{A}[\![\ \lambda x\colon loc.\ \lambda y\colon val.\ \mathcal{C}[\![P_1]\!]\ ]\!]\eta\ \texttt{in}$$
$$\mathcal{C}[\![P_2]\!]\eta[p \mapsto f]$$

Since the main properties of procedure declarations and calls are largely straightforward, following from properties of lambda abstraction and application, we leave the remaining development to the exercises.

Exercise 6.6.10 Show that denotational semantics of the program

$\texttt{let}\ inc(x\colon loc,\ y\colon val) = x := y + 1\ \texttt{in}\ inc(x, cont\, x)$

is a function on stores that increments the value stored in location x.

Exercise 6.6.11 Define a syntactic operation

$subst(x\colon loc,\ y\colon val,\ P_1, q, P_2)$

on programs so that $subst(x\colon loc,\ y\colon val,\ P_1, q, P_2)$ is a well-formed program not containing any procedure declaration that is not already in P_1 or P_2, and show the following equation between programs holds.

$\texttt{let}\ q(x\colon loc,\ y\colon val) = P_1\ \texttt{in}\ P_2 = subst(x\colon loc,\ y\colon val,\ P_1, q, P_2)$

Intuitively, $subst(x\colon loc,\ y\colon val,\ P_1, q, P_2)$ should be the result of substituting the procedure body P_1 for occurrences of q in P_2. In order to do this properly, it is necessary to know which location and value variables in P_1 are the formal parameters of the procedure. Illustrate your operation on the example program

$\texttt{let}\ q(x{:}\,loc,\ y{:}\,val) = x := y + (cont\ z)\ \texttt{in}$

$\quad \texttt{if}\ cont\ x > 1\ \texttt{then}\ q(w,\ cont\ z)$

$\quad \texttt{else}\ \texttt{let}\ r(z{:}\,loc,\ v{:}\,val) = q(z,\ v + 5)\ \texttt{in}\ r(x,\ y)$

Hint: Remember how $[cont_{x:=M}/cont]F$ is defined for first-order formula F.

Exercise 6.6.12 In the semantics given in this section, every procedure declaration is treated as a non-recursive declaration. Change one or both clauses, as needed, to allow recursive procedure declarations and explain why the lambda term you use has a meaning in the CPO model for *loc*, *val*, *bool*, *store* and $store_\perp$ that we have been using in the semantics of `while` programs.

6.6.4 Combining Blocks and Procedure Declarations

In programming practice, it is very common to declare local variables in a procedure body. This is not possible in the simple extensions of `while` programs we have considered so far, since one has procedures and the other has local variables. In the first part of this section, we combine the two and illustrate some of the different forms of parameter passing that developed along with the Algol family of programming languages. More specifically, we regard several parameter passing mechanisms as syntactic sugar for combinations of variable declarations and the two parameter forms considered in Section 6.6.3.

A denotational semantics for procedures and local variables may be formulated by combining the translations into lambda terms of the last two sections. However, this denotational semantics is not entirely satisfactory since many natural equations between programs do not hold. The main reason is that the set of accessible locations, easily determined from the syntax of a program without procedures, cannot be determined for an undeclared procedure. Since the successful treatment of variable declarations involves knowing the set of allocated locations, this poses a serious problem when it comes to allocating a "new" location that is not already accessible. Before discussing the technical problems with the semantics, we consider some of the positive features of this simplified imperative language.

Traditional *pass-by-reference* parameters are accurately modeled by the location parameters considered in Section 6.6.3. In the following example, we show how to model traditional *pass-by-value* using a combination of value parameters (as in Section 6.6.3) and variable declarations. Pass-by-value/result is considered in Exercise 6.6.14.

Example 6.6.13 This example shows how to treat pass-by-value parameters. Let us use the syntax

$\texttt{let}\ p(x{:}\,loc,\ y{:}\,\text{pass\_by\_value}) = P_1\ \texttt{in}\ P_2$

for the declaration of a procedure with one location parameter and one pass-by-value parameter. The procedure body is P_1 and the scope of the declaration is P_2. The difference between a pass-by-value parameter and a parameter of type *val* is that in traditional pass-by-value, the formal parameter y is initialized to the value of the actual parameter, and is assignable within the procedure body P_1. In our framework, this means that within P_1, the identifier y is used as if it has type *loc*. However, the final value of y is not passed back to the calling program on procedure return. (This is described in standard programming language textbooks, such as [Set89, Ten81].)

We assume that in the call $p(x, M)$ to a procedure declared as above, the actual pass-by-value parameter has type *val*. This allows us to treat the program form above as syntactic sugar for

$$\texttt{let}\ p(x\colon loc, z\colon val) = (\texttt{begin new}\ \ y := z;\ P_1\ \ \texttt{end})\ \texttt{in}\ P_2$$

where z is a fresh value variable not occurring in P_1. ■

For a `while` program with variable declarations, we define the set $access(P)$ of location variables accessed by P. This is used to formulate the notion of "appropriate environment and store," which is necessary to guarantee that new locations are really "new." We do not need to consider the set of accessible locations in the language with only procedures, but when we combine procedures with variable declarations, we must extend the definition of *access* to the two program forms not considered in Section 6.6.2, procedure declarations and calls. Let us attempt to do this by induction on the structure of programs. For a procedure declaration, the definition seems relatively natural,

$$access(\texttt{let}\ \ p(x\colon loc, y\colon val) = P_1\ \ \texttt{in}\ \ P_2) = access(P_2) \cup (access(P_1) - \{x\}).$$

Intuitively, the accessible locations are the locations named in P_2, plus those named in the procedure body P_1, except the formal location parameter. The reason the formal location parameter x is not an additional accessible location is that whenever the procedure is called, some other location already named in P_2 will be supplied. For example, in the execution of $\texttt{let}\ \ p(x\colon loc, y\colon val) = x := 5\ \ \texttt{in}\ \ p(z, cont\ w)$, the location z is passed to p. The location variable x is only a bound variable, and we can rename it to any other (except y) without changing the meaning of the program.

The problem now arises when we try to determine the accessible locations of a procedure call. Specifically, how do we define

$$access(p(x, M)) = \ldots?$$

If this call is contained in the block body of a program that declares p, then we can just let $access(p(x, M)) = access(M)$, since we will see the accessible locations of the procedure body when we look at the outer program. More specifically, the simple definition, which ignores the effect of the call to p, will give the right answer for any program of the form

... `let` $p(x\colon loc,\, y\colon val) = P_1$ `in` $\ldots p(x, M) \ldots\ldots$

since we count the accessible locations of P_1 when we determine *access* of the outer program. However, there is no obvious definition of $access(p(x, M))$ that gives the correct answer when p is not declared. One way to see that there is no easy solution is to notice that virtually any set of location variables is possible. In particular, there is a continuous function $loc \to val \to store \to store_\perp$ which, given a location, value and store s, returns a store that is different from s on *every* location. If we want a conservative estimate of the locations altered or accessed by a call $p(x, M)$, we must let $access(p(x, M))$ contain all locations. But then we cannot allocate a new location.

One way to see the problem in concrete terms is to consider the program

`begin new` $x := 3$; $p(y, 5)$; `if` $Eq?\,(cont\,x)\;3$ `then` *diverge* `else` *skip* `end`

where *diverge* is `while` *true* `do` *skip* `od`, or any other program that loops indefinitely. According to common sense, this program should be equal to *diverge*, as follows. If the call $p(y, 5)$ diverges, then the entire program diverges. If the call returns, then we should have $cont\,x$ equal to 3 since the location x must be different from y, and different from any global variable accessible to p. However, as mentioned above, there are continuous functions $loc \to val \to store \to store_\perp$ which return a store different from the one they are passed in all locations. For example, it is easy to see that the constant function returning the store with every location equal to 7 is continuous, and therefore a possible semantic value for the procedure identifier p. If the environment gives p this value, then the program above will halt from *every* store.

One solution to the problem of unruly semantic interpretations of undeclared procedure identifiers is simply to decide that we are only interested in reasoning about programs that declare all of their procedures. This is quite reasonable for many purposes. In particular, there is a Hoare logic that is sound and relatively complete for proving assertions about programs with variable declarations and all procedures declared within the program. This logic may be used to prove properties about many imperative algorithms. On the other hand, there are limitations to this point of view. One is that in many practical instances, we would like to know whether two program fragments are equal, for all possible surrounding programs. For example, we might be given a program to maintain, and see a way of improving one of the procedure declarations. If this declaration refers to global procedures, then we would like to be convinced that some modification does not change the observable behavior of the procedure at hand, without necessarily examining all of the global procedures in detail. A variation on this scenario arises in designing an optimizing compiler. In programming simple (or complex) manipulations of programs, it is important to have some way of understanding their correctness. A semantic model that accurately reflects the possible values of procedure identifiers, without requiring an enumeration of all possible syntactic procedure bodies, provides useful intuition for informal reasoning about programs, and a mathematical basis for formal reasoning.

How, then, might we change our semantic model to reflect the fact that every procedure, declared in the program or not, can only depend on and assign to a finite number of locations? In order to do this, we must construct a semantic model in which every function of type $loc \to val \to store \to store_\perp$ accesses a fixed, finite set of locations, independent of the actual store argument. On reflection, we can see that it suffices to guarantee that functions of type $store \to store_\perp$ have this "finite accessibility" property. We could try to modify the particular CPO for $store \to store_\perp$ and hope that if $\to$ is otherwise interpreted as meaning "all continuous functions," we would obtain a Henkin model with the appropriate fixed-point property. This would solve the problem for programming languages with procedures that do not have procedure parameters. However, to give reasonable semantics to programming languages that allow procedures to have procedure parameters, we must find a more uniform reinterpretation of $\to$.

Although this general problem remains a topic of continuing research, there does appear to be at least one promising general approach. This is the use of *Kripke-like structures,* which in category theory arise from so-called *functor categories.* Since we consider functor categories and Kripke-like models of typed lambda calculus in more detail in Chapter 7, we will only summarize the relevance of these general structures to the problem of accurate semantics for procedures with access to fixed sets of locations.

Intuitively, a Kripke-model, or "possible world semantics," is built around a set of what are generically called possible worlds. In logics that model belief, for example, a possible world might represent the intuitive concept of having a set of beliefs. In the semantics of imperative programs, a possible world is a finite set of locations. In general, possible worlds in a Kripke-like model are partially-ordered in some way. For beliefs, worlds are partially-ordered by containment, reflecting the intuitive fact that if we believe one set of propositions, the only possible sets of beliefs that seem possible are the ones that contain the propositions we now believe. For imperative programs, we may also order "possible worlds" by containment. Intuitively, we think of this ordering as reflecting the fact that if a procedure can be executed with one set of locations allocated, then the procedure can also be correctly executed with any larger set allocated. (Technically, we use a category instead of a partial order since there is more than one way of including a smaller set into a larger one.) The advantage of introducing the added structure of sets of allocated locations comes when we define functions from one set to another. The general notion of a set, or type, in a Kripke model, is a set for each possible world. The interpretation of a function symbol, at some possible world, is a function for each possible larger world, subject to a constraint relating the function at one world to the function at another. With locations as possible worlds, this constraint guarantees that if a procedure is allocated more locations than it needs, only the needed locations will be accessed. By following the usual interpretation of types and functions in Kripke models, we obtain a relatively natural mathematical structure in which each function of type $store \rightarrow store_{\perp}$ will depend on a finite set of locations. In addition, this structure is preserved at higher types, allowing a natural interpretation of imperative languages with higher-order procedures. The use of Kripke-like structures was initiated by Reynolds, in [Rey81], and further developed in [Ole82, Ole85, MS88, Ten86, O'H90, Ten91]. A good overview appears in [OT92].

Exercise 6.6.14 Another historical parameter-passing mechanism is called *pass by value-result* (or *copy-restore*). In value-result, the formal parameter is given a new storage location, which is initialized to the r-value of the actual parameter. After execution of the procedure body, the actual parameter is then assigned the r-value of the new location.

(a) Let us use the syntax

let $p(x\colon loc,\ y\colon \text{value-result}) = P_1$ in P_2

for the declaration of a procedure with one location parameter and one value-result parameter. Show how to treat this as syntactic sugar for some program of the form

let $p(x\colon loc,\ z\colon (\ldots)) =$ (begin new $(\ldots) := (\ldots);\ \ldots P_1 \ldots$ end) in P_2

(b) Explain your treatment of pass by value-result using the example

let $p(x\colon loc,\ y\colon \text{value-result}) =$

$y := cont\, x$; if $cont\, z = cont\, y$ then $z := 1$ else $z := 2$

in $p(3, z)$

What will be the final contents of z?

7 Categories and Recursive Types

7.1 Introduction

This chapter summarizes basic concepts from category theory, develops connections with lambda calculus, and uses a categorical generalization of domain concepts to present the semantics of recursive types. In outline, the main topics of the chapter are:

- Brief introduction to categories, functors and natural transformations.
- Cartesian closed categories, an alternative approach to both syntax and semantics of typed lambda calculus.
- Kripke lambda models, a class of a cartesian closed categories that are not Henkin models.
- Semantic models of typed lambda calculus with recursive types.

In comparison with other presentations of category theory, which is a broad mathematical subject intersecting algebra, mathematical logic and some areas of theoretical computer science, this chapter is only a brief overview of a few relevant topics. Some general reference books that provide more information are [AM75, AL91, BW90, FS90, Gol79, Joh77, LS86, Mac71, Pie91].

One aspect of category theory that may interest some readers is the correspondence between type theory, category theory and constructive logic. In broad terms, the formulas-as-types correspondence between typed lambda calculus and constructive logic may be completed to a three-way correspondence between typed lambda calculus, constructive logic and category theory. This correspondence yields some general insight into all three subjects, but is far too extensive to present here in any depth. For further information on the connection between lambda calculus and category theory, the reader may consult [AL91, LS86, MS89, Sco80a].

A general technique that seems fruitful in computer science is the categorical interpretation of logic, as described in [KR77, LS86, MR77, Pit99], for example. By interpreting logical formulas in categories, we may "relativize" classical constructions to other settings. Kripke lambda models, covered in Section 7.3, may be regarded as a worked example of this form. Another example, already presented in concrete terms without benefit of this general technique, is the development of "effective domains" in the category of modest sets (Sections 5.6.4). An interesting and readable short example from the literature is the formulation of fixed-point theory in an arbitrary CCC with finite limits and natural numbers object [Bar90]. A number of other examples appear in [Pit99].

This chapter draws on general properties of typed lambda calculus from Chapter 4 and refers, for examples, to model constructions given in Chapter 5. The material is independent of Chapter 6 and generally not required for later chapters of the book. An exception is the categorical generalization of logical relations in Section 8.6. Another use of categorical concepts appears in Section 9.3.2, where we use $\lambda^{\to,\forall}$ types and terms to represent categories and functors syntactically.

7.2 Cartesian Closed Categories

7.2.1 Category Theory and Typed Languages

An alternative approach to typed lambda calculus may be formulated using category theory. Cartesian closed categories (*CCC*'s) correspond closely to typed lambda calculus with pairing and a one-element type *unit*. These categories also provide models for any fragment of $\lambda^{unit,\times,\to}$, and may be extended to sums and other types. To a first approximation, we may read the definition of CCC as a summary of the properties of domains and continuous functions (or modest sets and recursive functions) that we use to demonstrate that every hierarchy of continuous functions forms a $\lambda^{unit,\times,\to}$ Henkin model. However, because of the way these properties are formulated, CCCs are more general than Henkin models. As a result, the traditional proof rules for typed lambda calculus are sound and complete for cartesian closed categories. Since we only achieve completeness for Henkin models by adding extra axioms for reasoning about empty or nonempty types, cartesian closed categories give us a more direct completeness theorem than Henkin models.

One useful aspect of the categorical view of typed lambda calculus is that CCCs seem as much an alternative formulation of syntax as they do semantics. This allows us to treat various syntactic and semantic notions uniformly. For example, an interpretation of terms in a model has the same character as a map between models. On the other hand, the useful distinction between syntax and semantics is less clear-cut in the categorical setting. In particular, arbitrary cartesian closed categories do not seem as "semantic" as Henkin models. One class of cartesian closed categories that are more general than Henkin models, yet seem more semantic than syntactic, are the Kripke lambda models discussed in Section 7.3. While there have been attempts to identify certain classes of categories as "models," we will not go into this topic since it involves more complex categorical properties. The interested reader may consult [LS86, Chap. 17] for more information.

7.2.2 Categories, Functors and Natural Transformations

Category theory is concerned with structures and the maps between them. In algebra (and many category theory books), the usual examples of structures are groups, rings or fields and the usual examples of maps are algebraic homomorphisms between them. In lambda calculus, the "structures" of interest are the type expressions of some calculus or their semantic interpretations, and the maps are terms, often modulo provable equality, or their semantic interpretations. Since some foundational claims about category theory in the literature invite comparisons with set theory, it is important to understand the fundamental differences. While set theory may be used to build (or prove the existence of) all of the usual mathematical objects, pure category theory cannot be used to build anything. More specifically, while set theory has axioms that guarantee the existence of certain sets, the basic axioms of category theory do not guarantee the existence of any categories. Instead, the axioms give properties that allow us to recognize that a collection of structures and maps form a category. In vague and informal terms, category theory is aimed at recognizing and utilizing general patterns among mathematical objects that are already known to exist. While it is possible to formulate a foundational theory based on category theory by postulating the existence of certain categories, we will not be concerned with that aspect of category theory here.

Formally, a *category*

$$\mathcal{C} = \langle C^o, C^a, dom, cod, id, comp \rangle$$

consists of two collections, C^o and C^a, and four maps,

$$\begin{aligned} dom &: C^a \to C^o \\ cod &: C^a \to C^o \\ id &: C^o \to C^a \\ comp &: C^a \times C^a \rightharpoonup C^a \end{aligned}$$

where "$\rightharpoonup$" indicates that *comp* is a partial function. Elements of C^o are called *objects* and elements of C^a are called *arrows* or *morphisms*. In many categories, the objects are sets with some kind of structure, and the morphisms are functions that preserve this structure. However, many other mathematical concepts yield categories. A number of examples appear below.

Intuitively, the maps *dom* and *cod* give the *domain* and *codomain* (or range) of a morphism, $id(a)$ is the identity map on object a, and *comp* is function composition. Formally, we require that for each object $a \in C^o$, the morphism $id(a)$ must have domain and codomain a. In addition, $id(a)$ must satisfy certain axioms given below. Although *comp* is generally partial, $comp(f, g)$ must be defined on any pair of morphisms $f, g \in C^a$ with $cod(g) = dom(f)$. In this case, the domain and codomain of $comp(f, g)$ are the domain of g and the codomain of f, respectively. The map *comp* must also satisfy the associativity axiom given below. It is conventional to write id_a for $id(a)$ and $f \circ g$ for $comp(f, g)$. We also write $f\colon a \to b$ for the pair of conditions $dom(f) = a$ and $cod(f) = b$. The category axioms are that each identity is a unit with respect to composition, and composition is associative. More precisely,

$$f = id_b \circ f = f \circ id_a$$

for every $f : a \to b$, and

$$f \circ (g \circ h) = (f \circ g) \circ h.$$

for every $h : a \to b$, $g : b \to c$ and $f : c \to d$.

Part of the culture of category theory is drawing pictures called *diagrams*. The diagram showing $f : a \to b$ is typically drawn

$$a \xrightarrow{\quad f \quad} b$$

The two equational axioms for categories (above) may be drawn as the following diagrams

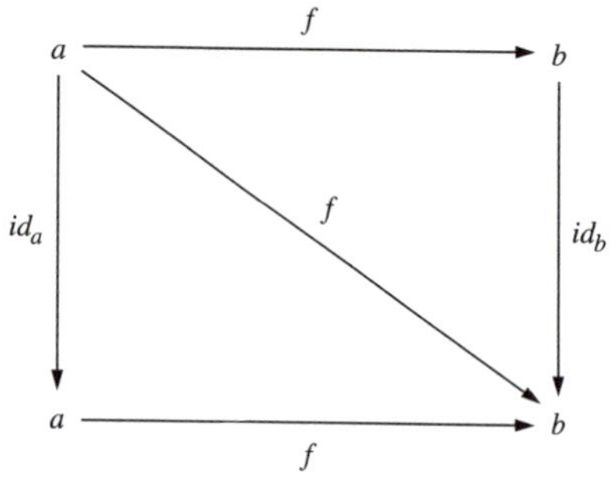

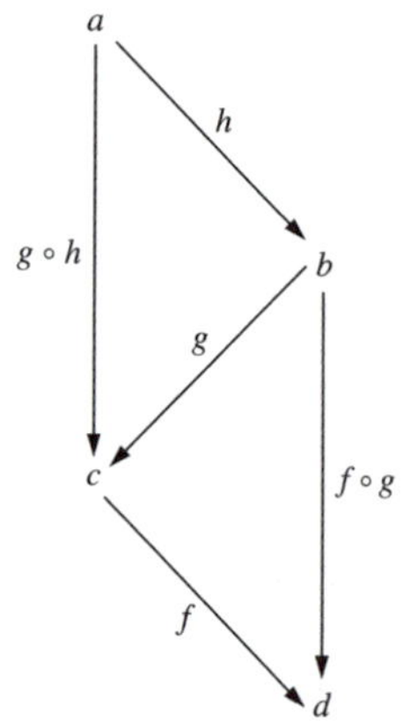

which make it unnecessary to state separately that $f : a \to b$, $g : b \to c$ and so on. The correspondence between the equations and their diagrams is described in the following paragraph.

A path in a diagram is interpreted as the composition of its arrows, with a diagram as a whole stating that any two compositions with common end points are equal. Since a single diagram may contain several paths with common endpoints, a diagram is a concise and pictorial way of stating one or more equations between compositions of morphisms. We say a diagram *commutes* if, for every pair of vertices, all compositions given by any path from the first to the second are the same morphism of the category.

It is a worthwhile exercise to compare each diagram to the corresponding equational category axiom above. It is easy to see that the first diagram is equivalent to the first equation. The second diagram seems as close as we can come to stating associativity diagrammatically. The difficulty is that interpreting a path as a composition of arrows is ambiguous unless we assume associativity to begin with. More specifically, since the zig-zag path could be either $f \circ (g \circ h)$ or $(f \circ g) \circ h$, the interpretation of the diagram itself assumes associativity. In comparing these diagrams with their equational counterparts, the reader may notice that the common order of composition, given by the usual definition $(f \circ g)\,x = f(g\,x)$ for ordinary functions, is not very convenient when working with diagrams. For this reason, many authors write composition in the opposite order. A common notation is $f; g$ for what is called *composition in diagrammatic order.* We may treat this as an abbreviation, $f; g \stackrel{\text{def}}{=} g \circ f$, for composition in the opposite order. Unfortunately, neither order is standard in the literature.

For any objects a and b of a category, the collection of all arrows $f : a \to b$ is often called a *hom-set,* since this is a set of homomorphisms in many common categories. It is conventional to write $Hom(a, b)$ for the collection of all arrows from a to b. Hom-sets play a central role in category theory; in fact, a category is determined by its hom-sets. If a and b are objects of category $\mathcal{C}$, then we often write $\mathcal{C}(a, b)$ for $Hom(a, b)$. This is particularly useful in discussions that refer to more than one category.

Example 7.2.1 The class $\mathcal{S}et$ of ordinary sets, with $\mathcal{S}et(A, B)$ all functions from A to B, forms a category. In $\mathcal{S}et$, id_a is the usual identity function, and composition is as usual. ■

Example 7.2.2 For any algebraic signature Σ, the class $\mathcal{A}lg_\Sigma$ of all Σ-algebras, with $\mathcal{A}lg_\Sigma(A, B)$ the set of all homomorphism from A to B, forms a category. It is easy to check that the identity map is a homomorphism and, by Lemma 3.5.4, the composition of two homomorphisms is a homomorphism.

For any set $\mathcal{E}$ of equations between Σ-terms, we also have a category $\mathcal{A}lg_{\Sigma,\mathcal{E}}$ whose objects are all Σ-algebras satisfying $\mathcal{E}$ and whose arrows are all homomorphisms. This general idea has many familiar examples, such as the category $\mathcal{G}$ of groups, with $\mathcal{G}(A, B)$ the collection of group homomorphisms from A to B. A category $\mathcal{A}lg_{\Sigma,\mathcal{E}}$ is called a *subcategory* of $\mathcal{A}lg_\Sigma$, since the objects of $\mathcal{A}lg_{\Sigma,\mathcal{E}}$ are a subset of the objects of $\mathcal{A}lg_\Sigma$, and similarly for the arrows. It is in fact a *full subcategory,* which means that $\mathcal{A}lg_\Sigma(A, B) = \mathcal{A}lg_{\Sigma,\mathcal{E}}(A, B)$ for all A, B that are objects of both categories. ■

Example 7.2.3 The class $\mathcal{M}od$ of modest sets, with $\mathcal{M}od(A, B)$ all recursive functions from A to B, forms a category, since identity functions and compositions of recursive functions are recursive. ■

Example 7.2.4 The class $\mathcal{C}po$ of CPOs, with $\mathcal{C}po(A, B)$ all continuous functions from A to B, form a category, since identity functions and compositions of continuous functions are continuous. The classes of PCPOs and BCPOs similarly form categories. Both are full subcategories of Cpo. ■

Example 7.2.5 For any typed lambda calculus signature Σ and Σ-Henkin model $\mathcal{A}$, there is a category $\mathcal{C}_{\mathcal{A}}$ whose objects are the type expressions over Σ and arrows from σ to τ are the elements of $A^{\sigma\to\tau}$. For each object σ, the identity is the meaning of the term $\lambda x{:}\sigma.\,x$ and composition is given similarly by the lambda term for composition. More specifically, if $f \in \mathcal{C}_{\mathcal{A}}(\tau,\rho)$ and $g \in \mathcal{C}_{\mathcal{A}}(\sigma,\tau)$ then $f \circ g$ is given by $\lambda x{:}\sigma.\, f\,(g\,x)$, using f and g as constants denoting these functions. We can check associativity of composition, for example, by calculating $(f \circ g) \circ h = \lambda x{:}\sigma.(f \circ g)(hx) = \lambda x{:}\sigma.(\lambda y{:}\tau.\, f(gy))(hx) =_{\beta} \lambda x{:}\sigma.\, f(g(hx))$ and similarly $f \circ (g \circ h) = \lambda x{:}\sigma.\, f(g(hx))$
■

Example 7.2.6 A single partial order $\mathcal{P} = \langle P, \leq\rangle$ may be regarded as a category whose objects are the elements of P and arrows are determined by $\leq$. Specifically, if $a, b \in P$, then $\mathcal{P}(a, b)$ is either empty, if $a \not\leq b$, or has the single element $\ell_{a,b}$, if $a \leq b$. The identity map $id_a{:}\, a \to a$ is $id_a = \ell_{a,a}$, which exists since $a \leq a$. We have composition since every partial order is transitive. It is easy that each partial order determines a unique category, and from any category obtained in this way, we may recover a unique partial order. More generally, categories with each hom-set containing at most one arrow correspond to preorders, and categories with the additional property that any pair of isomorphic objects (see below) are identical correspond to partial orders.

Viewing a preorder or partial order as a category may seem relatively abstract, since the arrows do not seem like functions, but more like "facts" or "relationships" between the objects. However, we will see that this is a useful technique. An important special case is that a CPO may be regarded as a category in exactly this way. ■

Two objects, a and b, of a category $\mathcal{C}$ are *isomorphic* if there are morphisms $a \to b$ and $b \to a$ whose compositions are the identities, as illustrated in the following diagram.

An isomorphism in Set means only that the two sets have the same cardinality. In $\mathcal{G}$ or Alg_{Σ}, this is the usual notion of group or algebraic isomorphism. In the category Mod of modest sets, an isomorphism is a recursive isomorphism and in Cpo, a continuous isomorphism.

A general construction on categories is the *product* of two categories. If $\mathcal{C}$ and $\mathcal{D}$ are categories, the objects of the product category $\mathcal{C} \times \mathcal{D}$ are pairs $\langle c, d\rangle$, where c is an object of $\mathcal{C}$ and d an object of $\mathcal{D}$. The arrows from $\langle c, d\rangle$ to $\langle c', d'\rangle$ are pairs $\langle f, g\rangle$ with $f: c \to c'$ and $g: d \to d'$. The identity on $\langle c, d\rangle$ is $\langle id_c, id_d\rangle$, with composition defined by

$$\langle f, g\rangle \circ \langle f', g'\rangle = \langle f \circ g, f' \circ g'\rangle.$$

It is easy to verify the category axioms for the product category. An interesting example, given in Exercise 7.2.9, is the product of two CPOs (regarding each as a category).

Another useful construction is to reverse all the arrows of a category. This is not very intuitive, since we tend to think of the arrows of a category as functions, and functions are not usually "reversible" or "invertible" in any natural sense. However, we will see that this construction is formally very useful for either applying some construction "backwards" or observing that some operation works in the opposite direction of another. To be precise, if $\mathcal{C} = \langle C^o, C^a, dom, cod, id, comp\rangle$ is a category, then the *opposite category*

$$\mathcal{C}^{op} = \langle C^o, C^a, cod, dom, id, comp^{op}\rangle$$

is just like $\mathcal{C}$, but with the domain and codomain of each arrow interchanged, and *comp* reversed accordingly, *i.e.*, $comp^{op}\ f\ g = comp\ g\ f$.

As presented, categories "almost" have an equational axiomatization. A category $\mathcal{C}$ is a two-sorted algebra, with four functions satisfying a set of equational axioms, *except* that *comp* is not required to be a total function. This exception notwithstanding, it is often useful to think of categories as two-sorted algebras. An alternative and occasionally useful presentation of categories *is* equational. Instead of using two sorts, one for objects and one for arrows, we may describe a single category using one sort for each hom-set (or, equivalently, pair of objects). In this alternative, we need a constant id_a for each object, and a composition map $comp_{a,b,c}$ for each triple of objects. Note that in this presentation, the signature depends on the set of objects. While the category axioms become equational, the alternative presentation does not suggest the definition of functor as clearly as the definition just described. In addition, our first view provides better guidance when it comes to studying functors that respect additional structure, such as cartesian closedness.

A category is *small* if the collections of objects and arrows are sets (as opposed to proper classes). The distinction between small categories and categories that are not small is occasionally needed to avoid inadvertently making paradoxical statements about sets. For example, since there is no set of all sets, we must be careful about defining a category of all categories. However, we will only have very occasional need to mention small categories, so if you are not familiar with the distinction between sets and classes, do not worry about it.

Two central notions in category theory are functors and natural transformations. Remembering that categories are "almost" two-sorted algebras, we may derive the definition of functor from the standard notion of homomorphism on multi-sorted algebras. The only detail that requires attention is the preservation of composition, since composition is a partial instead of total operation on arrows. More precisely, a *functor* from $\mathcal{C}$ to $\mathcal{D}$ is a pair of maps $F = \langle F^o, F^a \rangle$ with

- $F^o: C^o \to D^o$ mapping objects to objects
- $F^a: C^a \to D^a$ mapping arrows to arrows, such that
- if $f: a \to b$, then $F^a(f): F^o(a) \to F^o(b)$,
- $F^a(id_a) = id_{F^o(a)}$,
- $F^a(f \circ g) = F^a(f) \circ F^a(g)$.

It is common to omit superscripts from the maps F^o and F^a. Following this convention, we may write $F(f): F(a) \to F(b)$, for example.

Some important functors are the type operations on categories that form Henkin models. We describe product and function space functors first for Cpo, along with lifting, then consider the generalization of each to other categories.

Example 7.2.7 Lifting, product and function space constructors on CPOs, discussed in Section 5.2, are functors. The simplest, lifting, is a functor from the category Cpo to itself. The object map takes a CPO D to the CPO $D_\perp$ and the map on arrows takes a continuous function $f: D \to E$ to the strict continuous function $f_\perp: D_\perp \to E_\perp$ on pointed CPOs. We may also regard lifting as a functor from Cpo to the category $Cpo_\perp$ of pointed CPOs and strict continuous functions.

To view product and function constructions as functors, we must consider the product and opposite constructions on categories. The product functor, which we will write $\times$, is a functor from $Cpo \times Cpo$ to Cpo. (Note that we have used the symbol $\times$ for both the product operation on categories and for the product functor from $Cpo \times Cpo$ to Cpo.) The object map of the product functor takes a pair of CPOs, $\langle C, D \rangle$, to the product CPO, $C \times D$, while the arrow map takes a pair $\langle f, g \rangle$ of continuous functions with $f: C \to C'$ and $g: D \to D'$ to the function $f \times g: (C \times D) \to (C' \times D')$ given by

$$(f \times g)\langle x, y \rangle = \langle fx, gy \rangle.$$

It is easy to see that this map preserves identities and composition.

The function space constructor, $\to$, is more complicated. The object map of the function space functor maps a pair $\langle C, D \rangle$ of CPOs to the CPO $C \to D$ of continuous functions.

However, $\rightarrow$ is a functor from $Cpo^{op} \times Cpo$ to Cpo, not $Cpo \times Cpo \longrightarrow Cpo$. The reason we must reverse the arrows in the first argument is that otherwise there is no obvious way to form an arrow map. More specifically, if $\rightarrow$ were a functor, we would have to map a pair of continuous functions $f\colon A \rightarrow C$ and $g\colon B \rightarrow D$ to a function from $A \rightarrow B$ to $C \rightarrow D$. The problem with this may be visualized using the square on the left below.

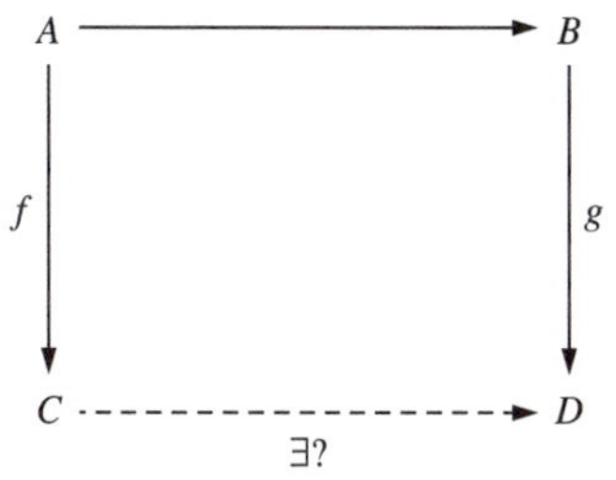

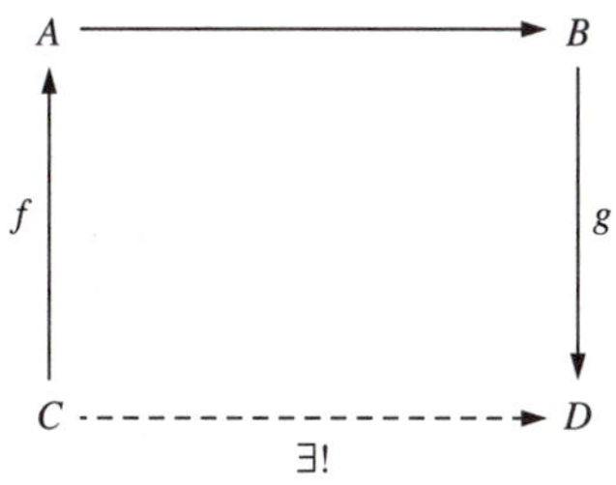

Given functions f and g as drawn, and a function $A \rightarrow B$ across the top, we need to be able to define a function $C \rightarrow D$ across the bottom. This does not seem possible, in general, but it would be if f were oriented in the opposite direction. We therefore work with the opposite category Cpo^{op} whose morphisms are continuous functions "drawn backwards." A functor $Cpo^{op} \times Cpo \longrightarrow Cpo$ must map a pair of continuous functions $f^{op}\colon A \rightarrow C$ and $g\colon B \rightarrow D$ to a function from $A \rightarrow B$ to $C \rightarrow D$. Since a morphism $f^{op}\colon A \rightarrow C$ of Cpo^{op} is (by definition) a continuous function $f\colon C \rightarrow A$, we can define the arrow map by completing the square on the right above. Given $f^{op}\colon A \rightarrow C$ and $g\colon B \rightarrow D$, we map a function $h\colon A \rightarrow B$ to

$$(f \rightarrow g)\, h = g \circ h \circ f : C \rightarrow D$$

by traversing the three given sides of the square above from C up, across and down to D. The reader may verify that product and functions space constructions are functors in Exercise 7.2.12. This is worth doing, since the way that $\rightarrow$ preserves composition requires some attention to the direction of arrows. ■

Categories and functors form a category. More specifically, the objects of the category Cat are all small categories and the arrows from $\mathcal{C}$ to $\mathcal{D}$ are all functors. We have an identity functor for each category (mapping each object or arrow to itself), and the composition of two functors (defined by composing object and arrow maps separately) is a functor. It is easy to check that all of the conditions are satisfied. Since the category axioms are "almost" equational, this is "almost" a special case of Example 7.2.2.

Perhaps the main historical motivation for the development of category theory was the desire to apply a single construction to a variety of examples or analogous algebraic settings. We consider two examples that are relevant to lambda calculus, products and function spaces. (Initial and terminal objects are considered in Exercise 7.2.8.) By showing how to define cartesian products in a categorical manner, we give a single definition that identifies the product of two sets, the product of two CPOs, the product of two modest sets, and so on. Since the standard language of category theory is diagrams, we will write the definitions in a diagrammatic way. Like many basic definitions in category theory, the definition of product tells us how to recognize a cartesian product if we have one (or someone else claims to be giving one). It does not tell us how to construct a product in any particular category.

If a, b, $[a \times b]$ and c are objects of category $\mathcal{C}$, then $[a \times b]$ *is a product of* a *and* b if there are arrows $p_1 : [a \times b] \longrightarrow a$ and $p_2 : [a \times b] \longrightarrow b$ such that for all f, g as indicated below, there is a unique h such that the following diagram commutes.

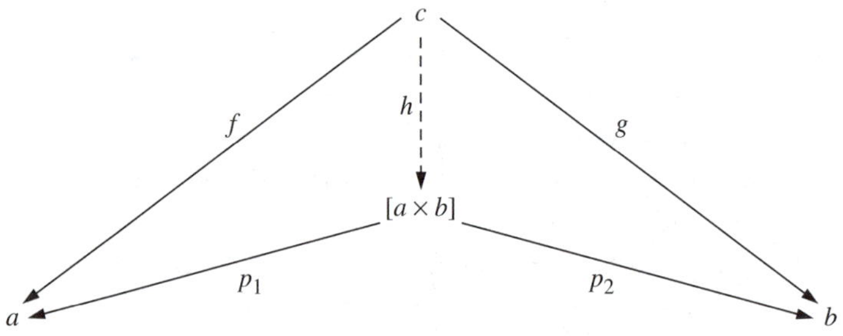

In this diagram, we have followed the categorical convention of writing existentially-quantified arrows with dashed instead of solid lines. According to convention, this diagram "says" that given f, g, p_1 and p_2 as indicated, there exists h satisfying the conditions imposed by the diagram. Exercise 7.2.10 shows that any two products of a and b are isomorphic, and also shows how to define sums (also called coproducts) by reversing all the arrows of this diagram.

A second categorical definition that is relevant to lambda calculus is the definition of *function object,* traditionally called an *exponential* in the category-theoretic literature. This definition assumes that we have product objects, written below without square brackets. If a, b, $[a \to b]$ and c are objects of category $\mathcal{C}$, then $[a \to b]$ *is a function object of* a *and* b if there is an arrow $apply : [a \to b] \times a \longrightarrow b$ such that for all $f : c \times a \longrightarrow b$ as indicated below, there is a unique $h : c \longrightarrow [a \to b]$ such that the following diagram commutes.

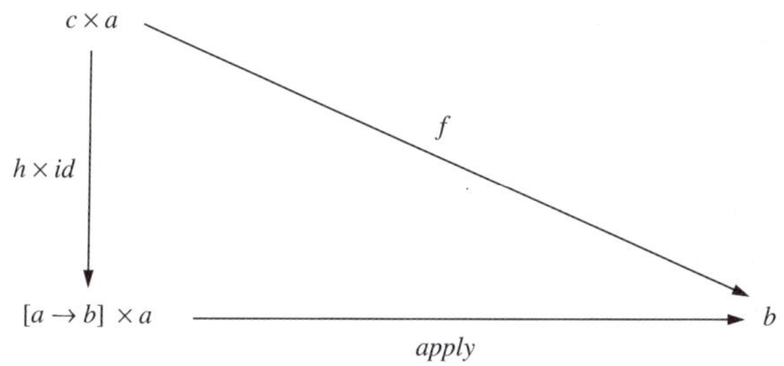

Intuitively, h is meant to be the curried form of function f and *apply* is function application. Speaking of the objects as sets of some kind, we may read the diagram in the following way. The function $h \times id$ maps a pair $\langle x, y\rangle$ to a pair $\langle hx, y\rangle$ consisting of a function from a to b and an element of a. If we apply *apply* to this pair, we obtain hxy, which, if h is to be the curried form of f, must be equal to $f\,\langle x, y\rangle$. Exercise 7.2.11 shows that any two function spaces of a and b are isomorphic, which is a way of showing that the formal definition by diagram is sufficiently powerful to characterize function spaces. The exercise also verifies that function CPOs and modest sets satisfy the definition.

As described in Example 7.2.7 (and generalized in Exercise 7.2.12), the function space functor on $\mathcal{C}$, mapping a and b to $a \to b$, is a functor from $\mathcal{C}^{op} \times \mathcal{C}$ to $\mathcal{C}$. In general, a functor from $\mathcal{C}$ to $\mathcal{D}$ may be called a *covariant functor,* to distinguish it from a functor $\mathcal{C}^{op} \to \mathcal{D}$. A functor from $\mathcal{C}^{op}$ to $\mathcal{D}$ is often referred to as a *contravariant functor* on $\mathcal{C}$. Using this terminology, it is often said that the function space functor is contravariant in its first argument and covariant in its second.

The final concept in this section is natural transformation. Intuitively, a natural transformation is a "map" between functors with the same domain and range. Since a functor is not a collection, it may take some time to get used to this idea.

Formally, a *natural transformation* $\nu : F \to G$ between functors $F, G : \mathcal{C} \to \mathcal{D}$ is a map from objects of $\mathcal{C}$ to arrows of $\mathcal{D}$ satisfying the following two conditions:

- for every $a \in \mathcal{C}^o$, we have $\nu(a)$: $F(a) \to G(a)$,
- for every f in $\mathcal{C}$ as indicated to the left, the diagram on the right commutes.

$$\begin{array}{cccc}
a & F(a) & \xrightarrow{\;\nu(a)\;} & G(a) \\
f\downarrow & F(f)\downarrow & & \downarrow G(f) \\
b & F(b) & \xrightarrow[\;\nu(b)\;]{} & G(b)
\end{array}$$

We can read this commutative diagram as saying that ν translates F's image $F(f)\colon F(a) \to F(b)$ of the arrow $f\colon a \to b$ from $\mathcal{C}$ to G's image $G(f)\colon G(a) \to G(b)$ of the same arrow from $\mathcal{C}$. A vague but helpful elaboration of this intuition involves thinking of a functor as providing a "view" of a category. To simplify the picture, let us assume that $F, G : \mathcal{C} \to \mathcal{D}$ are functors that are both injective (one-to-one) on objects and arrows. We may think of drawing F by drawing its image (a subcategory of $\mathcal{D}$), with each object and arrow labeled by its pre-image in $\mathcal{C}$. We may draw G similarly. This gives us two subcategories of $\mathcal{D}$ labeled in two different ways. A natural transformation from F to G is a "translation" from one picture to another, given by a family of arrows in $\mathcal{D}$. Specifically, for each object a of $\mathcal{C}$, a natural transformation selects an arrow from $F(a)$ to $G(a)$. The conditions of the definition guarantee that this collection of arrows respects the structure of "F's picture of $\mathcal{C}$." In other words, since functors F and G must preserve identities and composition, a natural transformation $\nu : F \to G$ may be regarded as a translation of any diagram in the image of F.

For any pair of categories, $\mathcal{C}$ and $\mathcal{D}$, we have the *functor category* $\mathcal{D}^{\mathcal{C}}$ whose objects are functors from $\mathcal{C}$ to $\mathcal{D}$, with natural transformations as arrows. The identity natural transformation just maps each object a to the identity arrow id_a. The standard composition of natural transformations $\mu\colon F \to G$ and $\nu\colon G \to H$, for functors $F, G, H\colon \mathcal{C} \to \mathcal{D}$, is to compose $\mu(a)\colon F(a) \to G(a)$ with $\nu(a)\colon G(a) \to H(a)$. This composition is sometimes called "vertical" composition of natural transformations, to distinguish it from another "horizontal" form of composition. We will not use horizontal composition in this book; the definition and examples may be found in standard texts [BW90, Mac71]. A worthwhile exercise on functor categories is 7.3.11, the Yoneda embedding.

Exercise 7.2.8 An object a of category $\mathcal{C}$ is *initial* if, for every object b in $\mathcal{C}$, there is a unique morphism from a to b. An object a of $\mathcal{C}$ is *terminal* if, for every b, there is a unique morphism from b to a.

(a) Show that if a and a' are both initial objects of $\mathcal{C}$, then they are isomorphic.

(b) Show that a is initial in $\mathcal{C}$ iff a' is terminal in $\mathcal{C}^{op}$.

(c) Show that if a and a' are both terminal objects of $\mathcal{C}$, then they are isomorphic.

(d) Show that if a is initial and b is terminal in $\mathcal{C}$, and there is an arrow from b to a, then a and b are isomorphic. Show that in this case, all objects of the category are isomorphic.

Exercise 7.2.9 Let $\mathcal{C}$ and $\mathcal{D}$ be CPOs. Show that if we regard both as categories, as described in Example 7.2.6, the product category $\mathcal{C} \times \mathcal{D}$ is the same as the product CPO, defined in Section 5.2. Show that the functor category $\mathcal{D}^{\mathcal{C}}$ is also a partial order. How is it similar to the function CPO $\mathcal{C} \to \mathcal{D}$ and how does it differ?

Exercise 7.2.10 This exercise asks you to verify properties of the categorical definitions of products and coproducts. Suppose that a, b and c are objects of some category $\mathcal{C}$.

(a) Show that if $[a \times b]$ and $[a \times b]'$ are products of a and b, then these are isomorphic.

(b) Show that the product of two CPOs is the categorical product (*i.e.*, satisfies the definition given in this section).

(c) Show that in any category with products and a terminal object, *unit*, there is an isomorphism $a \times unit \cong a$ for each object a.

(d) A quick way to define sums, or coproducts, is to say that *d is a coproduct of a and b* if d is a product of a and b in $\mathcal{C}^{op}$. This is an instance of *categorical duality,* which involves defining dual notions by applying a definition to the opposite category. Write a direct definition of coproduct along the lines of the definition of product in this section.

(e) Show that the sum CPO is the categorical coproduct and describe the categorical coproduct for the category $Cpo_{\bot}$ of pointed CPOs and strict functions. (*Hint:* See Exercise 5.2.33.)

Exercise 7.2.11 Show that if $[a \to b]$ and $[a \to b]'$ are function objects for a and b, then these are isomorphic. Check that function CPOs and modest sets are categorical function objects.

Exercise 7.2.12 Product and function space functors are defined for *Cpo* in Example 7.2.7. However, these definitions may be generalized to any category with products and function objects. Show that for any such category, these maps are indeed functors by checking that identities and composition are preserved. You may wish to write this out for *Cpo* first, then look to see what properties of *Cpo* you have used.

Exercise 7.2.13 Let $\mathcal{P} = \langle P, \leq \rangle$ be a partial order and let $F, G \colon \mathcal{P} \to Set$ be two functors into the category of sets.

(a) Show that if $a \leq b$ and $F(b)$ is empty, then $F(a)$ must also be the empty set.

(b) Show that if ν is a natural transformation from F to G, and $G(a)$ is empty, then $F(a)$ must also be the empty set.

(c) Let $\mathcal{O} \colon \mathcal{P} \to Set$ be the functor mapping each $a \in P$ to a one element set, $\{*\}$. By composition, each natural transformation $\nu \colon F \to G$ from F to G gives us way of mapping each natural transformation $\mu \colon \mathcal{O} \to F$ to a natural transformation $\nu \circ \mu \colon \mathcal{O} \to G$. Show, however, that there exist F and G such that there are many natural transformations from from F to G, but no natural transformations from $\mathcal{O}$ to F or $\mathcal{O}$ to G.

Exercise 7.2.14 An *equalizer* of two arrows

$$a \overset{f}{\underset{g}{\rightrightarrows}} b$$

consists of an object c and an arrow $h: c \to a$ with $f \circ h = g \circ h$ such that for any $h': c' \to a$ with $f \circ h' = g \circ h'$, there is a unique arrow $c' \to c$ forming a commuting triangle with h and h'. In $\mathcal{S}et$, we may let the equalizer of $f, g : a \to b$ be the subset $c = \{x \in a \mid f(x) = g(x)\}$ of a, together with the function $c \to a$ mapping each element of c to the same element in a. (This function is called the *inclusion* of c into a.)

(a) Show that $\mathcal{C}po$ has equalizers but $\mathcal{C}ppo$ does not. To do this, show that if $f, g : A \to B$ are continuous functions on CPOs, then $\{x \in A \mid f(x) = g(x)\}$ is a CPO (when ordered as in A), but not necessarily pointed even when A and B are pointed.

(b) Show that the category $\mathcal{M}od$ of modest sets and total recursive functions has equalizers.

(c) Show that for any category $\mathcal{C}$, the functor category $\mathcal{S}et^{\mathcal{C}}$ has equalizers. If $F, G : \mathcal{C} \longrightarrow \mathcal{S}et$ are functors (objects of $\mathcal{S}et^{\mathcal{C}}$), with natural transformations $\mu, \nu : F \longrightarrow G$, then consider the functor $H : \mathcal{C} \longrightarrow \mathcal{S}et$ with $H(A) = \{x \in F(A) \mid \mu_A(x) = \nu_A(x)\}$ and the inclusion natural transformation $\iota :: H \longrightarrow F$ mapping each object A of $\mathcal{C}$ to the inclusion of $H(A)$ into $F(A)$.

7.2.3 Definition of Cartesian Closed Category

In this section, we define cartesian closed categories (CCC's), which are the categorical analog to Henkin models. A category theorist might simply say that a *cartesian closed category* is a category with specified terminal object, products and exponentials (function objects). These three parts may be defined in several ways, differing primarily in the amount of category theory that they require. The word "specified" in this definition means that a CCC is a structure consisting of a category and a specific choice of terminal object, products and function objects, much the way a partial order is a set together with a specific order relation. As a result, there may be more than one way to view a category as a CCC. However, as shown in Exercises 7.2.8, 7.2.10 and 7.2.11, the choice of each part is determined up to isomorphism.

Since the concept of CCC is central to the study of categories and lambda calculus, we will give three definitions. Each definition has three parts, requiring terminal objects, products and function objects (respectively), but the way these three requirements are expressed will differ. The first definition is an approximation to a definition using adjunctions. Although adjunctions are among the most useful concepts in category theory, they involve slightly more category theory than will be needed in the rest of this book. Therefore, we consider adjunctions only in Exercise 7.2.25. The second definition is purely equational, while the third uses diagrams from Section 7.2.2 in a manner more common in the category-theoretic literature. It is a useful exercise, for the serious student, to work out the equivalence of these definitions in detail (see Exercises 7.2.21 and 7.2.25).

First definition of CCC A *cartesian closed category* (CCC) is a category with a specified object *unit* and specified binary maps $\times$ and $\rightarrow$ on objects such that for all objects a, b, and c,

- $Hom(a, unit)$ has exactly one element,
- $Hom(a, b) \times Hom(a, c) \cong Hom(a, b \times c)$,
- $Hom(a \times b, c) \cong Hom(a, b \rightarrow c)$,

where the first "$\times$" in the second line is ordinary cartesian product of sets, and the isomorphisms must be "natural" in a, b and c. The naturality conditions, which we will not spell out in detail here, may be made precise using the concept of adjunction. (See Exercise 7.2.25, which defines comma category and adjunction in general.) Intuitively, the naturality conditions ensure that these isomorphisms preserve composition in the manner described below.

The intuitive idea behind the definition of CCC is that we have a one-element type, *unit*, and given any two types, we also have their cartesian product and the collection of functions from one to the other. Each of these properties is stated axiomatically, by referring to collections of arrows. Since objects are not really sets, we do not say "*unit* has only one element" directly. However the condition that $Hom(a, unit)$ has only one element is equivalent in many categories. For example, in the category of sets, if there is only one map from B to A, for all B, then A must have only one element. In a similar way, the axiom that $Hom(a, b \times c)$ is isomorphic to the set of pairs of arrows $Hom(a, b) \times Hom(a, c)$ says that $b \times c$ is the collection of pairs of elements from b and c. The final axiom, $Hom(a \times b, c) \cong Hom(a, b \rightarrow c)$, says that the object $b \rightarrow c$ is essentially the collection of all arrows from b to c. A special case of the axiom which illustrates this point is $Hom(unit \times b, c) \cong Hom(unit, b \rightarrow c)$. Since *unit* is intended to be a one-element collection, it should not be surprising that $b \cong unit \times b$ in every CCC. Hence $Hom(unit \times b, c)$ is isomorphic to $Hom(b, c)$. From this, the reader may see that the hom-set $Hom(b, c)$ is isomorphic to $Hom(unit, b \rightarrow c)$. Since any set A is in one-to-one correspondence with the collection of functions from a one-element set into A, the isomorphism $Hom(b, c) \cong Hom(unit, b \rightarrow c)$ is a way of saying that the object $b \rightarrow c$ is a representation of $Hom(b, c)$ inside the category.

The first definition is not a complete definition since it does not state the additional "naturality conditions" precisely. Rather than spell these all out, we consider an example, motivating a slightly different set of operations that make it easier to define CCC's by a set of equations. The isomorphism involving products, in the definition above, requires a "pairing function"

$$\langle\cdot,\cdot\rangle^{a,b,c} : Hom(a,b) \times Hom(a,c) \to Hom(a, b \times c),$$

and a corresponding inverse function from $Hom(a, b \times c)$ to pairs of arrows, for all objects a, b and c. If $f \in Hom(a, b \times c)$, then we will write $\pi_1 f$ and $\pi_2 f$ for the elements of $Hom(a,b)$ and $Hom(a,c)$ given by this isomorphism. One of the "naturality conditions" is that when $f \circ g \in Hom(a, b \times c)$, we must have

$$\pi_i(f \circ g) = (\pi_i f) \circ g.$$

This gives us a way of replacing π_i, which is a map from one hom-set to another, by arrow of the category. Specifically, if we let $\mathbf{Proj}_i^{b,c} = \pi_i(id_{b\times c})$, then we have

$$\pi_i f = \pi_i(id_{b\times c} \circ f) = \mathbf{Proj}_i^{b,c} \circ f.$$

We may also derive an analogous arrow, $\mathbf{App}^{b,c} : (b \to c) \times b \longrightarrow c$, by applying the isomorphism from $Hom(a, b \to c)$ to $Hom(a \times b, c)$ to the identity on $b \to c$. Using $\mathbf{Proj}_1$, $\mathbf{Proj}_2$ and $\mathbf{App}$, we may write an equational definition of CCC directly without any additional naturality conditions.

Second definition of CCC A *cartesian closed category* is a category with the following extra structure

- An object *unit* with unique arrow $\mathbf{One}^a : a \longrightarrow unit$, for each object a,
- A binary object map $\times$ such that, for all objects a, b and c, there is a specified function $\langle\cdot,\cdot\rangle^{a,b,c} : Hom(a,b) \times Hom(a,c) \longrightarrow Hom(a, b \times c)$ and specified arrows $\mathbf{Proj}_1^{b,c} : b \times c \longrightarrow b$ and $\mathbf{Proj}_2^{b,c} : b \times c \longrightarrow c$ satisfying

$$\mathbf{Proj}_i \circ \langle f_1, f_2\rangle = f_i \quad \text{and} \quad \langle \mathbf{Proj}_1 \circ g, \mathbf{Proj}_2 \circ g\rangle = g$$

for all objects a, b, c and arrows $f_1 : a \longrightarrow b$, $f_2 : a \longrightarrow c$, and $g : a \longrightarrow b \times c$,

- A binary object map $\to$ such that, for all objects a, b and c, there is a specified function $\mathbf{Curry}^{a,b,c} : Hom(a \times b, c) \longrightarrow Hom(a, b \to c)$ and arrow $\mathbf{App}^{b,c} : (b \to c) \times b \longrightarrow c$ satisfying

$$\mathbf{App} \circ \langle \mathbf{Curry}(h) \circ \mathbf{Proj}_1, \mathbf{Proj}_2\rangle = h \quad \text{and} \quad \mathbf{Curry}(\mathbf{App} \circ \langle k \circ \mathbf{Proj}_1, \mathbf{Proj}_2\rangle) = k$$

for all objects a, b, c and arrows $h : a \times b \longrightarrow c$ and $k : a \longrightarrow (b \to c)$,

If we write $f \times g$ for the arrow $\langle f \circ \mathbf{Proj}_1, g \circ \mathbf{Proj}_2\rangle$, then we can write the last two equations of the definition above as

$$\mathbf{App} \circ (\mathbf{Curry}(h) \times id) = h \quad \text{and} \quad \mathbf{Curry}(\mathbf{App} \circ (k \times id)) = k$$

for all arrows h and k as described above.

If we view categories as two-sorted algebras, then we may write the second definition (above) using equational axioms over the expanded signature with function symbols **One**, $\times$, $\langle \cdot, \cdot \rangle$, and so on. In the third definition (below), we define CCC's using diagrams instead of equations. In doing so, we will also state that certain arrows are unique; this eliminates the need for some of the equations that appear in the second definition, as the reader may verify in Exercise 7.2.21.

Third definition of CCC A *cartesian closed category* is a category with the following extra structure:

- An object *unit* with unique arrow $\mathbf{One}^a : a \longrightarrow unit$ for each object a,
- A binary object map $\times$ such that, for all objects a, b and c, there is a specified function $\langle \cdot, \cdot \rangle^{a,b,c} : Hom(a, b) \times Hom(a, c) \longrightarrow Hom(a, b \times c)$ and specified arrows $\mathbf{Proj}_1^{b,c}$ and $\mathbf{Proj}_2^{b,c}$ such that for every $f_1 : a \longrightarrow b$ and $f_2 : a \longrightarrow c$, the arrow $\langle f_1, f_2 \rangle^{a,b,c} : a \longrightarrow b \times c$ is the unique g satisfying

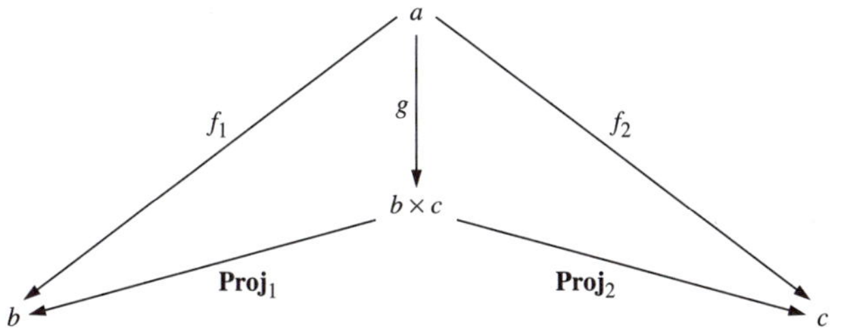

- A binary object map $\to$ such that, for all objects a, b and c, there is a specified function $\mathbf{Curry}^{a,b,c} : Hom(a \times b, c) \longrightarrow Hom(a, b \to c)$ and arrow $\mathbf{App}^{b,c}$ such that for every $h : a \times b \longrightarrow c$, the arrow $\mathbf{Curry}^{a,b,c}(h)$ is the unique $k : a \longrightarrow (b \to c)$ satisfying

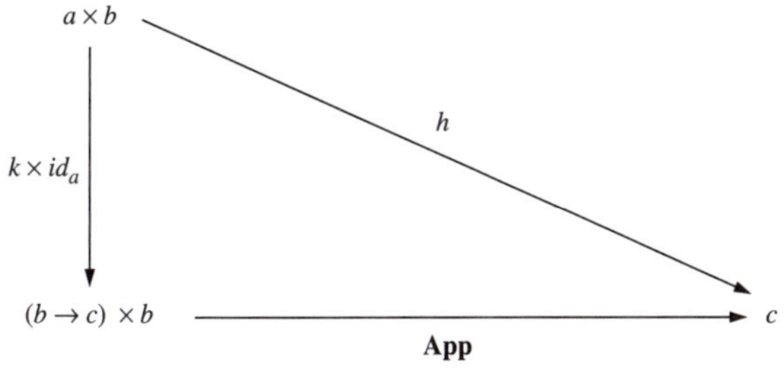

Example 7.2.15 The categories $\mathcal{S}et$ of sets, $\mathcal{M}od$ of modest sets, and $\mathcal{C}po$ of CPOs are all cartesian closed, with *unit*, $a \times b$ and $a \to b$ all interpreted as in the Henkin models based on sets (the full classical hierarchy), modest sets and CPOs.

Example 7.2.16 For any typed lambda calculus signature Σ and Σ-Henkin model $\mathcal{A}$, the category $\mathcal{C}_{\mathcal{A}}$ whose objects are the type expressions over Σ and arrows from σ to τ are the elements of $A^{\sigma\to\tau}$ is described in Example 7.2.5. If $\mathcal{A}$ is a $\lambda^{unit,\times,\to}$ Henkin model, this category is cartesian closed. The terminal object of $\mathcal{C}_{\mathcal{A}}$ is the type *unit*, the product of objects σ and τ is $\sigma \times \tau$, and the function object for σ and τ is $\sigma \to \tau$. Writing elements of the model as constants (*i.e.*, using the signature in which there is a constant for each element of the model), we let

$$\hat{c} = \lambda z\colon unit.\, c$$

$$\mathbf{One}^{\sigma} = \lambda x\colon \sigma.\, *$$

$$\mathbf{Proj}_i^{\sigma,\tau} = \lambda p\colon \sigma \times \tau.\, \mathbf{Proj}_i\, p$$

$$\langle f, g\rangle = \lambda x\colon \rho.\langle fx, gx\rangle : \rho \to (\sigma \times \tau)$$

$$\mathbf{App}^{\sigma,\tau} = \lambda p\colon (\sigma \to \tau) \times \sigma.(\mathbf{Proj}_1 p)(\mathbf{Proj}_2 p)$$

$$\mathbf{Curry}(f) = \lambda x\colon \rho.\, \lambda y\colon \sigma.\, f\,\langle x, y\rangle : \rho \to \sigma \to \tau$$

Exercise 7.2.23 asks you to verify that the equations given in the second definition of CCC are satisfied. ∎

Example 7.2.17 If $\mathcal{C}$ is any small category (*i.e.*, the collections of objects and arrows are sets), then the functor category $\mathcal{S}et^{\mathcal{C}}$ is cartesian closed. Since we discuss the special case $\mathcal{S}et^{\mathcal{P}}$, where $\mathcal{P}$ is a poset, in connection with Kripke lambda models in Section 7.3, we will not explain the cartesian closed structure of $\mathcal{S}et^{\mathcal{C}}$ here. However, it is worth mentioning that there exist cartesian closed categories of functors that are not equivalent to any category obtained by regarding a Henkin model as a CCC. ∎

Example 7.2.18 The category $\mathcal{C}at$ of small categories and functors is cartesian closed (but not a small category). The terminal object of $\mathcal{C}at$ is the category with one object and one arrow (which is the identity on this object). The product in $\mathcal{C}at$ is the product operation on categories and the function object $\mathcal{C} \to \mathcal{D}$ for categories $\mathcal{C}$ and $\mathcal{D}$ is the functor category $\mathcal{D}^{\mathcal{C}}$. ∎

Example 7.2.19 For any $\lambda^{unit,\times,\to}$ signature Σ and set $\mathcal{E}$ of equations between Σ-terms, we may construct a CCC $\mathcal{C}_{\Sigma}(\mathcal{E})$, called the $\lambda^{unit,\times,\to}$ *term category generated by* $\mathcal{E}$. The objects of $\mathcal{C}_{\Sigma}(\mathcal{E})$ are the types over Σ and the arrows are equivalence classes of terms, modulo provable equality from $\mathcal{E}$. To eliminate problems having to do with the names of free variables, it is simplest to choose one variable of each type, and define the arrows from σ to τ using terms over the chosen free variable of type σ. We will write $[z\colon\sigma \triangleright M\colon\tau]_{\mathcal{E}}$ for the arrow of $\mathcal{C}_\Sigma(\mathcal{E})$ given by the term $z\colon\sigma \triangleright M\colon\tau$, modulo $\mathcal{E}$. In more detail, $[z\colon\sigma \triangleright M\colon\tau]_{\mathcal{E}}$ is the set of typed terms

$$[z\colon\sigma \triangleright M\colon\tau]_{\mathcal{E}} = \{z\colon\sigma \triangleright N\colon\tau \mid \mathcal{E} \vdash z\colon\sigma \triangleright M = N\colon\tau\}.$$

The definition of the unique arrow $\mathbf{One}^\sigma\colon\sigma \longrightarrow unit$, and operations $\mathbf{Proj}_1$, $\mathbf{Proj}_2$, $\langle\ \rangle$, **App**, **Curry** are straightforward. For example, **One**, $\mathbf{Proj}_i$, $\langle\ \rangle$ and **Curry** are defined by

$$\begin{aligned}
\mathbf{One}^\sigma &= [z\colon\sigma \triangleright *\colon unit]\\
\mathbf{Proj}_i^{\sigma_1,\sigma_2} &= [z\colon\sigma_1 \times \sigma_2 \triangleright \mathbf{Proj}_i^{\sigma_1,\sigma_2} z\colon\sigma_i]\\
\langle [x\colon\sigma \triangleright M\colon\rho],\ [x\colon\sigma \triangleright N\colon\tau]\rangle &= [x\colon\sigma \triangleright \langle M, N\rangle\colon\rho \times \tau]\\
\mathbf{Curry}^{\sigma,\tau,\rho}([z\colon\sigma \times \tau \triangleright M\colon\rho]) &= [x\colon\sigma \triangleright \lambda y\colon\tau.[\langle x, y\rangle/z]M\colon\rho]
\end{aligned}$$

Composition in the term category is defined by substitution, as follows.

$$[x\colon\sigma \triangleright M\colon\tau]_{\mathcal{E}}\,;\,[y\colon\tau \triangleright N\colon\rho]_{\mathcal{E}} = [x\colon\sigma \triangleright [M/y]N\colon\rho]_{\mathcal{E}}$$

We sometimes omit the signature, writing $\mathcal{C}(\mathcal{E})$ instead of $\mathcal{C}_\Sigma(\mathcal{E})$, when Σ is either irrelevant or clear from context. Exercise 7.2.24 asks you to verify that this category is cartesian closed. The term category is used to prove completeness in Exercise 7.2.39. ∎

An interesting fact about cartesian closed categories that is relevant to lambda calculus with fixed-point operators is that any CCC with coproducts (sums; see Exercise 7.2.10) and a fixed-point operator $fix_a\colon(a \to a) \longrightarrow a$ for *every* object a is preorder. This is the categorical version of the statement that if we add sum types to PCF, as described in Section 2.6.2, then we can prove any two terms of the same type equal. The proof for CCC's is essentially the same as for PCF with sums, given in Exercise 2.6.4. We can see how each of the usual categories of CPOs and continuous functions skirts this problem:

Cpo The category *Cpo* of CPOs and continuous functions is cartesian closed and has coproducts (Exercise 7.2.10). But if the CPO D is not pointed, then a continuous function $f\colon D \to D$ may not have a fixed point.

$Cpo_\perp$ The category $Cpo_\perp$ of pointed CPOs and strict continuous functions has coproducts (Exercise 7.2.10) and fixed point operators on every object. However, this category is not cartesian closed.

Cppo The category *Cppo* of complete, pointed partial orders and (arbitrary) continuous functions is cartesian closed and has fixed point operators on every object but does not have coproducts.

Each of these claims may be verified by process of elimination. For example, we know by Lemma 5.2.20 that $Cpo_{\perp}$ has fixed points, and Exercise 7.2.10 shows that $Cpo_{\perp}$ has coproducts. Therefore, $Cpo_{\perp}$ cannot be cartesian closed. For *Cppo*, we again have fixed points by Lemma 5.2.20, and can see that *Cppo* is cartesian closed since the terminal object (one-element CPO) of *Cpo* is pointed, and product and function space constructions preserve pointedness.

The collection of cartesian closed categories forms a category. More precisely, the category CCC is the category whose objects are cartesian closed categories and morphisms are functors preserving cartesian closed structure. The morphisms of CCC are called *cartesian closed functors,* sometimes abbreviated to *cc-functors.* Another name for these functors that appears in the literature is *representation of cartesian closed category.* Since *unit*, $\times$, $\rightarrow$, and associated maps are specified as part of each CCC, we require that cc-functors preserve these. In more detail, if $\mathcal{C}$ and $\mathcal{D}$ are CCC's, then a functor $F\colon \mathcal{C} \rightarrow \mathcal{D}$ is a cc-functor if $F(unit_{\mathcal{C}}) = unit_{\mathcal{D}}$, $F(a \times b) = F(a) \times F(b)$, and similarly for function spaces. In addition, we require $F(\mathbf{One}^{a}) = \mathbf{One}^{F(a)}$, $F(\mathbf{Proj}_i^{a,b}) = \mathbf{Proj}_i^{F(a),F(b)}$, $F(\mathbf{App}^{a,b}) = \mathbf{App}^{F(a),F(b)}$, and the operations $\langle\ \rangle$, and **Curry** must be preserved. For **Curry**, for example, this means that $F(\mathbf{Curry}^{a,b,c}(g)) = \mathbf{Curry}^{F(a),F(b),F(c)}(F(g))$.

In the remainder of this section, we prove two useful identities that hold in all cartesian closed categories. They are

$$\langle f, g\rangle \circ h = \langle f \circ h, g \circ h\rangle$$

$$\mathbf{Curry}(f) \circ h = \mathbf{Curry}(f \circ (h \times id))$$

where $f\colon c \longrightarrow a$, $g\colon c \longrightarrow b$ and $h\colon d \longrightarrow c$ in the first equation and $f\colon a \times b \longrightarrow c$ and $h\colon d \longrightarrow a$ in the second. These equations, which are part of the "naturality conditions" associated with the first definition, may be proved using either the equations given in the second definition or the diagrams given in the third definition. To give an example of reasoning with pictures, we will prove these using diagrams.

The first equation may be proved using the diagram

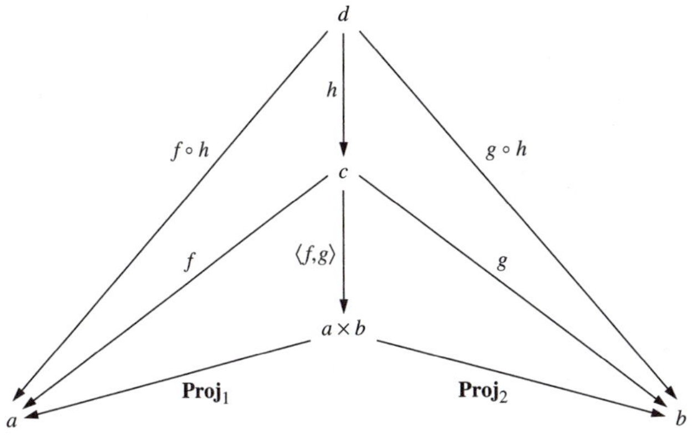

which is obtained from the "defining diagram" for $\langle f, g\rangle$ by adding an arrow h into c at the top of the picture and drawing both of the compositions with h that appear in the equation. Ignoring the two arrows for f and g, we have a triangle of the form that appears in the third definition of CCC, and in the definition of product object from the previous section. The conditions on this diagram are that for every pair of outside arrows, in this case $f \circ h$ and $g \circ h$, there is a unique arrow, $\langle f \circ h, g \circ h\rangle$, from d into $a \times b$ that commutes with the projection functions. But since the arrow $\langle f, g\rangle \circ h$, appearing as a path from d to $a \times b$ in this picture, also commutes with $f \circ h$, $g \circ h$ and the projection functions, it must be that $\langle f, g\rangle \circ h = \langle f \circ h, g \circ h\rangle$.

The second equation is proved by similar reasoning, using the diagram

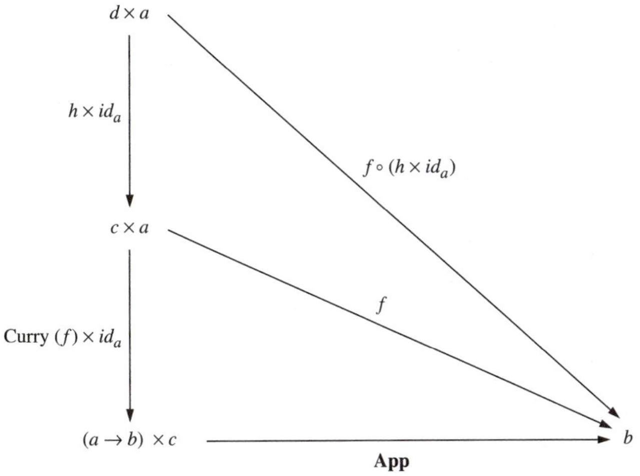

obtained by assuming an arrow $h: d \longrightarrow c$ and putting $h \times id_a$ at the top of the "defining diagram" for function objects. Here the composition of $h \times id$ with f forms the hypotenuse of the new (larger) right triangle. The defining condition for function objects says that given $f \circ (h \times id)$ and **App**, the unique arrow $k: d \longrightarrow (a \rightarrow b)$ such that $k \times id$ forms a commuting (larger) triangle is $k = \mathbf{Curry}(f \circ (h \times id))$. But since

$$(\mathbf{Curry}(f) \times id) \circ (h \times id) = (\mathbf{Curry}(f) \circ h) \times id$$

also forms a commuting triangle, we must have $\mathbf{Curry}(f) \circ h = \mathbf{Curry}(f \circ (h \times id))$ (see Exercise 7.2.20).

Exercise 7.2.20 Show that the following implications hold in every CCC, assuming each arrow has an appropriate domain and codomain.

(a) If $f \circ \mathbf{Proj}_1 = g \circ \mathbf{Proj}_1$, then $f = g$. (And similarly if $f \circ \mathbf{Proj}_2 = g \circ \mathbf{Proj}_2$.)

(b) If $(f \times id) \circ (g \times id) = (h \times id)$, then $f \circ g = h$. (*Hint:* Begin by writing $k \times id$ as $\langle k \circ \mathbf{Proj}_1, \mathbf{Proj}_2 \rangle$.)

Exercise 7.2.21 Show that the second and third definitions of CCC are equivalent and that either of these implies the isomorphisms given in the first definition of CCC.

Exercise 7.2.22 The product of two CCC's, in CCC, is the ordinary product of two categories. Show that CCC has function objects.

Exercise 7.2.23 The category $\mathcal{C}_{\mathcal{A}}$ derived from a Henkin model $\mathcal{A}$ is described in Examples 7.2.5 7.2.16. Show that for any $\lambda^{unit,\times,\rightarrow}$ Henkin model $\mathcal{A}$, the category $\mathcal{C}_{\mathcal{A}}$ is cartesian closed, using the second definition of CCC.

Exercise 7.2.24 Show that for any $\lambda^{unit,\times,\rightarrow}$ signature Σ and theory $\mathcal{E}$ between Σ-terms, the category $\mathcal{C}(\mathcal{E})$ generated by $\mathcal{E}$ is cartesian closed. This category is described in Example 7.2.19. First write out the conditions you must check, such as if $f: \sigma \rightarrow unit$ in $\mathcal{C}(\mathcal{E})$ then $f = \mathbf{One}^{\sigma}$. Then verify each condition.

Exercise 7.2.25 Adjoint situations occur commonly in mathematics and may be used to define terminal object, cartesian product, and function object succinctly. While there are several ways to define adjoint situations, the simplest and easiest to remember uses the *comma category* construction. If $\mathcal{A}$, $\mathcal{B}$ and $\mathcal{C}$ are categories, with functors $\mathcal{F}: \mathcal{A} \longrightarrow \mathcal{B}$ and $\mathcal{G}: \mathcal{C} \longrightarrow \mathcal{B}$, then the comma category $(\mathcal{F} \downarrow \mathcal{G})$ is defined as follows. (The original notation was $(\mathcal{F}, \mathcal{G})$ instead of $(\mathcal{F} \downarrow \mathcal{G})$.) The objects of $(\mathcal{F} \downarrow \mathcal{G})$ are triples $\langle a, h, c \rangle$ where a is an object of $\mathcal{A}$, c is an object of $\mathcal{C}$, and $h: F(a) \longrightarrow G(c)$ is a morphism of $\mathcal{B}$. A morphism $\langle a, h, c \rangle \longrightarrow \langle a', h', c' \rangle$ in $(\mathcal{F} \downarrow \mathcal{G})$ is pair of morphisms $\langle f, g \rangle$ with $f: a \longrightarrow a'$ in $\mathcal{A}$ and

$g\colon c \longrightarrow c'$ in $\mathcal{C}$ such that

$$\begin{array}{ccc}
F(a) & \xrightarrow{\quad F(f) \quad} & F(a') \\
{\scriptstyle h}\downarrow & & \downarrow{\scriptstyle h'} \\
G(c) & \xrightarrow[\quad G(g) \quad]{} & G(c')
\end{array}$$

A useful convention is to use the name of a category as the name of the identity functor on it. For example, we will use $\mathcal{A}$ as the name of the identity functor $\mathcal{A} : \mathcal{A} \longrightarrow \mathcal{A}$.

Using comma categories and the notation above, an *adjoint situation* consists of two categories, $\mathcal{A}$ and $\mathcal{B}$, two functors $\mathcal{F}\colon \mathcal{A} \longrightarrow \mathcal{B}$ and $\mathcal{U}\colon \mathcal{B} \longrightarrow \mathcal{A}$, and a functor $\mathcal{Q}\colon (\mathcal{F} \downarrow \mathcal{B}) \longrightarrow (\mathcal{A} \downarrow \mathcal{U})$ with inverse $\mathcal{Q}^{-1}$ such that

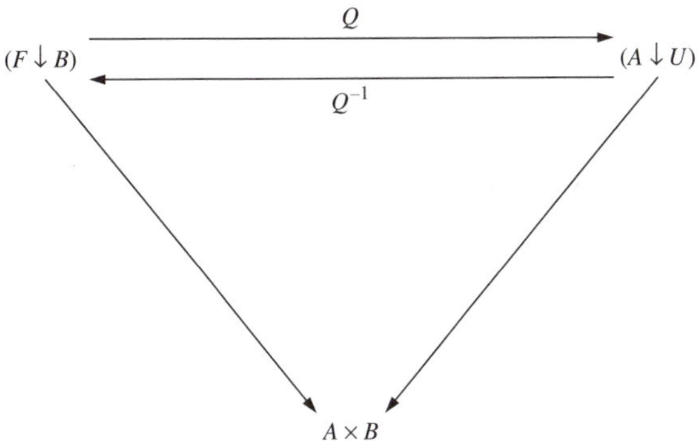

where the arrows into the product category $\mathcal{A} \times \mathcal{B}$ are the projections mapping an object $\langle a, h, b\rangle$ of either comma category to $\langle a, b\rangle$ and morphism $\langle f, g\rangle$ to $\langle f, g\rangle$. The functors into $\mathcal{A} \times \mathcal{B}$ force $\mathcal{Q}$ to map an object $\langle a, h, b\rangle$ of $(\mathcal{F} \downarrow \mathcal{B})$ to an object $\langle a, j, b\rangle$ with the same first and last components, and similarly for $\mathcal{Q}^{-1}$. When such an adjoint situation exists, F is called the *left adjoint* of U and U the *right adjoint* of F. The names "F" and "U" come from the traditional examples in algebra where $F(a)$ produces the *free* algebra over a, and $U(b)$ returns the *underlying* set of the algebra b.

(a) The terminal category $\mathcal{T}$ has one object, $*$, and one morphism, id_*. A category $\mathcal{C}$ *has a terminal object* iff the functor $\mathcal{F}\colon \mathcal{C} \longrightarrow \mathcal{T}$ (there is only one possible functor) has a right adjoint U. Show that $\mathcal{Q} : (\mathcal{F} \downarrow \mathcal{T}) \cong (\mathcal{C} \downarrow \mathcal{U})$ with inverse $\mathcal{Q}^{-1}$ gives an isomorphism of hom-sets $\mathcal{T}(*, *) \cong \mathcal{C}(c, U(*))$ for every object c of $\mathcal{C}$. Define a terminal object of $\mathcal{C}$ and morphism $\mathbf{One}^c$ from $\mathcal{T}$ and the functors involved in this adjoint situation and show that they have the properties required in either the second or third definition of CCC.

(b) A category $\mathcal{C}$ has products if there is a right adjoint $\mathcal{U}$ to the *diagonal functor* $\Delta: \mathcal{C} \longrightarrow \mathcal{C} \times \mathcal{C}$ mapping object c to $\langle c, c\rangle$ and similarly morphism f to $\langle f, f\rangle$. Show how such an adjoint situation gives an isomorphism of hom-sets $\mathcal{C}(a, b) \times \mathcal{C}(a, c) \cong \mathcal{C}(a, b \times c)$ for any objects a, b and c of $\mathcal{C}$. Define pairing, projection morphisms (as in the second and third definitions of CCC) and the product functor $\mathcal{C} \times \mathcal{C} \longrightarrow \mathcal{C}$ from the functors involved in this adjoint situation and show that they have the required properties.

(c) Assuming a category $\mathcal{C}$ has products, which we will write in the usual way, $\mathcal{C}$ has function spaces if, for every object b of $\mathcal{C}$, there is a right adjoint to the the functor $F_b: \mathcal{C} \longrightarrow \mathcal{C}$ with $F(a) = a \times b$. Show how such an adjoint situation gives an isomorphism of hom-sets $\mathcal{C}(a \times b, c) \cong \mathcal{C}(a, b \to c)$ for any objects a and c of $\mathcal{C}$. Define currying and application morphism (as in the second and third definitions of CCC) and the function space functor $\mathcal{C} \longrightarrow \mathcal{C}$ mapping c to $b \to c$ from the functors involved in this adjoint situation and show that they have the required properties. Note that the problem only asks for a covariant functor mapping c to $b \to c$, not a full contra/covariant functor mapping b and c to $b \to c$.

7.2.4 Soundness and the Interpretation of Terms

We may interpret $\lambda^{unit,\times,\to}$ terms over any signature in any CCC, once we have chosen an object of the category for each type constant and a morphism for each term constant. More specifically, given some $\lambda^{unit,\times,\to}$ signature Σ, and an object for type constant, we use *unit* and object maps $\times$ and $\to$ to interpret each $\lambda^{unit,\times,\to}$ type expression as some object of the category. Writing $[\![\sigma]\!]$ for the object named by type expression σ, we must also choose, for each term constant $c: \sigma$ of Σ, an arrow $\hat{c}: unit \to [\![\sigma]\!]$. We will call a CCC, together with interpretations for type constants and term constants from Σ, a Σ-*CCC*. This is similar to the terminology we use for algebra in Chapter 3, where we refer to an algebra with an interpretation for symbols from algebraic signature Σ as a Σ-algebra.

Although the interpretation of type expressions as objects of a CCC may be clear from the brief description in the preceding paragraph, we give a full inductive definition to eliminate any confusion. Given a $\lambda^{unit,\times,\to}$ signature Σ and Σ-CCC $\mathcal{C}$, we define the interpretation $\mathcal{C}[\![\sigma]\!]$ of type expression σ over Σ in CCC $\mathcal{C}$ as follows.

$$\begin{aligned}
\mathcal{C}[\![unit]\!] &= unit,\\
\mathcal{C}[\![b]\!] &= \hat{b}, \text{ given as part of the } \Sigma\text{-CCC } \mathcal{C},\\
\mathcal{C}[\![\sigma \times \tau]\!] &= \mathcal{C}[\![\sigma]\!] \times \mathcal{C}[\![\tau]\!],\\
\mathcal{C}[\![\sigma \to \tau]\!] &= \mathcal{C}[\![\sigma]\!] \to \mathcal{C}[\![\tau]\!].
\end{aligned}$$

As with other interpretation functions, we often omit the name of the category, writing $[\![\sigma]\!]$

instead of $\mathcal{C}[\![\sigma]\!]$ when the category $\mathcal{C}$ is clear from context. It is also sometimes convenient to omit the double brackets and use type expressions as names for objects of the category.

If $\Gamma \triangleright M\colon\sigma$ is a typed $\lambda^{unit,\times,\rightarrow}$ term, then the interpretation of this term in $\mathcal{C}$ will be an arrow from the types of its free variables to the semantic type of the term, $[\![\sigma]\!]$. This is analogous to the Henkin-model meaning of a term as a map from environments, which give the values of the free variables, to the semantic type of the term. One way of making "the type of the free variables" precise is to write the term with only one free variable, using cartesian products. More precisely, if $\Gamma = \{x_1\colon\sigma_1, \ldots, x_k\colon\sigma_k\}$, we may transform a term $\Gamma \triangleright M\colon\sigma$ into an essentially equivalent term $y\colon(\sigma_1 \times \ldots \times \sigma_k) \triangleright M'\colon\sigma$, where M' is obtained from M by replacing each free variable x_i by the appropriate combination of projection functions applied to y. This approach has been used to some extent in the literature. Instead of following it here, we will give a direct interpretation of arbitrary terms that has exactly the same result.

We formalize "the type of the free variables" of a term by interpreting each typing context as an object. The interpretation $\mathcal{C}[\![\Gamma]\!]$ of typing context Γ is defined by induction on the length of the context:

$$\mathcal{C}[\![\emptyset]\!] = unit,$$

$$\mathcal{C}[\![\Gamma, x\colon\sigma]\!] = \mathcal{C}[\![\Gamma]\!] \times \mathcal{C}[\![\sigma]\!].$$

It is easy to see that if $\Gamma = \{x_1\colon\sigma_1, \ldots, x_k\colon\sigma_k\}$, then $[\![\Gamma]\!] = unit \times [\![\sigma_1]\!] \times \ldots \times [\![\sigma_k]\!]$, with $\times$ associated to the left. This is the opposite of the way we associated products in Section 2.5.1; the reason is that the interpretation of lambda abstraction works out more easily this way. While it might seem more natural to let $[\![\Gamma]\!] = [\![\sigma_1]\!] \times \ldots \times [\![\sigma_k]\!]$, the use of *unit* avoids some special cases in the interpretation of terms. Since $a \times unit \cong a$, for any object a in a category with products and a terminal type (see Exercise 7.2.10), there is no harm in including *unit* in the interpretation of contexts.

A technical complication is that our contexts are sets of associations between term variables and types, not ordered sequences. However, the interpretation given above depends on the order in which we write a context. As a consequence, the meaning function on contexts is not well-defined, strictly speaking. The simplest repair is to reformulate the syntax of typed lambda terms so that contexts are sequences instead of sets. Other than interpreting the contexts in all of the typing rules as ordered sequences instead of sets, the only change is to rewrite the *(add var)* rule in a more general form that allows a variable to be added anywhere in the context,

$$\frac{\Gamma_1, \Gamma_2 \triangleright M\colon\sigma}{\Gamma_1, x\colon\tau, \Gamma_2 \triangleright M\colon\sigma}. \qquad \textit{(add var)}$$

It is easy to see that if contexts are unordered sets, then this is equivalent to the earlier form of the rule. In the remainder of this section, we will assume that lambda terms are typed using ordered type assignments and that typing derivations may use the more general form of (*add var*) rule given here. It is shown in Exercise 7.2.33 that this does not change the set of typable terms.

We will characterize the semantic effect of permuting variables or dropping unnecessary ones from a typing context using injective functions on natural numbers. (Similar but slightly different techniques are used in [Koy82, Gun92].) For natural numbers m and n, we say f is an *m, n-function* if f is a one-to-one function

$$f\colon \{1, \ldots, m\} \to \{1, \ldots, n\}.$$

In the special case that $m = n$, the m, n-functions are exactly the permutations on n elements. If f is an m, n-function and $\Gamma = x_1\colon\sigma_1, \ldots, x_n\colon\sigma_n$ is an ordered type assignment of length n, we define the ordered type assignment Γ_f of length m by

$$\Gamma_f = x_{f(1)}\colon\sigma_{f(1)},\ \ldots,\ x_{f(m)}\colon\sigma_{f(m)}.$$

If $\Gamma \triangleright M\colon\sigma$ is a well-typed term, and Γ_f contains all of the free variables of M, then we can relate the meaning of $\Gamma_f \triangleright M\colon\sigma$ to the meaning of $\Gamma \triangleright M\colon\sigma$ using a combination of pairing and projection functions. Intuitively, the function

$$\chi_f^{[\![\Gamma]\!]} : [\![\Gamma]\!] \longrightarrow [\![\Gamma_f]\!]$$

reorganizes a tuple so that the $f(i)$ component of the argument becomes the ith component of the result. We need a few notational conventions to write this out directly. If $h_i\colon a \longrightarrow a_i$ is a morphism from object a to a_i, for $1 \le i \le n$, then we will write $\langle h_1, \ldots, h_n\rangle$ for the morphism

$$\begin{aligned}\langle h_1, \ldots, h_n\rangle &= \langle\langle\langle h_1,\ h_2\rangle,\ h3\rangle \ldots\rangle \\ &\quad\ \colon a \longrightarrow (((a_1 \times a_2) \times a_3)\ \ldots)\end{aligned}$$

and write

$$\mathbf{Proj}_i^{a_1 \times \ldots \times a_n} : a_1 \times \ldots \times a_n \longrightarrow a_i$$

for the appropriate composition of $\mathbf{Proj}_1^{b,c}$ and $\mathbf{Proj}_2^{b,c}$ projection morphisms so that

$$\mathbf{Proj}_i^{a_1 \times \ldots \times a_n} \circ \langle h_1, \ldots, h_n\rangle \ = \ h_i.$$

(Further details appear in Exercise 7.2.34.) If f is an m, n-function, then we may define $\chi_f^{unit \times a_1 \times \ldots \times a_n}$ by

$$\chi_f^{unit \times a_1 \times \ldots \times a_n} = \langle \mathbf{One}^{unit \times a_1 \times \ldots \times a_n}, \mathbf{Proj}_{f(1)+1}^{unit \times a_1 \times \ldots \times a_n}, \ldots, \mathbf{Proj}_{f(m)+1}^{unit \times a_1 \times \ldots \times a_n} \rangle$$

$$: unit \times a_1 \times \ldots \times a_n \longrightarrow unit \times a_{f(1)} \times \ldots \times a_{f(m)}.$$

The reason we include *unit* in the type of χ_f is so that $\chi_f^{[\![\Gamma]\!]} : [\![\Gamma]\!] \longrightarrow [\![\Gamma_f]\!]$. We will use functions of this form in defining the meaning of terms and in subsequent lemmas about the meaning function.

The meaning $\mathcal{C}[\![\Gamma \triangleright M\colon \tau]\!]$ of a well-typed term is a morphism from $\mathcal{C}[\![\Gamma]\!]$ to $\mathcal{C}[\![\sigma]\!]$, defined by induction on the proof of the typing judgement $\Gamma \triangleright M\colon \tau$. This is given using the pairing, projection, application, and currying operations that appear in the second and third definitions of cartesian closed category. The clause for (*add var*), which appears last, uses a function $\chi_f^{[\![\Gamma_1, x:\sigma, \Gamma_2]\!]}$ of the form defined above. For notational simplicity, we omit $\mathcal{C}[\![\ ]\!]$ from types, writing type expressions as names of objects of $\mathcal{C}$.

$$\mathcal{C}[\![x\colon \sigma \triangleright x\colon \sigma]\!] = \mathbf{Proj}_2^{unit,\sigma}$$

$$\mathcal{C}[\![\emptyset \triangleright *\colon unit]\!] = \mathbf{One}^{unit}$$

$$\mathcal{C}[\![\emptyset \triangleright c\colon \sigma]\!] = \hat{c} \text{ where } \hat{c}\colon unit \longrightarrow [\![\sigma]\!] \text{ is given}$$

$$\mathcal{C}[\![\Gamma \triangleright \mathbf{Proj}_1^{\sigma,\tau} M\colon \sigma]\!] = \mathbf{Proj}_1^{\sigma,\tau} \circ \mathcal{C}[\![\Gamma \triangleright M\colon \sigma \times \tau]\!]$$

$$\mathcal{C}[\![\Gamma \triangleright \mathbf{Proj}_2^{\sigma,\tau} M\colon \tau]\!] = \mathbf{Proj}_2^{\sigma,\tau} \circ \mathcal{C}[\![\Gamma \triangleright M\colon \sigma \times \tau]\!]$$

$$\mathcal{C}[\![\Gamma \triangleright \langle M, N\rangle\colon \sigma \times \tau]\!] = \langle \mathcal{C}[\![\Gamma \triangleright M\colon \sigma]\!], \mathcal{C}[\![\Gamma \triangleright N\colon \tau]\!]\rangle$$

$$\mathcal{C}[\![\Gamma \triangleright MN\colon \tau]\!] = \mathbf{App}^{\sigma,\tau} \circ \langle \mathcal{C}[\![\Gamma \triangleright M\colon \sigma \to \tau]\!], \mathcal{C}[\![\Gamma \triangleright N\colon \sigma]\!]\rangle$$

$$\mathcal{C}[\![\Gamma \triangleright \lambda x\colon \sigma.M\colon \sigma \to \tau]\!] = \mathbf{Curry}\,(\mathcal{C}[\![\Gamma, x\colon \sigma \triangleright M\colon \tau]\!])$$

$$\mathcal{C}[\![\Gamma_1, x\colon \sigma, \Gamma_2 \triangleright M\colon \tau]\!] = \mathcal{C}[\![\Gamma_1, \Gamma_2 \triangleright M\colon \tau]\!] \circ \chi_f^{[\![\Gamma_1, x:\sigma, \Gamma_2]\!]} \text{ where } f \text{ is the } n, (n+1)\text{-function such that } (\Gamma_1, x\colon \sigma, \Gamma_2)_f = \Gamma_1, \Gamma_2$$

This interpretation of terms should seem at least superficially natural, since each term is interpreted using the part of the CCC that is intended for this purpose. For example, we have a terminal object so that we can interpret $*$, and the morphisms associated with a terminal object are indeed used to interpret $*$. Similarly, $\mathbf{Proj}_i$ and $\langle\ ,\ \rangle$ are associated with product objects, and these are used directly to interpret term forms associated with product types. While one might expect the interpretation of a variable $x\colon \sigma \triangleright x\colon \sigma$ to be the identity morphism, a morphism $unit \times \sigma \longrightarrow \sigma$ is used instead since the interpretation of context $x\colon \sigma$ is $unit \times \sigma$. Perhaps the most interesting aspect of this interpretation of terms is that lambda abstraction is interpreted as Currying. This makes intuitive sense if we remember that we form $\Gamma \triangleright \lambda x{:}\,\sigma.\, M$ from $\Gamma, x{:}\,\sigma \triangleright M$. If we view M as a function of $\Gamma, x{:}\,\sigma$, the domain of this function is $[\![\Gamma]\!] \times [\![\sigma]\!]$. When we change x from a free to a lambda-bound variable, we obtain a term whose meaning depends only on $[\![\Gamma]\!]$ and, for any values for the free variables, determines a function from $[\![\sigma]\!]$ to the type of M. Thus the passage from $\Gamma, x{:}\,\sigma \triangleright M$ to $\Gamma \triangleright \lambda x{:}\,\sigma.\, M$ is exactly Currying. The clause for (*add var*) is discussed below.

It is a worthwhile exercise to check that for every typable term, we have

$$[\![\Gamma \triangleright M{:}\,\sigma]\!] \quad : \quad [\![\Gamma]\!] \longrightarrow [\![\sigma]\!].$$

In words, the meaning of a term $\Gamma \triangleright M{:}\,\sigma$ in a cartesian closed category is a morphism from $[\![\Gamma]\!]$ to $[\![\sigma]\!]$. We have already seen, in Examples 7.2.5 and 7.2.16, that every Henkin model $\mathcal{A}$ determines a cartesian closed category $\mathcal{C}_{\mathcal{A}}$. It is shown in Exercise 7.2.38 that the meaning of a term $x_1{:}\,\sigma_1, \ldots, x_k{:}\,\sigma_k \triangleright M{:}\,\sigma$ in the cartesian closed category $\mathcal{C}_{\mathcal{A}}$, determined according to the definition above, corresponds to the meaning of the closed term $\lambda\langle z{:}\,unit, x_1{:}\,\sigma_1, \ldots, x_k{:}\,\sigma_k\rangle.\, M$ in the Henkin model $\mathcal{A}$.

Unlike the Henkin model interpretation of (*add var*), the CCC interpretation of this typing rule is nontrivial. The reason is that this rule changes the context, and therefore changes the "type" of the meaning of the term. Intuitively, since a new variable added to a context must not appear free in the term, the meaning of $\Gamma_1, x{:}\,\sigma, \Gamma_2 \triangleright M{:}\,\tau$ is obtained by composing the meaning of $\Gamma_1, \Gamma_2 \triangleright M{:}\,\tau$ with a combination of projection functions that "throw away" the value of free variable x and keep the values of the variables listed in Γ_1, Γ_2. A special case of the clause above (see Exercise 7.2.34) is

$$\mathcal{C}[\![\Gamma, x{:}\,\sigma \triangleright M{:}\,\tau]\!] = \mathcal{C}[\![\Gamma \triangleright M{:}\,\tau]\!] \circ \mathbf{Proj}_1^{[\![\Gamma]\!], \sigma}.$$

We give some intuition for the interpretation of (*add var*), using this special case, in the following example.

Example 7.2.26 As stated in Lemma 7.2.29 below, the meaning of a constant satisfies the condition

$$[\![\Gamma \triangleright c{:}\,\tau]\!] = \hat{c} \circ \mathbf{One}^{[\![\Gamma]\!]}$$

where $\hat{c}{:}\,unit \longrightarrow [\![\tau]\!]$ is given as part of the Σ-CCC. Intuitively, since the meaning of a constant does not depend on the values of any variables, we compose the map $\hat{c}{:}\,unit \longrightarrow [\![\tau]\!]$ with some constant function $\mathbf{One}^{[\![\Gamma]\!]}{:}\,[\![\Gamma]\!] \longrightarrow unit$ that does not depend on the value of type $[\![\Gamma]\!]$. We will work out a typical example with $\Gamma = \{x{:}\,\sigma,\ y{:}\,\rho\}$.

The only way to prove the typing assertion $\Gamma \triangleright c{:}\,\tau$, using our typing rules, is to begin with $\emptyset \triangleright c{:}\,\tau$ and use (*add var*) twice. Let us assume we derive $x{:}\,\sigma \triangleright c{:}\,\tau$ first, and then

$x\colon\sigma,\ y\colon\rho \rhd c\colon\tau$. The meaning of the term in a CCC is

$$
\begin{aligned}
[\![x\colon\sigma,\ y\colon\rho \rhd c\colon\tau]\!] &= [\![x\colon\sigma \rhd c\colon\tau]\!] \circ \mathbf{Proj}_1^{unit\times\sigma,\ \rho} \\
&= ([\![\emptyset \rhd c\colon\tau]\!] \circ \mathbf{Proj}_1^{unit,\ \sigma}) \circ \mathbf{Proj}_1^{unit\times\sigma,\ \rho} \\
&= (\hat{c} \circ \mathbf{Proj}_1^{unit,\ \sigma}) \circ \mathbf{Proj}_1^{unit\times\sigma,\ \rho}
\end{aligned}
$$

By the associativity of composition, we can write this as $\hat{c} \circ (\mathbf{Proj}_1^{unit,\ \sigma} \circ \mathbf{Proj}_1^{unit\times\sigma,\ \rho})$, where

$$\mathbf{Proj}_1^{unit,\ \sigma} \circ \mathbf{Proj}_1^{unit\times\sigma,\ \rho} \ = \ \mathbf{One}^{(unit\times\sigma)\times\rho} : (unit \times \sigma) \times \rho \longrightarrow unit$$

since the definition of CCC guarantees that there is only one arrow from $(unit \times \sigma) \times \rho$ to $unit$. ∎

Example 7.2.27 The term $\lambda x\colon\sigma \to \tau.\,\lambda y\colon\sigma.\,xy$ is one of the simplest that requires all but the typing rule for constants. We will work out its meaning and see that it is equal to the lambda term for the identity. Working out the meaning of each subterm, we have the following calculation.

$$
\begin{aligned}
&[\![\emptyset \rhd \lambda x\colon\sigma \to \tau.\,\lambda y\colon\sigma.\,xy]\!] = \mathbf{Curry}\,(\,\mathbf{Curry}\,(\,[\![x\colon\sigma \to \tau,\ y\colon\sigma \rhd xy\colon\tau]\!]\,)\,) \\
&[\![x\colon\sigma \to \tau,\ y\colon\sigma \rhd xy\colon\tau]\!] \quad = \mathbf{App}^{\sigma,\tau} \circ \langle [\![x\colon\sigma \to \tau,\ y\colon\sigma \rhd x]\!],\ [\![x\colon\sigma \to \tau,\ y\colon\sigma \rhd y]\!]\rangle \\
&[\![x\colon\sigma \to \tau,\ y\colon\sigma \rhd x]\!] \quad = [\![x\colon\sigma \to \tau \rhd x]\!] \circ \mathbf{Proj}_1^{(unit\times\sigma\to\tau),\sigma} \\
&\qquad = \mathbf{Proj}_2^{unit,\sigma\to\tau} \circ \mathbf{Proj}_1^{(unit\times\sigma\to\tau),\sigma} \\
&\qquad : \ (unit \times \sigma \to \tau) \times \sigma \longrightarrow (\sigma \to \tau) \\
&[\![x\colon\sigma \to \tau,\ y\colon\tau \rhd y]\!] \quad = \mathbf{Proj}_2^{(unit\times\sigma\to\tau),\sigma} \\
&\qquad : \ (unit \times \sigma \to \tau) \times \sigma \longrightarrow \sigma
\end{aligned}
$$

This gives us the final result

$$\mathbf{Curry}\,(\,\mathbf{Curry}\,(\,\mathbf{App}^{\sigma,\tau} \circ \langle \mathbf{Proj}_2^{unit,\sigma\to\tau} \circ \mathbf{Proj}_1^{(unit\times\sigma\to\tau),\sigma},\ \mathbf{Proj}_2^{(unit\times\sigma\to\tau),\sigma}\rangle\,)\,)$$

If we recognize that sequences of projection functions are used to give the meaning of a variable, as a function of the tuple of variables in the typing context, then we can begin to recognize the form of the term from its interpretation. Specifically, from the way the meaning of the term is written, we can see that the term must have the form

λ*–abstraction* (λ*–abstraction* (*application* ⟨*variable*, *variable*⟩)).

Intuitively, the direct correspondence between the interpretation of a term, expressed using the basic operations given as part of a CCC, and the lambda calculus syntax, demonstrates the close connection between the two systems. It is interesting to note that unlike the Henkin model meaning of a term, the variable names never appear in the calculation. This makes it easy to see that α-conversion does not change the meaning of a term.

We can compare the term above with $\emptyset \triangleright \lambda x\colon \sigma \to \tau .\, x$, whose meaning in a CCC is directly calculated as

$$\begin{aligned}
[\![\emptyset \triangleright \lambda x\colon \sigma \to \tau .\, x]\!] &= \mathbf{Curry}\,(\,[\![x\colon \sigma \to \tau \triangleright x\colon \sigma \to \tau]\!]\,) \\
&= \mathbf{Curry}\,(\,\mathbf{Proj}_2^{unit, \sigma \to \tau}\,) \\
&: \ unit \longrightarrow ((\sigma \to \tau) \to (\sigma \to \tau))
\end{aligned}$$

These two meanings are in fact the same morphism, which may be easily verified using the equations given in the second definition of CCC. Specifically, this is an immediate consequence of the equation

$$\mathbf{Curry}(\mathbf{App} \circ \langle k \circ \mathbf{Proj}_1, \mathbf{Proj}_2 \rangle) = k$$

which may be regarded as stating the soundness of η-conversion in a CCC. (The other equation associated with with function objects in the second definition of CCC similarly ensures soundness of β-conversion.) ■

It is worth noting that in defining the meaning of a term in a CCC, we do not need an extra condition, such as in the environment model condition for Henkin models, stating that every typed term must have a meaning. In essence, the definition of CCC is similar to the combinatory form of Henkin model definition. A CCC is required to have a set of operations which, together, allow us to interpret each term. In fact, we may regard the basic operations **One**, $\langle \cdot , \cdot \rangle$, $\mathbf{Proj}_i$, **Curry**, and **App** as an alternate set of combinators for typed lambda calculus, with the translation of lambda terms into combinators given by the meaning function above. The use of these *categorical combinators* is explored in [Cur86] and the references given there.

As shown in Exercise 7.2.38, every Henkin model can be regarded as a CCC, with the two meaning functions giving the same interpretation of terms. Therefore, CCC's may be regarded as a generalization of Henkin models. (Further discussion appears in Section 7.2.5.)

Since we have generalized the semantics of lambda terms, we must reprove the basic facts about the meanings of terms, such as the substitution lemma and fact that the meaning of term depends only on its free variables. Many of these are routine, often using essentially the same arguments as we used for Henkin models in Chapter 4. An important property that is *not* routinely proved by essentially the same argument is the *coherence* of the meaning function for CCC's. Specifically, we must show that for any term $\Gamma \triangleright M\colon\sigma$, the meanings we obtain using different proofs of the typing assertion $\Gamma \triangleright M\colon\sigma$ are all identical. The reason why this is more complicated for CCC's than for Henkin models is that we have used relatively complicated sequences of projection functions to correctly account for the dependence of a variable on the typing context.

Example 7.2.28 We can see the importance of coherence by working out the interpretation of $y\colon\sigma \triangleright (\lambda x\colon\sigma.\,x)y\colon\sigma$ and comparing it to the β-equivalent term $y\colon\sigma \triangleright y\colon\sigma$.

$$[\![y\colon\sigma \triangleright (\lambda x\colon\sigma.\,x)y]\!] = \mathbf{App} \circ \langle [\![y\colon\sigma \triangleright \lambda x\colon\sigma.\,x]\!],\ [\![y\colon\sigma \triangleright y]\!]\rangle$$

$$[\![y\colon\sigma \triangleright y]\!] = \mathbf{Proj}_2^{unit,\sigma}$$

$$:\ unit \times \sigma \longrightarrow \sigma$$

There are two ways we might calculate the meaning of $y\colon\sigma \triangleright \lambda x\colon\sigma.\,x$, the first is to assume that this term is typed by adding $y\colon\sigma$ to the closed term $\lambda x\colon\sigma.\,x$ with no free variables. The second involves adding the variable y to the context before doing the lambda abstraction. We work both of these out below.

$$[\![y\colon\sigma \triangleright \lambda x\colon\sigma.\,x]\!] = [\![\emptyset \triangleright \lambda x\colon\sigma.\,x]\!] \circ \mathbf{Proj}_1^{unit,\sigma}$$

$$= \mathbf{Curry}(\mathbf{Proj}_2^{unit,\sigma}) \circ \mathbf{Proj}_1^{unit,\sigma}$$

$$:\ unit \times \sigma \longrightarrow (\sigma \to \sigma)$$

$$[\![y\colon\sigma \triangleright \lambda x\colon\sigma.\,x]\!] = \mathbf{Curry}([\![y\colon\sigma,\, x\colon\sigma \triangleright x]\!])$$

$$= \mathbf{Curry}(\mathbf{Proj}_2^{unit\times\sigma,\sigma})$$

If we use the first, then the interpretation of the original term is written

$$[\![y\colon\sigma \triangleright (\lambda x\colon\sigma.\,x)y]\!] = \mathbf{App} \circ \langle \mathbf{Curry}(\mathbf{Proj}_2^{unit,\sigma}) \circ \mathbf{Proj}_1^{unit,\sigma},\ \mathbf{Proj}_2^{unit,\sigma}\rangle$$

which is equal to $\mathbf{Proj}_2^{unit,\sigma}$ by the general equation $\mathbf{App} \circ \langle \mathbf{Curry}(h) \circ \mathbf{Proj}_1, \mathbf{Proj}_2\rangle = h$ given in the second definition of CCC. Thus this part of the definition of CCC corresponds directly to the soundness of β-conversion. The reader may verify that the second interpretation of the subterm $y\colon\sigma \triangleright \lambda x\colon\sigma.\,x$ is equal to the first in Exercise 7.2.35. ■

Rather than prove coherence directly, we will prove simultaneously that the meaning of a term does not depend on which typing derivation we use and that permuting or dropping unnecessary variables from the typing context changes the meaning in a predictable way. By characterizing the effect of permutation, we will be able to treat typing contexts in equations as unordered. This allows us to continue to use unordered typing contexts in the equational proof system. In addition, we will use properties of permuting or dropping variables in the coherence proof.

Lemma 7.2.29 Let $\mathcal{C}$ be a Σ-CCC. The meaning function $\mathcal{C}[\![\ ]\!]$ on typed terms over signature Σ has the following properties:

(i) For any m, n-function f, and ordered type assignment $\Gamma = x_1{:}\,\sigma_1, \ldots, x_n{:}\,\sigma_n$ of length n such that $\Gamma \rhd M{:}\,\sigma$ is well-typed and Γ_f contains all free variables of M, we have

$$\mathcal{C}[\![\Gamma \rhd M{:}\,\sigma]\!] = \mathcal{C}[\![\Gamma_f \rhd M{:}\,\sigma]\!] \circ \chi_f^{[\![\Gamma]\!]}.$$

(ii)

$$\begin{aligned}
\mathcal{C}[\![x_1{:}\,\sigma_1, \ldots, x_n{:}\,\sigma_n \rhd x_i{:}\,\sigma_i]\!] &= \mathbf{Proj}_{i+1}^{unit\times\sigma_1\times\ldots\times\sigma_n}\\
\mathcal{C}[\![\Gamma \rhd *{:}\,unit]\!] &= \mathbf{One}^{[\![\Gamma]\!]}\\
\mathcal{C}[\![\Gamma \rhd c{:}\,\tau]\!] &= \hat{c} \circ \mathbf{One}^{[\![\Gamma]\!]}\\
\mathcal{C}[\![\Gamma \rhd \mathbf{Proj}_1^{\sigma,\tau} M{:}\,\sigma]\!] &= \mathbf{Proj}_1^{\sigma,\tau} \circ \mathcal{C}[\![\Gamma \rhd M{:}\,\sigma \times \tau]\!]\\
\mathcal{C}[\![\Gamma \rhd \mathbf{Proj}_2^{\sigma,\tau} M{:}\,\tau]\!] &= \mathbf{Proj}_2^{\sigma,\tau} \circ \mathcal{C}[\![\Gamma \rhd M{:}\,\sigma \times \tau]\!]\\
\mathcal{C}[\![\Gamma \rhd \langle M, N\rangle{:}\,\rho \times \tau]\!] &= \langle \mathcal{C}[\![\Gamma \rhd M{:}\,\sigma]\!], \mathcal{C}[\![\Gamma \rhd N{:}\,\tau]\!]\rangle\\
\mathcal{C}[\![\Gamma \rhd MN{:}\,\tau]\!] &= \mathbf{App}^{\sigma,\tau} \circ \langle \mathcal{C}[\![\Gamma \rhd M{:}\,\sigma \to \tau]\!], \mathcal{C}[\![\Gamma \rhd N{:}\,\sigma]\!]\rangle\\
\mathcal{C}[\![\Gamma \rhd \lambda x{:}\,\sigma.M{:}\,\sigma \to \tau]\!] &= \mathbf{Curry}\,(\mathcal{C}[\![\Gamma_f, x{:}\,\sigma \rhd M{:}\,\tau]\!]) \circ \chi_f^{[\![\Gamma]\!]}
\end{aligned}$$

for any f such that Γ_f contains

every $y \in FV(M)$ but not x

Proof We prove conditions (i) and (ii) simultaneously, by a single induction on the structure of terms (not their typing derivations). The general pattern is to prove (ii) first, using the induction hypothesis (i) for simpler terms, then check that (i) holds for the term itself.

For a variable, $x_1{:}\,\sigma_1, \ldots, x_n{:}\,\sigma_n \rhd x_i{:}\,\sigma_i$, the only typing derivations begin with axiom (*var*), followed by $n-1$ uses of the (*add var*) typing rule. We prove (ii) by a subinduction on the number of times (*add var*) is used. The base case is

$$[\![x_i{:}\,\sigma_i \rhd x_i{:}\,\sigma_i]\!] = \mathbf{Proj}_2^{unit,\,\sigma_i},$$

which satisfies the condition of the lemma. For the induction step, suppose $x_1{:}\,\sigma_1, \ldots, \ldots,$

$x_n\colon \sigma_n \triangleright x_i\colon \sigma_i$ is derived by adding the variable x_k. Then we have

$$[\![\ldots, x_{k-1}\colon \sigma_{k-1}, x_k\colon \sigma_k, x_{k+1}\colon \sigma_{k+1}, \ldots \triangleright x_i\colon \sigma_i]\!]$$

$$= \quad [\![\ldots, x_{k-1}\colon \sigma_{k-1}, x_{k+1}\colon \sigma_{k+1}, \ldots \triangleright x_i\colon \sigma_i]\!] \circ \chi_f^{unit\times\sigma_1\times\ldots\times\sigma_n}$$

where f is the $(n-1), n$-function mapping each $j < k$ to j and each $j \geq k$ to $j+1$. If $i < k$, then by the the hypothesis of the subinduction,

$$[\![x_1\colon \sigma_1, \ldots, x_k\colon \sigma_k, \ldots, x_n\colon \sigma_n \triangleright x_i\colon \sigma_i]\!]$$

$$= \quad \mathbf{Proj}_{i+1}^{unit\times\sigma_1\times\ldots\times\sigma_{k-1}\,\times\,\sigma_{k+1}\times\ldots\times\sigma_n} \circ \chi_f^{unit\times\sigma_1\times\ldots\times\sigma_n}$$

$$= \quad \mathbf{Proj}_{i+1}^{unit\times\sigma_1\times\ldots\times\sigma_{k-1}\times\sigma_k\times\sigma_{k+1}\times\ldots\times\sigma_n}$$

The case $i > k$ is similar, completing the proof of condition (ii). Given this, it is easy to check (i), which we leave to the reader.

For the constant $*$, or any constant from the signature, we prove (ii) by reasoning as in Example 7.2.26. This may be used to check (i).

For $\Gamma \triangleright \mathbf{Proj}_1^{\sigma,\tau} M\colon \sigma$, we assume some typing derivation that ends with typing rule ($\times$ Elim) followed by k uses of (*add var*). If Γ has n variables, is easy to see that the conclusion of rule ($\times$ Elim) must have the form $\Gamma_g \triangleright \mathbf{Proj}_1 M\colon \sigma$, where g is an appropriate $(n-k), n$-function. As in the variable case, we have

$$[\![\Gamma \triangleright \mathbf{Proj}_1^{\sigma,\tau} M\colon \sigma]\!] = [\![\Gamma_g \triangleright \mathbf{Proj}_1 M\colon \sigma]\!] \circ \chi_g^{[\![\Gamma]\!]}.$$

Expanding the definition of the meaning of $\Gamma_g \triangleright \mathbf{Proj}_1 M\colon \sigma$ and associating composition to the right gives us

$$[\![\Gamma \triangleright \mathbf{Proj}_1^{\sigma,\tau} M\colon \sigma]\!] = \mathbf{Proj}_1^{\sigma,\tau} \circ ([\![\Gamma_g \triangleright M\colon \sigma \times \tau]\!] \circ \chi_g^{[\![\Gamma]\!]}),$$

which by the induction hypothesis (i) for M gives us (ii) for $\Gamma \triangleright \mathbf{Proj}_1^{\sigma,\tau} M\colon \sigma$. It is straightforward to verify (i) using associativity of composition and the induction hypothesis.

The other projection case, pairing, and the application case are all similar, using the identity

$$\langle f, g\rangle \circ h = \langle f \circ h, g \circ h\rangle$$

proved at the end of Section 7.2.3 in the pairing and application cases.

The remaining case is a lambda abstraction. Again, we assume some typing derivation for $\Gamma \triangleright \lambda x\colon \sigma.M\colon \sigma \to \tau$, ending with rule ($\to$ Intro), followed by $n - m$ uses of rule (*add var*). The conclusion of rule ($\to$ Intro) must have the form $\Gamma_g \triangleright \lambda x\colon \sigma.M\colon \sigma \to \tau$, where g is an appropriate m, n-function. As in the previous cases, we have

$$[\![\Gamma \triangleright \lambda x{:}\sigma.M{:}\sigma \to \tau]\!] = [\![\Gamma_g \triangleright \lambda x{:}\sigma.M{:}\sigma \to \tau]\!] \circ \chi_g^{[\![\Gamma]\!]}.$$

Since $\Gamma_g \triangleright \lambda x{:}\sigma.M{:}\sigma \to \tau$ is typed using ($\to$ Intro), we have

$$[\![\Gamma \triangleright \lambda x{:}\sigma.M{:}\sigma \to \tau]\!] = \mathbf{Curry}(\,[\![\Gamma_g, x{:}\sigma \triangleright M{:}\tau]\!]\,) \circ \chi_g^{[\![\Gamma]\!]}.$$

This does not establish (ii), since g was not chosen arbitrarily, but it does get us half way there.

Before proceeding, it is helpful to recall the identity

$$\mathbf{Curry}(h) \circ k = \mathbf{Curry}(h \circ (k \times id))$$

from the end of Section 7.2.3. If f is any m, n-function, then let us write f' for the $(m+1), (n+1)$-function that extends f by mapping $(m+1)$ to $(n+1)$. This gives us $\chi_f^{[\![\Gamma]\!]} \times id = \chi_{f'}^{[\![\Gamma, x:\sigma]\!]}$. Combining these two, we have, for example,

$$\mathbf{Curry}(\,[\![\Gamma_g, x{:}\sigma \triangleright M{:}\tau]\!]\,) \circ \chi_g^{[\![\Gamma]\!]} = \mathbf{Curry}(\,[\![\Gamma_g, x{:}\sigma \triangleright M{:}\tau]\!] \circ \chi_{g'}^{[\![\Gamma]\!]}\,).$$

We will need this form of reasoning below.

Let f be any k, n-function such that Γ_f contains precisely the variables $FV(M) - \{x\}$. Since Γ_g must contain all the variables that appear in Γ_f, in some order, we have $k \le m$. In addition, there must be some k, m-function h such that $f = h \circ g$. It follows that $f' = h' \circ g'$. Applying the inductive hypothesis (i), we have

$$[\![\Gamma_g, x{:}\sigma \triangleright M{:}\tau]\!] = [\![\Gamma_f, x{:}\sigma \triangleright M{:}\tau]\!] \circ \chi_{h'}.$$

This gives us

$$\begin{aligned}[\![\Gamma \triangleright \lambda x{:}\sigma.M{:}\sigma \to \tau]\!] &= \mathbf{Curry}(\,[\![\Gamma_f, x{:}\sigma \triangleright M{:}\tau]\!] \circ \chi_{h'}^{[\![\Gamma]\!]}\,) \circ \chi_g^{[\![\Gamma]\!]}\\ &= \mathbf{Curry}(\,[\![\Gamma_f, x{:}\sigma \triangleright M{:}\tau]\!]\,) \circ \chi_h^{[\![\Gamma]\!]} \circ \chi_g^{[\![\Gamma]\!]}\\ &= \mathbf{Curry}(\,[\![\Gamma_f, x{:}\sigma \triangleright M{:}\tau]\!]\,) \circ \chi_f^{[\![\Gamma]\!]},\end{aligned}$$

which concludes the proof of (ii). Similar reasoning may be used to check (i), completing the proof of the lemma. ∎

Since the substitution lemma for Henkin models is stated using environments, and environments are not used in the CCC-interpretation of terms, we must state the substitution lemma in a different way.

Lemma 7.2.30 (CCC Substitution) If $\Gamma, x{:}\sigma \triangleright M{:}\tau$ and $\Gamma \triangleright N{:}\sigma$ are well-typed terms, then

$$[\![\Gamma \rhd [N/x]M\colon \tau]\!] = [\![\Gamma, x\colon \sigma \rhd M\colon \tau]\!] \circ \langle id_{[\![\Gamma]\!]}, [\![\Gamma \rhd N\colon \sigma]\!]\rangle.$$

Like the substitution lemmas for algebra (Lemma 3.3.11) and Henkin models (Lemma 4.5.16), this lemma says that the effect of syntactically substituting an expression N for x is the same as letting x denote the semantic meaning of N. Intuitively, the way that we "let x denote the semantic meaning of N" is by composing the meaning of M with a function that supplies the meaning of N as the value of x.

Proof The proof of Lemma 7.2.30 is largely a routine induction on the typing derivation of $\Gamma, x\colon \sigma \rhd M\colon \tau$. The only difficult case is lambda abstraction, since this changes the list of free variables and the induction hypothesis applies only to the last variable in the ordered type assignment. However, we may circumvent this problem using the permutation functions of Lemma 7.2.29.

Suppose $\Gamma, x\colon \sigma \rhd \lambda y\colon \rho.\, M\colon \rho \to \tau$ is typed from $\Gamma, x\colon \sigma, y\colon \rho \rhd M\colon \tau$ by typing rule ($\to$ Intro). Then the meaning of the lambda term is $\mathbf{Curry}([\![\Gamma, x\colon \sigma, y\colon \rho \rhd M\colon \tau]\!])$ and we may derive $\Gamma \rhd \lambda y\colon \rho.[N/x]M\colon \rho \to \tau$ from $\Gamma, y\colon \rho \rhd [N/x]M\colon \tau$ by ($\to$ Intro).

The inductive hypothesis gives us

$$[\![\Gamma, y\colon \rho \rhd [N/x]M\colon \tau]\!] = [\![\Gamma, y\colon \rho, x\colon \sigma \rhd M\colon \tau]\!] \circ \langle id_{[\![\Gamma]\!]}, [\![\Gamma \rhd N\colon \sigma]\!]\rangle.$$

To apply this usefully, suppose Γ has n variables and let f be the $(n+2)$, $(n+2)$-function that permutes $n+1$ and $n+2$, leaving all other numbers fixed, so that $(\Gamma, y\colon \rho, x\colon \sigma)_f = \Gamma, x\colon \sigma, y\colon \rho$. By Lemma 7.2.29, we have

$$[\![\Gamma, y\colon \rho, x\colon \sigma \rhd M\colon \tau]\!] = [\![\Gamma, x\colon \sigma, y\colon \rho \rhd M\colon \tau]\!] \circ \chi_f^{[\![\Gamma, y:\rho, x:\sigma]\!]}.$$

Using this, we may prove the lambda abstraction case by the following calculation,

$$\begin{aligned}
[\![\Gamma \rhd \lambda y\colon \rho.[N/x]M\colon \rho \to \tau]\!] &= \mathbf{Curry}([\![\Gamma, y\colon \rho \rhd [N/x]M\colon \tau]\!]) \\
&= \mathbf{Curry}([\![\Gamma, y\colon \rho, x\colon \sigma \rhd M\colon \tau]\!] \circ \langle id_{[\![\Gamma, y:\rho]\!]}, [\![\Gamma \rhd N\colon \sigma]\!]\rangle) \\
&= \mathbf{Curry}([\![\Gamma, x\colon \sigma, y\colon \rho \rhd M\colon \tau]\!] \circ \chi_f^{[\![\Gamma, y:\rho, x:\sigma]\!]} \circ \langle id_{[\![\Gamma, y:\rho]\!]}, \\
&\qquad [\![\Gamma \rhd N\colon \sigma]\!]\rangle) \\
&= \mathbf{Curry}([\![\Gamma, x\colon \sigma, y\colon \rho \rhd M\colon \tau]\!] \circ (\langle id_{[\![\Gamma]\!]}, [\![\Gamma \rhd N\colon \sigma]\!]\rangle \times id)) \\
&= \mathbf{Curry}([\![\Gamma, x\colon \sigma, y\colon \rho \rhd M\colon \tau]\!]) \circ \langle id_{[\![\Gamma]\!]}, [\![\Gamma \rhd N\colon \sigma]\!]\rangle \\
&= [\![\Gamma, x\colon \sigma \rhd \lambda y\colon \rho.\, M\colon \tau]\!] \circ \langle id_{[\![\Gamma]\!]}, [\![\Gamma \rhd N\colon \sigma]\!]\rangle
\end{aligned}$$

where the step simplifying $\chi_f^{[\![\Gamma, y:\rho, x:\sigma]\!]} \circ \langle id_{[\![\Gamma, y:\rho]\!]}, [\![\Gamma \rhd N\colon \sigma]\!]\rangle$ is a routine calculation involving pairing and projection morphisms. The remaining cases are left to the reader. ∎

Finally, we come to equations and cartesian closed categories. Although we must order a type assignment to give meaning to terms, Lemma 7.2.29 allows us to return to unordered type assignments for equations. The reason is that, if $\Gamma \rhd M = N\colon\sigma$ is a typed equation, the terms $\Gamma \rhd M\colon\sigma$ and $\Gamma \rhd N\colon\sigma$ denote the same morphism for one ordering of Γ iff they denote the same morphism for all orderings. Therefore, we say a Σ-CCC $\mathcal{C}$ *satisfies* an equation $\Gamma \rhd M = N\colon\sigma$ if, for any ordering of the set Γ, the terms $\Gamma \rhd M\colon\sigma$ and $\Gamma \rhd N\colon\sigma$ over signature Σ denote the same morphism of $\mathcal{C}$. Using the lemmas and examples of this section, it is not hard to prove the following soundness theorem for equational proofs.

Theorem 7.2.31 (Soundness) If $\mathcal{E} \vdash \Gamma \rhd M = N\colon\sigma$, then every CCC satisfying $\mathcal{E}$ also satisfies $\Gamma \rhd M = N\colon\sigma$.

Proof Like the proof of soundness for Henkin models (Theorem 4.5.17), the soundness proof for CCC's proceeds by induction on equational proofs from $\mathcal{E}$. The base cases are that $E \in \mathcal{E}$ or E is one of the axioms (*ref*),(*unit*), (α), (β), or (η). The case $E \in \mathcal{E}$, (*ref*) and (*unit*) are trivial. The soundness of (α) is left as Exercise 7.2.36, with the pairing and projection axioms considered in Exercise 7.2.37. The proof for (η) is essentially the same as the argument given in Example 7.2.27. Although a special case of (β) is given in Example 7.2.28, we give the general case here since this requires the substitution lemma and substitution was not considered in the example.

For (β), we use the substitution lemma, as follows. The meaning of an application is

$$[\![\Gamma \rhd (\lambda x\colon\sigma.\, M)N\colon\tau]\!] = \mathbf{App} \circ \langle \mathbf{Curry}([\![\Gamma, x\colon\sigma \rhd M\colon\tau]\!]),\ [\![\Gamma \rhd N\colon\sigma]\!]\rangle$$

We must show that this is the same as the meaning of the result of β-reduction, which by the substitution lemma (Lemma 7.2.30) may be written as

$$[\![\Gamma \rhd [N/x]M\colon\tau]\!] = [\![\Gamma, x\colon\sigma \rhd M\colon\tau]\!] \circ \langle id,\ [\![\Gamma \rhd N\colon\sigma]\!]\rangle.$$

The trick is to use $\langle f, g\rangle = (f \times id) \circ \langle id, g\rangle$, which is easily verified, to see that

$$[\![\Gamma \rhd (\lambda x\colon\sigma.\, M)N\colon\tau]\!] = \mathbf{App} \circ (\mathbf{Curry}([\![\Gamma, x\colon\sigma \rhd M\colon\tau]\!]) \times id) \circ \langle id,\ [\![\Gamma \rhd N\colon\sigma]\!]\rangle.$$

By the general equation $\mathbf{App} \circ (\mathbf{Curry}(h) \times id) = h$ given in the second definition of CCC's, we can see that this is equal to $[\![\Gamma \rhd [N/x]M\colon\tau]\!]$, concluding the proof of this case.

There are inductive steps for inference rules (*sym*), (*trans*), (ξ) and (ν). The (*sym*) and (*trans*) cases are trivial and the (ξ) and (ν) cases follow directly from the fact that **Curry** and pairing, $\langle\,\cdot\,,\,\cdot\,\rangle$, are both functions. This completes the proof. ∎

For algebra, lambda calculus, and other forms of logic, there are three main forms of completeness. These are discussed in Section 3.4.4. The simplest form is that every valid formula is provable, the next is deductive completeness, and the third is sometimes called "least model" completeness. As we shall see in Theorem 7.2.41, every Henkin model determines a CCC that satisfies exactly the same equations. Therefore, there is a CCC that satisfies exactly the valid equations of any signature. However, as discussed in Section 4.5.5, we only have deductive completeness for Henkin models if we add proof rules to the basic system. In contrast, we can prove the stronger "least model" form of completeness for CCC's, without adding any axioms or proof rules to the standard equational proof system.

Theorem 7.2.32 (Completeness) Let $\mathcal{E}$ be any $\lambda^{unit,\times,\to}$ theory, not necessarily closed under (nonempty) or (empty I) and (empty E). There is a CCC satisfying precisely the equations belonging to $\mathcal{E}$.

This theorem, which clearly illustrates the difference between CCC's and Henkin models, is proved as Exercise 7.2.39. By Proposition 4.4.24, completeness for $\lambda^{\to}$ follows. It is also possible to prove completeness for $\lambda^{\to}$ directly, by the construction described in Exercise 7.2.40. These proofs all use term categories. Since arbitrary cartesian closed categories seem rather abstract, we also want completeness theorems for particular classes of CCC's. This issue is considered in Sections 7.3.6 and 7.3.7, where completeness for Kripke models and full functor categories are considered.

Exercise 7.2.33 Let Γ be an unordered type assignment and suppose that $\Gamma \triangleright M\colon\sigma$ is derivable using the typing rules for unordered type assignments. Show that for any ordered type assignment Γ' containing all the *variable*: *type* pairs of Γ_M, we can derive $\Gamma \triangleright M\colon\sigma$ using the typing rules for ordered type assignments. (Recall that Γ_M is the set of *variable*: *type* pairs $x\colon\sigma$ from Γ with $x \in FV(M)$ and that $\Gamma \triangleright M\colon\sigma$ is derivable iff $\Gamma_M \triangleright M\colon\sigma$ is.)

Exercise 7.2.34 We define tupling and the projection morphisms by

$$\langle f \rangle = f$$

$$\langle f_1 \ldots, f_n, g\rangle = \langle\langle f_1 \ldots, f_n\rangle, g\rangle$$

$$\mathbf{Proj}_1^{a} = id_a$$

$$\mathbf{Proj}_n^{a_1\times\ldots\times a_n} = \mathbf{Proj}_2^{(a_1\times\ldots\times a_{n-1}),a_n} \qquad n > 1$$

$$\mathbf{Proj}_i^{a_1\times\ldots\times a_n} = \mathbf{Proj}_i^{a_1\times\ldots\times a_{n-1}} \circ \mathbf{Proj}_1^{(a_1\times\ldots\times a_{n-1}),a_n} \qquad 1 \le i < n$$

Show that the following equations hold in any category with products.

(a) $\mathbf{Proj}_i \circ \langle f_1, \ldots, f_n\rangle = f_i$

(b) $\langle f_1, \ldots, f_n\rangle \circ h = \langle f_1 \circ h, \ldots, f_n \circ h\rangle$

(c) $\langle \mathbf{Proj}_1^{a_1\times\ldots\times a_{n+1}}, \ldots, \mathbf{Proj}_n^{a_1\times\ldots\times a_{n+1}}\rangle$
$= \langle \mathbf{Proj}_1^{a_1\times\ldots\times a_n}, \ldots, \mathbf{Proj}_n^{a_1\times\ldots\times a_n}\rangle \circ \mathbf{Proj}_1^{(a_1\times\ldots\times a_n),a_{n+1}}$

(d) $\langle \mathbf{Proj}_1^{a_1\times\ldots\times a_n}, \ldots, \mathbf{Proj}_n^{a_1\times\ldots\times a_n}\rangle = id_{a_1\times\ldots\times a_n}$

(e) $\langle \mathbf{Proj}_1^{a_1\times\ldots\times a_{n+1}}, \ldots, \mathbf{Proj}_n^{a_1\times\ldots\times a_{n+1}}\rangle = \mathbf{Proj}_1^{(a_1\times\ldots\times a_n),a_{n+1}}$

Exercise 7.2.35 In Example 7.2.28, we see that the interpretation of $y{:}\,\sigma \triangleright \lambda x{:}\,\sigma.\, x{:}\,\sigma$ can be written as either $\mathbf{Curry}(\mathbf{Proj}_2^{unit,\sigma}) \circ \mathbf{Proj}_1^{unit,\sigma}$ or $\mathbf{Curry}(\mathbf{Proj}_2^{unit\times\sigma,\sigma})$. Show directly, without using coherence (Lemma 7.2.29), that these are equal.

Exercise 7.2.36 Use induction on the structure of terms to prove that α-equivalent terms have the same interpretation in any CCC. You will probably want to prove the following stronger statement: If $x_1{:}\,\sigma_1, \ldots, x_k{:}\,\sigma_k \triangleright M{:}\,\sigma$ and $y_1{:}\,\sigma_1, \ldots, y_k{:}\,\sigma_k \triangleright N{:}\,\sigma$ are well-typed, with $N \equiv_\alpha [y_1, \ldots, y_k/x_1, \ldots, x_k]M$, then

$$[\![x_1{:}\,\sigma_1, \ldots, x_k{:}\,\sigma_k \triangleright M{:}\,\sigma]\!] = [\![y_1{:}\,\sigma_1, \ldots, y_k{:}\,\sigma_k \triangleright N{:}\,\sigma]\!].$$

(*Hint:* Use Lemma 7.2.29.)

Exercise 7.2.37 Show that the following equations hold in any CCC, proving soundness of the pairing and projection axioms.

(a) $[\![\Gamma \triangleright \mathbf{Proj}_i\langle M_1, M_2\rangle{:}\,\sigma_i]\!] = [\![\Gamma \triangleright M_i{:}\,\sigma_i]\!]$

(b) $[\![\Gamma \triangleright \langle \mathbf{Proj}_1\, M, \mathbf{Proj}_2\, M\rangle{:}\,\sigma \times \tau]\!] = [\![\Gamma \triangleright M{:}\,\sigma \times \tau]\!]$

Exercise 7.2.38 The category $\mathcal{C}_\mathcal{A}$ derived from a Henkin model $\mathcal{A}$ is described in Examples 7.2.5 and 7.2.16 and proved to be a CCC in Exercise 7.2.23. This exercise asks you to show that for any $\lambda^{unit,\times,\rightarrow}$ Henkin model $\mathcal{A}$, the meaning of a term $x_1{:}\,\sigma_1, \ldots, x_n{:}\,\sigma_n \triangleright M{:}\,\tau$ in the CCC $\mathcal{C}_\mathcal{A}$ is the same as the meaning of the closed term $\lambda\langle z{:}\, unit, x_1{:}\,\sigma_1, \ldots, x_n{:}\,\sigma_n\rangle.\, M$ in the Henkin model $\mathcal{A}$, with tupling associated to the left as described in part (a) below. It follows that $\mathcal{C}_\mathcal{A}$ satisfies exactly the same equations as $\mathcal{A}$.

(a) Since we will need tupling associated to the left in lambda terms, we will write $\langle y_1, \ldots, y_n\rangle$ for $\langle\langle y_1, y_2\rangle \ldots, y_n\rangle$. If Γ is the sequence $x_1{:}\,\sigma_1, \ldots, x_n{:}\,\sigma_n$ and $\Gamma \triangleright M{:}\,\tau$ is a well-typed, then let $\lambda\langle\Gamma\rangle.\, M \stackrel{\text{def}}{=} \lambda\langle z{:}\, unit, x_1{:}\,\sigma_1, \ldots, x_n{:}\,\sigma_n\rangle.\, M$, where

$$\lambda\langle y_1{:}\,\sigma_1, \ldots, y_n{:}\,\sigma_n\rangle.\, M$$

$$\stackrel{\text{def}}{=} \quad \lambda p{:}\,(\ldots(\sigma_1 \times \sigma_2) \times \ldots \times \sigma_n).[\mathbf{Proj}_1^{\sigma_1\times\ldots\times\sigma_n} p, \ldots, \mathbf{Proj}_n^{\sigma_1\times\ldots\times\sigma_n} p \,/\, y_1, \ldots, y_n]M,$$

and $\mathbf{Proj}_i^{\sigma_1\times\ldots\times\sigma_n}$ is any lambda term such that $\mathbf{Proj}_i^{\sigma_1\times\ldots\times\sigma_n}\langle y_1,\ldots,y_n\rangle = y_i$ and $\langle \mathbf{Proj}_1^{\sigma_1\times\ldots\times\sigma_n} p,\ldots,\mathbf{Proj}_n^{\sigma_1\times\ldots\times\sigma_n} p\rangle = p$. If we use the form $\lambda\langle\Gamma\rangle.\ldots\langle\Gamma\rangle\ldots$ as short-hand for $\lambda\langle z{:}\,unit, x_1{:}\,\sigma_1,\ldots,x_n{:}\,\sigma_n\rangle.\ldots\langle z, x_1\ldots,x_n\rangle\ldots$, then show that

$$\lambda\langle\Gamma\rangle.\ldots(\lambda\langle\Gamma\rangle.\,M)\langle\Gamma\rangle\ldots = \lambda\langle\Gamma\rangle.\ldots M\ldots$$

(b) Show that if Γ is an ordered type assignment of length n and f is any m,n-function, then the morphism $\chi_f^{[\![\Gamma]\!]}$ in category $\mathcal{C}_{\mathcal{A}}$ is the meaning of the lambda term

$$\chi_f^{[\![\Gamma]\!]} = \lambda\langle\Gamma\rangle.\langle *, \mathbf{Proj}_{f(1)+1}^{unit\times\sigma_1\times\ldots\times\sigma_n}\langle\Gamma\rangle,\ldots,\mathbf{Proj}_{f(m)+1}^{unit\times\sigma_1\times\ldots\times\sigma_n}\langle\Gamma\rangle\rangle$$

(c) Show by induction on typing derivations that for any term $\Gamma\rhd M{:}\,\tau$, we have

$$\mathcal{C}_{\mathcal{A}}[\![\Gamma\rhd M{:}\,\tau]\!] = \mathcal{A}[\![\lambda\langle\Gamma\rangle.\,M]\!].$$

Exercise 7.2.39 Let $\mathcal{E}$ be a theory over $\lambda^{unit,\times,\rightarrow}$ signature Σ. The $\lambda^{unit,\times,\rightarrow}$ term category generated by $\mathcal{E}$ is described in Example 7.2.19. Exercise 7.2.24 asks you to verify that this category is cartesian closed. Using the results of Exercise 7.2.24, prove Theorem 7.2.32 by showing that $\mathcal{C}_{\mathcal{E}}$ is a CCC with

$$\mathcal{C}_{\mathcal{E}}\models x{:}\,\sigma\rhd M = N{:}\,\tau \quad\text{iff}\quad \mathcal{E}\vdash x{:}\,\sigma\rhd M = N{:}\,\tau$$

for all $\lambda^{unit,\times,\rightarrow}$ terms $x{:}\,\sigma\rhd M,\ N{:}\,\tau$. You may do this in the following steps.

(a) If $\Gamma = x_1{:}\,\sigma_1,\ldots,x_n{:}\,\sigma_n$ is an ordered type assignment, then let S_Γ^z be the substitution

$$S_\Gamma^z = [\mathbf{Proj}_2^{unit\times\sigma_1\times\ldots\times\sigma_n} z,\ldots,\mathbf{Proj}_{n+1}^{unit\times\sigma_1\times\ldots\times\sigma_n} z/x_1,\ldots,x_n]$$

Use induction on terms to show that for any $\Gamma\rhd M{:}\,\tau$, the meaning of this term in $\mathcal{C}(\mathcal{E})$ is the equivalence class of $z{:}\,unit\times\sigma_1\times\ldots\times\sigma_n\rhd S_\Gamma^z M{:}\,\tau$. (*Hint:* Don't forget to use Lemma 7.2.29.)

(b) Show that if $\mathcal{E}\vdash\emptyset\rhd M = N{:}\,\sigma$, then $\mathcal{C}(\mathcal{E})\models\emptyset\rhd M = N{:}\,\sigma$. (Be sure you understand why we only need to consider equations between closed terms.)

(c) Show that if $\mathcal{C}(\mathcal{E})\models\emptyset\rhd M = N{:}\,\sigma$, then $\mathcal{E}\vdash\emptyset\rhd M = N{:}\,\sigma$.

Exercise 7.2.40 An alternative to the term category used in Exercise 7.2.39 is a construction using $\lambda^{\rightarrow}$ instead of $\lambda^{unit,\times,\rightarrow}$. This allows us to prove completeness for $\lambda^{\rightarrow}$ directly without introducing the extra terms associated with $\lambda^{unit,\times,\rightarrow}$. Let $\mathcal{E}$ be a $\lambda^{\rightarrow}$ theory over signature Σ. The objects of the $\lambda^{\rightarrow}$ *term category* $\mathcal{C}_{\mathcal{E}}$ are sequences of type expressions over Σ. Intuitively, a sequence $\sigma_1,\ldots,\sigma_k$ is the product of these types. To simplify notation, we will write $\vec{x}_k$ for a sequence $x_1,\ldots,x_k$ of k variables, similarly $\vec{\sigma}_k$ for a sequence of k type expressions, and $\vec{x}_k{:}\,\vec{\sigma}_k$ for $x_1{:}\,\sigma_1,\ldots,x_k{:}\,\sigma_k$, omitting the length (subscript) when irrelevant or clear from context. The arrows from $\vec{\sigma}_j$ to $\vec{\tau}_k$ are given by k-tuples of terms over j free variables. To avoid details with names of free variables, we choose some fixed enumeration $x_1, x_2, x_3, \ldots$ and always use these in every term. An arrow $\vec{\sigma}_j \longrightarrow \vec{\tau}_k$ is an equivalence class of tuples of terms,

$$[\Gamma \triangleright M_1 \colon \tau_1, \ldots, \Gamma \triangleright M_k \colon \tau]_{\mathcal{E}}$$
$$= \{\langle \Gamma \triangleright N_1 \colon \tau_1, \ldots, \Gamma \triangleright N_k \colon \tau \rangle$$
$$\mid \mathcal{E} \vdash \Gamma \triangleright M_i = N_i \colon \tau \text{ for } 1 \le i \le k\},$$

where $\Gamma = \vec{x}_j \colon \vec{\sigma}_j$. Composition in this category is defined by substitution, as follows.

$$[\vec{x}_k \colon \vec{\tau}_k \triangleright N_1 \colon \rho_1, \ldots, \vec{x}_k \colon \vec{\tau}_k \triangleright N_\ell \colon \rho_\ell]_{\mathcal{E}} \circ [\vec{x}_j \colon \vec{\sigma}_j \triangleright M_1 \colon \tau_1, \ldots, \vec{x}_j \colon \vec{\sigma}_j \triangleright M_k \colon \tau]_{\mathcal{E}}$$
$$= [\vec{x}_j \colon \vec{\sigma}_j \triangleright [\vec{M}_k/\vec{x}_k]N_1 \colon \rho_1, \ldots, \vec{x}_j \colon \vec{\sigma}_j \triangleright [\vec{M}_k/\vec{x}_k]N_\ell \colon \rho_\ell]_{\mathcal{E}}$$

The terminal type, *unit*, is the empty sequence of types and the cartesian product of $\sigma_1, \ldots, \sigma_j$ and $\tau_1, \ldots, \tau_k$ is their concatenation, $\sigma_1, \ldots, \sigma_j, \tau_1, \ldots, \tau_k$. Show that $\mathcal{C}_{\mathcal{E}}$ is a CCC with

$$\mathcal{C}_{\mathcal{E}} \models x \colon \sigma \triangleright M = N \colon \tau \quad \text{iff} \quad \mathcal{E} \vdash x \colon \sigma \triangleright M = N \colon \tau$$

for all $\lambda^{\rightarrow}$ terms $x \colon \sigma \triangleright M, N \colon \tau$, by the following steps.

(a) Identify the unique arrow $\mathbf{One}^{\sigma} \colon \sigma \longrightarrow \mathit{unit}$, operations $\mathbf{Proj}_1$, $\mathbf{Proj}_2$, $\langle\,\rangle$, **App**, **Curry** and show that $\mathcal{C}_{\mathcal{E}}$ is cartesian closed.

(b) Use induction on terms and Lemma 7.2.29 to show that for any $x_1 \colon \sigma_1, \ldots, x_n \colon \sigma_n \triangleright M \colon \tau$, the meaning of this term in $\mathcal{C}(\mathcal{E})$ is the equivalence class of $x_0 \colon \mathit{unit}, x_1 \colon \sigma_1, \ldots, x_n \colon \sigma_n \triangleright M \colon \tau$.

(c) Show that if $\mathcal{E} \vdash \emptyset \triangleright M = N \colon \sigma$, then $\mathcal{C}(\mathcal{E}) \models \emptyset \triangleright M = N \colon \sigma$. (Be sure you understand why we only need to consider equations between closed terms.)

(d) Show that if $\mathcal{C}(\mathcal{E}) \models \emptyset \triangleright M = N \colon \sigma$, then $\mathcal{E} \vdash \emptyset \triangleright M = N \colon \sigma$.

7.2.5 Henkin Models as CCCs

Henkin models may be regarded as a special case of cartesian closed categories, since every Henkin model determines a cartesian closed category with the same equational theory. However, as we shall see in this section, Henkin models only correspond to CCC's that have an easily stated "well-pointedness" property.

As described in Example 7.2.5, a Henkin model, $\mathcal{A}$, determines a cartesian closed category, $\mathcal{C}_{\mathcal{A}}$, whose objects are the type expressions of the signature and whose arrows from σ to τ are the elements of $A^{\sigma \to \tau}$. This construction has the property that the meaning of an open term in $\mathcal{C}_{\mathcal{A}}$, according to the usual meaning function for CCC's, corresponds to the meaning of an associated closed term in $\mathcal{A}$, according to the usual meaning function for Henkin models (see Exercise 7.2.38). As a consequence, $\mathcal{A}$ and $\mathcal{C}_{\mathcal{A}}$ satisfy exactly the same equations between lambda terms. However, the reverse mapping from cartesian closed categories to Henkin models is more complicated, as we shall see below.

We may construct a typed applicative structure from any cartesian closed category. If we begin with a cartesian closed category constructed from a Henkin model, this applicative structure will be isomorphic to the original Henkin model. However, we do not obtain a Henkin model from every CCC. This is not an accident of the construction, but a result of the fundamental difference between Henkin models and CCC's. Specifically, the completeness theorems for CCC's show that there are CCC's whose theories differ from the lambda theory of any Henkin model. It follows that there is no map from arbitrary CCC's to Henkin models that preserves equations between lambda terms.

Given a Σ-CCC $\mathcal{C}$, we form a Σ-applicative structure $\mathcal{A}_{\mathcal{C}}$ by letting $A^{\sigma} = \mathcal{C}(\mathit{unit}, \mathcal{C}[\![\sigma]\!])$ and $\mathit{Const}(c) = \hat{c}$. For notational simplicity, we will write σ for $\mathcal{C}[\![\sigma]\!]$. Application,

$$\mathbf{App}_{\mathcal{A}} : A^{\sigma\to\tau} \to A^{\sigma} \to A^{\tau},$$

in the applicative structure $\mathcal{A}_{\mathcal{C}}$ is defined by composition with the arrow $\mathbf{App}_{\mathcal{C}}$ of the category $\mathcal{C}$ according to

$$\mathbf{App}_{\mathcal{A}}^{\sigma,\tau}\, f\, x \;=\; \mathbf{App}_{\mathcal{C}}^{\sigma,\tau} \circ \langle f, x\rangle,$$

where $\langle f, x\rangle : \mathit{unit} \longrightarrow (\sigma \to \tau) \times \sigma$ in $\mathcal{C}$. Projections are defined similarly. Since every term over Σ has a meaning in $\mathcal{C}$, we may show that $\mathcal{A}_{\mathcal{C}}$ is a combinatory algebra. (This is Exercise 7.2.42.) The structure also satisfies the axioms for lambda algebras given in Section 4.5.8. However, $\mathcal{A}_{\mathcal{C}}$ may not be extensional. Specifically, $\mathcal{A}_{\mathcal{C}}$ is extensional only if $f = g : \mathit{unit} \longrightarrow (\sigma \to \tau)$ in $\mathcal{C}$ whenever

$$\mathbf{App}_{\mathcal{C}}^{\sigma,\tau} \circ \langle f, x\rangle = \mathbf{App}_{\mathcal{C}}^{\sigma,\tau} \circ \langle g, x\rangle$$

for all arrows $x : \mathit{unit} \longrightarrow \sigma$ in $\mathcal{C}$. There is no reason to expect this to hold in every CCC, and in fact this fails in functor categories (Exercise 7.2.43), including Kripke lambda models, and term categories (Exercise 7.2.44). This may seem puzzling, since we may interpret any term $x{:}\sigma \rhd M{:}\tau$ as an arrow $\mathit{unit} \times \sigma \to \tau$ of $\mathcal{C}$, and therefore an element of $A_{\mathcal{C}}^{\mathit{unit}\times\sigma\to\tau}$. However, this element of $A_{\mathcal{C}}^{\mathit{unit}\times\sigma\to\tau}$ is not determined according to the standard meaning function for the Henkin model $\mathcal{A}_{\mathcal{C}}$. In particular, it may not be the only element of $A_{\mathcal{C}}^{\mathit{unit}\times\sigma\to\tau}$ that has the correct functional behavior to be the meaning of M. Intuitively, the reason extensionality fails is that in only using arrows from unit to construct $\mathcal{A}_{\mathcal{C}}$, some of the structure of $\mathcal{C}$ is lost. Arrows from an object a that may behave differently in composition with arbitrary arrow from b into a may happen to behave identically in composition with arrows from *unit* into a. By only using arrows from *unit* in $\mathcal{A}_{\mathcal{C}}$, we limit the "domain" of elements in such a way that the structure is not extensional.

We may identify the CCCs that correspond to Henkin models using a concept that goes by many names. A relatively neutral term, suggested by Peter Freyd, is that a category $\mathcal{C}$ is *well-pointed* if, for all arrows $f, g : a \longrightarrow b$,

$$\text{if } f \circ h = g \circ h \text{ for all } h : unit \longrightarrow a, \text{ then } f = g. \qquad (\textit{well-pointed})$$

The name comes from the fact that arrows $h : unit \longrightarrow a$ are often called the *points* of a. An alternative word for point is *global element.* In the literature, several synonyms for well-pointed are used, such as "having enough points" or "having *unit* as a generator." A term that is used in some of the computer science literature is "concrete," which is problematic since concrete does not always mean well-pointed in the category-theoretic literature. The correspondence between well-pointed CCC's and Henkin models is given in the following proposition.

Theorem 7.2.41 Every Henkin model for $\lambda^{unit,\times,\rightarrow}$ signature Σ determines a well-pointed Σ-CCC and conversely, every well-pointed Σ-CCC determines a Henkin model. The maps between Henkin models and well-pointed CCC's are inverses, and preserve the meanings of terms.

The proof follows easily from Exercises 7.2.38 and 7.2.45.

Since the applicative structure determined from an arbitrary cartesian closed category may not be extensional, many researchers have concluded that cartesian closed categories are "less extensional" than Henkin models. This is correct in the sense that when we try to build a Henkin model from a cartesian closed category, we do not always obtain an extensional structure. However, there are some subtleties that must be taken into consideration. The first is that, by the soundness theorem for CCC's, all CCC's satisfy all of the axioms and inference rules of typed lambda calculus, including extensionality (axiom (η) and rule (ξ)). Secondly, there is an "internal" sense in which all CCC's may be considered extensional. More specifically, any CCC $\mathcal{C}$ may be embedded in another category $\mathcal{D}$ that is a model of predicate logic in a way that preserves the interpretation of terms. When the quantified formula expressing extensionality of $\mathcal{C}$ is interpreted in the model $\mathcal{D}$, the formula is true. However, $\mathcal{D}$ may only be a model of intuitionistic logic, not classical logic. Thus, in rough terms, CCC's are "intuitionistically extensional" but not necessarily "classically" so. (The embedding of $\mathcal{C}$ into $\mathcal{D}$, called the *Yoneda embedding*, may be found in Section 7.3.7.)

Exercise 7.2.42 Let $\mathcal{C}$ be any CCC and let $\mathcal{A}_{\mathcal{C}}$ be a $\lambda^{\rightarrow}$ applicative structure defined from $\mathcal{C}$ as described in this section. (Although we may define a $\lambda^{unit,\times,\rightarrow}$ applicative structure, we do not need *unit* or products for this exercise.) Show that $\mathcal{A}_{\mathcal{C}}$ is a combinatory algebra.

Exercise 7.2.43 A simple CCC that is not well-pointed is the following functor category. Let $\mathcal{P} = \langle\{0, 1\}, \leq\rangle$ be the poset with two elements 0 and 1, ordered so that $0 \leq 1$, and let $Set^{\mathcal{P}}$ be the category of functors from $\mathcal{P}$ to sets. A terminal object, *unit*, of this category is the functor mapping both 0 and 1 to a one-element set, $\{*\}$. Let F be the functor $F(0) = \emptyset$ and $F(1) = \mathcal{N}$, where $\mathcal{N}$ is the set of natural numbers. Find two different natural transformations $\mu, \nu \colon F \rightarrow F$ that are equal when composed with every natural transformation from *unit* to F.

Exercise 7.2.44 A term category, with the arrows from σ to τ equivalence classes of terms as in Example 7.2.19, may not be well-pointed. In a term category $\mathcal{C}(\mathcal{E})$ constructed using theory $\mathcal{E}$,

$$\mathbf{App}_{\mathcal{C}}^{\sigma,\tau} \circ \langle [x\colon unit \triangleright M\colon \sigma \rightarrow \tau], [x\colon unit \triangleright P\colon \sigma]\rangle = [x\colon unit \triangleright MP\colon \tau].$$

Show that $\mathcal{C}(\mathcal{E})$ may not be well-pointed by choosing a signature Σ and theory $\mathcal{E}$ such that when terms are considered modulo provability from $\mathcal{E}$, we may have

$$\mathcal{E} \vdash x\colon unit \triangleright MP = NP\colon \tau$$

for every term $x\colon unit \triangleright P\colon \sigma$, without being able to prove $x\colon unit \triangleright M = N\colon \sigma \rightarrow \tau$ from $\mathcal{E}$.

Exercise 7.2.45 This exercise asks you to complete the proof that if $\mathcal{C}$ is well-pointed, then $\mathcal{A}_{\mathcal{C}}$ is a Henkin model with the same equational theory. (You may assume the results of Exercise 7.2.42.)

(a) Show that if $\mathcal{C}$ is well-pointed, then the applicative structure $\mathcal{A}_{\mathcal{C}}$ is extensional.

(b) Show that when $\mathcal{A}_{\mathcal{C}}$ is a Henkin model, the meaning of $\Gamma \triangleright M\colon \tau$ in $\mathcal{A}_{\mathcal{C}}$ at environment η is the composition of the meaning of this term in $\mathcal{C}$ and an arrow $unit \longrightarrow [\![\Gamma]\!]$ determined from $\eta(x)$.

(c) Conclude that $\mathcal{C}$ and $\mathcal{A}_{\mathcal{C}}$ satisfy the same equations between closed terms, and therefore have the same equational theory.

7.2.6 Categorical Characterization of Meaning Function

In this section, we consider categorical properties of the interpretation of lambda terms in a CCC. If we wish to view the meaning function in a categorical way, then we must begin by making the set of terms into a category. One plausible approach might be to let the type expressions over some signature be the objects of the category and the terms of type σ over some type assignment be arrows from a product type to σ. While this construction does produce a category, with composition given by substitution, it does not seem to have the categorical structure needed to identify properties of the meaning function from terms to a CCC. In particular, this category is not cartesian closed. However, if we select some theory and consider the CCC generated by this theory, as described in Example 7.2.19, then the equivalence classes of terms give rise to a CCC, as shown in Exercise 7.2.24. The main idea in this section is that meaning functions for CCC's correspond to cartesian closed functors.

We begin by showing how the meaning function for a Σ-CCC $\mathcal{D}$ determines a cartesian closed functor from any term category $\mathcal{C}_\Sigma(\mathcal{E})$, provided $\mathcal{E}$ does not equate terms that are unequal in $\mathcal{D}$. Suppose we have a $\lambda^{unit,\times,\rightarrow}$ signature Σ and a Σ-CCC $\mathcal{D}$, with the meaning function $[\![\cdot]\!]$ mapping terms over Σ to morphisms of $\mathcal{D}$. This determines a lambda theory, $Th(\mathcal{D})$, consisting of precisely the equations satisfied by $\mathcal{D}$. If we construct the cartesian closed term category $\mathcal{C}_\Sigma(\mathcal{E})$, for any theory $\mathcal{E} \subseteq Th(\mathcal{D})$, then we may see that the meaning function determines a cartesian closed functor $F_{[\![\cdot]\!]}\colon \mathcal{C}_\Sigma(\mathcal{E}) \longrightarrow \mathcal{D}$ defined as follows. For types, the objects of $\mathcal{C}_\Sigma(\mathcal{E})$, we let $F_{[\![\cdot]\!]}(\sigma)$ be the interpretation of σ in $\mathcal{D}$. For an arrow

$$[x\colon \sigma \rhd M\colon \tau]_{\mathcal{E}} : \sigma \longrightarrow \tau$$

we let

$$F_{[\![\cdot]\!]}([x\colon \sigma \rhd M\colon \tau]_{\mathcal{E}}) = \mathcal{D}[\![x\colon \sigma \rhd M\colon \tau]\!] : F_{[\![\cdot]\!]}(\sigma) \longrightarrow F_{[\![\cdot]\!]}(\tau)$$

By Theorem 7.2.31, the functor $F_{[\![\cdot]\!]}$ is well-defined. Exercise 7.2.49 asks you to use properties of $[\![\cdot]\!]$ to check that $F_{[\![\cdot]\!]}$ is the unique a cartesian closed functor from Σ-CCC $\mathcal{C}_\Sigma(\mathcal{E})$ to $\mathcal{D}$. This gives us the following proposition.

Proposition 7.2.46 Let $[\![\cdot]\!]$ be the meaning function from $\lambda^{unit,\times,\rightarrow}$ terms over signature Σ into CCC $\mathcal{D}$, and let $\mathcal{E} \subseteq Th(\mathcal{D})$ be any subset of the induced lambda theory that is closed under the proof rules. Then $F_{[\![\cdot]\!]}\colon \mathcal{C}_\Sigma(\mathcal{E}) \longrightarrow \mathcal{D}$ is the unique cartesian closed functor from the Σ-CCC generated by $\mathcal{E}$ into $\mathcal{D}$.

In categorical terms, this proposition shows that the category $\mathcal{C}_\Sigma(\mathcal{E})$ is initial in the category whose objects are Σ-CCC's satisfying $\mathcal{E}$ and whose morphisms are cartesian closed functors preserving the interpretation of symbols from the signature Σ. Recall from Section 3.5.2 that an algebra $\mathcal{A}$ is initial in some class $\mathcal{K}$ if $\mathcal{A} \in \mathcal{K}$ and, for every $\mathcal{B} \in \mathcal{K}$, there is a unique homomorphism from $\mathcal{A}$ to $\mathcal{B}$. More generally, as stated in Exercise 7.2.8, an object a of category $\mathcal{K}$ is initial if there is a unique morphism of the category from a to any object b. Just as the term algebra over an algebraic signature is initial, with the unique homomorphism given by the interpretation of terms, Proposition 7.2.46 shows that the term CCC is initial, with the unique cc-functor given by the interpretation of terms.

While this lemma shows that the interpretation of lambda terms into a CCC determines a cartesian closed functor, we would also like to be able to recover the meaning function from the resulting cartesian closed functor. In rough terms, the meaning function $[\![\cdot]\!]$ is the composition of $F_{[\![\cdot]\!]}$ and the process of collapsing terms modulo $\mathcal{E}$. However, in order to make this more precise, we must address some differences between terms over signature Σ and arrows of $\mathcal{C}_\Sigma(\mathcal{E})$.

Suppose $[\![\cdot]\!]$ is the meaning function into $\mathcal{D}$, and let $\mathcal{E} = Th(\mathcal{D})$ be the induced theory. By substituting projections of z for variables $x_1, \ldots, x_k$, we can transform any Σ-term $x_1{:}\,\sigma_1, \ldots, x_k{:}\,\sigma_k \triangleright M{:}\,\tau$ into a term $z{:}\,(\sigma_1 \times \ldots \times \sigma_k) \triangleright M'{:}\,\tau$ of the same type, with one free variable, and such that

$$[\![x_1{:}\,\sigma_1, \ldots, x_k{:}\,\sigma_k \triangleright M{:}\,\tau]\!] = [\![z{:}\,(\sigma_1 \times \ldots \times \sigma_k) \triangleright M'{:}\,\tau]\!].$$

Since the name of the free variable (z above) may be chosen arbitrarily, we can define a map i_Σ on Σ-terms mapping each term to a term with the one free variable of the appropriate type used to construct $\mathcal{C}_\Sigma(\mathcal{E})$. We can then map the term $i_\Sigma(\Gamma \triangleright M{:}\,\tau) = z{:}\,(\sigma_1 \times \ldots \times \sigma_k) \triangleright M'{:}\,\tau$ to its equivalence class, modulo $\mathcal{E}$. Let $j_\mathcal{E}$ be the map from terms to equivalence classes taking $\Gamma \triangleright M{:}\,\tau$ to the equivalence class $[i_\Sigma(\Gamma \triangleright M{:}\,\tau)]_\mathcal{E}$. Then we may write $[\![\cdot]\!]$ as the composition of the function $j_\mathcal{E}$ and the cartesian closed functor $F_{[\![\cdot]\!]}$ as stated in the following lemma.

Lemma 7.2.47 Let $[\![\cdot]\!]$ be the meaning function from terms over signature Σ into a Σ-CCC $\mathcal{D}$, and let $\mathcal{E}$ be the induced lambda theory. Then $[\![\cdot]\!]$ is the composition

$$[\![\cdot]\!] = F_{[\![\cdot]\!]} \circ j_\mathcal{E}$$

of the map $j_\mathcal{E}$ taking terms to equivalence classes and the cc-functor $F_{[\![\cdot]\!]}$ from $\mathcal{C}_\Sigma(\mathcal{E})$ into $\mathcal{D}$.

Using initiality, we can also show that every cartesian closed functor $F : \mathcal{C}_\Sigma(\mathcal{E}) \longrightarrow \mathcal{D}$ determines a meaning function, for some way of regarding $\mathcal{D}$ as a Σ-CCC. As mentioned in Section 7.2.3, cartesian closedness of a functor F means that *unit*, $\times$ and $\rightarrow$ are preserved, so that $F(unit_{\mathcal{C}(\mathcal{E})}) = unit_\mathcal{D}$, $F(\sigma \times_{\mathcal{C}(\mathcal{E})} \tau) = F(\sigma) \times_\mathcal{D} F(\tau)$, and similarly for function spaces. In addition, the term formation operations $\mathbf{Proj}_1$, $\mathbf{Proj}_2$, $\langle\ \rangle$, **App** and **Curry** must be preserved. For **App**, for example, this means that

$$\begin{aligned} F([z{:}\,\sigma \triangleright M \cdot_\rho N{:}\,\tau]_\mathcal{E}) &= F(\mathbf{App} \circ \langle [z{:}\,\sigma \triangleright M{:}\,\rho \rightarrow \tau]_\mathcal{E},\ [z{:}\,\sigma \triangleright N{:}\,\rho]_\mathcal{E}\rangle) \\ &= \mathbf{App} \circ \langle F([z{:}\,\sigma \triangleright M{:}\,\rho \rightarrow \tau]_\mathcal{E}),\ F([z{:}\,\sigma \triangleright N{:}\,\rho]_\mathcal{E})\rangle \end{aligned}$$

Writing $[\![\ ]\!]$ for the composition of F and j, we have as a consequence

$$[\![\Gamma \triangleright M \cdot_{\rho} N\colon \tau]\!] = \mathbf{App} \circ \langle [\![\Gamma \triangleright M\colon \rho \to \tau]\!],\ [\![\Gamma \triangleright N\colon \rho]\!]\rangle.$$

The other conditions work out similarly, giving us the following theorem.

Theorem 7.2.48 Let $F : \mathcal{C}_{\Sigma}(\mathcal{E}) \longrightarrow \mathcal{D}$ be any cartesian closed functor from the category generated by theory $\mathcal{E}$ over Σ-terms into a CCC $\mathcal{D}$. Then the function $[\![\cdot]\!]$ from Σ-terms into $\mathcal{D}$ given by composing F with the map $j_{\mathcal{E}}$ from terms to equivalence classes modulo $\mathcal{E}$ is a meaning function for some Σ-CCC obtained from $\mathcal{D}$ by choosing interpretations for type and term constants of Σ. Furthermore, the theory $\mathcal{E}'$ induced by $[\![\cdot]\!]$ is an extension of $\mathcal{E}$, with $\mathcal{E}' = \mathcal{E}$ if F is one-to-one.

Exercise 7.2.49 Prove Proposition 7.2.46

7.3 Kripke Lambda Models and Functor Categories

7.3.1 Overview

We have seen that Henkin models correspond to a special case of cartesian closed category, namely, well-pointed CCC's. In this section, we consider a more general class of models, called Kripke lambda models. These models provide an intuitive class of CCC's, based on functor categories, that differ from Henkin models. Structurally, the difference between a Kripke lambda model and a Henkin model is roughly the same as the difference between a Kripke model of first-order logic and an ordinary model: instead of a set of elements for each type, a Kripke model has a family of sets indexed by a partially-ordered set of "possible worlds." By working through the definition of Kripke lambda model, and seeing the connection with functor categories, the reader may develop better intuition for the logical properties of cartesian closed categories in general, and functor categories in particular.

A technical reason for studying Kripke models is that we may prove "least model" completeness for the standard equational proof system of typed lambda calculus. Since Kripke lambda models are a special case of cartesian closed categories, this gives a completeness theorem for CCC's as a corollary. Since we obtain completeness for Henkin models only by adding extra inference rules, the Kripke completeness theorem clearly illustrates the difference between Henkin models and arbitrary CCC's. Some applications of Kripke models are discussed in Section 6.6.4, in connection with the semantics of block-structured imperative languages. The general development here is based on [MM91].

7.3.2 Possible Worlds

A Kripke lambda model will include a partially-ordered set of "possible worlds." Instead of having a set of elements of each type, a Kripke lambda model will have a set of elements of each type at each possible world. The relationship between elements of type σ at worlds w and w', if $w \leq w'$, is that every $a\colon \sigma$ *at* w is associated with some unique $a'\colon \sigma$ *at* w'. Informally, using the common metaphor of $\leq$ as relation in time, this means that every element of σ at w will continue to be an element of σ in every possible $w' \geq w$. As we move from w to a possible future world w', two things might happen: we may acquire more elements, and distinct elements may become identified. These changes may be explained in a philosophical way by saying that as time progresses, we may become aware of (or construct) more elements of the universe, and we may come to know more "properties" of elements. In the case of lambda calculus, the properties of interest are equations, and so we may have more equations in future worlds. Since a type σ may be empty at some world w and then become nonempty at $w' \geq w$, some types may be neither "globally" empty nor nonempty. This is one property that distinguishes Kripke models from Henkin models, since A^σ is either empty or nonempty in a Henkin model $\mathcal{A}$.

7.3.3 Applicative Structures

Kripke lambda models may be defined using a Kripke form of applicative structure. For simplicity, we treat $\lambda^\rightarrow$ here and add *unit* and product types in Section 7.3.7. A *Kripke applicative structure*

$$\mathcal{A} = \langle \mathrm{W}, \leq, \{A_w^\sigma\}, \{\mathbf{App}_w^{\sigma,\tau}\}, \{i_{w,w'}^\sigma\}, \mathit{Const}\rangle$$

for $\lambda^\rightarrow$ signature Σ consists of

- a set $\mathcal{W}$ of "possible worlds" partially-ordered by $\leq$,
- a family $\{A_w^\sigma\}$ of sets indexed by type expressions σ over signature Σ and worlds $w \in \mathcal{W}$,
- a family $\{\mathbf{App}_w^{\sigma,\tau}\}$ of "application maps" $\mathbf{App}_w^{\sigma,\tau}\colon A_w^{\sigma\rightarrow\tau} \times A_w^\sigma \rightarrow A_w^\tau$ indexed by pairs of type expressions σ, τ and worlds $w \in \mathcal{W}$,
- a family $\{i_{w,w'}^\sigma\}$ of "transition functions" $i_{w,w'}^\sigma\colon A_w^\sigma \rightarrow A_{w'}^\sigma$ indexed by type expressions σ and pairs of worlds $w \leq w'$
- a function *Const* from term constants of the signature Σ to *global elements* (defined below) of the appropriate type

subject to the following conditions. We want the transition from A_w^σ to A_w^σ to be the identity

$i^{\sigma}_{w,w}\colon A^{\sigma}_{w} \to A^{\sigma}_{w}$ is the identity, *(id)*

and other transition functions to compose

$$i^{\sigma}_{w',w''} \circ i^{\sigma}_{w,w'} = i^{\sigma}_{w,w''} \quad \text{for all } w \le w' \le w'' \qquad (comp)$$

so that there is exactly one mapping of A^{σ}_{w} into $A^{\sigma}_{w'}$ given for $w \le w'$. We also require that application and transition commute in a natural way

$$\begin{array}{l} \forall f \in A^{\sigma\to\tau}_{w}. \forall a \in A^{\sigma}_{w}. \\ i^{\tau}_{w,w'}(\mathbf{App}^{\sigma,\tau}_{w}(f, a)) = \mathbf{App}^{\sigma,\tau}_{w'}((i^{\sigma\to\tau}_{w,w'} f), (i^{\sigma}_{w,w'} a)), \end{array} \qquad (nat)$$

which may be drawn

$$\begin{array}{ccc} A^{\sigma\to\tau}_{w'} \times A^{\sigma}_{w'} & \xrightarrow{\mathbf{App}^{\sigma,\tau}_{w'}} & A^{\tau}_{w'} \\ {\scriptstyle i^{\sigma\to\tau}\times i^{\sigma}}\uparrow & & \uparrow{\scriptstyle i^{\tau}} \\ A^{\sigma\to\tau}_{w} \times A^{\sigma}_{w} & \xrightarrow[\mathbf{App}^{\sigma,\tau}_{w}]{} & A^{\tau}_{w} \end{array}$$

and will be described informally below.

Intuitively, a global element $\mathbf{a}$ of type σ is a "consistent" family of elements $a_w \in A^{\sigma}_{w}$, one for each $w \in \mathcal{W}$. More precisely, a *global element of type* σ is a map $\mathbf{a} : \mathcal{W} \to \bigcup_{w\in\mathcal{W}} A^{\sigma}_{w}$ such that $\mathbf{a}(w) \in A^{\sigma}_{w}$ and, whenever $w \le w'$, we have $\mathbf{a}(w') = i^{\sigma}_{w,w'}\mathbf{a}(w)$. It is conventional to write $\mathbf{a}_w$ for $\mathbf{a}(w)$. This completes the definition of Kripke applicative structure.

Although we have defined Kripke applicative structures with $\mathbf{App}^{\sigma,\tau}_{w}\colon A^{\sigma\to\tau}_{w} \times A^{\sigma}_{w} \to A^{\tau}_{w}$ for technical convenience, we will also use $\mathbf{App}$ as a curried function when convenient.

If $a \in A^{\sigma}_{w}$ and $w \le w'$, then we can read $i^{\sigma}_{w,w'}a \in A^{\sigma}_{w'}$ as "a viewed at world w'." The purpose of the application map $\mathbf{App}^{\sigma,\tau}_{w}$ is to associate a function $\mathbf{App}^{\sigma,\tau}_{w} f$ from A^{σ}_{w} to A^{τ}_{w} with each element $f \in A^{\sigma\to\tau}_{w}$. Since we can view $f \in A^{\sigma\to\tau}_{w}$ as an element at any future world $w' \ge w$, the application map at world w' also associates a function with $i^{\sigma\to\tau}_{w,w'} f$ at w'. The condition *(nat)* is intended to give a degree of coherence to the functions associated with different views of f. Basically, *(nat)* says that if we apply f to argument a at world w, and then view the result at a later world $w' \ge w$, we see the same value as when we view f and a as elements of world w', and apply f to a there.

Kripke applicative structures can be defined using category-theoretic concepts. The usual definition of applicative structure may be interpreted in any cartesian category (category with terminal object and products), as follows. An ordinary applicative structure may be defined as a structure $\langle\{A^{\sigma}\}, \{\mathbf{App}^{\sigma,\tau}\}, Const\rangle$, where $\{A^{\sigma}\}$ is a family of sets indexed by type expressions over the signature, $\{\mathbf{App}^{\sigma,\tau}\}$ is a family of application functions

$$\mathbf{App}^{\sigma,\tau}\colon A^{\sigma\to\tau} \times A^{\sigma} \to A^{\tau}$$

indexed by pairs of type expressions, and *Const* is a map from constants of the signature to elements of the model. We may interpret this definition "in" a category $\mathcal{C}$ with products and terminal object by regarding the word "set" as meaning "object from $\mathcal{C}$," the word "function" as meaning "morphism from $\mathcal{C}$" and the word "element" as meaning "point," or "global element" of the category (morphism from *unit*). Thus products are used to give $\mathbf{App}^{\sigma,\tau}$ an appropriate domain and a terminal object is used to define global elements. Summarizing this description, an *applicative structure in a category $\mathcal{C}$ with products and terminal object* is a collection of objects $\{C^{\sigma}\}$ indexed by type expressions of the signature, a collection of morphisms $\{\mathbf{App}^{\sigma,\tau}\}$ indexed by pairs of type expressions (such that $\mathbf{App}^{\sigma,\tau}$ has the domain and codomain given above) and a map *Const* from constants to global elements of the appropriate types. To derive our definition of Kripke applicative structure from this general idea, we regard a poset $\langle \mathcal{W}, \leq\rangle$ as a category as in Example 7.2.6, and consider the category $\mathit{Set}^{\langle \mathcal{W}, \leq\rangle}$ of functors from $\langle \mathcal{W}, \leq\rangle$ to sets. If we work out what *applicative structure* means in a category of the form $\mathit{Set}^{\langle \mathcal{W}, \leq\rangle}$, then "sets" will be functors, "functions" natural transformations and "elements" will determine global elements. In short, we end up with the definition of applicative structure spelled out explicitly above, with $w \mapsto A^{\sigma}_{w}$ the object map of a functor and $\ell_{w,w'} \mapsto i^{\sigma}_{w,w'}$ the morphisms map of this functor. The details are taken up in Exercise 7.3.1.

A second connection between Kripke lambda models and category theory is that each Kripke lambda model forms a CCC. This is discussed in Section 7.3.7.

Exercise 7.3.1 If $\mathcal{C}$ is a category with terminal objects and product, then an applicative structure in $\mathcal{C}$ is a tuple $\langle\{C^{\sigma}\}, \{\mathbf{App}^{\sigma,\tau}, \mathit{Const}\rangle$ as described in this section.

(a) Show that for any partial order $\langle \mathcal{W}, \leq\rangle$, the functor category $\mathit{Set}^{\langle \mathcal{W}, \leq\rangle}$ has products and a terminal object.

(b) Show that an applicative structure in $\mathit{Set}^{\langle \mathcal{W}, \leq\rangle}$ is precisely a Kripke applicative structure over possible worlds $\langle \mathcal{W}, \leq\rangle$.

7.3.4 Extensionality, Combinators and Functor Categories

A classical applicative structure may fail to be a model for two reasons; both apply to Kripke applicative structures as well. The first possibility is that we may not have enough elements. For example, $\sigma \to \sigma$ might be empty, making it impossible to give meaning to the identity function $\lambda x\colon \sigma.\, x$. The second problem is that application may not be extensional, *i.e.*, we may have two distinct elements of functional type with the same functional behavior. Consequently, the meaning of a lambda term $\lambda x\colon\sigma.\, M$ may not be determined uniquely.

The usual statement of extensionality is that $f = g$ whenever $fx = gx$ for all x of the appropriate type. In Kripke applicative structures, we are concerned not only with the behavior of elements $f, g \in A_w^{\sigma\rightarrow\tau}$ as functions from A_w^σ to A_w^τ, but also as functions from $A_{w'}^\sigma$ to $A_{w'}^\tau$ for all $w' \geq w$. Therefore, we say a Kripke applicative structure $\mathcal{A}$ is *extensional* if, for all $f, g \in A_w^{\sigma\rightarrow\tau}$,

$f = g$ whenever

$$\forall w' \geq w. \forall a \in A_{w'}^\sigma.\ \mathbf{App}_{w'}^{\sigma\rightarrow\tau}(i_{w,w'}^{\sigma\rightarrow\tau} f)\, a = \mathbf{App}_{w'}^{\sigma\rightarrow\tau}(i_{w,w'}^{\sigma\rightarrow\tau} g)\, a.$$

This can also be stated using the standard interpretation of predicate logic in Kripke structures. However, since this requires extra machinery, we will not go into predicate logic here. The main point that may be of interest to the general reader is that the statement above is exactly the result of interpreting the usual formula for extensionality (not mentioning possible worlds at all) in a Kripke model.

There are two ways to identify the extensional applicative structures that have enough elements to be models. As with ordinary applicative structures, the environment and combinatory model definitions are equivalent. Since the combinatory condition is simpler, we will use it here. For all types σ, τ and ρ, we need global elements $\mathbf{K}_{\sigma,\tau}$ of type $\sigma \rightarrow \tau \rightarrow \sigma$ and $\mathbf{S}_{\sigma,\tau,\rho}$ of type $(\rho \rightarrow \sigma \rightarrow \tau) \rightarrow (\rho \rightarrow \sigma) \rightarrow \rho \rightarrow \tau$. The equational condition on $\mathbf{K}_{\sigma,\tau}$ is that for $a \in A_w^\sigma$, $b \in A_w^\tau$, we must have $(\mathbf{K}_{\sigma,\tau})_w\ a\ b = a$. The condition for $\mathbf{S}$ is derived from the equational axiom in Section 4.5.7 similarly.

We define a *Kripke lambda model* to be a Kripke applicative structure $\mathcal{A}$ that is extensional and has combinators.

As mentioned in the last section, the interpretation of each type in a Kripke model is a functor from a partial order of possible worlds into $\mathcal{S}et$. The *full* $\lambda^{\rightarrow}$ *Kripke model* over any given functors $F_1, \ldots, F_n : \mathcal{P} \longrightarrow \mathcal{S}et$ is the full subcategory of $\mathcal{S}et^{\mathcal{P}}$ whose objects are all functors definable from $F_1, \ldots, F_n$ using $\rightarrow$ and whose arrows are all natural transformations between these functors. Since we did not define function objects in $\mathcal{S}et^{\mathcal{P}}$ in Example 7.2.17, we do so after the following example.

Example 7.3.2 This example describes part of a Kripke lambda model and shows that $A_w^{\sigma\rightarrow\tau}$ may be nonempty, even if A_w^σ and A_w^τ are both empty. Let $\mathcal{P} = \{0, 1, 2\}$ with $0 \leq 1 \leq 2$. We are interested in the Kripke lambda model $\mathcal{A}$ with a single type constant a interpreted as the functor $F : \mathcal{P} \longrightarrow \mathcal{S}et$ with $F(0) = \emptyset$, $F(1) = \{c_1, c_2\}$ and $F(2) = \{c\}$. (This means that $A_i^a = F(i)$ for $i \in \{0, 1, 2\}$; each $i_{w,w'}^a = F(\ell_{w,w'})$ is uniquely determined.)

A natural transformation $\nu : F \longrightarrow F$ must satisfy the diagram

$$\begin{array}{ccc}
\{c\} & \xrightarrow{\nu(2)} & \{c\} \\
{\scriptstyle i^a_{1,2}}\uparrow & & \uparrow{\scriptstyle i^a_{1,2}} \\
\{c_1, c_2\} & \xrightarrow{\nu(1)} & \{c_1, c_2\} \\
{\scriptstyle i^a_{0,1}}\uparrow & & \uparrow{\scriptstyle i^a_{0,1}} \\
\emptyset & \xrightarrow[\nu(0)]{} & \emptyset
\end{array}$$

Since $\nu(0)$ and $\nu(1)$ are uniquely determined and any map from $\{c_1, c_2\}$ to $\{c_1, c_2\}$ will do for $\nu(1)$, there are four natural transformations from F to F. Let us call these ν, ν', ν'', ν'''.

The function type $A^{a\to a}$ should represent all natural transformations from F to G. However, by extensionality, we may only have as many elements of $A^{a\to a}_w$ as there are natural transformations when we consider the possible worlds that are $\geq w$. In particular, $A^{a\to a}_2$ may only have one element, since there is only one possible mapping from A^a_2 to A^a_2 and there are no other worlds ≥ 2. Let us write $\nu|_w$ for the result of restricting ν to worlds $\geq w$. In other words, $\nu|_w$ is the function with domain $\{w' \mid w' \geq w\}$ such that $\nu|_w(w') = \nu(w')$. Using this notation, we may define $A^{a\to a}$ by

$$A^{a\to a}_2 = \{\nu|_2, \nu'|_2, \nu''|_2, \nu'''|_2\}$$

$$A^{a\to a}_1 = \{\nu|_1, \nu'|_1, \nu''|_1, \nu'''|_1\}$$

$$A^{a\to a}_0 = \{\nu, \nu', \nu'', \nu'''\}$$

Note, however, that $\nu|_2 = \nu'|_2 = \nu''|_2 = \nu'''|_2$ since there is only one function from A^a_2 to A^a_2. Application is given by

$$\mathbf{App}^{\sigma,\tau}_w\ \nu\, x = \nu(w)(x),$$

which is the general definition for any full Kripke lambda model where the elements of function type are natural transformations. The reader is encouraged to verify that this is an extensional interpretation of $a \to a$ with four elements of $A^{a\to a}_0$, four elements of $A^{a\to a}_1$, and one element of $A^{a\to a}_2$. ■

As mentioned in Example 7.2.17, the category $\mathit{Set}^{\mathcal{C}}$ of functors from $\mathcal{C}$ into Set is cartesian closed, for any small category $\mathcal{C}$. Any functor F with each $F(c)$ a one-element set will be a terminal object of $\mathit{Set}^{\mathcal{C}}$. The product of functors $F, G : \mathcal{C} \longrightarrow \mathit{Set}$ is given by

$$(F \times G)(c) = F(c) \times G(c),$$

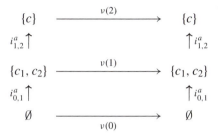

with the arrow may of $F \times G$ taking an arrow f to $F(f) \times G(f)$. The function object $(F \to G) : \mathcal{C} \longrightarrow Set$ defined using the *Hom* functor with $Hom(a, \_) : \mathcal{C} \longrightarrow Set$ taking object c to the set $Hom(a, c)$ and acting on morphisms by composition. Using *Hom*, the functor $F \to G$ is defined as follows:

$(F \to G)(c)$ = the set of all natural transformations from $Hom(c, \_) \times F$ to G

$(F \to G)(f : a \to b)$ = the map taking natural transformation

$\nu : Hom(a, \_) \times F \longrightarrow G$

to $\mu = (F \to G)(f)(\nu) : Hom(b, \_) \times F \longrightarrow G$

according to the diagram below, for each object c of $\mathcal{C}$.

$$
\begin{array}{cccc}
b & Hom(b, c) \times F(c) & \xrightarrow{\quad \mu(c) \quad} & G(c) \\
f \uparrow & (\_ \circ f) \times id \downarrow & & \uparrow id \\
a & Hom(a, c) \times F(c) & \xrightarrow[\quad G(g) \quad]{} & G(c)
\end{array}
$$

where the function $(\_ \circ f) : Hom(b, c) \longrightarrow Hom(a, c)$ maps h to $h \circ f$.

In the special case of $Set^{\mathcal{P}}$, where $\mathcal{P}$ is a partial order, each of the hom-sets have at most one element. This allows us to simplify the definition of $F \to G$ considerably. If w is an object of the partial order $\mathcal{P}$, it will be convenient to write $\mathcal{P}_{\geq w}$ for the full subcategory of $\mathcal{P}$ containing exactly the objects that are $\geq w$ in the partial order. If $F : \mathcal{P} \longrightarrow Set$, then we similarly write $F_{\geq w}$ for the functor from $\mathcal{P}_{\geq w}$ into Set obtained by restricting f to $\mathcal{P}_{\geq w}$. For any $F, G : \mathcal{P} \longrightarrow Set$, we can simplify the definition above as follows.

$(F \to G)(w)$ = the set of all natural transformations from $F_{\geq w}$ to G

$(F \to G)(\ell_{w,w'})$ = the map taking natural transformation $\nu : F_{\geq w} \longrightarrow G$

to $\mu = (F \to G)(f)(\nu) : F_{\geq w'} \longrightarrow G$

according to the diagram below, for each object $w'' \geq w' \geq w$ in $\mathcal{P}$.

$$
\begin{array}{cccc}
w' & F_{\geq w}(w'') & \xrightarrow{\quad \mu(w) \quad} & G(w) \\
\ell_{w,w'} \uparrow & id \downarrow & & \uparrow id \\
w & F_{\geq w}(w'') & \xrightarrow[\quad \nu(w) \quad]{} & G(w)
\end{array}
$$

In other words, $(F \to G)(f)(\nu)$ is identical to ν, restricted to the subcategory $\mathcal{P}_{\geq w'}$. Put in the notation of Kripke lambda models, if types σ and τ are interpreted as functors

$F, G : \mathcal{P} \longrightarrow Set$ by $A^{\sigma}_{w} = F(w)$, $A^{\tau}_{w} = G(w)$ then the interpretation of $\sigma \rightarrow \tau$ in the full Kripke lambda model is the functor $A^{\sigma\rightarrow\tau} = F \rightarrow G$ with

$A^{\sigma\rightarrow\tau}_{w}$ = the set of all natural transformations from $F_{\geq w}$ to G

$i^{\sigma\rightarrow\tau}_{w,w'}$ = the map restricting $\nu: F_{\geq w} \longrightarrow G$ to $F_{\geq w'}$.

Exercise 7.3.3 Describe $A^{a\rightarrow a\rightarrow a}_{0}$ and $A^{a\rightarrow a\rightarrow a}_{1}$ in the full Kripke model of Example 7.3.2.

7.3.5 Environments and Meanings of Terms

An *environment* η for a Kripke applicative structure $\mathcal{A}$ is a partial mapping from variables and worlds to elements of $\mathcal{A}$ such that

If $\eta x w \in A^{\sigma}_{w}$ and $w' \geq w$, then $\eta x w' = i^{\sigma}_{w,w'}(\eta x w)$. (*env*)

Intuitively, an environment η maps a variable x to a "partial element" ηx that may exist (or be defined) at some worlds, but not necessarily all worlds. Since a type may be empty at one world and then nonempty later, we need to have environments such that $\eta x w$ is undefined at some w, and then "becomes" defined at a later $w' \geq w$. We will return to this point after defining the meanings of terms.

If η is an environment and $a \in A^{\sigma}_{w}$, we write $\eta[x \mapsto a]$ for the environment identical to η on variables other than x, and with

$(\eta[x \mapsto a])x w' = i^{\sigma}_{w,w'} a$

for all $w' \geq w$. We take $(\eta[x \mapsto a])x w'$ to be undefined if w' is not greater than or equal to w. Note that the definition of $\eta[x \mapsto a]$ actually depends on w if the A^{σ}_{w} are not disjoint. If η is an environment for applicative structure $\mathcal{A}$, and Γ is a type assignment, we say η *satisfies* Γ *at* w, written $\eta, w \models \Gamma$ if

$\eta x w \in A^{\sigma}_{w}$ for all $x{:}\,\sigma \in \Gamma$.

Note that if $\eta, w \models \Gamma$ and $w' \geq w$, then $\eta, w' \models \Gamma$.

For any Kripke model $\mathcal{A}$, world w and environment η with $\eta, w \models \Gamma$, we define the meaning $\mathcal{A}[\![\Gamma \triangleright M{:}\,\sigma]\!]\eta w$ of term $\Gamma \triangleright M{:}\,\sigma$ in environment η at world w by induction on typing derivations, as for standard Henkin models. For notational simplicity, we write $[\![\ldots]\!]\ldots$ in place of $\mathcal{A}[\![\ldots]\!]\ldots$ Since the clause for (*add var*) is trivial, it is omitted.

$$[\![\Gamma \triangleright x\colon\sigma]\!]\eta w \qquad = \eta x w$$

$$[\![\Gamma \triangleright c\colon\sigma]\!]\eta w \qquad = Const(c)_w$$

$$[\![\Gamma \triangleright MN\colon\tau]\!]\eta w \qquad = \mathbf{App}_w^{\sigma,\tau}\ ([\![\Gamma \triangleright M\colon\sigma\to\tau]\!]\eta w)\ ([\![\Gamma \triangleright N\colon\sigma]\!]\eta w)$$

$$[\![\Gamma \triangleright \lambda x\colon\sigma.M\colon\sigma\to\tau]\!]\eta w = \text{the unique } d \in A_w^{\sigma\to\tau}$$

$$\text{such that for all } w' \geq w \text{ and } a \in A_{w'}^{\sigma},$$

$$\mathbf{App}_{w'}^{\sigma,\tau}(i_{w,w'}^{\sigma\to\tau} d)a = [\![\Gamma, x\colon\sigma \triangleright M\colon\tau]\!]\eta[x \mapsto a]\, w'$$

Combinators and extensionality guarantee that in the $\Gamma \triangleright \lambda x\colon\sigma.M\colon\sigma\to\tau$ case, d exists and is unique. This is proved as in the standard Henkin setting, using translation into combinators as in Section 4.5.7 for existence, and extensionality for uniqueness.

We say an equation $\Gamma \triangleright M = N\colon\sigma$ *holds at* w *and* η, written

$$\eta, w \Vdash (\Gamma \triangleright M = N\colon\sigma)$$

if, whenever $\eta, w \models \Gamma$, we have

$$[\![\Gamma \triangleright M\colon\sigma]\!]\eta w = [\![\Gamma \triangleright N\colon\sigma]\!]\eta w.$$

A model $\mathcal{A}$ *satisfies* $\Gamma \triangleright M = N\colon\sigma$, written $\mathcal{A} \models \Gamma \triangleright M = N\colon\sigma$, if every η and w of $\mathcal{A}$ satisfy the equation.

Example 7.3.4 As an application of Kripke models, we will show how to construct a counter-model to an implication that holds over Henkin models. Let E_1 and E_2 be the equations

$$E_1 \stackrel{\text{def}}{=} \lambda x\colon a.f P_1 = \lambda x\colon a.f P_2 \quad\text{and}\quad E_2 \stackrel{\text{def}}{=} f P_1 = f P_2,$$

where $f\colon(a \to a \to a) \to b$, $P_1 \stackrel{\text{def}}{=} \lambda x\colon a.\lambda y\colon a.x$ and $P_2 \stackrel{\text{def}}{=} \lambda x\colon a.\lambda y\colon a.y$. Exercise 4.5.24 shows how rule (*nonempty*) can be used to prove E_2 from E_1 and Exercise 4.5.29 how to prove E_2 from E_1 using rules (*empty I*) and (*empty E*). Since E_1 does not semantically imply E_2 over Kripke models, it follows that we cannot prove E_2 from E_1 without using one of these extensions to the proof system. Furthermore, neither (*nonempty*) nor (*empty I*) and (*empty E*) are sound for Kripke lambda models.

We must construct a Kripke lambda model $\mathcal{A}$ for type constants a and b and term constant f that satisfies E_1 but not E_2. If there is a global element of type a, then we could apply both functions in E_1 to this element and obtain E_2. If A^a is empty at all possible worlds, then the argument given in Exercise 4.5.29 shows that E_1 implies E_2. Therefore, we must let A^a be empty at some world and nonempty at another. Since it suffices to have two possible worlds, we let $\mathcal{W} = \{0, 1\}$ with $0 \le 1$ and take $A^a_0 = \emptyset$. Since we need P_1 and P_2 to be different, we let A^a_1 have a two distinct elements, c_1 and c_2.

Equation E_1 will hold at world 0, since a is empty. To make $f\,P_1 = f\,P_2$ equal at world 1, we let A^b_1 have only one element, say d. Without committing to A^b_0, we can see that E_1 must hold at both worlds: the two terms of type $a \to b$ are equal at world 0 since $A^a_0 = \emptyset$ and equal at world 1 since A^b_1 has only one element. We let A^b_0 have two elements, d_1 and d_2, so that E_2 may fail at world 0.

Our counter-model is the full Kripke lambda model over the two functors A^a and A^b. As described in Example 7.3.2 and Exercise 7.3.3, $A^{a \to a}$ and therefore $A^{a \to a \to a}$ are nonempty at world 0. If we let $f^{\mathcal{A}}_0$ map $[\![P_1]\!]$ to d_1 and $[\![P_1]\!]$ to d_2, then the equation E_2 fails at world 0. Since E_2 holds in $\mathcal{A}$ only if it holds at all possible worlds of $\mathcal{A}$, we can see that $\mathcal{A} \models E_1$ but $\mathcal{A} \not\models E_2$.

Exercise 7.3.5 We may consider classical applicative structures as a special case of Kripke applicative structures, using any partial order. To be specific, let $\mathcal{A} = \langle \{A^\sigma\}, \{App^{\sigma,\tau}\} \rangle$ be a classical applicative structure, *i.e.*, $\{A^\sigma\}$ is a collection of sets indexed by types and $\{\mathbf{App}^{\sigma,\tau}\}$ is a collection of application functions. We define the Kripke structure

$$\mathcal{A}^{\mathcal{W}} = \langle \mathrm{W}, \le, \{A^\sigma_w\}, \{\mathbf{App}^{\sigma,\tau}_w\}, \{i^\sigma_{w,w'}\}, Const \rangle$$

by taking sets $A^\sigma_w = A^\sigma$, application functions $\mathbf{App}^{\sigma,\tau}_w = \mathbf{App}^{\sigma,\tau}$ and each transition function $i^\sigma_{w,w'}$ to be the identity. In categorical terms, $\mathcal{A}^{\mathcal{W}}$ could be called an applicative structure of constant presheaves. Show that if $\mathcal{A}$ is a classical lambda model then $\mathcal{A}^{\mathcal{W}}$ is a Kripke lambda model by checking extensionality and using induction on terms to prove that the meaning of a term M in $\mathcal{A}^{\mathcal{W}}$ is the same as the meaning of M in $\mathcal{A}$, in any environment.

7.3.6 Soundness and Completeness

We have soundness and completeness theorems for Kripke lambda models.

Lemma 7.3.6 (Soundness) Let $\mathcal{E}$ be a set of well-typed equations. If $\mathcal{E} \vdash \Gamma \triangleright M = N\colon \sigma$, then every model satisfying $\mathcal{E}$ also satisfies $\Gamma \triangleright M = N\colon \sigma$.

A direct proof is given as Exercise 7.3.8. An alternate proof may be obtained using the correspondence between Kripke models and CCC's discussed in Section 7.3.7.

Theorem 7.3.7 (Completeness for Kripke Models) For every lambda theory $\mathcal{E}$, there is a Kripke lambda model satisfying precisely the equations belonging to $\mathcal{E}$.

Proof The completeness theorem is proved by constructing a term model

$$\mathcal{A} = \langle \mathrm{W}, \leq, \{A_w^\sigma\}, \{\mathbf{App}_w^{\sigma,\tau}\}, \{i_{w,w'}^\sigma\}, Const\rangle$$

of the following form.

- $\mathcal{W}$ is the poset of finite type assignments Γ ordered by inclusion. In what follows, we will write Γ for an arbitrary element of $\mathcal{W}$.
- A_Γ^σ is the set of all $[\Gamma \triangleright M\colon\sigma]$, where $\Gamma \triangleright M\colon\sigma$ is well-typed, and the equivalence class of $\Gamma \triangleright M\colon\sigma$ with respect to $\mathcal{E}$ is

$$[\Gamma \triangleright M\colon\sigma] = \{\Gamma \triangleright N\colon\sigma \mid \mathcal{E} \vdash \Gamma \triangleright M = N\colon\sigma\}.$$

- $\mathbf{App}_\Gamma^{\sigma,\tau}([\Gamma \triangleright M\colon\sigma \to \tau], [\Gamma \triangleright N\colon\sigma]) = [\Gamma \triangleright MN\colon\tau]$
- $i_{\Gamma,\Gamma'}^\sigma([\Gamma \triangleright M\colon\sigma]) = [\Gamma' \triangleright M\colon\sigma]$ for $\Gamma \subseteq \Gamma'$

It is easy to check that the definition makes sense, and that we have global elements **K** and **S** at all appropriate types. For example,

$$\mathbf{K}_\Gamma = [\lambda x\colon\sigma.\lambda y\colon\tau.x]$$

Since the required properties of **K** and **S** are easily verified, the term applicative structure is a Kripke combinatory algebra.

The proof of extensionality illustrates the difference between Kripke models and ordinary Henkin models. Suppose that $[\Gamma \triangleright M\colon\sigma \to \tau]$ and $[\Gamma \triangleright N\colon\sigma \to \tau]$ have the same functional behavior, *i.e.*, for all $\Gamma' \geq \Gamma$ and $\Gamma' \triangleright P\colon\sigma$, we have

$$[\Gamma' \triangleright MP\colon\tau] = [\Gamma' \triangleright NP\colon\tau]$$

Then, in particular, for $\Gamma' \equiv \Gamma, x\colon\sigma$ with x not in Γ, we have

$$[\Gamma, x\colon\sigma \triangleright Mx\colon\tau] = [\Gamma, x\colon\sigma \triangleright Nx\colon\tau]$$

and so by rule (ξ) and axiom (η), we have $[\Gamma \triangleright M\colon\sigma \to \tau] = [\Gamma \triangleright N\colon\sigma \to \tau]$. Thus $\mathcal{A}$ is a Kripke lambda model. This argument may be compared with the step in the proof of Lemma 8.3.1 showing that if $\mathcal{E} \vdash \Gamma \triangleright MN = M'N'\colon\tau$ for every N, N' with $\mathcal{E} \vdash \Gamma \triangleright N = N'\colon\sigma$, then $\mathcal{E} \vdash \Gamma \triangleright M = M'\colon\sigma \to \tau$ using the assumption that $\mathcal{H}$ provides infinitely many variables of each type.

It remains to show that $\mathcal{A}$ satisfies precisely the equations belonging to $\mathcal{E}$. We begin by relating the interpretation of a term to its equivalence class. If Γ is any type assignment, we may define an environment η by

$$\eta x \Gamma' = \begin{cases} [\Gamma' \triangleright x\colon\sigma] & \text{if } x\colon\sigma \in \Gamma \subseteq \Gamma' \\ \textit{undefined} & \text{otherwise} \end{cases}$$

A straightforward induction on terms shows that for any $\Gamma'' \supseteq \Gamma' \supseteq \Gamma$, we have

$$[\![\Gamma' \triangleright M\colon \sigma]\!]\eta\Gamma'' = [\Gamma'' \triangleright M\colon \sigma]$$

In particular, whenever $\mathcal{A}$ satisfies an equation $\Gamma \triangleright M = N\colon \sigma$, we have $\eta, \Gamma \models \Gamma$ by construction of η, and so

$$[\Gamma \triangleright M\colon \sigma] = [\Gamma \triangleright N\colon \sigma]$$

Since this reasoning applies to every Γ, every equation satisfied by $\mathcal{A}$ must be provable from $\mathcal{E}$.

While it is possible to show that $\mathcal{A}$ satisfies every equation in $\mathcal{E}$ directly, by similar reasoning, certain complications may be avoided by restricting our attention to closed terms. There is no loss of generality in doing so, since it is easy to prove the closed equation

$$\emptyset \triangleright \lambda x_1\colon \sigma_1 \ldots . \lambda x_k\colon \sigma_k.M = \lambda x_1\colon \sigma_1 \ldots . \lambda x_k\colon \sigma_k.N$$

from the equation

$$x_1\colon \sigma_1 \ldots . \lambda x_k\colon \sigma_k \triangleright M = N$$

between open terms, and vice versa. For any closed equation $\emptyset \triangleright M = N\colon \tau \in \mathcal{E}$, we have

$$\mathcal{E} \vdash \Gamma \triangleright M = N\colon \tau$$

for any Γ, by rule (*add var*). Therefore, for every world Γ of $\mathcal{A}$, the two equivalence classes $[\Gamma \triangleright M\colon \tau]$ and $[\Gamma \triangleright N\colon \tau]$ will be identical. Since the meaning of $\emptyset \triangleright M\colon \tau$ in any environment η at world Γ will be $[\Gamma \triangleright M\colon \tau]$, and similarly for $\emptyset \triangleright N\colon \tau$, it follows that $\mathcal{A}$ satisfies $\emptyset \triangleright M = N\colon \tau$. This proves the theorem.

Exercise 7.3.8 Prove Lemma 7.3.6 by induction on equational proofs.

7.3.7 Kripke Lambda Models as Cartesian Closed Categories

In this section, we will see that any Kripke model $\mathcal{A}$ with products and a terminal type determines a cartesian closed category $\mathcal{C}_{\mathcal{A}}$. As one would hope, the categorical interpretation of a term in $\mathcal{C}_{\mathcal{A}}$ coincides with the meaning of the term in the Kripke model $\mathcal{A}$.

It is easy to extend the definitions of Kripke applicative structure and Kripke lambda model to include cartesian product types $\sigma \times \tau$ and a terminal type *unit*. The main ideas are the same as for Henkin models, outlined in Section 4.5.9. Specifically, a $\lambda^{unit,\times,\rightarrow}$ applicative structure is just like a $\lambda^{\rightarrow}$ structure, but with additional operations

$$\mathbf{Proj}_1^{\sigma,\tau}{}_w \colon A_w^{\sigma\times\tau} \longrightarrow A_w^\sigma$$

$$\mathbf{Proj}_2^{\sigma,\tau}{}_w \colon A_w^{\sigma\times\tau} \longrightarrow A_w^\tau$$

at each possible world w. An extensional structure, and therefore model, must satisfy the conditions that $A_w^{\sigma\to unit}$ must have exactly one element at each world, and

$$\forall p, q \in A_w^{\sigma\times\tau}. (\mathbf{Proj}_1^{\sigma,\tau}{}_w p = \mathbf{Proj}_1^{\sigma,\tau}{}_w q \wedge \mathbf{Proj}_2^{\sigma,\tau}{}_w p = \mathbf{Proj}_2^{\sigma,\tau}{}_w q) \supset p = q$$

at each world. The interpretation of combinators $*$ and **Pair**, as described in Section 4.5.9, give a name to the unique global element of $A^{\sigma\to unit}$ and force there to be a pairing function.

To construct a CCC $\mathcal{C}_\mathcal{A}$ from $\lambda^{unit,\times,\to}$ Kripke model $\mathcal{A}$, we regard a partially-ordered set $\langle \mathcal{W}, \leq \rangle$ of possible worlds from $\mathcal{A}$ as a category as in Example 7.2.6. Recall that the objects of this category are the elements of $\mathcal{W}$ and there is a unique "less-than-or-equal-to" arrow $\ell_{w,w'}$ from w to w' iff $w \leq w'$. Since a category must have identities and be closed under composition, $\ell_{w,w}$ is the identity on w and composition satisfies

$$\ell_{w',w''} \circ \ell_{w,w'} = \ell_{w,w''}.$$

It is easy to see that each type σ determines a functor Φ^σ from $\langle \mathcal{W}, \leq \rangle$ to sets. Specifically, we take

$$\Phi^\sigma(w) \quad = A_w^\sigma$$

$$\Phi^\sigma(\ell_{w,w'}) = i_{w,w'}^\sigma$$

and use conditions (*id*) and (*comp*) in the definition of Kripke applicative structure to show that this map is functorial. While it may seem simplest to use functors of the form Φ^σ as objects of $\mathcal{C}_\mathcal{A}$, this may identify types in the case where σ and τ are different but A_w^σ and A_w^τ happen to be the same set (for all w). We therefore use the type expressions of the signature as the objects of $\mathcal{C}_\mathcal{A}$.

Since each type determines a functor from $\langle \mathcal{W}, \leq \rangle$ into $\mathcal{S}et$, we will use natural transformations as the morphisms of $\mathcal{C}_\mathcal{A}$. For every pair of types σ and τ, condition (*nat*) in the definition of Kripke applicative structure says that the map $w \mapsto \mathbf{App}_w^{\sigma,\tau}$, which we shall write simply as $\mathbf{App}^{\sigma,\tau}$, is a natural transformation from $\Phi^{\sigma\to\tau} \times \Phi^\sigma$ to Φ^τ. Using $\mathbf{App}^{\sigma,\tau}$, we can see that every global element $\mathbf{a}$ of type $\sigma \to \tau$ induces a natural transformation ν from Φ^σ to Φ^τ, namely

$$\nu_w = \mathbf{App}_w^{\sigma,\tau}(a_w, \cdot)$$

For extensional applicative structures (and hence models), it is easy to see that if two global elements **a** and **b** determine the same natural transformation, then $a_w = b_w$ at every world w and hence $\mathbf{a} = \mathbf{b}$. We therefore let the morphisms from σ to τ in $\mathcal{C}_{\mathcal{A}}$ be all natural transformations $\nu : \Phi^\sigma \to \Phi^\tau$ induced by global elements of $\mathcal{A}$ of type $\sigma \to \tau$. For composition of morphisms, we use ordinary composition of natural transformations in $Set^{\langle \mathcal{W}, \leq \rangle}$, described in Section 7.2.2. Exercise 7.3.10 asks you to establish the main properties of this construction.

The construction of CCC $\mathcal{C}_{\mathcal{A}}$ from Kripke lambda model $\mathcal{A}$ can be composed with the completeness proof for Kripke lambda models described in Section 7.3.6 to give us an alternate proof of completeness for CCC's. In fact, it gives us the following stronger completeness theorem.

Theorem 7.3.9 Every $\lambda^{unit,\times,\to}$-theory is the theory of a CCC $\mathcal{C}$ that is a subcategory of a functor category $Set^{\mathcal{W}}$ where the category $\mathcal{W}$ is a partial order. The terminal object and products of $\mathcal{C}$ are the same as in $Set^{\mathcal{W}}$, but the function objects may not be the same in both categories.

There are also other proofs of this theorem, as we shall see below. The relationship between the CCC $\mathcal{C}$ mentioned in the theorem above and the functor category $Set^{\mathcal{W}}$ is the same as the relationship between a Henkin model and the category Set. The terminal object and products in a Henkin model may be taken to be the same as in Set, but the interpretation $A^{\sigma\to\tau}$ of a function type $\sigma \to \tau$ in Henkin model $\mathcal{A}$ may be a proper subset of the set of all functions from A^σ to A^τ.

Theorem 7.3.9 may also be proved using standard categorical constructions. Beginning with the term category $\mathcal{C} = \mathcal{C}_\Sigma(\mathcal{E})$ for some lambda theory $\mathcal{E}$, there is a standard embedding into the functor category $Set^{\mathcal{C}^{op}}$. This is called the *Yoneda embedding*. Since the embedding is a cc-functor, the image of $\mathcal{C}$ in $Set^{\mathcal{C}^{op}}$ is a full subcategory of $Set^{\mathcal{C}^{op}}$ satisfying the same equations as $\mathcal{C}$. Once we have a functor category $Set^{\mathcal{C}^{op}}$, there is a second, less well-known construction that produces an embedding into a functor category $Set^{P^{op}}$ where P (and therefore P^{op}) is a partial order. The embedding of $Set^{\mathcal{C}^{op}}$ into P^{op}, called the *Diaconescu cover*, is not a cc-functor since it does not preserve function objects. However, it does preserve structure that is first-order definable, in a technical sense that we shall not explore. This is sufficient to guarantee that the functor preserves terminal object, products and equations between lambda terms. In summary, we can prove Theorem 7.3.9 using the term category construction and the composition of two categorical constructions. As a diagram, this may be drawn

$$\mathcal{C}_\Sigma(\mathcal{E}) \xrightarrow{Y} Set^{\mathcal{C}_\Sigma(\mathcal{E})^{op}} \xrightarrow{D} Set^{P^{op}}$$

where Y is the *Yoneda embedding* and D is the *Diaconescu cover.* A related two-step construction for higher-order logic appears in [LS86, Theorems 19.1, 19.2], where every unprovable formula fails in a Kripke model $Set^{P^{op}}$, where P is a poset of pairs $\langle X, F\rangle$, with X a type assignment and F a filter of propositions.

The Yoneda construction and embedding are described in Exercise 7.3.11 below. For the Diaconescu cover, the reader may consult [Joh77]. The poset P used in the Diaconescu cover is the poset of composable sequences of $\mathcal{C}(\mathcal{E})$ morphisms, ordered such that $u \leq v$ iff v is an initial segment of u.

Exercise 7.3.10
(a) Show that if $\mathcal{A}$ is a Kripke lambda model for signature Σ, then $\mathcal{C}_{\mathcal{A}}$ is a category with an object for each type over Σ and, in addition, there is a one-one correspondence between global elements of type $\sigma \to \tau$ in $\mathcal{A}$ and morphisms from σ to τ in $\mathcal{C}_{\mathcal{A}}$.

(b) Assuming that $\mathcal{A}$ has products and a terminal type, show that $\mathcal{C}_{\mathcal{A}}$ is cartesian closed.

(c) Show that meaning is preserved. More specifically, show that for any term $\Gamma \rhd M{:}\,\sigma$, with $\Gamma = x_1{:}\,\sigma_1, \ldots, x_k{:}\,\sigma_k$, we have

$$\mathcal{C}[\![\Gamma \rhd M{:}\,\sigma]\!] \;=\; \mathcal{A}[\![\lambda z{:}\, unit \times \sigma_1 \times \ldots \times \sigma_k.\, S^z_\Gamma M]\!]$$

where the substitution S^z_Γ is as in Exercise 7.2.39.

Exercise 7.3.11 Let $\mathcal{C}$ be a small and let $\mathcal{D} = Set^{\mathcal{C}^{op}}$ be the category of functors from the opposite of $\mathcal{C}$ into the category of sets. (We could also describe $\mathcal{D}$ as a category of contravariant functors from $\mathcal{C}$ into Set.) The *Yoneda lemma* states that the functor $F : \mathcal{C} \to \mathcal{D}$ mapping object A to the functor $\mathcal{C}(\cdot\,, A)$ defined below is full and faithful.

(a) For any object A from $\mathcal{C}$, there is a functor we will write $\mathcal{C}(\cdot\,, A)$ from $\mathcal{C}^{op}$ to Set mapping object B to the hom-set $\mathcal{C}(B, A)$, *i.e.*, the set of all morphisms from B to A. The functor $\mathcal{C}(\cdot\,, A)$ maps a morphism $f{:}\, C \to B$ in $\mathcal{C}$ to the function from $\mathcal{C}(B, A)$ to $\mathcal{C}(C, A)$ determined by composition with f, *i.e.*, if $g \in \mathcal{C}(B, A)$, then $\mathcal{C}(\cdot\,, A)(f)(g) = g \circ f \in \mathcal{C}(C, A)$. Verify that each $\mathcal{C}(\cdot\,, A)$ is a functor from $\mathcal{C}^{op}$ to Set.

(b) The Yoneda embedding is a functor $F : \mathcal{C} \to \mathcal{D}$ mapping each object A of $\mathcal{C}$ to the functor $\mathcal{C}(\cdot\,, A)$ and mapping an arrow $A \to B$ to a natural transformation from $\mathcal{C}(\cdot\,, A)$ to $\mathcal{C}(\cdot\,, B)$ determined using composition. Define the mapping $F(f)$, for $f{:}\, A \to B$, and verify that it is a natural transformation from $\mathcal{C}(\cdot\,, A)$ to $\mathcal{C}(\cdot\,, B)$.

(c) Show that the Yoneda embedding is faithful. More specifically, if $F(f) = F(g)$ for some $f, g{:}\, A \to B$ in $\mathcal{C}$ then $f = g$.

(d) Show that the Yoneda embedding is full. More specifically, for any objects A and B

of $\mathcal{C}$, every natural transformation from $\mathcal{C}(\cdot, A)$ to $\mathcal{C}(\cdot, B)$ has the form $F(f)$ for some $f: A \to B$ in $\mathcal{C}$. This is the most surprising part of the Yoneda lemma.

7.4 Domain Models of Recursive Types

7.4.1 A Motivating Example

This section describes a traditional approach to recursive types, pioneered by Dana Scott and codified and studied in [SP82]. The main idea is to interpret a recursive type $\mu t.\, \sigma$ as the least fixed point of a functor representing the way that σ depends on t. For example, $\mu t.\, unit + t$ is the least fixed point of a functor $F(t) = unit + t$, defined using the initial object, *unit*, and coproduct, $+$, on some category. However, some care must be taken in choosing the category and in working with contravariant functors such as function space. For example, rather than working with the category *Cpo* of CPOs and continuous functions, we must work with a related category Cpo^E whose objects are CPOs but whose morphisms are "embeddings." One reason for using a different class of morphisms is to obtain a category whose structure is closer to a CPO; we want the morphisms of the category to represent a kind of "ordering" between objects so that the least fixed point with respect to this order is the appropriate interpretation of the recursive type. A second reason is that some technical properties of embeddings will be essential for types that involve contravariant functors.

Before proceeding, we will consider some general issues by example. One of the most commonly used recursive types is the type of lists. For simplicity, let us consider lists of booleans, defined syntactically by the recursive type expression

$$bool\_list \stackrel{\text{def}}{=} \mu t.\, unit + bool \times t.$$

As discussed in Section 2.6.3, this means that *bool_list* is a type satisfying the isomorphism

$$bool\_list \cong unit + bool \times bool\_list.$$

Intuitively, this recursive type gives us the type of finite lists of booleans since the elements of this type are either the single element of type *unit*, which we think of as representing the empty list, or a pair consisting of a boolean (the first element of the list) and a list (the remaining elements of the list).

It is useful to review some general points about set definitions using the boolean list example. Writing $\mathcal{B} = \{true, false\}$ for the set of booleans, a common mathematical definition of the set L of boolean lists might be written

is positive. If we try to write the second, improper recursive definition as an operation on sets, we can see that it requires a fixed-point of the operator

$$G(A) = \mathcal{N} - A,$$

where $-$ is set difference. This operator is not monotonic with respect to set containment, and therefore is not a functor on $Set^{\subseteq}$.

At this point, we have a functor $F\colon Set^{\subseteq} \to Set^{\subseteq}$ on a category whose objects are the ones of interest (sets), but whose morphisms are chosen so as to make an ordering on objects explicit. We wish to find the least fixed point of F. Following the usual method for finding least fixed points of functions, we begin with the initial object of the category (least element of the partial order), which is the empty set, and apply the functor repeatedly. We have $\emptyset \subseteq F(\emptyset)$ since $\emptyset$ is the initial object of $Set^{\subseteq}$. Since F is a functor, we have $F(\emptyset) \subseteq F(F(\emptyset))$ and so, by induction,

$$\emptyset \subseteq F(\emptyset) \subseteq F^2(\emptyset) \subseteq \ldots \subseteq F^k(\emptyset) \subseteq \ldots$$

The least upper bound of this countable sequence of sets, with respect to containment, is the union

$$L = \cup_{n \geq 0} F^n(\emptyset),$$

which is the set of all finite lists of booleans. We can explain why this set must satisfy the equation $L = F(L)$ by observing that $Set^{\subseteq}$ is a complete partial order, showing that F is continuous, and using the general properties of fixed points of continuous functions given in Chapter 4.

The straightforward interpretation of boolean lists, as the least fixed point of a functor on $Set^{\subseteq}$, can be extended easily to similar categories whose objects are CPOs or modest sets. In all three cases, the result is essentially the same: $\mu t.\, unit + bool \times t$ denotes the collection of finite lists of booleans. However, the situation is much more complicated for recursive types involving $\to$, the function-space functor. Since a functor like $F(t) = t \to bool$ is not covariant, we cannot use standard methods for monotonic operators. In fact, by Cantor's theorem from set theory, there is no solution to $A \cong A \to bool$ in Set since $A \to bool$ always has a larger cardinality than A. Therefore, if we wish to interpret recursive types involving $\to$, we must abandon sets and use other categories. While the isomorphism $A \cong A \to bool$ has solutions in both the category of modest sets and the category of CPOs, we will focus on CPOs, since the treatment of contravariant uses of $\to$ in CPOs is more thoroughly studied.

Since our general arguments for fixed points involve monotonic, or covariant, operations, it seems natural to approach contravariant functors using some category where the morphisms are "reversible" in some way. This would allow us to turn contravariant functors into covariant ones, and therefore to regard operators such as $F(t) = t \to t$ (which is not usually any kind of functor) as covariant. At the same time, as illustrated above by the passage from *Set* to $Set^{\subseteq}$, we would like the morphism of the category to impose a natural order structure of some kind. It turns out to be too much to ask that the resulting category be a partial order; there will often be more than one morphism between a pair of objects. But, for categories in which the hom-sets have a CPO structure, we can choose a class of "reversible" maps so that the resulting structure is a reasonable categorical generalization of a complete partial order. This will allow us to interpret arbitrary recursive types involving *unit*, $+$, $\times$, $\to$ and other familiar functors in an acceptable way.

To summarize, there are several important steps in the interpretation of recursive types.

- Generalize the notions of fixed point and least upper bound from partial orders to categories. (This is covered in Sections 7.4.2–7.4.4.)
- Restrict our attention to categories with a CPO-like structure on the hom-sets. (These are **O**-categories, defined in Section 7.4.5.)
- Choose a class of morphisms such that each is reversible in some sense and so that the resulting category has an "order" structure. (Section 7.4.5.)
- Show that we have least upper bounds, for an appropriate analog of direct sets of objects. (Section 7.4.6.)
- Identify a class of functors that can be proved continuous, with respect to the "order structure" of the category, and that can be made covariant. Show that functors of interest, such as $+$, $\times$ and $\to$, are in this class. (Section 7.4.7.)

The reader should be warned that the proofs in this section are among the most difficult in the book.

Exercise 7.4.1 Let us write $+$ for the coproduct in *Set*, which is given by disjoint union, $A \uplus B = (\{0\} \times A \cup (\{1\} \times B)$. Characterize the least fixed point of the functor $F(t) = unit + t$ on $Set^{\subseteq}$. More specifically, show that F is a functor on $Set^{\subseteq}$, describe the sets $F^i(\emptyset)$ for $i \geq 0$, and show that the least fixed point of F is isomorphic to the natural numbers. What operation on $\mu t.\, unit + t$ corresponds to successor? Is $\uplus$ coproduct in $Set^{\subseteq}$?

7.4.2 Diagrams, Cones and Limits

Our first step is to generalize the definition of least upper bound from partial orders to categories. This requires some subsidiary definitions. In keeping with standard categorical terminology, we consider the generalization of greatest lower bound before least upper bound.

A *diagram* D in a category $\mathcal{C}$ is a directed graph whose vertices are labeled by objects of $\mathcal{C}$ and arcs are labeled by morphisms such that if the edge e is labeled by an arrow f from a to b, then the labels on the endpoints of e must be a and b. Some examples of diagrams are the squares and triangles that were drawn in earlier sections. If a vertex of D is labeled by object a, we will often ambiguously refer to both the vertex and its label as a, when no confusion seems likely to result, and similarly for morphisms and arcs. If D is a diagram in $\mathcal{C}$, then D^{op} is the diagram in the opposite category $\mathcal{C}^{op}$ obtained by reversing the direction of each of the arcs (arrows). As explained in Section 7.2.2, a diagram *commutes* if, for every pair of vertices, all compositions given by a path from the first vertex to the second are equal morphisms of the category.

The reason for defining diagrams formally is to define limits; the definition of limit, in turn, requires the definition of cone. A *cone* $\langle c, \{f_d : c \to d\}_{d \; in \; D}\rangle$ over commuting diagram D consists of an object c together with a morphism $f_d : c \to d$ for each vertex d of D such that the diagram obtained by adding c and all $f_d : c \to d$ to D commutes.

A morphism of cones, $\langle c, \{f_d : c \to d\}_{d \; in \; D}\rangle \to \langle c', \{g_d : c' \to d\}_{d \; in \; D}\rangle$, both over the same diagram D, is a morphism $h : c \to c'$ such that the entire diagram combining h, both cones, and D commutes. Since we assume each cone commutes, it suffices to check that for each d in D, the triangle asserting $f_d = g_d \circ h$ commutes. This is illustrated in Figure 7.1. It is easy to check that cones and their morphisms form a category.

A *limit of a diagram* D is a terminal cone over D. In other words, a limit is a cone $\langle c, \{f_d : c \to d\}\rangle$ such that for any cone $\langle c', \{g_d : c' \to d\}\rangle$ over the same diagram, there is a unique morphism of cones from c' to c. The dual notion is *colimit:* a colimit of D is a limit of the diagram D^{op} in the opposite category $\mathcal{C}^{op}$. It follows from Exercise 7.2.8, showing that initial and terminal objects are unique up to isomorphism, that any two limits or colimits of a diagram are isomorphic in the category of cones or cocones. It is easy to see that if $h : c \cong c'$ is an isomorphism of cones or cocones, it is also an isomorphism of c and c' in the underlying category.

Example 7.4.2 The limit of a discrete diagram $D = \{d_1, d_2\}$, with two objects and no arrows, is the product, $d_1 \times d_2$, with projection functions $\mathbf{Proj}_i : d_1 \times d_2 \longrightarrow d_i$. (See Exercise 7.4.4.) ■

Example 7.4.3 Let $\mathcal{C}$ be a partial order, regarded as a category in the usual way (Example 7.2.6) and let D be set of objects from $\mathcal{C}$. We may regard D as a diagram by including all of the "less-than-or-equal-to" arrows between elements of D. Since all diagrams in $\mathcal{C}$ commute, a cone over D is any lower bound of D, and the limit of D is the greatest lower

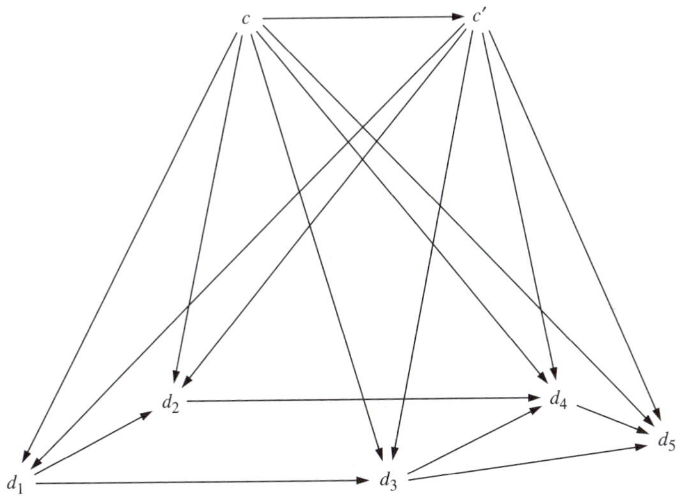

Figure 7.1
Morphism of cones.

bound of D. We can also describe least upper bounds as limits using the opposite category $\mathcal{C}^{op}$. Specifically, the least upper bound of D is the limit of D^{op} in $\mathcal{C}^{op}$ or, equivalently, the colimit of D in $\mathcal{C}$. ∎

Example 7.4.3 shows that least upper bounds are a special case of colimits. The way we will obtain recursively-defined objects is by generalizing the least fixed-point construction to obtain colimits of certain diagrams. Since we will therefore have more occasion to work with colimits than limits, it is useful to have a direct definition of colimits using cocones instead of opposite categories. A *cocone* $\langle c, \{f_d: d \to c\}_{d\ in\ D}\rangle$ *over diagram* D consists of an object c together with a morphism $f_d: d \to c$ for each vertex d of D such that the diagram obtained by adding c and all $f_d: d \to c$ to D commutes. A morphism of cocones, $\langle c, \{f_d: d \to c\}\rangle \longrightarrow \langle c', \{g_d: d \to c'\}\rangle$, is a morphism $h : c \to c'$ such that the entire diagram combining h, both cocones, and D commutes.

If Δ is a diagram, a common notation is to write $\mu: c \to \Delta$ for a cone $\mu = \langle c, \{\mu_d: c \to d\}_{d\ in\ D}\rangle$ and $\mu: \Delta \to c$ for a cocone $\mu = \langle c, \{\mu_d: d \to c\}_{d\ in\ D}\rangle$, since these highlight the directions of the arrows involved.

Exercise 7.4.4 Show that the limit of a discrete diagram $D = \{d_1, d_2\}$, as described in Example 7.4.2, if it exists, is the product $d_1 \times d_2$.

Exercise 7.4.5 If $f, g: a \to b$, then an *equalizer* of f and g is a limit of the diagram

$$a \underset{g}{\overset{f}{\rightrightarrows}} b.$$

Show that an equalizer is determined by an arrow $h: c \to a$ and that, in *Set*, the image of h is $\{x \in a \mid f(x) = g(x)\}$.

7.4.3 F-algebras

We will interpret a recursively-defined type as a "least fixed point" of an appropriate functor. In this section, we show that the least fixed point of a functor F is the initial object in the category of F-algebras, which are also defined below. We will show in the next section that an initial F-algebra is also the colimit of an appropriate diagram.

The ordinary algebras (as in Chapter 3) for an algebraic signature may be characterized as F-algebras in the category of sets. To illustrate this concretely, let us take the signature Σ with one sort, s, and three function symbols,

$$f_1 : s \times s \to s, \quad f_2 : s \times s \times s \to s, \quad f_3 : s.$$

Recall that a Σ-algebra $\mathcal{A}$ consists of a set, A, together with functions f_1^A, f_2^A and f_3^A of the appropriate type. If we use a one-element set *unit*, products and sums (disjoint unions), we can reformulate any Σ-algebra as a set, A, together with a single function

$$f^A : (A \times A) + (A \times A \times A) + unit \to A,$$

since f_1^A, f_2^A and f_3^A can all be recovered from f^A using injection functions. Since any composition of products, sums and constant functors yields a functor, we may define a functor,

$$F_\Sigma(s) = (s \times s) + (s \times s \times s) + unit,$$

and say that a Σ-algebra is a pair $\langle A, f \rangle$ consisting of a set A and a function $f : F_\Sigma(A) \to A$. It is easy to formulate a general definition of functor F_Σ, for any algebraic signature Σ. This allows us to define of the class of algebras with a given signature using categorical concepts.

If $\mathcal{C}$ is a category and $F : \mathcal{C} \to \mathcal{C}$ is a functor, then an *F-algebra* is a pair $\langle a, f \rangle$ consisting of an object a and a morphism $f : F(a) \to a$ in $\mathcal{C}$. This is equivalent to the definition in Chapter 3. More precisely, for any algebraic signature Σ, the F_Σ-algebras in *Set* are exactly the Σ-algebras of universal algebra. We can also use the definition for categories other than *Set*, which is one of the advantages of using categorical terminology.

The curious reader may wonder why the definition of F-algebra requires that F be a functor, instead of just a function from objects to objects. After all, in establishing a correspondence with the definition of Σ-algebra, we only use the object part of F_Σ. The answer to this question is that, using functors, we may give a straightforward definition of algebraic homomorphism, as verified in Exercise 7.4.7. Specifically, a *morphism of F-algebras* from $\langle a, f\rangle$ to $\langle b, g\rangle$ is a morphism $h : a \to b$ satisfying the commuting diagram

$$\begin{array}{ccc} F(a) & \xrightarrow{F(h)} & F(b) \\ {\scriptstyle f}\downarrow & & \downarrow{\scriptstyle g} \\ a & \xrightarrow[h]{} & b \end{array}$$

Since F-algebras and F-algebra morphisms form a category, we write $h : \langle a, f\rangle \to \langle b, g\rangle$ to indicate that h is a morphism of F-algebras.

An F-algebra $\langle a, f\rangle$ is a *fixed point of F* if $f : F(a) \to a$ is an isomorphism. The category of fixed points of F form a subcategory of the category of F-algebras, using F-algebra morphisms as morphisms between fixed points.

In the special case that $\mathcal{C}$ is a CPO and a functor is a monotonic function $f : \mathcal{C} \to \mathcal{C}$, the definition of fixed point just given is equivalent to the definition in Chapter 4, by antisymmetry. An f-algebra, in the case that $\mathcal{C}$ is a CPO, is called a pre-fixed-point of f, as described in Exercise 5.2.31.

The following lemma identifies fixed points of a functor F within the category of F-algebras and shows that an initial F-algebra is a fixed point of F. For the special case of a CPO as a category, this shows that the least pre-fixed-point is the least fixed point, which is part (b) of Exercise 5.2.31. Since F-algebra morphisms are a generalization of standard algebraic homomorphisms (when some category other than *Set* is used), initial F-algebras are also a generalization of the the initial algebras described in Chapter 3. In particular, the discussion of initiality in Sections 3.5.2 and 3.6.2 provides some useful intuition for F-algebras in arbitrary categories.

Lemma 7.4.6 If $\langle a, f\rangle$ is an initial F-algebra, then $\langle a, f\rangle$ is an initial fixed point of F.

Proof Suppose $\langle a, f\rangle$ is initial. We show $\langle a, f\rangle$ is a fixed point using the diagram

$$\begin{array}{ccc} F(F(a)) & \xrightarrow{F(f)} & F(a) \\ {\scriptstyle F(f)}\downarrow & & \downarrow{\scriptstyle f} \\ F(a) & \xrightarrow[f]{} & a \end{array}$$

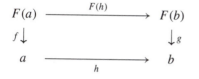

which shows that f is an F-algebra morphism from $\langle F(a), F(f)\rangle$ to $\langle a, f\rangle$. Since $\langle a, f\rangle$ is initial, we also have an F-algebra morphism $g : \langle a, f\rangle \to \langle F(a), F(f)\rangle$ in the opposite direction. Since the only morphism from an initial objects to itself (in any category) is the identity, it is easy to see that $f \circ g = id_a$. Since F is a functor, it follows $F(f) \circ F(g) = id_{F(a)}$.

The remaining identity is proved by adding g and $F(g)$ horizontally and vertically to the square above. Since the result commutes, and $F(f) \circ F(g) = id_{F(a)}$ as noted above, we may conclude $g \circ f = id_{F(a)}$. This shows $\langle a, f\rangle$ is a fixed point. Since the fixed points form a subcategory of the category of F-algebras, it follows that $\langle a, f\rangle$ is initial in the category of fixed point of F. ■

Exercise 7.4.7 Using the example signature Σ and functor F_Σ above, verify that morphisms of F_Σ algebras (in $\mathcal{S}et$) are precisely ordinary homomorphisms of Σ-algebras.

Exercise 7.4.8 Let $F : \mathcal{C}po \rightarrow \mathcal{C}po$ be the *lifting functor,* with $F(A) = A_\perp$ and, for $f : A \rightarrow B$, $F(f) = f_\perp : A_\perp \rightarrow B_\perp$. Describe the initial F-algebra and explain, for any other F-algebra, the unique F-algebra morphism.

Exercise 7.4.9 In $\mathcal{C}po$ or $\mathcal{S}et$, let F be the functor $F(A) = unit + A$.

(a) Describe the initial F-algebra $\langle A, f\rangle$ and explain, for any other F-algebra $\langle B, g\rangle$, the unique F-algebra morphism $h_{B,g} : A \rightarrow B$.

(b) If we think of the unique $h_{B,g} : A \rightarrow B$ as a function of g, for each B, we obtain a function $h_B : ((unit + B) \rightarrow B) \rightarrow B$. What standard operation from recursive function theory does this provide? (*Hint:* A function $(unit + B) \rightarrow B$ is equivalent to a pair $B \times (B \rightarrow B)$; see Exercise 2.5.7.)

(c) Why is the initial F-algebra the same in $\mathcal{C}po$ and $\mathcal{S}et$?

7.4.4 ω-Chains and Initial F-algebras

As discussed earlier, we are interested in finding least fixed-points of functors. The main lemma in this section shows that under certain completeness and continuity assumptions, colimits of the appropriate diagrams are also initial F-algebras and therefore, by Lemma 7.4.6, initial (or least) fixed points. Although we used directed sets to define complete partial orders, we will use chains instead for categories. (Exercise 5.2.6 compares chains and directed sets for CPOs).

An *ω-chain* is a diagram Δ of the form

$$\Delta = d_0 \xrightarrow{f_0} d_1 \xrightarrow{f_1} d_2 \xrightarrow{f_2} \dots,$$

written in symbols as $\Delta = \langle d_i, f_i\rangle_{i \geq 0}$. In any such ω-chain, there is a unique composition of arrows leading from d_i to d_j, when $i \leq j$. To be precise, and to give this a name, we define the morphism $f_{i,j} : d_i \rightarrow d_j$ by

$$f_{i,i} \quad = id_{d_i}$$

$$f_{i,j+1} = f_j \circ f_{i,j}$$

For an ω-chain Δ as indicated above, we write Δ^- for the ω-chain obtained by dropping the first object and arrow,

$$\Delta^- = d_1 \stackrel{f_1}{\longrightarrow} d_2 \stackrel{f_2}{\longrightarrow} d_3 \stackrel{f_3}{\longrightarrow} \ldots$$

and, if $F: \mathcal{C} \to \mathcal{C}$ is a functor on the category containing Δ, we also define the diagram $F(\Delta)$ by

$$F(\Delta) = F(d_0) \stackrel{F(f_0)}{\longrightarrow} F(d_1) \stackrel{F(f_1)}{\longrightarrow} F(d_2) \stackrel{F(f_2)}{\longrightarrow} \ldots$$

If $\mu = \langle c, \{\mu_i : d_i \to c\}_{i \geq 0} \rangle : c \to \Delta$ is a cocone of Δ, we similarly write μ^- for the cocone $\langle c, \{\mu_i : d_i \to c\}_{i \geq 1} \rangle$ of Δ^- and $F(\mu)$ for the cocone $\langle F(c), \{F(\mu_i) : F(d_i) \to F(c)\}_{i \geq 0} \rangle$ of $F(\Delta)$.

A familiar example of an ω-chain arises in a CPO, regarded as a category $\mathcal{C}$ with a morphism $a \to b$ iff $a \leq b$. If $f: \mathcal{C} \to \mathcal{C}$ is continuous, then the colimit of the ω-chain

$$\bot \stackrel{\leq}{\longrightarrow} f(\bot) \stackrel{\leq}{\longrightarrow} f^2(\bot) \stackrel{\leq}{\longrightarrow} \ldots$$

is the least fixed point of f.

We can construct a similar diagram for any functor $F: \mathcal{C} \to \mathcal{C}$, if $\mathcal{C}$ has an initial object. To emphasize the analogy with finding the least fixed point in a CPO, we write $\bot_C$ for the initial object of $\mathcal{C}$. We write $!_a : \bot_C \to a$ for the unique morphism from the initial object, omitting the subscripts C and a when unnecessary or clear from context. If $F: \mathcal{C} \to \mathcal{C}$ and $\mathcal{C}$ has an initial object, we let Δ_F be the diagram

$$\Delta_F \quad = \bot \stackrel{!}{\longrightarrow} F(\bot) \stackrel{F(!)}{\longrightarrow} F^2(\bot) \stackrel{F^2(!)}{\longrightarrow} \ldots$$

In the categorical analog of a CPO, defined below, every such diagram has a colimit.

A category, $\mathcal{C}$, is an *ω-complete pointed category,* or *ω-category* for short, if it has an initial object and every ω-chain has a colimit. If $\mathcal{C}$ and $\mathcal{D}$ are ω-categories, then a functor $F: \mathcal{C} \to \mathcal{D}$ is *ω-continuous* if it preserves ω-colimits, *i.e.*, if Δ is an ω-chain and $\mu: \Delta \to a$ is a colimit, then $F(\mu): F(\Delta) \to F(a)$ is also a colimit. We can show, as stated in Exercise 7.4.11, that functors such as products and coproducts are ω-continuous, as well as any composition of ω-continuous functors. However, we will need to put some effort into constructing a continuous function space functor. This is taken up in the Section 7.4.7, where Theorem 7.4.27 gives a general method for obtaining ω-continuous functors on certain categories.

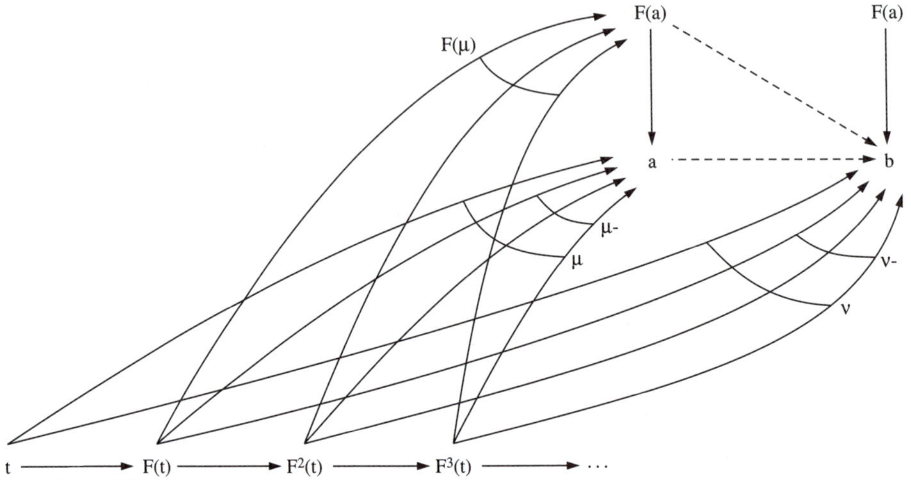

Figure 7.2
F-algebras and unique morphisms of cocones.

If $F: \mathcal{C} \to \mathcal{C}$, for ω-category $\mathcal{C}$, then the following lemma shows that how to derive an initial F-algebra from a colimit of Δ_F. In the special case that $\mathcal{C}$ is a CPO C and the functor $f: C \to C$ is a continuous function, this lemma states that the least upper bound of $\{f^i(\bot) \mid i \geq 0\}$ is the least fixed point of f. For this reason, the reader may wish to look back at Lemma 5.2.20 and its proof, which is considerably simpler than the proof below.

Lemma 7.4.10 Let $\mathcal{C}$ be an ω-category and suppose $F: \mathcal{C} \to \mathcal{C}$ is ω-continuous, with colimit $\mu: \Delta_F \to a$. Then $\langle a, f\rangle$ is an initial F-algebra, where $f: F(a) \to a$ is the unique morphism of cocones from $F(\mu)$ to μ^-.

Proof Since F is ω-continuous and $\mu: \Delta_F \to a$ is a colimit, $F(\mu): F(\Delta_F) \to F(a)$ is also a colimit (initial cocone). Since $F(\mu)$ and μ^- are cocones over $F(\Delta) = \Delta^-$, there is a unique cocone morphism $f: F(\mu) \to \mu^-$ as written in the statement of the lemma. Let $\langle b, g\rangle$ be any F-algebra. We construct a cocone $\nu: \Delta \to b$ and use the cocone morphism $\mu \to \nu$, resulting from the fact that a colimit is an initial cocone, to show that there is a unique F-algebra morphism from $\langle a, f\rangle$ to $\langle b, g\rangle$. A diagram showing the cocones and morphism that are essential to the proof appears in Figure 7.2. The arrows in this diagram are discussed below.

A cocone $\nu\colon \Delta_F \to b$ requires of a family of morphisms, $\nu_i\colon d_i \to b$, for each $i \geq 0$, where $d_i = F^i(\bot)$. Since $d_0 = \bot$, we let $\nu_0 = !_b$. Using $F(F^i(\bot)) \xrightarrow{F(\nu_i)} F(b) \xrightarrow{g} b$, it is easy to continue by defining $\nu_{i+1} = g \circ F(\nu_i)$. An induction on i, left as Exercise 7.4.12, shows that

$$\nu_i = \nu_{i+1} \circ F^i(!_{F(\bot)})$$

for all $i \geq 0$. This establishes that $\nu\colon \Delta_F \to b$ is a cocone of Δ_F.

The cocones μ, μ^-,$F(\mu)$,ν and ν^- all appear in Figure 7.2. The dotted arrow from $F(a)$ to a is f, the unique cocone morphism from $F(\mu)$ to μ^-. The dotted arrow from a to b is the unique cocone morphism from μ to ν and the diagonal dotted arrow from $F(a)$ to b is the unique cocone morphism $F(\mu)$ to ν^-.

We show that the unique cocone morphism $h\colon \mu \to \nu$ is an F-algebra morphism $h\colon \langle a, f\rangle \to \langle b, g\rangle$. Since $h\colon \mu \to \nu$, we have $\nu_i = h \circ \mu_i$ for all $i \geq 0$. We must verify that $h \circ f = g \circ F(h)$. We do this by showing that both are cocone morphisms from $F(\mu)$ to ν^-, *i.e.*, when composed with $F(\mu_i)$, each yields ν_{i+1}, for all i. This is accomplished in the following calculations.

$$\begin{aligned}(h \circ f) \circ F(\mu_i) &= h \circ \mu_{i+1}\\ &= \nu_{i+1}\\ (g \circ F(h)) \circ F(\mu_i) &= g \circ F(h \circ \mu_i)\\ &= g \circ F(\nu_i)\\ &= \nu_{i+1}\end{aligned}$$

Since $F(\mu)\colon F(\Delta_F) \to F(a)$ is a colimit (initial cocone), by hypothesis of the lemma, the two cocone morphisms $h \circ f$ and $g \circ F(h)$ must be equal.

The final step of the proof is to show that the F-algebra morphism $h\colon \langle a, f\rangle \to \langle b, g\rangle$ is unique, since this establishes that $\langle a, f\rangle$ is initial. An induction left as Exercise 7.4.13 shows that if $k\colon \langle a, f\rangle \to \langle b, g\rangle$, then $\nu_i = k \circ \mu_i$ for each $i \geq 0$. From this it follows that k is a cocone morphism from μ to ν. Since μ is a colimit, it follows that there is only one $k\colon \langle a, f\rangle \to \langle b, g\rangle$. This concludes the proof. ■

We will occasionally use the dual of an ω-chain, which is called an ω^{op}-chain. As a special case of the general definition of the opposite of a diagram, an *ω^{op}-chain* in $\mathcal{C}$ is an ω-chain in $\mathcal{C}^{op}$. Drawn in $\mathcal{C}$, an ω^{op}-chain is a diagram of the form

$$d_0 \xleftarrow{f_0} d_1 \xleftarrow{f_1} d_2 \xleftarrow{f_2} \cdots$$

Exercise 7.4.11 Show that if $\mathcal{C}$ is an ω-category with products, then the product functor $\mathcal{C} \to \mathcal{C}$ is ω-continuous. In general, show that any composition of ω-continuous functors is ω-continuous.

Exercise 7.4.12 Use induction on i to show that

$$\nu_i = \nu_{i+1} \circ F^i(!_{F(\perp)})$$

for all $i \geq 0$, where all symbols are defined as in the proof of Lemma 7.4.10.

Exercise 7.4.13 Use induction on i to show that if $k: \langle a, f\rangle \to \langle b, g\rangle$, then $\nu_i = k \circ \mu_i$ for each $i \geq 0$, where all symbols are defined as in the proof of Lemma 7.4.10. (*Hint:* The definition of f as the unique morphism $F(\mu) \to \mu$ implies $\mu_{i+1} = f \circ F(\mu_i)$. In the induction step, begin by writing $k \circ \mu_{i+1} = k \circ f \circ F(\mu_i)$. In addition to the assumption that k is an F-algebra morphism, you will have to use the definition of ν by $\nu_{i+1} = g \circ F(\nu_i)$.)

7.4.5 O-categories and Embeddings

The main goal of this and the following two sections is to develop conditions allowing our general results on colimits in ω-categories to be applied to functors arising from recursive types involving $+$, $\times$, $\to$ and other standard operations. The dominant theme is to relate "global" conditions on a category as a whole, such as ω-completeness, to "local" conditions on hom-sets that are easier to establish and that are satisfied in important examples. In this section, we identify a class of morphisms that provide a useful "ordering" on objects of CPO-like categories.

An ***O**-category* is a category in which each hom-set is a CPO and composition is continuous with respect to the ordering on hom-sets. An example is the category $\mathcal{C}po$ of CPOs, with the hom-set $\mathcal{C}po(a, b)$ consisting of all continuous functions from a to b, partially ordered in the usual point-wise way. Other examples include CPOs with strict continuous functions or partial continuous functions. It is easy to check that if $\mathcal{C}$ is an **O**-category, then so is $\mathcal{C}^{op}$, ordered by $f \leq g$ in $\mathcal{C}^{op}$ iff $f \leq g$ in $\mathcal{C}$. Moreover, the product of any number of **O**-categories is an **O**-category, with tuples of morphisms ordered component-wise. The difference between an ω-category and an **O**-category is that an ω-category has colimits of diagrams while an **O**-category has least upper bounds in each hom-set. However, we will see that there are useful connections between these two definitions.

Our immediate goal is to show how certain **O**-categories yield ω-categories. The guiding intuition is to think of an ω-category as a generalization of a CPO, with more than one way for an object to be "less than" another. However, just as we passed from $\mathcal{S}et$ to

$Set^{\subseteq}$ to obtain a category with a CPO structure in Section 7.4.1, we must select a subset of the morphisms to obtain a suitable ω-category from an arbitrary **O**-category. An arbitrary continuous function from a to b does not imply that "a is an approximation of b" in any intuitive sense. However, using the ordering on hom-sets, we may identify a class of "embeddings" that capture an intuitive idea of "approximation" between objects. A very important aspect of embeddings is that they are "reversible" in a precise sense. This is used later to convert contravariant functors into covariant ones.

An *embedding-projection pair* from a to b in an **O**-category $\mathcal{C}$ is pair consisting of a morphism $e: a \to b$, called the *embedding,* and a morphism $p: b \to a$, called the *projection,* with the properties that $p \circ e = id$ and $e \circ p \leq id$. Some illustrations appear in Example 7.4.14 below. It is easy to check that if $\langle e, p\rangle$ and $\langle e', p'\rangle$ are embedding-projection pairs from a to b, then $e \leq e'$ iff $p \geq p'$ (see Exercise 7.4.16). It follows that if $\langle e, p\rangle$ and $\langle e', p'\rangle$ are embedding-projection pairs with $e = e'$, then $p = p'$, and conversely. Therefore, if f is an embedding we may unambiguously write f^{prj} for the corresponding projection. If f is a projection we similarly write f^{emb} for the corresponding embedding. It is also convenient to extend this notation to diagrams, writing Δ^{prj}, for example, for the diagram obtained by replacing every morphism f in a diagram Δ in $\mathcal{C}^E$ with the associated projection f^{prj}.

Exercise 7.4.18 shows that if A and B are CPOs with an embedding-projection pair $\langle e, p\rangle: A \to B$ and A is pointed, then B must be pointed and both e and p must be strict.

Example 7.4.14 If A and B are CPOs, then $e: A \to B$ and $p: B \to A$ form an embedding-projection pair only if $p \circ e = id$. This equation, which is often read, "p is a *left inverse* of e," may be satisfied only if e is injective (one-to-one). Since we only consider continuous functions in the category Cpo, an embedding in Cpo must be an injective, continuous function with a left-inverse. Using the CPOs $\{0, 1\}$ to $\{0, 1, 2\}$, with $0 < 1 < 2$ in both cases, we will compare continuous functions that have a left-inverse with embeddings and see that not all continuous functions with a left-inverse are embeddings. Recall that on finite CPOs, a function is continuous iff it is monotonic.

The three injective, monotone functions are drawn below as solid arrows, the second one repeated twice since there are two monotone left inverses. If an injective function is an embedding, then the corresponding projection is clearly determined on the image of the embedding; the map from right to left must reverse each of the solid arrows from left to right. However, for the one element of $\{0, 1, 2\}$ that is not in the image of the embedding, there may be one or more plausible elements of $\{0, 1\}$ that yield a monotone, left inverse. This gives us four candidate embedding-projection pairs from $\{0, 1\}$ to $\{0, 1, 2\}$, sketched below with each CPO drawn vertically.

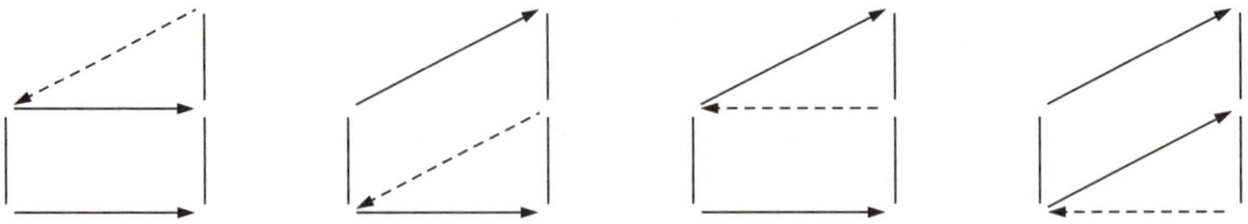

Further examination shows that only the first two are embedding-projection pairs. The reason the third one fails is that the middle element, 1, of $\{0, 1, 2\}$ projects and then embeds to 2. Thus the condition $e \circ p \leq id$ fails. This condition also fails for similar reasons in the fourth picture. ■

If $\mathcal{C}$ is an **O**-category, then the *category* $\mathcal{C}^E$ *of* $\mathcal{C}$*-embeddings* has the same objects as $\mathcal{C}$, but only the embeddings of $\mathcal{C}$ as morphism. The *category* $\mathcal{C}^P$ *of* $\mathcal{C}$*-projections* is defined similarly. It is easy to see that if $e_1 \colon a \to b$ and $e_2 \colon b \to c$ are embeddings, then $e_2 \circ e_1$ is an embedding with $(e_2 \circ e_1)^{prj} = e_1^{prj} \circ e_2^{prj}$. It is worth noting that neither $\mathcal{C}^E$ nor $\mathcal{C}^P$ is necessarily an **O**-category.

The following lemma suggests some of the connections between an **O**-category $\mathcal{C}$ and its category of embeddings, $\mathcal{C}^E$. Note that the hypotheses hold for $Cpo_\perp$, the category of pointed CPOs and strict functions, as well as the category $Cppo$ of pointed CPOs with arbitrary continuous functions. The terminal object of both categories is the one-element CPO, $\{\perp\}$, and in fact $Cpo_\perp^E$ and $Cppo^E$ are the same category.

Lemma 7.4.15 Let $\mathcal{C}$ be an **O**-category with terminal object $\perp$ such that each hom-set $\mathcal{C}(a, b)$ has a least element, $\perp_{a,b}$. If $\perp_{b,c} \circ f = \perp_{a,c}$ for every morphism $f \colon a \to b$, then $\perp$ is an initial object of $\mathcal{C}^E$.

The proof is left as Exercise 7.4.20. The main idea is that $\perp$ becomes initial in $\mathcal{C}^E$ because there is only one projection into $\perp$ and an embedding f is determined by the projection f^{prj}. This lemma is a useful sufficient condition for finding initial objects with respect to embeddings.

In Lemma 7.4.15, it is necessary to assume that every hom-set has a least element. This hypothesis fails in Cpo, since $Cpo(a, b)$ may have no least element if b has no least element. Although Cpo has an initial object (the empty CPO) and a terminal object (the one-element CPO), Cpo^E has no initial object. Specifically, the empty CPO cannot be initial in Cpo^E, since there are no projections from a nonempty CPO into it, and the one-element CPO is not initial since it has no embedding into the empty CPO. For this reason, the basic theory is more easily applied to the categories $Cppo$ and $Cpo_\perp$ than Cpo. Another possibility is the category $Cpo_\rightharpoonup$ of CPOs and partial continuous functions. While $Cpo_\rightharpoonup^E$ is an **O**-category with an initial object, $Cpo_\rightharpoonup$ is not cartesian closed and the treatment of total function spaces in $Cpo_\rightharpoonup$ involves complications similar to those associated with recursive types in Cpo. To give some flavor of both Cpo and $Cpo_{\rightharpoonup}$, with fewer complications, the main examples of this section will be $Cpo_\perp$ and Pfn, the category of sets and partial functions.

Exercise 7.4.16 Show that if $\langle e, p\rangle$ and $\langle e', p'\rangle$ are embedding-projection pairs from a to b, then $e \le e'$ iff $p \ge p'$. Use this to verify that if $\langle e, p\rangle$ and $\langle e', p'\rangle$ are embedding-projection pairs with $e = e'$, then $p = p'$, and similarly $p = p'$ implies $e = e'$.

Exercise 7.4.17 Describe all of the embedding-projection pairs from $\mathcal{B}_\perp$ to $\mathcal{B}_\perp \times \mathcal{B}_\perp$, where $\mathcal{B} = \{true, false\}$.

Exercise 7.4.18 Shows that if A and B are CPOs with an embedding-projection pair $\langle e, p\rangle: A \to B$ and A is pointed, then B must be pointed and both e and p must be strict.

Exercise 7.4.19 Show that if $\langle e, p\rangle: A \to B$ is an embedding-projection pair from CPO A to B, then for all $y \in B$, we have $p(y) = \bigvee\{x \in A \mid e(x) \le y\}$. Give a similar characterization of e in terms of p.

Exercise 7.4.20 Prove Lemma 7.4.15.

7.4.6 Colimits and O-colimits

The first important aspect of **O**-categories is that we may use the order structure on hom-sets to identify embedding-projection pairs, which give us a form of "partial order" on the objects of the category. The next property of **O**-categories, considered in this section, is that we may relate a colimit to the least upper bounds of a set of morphisms. This allows us to use the CPO structure of hom-sets to show the existence of certain colimits. This is essential to the interpretation of recursive types since least fixed points of functors are colimits of ω-diagrams.

If $\mathcal{C}$ is an **O**-category, Δ is an ω-chain in $\mathcal{C}^E$ and $\mu: \Delta \to a$ is a cocone in $\mathcal{C}^E$, then μ *is an **O**-colimit of* Δ if the sequence

$$\langle \mu_i \circ \mu_i^{prj}\rangle_{i\ge 0} = \langle \mu_0 \circ \mu_0^{prj}, \mu_1 \circ \mu_1^{prj}, \mu_2 \circ \mu_2^{prj}, \ldots\rangle$$

is increasing in $\mathcal{C}(a, a)$ and $\bigvee_{i\ge 0} \mu_i \circ \mu_i^{prj} = id_a$. This is different from the definition of colimit since it requires a least upper bound in a single hom-set instead of a unique morphism to every cocone.

The definition of **O**-colimit may be understood by realizing that if $\langle e, p\rangle$ is an embedding-projection pair from a to b, in $Cpo_\perp$ for example, then a is isomorphic (as a CPO) to the image of $e \circ p$, which is a subset of b. Therefore, if $\mu: \Delta \to a$ is a cocone in $Cpo_\perp^E$, with $\Delta = \langle d_i, \delta_i\rangle_{i\ge 0}$, the objects $d_0, d_1, d_2, \ldots$ are isomorphic to the images of $\mu_0 \circ \mu_0^{prj}, \mu_1 \circ \mu_1^{prj}, \mu_2 \circ \mu_2^{prj}, \ldots$ in a. This gives us a correspondence between cocones and maps that are $\le id$. If $\bigvee_{i\ge 0} \mu_i \circ \mu_i^{prj} = id_a$, then we can see that the images of $\mu_0 \circ$

$\mu_0^{prj}, \mu_1 \circ \mu_1^{prj}, \mu_2 \circ \mu_2^{prj}, \ldots$ approach a. This suggests that an **O**-colimit should be a colimit, which is proved in the following lemma.

Lemma 7.4.21 Let $\mathcal{C}$ be an **O**-category and Δ an ω-chain in $\mathcal{C}^E$. If $\mu: \Delta \to a$ is an **O**-colimit then μ is a colimit in $\mathcal{C}$ and in $\mathcal{C}^E$.

Proof Let $\nu: \Delta \to b$ be any cocone in $\mathcal{C}$. We first show that there is at most one cocone morphism $f: \mu \to \nu$, then prove the existence of such a morphism.

If $f: \mu \to \nu$, then by definition of cocone morphism we have $f \circ \mu_i = \nu_i$. Since μ is an **O**-colimit, we have $\bigvee_{i \geq 0}(\mu_i \circ \mu_i^{prj}) = id$ and therefore

$$f = f \circ \bigvee_{i \geq 0}(\mu_i \circ \mu_i^{prj}) = \bigvee_{i \geq 0}(f \circ \mu_i \circ \mu_i^{prj}) = \bigvee_{i \geq 0}(\nu_i \circ \mu_i^{prj}).$$

Since the rightmost expression does not contain f, this shows that f is uniquely determined.

We show the existence of $f: \mu \to \nu$ by showing that $\langle \nu_i \circ \mu_i^{prj} \rangle_{i \geq 0}$ is increasing and checking that $f = \bigvee_{i \geq 0}(\nu_i \circ \mu_i^{prj})$ is actually a morphism of cocones. If $\Delta = \langle d_i, \delta_i \rangle_{i \geq 0}$, then we have

$$\nu_i \circ \mu_i^{prj} = (\nu_{i+1} \circ \delta_i) \circ (\mu_{i+1} \circ \delta_i)^{prj} = \nu_{i+1} \circ (\delta_i \circ \delta_i^{prj}) \circ \mu_{i+1}^{prj} \leq \nu_{i+1} \circ \mu_{i+1}^{prj}.$$

This allows us to define $f = \bigvee_{i \geq 0}(\nu_i \circ \mu_i^{prj})$ and calculate

$$f \circ \mu_i = (\bigvee_{j \geq i}(\nu_j \circ \mu_j^{prj})) \circ \mu_i = \bigvee_{j \geq i}(\nu_j \circ \mu_j^{prj} \circ \mu_j \circ \delta_{i,j}) = \bigvee_{j \geq i}(\nu_j \circ \delta_{i,j}) = \nu_i$$

where $\delta_{i,j}$ is the unique composition of arrows in Δ leading from d_i to d_j. This shows that f is a cocone morphism from μ to ν and completes the proof that μ is a colimit in $\mathcal{C}$.

The last step is to show that if ν is a cocone in $\mathcal{C}^E$, then $f: \mu \to \nu$ as defined above is an embedding. The brief calculation showing that $\langle \nu_i \circ \mu_i^{prj} \rangle_{i \geq 0}$ is increasing may also be used to show that $\langle \mu_i \circ \nu_i^{prj} \rangle_{i \geq 0}$ is increasing. We let $g = \bigvee_{i \geq 0}(\mu_i \circ \nu_i^{prj})$ and show that $\langle f, g \rangle$ is an embedding-projection pair. This is accomplished in the following calculations, which complete the proof of the lemma:

$$\bigvee_{i \geq 0}(\mu_i \circ \nu_i^{prj}) \circ \bigvee_{i \geq 0}(\nu_i \circ \mu_i^{prj}) = \bigvee_{i \geq 0}\mu_i \circ (\nu_i^{prj} \circ \nu_i) \circ \mu_i^{prj} = \bigvee_{i \geq 0}\mu_i \circ \mu_i^{prj} = id,$$

$$\bigvee_{i \geq 0}(\nu_i \circ \mu_i^{prj}) \circ \bigvee_{i \geq 0}(\mu_i \circ \nu_i^{prj}) = \bigvee_{i \geq 0}\nu_i \circ (\mu_i^{prj} \mu_i) \circ \nu_i^{prj} = \bigvee_{i \geq 0}\nu_i \circ \nu_i^{prj} \leq id. \blacksquare$$

We may also prove a partial converse to Lemma 7.4.21. Since we will use this (in the proof of Theorem 7.4.23) for limits of ω^{op}-chains instead of colimits of ω-chains, we state and prove the lemma for limits. A dual statement and further discussion appear following the proof.

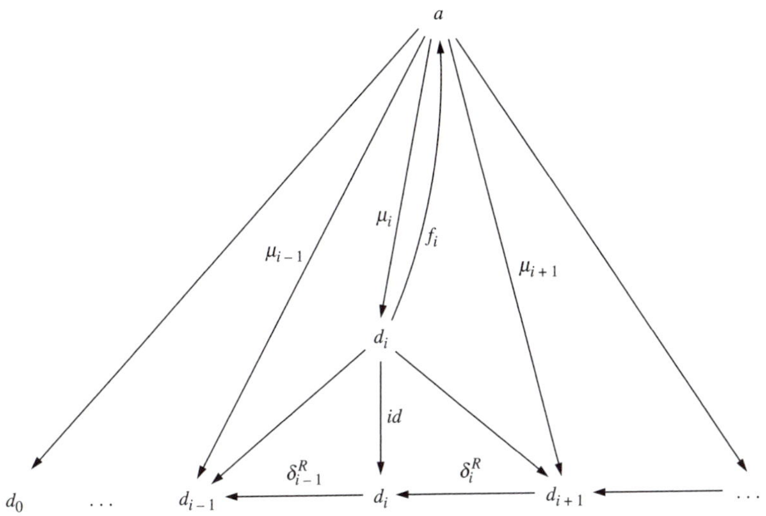

Figure 7.3
Unique morphism from $\nu^{(i)}$ into limit cone μ over Δ^{prj}.

Lemma 7.4.22 Let $\mathcal{C}$ be an **O**-category with ω-chain Δ in $\mathcal{C}^E$. If $\mu: a \to \Delta^{prj}$ is a limit in $\mathcal{C}$ then each μ_i is a projection and μ is an **O**-limit of Δ^{prj}.

Proof Suppose $\Delta = \langle d_i, \delta_i \rangle_{i \geq 0}$ with $\delta_i : d_i \to d_{i+1}$. Recall that if $i \leq j$, then $\delta_{i,j}$ is the composition of arrows in Δ leading from d_i to d_j. For each object d_i in the diagram Δ, we define a cone $\nu^{(i)}: d_i \to \Delta$ by

$$\nu^{(i)}_j : d_i \to d_j = \begin{cases} \delta_{i,j} & \text{if } i \leq j, \\ (\delta_{i,j})^{prj} & \text{if } i > j. \end{cases}$$

To show that $\nu^{(i)}$ is a cone, we must verify that for all $j \geq 0$, $\delta^{prj}_j \circ \nu^{(i)}_{j+1} = \nu^{(i)}_j$. This is an easy case analysis, considering $i \leq j$ and $i \geq j+1$ separately. For $i \leq j$, we have

$$d_i \overset{\delta^{prj}_i}{\longleftarrow} \cdots \overset{\delta^{prj}_{j-1}}{\longleftarrow} d_j \overset{\delta^{prj}_j}{\longleftarrow} d_{j+1}$$

with $\delta^{prj}_j \circ \nu^{(i)}_{j+1} = \delta^{prj}_j \circ \delta_{i,j+1} = \delta_{i,j} = \nu^{(i)}_j$ since δ_j is an embedding. The case for $i \geq j+1$ is similar.

Since μ is a limit, there is a unique arrow $f_i: d_i \to a$ that is a cone morphism $f_i: \nu^{(i)} \to \mu$. This is shown in Figure 7.3. In the remaider of the proof, we will establish that for each i, $\langle f_i, \mu_i \rangle$ is an embedding-projection pair and $\bigvee_{i \geq 0} f_i \circ \mu_i = id$. This will prove the lemma, since then μ is an **O**-limit of Δ^{prj}.

Since f_i is a cone morphism from $\nu^{(i)}$ to μ, we have $\mu_j \circ f_i = \nu^{(i)}_j$. In the special case that $i = j$, this gives us $\mu_i \circ f_i = id_{d_i}$, which is half of showing that $\langle f_i, \mu_i \rangle$ is an embedding-projection pair. We may also show that $(f_{i+1} \circ \delta_i)\colon \nu^{(i)} \to \mu$ is a morphism of cones, by noting

$$\mu_j \circ (f_{i+1} \circ \delta_i) = \nu_j^{(i+1)} \circ \delta_i = \nu_j^{(i)}.$$

This follows from the fact that $f_{i+1}\colon \nu^{(i+1)} \to \mu$ is a cone morphism and is easy to see if you pencil $\nu^{(i+1)}$ into Figure 7.3 over d_{i+1}. Since the morphism from $\nu^{(i)}$ to μ is unique, it follows that $f_i = f_{i+1} \circ \delta_i$. This allows us to show that the sequence $\langle f_i \circ \mu_i \rangle_{i \geq 0}$ is increasing by

$$f_i \circ \mu_i = (f_{i+1} \circ \delta_i) \circ (\delta_i^{prj} \circ \mu_{i+1}) \leq f_{i+1} \circ \mu_{i+1}.$$

If we define $f\colon a \to a$ by $f = \bigvee_{i \geq 0} f_i \circ \mu_i$, then the lemma may be proved by showing $f = id_a$. Since μ is a limit, it suffices to show that $f\colon \mu \to \mu$ is a morphism of cones, which is verified by the following calculation:

$$\mu_j \circ f = \mu_j \circ (\bigvee_{i \geq j} f_i \circ \mu_i) = \bigvee_{i \geq j} (\mu_j \circ f_i) \circ \mu_i = \bigvee_{i \geq j} \nu_j^{(i)} \circ \mu_i = \bigvee_{i \geq j} \delta_{i,j}^{prj} \circ \mu_i = \mu_j$$

Since $f_i \circ \mu_i \leq f = id$, we have also shown that each $\langle f_i, \mu_i \rangle$ is an embedding-projection pair. This completes the proof. ∎

The dual of Lemma 7.4.22 is that if $\mu\colon \Delta \to a$ is a colimit in $\mathcal{C}$, then each μ_i is an embedding and μ is an **O**-colimit. This is not the converse of Lemma 7.4.21 since the hypothesis is that μ is a colimit in $\mathcal{C}$ rather than a colimit in $\mathcal{C}^E$. Since we wish to have a stronger connection between **O**-colimits and colimits in $\mathcal{C}^E$, we make the following definition.

If $\mathcal{C}$ is an **O**-category, we say that $\mathcal{C}^E$ has *locally determined ω-colimits* if, for every ω-chain Δ in $\mathcal{C}^E$, a cocone $\mu\colon \Delta \to a$ is a colimit in $\mathcal{C}^E$ iff μ is an **O**-colimit. The following theorem, whose proof uses both Lemmas 7.4.21 and 7.4.22, is useful for finding ω-categories with locally determined colimits.

Theorem 7.4.23 If every ω^{op}-chain in an **O**-category $\mathcal{C}$ has a limit, then $\mathcal{C}^E$ is an ω-category with locally determined ω-colimits.

Proof We show that $\mathcal{C}^E$ is an ω-category by proving that every ω-chain in $\mathcal{C}^E$ has an **O**-colimit that is consequently a colimit. Let Δ be any ω-chain in $\mathcal{C}^E$. Since Δ^{prj} is an ω^{op} chain in $\mathcal{C}$, Δ^{prj} has a limit $\nu\colon b \to \Delta^{prj}$ in $\mathcal{C}$, by hypothesis. By Lemma 7.4.22, ν is an **O**-limit of Δ^{prj} or, equivalently, $\nu^{emb}\colon \Delta \to b$ is an **O**-colimit of Δ. It follows by Lemma 7.4.21 that ν^{emb} is a colimit in $\mathcal{C}^E$.

To show that $\mathcal{C}^E$ has locally determined ω-colimits, we suppose $\mu\colon \Delta \to a$ is any colimit of Δ in $\mathcal{C}^E$. Since ν^{emb}, as described above, and μ are both colimits of Δ in $\mathcal{C}^E$, they must be isomorphic cocones. However, we have shown that $\nu^{emb}\colon \Delta \to b$ is an **O**-colimit.

Therefore, the isomorphic cocone μ must be an **O**-colimit. The converse, that any **O**-colimit is a colimit, follows from Lemma 7.4.21. This concludes the proof. ∎

Example 7.4.24 The category P*fn* has arbitrary sets as objects and partial functions as morphisms. The partial functions from a to b, represented as sets of ordered pairs in the usual way, form a CPO when partially ordered by set containment (see Exercise 5.2.5). We can use Theorem 7.4.23 to show that $\mathcal{P}fn^E$ is an ω-category with locally determined colimits.

An ω^{op} diagram in P*fn* has the form

$$\Delta = D_0 \overset{\delta_0}{\leftharpoonup} D_1 \overset{\delta_1}{\leftharpoonup} D_2 \overset{\delta_2}{\leftharpoonup} \cdots$$

where each D_i is a set and each δ_i is a partial function. A cone of Δ consists of a set and a partial function into each D_i. We may construct a limit using the set

$$D = \{a \in \prod_i D_i \mid \forall i.\, a_i = \delta_i(a_{i+1})\},$$

where $\prod_i D_i$ is the set of infinite sequences $a = \langle a_0, a_1, a_2, \ldots\rangle$ with $a_i \in D_i$. An obvious partial function from D to D_i is the projection $a \mapsto a_i$. The set D and collection of all such projections form a cone, as is easily verified. It is also easy to check that D and the projection functions form a terminal cone since, if $\langle C, \{f_i \colon C \to D_i\}\rangle$ is any other cone over Δ, we can define a cone morphism $g \colon C \to D$ by mapping $c \in C$ to the infinite sequence $\langle f_0(c), f_1(c), f_2(c), \ldots\rangle \in D$. Since every ω^{op} diagram in P*fn* therefore has limit, $\mathcal{P}fn^E$ is an ω-category with locally determined colimits. ∎

Example 7.4.25 We can similarly use Theorem 7.4.23 to show that the category $\mathcal{C}po_\perp^E$ is an ω-category with locally determined colimits. An ω^{op} diagram in $\mathcal{C}po_\perp$ has the form

$$\Delta = D_0 \overset{\delta_0}{\longleftarrow} D_1 \overset{\delta_1}{\longleftarrow} D_2 \overset{\delta_2}{\longleftarrow} \cdots$$

where each D_i is a pointed CPO and each δ_i is a strict continuous function. A cone over Δ consists of a pointed CPO and a continuous function into each D_i. A limit is

$$D = \{a \in \prod_i D_i \mid \forall i.\, a_i = \delta_i(a_{i+1})\},$$

with projection functions as in Example 7.4.24 above. This set may be partially ordered using the coordinate-wise ordering, $a \le b$ iff $a_i \le b_i$ for all $i \ge 0$. It is easy to check that D is a CPO with least element $\langle \perp, \perp, \ldots\rangle$ under this order. The proof that D and the projection functions form a terminal cone in $\mathcal{C}po_\perp$ is essentially the same as in Example 7.4.24, since all of the necessary functions are easily seen to be total, continuous and strict. Since every ω^{op} diagram in $\mathcal{C}po_\perp$ has a limit, $\mathcal{C}po_\perp^E$ is an ω-category with locally determined colimits. ∎

7.4.7 Locally Continuous Functors

Working with **O**-categories that yield ω-categories with locally determined colimits, we turn our attention to local conditions guaranteeing ω-continuity of functors. The essential properties are local monotonicity and local continuity on arrows. The main theorem of this section shows that a functor that may be both covariant and contravariant, such as the function-space functor, determines a purely covariant and continuous one with the same action on objects. The "trick" here is that if we begin with a contravariant functor on a category $\mathcal{C}$, we obtain a covariant one on $\mathcal{C}^E$ using the fact that every embedding a corresponding projection in the opposite direction.

We are interested in functors of several arguments, possibly covariant in some and contravariant in others. If we rearrange the order of arguments, such a functor can be written in the form $F\colon \mathcal{B}^{op} \times \mathcal{C} \to \mathcal{D}$, where $\mathcal{B}$ is a product category representing the contravariant arguments and $\mathcal{C}$ a product category representing the covariant arguments. For example, if $F\colon \mathcal{D} \times \mathcal{D} \times \mathcal{D} \to \mathcal{D}$ is contravariant in the first two arguments and covariant in the third argument, we can see that F is a covariant functor of the form $F\colon (\mathcal{D} \times \mathcal{D})^{op} \times \mathcal{D} \to \mathcal{D}$. By taking either $\mathcal{B}$ or $\mathcal{C}$ in $\mathcal{B}^{op} \times \mathcal{C} \to \mathcal{D}$ to be a trivial, one-object category, we can also write purely contravariant functors and purely covariant functors in this form.

A functor $F\colon \mathcal{B}^{op} \times \mathcal{C} \to \mathcal{D}$ is *locally monotonic* if it is monotonic on hom-sets, *i.e.*, if $f \leq f'\colon b \to b'$ in $\mathcal{B}$ and $g \leq g'\colon c \to c'$ in $\mathcal{C}$, then $F(f, g) \leq F(f', g')$ in $\mathcal{D}$.

If $F\colon \mathcal{B}^{op} \times \mathcal{C} \to \mathcal{D}$ is locally monotonic, then we may define a *covariant* $F^E\colon \mathcal{B}^E \times \mathcal{C}^E \to \mathcal{D}^E$ by

$$F^E(b, c) = F(b, c) \quad \text{on objects,}$$

$$F^E(f, g) = F((f^{prj})^{op}, g) \quad \text{on arrows,}$$

as verified in the following lemma.

Lemma 7.4.26 If $F\colon \mathcal{B}^{op} \times \mathcal{C} \to \mathcal{D}$ is locally monotonic, then F^E is a covariant functor from $\mathcal{B}^E \times \mathcal{C}^E$ to $\mathcal{D}^E$.

Proof If $f\colon b \to b'$ in $\mathcal{B}$ and $g\colon c \to c'$ in $\mathcal{C}$, then we may show that $F^E(f, g) = F(f^{prj}, g)$ is an embedding with $(F^E(f, g))^{prj} = F(f, g^{prj})$ by the following calculation:

$$\begin{array}{lllllll} F(f, g^{prj}) \circ F(f^{prj}, g) & = & F(f \circ f^{prj}, g^{prj} \circ g) & = & F(id, id) & = & id_{F(b,c)}, \\ F(f^{prj}, g) \circ F(f, g^{prj}) & = & F(f^{prj} \circ f, g \circ g^{prj}) & \leq & F(id, id) & = & id_{F(b',c')}. \end{array}$$

Preservation of identities follows from the fact that $id^{prj} = id$ and composition is left as Exercise 7.4.28. ∎

A functor $F\colon \mathcal{B}^{op} \times \mathcal{C} \to \mathcal{D}$ is *locally continuous* if it is ω-continuous on hom-sets, *i.e.*, if $f_0 \le f_1 \le \ldots : b \to b'$ is an increasing sequence in $\mathcal{B}$ and $g_0 \le g_1 \le \ldots : c \to c'$ in $\mathcal{C}$, then $F(\bigvee_i f_i, \bigvee_i g_i) = \bigvee_i F(f_i, g_i)$.

It is easy to see that constant and projection functors are locally continuous and an exercise to show that the locally continuous functors are closed under composition, tupling, and taking the opposite of a functor (Exercise 7.4.29).

Theorem 7.4.27 If $F: \mathcal{B}^{op} \times \mathcal{C} \to \mathcal{D}$ is a locally continuous functor on **O**-categories and both $\mathcal{B}$ and $\mathcal{C}$ have locally determined colimits, then $F^E: \mathcal{B}^E \times \mathcal{C}^E \to \mathcal{D}^E$ is ω-continuous.

Proof Let

$$\Delta = \langle b_0, c_0\rangle \stackrel{\langle f_0, g_0\rangle}{\longrightarrow} \langle b_1, c_1\rangle \stackrel{\langle f_1, g_1\rangle}{\longrightarrow} \langle b_2, c_2\rangle \stackrel{\langle f_2, g_2\rangle}{\longrightarrow} \cdots$$

be an ω-chain in $\mathcal{B}^E \times \mathcal{C}^E$ with colimit $\mu: \Delta \to \langle b, c\rangle$ in $\mathcal{D}^E$. If we write each morphism $\mu_i: \langle b_i, c_i\rangle \to \langle b, c\rangle$ as $\mu_i = \nu_i \times \pi_i$, then $\nu: \Delta_1 \to b$ and $\pi: \Delta_2 \to c$ are colimits in $\mathcal{B}^E$ and $\mathcal{C}^E$, where $\Delta_i = \mathbf{Proj}_i(\Delta)$. It follows that $id_b = \bigvee_i \nu_i \circ \nu_i^{prj}$ and similarly $id_c = \bigvee_i \pi_i \circ \pi_i^{prj}$, with both sequences increasing.

We show that $F^E(\mu): F^E(\Delta) \to F^E(\langle b, c\rangle)$ is an **O**-colimit and conclude by Lemma 7.4.21 that $F^E(\mu): F^E(\Delta) \to F^E(\langle b, c\rangle)$ is a colimit in $\mathcal{D}^E$. The sequence $\langle F(\nu_i \circ \nu_i^{prj}, \pi_i \circ \pi_i^{prj})\rangle_{i\ge 0}$ is increasing since both $\langle \nu_i \circ \nu_i^{prj}\rangle_{i\ge 0}$ and $\langle \pi_i \circ \pi_i^{prj}\rangle_{i\ge 0}$ are increasing and F is locally monotonic. We must show that the least upper bound of the sequence $\langle F^E(\mu_i) \circ F^E(\mu_i)^{prj}\rangle_{i\ge 0}$ is id.

Since F^E treats its first argument in the opposite order from F, we have $F^E(\mu_i) = F^E(\nu_i, \mu_i) = F(\nu_i^{prj}, \mu_i)$. As shown in the proof of Lemma 7.4.26, we also have $(F(f^{prj}, g))^{prj} = F(f, g^{prj})$. This gives us

$$\begin{aligned} F^E(\mu_i) \circ F^E(\mu_i)^{prj} &= F(\nu_i^{prj}, \pi_i) \circ F(\nu_i^{prj}, \pi_i)^{prj} \\ &= F(\nu_i^{prj}, \pi_i) \circ F(\nu_i, \pi_i^{prj}) \\ &= F(\nu_i \circ \nu_i^{prj}, \pi_i \circ \pi_i^{prj}). \end{aligned}$$

Using this expression for each element of the sequence, we have

$$\begin{aligned} \bigvee_{i\ge 0} F^E(\mu_i) \circ F^E(\mu_i)^{prj} &= \bigvee_{i\ge 0} F(\nu_i \circ \nu_i^{prj}, \pi_i \circ \pi_i^{prj}) \\ &= F(\bigvee_{i\ge 0} \nu_i \circ \nu_i^{prj}, \bigvee_{i\ge 0} \pi_i \circ \pi_i^{prj}) \\ &= F(id_b, id_c) \\ &= id_{F(b,c)}. \end{aligned}$$

Table 7.1
Smyth-Plotkin method for finding fixed-points of functors.

Given category $\mathcal{C}$ and functors $F_1, \ldots, F_k$ with $F_i\colon (\mathcal{C}^{op})^{m_i} \times \mathcal{C}^{n_i} \to \mathcal{C}$, use the following steps to show that recursive type expressions over $F_1, \ldots, F_k$ may be interpreted in $\mathcal{C}$.
1. Show that $\mathcal{C}$ is an **O**-category with terminal object $\perp$ and left-strict composition. Conclude by Lemma 7.4.15 that $\mathcal{C}^E$ has initial object $\perp$.
2. Show that $\mathcal{C}$ has all ω^{op} limits. Conclude by Theorem 7.4.23 that $\mathcal{C}^E$ is an ω-category with locally determined colimits.
3. Show that each $F_i\colon (\mathcal{C}^{op})^{m_i} \times \mathcal{C}^{n_i} \to \mathcal{C}$ is locally continuous. Conclude by Theorem 7.4.27 that each $F_i^E\colon (\mathcal{C}^E)^{m_i} \times (\mathcal{C}^E)^{n_i} \to \mathcal{C}^E$ is an ω-continuous covariant functor.

This completes the proof. ■

Exercise 7.4.28 Show that if $F\colon \mathcal{B}^{op} \times \mathcal{C} \to \mathcal{D}$ is locally monotonic, then F^E preserves composition of morphisms, *i.e.*, $F^E(f \circ g, f' \circ g') = F^E(f, f') \circ F^E(g, g')$ for all appropriate morphisms f, g, f' and g'. (This completes the proof of Lemma 7.4.26.)

Exercise 7.4.29 Show that the locally continuous functors are closed under composition, tupling, and taking the opposite of a functor:

(a) Show that if F and G are locally continuous, then $F \circ G$ is a locally continuous functor.

(b) Show that if F and G are locally continuous, then $F \times G$ is a locally continuous functor.

(c) Show that if F is locally continuous, then F^{op} is a locally continuous functor.

7.4.8 Examples of the General Method

Lemma 7.4.15, Theorem 7.4.23 and Theorem 7.4.27 provide a standard method for interpreting recursive types over given basic functors. This is summarized in Table 7.1 and illustrated in the following two examples. Another useful class of examples are models of subtyping, polymorphism and recursive types, as in [AP90, BM92, Ros92], for example. An important observation about the method is that, starting with functor $F\colon \mathcal{C} \to \mathcal{C}$, we find an object a with $a \cong F^E(a)$ in $\mathcal{C}^E$ instead $a \cong F(a)$ in $\mathcal{C}$. However, since $\mathcal{C}^E$ is a subcategory of $\mathcal{C}$ and functor F^E is the same on objects as F, an isomorphism $a \cong F^E(a)$ in $\mathcal{C}^E$ implies $a \cong F(a)$ in $\mathcal{C}$. Therefore, when applicable, the method allows us to interpret recursive type expressions as desired.

Example 7.4.30 The category P*fn* of sets and partial functions is considered in Example 7.4.24, which shows that P*fn*^{E} is an ω-category with locally determined colimits. By Lemma 7.4.15, the initial object of P*fn*^{E} is the empty set, $\emptyset$.

A "product" functor, $P\colon \mathrm{P}fn \times \mathrm{P}fn \to \mathrm{P}fn$, is

$$P(A, B) \quad = A \times B,$$

$$P(f, g)\langle a, b\rangle = \begin{cases} \langle f(a), g(b)\rangle & \text{if both } f(a)\downarrow,\ g(b)\downarrow, \\ \text{undefined} & \text{otherwise.} \end{cases}$$

We can see that this is locally continuous by calculating $P(\bigvee S, \bigvee T)\langle a, b\rangle = \bigvee\{P(f, g)\langle a, b\rangle \mid f \in S, g \in T\} = (\bigvee\{P(f, g) \mid f \in S, g \in T\})\langle a, b\rangle$ for any directed sets $S \subseteq \mathrm{P}fn(A, A')$, $T \subseteq \mathrm{P}fn(B, B')$ and $\langle a, b\rangle \in A \times B$. Consequently, P^E is ω-continuous and we can find sets such as $A \cong nat \times A$ as the colimit of an ω-diagram (see Exercise 7.4.32). However, in Exercise 7.4.34 it is shown that P is not the categorical product in P*fn* and the categorical product in P*fn* is not locally continuous. More importantly, the function-space functor cannot be locally continuous, since cardinality constraints rule out finding any $A \cong bool \rightharpoonup A$, for example. Categorical coproducts (sums) in P*fn* are considered in Exercise 7.4.35. ∎

Example 7.4.31 We will apply the general method to $Cpo_\perp$, the category of pointed CPOs and strict continuous functions, and construct a CPO D satisfying $D \cong unit \langle+\rangle (D \to D)$, where $\langle+\rangle$ is separated sum.

The first step is to note that $Cpo_\perp$ is an **O**-category with terminal object $\perp$ and left-strict composition. (This is clear from our study of CPOs in Chapter 5.) It follows, by Lemma 7.4.15, that $Cpo_\perp^E$ has initial object $\{\perp\}$.

The second step is to show that $Cpo_\perp$ has all ω^{op} limits and conclude by Theorem 7.4.23 that $Cpo_\perp^E$ is an ω-category with locally determined colimits. This is done in Example 7.4.25.

The third step is to show that each $F_i\colon (Cpo_\perp^{op})^{m_i} \times Cpo_\perp^{n_i} \to Cpo_\perp$ of interest is locally continuous and conclude by Theorem 7.4.27 that each $F_i^E\colon (Cpo_\perp^E)^{m_i} \times (Cpo_\perp^E)^{n_i} \to Cpo_\perp^E$ is an ω-continuous covariant functor. This is where we see the most important difference between P*fn* and categories of CPOs. In particular, both C*ppo* and $Cpo_\perp$ have locally continuous function-space functors.

The main functors of interest on CPOs are lifting, product, function space, coproduct (sum) and variations that treat $\perp$ in different ways. The lifting, $(\ )_\perp$, categorical product, $\times$, and function space, $\to$, functors on C*ppo* are the same as for C*po* and are described in Example 7.2.7. The categorical product and coproduct of $Cpo_\perp$ are the smash product, $\otimes$, of Exercise 5.2.34 and the coalesced sum, $\oplus$, of Exercise 5.2.33. Although C*ppo* has no categorical coproduct, the separated sum, $\langle+\rangle$, of Exercise 5.2.33 is often used instead. It can be verified that all of these functors are locally monotonic and locally continuous and therefore give rise to ω-continuous functors on $Cpo_\perp^E = Cppo^E$.

An illustrative example is the initial F^E-algebra for $F(A) = unit \langle+\rangle (A \to A)$. This is a CPO $D \cong unit \langle + \rangle (D \to D)$ obtained as the colimit of the ω-diagram Δ_{F^E} in $Cpo_\perp^E$. We will construct D by following the proof that such a CPO exists.

The diagram Δ_{F^E} is

$$\Delta \;=\; \{\perp\} \xrightarrow{\;!\;} F^E(\perp) \xrightarrow{F^E(!)} (F^E)^2(\perp) \xrightarrow{(F^E)^2(!)} \ldots,$$

To make this generic diagram more concrete, we sketch out the first few CPOs.

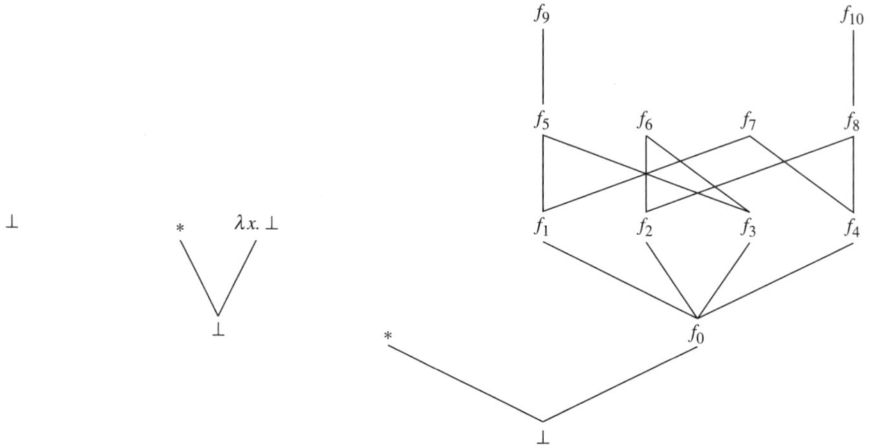

The reader is encouraged to work out the embeddings and projections, which are uniquely determined since there is only one embedding of the first CPO into the second. The second CPO is isomorphic to $\mathcal{B}_\perp$, the CPO of lifted booleans. As a result, the upper right portion of the third CPO is isomorphic to $\mathcal{B}_\perp \to \mathcal{B}_\perp$, which is discussed in Example 5.2.9 and shown in Figure 5.1. The fourth CPO in the series would be considerably larger, in fact too large to draw comfortably.

The general argument in Example 7.4.25 shows that Δ^{prj} has a limit in $Cpo_\perp$. This limit is a CPO of infinite sequences. However, what we want is a colimit of Δ in $Cpo_\perp^E$. We obtain this by working through the proof of Theorem 7.4.23. This theorem shows that if a category $\mathcal{C}$ has all ω^{op} limits, then $\mathcal{C}^E$ has all ω-colimits. The proof proceeds by showing that a limit of any Δ^{prj} in $\mathcal{C}$ is a colimit of Δ in $\mathcal{C}^E$. Therefore, this proof shows that the colimit of our diagram Δ in $Cpo_\perp^E$ above is the limit of Δ^{prj} from Example 7.4.25. Therefore, the colimit $\mu = \langle D, \{\pi_i \colon D \to D_i\}_{i \geq 0}\rangle$ consists of a CPO

$$D = \{a \in \prod_i D_i \mid \forall i.\, a_i = \delta_i^{prj}(a_{i+1})\},$$

where $D_i = (F^E)^i(\perp)$ and $\delta_i = (F^E)^i(\perp)$, together with projection functions $\pi_i \colon D \to D_i$

as described in Example 7.4.24. The ordering on D is the coordinate-wise order $a \leq b$ iff $a_i \leq b_i$ for all $i \geq 0$. The least element of D is therefore the infinite sequence $\langle \bot, \bot, \ldots \rangle$ that is $\bot$ in each coordinate.

Now that we have identified a CPO D that should satisfy $D \cong unit \langle + \rangle (D \rightarrow D)$, it is useful to verify this isomorphism. The existence of this isomorphism is given by Lemma 7.4.10, using the fact that F^E is locally continuous, by Theorem 7.4.27. From the Lemma 7.4.10, we can see that the isomorphism from $F(D)$ to D is the unique cocone morphism from $F(\mu)$ to μ^-. We can extract the cocone morphism from $F(\mu)$ to μ^- from the proof of Theorem 7.4.23, since the existence of this morphism follows from the initiality of μ in the category of cocones. Since Theorem 7.4.23 shows how to obtain an initial cocone in $Cpo_\bot^E$ from a terminal cone in $Cpo_\bot$, this in turn relies on the proof that Δ^{prj} has a limit in $Cpo_\bot$. The net result, however, can be understood directly from a picture of D and $F(D)$.

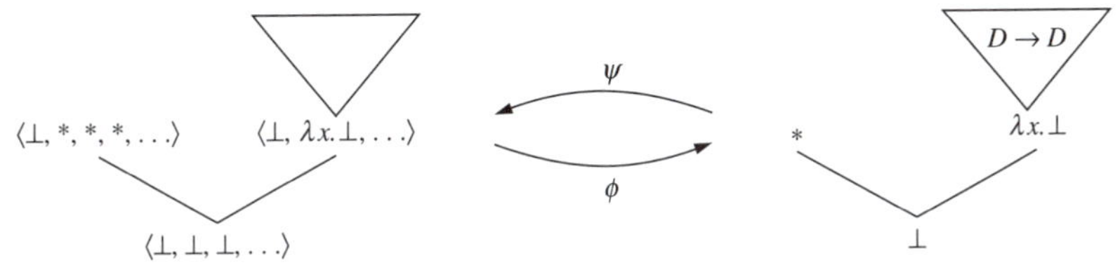

In the CPO D on the left, every element is an infinite sequence. Every sequence begins with $\bot$ since this is the only element of D_0. The least element is $\langle \bot, \bot, \ldots \rangle$, with two elements above it constant after the second element of the sequence. The elements of the triangle in the upper right all have the form $\langle \bot, f_1, f_2, f_3, \ldots \rangle$, where $f_{i+1} \colon D_i \rightarrow D_i$. Since $D_0 = \{\bot\}$, f_1 is always the function $\lambda x \in D_0.\ \bot$. However, since the D_i's grow rapidly in size, there are many possibilities for the later functions in the sequence. It is easy to guess from the picture that the isomorphism from D into $D \cong unit \langle + \rangle (D \rightarrow D)$ behaves as follows:

$$\phi(\langle \bot, \bot, \bot, \ldots \rangle) = \bot$$

$$\phi(\langle \bot, *, *, \ldots \rangle) = *$$

$$\phi(\langle \bot, f_1, f_2, f_3, \ldots \rangle) = \lambda \langle a_0, a_1, a_2, \ldots \rangle \in D. \langle f_1(a_0), f_2(a_1), f_3(a_2), \ldots \rangle$$

The only subtle point is the way that we regard each element in the upper-right triangle of D as a function from D to D. However, there is really only one reasonable thing to do with a sequence of functions, namely, apply each one to the element of the argument sequence that is in its domain. (Exercise 7.4.33 asks you to check that

$\langle f_1(a_0), f_2(a_1), f_3(a_2), \ldots\rangle \in D$.) Note that we can apply a sequence of functions to itself by this method: if $\langle \bot, f_1, f_2, f_3, \ldots\rangle$ is a sequence with $f_{i+1}\colon D_i \to D_i$, then f_i is in the domain of f_{i+1} and we can form the sequence $\langle f_1(f_0), f_2(f_1), f_3(f_2), \ldots\rangle \in D$.

The converse map is essentially

$$\psi(\bot) = \langle \bot, \bot, \bot, \ldots\rangle$$

$$\psi(*) = \langle \bot, *, *, \ldots\rangle$$

$$\psi(f\colon D \to D) = \langle \bot, \lambda x \in D_0.\, f(x), \lambda x \in D_1.\, f(x), \lambda x \in D_2.\, f(x), \ldots\rangle$$

In the definition of $\psi(f\colon D \to D)$, which is only approximately correct above, we use the embedding of each D_i into D. More specifically, since each $\pi_i\colon D \to D_i$ is a projection, there is a corresponding embedding $\pi_i^{emb}\colon D_i \to D$. Instead of writing $\lambda x \in D_i.\, f(x)$, we should use the function $\lambda x \in D_i.\, \pi_i(f(\pi_i^{emb}(x)))$ obtained by restricting f to $D_i \to D_i$ using π_i. Thus a more precise way of defining $\psi(f\colon D \to D)$ is

$$\psi(f\colon D \to D) = \langle \bot, \pi_0 \circ f \circ \pi_0^{emb}, \pi_1 \circ f \circ \pi_1^{emb}, \pi_2 \circ f \circ \pi_2^{emb}, \ldots\rangle$$

It is a worthwhile exercise for the reader to verify that ϕ and ψ are inverses of each other, as outlined in Exercise 7.4.33. ∎

Exercise 7.4.32 Describe the set $A \cong nat \times A$ derived from the colimit of an ω-diagram as explained in Example 7.4.30.

Exercise 7.4.33 Let D be the CPO constructed in Example 7.4.31. Show that ϕ and ψ are inverses of each other using the following steps. You will need to use the fact that a sequence $\langle a_0, a_1, a_2, a_3, \ldots\rangle$ with $a_i \in D_i$ is in D iff $a_i = \delta_i^{prj}(a_{i+1})$.

(a) If $f = \langle f^{emb}, f^{prj}\rangle\colon A \to B$ is a morphism in $Cpo_\bot^E$ then the functor F gives us the morphism $F(A) \to F(B)$ determined by the following embedding:

$$F(f)(*) = *$$

$$F(f)(\bot) = \bot$$

$$F(f)(g\colon A \to A) = f^{emb} \circ g \circ f^{prj} \quad : B \to B$$

Work out a similar characterization for the projection from $b \to B$ to $A \to A$. (Note that the diagram $\Delta = \Delta_{FE}$ of Example 7.4.31, $\delta_{i+1} = F(\delta_i)$.)

(b) The projection $\pi_i\colon D \to D_i$ is defined by $\pi_i(\langle a_0, a_1, \ldots\rangle) = a_i$. The corresponding embedding is $\pi_i^{emb}(a) = \langle a_0, a_1, \ldots\rangle$ where $a_i = a$, $a_j = \delta_j^{prj}(a_{j+1})$ for $j < i$ and $a_{j+1} = \delta_j^{emb}(a_j)$ for $j > i$. Show that for any $a \in D_i$, we have $\pi_i^{emb}(a) \in D$.

(c) Show that if $\langle a_0, a_1, a_2, a_3, \ldots \rangle, \langle f_0, f_1, f_2, f_3, \ldots \rangle \in D$ are sequences with $a_i = \delta^{prj}(a_{i+1})$, $f_i = \delta^{prj}(f_{i+1})$ and $f_{i+1}\colon D_i \to D_i$. Show that $\langle f_1(a_0), f_2(a_1), f_3(a_2), \ldots \rangle \in D$, *i.e.*, $f_{i+1}(a_i) = \delta^{prj}(f_{i+2}(a_{i+1}))$ for all $i \geq 0$.

(d) Show that $\psi \circ \phi = Id$ and $\phi \circ \psi = Id$.

Exercise 7.4.34 The functor P of Example 7.4.34 appears to be a form of product. An expert in category theory would recognize that P is left-adjoint to the *Hom* functor, as cartesian product would be in a CCC). However, P is what is called a "tensor" product.

(a) Show that P is not the categorical product in P*fn*.

(b) Show that the categorical product in P*fn* is not locally continuous.

Exercise 7.4.35 The the sum functor in P*fn* is $A + B = A \uplus B = (\{0\} \times A) \cup (\{1\} \times B)$ on objects and

$$(f+g)(c) = \begin{cases} \langle 0, f(a) \rangle & \text{if } c = \langle 0, a \rangle \text{ and } f(a)\downarrow, \\ \langle 0, g(b) \rangle & \text{if } c = \langle 1, b \rangle \text{ and } g(b)\downarrow, \\ \text{undefined} & \text{otherwise.} \end{cases}$$

on arrows (*c.f.* Exercise 5.2.33).

(a) Show that this functor is categorical coproduct in P*fn*.

(b) Prove that $+$ is locally continuous.

(c) Determine the set $A \cong unit + \mathcal{N} \times A$, where $\times$ is the non-categorical product in Example 7.4.30, and describe the unique embedding into any B with embedding $(unit + \mathcal{N} \times B) \to B$.

Exercise 7.4.36 Describe the solution to $D = (D \to D)_\perp$ in $Cpo_\perp$ in approximately the same detail as Example 7.4.31. Draw the first few CPOs and describe the embeddings and projections between them. Then sketch the orderings on D and $(D \to D)_\perp$ and give explicit definitions of the isomorphisms.

8 Logical Relations

8.1 Introduction to Logical Relations

Logical relations are an important tool in the study of typed lambda calculus. Essentially, a logical relation $\mathcal{R}$ is a collection $\{R^\sigma \mid \sigma \text{ a type}\}$ of typed relations with the relation $R^{\sigma\to\tau}$ for type $\sigma \to \tau$ determined from the relations R^σ and R^τ in a way that guarantees closure under application and lambda abstraction. The relation $R^{\sigma\times\tau}$ for type $\sigma \times \tau$ is determined from the relations R^σ and R^τ in a way that guarantees closure under pairing and projection, and similarly for sums (disjoint unions) and other types. Since logical relations are very general, some important algebraic concepts like homomorphisms and congruence relations lead to special classes of logical relations. However, logical relations lack many familiar properties of their algebraic analogs. For example, the composition of two logical relations may not be a logical relation, even in the special cases where both logical relations seem to act as homomorphisms or congruence relations. Logical relations are also closely related to partial equivalence relation models (Section 5.6).

The main topics in this chapter are:

• Definition of logical relation over typed applicative structure and the "basic lemma." For $\lambda^\to$, this lemma says that logical relations are closed under application and lambda abstraction. In particular, if $\mathcal{R}$ is a logical relation between models $\mathcal{A}$ and $\mathcal{B}$, and M is a closed term, then $\mathcal{R}$ relates the meaning of M in $\mathcal{A}$ to the meaning of M in $\mathcal{B}$.

• Completeness and reduction properties of typed lambda calculus and PCF using logical relations over the typed applicative structure of terms.

• Logical partial functions and partial equivalence relations, which are roughly similar to homomorphisms and congruence relations over algebraic structures. These are used to prove completeness of the equational axioms for particular models.

• Representation independence using logical relations. Intuitively, representation independence states that implementors of a programming language have some freedom in the way they implement data types. For example, in implementing a language based on $\lambda^\to$ with type constant *bool*, it does not matter whether *true* is represented by 1 and *false* by 0, or vice-versa, as long as operations like conditional behave properly.

• Special types of logical relations, such as those appropriate to domain-theoretic (CPO) models.

Logical relations for typed lambda calculus were developed by Howard, Tait, Friedman, Statman, Plotkin, and others. The main historical references are [How73, Tai67, Fri75, Plo73, Plo80] and the three papers by Statman [Sta82, Sta85b, Sta85a]. Many of the results presented in this chapter are proved in [Sta85b], using a slightly different framework, although our definition of relation over applicative structures that are not Henkin models is different from his. The uniform treatment of relations over models and terms, and the revised definition of "admissible," are based on [Mit86c].

There are many interesting properties of logical relations that we do not have sufficient space to go into. Among other things, logical relations have applications to strictness analysis [BHA86, Abr90], full abstraction [Mul87], and realizability semantics of constructive logics [Mit86a, MO86].

8.2 Logical Relations over Applicative Structures

8.2.1 Definition of Logical Relation

We will formulate the basic definitions using $\lambda^{\times,\rightarrow}$ applicative structures. Since the set of terms, as well as any model, forms a typed applicative structure, we will be able to use logical relations to prove syntactic as well as semantic results about typed lambda calculus.

Let $\mathcal{A} = \langle \{A^\sigma\}, \{\mathbf{Proj}_1^{\sigma,\tau}, \mathbf{Proj}_2^{\sigma,\tau}, \mathbf{App}_{\mathcal{A}}^{\sigma,\tau}\}, Const_{\mathcal{A}}\rangle$ and $\mathcal{B} = \langle \{B^\sigma\}, \{\mathbf{Proj}_1^{\sigma,\tau}, \mathbf{Proj}_2^{\sigma,\tau}, \mathbf{App}_{\mathcal{B}}^{\sigma,\tau}\}, Const_{\mathcal{B}}\rangle$ be $\lambda^{\times,\rightarrow}$ applicative structures for some signature Σ. A *logical relation* $\mathcal{R} = \{R^\sigma\}$ *over* $\mathcal{A}$ *and* $\mathcal{B}$ is a family of relations indexed by the type expressions over Σ such that

- $R^\sigma \subseteq A^\sigma \times B^\sigma$ for each type σ,
- $R^{\sigma\times\tau}(p, q)$ iff $R^\sigma(\mathbf{Proj}_1 p, \mathbf{Proj}_1 q)$ and $R^\tau(\mathbf{Proj}_2 p, \mathbf{Proj}_2 q)$,
- $R^{\sigma\rightarrow\tau}(f, g)$ iff $\forall x \in A^\sigma.\ \forall y \in B^\sigma. R^\sigma(x, y) \supset R^\tau(\mathbf{App}_{\mathcal{A}}\, f\, x, \mathbf{App}_{\mathcal{B}}\, g\, y)$,
- $R^\sigma(Const_{\mathcal{A}}(c), Const_{\mathcal{B}}(c))$ for every typed constant $c\colon \sigma$ of Σ.

For $\lambda^{\rightarrow}$, we drop the condition on $R^{\sigma\times\tau}$, and for extensions of $\lambda^{\times,\rightarrow}$, there is an additional condition for each type form. The central property for $\lambda^{\rightarrow}$ is that two functions, f and g, are logically related iff they map related arguments to related results. Given R^σ and R^τ, this determines $R^{\sigma\rightarrow\tau}$ uniquely, and similarly for $\sigma \times \tau$, and other types. We will often write $R(x, y)$ for $R^\sigma(x, y)$ when σ is either clear from context or irrelevant. We also write $\mathcal{R} \subseteq \mathcal{A} \times \mathcal{B}$ to indicate that $\mathcal{R}$ is a relation over $\mathcal{A}$ and $\mathcal{B}$.

Some trivial examples of logical relations are the identity and "true everywhere" relations.

If $\mathcal{A}$ is extensional, then the identity relation $\mathcal{I} = \{I^\sigma\} \subseteq \mathcal{A} \times \mathcal{A}$ with $I^\sigma(x, y)$ iff $x = y \in A^\sigma$ is logical.

For any applicative structures $\mathcal{A}$ and $\mathcal{B}$ of the same signature, the relation $\mathcal{R} \subseteq \mathcal{A} \times \mathcal{B}$ that relates every element of A^σ to every element of B^σ is logical.

When the signature Σ has no term constants, logical relations may be constructed by choosing arbitrary $R^b \subseteq A^b \times B^b$ for each type constant b and extending to higher types inductively. For signatures with term constants, it is sometimes more difficult to construct logical relations. However, if all constants have base type (*i.e.*, if $c\colon \sigma$ is a constant of the signature, then σ is a type constant), we may construct logical relations by choosing a relation for each type constant that respects the interpretation of all term constants. It is also relatively easy to accommodate first-order function constants (see Exercise 8.2.2). For higher-order constants such as $fix_{nat \to nat}\colon ((nat \to nat) \to (nat \to nat)) \to nat \to nat$, however, we must construct relations in a special way. For *fix* specifically, this is discussed in Section 8.6.2.

Binary logical relations illustrate the general properties of logical relations well and will be sufficient for most of our purposes. However, it is worth noting that the definition above generalizes easily to *k-ary* logical relations $\mathcal{R}$ over applicative structures $\mathcal{A}_1, \ldots, \mathcal{A}_k$, including the case $k = 1$. All of the results of this chapter generalize easily to relations of arbitrary arity; only the notation becomes more complicated. The reason is that logical relations of any arity may be viewed as unary logical relations. The reader may enjoy formulating the definition of logical predicate (unary logical relation) and proving that a logical relation $\mathcal{R} \subseteq \mathcal{A} \times \mathcal{B}$ is just a logical predicate over the straightforwardly-defined product applicative structure $\mathcal{A} \times \mathcal{B}$ (see Exercise 8.2.1).

Exercise 8.2.1 Let $\mathcal{A}$ and $\mathcal{B}$ be $\lambda^{\to}$ applicative structures. Write out a definition for the product structure

$$\mathcal{A} \times \mathcal{B} = \langle \{A^\sigma \times B^\sigma\}, \{\mathbf{App}^{\sigma,\tau}\}, Const \rangle,$$

with application defined component-wise. Show that a typed relation $\mathcal{R}$ is a binary logical relation over $\mathcal{A}$ and $\mathcal{B}$ iff $\mathcal{R}$ is a logical predicate (unary logical relation) over $\mathcal{A} \times \mathcal{B}$.

Exercise 8.2.2 Let Σ be a $\lambda^{\to}$ signature with type constant *nat* and term constants $0, 1\colon nat$ and $+, *\colon nat \to nat \to nat$. Describe the smallest logical relation $\mathcal{R} \subseteq \mathcal{A} \times \mathcal{A}$ over any Σ applicative structure $\mathcal{A}$.

Exercise 8.2.3 Let $\mathcal{A}$ be the full classical $\lambda^{\to}$ hierarchy for some signature Σ without term constants. For each type constant b of Σ, let π^b be some permutation on A^b. Let $\mathcal{R} \subseteq \mathcal{A} \times \mathcal{A}$ be the logical relation determined by

$$R^b(a, b) \text{ iff } \pi^b a = b.$$

Show that for every type τ, the relation R^τ is the graph of a permutation π^τ on A^τ, and that

$$\pi^{\sigma\to\tau} f = \pi^\tau \circ f \circ (\pi^\sigma)^{-1}.$$

A logical relation with this property is called a *hereditary permutation.*

Exercise 8.2.4 Let $\mathcal{A}$ be a $\lambda^\to$ typed applicative structure for some signature Σ without term constants and define the predicate $\mathcal{R} \subseteq \mathcal{A}$ by

$$R^\sigma = \begin{cases} A^\sigma & \text{if } \exists \text{ closed } M\colon\sigma, \\ \emptyset & \quad\text{otherwise.} \end{cases}$$

Use Lemma 4.3.14 to prove that $\mathcal{R}$ is a logical relation iff Σ has only one type constant. This shows that in proving properties of logical relations, it is *not* sufficient to consider only the special case with one type constant.

8.2.2 The Basic Lemma

The Basic Lemma establishes that the meaning of a term in one model is always logically related to its meaning in any other model. On the face of it, the Basic Lemma only seems to apply to models, since the meaning of a term is not necessarily defined in an arbitrary applicative structure. However, with a little extra work, we can also state a version of the lemma which will be useful in proving properties of applicative structures that are not models. We will take this up after stating the Basic Lemma for models. For simplicity, we restrict our attention to $\lambda^\to$.

An auxiliary definition will make the lemma easier to write down. A logical relation $\mathcal{R} \subseteq \mathcal{A} \times \mathcal{B}$ may be regarded as a relation on environments for $\mathcal{A}$ and $\mathcal{B}$, as follows. We say that *environments* η_a *for* $\mathcal{A}$ *and* η_b *for* $\mathcal{B}$, *satisfying* Γ, *are related by* $\mathcal{R}$, and write $R^\Gamma(\eta_a, \eta_b)$, if

$$R^\sigma(\eta_a(x), \eta_b(x))$$

for every $x\colon\sigma \in \Gamma$.

Lemma 8.2.5 (Basic Lemma, for models) Let $\mathcal{R} \subseteq \mathcal{A} \times \mathcal{B}$ be a logical relation and let η_a and η_b be environments for models $\mathcal{A}$ and $\mathcal{B}$ with $\eta_a, \eta_b \models \Gamma$ and $R^\Gamma(\eta_a, \eta_b)$. Then

$$\mathcal{R}(\mathcal{A}[\![\Gamma \triangleright M\colon\sigma]\!]\eta_a, \mathcal{B}[\![\Gamma \triangleright M\colon\sigma]\!]\eta_b)$$

for every typed term $\Gamma \triangleright M\colon\sigma$.

Proof We use induction on terms. Constants are straightforward, since we assume that any logical relation respects constants. For a variable $\Gamma \triangleright x\colon\sigma$, it is easy to see that $\mathcal{R}(\mathcal{A}[\![\Gamma \triangleright x\colon\sigma]\!]\eta_a, \mathcal{B}[\![\Gamma \triangleright x\colon\sigma]\!]\eta_b)$, since we have assumed $\mathcal{R}(\eta_a(x), \eta_b(x))$ for every variable x in Γ. For an application $\Gamma \triangleright MN\colon\tau$, we assume inductively that $R^{\sigma\to\tau}(\mathcal{A}[\![\Gamma \triangleright$

$M\colon\sigma\to\tau]\!]\eta_a, \mathcal{B}[\![\Gamma\rhd M\colon\sigma\to\tau]\!]\eta_b)$ and $R^\sigma(\mathcal{A}[\![\Gamma\rhd N\colon\sigma]\!]\eta_a, \mathcal{B}[\![\Gamma\rhd N\colon\sigma]\!]\eta_b)$. By the definition of logical relation, we have

$$R^\tau(\mathbf{App}\,\mathcal{A}[\![\Gamma\rhd M\colon\sigma\to\tau]\!]\eta_a\,\mathcal{A}[\![\Gamma\rhd N\colon\sigma]\!]\eta_a, \mathbf{App}\,\mathcal{B}[\![\Gamma\rhd M\colon\sigma\to\tau]\!]\eta_b\,\mathcal{B}[\![\Gamma\rhd N\colon\sigma]\!]\eta_b),$$

which implies that $\mathcal{A}[\![\Gamma\rhd MN\colon\tau]\!]\eta_a$ and $\mathcal{B}[\![\Gamma\rhd MN\colon\tau]\!]\eta_a$ are related.

For an abstraction $\Gamma\rhd\lambda x\colon\sigma.M\colon\sigma\to\tau$, we want to show that

$$\mathcal{R}(\mathcal{A}[\![\Gamma\rhd\lambda x\colon\sigma.M\colon\sigma\to\tau]\!]\eta_a, \mathcal{B}[\![\Gamma\rhd\lambda x\colon\sigma.M\colon\sigma\to\tau]\!]\eta_b)$$

whenever η_a and η_b are related. If η_a and η_b are related, then whenever $R^\sigma(a,b)$, the modified environments $\eta_a[x\mapsto a]$ and $\eta_b[x\mapsto b]$ are related. Therefore, by the inductive hypothesis, we have

$$\forall a,b.\ R^\sigma(a,b)\supset\mathcal{R}(\mathcal{A}[\![\Gamma, x\colon\sigma\rhd M\colon\tau]\!]\eta_a[x\mapsto a], \mathcal{B}[\![\Gamma, x\colon\sigma\rhd M\colon\tau]\!]\eta_b[x\mapsto b]).$$

But, since $\mathcal{A}[\![\Gamma, x\colon\sigma\rhd M\colon\tau]\!]\eta_a[x\mapsto a] = \mathbf{App}\,(\mathcal{A}[\![\Gamma\rhd\lambda x\colon\sigma.M\colon\sigma\to\tau]\!]\eta_a)\,a$, and similarly for $\mathcal{B}$, it follows from the definition of logical relation that $\mathcal{A}[\![\Gamma\rhd\lambda x\colon\sigma.M\colon\sigma\to\tau]\!]\eta_a$ and $\mathcal{B}[\![\Gamma\rhd\lambda x\colon\sigma.M\colon\sigma\to\tau]\!]\eta_b$ are related. ∎

The Basic Lemma may be generalized to applicative structures that are not models by including some hypotheses about the way terms are interpreted. If $\mathcal{A}$ is an applicative structure, a partial mapping $\mathcal{A}[\![\ ]\!]$ from terms and environments to $\mathcal{A}$ is *an acceptable meaning function* if

$$\mathcal{A}[\![\Gamma\rhd M\colon\sigma]\!]\eta\in A^\sigma \text{ whenever } \eta\models\Gamma$$

and the following conditions are satisfied:

$$\begin{aligned}
\mathcal{A}[\![\Gamma\rhd x\colon\sigma]\!]\eta &= \eta(x)\\
\mathcal{A}[\![\Gamma\rhd c\colon\sigma]\!]\eta &= Const(c)\\
\mathcal{A}[\![\Gamma\rhd MN\colon\tau]\!]\eta &= \mathbf{App}\,\mathcal{A}[\![\Gamma\rhd M\colon\sigma\to\tau]\!]\eta\,\mathcal{A}[\![\Gamma\rhd N\colon\sigma]\!]\eta\\
\mathcal{A}[\![\Gamma\rhd\lambda x\colon\sigma.M\colon\sigma\to\tau]\!]\eta &= \mathcal{A}[\![\Gamma\rhd\lambda y\colon\sigma.[y/x]M\colon\sigma\to\tau]\!]\eta\\
\mathcal{A}[\![\Gamma\rhd M\colon\sigma]\!]\eta_1 &= \mathcal{A}[\![\Gamma\rhd M\colon\sigma]\!]\eta_2 \text{ whenever } \eta_1(x)=\eta_2(x) \text{ all } x\in FV(M)\\
\mathcal{A}[\![\Gamma, x\colon\sigma\rhd M\colon\tau]\!]\eta &= \mathcal{A}[\![\Gamma\rhd M\colon\tau]\!]\eta \text{ for } x \text{ not in } \Gamma
\end{aligned}$$

Two important examples of acceptable meaning functions are meaning functions for models and substitution on applicative structures of terms. These and other examples appear following the next definition. The last three conditions of the definition above are not strictly necessary for the Basic Lemma. However, they are natural properties that hold of all the examples we consider.

In addition to acceptable meaning functions, we will need some assumptions about the behavior of a logical relation on lambda abstractions. A logical relation over models is necessarily closed under lambda abstraction, as a consequence of the way that lambda abstraction and application interact. However, in an arbitrary applicative structure, abstraction and application may not be "inverses," and so we need an additional assumption to prove the Basic Lemma.

If $\mathcal{R} \subseteq \mathcal{A} \times \mathcal{B}$ and $\mathcal{A}[\![\ ]\!]$, $\mathcal{B}[\![\ ]\!]$ are acceptable meaning functions, we say $\mathcal{R}$ is *admissible for* $\mathcal{A}[\![\ ]\!]$ and $\mathcal{B}[\![\ ]\!]$ if, for all related environments $\eta_a, \eta_b \models \Gamma$ and terms $\Gamma, x\!:\!\sigma \triangleright M\!:\!\tau$ and $\Gamma, x\!:\!\sigma \triangleright N\!:\!\tau$,

$$\forall a, b.\ R^{\sigma}(a, b) \supset R^{\tau}(\mathcal{A}[\![\Gamma, x\!:\!\sigma \triangleright M\!:\!\tau]\!]\eta_a[x \mapsto a], \mathcal{B}[\![\Gamma, x\!:\!\sigma \triangleright N\!:\!\tau]\!]\eta_b[x \mapsto b])$$

implies

$$\forall a, b.\ R^{\sigma}(a, b) \supset R^{\tau}(\mathbf{App}\,(\mathcal{A}[\![\Gamma \triangleright \lambda x\!:\!\sigma.M\!:\!\sigma \to \tau]\!]\eta_a)\,a,$$

$$\mathbf{App}\,(\mathcal{B}[\![\Gamma \triangleright \lambda x\!:\!\sigma.N\!:\!\sigma \to \tau]\!]\eta_b)\,b\,).$$

The definitions of acceptable meaning function and admissible logical relation are technical and motivated primarily by their use in applications of the Basic Lemma. To give some intuition, several examples are listed below.

Example 8.2.6 If $\mathcal{A}$ is a model, then the ordinary meaning function $\mathcal{A}[\![\ ]\!]$ is acceptable. It is clear that if $\mathcal{A}$ and $\mathcal{B}$ are models, then any logical $\mathcal{R} \subseteq \mathcal{A} \times \mathcal{B}$ is admissible, since then

$$\mathcal{A}[\![\Gamma, x\!:\!\sigma \triangleright M\!:\!\tau]\!]\eta_a[x \mapsto a] = \mathbf{App}\,(\mathcal{A}[\![\Gamma \triangleright \lambda x\!:\!\sigma.M\!:\!\sigma \to \tau]\!]\eta_a)\,a,$$

and similarly for $\Gamma, x\!:\!\sigma \triangleright N\!:\!\tau$. ■

Example 8.2.7 Let $\mathcal{T}$ be an applicative structure of terms M such that $\Gamma \triangleright M\!:\!\sigma$ for some $\Gamma \subseteq \mathcal{H}$, as in Example 4.5.1. An environment η for $\mathcal{T}$ is a mapping from variables to terms, which we may regard as a substitution. Let us write ηM for the result of substituting terms for free variables in M, and define a meaning function on $\mathcal{T}$ by

$$\mathcal{T}[\![\Gamma \triangleright M\!:\!\sigma]\!]\eta = \eta M.$$

It is a straightforward but worthwhile exercise to verify that $\mathcal{T}[\![\ ]\!]$ is an acceptable meaning function. We will see in Section 8.3.1 that every lambda theory $\mathcal{E}$ gives us an admissible logical relation $\mathcal{R}_{\mathcal{E}} \subseteq \mathcal{T} \times \mathcal{T}$. In short, $\mathcal{R}_{\mathcal{E}}$ relates any pair of terms that are provably equal from $\mathcal{E}$. The reason why $\mathcal{R}_{\mathcal{E}}$ is admissible is that we can prove $\Gamma \triangleright \lambda x\!:\!\sigma.\, M = \lambda x\!:\!\sigma.\, N\!:\!\sigma \to \tau$ immediately from $\Gamma, x\!:\!\sigma \triangleright M = N\!:\!\tau$. ■

Example 8.2.8 If $\mathcal{A}$ is a typed combinatory algebra, then $\mathcal{A}$ is an applicative structure with an acceptable meaning function. The standard acceptable meaning function for $\mathcal{A}$ is obtained by translation into combinators. More specifically, as described in Section 4.5.7, we may translate a typed term $\Gamma \triangleright M\colon \sigma$ into a combinatory term $\Gamma \triangleright \text{CL}(M)\colon \sigma$ that contains constants K and S of various types but does not involve lambda abstraction. Since any such combinatory term has a meaning in $\mathcal{A}$, we can take the meaning of $\Gamma \triangleright \text{CL}(M)\colon \sigma$ as the meaning of $\Gamma \triangleright M\colon \sigma$. It is easy to verify that this is an acceptable meaning function. However, recall that since a combinatory algebra need not be extensional, β-equivalent terms may have different meanings. It is shown in Exercise 8.2.16 that every logical relation over combinatory algebras is admissible. ■

Example 8.2.9 A special case of Example 8.2.8 that deserves to be singled out is that from any partial combinatory algebra $\mathcal{D}$, as defined in Section 5.6.2, we may construct a typed combinatory algebra $\mathcal{A}_{\mathcal{D}}$. In this structure, the interpretation of each typed term will be an element of the untyped partial combinatory algebra. We shall see in Sections 8.2.4 and 8.2.5 that the symmetric and transitive logical relations over $\mathcal{A}_{\mathcal{D}}$ correspond exactly to partial equivalence relation models over $\mathcal{D}$. ■

Using acceptable meaning functions and admissible relations, we have the following general form of the Basic Lemma.

Lemma 8.2.10 (Basic Lemma, general version) Let $\mathcal{A}$ and $\mathcal{B}$ be applicative structures with acceptable meaning functions $\mathcal{A}[\![\ ]\!]$ and $\mathcal{B}[\![\ ]\!]$ and let $\mathcal{R} \subseteq \mathcal{A} \times \mathcal{B}$ be an admissible logical relation. Suppose η_a and η_b are related environments satisfying the type assignment Γ. Then

$$\mathcal{R}(\mathcal{A}[\![\Gamma \triangleright M\colon \sigma]\!]\eta_a, \mathcal{B}[\![\Gamma \triangleright M\colon \sigma]\!]\eta_b)$$

for every typed term $\Gamma \triangleright M\colon \sigma$.

The proof is similar to the proof of the Basic Lemma for models, since the acceptability of $\mathcal{A}[\![\ ]\!]$ and $\mathcal{B}[\![\ ]\!]$, and the admissibility of $\mathcal{R}$, are just what we need to carry out the proof. We will go through the proof to see how this works.

Proof We use induction on terms. For a constant c, we assume $\mathcal{R}(Const_A(c), Const_B(c))$ as part of the definition of logical relation, so the lemma follows from the definition of acceptable meaning function. For a variable $\Gamma \triangleright x\colon \sigma$, we have $\mathcal{R}(\eta_a(x), \eta_b(x))$ by assumption. Since $\mathcal{A}[\![\ ]\!]$ is acceptable, $\mathcal{A}[\![\Gamma \triangleright x\colon \sigma]\!]\eta_a = \eta_a(x)$, and similarly for $\mathcal{B}[\![\ ]\!]$. Therefore $\mathcal{R}(\mathcal{A}[\![\Gamma \triangleright x\colon \sigma]\!]\eta_a, \mathcal{B}[\![\Gamma \triangleright x\colon \sigma]\!]\eta_b)$.

For an application $\Gamma \triangleright MN\colon \tau$, we assume inductively that $R^{\sigma\to\tau}(\mathcal{A}[\![\Gamma \triangleright M\colon \sigma \to \tau]\!]\eta_a, \mathcal{B}[\![\Gamma \triangleright M\colon \sigma \to \tau]\!]\eta_b)$ and $R^{\sigma}(\mathcal{A}[\![\Gamma \triangleright N\colon \sigma]\!]\eta_a, \mathcal{B}[\![\Gamma \triangleright N\colon \sigma]\!]\eta_b)$. Since $\mathcal{R}$ is logical, it follows that

$$R^\tau(\mathbf{App}\ \mathcal{A}[\![\Gamma \triangleright M\colon \sigma \to \tau]\!]\eta_a\ \mathcal{A}[\![\Gamma \triangleright N\colon \sigma]\!]\eta_a, \mathbf{App}\ \mathcal{B}[\![\Gamma \triangleright M\colon \sigma \to \tau]\!]\eta_b\ \mathcal{B}[\![\Gamma \triangleright N\colon \sigma]\!]\eta_b).$$

Since the meaning functions are acceptable, it follows that $\mathcal{A}[\![\Gamma \triangleright MN\colon \tau]\!]\eta_a$ and $\mathcal{B}[\![\Gamma \triangleright MN\colon \tau]\!]\eta_a$ are related.

For an abstraction $\Gamma \triangleright \lambda x\colon \sigma.M\colon \sigma \to \tau$, we want to show that

$$\mathcal{R}(\mathcal{A}[\![\Gamma \triangleright \lambda x\colon \sigma.M\colon \sigma \to \tau]\!]\eta_a, \mathcal{B}[\![\Gamma \triangleright \lambda x\colon \sigma.M\colon \sigma \to \tau]\!]\eta_b)$$

for related environments η_a and η_b. If η_a and η_b are related, then whenever $R^\sigma(a, b)$, the modified environments $\eta_a[x \mapsto a]$ and $\eta_b[x \mapsto b]$ are related. By the inductive hypothesis, we have

$$\forall a, b.\ R^\sigma(a, b) \supset \mathcal{R}(\mathcal{A}[\![\Gamma, x\colon \sigma \triangleright M\colon \tau]\!]\eta_a[x \mapsto a], \mathcal{B}[\![\Gamma, x\colon \sigma \triangleright M\colon \tau]\!]\eta_b[x \mapsto b]).$$

Since $\mathcal{R}$ is admissible, it follows that

$$\forall a, b.\ R^\sigma(a, b) \supset R^\tau(\mathbf{App}\ (\mathcal{A}[\![\Gamma \triangleright \lambda x\colon \sigma.M\colon \sigma \to \tau]\!]\eta_a)\, a,$$
$$\mathbf{App}\ (\mathcal{B}[\![\Gamma \triangleright \lambda x\colon \sigma.M\colon \sigma \to \tau]\!]\eta_b)\, b\,).$$

But by definition of logical relation, this implies that $\mathcal{A}[\![\Gamma \triangleright \lambda x\colon \sigma.M\colon \sigma \to \tau]\!]\eta_a$ and $\mathcal{B}[\![\Gamma \triangleright \lambda x\colon \sigma.M\colon \sigma \to \tau]\!]\eta_b$ are related. ■

The following lemma is useful for establishing that logical relations over term applicative structures are admissible. For simplicity, we state the lemma for logical predicates only.

Lemma 8.2.11 Let $\mathcal{T}$ be an applicative structure of terms with meaning function defined by substitution, as in Example 8.2.7. Let $\mathcal{P} \subseteq \mathcal{T}$ be a logical predicate. If

$$\forall N \in P^\sigma.\ P^b(([N/x]M)N_1 \dots N_k) \quad \text{implies} \quad \forall N \in P^\sigma.\ P^b((\lambda x\colon \sigma.M)NN_1 \dots N_k)$$

for any type constant b, term $\lambda x\colon \sigma.M$ in $T^{\sigma \to \tau_1 \to \dots \to \tau_k \to b}$ and terms $N_1 \in T^{\tau_1}, \dots, N_k \in T^{\tau_k}$, then $\mathcal{P}$ is admissible.

This lemma may be extended to $\lambda^{\times,\to}$ using elimination contexts in place of sequences of applications, as described in Section 8.3.4.

Proof For a term applicative structure $\mathcal{T}$, the definition of admissible simplifies to

$$\forall N \in P^\sigma.P^\tau([L_1, \dots, L_\ell, N/x_1, \dots, x_\ell, x]M) \quad \text{implies}$$
$$\forall N \in P^\sigma.P^\tau(([L_1, \dots, L_\ell/x_1, \dots, x_\ell]\lambda x\colon \sigma.M)N)$$

Since x is a bound variable in the statement of the lemma, we are free to choose x so as not to appear in any of the L_i. Therefore, it suffices to show that

$$\forall N \in P^{\sigma}.P^{\tau}([N/x]M) \quad \text{implies} \quad \forall N \in P^{\sigma}.P^{\tau}((\lambda x\colon\sigma.M)N)$$

for arbitrary M,x and τ. Since this follows immediately from condition

$$\forall N \in P^{\sigma}.P^{\tau}(([N/x]M)N_1 \ldots N_k) \quad \text{implies} \quad \forall N \in P^{\sigma}.P^{\tau}((\lambda x\colon\sigma.M)NN_1 \ldots N_k), \qquad (*)$$

it suffices to show $(*)$ by induction on τ. The base case is easy, since this is the hypothesis of the lemma.

For the inductive step, we assume $(*)$ for types τ_1 and τ_2 and assume

$$\forall N \in P^{\sigma}.P^{\tau_1\to\tau_2}(([N/x]M)N_1 \ldots N_k).$$

We must show that $[N/x]M$ may be replaced by $(\lambda x\colon\sigma.M)N$. Let $Q \in P^{\tau_1}$. By assumption and the fact that $\mathcal{P}$ is logical, we have

$$\forall N \in P^{\sigma}.P^{\tau_2}(([N/x]M)N_1 \ldots N_k Q)$$

By the inductive hypothesis, is follows that

$$\forall N \in P^{\sigma}.P^{\tau_2}((\lambda x\colon\sigma.M)NN_1 \ldots N_k Q).$$

Since this holds for all $Q \in P^{\tau_1}$, we may conclude that

$$\forall N \in P^{\sigma}.P^{\tau_1\to\tau_2}((\lambda x\colon\sigma.M)NN_1 \ldots N_k).$$

This completes the inductive step and the proof of the lemma. ∎

Our definition of "admissible" is similar to the definition given in [Sta85b], but slightly weaker. Using our definition we may prove strong normalization directly by a construction that does not seem possible in Statman's framework [Sta85b, Example 4].

Exercise 8.2.12 Let $\mathcal{A}$ be a Henkin model. We say that $a \in A^{\sigma}$ is *lambda definable from* $a_1 \in A^{\sigma_1}, \ldots, a_k \in A^{\sigma_k}$ if there is a term $\{x_1\colon\sigma_1, \ldots, x_k\colon\sigma_k\} \rhd M\colon\sigma$ such that $a = [\![M]\!]\eta$ in the environment η with $\eta(x_i) = a_i$. Use the Basic Lemma (for models) to show that if $\mathcal{R} \subseteq \mathcal{A} \times \mathcal{A}$ is a logical relation, $a \in A^{\sigma}$ is lambda definable from $a_1 \in A^{\sigma_1}, \ldots, a_k \in A^{\sigma_k}$, and $R^{\sigma_i}(a_i, a_i)$ for each i, then $R^{\sigma}(a, a)$.

Exercise 8.2.13 Complete Example 8.2.7 by showing that $\mathcal{T}[\![\Gamma \rhd M\colon\sigma]\!]\eta = \eta M$ is an acceptable meaning function for $\mathcal{T}$.

Exercise 8.2.14 Let $\mathcal{A}$ be a lambda model for some signature without constants. If a logical relation $\mathcal{R} \subseteq \mathcal{A} \times \mathcal{A}$ is a permutation at each type, then $\mathcal{R}$ is called a hereditary permutation (see Exercise 8.2.3). We say that an element $a \in A^\sigma$ is *permutation-invariant* if $\mathcal{R}(a, a)$ for every hereditary permutation $\mathcal{R} \subseteq \mathcal{A} \times \mathcal{A}$. Show that for every closed term M, its meaning $\mathcal{A}[\![M]\!]$ in $\mathcal{A}$ is permutation invariant.

Exercise 8.2.15 Let $\mathcal{A}$ be the full classical hierarchy over a signature with single type constant b, with $A^b = \{0, 1\}$.

(a) Find some function $f \in A^{b \to b}$ that is permutation invariant (see Exercise 8.2.14), but not the meaning of a closed lambda term. You may assume that every term has a unique normal form.

(b) Show that if $f \in A^{b \to b}$ has the property that $R(f, f)$ for every logical relation $\mathcal{R} \subseteq \mathcal{A} \times \mathcal{A}$, then f is the meaning of a closed lambda term. (This is not true for all types, but that is tricky to prove.)

Exercise 8.2.16 Prove the basic lemma for combinatory algebras. More specifically show that if $\mathcal{R} \subseteq \mathcal{A} \times \mathcal{B}$ is a logical relation over combinatory algebras $\mathcal{A}$ and $\mathcal{B}$ and η_a and η_b are related environments with $\eta_a, \eta_b \models \Gamma$, then

$$\mathcal{R}(\mathcal{A}[\![\Gamma \triangleright M\colon\sigma]\!]\eta_a,\ \mathcal{B}[\![\Gamma \triangleright M\colon\sigma]\!]\eta_b)$$

for every typed combinatory term $\Gamma \triangleright M\colon\sigma$. (Do not consider it part of the definition of logical relation that $R(K, K)$ and $R(S, S)$ for combinators K and S of each type.)

8.2.3 Partial Functions and Theories of Models

A logical relation $\mathcal{R} \subseteq \mathcal{A} \times \mathcal{B}$ is called a *logical partial function* if each R^σ is a partial function from A^σ to B^σ, *i.e.*,

$$R^\sigma(a, b_1) \text{ and } R^\sigma(a, b_2) \text{ implies } b_1 = b_2.$$

Logical partial functions are related to the theories of typed lambda models by the following lemma.

Lemma 8.2.17 If $\mathcal{R} \subseteq \mathcal{A} \times \mathcal{B}$ is a logical partial function from model $\mathcal{A}$ to model $\mathcal{B}$, then $Th(\mathcal{A}) \subseteq Th(\mathcal{B})$.

Proof Without loss of generality, we will only consider equations between closed terms. Let $\mathcal{R} \subseteq \mathcal{A} \times \mathcal{B}$ be a partial function and suppose $\mathcal{A}[\![M]\!] = \mathcal{A}[\![N]\!]$ for closed M, N. Writing $\mathcal{R}(\cdot)$ as a function, we have

$$\mathcal{R}(\mathcal{A}[\![M]\!]) = \mathcal{B}[\![M]\!] \text{ and } \mathcal{R}(\mathcal{A}[\![N]\!]) = \mathcal{B}[\![N]\!]$$

by the Basic Lemma. Thus $\mathcal{B}[\![M]\!] = \mathcal{B}[\![N]\!]$. ∎

By Corollary 4.5.23 (completeness for the pure theory of β, η-conversion) we know there is a model $\mathcal{A}$ satisfying $\Gamma \triangleright M = N : \sigma$ iff $\vdash \Gamma \triangleright M = N : \sigma$. Since the theory of this model is contained in the theory of every other model, we may show that a model $\mathcal{B}$ has the same theory by constructing a logical partial function $\mathcal{R} \subseteq \mathcal{B} \times \mathcal{A}$. This technique was first used by Friedman to show that β, η-conversion is complete for the full set-theoretic type hierarchy over any infinite ground types [Fri75, Sta85a].

Corollary 8.2.18 Let $\mathcal{A}$ be a model of the pure theory of β, η-conversion. If $\mathcal{R} \subseteq \mathcal{B} \times \mathcal{A}$ is a logical partial function and $\mathcal{B}$ is a model, then $Th(\mathcal{B}) = Th(\mathcal{A})$.

We use Friedman's technique, and extensions, in Section 8.4 to show completeness for full set-theoretic, recursive and continuous models.

Since logical partial functions are structure-preserving mappings, it is tempting to think of logical partial functions as the natural generalization of homomorphisms. This often provides useful intuition. However, the composition of two logical partial functions need not be a logical relation. It is worth noting that for a fixed model $\mathcal{A}$ and environment η, the meaning function $\mathcal{A}[\![\ ]\!]\eta$ from $\mathcal{T}$ to $\mathcal{A}$ is not necessarily a logical relation. In contrast, meaning functions in algebra are always homomorphisms.

Exercise 8.2.19 Find logical partial functions $\mathcal{R} \subseteq \mathcal{A} \times \mathcal{B}$ and $\mathcal{S} \subseteq \mathcal{B} \times \mathcal{C}$ whose composition $\mathcal{S} \circ \mathcal{R} = \{S^\sigma \circ R^\sigma\} \subseteq \mathcal{A} \times \mathcal{C}$ is not a logical relation. (*Hint:* Try $\mathcal{C} = \mathcal{A}$ and $\mathcal{S} = \mathcal{R}^{-1}$.)

8.2.4 Logical Partial Equivalence Relations

Another useful class of logical relations are the logical partial equivalence relations (logical pȩr's), which have many of the properties of congruence relations. If we regard typed applicative structures as multi-sorted algebras, we may see that logical partial equivalence relations are somewhat more than congruence relations. Specifically, any logical pȩr $\mathcal{R}$ is a congruence, since $\mathcal{R}$ is an equivalence relation closed under application, but $\mathcal{R}$ must also be closed under lambda abstraction.

Before looking at the definition of logical partial equivalence relation, it is worth recalling the definition of partial equivalence relation from Section 5.6.1. The first of two equivalent definitions is that a *partial equivalence relation on a set* A is an equivalence relation on some subset of A, *i.e.*, a pair $\langle A', R \rangle$ with $A' \subseteq A$ and $R \subseteq A' \times A'$ an equivalence relation. However, because R determines $A' = \{a \mid R(a, a)\}$ uniquely and R is an equivalence relation on A' iff R is symmetric and transitive on A, we may give a simpler definition.

A *logical partial equivalence relation on* $\mathcal{A}$ is a logical relation $\mathcal{R} \subseteq \mathcal{A} \times \mathcal{A}$ such that each R^σ is symmetric and transitive. We say a partial equivalence relation is *total* if each

R^σ is reflexive, *i.e.*, $R^\sigma(a, a)$ for every $a \in A^\sigma$. From the following lemma, we can see that there are many examples of partial equivalence relations.

Lemma 8.2.20 Let $\mathcal{R} \subseteq \mathcal{A} \times \mathcal{A}$ be a logical relation. If R^b is symmetric and transitive, for each type constant b, then every R^σ is symmetric and transitive.

The proof is given as Exercise 8.2.21.

Intuitively, this lemma shows that being a partial equivalence relation is a "hereditary" property; it is inherited at higher types. In contrast, being a total equivalence relation is not. Specifically, there exist logical relations which are total equivalence relations for each type constant, but not total equivalence relations at every type. This is one reason for concentrating on partial instead of total equivalence relations.

Exercise 8.2.21 Prove Lemma 8.2.20 for $\lambda^{\rightarrow}$ by induction on type expressions.

Exercise 8.2.22 Find a $\lambda^{\rightarrow}$ Henkin model $\mathcal{A}$ and logical relation $\mathcal{R} \subseteq \mathcal{A} \times \mathcal{A}$ such that R^b is reflexive, symmetric and transitive, for each type constant b, but some R^σ is not reflexive. (*Hint:* Almost any model will do.)

Exercise 8.2.23 Let Σ be a signature with type constants $B = \{b_0, b_1, \ldots\}$ and (for simplicity) no term constants. Let $\mathcal{D}$ be a partial combinatory algebra and let $\mathcal{A}_\mathcal{D}$ be a $\lambda^{\times,\rightarrow}$ combinatory algebra for signature Σ constructed using subsets of $\mathcal{D}$ as in Section 5.6.2. Let $\mathcal{R} \subseteq \mathcal{A}_\mathcal{D} \times \mathcal{A}_\mathcal{D}$ be any logical partial equivalence relation. Show that for all types σ and τ, the product per $R^\sigma \times R^\tau \subseteq \mathcal{D}$ is identical to the relation $R^{\sigma\times\tau}$, and similarly for $R^{\sigma\rightarrow\tau}$. (*Hint:* There is something to check here, since the definition of $R^{\sigma\times\tau}$ depends on $A^{\sigma\times\tau}$ but, regarding R^σ and R^τ as pers over $\mathcal{D}$, the definition of $R^\sigma \times R^\tau$ does not.)

8.2.5 Quotients and Extensionality

If $\mathcal{R}$ is a logical partial equivalence relation over applicative structure $\mathcal{A}$, then we may form a quotient structure $\mathcal{A}/\mathcal{R}$ of equivalence classes from $\mathcal{A}$. This is actually a "partial" quotient, since some elements of $\mathcal{A}$ may not have equivalence classes with respect to $\mathcal{R}$. However, to simplify terminology, we will just call $\mathcal{A}/\mathcal{R}$ a "quotient." One important fact about the structure $\mathcal{A}/\mathcal{R}$ is that it is always extensional. Another is that under certain reasonable assumptions, $\mathcal{A}/\mathcal{R}$ will be a model with the meaning of each term in $\mathcal{A}/\mathcal{R}$ equal to the equivalence class of its meaning in $\mathcal{A}$.

Let $\mathcal{R} \subseteq \mathcal{A} \times \mathcal{A}$ be a logical partial equivalence relation on the applicative structure $\mathcal{A} = \langle\{A^\sigma\}, \{\mathbf{App}^{\sigma,\tau}\}, \mathit{Const}\}\rangle$. The quotient applicative structure

$$\mathcal{A}/\mathcal{R} = \langle\{A^\sigma/\mathcal{R}\}, \{\mathbf{App}^{\sigma,\tau}/\mathcal{R}\}, \mathit{Const}/\mathcal{R}\rangle$$

is defined as follows. If $R^\sigma(a, a)$, then the *equivalence class* $[a]_\mathcal{R}$ *of a with respect to* $\mathcal{R}$ is defined by

$[a]_{\mathcal{R}} = \{a' \mid \mathcal{R}(a, a')\}.$

Note that $a \in [a]_{\mathcal{R}}$. We let $A^\sigma/\mathcal{R} = \{[a]_{\mathcal{R}} \mid R^\sigma(a, a)\}$ be the collection of all such equivalence classes and define application on equivalence classes by

$(\mathbf{App}^{\sigma,\tau}/\mathcal{R})\ [a]\ [b] = [\mathbf{App}^{\sigma,\tau}\ a\ b]$

The map $Const/\mathcal{R}$ interprets each constant c as the equivalence class $[Const(c)]_{\mathcal{R}}$. This completes the definition of $\mathcal{A}/\mathcal{R}$. It is easy to see that application is well-defined: if $R^{\sigma\to\tau}(a, a')$ and $R^\sigma(b, b')$, then since $\mathcal{R}$ is logical, we have $R^\tau(\mathbf{App}^{\sigma,\tau}\ a\ b, \mathbf{App}^{\sigma,\tau}\ a'\ b')$.

Lemma 8.2.24 If $\mathcal{R} \subseteq \mathcal{A} \times \mathcal{A}$ is a logical partial equivalence relation, then $\mathcal{A}/\mathcal{R}$ is an extensional applicative structure.

Proof Let $[a_1], [a_2] \in A^{\sigma\to\tau}/\mathcal{R}$ and suppose that for every $[b] \in A^\sigma/\mathcal{R}$, we have $\mathbf{App}/\mathcal{R}\ [a_1]\ [b] = \mathbf{App}/\mathcal{R}\ [a_2]\ [b]$. This means that for every $b_1, b_2 \in A^\sigma$, we have $R^\sigma(b_1, b_2) \supset R^\tau(\mathbf{App}\ a_1\ b_1, \mathbf{App}\ a_2\ b_2)$. Since $\mathcal{R}$ is logical, this gives us $R^{\sigma\to\tau}(a_1, a_2)$, which means that $[a_1] = [a_2]$. Thus $\mathcal{A}/\mathcal{R}$ is extensional. ∎

A special case of this lemma is the *extensional collapse*, $\mathcal{A}^E$, of an applicative structure $\mathcal{A}$; this is also called the *Gandy hull of* $\mathcal{A}$, and appears to have been discovered independently by Zucker [Tro73] and Gandy [Gan56]. The extensional collapse $\mathcal{A}^E$ is defined as follows. Given $\mathcal{A}$, there is at most one logical relation $\mathcal{R}$ with

$R^b(a_1, a_2)$ iff $a_1 = a_2 \in A^b$

for each type constant b. (Such an $\mathcal{R}$ is guaranteed to exist when the type of each constant is either a type constant or first-order function type.) If there is a logical relation $\mathcal{R}$ which is the identity relation for all type constants, then we define $\mathcal{A}^E = \mathcal{A}/\mathcal{R}$.

Corollary 8.2.25 (Extensional Collapse) Let $\mathcal{A}$ be an applicative structure for signature Σ. If there is a logical relation $\mathcal{R}$ that is the identity relation on each type constant, then the extensional collapse $\mathcal{A}^E$ is an extensional applicative structure for Σ.

In some cases, $\mathcal{A}/\mathcal{R}$ will not only be extensional, but also a Henkin model. This will be true if $\mathcal{A}$ is a model to begin with. In addition, since $\mathcal{A}/\mathcal{R}$ is always extensional, we would expect to have a model whenever $\mathcal{A}$ has "enough functions," and β-equivalent terms are equivalent modulo $\mathcal{R}$. If $\mathcal{A}[\![\ ]\!]$ is an acceptable meaning function, then this will guarantee that $\mathcal{A}$ has enough functions. When we have an acceptable meaning function, we can also express the following condition involving β-equivalence. We say $\mathcal{R}$ *satisfies* (β) *with respect to* $\mathcal{A}[\![\ ]\!]$ if, for every term $\Gamma, x{:}\sigma \triangleright M{:}\tau$ and environment $\eta \models \Gamma, x{:}\sigma$

with $R^{\Gamma,x:\sigma}(\eta,\eta)$, we have

$$\mathcal{R}(\mathcal{A}[\![\Gamma, x:\sigma \triangleright (\lambda x:\sigma.M)x]\!]\eta,\ \mathcal{A}[\![\Gamma, x:\sigma \triangleright M]\!]\eta).$$

It follows from properties of acceptable meaning function $\mathcal{A}$ that if $\mathcal{R}$ satisfies (β), then $\mathcal{R}$ relates β-equivalent terms (Exercise 8.2.28) and $\mathcal{R}$ is admissible (Exercise 8.2.29). In addition, if $\mathcal{A}$ is a combinatory algebra with standard meaning function as described in Example 8.2.8, then by Exercise 8.2.16 and the equational properties of combinators, every $\mathcal{R}$ over $\mathcal{A}$ satisfies (β).

To describe the meanings of terms in $\mathcal{A}/\mathcal{R}$, we will associate an environment $\eta_{\mathcal{R}}$ for $\mathcal{A}/\mathcal{R}$ with each environment η for $\mathcal{A}$ with $R^{\Gamma}(\eta,\eta)$. We define $\eta_{\mathcal{R}}$ by

$$\eta_{\mathcal{R}}(x) = [\eta(x)]_{\mathcal{R}},$$

and note that $\eta \models \Gamma$ iff $\eta_{\mathcal{R}} \models \Gamma$. Using these definitions, we can give useful conditions which imply that $\mathcal{A}/\mathcal{R}$ is a model, and characterize the meanings of terms in $\mathcal{A}/\mathcal{R}$.

Lemma 8.2.26 (Quotient Models) Let $\mathcal{R} \subseteq \mathcal{A} \times \mathcal{A}$ be a partial equivalence relation over applicative structure $\mathcal{A}$ with acceptable meaning function $\mathcal{A}[\![\ ]\!]$, and suppose that $\mathcal{R}$ satisfies (β). Then $\mathcal{A}/\mathcal{R}$ is a model such that for any $\mathcal{A}$-environment $\eta \models \Gamma$ with $R^{\Gamma}(\eta,\eta)$, we have

$$(\mathcal{A}/\mathcal{R})[\![\Gamma \triangleright M:\sigma]\!]\eta_{\mathcal{R}} = [\mathcal{A}[\![\Gamma \triangleright M:\sigma]\!]\eta]_{\mathcal{R}}.$$

In other words, under the hypotheses of the lemma, the meaning of a term $\Gamma \triangleright M:\sigma$ in $\mathcal{A}/\mathcal{R}$ is the equivalence class of the meaning of $\Gamma \triangleright M:\sigma$ in $\mathcal{A}$, modulo $\mathcal{R}$. Lemma 8.2.26 is similar to the "Characterization Theorem" of [Mit86c], which seems to be the first use of this idea (see Theorem 9.3.46).

Proof We use induction on the structure of terms. By Exercise 8.2.29, $\mathcal{R}$ is admissible. It follows from the general version of the Basic Lemma that the equivalence class $[\mathcal{A}[\![\Gamma \triangleright M:\sigma]\!]\eta]_{\mathcal{R}}$ of the interpretation of any term in $\mathcal{A}$ is nonempty. This is essential to the proof.

For any variable $\Gamma \triangleright x:\sigma$, it is clear that

$$(\mathcal{A}/\mathcal{R})[\![\Gamma \triangleright x:\sigma]\!]\eta_{\mathcal{R}} = \eta_{\mathcal{R}}(x) = [\eta(x)]_{\mathcal{R}} = [\,\mathcal{A}[\![\Gamma \triangleright x:\sigma]\!]\eta\,]_{\mathcal{R}}$$

by definition of $\eta_{\mathcal{R}}$ and acceptability of $\mathcal{A}[\![\ ]\!]$. The case for constants is similarly straightforward. The application case is also easy, using the definition of application in $\mathcal{A}/\mathcal{R}$. For the abstraction case, recall that

$$(\mathcal{A}/\mathcal{R})[\![\Gamma \triangleright \lambda x:\sigma.M:\sigma \to \tau]\!]\eta_{\mathcal{R}} = f,$$

where, by definition, f satisfies the equation

$$(\mathbf{App}/\mathcal{R})\ f\ [a]_{\mathcal{R}} = (\mathcal{A}/\mathcal{R})[\![\Gamma, x{:}\,\sigma \triangleright M{:}\,\tau]\!]\eta_{\mathcal{R}}[x \mapsto [a]]$$

for all $[a]_{\mathcal{R}} \in A^{\sigma}/R^{\sigma}$. We show that $[\mathcal{A}[\![\Gamma \triangleright \lambda x{:}\,\sigma.M{:}\,\sigma \to \tau]\!]\eta]_{\mathcal{R}}$ satisfies the equation for f, and hence the meaning of $\Gamma \triangleright \lambda x{:}\,\sigma.M{:}\,\sigma \to \tau$ exists in $\mathcal{A}/\mathcal{R}$. Since $\mathcal{A}/\mathcal{R}$ is extensional by Lemma 8.2.24, it follows that $\mathcal{A}/\mathcal{R}$ is a Henkin model.

For any $[a]_{\mathcal{R}} \in A^{\sigma}/R^{\sigma}$, we have

$$(\mathbf{App}/\mathcal{R})\ [\mathcal{A}[\![\Gamma \triangleright \lambda x{:}\,\sigma.M{:}\,\sigma \to \tau]\!]\eta]_{\mathcal{R}}\ [a]_{\mathcal{R}} = [\mathbf{App}\ (\mathcal{A}[\![\Gamma \triangleright \lambda x{:}\,\sigma.M{:}\,\sigma \to \tau]\!]\eta)\ a]_{\mathcal{R}}$$

by definition of application in $\mathcal{A}/\mathcal{R}$. Using the definition of acceptable meaning function, it is easy to see that

$$\mathcal{A}[\![\Gamma \triangleright \lambda x{:}\,\sigma.M{:}\,\sigma \to \tau]\!]\eta = \mathcal{A}[\![\Gamma, x{:}\,\sigma \triangleright \lambda x{:}\,\sigma.M{:}\,\sigma \to \tau]\!]\eta[x \mapsto a]$$

since x is not free in $\lambda x{:}\,\sigma.M$. Since $a = \mathcal{A}[\![\Gamma, x{:}\,\sigma \triangleright x{:}\,\sigma]\!]\eta[x \mapsto a]$, it follows from the definition of acceptable that

$$\mathbf{App}\ (\mathcal{A}[\![\Gamma \triangleright \lambda x{:}\,\sigma.M{:}\,\sigma \to \tau]\!]\eta)\ a = \mathcal{A}[\![\Gamma, x{:}\,\sigma \triangleright (\lambda x{:}\,\sigma.M)x{:}\,\tau]\!]\eta[x \mapsto a]$$

Therefore, using the assumption that $\mathcal{R}$ satisfies (β), we may conclude that

$$[\mathbf{App}\ (\mathcal{A}[\![\Gamma \triangleright \lambda x{:}\,\sigma.M{:}\,\sigma \to \tau]\!]\eta)\ a]_{\mathcal{R}} = [\mathcal{A}[\![\Gamma, x{:}\,\sigma \triangleright M{:}\,\tau]\!]\eta[x \mapsto a]\,]_{\mathcal{R}}$$

By the induction hypothesis, it follows that $[\mathcal{A}[\![\Gamma \triangleright \lambda x{:}\,\sigma.M{:}\,\sigma \to \tau]\!]\eta]_{\mathcal{R}}$ satisfies the equation for f. This proves the lemma. ■

A straightforward corollary, with application to per models, is that the quotient of any combinatory algebra by a partial equivalence relation is a Henkin model.

Corollary 8.2.27 Let $\mathcal{A}$ be a combinatory algebra and $\mathcal{R} \subseteq \mathcal{A} \times \mathcal{A}$ a logical partial equivalence relation. Then $\mathcal{A}/\mathcal{R}$ is a Henkin model, with the meaning of term $\Gamma \triangleright M{:}\,\sigma$ the equivalence class

$$\mathcal{A}/\mathcal{R}[\![\Gamma \triangleright M{:}\,\sigma]\!]\eta_R = [\,\mathcal{A}[\![\Gamma \triangleright \text{CL}(M){:}\,\sigma]\!]\eta\,]_{\mathcal{R}}$$

of the interpretation of the combinatory term $\text{CL}(M)$ in $\mathcal{A}$.

The proof is simply to apply Lemma 8.2.26 to combinatory algebras, with acceptable meaning function as described in Example 8.2.8, noting that by Exercise 8.2.16 and the equational properties of combinators, every relation over $\mathcal{A}$ satisfies (β).

Corollary 8.2.27 implies that any hierarchy of partial equivalence relations over a partial combinatory algebra (see Sections 5.6.1 and 5.6.2) forms a Henkin model. More specifically, for any partial combinatory algebra $\mathcal{D}$, any hierarchy of pers over $\mathcal{D}$ forms a logical partial equivalence relation over a typed (total) combinatory algebra $\mathcal{A}_{\mathcal{D}}$, as described in Exercise 8.2.23. Therefore, we may show that pers over $\mathcal{D}$ form a Henkin model by showing that the quotient $\mathcal{A}_{\mathcal{D}}/\mathcal{R}$ of a combinatory algebra by a logical partial equivalence relation $\mathcal{R} \subseteq \mathcal{A}_{\mathcal{D}} \times \mathcal{A}_{\mathcal{D}}$ is a Henkin model. This is immediate from Corollary 8.2.27. In addition, Corollary 8.2.27 shows that the interpretation of a lambda term is the equivalence class of its translation into combinators. Since the combinators of $\mathcal{A}_{\mathcal{D}}$ are exactly the untyped combinators of $\mathcal{D}$, according to the proof of Lemma 5.6.8, it follows that the meaning of a typed term in $\mathcal{A}_{\mathcal{D}}/\mathcal{R}$ is the equivalence class of the meaning of its translation into untyped combinators in $\mathcal{D}$.

Exercise 8.2.28 Show that if $\mathcal{R}$ satisfies (β) with respect to $\mathcal{A}[\![\ ]\!]$ then, for every pair of terms $\Gamma, x{:}\sigma \rhd M{:}\tau$ and $\Gamma \rhd N{:}\sigma$, and environment $\eta \models \Gamma$ with $R^{\Gamma}(\eta, \eta)$, we have

$$\mathcal{R}(\mathcal{A}[\![\Gamma \rhd (\lambda x{:}\sigma.M)N{:}\tau]\!]\eta,\ \mathcal{A}[\![\Gamma \rhd [N/x]M{:}\tau]\!]\eta).$$

Exercise 8.2.29 Show that if $\mathcal{R}$ satisfies (β) with respect to $\mathcal{A}[\![\ ]\!]$, then $\mathcal{R}$ is admissible.

Exercise 8.2.30 Let $\mathcal{A}$ be an applicative structure and let $\{x_1{:}\sigma_1, \ldots, x_k{:}\sigma_k\} \rhd M{:}\tau$ be a term without lambda abstraction. An element $a \in A^{\sigma_1\to\ldots\to\sigma_k\to\tau}$ *represents* M if $\mathcal{A} \models \{x_1{:}\sigma_1, \ldots, x_k{:}\sigma_k\} \rhd a x_1 \ldots x_k = M{:}\tau$, using a as a constant denoting a. Note that since M contains only applications, this equation makes sense in any applicative structure. Show that if $\mathcal{R} \subseteq \mathcal{A} \times \mathcal{A}$ is a logical partial equivalence relation and a represents $\Gamma \rhd M{:}\sigma$ in $\mathcal{A}$, then $[a]$ represents $\Gamma \rhd M{:}\sigma$ in $\mathcal{A}/\mathcal{R}$.

8.3 Proof-Theoretic Results

8.3.1 Completeness for Henkin Models

In universal algebra, we may prove equational completeness (assuming no sort is empty) by showing that any theory $\mathcal{E}$ is a congruence relation on the term algebra $\mathcal{T}$, and noting that $\mathcal{T}/\mathcal{E}$ satisfies an equation $M = N$ iff $M = N \in \mathcal{E}$. We may give similar completeness proofs for typed lambda calculus, using logical equivalence relations in place of congruence relations. We will illustrate the main ideas by proving completeness for models without empty types. A similar proof is given for Henkin models with possibly empty types in Exercise 8.3.3. It is also possible to present a completeness theorem for Kripke models (Section 7.3) in this form, using a Kripke version of logical relations.

Throughout this section, we let $\mathcal{T}$ be the applicative structure of terms typed using infinite type assignment $\mathcal{H}$, with meaning function $\mathcal{T}[\![\ ]\!]$ defined by substitution. (These are defined in Example 8.2.7.) We assume $\mathcal{H}$ provides infinitely many variables of each type, so each T^{σ} is infinite. If $\mathcal{E}$ is any set of equations, we define the relation $\mathcal{R}_{\mathcal{E}} = \{R^{\sigma}\}$ over $\mathcal{T} \times \mathcal{T}$ by taking

$R^\sigma(M, N)$ iff $\mathcal{E} \vdash \Gamma \triangleright M = N : \sigma$ for some finite $\Gamma \subseteq \mathcal{H}$.

Note that since $\mathcal{E} \vdash x : \sigma \triangleright x = x : \sigma$ for each $x : \sigma \in \mathcal{H}$, no R^σ is empty.

Lemma 8.3.1 For any theory $\mathcal{E}$, the relation $\mathcal{R}_\mathcal{E} \subseteq \mathcal{T} \times \mathcal{T}$ is a logical equivalence relation.

Proof It is easy to see that $\mathcal{R} = \mathcal{R}_\mathcal{E}$ is an equivalence relation. To show that $\mathcal{R}$ is logical, suppose that $R^{\sigma \to \tau}(M, M')$ and $R^\sigma(N, N')$. Then $\mathcal{E} \vdash \Gamma_1 \triangleright M = M' : \sigma \to \tau$ and $\mathcal{E} \vdash \Gamma_2 \triangleright N = N' : \sigma$, for some $\Gamma_1, \Gamma_2 \subseteq \mathcal{H}$. By (*add hyp*) and rule (ν) we have $\mathcal{E} \vdash \Gamma_1 \cup \Gamma_2 \triangleright MN = M'N' : \tau$. Therefore $R^\tau(MN, M'N')$. It remains to show that if $\mathcal{E} \vdash \Gamma \triangleright MN = M'N' : \tau$ for every N, N' with $\mathcal{E} \vdash \Gamma \triangleright N = N' : \sigma$, then $\mathcal{E} \vdash \Gamma \triangleright M = M' : \sigma \to \tau$. This is where we use the assumption that $\mathcal{H}$ provides infinitely many variables of each type.

Let x be a variable that is not free in M or M' and with $x : \sigma \in \mathcal{H}$. Since $\mathcal{E} \vdash \Gamma, x : \sigma \triangleright x = x : \sigma$, we have $\mathcal{E} \vdash \Gamma, x : \sigma \triangleright Mx = M'x : \tau$ with $\Gamma, x : \sigma \subseteq \mathcal{H}$. By ($\xi$), we have

$$\mathcal{E} \vdash \Gamma \triangleright \lambda x : \sigma . Mx = \lambda x : \sigma . M'x : \sigma \to \tau.$$

We now apply (η) to both sides of this equation to derive $\mathcal{E} \vdash \Gamma \triangleright M = M' : \sigma \to \tau$. By reflexivity, $\mathcal{R}$ respects constants. This proves the lemma. ∎

From Lemma 8.2.26, and the straightforward observation that any $\mathcal{R}_\mathcal{E}$ satisfies (β), we can form a quotient model from any theory. This allows us to prove "least model" completeness for Henkin models without empty types.

Theorem 8.3.2 (Henkin completeness without empty types) Let $\mathcal{E}$ be any theory closed under (*nonempty*), and let $\mathcal{A} = \mathcal{T}/\mathcal{R}_\mathcal{E}$. Then $\mathcal{A}$ is a Henkin model without empty types satisfying precisely the equations belonging to $\mathcal{E}$.

Proof By Lemma 8.3.1, the theory $\mathcal{E}$ determines a logical equivalence relation $\mathcal{R}_\mathcal{E}$ over $\mathcal{T}$. Since $\mathcal{R}_\mathcal{E}$ clearly satisfies (β), the relation $\mathcal{R}_\mathcal{E}$ is admissible by Exercise 8.2.29. Let us write $\mathcal{R}$ for $\mathcal{R}_\mathcal{E}$ and $\mathcal{A}$ for $\mathcal{T}/\mathcal{R}$. By Lemma 8.2.26, $\mathcal{A}$ is a model with $\mathcal{A}[\![\Gamma \triangleright M : \sigma]\!]\eta_\mathcal{R} = [\eta M]_\mathcal{R}$, for every $\mathcal{T}$-environment (substitution) η satisfying Γ. It remains to show that $\mathcal{A}$ satisfies precisely the equations belonging to $\mathcal{E}$.

Without loss of generality, we may restrict our attention to closed terms. The justification for this is that it is easy to prove the closed equation

$$\emptyset \triangleright \lambda x_1 : \sigma_1 . \dots \lambda x_k : \sigma_k . M = \lambda x_1 : \sigma_1 . \dots \lambda x_k : \sigma_k . N : \sigma_1 \to \dots \to \sigma_k \to \tau$$

from the equation

$$\{x_1 : \sigma_1 . \dots x_k : \sigma_k\} \triangleright M = N : \tau$$

between open terms, and vice versa. Let η be the identity substitution. Then for any closed equation $\emptyset \triangleright M = N\colon \tau \in \mathcal{E}$, since $\eta_{\mathcal{R}} \models \emptyset$, we have

$$\mathcal{A}[\![\emptyset \triangleright M\colon \tau]\!]\eta_{\mathcal{R}} = [M]_{\mathcal{R}} = [N]_{\mathcal{R}} = \mathcal{A}[\![\emptyset \triangleright N\colon \tau]\!]\eta_{\mathcal{R}}$$

This shows that $\mathcal{A}$ satisfies every equation in $\mathcal{E}$. Conversely, if $\mathcal{A}$ satisfies $\emptyset \triangleright M = N\colon \tau$, then $\mathcal{A}$ certainly must do so at environment $\eta_{\mathcal{R}}$. This implies $[M]_{\mathcal{R}} = [N]_{\mathcal{R}}$, which means $\mathcal{E} \vdash \Gamma \triangleright M = N\colon \tau$ for some $\Gamma \subseteq \mathcal{H}$. Since M and N are closed, we have $\emptyset \triangleright M = N\colon \tau \in \mathcal{E}$ by rule (*nonempty*). This proves the theorem. ■

Exercise 8.3.3 A quotient construction, like the one in this section for models without empty types, may also be used to prove deductive completeness of the extended proof system with proof rules (*empty I*) and (*empty E*) for models that may have empty types. (This system is described in Sections 4.5.5 and 4.5.6.) This exercise begins the model construction and asks you to complete the proof. To prove deductive completeness, we assume that $\Gamma_0 \triangleright M_0 = N_0\colon \sigma_0$ is not provable from some set $\mathcal{E}$ of typed equations and construct a model $\mathcal{A} = \mathcal{T}_{\mathcal{H}}/\mathcal{R}_{\mathcal{E}}$ with $\mathcal{A} \models \mathcal{E}$, but $\mathcal{A} \not\models \Gamma_0 \triangleright M_0 = N_0\colon \sigma_0$. The main new idea in this proof is to choose an infinite set of typed variables carefully so that some types may be empty.

We decide which types to make empty by constructing an infinite set $\mathcal{H}$ of typing hypotheses of the form $x\colon \sigma$ and emptiness assertions of the form $empty(\sigma)$ such that

(a) $\Gamma_0 \subseteq \mathcal{H}$,

(b) for every type σ, we either have $empty(\sigma) \in \mathcal{H}$ or we have $x\colon \sigma \in \mathcal{H}$ for infinitely many variables x (but not both),

(c) for every finite $\Gamma \subseteq \mathcal{H}$ containing all the free variables of M_0 and N_0, the equation $\Gamma \triangleright M_0 = N_0\colon \sigma_0$ is not provable from $\mathcal{E}$.

The set $\mathcal{H}$ is constructed in infinitely many stages, starting from $\mathcal{H}_0 = \Gamma_0$. If $\tau_0, \tau_1, \ldots$ is an enumeration of all type expressions, then $\mathcal{H}_{i+1}$ is determined from $\mathcal{H}_i$ by looking at equations of the form $\Gamma, x\colon \tau_i \triangleright M_0 = N_0\colon \sigma_0$, where $\Gamma \subseteq \mathcal{H}_i$ and x is not in $\mathcal{H}_i$ and not free in M_0 or N_0. If

$$\mathcal{E} \vdash^{(emptyI,E)} \Gamma, x\colon \tau_i \triangleright M_0 = N_0\colon \sigma_0$$

for any finite $\Gamma \subseteq \mathcal{H}_i$ with the above equation well-formed, then we let

$$\mathcal{H}_{i+1} = \mathcal{H}_i \cup \{empty(\tau_i)\}.$$

Otherwise, we take

$$\mathcal{H}_{i+1} = \mathcal{H}_i \cup \{x\colon \tau_i \mid \text{infinitely many fresh } x\}.$$

Let $\mathcal{H}$ be the union of all the $\mathcal{H}_i$.

Given $\mathcal{H}$, the model $\mathcal{A} = \mathcal{T}_{\mathcal{H}}/\mathcal{R}_{\mathcal{E}}$ is defined as in this section. As described in Example 4.5.1, $\mathcal{T}_{\mathcal{H}}$ is an applicative structure for any $\mathcal{H}$. However, while Lemma 8.3.1 does not require (*nonempty*), the proof does assume that $\mathcal{H}$ provides infinitely many variables of each type.

(a) Show that properties (i) and (ii) hold for $\mathcal{H}$.

(b) Show that $\mathcal{R}_{\mathcal{E}}$ is a logical equivalence relation, re-proving only the parts of Lemma 8.3.1 that assume $\mathcal{H}$ provides infinitely many variables of each type. (*Hint:* You will need to use proof rule (*empty I*).)

(c) Show that $\mathcal{A}$ does not satisfy $\Gamma_0 \triangleright M_0 = N_0 : \sigma_0$. (This is where you need to use rule (*empty E*). The proof that $\mathcal{A}$ satisfies $\mathcal{E}$ proceeds as before, so there is no need for you to check this.)

8.3.2 Normalization

Logical relations may also be used to prove various properties of reduction on typed terms. In this section, we show that every $\lambda^{\rightarrow}$ term is strongly normalizing. More precisely, we show that for every typed term $\Gamma \triangleright M : \sigma$, we have $SN(M)$, where SN is defined by

$SN(M)$ iff there is no infinite sequence of β, η-reductions from M.

While the proof works for terms with term constants, we state the results without term constants to avoid confusion with more general results in later sections. We generalize the argument to other reduction properties and product types in the next section and consider reductions associated with constants such as $+$ and *fix* in Section 8.3.4.

The normalization proof for $\lambda^{\rightarrow}$ has three main parts:

1. Define a logical predicate $\mathcal{P}$ on the applicative structure of terms.

2. Show that $P^{\sigma}(M)$ implies $SN(M)$.

3. Show that $\mathcal{P}$ is admissible, so that we may use the Basic Lemma to conclude that $P^{\sigma}(M)$ holds for every well-typed term $\Gamma \triangleright M : \sigma$.

Since the Basic Lemma is proved by induction on terms, the logical relation $\mathcal{P}$ is a kind of "induction hypothesis" for proving that all terms are strongly normalizing. To make the outline of the proof as clear as possible, we will give the main definition and results first, postponing the proofs to the end of the section.

Let $\mathcal{T} = \mathcal{T}_{\mathcal{H}}$ be an applicative structure of terms, as in Examples 4.5.1 and 8.2.7, where $\mathcal{H}$ provides infinitely many variables of each type. We define the logical predicate (unary logical relation) $\mathcal{P} \subseteq \mathcal{T}$ by taking P^b to be all strongly normalizing terms, for each type constant b, and extending to function types by

$$P^{\sigma\to\tau}(M) \quad \text{iff} \quad \forall N \in T^{\sigma}.\, P^{\sigma}(N) \supset P^{\tau}(MN).$$

It is easy to see that this predicate is logical. (If we have a signature with term constants, then it follows from Lemma 8.3.4 below that $\mathcal{P}$ is logical, as long as only β, η-reduction is used in the definition of *SN*.) The next step is to show that $\mathcal{P}$ contains only strongly normalizing terms. This is a relatively easy induction on types, as long as we take the correct induction hypothesis. The hypothesis we use is the conjunction of (i) and (ii) of the following lemma.

Lemma 8.3.4 For each type σ, the predicate P^{σ} satisfies the following two conditions.

(i) If $xM_1 \ldots M_k \in T^{\sigma}$ and $SN(M_1), \ldots SN(M_k)$, then $P^{\sigma}(xM_1 \ldots M_k)$.

(ii) If $P^{\sigma}(M)$ then $SN(M)$.

The main reason condition (i) is included in the lemma is to guarantee that each P^{σ} is non-empty, since this is used in the proof of condition (ii). Using Lemma 8.2.11, we may show that the logical predicate $\mathcal{P}$ is admissible.

Lemma 8.3.5 The logical predicate $\mathcal{P} \subseteq \mathcal{T}$ is admissible.

From the two lemmas above, and the Basic Lemma for logical relations, we have the following theorem.

Theorem 8.3.6 (Strong Normalization) For every well-typed term $\Gamma \triangleright M{:}\sigma$, we have $SN(M)$.

Proof of Theorem 8.3.6 Let $\Gamma \triangleright M{:}\sigma$ be a typed term and consider the applicative structure $\mathcal{T}$ defined using variables from $\mathcal{H}$ with $\Gamma \subseteq \mathcal{H}$. Let η_0 be the environment for $\mathcal{T}$ with $\eta_0(x) = x$ for all x. Then since $\mathcal{T}[\![\ ]\!]$ is acceptable and the relation $\mathcal{P}$ is admissible, by Lemma 8.3.5, we have $P^{\sigma}(\mathcal{T}[\![\Gamma \triangleright M{:}\sigma]\!]\eta_0)$, or, equivalently, $P^{\sigma}(M)$. Therefore, by Lemma 8.3.4, we conclude $SN(M)$. ■

Proof of Lemma 8.3.4 We prove both conditions simultaneously using induction on types. We will only consider variables in the proof of (i), since the constant and variable cases are identical. For a type constant b, condition (i) is straightforward, since $SN(xM_1 \ldots M_k)$ whenever $SN(M_i)$ for each i. Condition (ii) follows trivially from the definition of $\mathcal{P}$. So, we move on to the induction step.

For condition (i), suppose $xM_1 \ldots M_k \in T^{\sigma\to\tau}$ and for each M_i, we have $SN(M_i)$. Let $N \in T^{\sigma}$ with $P^{\sigma}(N)$. By the induction hypothesis (ii) for type σ, we have $SN(N)$.

Therefore, by the induction hypothesis (i) for type τ, we have $P^{\tau}(xM_1 \dots M_k N)$. Since this reasoning applies to every $N \in P^{\sigma}$, we conclude that $P^{\sigma\to\tau}(xM_1 \dots M_k)$.

We now consider condition (ii) for type $\sigma \to \tau$. Suppose $M \in T^{\sigma\to\tau}$ with $P^{\sigma\to\tau}(M)$ and $x \in T^{\sigma}$. By the induction hypothesis (i) we have $P^{\sigma}(x)$ and so $P^{\tau}(Mx)$. Applying the induction hypothesis (ii) we have $SN(Mx)$. However, this implies $SN(M)$, since any infinite sequence of reductions from M would give us an infinite sequence of reductions from Mx. ■

Proof of Lemma 8.3.5 This lemma is proved using Lemma 8.2.11, which gives us a straightforward test for each type constant. To show that $\mathcal{P}$ is admissible, it suffices to show that for each type constant b, term N and term $([N/x]M)N_1 \dots N_k$ of type b,

$$SN(N) \text{ and } SN(([N/x]M)N_1 \dots N_k) \text{ imply } SN((\lambda x{:}\sigma.M)NN_1 \dots N_k).$$

With this in mind, we assume $SN(N)$ and $SN(([N/x]M)N_1 \dots N_k)$ and consider the possible reductions from $(\lambda x{:}\sigma.M)NN_1 \dots N_k$. It is clear that there can be no infinite sequences of reductions solely within N, because $SN(N)$. Since $([N/x]M)N_1 \dots N_k$ is strongly normalizing, we may conclude $SN(M)$, and $SN(N_1), \dots, SN(N_k)$, since otherwise we could produce an infinite reduction sequence from $([N/x]M)N_1 \dots N_k$ by reducing one of its subterms. Therefore, if there is any infinite reduction sequence with β-reduction occurring at the left, the reduction sequence must have an initial segment of the form

$$(\lambda x{:}\sigma.M)NN_1 \dots N_k \twoheadrightarrow (\lambda x{:}\sigma.M')N'N_1' \dots N_k' \to ([N'/x]M')N_1' \dots N_k' \twoheadrightarrow \dots,$$

where $M \twoheadrightarrow M'$, $N \twoheadrightarrow N'$ and $N_i \twoheadrightarrow N_i'$ for $1 \le i \le k$. But then clearly we may reduce

$$([N/x]M)N_1 \dots N_k \twoheadrightarrow ([N'/x]M')N_1' \dots N_k' \twoheadrightarrow \dots$$

as well, giving us an infinite sequence of reductions from $([N/x]M)N_1 \dots N_k$. The other possibility is an infinite reduction sequence with η-reduction occurring at the left, which would have the form

$$(\lambda x{:}\sigma.M)NN_1 \dots N_k \twoheadrightarrow (\lambda x{:}\sigma.M'x)N'N_1' \dots N_k' \to M'N'N_1' \dots N_k' \twoheadrightarrow \dots$$

But since the last reduction shown could also have been carried out using β-reduction, we have already covered this possibility above. Since no infinite reduction sequence is possible, the lemma is proved. ■

Exercise 8.3.7 We can show weak normalization of β-reduction directly, using an argument devised by A.M. Turing sometime between 1936 and 1942 [Gan80]. For this exercise, the *degree* of a β-redex $(\lambda x{:}\sigma.\,M)N$ is the length of the type $\sigma \to \tau$ of $\lambda x{:}\sigma.\,M$

when written out as a string of symbols. The *measure* of a term M is the pair of natural numbers $\langle i, j \rangle$ such that the redex of highest degree in M has degree i, and there are exactly j redexes of degree i in M. These pairs can be ordered lexicographically by $\langle i, j \rangle < \langle i', j' \rangle$ iff either $i < i'$ or $i = i'$ and $j < j'$. The main idea is to show that every term not in normal form can be reduced in a way that decreases the measure of the term.

(a) Show that if $(\lambda x\colon\sigma.\, M)N$ has degree n, and no redex within this term has degree greater than $n - 1$, then $[N/x]M$ has no redex of degree greater than $n - 1$.

(b) Show that for any term M not in normal form, there is some reduction $M \to M'$ such that the measure of M' is less than the measure of M. Use this to conclude that every typed lambda term must have at least one normal form.

(c) Show that this assignment of measures to terms does not prove strong normalization by finding a term M and reduction $M \to M'$ with the measure of M' greater than the measure of M.

8.3.3 Confluence and Other Reduction Properties

We may also prove confluence and other properties of typed reduction using logical relations. While it is well-known that β, η-reduction is confluent on untyped lambda terms, this does not immediately carry over to typed reduction; some proof is necessary. In particular, with variables distinguished by type, α-conversion on typed terms is slightly different from untyped α-conversion. For this reason, β, η-reduction is *not* confluent on un-type-checked terms with typed variables, as discussed in Section 4.4.2. We will prove confluence using logical relations, discuss alternative proofs, and extend the method to $\lambda^{\times,\to}$ at the end of the section.

Many parts of the confluence proof are identical to the proof of strong normalization. Rather than simply repeat the lemmas of the last section, we will state a general theorem about properties of typed terms, based on [Mit86c]. To be precise, let $\mathcal{S}$ be a property of typed lambda terms, which we may regard as a typed predicate $\mathcal{S} = \{S^\sigma\}$ on a term applicative structure $\mathcal{T}$. (We do not assume that $\mathcal{S}$ is logical.) We say $\mathcal{S}$ is *type-closed* if the following three conditions are satisfied.

(a) If $\mathcal{S}(M_1), \ldots, \mathcal{S}(M_k)$, then $\mathcal{S}(xM_1 \ldots M_k)$, where x is any variable of the appropriate type,

(b) If $S^\tau(Mx)$ holds for every variable x of type σ, then $S^{\sigma\to\tau}(M)$,

(c) If $S^\sigma(N)$ and $S^b(([N/x]M)N_1 \ldots N_k)$, then $S^b((\lambda x\colon\sigma.M)NN_1 \ldots N_k)$ for each type constant b.

In verifying that a particular predicate satisfies (b), we generally assume $S(Mx)$ for x not free in M and show $S(M)$. (It easy to see that if there is some x such that $S^{\tau}(Mx)$ implies $S^{\sigma\to\tau}(M)$, then when $S^{\tau}(Mx)$ holds for all x, we must have $S^{\sigma\to\tau}(M)$.)

Theorem 8.3.8 If $\mathcal{S}$ is any type-closed property of typed $\lambda^{\to}$ terms, then $\mathcal{S}(M)$ for every term $\Gamma \triangleright M\colon\sigma$.

Proof The proof of this theorem follows the proof of strong normalization in the last section exactly, since all of the properties of strong normalization used in Section 8.3.2 are included in the definition of type-closed property. More specifically, we construct predicate $\mathcal{P} \subseteq \mathcal{T}$ from $\mathcal{S}$ and prove a variant of Lemma 8.3.4 with *SN* replaced by $\mathcal{S}$ in statements (i) and (ii) of the lemma. This shows that $\mathcal{P}$ is logical and that $\mathcal{P}(M)$ implies $\mathcal{S}(M)$. It is straightforward to show that $\mathcal{P}$ is admissible, using Lemma 8.2.11 as in the proof of Lemma 8.3.5, since the condition needed on $\mathcal{S}$ is part (c) of the definition of type-closed. It follows by the Basic Lemma that for any $\Gamma \triangleright M\colon\sigma$, we have $P^{\sigma}(M)$ and hence $S^{\sigma}(M)$. ∎

We may obtain strong normalization and confluence as relatively straightforward corollaries. In addition, as pointed out in [Sta85b], we may also prove termination of standard reduction, completeness of standard reduction and η-postponement, which are traditional topics in untyped lambda calculus, using logical relations. (See Exercise 8.3.13.) These are all corollaries of Theorem 8.3.8. In the rest of this section, we will prove confluence of β,η-reduction for $\lambda^{\to}$ and show how the method may be extended to $\lambda^{\times,\to}$.

Confluence for $\lambda^{\to}$

We may regard confluence as a predicate on typed $\lambda^{\to}$ terms by defining

$$CR(M) \text{ iff } \forall M_1, M_2[\, M \twoheadrightarrow M_1 \wedge M \twoheadrightarrow M_2 \supset \exists N.\, M_1 \twoheadrightarrow N \wedge M_2 \twoheadrightarrow N].$$

In verifying that *CR* is type-closed, the most difficult condition is (b). While it is easy to see that $SN(Mx) \supset SN(M)$, it is not immediate that $CR(Mx) \supset CR(M)$, since there may be reductions of Mx that do not apply to M. A general property that suggests confluence is more subtle than termination is that when a set of reduction rules is terminating, every subset must also be terminating. However, not every subset of a confluent system is confluent.

Lemma 8.3.9 The predicate *CR* is type-closed.

Proof Condition (a) is straightforward, since $CR(xM_1\ldots M_k)$ whenever $CR(M_i)$ for each i.

For condition (b), we let x be any variable not free in M and assume $CR(Mx)$. We must prove $CR(M)$. Suppose $M \twoheadrightarrow M_1$ and $M \twoheadrightarrow M_2$. Then clearly $Mx \twoheadrightarrow M_1x$ and

$Mx \twoheadrightarrow M_2x$, so by $CR(Mx)$ there is a term N with $M_1x \twoheadrightarrow N$ and $M_2x \twoheadrightarrow N$. We will use these reductions to construct a common reduct of M_1 and M_2.

There are two cases to consider for the reduction path $M_1x \twoheadrightarrow N$. The first case is that no reduction involves x, which implies $N \equiv N'x$ and $M_1 \twoheadrightarrow N'$. The second case is that

$$M_1x \twoheadrightarrow (\lambda y\colon \rho.M_3)x \xrightarrow{\beta} [x/y]M_3 \twoheadrightarrow N.$$

It is easy to see that in this case, $\lambda y\colon \rho.M_3 \twoheadrightarrow \lambda x\colon \sigma.N$, since the typing rules guarantee $\sigma = \rho$. Therefore, we have

$$M_1 \twoheadrightarrow \lambda y\colon \rho.M_3 \twoheadrightarrow \lambda x\colon \sigma.N.$$

The same two cases apply for $M_2x \twoheadrightarrow N$.

We now find a common reduct for M_1 and M_2, depending on the forms of the reduction paths $M_1x \twoheadrightarrow N$ and $M_2x \twoheadrightarrow N$. If neither involves x, then we have $M_1 \twoheadrightarrow N'$ and $M_2 \twoheadrightarrow N'$, while if both paths contain a reduction with x, we have $M_1 \twoheadrightarrow \lambda x\colon \sigma.N$ and $M_2 \twoheadrightarrow \lambda x\colon \sigma.N$. The remaining case is $M_1 \rightarrow N'$ and $M_2 \twoheadrightarrow \lambda x\colon \sigma.N \equiv \lambda x\colon \sigma.N'x$. Recall that x was chosen not to occur in M, and so x cannot be free in the reduct N' of M. Therefore $\lambda x\colon \sigma.N'x \xrightarrow{\eta} N'$, and condition (b) is established.

To prove condition (c), we assume $CR(([N/x]M)N_1 \ldots N_k)$ and show $CR((\lambda x\colon \sigma.M) NN_1 \ldots N_k)$. The main idea is to show that if P may be obtained from $(\lambda x\colon \sigma.M)NN_1 \ldots N_k$ by reduction, then we may reduce P to some term that may be obtained from $([N/x]M)N_1 \ldots N_k$. This gives us $CR((\lambda x\colon \sigma.M)NN_1 \ldots N_k)$ as a consequence of $CR(([N/x]M)N_1 \ldots N_k)$.

There are three cases to consider. First, suppose we have a reduction sequence

$$(\lambda x\colon \sigma.M)NN_1 \ldots N_k \;\twoheadrightarrow\; (\lambda x\colon \sigma.M')N'N_1' \ldots N_k'$$

which does not involve λx. We wish to show that $(\lambda x\colon \sigma.M')N'N_1' \ldots N_k'$ and $([N/x]M) N_1 \ldots N_k$ reduce to a common term. But clearly both reduce to $([N'/x]M')N_1' \ldots N_k'$. The second case is that we have a reduction sequence

$$(\lambda x\colon \sigma.M)NN_1 \ldots N_k \;\twoheadrightarrow\; (\lambda x\colon \sigma.M')N'N_1' \ldots N_k' \xrightarrow{\beta} ([N'/x]M')N_1' \ldots N_k' \;\twoheadrightarrow\; P$$

which eliminates λx by β-reduction. Reasoning as above, we also have $([N/x]M)N_1 \ldots N_k \twoheadrightarrow P$. The last possibility is a reduction sequence

$$(\lambda x\colon \sigma.M)NN_1 \ldots N_k \;\twoheadrightarrow\; (\lambda x\colon \sigma.M'x)N'N_1' \ldots N_k' \xrightarrow{\eta} M'N'N_1' \ldots N_k' \;\twoheadrightarrow\; P$$

eliminating λx by η-reduction. In this case, we have $[N/x]M \twoheadrightarrow M'N'$ and so $([N/x]M) N_1 \ldots N_k \twoheadrightarrow P$. This proves the lemma. ∎

Combining Lemma 8.3.9 with Theorem 8.3.8, we have confluence of β, η-reduction.

Theorem 8.3.10 (Confluence) β, η-Reduction is confluent on typed lambda terms.

This is not the only way to prove that typed β, η-reduction is confluent. An alternative proof involves the subject reduction theorem (Lemma 4.4.16), and inspection the proof of confluence for untyped lambda calculus. Specifically, one begins by observing that if the variables of untyped lambda calculus are partitioned into infinite disjoint sets, and α-conversion is restricted to variables in the same equivalence class, then untyped lambda calculus remains confluent. Confluence of typed reduction then follows by the subject reduction theorem.

Another proof of confluence involves verifying local confluence directly, by case analysis. Recall that *local confluence,* also called the *weak Church-Rosser property,* is

$M \rightarrow M_1 \wedge M \rightarrow M_2$ implies $\exists N.\ M_1 \twoheadrightarrow N \wedge M_2 \twoheadrightarrow N.$

which we regard as a predicate by defining

$WCR(M)$ iff $\forall M_1, M_2.\ M \rightarrow M_1 \wedge M \rightarrow M_2 \supset \exists N.\ M_1 \twoheadrightarrow N \wedge M_2 \twoheadrightarrow N.$

By the Newman's Lemma (Proposition 3.7.32), we may prove confluence by establishing $WCR(M)$ for every well-typed term M. This may be done directly, by a case analysis. On the other hand, if we try to prove local confluence by logical relations, it seems difficult to show directly that WCR is type-closed. The problem lies in condition (c), where the hypothesis that $WCR(([N/x]M)N_1 \ldots N_k)$ does not seem strong enough to show $WCR((\lambda z{:}\,\sigma.M)N N_1 \ldots N_k)$. In contrast, as noted above, this is straightforward for CR.

Since η-reduction is used in verifying condition (b), in the proof of Lemma 8.3.9, the method of logical relations and type-closed properties does not appear to yield confluence of β-reduction alone. However, with β-reduction only, we have termination by the logical relations proof and therefore, by Newman's Lemma (Proposition 3.7.32), it suffices to check local confluence. This is quite easy for β-reduction alone.

Extension to Cartesian Products

We may extend Theorem 8.3.8 to $\lambda^{\times,\rightarrow}$ using an extension of the definition of type-closed to product types. A useful auxiliary concept is an *elimination context,* which was also mentioned in Exercise 5.4.21. The name comes from the fact that elimination contexts only involves term forms that arise from elimination rules for types. For $\lambda^{\times,\rightarrow}$, the elimination forms are application and projection, given in typing rules ($\rightarrow$ Elim) and ($\times$ Elim). To be precise, we define elimination contexts by the following grammar:

$$\mathcal{E}[\,] \ ::= \ [\,] \mid \mathcal{E}[[\,]M] \mid \mathcal{E}[\mathbf{Proj}_i\,[\,]]$$

Elimination contexts can be typed according to the kind of term that may be inserted and the type of term produced. We say $\mathcal{E}[\ ]$ is a σ, τ*-context* if, whenever $M\colon\sigma$, we have $\mathcal{E}[M]\colon\tau$. It is easy to see from the form of elimination contexts that if $\mathcal{E}[\ ]$ is a σ, τ-context, then τ must be a subexpression of σ.

As a convenient shorthand, we write $\mathcal{S}(\mathcal{E}[\ ])$ to mean that $\mathcal{S}$ holds for each term that appears in $\mathcal{E}[\ ]$. For example, if $\mathcal{E}[\ ] \equiv (\mathbf{Proj}_1([\ ]\, N_1))N_2$, then $\mathcal{S}(\mathcal{E}[\ ])$ is short for $S^{\sigma_1}(N_1) \wedge S^{\sigma_2}(N_2)$.

A property $\mathcal{S}$ of $\lambda^{\times,\rightarrow}$ terms is *type-closed* if the following conditions are satisfied.

(a) $\mathcal{S}(\mathcal{E}[\ ])$ implies $S^{\rho}(\mathcal{E}[x])$, for any variable x of the appropriate type,

(b) If $S^{\tau}(Mx)$ for every variable x of type σ, then $S^{\sigma\rightarrow\tau}(M)$,

(c) If $S^{b}(\mathcal{E}[[N/x]M])$ and $S^{\sigma}(N)$, then $S^{b}(\mathcal{E}[(\lambda x\colon\sigma.\, M)N])$,

(d) If $S^{\sigma_i}(\mathbf{Proj}_i M)$, for $i = 1, 2$, then $S^{\sigma_1\times\sigma_2}(M)$,

(e) If $S^{b}(\mathcal{E}[M])$ and $S^{\sigma}(N)$, then $S^{b}(\mathcal{E}[\mathbf{Proj}_1\langle M, N\rangle])$ and $S^{b}(\mathcal{E}[\mathbf{Proj}_2\langle N, M\rangle])$.

We have the following extension of Theorem 8.3.8 to $\lambda^{\times,\rightarrow}$.

Theorem 8.3.11 If a property $\mathcal{S}$ of $\lambda^{\times,\rightarrow}$ terms is type-closed, then $\mathcal{S}(M)$ holds for every well-typed term M of $\lambda^{\times,\rightarrow}$.

Proof Since the proof is similar to the proof of Theorem 8.3.8, many of the details are omitted. We define a typed predicate $\mathcal{P} = \{P^{\sigma}\}$ by

$$P^{b}(M) \text{iff} \mathcal{S}(M)$$

$$P^{\sigma\times\tau}(M) \text{iff} P^{\sigma}(\mathbf{Proj}_1 M) \text{ and } P^{\tau}(\mathbf{Proj}_2 M)$$

$$P^{\sigma\rightarrow\tau}(M) \text{iff} \forall N.\ P^{\sigma}(N) \text{ implies } P^{\tau}(MN)$$

and show that $\mathcal{P}(M)$ implies $\mathcal{S}(M)$ by a variant of Lemma 8.3.4. More specifically, we show the two conditions

(i) If $\mathcal{E}[x] \in T^{\sigma}$ and $\mathcal{S}(\mathcal{E}[\ ])$ then $P^{\sigma}(\mathcal{E}[x])$, for any variable x of the appropriate type,

(ii) If $P^{\sigma}(M)$ then $S^{\sigma}(M)$.

simultaneously by induction on types. The base case and induction step for function types are as in the proof of Lemma 8.3.4. The induction step for cartesian products is straightforward and left to the reader.

The next step is to prove that $\mathcal{P}$ is admissible by an argument similar to Lemma 8.2.11. Specifically, *admissible* with product types requires that if $P^{\tau_1}(\mathcal{A}[\![M_1]\!]\eta)$ and P^{τ_2}

$(\mathcal{A}[\![M_2]\!]\eta)$, then $P^{\tau_1\times\tau_2}(\mathcal{A}[\![\langle M_1, M_2\rangle]\!]\eta)$, in addition to the condition on lambda abstractions used as the definition of admissible for $\lambda^{\rightarrow}$. Admissibility may be proved by showing

- If $P^{\rho}(\mathcal{E}[[N/x]M])$ and $P^{\sigma}(N)$, then $P^{\rho}(\mathcal{E}[(\lambda x\colon\sigma.\, M)N])$,
- If $P^{\rho}(\mathcal{E}[M])$ and $P^{\sigma}(N)$, then $P^{\rho}(\mathcal{E}[\mathbf{Proj}_1\langle M, N\rangle])$ and $P^{\rho}(\mathcal{E}[\mathbf{Proj}_2\langle N, M\rangle])$.

by induction on types. The first is the generalization of the induction hypothesis of Lemma 8.2.11 to elimination contexts for $\lambda^{\times,\rightarrow}$, while the second is the analogous condition for products. The base case of the induction is immediate from properties (c) and (e) of type-closed $\mathcal{S}$. The induction steps are similar to the proof of Lemma 8.2.11. ■

Termination and confluence of $\beta, \eta, proj, sp$-reduction on $\lambda^{\times,\rightarrow}$ terms are shown in Exercises 8.3.14 and 8.3.15.

Exercise 8.3.12 Show by direct argument that under the typing assumptions $\Gamma \rhd x\colon\sigma$ and $\Gamma \rhd M\colon\tau$, if $CR(M)$, then $CR(\lambda x\colon\sigma.M)$. Remember that M might have the form $M \equiv (\lambda y\colon\rho.M_1)x$ with $x \notin FV(\lambda y\colon\rho.M_1)$.

Exercise 8.3.13 We say *η-postponement holds from M*, and write $EP(M)$ if, whenever $M \twoheadrightarrow N$, there is some term P with $M \stackrel{\beta}{\twoheadrightarrow} P$ and $P \stackrel{\eta}{\twoheadrightarrow} N$. Show that EP is type-closed and conclude, by Theorem 8.3.8, that $EP(M)$ for every $\lambda^{\rightarrow}$ term $\Gamma \rhd M\colon\sigma$.

Exercise 8.3.14 Using Theorem 8.3.11, we can prove termination of $\beta, \eta, proj, sp$-reduction on $\lambda^{\times,\rightarrow}$ terms by showing that the property SN defined as in Section 8.3.2 (but for $\beta, \eta, proj, sp$-reduction on $\lambda^{\times,\rightarrow}$ terms) is type-closed. This means we must check conditions (a)–(e) of the definition. Since conditions (a)–(c) are verified essentially as in the proofs of Lemmas 8.3.4 and 8.3.5, this exercise only asks you to prove conditions (d) and (e).

(a) Show that if $M\colon\sigma_1 \times \sigma_2$ and $SN(\mathbf{Proj}_i M)$, for $i = 1, 2$, then $SN(M)$.

(b) Show that if $SN(\mathcal{E}[M])$ and $SN(N)$, then $SN(\mathcal{E}[\mathbf{Proj}_1\langle M, N\rangle])$ and $SN(\mathcal{E}[\mathbf{Proj}_2 \langle N, M\rangle])$.

Exercise 8.3.15 Using Theorem 8.3.11, we can prove confluence of $\beta, \eta, proj, sp$-reduction on $\lambda^{\times,\rightarrow}$ terms by showing that the property CR defined as in Section 8.3.3 (but for $\beta, \eta, proj, sp$-reduction on $\lambda^{\times,\rightarrow}$ terms) is type-closed. This means we must check conditions (a)–(e) of the definition. Since conditions (a)–(c) are verified essentially as in the proof of Lemma 8.3.9, this exercise only asks you to prove conditions (d) and (e). Since (e) is easier, you are asked to prove this first. (The next line is part (a) of this exercise. Parts (b)–(d) follow after further explanation.)

(a) Show that if $CR(\mathcal{E}[M])$ and $CR(N)$, then $CR(\mathcal{E}[\mathbf{Proj}_1\langle M, N\rangle])$ and $CR(\mathcal{E}[\mathbf{Proj}_2 \langle N, M\rangle])$.

Condition (d) is divided into cases, in the remaining parts of this question, with symmetric possibilities omitted. Assume $M\colon \sigma_1 \times \sigma_2$ and $CR(\mathbf{Proj}_i M)$ for $i = 1, 2$. Suppose $N \twoheadleftarrow M \twoheadrightarrow P$. It follows that $\mathbf{Proj}_i N \twoheadleftarrow \mathbf{Proj}_i M \twoheadrightarrow \mathbf{Proj}_i P$ for $i = 1, 2$ and therefore, by assumption, there exist terms Q_1, Q_2 with $\mathbf{Proj}_i N \twoheadrightarrow Q_i \twoheadleftarrow \mathbf{Proj}_i P$. Show that $N \twoheadrightarrow \circ \twoheadleftarrow P$ in each of the following cases.

(b) Suppose that $\mathbf{Proj}_1 N \twoheadrightarrow Q_1 \equiv \mathbf{Proj}_1 Q'_1$ and similarly $\mathbf{Proj}_1 P \twoheadrightarrow Q_1 \equiv \mathbf{Proj}_1 Q'_1$, with neither reduction involving *proj*-reduction on the left-most $\mathbf{Proj}_1$ in any term.

(c) Suppose that the reductions to Q_1 and Q_2 have the forms

$$\mathbf{Proj}_1 N \twoheadrightarrow \mathbf{Proj}_1\langle N_1, N_2\rangle \rightarrow N_1 \twoheadrightarrow Q_1$$

$$\mathbf{Proj}_1 P \twoheadrightarrow \mathbf{Proj}_1\langle P_1, P_2\rangle \rightarrow P_1 \twoheadrightarrow Q_1$$

$$\mathbf{Proj}_2 N \twoheadrightarrow \mathbf{Proj}_2\langle N_3, N_4\rangle \rightarrow N_4 \twoheadrightarrow Q_2$$

$$\mathbf{Proj}_2 P \twoheadrightarrow \mathbf{Proj}_2\langle P_3, P_4\rangle \rightarrow P_4 \twoheadrightarrow Q_2$$

where the reductions prior to the indicated *proj*-reduction do not involve *proj*-reduction on the left-most $\mathbf{Proj}_i$ in any term. (*Hint:* Since $\langle Q_1, N_2\rangle \twoheadleftarrow M \twoheadrightarrow \langle N_1, Q_2\rangle$, the assumption $CR(\mathbf{Proj}_1 M)$ implies $Q_1 \twoheadrightarrow \circ \twoheadleftarrow N_1$, for example.)

(d) Suppose we have reductions of the form

$$\mathbf{Proj}_1 N \twoheadrightarrow \mathbf{Proj}_1\langle N_1, N_2\rangle \rightarrow N_1 \twoheadrightarrow Q_1$$

$$\mathbf{Proj}_1 P \twoheadrightarrow Q_1 \equiv \mathbf{Proj}_1 Q'_1$$

where the reduction from $\mathbf{Proj}_1 P$ does not involve *proj*-reduction on the left-most $\mathbf{Proj}_i$. If there is another reduction $\mathbf{Proj}_1 P \twoheadrightarrow \mathbf{Proj}_1\langle P_1, P_2\rangle$, then we may proceed as in the previous case, so assume that there are no terms P_1, P_2 such that $P \twoheadrightarrow \langle P_1, P_2\rangle$. It follows that we may assume without loss of generality that $N_2 \twoheadrightarrow Q_2$ and $\mathbf{Proj}_2 P \twoheadrightarrow Q_2 \equiv \mathbf{Proj}_2 Q'_2$. (*Hint:* Explain why it suffices to show $Q'_1 \twoheadrightarrow \circ \twoheadleftarrow Q'_2$ and use $\mathbf{Proj}_i Q'_1 \twoheadleftarrow \mathbf{Proj}_i M \twoheadrightarrow \mathbf{Proj}_i Q'_2$.)

8.3.4 Reduction with *Fix* and Additional Operations

In this section, we analyze reduction for typed lambda calculus with *fix* and other operations, of the form used in PCF, for example. We include product types so that these results apply to PCF as formulated in Chapter 2. Some important consequences of the general theorems here, mentioned in earlier chapters, are the confluence of PCF, confluence and termination of labeled PCF reduction, and the completeness of left-most reduction for finding PCF normal forms. An important idea for handling *fix* is to label each occurrence of a fixed-point operator in a term with a bound on the number of reductions that may be applied. This produces a confluent and terminating reduction relation. We use confluence of labeled reduction to prove this property for unlabeled reduction and termination of labeled reduction to prove the completeness of left-most reduction for unlabeled reduction. All of the results in this section hold with or without products and *proj*-reduction.

Labeled Reduction

Labeled terms and labeled reduction were described briefly in Section 5.4.1. We will consider two versions of labeled reduction here, one needed to prove the semantic results in Section 5.4.1, and the other used to prove the syntactic reduction properties considered in the rest of this section. Similar labeling techniques for untyped lambda calculus were developed by Hyland, Lévy and Wadsworth [Bar84, Hyl76, Lév75, Wad76].

If we begin with simply-typed lambda calculus over signature Σ, containing fixed-point constants at some types, then the labeled terms over Σ are defined using the extended signature $\Sigma_{lab} \supseteq \Sigma$ obtained by adding a constant, fix_σ^n, for each type σ that has a fixed point operator in Σ and for each natural number $n \geq 0$. The constant fix_σ^n is called the *labeled fixed-point operator with label n*. For the semantic results in Section 5.4.1, we also add a constant $\perp_\sigma$ for each type σ that has a fixed-point operator. We use the notation $\Sigma_{lab,\perp}$ for the signature $\Sigma_{lab,\perp} \supseteq \Sigma_{lab} \supseteq \Sigma$ with labeled fixed-point operators and constants $\perp_\sigma$ at appropriate types. We say M is a *labeled term over* Σ if M is a well-typed term over $\Sigma_{lab,\perp}$ and M does not contain any *fix* without a label. We write $lab(M)$ for the set of labeled terms that become syntactically identical to M when we replace each fix_σ^n by fix_σ.

The two forms of labeled reduction for typed lambda terms containing labeled fixed-point operators are defined using the following reduction axioms:

$$fix_\sigma^{n+1} \rightarrow \lambda f\colon \sigma \rightarrow \sigma.\, f\,(fix_\sigma^n\, f),$$

$$fix_\sigma^0 \quad \rightarrow \lambda f\colon \sigma \rightarrow \sigma.\, \perp_\sigma .$$

We will call reduction using the first reduction axiom *positive labeled reduction*, and refer to this using the symbol lab_+. The second reduction will be indicated by lab_0. Reduction with both reduction axioms will be called *labeled reduction* and denoted $lab_{+,0}$. We use $lab_{+(0)}$ for either lab_+ or $lab_{+,0}$. It is also possible to add reduction rules for $\perp$, such as $(\perp_{\sigma\rightarrow\tau}\, M) \rightarrow \perp_\tau$, but we will not need them.

In semantic analysis, we wish to treat fix_σ as one of its semantic approximants, $\lambda f\colon \sigma \rightarrow \sigma.\, f^n(\perp)$. This is precisely what happens if we label an occurrence of fix_σ with the number n and use $lab_{+,0}$ reduction. The problem with full $lab_{+,0}$ reduction, for the purpose of analyzing reduction without labels, is that the reduction of $fix_\sigma^0\, M$ to

$(\lambda f\colon \sigma \to \sigma.\ \bot_\sigma)\, M$ allows us to discard the subterm M on subsequent β-reduction. This make it impossible to use confluence of β, $lab_{+,0}$-reduction to prove confluence of β, fix-reduction, for example, in any direct way. Therefore, we need both forms reduction.

In PCF, we also have reduction axioms for operations like addition and conditional. We develop some general connections between labeled reduction and unlabeled reduction below, in a setting that allows for a set $\mathcal{R}$ of additional rewrite axioms. Like the rewrite axioms for PCF addition and conditional, these must be left-linear (see Section 3.7.5). Just to clarify notation, we write $\mathcal{R}, \beta, \mathit{proj}, lab_+$ for the combination of reduction given by a set $\mathcal{R}$ of reduction axioms, β-reduction, *proj*-reduction, and positive labeled reduction lab_+. Since this long string of names does not fit very well over an arrow, we will abbreviate *proj* to p and write $\xrightarrow{\mathcal{R},\beta,p,lab_+}\!\!\!\!\rightarrow$, for example. Two basic and useful connections are given in the following lemmas.

Lemma 8.3.16 Suppose $\mathcal{R}$ is left-linear and $M \xrightarrow{\mathcal{R},\beta,p,\mathit{fix}}\!\!\!\!\rightarrow N$. There is a natural number k such that if $M^* \in lab(M)$, with each label in M^* at least k, then $M^* \xrightarrow{\mathcal{R},\beta,p,lab_+}\!\!\!\!\rightarrow N^*$ for some $N^* \in lab(N)$.

Lemma 8.3.17 If $M^* \xrightarrow{\mathcal{R},\beta,p,lab_+}\!\!\!\!\rightarrow N^*$, where $M^* \in lab(M)$ and $N^* \in lab(N)$, then $M \xrightarrow{\mathcal{R},\beta,p,\mathit{fix}}\!\!\!\!\rightarrow N$.

Both are proved by easy inductions on the length of reduction sequences. In Lemma 8.3.16, the number k is essentially the length of the reduction sequence from M to N, since any single reduction could be carried out by labeling any *fix* that is reduced with any number at least 1. The importance of assuming that $\mathcal{R}$ is left-linear is discussed below. Since $lab_{+,0}$ contains lab_+, the first lemma also holds for $\mathcal{R}, \beta, \mathit{proj}, lab_{+,0}$. However, Lemma 8.3.17 fails for $lab_{+,0}$, since the rule for fix^0 cannot be simulated using unlabeled *fix*. These two lemmas are used to prove the basic connection between confluence of labeled and unlabeled reduction.

Proposition 8.3.18 If $\mathcal{R}, \beta, \mathit{proj}, lab_+$-reduction is confluent on labeled terms, and $\mathcal{R}$ is left-linear, then $\mathcal{R}, \beta, \mathit{proj}, \mathit{fix}$-reduction is confluent on unlabeled terms.

Proof Suppose $N \twoheadleftarrow^{\mathcal{R},\beta,p,\mathit{fix}} M \xrightarrow{\mathcal{R},\beta,p,\mathit{fix}}\!\!\!\!\rightarrow P$. By Lemma 8.3.16, there are labeling M^*, N^*, and P^* of these terms (respectively) such that $N^* \twoheadleftarrow^{\mathcal{R},\beta,p,lab_+} M^* \xrightarrow{\mathcal{R},\beta,p,lab_+}\!\!\!\!\rightarrow P^*$. Since $\mathcal{R}, \beta, \mathit{proj}, lab_+$-reduction is confluent, N^* and P^* must have a common reduct Q^*. By Lemma 8.3.17, we may erase labels to obtain $N \xrightarrow{\mathcal{R},\beta,p,\mathit{fix}}\!\!\!\!\rightarrow Q \twoheadleftarrow^{\mathcal{R},\beta,p,\mathit{fix}} P$. This shows that $\mathcal{R}, \beta, \mathit{proj}, \mathit{fix}$-reduction is confluent. ∎

It is important to understand how left-linearity is used in the proof of Lemma 8.3.16. The critical step is the base case for a reduction from $\mathcal{R}$. The property that we may choose labels arbitrarily, as long as they are all big enough, may fail if we have a non-linear rule, since some reduction rule may be applicable only if two subterms have the same label. For example, consider the following algebraic rewrite rules for $Eq?\colon nat \to nat \to bool$, $succ\colon nat \to nat$ and $true, false\colon nat$.

$$Eq?\,x\,x \to true$$

$$Eq?\,x\,(succ\,x) \to false$$

Lemma 8.3.16 fails if $\mathcal{R}$ consists solely of either one of these rules, or both of them. These rules also provide a counter-example to Proposition 8.3.18, if we drop the assumption that $\mathcal{R}$ is left-linear, since we may reduce $Eq?\,(fix\,succ)\,(fix\,succ)$ to both $true$ and $false$. The first reduction is immediate, while the second proceeds by

$$Eq?\,(fix\,succ)\,(fix\,succ) \twoheadrightarrow Eq?\,(fix\,succ)\,(succ\,(fix\,succ)).$$

If we label $Eq?\,(fix\,succ)\,(fix\,succ)$ in any way, then at most one of these reductions will be possible.

A related phenomenon occurs with surjective pairing, as discussed in Section 4.4.3.

Extend Type-closed Method to Constants

We prove properties of labeled and other reduction by extending the "type-closed" method of the last section to $\lambda^{\times,\to}$ terms with constants. With constants, the proof that every term has a type-closed property $\mathcal{S}$ has four main parts:

1. Define a predicate $\mathcal{P}$ on the applicative structure of terms, from $\mathcal{S}$, by

$$P^b(M) \quad \text{iff } \mathcal{S}(M)$$

$$P^{\sigma\times\tau}(M) \text{ iff } P^\sigma(\mathbf{Proj}_1 M) \text{ and } P^\tau(\mathbf{Proj}_2 M)$$

$$P^{\sigma\to\tau}(M) \text{ iff } \forall N.\, P^\sigma(N) \text{ implies } P^\tau(MN)$$

2. Show that $P^\sigma(M)$ implies $\mathcal{S}(M)$.

2′. Show that $P^\sigma(c)$ for each term constant $c\colon\sigma$.

3. Show that $\mathcal{P}$ is admissible, so that we may use the Basic Lemma to conclude that $P^\sigma(M)$ holds for every well-typed term $\Gamma \rhd M\colon\sigma$.

The main idea is that in treating constant c, we may need some properties of $\mathcal{P}$ in proving $P^\sigma(c)$. We therefore insert an extra step (2′) in the middle of the proof to accommodate constants.

Rather that try to identify a sufficient condition for step 2′ to succeed, we simply state a theorem that says the method works when it works. We will illustrate this below using labeled PCF reduction.

Theorem 8.3.19 Let $\mathcal{S}$ be a type-closed property of $\lambda^{\times,\rightarrow}$ terms and let $\mathcal{P}$ be the predicate on terms defined from $\mathcal{S}$ as above. If $P(c_1), \ldots, P(c_k)$, for term constants $c_1, \ldots, c_k$, then $\mathcal{S}(M)$ holds for every well-typed $\lambda^{\times,\rightarrow}$ term M over $c_1, \ldots, c_k$.

Proof The proof is identical to the proof of Theorem 8.3.11, except for the addition of term constants. However, the only way that constants affect the proof is that we need to know $P(c)$ for each constant c in order to conclude that $\mathcal{P}$ is logical. Since this is stated explicitly in the hypothesis of the theorem, the proof goes through essentially unchanged.
■

Termination of Labeled Reduction and Its Corollaries

As an application of the Theorem 8.3.19, we show that labeled PCF is strongly normalizing. We use *pcf* to indicate reduction using the axioms of PCF, and pcf_+ for PCF reduction with lab_+ replacing *fix*-reduction. It is a simple matter to extend the argument to show that $pcf_{+,0}$-reduction, with lab_0 added, is terminating.

We begin by defining the property we wish to establish, namely

$\mathcal{S}(M)$ iff pcf_+-reduction is terminating from M

where M may be any labeled PCF term, *i.e.*, any $\lambda^{\times,\rightarrow}$ term over the signature type constants *nat* and *bool*, numerals, boolean constants *true* and *false*, addition, equality test *Eq*? on *nat*, conditional on each type, and labeled fixed point constants fix_σ^n for each type σ and all $n \geq 0$. Let $\mathcal{T}$ be the term applicative structure over this signature, constructed using infinitely many variables at each type.

Let $\mathcal{P} \subseteq \mathcal{T}$ be the typed predicate defined from $\mathcal{S}$ as above. It is easy to see that this is a logical predicate, provided we can establish $\mathcal{P}(c)$ for each constant of the signature. The numerals and boolean constants are covered by the fact that $P^b(c)$ iff $\mathcal{S}(c)$, since all of these constants are normal forms. It remains to show that $\mathcal{P}$ holds for each of the remaining constants.

A useful fact to notice is that by Theorem 8.3.11, we have $\mathcal{P}(M)$ for every term without constants. A consequence is that for every type σ, there is a σ, b-elimination context $\mathcal{E}[\ ]$ with $\mathcal{P}(\mathcal{E}[\ ])$ and therefore $\mathcal{S}(\mathcal{E}[\ ])$. This is easily verified by induction on types, using a variable wherever we need a term M with $P^\sigma(M)$.

The following lemma will be useful in reasoning about constants. The first two parts do not depend on the choice of $\mathcal{S}$, only the definition of $\mathcal{P}$ from $\mathcal{S}$. Part (iii) relies only on the fact that $\mathcal{S}$ is closed under reduction.

Lemma 8.3.20 Let $M \in T^\sigma$ and let b be *nat* or *bool*.

(i) If $P^b(\mathcal{E}[M])$ for every σ, b-context $\mathcal{E}[\ ]$ with $\mathcal{P}(\mathcal{E}[\ ])$, then $P^\sigma(M)$.

(ii) If $P^\sigma(M)$ and $\mathcal{E}[\ ]$ is a σ, b-context with $\mathcal{P}(\mathcal{E}[\ ])$, then $P^b(\mathcal{E}[M])$.

(iii) If $P^\sigma(M)$ and $M \xrightarrow{pcf_+}\!\!\!\!\!\rightarrow N$, then $P^\sigma(N)$.

Proof We prove (i) by induction on the type of M. If $M\colon b$, then the only b, b-elimination context is $\mathcal{E}[\ ] = [\ ]$ and the lemma clearly holds. If $M\colon \sigma \to \tau$, then every relevant $\sigma \to \tau, b$-elimination context has the form $\mathcal{E}[[\ ]N_0]$, where $P^\sigma(N_0)$ and $\mathcal{E}[\ ]$ is a τ, b-elimination context with $\mathcal{P}(\mathcal{E}[\ ])$. Let $N \in T^\sigma$ be any term with $P^\sigma(N)$, and consider any τ, b-elimination context $\mathcal{E}[\ ]$ with $\mathcal{P}(\mathcal{E}[\ ])$. By the inductive hypothesis for $MN \in T^\tau$, we have $P^\tau(MN)$. Since N was chosen arbitrarily, if follows that $P^{\sigma\to\tau}(M)$. The proof for term $M\colon \sigma \times \tau$ is similar. This proves (i). Part (ii) may be proved by an easy induction on types.

We prove part (iii) from (i) and (ii) using the fact that if $\mathcal{S}(M)$ and $M \xrightarrow{pcf_+}\!\!\!\!\!\rightarrow N$, then $\mathcal{S}(N)$. More specifically, suppose $P^\sigma(M)$ and let $\mathcal{E}[\ ]$ be any σ, b-elimination context with $\mathcal{P}(\mathcal{E}[\ ])$. By (ii), we have $P^b(\mathcal{E}[M])$. If $M \xrightarrow{pcf_+}\!\!\!\!\!\rightarrow N$, then $\mathcal{E}[M] \xrightarrow{pcf_+}\!\!\!\!\!\rightarrow \mathcal{E}[N]$. Since $P^b(Q)$ iff $Q \in \mathcal{S}$, we therefore have $P^b(\mathcal{E}[N])$. Since this is true for every σ, b-context $\mathcal{E}[\ ]$ with $\mathcal{P}(\mathcal{E}[\ ])$, we have $P^\sigma(N)$ by (i). This proves the lemma. ∎

Lemma 8.3.21 For $\mathcal{P}$ defined from strong normalization of pcf_+-reduction, we have $P(+)$, $P(Eq?)$, $P($`if then else`$)$, and $P(fix^n_\sigma)$ for each type σ and natural number $n \geq 0$.

Proof For addition, we assume $P^{nat}(M)$ and $P^{nat}(N)$ and show $P^{nat}(M+N)$. It suffices to show that $M + N$ is strongly normalizing. However, this follows immediately since M and N are both strongly normalizing and the reduction axioms for $+$ only produce a numeral from two numerals. The proof for equality test, *Eq?*, is essentially the same.

For conditional, we assume $P^{bool}(B)$, $P^\sigma(M)$, $P^\sigma(N)$ and demonstrate $P^\sigma($`if` B `then` M `else` $N)$. By Lemma 8.3.20, it suffices to show that if $\mathcal{E}[$`if` B `then` M `else` $N] \in T^b$, for $\mathcal{P}(\mathcal{E}[\ ])$ and $b \equiv nat$ or $b \equiv bool$, then $\mathcal{E}[$`if` B `then` M `else` $N]$ is strongly normalizing. However, this is an easy case analysis, according to whether $B \xrightarrow{pcf_+}\!\!\!\!\!\rightarrow true$, $B \xrightarrow{pcf_+}\!\!\!\!\!\rightarrow false$, or neither, using (ii) of Lemma 8.3.20.

The remaining case is a labeled fixed-point constant fix^n_σ. For this, we use induction on the label. The base case, for fix^0_σ, is easy since there is no associated reduction. For fix^{n+1}_σ, we assume $P^{\sigma\to\sigma}(M)$ and let $\mathcal{E}[\ ]$ be any elimination context with $\mathcal{P}(\mathcal{E}[\ ])$ and $\mathcal{E}[fix^{n+1}_\sigma M] \in T^b$. We prove the lemma by showing that $\mathcal{E}[fix^{n+1}_\sigma M]$ is strongly normalizing. If there is an infinite reduction sequence from this term, it must begin with steps of the form

$$\mathcal{E}[\mathit{fix}_\sigma^{n+1} M] \xrightarrow{pcf_+} \mathcal{E}'[\mathit{fix}_\sigma^{n+1} M'] \xrightarrow{lab_+} \mathcal{E}'[(\lambda f\colon \sigma \to \sigma.\, f(\mathit{fix}_\sigma^n f))M']$$

$$\xrightarrow{pcf_+} \mathcal{E}''[(\lambda f\colon \sigma \to \sigma.\, f(\mathit{fix}_\sigma^n f))M''] \xrightarrow{\beta} \mathcal{E}''[M''(\mathit{fix}_\sigma^n M'')] \xrightarrow{pcf_+} \cdots$$

However, by the induction hypothesis and (ii) of Lemma 8.3.20, we have $P^{\sigma\to\sigma}(M'')$, $P^{\sigma}(\mathit{fix}_\sigma^n M'')$ and $\mathcal{P}(\mathcal{E}''[\ ])$, which implies that an infinite reduction sequence of this form is impossible. This completes the induction step and proves the lemma. ∎

Since Lemma 8.3.21 is easily extended to $pcf_{+,0}$, we have the following corollary of Theorem 8.3.19.

Theorem 8.3.22 Both pcf_+ and $pcf_{+,0}$-reduction are strongly normalizing on labeled PCF terms.

We also wish to show that both forms of labeled PCF reduction are confluent. A general theorem that could be applied, if we did not have conditional at all types, is given in [BT88, BTG89] (see Exercise 8.3.29). The general theorem is that if typed lambda calculus is extended with a confluent, algebraic rewrite system, the result is confluent. The proof of this is nontrivial, but is substantially simplified if we assume that $\mathcal{R}$ is left-linear. That is in fact the case we are interested in, since left-linearity is essential to Proposition 8.3.18 anyway. An adaptation of this proof to typed lambda calculus with labeled fixed-point operators has been carried out in [HM90, How92]. For the purposes of proving our desired results as simply as possible, however, it suffices to prove weak confluence, since confluence then follows by Proposition 3.7.32. To emphasize the fact that the argument does not depend heavily on the exact natural number and boolean operations of PCF, we show that adding $\beta, \mathit{proj}, \mathit{lab}_{+(0)}$ to any weakly confluent reduction system preserves weak confluence, as long as there are no symbols in common between $\mathcal{R}$ and the reduction axioms of $\beta, \mathit{proj}, \mathit{lab}_{+(0)}$. This is essentially an instance of *orthogonal rewrite systems,* as they are called in the literature on algebraic rewrite systems [Toy87], except that application is shared. A related confluence property of untyped lambda calculus is Mitschke's δ-reduction theorem [Bar84], which shows that under certain syntactic conditions on $\mathcal{R}$, untyped $\mathcal{R}, \beta$-reduction is confluent.

Lemma 8.3.23 Let $\mathcal{R}$ be a set of reduction axioms of the form $L \to R$, where L and R are lambda terms of the same type and L does not contain an application xM of a variable to an argument or any of the symbols λ, $\mathbf{Proj}_i$, fix or any fix_σ^n. If $\mathcal{R}$ is weakly confluent, then $\mathcal{R}, \beta, \mathit{proj}, \mathit{lab}_{+(0)}$ is weakly confluent.

Proof The proof is a case analysis on pairs of redexes. We show two cases involving β-reduction and reduction from $\mathcal{R}$. The significance of the assumptions on the form of L is that these guarantee that if a subterm of a substitution instance $[M_1, \ldots, M_k/x_1, \ldots, x_k]L$ of some left-hand-side contains a $\beta, proj, lab_{+(0)}$ redex, then this redex must be entirely within one of $M_1, \ldots, M_k$. The lemma would also hold with any other hypotheses guaranteeing this property.

The first case is an $\mathcal{R}$-redex inside a β-redex. This gives a term of the form

$$(\lambda y\colon \sigma.(\ldots [M_1, \ldots, M_k/x_1, \ldots, x_k]L \ldots))N$$

reducing to either of the terms

$$(\ldots [N/y][M_1, \ldots, M_k/x_1, \ldots, x_k]L \ldots)$$

$$(\lambda y\colon \sigma.(\ldots [M_1, \ldots, M_k/x_1, \ldots, x_k]R \ldots))N$$

the first by β-reduction and the second by an axiom $L \to R$ from $\mathcal{R}$. It is easy to see that both reduce in one step to

$$(\ldots [N/y][M_1, \ldots, M_k/x_1, \ldots, x_k]R \ldots)$$

The other possible interaction between β-reduction and $\mathcal{R}$ begins with a term of the form

$$(\ldots [M_1, \ldots, M_k/x_1, \ldots, x_k]L \ldots)$$

where one of $M_1, \ldots, M_k$ contains a β-redex. If $M_i \to M_i'$, then this term reduces to either of the two terms

$$(\ldots [M_1, \ldots, M_i', \ldots, M_k/x_1, \ldots, x_k]L \ldots)$$

$$(\ldots [M_1, \ldots, M_i, \ldots, M_k/x_1, \ldots, x_k]R \ldots)$$

in one step. We can easily reduce the first to

$$(\ldots [M_1, \ldots, M_i', \ldots, M_k/x_1, \ldots, x_k]R \ldots)$$

by one $\mathcal{R}$ step. Since we can also reach this term by some number of β-reductions, one for each occurrence of x_i in R, local confluence holds. The cases for other reductions in a substitution instance of the left-hand-side of an $\mathcal{R}$ axiom are very similar. ■

By Lemma 3.7.32, it follows that pcf_+ and $pcf_{+,0}$ are confluent. We may use Proposition 8.3.18 to derive confluence of pcf-reduction from confluence of pcf_+. This gives us the following theorem.

Theorem 8.3.24 The reductions pcf_+ and $pcf_{+,0}$ are confluent on labeled PCF terms and pcf-reduction is confluent on ordinary (unlabeled) PCF terms.

Completeness of Leftmost Reduction

The final result in this section is that if $\mathcal{R}$ is a set of "left-normal" rules (defined below), and $\mathcal{R}, \beta, proj, lab_+$ is confluent and terminating, then the leftmost reduction strategy defined in Section 2.4.3 is complete for finding $\mathcal{R}, \beta, proj, fix$-normal forms. Since the PCF rules are left-normal, it follows from Proposition 2.4.15 that lazy reduction is complete for finding normal forms of PCF programs.

A reduction axiom is *left-normal* if all the variables in the left-hand side of the rule appear to the right of all the term constants. For example, all of the PCF rules for natural numbers and booleans are left-normal. If we permute the arguments of conditional, however, putting the boolean argument at the end, then we would have reduction axioms

$$cond\ x\ y\ true \longrightarrow x,$$

$$cond\ x\ y\ false \longrightarrow y.$$

These are not left-normal since x and y appear to the left of the constants *true* and *false*. Intuitively, if we have left-normal rules, then may safely evaluate the arguments of a function from left to right. In many cases, it is possible to replace a set of rules with essentially equivalent left-normal ones by either permuting arguments or introducing auxiliary function symbols (see Exercise 8.3.28). However, this is not possible for inherently "non-sequential" functions such as parallel-or.

We will prove the completeness of left-most reduction using strong normalization and confluence of positive labeled reduction, and the correspondence between labeled and unlabeled reduction. Since labeled *fix* reduction may terminate with fix^0 where unlabeled *fix* reduction could continue, our main lemma is that any fix^0 occurring to the left of the left-most redex will remain after reducing the left-most redex.

Lemma 8.3.25 Let $\mathcal{R}$ be a set of left-normal reduction axioms with no left-hand-side containing fix^0. If $M \xrightarrow{\mathcal{R},\beta,p,lab_+} N$ by the left-most reduction step, and fix^0 occurs to the left of the left-most redex of M, then fix^0 must also occur in N, to the left of the left-most redex if N is not in normal form.

Proof Suppose $M \equiv \mathcal{C}[L] \rightarrow \mathcal{C}[R] \equiv N$ by contracting the left-most $\mathcal{R}, \beta, proj, lab_+$-redex and assume fix^0 occurs in $\mathcal{C}[\ ]$ to the left of $[\ ]$. If $N \equiv \mathcal{C}[R]$ is in normal form, then fix^0 occurs in N since fix^0 occurs in $\mathcal{C}[\ ]$. We therefore assume N is not in normal form and show that fix^0 occurs to the left of the left-most redex in N.

Suppose, for the sake of deriving a contradiction, that fix^0 occurs within, or to the right of, the left-most redex of N. Since a term beginning with fix^0 is not a redex, the left-most redex of N must begin with some symbol to the left of fix^0, which is to the left of R when we write N as $\mathcal{C}[R]$. The proof proceeds by considering each possible form of redex.

Suppose the left-most redex in N is $\mathbf{Proj}_i \langle N_1, N_2 \rangle$, with fix^0 and therefore R occurring to the right of $\mathbf{Proj}_i$. Since fix^0 must occur between $\mathbf{Proj}_i$ and R, R cannot be $\langle N_1, N_2\rangle$, and so a redex of the form $\mathbf{Proj}_i\langle\_, \_\rangle$ must occur in M to the left of L. This contradicts the assumption that L is the leftmost redex in M. Similar reasoning applies to a β-redex; the *fix* case is trivial.

It remains to consider a redex SL' with S some substitution and $L' \to R'$ in $\mathcal{R}$. We assume fix^0 and therefore R occur to the right of the first symbol of SL'. Since fix^0 is not in L', by hypothesis, and the rule is left-normal, all symbols to the right of fix^0, including R if it occurs within L', must be the result of substituting terms for variables in L'. It follows that we have a redex in M to the left of L, again a contradiction. This proves the lemma. ∎

Theorem 8.3.26 Suppose $\mathcal{R}, \beta, \mathit{proj}, \mathit{lab}_+$ is confluent and terminating, with $\mathcal{R}$ left-linear and left-normal. If $M \overset{\mathcal{R},\beta,p,\mathit{fix}}{\twoheadrightarrow} N$ and N is a normal form, then there is a $\mathcal{R}, \beta, \mathit{proj}$, *fix*-reduction from M to N that contracts the leftmost redex at each step.

Proof If $M \overset{\mathcal{R},\beta,p,\mathit{fix}}{\twoheadrightarrow} N$ then, by Lemma 8.3.16 there exist labelings M^* and N^* of these terms such that $M^* \overset{\mathcal{R},\beta,p,\mathit{lab}_+}{\twoheadrightarrow} N^*$. Since $\mathcal{R}, \beta, \mathit{proj}, \mathit{lab}_+$-reduction is confluent and terminating, we may reduce M^* to N^* by reducing the left-most redex at each step.

We show that the left-most $\mathcal{R}, \beta, \mathit{proj}, \mathit{lab}_+$-reduction of M^* to N^* is also the left-most $\mathcal{R}, \beta, \mathit{proj}, \mathit{fix}$-reduction of M to N (when labels are removed). It is easy to see that this is the case if no term in the reduction sequence has fix^0 to the left of the left-most redex, since this is the only term that would be an unlabeled redex without being a labeled one. Therefore, we assume that the final k steps of the reduction have the form

$$M_k^* \equiv \mathcal{C}[L] \to \mathcal{C}[R] \equiv M_{k-1}^* \to M_{k-2}^* \to \ldots \to N^*,$$

where fix^0 occurs to the left of L in M_k. But by Lemma 8.3.25 and induction on k, fix^0 must also be present in N^*, which contradicts the fact that N is a $\mathcal{R}, \beta, \mathit{proj}, \mathit{fix}$-normal form. It follows from Lemma 8.3.16 that by erasing labels we obtain a leftmost reduction from M to N. ∎

A related theorem in [Klo80] shows that left-most reduction is normalizing for the untyped lambda calculus extended with any left-normal, linear and non-overlapping term rewriting system. Our proof is simpler since we assume termination, and since type restrictions make *fix* the only source of potential nontermination.

Since the rules of PCF satisfy all the conditions above, Theorem 8.3.26 implies the completeness of leftmost reduction for finding PCF normal forms. This was stated as Proposition 2.4.12 in Section 2.4.3.

Exercise 8.3.27 Gödel's system $\mathcal{T}$ of primitive recursive functionals is $\lambda^{\to}$ over type constant *nat* and term constants

$0 \quad : nat$

$succ : nat \to nat$

$R_\sigma \quad : \sigma \to (\sigma \to nat \to \sigma) \to nat \to \sigma$

for each type σ, with the following reduction axioms

$R_\sigma M N 0 \to M$

$R_\sigma M N (succ\, x) \to N (R_\sigma M N x) x$

The primitive recursion operator R_σ of type σ is essentially the same as $prim_\sigma$ of Exercise 2.5.7, with cartesian products eliminated by currying.

Extend the proof in this section to show that Gödel's $\mathcal{T}$ is strongly normalizing. You need not repeat proof steps that are given in the text. Just point out where additional arguments are needed and carry them out. Historically, Gödel's $\mathcal{T}$ was used to prove the consistency of first-order Peano arithmetic [Göd58], by a reduction also described in [HS86, Tro73] and mentioned briefly in [Bar84, Appendix A.2]. It follows from this reduction that the proof of strong normalization of $\mathcal{T}$ cannot be formalized in Peano arithmetic. Given this, it is particularly surprising that the proof for $\mathcal{T}$ involves only the same elementary reasoning used for $\lambda^{\to}$.

Exercise 8.3.28 Consider the following set of algebraic reduction axioms.

$f\ true\ true\ y \longrightarrow true$

$f\ true\ false\ y \longrightarrow false$

$f\ false\ x\ true \longrightarrow false$

$f\ false\ x\ false \longrightarrow true.$

This system is not left-normal. Show that by adding a function symbol *not* with axioms

$not\ true \longrightarrow false$

$not\ false \longrightarrow true.$

we may replace the four reduction axioms by two left-normal ones in a way that gives exactly the same truth-table for f.

Exercise 8.3.29 This exercise is concerned with adding algebraic rewrite rules to typed lambda calculus. Recall from Section 4.3.2 that if $\Sigma_{alg} = \langle S, F \rangle$ is an algebraic signature, we may construct a similar $\lambda^{\to}$ signature $\Sigma = \langle B, F' \rangle$ by taking the sorts of Σ_{alg} as base types, and letting each algebraic function have the corresponding curried type. This allows us to view algebraic terms as a special case of typed lambda terms.

Let $\mathcal{R}$ be an algebraic rewrite system over Σ_{alg}. Thinking of $\mathcal{R}$ as a set of rewrite rules for $\lambda^{\rightarrow}$ terms over Σ, it makes sense to ask whether the reduction system consisting of $\mathcal{R}$ together with the usual reduction rules $(\beta)_{red}$ and $(\eta)_{red}$ of typed lambda calculus is confluent. This turns out to be quite tricky in general, but it gets much simpler if we drop $(\eta)_{red}$ and just consider $\mathcal{R}$ plus β-reduction (modulo α-conversion of terms). We call the combination of $\mathcal{R}$ and β-reduction *$\mathcal{R}, \beta$-reduction*. The problem is to prove that if $\mathcal{R}$ is confluent (as an algebraic rewrite system), then $\mathcal{R}, \beta$-reduction is confluent on typed lambda terms over Σ. (This also holds with *proj*-reduction added [HM90, How92].)

Some useful notation is to write $\twoheadrightarrow_{\mathcal{R}}$ for reduction using rules from $\mathcal{R}$, similarly $\twoheadrightarrow_{\mathcal{R},\beta}$ for $\mathcal{R}, \beta$-reduction, and $\beta nf(M)$ for the normal form of$M$ under β-reduction. Note that $\beta nf(M)$ may still be reducible using rules from $\mathcal{R}$. You may assume the following facts, for all $\Gamma \triangleright M{:}\,\sigma$ and $\Gamma \triangleright N{:}\,\sigma$.

1. If $\mathcal{R}$ is confluent on algebraic terms over signature Σ_{alg}, then $\twoheadrightarrow_{\mathcal{R}}$ is confluent on typed lambda terms over Σ.
2. If M is a β-normal form and $M \twoheadrightarrow_{\mathcal{R}} N$, then N is a β-normal form.
3. If $M \twoheadrightarrow_{\mathcal{R},\beta} N$, then $\beta nf(M) \twoheadrightarrow_{\mathcal{R}} \beta nf(N)$.

The problem has two parts.

(a) Using 1–3 above, show that if $\mathcal{R}$ is confluent (as an algebraic rewrite system), then $\mathcal{R}, \beta$-reduction is confluent on typed lambda terms over Σ. (This problem has a 4 or 5-sentence solution, using a picture involving $\twoheadrightarrow_{\mathcal{R}}$, $\twoheadrightarrow_{\mathcal{R},\beta}$ and ordinary β-reduction $\twoheadrightarrow_{\beta}$.)

(b) Show that (a) fails if we add *fix*-reduction. Specifically, find a confluent algebraic rewrite system $\mathcal{R}$ such that $\mathcal{R}, \beta, \mathit{fix}$-reduction on typed lambda terms over signature $\Sigma \cup \{\mathit{fix}_{\sigma}{:}\, (\sigma \rightarrow \sigma) \rightarrow \sigma\}$ is not confluent. (Hint: try to find some algebraic equations that become inconsistent when fixed points are added.)

8.4 Partial Surjections and Specific Models

In Sections 8.4.1–8.4.3, we prove completeness of β, η-conversion for three specific models, the full classical, recursive and continuous hierarchies. These theorems may be contrasted with the completeness theorems of Section 8.3.1, which use term models to show that provability coincides with semantic implication. The completeness theorems here show that the specific theory of β, η-conversion captures semantic equality between pure typed lambda terms in three specific, non-syntactic models.

One way of understanding each of these theorems is to consider a specific model as characterizing a specific form of "distinguishability." Suppose we have two terms,

$M, N: (b \to b) \to b$, for example. These will be equal in the full classical hierarchy if the functions defined by M and N produce equal values of type b for all possible function arguments. On the other hand, in a recursive model $\mathcal{A}$ where $A^{b \to b}$ only contains recursive functions, these terms will be equal if the functions they define produce equal values when applied to all recursive functions. Since not all set-theoretic functions are recursive, there may be some equations (at this type) that hold in the recursive model but not in the full set-theoretic hierarchy. Surprisingly, the completeness theorems show that these two forms of semantic equivalence are the same, at least for pure typed lambda terms without constants. The third case, the full continuous hierarchy, is also interesting for its connection with PCF extended with parallel-or. Specifically, we know from Theorem 5.4.14 that two terms of PCF $+$ *por* are equal in the continuous hierarchy over *nat* and *bool* iff they are operationally equivalent. In other words, two lambda terms are equal in the continuous model iff they are indistinguishable by PCF program contexts. Therefore, our completeness theorem for the full continuous hierarchy shows that β, η-conversion captures PCF operational equivalence for pure typed lambda terms without the term constants of PCF. A technical point is that this only holds for terms whose types involve only *nat* and $\to$; with *bool*, the theorem does not apply since we only prove completeness of β, η-conversion for the full continuous hierarchy over *infinite* CPOs.

A more general theorem, which we do not consider, is Statman's so-called *1-section theorem* [Rie94, Sta85a, Sta82]. Briefly, Statman's theorem gives a sufficient condition on a Henkin model $\mathcal{A}$ implying that two terms have the same meaning in $\mathcal{A}$ iff the terms are β, η-convertible. It is called the "1-section theorem" since the condition only involves the first-order functions of $\mathcal{A}$. Although the 1-section theorem implies all of the three completeness theorems here, the proof is more complex and combinatorial than the logical relations argument used here, and the generalization to other lambda calculi is less clear.

We will work with $\lambda^{\to}$, and type frames instead of arbitrary applicative structures. Recall that a $\lambda^{\to}$ type frame is an extensional applicative structure $\mathcal{A}$ such that the elements of $A^{\sigma \to \tau}$ are functions from A^{σ} to A^{τ} and **App** $f\,x = f(x)$. We therefore write fx in place of **App** $f\,x$.

8.4.1 Partial Surjections and the Full Classical Hierarchy

It is tempting to think of any $\lambda^{\to}$ type frame $\mathcal{B}$ as a "subframe" of the full classical hierarchy $\mathcal{P}$ with the same interpretation of type constants. This seems quite natural, since at every type $\sigma \to \tau$, the set $B^{\sigma \to \tau}$ is a subset of the set of all functions from B^{σ} to B^{τ}. However, we do not have $B^{\sigma \to \tau} \subseteq P^{\sigma \to \tau}$ in general. This is because B^{σ} may be a proper subset of P^{σ} if σ is a functional type, and so the domain of a function in $B^{\sigma \to \tau}$ is different from a function in $P^{\sigma \to \tau}$. However, the intuitive idea that $\mathcal{P}$ "contains" $\mathcal{B}$ is reflected in a certain kind a logical relation between $\mathcal{P}$ and $\mathcal{B}$. Specifically, a logical relation $\mathcal{R} \subseteq \mathcal{A} \times \mathcal{B}$ is called a *partial surjection* if each R^σ is a partial surjection, *i.e.*, $\mathcal{R}$ is a partial function and for each $b \in B^\sigma$ there is some $a \in A^\sigma$ with $R^\sigma(a, b)$.

In this section, we prove that if we begin with partial surjections $R^b \colon P^b \to B^b$ for each type constant b of some frame $\mathcal{B}$, then the induced logical relation from the full classical hierarchy $\mathcal{P}$ to $\mathcal{B}$ is a partial surjection. By choosing $\mathcal{B}$ isomorphic to a β, η-term model, we may conclude that any full classical $\mathcal{P}$ with each P^b large enough has the same theory as $\mathcal{B}$. Consequently, an equation $\Gamma \rhd M = N \colon \sigma$ holds in the full classical hierarchy over any infinite types iff M and N are β, η-convertible. This was first proved in [Fri75].

Lemma 8.4.1 (Surjections for Classical Models) Let $\mathcal{R} \subseteq \mathcal{P} \times \mathcal{B}$ be a logical relation over a full classical hierarchy $\mathcal{P}$ and type frame $\mathcal{B}$. If $R^b \subseteq P^b \times B^b$ is a partial surjection for each type constant b, then $\mathcal{R}$ is a partial surjection.

Proof We assume R^σ and R^τ are partial surjections and show that $R^{\sigma\to\tau}$ is also a partial surjection. Recall that

$$R^{\sigma\to\tau} = \{\langle a, b\rangle \mid R^\sigma(a', b') \supset R^\tau(aa', bb')\}.$$

We first show that $R^{\sigma\to\tau}$ is onto by letting $b \in B^{\sigma\to\tau}$ and finding $a \in P^{\sigma\to\tau}$ related to b. Writing R^σ and R^τ as functions, a can be any function satisfying

$$aa_1 \in (R^\tau)^{-1}(b(R^\sigma a_1)) \text{ all } a_1 \in Dom(R^\sigma).$$

Since $\mathcal{P}$ is the full type hierarchy, R^σ is a function on its domain $Dom(R^\sigma)$ and R^τ is onto, there is at least one such $a \in P^{\sigma\to\tau}$.

To see that $R^{\sigma\to\tau}$ is a partial function, we suppose that $R^{\sigma\to\tau}(a, b_1)$ and $R^{\sigma\to\tau}(a, b_2)$. Let $f \colon B^\sigma \to P^\sigma$ be any "choice function" satisfying

$$R^\sigma(fb', b') \text{ all } b' \in B^\sigma.$$

Then for every $b' \in B^\sigma$, we have $R^\tau(a(fb'), b_ib')$ for $i = 1, 2$. But since R^τ is a function, it follows that $b_1b' = b_2b'$ for every $b' \in B^\sigma$. Thus, by extensionality of $\mathcal{B}$, we have $b_1 = b_2$. This proves the lemma. ∎

It is now an easy matter to prove the completeness of β, η-conversion for the full classical hierarchy over any infinite sets.

Theorem 8.4.2 (Completeness for Classical Models) Let $\mathcal{P}$ be the full classical $\lambda^\to$ hierarchy over any infinite sets. Then for any pure lambda terms, $\Gamma \rhd M, N \colon \sigma$ without constants, we have $\mathcal{P} \models \Gamma \rhd M = N \colon \sigma$ iff M and N are β, η-convertible.

Proof Let $\mathcal{B} \cong \mathcal{T}/\mathcal{R}_{\mathcal{E}}$ be isomorphic to a Henkin model of equivalence classes of terms, as in Theorem 8.3.2, where $\mathcal{E}$ is the pure theory of β, η-conversion. Let $\mathcal{R} \subseteq \mathcal{P} \times \mathcal{B}$ be a logical relation with R^b a partial surjection. We know this is possible since P^b is infinite and each B^b is countably infinite. By Lemma 8.4.1, $\mathcal{R}$ is a partial surjection. Consequently, by Lemma 8.2.17, $Th(\mathcal{P}) \subseteq Th(\mathcal{B})$. But since every theory contains $Th(\mathcal{B})$, it follows that $Th(\mathcal{P}) = Th(\mathcal{B})$. ∎

8.4.2 Full Recursive Hierarchy

In this subsection, we prove a surjection theorem for modest sets. Just as any frame $\mathcal{A}$ with an arbitrary collection of functions is the partial surjective image of a full classical hierarchy, we can show that any frame $\mathcal{A}$ containing only recursive functions is the partial surjective image of a full recursive hierarchy. Since we may view the term model as a recursive model, the surjection lemma for recursive models also implies that β, η-conversion is complete for recursive models with infinite interpretation of each type constant.

In order to carry out the inductive proof of the surjection lemma, we need to be able to show that for every function in a given recursive frame $\mathcal{B}$, we can find some related recursive function in the full recursive hierarchy $\mathcal{A}$. The way we will do this is to establish that for every type, we have functions that "recursively demonstrate" that the logical relation $\mathcal{R}$ is a partial surjection. Following the terminology of Kleene realizability [Kle71], we say that a function f_σ *realizes* R^σ *is surjective* by computing $f_\sigma b$ with $R^\sigma(f_\sigma b, b)$ for every element $b \in B^\sigma$. Similarly, a recursive function g_σ *realizes* R^σ *is a partial function* by computing the unique $g_\sigma a = b$ with $R^\sigma(a, b)$ from any a in the domain of R^σ. We adapt the classical proof to modest sets by showing that the inductive hypothesis is realized by recursive functions.

The assumption we will need for the interpretation of type constants is a form of "recursive embedding." If $\langle A, e_A \rangle$ and $\langle B, e_b \rangle$ are modest sets, then we say $\langle f, g \rangle$ is a *recursive embedding of* $\langle B, e_b \rangle$ *into* $\langle A, e_A \rangle$ if f and g are recursive functions

$$f\colon \langle B, e_b \rangle \to \langle A, e_A \rangle \quad \text{and} \quad g\colon \langle A, e_A \rangle \to \langle B, e_b \rangle$$

whose composition $g \circ f = id_B$ is the identity function on B. We incorporate such functions into a form of logical relation with the following definition. Let $\mathcal{A}$ and $\mathcal{B}$ be type frames with each type interpreted as a modest set. We say a family $\{R^\sigma, f_\sigma, g_\sigma\}$ of relations and functions is a *recursive partial surjection from* $\mathcal{A}$ *to* $\mathcal{B}$ if $\mathcal{R} \subseteq \mathcal{A} \times \mathcal{B}$ is a logical partial surjection, and

$$f_\sigma\colon \langle B^\sigma, e'_\sigma \rangle \to \langle A^\sigma, e_\sigma \rangle, \quad g_\sigma\colon \langle A^\sigma, e_\sigma \rangle \to \langle B^\sigma, e'_\sigma \rangle$$

are recursive functions with f_σ realizing that R^σ is surjective and g_σ realizing that R^σ is a partial function.

Lemma 8.4.3 (Surjections for Recursive Models) Let $\mathcal{A}, \mathcal{B}$ be frames of recursive functions and modest sets, for a signature without term constants, with $\mathcal{A}$ a full recursive hierarchy. If B^b is recursively embedded in A^b for each type constant b, then there is a recursive partial surjection $\{R^\sigma, f_\sigma, g_\sigma\}$ from $\mathcal{A}$ to $\mathcal{B}$.

Proof For each type constant b, we define R^b from the recursive embedding $\langle f_b, g_b\rangle$ by $R^b(x, y)$ iff $g_b x = y$. It is easy to check that $\langle R^b, f_b, g_b\rangle$ has the required properties. We define the logical relation $\mathcal{R} \subseteq \mathcal{A} \times \mathcal{B}$ by extending to higher types inductively.

For the inductive step of the proof, we have three conditions to verify, namely

(i) $R^{\sigma\to\tau}$ is a surjective partial function,

(ii) There is a recursive $f_{\sigma\to\tau}\colon \langle B^{\sigma\to\tau}, e'_{\sigma\to\tau}\rangle \to \langle A^{\sigma\to\tau}, e_{\sigma\to\tau}\rangle$ with $R^{\sigma\to\tau}(fb, b)$ for all $b \in B^{\sigma\to\tau}$, and

(iii) There is a recursive $g_{\sigma\to\tau}\colon \langle A^{\sigma\to\tau}, e_{\sigma\to\tau}\rangle \to \langle B^{\sigma\to\tau}, e'_{\sigma\to\tau}\rangle$ with $R^{\sigma\to\tau}(a, ga)$ for all $a \in Dom(R^{\sigma\to\tau})$.

Since (i) follows from (ii) and (iii), we check only (ii) and (iii), beginning with (ii). Given $b \in B^{\sigma\to\tau}$, we must find some recursive function $a \in A^{\sigma\to\tau}$ with $R^{\sigma\to\tau}(a, b)$. Writing $R(\cdot)$ as a function, a must have the property

$$aa_1 \in (R^\tau)^{-1}(b(R^\sigma a_1))$$

for all $a_1 \in Dom(R^\sigma)$. It is easy to see that this condition is satisfied by taking $a = f_\tau \circ b \circ g_\sigma$, since g_σ computes the function R^σ and f_τ chooses an element $f_\tau(b(R^\sigma a_1)) \in (R^\tau)^{-1}(b(R^\sigma a_1))$ whenever there is one. We can also compute a as a function of b by composing with recursive functions.

For condition (iii), we assume $a \in Dom(R^{\sigma\to\tau})$ so that $R^{\sigma\to\tau}(a, b)$ for some b. We need to show how to compute b uniquely from a. It suffices to show how to compute the function value bb_1 for every $b_1 \in B^\sigma$, and that the value bb_1 is uniquely determined by a and b_1. If $b_1 \in B^\sigma$, then $R^\sigma(f_\sigma b_1, b_1)$ and so we have $R^\tau(a(f_\sigma b_1), bb_1)$. Therefore $g_\tau(a(f_\sigma b_1)) = bb_1$ and this equation determines the value bb_1 uniquely. Thus we take $g_{\sigma\to\tau}a = g_\tau \circ a \circ f_\sigma$, which, as we have just seen, gives the correct result for every $a \in Dom(R^{\sigma\to\tau})$. ■

The completeness theorem is now proved exactly as for the full classical hierarchy, with Lemma 8.4.3 in place of Lemma 8.4.1, and with the term model viewed as a frame

The completeness theorem is now proved exactly as for the full recursive hierarchy, with Lemma 8.4.5 in place of Lemma 8.4.3.

Theorem 8.4.6 (Completeness for Continuous Models) Let $\mathcal{A}$ be the full recursive type hierarchy over any CPOs $\langle A^{b_0}, \leq_0\rangle, \ldots$ with infinite discrete retractions. Then for any pure lambda terms, $\Gamma \triangleright M, N\colon\sigma$ without constants, we have $\mathcal{A} \models \Gamma \triangleright M = N\colon\sigma$ iff M and N are β, η-convertible.

8.5 Representation Independence

8.5.1 Motivation

One pragmatic motivation for type checking in programming languages is to keep certain implementation details from affecting the behavior of programs. This is important for program portability, for example. If the difference between one's complement and two's complement representation of negative integers (with -1 represented as $1\ldots10_2$ or $1\ldots11_2$, respectively) were immediately apparent to any program, it could prove difficult to transport programs written on a one's complement machine to a two's complement machine. In an "untyped" programming language allowing bit-string operations on integers, a program could distinguish a one's complement implementation from two's complement. However, if bit-strings and integers are separate types, then we can show that one's complement and two's complement are indistinguishable by proving a "representation independence" theorem.

Intuitively, representation independence is the property that programs do not depend on the way data types are represented, only on the behavior of data types with respect to the operations that are provided. In addition to the portability issue mentioned above, this allows the implementation of a user-defined data type to be optimized after a program using it has been completed. For example, representation independence would guarantee that stacks could be implemented using arrays or linked lists, as long as the *push* and *pop* operations give the correct results. In this case, the implementation of stacks could be changed from arrays to linked lists, or vice versa, without altering the correctness of any program that uses stacks.

The intent of a representation independence theorem is to characterize the kinds of implementation decisions that do not effect the meanings of programs. Various formal statements of the property have been proposed in the literature [Don79, Hay84, Rey83, MM85, Mit86b, Mit91a]. Essentially, all of these have the following general form.

If two interpretations $\mathcal{A}$ and $\mathcal{B}$ are related in a certain way, then the meaning $\mathcal{A}[\![M]\!]$ of any closed term M in $\mathcal{A}$ is related to the meaning $\mathcal{B}[\![M]\!]$ in $\mathcal{B}$ in the same certain way.

We generally choose the correspondence between $\mathcal{A}$ and $\mathcal{B}$ to be the identity for observables such as natural numbers, strings and booleans. The pragmatic consequence of this sort of theorem is that if two programming language interpreters are related in this "certain way," then the result of executing any program using one interpreter will correspond to the result of executing the same program using the other interpreter. Thus the precise statement of the theorem describes the kind of implementation decisions that do not effect the meanings of programs. Of course, the kinds of relations we are interested in will turn out to be logical relations. The main ideas seem best illustrated by example.

8.5.2 Example Language

We will consider multisets of natural numbers, assuming that we observe the behavior of programs by computing natural numbers. Since we do not have type declarations in $\lambda^{\rightarrow}$, we will compare implementations of multisets by assuming the implementations are provided as part of the semantics of a simple programming language. However, the main ideas may also be applied to languages with abstract data type declarations (Section 9.4).

To study programs with multisets, we let Σ be the $\lambda^{\rightarrow}$ signature with type constants *nat* (for natural numbers) and *s* (for multisets), term constants

$$0, 1\colon nat, \quad +\colon nat \rightarrow nat \rightarrow nat$$

to provide arithmetic, and constants

$$empty\colon s, \quad insert\colon nat \rightarrow s \rightarrow s, \quad count\colon s \rightarrow nat \rightarrow nat$$

for multiset operations. Informally, *empty* is the empty multiset, *insert* adds an element to a multiset, and *count* returns the multiplicity of a multiset element. (An algebraic specification of multisets appears in Table 3.2; see also Exercise 3.4.20.)

In this language, we intend to write programs with natural number inputs and outputs. Multisets and function expressions may occur in programs, but are used only at "intermediate stages." Our goal is to describe the conditions under which different representations (or implementations) of multisets are indistinguishable by programs. Since our definition will involve quantifying over the collection of all programs, it suffices to consider programs with no input, and only one output. Therefore, we let the *programs over* Σ be the closed terms $M\colon nat$ of type natural number, as for PCF in Section 2.3.1.

We will compare different representations of multisets by examining the values of programs over appropriate models. Since we consider natural numbers the "printable output," we will assume that each model interprets *nat* as the usual natural numbers $0, 1, 2, \ldots$. For the purposes of this discussion, we define an *implementation for* Σ to be a model

$$\mathcal{A} = \langle \{A^{\sigma}\}, 0, 1, +, empty^{\mathcal{A}}, insert^{\mathcal{A}}, count^{\mathcal{A}} \rangle$$

with A^{nat} and $0, 1, +$ standard, but A^s and operations *empty*, *insert*, *count* arbitrary.

Two compilers or interpreters for a programming language would generally be considered equivalent if every program produces identical results on either one. We say that implementations $\mathcal{A}$ and $\mathcal{B}$ for Σ are *observationally equivalent* if, for any program $M\colon nat$, we have

$$\mathcal{A}[\![M\colon nat]\!] = \mathcal{B}[\![M\colon nat]\!]$$

i.e., the meaning of $M\colon nat$ in $\mathcal{A}$ is the same as the meaning of $M\colon nat$ in $\mathcal{B}$. The rest of this section is devoted to characterizing observational equivalence of implementations.

A first guess might be that $\mathcal{A}$ and $\mathcal{B}$ are observationally equivalent iff there exists some kind of mapping between multisorted first-order structures

$$\langle A^{nat}, A^s, 0, 1, +, empty^{\mathcal{A}}, insert^{\mathcal{A}}, count^{\mathcal{A}}\rangle$$

and

$$\langle B^{nat}, B^s, 0, 1, +, empty^{\mathcal{B}}, insert^{\mathcal{B}}, count^{\mathcal{B}}\rangle,$$

say a homomorphism preserving 0, 1 and +. This is partly correct, since a first-order homomorphism lifts to a logical relation, and therefore the Basic Lemma guarantees equivalent results for any program. However, there are two reasons why homomorphisms are not an exact characterization. These are worth discussing, since they will sharpen our intuition for observational equivalence of implementations. The first reason has to do with the fact that elements of A^s and B^s that are not definable by terms are irrelevant. For example, suppose $\mathcal{B}$ contains only definable, finite multisets and $\mathcal{A}$ is derived from $\mathcal{B}$ by adding some "nonstandard" multiset a with the property

$$insert\ x\ a = a \quad \text{for all } x.$$

This will not keep $\mathcal{A}$ and $\mathcal{B}$ from being observationally equivalent unless the multiset a is definable by some expression. However, there can be no homomorphism h since there is no reasonable choice for $h(a)$.

Another shortcoming of homomorphisms may be explained by describing straightforward computer implementations of multisets. One way of representing a multiset is as a linked list of pairs of the form

$$\langle element, count\rangle$$

where the natural number *count* is the number of times *element* has been inserted. The *empty* multiset is then the empty linked list, *insert* adds a new pair or increments the appropriate count, and the function *count* searches the list and returns the appropriate count.

An alternative representation makes sense if we assume that small numbers $1, \ldots, 10$ will occur quite frequently, with other numbers much less likely. In this case, we might use an array of length 10 to count the number of times $1, \ldots, 10$ are inserted, together with a simple list of other insertions in the order they occur. Note that repeatedly inserting 12, for example, will result in 12 appearing several times in the list. With *insert* and *count* implemented properly, these two representations will be observationally equivalent. However, there can be no homomorphism from the first implementation to the second. To see why this is so, consider the result of inserting three elements into the empty multiset. To simplify notation, we will use the abbreviation

$$\mathit{insert}^3\ x\ y\ z \stackrel{\text{def}}{=} \mathit{insert}\ x\ (\mathit{insert}\ y\ (\mathit{insert}\ z\ \mathit{empty})).$$

In the first representation, assuming $x, y > 10$, we have

$$\mathit{insert}^3\ x\ y\ x = \mathit{insert}^3\ x\ x\ y = \langle\langle x, 2\rangle, \langle y, 1\rangle\rangle$$

whereas in the second representation.

$$\mathit{insert}^3\ x\ y\ x = \mathit{Array};\ \langle x, y, x\rangle \neq \mathit{Array};\ \langle x, x, y\rangle = \mathit{insert}^3\ x\ x\ y.$$

Any homomorphism h from the first representation to the second would have to map the list of pairs $\langle\langle x, 2\rangle, \langle y, 1\rangle\rangle$ to two values, but this is impossible. Conversely,

$$\mathit{insert}^3\ 1\,2\,3 = \mathit{insert}^3\ 3\,2\,1$$

in the second representation, since both set $\mathit{Array}[1] = \mathit{Array}[2] = \mathit{Array}[3] = 1$. However, in the first representation using lists of $\langle \mathit{element},\mathit{count}\rangle$ pairs, $\mathit{insert}^3\ 1\,2\,3$ and $\mathit{insert}^3\ 3\,2\,1$ yield lists in different orders. So there is no homomorphism in either direction.

As the discussion illustrates, the correct characterization must be a combination of homomorphism and quotient of a subset, which is exactly what a logical relation provides. We state this as the following proposition.

Proposition 8.5.1 Implementations $\mathcal{A}$ and $\mathcal{B}$ for signature Σ with natural number multisets are observationally equivalent with respect to the natural numbers iff there is a logical relation $\mathcal{R} \subseteq \mathcal{A} \times \mathcal{B}$ such that R^{nat} is the identity relation on the natural numbers.

We may derive Proposition 8.5.1 as a corollary of Theorem 8.5.4, which is proved in the next section. In general, when implementations $\mathcal{A}$ and $\mathcal{B}$ are observationally equivalent, there may be more than one logical relation $\mathcal{R} \subseteq \mathcal{A} \times \mathcal{B}$ with R^{nat} the identity relation on the natural numbers.

Exercise 8.5.2 If we choose basic operations that treat integers as booleans, then we have less flexibility in reimplementing integers than if integers and booleans were separate types. To make this precise, consider the $\lambda^{\rightarrow}$ signature with

$$0, 1 \colon int$$

$$+, -, Eq? \colon int \rightarrow int \rightarrow int$$

$$cond \colon int \rightarrow int \rightarrow int \rightarrow int$$

so that, writing `if ... then ... else ...` for *cond* as usual, we have the implied typing rule

$$\frac{M \colon int,\ N \colon int,\ P \colon int}{\texttt{if}\ M\ \texttt{then}\ N\ \texttt{else}\ P \colon int}$$

Describe two implementations (algebras)

$$\mathcal{A} = \langle A^{int}, 0, 1, +, -, Eq?^{\mathcal{A}}, cond^{\mathcal{A}} \rangle$$

$$\mathcal{B} = \langle B^{int}, 0, 1, +, -, Eq?^{\mathcal{B}}, cond^{\mathcal{B}} \rangle$$

that both interpret $0, 1, +, -$ in the usual way, interpret $\texttt{if}\ Eq?\,u\,v\ \texttt{then}\ x\ \texttt{else}\ y$ as x when u, v are equal and y when they are not, yet give different positive integer values to some integer expression without variables. This is similar to the situation for C [KR78], where integers, booleans and pointers are all given the same type. Although C is a typed programming language (with some type checks omitted in most implementations), even programs that do not take advantages of type loopholes such as type casts are more implementation dependent than would be the case if integers, booleans and pointers were separate types.

Exercise 8.5.3 Let $\mathcal{A}_0$ and $\mathcal{B}_0$ be multisorted algebras

$$\mathcal{A}_0 = \langle A^{nat}, A^s, 0, 1, +, empty^{\mathcal{A}}, insert^{\mathcal{A}}, count^{\mathcal{A}} \rangle$$

$$\mathcal{B}_0 = \langle B^{nat}, B^s, 0, 1, +, empty^{\mathcal{B}}, insert^{\mathcal{B}}, count^{\mathcal{B}} \rangle$$

for natural numbers and multisets, with $A^{nat} = B^{nat} = \mathcal{N}$ and A^s derived from B^s by adding a single multiset element a with the property

$$insert\ x\ a = a \quad \text{for all } x \in \mathcal{N}.$$

Let $\mathcal{A}$ and $\mathcal{B}$ be the lambda models defined from $\mathcal{A}_0$ and $\mathcal{B}_0$ by letting $A^{\sigma \rightarrow \tau}$ be all total functions from A^σ to A^τ, and similarly for $B^{\sigma \rightarrow \tau}$. Describe a logical relation $\mathcal{R} \subseteq \mathcal{A} \times \mathcal{B}$ with R^{nat} the identity relation. Is there more than one such relation? Explain.

8.5.3 General Representation Independence

We may generalize Proposition 8.5.1, stated for natural numbers and multisets, to any other data type, or collection of related data types. However, there are two aspects of natural numbers and multisets that are essential to the proposition as stated. The first is that all functions are first-order, which means that none of the function constants associated with natural numbers or multisets take function arguments. This is important, since characterizing observational equivalence of implementations becomes much more complicated with higher-order function constants, as illustrated in Exercise 8.5.6. The second factor is that we need a closed term naming each natural number (*i.e.*, each element of observable type). The general situation is summarized in the following theorem about any signature giving a collection of possibly interdependent types and operations.

Theorem 8.5.4 Let Σ be some signature with type constant *nat* and let $\mathcal{A}$ and $\mathcal{B}$ be models, with $A^{nat} = B^{nat} = \mathcal{N}$. If there is a logical relation $\mathcal{R} \subseteq \mathcal{A} \times \mathcal{B}$ with R^{nat} the identity relation on natural numbers, then $\mathcal{A}$ and $\mathcal{B}$ are observationally equivalent. Conversely, if $\mathcal{A}$ and $\mathcal{B}$ are observationally equivalent, Σ provides a closed term for each element of $\mathcal{N}$, and Σ only contains first-order functions, then there is a logical relation $\mathcal{R} \subseteq \mathcal{A} \times \mathcal{B}$ with R^{nat} the identity relation.

Proof The first part of the theorem follows directly from the Basic Lemma (8.2.5). For the proof of the second part, we must construct a logical relation $\mathcal{R} \subseteq \mathcal{A} \times \mathcal{B}$. For each type constant s, we let $R^s \subseteq A^s \times B^s$ be the relation containing pair $\langle a, b\rangle$ iff there is a closed term M of type s whose meaning in $\mathcal{A}$ is a and whose meaning in $\mathcal{B}$ is b. We must show that for any function symbol $f\colon s_1 \times \ldots \times s_k \to s$ from Σ, if $\langle a_i, b_i\rangle \in R^{s}_{i}$ for $i = 1, \ldots, k$, then $\langle f^{\mathcal{A}}(a_1, \ldots, a_k), f^{\mathcal{B}}(b_1, \ldots, b_k)\rangle \in R^s$. This follows easily from the definition of R^s. Since Σ provides a closed term for each element of $\mathcal{N}$, it is easy to see that R^{nat} is the identity relation. ■

Exercise 8.5.5 Let Σ be a $\lambda^{\to}$ signature with type constants $nat, s_1, \ldots, s_k$ and only first-order function symbols. Let $\mathcal{A}$ and $\mathcal{B}$ be Henkin models for Σ with $A^{nat} = B^{nat} = \mathcal{N}$ and assume that every natural number is definable in $\mathcal{A}$ and $\mathcal{B}$ by some expression. Suppose $\mathcal{A}$ and $\mathcal{B}$ are observationally equivalent, let

$$\mathcal{A}_0 = \langle A^{nat}, A^{s_1}, \ldots, A^{s_k}, f_1^{\mathcal{A}}, \ldots f_n^{\mathcal{A}}\rangle$$

be the algebra with the same interpretation of type constants and function symbols as $\mathcal{A}$, and define the algebra $\mathcal{B}_0$ from $\mathcal{B}$ similarly. Let $\sim^s_{\mathcal{A}} \subseteq A^s \times A^s$ be the least transitive relation such that if $\exists b.\, R(a, b) \wedge R(a', b)$ then $a \sim^s_{\mathcal{A}} a'$. Define $\sim^s_{\mathcal{B}} \subseteq B^s \times B^s$ similarly.

(a) Show that $\{\sim^s_A\}$ is a partial congruence relation on $\mathcal{A}$, as defined in Exercise 3.4.27. (You need not repeat the argument for $\{\sim^s_B\}$.)

(b) Show that the two partial quotients $\mathcal{A}_0/\sim_A$ and $\mathcal{B}_0/\sim_B$ are isomorphic.

(c) Show that $\sim^{nat}_A$ and $\sim^{nat}_B$ are both the identity relation on the natural numbers.

Exercise 8.5.6 Let Σ be a $\lambda^{\rightarrow}$ signature with type constant *nat* and with term constants $0, 1, 2, 3, \ldots : nat$, $+ : nat \rightarrow nat \rightarrow nat$ and and $f : (nat \rightarrow nat) \rightarrow nat$. Let $\mathcal{A}$ be the full classical hierarchy over $A^{nat} = \mathcal{N}$ with $0, 1, 2, 3, \ldots$ and $+$ interpreted in the standard way and the interpretation of f to be determined. Let $\mathcal{B}$ be the same as $\mathcal{A}$, except possibly for the interpretation of f. Show that we can choose $f^{\mathcal{A}}$ and $f^{\mathcal{B}}$ so that $\mathcal{A}$ and $\mathcal{B}$ are observationally equivalent, but there is no logical relation of the form described in Theorem 8.5.4, as follows:

(a) Assume we choose $f^{\mathcal{A}}$ so that for all computable $g \in A^{nat \rightarrow nat}$ we have $f^{\mathcal{A}}(g) = 0$. Prove that for every term $x_1 : nat, \ldots, x_k : nat \triangleright M : nat$ over Σ, the meaning of M is a computable function of the values of $x_1, \ldots, x_k$. (*Hint:* Use induction on terms given by the grammar $M \ ::= \ x \mid 0 \mid \ldots \mid M + M \mid f(\lambda x : nat.\, M)$.)

(b) Show that if both $f^{\mathcal{A}}$ and $f^{\mathcal{B}}$ are interpreted as explained in (a), then $\mathcal{A}$ and $\mathcal{B}$ are observationally equivalent.

(c) Show that there is a choice for $f^{\mathcal{A}}$ and $f^{\mathcal{B}}$ so that $\mathcal{A}$ and $\mathcal{B}$ are observationally equivalent but any possible logical relation $\mathcal{R} \subseteq \mathcal{A} \times \mathcal{B}$ with R^{nat} the identity fails to relate $f^{\mathcal{A}}$ and $f^{\mathcal{B}}$.

8.6 Generalizations of Logical Relations

8.6.1 Introduction

We have seen that logical relations are useful for proving a variety of theorems about typed lambda calculus and for carrying out certain model-theoretic constructions. One reason to consider variations on the definition used so far in this chapter is that for languages with function constants, we need methods for constructing logical relations that respect the constants. An important example is a fixed-point constant interpreted over CPOs as the least-fixed point operator. Since the fixed-point constants are interpreted systematically, we may develop a specialized version of logical relations over CPOs that are guaranteed to respect fixed-point operators. We will see that a class of directed-complete relations serve this purpose. Another reason to generalize the definition is that it only applies to Henkin models or applicative structures, but not arbitrary CCCs. There are other forms of models, such as Kripke lambda models, where it is useful to have a form of logical relation. Therefore, we would like some general notion of "logical relation over a cartesian closed category" that would give us directed-complete and Kripke logical relations as special cases.

In the general theory we develop in this section, we form "logical relations" over a cartesian closed category $\mathbf{C}$ using a functor $\mathbf{F}$ into another category $\mathbf{C}'$. There are two reasons for the functor $\mathbf{F} : \mathbf{C} \to \mathbf{C}'$. The first is that the categorical structure of $\mathbf{C}'$ affects the kind of relation we obtain. For example, if we form relations using the functor $|\cdot| : Cpo \to Set$ explained below, then we obtain standard logical relations over CPOs. However, if we form relations using a particular functor $\mathbf{F} : Cpo \to Cpo$, then the CPO structure on the target category forces our relations to be closed under limits of directed sets. This gives us the directed-complete relations. The second reason we use a functor from the category $\mathbf{C}$ of interest to some auxiliary category $\mathbf{C}'$ is that we need to be able to do certain operations on relations (or subsets, in the unary case). If $\mathbf{C}$ does not have sufficient structure, then we must construct our relations or subsets of objects of $\mathbf{C}$ in another category. The kind of categorical structure we need is that $\mathbf{C}'$ must have equalizers (see Exercises 7.2.14 and 7.4.5).

The construction of "categorical logical relations" is motivated in Section 8.6.2, where we describe directed-complete relations over CPOs, a natural form of Kripke logical relation and show a brief glimpse of their applications. The main mathematical tool is the category-theoretic method of *sconing,* described in Section 8.6.3. In a sense, the sconing construction gives a mathematical explanation for the definition of logical relation. More specifically, the definition in Section 8.2.1 appears to come out of thin air. We can see, from the list of applications of the Basic Lemma, that the definition is useful. However, it is not at all clear why this definition serves this purpose, or whether another definition would serve equally well. What sconing shows is that if we begin with a category $\mathbf{C}$ and try to construct a category of relations or predicates over $\mathbf{C}$ (using a functor $\mathbf{C} \to \mathbf{C}'$), then the conditions we use in the definition of logical relation are exactly the definitions of product and function objects in the category of relations or predicates. Since products and function objects are unique (up to isomorphism) in any cartesian closed category, any other definition with the same uses would have to be isomorphic, in the categorical setting. This shows that there is something mathematical and canonical about the definition of logical relation. This explanation cannot be given using Henkin models alone, it seems, since the category of predicates or relations over a Henkin model is necessarily cartesian closed, but not necessarily a Henkin model (or well-pointed CCC). An interesting open problem is that we have no categorical explanation for logical relations over applicative structures that are not cartesian closed categories, such as the structure of typed lambda terms. The general development can be extended to polymorphic types, however. In treating polymorphic types, a central role is played by *relators*, which are maps that take objects to objects and relations to relations. The categorical ideas developed here may be used to express relators as functors.

Kripke logical relations over ordinary Henkin models were first used in [Plo80] in a characterization of lambda definability. Kripke logical relations were then adapted to Kripke lambda models in [MM91]. Inclusive relations (as well as strict inclusive relations) are widely used in relating denotational semantics and in proofs by fixed-point induction [MS76, Rey74a, CP92]. This section is based on [MS93], with many of the main ideas developed independently in [MR92]. Some applications may be found in [AJ91, BFSS89, Rey83, Wad89, OT93]. Sconing is described in general in [FS90]; it is called gluing or Freyd cover in [LS86, SS82].

8.6.2 Motivating Examples: Complete Partial Orders and Kripke Models

Logical Relations for Complete Partial Orders

We would like a class of logical relations over CPOs that respect terms with least fixed-point operators. By the Basic Lemma, it suffices to find logical relations that relate fixed-point operators fix_σ for each σ. Since we often construct logical relations by choosing a relation for each type constant, and then extending to all types inductively, we would like a condition that may be applied easily on the interpretation of a type constant. We may achieve this using conditions that resemble the conditions used to define CPOs, completeness and (since we are interested in least fixed-points) pointedness.

A logical predicate $\mathcal{R} \subseteq \mathcal{A}$ over an applicative structure of CPOs is *directed complete,* or *complete* for short, if each R^σ is closed under limits of directed sets, *i.e.*,

if $S \subseteq R^\sigma$ is directed, then $\bigvee S \in R^\sigma$.

A logical predicate $\mathcal{R} \subseteq \mathcal{A}$ over an applicative structure of CPOs is *pointed at type* σ if $R^\sigma(\bot)$. Both conditions extend to binary logical relations by considering $\mathcal{R} \subseteq \mathcal{A} \times \mathcal{B}$ as a unary logical predicate over the product structure $\mathcal{A} \times \mathcal{B}$ with $(A \times B)^\sigma = A^\sigma \times B^\sigma$ the product CPO. In the literature, the term *directed complete* is often used to mean "pointed and directed-complete" since, historically, it has been common to include pointedness in the definition of CPO [MS76, Rey74a].

Lemma 8.6.1 Let $\mathcal{R} \subseteq \mathcal{A} \times \mathcal{B}$ be a logical relation over full continuous hierarchies $\mathcal{A}$ and $\mathcal{B}$. If R^σ and R^τ are complete, then so is $R^{\sigma\to\tau}$. Moreover, if A^τ, B^τ and $R^\tau \subseteq A^\tau \times B^\tau$ are pointed, then $R^{\sigma\to\tau}$ is pointed.

Proof Suppose R^σ and R^τ are complete and let $S \subseteq R^{\sigma\to\tau} \subseteq A^{\sigma\to\tau} \times B^{\sigma\to\tau}$ be a directed set of pairs of continuous functions. We must show that $\bigvee S \in R^{\sigma\to\tau}$, where by Lemma 5.2.2, $\bigvee S = \langle \bigvee S_1, \bigvee S_2 \rangle$, with $S_i = \mathbf{Proj}_i S$.

Let $\langle a, b\rangle \in R^\sigma \subseteq A^\sigma \times B^\sigma$. It suffices to show that $\langle (\bigvee S_1)a, (\bigvee S_2)b\rangle \in R^\tau$. For each $\langle f, g\rangle \in S$, we have $\langle fa, gb\rangle \in R^\tau$. Since $\{\langle fa, gb\rangle \mid \langle f, g\rangle \in S\}$ is easily seen to be directed, we have

$$\bigvee\{\langle fa, gb\rangle \mid \langle f, g\rangle \in S\} \in R^\tau.$$

It follows by Lemmas 5.2.2 and 5.2.10 that this least upper bound is equal to $\langle (\bigvee S_1)a$, $(\bigvee S_2)b\rangle$ and the first part of the lemma follows.

If $R^\tau(\bot, \bot)$, then since $\bot_{\sigma\to\tau} = \lambda x{:}\,\sigma.\ \bot_\tau$, we can easily see that $R^{\sigma\to\tau}(\bot, \bot)$. ∎

An easy argument shows that every complete logical relation which is pointed at the appropriate types preserves least fixed-point operators.

Lemma 8.6.2 Let $\mathcal{R} \subseteq \mathcal{A} \times \mathcal{B}$ be a complete logical relation over full continuous hierarchies $\mathcal{A}$ and $\mathcal{B}$. If A^σ, B^σ and $R^\sigma \subseteq A^\sigma \times B^\sigma$ are pointed, then $R^{(\sigma\to\sigma)\to\sigma}(\mathit{fix}^{\mathcal{A}}_\sigma, \mathit{fix}^{\mathcal{B}}_\sigma)$, where $\mathit{fix}^{\mathcal{A}}_\sigma$ is the least fixed point operator on $A^{\sigma\to\sigma}$, and similarly for $\mathit{fix}^{\mathcal{B}}_\sigma$.

As a consequence, complete logical relations, appropriately pointed, relate the meanings of terms with *fix*.

Proof For simplicity, we prove the unary case, $\mathcal{R} \subseteq \mathcal{A}$; this easily generalizes to n-ary relations using Lemmas 5.2.2 and 5.2.10 as in the proof of Lemma 8.6.1 above.

We must show that, under the conditions of the lemma, if $R^{\sigma\to\sigma}(f)$, then $R^\sigma(\mathit{fix}\ f)$. By hypothesis, $R^\sigma(\bot)$ and hence $R^\sigma(f\ \bot)$. An easy induction shows $R^\sigma(f^n\ \bot)$ for all $n \geq 0$ and so by completeness and $\mathit{fix}\ f = \bigvee\{f^n(\bot)\}$ we have $R^\sigma(\mathit{fix}\ f)$. ∎

It follows from these two lemmas that if we wish to construct a logical relation between CPO models for a signature including *fix* at one or more types, it suffices to construct a complete logical relation, pointed appropriately, and check that it preserves all constants other than *fix*. This is illustrated in the following example, which gives a deceptively simple proof that parallel-or is not definable in PCF (Theorem 2.5.19). The argument is due to Plotkin (see [AC80]), and Sieber [Sie92], independently.

Example 8.6.3 There is a ternary logical relation $\mathcal{R} \subseteq \mathcal{A}_{\text{PCF}} \times \mathcal{A}_{\text{PCF}} \times \mathcal{A}_{\text{PCF}}$ over the CPO model of PCF (given in Section 5.2.5) which demonstrates that parallel-or is not definable. For $b = \mathit{nat}, \mathit{bool}$, we let $R^b(x, y, z)$ iff either $x = y = z$ or at least one of x, y or z is $\bot$ and extend this relation to product and function types inductively. Since each R^b is complete and pointed, so is every R^σ, by Lemma 8.6.1.

To show that $\mathcal{R}$ is a logical relation for PCF, we must check that $R(c, c, c)$ for each constant of the signature. From Lemma 8.6.2, we have $R(\mathit{fix}_\sigma, \mathit{fix}_\sigma, \mathit{fix}_\sigma)$ for each type σ. The remaining constants are $+$, *Eq*? and conditional.

For addition, we must show that if $R^{nat}(x_1, y_1, z_1)$ and $R^{nat}(x_2, y_2, z_2)$, then $R^{nat}(x_1 + x_2, y_1 + y_2, z_1 + z_2)$, where for notational simplicity we write $+$ for the strict extension of addition to $\mathcal{N}_\bot \times \mathcal{N}_\bot$. If any x_i, y_i or z_i is $\bot$, then clearly one of the sums is $\bot$. The remaining case, $x_1 = y_1 = z_1$ and $x_2 = y_2 = z_2$, is immediate. The argument for *Eq*? is identical, since this is also a strict function. The argument for `if ... then ... else ...` is slightly more interesting, and left as Exercise 8.6.10.

Now suppose that parallel-or is definable by a closed term *POR*. By the Basic Lemma, it follows that $R^{(bool \times bool) \to bool}(POR, POR, POR)$. But since $R^{bool}(\mathit{true}, \bot, \mathit{false})$ and $R^{bool}(\bot, \mathit{true}, \mathit{false})$, we must have

$$R^{bool}(POR\,\mathit{true}\,\bot,\ \ POR\,\bot\,\mathit{true},\ \ POR\,\mathit{false}\,\mathit{false}),$$

or $R^{bool}(\mathit{true},\ \mathit{true},\ \mathit{false})$, which is a contradiction. ■

More complicated methods are required for constructing directed-complete logical relations between recursively-defined domains. Some historical references on this topic are [MS76, Rey74a].

Kripke Logical Relations

While Kripke structures are not ordinary applicative structures, it is relatively easy to generalize logical relations to Kripke structures. The reason is that Kripke applicative structures are not only models of typed lambda calculus, but also provide a natural interpretation of logic. (This is the interpretation used in Kripke models of intuitionistic logic). In effect, we apply this interpretation of logic to the sentences used to define logical relations at function or product types. The main ideas for Kripke logical relations over ordinary Henkin models were first outlined in [Plo80], and then adapted to Kripke lambda models in [MM91]. We will show that every lambda theory is the theory of a Kripke quotient of a classical (ordinary Henkin) model, but not every Kripke lambda model is isomorphic to such a model.

Instead of having a relation for each type, we have a relation for each type and possible world, with the main condition quantifying over all possible future worlds. Specifically, a *Kripke logical relation* over Kripke applicative structures $\mathcal{A}$ and $\mathcal{B}$ sharing the same structure $\langle \mathcal{W}, \leq \rangle$ of possible worlds is a family $\mathcal{R} = \{R^\sigma_w\}$ of relations $R^\sigma_w \subseteq A^\sigma_w \times B^\sigma_w$ indexed by types σ and worlds $w \in \mathcal{W}$ satisfying the following three conditions. The first is a "monotonicity" condition

$$R^{\sigma}_{w}(a, b) \text{ implies } R^{\sigma}_{w'}(i^{\sigma}_{w,w'}a, i^{\sigma}_{w,w'}b) \text{ for all } w' \geq w, \qquad (mon)$$

which says that when $w \leq w'$, the relation R^{σ}_{w} is contained in $R^{\sigma}_{w'}$, modulo the transition functions. The second condition

$$R^{\sigma\to\tau}_{w}(f, g) \text{ iff } \forall w' \geq w. \forall a, b.\ R^{\sigma}_{w'}(a, b) \text{ implies } R^{\tau}_{w'}((i^{\sigma\to\tau}_{w,w'} f)a, (i^{\sigma\to\tau}_{w,w'} g)b), \qquad (compre)$$

called "comprehension," says that the relation $R^{\sigma\to\tau}_{w}$ contains all functions mapping related arguments to related results. The third condition is that constants of the language must be related at every possible world. This completes the definition.

It is easy to show that if (*mon*) holds for each type constant, it holds for all types (Exercise 8.6.11.) We say environments η_a, η_b are *related by $\mathcal{R}$ on Γ at w* if $R^{\tau}_{w}(\eta_a x w, \eta_b x w)$ for all $x\colon\tau$ in Γ. The following Basic Lemma is proved by induction on terms in Exercise 8.6.12.

Lemma 8.6.4 (Basic Lemma for Kripke logical relations) If $\mathcal{R} \subseteq \mathcal{A} \times \mathcal{B}$ is a Kripke logical relation over models $\mathcal{A}$ and $\mathcal{B}$, and environments η_a, η_b are related by $\mathcal{R}$ on Γ at w, then for every term $\Gamma \triangleright M\colon\sigma$, we have $R^{\sigma}_{w}(\mathcal{A}[\![\Gamma \triangleright M\colon\sigma]\!]\eta_a w, \mathcal{B}[\![\Gamma \triangleright M\colon\sigma]\!]\eta_b w)$

We can form quotients of Kripke lambda models using Kripke partial equivalence relations. Like logical partial equivalence relations, a *Kripke logical partial equivalence relation* $\mathcal{R} \subseteq \mathcal{A} \times \mathcal{A}$ is a Kripke logical relation such that each R^{σ}_{w} is symmetric and transitive. We will abbreviate the cumbersome phrase "Kripke logical partial equivalence relation" to klper. The following lemma, proved as Exercise 8.6.13, shows that klper's may be constructed by choosing relations at base types.

Lemma 8.6.5 Let $\mathcal{R} \subseteq \mathcal{A} \times \mathcal{A}$ be a Kripke logical relation. If each R^{c}_{w} is symmetric and transitive, for each base type c and world $w \in \mathcal{W}$, then every R^{σ}_{w} is symmetric and transitive.

If

$$\mathcal{A} = \langle \mathrm{W}, \leq, \{A^{\sigma}_{w}\}, \{\mathbf{App}^{\sigma,\tau}_{w}\}, \{i^{\sigma}_{w,w'}\}, Const\rangle$$

is a Kripke applicative structure and $\mathcal{R} \subseteq \mathcal{A} \times \mathcal{A}$ is a klper, then the *quotient applicative structure*

$$\mathcal{A}/\mathcal{R} = \langle \mathcal{W}, \leq, \{A^{\sigma}_{w}/R^{\sigma}_{w}\}, \{App^{\sigma,\tau}_{w}/\mathcal{R}\}, \{i^{\sigma}_{w,w'}/\mathcal{R}\}\rangle$$

is defined as follows:

$A_w^\sigma / R_w^\sigma = \{[a]_{\mathcal{R}} \mid R_w^\sigma(a, a)\}$, where $[a]_{\mathcal{R}}$ is the *equivalence* class

$[a]_{\mathcal{R}} = \{a' \in A_w^\sigma \mid R_w^\sigma(a, a')\}$

$(App_w^{\sigma,\tau} / \mathcal{R})\ [a]_{\mathcal{R}}\ [b]_{\mathcal{R}} = [App_w^{\sigma,\tau}\ a\ b]_{\mathcal{R}}$

$(i_{w,w'}^\sigma / \mathcal{R})\ [a]_{\mathcal{R}} = [i_{w,w'}^\sigma\ a]_{\mathcal{R}}$

It is a simple exercise, similar to the proof of Lemma 8.2.24, to verify that the quotient structure is well-defined, and a Kripke applicative structure.

Lemma 8.6.6 If $\mathcal{R} \subseteq \mathcal{A} \times \mathcal{A}$ is a Kripke partial equivalence relation over Kripke applicative structure $\mathcal{A}$, then $\mathcal{A}/\mathcal{R}$ satisfies the Kripke extensionality condition *(ext)*.

A straightforward induction on terms similar to the proof of Lemma 8.2.26, may be used to prove the following "quotient model" theorem.

Lemma 8.6.7 If $\mathcal{R} \subseteq \mathcal{A} \times \mathcal{A}$ is a klper over Kripke lambda *model* $\mathcal{A}$, then $\mathcal{A}/\mathcal{R}$ is a Kripke lambda model such that for every environment η with $R_w^\tau(\eta x w, \eta x w)$ for all $x\colon \tau$ in Γ, we have

$$(\mathcal{A}/\mathcal{R})[\![\Gamma \triangleright M\colon \sigma]\!]\eta_{\mathcal{R}} w = [\,\mathcal{A}[\![\Gamma \triangleright M\colon \sigma]\!]\eta w\,]_{\mathcal{R}},$$

where the environment $\eta_{\mathcal{R}}$ for $\mathcal{A}/\mathcal{R}$ is defined by taking $\eta_{\mathcal{R}} x w = [\eta x w]_{\mathcal{R}}$ for all x and w.

In short, the meaning of a term M in the quotient model $\mathcal{A}/\mathcal{R}$ is the equivalence class of the meaning of M in $\mathcal{A}$.

We now consider Kripke logical relations over classical applicative structures. The simplest way to do this is to regard classical structures as a special case of Kripke structures, as illustrated in Exercise 7.3.5. We say $\mathcal{R} = \{R_w^\sigma\}$ is a *Kripke logical relation over classical applicative structures* $\mathcal{A}$ and $\mathcal{B}$ if $\mathcal{R}$ is a Kripke logical relation over the Kripke models $\mathcal{A}^{\mathcal{W}}$ and $\mathcal{B}^{\mathcal{W}}$ defined in Exercise 7.3.5. By Lemma 8.6.7, we can produce Kripke models by taking Kripke quotients of classical models. This gives us a fairly simple class of models with intuitionistic properties. In fact, we can show that every lambda theory is the theory of a model of this form.

Theorem 8.6.8 Let $\mathcal{E}$ be any set of equations closed under $\vdash$. There exists an ordinary (classical) Henkin model $\mathcal{A}$ and a Kripke partial equivalence relation $\mathcal{R} \subseteq \mathcal{A} \times \mathcal{A}$ such that $\mathcal{A}/\mathcal{R}$ satisfies precisely those equations that belong to $\mathcal{E}$.

Proof Let $\mathcal{B}$ be the Kripke term model for $\mathcal{E}$, as in the proof of Theorem 7.3.7. Since $\mathcal{B}$ satisfies precisely the equations in $\mathcal{E}$, we will show that $\mathcal{B}$ is isomorphic to a Kripke quotient of the classical term model $\mathcal{A}$ of β, η-conversion, which is summarized in the proof of Theorem 4.5.22.

For the specific theory of β, η-conversion, the classical term model $\mathcal{A}$ is constructed by choosing an infinite set $\mathcal{H}$ of variable typings $x: \sigma$ with two properties. There must be infinitely many variables of each type and no variable may appear twice. We define the equivalence class $[M]$ of M by

$$[M] = \{N \mid \vdash \Gamma \triangleright M = N: \tau, \text{ some finite } \Gamma \subseteq \mathcal{H}\}$$

and let A^τ be the collection of all $[M]$ with $\Gamma \triangleright M: \tau$ for some $\Gamma \subseteq \mathcal{H}$. This gives us an applicative structure, with

$$\mathbf{App}\,[M]\,[N] = [MN].$$

As clarified in Section 8.3.1, this is a model with the meaning of a term obtained by substitution.

Using $\mathcal{E}$, we can define a klper $\mathcal{R}$ over $\mathcal{A}$. Our goal is to define $\mathcal{R}$ so that the quotient $\mathcal{A}/\mathcal{R}$ is isomorphic to the Kripke term model $\mathcal{B}$. Since the possible worlds of $\mathcal{B}$ are type assignments, we will use type assignments as the worlds of $\mathcal{R}$.

For each σ and Γ, we define the relation $R^\sigma_\Gamma \subseteq A^\sigma \times A^\sigma$ by

$$R^\sigma_\Gamma([M], [N]) \text{ iff } \mathcal{E} \vdash \Gamma \triangleright M^0 = N^0: \sigma,$$

where M^0 is the β, η-normal form of M, and similarly for N^0. This is well defined since each $[M]$ has a unique β, η-normal form. Since provable equality is symmetric and transitive with respect to any Γ, $\mathcal{R}$ is clearly a partial equivalence relation. (In general, R^σ_Γ will not be reflexive on B^σ, since some M^0 may require variables not in in Γ.) By rule *(add var)*, $\mathcal{R}$ satisfies the monotonicity condition *(mon)*. The proof that $\mathcal{R}$ satisfies *(compre)* is similar to the proof that Kripke term models are extensional.

It remains easy to show that $\mathcal{B}$ is isomorphic to $\mathcal{A}/\mathcal{R}$. Every A^σ/R^σ_Γ equivalence class is characterized by a collection of normal forms that are all well-typed in Γ and provably equal using $\mathcal{E}$. Thus for each A^σ/R^σ_Γ equivalence class $[M]/R^\sigma_\Gamma$, there is a unique $[\Gamma \triangleright M^0: \sigma] \in B^\sigma_\Gamma$. Conversely, all of the β, η-normal forms in any $[\Gamma \triangleright M^0: \sigma]$ will be equivalent modulo R^σ_Γ, and so we have a straightforward bijection between B^σ and A^σ/R^σ_Γ. It is easy to show that application behaves appropriately, and so we have an isomorphism between $\mathcal{A}$ and $\mathcal{B}/\mathcal{R}$. This proves the theorem. ∎

However, we can show that some Kripke lambda models are not isomorphic to any Kripke quotient of any classical applicative structure.

Theorem 8.6.9 There is a Kripke lambda model $\mathcal{B}$ which is not isomorphic to $\mathcal{A}/\mathcal{R}$, for any classical applicative structure $\mathcal{A}$ and Kripke partial equivalence relation $\mathcal{R}$. In fact, $\mathcal{B}$ is distinguished from all $\mathcal{A}/\mathcal{R}$ by a formula of predicate logic.

Proof The main idea is relatively simple. Suppose $\mathcal{R} \subseteq \mathcal{A} \times \mathcal{A}$ is a Kripke logical partial equivalence relation over a classical applicative structure, and suppose we have two type constants a and b with R^a_w empty at all possible worlds. Then $R^{a\to b}_w(f, g)$ for all worlds w and all $f, g \in A^{a\to b}$, since the implication

$R^a_w(x, y)$ implies $R^b_w(\mathbf{App}\,fx, \mathbf{App}\,gy)$

holds vacuously. In particular, if A^b/R^b is non-empty at any world, so that $A^{a\to b}$ is non-empty, then $A^{a\to b}/R^{a\to b}$ is nonempty at all possible worlds. Those familiar with the intuitionistic interpretation of predicate logic in Kripke structures will easily see that this property of Kripke quotients of classical structures can be expressed by a formula

- if $empty(a)$ and $\neg empty(a \to b)$, then $inhabited(a \to b)$,

where $inhabited(\tau) \equiv (\exists x\colon \tau.x = x)$ and $empty(\tau) \equiv \neg inhabited(\tau)$.

To show that this property fails in some models, we consider the following Kripke lambda model $\mathcal{B}$ defined by:

- $\mathcal{W}$ is the poset with two elements $0 < 1$,
- $\mathcal{B}$ at 1 is the full classical hierarchy over $B^a = \emptyset$ and $B^b = \mathcal{N}$,
- $\mathcal{B}$ at 0 is the set of lambda-definable elements from $\mathcal{B}$ at 1, *i.e.*, the applicative structure whose elements are interpretations of closed λ-terms,
- the transition function $i_{0,1}$ is the inclusion.

Then $A^{a\to b}_1$ contains exactly one element (the empty function), and therefore $\mathcal{B}$ satisfies $\neg empty(a \to b)$; but $A^{a\to b}_0$ is empty (because there are no closed terms of that type), so $\mathcal{B}$ does not satisfy $inhabited(a \to b)$. ∎

Exercise 8.6.10 Show that for the logical relation $\mathcal{R} \subseteq \mathcal{A}_{\text{PCF}} \times \mathcal{A}_{\text{PCF}} \times \mathcal{A}_{\text{PCF}}$ given in Example 8.6.3, if one of $x, y, z \in A^\sigma$ is $\bot_\sigma$, then $R^\sigma(x, y, z)$. Use this to show that

$R^{(bool\times\sigma\times\sigma)\to\sigma}(cond, cond, cond)$.

where $cond\,x\,y\,z\ =\ \texttt{if}\ x\ \texttt{then}\ y\ \texttt{else}\ z$.

Exercise 8.6.11 Let $\mathcal{R} \subseteq \mathcal{A} \times \mathcal{B}$ be a family $\mathcal{R} = \{R^\sigma_w\}$ of relations $R^\sigma_w \subseteq A^\sigma_w \times B^\sigma_w$ indexed by types σ and worlds $w \in \mathcal{W}$ of Kripke models $\mathcal{A}$ and $\mathcal{B}$ satisfying (mon) for type constants only, and (*compre*) and preserving all constants. Show that $\mathcal{R}$ is a Kripke logical relation by showing that $\mathcal{A}$ satisfies (*mon*) at all types.

Exercise 8.6.12 Prove the Basic Lemma for Kripke logical relations by induction on terms.

Exercise 8.6.13 Prove Lemma 8.6.5 by induction on types.

8.6.3 Sconing and Relations

As explained in Section 8.6.1, we develop a general form of logical relation over a category $\mathbf{C}$ using a functor $\mathbf{F}: \mathbf{C} \longrightarrow \mathbf{C}'$, forming the relations or predicates in $\mathbf{C}'$ in some way. Thinking only about the unary case, with predicates, for the moment, we can see that $\mathbf{C}'$ must have a "set-like" character so that we can identify subsets easily and do certain constructions on subsets. For concreteness, we begin by choosing a specific functor into $\mathcal{S}et$, definable from any $\mathbf{C}$ with a terminal object. This simplifies the problem of subset operations and lets us focus on the relationship between the category $\mathbf{C}$ of interest and the category of subsets of $\mathbf{C}$. We generalize to other categories in Section 8.6.5.

Assuming that $\mathbf{C}$ is a category with a terminal object *unit*, we will use the functor $|\cdot|$ from $\mathbf{C}$ to $\mathcal{S}et$ which maps each object to its set of *global elements*. This functor is defined by

$|A|$ = the set of all morphisms $unit \longrightarrow A$ in $\mathbf{C}$

$|x|$ = the function $|A| \longrightarrow |A'|$ defined by composition according to

the diagram below, for any morphism $x: A \longrightarrow A'$ in $\mathbf{C}$

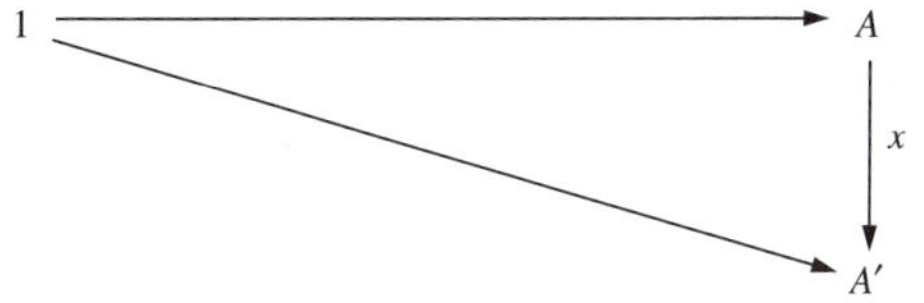

It is not hard to see that this functor preserves products up to isomorphism, which means that $|A \times B| \cong |A| \times |B|$; see Exercise 8.6.16. The functor also preserves equalizers up to isomorphism, but we will not need this fact. However, equalizers will come into play in the general construction. (Some properties of equalizers are given in Exercise 7.4.5.)

The category $\hat{\mathbf{C}}$, called the *scone of* $\mathbf{C}$, is defined as follows. Intuitively, the scone of $\mathbf{C}$ is the category of "set preimages" of objects of $\mathbf{C}$, where "set preimages" are determined after applying the functor $|\cdot|$ into $\mathcal{S}et$. We will specialize this construction below from "preimages" to subsets. The objects of $\hat{\mathbf{C}}$ are triples $\langle S, f, A\rangle$, where S is a set, A is an object of $\mathbf{C}$, and $f: S \longrightarrow |A|$ is a function (in $\mathcal{S}et$). The morphisms $\langle S, f, A\rangle \longrightarrow \langle S', f', A'\rangle$ in $\hat{\mathbf{C}}$ are pairs $\langle t, x\rangle$, where $t: S \longrightarrow S'$ is a function and $x: A \longrightarrow A'$ is a morphism in $\mathbf{C}$ such that:

$$\begin{array}{ccc} S & \xrightarrow{\quad t \quad} & S' \\ {\scriptstyle f}\downarrow & & \downarrow{\scriptstyle f'} \\ |A| & \xrightarrow[\quad |x| \quad]{} & |A'| \end{array}$$

The reader may easily check that $\langle |unit|, id, unit\rangle$ is a terminal object in $\hat{\mathbf{C}}$. There is a canonical "forgetful" functor $\pi: \hat{\mathbf{C}} \longrightarrow \mathbf{C}$ which takes $\langle S, f, A\rangle$ to A and $\langle t, x\rangle$ to x. Category theorists will recognize the scone as a special case of a *comma category*, namely $\hat{\mathbf{C}} = (id \downarrow |\cdot|)$, where *id* is the identity functor on $\mathcal{S}et$ (see Exercise 7.2.25). It is common to overload notation and use the symbol $\mathcal{S}et$ for the identity functor from sets to sets (and similarly for other categories). With this convention, we may write $\hat{\mathbf{C}} = (\mathcal{S}et \downarrow |\cdot|)$.

A remarkable feature of *sconing* in general is that it preserves almost any additional categorical structure that $\mathbf{C}$ might have. Since we are interested in cartesian closed structure, we show that sconing preserves terminal object, products and function objects (exponentials).

Lemma 8.6.14 If $\mathbf{C}$ is a cartesian closed category, then $\hat{\mathbf{C}}$ is cartesian closed and the canonical functor $\pi: \hat{\mathbf{C}} \longrightarrow \mathbf{C}$ is a cartesian closed functor. ■

Proof Let $X = \langle S, f, A\rangle$ and $Y = \langle S', f', A'\rangle$ be objects of $\hat{\mathbf{C}}$. Then the object

$$X \times Y = \langle S \times S', f \times f', A \times A'\rangle,$$

is a product of X and Y, where $(f \times f')\langle s, s'\rangle = \langle f(s), f'(s')\rangle$. A function object of X and Y is given by

$$X \to Y = \langle M, h, A \to A'\rangle,$$

where M is the set of morphisms $X \longrightarrow Y$ in $\hat{\mathbf{C}}$ and $h(\langle t, x\rangle): unit \longrightarrow A \to A'$ is the morphism in $\mathbf{C}$ obtained from $x: A \longrightarrow A'$ by currying, *i.e.*, $h(\langle t, x\rangle) = \mathbf{Curry}\,x$. We leave it to the reader, in Exercise 8.6.17, to check that $\pi: \hat{\mathbf{C}} \longrightarrow \mathbf{C}$ is a cartesian closed functor.
■

In order to make a connection with logical predicates or relations, we will be interested in a subcategory $\tilde{\mathbf{C}}$ of the scone which we call the *subscone* of $\mathbf{C}$. The objects of the subscone $\tilde{\mathbf{C}}$ are the triples $\langle S, f, A\rangle$ with $f: S \hookrightarrow |A|$ an inclusion of sets. It is possible to let $f: S \hookrightarrow |A|$ be any one-to-one map. But, since we are really more interested in the map $|x|: |A| \longrightarrow |A'|$ in the diagram above than $|t|: S \longrightarrow S'$, for reasons that will become clear, we will assume that if $\langle S, f, A\rangle$ is an object of $\tilde{\mathbf{C}}$, then $S \subseteq |A|$ is an ordinary set-theoretic subset and $f: S \to |A|$ is the identity map sending elements of S into the larger set $|A|$. The morphisms $\langle S, f, A\rangle \longrightarrow \langle S', f', A'\rangle$ of $\tilde{\mathbf{C}}$ are the same as for $\hat{\mathbf{C}}$, so $\tilde{\mathbf{C}}$ is a *full* subcategory of $\hat{\mathbf{C}}$. If $\langle t, x\rangle$ is a morphism from $\langle S, f, A\rangle$ to $\langle S', f', A'\rangle$ in $\tilde{\mathbf{C}}$, then the set function $t: S \longrightarrow S'$ is uniquely determined by x and S. Specifically, t is the restriction of $|x|: |A| \longrightarrow |A'|$ to the subset $S \subseteq |A|$.

The subcategory $\tilde{\mathbf{C}}$ inherits the cartesian closed structure of $\hat{\mathbf{C}}$, up to isomorphism. More precisely, $\tilde{\mathbf{C}}$ is a subcategory of $\hat{\mathbf{C}}$ that is also cartesian closed. However, given two objects, X and Y, from $\tilde{\mathbf{C}}$, the function object $X \to Y = \langle M, h, A \to A'\rangle$ given in the proof of Lemma 8.6.14 is not an object of $\tilde{\mathbf{C}}$ since M is not a subset of $|A \to A'|$. However, the function object for X and Y in $\tilde{\mathbf{C}}$ is isomorphic to the function object in $\hat{\mathbf{C}}$. Instead of describing function objects in $\tilde{\mathbf{C}}$ directly for arbitrary $\mathbf{C}$, we will take this up in the illustrative special case that $\mathbf{C}$ is a product of two CCCs.

Let us suppose we have a product category $\mathbf{C} = \mathbf{A} \times \mathbf{B}$, where both categories $\mathbf{A}$ and $\mathbf{B}$ have a terminal object. Recall that the objects of $\mathbf{A} \times \mathbf{B}$ are ordered pairs of objects from $\mathbf{A}$ and $\mathbf{B}$ and the morphisms $\langle A, B\rangle \longrightarrow \langle A', B'\rangle$ are pairs $\langle x, y\rangle$, where $x: A \longrightarrow A'$ is a morphism in $\mathbf{A}$ and $y: B \longrightarrow B'$ is a morphism in $\mathbf{B}$. It is easy to see that when $\mathbf{A}$ and $\mathbf{B}$ are cartesian closed, so is $\mathbf{A} \times \mathbf{B}$, with coordinate-wise cartesian closed structure. For example, a terminal object of $\mathbf{A} \times \mathbf{B}$ is $\langle unit, unit\rangle$. It is easy to see that $|\langle A, B\rangle|_{\mathbf{C}} = |A|_{\mathbf{A}} \times |B|_{\mathbf{B}}$, where the cartesian product of $|A|_{\mathbf{A}}$ and $|B|_{\mathbf{B}}$ is taken in sets. We will often omit the subscripts from various $| \cdot |$'s, since these are generally clear from context.

The objects of the scone $\widehat{\mathbf{A}\times\mathbf{B}}$ may be described as tuples $\langle S, f, g, A, B\rangle$, with S a set, A an object in $\mathbf{A}$, B an object in $\mathbf{B}$, and f and g functions that form a so-called *span:*

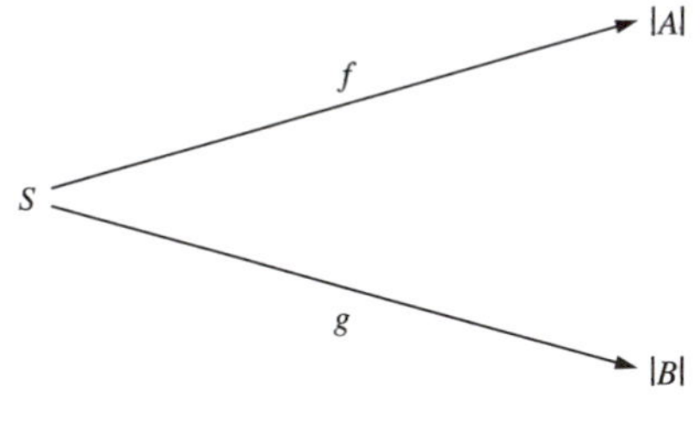

The morphisms $\langle S, f, g, A, B\rangle \longrightarrow \langle S', f', g', A', B'\rangle$ in $\widehat{\mathbf{A}\times\mathbf{B}}$ may be described as tuples $\langle t, x, y\rangle$, with $x: A \longrightarrow A'$ a morphism in $\mathbf{A}$, $y: B \longrightarrow B'$ a morphism in $\mathbf{B}$, and $t: S \longrightarrow S'$ a function such that:

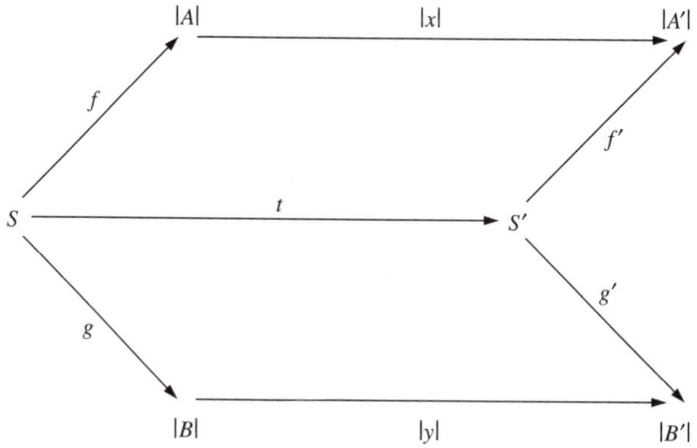

Let us now look at the subcategory $\widetilde{\mathbf{A}\times\mathbf{B}}$ of $\widehat{\mathbf{A}\times\mathbf{B}}$. Working through the definition of $\widetilde{\mathbf{A}\times\mathbf{B}}$, we may regard the objects of this subcategory as tuples $\langle S, f, g, A, B\rangle$, where f and g provide an inclusion $S \hookrightarrow |A| \times |B|$. Since S, f and g determine a subset of $|A| \times |B|$, as before, an object $\langle S, f, g, A, B\rangle$ may be expressed more simply as a triple $\langle S, A, B\rangle$ with S an ordinary binary relation on $|A| \times |B|$. For any morphisms $\langle t, x, y\rangle$ between objects of $\widetilde{\mathbf{A}\times\mathbf{B}}$, the set map t is again uniquely determined by $\mathbf{A}$ and $\mathbf{B}$ maps x and y and the relation S. Specifically, t is the restriction of the product map $|x| \times |y|$ to the subset S. This allows us to simply write morphisms as pairs, instead of triples. It is easy to see that $\langle x, y\rangle$ forms a morphism from $\langle S, A, B\rangle$ to $\langle S', A', B'\rangle$ exactly if, for all morphisms $a\colon \mathit{unit} \longrightarrow A$ in $\mathbf{A}$ and $b\colon \mathit{unit} \longrightarrow B$ in $\mathbf{B}$, we have

$a\ S\ b$ implies $(x \circ a)\ S'\ (y \circ b)$,

where we use relational notation $a\ S\ b$ to indicate that S relates a to b , and similarly for S'.

With some additional notation, we can express the definition of morphism in $\widetilde{\mathbf{A}\times\mathbf{B}}$ as a form of "commuting square." To begin with, let us write $S\colon |A| \longrightarrow\!\!\!\!\!\times\ |B|$ to indicate that S is a binary relation on $|A| \times |B|$. The definition of morphism now has an appealing diagrammatic presentation as a pair $\langle x, y\rangle$ satisfying

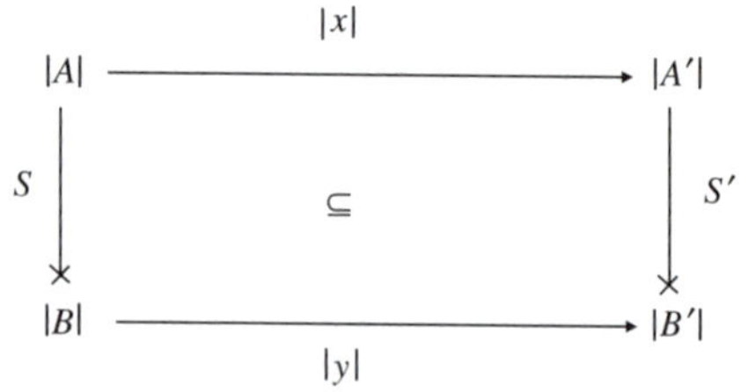

where "$\subseteq$" in this diagram means that the relation $|y| \circ S$ is included in the relation $S' \circ |x|$.

It is instructive to write out the function objects (exponentials) in the cartesian closed category $\widetilde{\mathbf{A}\times\mathbf{B}}$. The function object $\langle S, A, B\rangle \to \langle S', A', B'\rangle$ may be written $\langle R, A \to A', B \to B'\rangle$, where $R\colon |A \to A'| \longrightarrow\!\!\!\!\!\times\ |B \to B'|$ is the binary relation such that for all morphisms $e\colon unit \longrightarrow A \to A'$ in $\mathbf{A}$ and $d\colon unit \longrightarrow B \to B'$ in $\mathbf{B}$, we have

$$e\ R\ d \text{ iff } a\ S\ b \text{ implies } \mathbf{App} \circ \langle e, a\rangle\ S'\ \mathbf{App} \circ \langle d, b\rangle$$

$$\text{for all } a\colon unit \longrightarrow A \text{ in } \mathbf{A},\ b\colon unit \longrightarrow B \text{ in } \mathbf{B}.$$

We may also express products in a similar fashion. As in the general case, the subscone $\tilde{\mathbf{C}}$ is a CCC and a full subcategory of $\hat{\mathbf{C}}$, and the restriction of the forgetful functor $\hat{\mathbf{C}} \longrightarrow \mathbf{C}$ to $\tilde{\mathbf{C}}$ is also a cartesian closed functor. The main properties of $\widetilde{\mathbf{A}\times\mathbf{B}}$ are summarized in the following proposition, whose proof is left as Exercise 8.6.18.

Proposition 8.6.15 Let $\mathbf{C} = \mathbf{A} \times \mathbf{B}$ be the cartesian product of two CCCs. Then $\tilde{\mathbf{C}}$ is a cartesian closed category, with canonical functor $\tilde{\mathbf{C}} \longrightarrow \mathbf{C}$ a cartesian closed functor. Products and function objects in $\tilde{\mathbf{C}}$ are given by

$$\langle S, A, B\rangle \times \langle S', A', B'\rangle = \langle S \times S', A \times A', B \times B'\rangle,$$

$$\langle S, A, B\rangle \to \langle S', A', B'\rangle = \langle S \to S', A \to A', B \to B'\rangle,$$

where the relations $S \times S'$ and $S \to S'$ have the following characterizations:

$$a\ (S \times S')\ b \text{ iff } (\mathbf{Proj}_1 \circ a)\ S\ (\mathbf{Proj}_1 \circ b) \text{ and } (\mathbf{Proj}_2 \circ a)\ S'\ (\mathbf{Proj}_2 \circ b)$$

$$e\ (S \to S')\ d \text{ iff } \forall a\colon unit \longrightarrow A.\, \forall b\colon unit \longrightarrow B.\ a\ S\ b \text{ implies } \mathbf{App} \circ \langle e, a\rangle\ S'\ \mathbf{App} \circ \langle d, b\rangle.$$

At this point, it may be instructive to look back at the definition of logical relations in Section 8.2.1 and see the direct similarity between the descriptions of products and function objects in this proposition and the definition of logical relations over an applicative structure or Henkin model. The difference is that here we have generalized the definition to any cartesian closed category, forming relations in *Set* after applying the functor $|\cdot|$.

Exercise 8.6.16 Show that for any category $\mathbf{C}$ with products and terminal object, the functor $|\cdot|$ from $\mathbf{C}$ to *Set* preserves products up to isomorphism, *i.e.*, $|A \times B| \cong |A| \times |B|$ for all objects A and B of $\mathbf{C}$.

Exercise 8.6.17 Show that for any CCC $\mathbf{C}$, the map $\pi\colon \hat{\mathbf{C}} \longrightarrow \mathbf{C}$ defined in this section is a functor that preserves terminal object, products and function objects. Begin by showing that π is a functor, then check that $\pi(X \times Y) = \pi X \times \pi Y$ for all objects $X = \langle S, f, A \rangle$ and $Y = \langle S', f', A' \rangle$ of $\hat{\mathbf{C}}$, and similarly for function objects and the terminal object.

Exercise 8.6.18 Prove Proposition 8.6.15.

(a) Show that $\langle S, A, B \rangle \times \langle S', A', B' \rangle = \langle S \times S', A \times A', B \times B' \rangle$ is a product in $\tilde{\mathbf{C}}$.

(b) Show that $\langle S, A, B \rangle \to \langle S', A', B' \rangle = \langle S \to S', A \to A', B \to B' \rangle$ is a function object in $\tilde{\mathbf{C}}$.

(c) Show that the functor $\pi\colon \tilde{\mathbf{C}} \longrightarrow \mathbf{C}$ is a cartesian closed functor.

Exercise 8.6.19 Show that if $\mathbf{C}$ is a well-pointed category, then so is $\tilde{\mathbf{C}}$.

8.6.4 Comparison with Logical Relations

In this section, we describe the connection between logical relations and subscones, for the special case of cartesian closed categories determined from Henkin models, and show how the Basic Lemma may be derived from a simple categorical properties of the subscone. Since a logical predicate $\mathcal{P} \subseteq \mathcal{A}$ is a family of predicates $\{P^\sigma\}$ indexed by the types over the signature of $\mathcal{A}$, we can think of a logical predicate as a mapping from types over some signature to subsets of some structure. We will see that a mapping of this form is determined by the categorical interpretation of lambda terms in the subscone of a CCC.

In discussing the interpretation of terms in cartesian closed categories in Section 7.2.4, we used a structure called a Σ-CCC, where Σ may be any $\lambda^{unit,\times,\to}$ signature. The difference between a CCC and a Σ-CCC is that a Σ-CCC $\mathbf{A}$ is equipped with a specific choice of object A^b for each type constant b of Σ, and a morphism $\hat{c}\colon unit \longrightarrow A$ for each term constant of Σ. Since a Σ-CCC associates an object or arrow with each symbol in Σ, we can think of a Σ-CCC as a cartesian closed category $\mathbf{A}$ together with a mapping $\Sigma \longrightarrow \mathbf{A}$ from the signature into the category.

For any $\lambda^{unit,\times,\to}$ signature Σ and set $\mathcal{E}$ of equations between Σ-terms, there is a CCC $\mathcal{C}_\Sigma(\mathcal{E})$ called the term category generated by $\mathcal{E}$, as described in Example 7.2.19. There is a canonical mapping $\Sigma \longrightarrow \mathcal{C}_\Sigma(\mathcal{E})$ presenting $\mathcal{C}_\Sigma(\mathcal{E})$ as a Σ-CCC, namely, the function mapping each type constant to itself and each term constant to its equivalence class, modulo $\mathcal{E}$. As shown in Proposition 7.2.46, there is a unique cartesian closed functor from $\mathcal{C}_\Sigma(\emptyset)$ to any other Σ-CCC $\mathbf{D}$. (The categorical name for this is that $\mathcal{C}_\Sigma(\emptyset)$ is the free cartesian closed category over signature Σ.) If we draw in the mappings from Σ, then such a cartesian closed functor forms a commuting triangle

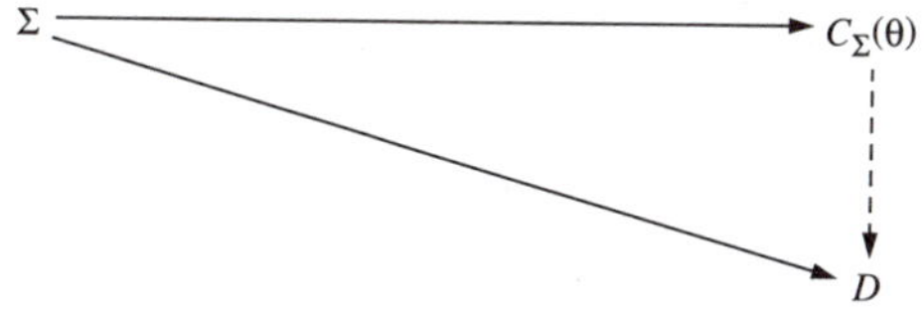

since the interpretation of a type or term constant is determined by the way that **D** is regarded as a Σ-CCC. As explained in Section 7.2.6, the cartesian closed functor from $\mathcal{C}_\Sigma(\emptyset)$ into a Σ-CCC **D** is the categorical equivalent of the meaning function associated with a Henkin model.

It is really only a matter of unraveling the definitions, and using Proposition 8.6.15, to see that the logical predicates over a Henkin model $\mathcal{A}$ for signature Σ correspond to ways of regarding the subscone of the category $\mathcal{C}_\mathcal{A}$ determined $\mathcal{A}$ as a Σ-CCC. More specifically, let $\mathbf{C} = \mathcal{C}_\mathcal{A}$ be the cartesian closed category determined by Henkin model $\mathcal{A}$, as explained in Section 7.2.5, regarded as a Σ-CCC in the way that preserves the meaning of terms. By Theorem 7.2.41, **C** is a well-pointed cartesian closed category, with the morphisms $unit \longrightarrow \sigma$ exactly the elements of A^σ from the Henkin model $\mathcal{A}$. If we consider a cartesian closed functor **F** from the term category $\mathcal{C}_\Sigma(\emptyset)$ into the subscone $\tilde{\mathbf{C}}$ of **C**, then the object map of this functor designates an object $\mathbf{F}(\sigma) = \langle P^\sigma, \sigma\rangle$, with $P \subseteq |\sigma|$ for each type σ. But since $|\sigma| = A^\sigma$, a meaning function into the subscone chooses a subset of the Henkin model at each type. It is easy to see from Proposition 8.6.15 that the family of predicates determined by the object map of a cartesian closed functor $\mathcal{C}_\Sigma(\emptyset) \to \tilde{\mathbf{C}}$ is in fact a logical relation. This gives us the following proposition.

Proposition 8.6.20 Let $\mathbf{C} = \mathcal{C}_\mathcal{A}$ be the well-pointed Σ-CCC determined by the Henkin model $\mathcal{A}$ for signature Σ. Then a logical predicate on $\mathcal{A}$ is exactly the object part of a cartesian closed functor from the term category $\mathcal{C}_\Sigma(\emptyset)$ over Σ into the Σ-CCC $\tilde{\mathbf{C}}$.

Using product categories, Proposition 8.6.20 gives us a similar characterization of logical relations over any number of models. For example, if $\mathbf{C} = \mathcal{C}_\mathcal{A} \times \mathcal{C}_\mathcal{B}$ is determined from Henkin models $\mathcal{A}$ and $\mathcal{B}$, then **C** and $\tilde{\mathbf{C}}$ are again well-pointed cartesian closed categories (see Exercise 8.6.19) and a meaning function into $\tilde{\mathbf{C}}$ is a logical relation over Henkin models $\mathcal{A}$ and $\mathcal{B}$.

Using the correspondence given in Proposition 8.6.20, we can see that the Basic Lemma for logical relations is a consequence of the commuting diagram given in the following proposition.

Proposition 8.6.21 Let Σ be a $\lambda^{unit,\times,\rightarrow}$ signature and let $\mathbf{C}$ be a cartesian closed category. Consider any mapping $\Sigma \rightarrow \tilde{\mathbf{C}}$ presenting $\tilde{\mathbf{C}}$ as a Σ-CCC. Composing with the canonical functor $\tilde{\mathbf{C}} \longrightarrow \mathbf{C}$, we obtain a corresponding map $\Sigma \rightarrow \mathbf{C}$ and, by the natural embedding of symbols into the term category, we have a similar map $\Sigma \rightarrow \mathcal{C}_\Sigma(\emptyset)$ into the term category. Given these three maps from Σ, there exist unique cartesian closed functors from $\mathcal{C}_\Sigma(\emptyset)$ into $\mathbf{C}$ and $\tilde{\mathbf{C}}$ commuting with the canonical functor $\tilde{\mathbf{C}} \longrightarrow \mathbf{C}$ as follows:

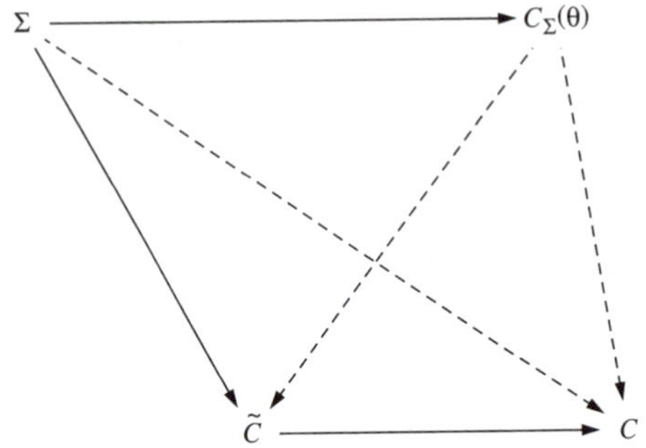

Proof Let functions from Σ to objects of the CCCs $\mathbf{C}$, $\tilde{\mathbf{C}}$ and $\mathcal{C}_\Sigma(\emptyset)$ be given as in the statement of the proposition. It is a trivial consequence of the definitions that the triangle involving Σ, $\tilde{\mathbf{C}}$ and $\mathbf{C}$ commutes. By Proposition 7.2.46, the cartesian closed functors $\mathcal{C}_\Sigma(\emptyset) \rightarrow \mathbf{C}$ and $\mathcal{C}_\Sigma(\emptyset) \rightarrow \tilde{\mathbf{C}}$ are uniquely determined. This implies that the two triangles with vertices Σ, $\mathcal{C}_\Sigma(\emptyset)$ and either $\tilde{\mathbf{C}}$ or $\mathbf{C}$ commute. Finally, since the canonical functor $\pi: \tilde{\mathbf{C}} \longrightarrow \mathbf{C}$ is a cartesian closed functor (see Proposition 8.6.15), the two uniquely determined cartesian closed functors from $\mathcal{C}_\Sigma(\emptyset)$ must commute with this functor. ■

It is again a matter of unraveling definitions to see how the Basic Lemma follows from this diagram. Let us consider the binary case with $\mathbf{A}$ and $\mathbf{B}$ given by Henkin models $\mathcal{A}$ and $\mathcal{B}$ of simply typed lambda calculus. Then both $\mathbf{C} = \mathbf{A} \times \mathbf{B}$ and $\tilde{\mathbf{C}}$ are well-pointed cartesian closed categories. The cartesian closed functor $\mathcal{C}_\Sigma(\emptyset) \rightarrow \mathbf{C}$ maps a typed lambda term $x{:}\sigma \triangleright M{:}\tau$ to the pair of morphisms giving the meaning of M in $\mathcal{A}$ and, respectively, the meaning of M in $\mathcal{B}$. The cartesian closed functor $\mathcal{C}_\Sigma(\emptyset) \rightarrow \tilde{\mathbf{C}}$ maps a typed lambda term $x{:}\sigma \triangleright M{:}\tau$ to a morphism from some subset $S \subseteq |\mathcal{C}_\mathcal{A}[\![\sigma]\!] \times \mathcal{C}_\mathcal{B}[\![\sigma]\!]| = A^\sigma \times B^\sigma$ to a subset $S' \subseteq |\mathcal{C}_\mathcal{A}[\![\tau]\!] \times \mathcal{C}_\mathcal{B}[\![\tau]\!]| = A^\tau \times B^\tau$, where $\mathcal{C}_\mathcal{A}[\![\sigma]\!]$ is the object of $\mathbf{A}$ named type expression σ, and similarly for $\mathcal{C}_\mathcal{B}[\![\sigma]\!]$ and so on. As noted in Section 8.6.3, such a morphism in the subscone is a product map $f \times g$ with $f: \mathcal{C}_\mathcal{A}[\![\sigma]\!] \longrightarrow \mathcal{C}_\mathcal{A}[\![\tau]\!]$ and $g: \mathcal{C}_\mathcal{B}[\![\sigma]\!] \longrightarrow \mathcal{C}_\mathcal{B}[\![\tau]\!]$ which maps a pair $\langle u, v\rangle$ with $u\ S\ v$ to a pair $\langle f(u), g(v)\rangle$ with $f(u)\ S'\ g(v)$. Because the two cartesian closed functors of $\mathcal{C}_\Sigma(\emptyset)$ commute with the functor $\pi: \tilde{\mathbf{C}} \rightarrow \mathbf{C}$, f must be the meaning $f = \mathcal{A}[\![x{:}\sigma \triangleright M{:}\tau]\!]$ of the term M in $\mathcal{A}$, regarded as a function of the free variable x, and similarly $g = \mathcal{B}[\![x:\sigma \triangleright M:\tau]\!]$. Because the term $x:\sigma \triangleright M:\tau$ was arbitrary, and σ may be a cartesian product of any types, we have shown that given logically related interpretations of the free variables, the meaning of any term in $\mathcal{A}$ is logically related to the meaning of this term in $\mathcal{B}$. This is precisely the Basic Lemma for logical relations over Henkin models.

8.6.5 General Case and Applications to Specific Categories

The definition of scone and subscone of a category $\mathbf{C}$ rely on the functor $|\cdot|$ from $\mathbf{C}$ into $\mathcal{S}et$. However, since relatively few properties of $\mathcal{S}et$ are used, we can generalize the construction and associated theorems to other functors and categories. We begin by stating the basic properties of the "generalized scone" and "subscone," then continue by deriving Kripke logical relations and directed-complete logical relations (from Section 8.6.2) as special cases.

Proposition 8.6.14 holds in a more general setting with $\mathcal{S}et$ replaced by any cartesian closed category $\mathbf{C}'$ with equalizers and the functor $|\cdot|: \mathbf{C} \longrightarrow \mathcal{S}et$ replaced by any functor $\mathbf{F}: \mathbf{C} \longrightarrow \mathbf{C}'$ that preserves products up to isomorphism, by essentially the same proof. This takes us from the specific comma category $\hat{\mathbf{C}} = (\mathcal{S}et \downarrow |\cdot|)$ to a more general case of the form $(\mathbf{C}' \downarrow \mathbf{F})$.

Proposition 8.6.22 Let $\mathbf{C}$ and $\mathbf{C}'$ be cartesian closed categories and assume $\mathbf{C}'$ has equalizers. Let $\mathbf{F}: \mathbf{C} \longrightarrow \mathbf{C}'$ be a functor that preserves finite products up to isomorphism. Then the comma category $(\mathbf{C}' \downarrow \mathbf{F})$ is a cartesian closed category and the canonical functor $\pi: (\mathbf{C}' \downarrow \mathbf{F}) \longrightarrow \mathbf{C}$ is a cartesian closed functor.

The next step is to identify generalizations of the subscone. The proof of Proposition 8.6.21 actually establishes the general version where instead of $\tilde{\mathbf{C}}$, we may consider any CCC $\mathbf{D}$ that has a cartesian closed functor into $\mathbf{C}$. We will be interested in situations where $\mathbf{D}$ is a subcategory of a comma category $(\mathbf{C}' \downarrow \mathbf{F})$, such that the restriction of the canonical cartesian closed functor $\pi: (\mathbf{C}' \downarrow \mathbf{F}) \longrightarrow \mathbf{C}$ to $\mathbf{D}$ is a cartesian closed functor.

Proposition 8.6.23 Let $\mathbf{C}$ and $\mathbf{C}'$ be cartesian closed categories and assume $\mathbf{C}'$ has equalizers. Let $\mathbf{F}: \mathbf{C} \longrightarrow \mathbf{C}'$ be a functor that preserves products and let $\mathbf{D}$ be a sub-cartesian-closed category of the comma category $(\mathbf{C}' \downarrow \mathbf{F})$. Let Σ be a $\lambda^{unit,\times,\rightarrow}$ signature and consider any mapping $\Sigma \rightarrow \mathbf{D}$ presenting $\mathbf{D}$ as a Σ-CCC. Composing with the canonical functor $\mathbf{D} \longrightarrow \mathbf{C}$, we obtain a corresponding map $\Sigma \rightarrow \mathbf{C}$ and, by the natural embedding of symbols into the term category, we have a similar map $\Sigma \rightarrow \mathcal{C}_\Sigma(\emptyset)$ into the term category. Given these three maps from Σ, there exist unique cartesian closed functors from $\mathcal{C}_\Sigma(\emptyset)$ into $\mathbf{C}$ and $\mathbf{D}$ commuting with the canonical functor $\mathbf{D} \longrightarrow \mathbf{C}$ as follows:

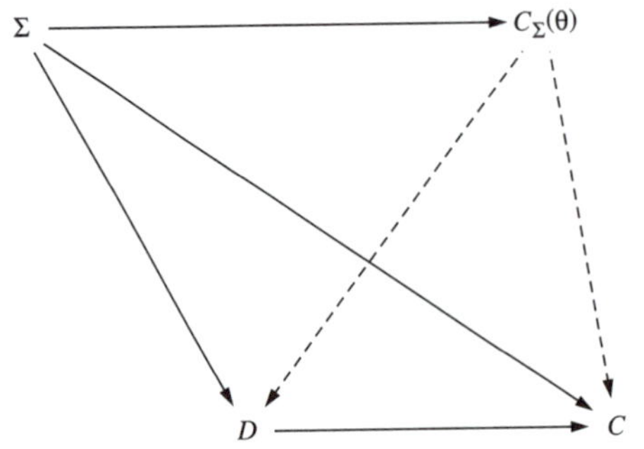

Sconing with Kripke Models

If $\mathcal{P}$ is a partially ordered set, then we may consider $\mathcal{P}$ as a category whose objects are the elements of $\mathcal{P}$ and morphisms indicate when one element is less than another, as described in Example 7.2.6. As shown in Section 7.3.7, each Kripke lambda model with $\mathcal{P}$ as the set of "possible worlds" determines a cartesian closed category $\mathbf{C}$ that is a subcategory of the functor category $Set^{\mathcal{P}}$. The inclusion $\mathbf{F}$ of $\mathbf{C}$ into category $Set^{\mathcal{P}}$ preserves products, since the interpretation of a product type in a Kripke lambda model is the same as cartesian product in $Set^{\mathcal{P}}$. By Exercise 7.2.14, $Set^{\mathcal{P}}$ has equalizers and we can apply Propositions 8.6.22 and 8.6.23

For the appropriate analog of subscone, we take the subcategory with an inclusion at each "possible world." More specifically, let $\mathbf{D}$ be the full subcategory of the comma category $(Set^{\mathcal{P}} \downarrow \mathbf{F})$ that consists of objects $\langle S, f, A\rangle$ with $f_p \colon S(p) \hookrightarrow \mathbf{F}(A)(p)$ an inclusion for each p in $\mathcal{P}$. By assuming these are ordinary subsets, we may omit f when referring to objects of $\mathbf{D}$. It may be shown that $\mathbf{D}$ is a CCC (Exercise 8.6.24). In describing function objects (exponentials) in $\mathbf{D}$ we may use natural transformations $\mathbf{F}(app_{A,A'})\colon \mathbf{F}(A \to A') \times \mathbf{F}(A) \longrightarrow \mathbf{F}(A')$ because the functor $\mathbf{F}$ preserves binary products. For each object C in $\mathbf{C}$ and each $p \le p'$ in $\mathcal{P}$, we also use the transition function $\mathbf{F}(C)(p \le p')\colon \mathbf{F}(C)(p) \to \mathbf{F}(C)(p')$ given by the action of the functor $\mathbf{F}(C)\colon \mathcal{P} \to Set$ on the order of $\mathcal{P}$. Specifically, $\langle S, A\rangle \to \langle S', A'\rangle$ may be given as $\langle P, A \to A'\rangle$, where $A \to A'$ is taken in $\mathbf{C}$ and $P\colon \mathcal{P} \to Set$ is the functor such that the set $P(p)$ consists of all t in $\mathbf{F}(A \to A')(p)$ for which for all $p' \ge p$ and all a in $\mathbf{F}(A)(p')$, if a belongs to $S(p')$, then the element $\mathbf{F}(app_{A,A'})_{p'}(\mathbf{F}(A \to A')(p \le p')(t), a)$ in $\mathbf{F}(A')(p')$ belongs to $S'(p')$. In other words, the object parts of the unique cartesian closed functor from the term category into $\mathbf{D}$ in this case amount to the Kripke logical predicates on the Kripke lambda model that corresponds to $\mathbf{F}$.

In the binary case, we let **A** and **B** be cartesian closed categories and let $\mathbf{F}: \mathbf{A} \to Set^{\mathcal{P}}$ and $\mathbf{G}: \mathbf{A} \to Set^{\mathcal{P}}$ finite product preserving functors given by Kripke lambda models $\mathcal{A}$ and $\mathcal{B}$, each with $\mathcal{P}$ as the poset of possible worlds. Let $\mathbf{H}: \mathbf{A} \times \mathbf{B} \to Set^{\mathcal{P}}$ be the functor given by $\mathbf{H}(A, B) = \mathbf{F}(A) \times \mathbf{G}(B)$. Continuing as above, with $\mathbf{C} = \mathbf{A} \times \mathbf{B}$ and with $\mathbf{H}$ instead of $\mathbf{F}$, we can see that the object parts of the cartesian closed functors into $\mathbf{D}$ are exactly the Kripke logical relations on Kripke lambda models $\mathcal{A}$ and $\mathcal{B}$.

Sconing with CPOs

Since *Cpo* is a cartesian closed category with equalizers (by Exercise 7.2.14), we may also form a generalized scone using functors into *Cpo*. This is like the case for Kripke models, except that we have the added complication of treating pointed CPOs properly; our relations must preserve the bottom element in order to preserve fixed points, as illustrated in Section 8.6.2. It might seem reasonable to work with the category *Cppo* of pointed CPOs instead, since relations taken in *Cppo* would have to have least elements. However, the category *Cppo* does not have equalizers (by Exercise 7.2.14). Moreover, we may wish to construct logical relations which are closed under limits at all types, but which are only pointed where needed to preserve fixed points. A general approach would be to use lifted types, and extend the lifting functor from *Cpo* to the appropriate comma category. This would give "lifted relations" on lifted types, which would necessarily preserve least elements. A less general alternative, which we will describe below, is to simply work with subcategories where predicates or relations are pointed when needed. This is relatively ad hoc, but is technically simpler and (hopefully) illustrates the main ideas.

Since we are interested in preserving fixed-point operators, we let the signature Σ be a signature that may include fixed-point constants at one or more types, and let $\mathcal{E}_{fix}$ be the set of equations of the form $fix_\sigma = \lambda f\colon \sigma \to \sigma.\, f(fix\ f)$ for each type σ that has a fixed-point operator in Σ. The category $\mathcal{C}_\Sigma(\mathcal{E}_{fix})$ is the term category of simply typed lambda calculus with with one or more fixed-point constants, each with its associated equational axiom. By Proposition 7.2.46, there is a unique cartesian closed functor $\mathcal{C}_\Sigma(\mathcal{E}_{fix}) \longrightarrow \mathbf{C}$ from $\mathcal{C}_\Sigma(\mathcal{E}_{fix})$ to any Σ-CCC satisfying the fixed-point equations. In particular, there is a unique such functor into any Σ-CCC of CPOs.

If we use $|\cdot|\colon Cpo \longrightarrow Set$, then the scone $(Set \downarrow |\cdot|)$ allows us to form logical predicates or relations over CPOs. However, these relations will not be directed complete. Instead, we let **I** be the identity functor on *Cpo* and consider the comma category $(Cpo \downarrow \mathbf{I})$. This could also be written $(Cpo \downarrow Cpo)$, since we are using *Cpo* as a convenient shorthand for the identity functor on *Cpo*. To form the subscone, we consider the full subcategory **D** with objects of the form $\langle P, f, A\rangle$, where f is an inclusion $P \hookrightarrow A$. In other words, P is a sub-CPO of A, and therefore closed under limits of directed sets. By generalizing Proposition 8.6.15, we can see that **D** provides logical predicates over CPO models that are closed under limits. However, there is no reason for predicates taken in *Cpo* to preserve least elements – we have objects $\langle P, f, A\rangle$ where A is pointed and P is not. This is not a problem in general, but if we wish to have a predicate preserve a fixed-point operator on pointed A, we will need for P to be a pointed subset of A.

In order to preserve fixed points, we consider a further subcategory. Assume we have a map $\Sigma \longrightarrow Cpo$ identifying certain CPOs on which we wish to have fixed-point operators. For this to make sense, we assume that if σ is a type over Σ with a constant $fix_\sigma\colon (\sigma \to \sigma) \to \sigma$, then our mapping from types to CPOs will guarantee that the interpretation of σ is a pointed CPO. In this case, we are interested in subcategories of $\mathbf{D}$ whose objects are of the form $\langle P, A\rangle$, where if A is the interpretation of a type with a fixed-point constant, then the inclusion $P \hookrightarrow A$ is strict. In particular, P must have a least element. The CCC structure of this subcategory remains the same, but in $\mathbf{D}$ we also get fixed-point operators where required, and the forgetful functor $\mathbf{D} \to Cpo$ preserves them. The object parts of the unique cartesian closed functor from $\mathcal{C}_\Sigma(\mathcal{E}_{fix})$ into $\mathbf{D}$ are exactly the inclusive logical predicates described in Section 8.6.2, pointed where required by the choice of fixed-point constants. In the binary case, we let $\mathbf{D}$ be the full subcategory of $(Cpo \times Cpo \downarrow Cpo \times Cpo)$ whose objects are of the form $\langle S, A, B\rangle$, where S is a sub-CPO of $A \times B$, and force pointed relations as required.

Exercise 8.6.24 Suppose $\mathcal{P}$ is a partially ordered set and $\mathbf{C}$ is a Kripke lambda model with $\mathcal{P}$ as the set of "possible worlds." Let $\mathbf{F}\colon \mathbf{C} \longrightarrow Set^{\mathcal{P}}$ be the inclusion of $\mathbf{C}$ into the category category $Set^{\mathcal{P}}$. Show that the full subcategory $\mathbf{D}$ of the comma category $(Set^{\mathcal{P}} \downarrow \mathbf{F})$ consisting of objects $\langle S, f, A\rangle$ with $f_p\colon S(p) \hookrightarrow \mathbf{F}(A)(p)$ an inclusion for each p in $\mathcal{P}$ is cartesian closed.

9 Polymorphism and Modularity

9.1 Introduction

9.1.1 Overview

This chapter presents type-theoretic concepts underlying polymorphism and data abstraction in programming languages. These concepts are relevant to language constructs such as Ada packages and generics [US 80], C++ templates [ES90], and polymorphism, abstract types, and modules in ML [MTH90, MT91, Ull94] and related languages Miranda [Tur85] and Haskell [HF92, H^+92]. As a rule, the typed lambda calculi we use to formalize and study polymorphism and data abstraction are more flexible than their implemented programming language counterparts. In some cases, the implemented languages are restricted due to valid implementation or efficiency considerations. However, there are many ideas that have successfully progressed from lambda calculus models into implemented programming languages. For example, it appears from early Clu design notes [L^+81] that the original discovery that polymorphic functions could be type-checked at compile time came about through Reynolds' work on polymorphic lambda calculus [Rey74b]. Another example is the Standard ML module system, which was heavily influenced by a type-theoretic perspective [Mac85]. The main topics of this chapter are:

• Syntax of polymorphic type systems, including predicative, impredicative and *type*: *type* versions.

• Predicative polymorphic lambda calculus, with discussion of relationship to other systems, semantic models, reduction and polymorphic declarations.

• Survey of impredicative polymorphic lambda calculus, focusing on expressiveness, strong normalization and construction of semantic models. This section includes discussion of representation of natural numbers and other data by pure terms, a characterization of theories by contexts, including the maximum consistent theory, parametricity, and formal category theory.

• Data abstraction and existential types.

• General products and sums and their relation to module systems for Standard ML and related languages.

Most of the topics are covered in a less technical manner than earlier chapters, with emphasis on the intuitive nature and expressiveness of various languages. An exception is the more technical study of semantics and reduction properties of impredicative polymorphism.

9.1.2 Types as Function Arguments

In the simply-typed lambda calculus and programming languages with similar typing constraints, static types serve a number of purposes. For example, the type soundness theorem (Lemma 4.5.13) shows that every expression of type $\sigma \rightarrow \tau$ determines a function from type σ to τ, in every Henkin model. Since every term has meaning in every Henkin model, it follows that no typed term contains a function of type $nat \rightarrow nat$, say, applied to an argument of type $bool$. This may be regarded as a precise way of saying that simply-typed lambda calculus does not allow type errors. Simply-typed lambda calculus also enjoys a degree of representation independence, as discussed in Section 8.5. However, the typing constraints of simply-typed lambda calculus have some obvious drawbacks: there are many useful and computationally meaningful expressions that are not well-typed. In this chapter, we consider static type systems that may be used to support more flexible styles of typed programming, generally without sacrificing the type security of more restricted languages based on simply-typed lambda calculus.

Some of the inconvenience of simple type structure may be illustrated by considering sorting functions in a language like C or Pascal. The reader familiar with a variety of sorting algorithms will know that most may be explained without referring to the kind of data to be sorted. We typically assume that we are given an array of pointers to records, and that each record has an associated *key*. It does not matter what type of value the key is, as long as we have a "comparison" function that will tell which of two keys should come first in the sorted list. Most sorting algorithms simply compare keys using the comparison function and swap records by resetting pointers accordingly. Since this form of sorting algorithm does not depend on the type of the data, we should be able to write a function *Sort* that sorts any type of records, given a comparison function as a actual parameter. However, in a language such as Pascal, every *Sort* function must have a type of the form

$$Sort : (t \times t \rightarrow bool) \times Array[ptr\ t] \rightarrow Array[ptr\ t]$$

for some fixed type t. (This is the type of function which, given a binary relation on t and an array of pointers to t, return an array of pointers to t). This forces us to write a separate procedure for each type of data, even though there is nothing inherent in the sorting algorithm to require this. From a programmer's point of view, there are several obvious disadvantages. The first is that if we wish to build a program library, we must anticipate in advance the types of data we wish to sort. This is unreasonably restrictive. Second, even if we are only sorting a few types of data, it is a bothersome chore to duplicate a procedure declaration several times. Not only does this consume programming time, but having several copies of a procedure may increase debugging and maintenance time. It is far more convenient to use a language that allows one procedure to be applied to many types of data.

One family of solutions to this problem may be illustrated using function composition, which is slightly simpler than sorting. The $\lambda^{\rightarrow}$ function

$$compose_{nat,nat,nat} \stackrel{\text{def}}{=} \lambda f\colon nat \rightarrow nat.\lambda g\colon nat \rightarrow nat.\lambda x\colon nat.f(gx)$$

composes two natural number functions. Higher-order functions of type $nat \rightarrow (nat \rightarrow nat)$ and $(nat \rightarrow nat) \rightarrow nat$ may be composed using the function

$$compose_{nat,nat\rightarrow nat,nat} \stackrel{\text{def}}{=} \lambda f\colon (nat \rightarrow nat) \rightarrow nat.\lambda g\colon nat \rightarrow (nat \rightarrow nat).\lambda x\colon nat.f(gx).$$

It is easy to see that these two composition functions differ only in the types given to the formal parameters. Since these functions compute their results in precisely the same way, we might expect both to be "instances" of some general composition function.

A *polymorphic function* is a function that may be applied to many types of arguments. (This is not a completely precise definition, in part because "many" is not specified exactly, but it does give the right general idea.) We may extend $\lambda^{\rightarrow}$ to include polymorphic functions by extending lambda abstraction to type variables. Using type variables r, s and t, we may write a "generic" composition function

$$compose_{r,s,t} \stackrel{\text{def}}{=} \lambda f\colon s \rightarrow t.\lambda g\colon r \rightarrow s.\lambda x\colon r.f(gx).$$

It should be clear that $compose_{r,s,t}$ denotes a composition function of type $(s \rightarrow t) \rightarrow (r \rightarrow s) \rightarrow (r \rightarrow t)$, for any semantic values of type variables r, s and t. In particular, when all three type variables are interpreted as the type of natural numbers, the meaning of $compose_{r,s,t}$ is the same as $compose_{nat,nat,nat}$. By lambda abstracting r, s and t, we may write a function that produces $compose_{nat,nat,nat}$ when applied to type arguments nat, nat and nat. To distinguish type variables from ordinary variables, we will use the symbol T for some collection of types. As we shall see shortly, there are several possible interpretations for T. Since these are more easily considered after presenting abstraction and application for type variables, we will try to think of T as some collection of types that at least includes all the $\lambda^{\rightarrow}$ types, and perhaps other types not yet specified. There is no need to think of T itself as a "type," in the sense of "element of T." In particular, we do not need T to include itself as a member.

Using lambda abstraction over types, which we will call *type abstraction,* we may define a polymorphic composition function

$$compose \stackrel{\text{def}}{=} \lambda r\colon T.\,\lambda s\colon T.\,\lambda t\colon T.\,compose_{r,s,t}.$$

This function requires three type parameters before it may be applied to an ordinary function. We will refer to the application of a polymorphic function to a type parameter as *type application.* Type applications may be simplified using a version of β-reduction, with the type argument substituted in place of the bound type variable. If we want to apply *compose* to two numeric functions $f, g : nat \rightarrow nat$, then we first apply *compose* to type arguments *nat*, *nat* and *nat*. Using β-reduction for type application, this gives us

$$\begin{aligned} compose\ nat\ nat\ nat &= (\lambda r\colon T.\lambda s\colon T.\lambda t\colon T.\lambda f\colon s \rightarrow t.\lambda g\colon r \rightarrow s.\lambda x\colon r.f(gx))\ nat\ nat\ nat \\ &= \lambda f\colon nat \rightarrow nat.\lambda g\colon nat \rightarrow nat.\lambda x\colon nat.f(gx). \end{aligned}$$

In other words, $compose\ nat\ nat\ nat = compose_{nat,nat,nat}$. By applying *compose* to other type arguments, we may obtain composition functions of other types.

In a typed function calculus with type abstraction and type application, we must give types to polymorphic functions. A polymorphic function that illustrates most of the typing issues is the *polymorphic identity*

$$Id \stackrel{\text{def}}{=} \lambda t\colon T.\lambda x\colon t.x.$$

It should be clear from the syntax that the domain of *Id* is T. The range is somewhat more difficult to describe. Two common notations for the type of *Id* are $\Pi t\colon T.t \rightarrow t$ and $\forall t\colon T.t \rightarrow t$. In these expressions, Π and $\forall$ bind t. The $\forall$ notation allows informal readings such as, "the type of functions which, *for all* $t\colon T$, give us a map from t to t." The Π notation is closer to standard mathematical usage, since a product $\prod_{i \in I} A_i$ over an infinite index set I consists of all functions $f\colon I \rightarrow \cup_{i \in I} A_i$ such that $f(i) \in A_i$. Since $Id\ t : t \rightarrow t$ for every $t \in T$, the polymorphic identity has the correct functional behavior to belong to the infinite product $\prod_{t:T} t \rightarrow t$, and we may write $Id\colon \Pi t.t \rightarrow t$. We will use Π notation in the first polymorphic lambda calculus we consider and $\forall$ in a later system, primarily as a way of distinguishing the two systems.

Just as we can determine the type of an ordinary function application fx from the types of f and x, we can compute the type of a type application from the type of the polymorphic function and the type argument. For the type application $Id\ \tau$, for example, the type of *Id* is $\Pi t.t \rightarrow t$. The type of $Id\ \tau$ is obtained by substituting τ for the bound variable t in $t \rightarrow t$. While this substitution may seem similar to some kind of β-reduction (with Π in place of λ), it is important to notice that this substitution is done only on the type of *Id*, not the function itself. In other words, we can type-check applications of polymorphic functions by without evaluating the applications. In a programming language based on this form of polymorphism, this type operation be carried out by a compile-time type checker (except in the case for *type*: *type* polymorphism described below, where it is difficult to separate compile-time from run-time).

Having introduced types for polymorphic functions, we must decide how these types fit into the type system. At the point we introduced T, we had only defined non-polymorphic types. With the addition of polymorphic types, there are three natural choices for T. We may choose to let T contain only the simple types defined using $\rightarrow$, $+$ and/or $\times$, say, and some collection of type constants. This leads us to a semantically straightforward calculus of what is called *predicative polymorphism.* The word "predicative" refers to the fact that T is introduced only after we have defined all of the members of T. In other words, the collection T does not contain any types that rely on T for their definition. An influential predicative calculus is Martin-Löf's constructive type theory [Mar73, Mar82, Mar84], which provides the basis for the Nuprl proof development system [C^+86].

A second form of polymorphism is obtained by letting T also contain all the polymorphic types (such as $\Pi t{:}\, T.t \rightarrow t$), but not consider T itself a type. This T is "impredicative," since we assume T is closed under type definitions that refer to the entire collection T. The resulting language, formulated independently by Girard [Gir71, Gir72] and Reynolds [Rey74b], is variously called the *second-order lambda calculus, System F,* or the calculus of *impredicative polymorphism.* (It is also referred to as the *polymorphic lambda calculus*, but we will consider this phrase ambiguous.) The final alternative is to consider T a type, and let T contain all types, including itself. This may seem strange, since assumptions like "there is a set of all sets" are well-known to lead to foundational problems (see Section 1.6). However, from a computational point of view, it is not immediately clear that there is anything wrong with introducing a "type of all types."

Some simple differences between these three kinds of polymorphism may be illustrated by considering uses of *Id*, since the domain of *Id* is T. If we limit T to the collection of all $\lambda^{\rightarrow}$ types, we may only apply *Id* to a non-polymorphic type such as *nat* or $(nat \rightarrow nat) \rightarrow (nat \rightarrow bool)$. If we are only interested polymorphic functions as a means for defining functions with $\lambda^{\rightarrow}$ types, then this seems sufficient. A technical property of this restricted language is that any model of $\lambda^{\rightarrow}$ may be extended to a model of predicative polymorphism. In particular, there are classical set-theoretic models of predicative polymorphism. A second advantage of predicative polymorphism is the way that modularity constructs may be integrated into the type system, as discussed in Section 9.5. Predicativity may also be useful in the development of type inference algorithms. These algorithms allow a programmer to obtain the full benefit of a static type system without having to explicitly declare the type of each variable in a program. The type inference algorithm used in the programming language ML is discussed in Chapter 11.

If we let T be the collection of all types, then the polymorphic identity may be applied to any type, including its own. By β-reduction on types, the result of this application is an identity function

$$Id\,(\Pi t\colon T.t \rightarrow t) = \lambda x\colon (\Pi t\colon T.t \rightarrow t).\, x$$

which we may apply to *Id* itself. This gives a form of "self-application" reminiscent of Russell's paradox (Exercise 4.1.1). In the impredicative calculus, it is impossible to interpret every polymorphic lambda term as a set-theoretic function and every type as the set of all functions it describes. The reason is that the interpretation of *Id* would have to be a function whose domain contains a set (the meaning of $\Pi t\colon T.t \rightarrow t$) which contains *Id*. The reader may find it amusing to draw a Venn diagram of this situation. If we think of a function as a set of ordered pairs (as described in Section 1.6.2) then we begin with a circle for the set *Id* of ordered pairs $Id = \{\langle \tau, \lambda x\colon \tau.x \rangle \mid \tau \in T\}$. But one of the elements of *Id* is the pair $\langle (\Pi t\colon T.t \rightarrow t), \lambda x\colon (\Pi t\colon T.t \rightarrow t).x \rangle$ allowing the function to be applied to its own type. One of the components of this ordered pair is a set which contains *Id*, giving us a picture with circularly nested sets. This line of reasoning may be used to show that a naive interpretation of the impredicative second-order calculus conflicts with basic axioms of set theory. A more subtle argument, discussed in Section 9.3.2, shows that it is not even possible to have a semantic model with classical set-theoretic interpretation of all function types. The semantics of impredicative polymorphism has been a popular research topic in recent years, and several appealing models have been found.

In the final form of polymorphism, we let T be a type which contains all types, including itself. This design is often referred to as *type*: *type*. One effect of *type*: *type* is to allow polymorphic functions such as *Id* to act as functions from types to types, as well as functions from types to elements of types. For example, the application $Id\,T$ is considered meaningful, since $T\colon T$. By β-reduction on types, we have $Id\,T = \lambda x\colon T.x$ and so $(Id\,T)\colon T \rightarrow T$ is a function from types to types. We may also write more complicated functions from T to T and use these in type expressions. While languages based on the other two choices for T are strongly normalizing (unless we add fixed-point operators) and have efficiently decidable typing rules, strong normalization fails for most languages with *type*: *type*. In fact, it may be shown that the set of provable equations in a minimal language with *type*: *type* is undecidable ([MR86]; see also [Mar73, Coq86, How87]). Since arbitrarily complex expressions may be incorporated into type expressions, this makes the set of well-typed term undecidable. Historically, a calculus with a type of all types was proposed as a foundation for constructive mathematics by Martin-Löf, until an inconsistency was found by Girard in the early 1970's [Mar73]. While compile-time type checking may be impossible for a language with a type of all types, we will see in Section 9.3.5 that there are insightful and non-trivial semantic models for polymorphism with a type of all types.

In Sections 9.1.3 and 9.1.4, we summarize some extensions of polymorphic type systems. In Section 9.2, we return to the predicative polymorphic calculus and give a precise definition of the syntax, equational proof rules and semantics of this typed lambda calculus. We also show how impredicative and *type*: *type* polymorphism may be derived by adding rules to the predicative type system.

All of the systems described in this chapter use what is called *parametric polymorphism.* This term, coined by Strachey [Str67], refers to the fact that every polymorphic function uses "essentially the same algorithm" at each type. For example, the composition function given earlier in this section composes two functions f and g in essentially the same way, regardless of the types of f and g. Specifically, $compose\,\rho\,\sigma\,\tau\,f\,g\,x$ is always computed by first applying g to x and then applying f to the result. This may be contrasted with what Strachey termed *ad hoc polymorphism.* An ad hoc polymorphic function might, for example, test the value of a type argument and then branch in some way according to the form of this type. If we added a test for type equality, we could write the following form of "composition" function:

$$add\_hoc\_compose \stackrel{\text{def}}{=} \lambda r\colon T.\,\lambda s\colon T.\,\lambda t\colon T.\,\lambda f\colon s \to t.\lambda g\colon r \to s.\lambda x\colon r$$

$$\texttt{if } Eq?\,s\,t \texttt{ then } f(f(gx)) \texttt{ else } f(gx)$$

This function clearly composes f and g in a manner that depends on the type of f. This kind function is considered briefly in Section 9.3.2. It appears that ad hoc polymorphism is consistent with predicative polymorphism, as explored in [HM95a]. However, ad hoc operators destroy some of the desirable properties of impredicative polymorphic calculus. Some research papers on parametricity, which has been studied extensively if not conclusively, are [BFSS89, FGSS88, Rey83, MR92, Wad89].

9.1.3 General Products and Sums

There are a number of variations and extensions of the polymorphic type systems described in this chapter. An historically important series of typed lambda calculi are the Automath languages, used in a project to formalize mathematics [DB80]. Some conceptual descendants of the Automath languages are Martin-Löf's intuitionistic type theory [Mar73, Mar82, Mar84] and the closely related Nuprl system for program verification and formal mathematics [C$^+$86]. Two important constructs in these predicative type systems are the "general" product and sum types, written using Π and Σ, respectively.

Intuitively, general sums and products may be viewed as straightforward set-theoretic constructions. If A is an expression defining some collection (either a type or collection of types, for example), and B is an expression with free variable x which defines a collection for each x in A, then $\Sigma x\colon A.B$ and $\Pi x\colon A.B$ are called the *sum* and *product of the family B over the index set A*, respectively. In set-theoretic terms, the product $\Pi x\colon A.B$ is the Cartesian product of the family of sets $\{B(x) \mid x \in A\}$. The elements of this product are functions f such that $f(a) \in [a/x]B$ for each $a \in A$. The sum $\Sigma x\colon A.B$ is the disjoint union of the family $\{B(x) \mid x \in A\}$. Its members are ordered pairs $\langle a, b\rangle$ with $a \in A$ and $b \in [a/x]B$. Since the elements of sum types are pairs, general sums have projection functions *first* and *second* for first and second components.

A polymorphic type $\Pi t\colon T.\sigma$ or $\forall t\colon T.\sigma$ is a special case of general products. Another use of general products is in so-called "first-order dependent products." An example from programming arises in connection with arrays of various lengths. For simplicity, let us consider the type constructor *vector* which, when applied to an integer n, denotes the type of integer arrays indexed from 1 to n. If we have a function *zero_vector* that, given an integer n, returns the zero-vector (array with value 0 in each location) of length n, then we can write the type of this function as a general product type

$$zero\_vector : \Pi n\colon int.\, vector\, n$$

In words, the type $\Pi n\colon int.\, vector\, n$ is the type of functions which, on argument n, return an element of the type $vector\, n$. An interesting and sometimes perplexing impredicative language with general products is the Calculus of Constructions [CH88], which extends the impredicative polymorphic calculus.

Existential types, described in Section 9.4, provide a type-theoretic account of abstract data types. These types are similar to general sums, but restricted in a significant way. Intuitively, in a program with an abstract data type of stacks, for example, stacks would be implemented using some type (such as records consisting of an array and an array index) for representing stacks, and functions for manipulating stacks. Thus an implementation of stacks is a pair consisting of a type and a tuple of elements of a related type (in this case, a tuple of functions). If σ is a type expression describing the signature of the tuple of functions associated with stacks, then the type of all stack implementations is the *existential type* $\exists t\colon T.\sigma$. This differs from the general sum type $\Sigma t\colon T.\sigma$ in the following way. If $\langle a, b\rangle\colon \Sigma x\colon A.B$, then $first\langle a, b\rangle$ is an expression for an element of A with $first\langle a, b\rangle = a$. However, if $\langle t = \tau, M\colon \sigma\rangle\colon \exists t.\sigma$, the we do not want any program to be able to access the first component, τ, since this is the representation of an abstract type. This restriction follows from the goals of data abstraction, but may seem unnecessarily restrictive in other contexts, such as for ML-style modules. We discuss existential types in more detail in Section 9.4

Exercise 9.1.1 Show that if x does not occur free in B, then $\Pi x\colon A.B$ is the set of functions from A to B and $\Sigma x\colon A.B$ is the set of ordered pairs $A \times B$.

9.1.4 Types as Specifications

The more expressive type systems mentioned in Section 9.1.3 all serve dual purpose, following what is called the *formulas-as-types* correspondence, or sometimes the *Curry-*

Howard isomorphism. This general correspondence between typed lambda calculi and constructive logics allows us to regard lambda terms (or programs) as proofs and types as specifications. In simple type systems without variables or binding operators in types, the logic of types is just propositional logic. With polymorphism and data abstraction, however, we may develop type systems of quantified logics, capable of specifying more subtle properties of programs. This approach is used in the the Nuprl system for program verification [C+86] and other conceptual descendents of the Automath languages [DB80]. Some related systems for checking proofs via type checking are the Edinburgh Logical Framework [HHP87] and PX [HN88], which is based on Feferman's logical system [Fef79].

Section 4.3.4 contains a basic explanation of natural deduction and the formulas-as-types correspondence for propositional logic. The main idea in extending this correspondence to universal quantification is that a constructive proof of $\forall x\colon A.\phi$ must be some kind of construction which, given any $a \in A$, produces a proof of $[a/x]\phi$. If we identify proofs of the formula $[a/x]\phi$ with elements of a type that we also write $[a/x]\phi$, then proofs of $\forall x\colon A.\phi$ must be functions from A to $\cup_{a\in A}[a/x]\phi$ which, given any $a \in A$, produce an element of $[a/x]\phi$. Therefore, the constructive proofs of $\forall x\colon A.\phi$ are precisely the elements of the general product type $\Pi x\colon A.\phi$.

The correspondence between $\forall x\colon A.\phi$ and $\Pi x\colon A.\phi$ can also be seen in the proof rules for universal quantification. The natural deduction rules for universal quantifiers, found in [Pra65], for example, are universal generalization and instantiation.

$$\frac{\phi}{\forall x\colon A.\phi} \qquad \begin{array}{l} x\colon A \text{ not free in} \\ \text{any assumption} \end{array} \qquad \frac{\forall x\colon A.\phi \quad a\colon A}{[a/x]\phi}$$

(The condition in the middle is a side condition for the first rule.) The first rule gives us a typing rule for lambda abstraction. Specifically, if we have a term giving a proof of ϕ, we can lambda abstract a free variable x of type A in M to obtain a proof of $\forall x\colon A.\phi$. In lambda calculus terminology, the side condition is that x may not appear in the type of any free variable of M. This does not arise in simply-typed lambda calculus since term variables cannot appear in type expressions. However, in polymorphic calculi, this becomes an important restriction on lambda abstraction of type variables. In summary, the logical rule of universal generalization leads to the (Π Intro) rule

$$\frac{\Gamma, x\colon A \triangleright M\colon \sigma}{\Gamma \triangleright \lambda x\colon A.\, M\colon \Pi x\colon A.\sigma}\ x \text{ not free in } \Gamma \qquad (\Pi\ \text{Intro})$$

explained in more detail for $A = U_1$, a "universe of types," in Section 9.2.1. The second proof rule, universal instantiation, corresponds to function application. More specifically, if a proof of $\forall x\colon A.\phi$ is a function of type $\Pi x\colon A.\phi$, and $a\colon A$, then we may obtain a proof of $[a/x]\phi$ by applying the function to argument a. This leads to the (Π Elim) rule

$$\frac{\Gamma \triangleright M\colon \Pi x\colon A.\sigma \quad \Gamma \triangleright N\colon A}{\Gamma \triangleright MN\colon [N/x]\sigma} \qquad (\Pi\ \text{Elim})$$

explained for $A = U_1$ in Section 9.2.1.

The situation is similar for existential quantification and general sums. The logical rules of existential generalization and instantiation are

$$\frac{[a/x]\phi \quad a\colon A}{\exists x\colon A.\phi} \qquad \frac{\exists x\colon A.\phi \quad \begin{array}{c}[y/x]\phi \\ \vdots \\ \psi\end{array}}{\psi} \qquad \begin{array}{l} y \text{ not free in any} \\ \text{other assumption}\end{array}$$

In the first rule, we prove $\exists x\colon A.\phi$ by showing that ϕ holds for some specific $a\colon A$. In the second rule, the second hypothesis is meant to indicate a proof of ψ from an assumption of a formula of the form $[y/x]\phi$, with some "fresh" variable y used to stand for some arbitrary element satisfying the property ϕ. In other words, the formula $\exists x\colon A.\phi$ says that "ϕ holds for some x." We can use this to prove another formula ψ by choosing some arbitrary name y for "some x." This rule discharges the assumption $[y/x]\phi$, which means that although the proof of ψ above the line depends on this hypothesis, the proof of ψ resulting from the use of this rule does not depend on this assumption. (See Section 4.3.4 for a discussion of how natural deduction rules may introduce or discharge assumptions.) The term formation rules associated with general sums and existential quantification are given in Section 9.4.

In logic, there is a fundamental distinction between first-order logic and second- and higher-order logics. Since a general product $\Pi x\colon A.B$ provides universal quantification over A, we can obtain first-order, second-order or higher-order type systems by specifying the kind of type A that may appear in a product $\Pi x\colon A.B$. The first-order dependent products of the last subsection usually correspond to first-order quantification, since we are quantifying over elements of a type. Polymorphism arises from products of the form $\Pi x\colon T.B$, where T is some collection of types, providing universal quantification over propositions. Similarly, a general sum $\Sigma x\colon A.B$ provides existential quantification over A while the general sums $\Sigma x\colon T.B$ associated with data abstraction provide existential quantification over propositions. With general products and sums of all kinds, we can develop logic with universal and existential quantification over each type, as well as quantification over collections of types. In a predicative system, quantification over propositions is restricted to certain subcollections, while in an impredicative system, we can quantify over the class of all propositions.

Another aspect of formulas-as-types is that in most type systems, common atomic formulas such as equality do not appear as basic types. Therefore, in order to develop type systems that allow program specification and verification, we must also introduce types that correspond to atomic formulas. To give some idea of how atomic formulas may be added, we will briefly summarize a simple encoding of equality between terms. Since types represent propositions, we need a type representing the proposition that two terms are equal, together with a way of writing terms of the resulting "equality type." For any terms $M, N\colon A$, we could introduce a type of the form $Eq_A(M, N)$ to represent the atomic formula $M = N$. The terms of type $Eq_A(M, N)$ would correspond to the ways of establishing that $M = N$. Since equality is reflexive, we might have a term formation rule so that for any $M\colon A$, there is a term $\mathit{refl}_A(M)\colon Eq_A(M, M)$. In other words, for every $M\colon A$, there is a "proof" $\mathit{refl}_A(M)$ of the formula $Eq_A(M, M)$. To account for symmetry, we would have another term formation rule such that for any $M\colon Eq_A(N, P)$, representing a proof that $N = P$, there is also a term $\mathit{sym}_A(M)\colon Eq_A(P, N)$ representing a proof that $P = N$. In addition, we would expect term forms for transitivity and possibly other properties of equality such as substitutivity of equivalents. In a language like this, we could write a term of type $Eq_A(M, N)$ whenever M and N are provably equal terms of type A.

To see how we may regard types as "program specifications" and well-typed terms as "verified programs," we will give a concrete example. Suppose $\mathit{prime}(x)$ is a type corresponding to the assertion that $x\colon \mathit{nat}$ is prime, and $\mathit{divides}(x, y)$ is a type "saying" that x divides y. These would not necessarily be atomic types of the language, but could be complicated type expressions with free natural number variables x and y. Then we would expect a term of type

$$\Pi x\colon \mathit{nat}.(x > 1 \to \Sigma y\colon \mathit{nat}.(\mathit{prime}(y) \times \mathit{divides}(y, x)))$$

to define a function which, given any natural number x, takes a proof of $x > 1$ and returns a pair $\langle N, M\rangle$ with $N\colon \mathit{nat}$ and M proving that N is a prime number dividing x. Based on this general idea of types as logical assertions, Automath, Nuprl and the Calculus of Constructions have all been proposed as systems for verifying programs.

9.2 Predicative Polymorphic Calculus

9.2.1 Syntax of Types and Terms

In this section, we define the predicative polymorphic lambda calculus $\lambda^{\to,\Pi}$. By itself, pure $\lambda^{\to,\Pi}$ is not a very significant extension of $\lambda^{\to}$ since the only operations we may perform on an expression of polymorphic type are type abstraction and application. Since we do not have lambda abstraction over term variables with polymorphic types, we cannot pass polymorphic functions as arguments or model polymorphic function declarations. However, $\lambda^{\rightarrow,\Pi}$ illustrates some of the essential features common to all languages with type abstraction and forms the core fragment of several useful languages. For example, by adding a declaration form for polymorphic functions, we obtain a language resembling a core fragment of the programming language ML as explained in Section 9.2.5. With additional typing rules that eliminate the distinctions imposed by predicativity, we obtain the Girard–Reynolds calculus of impredicative polymorphism, explored in Section 9.3. With one more typing assumption, we obtain *type*: *type*. It is straightforward to extend any of these systems with other simple types such as *null*, *unit*, $+$ and $\times$, using the term forms and equational rules in Chapter 4.

The types of $\lambda^{\rightarrow,\Pi}$ fall into two classes, corresponding to the $\lambda^{\rightarrow}$ types and the polymorphic types constructed using Π. Following the terminology that originated with Martin-Löf's type theory, we will call these classes *universes.* The universe of function types over some collection of given types (such as *nat* and *bool*) will be written U_1 and the universe of polymorphic types U_2. If we were to extend the language with cartesian product types, we would put the cartesian product of two U_1 types in U_1, and the cartesian product of two U_2 types (if desired) in U_2. To give the universes simple names, we sometimes call U_1 and U_2 the "small" and "large" types, respectively. Although we will later simplify the syntax of $\lambda^{\rightarrow,\Pi}$ by introducing some meta-linguistic conventions, we will begin by giving explicit syntax rules for both type expressions and terms. The reasons for giving a detailed treatment of syntax are: (i) this makes membership in each type and universe as clear as possible, (ii) this gives an introduction to the general method used to define the syntax of more general type systems, and (iii) this makes it easier to see precisely how impredicative and *type*: *type* polymorphism are derivable from predicative polymorphism by imposing additional relationships between U_1 and U_2.

In a general type system, the syntax of each class of expressions is given by a proof system for assertions that are commonly called "syntactic judgements." Like the type derivation system for simply-typed lambda calculus in Chapter 4, the proof system for syntactic judgements may be understood as an axiomatic presentation of a type checker for the language. In our general presentation of $\lambda^{\rightarrow,\Pi}$, we will use judgements of the form $\Gamma \triangleright A\colon B$, where Γ is a context (like the sort assignments of Chapter 3 and type assignments of Chapter 4) indicating the type or universe of each variable, A is the expression whose type or universe is being asserted, and B is either U_1, U_2 or a type expression. The judgement $\Gamma \triangleright A\colon B$ is read, "in context Γ, A is a well-formed expression defining an element of type or universe B." A useful property of the syntax rules is that if $\Gamma \triangleright A\colon B$ is derivable, then all of the free variables of A and B must appear in Γ.

A *context* is an ordered sequence

$$\Gamma = v_1: A_1, \ldots, v_k: A_k$$

giving types or universes to variables $v_1, \ldots, v_k$. In order to make sense, no v_i may occur twice in this sequence, and each A_i must be provably well-formed assuming only $v_1: A_1, \ldots, v_{i-1}: A_{i-1}$. We will put this formally using axioms and inference rules for judgements of the form "Γ context," which say that "Γ is a well-formed context." The order of assertions in a context is meant to reflect the order of declarations in an expression, including declarations of the types of formal parameters. For example, in showing that a term such as

$$\lambda t: U_1. \lambda x: t \to t. \lambda y: t. xy$$

is well-typed, we would show that the function body, xy, is well-typed in the context $t: U_1, x: t \to t, y: t$. In this context, it is important that $t: U_1$ precedes $x: t \to t$ and $y: t$ since we need to declare that t is a type variable before we write type expressions $t \to t$ and t. The context would make sense with x and y declared in either order, but only one order is useful for deriving a type for this term.

The context axiom

$$\emptyset \text{ context} \qquad (\textit{empty context})$$

says that the empty sequence is a well-formed context. We can add an assertion $x: A$ to a context if A is either a universe or a well-formed type expression. Although it would be entirely reasonable to have U_2 variables in an extension of $\lambda^{\to,\Pi}$, we will only use U_1 variables, for reasons that are outlined below. We therefore have one rule for adding U_1 variables and one for adding variables with U_i types to contexts.

$$\frac{\Gamma \text{ context}}{\Gamma, t: U_1 \text{ context}}\ t \text{ not in } \Gamma \qquad (U_1\ \textit{context})$$

$$\frac{\Gamma \rhd \sigma: U_i}{\Gamma, x: \sigma \text{ context}}\ x \text{ not in } \Gamma \qquad (U_i\ \textit{type context})$$

The second rule (for adding a variable ranging over a specific type) illustrates a general convention in formal presentation of type systems: we omit conditions that will be guaranteed by simple properties of the syntax rules. In this case, we do not explicitly assume "Γ context" in the hypothesis of this rule since it will be a property of the syntax rules that we can only derive $\Gamma \rhd \sigma: U_i$ when Γ is a well-formed context.

Along with forming contexts, there are two other general rules that apply to a variety of type systems. The first is the rule for making use of assumptions in contexts.

$$\frac{\Gamma, x\colon A \text{ context}}{\Gamma, x\colon A \rhd x\colon A} \qquad (var)$$

This is essentially the converse of the rules for adding an assertion $x\colon A$ to a context. The rule is useful both when A is U_1 and when A is a type belonging to U_1 or U_2. We also have a general rule for adding hypotheses to a syntactic judgement.

$$\frac{\Gamma \rhd A\colon B \qquad \Gamma, x\colon C \text{ context}}{\Gamma, x\colon C \rhd A\colon B} \qquad (add\ var)$$

This is needed to derive a judgement such as $x\colon A,\ y\colon B \rhd x\colon A$ where the variable on the right of the "$\rhd$" is not the last variable in the context. We give these rules the same names, (*var*) and (*add var*), as the axiom and inference rule in the definition of simply-typed lambda calculus, since these are the natural generalizations.

A $\lambda^{\rightarrow,\Pi}$ *signature* consists of a set of type constants (which we restrict to U_1) and a set of term constants. Each term constant must be assigned a closed type expression (without free variables) over the type constants of the signature.

We now give syntax rules for U_1 and U_2 type expressions. The first universe U_1 is essentially the predicative T of the last section. The U_1 type expressions are given by variable rule (*var*), applied to U_1 variables, the axiom

$$\emptyset \rhd b\colon U_1 \qquad (cst\ U_1)$$

for type constant b of the signature, and inference rule

$$\frac{\Gamma \rhd \tau\colon U_1 \quad \Gamma \rhd \tau'\colon U_1}{\Gamma \rhd \tau \rightarrow \tau'\colon U_1} \qquad (\rightarrow\ U_1)$$

giving us function type expressions. The second universe U_2 contains the U_1 types and types of polymorphic functions.

$$\frac{\Gamma \rhd \tau\colon U_1}{\Gamma \rhd \tau\colon U_2} \qquad (U_1 \subseteq U_2)$$

$$\frac{\Gamma, t\colon U_1 \rhd \sigma\colon U_2}{\Gamma \rhd \Pi t\colon U_1 . \sigma\colon U_2} \qquad (\Pi\ U_2)$$

Since the $(U_1 \subseteq U_2)$ rule makes every type of the first universe a type of the second, we describe the relationship between universes by writing $U_1 \subseteq U_2$.

Example 9.2.1 A simple example of a typing derivation is the proof that $\Pi t\colon U_1 . t \rightarrow t$ is a well-formed U_2 type expression.

$\emptyset$ context	by axiom (*empty context*)
$t\colon U_1$ context	by (U_1 *context*)
$t\colon U_1 \rhd t\colon U_1$	(*var*)
$t\colon U_1 \rhd t \to t\colon U_1$	($\to\ U_1$)
$t\colon U_1 \rhd t \to t\colon U_2$	($U_1 \subseteq U_2$)
$\emptyset \rhd (\Pi t\colon U_1.t \to t)\colon U_2(\Pi\ U_2)$	

The reader may wish to stop and work out the similar proof that $\Pi s\colon U_1.\, \Pi t\colon U_1.\, s \to t$ is a well-formed U_2 type expression. The only tricky point in this proof is using (*add var*) to derive $s\colon U_1, t\colon U_1 \rhd s\colon U_1$ from $s\colon U_1 \rhd s\colon U_1$. Although all these proof rules for syntax may seem like much ado about nothing, it is important to be completely clear about which expressions are well-formed and which are not. In addition, with a little practice, syntax proofs become second nature and require very little thought. ∎

While we have expressions for U_2 types, we do not have variables ranging over U_2. The reason is that since we do not have binding operators for U_2 variables, it seems impossible to use U_2 variables for any significant purpose. If we were to add variables and lambda abstraction over U_2, this would lead us to types of the form $\Pi t\colon U_2.\, \sigma$, which would belong to a third universe U_3. Continuing in this way, we might also add universes U_4, U_5, U_6 and so on. Several systems of this form may be found in the literature [C+86, Mar73, Mar82, Mar84], but we do not investigate these in this book.

The terms of $\lambda^{\to,\Pi}$ may be summarized by defining the set of "pre–terms," or expressions which look like terms but are not guaranteed to satisfy all the typing constraints. The un–checked *pre–terms* of $\lambda^{\to,\Pi}$ are given by the grammar

$$M \ ::= \ x \mid \lambda x\colon \tau.M \mid MM \mid \lambda t\colon U_1.\, M \mid M\tau$$

where in each case τ must be a U_1 type. Every term of $\lambda^{\to,\Pi}$ must have one of the forms given by this grammar, but not all expressions generated by the grammar are well-typed $\lambda^{\to,\Pi}$ terms.

The precise typing rules for terms include axiom (*var*) for variables and rule (*add var*) for adding hypotheses about additional variables to judgements. We also have an axiom

$$\emptyset \rhd c\colon \sigma \qquad (cst)$$

for each term constant of the signature. For lambda abstraction and application, we have rules ($\to$ Intro) and ($\to$ Elim) as in $\lambda^{\to}$, reformulated as follows to include type variables and explicit universe assumptions.

$$\frac{\Gamma, x{:}\,\tau \rhd M{:}\,\tau' \quad \Gamma \rhd \tau{:}\,U_1 \quad \Gamma \rhd \tau'{:}\,U_1}{\Gamma \rhd (\lambda x{:}\,\tau.M){:}\,\tau \to \tau'} \qquad (\to \text{ Intro})$$

$$\frac{\Gamma \rhd M{:}\,\tau \to \tau' \quad \Gamma \rhd N{:}\,\tau}{\Gamma \rhd MN{:}\,\tau'} \qquad (\to \text{ Elim})$$

In rule ($\to$ Elim), It is not necessary to specify that $\tau{:}\,U_1$ since $\tau \to \tau'$ will only be well formed when both τ and τ' are in U_1. Since we have repeated all the typing rules from $\lambda^{\to}$, it is easy to check that any $\lambda^{\to}$ term, perhaps containing type variables in place of type constants, is a term of $\lambda^{\to,\Pi}$.

Type abstractions and applications are formed according to the following rules:

$$\frac{\Gamma, t{:}\,U_1 \rhd M{:}\,\sigma}{\Gamma \rhd \lambda t{:}\,U_1.\,M{:}\,\Pi t.\sigma} \qquad (\Pi \text{ Intro})$$

$$\frac{\Gamma \rhd M{:}\,\Pi t{:}\,U_1.\sigma \quad \Gamma \rhd \tau{:}\,U_1}{\Gamma \rhd M\tau{:}\,[\tau/t]\sigma} \qquad (\Pi \text{ Elim})$$

In (Π Elim), the type $[\tau/t]\sigma$ will belong to U_1 if $\sigma{:}\,U_1$, and belong only to U_2 otherwise. The final rule is a type equality rule

$$\frac{\Gamma \rhd M{:}\,\sigma_1 \quad \Gamma \rhd \sigma_1 = \sigma_2{:}\,U_i}{\Gamma \rhd M{:}\,\sigma_2} \qquad (\textit{type eq})$$

which allows us to replace the type of a term by an equal type. In pure $\lambda^{\to,\Pi}$, the only equations between types will be consequences of α-conversion. However, in extensions of the language, there may be more complicated type equations and so we give the general rule here.

We say M *is a term of* $\lambda^{\to,\Pi}$ *with type* σ *in context* Γ if $\Gamma \rhd M : \sigma$ is derivable from the axioms and $\lambda^{\to,\Pi}$ typing rules.

Example 9.2.2 Let Σ be a signature with type constant *nat* and term constant $3{:}\,nat$. We will show that $(\lambda t{:}\,U_1.\,\lambda x{:}\,t.\,x)\,nat\,3$ has type *nat*. This is a relatively simple term, but the typing derivation involves many of the proof rules. Since the term begins with lambda bindings for $t{:}\,U_1, x{:}\,t$, we begin by showing "$t{:}\,U_1, x{:}\,t$ context."

$\emptyset$ context	by axiom(*empty context*)
$t{:}\,U_1$ context	by (U_1 *context*)
$t{:}\,U_1 \rhd t{:}\,U_1$	(*var*)
$t{:}\,U_1, x{:}\,t$ context	(U_i *type context*)

We next observe that the judgement

$t: U_1, x: t \triangleright t: U_1$

follows from the last two lines above by (*add var*) while

$t: U_1, x: t \triangleright x: t$

follows from $t: U_1, x: t$ context by (*var*). The remaining steps use the term-formation rules. For simplicity, we omit the judgement $nat: U_1$, used below as the second hypothesis for rules ($\rightarrow$ Intro) and (Π Elim).

$t: U_1, x: t \triangleright x: t$	from above
$t: U_1 \triangleright \lambda x: t.\, x: t \rightarrow t$	($\rightarrow$ Intro)
$\emptyset \triangleright \lambda t: U_1.\, \lambda x: t.\, x: \Pi t.t \rightarrow t$	(Π Intro)
$\emptyset \triangleright (\lambda t: U_1.\, \lambda x: t.\, x)\ nat: nat \rightarrow nat$	(Π Elim)
$\emptyset \triangleright 3: nat$	axiom (*cst*)
$\emptyset \triangleright (\lambda t: U_1.\, \lambda x: t.\, x)\, nat\, 3: nat$	($\rightarrow$ Elim) ■

One potentially puzzling design decision is the containment $U_1 \subseteq U_2$. The main reason for this rule is that it simplifies both the use of the language, and a number of technical details in its presentation. For example, by putting every $\tau: U_1$ into U_2 as well, we can write a single Π-formation rule, instead of giving two separate cases for types starting in U_1 or U_2. An important part of this design decision is that $U_1 \subseteq U_2$ places no additional semantic constraints on the language. More specifically, if we remove the $(U_1 \subseteq U_2)$ rule from the language definition, we are left with a system in which every U_1 type is represented as a U_2 type. This allows us to faithfully translate $\lambda^{\rightarrow,\Pi}$ into the weaker version without $U_1 \subseteq U_2$. This is made more precise in Exercises 9.2.5 and 9.2.11, which uses the equational axiom system.

Another possible relationship that we do not impose is $U_1: U_2$, which would mean that "the universe of small types is itself a large type." Since $\lambda^{\rightarrow,\Pi}$ does not have any significant operations on arbitrary U_2 types, there does not seem to be any reason to take $U_1: U_2$. However, in predicative extensions of $\lambda^{\rightarrow,\Pi}$, it would be a reasonable language design to put $U_1: U_2$. In an impredicative system with $U_1 = U_2$, the further assumption that $U_1: U_2$ would lead to *type*: *type*, which is often considered undesirable. However, we will see in Section 9.5.4 that with the σ type-binding operator, used for writing ML "signatures," we will essentially be forced to have U_1 as a member of U_2.

Exercise 9.2.3 An alternate (*var*) rule is

$$\frac{\Gamma \text{ context} \quad x\colon\sigma \in \Gamma}{\Gamma \triangleright x\colon\sigma} \qquad (var)_{alt}$$

Show that this is a derivable rule, given (*var*), (*add var*) and the other rules listed in this section.

Exercise 9.2.4 Sketch derivations of the following typing judgements.

(a) $\emptyset \triangleright \lambda s\colon U_1.\, \lambda t\colon U_1.\, \lambda x\colon s \to t.\, \lambda y\colon s.\, xy\colon \Pi s\colon U_1.\, \Pi t\colon U_1.\, (s \to t) \to s \to t$

(b) $s\colon U_1,\ x\colon s,\ y\colon s \to s \triangleright \lambda z\colon s \to s \to s.\, zxy\colon (s \to s \to s) \to s$

(c) $s\colon U_1,\ x\colon s \to s \triangleright (\lambda y\colon s \to s.\, x)\, (\lambda x\colon s.\, x)\colon s \to s$

Exercise 9.2.5 This exercise asks you to show that for the purpose of typing terms, we have $U_1 \subseteq U_2$ even if we reformulate the system without the $(U_1 \subseteq U_2)$ rule. If we drop the $(U_1 \subseteq U_2)$ rule, then we need two $(\Pi\ U_2)$ rules, one for a U_1 type and one for a U_2 type:

$$\frac{\Gamma, t\colon U_1 \triangleright \tau\colon U_1}{\Gamma \triangleright \Pi t\colon U_1.\, \tau : U_2} \qquad \frac{\Gamma, t\colon U_1 \triangleright \sigma\colon U_2}{\Gamma \triangleright \Pi t\colon U_1.\, \sigma : U_2}$$

(These could be written as a single rule using a meta-variable i representing either 1 or 2.) We should also rewrite the (Π Intro) rule as two rules:

$$\frac{\Gamma, t\colon U_1 \triangleright M\colon \tau \quad \Gamma, t\colon U_1 \triangleright \tau\colon U_1}{\Gamma \triangleright \lambda t\colon U_1.\, M\colon \Pi t.\tau} \qquad \frac{\Gamma, t\colon U_1 \triangleright M\colon \sigma \quad \Gamma, t\colon U_1 \triangleright \sigma\colon U_2}{\Gamma \triangleright \lambda t\colon U_1.\, M\colon \Pi t.\sigma}$$

Show that with these changes to $(\Pi\ U_2)$ and (Π Intro), any typing assertion $\Gamma \triangleright M\colon\sigma$ that can be derived using $(U_1 \subseteq U_2)$ can also be derived without $(U_1 \subseteq U_2)$.

9.2.2 Comparison with Other Forms of Polymorphism

Both the impredicative typed lambda calculus and the "*type*: *type*" calculus may be viewed as special cases of the predicative polymorphic calculus. The first arises by imposing the "universe equation" $U_1 = U_2$ and the second by imposing both the equation $U_1 = U_2$ and the condition $U_1\colon U_2$. This way of relating the three calculi is particularly useful when it comes to semantics, since it allows us to use the same form of structure as models for all three languages. We conclude this section with a simplified syntax for $\lambda^{\to,\Pi}$ that eliminates the need for type variables in contexts. This simplified syntax may also be used for the impredicative calculus, but breaks down with either *type*: *type* or the general product and sum operations added to $\lambda^{\to,\Pi}$ in Section 9.5.

Impredicative Calculus

Since we already have $U_1 \subseteq U_2$ in $\lambda^{\rightarrow,\Pi}$, we may obtain $U_1 = U_2$ by adding a syntax rule that forces the reverse inclusion, $U_2 \subseteq U_1$. The following rule accomplishes this.

$$\frac{\Gamma \rhd \sigma : U_2}{\Gamma \rhd \sigma : U_1} \qquad (U_2 \subseteq U_1)$$

Example 9.2.6 A simple example which illustrates the effect of this rule is the term $(I\,(\Pi t.t \rightarrow t))\,I$, where $I \stackrel{\text{def}}{=} \lambda t\colon U_1.\lambda x\colon t.x$ is the polymorphic identity. We will prove the syntactic judgement

$$\emptyset \rhd (I\,(\Pi t.t \rightarrow t))\,I\colon \Pi t.t \rightarrow t.$$

As illustrated in Example 9.2.2, we can derive the typing judgement $\emptyset \rhd I\colon (\Pi t.t \rightarrow t)$ using the typing rules of $\lambda^{\rightarrow,\Pi}$, with $(\Pi t.t \rightarrow t)\colon U_2$. Using the impredicative rule $(U_2 \subseteq U_1)$, we may now derive $(\Pi t.t \rightarrow t)\colon U_1$. This allows us to apply the polymorphic identity to the type $\Pi t.t \rightarrow t$. According to the (Π Elim) typing rule, the type application $I\,(\Pi t.t \rightarrow t)$ has type $[(\Pi t.t \rightarrow t)/t](t \rightarrow t)$, which is $(\Pi t.t \rightarrow t) \rightarrow (\Pi t.t \rightarrow t)$. Notice that this would not be a well-formed type expression in predicative $\lambda^{\rightarrow,\Pi}$, but it is a type expression of both universes (since they are the same) when we have $(U_2 \subseteq U_1)$. Finally, by rule ($\rightarrow$ Elim) the application $(I\,(\Pi t.t \rightarrow t))\,I$ has type $\Pi t.t \rightarrow t$. ∎

Type : Type

The second extension of predicative polymorphism is to add both $U_2 = U_1$ and $U_1\colon U_2$. We have already seen that the syntax rule $(U_2 \subseteq U_1)$ is sufficient to achieve $U_2 = U_1$. To make U_1 an element of U_2, we may add the typing axiom

$$\emptyset \rhd U_1\colon U_2 \qquad (U_1\colon U_2)$$

Since there is no reason to distinguish between U_1 and U_2, we will often simply write U for either universe. There is some lack of precision in doing this, but the alternative involves lots of arbitrary decisions of when to write U_1 and when to write U_2.

There is much more complexity to the syntax of this language than initially meets the eye. In particular, since the distinction between types and terms that have a type is blurred, the equational proof rules may enter into typing derivations in relatively complicated ways. Some hint of this is given in the following example.

Example 9.2.7 An example which illustrates the use of the *type*: *type* rule is the term

$$(\lambda f\colon U \rightarrow (U \rightarrow U).\, \lambda s\colon U.\, \lambda t\colon U.\, \lambda x\colon (f\,s\,t).\, x)\ \ (\lambda s\colon U.\lambda t\colon U.s)\ \mathit{nat}\ \mathit{bool}\ 3$$

where we assume *nat*, *bool*: U_1 and 3: *nat*. Intuitively, the first part of this term is an identity function whose type depends on three parameters, the type function $f\colon U \to (U \to U)$ and two type arguments $s, t\colon U$. This is applied to the type function $\lambda s\colon U.\lambda t\colon U.s$, two type arguments, and a natural number argument. The most interesting part of the type derivation is the way that equational reasoning is used.

We begin by typing the left-most function. The type derivation for this subterm begins by showing that $U_1 \to U_1 \to U_1$ is a type, introducing a variable f and adding variables s and t to the context.

$\emptyset \rhd U_1\colon U_2$	by axiom ($U_1\colon U_2$)
$\emptyset \rhd U_1\colon U_1$	($U_2 \subseteq U_1$)
$\emptyset \rhd U_1 \to U_1\colon U_1$	($\to U_1$)
$\emptyset \rhd U_1 \to U_1 \to U_1\colon U_1$	($\to U_1$)
$f\colon U_1 \to U_1 \to U_1$ context	(U_i *type context*)
$f\colon U_1 \to U_1 \to U_1 \rhd f\colon U_1 \to U_1 \to U_1$	(*var*)
$f\colon U_1 \to U_1 \to U_1, s\colon U$ context	(U_1 *context*)
$f\colon U_1 \to U_1 \to U_1, s\colon U \rhd f\colon U_1 \to U_1 \to U_1$	(*add var*)
$f\colon U_1 \to U_1 \to U_1, s\colon U, t\colon U$ context	(U_1 *context*)
$f\colon U_1 \to U_1 \to U_1, s\colon U, t\colon U \rhd f\colon U_1 \to U_1 \to U_1$	(*add var*)

We may derive $s\colon U_1$ and $t\colon U_1$ in the same context similarly, and use ($\to$ Elim) twice to show

$$f\colon U_1 \to U_1 \to U_1, s\colon U, t\colon U \rhd fst\colon U_1$$

It is then straightforward to form the identity function of this type, and lambda abstract the three variables in the context to obtain

$$\emptyset \rhd \lambda f\colon U_1 \to U_1 \to U_1.\, \lambda s\colon U.\, \lambda t\colon U.\, \lambda x\colon fst.\, x\colon$$
$$\Pi f\colon U_1 \to U_1 \to U_1.\, \Pi s\colon U_1.\, \Pi t\colon U_1.\, (fst) \to (fst)$$

The interesting step is now that after applying to arguments $(\lambda s\colon U_1.\lambda t\colon U_1.s)\colon U_1 \to U_1 \to U_1$, *nat*: U_1 and *bool*: U_1 to obtain

$$\emptyset \rhd (\lambda f\colon U_1 \to U_1 \to U_1.\, \lambda s\colon U_1.\, \lambda t\colon U_1.\, \lambda x\colon fst.\, x)(\lambda s\colon U_1.\lambda t\colon U_1.s)\mathit{nat}\ \mathit{bool}\colon$$
$$((\lambda s\colon U_1.\lambda t\colon U_1.s)\mathit{nat}\ \mathit{bool}) \to ((\lambda s\colon U_1.\lambda t\colon U_1.s)\mathit{nat}\ \mathit{bool})$$

We must use equational reasoning to simplify both occurrences of $(\lambda s\colon U_1.\lambda t\colon U_1.s)\mathit{nat}$

bool in the type of this application to *nat*. This is done using β-reduction to obtain

$$\emptyset \triangleright (\lambda s\colon U_1.\lambda t\colon U_1.s)\mathit{nat}\ \mathit{bool} = \mathit{nat}\colon U_1$$

followed by the type equality rule (*type eq*). Once we have the resulting typing assertion,

$$\emptyset \triangleright (\lambda f\colon U_1 \to U_1 \to U_1.\,\lambda s\colon U_1.\,\lambda t\colon U_1.\,\lambda x\colon fst.\,x)(\lambda s\colon U_1.\lambda t\colon U_1.s)\mathit{nat}\ \mathit{bool}\colon \mathit{nat} \to \mathit{nat}$$

it is clear that we may apply this function to $3\colon \mathit{nat}$. The important thing to notice is that the type function $\lambda s\colon U_1.\lambda t\colon U_1.s$ could have been replaced by a much more complicated expression, and that type checking requires the evaluation of a type function applied to type arguments. ■

Example 9.2.7 shows how equational reasoning enters into *type*: *type* typing derivations. Although we will not go into the proof, it can be shown by a rather subtle argument [Mar73, MR86] that with *type*: *type*, we may write very complex functions of type $U_1 \to U_1 \to U_1$, for example. This allows us to construct functions like the one given in Example 9.2.7 where evaluating the actual function is very simple, but deciding whether it is well-typed is very complicated. Using essentially this idea, it may be shown that the set of well-typed terms with *type*: *type* is in fact undecidable [Mar73, MR86]. This definitely rules out an efficient compile-time type checking algorithm for any programming language based on the *type*: *type* calculus.

Simplified Syntax of $\lambda^{\to,\Pi}$

A simplifying syntactic convention is to use two sorts of variables, distinguishing term variables $x, y, z, \ldots$ from type variables $r, s, t, \ldots$ by using different letters of the alphabet. In the simplified presentation of $\lambda^{\to,\Pi}$, we assume that all type variables denote U_1 types. A second convention is to use $\tau, \tau', \tau_1, \ldots$ for U_1 types and $\sigma, \sigma', \sigma_1, \ldots$ for U_2 types. This allows us to give the syntax of U_1 and U_2 type expressions by the following grammar:

$$\tau \ ::= \ t \mid b \mid \tau \to \tau$$

$$\sigma \ ::= \ \tau \mid \Pi t.\sigma$$

When we simplify the presentation of type expressions, we no longer need to include type variables in contexts, and we can drop the ordering on assumptions in contexts.

The typing rules for $\lambda^{\to,\Pi}$ terms may now be written using contexts of the form

$$\Gamma = \{x_1, \sigma_1, \ldots, x_k\colon \sigma_k\}$$

consisting of pairs $x\colon\sigma$ that each associate a type with a distinct variable. The rules for terms remain essentially the same as above, except that we may drop the explicit assumptions involving universes since these follow from our notational conventions. To be absolutely clear, we give the entire simplified rules below.

$$\{x\colon \sigma\} \rhd x\colon \sigma \qquad (var)$$

$$\emptyset \rhd c\colon \sigma \qquad (cst)$$

$$\frac{\Gamma, x\colon \tau \rhd M\colon \tau'}{\Gamma \rhd (\lambda x\colon \tau.M)\colon \tau \to \tau'} \qquad (\to \text{Intro})$$

$$\frac{\Gamma \rhd M\colon \tau \to \tau', \;\; \Gamma \rhd N\colon \tau}{\Gamma \rhd MN\colon \tau'} \qquad (\to \text{Elim})$$

$$\frac{\Gamma \rhd M\colon \sigma}{\Gamma \rhd \lambda t.M\colon \Pi t.\sigma} \quad (t \text{ not free in } \Gamma) \qquad (\Pi\ \text{Intro})$$

$$\frac{\Gamma \rhd M\colon \Pi t.\sigma}{\Gamma \rhd M\tau\colon [\tau/t]\sigma} \qquad (\Pi\ \text{Elim})$$

The restriction "t not free in Γ" in (Π Intro) is derived from the ordering on contexts in the detailed presentation of syntax. Specifically, if we use the detailed presentation of syntax, then a term may contain a free type variable t only if the context contains $t\colon U_1$. Since (Π Intro) for ordered contexts only applies when $t\colon U_1$ occurs last in the context, we are guaranteed that t does not occur elsewhere in the context. In order for the simplified syntax to be accurate, we therefore need the side condition in (Π Intro) above. This side condition prevents meaningless terms such as $\{x\colon t\} \rhd \lambda t.x$, in which it is not clear whether t is free or bound (see Exercise 9.2.10).

Exercise 9.2.8 Use induction on typing derivations to show that if $\Gamma \rhd M\colon \sigma$ is derivable, then so is $[\tau/t]\Gamma \rhd [\tau/t]M\colon [\tau/t]\sigma$.

9.2.3 Equational Proof System and Reduction

We will write terms using the simplified syntax presented at the end of the last section.

Like other typed equations, $\lambda^{\to,\Pi}$ equations have the form $\Gamma \rhd M = N\colon \sigma$, where M and N are terms of type σ in context Γ. The equational inference system for $\lambda^{\to,\Pi}$ is an extension of the $\lambda^{\to}$ proof system, with additional axioms for type abstraction and application.

$$\Gamma \rhd \lambda t.M = \lambda s.[s/t]M\colon \Pi t.\sigma \qquad (\alpha)_\Pi$$

$$\Gamma \rhd (\lambda t.M)\tau = [\tau/t]M\colon [\tau/t]\sigma \qquad (\beta)_\Pi$$

$$\Gamma \triangleright \lambda t.Mt = M\colon \Pi t.\sigma \quad t \text{ not free in } M \qquad (\eta)_\Pi$$

Reduction rules are defined from $(\beta)_\Pi$ and $(\eta)_\Pi$ by directing these axioms from left to right.

The proof system includes a reflexivity axiom and symmetry and transitivity rules to make provable equality an equivalence relation. Additional inference rules make provable equality a congruence with respect to all of the term-formation rules. For ordinary lambda abstraction and application, the appropriate axioms are given in Chapter 4. For type abstraction and application we have the following congruence rules.

$$\frac{\Gamma \triangleright M = N\colon \sigma}{\Gamma \triangleright \lambda t.M = \lambda t.N\colon \Pi t.\sigma} \qquad (\xi)_\Pi$$

$$\frac{\Gamma \triangleright M = N\colon \Pi t.\sigma}{\Gamma \triangleright M\tau = N\tau\colon [\tau/t]\sigma} \qquad (\nu)_\Pi$$

We consider type expressions that only differ in the names of bound variables to be equivalent. As a result, we do not use an explicit rule for renaming bound type variables in types that occur in equations or terms.

As for other forms of lambda calculus, we can orient the equational axioms from left to right to obtain a reduction system. In more detail, we say that $\lambda^{\rightarrow,\Pi}$ term M *reduces to* N and write $M \rightarrow N$ if N may be obtained by applying any of the reduction rules (β), (η), $(\beta)_\Pi$, $(\eta)_\Pi$ to some subterm of M. For example, we have the reduction sequence

$$(\lambda t.\lambda x\colon t.x)\, \tau\, y \rightarrow (\lambda x\colon \tau.x)\, y \rightarrow y,$$

the first by $(\beta)_\Pi$ reduction and the second by ordinary (β) reduction. It is generally convenient to refer to both ordinary (β) and $(\beta)_\Pi$ as β-reduction, and similarly for η-reduction.

Most of the basic theorems about reduction in simply-typed lambda calculus generalize to $\lambda^{\rightarrow,\Pi}$. For example, we may prove confluence and strong normalization for reduction polymorphic $\lambda^{\rightarrow,\Pi}$ terms. (See Exercise 9.2.12 below for an easy proof of strong normalization; confluence follows from an easy check for local confluence, using Lemma 3.7.32.) An important reduction property of $\lambda^{\rightarrow,\Pi}$, *subject reduction,* is that reduction preserves the type of a term.

Proposition 9.2.9 (Subject Reduction) Suppose $\Gamma \triangleright M\colon \sigma$ is a well-typed $\lambda^{\rightarrow,\Pi}$ term and $M \twoheadrightarrow N$ by any number of β, η, β_Π, η_Π-reduction steps. Then $\Gamma \triangleright N\colon \sigma$, *i.e.*, N is a well-typed term of the same type.

The proof is similar to the proof of Lemma 4.4.16. The main lemmas are preservation of typing under term substitution (as in Lemma 4.3.6) and an analogous property of type substitution given as Exercise 9.2.8.

Exercise 9.2.10 Show that if the side condition "t not free in Γ" is dropped from rule (Π Intro), the Subject Reduction property fails. (*Hint:* Consider a term of the form $(\lambda t.\, M)\tau$ where t is not free in M.)

Exercise 9.2.11 Exercise 9.2.5 shows that for the purpose of typing terms, the rule ($U_1 \subseteq U_2$) is unnecessary, provide we reformulate (Π U_2) and (Π Intro) appropriately. This exercise asks you to show that under the same modifications of (Π U_2) and (Π Intro), we will essentially have $U_1 \subseteq U_2$, *i.e.*, for every U_1 type there is an "essentially equivalent" U_2 type.

Let $\tau\colon U_1$ be any type from the first universe, and let t be a variable that is not free in τ. Let *unit* be any U_1 type that has a closed term $*\colon unit$. For any term M, let t_M be a type variable that does not occur free in M. The mappings $i[\,]$ and $j[\,]$ on terms are defined by $i[M] \stackrel{\text{def}}{=} \lambda t_M\colon U_1.\, M$ and $j[M] \stackrel{\text{def}}{=} M unit$.

(a) Show that $\Gamma \rhd i[M] : \Pi t\colon U_1.\tau$ whenever $\Gamma \rhd M : \tau$.

(b) Show that $\Gamma \rhd j[M] : \tau$ whenever $\Gamma \rhd M : \Pi t\colon U_1.\tau$.

(c) Show that $\Gamma \rhd j[i[M]] = M : \tau$ for all $\Gamma \rhd M : \tau$.

(d) Using $i[\,]$ and $j[\,]$, sketch a translation from $\lambda^{\rightarrow,\Pi}$ with $U_1 \subseteq U_2$ into an equivalent expression that is typed without using $U_1 \subseteq U_2$. Explain briefly why this translation preserves equality and the structure of terms.

Exercise 9.2.12 Use the strong normalization property of the simply typed lambda calculus $\lambda^{\rightarrow}$ to prove that $\lambda^{\rightarrow,\Pi}$ reduction is strongly normalizing. It may be useful to show first that if a $\lambda^{\rightarrow,\Pi}$ term M has a subterm of the form $x\tau$, then x must be a free variable of M.

9.2.4 Models of Predicative Polymorphism

It is basically straightforward to extend the definitions of $\lambda^{\rightarrow}$ applicative structure and Henkin model to $\lambda^{\rightarrow,\Pi}$ and to prove analogous type soundness, equational soundness and equational completeness theorems. In this section, we give a short presentation of $\lambda^{\rightarrow,\Pi}$ applicative structures and Henkin models, leaving it to the reader to prove soundness and completeness theorems if desired. Since impredicative and *type*: *type* polymorphism are derivable from predicative polymorphism by imposing additional relationships between universes, models of impredicative and *type*: *type* calculi are special cases of the more general predicative structures defined below. A category-theoretic framework for polymorphism may be developed using *hyperdoctrines, relatively cartesian closed categories*

[Tay87], or *locally cartesian closed* categories [See84]. However, none of the connections between these categories and polymorphic calculi are as straightforward as the categorical equivalence between $\lambda^{unit,\times,\rightarrow}$ and CCCs described in Chapter 7.

An interesting choice in giving semantics to $\lambda^{\rightarrow,\Pi}$ lies in the interpretation of the containment $U_1 \subseteq U_2$. While it seems syntactically simpler to view every element of U_1 as an element of U_2, there may be some semantic advantages of interpreting $U_1 \subseteq U_2$ as meaning that U_1 may be embedded in U_2. With appropriate assumptions about the inclusion mapping from U_1 to U_2, this seems entirely workable, and leads to a more flexible model definition than literal set-theoretic interpretation of $U_1 \subseteq U_2$. For simplicity, however, we will interpret $U_1 \subseteq U_2$ semantically as literal set-theoretic containment. This assumption is convenient when we come to impredicative and *type*: *type* calculi, since in both cases we will assume $U_1 = U_2$ anyway.

Henkin Models for Polymorphic Calculi

Since $\lambda^{\rightarrow,\Pi}$ has two collections of types, U_1 and U_2, with $U_1 \subseteq U_2$, a $\lambda^{\rightarrow,\Pi}$ model $\mathcal{A}$ will have two sets $U_1^{\mathcal{A}}$ and $U_2^{\mathcal{A}}$ with $U_1^{\mathcal{A}} \subseteq U_2^{\mathcal{A}}$. For each element $a \in U_2^{\mathcal{A}}$, we will also have a set Dom^a of elements of type a. This also gives us a set Dom^a for each $a \in U_1^{\mathcal{A}}$. In addition, we need some way to interpret type expressions with $\rightarrow$ and $\forall$ as elements of U_1 or U_2, and some machinery to interpret function application. The following model definition is in the same spirit as the Henkin models for impredicative calculus developed in [BMM90].

A $\lambda^{\rightarrow,\Pi}$ *applicative structure* $\mathcal{A}$ is a tuple

$$\mathcal{A} = \langle \mathcal{U}, \mathrm{dom}, \{\mathbf{App}^{a,b}, \mathbf{App}^f\}, \mathcal{I} \rangle,$$

where

- $\mathcal{U} = \{U_1^{\mathcal{A}}, U_2^{\mathcal{A}}, [U_1^{\mathcal{A}} \rightarrow U_2^{\mathcal{A}}], \rightarrow^{\mathcal{A}}, \Pi^{\mathcal{A}}, \mathcal{I}_{type}\}$ specifies sets $U_1^{\mathcal{A}} \subseteq U_2^{\mathcal{A}}$, a set $[U_1^{\mathcal{A}} \rightarrow U_2^{\mathcal{A}}]$ of functions from $U_1^{\mathcal{A}}$ to $U_2^{\mathcal{A}}$, a binary operation $\rightarrow^{\mathcal{A}}$ on $U_1^{\mathcal{A}}$, a map $\Pi^{\mathcal{A}}$ from $[U_1^{\mathcal{A}} \rightarrow U_2^{\mathcal{A}}]$ to $U_2^{\mathcal{A}}$, and a map $\mathcal{I}_{type}$ from type constants to $U_1^{\mathcal{A}}$.
- $\mathrm{dom} = \{\mathrm{Dom}^a \mid a \in U_2^{\mathcal{A}}\}$ is a collection of sets indexed by types of the structure.
- $\{\mathbf{App}^{a,b}, \mathbf{App}^f\}$ is a collection of application maps, with one $\mathbf{App}^{a,b}$ for every pair of types $a, b \in U_1^{\mathcal{A}}$ from the first universe, and one $\mathbf{App}^f$ for every function $f \in [U_1^{\mathcal{A}} \rightarrow U_2^{\mathcal{A}}]$ mapping the first universe to the second. Each $\mathbf{App}^{a,b}$ must be a function

$$\mathbf{App}^{a,b} : \mathrm{Dom}^{a \rightarrow b} \longrightarrow (\mathrm{Dom}^a \longrightarrow \mathrm{Dom}^b)$$

from $\mathrm{Dom}^{a\rightarrow b}$ to functions from Dom^a to Dom^b. Similarly, each $\mathbf{App}^f$ must be a function

$$\mathbf{App}^f : \mathrm{Dom}^{\Pi f} \longrightarrow \prod_{a \in U_1} \mathrm{Dom}^{f(a)}$$

from $\mathit{Dom}^{\Pi f}$ into the cartesian product $\prod_{a \in U_1} \mathit{Dom}^{f(a)}$.

• $\mathcal{I} : \mathit{Constants} \to \bigcup_{a \in U_2} \mathit{Dom}^a$ assigns a value to each constant symbol, with $\mathcal{I}(c) \in \mathit{Dom}^{[\![\tau]\!]}$ if c is a constant of type τ. Here $[\![\tau]\!]$ is the meaning of type expression τ, defined below. Recall that the type of a constant must not contain any free type variables.

This concludes the definition. An applicative structure is *extensional* if every $\mathbf{App}^{a,b}$ and $\mathbf{App}^f$ is one-to-one.

As in Chapter 4, we define Henkin models by placing an additional constraint on extensional applicative structures. Specifically, we give inductive definitions of the meanings of type expressions and terms below. If, for all type expression, term and environment, these clauses define a total meaning function, then we say that the structure is a Henkin model.

If $\mathcal{A}$ is a $\lambda^{\to,\Pi}$ frame, then an $\mathcal{A}$-environment is a mapping

$$\eta : \mathit{Variables} \longrightarrow (U_1^{\mathcal{A}} \cup \bigcup_{a \in U_2^{\mathcal{A}}} \mathit{Dom}^a)$$

such that for every type variable t, we have $\eta(t) \in U_1^{\mathcal{A}}$. The meaning $[\![\sigma]\!]\eta$ of a type expression σ in environment η is defined inductively as follows:

$$[\![t]\!]\eta = \eta(t)$$

$$[\![b]\!]\eta = \mathcal{I}_{type}(b)$$

$$[\![\tau \to \tau']\!]\eta = [\![\tau]\!]\eta \to^{\mathcal{A}} [\![\tau']\!]\eta$$

$$[\![\Pi t.\sigma]\!]\eta = \Pi^{\mathcal{A}}(\lambda a \in U_1^{\mathcal{A}}.\, [\![\sigma]\!]\eta[a/t])$$

In the Π case, recall that $\Pi^{\mathcal{A}}$ is a map from $[U_1^{\mathcal{A}} \to U_2^{\mathcal{A}}]$ to $U_2^{\mathcal{A}}$. For a frame to be a model, the domain $[U_1^{\mathcal{A}} \to U_2^{\mathcal{A}}]$ of $\Pi^{\mathcal{A}}$ must contain, for each type expression σ and environment η, the function $\lambda a \in U_1^{\mathcal{A}}.\, [\![\sigma]\!]\eta[a/t]$ obtained by treating σ as a function of t.

If Γ is a context, then η *satisfies* Γ, written $\eta \models \Gamma$, if $\eta(x) \in \mathit{Dom}^{[\![\sigma]\!]\eta}$ for every $x\!:\!\sigma \in \Gamma$. The meaning of a term $\Gamma \triangleright M\!:\!\sigma$ in environment $\eta \models \Gamma$ is defined by induction as follows:

$$[\![\Gamma \triangleright x\!:\!\sigma]\!]\eta = \eta(x)$$

$$[\![\Gamma \triangleright MN\!:\!\tau]\!]\eta = \mathbf{App}^{a,b}[\![\Gamma \triangleright M\!:\!\tau' \to \tau]\!]\eta\; [\![\Gamma \triangleright N\!:\!\tau']\!]\eta,$$

$$\text{where } a = [\![\tau']\!]\eta \text{ and } b = [\![\tau]\!]\eta$$

$$
\begin{aligned}
[\![\Gamma \rhd \lambda x\colon \sigma.M\colon \sigma \to \tau]\!]\eta &= \text{the unique } f \in \mathrm{Dom}^{a\to b} \text{ with} \\
&\quad \mathbf{App}^{a,b} f d = [\![\Gamma, x\colon \sigma \rhd M : \tau]\!]\eta[x \mapsto d] \text{ all } d \in \mathrm{Dom}^{a}, \\
&\quad \text{where } a = [\![\sigma]\!]\eta \text{ and } b = [\![\tau]\!]\eta \\
[\![\Gamma \rhd M\tau\colon [\tau/t]\sigma]\!]\eta &= \mathbf{App}^{f}\ [\![\Gamma \rhd M\colon \Pi t.\sigma]\!]\eta\ [\![\tau]\!]\eta, \\
&\quad \text{where } f(a) = [\![\sigma]\!]\eta[a/t] \text{ all } a \in U_1^{\mathcal{A}}, \\
[\![\Gamma \rhd \lambda t\colon U_1.M\colon \Pi t.\sigma]\!]\eta &= \text{the unique } g \in \mathrm{Dom}^{\Pi f} \text{ with} \\
&\quad \mathbf{App}^{f} g a = [\![\Gamma \rhd M : \sigma]\!]\eta[a/t] \text{ all } a \in U_1^{\mathcal{A}}, \\
&\quad \text{where } f(a) = [\![\sigma]\!]\eta[a/t] \text{ all } a \in U_1^{\mathcal{A}}.
\end{aligned}
$$

An extensional $\lambda^{\to,\Pi}$ applicative structure is a *Henkin model* if $[\![\Gamma \rhd M\colon \sigma]\!]\eta$ exists, as defined above, for every well-typed term $\Gamma \rhd M\colon \sigma$ and every $\eta \models \Gamma$.

An *impredicative applicative structure* or *Henkin model* is one with $U_1^{\mathcal{A}} = U_2^{\mathcal{A}}$.

A *type:type applicative structure* or *Henkin model* is one with $\mathrm{Dom}^{a} = U_1^{\mathcal{A}} = U_2^{\mathcal{A}}$ for some specified $a \in U_1^{\mathcal{A}} = U_2^{\mathcal{A}}$.

Soundness and Completeness

It is easy to show that in every model, the meaning of each term has the correct semantic type.

Lemma 9.2.13 (Type Soundness) Let $\mathcal{A}$ be a $\lambda^{\to,\Pi}$ model, $\Gamma \rhd M\colon \sigma$ a well-typed term, and $\eta \models \Gamma$ an environment. Then

$$[\![\Gamma \rhd M\colon \sigma]\!]\eta \ \in \mathrm{Dom}^{[\![\sigma]\!]\eta}.$$

A straightforward induction shows that the equational proof system is sound and term model constructions may be used to show that the equational proof system is complete (when a (*nonempty*) rule as in Chapter 4 is added) for models that do not have empty types. Additional equational completeness theorems may be proved for models that may have empty types [MMMS87], and for Kripke-style models.

Predicative Model Construction

We will see additional examples of models in Section 9.3, which is concerned with impredicative and *type*: *type* models. One difference between the predicative, impredicative and *type*: *type* languages is that $\lambda^{\to,\Pi}$ has classical set-theoretic models, while the other languages do not (see Section 9.3.2). In fact, any model of the simply-typed lambda calculus, $\lambda^{\rightarrow}$, may be extended to a model of $\lambda^{\rightarrow,\Pi}$ by the following simple set-theoretic construction.

If we begin with some model $\mathcal{A} = \langle U_1^{\mathcal{A}}, \rightarrow^{\mathcal{A}}, \{\mathrm{Dom}^a \mid a \in U_1^{\mathcal{A}}\}, \mathcal{I}\rangle$ for the U_1 types and terms, we can extend this to a model for all of $\lambda^{\rightarrow,\Pi}$ using standard set-theoretic cartesian product. For any ordinal α, we define the set $[U_2]_\alpha$ as follows

$$[U_2]_0 \quad = U_1$$

$$[U_2]_{\beta+1} = [U_2]_\beta \cup \{\prod_{a \in U_1} . f(a) \mid f : U_1^{\mathcal{A}} \rightarrow [U_2]_\beta\}$$

$$[U_2]_\alpha \quad = \bigcup_{\beta<\alpha} [U_2]_\beta \text{ for limit ordinal } \alpha$$

Note that for any α, the set $[U_2]_\alpha$ contains all cartesian products indexed by functions from

$$[U_1 \rightarrow U_2]_\alpha = \bigcup_{\beta<\alpha} U_1 \longrightarrow [U_2]_\beta.$$

The least limit ordinal ω actually gives us a model. The reason for this is that every U_2 type expression σ of $\lambda^{\rightarrow,\Pi}$ is of the form $\sigma \equiv \Pi t_1 \colon U_1 \ldots \Pi t_k \colon U_1.\tau$ for some $\tau \colon U_1$. It is easy to show that any type with k occurrences of Π has a meaning in $[U_2]_k$. Consequently, every type expression has a meaning in $[U_2]_\omega$. This is proved precisely in the lemma below. To shorten the statement of the lemma, we let $\mathcal{A}_n$ be the structure obtained from a U_1 model $\mathcal{A}$ by taking

$$[U_1 \rightarrow U_2]_n = \bigcup_{k<n} U_1 \rightarrow [U_2]_k$$

and $U_2 = [U_2]_n$

Lemma 9.2.14 Let $\Gamma \triangleright M \colon \sigma$ be any well-typed $\lambda^{\rightarrow,\Pi}$ expression such that in the derivation of $\Gamma \triangleright M \colon \sigma$, every type of every subterm has no more that n occurrences of the quantifier Π. Then for any environment η mapping variables into a U_1 structure $\mathcal{A}$, the meaning $[\![\Gamma \triangleright M \colon \sigma]\!]\eta$ exists and is well-defined in the structure $\mathcal{A}_n$.

The lemma is proved by first showing that every $\sigma \equiv \Pi t_1 \ldots \Pi t_k.\tau$ with $k < n$ has a meaning in $\mathcal{A}_n$, and then using induction on terms to prove the lemma.

While stage ω yields a model in which $\Pi t \colon U_1.\sigma$ is interpreted as ordinary set-theoretic cartesian product over U_1, the set of functions $[U_1 \rightarrow U_2]_\omega$ is not necessarily all set-theoretic functions from U_1 to $U_2 = [U_2]_\omega$. In order to get a truly full set-theoretic model, we may have to consider much larger ordinals. However, this is not much of a problem, and it is easy to see that induction up to an inaccessible cardinal (which must be larger than the cardinality of any set in the given U_1 model, including U_1 itself) yields a full set-theoretic model.

9.2.5 ML-style Polymorphic Declarations

Although the programming language ML [MTH90, MT91, Ull94] uses a type inference algorithm to determine the types of untyped expressions, the type system of ML may be viewed as an extension of $\lambda^{\rightarrow,\Pi}$. (This perspective, originally proposed in [Mac86, MH88], is discussed in Section 11.3.) The primary typing difference between $\lambda^{\rightarrow,\Pi}$ and an explicitly-typed version of the core ML expression language is that ML includes a polymorphic `let` declaration. The form of this declaration may be motivated by considering the use of polymorphic functions in $\lambda^{\rightarrow,\Pi}$.

In $\lambda^{\rightarrow,\Pi}$, we may write a polymorphic identity function

$$Id \stackrel{\text{def}}{=} \lambda t.\lambda x\colon t.x$$

of type $\Pi t.t \rightarrow t$. Using type application, we may apply Id to any argument belonging to a U_1 type. For example, the expressions $Id\, nat\, 3$ and $Id\, bool\, true$ are well-typed in any signature with $3\colon nat$ and $true\colon bool$. However, we cannot lambda-bind variables of type $\Pi t.t \rightarrow t$, since the ($\rightarrow$ Intro) rule is restricted to variables with U_1 types. As a consequence, we cannot write terms of the form

$$(\lambda f\colon (\Pi t.t \rightarrow t). \ldots f\, nat\, 3 \ldots f\, bool\, true)\ \lambda t.\lambda x\colon t.x$$

in which the polymorphic identity occurs only once, but will be applied to values of different types when the term is reduced. Introducing lambda abstraction over variables with U_2 types would allow us to write the function above. However a more limited form of variable-binding for U_2 types is also sufficient for much practical programming with polymorphic functions.

ML polymorphism is illustrated using the language $\lambda^{\rightarrow,\Pi,\mathtt{let}}$, which extends $\lambda^{\rightarrow,\Pi}$ with polymorphic declarations. Intuitively, the value of the expression

$$\mathtt{let}\ x\colon \sigma = N\ \mathtt{in}\ M$$

is the value of M when x is given the value of N. The following typing rule for this expression is based on the presentation of ML given in [DM82].

$$\frac{\Gamma, x\colon \sigma \rhd M\colon \tau,\quad \Gamma \rhd N\colon \sigma}{\Gamma \rhd (\mathtt{let}\ x\colon \sigma = N\ \mathtt{in}\ M)\colon \tau} \qquad (let)$$

This particular rule follows [DM82] in restricting the type of a `let` expression to U_1.

However, it would not change the set of typable terms substantially to replace the type τ by a type scheme σ in this rule.

The intuitive description of the value of a `let` expression is reflected in the equational axiom

$$\Gamma \triangleright (\texttt{let}\ x{:}\sigma = N\ \texttt{in}\ M) \;=\; [N/x]M{:}\tau \qquad (let)_{eq}$$

We may derive the reduction rule from this axiom by reading the equation from left to right. Note that $\texttt{let}\ x = M\ \texttt{in}\ N$ and $(\lambda x.N)M$ are both semantically equal to $[M/x]N$. However, they are typed differently, as we see below.

One distinction between $\lambda^{\rightarrow,\Pi}$ and $\lambda^{\rightarrow,\Pi,\texttt{let}}$ may be illustrated using any $\lambda^{\rightarrow,\Pi}$ term in which a polymorphic subterm occurs several times. For concreteness, let us consider a specific polymorphic function, say *compose*: $\Pi r.\Pi s.\Pi t.\tau$, where $\tau = (s \rightarrow t) \rightarrow (r \rightarrow s) \rightarrow r \rightarrow t$. If we use *compose* several times in one expression, we might prefer to follow standard programming practice and write the function body only once. Given any expression $[compose/x]M$ of $\lambda^{\rightarrow,\Pi}$, we may use `let` to write a $\lambda^{\rightarrow,\Pi,\texttt{let}}$ expression

$$\texttt{let}\ x{:}(\Pi r.\Pi s.\Pi t.\tau) = compose\ \texttt{in}\ M$$

with only one occurrence of *compose*. The equational axiom for `let` specifies that

$$\Gamma \triangleright (\texttt{let}\ x{:}(\Pi r.\Pi s.\Pi t.\tau) = compose\ \texttt{in}\ M) \;=\; [compose/x]M{:}\sigma$$

so the `let` expression may be viewed as a more concise way of writing $[compose/x]M$. However, since $\Gamma, x{:}(\Pi r.\Pi s.\Pi t.\tau) \triangleright M{:}\sigma$ has a free polymorphic variable, we cannot even type this term in $\lambda^{\rightarrow,\Pi}$. Therefore, due to typing constraints, we cannot hope to "simulate" `let` in $\lambda^{\rightarrow,\Pi}$ in any general way. This shows that $\lambda^{\rightarrow,\Pi,\texttt{let}}$ is indeed more flexible than $\lambda^{\rightarrow,\Pi}$. Of course, $\lambda^{\rightarrow,\Pi,\texttt{let}}$ also has its limitations. For example, since we may write expressions of the form $\Gamma, x{:}(\Pi r.\Pi s.\Pi t.\tau) \triangleright M{:}\sigma$, we might wish to lambda abstract the polymorphic variable $x{:}\,\Pi r.\Pi s.\Pi t.\tau$. However, since the resulting function would have a type that does not belong to U_2, this is not possible in $\lambda^{\rightarrow,\Pi,\texttt{let}}$.

In studying the ML type inference problem, it will be useful to have some understanding of pure `let` reduction, axiomatized by

$$\texttt{let}\ x = M\ \texttt{in}\ N \xrightarrow{\text{let}} [M/x]N. \qquad (let)_{red}$$

We say M' `let`-*reduces to* N', and write $M' \overset{\text{let}}{\twoheadrightarrow} N'$, if we can obtain N' from M' by repeatedly applying rule (*let*) to subexpressions, and renaming bound variables. An interesting fact about `let`-reduction (alone) is that it is confluent and terminating (even on untyped terms). The following proposition is essentially the uniqueness and finiteness of developments for untyped lambda calculus. The idea is that $\texttt{let}\ x = M\ \texttt{in}\ N$ may be regarded as the *marked* redex $(\lambda x.N)^1 M$, where the superscript 1 indicates that this redex may be contracted. The reader is referred to [Bar84] for further discussion and proof.

Proposition 9.2.15 Let M be any untyped λ, `let`-term. There is a unique `let`-free expression N such that every maximal sequence of `let`-reductions starting from M terminates at N. In particular, there are no infinite sequences of `let`-reductions.

If N is a `let`-free expression obtained from M by repeated `let`-reduction, then we say N is the `let` *normal form* of M. By Proposition 9.2.15, `let` normal forms exist and are unique.

In general, the length of a term may increase exponentially as a result of `let`-reduction. We can give a more precise description of the increase by considering the way that `let`'s occur. We define the `let`-*depth*, $\ell d(M)$, *of* M inductively as follows:

$$\begin{aligned}
\ell d(x) &= 1\\
\ell d(MN) &= \max\{\ell d(M), \ell d(N)\}\\
\ell d(\lambda x{:}\,\tau.M) &= \ell d(M)\\
\ell d(\texttt{let}\ x{:}\sigma = M\ \texttt{in}\ N) &= \ell d(M) + \ell d(N)
\end{aligned}$$

In the common special case that M is `let`-free, the `let`-depth of $\texttt{let}\ x = M\ \texttt{in}\ N$ is $1 + \ell d(N)$. Lest there be any confusion, we also define the *length* $|M|$ of an expression M inductively as follows.

$$\begin{aligned}
|a| &= 1 && \text{if } a \text{ is a variable or constant}\\
|MN| &= |M| + |N| + 1\\
|\lambda x{:}\,\tau.N| &= |N| + 1\\
|\texttt{let}\ x{:}\sigma = M\ \texttt{in}\ N| &= |M| + |N| + 1
\end{aligned}$$

Note that we do not count the type expressions in the size of a term.

Lemma 9.2.16 Let M' be the `let` normal form of M. Then $|M'| \leq |M|^{\ell d(M)}$.

Proof By Proposition 9.2.15, the `let` normal form is always defined and is unique. This lets us choose any order of `let`-reductions we wish in reasoning about a term. We proceed by a straightforward induction on the syntax of expressions, only considering `let`-reduction directly in the `let` case.

The lemma is trivially true for a variable or constant. The proof is straightforward for application and abstraction. We illustrate the flavor of these arguments by proving the application case. For application MN, the `let` normal form is $M'N'$, where M' and N' are the `let` normal forms of M and N, respectively.

$$\begin{aligned}
|(MN)'| &= |M'N'| \\
&= |M'| + |N'| + 1 \\
&\le |M|^{\ell d(M)} + |N|^{\ell d(N)} + 1 \qquad \text{by inductive hypothesis} \\
&\le |M|^{\max\{\ell d(M),\ell d(N)\}} + |N|^{\max\{\ell d(M),\ell d(N)\}} + 1 \\
&\le (|M| + |N| + 1)^{\max\{\ell d(M),\ell d(N)\}} \\
&\le |MN|^{\ell d(MN)}.
\end{aligned}$$

The remaining case is $\mathtt{let}\ x = M\ \mathtt{in}\ N$, where we apply the outer-most `let`-reduction.

$$\begin{aligned}
|(\mathtt{let}\ x{:}\sigma = M\ \mathtt{in}\ N)'| &= |(\mathtt{let}\ x = M'\ \mathtt{in}\ N')'| \\
&= |[M'/x]N'| \\
&\le |M'| \cdot |N'| \\
&\le |M|^{\ell d(M)} \cdot |N|^{\ell d(N)} \qquad \text{by inductive hypothesis} \\
&\le (|M| + |N| + 1)^{\ell d(M)+\ell d(N)} \\
&\le |\mathtt{let}\ x{:}\sigma = M\ \mathtt{in}\ N|^{\ell d(\mathtt{let}\ x=M\ \mathtt{in}\ N)}.
\end{aligned}$$

This proves the lemma. ∎

Exercise 9.2.17 Use `let`-reduction and type β-reduction to transform the term

$\mathtt{let}\ \mathit{twice}{:}\ \Pi t.\,(t \to t) \to t \to t = \lambda t.\,\lambda f{:}t \to t.\,\lambda x{:}t.\,f(fx)$
  $\mathtt{in\ if}\ \mathit{twice\, bool\, not})\ \mathit{true}$
    $\mathtt{then}\ (\mathit{twice\, nat}\ \lambda x{:}\,\mathit{nat}.\,x + 1)\ 2$
    $\mathtt{else}\ (\mathit{twice\, nat}\ \lambda x{:}\,\mathit{nat}.\,x + 3)\ 4$

where $\mathit{not} \stackrel{\text{def}}{=} \lambda x{:}\,\mathit{bool}.\,\mathtt{if}\ x\ \mathtt{then}\ \mathit{false}\ \mathtt{else}\ \mathit{true}$ to a simply-typed $\lambda^{\to}$ term without polymorphic subterms.

9.3 Impredicative Polymorphism

9.3.1 Introduction

The impredicative polymorphic lambda calculus was developed independently by Girard [Gir71, Gir72] and Reynolds [Rey74b]. Girard used the calculus to prove the consistency of second-order Peano arithmetic while Reynolds proposed the calculus as a model of polymorphic type structure in programming languages. In the terminology of this chapter, the Girard/Reynolds calculus, which we shall denote by $\lambda^{\rightarrow,\forall}$, may be obtained from the predicative $\lambda^{\rightarrow,\Pi}$ by dropping the distinction between universes U_1 and U_2. More precisely, the usual syntactic presentation of $\lambda^{\rightarrow,\forall}$ may be obtained from our definition of $\lambda^{\rightarrow,\Pi}$ by replacing U_1 and U_2 by a single collection T of all types. To distinguish the impredicative system from the predicative one, we will use $\forall$ in place of Π, giving us the name $\lambda^{\rightarrow,\forall}$. Thus the type of the impredicative polymorphic identity is written $\forall t.\, t \rightarrow t$. To keep the distinction between systems straight, the reader may think of Π as standing for "p" in "predicative." Another justification for the choice of notation is the formulas-as-types analogy, discussed below.

In $\lambda^{\rightarrow,\forall}$, types are formed according to the grammar

$$\sigma \quad ::= \quad b \mid t \mid \sigma \rightarrow \sigma \mid \forall t.\sigma$$

and terms are formed according to axioms (*var*) and (*cst*) for variables and constants, rule (*add hyp*) to add hypotheses about the types of free variables, and rules ($\rightarrow$ Intro), ($\rightarrow$ Elim), (Π Intro) and (Π Elim), writing $\forall$ in place of Π and without restrictions related to type universes. (See Section 9.2.2 for these rules.)

The impredicative calculus is probably the most widely studied of the three forms of polymorphism outlined in Section 9.1, primarily because of its syntactic simplicity, programming flexibility, and semantic complexity. The language is syntactically simpler than $\lambda^{\rightarrow,\Pi}$, since there are no universe restrictions, but it is substantially more difficult to prove strong normalization or to provide intuitive and mathematically rigorous semantics.

From a programming point of view, $\lambda^{\rightarrow,\forall}$ provides a very flexible polymorphic type system. The polymorphic features of languages such as Ada, CLU and ML may all be regarded as restrictions of $\lambda^{\rightarrow,\forall}$ polymorphism. For example, we may mimic ML `let` using lambda abstraction in $\lambda^{\rightarrow,\forall}$ as follows. Suppose $\Gamma \triangleright M\colon \forall t.\sigma$ is a polymorphic expression and $\Gamma, x\colon \forall t.\sigma \triangleright N\colon \tau$ is a term which may have several occurrences of a polymorphic variable. We might consider extending $\lambda^{\rightarrow,\forall}$ with a `let` declaration form which would allow us to write

$$\Gamma \triangleright \texttt{let}\ x\colon \forall t.\sigma = M\ \texttt{in}\ N\colon \tau.$$

However, this is not necessary, since the `let` expression may be considered an abbreviation for the term

$\Gamma \triangleright (\lambda x\colon \forall t.\sigma.N)M\colon \tau$

with the same type, same meaning, and same immediate subterms. This illustrates some of the programming flexibility that results from dropping the universe restrictions of $\lambda^{\rightarrow,\Pi}$. However, as suggested in Section 9.1, the semantics of $\lambda^{\rightarrow,\forall}$ is rather complicated. Since the polymorphic identity may be applied to its own type, we cannot interpret types as sets of ordinary set-theoretic functions on these sets.

In the formulas-as-types analogy, discussed in Sections 4.3.4 and 9.1.4, the calculus $\lambda^{\rightarrow,\forall}$ corresponds to propositional intuitionistic logic with implication and universal quantification over propositions. This logic is undecidable [Gab81, Löb75] and sufficient to express intuitionistic existential quantification and the other propositional connectives [Pra65]. Moreover, the normalization theorem for $\lambda^{\rightarrow,\forall}$ implies normalization for second-order Peano arithmetic and therefore implies consistency. It follows from Gödel's incompleteness theorem that the normalization theorem for $\lambda^{\rightarrow,\forall}$, first proved by Girard [Gir71, Gir72], cannot be formalized in second-order arithmetic. It is also shown in [Gir72] that the numeric functions definable in pure $\lambda^{\rightarrow,\forall}$ are precisely the partial recursive functions that may be proved total in second-order arithmetic (see also [FLO83, Sta81]). This representability theorem may be extended to higher-order functionals [FS87, Sce88]. We will discuss the expressiveness of the calculus in Section 9.3.2 and give a version of Girard's normalization proof in Section 9.3.3. A good general reference on logical properties of polymorphic lambda calculus is [GLT89].

9.3.2 Expressiveness and Properties of Theories

There are several ways to assess the expressive power of impredicative polymorphic lambda calculus. The technical results presented in this section distinguish the impredicative calculus from other lambda calculi and are mathematically interesting in their own right. The four subsections of this section are

- Number-theoretic functions
- Parametricity
- Maximum consistent theory
- Formal category theory

Numeric Functions and Church Numerals

As mentioned earlier, every number-theoretic function that is provably total in second-order Peano arithmetic is definable. More specifically, we know from standard coding results used in the proof of Gödel's incompleteness theorem (see [End72], for example) that for every partial recursive function f, there is a formula $\phi(x, y)$ with free variables x and y representing f in the following sense: for any pair of numerals $\bar{n}$ and $\bar{m}$, we can prove $\phi(\bar{n}, \bar{m})$ in Peano arithmetic iff $f(n) = m$. In the case that f is a total function, we can ask whether the formula $\forall x \exists y \phi(x, y)$ stating "f is total" is provable in Peano arithmetic. If so, we say f is *provably total.* Since the set of total recursive functions is not recursively enumerable (and the theorems of Peano arithmetic are), there are some total functions that are not provably total. It is a deep fact that the recursive functions which are provably total in second-order Peano arithmetic are exactly the numeric functions definable in impredicative polymorphic lambda calculus. This is part of the larger connection between the polymorphic lambda calculus and the proof-theory of second-order logic. Since this topic is covered well in another book [GLT89], we will only sketch some aspects of the representation of numeric functions.

Before proceeding, we consider the general notion of "encoding" for typed languages. In PCF, we defined numeric functions using the type *nat*, with numerals $0, 1, 2, 3, \ldots$. From a general perspective, the important properties of *nat* are that we have an expression of this type for every natural number, and that these are exactly the normal form expressions of the type. It follows from these properties that we can associate each term of type $nat \rightarrow nat$ with a partial or total function on the natural numbers. In the case of PCF, the terms of type $nat \rightarrow nat$ define partial functions (as discussed in Section 2.5.5) since there are terms without normal forms. If we replace *fix* by some primitive recursion operator, then every term of weakened PCF would have a normal form, and every expression of type $nat \rightarrow nat$ would define a total function on the natural numbers.

In pure $\lambda^{\rightarrow,\forall}$ without type constants, there is a natural choice for a type of natural numbers. This may be motivated by considering the common unary representation for natural numbers often used in formal logic. Specifically, if we have constants $zero\colon nat$ and $succ\colon nat \rightarrow nat$, then we can write the number n as the expression

$$\underbrace{succ(succ \ldots (succ}_{n}\ zero) \ldots)$$

with n occurrences of the function *succ*. We do not have constants *zero* and *succ* in pure $\lambda^{\rightarrow,\forall}$, but we can treat these symbols as variables and lambda abstract them. This gives us expressions of the form

$$\lambda zero\colon nat.\, \lambda succ\colon nat \rightarrow nat.\, succ(succ \ldots (succ\ zero) \ldots)$$

However, this term contains the type name *nat*, which would have to be chosen arbitrarily. Again, the path that leads to a useful representation of the natural numbers is to treat this symbol as a variable and lambda abstract it. Finally, we obtain pure closed terms of the form

$\lambda nat.\, \lambda zero{:}\, nat.\, \lambda succ{:}\, nat \to nat.\, succ(succ \ldots (succ\, zero) \ldots)$

more commonly written with simpler variable names. This leads us to define the *Church numeral* $\bar{n}$ representing the natural number n by

$$\bar{n} \stackrel{\text{def}}{=} \lambda t.\, \lambda f{:}\, t \to t.\, \lambda x{:}\, t.\; f^n x,$$

where $f^n x$ is the term $f(f...(fx)...)$ with n occurrences of f. The name "Church numeral" comes from the fact that similar untyped terms were used by Alonzo Church to represent the natural numbers in untyped lambda calculus. There are also many other systems of untyped numerals [Bar84], as well as several other choices for numerals in the polymorphic lambda calculus. All of the Church numerals have type

$$nat \stackrel{\text{def}}{=} \forall t.\, (t \to t) \to t \to t,$$

and it is shown in Exercise 9.3.2 that the normal forms of type $\forall t.\, (t \to t) \to t \to t$ are exactly the Church numerals.

Addition and multiplication operations on polymorphic Church numerals are forms of composition functions. The terms for these operations are:

$$mult \stackrel{\text{def}}{=} \lambda x{:}\, nat.\, \lambda y{:}\, nat.\, \lambda t.\, \lambda f{:}\, t \to t.\, xt(ytf)$$

$$add \stackrel{\text{def}}{=} \lambda x{:}\, nat.\, \lambda y{:}\, nat.\, \lambda t.\, \lambda f{:}\, t \to t.\, \lambda z{:}\, t.\, xtf(ytfz)$$

Exercise 9.3.3 asks you to verify that both work properly.

In addition to natural numbers, we can represent booleans by a type with exactly two normal forms. Intuitively, if we are given two arguments $x{:}\, t$ and $y{:}\, t$ of an arbitrary type t, then there are two ways to return a result of type t: return x or return y. This leads us to consider the type

$$bool \stackrel{\text{def}}{=} \forall t.\, t \to t \to t$$

for encoding booleans. The proof that this type has exactly two normal forms is the essentially the same as for *nat*. Since we may refer to these later, we name the two normal forms:

$$true \stackrel{\text{def}}{=} \lambda t.\, \lambda x{:}\, t.\, \lambda y{:}\, t.\, x$$

$$false \stackrel{\text{def}}{=} \lambda t.\, \lambda x{:}\, t.\, \lambda y{:}\, t.\, y$$

We can define a zero-test operation by a simple but useful trick. A numeral $\bar{n}$ is a function that applies its first argument to its second argument some number of times. If the first argument is a constant function, then all numerals greater than zero will give the same result. More specifically, it is easy to check that

$\bar{n}\ bool\ (\lambda x\colon bool.\, false)\ true$

will reduce to *true* if $n = 0$, and false otherwise. Therefore, we define the zero-test function by

$zero? \stackrel{\text{def}}{=} \lambda x\colon nat.\, x\ bool\ (\lambda x\colon bool.\, false)\ true$

Exercise 9.3.4 asks you to define conditional and equality test.

Another trick allows us to represent pairs. For any types σ and τ, we can represent the cartesian product by

$\sigma \times \tau \stackrel{\text{def}}{=} \forall t.\, (\sigma \to \tau \to t) \to t$

where t is some type variable that does not occur free in σ or τ. The pairing function $pair : \forall r.\, \forall s.\, r \to s \to (r \times s)$ is

$pair \stackrel{\text{def}}{=} \lambda r.\, \lambda s.\, \lambda x\colon r.\, \lambda y\colon s.\ \ \lambda t.\, \lambda f\colon r \to s \to t.\, fxy$

Exercise 9.3.4 asks you to devise projection functions.

Example 9.3.1 Using the functions given above, together with the ones in Exercise 9.3.4, it is relatively straightforward to define primitive recursion operators at all types. Changing the binary function of Exercise 2.5.7 to curried form (as in Exercise 8.3.27), the primitive recursion operator R_σ with type

$R_\sigma : \sigma \to (\sigma \to nat \to \sigma) \to nat \to \sigma$

must have the property

$$R_\sigma M N \bar{0} \twoheadrightarrow M$$

$$R_\sigma M N \overline{n+1} \twoheadrightarrow N(R_\sigma M N \bar{n})\bar{n}$$

We can define a single polymorphic primitive recursion operator $R\colon \forall t.\, t \to (t \to nat \to t) \to nat \to t$ with $R\sigma = R_\sigma$ for any type σ. The main idea is to define a function *step* that maps the pair $\langle R_\sigma M N \bar{k},\ \bar{k}\rangle$ to $\langle R_\sigma M N \overline{k+1},\ \overline{k+1}\rangle$. The reason we use pairs is that we need $\bar{k}$ to compute $R_\sigma M N \overline{k+1}$ from $R_\sigma M N \bar{k}$. If we apply this function n times to the pair $\langle M, 0\rangle$, the result should be the pair $\langle R_\sigma M N \bar{n},\ \bar{n}\rangle$ whose first component is the answer we want. The function *step*, which depends implicitly on the type t of M and the term $N\colon t \to nat \to t$, may be written

$$step_{t,N}: (t \times nat) \to (t \times nat)$$

$$\stackrel{\text{def}}{=} \lambda p: (t \times nat).\, pair\, t\, nat\, (N (proj_1\, t\, nat\, p)(proj_2\, t\, nat\, p))\, (succ\, (proj_2\, t\, nat\, p))$$

This allows us to define the primitive recursion operator R by

$$R \stackrel{\text{def}}{=} \lambda t.\, \lambda x{:}\, t.\, \lambda y{:}\, t \to nat \to t.\, \lambda z{:}\, nat.$$

$$(proj_1\, t\, nat\, (z\ (t \times nat)\ step_{t,y}\ (pair\, t\, nat\, x\, \bar{0})))$$

It is a useful exercise for the serious reader to try an example, such as $R\, nat\, \bar{0}\, (\lambda x{:}\, nat.\, succ(succ\, x))$, which should be a function on numerals that doubles its argument. ∎

Exercise 9.3.2 Show that the β-normal forms of type $\forall t.\, (t \to t) \to t \to t$ are precisely the Church numerals. For this to hold with β, η-normal forms, we must redefine the numeral for 1 to be the β, η-normal form $\bar{1} = \lambda t.\, \lambda f{:}\, t \to t.\, f$.

Exercise 9.3.3 Show that for any polymorphic Church numerals $\bar{m}$ and $\bar{n}$, we have

(a) $add\, \bar{m}\, \bar{n} \twoheadrightarrow \overline{m + n}$

(b) $mult\, \bar{m}\, \bar{n} \twoheadrightarrow \overline{m * n}$

Exercise 9.3.4 Write closed polymorphic lambda terms for the functions

(a) $cond{:}\, \forall t.\, bool \to t \to t \to t$ with $cond\, t\, true\, x\, y \twoheadrightarrow x$ and $cond\, t\, false\, x\, y \twoheadrightarrow y$.

(b) $proj_i{:}\, \forall t_1.\forall t_2.\, (t_1 \times t_2) \to t_i$ with $proj_i\, A\, B\, (pair\, A\, B\, M_1 M_2) \twoheadrightarrow M_i$.

(c) $pred{:}\, nat \to nat$ with $pred\, \bar{0} \twoheadrightarrow \bar{0}$ and $pred\, \overline{n + 1} \twoheadrightarrow \bar{n}$. *Hint:* Consider the function

$$\lambda p{:}\, bool \times nat.\, cond\, (bool \times nat)$$

$$(proj_1\, bool\, nat\, p)$$

$$(pair\, bool\, nat\, false\, \bar{0})$$

$$(pair\, bool\, nat\, false\ (succ\, (proj_2\, bool\, nat\, p)))$$

What if we apply this function n times to $pair\, bool\, nat\, true\, \bar{0}$?

(d) $Eq?{:}\, nat \to nat \to bool$ with $Eq?\, \bar{m}\, \bar{n} \twoheadrightarrow true$ iff $m = n$.

Exercise 9.3.5 Exercise 2.3.2 shows that adding the equation $true = false$ to PCF is inconsistent. Show that the equation $true = false$ is inconsistent in $\lambda^{\to,\forall}$, where $true$ and $false$ are the terms of type $bool \equiv \forall t.\, t \to t \to t$ given in this section.

Parametricity

An aspect of polymorphism that has received substantial attention is "parametricity," a term coined by Strachey [Str67] and taken up in earnest by Reynolds [Rey74b, Rey83, Rey84]. This is discussed intuitively in Section 9.1.2, where it is noted that adding a simple non-parametric operation to the impredicative calculus causes normalization to fail. We will discuss some non-parametric functions and demonstrate the failure of normalization. Although we will not go into the technical details, we also note that non-parametric operations may be added to the predicative calculus without destroying normalization.

We begin with a relatively general "type equality" test and then explore some variations and specialized usages of this operation. A simple test for type equality might take the form

$$\mathit{TypeEq} : \forall s.\, \forall t.\, \mathit{bool}$$

with $\mathit{TypeEq}\, \sigma\, \tau = \mathit{true}$ if σ and τ are the same type, and *false* otherwise. By itself, this test is weaker than one might expect, due to the typing constraints of $\lambda^{\rightarrow,\forall}$. For example, we could write a polymorphic function that returns a different number on the type argument *nat* than other types,

$$\lambda t.\, \texttt{if}\ \mathit{TypeEq}\, t\, \mathit{nat}\ \texttt{then}\ 1\ \texttt{else}\ 2 : \forall t.\, \mathit{nat}$$

but we cannot use the fact that two types are equal in type checking. The consequences of adding only *TypeEq* to $\lambda^{\rightarrow,\forall}$ do not appear to have been studied in any depth.

A more expressive non-parametric primitive is motivated by expressions such as

$$\lambda x{:}s.\, \lambda y{:}t.\, \texttt{if}\ \mathit{TypeEq}\, s\, t\ \texttt{then}\ x\ \texttt{else}\ y$$

where we must reason by cases about the type of the expression. Intuitively this function has type $s \rightarrow t \rightarrow t$, for the following reason. If types s and t are equal, then the result x has type s, which is equal to t. Otherwise the result y has type t. However, we cannot formalize this type reasoning without using the equation $s = t$. This leads us to consider a type-conditional operation *TypeCond* with the typing rule

$$\frac{\Gamma, \sigma = \tau \rhd M{:}\, \rho \qquad \Gamma \rhd N{:}\, \rho}{\Gamma \rhd \mathit{TypeCond}\, \sigma\, \tau\, M\, N{:}\, \rho} \qquad (\mathit{TypeCond})$$

Since we will only be interested in simple examples illustrating the main ideas, we will not formalize the additional typing rules associated with equality assumptions in contexts.

There are two natural equational axioms or reduction rules for *TypeCond*. However, some care must be taken to avoid a problem with type expressions that contain free variables, as discussed below. The reduction rules are

$$TypeCond\ \sigma\ \sigma\ M\ N \to M$$

$$TypeCond\ \sigma\ \tau\ M\ N \to N \qquad \sigma,\ \tau \text{ distinct, closed}$$

Without the side condition on the second rule, the system would be non-confluent and, more importantly, inconsistent. This may be understood by considering the term

$$(\lambda t.\, TypeCond\ s\ t\ true\ false\,)\ s$$

where *true*, *false* are the encodings of truth values with types $bool \equiv \forall t.\, t \to t \to t$. This term would have normal forms *true* and *false* if we drop the side condition requiring closed type expressions, the first obtained starting with the outermost reduction

$$(\lambda t.\, TypeCond\ s\ t\ true\ false)\ s \ \to\ TypeCond\ s\ s\ true\ false \to\ true$$

and the second beginning with the inner-most reduction

$$(\lambda t.\, TypeCond\ s\ t\ true\ false)\ s \ \to\ (\lambda t.\, false)\ s \ \to\ false$$

Since it is inconsistent to have $true = false$, by Exercise 9.3.5, we cannot use reduction or equational reasoning without requiring closed types in the second reduction rule, or the corresponding equational axiom, for *TypeCond*.

One way of understanding *TypeCond* is to consider writing a function that does multiplication on natural numbers and a component-wise multiplication on pairs of natural numbers. In other words, we would like to combine functions

$$\begin{aligned} mult_N &\stackrel{\text{def}}{=} \lambda x\colon nat.\, \lambda y\colon nat.\, x * y \\ &:\ nat \to nat \to nat \\ mult_{N,N} &\stackrel{\text{def}}{=} \lambda x\colon nat \times nat.\, \lambda y\colon nat \times nat.\langle \mathbf{Proj}_1 x * \mathbf{Proj}_1 y, \mathbf{Proj}_2 x * \mathbf{Proj}_2 y\rangle \\ &:\ nat \times nat \to nat \times nat \to nat \times nat \end{aligned}$$

The best $\lambda^{\to,\forall}$-type for the combined function is $\forall t.\, t \to t \to t$, since the type of each individual function is a substitution instance of $t \to t \to t$. Using *TypeCond*, we can combine the two multiplication functions into a single function with this type by writing

$$\begin{aligned} mult &\stackrel{\text{def}}{=} \lambda s.\, \lambda x\colon s.\, \lambda y\colon s. \\ &\qquad TypeCond\ s\ nat\ (mult_N x y) \\ &\qquad\ \ TypeCond\ s\ (nat \times nat)\ (mult_{N,N} x y) \\ &\qquad\qquad x \\ &:\ \forall t.\, t \to t \to t \end{aligned}$$

The function *mult* takes arguments x and y of the same type. If the type is *nat*, the result is $mult_N xy$, else if the type is $nat \times nat$, the result is $mult_{N,N} xy$, else the result is x. Note that to produce a term of type $\forall t.\, t \to t \to t$, we need to have some way of computing a result of the right type, for all possible argument types.

A technical problem with *TypeCond* is the unusual typing rule using type equations. We can write polymorphic functions such as *mult* using a simpler "patch" function

$$patch_{\forall t.\sigma} : (\forall t.\sigma) \to \forall t.\,(\sigma \to \forall t.\sigma)$$

Intuitively, $patch_{\forall t.\sigma}\; x\; \tau\; y$ is just like the polymorphic value $x{:}\,\forall t.\sigma$, except at type τ, where the value is y. This is definable from *TypeCond* using

$$patch_{\forall t.\sigma} \stackrel{\text{def}}{=} \lambda x{:}\,\forall t.\sigma.\, \lambda r.\, \lambda y{:}\,[r/t]\sigma.\, \lambda s.\, TypeCond\; s\; r\; y\; (xs)$$

However, reasonable uses of *patch* can be typed using the standard typing rule without type equations, as illustrated in Exercise 9.3.6.

The reduction rules for *patch* are

$$patch_{\forall t.\sigma}\; M\; \tau\; N\; \tau \to M$$

$$patch_{\forall t.\sigma}\; M\; \tau\; N\; \sigma \to N\; \sigma \qquad \sigma, \tau \text{ distinct, closed}$$

In a 1971 paper, Girard discusses parametricity and gives an example showing that if we add a non-parametric operator to $\lambda^{\to,\forall}$, normalization fails [Gir71]. This example has been interpreted as a demonstration that $\lambda^{\to,\forall}$ is inherently a calculus of parametric functions. Specifically, since adding a non-parametric operator alters a fundamental property of the system, we can conclude the non-parametric operator cannot be definable in $\lambda^{\to,\forall}$. Girard's original example is given in Exercise 9.3.7.

We can use a variant of Girard's construction to show that *patch* violates strong normalization. The main idea is that we give a "self-application function" a simpler type than it would have in pure $\lambda^{\to,\forall}$ without *patch*. This allows us to apply the self-application function to itself. Let D be the "self-application function"

$$D \stackrel{\text{def}}{=} \lambda x{:}\,\forall t.\, t \to t.\, (x\; \forall t.\, t \to t)\; x$$

and let $Id \stackrel{\text{def}}{=} \lambda t.\, \lambda x{:}\, t.\, x$ be the polymorphic identity function as usual. Combining these two functions at type $\forall t.\, t \to t$, we have the term

$$X \stackrel{\text{def}}{=} patch_{\forall t.\, t \to t}\; Id\; (\forall t.\, t \to t)\; D$$

$$:\; \forall t.\, t \to t$$

Since $X{:}\,\forall t.\, t \to t$ we can type $X\,(\forall t.\, t \to t)\,X$. However, this term has no normal form, as illustrated by the reduction

$$X(\forall t.\, t \to t)X \;\twoheadrightarrow\; DX \;\twoheadrightarrow\; X(\forall t.\, t \to t)X$$

Although the identity does not participate in this reduction, the type of *Id* is important since it allows us to "hide" the term D of type $(\forall t.\, t \to t) \to (\forall t.\, t \to t)$ inside a term with the simpler type $\forall t.\, t \to t$.

Girard's original example used constants $0\colon \forall t.t$ and $J\colon \forall s.\, \forall t.\, s \to t$, given in Exercise 9.3.7. The function J is similar to *patch*, except that it "patches" the polymorphic value 0 instead of an arbitrary value passed as an argument. Therefore, the real difference between Girard's example and the functions used here is the constant $0\colon \forall t.t$. A debatable issue surrounding $0\colon \forall t.t$ is that this constant gives us a way of defining an element of each type. This destroys the formulas-as-types correspondence, since it makes every formula "provable". However, it is not clear what real consequence $0\colon \forall t.t$ would have for programming languages. The one technical issue that can be identified is that adding only *patch* to $\lambda^{\to,\forall}$, there is an easy proof that no polymorphic fixed-point operator $Y : \forall t.\, (t \to t) \to t$ is definable (see Exercise 9.3.8). In contrast, it is conceivable that a polymorphic fixed-point is definable from J and 0.

Two related non-parametric operators appear in the more recent literature. The difference between these operators highlights the role of impredicativity in the examples we have considered so far. The first operator a *typecase* construct, associated with a type *Dynamic* used to provide dynamic type checking in a statically-typed language [ACPP91, ACP$^+$92]. The motivations for this operator include writing typed values to a persistent memory or heap. As pointed out by Abadi *et al.* [ACPP91], a fixed point combinator of a specific type such as $((nat \to nat) \to (nat \to nat)) \to (nat \to nat)$ is definable in the simply-typed λ-calculus enriched with the type *Dynamic*. Since we may regard the type *Dynamic* as an abbreviation for the quantified type $\exists t.t$, considered in Section 9.4, the existence of fixed point combinators may be traced to the combination of non-parametric polymorphism and impredicative quantified types. In particular, the definition of a fixed-point operator involves embedding functions of type $Dynamic \to \sigma \to \tau$ into type *Dynamic*, which would not be allowed if *Dynamic* were considered a member of a different universe from the types σ and τ where we wish to construct a fixed point.

In a second use of non-parametricity, Harper and Morrisett [HM95a] consider a *typerec* for defining primitive recursive functions on types. This includes a form of type conditional and equality test. However, the surrounding language is predicative. This makes it possible to prove strong normalization property and show that no fixed-point operator is definable from *typerec*.

Exercise 9.3.6 Write the non-parametric *mult* function in this section using the *patch* operation instead of *TypeCond* and show that the function can be typed using ordinary typing rules without type equations.

Exercise 9.3.7 The original example of [Gir71] used a polymorphic constant $0\colon \forall t.t$ and an operator $J\colon \forall s.\forall t.\, s \to t$ that is definable from 0 and *patch* by $J \stackrel{\text{def}}{=} \lambda t.\, \lambda x\colon t.\, patch\, 0\; t\, x$. Let

$$X \stackrel{\text{def}}{=} \lambda t.\, J\, t\, (\forall t.t) \to (\forall t.t)\, D'$$

where $D' \stackrel{\text{def}}{=} \lambda x\colon \forall t.t.\, x\, ((\forall t.t) \to (\forall t.t))\, x$. Show that reduction of $X\, ((\forall t.t) \to (\forall t.t))\, X$ does not terminate.

Exercise 9.3.8 Use the formulas-as-types analogy to show that if $Op : \sigma$ and there exists a pure closed term of type σ, then there exists a closed term of type τ containing *Op* iff there exists a pure closed term of type τ not containing *Op*. Use this to prove that no fixed-point operator of type $\forall t.(t \to t) \to t$ is definable from *patch*. In light of various studies relating logical paradoxes and fixed-point operators [MR86, Coq86, CH94a], it does not seem easy to establish that no fixed-point operator or similar "looping combinator" is definable from J.

Maximum consistent theory

One general proof-theoretic method for studying lambda theories is presented in Section 4.4.4 using simply-typed lambda calculus. To illustrate another general method, we develop a characterization of theories using contexts and sets of indistinguishables. As an application, we show that there is a maximum consistent $\lambda^{\to,\forall}$-theory.

Contexts, which are terms with holes indicated by empty square brackets [ ], are defined elsewhere. For the purposes of this section, we write type assignments as part of contexts (to specify the types of free variables) and give them types. We say a context $\Gamma \rhd \mathcal{C}[\;]\colon \sigma$ is a $\Gamma' \rhd \tau$*-context* if $\Gamma \rhd \mathcal{C}[M]\colon \sigma$ is well-typed whenever $\Gamma' \rhd M\colon \tau$ is well-typed. A straightforward induction on the structure of contexts gives us the following lemma.

Lemma 9.3.9 Let $\Gamma \rhd \mathcal{C}[\;]\colon \sigma$ be any $\Gamma' \rhd \tau$ context and let $\Gamma' \rhd M = N\colon \tau$ be any equation. Then

$$\Gamma' \rhd M = N\colon \tau \vdash \Gamma \rhd \mathcal{C}[M] = \mathcal{C}[N]\colon \sigma.$$

Using typed contexts, we can characterize any theory by selecting a set of "indistinguishable" terms. Let S be any set of $\lambda^{\to,\forall}$-terms $\Gamma \rhd M\colon \tau$ closed under conversion. In other words, we assume that if $\Gamma \rhd M\colon \tau \in S$ and $\Gamma \rhd M \leftrightarrow N\colon \tau$ then $\Gamma \rhd N\colon \tau \in S$. The *contextual theory $T(S)$ determined by S* is the following set of equations:

$T(S) = \{\Gamma \triangleright M = N : \sigma \mid$ for every $\Gamma \triangleright \sigma$ context $\Gamma' \triangleright \mathcal{C}[\ ] : \tau$

we have $\Gamma' \triangleright \mathcal{C}[M] : \tau \in S$ iff $\Gamma' \triangleright \mathcal{C}[N] : \tau \in S.\}$

We first show that for any S closed under conversion, $T(S)$ is a $\lambda^{\rightarrow,\forall}$-theory, then show that every $\lambda^{\rightarrow,\forall}$-theory can be characterized in this way.

Lemma 9.3.10 If S is closed under conversion, then $T(S)$ contains all instances of axioms (α), (β) and (η).

Proof Since S is closed under conversion, whenever $\Gamma \triangleright M : \sigma$ is convertible to $\Gamma \triangleright N : \sigma$, we have $\vdash \Gamma' \triangleright \mathcal{C}[M] = \mathcal{C}[N] : \tau$ and consequently $\Gamma \triangleright M = N : \sigma$ is in $T(S)$. ∎

Lemma 9.3.11 If S is closed under conversion, then $T(S)$ is closed under the *(add var)* rule

$$\frac{\Gamma \triangleright M = N : \sigma}{\Gamma, x : \tau \triangleright M = N : \sigma}$$

Proof Suppose that $\Gamma \triangleright M = N : \sigma$ is in $T(S)$ and let $\Gamma' \triangleright \mathcal{C}[\ ] : \tau$ be any $\Gamma, x : \tau \triangleright \sigma$ context. Then since $\Gamma' \triangleright \mathcal{C}[\ ] : \tau$ is also an $\Gamma \triangleright \sigma$ context, we have $\Gamma' \triangleright \mathcal{C}[M] : \tau \in S$ iff $\Gamma' \triangleright \mathcal{C}[N] : \tau \in S$. Therefore, $\Gamma, x : \tau \triangleright M = N : \sigma \in T(S)$. ∎

The proof of the following lemma is left as Exercise 9.3.17.

Lemma 9.3.12 $T(S)$ is closed under symmetry, transitivity and congruence with respect to application and abstraction.

Theorem 9.3.13 For any set S of terms closed under conversion, $T(S)$ is a $\lambda^{\rightarrow,\forall}$-theory. Furthermore, $T(S)$ is consistent iff there exist well-typed terms $\Gamma \triangleright M : \tau$ and $\Gamma \triangleright N : \tau$ with $\Gamma \triangleright M : \tau \in S$ and $\Gamma \triangleright N : \tau \notin S$.

Proof The preceding lemmas establish that $T(S)$ is a $\lambda^{\rightarrow,\forall}$-theory. Therefore, we need only prove the statement about consistency. If $\Gamma \triangleright M : \tau \in S$ and $\Gamma \triangleright N : \tau \notin S$, then we can use the empty context to show that $\Gamma \triangleright M = N : \tau \notin S$. For the converse, suppose that $T(S)$ is consistent. Then there must be some equation $\Gamma \triangleright M = N : \sigma$ not in $T(S)$. By definition of $T(S)$, there must be some $\Gamma \triangleright \sigma$ context $\Gamma' \triangleright \mathcal{C}[\ ] : \tau$ with $\Gamma' \triangleright \mathcal{C}[M] : \tau \in S$ and $\Gamma' \triangleright \mathcal{C}[N] : \tau \notin S$. This proves the lemma. ∎

We also have a converse. Namely, every theory may be presented by giving a set S of terms closed under conversion.

Theorem 9.3.14 Every $\lambda^{\rightarrow,\forall}$-theory *Th* may be written $Th = T(S)$ for some set S of terms closed under conversion.

Proof The proof uses pairing and projection. We only need to assume that for each type τ, we have the product type $\tau \times \tau$ with pairing and projection. (Since we do not need general pairing $\sigma \times \tau$ for all σ and τ, the argument can be carried out for the simply typed lambda calculus using $\langle M, N\rangle = \lambda x\colon (\tau \to \tau \to \tau) \to \tau .\, xMN$.)

If *Th* is any $\lambda^{\to,\forall}$-theory, then we define the set S_{Th} by

$$S_{Th} = \{\Gamma \triangleright M\colon \tau \times \tau \mid \exists P, Q.\, Th \vdash \Gamma \triangleright M = \langle P, Q\rangle\colon \tau \times \tau \text{ and } Th \vdash \Gamma \triangleright P = Q\colon \tau\}$$

We first show that $T(S)$ contains *Th*. Suppose $Th \vdash \Gamma \triangleright M = N\colon \tau$ and $\Gamma' \triangleright \mathcal{C}[\;]\colon \sigma \times \sigma$ is an $\Gamma \triangleright \tau$ context with $\Gamma' \triangleright \mathcal{C}[M]\colon \sigma \times \sigma$ in S. Then by definition of S, we know

$$Th \vdash \Gamma' \triangleright \mathcal{C}[M] = \langle P, Q\rangle\colon \tau \times \tau \text{ and } Th \vdash \Gamma \triangleright P = Q\colon \tau$$

Since $Th \vdash \Gamma \triangleright M = N\colon \tau$, we also have $Th \vdash B \triangleright \mathcal{C}[M] = \mathcal{C}[N]\colon \sigma \times \sigma$ by Lemma 9.3.9 and so it is easy to see that $\Gamma \triangleright M = N\colon \tau$ is in $T(S)$.

Now suppose $\Gamma \triangleright M = N\colon \tau$ is not in *Th* and consider the $\Gamma \triangleright \tau$ context $\Gamma \triangleright \langle M, [\;]\rangle\colon \tau \times \tau$. Clearly $\Gamma \triangleright \langle M, M\rangle\colon \tau \times \tau$ is in S, so we need only to show that $\Gamma \triangleright \langle M, N\rangle\colon \tau \times \tau$ is not in S. If $\Gamma \triangleright \langle M, N\rangle\colon \tau \times \tau$ is in S, then there exist P, Q with $Th \vdash \Gamma \triangleright \langle M, N\rangle = \langle P, Q\rangle\colon \tau \times \tau$ and $Th \vdash \Gamma \triangleright P = Q\colon \tau$, from which it follows (by use of projection functions and congruence) that $Th \vdash \Gamma \triangleright M = N\colon \tau$. Since this is a contradiction, it must be that $\Gamma \triangleright \langle M, N\rangle\colon \tau \times \tau$ is not in S, and hence $\Gamma \triangleright M = N\colon \tau$ is not in $T(S)$. ∎

This completes the general results on context presentations of theories. The maximum consistent theory is characterized by taking

$$S_{true} = \{\emptyset \triangleright M\colon bool \mid M \twoheadrightarrow true\}$$

where $true \equiv \lambda t.\, \lambda x\colon t.\, \lambda y\colon t.\, x$ is the pure $\lambda^{\to,\forall}$ term of type $bool \equiv \forall t.\, t \to t \to t$.

Lemma 9.3.15 If $\Gamma \triangleright M = N\colon \sigma$ is not in $T(S_{true})$, then

$$(\Gamma \triangleright M = N\colon \sigma) \vdash (\emptyset \triangleright true = false\colon bool).$$

Proof Suppose $\Gamma \triangleright M = N\colon \sigma$ is not in $T(S_{true})$ and let $\mathcal{C}[\;]\colon bool$ be some $\Gamma \triangleright \sigma$ context with $\mathcal{C}[M] \in S$ and $\mathcal{C}[N] \notin S$. By choice of S_{true}, and the fact that *true* and *false* are the only closed terms of type *bool*, we must have $\mathcal{C}[M] \twoheadrightarrow true$ and $\mathcal{C}[N] \twoheadrightarrow false$ (or vice versa). Therefore, by Lemma 9.3.9, we conclude that $\Gamma \triangleright M = N\colon \sigma$ proves $\emptyset \triangleright true = false\colon bool$. ∎

The proof of the following corollary is left as Exercise 9.3.18.

Corollary 9.3.16 $T(S_{true})$ is the maximum consistent theory.

Exercise 9.3.17 Prove Lemma 9.3.12. Since symmetry and transitivity are trivial, you need only prove the cases for application and abstraction.

Exercise 9.3.18 Prove Corollary 9.3.16. (Do not forget Exercise 9.3.5.)

Formal Category Theory

In Section 9.1.2, it was pointed out that we cannot give impredicative $\lambda^{\rightarrow,\forall}$ a straightforward set-theoretic interpretation. This is a relatively subtle point, however. In any model of $\lambda^{\rightarrow,\forall}$ using sets, we would like each type to denotes a set and each term to denote an element of the appropriate type-set. All three forms of polymorphic lambda calculus, predicative, impredicative and *type*: *type* have models of this form. We have already seen this in Section 9.2.4 for the predicative calculus; models of $\lambda^{\rightarrow,\forall}$ and *type*: *type* are discussed in Section 9.3.4. The discussion in Section 9.1.2 shows that we cannot have a model of $\lambda^{\rightarrow,\forall}$ satisfying the following two *additional* conditions:

- The elements of $\sigma \rightarrow \tau$ are functions from σ to τ,
- The elements of $\forall t.\sigma$ are functions from the collection of types to elements of types.

A more subtle negative result is that we cannot have a set-theoretic model satisfying only a strong version of the first of the two conditions above, namely, $\sigma \rightarrow \tau$ is the set of all functions from σ to τ, regardless of how we interpret polymorphic types. This was first proved by Reynolds [Rey84]. The proof is clarified in [RP93] and generalized in [Pit87, Pit89]. An interesting clarification from Pitts' work is that if we work in intuitionistic instead of classical logic, then it *is* possible to give set-theoretic semantics to $\lambda^{\rightarrow,\forall}$. The reason why this is possible is that fewer functions can be proved to exist in intuitionistic logic than classical logic.

The proof that there are no set-theoretic models of a certain form uses ideas from Section 7.4 on the interpretation of recursive types. The main idea is to show that certain functors are representable by $\lambda^{\rightarrow,\forall}$-terms and, in addition, show that every representable functor F has a "weakly initial" F-algebra. As described in Section 7.4, an initial F-algebra is a solution to the isomorphism $A \cong F(A)$. A weakly initial F-algebra A does not provide an isomorphism between A and $F(A)$, but an isomorphism can be constructed using subsets of the semantic interpretations of the $\lambda^{\rightarrow,\forall}$-types A and $F(A)$ in a set-theoretic model. This leads to a contradiction, however, since there can be no solution to $A \cong (A \rightarrow bool) \rightarrow bool$ in any model where $\sigma \rightarrow \tau$ is all functions from σ to τ. While we will not go through the complete proof, we can get some feel for the kind of argument involved by developing a form of "formal category theory" in $\lambda^{\rightarrow,\forall}$. While it takes several steps to show that every definable functor has a weakly initial algebra, the benefit will be a systematic way of deriving encodings for many kinds of data types.

Our starting point is a categorical view of typed languages. Specifically, we will think of the syntax of $\lambda^{\rightarrow,\forall}$ as a category $\mathcal{C}_{\rightarrow,\forall}$ as follows:

- Types of the calculus are objects of the category,
- Closed terms of type $\sigma \rightarrow \tau$ are morphisms from $\sigma \rightarrow \tau$, with the understanding that provably equal terms name the same morphism.

This general idea can be applied to a variety of typed languages. However, the polymorphism of $\lambda^{\rightarrow,\forall}$ is particularly useful for representing functors and natural transformations.

With this view of a typed language as a category, we can see that a functor has two parts, a map from types to types and a map from terms to terms with a certain special kind of type. It is convenient to extend $\lambda^{\rightarrow,\forall}$ with lambda abstraction in type expressions, writing $\Phi = \lambda t.\, \sigma$ for a function mapping type τ to $[\tau/t]\sigma$. With this notation, we say a *definable functor in* $\lambda^{\rightarrow,\forall}$ is a pair $\langle \Phi, F \rangle$ consisting of a definable function $\Phi = \lambda t.\, \sigma$ representing a map on objects and a term

$$F : \forall s.\, \forall t.\, (s \rightarrow t) \rightarrow (\Phi s \rightarrow \Phi t)$$

representing a map on arrows. The arrow map must satisfy the two equations

$$F\, s\, s\, (\lambda x{:}\, s.\, x) = \lambda x{:}\, \sigma.\, x \qquad F\, r\, t\, (f \circ g) = (F\, s\, t\, g) \circ (F\, r\, s\, g)$$

where f and g are variables of types $g{:}\, r \rightarrow s$ and $f{:}\, s \rightarrow t$. (Composition $f \circ g$ is shorthand for the lambda term $\lambda x{:}\, r.\, f(gx) : r \rightarrow t$.) These equations are the straightforward translations into $\lambda^{\rightarrow,\forall}$ of the conditions that a functor must preserve identities and composition.

Example 9.3.19 While $\lambda^{\rightarrow,\forall}$ does not have cartesian products, we have seen that pairing and projection functions are representable in the calculus (see Exercise 9.3.4). This is actually a "weak" version of cartesian products, since we have $\mathbf{Proj}_i \langle M_1, M_2 \rangle = M_i$, but not the surjective pairing equation $\langle \mathbf{Proj}_1 P, \mathbf{Proj}_2 P \rangle = P$.

With this weak encoding, we can define a weak form of cartesian product functor $\mathit{Prod} : \mathcal{C}_{\rightarrow,\forall} \times \mathcal{C}_{\rightarrow,\forall} \rightarrow \mathcal{C}_{\rightarrow,\forall}$; for simplicity, we will give it in Curried form. The map on objects is determined by treating $s \times t \equiv \forall r.\, (s \rightarrow t \rightarrow r) \rightarrow r$ as a function of s and t. The map on morphisms, or terms, is given by the polymorphic function

$$\begin{aligned}
\mathit{Prod} \;&\stackrel{\text{def}}{=}\; \lambda s_1.\, \lambda t_1.\, \lambda s_2.\, \lambda t_2.\\
&\qquad \lambda f_1{:}\, s_1 \rightarrow t_1.\, \lambda f_2{:}\, s_2 \rightarrow t_2.\, \lambda p{:}\, s_1 \times s_2.\langle \mathbf{Proj}_1 p,\ \mathbf{Proj}_2 p \rangle\\
&:\; \forall s_1.\, \forall t_1.\, \forall s_2.\, \forall t_2.\\
&\qquad (s_1 \rightarrow t_1) \rightarrow (s_2 \rightarrow t_2) \rightarrow (s_1 \times s_2) \rightarrow (t_1 \times t_2)
\end{aligned}$$

Exercise 9.3.22 asks you to verify that when we use the encoding of product in $\lambda^{\rightarrow,\forall}$, this is actually a functor. ∎

As discussed in general in Section 7.4, a $\langle \Phi, F \rangle$-algebra consists of an object τ and morphism $M : \Phi\tau \rightarrow \tau$. An F-algebra morphism from $\langle \tau, M \rangle$ to $\langle \tau', M' \rangle$ is a term $N : \tau \rightarrow \tau'$ satisfying the equation

$$N \circ M = M' \circ (F\tau\tau' N) : \Phi\tau \rightarrow \tau'$$

corresponding to a commuting diagram given in Section 7.4.3. Recall that $\langle \tau, M \rangle$ is an initial $\langle \Phi, F \rangle$-algebra if there is a *unique* $\langle \Phi, F \rangle$-algebra morphism to each $\langle \Phi, F \rangle$-algebra. We say $\langle \tau, M \rangle$ is *weakly initial* if there is some morphism from $\langle \tau, M \rangle$ to each algebra; the morphism need not be unique.

It takes several steps to show that every definable functor $\langle \Phi, F \rangle$ has a weakly initial algebra. The result is a syntactic way of deriving encodings of all manner of data types, since weak initiality is generally enough for computational purposes.

Given any definable functor $\langle \Phi, F \rangle$, there is a uniform way of choosing a weakly initial algebra. This algebra $\langle \tau, M \rangle$ has the property that there is a term N which, given any $\langle \Phi, F \rangle$-algebra $\langle \tau', M' \rangle$, produces a morphism from $\langle \tau, M \rangle$ to $\langle \tau', M' \rangle$. The definition of $\langle \tau, M \rangle$ from $\langle \Phi, F \rangle$ can be motivated by considering how such a term N might work. Given $\langle \tau', M' \rangle$, we want the following diagram to commute:

$$\begin{array}{ccc}
\Phi\tau & \xrightarrow{\quad F_{\tau\tau'}(N_{\tau}{}'M') \quad} & \Phi_{\tau}{}' \\
M(f)\big\downarrow & & \big\downarrow M' \\
\tau & \xrightarrow[\quad N_{\tau}{}'M' \quad]{} & \tau'
\end{array}$$

This tells us that N should have the type

$$N : \forall s.\, (\Phi s \rightarrow s) \rightarrow \tau \rightarrow s$$

where τ is yet to be determined. Without loss of generality, we can assume that N will have the form

$$N = \lambda s.\, \lambda f : \Phi s \rightarrow s.\, \lambda x : \tau.\, N'$$

where $N' : s$ has only s, f and x free. We can make the problem of finding a term N' easy by choosing the type τ of x properly. Specifically, since we want to use x to build a term of type s from s and f, we can just take

$$\tau \stackrel{\text{def}}{=} \forall s.\, (\Phi s \rightarrow s) \rightarrow s$$

and let

$$N \stackrel{\text{def}}{=} \lambda s.\,\lambda f\colon \Phi s \to s.\,\lambda x\colon \tau.\,xsf$$

This solves half our problem, but we still need a function M for the weakly initial algebra $\langle \tau, M\rangle$. Since we have chosen three sides of the commuting square, the obvious approach is to write a few equations and "solve" for M. Since τ' and $M'\colon \Phi\tau' \to \tau'$ will vary, we use type variable s and term variable $f\colon \Phi s \to s$. The square above then gives us the equation

$$Nsf \circ M \;=\; f \circ (F\tau s(Nsf))$$

Using the term above for N and expanding the definition of composition, we have

$$Nsf \circ M \qquad = \lambda x\colon \Phi\tau.\,Mxsf$$

$$f \circ (F\tau s(Nsf)) = \lambda x\colon \Phi\tau.\,f(F\tau s(\lambda x'\colon \Phi\tau.\,x'sf)x)$$

which together give us

$$Mxsf \;=\; f(F\tau s(\lambda x'\colon \Phi\tau.\,x'sf)x)$$

This suggests the definition

$$M \stackrel{\text{def}}{=} \lambda x\colon \Phi\tau.\,\lambda s.\,\lambda f\colon \Phi s \to s.\,f(F\tau s(\lambda x'\colon \Phi\tau.\,x'sf)x)$$

Exercise 9.3.23 asks you to check that the diagram above in fact commutes. This gives us the following proposition.

Proposition 9.3.20 For every definable functor $\langle \Phi, F\rangle$, there is a weakly initial algebra $\langle \tau, M\rangle$ and term $N\colon \forall s.\,(\Phi s \to s) \to \tau \to s$ which, given any $\langle \Phi, F\rangle$-algebra $\langle \tau', M'\rangle$, produces a morphism $N\tau'M'$ from $\langle \tau, M\rangle$ to $\langle \tau', M'\rangle$.

An application of this proposition illustrates the usefulness of weakly initial algebras.

Example 9.3.21 An initial algebra for the functor $F(D) = \mathit{unit} + D$ would give us the natural numbers, as illustrated in Section 2.6.3. We will see that a weakly inital algebra is almost as good. In fact, computing the weakly inital algebra according to Proposition 9.3.20 gives us a systematic way of deriving a representation of the natural numbers that is very similar (and provably isomorphic) to the polymorphic Church numerals. To make this as simple as possible, we assume we have a type *unit* and sum types $\sigma + \tau$ with **Inleft**, **Inright** and **Case** expressions essentially as in Section 2.6.2, but with polymorphic types

Inleft : $\forall s.\, \forall t.\, s \rightarrow (s + t)$

Inright : $\forall s.\, \forall t.\, t \rightarrow (s + t)$

Case : $\forall s.\, \forall t.\, \forall r.\, (s + t) \rightarrow (s \rightarrow r) \rightarrow (t \rightarrow r) \rightarrow r$

The functor we are interested is definable in $\lambda^{\rightarrow,\forall}$ by

$\Phi = \lambda t.\, unit + t$

$F = \lambda s.\, \lambda t.\, \lambda f\colon s \rightarrow t.\, \lambda x\colon unit + s.$

$\quad$ **Case** $unit\; s\; (1 + t)\; x$ (**Inleft** $unit\; t$) ($\lambda z\colon s.$ **Inright** $unit\; t\; (f z)$)

It is easy to check that F preserves identities and compositions, showing that this is indeed a functor.

The weakly inital algebra $\langle \tau, M \rangle$ for this functor, determined from Proposition 9.3.20, is given by the following terms

$\tau \;= \forall t.\, ((unit + t) \rightarrow t) \rightarrow t$

$M = \lambda x\colon unit + \tau.\, \lambda s.\, \lambda f\colon (unit + s) \rightarrow s.$

$\qquad f(F \tau s (\lambda x'\colon \tau.\, x' s f) x)$

$\quad = \lambda x\colon unit + \tau.\, \lambda s.\, \lambda f\colon (unit + s) \rightarrow s.$

$\qquad f$ (**Case** $unit\; \tau\; (unit + s)\; x$ (**Inleft** $unit\; t$) ($\lambda z\colon \tau.$ **Inright** $unit\; t\; (z s f)$)))

Proceeding as if we had an initial algebra, and therefore an interpretation for the recursive type $\mu t.\, unit + t$, the natural numbers are defined by taking $0 \overset{\text{def}}{=} M$(**Inleft** $unit\; \tau\; *$) and successor $succ \overset{\text{def}}{=} M \circ$ (**Inleft** $unit\; \tau$). This gives us the following numerals:

$0 = \lambda s.\, \lambda f\colon (unit + s) \rightarrow s.\, f$(**Inleft** $unit\; \tau\; *$)

$1 = \lambda s.\, \lambda f\colon (unit + s) \rightarrow s.\, f$ (**Inright** $unit\; s\; f$(**Inleft** $unit\; \tau\; *$))

$2 = \lambda s.\, \lambda f\colon (unit + s) \rightarrow s.\, f$ (**Inright**(f (**Inright** $unit\; s\; f$(**Inleft** $unit\; \tau\; *$))

These terms bear a strong resemblance to the Church numerals described earlier in this section. In fact, as outlined in Exercise 9.3.24, the type τ is provably isomorphic to the type $\forall t.\, (t \rightarrow t) \rightarrow t \rightarrow t$ of the Church numerals. As the interested reader may verify, the term N giving a morphism from $\langle \tau, M \rangle$ to any $\langle \Phi, F \rangle$-algebra $\langle \tau', M' \rangle$ gives a polymorphic primitive recursion operator (see Exercise 7.4.9). ∎

Exercise 9.3.22 Show that the pair $\langle \lambda s.\, \lambda t.\, s \times t,\ Prod \rangle$ given in Example 9.3.19 satisfy the two equations given in the definition of definable functor. Use the encoding of products in $\lambda^{\rightarrow,\forall}$ given earlier in this section.

Exercise 9.3.23 Prove Lemma 9.3.20 by showing that the associated square commutes for any definable functor $\langle \Phi, F \rangle$, algebra $\langle \tau', M' \rangle$ and specific types and and terms τ, M, N given above.

Exercise 9.3.24 A general property of sum is that the maps $(a + b) \rightarrow c$ are in one-to-one correspondence with pairs of maps $(a \rightarrow c) \times (b \rightarrow c)$. In particular, since $(unit \rightarrow t) \cong t$, we would expect

$$(t \rightarrow t) \rightarrow t \rightarrow t \;\cong\; ((t \rightarrow t) \times t) \rightarrow t \;\cong\; ((unit + t) \rightarrow t) \rightarrow t$$

for any type t, the first isomorphism by Currying. Show that the type $\tau = \forall t.\, ((unit + t) \rightarrow t) \rightarrow t$ of numerals used in Example 9.3.21 is isomorphic to the type $\nu = \forall t.\, (t \rightarrow t) \rightarrow t \rightarrow t$ of the Church numerals. Do this by giving $\lambda^{\rightarrow,\forall}$-terms of types $\tau \rightarrow \nu$ and $\nu \rightarrow \tau$ which are provably inverses of each other. Show that your isomorphism maps the Church numeral for 0 to the term for 0 in Example 9.3.21, and similarly for 1 and 2.

9.3.3 Termination of Reduction

In this section, we show strong normalization of type β-reduction and ordinary β-reduction on $\lambda^{\rightarrow,\forall}$-terms. The proof is a variant of Girard's original argument [Gir71, Gir72], developed in [Mit86c]. The main idea is to set up a form of "interpretation" for typing assertions about *untyped* lambda terms, and cast normalization as a form of type soundness property. The use of untyped terms simplifies a number of arguments, since we do not have to worry about static typing conditions on terms. On the other hand, it requires some connections between typed and untyped reduction. Although the proof may be extended to β, η-reduction on $\lambda^{\rightarrow,\forall}$-terms, we will not do so. Many of the main ideas will seem similar to the logical relations proof of strong normalization for $\lambda^{\rightarrow}$ in Section 8.3.2. The construction of an "interpretation" of types over the structure of untyped terms is also similar to the view of PER models as logical relations over an untyped partial combinatory algebra, explained in Example 8.2.9 and Sections 8.2.4 and 8.2.5, except that since we are only interested in type membership, not term equality, we use predicates instead of partial equivalence relations.

A useful tool for comparing typed and untyped terms is the *Erase* function which erases types from terms. Recall that the unchecked *pre-terms* of $\lambda^{\rightarrow,\forall}$ are defined by

$$M ::= c \mid x \mid MN \mid \lambda x{:}\sigma.M \mid M\sigma \mid \lambda t.M$$

while the *untyped lambda terms* are given by

$U ::= c \mid x \mid UV \mid \lambda x.U$

In both definitions, c may be any constant and x any ordinary variable (ordinary variables $x, y, z, \ldots$ are assumed distinct from type variables $r, s, t, \ldots$). The *Erase* function from pre-terms to untyped terms has a straightforward inductive definition; the nontrivial clauses are

$$Erase(\lambda x{:}\,\sigma.M) = \lambda x.Erase(M)$$

$$Erase(M\sigma) \quad = Erase(M)$$

$$Erase(\lambda t.M) \quad = Erase(M)$$

(See Section 11.1 for further discussion of erasure functions.)

We may give inference rules for deriving "implicit" typings of untyped terms. (Algorithmic issues and other aspects of this general idea are explored in Chapter 11.) The implicit rules are easily constructed from the explicit rules by applying *Erase* to the antecedent and consequent of each rule. For example, the implicit (∀ Elim) rule is

$$\frac{\Gamma \triangleright Erase(M){:}\,\forall t.\sigma}{\Gamma \triangleright Erase(M\tau){:}\,[\tau/t]\sigma} \qquad (\forall\ \text{Elim})_{imp}$$

or, simplifying the applications of *Erase*,

$$\frac{\Gamma \triangleright U{:}\,\forall t.\sigma}{\Gamma \triangleright U{:}\,[\tau/t]\sigma} \qquad (\forall\ \text{Elim})_{imp}$$

A useful property of implicit typing is that $\Gamma \triangleright U{:}\,\sigma$ is derivable in the implicit typing system iff there is some explicitly typed M with $\Gamma \triangleright M{:}\,\sigma$ and $Erase(M) = U$. (See Lemmas 11.2.15 and 11.3.1.)

Lambda Interpretations

The first step in setting up a semantic framework for interpreting typing assertions $\Gamma \triangleright U{:}\,\sigma$ about untyped lambda terms is to adopt some interpretation of lambda terms. We use the following very general structure, which allows the set of terms as a special case.

A *lambda interpretation* is a triple

$$\mathcal{D} = \langle D, \cdot, [\![\ ]\!] \rangle$$

where D is a set, $\cdot$ is a binary operation on D and $[\![\ ]\!]$ is a mapping from untyped lambda terms and environments to D such that

$$
\begin{array}{lll}
(i) & [\![x]\!]\eta & = \eta(x) \\
(ii) & [\![UV]\!]\eta & = [\![U]\!]\eta \cdot [\![V]\!]\eta \\
(iii) & [\![\lambda x.U]\!]\eta & = [\![\lambda y.[y/x]U]\!]\eta \\
(iv) & [\![\lambda x.U]\!]\eta & = [\![\lambda x.V]\!]\eta \\
 & & \quad \text{if } [\![U]\!]\eta[x \mapsto d] = [\![V]\!]\eta[x \mapsto d] \text{ all } d \in D \\
(v) & [\![M]\!]\eta & = [\![M]\!]\eta' \text{ if } \eta(x) = \eta'(x) \text{ for all } x \in FV(M)
\end{array}
$$

Hindley and Longo [Bar84, HL80] define models of untyped lambda calculus as lambda interpretations that satisfy the additional condition

$$(vi) \qquad [\![\lambda x.U]\!]\eta \cdot d = [\![U]\!]\eta[x \mapsto d] \text{ all } d \in D.$$

It is easy to see that if $\mathcal{D}$ satisfies all instances of the axiom scheme

$$(\lambda x.U)V = [V/x]U \qquad (\beta)$$

then (vi) holds and $\mathcal{D}$ is a lambda model.

Example 9.3.25 A simple lambda interpretation

$$\mathcal{D}_\alpha = \langle D, \cdot, [\![\ ]\!] \rangle$$

may be constructed using α-equivalence classes of lambda term. For each lambda term U, let $\langle U \rangle$ denote the set of terms V that differ from U only in the names of bound variables. Let D be the set of all $\langle U \rangle$ and define $\langle U \rangle \cdot \langle V \rangle$ to be the set of terms $\langle UV \rangle$. It is not hard to see that $\cdot$ is well-defined. We define $[\![\ ]\!]$ using substitution. An environment η for D is a mapping from terms to equivalence classes of terms. Any environment η may be viewed as a substitution mapping each variable x to any element of the set $\eta(x)$ of α-equivalent terms. We define $[\![\ ]\!]$ by

$$[\![U]\!]\eta = \langle \eta U \rangle.$$

It is not hard to check that $[\![U]\!]\eta$ is a well-defined function of U and η and that $[\![\ ]\!]$ satisfies conditions (i) through (v). ■

Example 9.3.26 Any model of untyped lambda calculus is a lambda interpretation. ■

A straightforward axiom system, essentially comprising the usual rules, but without (β), is easily shown to be sound and complete for proving equations between untyped lambda terms that hold in λ-interpretations.

Subset Interpretation

We interpret typing statements over subset interpretations. A $\lambda^{\to,\forall}$ *subset interpretation* $\mathcal{A}$ is a tuple

$\mathcal{A} = \langle \mathcal{U}, \mathcal{D}, Sub, \mathcal{I} \rangle,$

where

- $\mathcal{U} = \{T^{\mathcal{A}}, \to^{\mathcal{A}}, \forall^{\mathcal{A}}, \mathcal{I}_{type}\}$ specifies set $T^{\mathcal{A}}$, a binary operation $\to^{\mathcal{A}}$ on $T^{\mathcal{A}}$, a map $\forall^{\mathcal{A}}$ from functions $T^{\mathcal{A}} \to T^{\mathcal{A}}$ to $T^{\mathcal{A}}$, and a map $\mathcal{I}_{type}$ from type constants to $T^{\mathcal{A}}$,
- $\mathcal{D} = \langle D, \cdot, [\![\ ]\!] \rangle$ is a lambda interpretation,
- $Sub: T^{\mathcal{A}} \to 2^{D}$ is a map assigning a subset of D to each type, satisfying the following conditions:

(*Arrow*.1) If $d \in Sub(a \to b)$ and $e \in Sub(a)$ then $d \cdot e \in Sub(b)$.

(*Arrow*.2) If $[\![U]\!]\eta[x \mapsto d] \in Sub(b)$ for all $d \in Sub(a)$, then $[\![\lambda x.U]\!]\eta \in Sub(a \to b)$.

(*ForAll*) $Sub(\forall f) = \bigcap_{a \in U^{\mathcal{I}}} Sub(f(a))$.

If $\mathcal{D}$ is a λ-model, then (Arrow.2) may be simplified to

($Arrow.2_{model}$) If $d \cdot e \in Sub(b)$ for all $e \in Sub(a)$, then $[\![\lambda x \lambda y.xy]\!] \cdot d \in Sub(a \to b)$.

- $\mathcal{I}$: *Constants* $\to D$ assigns a value to each constant symbol, with $\mathcal{I}(c) \in Sub([\![\tau]\!])$ if c is a constant of type τ. The interpretation $[\![\tau]\!]$ of τ in $\mathcal{U}$ is defined below.

This concludes the definition. It is sometimes convenient to write D^{a} for $Sub(a)$.

We interpret typing statements using environments that map type variables to elements of $T^{\mathcal{A}}$ and ordinary variables to elements of D. The meaning of a type expression σ in an environment η for interpretation $\mathcal{A} = \langle \mathcal{U}, \mathcal{D}, Sub \rangle$ is defined by induction on σ as follows.

$$[\![t]\!]\eta = \eta(t),$$

$$[\![\sigma \to \tau]\!]\eta = \to^{\mathcal{A}} ([\![\sigma]\!]\eta)([\![\tau]\!]\eta),$$

$$[\![\forall t.\sigma]\!]\eta = \forall^{\mathcal{A}}(\lambda a \in T.[\![\sigma]\!]\eta[t \mapsto a]),$$

where $\eta[t \mapsto a]$ denotes the environment η modified so that $(\eta[t \mapsto a])(t) = a$. This is the same as the interpretation of type expressions given in Section 9.2.4, simplified for a single impredicative collection T of types.

An environment η for interpretation $\langle \mathcal{U}, \mathcal{D}, Sub \rangle$ satisfies a typing $U\!:\!\sigma$, written $\eta \models U\!:\!\sigma$, if

$$[\![U]\!]\eta \in D^{[\![\sigma]\!]\eta}.$$

An environment η satisfies type assignment Γ, written $\eta \models \Gamma$, if $\eta \models x\!:\!\sigma$ for all $x\!:\!\sigma \in \Gamma$. The soundness of the implicit type inference is proved by induction on derivations.

Lemma 9.3.27 (Type Soundness) If $\Gamma \rhd U\!:\!\sigma$ is derivable and $\eta \models \Gamma$, then $\eta \models U\!:\!\sigma$.

The proof is left as Exercise 9.3.35. A general completeness theorem for typing assertions can also be proved [Mit88], but we do not need to go into this here.

Type-closed Properties

The next step is to show that for any "type-closed" set S of untyped lambda terms, there is a subset interpretation in which every typable term is an element of S. The definition of "type-closed" is relatively subtle, and would be more complicated if we used typed instead of untyped terms. The main idea is the same as in Section 8.3.3.

Let S be a set of untyped lambda terms. A subset $B \subseteq S$ is a *type set relative to* S if

(i) $\quad xU_1 \ldots U_k \in B$ whenever $U_1, \ldots, U_k \in S$,

(ii) $\quad (\lambda x.U)V_0 \ldots V_k \in B$ whenever $([V_0/x]U)V_1 \ldots V_k \in B$ and $V_0 \in S$.

A set S of lambda terms is *type-closed* if S is a type set relative to S and we have $U \in S$ whenever $UV \in S$.

If S is type-closed, we define the subset interpretation

$$\mathcal{A}_S = \langle \mathcal{U}, \mathcal{D}, Sub \rangle$$

by

• $\mathcal{U} = \{T^{\mathcal{A}}, \rightarrow^{\mathcal{A}}, \forall^{\mathcal{A}}, \mathcal{I}_{type}\}$ where $T^{\mathcal{A}}$ is the set of all type sets relative to S, and operations $\rightarrow^{\mathcal{A}}$ and $\forall^{\mathcal{A}}$ are given by

$$A \rightarrow^{\mathcal{I}} B = \{U \mid V \in A \text{ implies } UV \in B\} \qquad \forall^{\mathcal{I}}(f) = \cap_{A \in U^{\mathcal{I}}} f(A)$$

• $\mathcal{D} = \langle D, \cdot, [\![\ ]\!] \rangle$ is the lambda interpretation of α-equivalence classes of terms,

• $Sub\colon T^{\mathcal{A}} \rightarrow 2^D$ is the identity may on type sets relative to S, mapping each type set to itself.

Lemma 9.3.28 If S is type closed, then $\mathcal{I}_S$ is a subset interpretation.

It follows from type soundness that every typable term belongs to every type-closed set of untyped terms.

Theorem 9.3.29 If S is a type closed set of untyped lambda terms and $\Gamma \triangleright M\colon\sigma$, then $Erase(M) \in S$.

The proof of Lemma 9.3.28 is left as Exercise 9.3.36. Theorem 9.3.29 follows immediately from the lemma and the definition of $\mathcal{I}_S$.

Strong Normalization for Pure Terms

We show that the set of strongly-normalizing terms is "type-closed" and apply type soundness to conclude that whenever $\Gamma \triangleright M\colon\sigma$, the term $Erase(M)$ is strongly normalizing. From this we can also conclude that M is strongly normalizing.

Lemma 9.3.30 The set of strongly normalizing untyped lambda terms is type-closed.

This gives us the following normalization theorem.

Corollary 9.3.31 If $\Gamma \triangleright M\colon\sigma$, then $Erase(M)$ is a strongly normalizing untyped term.

We prove strong normalization for typed $\lambda^{\rightarrow,\forall}$-terms by establishing a correspondence between typed and untyped reductions.

Lemma 9.3.32 If explicitly-typed term $(\lambda t.\, M)\sigma$ reduces to $[\sigma/t]M$ by type β-reduction, then $[\sigma/t]M$ has one less type abstraction than $(\lambda t.\, M)\sigma$.

Lemma 9.3.33 If explicitly-typed term $(\lambda x\colon\sigma.\, M)N$ β-reduces to $[N/x]M$ then $Erase((\lambda x\colon\sigma.\, M)N)$ β-reduces to $Erase([N/x]M)$ by one untyped β-reduction.

It is easy to see that type β-reductions, $(\lambda t.\, M)\tau \rightarrow [\tau/t]M$, do not change the erasure of a term. Therefore, if there is an infinite sequence of type β-reductions and ordinary β-reductions starting from the explicitly-typed term M, there must be an infinite sequence of untyped β-reductions starting from $Erase(M)$. Using Lemmas 9.3.32 and 9.3.33, we have

Corollary 9.3.34 If $\Gamma \triangleright M\colon\sigma$, then M is a strongly normalizing typed term.

The similarities between proofs of strong normalization and other reduction properties are discussed in Section 8.3.3. Some other type-closed sets are the set of terms M from which all reductions are confluent and the set of terms M for which standard reduction reaches a normal form. Thus the theorem above has the Church-Rosser theorem for typable terms and the completeness of standard reduction for typable terms as corollaries. However, in these other cases, it is more difficult to derive properties of M from properties of $Erase(M)$.

Exercise 9.3.35 Prove Lemma 9.3.27 by induction in typing derivations. Use the implicit typing rules for assigning $\lambda^{\to,\forall}$-types to untyped lambda terms.

Exercise 9.3.36 Prove Lemma 9.3.28.

9.3.4 Summary of Semantic Models

In this section, we discuss models of $\lambda^{\to,\forall}$ in general and take a look at two kinds of models that are constructed from untyped structures. In the first class of models, types are represented by elements of a "universal domain," a CPO constructed in a special way that allows elements of the domain to represent sub-CPOs. This allows us to use untyped lambda terms to define operations on types. In the second class of models, types are quotients of subsets of an untyped partial combinatory algebra (Section 5.6.2), such as the natural numbers with recursive function application. Models of this kind are often referred to as *per models* since a quotient of a subset is given by a partial equivalence relation (see Section 5.6.1). In passing, we prove that there are no nontrivial models of $\lambda^{\to,\forall}$ that are finite at each type. The reader may also wish to consult Section 9.3.2 for a discussion of the fact that there are no set-theoretic models of a certain form.

Henkin Models

As pointed out in Section 9.2.4, an *impredicative applicative structure* or *Henkin model* is a $\lambda^{\to,\Pi}$-structure $\mathcal{A}$ with the added property that $U_1^{\mathcal{A}} = U_2^{\mathcal{A}}$. In other words, a predicative $\lambda^{\to,\Pi}$-applicative structure (or Henkin model) has interpretations $U_1^{\mathcal{A}}$ and $U_2^{\mathcal{A}}$ of the two universes of $\lambda^{\to,\Pi}$. The impredicative calculus $\lambda^{\to,\forall}$ differs from $\lambda^{\to,\Pi}$ only in that the two universes are identified in a single collection of types. Simplifying the definition of applicative structure from Section 9.2.4 to the impredicative case with only one universe, which we shall refer to as T instead of U_1 or U_2, we have the following definition.

A $\lambda^{\to,\forall}$-*applicative structure* $\mathcal{A}$ is a tuple

$$\mathcal{A} = \langle \mathcal{U}, Dom, \{\mathbf{App}^{a,b}, \mathbf{App}^f\}, \mathcal{I}\rangle$$

where

- $\mathcal{U} = \{T^{\mathcal{A}}, [T^{\mathcal{A}} \to T^{\mathcal{A}}], \to^{\mathcal{A}}, \forall^{\mathcal{A}}, \mathcal{I}_{type}\}$ specifies set $T^{\mathcal{A}}$, a set $[T^{\mathcal{A}} \to T^{\mathcal{A}}]$ of functions from $T^{\mathcal{A}}$ to $T^{\mathcal{A}}$, a binary operation $\to^{\mathcal{A}}$ on $T^{\mathcal{A}}$, a map $\forall^{\mathcal{A}}$ from $[T^{\mathcal{A}} \to T^{\mathcal{A}}]$ to $T^{\mathcal{A}}$, and a map $\mathcal{I}_{type}$ from type constants to $T^{\mathcal{A}}$,
- $Dom = \{Dom^a \mid a \in T^{\mathcal{A}}\}$ is a collection of sets indexed by types of the structure,
- $\{\mathbf{App}^{a,b}, \mathbf{App}^f\}$ is a collection of application maps, with one $\mathbf{App}^{a,b}$ for every pair of types $a, b \in T^{\mathcal{A}}$ and one $\mathbf{App}^f$ for every function $f \in [T^{\mathcal{A}} \to T^{\mathcal{A}}]$ from types to types. Each $\mathbf{App}^{a,b}$ must be a function

$$\mathbf{App}^{a,b} : Dom^{a \to b} \longrightarrow (Dom^a \longrightarrow Dom^b)$$

and each $\mathbf{App}^f$ must be a function

$$\mathbf{App}^f : Dom^{\forall f} \longrightarrow \prod_{a \in U_1} Dom^{f(a)}$$

as in Section 9.2.4,

- $\mathcal{I} : Constants \to \bigcup_{a \in T} Dom^a$ assigns a value to each constant symbol, with $\mathcal{I}(c) \in Dom^{[\![\tau]\!]}$ if c is a constant of type τ. Here $[\![\tau]\!]$ is the meaning of type expression τ, defined below. Recall that the type of a constant must not contain any free type variables.

This concludes the definition.

As in Section 9.2.4, we say a $\lambda^{\to,\forall}$-applicative structure is *extensional* if every $\mathbf{App}^{a,b}$ and $\mathbf{App}^f$ is one-to-one and a *Henkin model* if every term has a meaning in every environment. The interpretation of terms in a $\lambda^{\to,\forall}$-model is the same as for a predicative $\lambda^{\to,\Pi}$-model. It is easy to check that any model $\mathcal{D}$ of the untyped λ-calculus may be viewed as a $\lambda^{\to,\forall}$ model by taking $\mathcal{D}$ as the single element of $T^{\mathcal{A}}$.

Sections 4.5.5 and 4.5.6 discuss the implications of empty types for equational reasoning in $\lambda^{\to}$. Essentially the same proof rules and completeness theorems hold for $\lambda^{\to,\forall}$. More specifically, with the rule for models without empty types in Section 4.5.5, we have completeness for Henkin models without empty types [BMM90], and similarly for the rules in Section 4.5.6 and empty types [MMMS87]. We will not go into any of the completeness proofs, however, since they involve essentially the same kind of syntactic model constructions as for $\lambda^{\to}$. Exercise 9.3.51 and Examples 9.3.43 and 9.3.44 give some information about the existence of empty types in various models of $\lambda^{\to,\forall}$.

Some interesting domain-theoretic models are presented in [Gir86] and [CGW89], the latter also appearing in [Gun92]. The reader may consult [FS87, Pit87, Mes89, See87] for discussion of categorical approaches to semantics.

Impossibility of Finite Models

One distinction between untyped lambda calculus and simply-typed lambda calculus is that typed lambda calculus has nontrivialmodels in which all types are finite, but the untyped lambda calculus has no finite models [Bar84, Proposition 5.1.15]. A simple argument shows that there are no nontrivial models of $\lambda^{\to,\forall}$ in which all types are finite. (A model is trivial if it has at most one element of each type.) The main idea is essentially similar to Exercise 5.2.43; both use the basic fact that if equality on the natural numbers is definable by some term $Eq? : nat \to nat \to bool$, then $true = false$ in any model where the interpretation of nat is finite. In applying this observation to $\lambda^{\to,\forall}$, we may use the encodings of natural numbers and booleans as pure polymorphic terms.

As discussed in Section 9.3.2, the polymorphic Church numerals are terms of the form

$$\bar{n} \stackrel{\text{def}}{=} \lambda t.\, \lambda f\colon t \to t.\, \lambda x\colon t.\, f^n x,$$

where $f^n x$ is the term $f(f\ldots(fx)\ldots)$ with n occurrences of f. All of the Church numerals have type $nat \stackrel{\text{def}}{=} \forall t.\,(t \to t) \to t \to t$. We also have representations *true*, *false*: *bool* of the booleans by closed terms, where $bool \stackrel{\text{def}}{=} \forall t.\, t \to t \to t$. An important theorem mentioned in Section 9.3.2 is that every numeric function that can be proved total recursive in second-order Peano arithmetic is definable in $\lambda^{\to,\forall}$. It follows that there is a term $Eq? : nat \to nat \to bool$ with

$$\vdash Eq?\, \bar{m}\, \bar{n} = true \quad \text{if } m = n$$

$$\vdash Eq?\, \bar{m}\, \bar{n} = false \quad \text{if } m \neq n$$

for all natural numbers m and n. The term *Eq?* can also be constructed explicitly as outlined in Exercise 9.3.4.

If $\mathcal{A}$ is finite at each type, then $\mathcal{A} \models \bar{m} = \bar{n}$ for some $m \neq n$, since there are only finitely many elements of type $\forall t.\,(t \to t) \to t \to t$. It follows that

$$\mathcal{A} \models false = Eq?\, \bar{m}\, \bar{n} = Eq?\, \bar{n}\, \bar{n} = true.$$

However, Exercise 9.3.5 shows that if *true* = *false*, then every equation holds in $\mathcal{A}$. Therefore, $\mathcal{A}$ is a trivial model. In fact, we have shown that if $\forall t.\,(t \to t) \to t \to t$ is finite in some $\lambda^{\to,\forall}$-model, then the model must be trivial.

9.3.5 Models Based on Universal Domains

Universal domain models may be constructed using closures, finitary retracts, or finitary projections of certain domains. In each case, certain elements of the domain also represents a type (or subset) of the domain. We discuss the closure model and refer to the literature on finitary retracts and projections. Some terminology associated with these structures is that a *retraction* is a function f with the property that $f \circ f = f$ and the range of a retraction is called a *retract*. In the retract models, the types are retracts, represented by continuous retractions from the domain.

In this section, we will look at a model based on Scott's $\mathcal{P}\omega$ model of untyped lambda calculus [Sco76], with types represented by a special class of retractions called closures. This model was first worked out by McCracken [McC79], drawing heavily from [Sco76]. An important property of this models is that a rich class of retractions is itself a retract of $\mathcal{P}\omega$. Although we will not verify this, the retract of all retractions gives us a model of the *type*: *type* calculus discussed earlier in this chapter. At the end of the section, we mention two related models that differ primarily in the class of retractions used as types.

We will need some basic facts about the $\mathcal{P}\omega$ model of the untyped lambda calculus [Sco76]. Briefly, the elements of $\mathcal{P}\omega$ are subsets of the natural numbers; the name "$\mathcal{P}\omega$" comes from the common mathematical use of $\mathcal{P}$ for powerset and ω for the set of natural numbers. It is easy to see that this is a CPO under the subset ordering. One of the creative ideas behind the structure is a method for regarding a set of natural numbers as a function on sets. We can regard each natural number n as coding a finite set e_n by

$$e_n = \{k_0, k_1, \ldots, k_m\} \quad \text{if} \quad k_0 < k_1 < \ldots < k_m \text{ and } n = \sum_{i \le m} 2^{k_i}$$

In words, we can calculate e_n from n by writing n in binary and looking at the positions where 1's occur. For example, $n = 100101_2$ codes the set $e_n = \{0, 2, 5\}$ since 1's occur in positions 0,2 and 5, counting from the right. It is easy to see that simple operations on finite sets such as membership test and union are computable, *e.g.*, there is a computable function $f : \mathcal{N} \times \mathcal{N} \to \mathcal{N}$ such that $e_n \cup e_m = e_p$ iff $p = f(n, m)$. Combining this codings of sets with the coding of pairs given in Exercise 2.5.13 (see also Section 5.5.1), we can regard any natural number n as coding a pair $n = \langle n_1, n_2 \rangle$ and hence a pair

$$n = \langle \{k_0, k_1, \ldots, k_i\}, n_2 \rangle$$

where $e_{n_1} = \{k_0, k_1, \ldots, k_i\}$. We can think of this pair as the "instruction" that says, "when presented with all of the numbers $k_0, k_1, \ldots, k_i$, output number n_2." We apply one set of natural numbers, a, to another, b, by executing all of the instructions in a on input b and collecting the results, *i.e.*,

$$\mathbf{App}\, a\, b \;=\; \{n_2 \mid n = \langle n_1, n_2 \rangle \in a \text{ and } e_{n_1} \subseteq b\}$$

Exercise 9.3.39 asks you to show that application is continuous and that for every continuous $f : \mathcal{P}\omega \to \mathcal{P}\omega$ there is a set $a = \Psi(f)$ with $f(b) = \mathbf{App}\, a\, b$ for every $b \in \mathcal{P}\omega$. In addition, the composition $\mathbf{App} \circ \Psi$ is the identity on the set $[\mathcal{P}\omega \to \mathcal{P}\omega]$ of continuous functions on $\mathcal{P}\omega$. It follows that the CPO of continuous functions on $\mathcal{P}\omega$ is a retract of $\mathcal{P}\omega$.

We can interpret untyped lambda terms in P_ω by,

$$[\![x]\!]\eta \quad = \eta(x)$$

$$[\![UV]\!]\eta \quad = \mathbf{App}\ [\![U]\!]\eta\ [\![V]\!]\eta$$

$$[\![\lambda x.\, V]\!]\eta = \Psi(\lambda a \in P_\omega . [\![V]\!]\eta[x \mapsto a])$$

$P\omega$ is a non-extensional model of untyped lambda calculus, which means that this interpretation satisfies untyped lambda calculus axioms (α) and (β) but not (η). Additional information may be found in [Bar84, Sco76]. We will simplify notation by writing untyped lambda terms for elements of $\mathcal{P}\omega$ and adopting the abbreviations

$$ab \stackrel{\text{def}}{=} \mathbf{App}\, a\, b$$

$$a \circ b \stackrel{\text{def}}{=} \lambda x.a(bx)$$

for any $a, b \in \mathcal{P}\omega$. A *retraction in* $\mathcal{P}\omega$ is an element $\Psi(f) \in \mathcal{P}\omega$ such that the function $f\colon \mathcal{P}\omega \to \mathcal{P}\omega$ is a retraction. This is equivalent to saying that a retraction in $\mathcal{P}\omega$ is an element $a \in \mathcal{P}\omega$ with $a \circ a = a$, in the notation above.

We may build a $\lambda^{\to,\forall}$-model $\mathcal{A} = \mathcal{A}_{\mathcal{P}\omega}$ from $\mathcal{P}\omega$ using a special class of retractions as types. A retraction $a \in \mathcal{P}\omega$ is a *closure* if $ad \supseteq d$ for all $d \in \mathcal{P}\omega$. Intuitively, we can think of a closure as mapping an arbitrary $d \in \mathcal{P}\omega$ to the least superset of d satisfying some property. For example, the function mapping any set $a \in \mathcal{P}\omega$ of natural numbers to the set of all multiples of elements of a is a closure. We let

$$T^{\mathcal{A}} = \{a \in \mathcal{P}\omega \mid a \text{ is a closure}\}$$

so that the types of $\mathcal{A}$ are the closures of $\mathcal{P}\omega$. The elements of type a are the elements in the range of a, *i.e.*,

$$Dom^a = \{ad \mid d \in \mathcal{P}\omega\}.$$

for any $a \in T^{\mathcal{A}}$. Identifying closures and their images, we may think of the closure a as coercing untyped elements of $\mathcal{P}\omega$ to elements of type a. Since any closure a is a retraction, this coercion leaves elements of type a unchanged.

As shown in [Sco76], there is a closure $V \in T^{\mathcal{A}}$ of all closures, giving us $Dom^V = T^{\mathcal{A}}$. We let $[T^{\mathcal{A}} \to T^{\mathcal{A}}] = Dom^{V \to V}$, with the closure $V \to V$ defined below. Intuitively, Va is the least closure containing a. More precisely, the closure V may be defined by

$$Vab = \bigcap\{y \mid b \subseteq y \text{ and } ay \subseteq y\}$$

Another expression that is sometimes more useful in reasoning about expressions containing V is given in Exercise 9.3.42. The existence of V is a very specific property of closures and $\mathcal{P}\omega$. In particular, the collection of all retractions in $\mathcal{P}\omega$ is not a retract of $\mathcal{P}\omega$ [Sco76].

If a is a closure, then it is convenient to write $d\colon a$ for $d = ad$, which is another way of saying that $d \in Dom^a$. Another useful abbreviation is

$$\lambda x\colon a.\, M \stackrel{\text{def}}{=} \lambda y.[ay/x]M$$

Intuitively, $\lambda x\colon a.\, M$ is the function $\lambda x.\, M$, restricted to the range of closure a. More precisely, using (β), it is easy to see that $\lambda x\colon a.\, M = (\lambda x.\, M) \circ a$.

If a and b are closures, then we want $a \to b$ to be a closure which coerces every element d of $\mathcal{P}\omega$ to a mapping from Dom^a to Dom^b. In addition, we would like to have each continuous function from Dom^a to Dom^b represented exactly once in the range of $a \rightarrow b$, so that $Dom^{a \rightarrow b}$ is an extensional type of functions. As we show below, both of these goals may be accomplished by taking

$$a \rightarrow b = \lambda x. b \circ x \circ a.$$

Intuitively, $a \rightarrow b$ works by taking any element d and producing the element $b \circ d \circ a$ which, when used as a function, first coerces its argument to an element of type a, then applies d, and then coerces the result to type b. It is easy to see that if $x{:}\, a$, then $((b \circ d \circ a)x){:}\, b$, so $(b \circ d \circ a)$ represents a function from Dom^a to Dom^b. In addition, if d already represents a function from Dom^a to Dom^b, so $dx{:}\, b$ whenever $x{:}\, a$, then $(b \circ d \circ a)x = dx$ for all $x{:}\, a$.

We show the model is extensional by showing that for any closures a and b, if $(b \circ d_1 \circ a)x = (b \circ d_2 \circ a)x$ for all $x{:}\, a$, then $b \circ d_1 \circ a = b \circ d_2 \circ a$. This is proved by noticing that the restriction to $x{:}\, a$ is inessential, and so $(b \circ d_1 \circ a)x = (b \circ d_2 \circ a)x$ holds in $\mathcal{P}\omega$. Therefore $\lambda x.(b \circ d_1 \circ a)x = \lambda x.(b \circ d_2 \circ a)x$. Working out the definition of $\circ$ gives the desired equation. This means that range of $a \rightarrow b$ contains exactly one representative for each continuous function on $\mathcal{P}\omega$ that maps Dom^a into Dom^b. Based on this discussion, we let

$$\rightarrow = \lambda a{:}\, V. \lambda b{:}\, V.(\lambda x. b \circ x \circ a)$$

and write $\rightarrow$ as an infix operator, as in $a \rightarrow b$. Exercise 9.3.40 asks you to verify that for any $a, b \in \mathcal{P}\omega$, the element $a \rightarrow b$ is a closure.

The intuition behind $\forall$ is relatively straightforward. If $f{:}\, V \rightarrow V$ is a function from closures to closures, then every element $x{:}\, \forall f$ should map each closure (type) $t{:}\, V$ to some element xt of type ft. Therefore, $\forall f$ should be a function that coerces any $x \in \mathcal{P}\omega$ to a function which, given any $t{:}\, V$, returns an element $xt{:}\, ft$. Writing this out as a lambda term (including the type assumptions), we are led to the definition

$$\forall = \lambda f{:}\, V \rightarrow V. \lambda x. \lambda t{:}\, V.(ft)(xt).$$

Recall that $xt{:}\, ft$ is an abbreviation for $xt = (ft)(xt)$, so we have used $(ft)(xt)$ in the definition of $\forall$. Exercise 9.3.41 asks you to verify that if $f \in Dom^{V \rightarrow V}$, then $\forall f \in Dom^V = T^{\mathcal{A}}$.

To complete the definition of a $\lambda^{\rightarrow,\forall}$-applicative structure, we must define $\mathbf{App}^{a,b}$ and $\mathbf{App}^f$ for every $a, b \in T^{\mathcal{A}} = Dom^V$ and $f \in Dom^{V \rightarrow V}$. Surprisingly, all of these may be obtained as restrictions of the untyped $\mathbf{App}$ mapping $\mathcal{P}\omega$ to the set $[\mathcal{P}\omega \rightarrow \mathcal{P}\omega]$ of continuous functions on $\mathcal{P}\omega$. For all $a, b \in T^{\mathcal{A}}$, $d \in Dom^{a \rightarrow b}$, $e \in Dom^a$, $f \in Dom^{V \rightarrow V}$, and $d' \in Dom^{\forall f}$, we let

$$\mathbf{App}^{a,b}(d)(e) = \mathbf{App}(d)(e) \quad \text{and} \quad \mathbf{App}^{f}(d')(a) = \mathbf{App}(d')(a).$$

Some properties of these restrictions of the untyped application function are given in the following lemma.

Lemma 9.3.37

(i) $\mathbf{App}^{a,b}$ is a one-to-one and onto function from $Dom^{a \to b}$ to $[Dom^{a} \to Dom^{b}]$, where $[Dom^{a} \to Dom^{b}]$ is the set of continuous functions from Dom^{a} to Dom^{b}.

(ii) $\mathbf{App}^{f}$ is a one-to-one and onto function from $Dom^{\forall(f)}$ to $[\Pi_{a \in T^{\mathcal{A}}} Dom^{f(a)}]$, where $[\Pi_{a \in T^{\mathcal{A}}} Dom^{f(a)}]$ is the set of continuous functions in $\Pi_{a \in T^{\mathcal{A}}} Dom^{f(a)}$.

Proof For (i), note that $d \in Dom^{a \to b}$ implies $d = b \circ d \circ a$. Thus $\mathbf{App}(d)(e) = b(d(ae)) \in Dom^{b}$. It can also be shown that the range of $\mathbf{App}^{a,b}$ is all of $[Dom^{a} \to Dom^{b}]$. Suppose there are $d_1, d_2 \in Dom^{a \to b}$ such that $\mathbf{App}^{a,b}(d_1) = \mathbf{App}^{a,b}(d_2)$. It is then easy to show that $\mathbf{App}(d_1) = \mathbf{App}(d_2)$. Hence, $\Psi(\mathbf{App}(d_1)) = \Psi(\mathbf{App}(d_2))$. However $d_1, d_2 \in Dom^{a \to b}$ implies $d_i = b \circ d_i \circ a$ for $i = 1, 2$, and therefore $\Psi(\mathbf{App}(d_i)) = \Psi(\mathbf{App}(b \circ d_i \circ a)) = b \circ d_i \circ a = d_i$, where the middle equation holds since $b \circ d_i \circ a$ is of the form $\Psi(g)$ and $\Psi(\mathbf{App}(\Psi(g))) = \Psi(g)$. Thus $d_1 = \Psi(\mathbf{App}(d_1)) = \Psi(\mathbf{App}(d_2)) = d_2$, and it follows that $\mathbf{App}^{a,b}$ is one to one. The proof of (ii) is similar. ∎

This shows that $\mathcal{A}_{\mathcal{P}\omega}$ is a $\lambda^{\to,\forall}$-applicative structure. Since $[Dom^{a} \to Dom^{b}]$ and $[\Pi_{a \in T^{\mathcal{A}}} Dom^{f(a)}]$ consist of all continuous functions of the appropriate functionality, we can show that every term has an interpretation in $\mathcal{A}_{\mathcal{P}\omega}$. The main idea is the same as in the proof of Lemma 5.2.25 for $\lambda^{\to}$.

Theorem 9.3.38 $\mathcal{A}_{\mathcal{P}\omega} = \langle \mathcal{U}_{\mathcal{P}\omega}, Dom_{\mathcal{P}\omega}, \mathbf{App}^{a,b}, \mathbf{App}^{f} \rangle$, as defined above, is a $\lambda^{\to,\forall}$-Henkin model.

The model $\mathcal{A}_{\mathcal{P}\omega}$ has several interesting features. Perhaps most interesting is that $T^{\mathcal{A}} \in Dom$, giving the set of types a very rich structure. In particular we can interpret recursive types using the untyped least fixed-point operator of $\mathcal{P}\omega$. Somewhat surprisingly, given the definition of $T^{\mathcal{A}}$, the correspondence between $T^{\mathcal{A}}$ and Dom is bijective, *i.e.*, $a = b$ iff $Dom^{a} = Dom^{b}$.

A similar development yields a model whose types are finitary retracts [McC84, Sco80b]. More specifically, a retraction r is *finitary* if the range of r is an ω-algebraic, consistently complete CPO. The finitary retract model is built from a domain model of untyped lambda calculus by taking finitary retracts as types. While similar to the closure model described above (*e.g.*, in the definitions of $\to$ and $\forall$), there are some differences.

An easy one to identify is that the relation between $T^{\mathcal{A}}$ and *Dom* is not bijective. A similar extensional model using finitary projections appears in [ABL86]. The ideas behind the finitary projection model also appear in several papers of Scott. The finitary projection model is again bijective in the relationship between $T^{\mathcal{A}}$ and *Dom*. In [ABL86] it is shown how to solve higher-order recursive domain equations in this model. The same paper also shows that the type structures of all three models are very similar.

Exercise 9.3.39

(a) Show that in $\mathcal{P}\omega$, $\mathbf{App}\, a\, b$ is monotonic and continuous in a and b.

(b) Show that for every continuous $f : \mathcal{P}\omega \to \mathcal{P}\omega$ there is a set $a = \Psi(f)$ with $f(b) = \mathbf{App}\, a\, b$ for all $b \in \mathcal{P}\omega$. You may use the fact that if f is continuous, then $f(b) = \cup\{f(e) \mid e \subseteq b \text{ finite}\}$.

Exercise 9.3.40 Show that for any $a, b \in \mathcal{P}\omega$, the element $a \to b$ is a closure. You may use that fact that for any a, $V a$ is a closure.

Exercise 9.3.41 Show that for any $f \in Dom^{V \to V}$, we have $\forall f \in Dom^{V} = T^{\mathcal{A}}$. You may use that fact that for any a, $V a$ is a closure.

Exercise 9.3.42 One way of finding a precise difference between the closure model and other models is to examine the elements of $\forall t.t$. This exercise asks you to show there exist two distinct elements of this type. In contrast, Example 9.3.43 shows that $\forall t.t$ may be empty in a per model.

(a) Show that $\forall t.t = \lambda x.[\lambda y.(V y)(x(V y))$.

(b) Use the expression $V = \lambda f.\, \lambda x.\, \cup_i f^i x$ for V to simplify $(\forall t.t)(\lambda x.\, \lambda y.\, \lambda z.\, y)$ and $(\forall t.t)(\lambda x.\, \lambda y.\, \lambda z.\, z)$ to the form $\lambda f.\, \cup_i f^i(\ldots)$ where the expression $(\ldots)$ does not contain f.

(c) Show that $(\forall t.t)(\lambda x.\, \lambda y.\, \lambda z.\, y)$ and $(\forall t.t)(\lambda x.\, \lambda y.\, \lambda z.\, z)$ must be different elements of $\mathcal{P}\omega$ by finding some untyped lambda term W with $(\forall t.t)(\lambda x.\, \lambda y.\, \lambda z.\, y)W \neq (\forall t.t)(\lambda x.\, \lambda y.\, \lambda z.\, z)W$.

9.3.6 Partial Equivalence Relation Models

Modest set and partial equivalence relation (per) models for $\lambda^{\to}$ are described in Sections 5.5 and 5.6. Those sections introduce a form of computability on sets equipped with partial enumeration functions and develop an alternative presentation of the same mathematical structures using partial equivalence relations (pers). As explained in Section 5.6.2, per models of $\lambda^{\to}$ can be defined over any partial combinatory algebra, including the natural numbers (regarded as Gödel numbers of partial recursive functions) and syntactic structures such combinatory terms (Example 5.6.6) or untyped lambda terms (Example 5.6.7). In this section, we show how any such per model can be extended to $\lambda^{\rightarrow,\forall}$ and discuss some properties and variants of these models. In particular, we give a "characterization theorem" showing that the meaning of any polymorphic term is the equivalence class of the meaning of an untyped combinatory term obtained by erasing types (generalizing Lemma 8.2.26).

Historically, the per model HEO_2 over the natural numbers was the first semantic model of $\lambda^{\rightarrow,\forall}$ [Gir72, Tro73]. The structure HEO_2 was also discovered independently by Moggi and Plotkin (personal communication, 1985). The characterization theorem and equational completeness theorems for partial equivalence relation models are taken from [Mit86c].

For concreteness, we begin with Girard's model HEO_2. As in Section 5.5, we assume some enumeration of all partial recursive functions and write $n \cdot m \stackrel{\text{def}}{=} \phi_n(m)$ for the application of the n-th recursive function to m. It is possible to assume that the recursive functions are numbered so that $\phi_0(m) = 0$ for every integer m. However, we will only make this assumption in Example 9.3.43.

The main idea in extending a per model of $\lambda^{\rightarrow}$ to $\lambda^{\rightarrow,\forall}$ is to interpret $\forall t.\sigma$ as the intersection of all pers defined by σ, as t ranges over pers. Intuitively, two numbers code the same element of a polymorphic type $\forall t.\sigma$ exactly when they code the same element of each type obtained by assigning t a specific per. Mixing syntax and semantics, we can write this as $m\ \forall t.\sigma\ n$ iff $m\ [R/t]\sigma\ n$ for every type (per) R. An alternate but closely related interpretation of universal quantification is described at the end of this section.

A useful way to think about intersection of pers is to return to the idea of a per as a membership predicate and an equivalence relation. More specifically, a per $R \subseteq \mathcal{N} \times \mathcal{N}$ is an equivalence relation on the subset $|R| = \{n \mid n\ R\ n\}$; the "elements" of this per are the equivalence classes $[n]_R = \{m \mid n\ R\ m\}$ with $n \in |R|$. This is reflected in the development of Sections 5.5 and 5.6, where we regard a per R as a technical device for representing a modest set whose elements are the equivalence classes $[n]_R$ for $n \in |R|$. If we intersect two pers R and S, then the elements of $R \cap S$ are the equivalence classes

$$[n]_{R\cap S} = \{m \mid n\ R\ m \text{ and } n\ S\ m\}$$

for $n \in |R| \cap |S|$. There is no straightforward relationship between the cardinalities of R, S and $R \cap S$. In some cases, $R \cap S$ may have fewer equivalence classes since we only consider $n \in |R| \cap |S|$. On the other hand, as pointed out in Exercise 9.3.49, each equivalence class may be smaller, since $m \in [n]_{R\cap S}$ only if both $n\ R\ m$ and $n\ S\ m$.

The first step in defining the $\lambda^{\rightarrow,\forall}$-model

$$\mathrm{HEO}_2 = \langle \mathcal{U}, Dom, \{\mathbf{App}^{a,b}, \mathbf{App}^{f}\}, \mathcal{I}\rangle$$

is to define the interpretation $\mathcal{U} = \{T^H, [T^H \to T^H], \to, \forall, \mathcal{I}_{type}\}$ of types and type operations. We let T^H be the set of all partial equivalence relations over the natural numbers. For any $R, S \in T^H$, we let $R \to S$ be the relation

$$R \to S = \{\langle n_1, n_2\rangle \mid \text{ if } \langle m_1, m_2\rangle \in R \text{ then } \langle n_1 \cdot m_1, n_2 \cdot m_2\rangle \in S\}$$

as in Section 5.6.1. We let $[T^H \to T^H]$ be the set of all functions from pers to pers. If $f : T^H \to T^H$, then we let

$$\forall f = \cap_{R \in T^H} f(R).$$

It is easy to check that the intersection of any collection of pers is a per, giving us $\forall f \in T^H$. If we are interested in interpreting a signature with type constants, we may choose $\mathcal{I}_{type}$ as desired (see Example 5.6.1).

For any $R \in T^H$ and integer n with $\langle n, n\rangle \in R$, we let the set Dom^R of "elements of type R" be the collection of all nonempty equivalence classes

$$Dom^R = \{[n]_R \mid \langle n, n\rangle \in R\}$$

and let $Dom = \{Dom^R \mid R \in T^H\}$.

The application functions $\mathbf{App}^{R,S}$ and $\mathbf{App}^f$ are defined by

$$\mathbf{App}^{R,S}\ [n]_{R \to S}\ [m]_R = [n \cdot m]_S$$

$$\mathbf{App}^f\ [n]_{\forall f}\ R = [n]_{f(R)}$$

It is easy to see that both are well-defined on equivalence classes. Although $\mathbf{App}^f$ may look trivial, it is not since $[n]_{f(R)}$ will generally be a larger equivalence class than $[n]_{\forall f}$. If we are interested in a signature with term constants, we may choose $\mathcal{I}$ as desired. This completes the definition of the $\lambda^{\to,\forall}$-applicative structure HEO_2. An essentially straightforward extension of Theorem 5.5.10 shows that every term has a meaning and therefore HEO_2 is a $\lambda^{\to,\forall}$-Henkin model.

The definition of HEO_2 is easily generalized to any partial combinatory algebra. Many of the main ideas are described in Section 5.6.2. Essentially, all that is needed beyond a model of $\lambda^{\to}$ is to interpret $\forall$ as intersection. We say a $\lambda^{\to,\forall}$-model $\mathcal{A}$ is a *per model* if there is some partial combinatory algebra $\mathcal{D} = \langle D, \cdot, K, S\rangle$ such that every type Dom^a of $\mathcal{A}$ is determined by a per $R \subseteq D \times D$ with $\to$ and $\forall$ defined as above for the partial combinatory algebra of natural numbers and partial recursive function applications.

Example 9.3.43 In HEO_2, the type $\forall t.t$ is empty. This is an obvious consequence of the fact that $[\![\forall t.t]\!]$ is the intersection of all pers and there exist disjoint pers over the natural numbers. This may be contrasted with the situation for continuous models such as the closure model, where $\forall t.t$ is nonempty (see Exercise 9.3.42). ■

Example 9.3.44 We can construct variants of HEO_2 in which $\forall t.t$ is non-empty. The simplest approach is the one originally used by Girard. (A generalization is given in Exercise 9.3.50.) As mentioned earlier, it is possible to assume that the recursive functions are numbered so that $\phi_0(m) = 0$ for every integer m. With this assumption on the coding of recursive functions, we may build a per model such that 0 has a nonempty equivalence class at every type. More specifically, we modify the definition of HEO_2 so that T^H is the set of all pers R over the natural numbers with $0\ R\ 0$. It is easy (and instructive) to check that $0\ (R \to S)\ 0$ whenever $0\ S\ 0$. It is also quite easy to see that $0\ (\forall f)\ 0$ when $\forall f$ is an intersection of relations containing the pair $\langle 0, 0\rangle$. In this version of HEO_2, the type $\forall t.t$ contains is exactly the singleton $\{\langle 0, 0\rangle\}$ since there are relations in T^H whose only overlap is this pair. ■

Example 9.3.45 It is relatively easy to show that the type $\forall t.\, t \to t$ contains only the identity function in HEO_2. This is left to the reader as Exercise 9.3.52. A relatively complicated argument shows that the type $\forall t.\, (t \to t) \to t \to t$ contains only the Church numerals (*i.e.*, the indexes of recursive functions $\lambda f.\, \lambda x.\, f^n x$) [Fre88]. Instead of examining this argument, we will show that in a per model based on untyped lambda terms, $\forall t.\, (t \to t) \to t \to t$ contains only the Church numerals. More specifically, we use the variant of HEO_2 based on the partial combinatory algebra whose elements are untyped lambda terms over infinitely many variables, modulo β, η-conversion, as described in Example 5.6.7.

We prove that $\forall t.\, (t \to t) \to t \to t$ contains only the untyped Church numerals by assuming that untyped term $U \in |\forall t.\, (t \to t) \to t \to t|$. This means that for any per R, if $f\ R \to R\ f$ and $x\ R\ x$, then $(Ufx)\ R\ (Ufx)$. In particular, let f and x be two distinct variables of the untyped lambda calculus and consider the relation

$$R \stackrel{\text{def}}{=} \{\langle U_1, U_2\rangle \mid \exists n \in \mathcal{N} \text{ such that } U_1 \twoheadrightarrow f^n x \text{ and } U_2 \twoheadrightarrow f^n x\}$$

Clearly $f\ R \to R\ f$ and $x\ R\ x$. Therefore, from our assumption that $U \in |\forall t.\, (t \to t) \to t \to t|$, we conclude that there is some $n \in \mathcal{N}$ such that $Ufx \twoheadrightarrow f^n x$. Therefore $\lambda f.\, \lambda x.\, Ufx \twoheadrightarrow U \twoheadrightarrow \lambda f.\, \lambda x.\, f^n x$ and U is β, η-equivalent to a Church numeral. ■

Using essentially the same ideas as in Section 8.2.5, we may establish a connection between the meaning of a typed term in a per model and an associated untyped combinatory term in the underlying partial combinatory algebra. The *erasure function Erase* from typed $\lambda^{\to,\forall}$-terms to untyped lambda terms is described in Section 9.3.3. (Additional discussion, for $\lambda^{\rightarrow}$, appears in Section 11.1.) The main idea is that *Erase*(M) is an untyped term similar to M, but with type annotations on lambda-bound variables, type abstractions and type applications removed. The resulting untyped lambda term may be converted to an untyped combinatory term following the procedure given for typed terms in Section 4.5.7. Combining these two translations, we can convert any typed $\lambda^{\rightarrow,\forall}$-term $\Gamma \triangleright M\colon\sigma$ to an untyped combinatory term $\text{CL}(\mathit{Erase}(M))$, written using application and constants K and S, which may be interpreted in any partial combinatory algebra (see Section 5.6.2).

We show below that the meaning of $\Gamma \triangleright M\colon\sigma$ in a per model over partial combinatory algebra $\mathcal{D} = \langle D, \cdot, K, S\rangle$ is the equivalence class of the interpretation of $\text{CL}(\mathit{Erase}(M))$ in $\mathcal{D}$, modulo the partial equivalence relation given by its type, σ. We state this precisely using a correspondence between environments for a per model $\mathcal{A}$ and environments for the partial combinatory algebra $\mathcal{D}$ whose partial equivalence relations form the types of $\mathcal{A}$. Specifically, suppose η_1 is an environment for $\mathcal{D}$ and η_2 is a mapping from type variables to types of $\mathcal{A}$ such that $\eta_1(x) \in |[\![\sigma]\!]\eta_2|$ for every $x\colon\sigma \in \Gamma$. We let the environment $\eta_{1,2}$ for $\mathcal{A}$ be any environment satisfying

$$\eta_{1,2}(t) = \eta_2(t)$$

for any type variable t, and

$$\eta_{1,2}(x) = [\eta_1(x)]_{[\![\sigma]\!]\eta_2}$$

for any term variable x with $x\colon\sigma \in \Gamma$. With this notation, we can state the following theorem.

Theorem 9.3.46 (Characterization Theorem) Let $\mathcal{A}$ be a per model with every Dom^R given by a partial equivalence relation R over partial combinatory algebra $\mathcal{D}$. Suppose $\Gamma \triangleright M\colon\sigma$ is a well-typed $\lambda^{\rightarrow,\forall}$-term, η_1 is an environment for $\mathcal{D}$ and η_2 is a mapping from type variables to types of $\mathcal{A}$ with $\eta_1(x) \in |[\![\sigma]\!]\eta_2|$ for every $x\colon\sigma \in \Gamma$. Then

$$\mathcal{A}[\![\Gamma \triangleright M\colon\sigma]\!]\eta_{1,2} = [\mathcal{D}[\![\text{CL}(\mathit{Erase}(M))]\!]\eta_1]_{[\![\sigma]\!]\eta_2}.$$

In other words, the meaning of $\Gamma \triangleright M\colon\sigma$ in $\mathcal{A}$ is the equivalence class of the untyped meaning of the untyped combinatory term $\text{CL}(\mathit{Erase}(M))$ in $\mathcal{D}$. In the special case that $\mathcal{D}$ is an untyped lambda model, we may omit the translation CL from untyped lambda terms to combinatory terms.

Proof The proof is essentially the same as for Lemma 8.2.26, with extra cases for type abstraction and application. We illustrate the main ideas by proving the induction steps for lambda abstraction. The cases for application are similar.

Let $\Gamma, x\colon\sigma \triangleright M\colon\tau$ be a typed $\lambda^{\rightarrow,\forall}$-term and let $U = \textsc{cl}(Erase(M))$ be the corresponding untyped combinatory term. We assume that

$$\mathcal{A}[\![\Gamma, x\colon\sigma \triangleright M\colon\tau]\!]\eta_{1,2}[x \mapsto [d]] = [\,\mathcal{D}[\![U]\!]\eta_1[x \mapsto d]\,]_{[\![\tau]\!]\eta_2}$$

for any $d \in |[\![\sigma]\!]\eta_2|$. Let $\langle x\rangle U$ be the combinatory term representing $\lambda x.\, U$, as described in Section 4.5.7. It may be proved that in any partial combinatory algebra, we have $(\langle x\rangle U)\cdot V \cong [V/x]U$ for any partial combinatory term V. We show that

$$\mathcal{A}[\![\Gamma \triangleright \lambda x\colon\sigma.\, M\colon\sigma \to \tau]\!]\eta_{1,2} = [\,\mathcal{D}[\![\langle x\rangle U]\!]\eta_1\,]_{[\![\sigma\to\tau]\!]\eta_2}$$

by extensionality and a calculation involving application. Specifically, for any $d \in |[\![\sigma]\!]\eta_2|$, so that $[d]_{[\![\sigma]\!]\eta_2}$ is nonempty, we have

$$\begin{aligned}\textbf{App}\ \mathcal{A}[\![\Gamma \triangleright \lambda x\colon\sigma.\, M\colon\sigma \to \tau]\!]\eta_{1,2}\ [d] &= \mathcal{A}[\![\Gamma, x\colon\sigma \triangleright M\colon\tau]\!]\eta_{1,2}[x \mapsto [d]]\\ &= [\,\mathcal{D}[\![U]\!]\eta_1[x \mapsto d]\,]_{[\![\tau]\!]\eta_2}\\ &= [\,\mathcal{D}[\![\langle x\rangle U]\!]\eta_1 \cdot d\,]_{[\![\tau]\!]\eta_2}\\ &= \textbf{App}\ [\,\mathcal{D}[\![\langle x\rangle U]\!]\eta_1\,]_{[\![\sigma\to\tau]\!]\eta_2}\ [d]_{[\![\sigma]\!]\eta_2}\end{aligned}$$

the first step by the substitution lemma for $\lambda^{\rightarrow,\forall}$-models, the second by the induction hypothesis, the third by the substitution lemma for partial combinatory algebras, and the final steps by properties of psuedo-abstraction and the definition of lambda abstraction in per models.

For type abstraction, we have a similar but simpler calculation, namely,

$$\begin{aligned}\textbf{App}\ \mathcal{A}[\![\Gamma \triangleright \lambda t.\, M\colon\forall t.\sigma]\!]\eta_{1,2}\ R &= \mathcal{A}[\![\Gamma \triangleright M\colon\sigma]\!]\eta_{1,2}[t \mapsto R]\\ &= [\,\mathcal{D}[\![U]\!]\eta_1\,]_{[\![\sigma]\!]\eta_2[t\mapsto R]}\\ &= \textbf{App}\ [\,\mathcal{D}[\![U]\!]\eta_1\,]_{[\![\forall t.\sigma]\!]\eta_2}\ R\end{aligned}$$

This proves the theorem. ∎

The characterization theorem shows that if $\Gamma \triangleright M\colon\sigma$ and $\Gamma \triangleright N\colon\sigma$ have the same type and $Erase(M) = Erase(N)$, then $\Gamma \triangleright M = N\colon\sigma$ holds in every per model, regardless of the partial combinatory algebra used to construct the model. For example, the equation

$$\lambda x\colon(\forall t.t).\, x = \lambda x\colon(\forall t.t).(x\ \forall t.t) : (\forall t.t) \to (\forall t.t)$$

holds in every per model. Similarly, if $[\tau_1/s]\sigma_1 = [\tau_2/t]\sigma_2$ and $[\rho_1/s]\sigma_1 = [\rho_2/t]\sigma_2$, then the equation

$$\lambda x\colon \forall s(\sigma_1 \to r).\, \lambda y\colon \forall t.\sigma_2.(x\tau_1)(y\tau_2) = \lambda x\colon \forall s(\sigma_1 \to r).\, \lambda y\colon \forall t.\sigma_2.(x\rho_1)(y\rho_2)$$

holds in every per model. However, there is a completeness theorem showing that this is the only kind of unprovable equation that holds in all per models.

Theorem 9.3.47 (Completeness) Let *Th* be any $\lambda^{\to,\forall}$-theory containing every well-typed equation $\Gamma \rhd M = N\colon\sigma$ with $Erase(M) = Erase(N)$ and closed under rule (*nonempty*) from Section 4.5.5. Then there is a per model without empty types satisfying exactly the equations in *Th*.

The theorem is proved using a syntactic construction over the partial combinatory algebra of untyped lambda terms from Example 5.6.7 (also used in Example 9.3.45). The types of the model are all pers definable by type expressions, with $\langle U, V\rangle$ in the relation for type σ if there is a typed equation $\Gamma \rhd M = N\colon\sigma$ in *Th*, for $\Gamma \subseteq \mathcal{H}$, with $Erase(M) \equiv U$ and $Erase(N) \equiv V$. The infinite type assignment $\mathcal{H}$ provides infinitely many variables of each type (as in Section 8.3.1), forcing each type to be nonempty. We will not go into the details of the proof since many of the ideas are illustrated the proof of Theorem 10.4.25 and in the following example. A similar construction proves the analogous theorem for theories closed under rules (*empty I*) and (*empty E*) from Sections 4.5.6 and models with some types empty (see Exercise 8.3.3 for the main ideas).

Example 9.3.48 There is a straightforward syntactic method for embedding any multi-sorted algebra in a per model. We illustrate this using the algebra $\mathcal{A}_{pcf}$ of natural numbers and booleans from Section 3.3.1. The general method requires a signature that provides a constant symbol for each element of each sort of the algebra. For $\mathcal{A}_{pcf}$, we may use the natural number and boolean constants of PCF. More specifically, we embed equivalence classes of terms into a combinatory algebra and then form a per model.

The first step is to construct a partial combinatory algebra containing $\mathcal{A}_{pcf}$. We do this by extending the signature of combinatory logic, given in Example 3.7.31, with constants for each of the functions ane elements of the multi-sorted algebra. Since a partial combinatory algebra is a single-sorted structure, we give all of the constant symbols the same sort. In addition, we write equational axioms for the graph of each function from $\mathcal{A}_{pcf}$. This leads us to the following algebraic specification, which also includes conditional:

sorts:ι

fctns:$S, K, I: \iota$

$ap: \iota \to \iota \to \iota$

$0, 1, 2, 3, \ldots: \iota$

$true, false: \iota$

$+, Eq?, cond: \iota$

eqns:$ap\ (ap\ (ap\ S\ x)\ y)\ z = ap\ (ap\ x\ z)\ (ap\ y\ z)$

$ap\ (ap\ K\ x)\ y = x$

$ap\ I\ x = x$

$ap(ap + 0)\ 0 = 0$

$ap(ap + 0)\ 1 = 1$

$ap(ap + 0)\ 2 = 2$

$\ldots$

$ap(ap + 2)\ 3 = 5$

$\ldots$

$Eq?\ 0\ 0 = true$

$Eq?\ 0\ 1 = false$

$\ldots$

$cond\ true = K$

$cond\ false = \langle x \rangle \langle y \rangle y$

where $\langle x \rangle \langle y \rangle y$ is an abbreviation for an applicative combination of K, S and I as defined in Section 4.5.7. For each function f and sequence of arguments $a_1, \ldots, a_k$, we have a closed combinatory term representing $f(a_1, \ldots, a_k)$ and equation giving the value of f on these arguments. This equation does not contain any variables, only constant symbols representing elements of the multi-sorted algebra we started with. For *cond*, we have deviated from the standard pattern, using more general axioms that will give us a polymorphic conditional of type $\forall t.\, bool \to t \to t \to t$ in the final per model. The axioms for *cond* are designed to give us $cond\ true\ x\ y = x$ and $cond\ false\ x\ y = y$.

It is easy to check that if we orient each equational axiom from left to right, we obtain a left-linear, non-overlapping rewrite system $\mathcal{R}$. By Proposition 3.7.29, $\twoheadrightarrow_{\mathcal{R}}$ is confluent. It follows that we can prove $M = N$ from our algebraic specification iff M and N reduce to a common term. In particular, since each constant naming a function or element of our original multi-sorted algebra is a normal form, none of these are provably equal. Therefore, when we form the term algebra of equivalence classes modulo this specification, each function or element of our original multi-sorted algebra corresponds to a distinct equivalence class. Moreover, it follows easily from the design of the specification that if $f(a_1, \ldots, a_k) = a$ in the algebra, then

$$[ap]\,([ap]\,([ap]\,[f]\,[a_1])\ \ldots)\,[a_k] = [a]$$

in the quotient algebra.

We now form a per model over the term combinatory algebra by taking all pers as types. Each function symbol from the algebraic signature can be interpreted as its equivalence class in the term algebra. For example, the obvious interpretation of a term constant 0 is the equivalence class [0]. For type *nat*, we use the identity relation on the equivalence classes of numerals 0, 1, 2, ..., and similarly for *bool*. It is essentially straightforward to verify that this gives us a per model for $\lambda^{\rightarrow,\forall}$ with an isomorphic copy of the chosen multi-sorted algebra. ■

Some authors have used an alternative interpretation of $\forall$ derived from topos theory (see [BL90], for example). Specifically, we may interpret $\forall f$ as a set of functions returning elements of the intersection using the definition

$$\forall f = \{\langle d, d' \rangle \mid \forall a \in D. \forall R \in T^{\mathcal{A}}.\ d \cdot a\ f(R)\ d \cdot a\}$$

in place of intersection and defining application of polymorphic functions by

$$\mathbf{App}^f\ [d]_{\forall f}\ R = [n \cdot a]_{f(R)}$$

where a may be any element of D. Theorem 9.3.46 may be adapted to this setting by letting $Erase(\lambda t.\, M) = \lambda t'.\, Erase(M)$ where t' does not occur free in $Erase(M)$.

Exercise 9.3.49 For each part of this problem, find *nonempty* pers $R, S, \subseteq \{1, \ldots, 4\} \times \{1, \ldots, 4\}$ such that

(a) $R \cap S = \emptyset$.

(b) $|R \cap S| = |R| = |S|$ and $R \cap S$ has more equivalence classes than either R or S.

(c) $R \cap S \neq \emptyset$ has fewer equivalence classes than either R or S.

Exercise 9.3.50 Suppose $\mathcal{D} = \langle D, \cdot, K, S \rangle$ is a partial combinatory algebra. In building a per model over $\mathcal{D}$, we can make all types nonempty by choosing any set $Z \subseteq D$ such that for all $z \in Z$ and $d \in D$, we have $z \cdot d \in Z$. We then let the types of the per model be all pers R containing $Z \times Z$. It is trivial to check that the set of such pers is closed under intersection. Show that if R and S are pers with $S \supseteq Z \times Z$, then $R \to S \supseteq Z \times Z$.

Exercise 9.3.51 Show that in any per model, there exists an empty type iff the type $\forall t.t$ is empty. Would this also hold in closure, finitary retract and finitary projection models?

Exercise 9.3.52 Show that in HEO_2, the type $\forall t.\, t \to t$ contains only the identity function. More specifically, show that if $\langle n, n\rangle \in \bigcap_R R \to R$, then $n \cdot m = m$ for every natural number $m \in \mathcal{N}$.

9.4 Data Abstraction and Existential Types

Data abstraction and associated notions of program specification and modularity are probably the most influential programming language developments of the 1970's, leading in part to the popularity and acceptance of object-oriented systems in the 1980's and 90's. Abstract data type declarations, a language facility that supports data abstraction, appear in a number of programming languages, including Ada, Clu and ML [US 80, L+81, Mil85a, MTH90, MT91, Ull94]. Without going into all of the pragmatic issues associated with data abstraction and program structure, we investigate a general form of data type declaration that may be incorporated into any language with type variables, including the three versions of polymorphic typed lambda calculus introduced in Section 9.1. The main ideas are taken from [MP88].

We begin with a slightly more general form of `abstype` declaration than necessary, since this makes it easier to describe intuitive examples. We then reduce the general form to a special case (using cartesian products) when we come to formal typing rules. The declaration form

$$\texttt{abstype}\ t\ \texttt{with}\ x_1{:}\sigma_1, \ldots, x_k{:}\sigma_k\ \texttt{is}\ \langle \tau, M_1, \ldots, M_k\rangle\ \texttt{in}\ N$$

declares an abstract type t with "operations" $x_1, \ldots, x_k$ and implementation $\langle \tau, M_1, \ldots, M_k\rangle$. The scope of this declaration is N. We can illustrate this general construct using integer streams, which are a form of infinite list. For simplicity, we will consider streams with only two operations, one that selects the first element from a stream, and another that returns the stream of remaining elements. The expression

$$\begin{array}{l}\texttt{abstype}\ \mathit{stream}\ \texttt{with}\\ \qquad s{:}\ \mathit{stream},\\ \qquad \mathit{first}{:}\ \mathit{stream} \to \mathit{nat},\\ \qquad \mathit{rest}{:}\ \mathit{stream} \to \mathit{stream}\end{array}$$

`is`

$\langle \tau, M_1, M_2, M_3 \rangle$

`in`

N

declares an abstract data type *stream* with distinguished element s: *stream* and functions *first* and *rest* for operating on streams. Within the scope N of the declaration, the stream s and operations *first* and *rest* may be used to compute streams, natural numbers or other results. However, the type of N may not be *stream,* since this type is local to the expression. In computational terms, the elements of the abstract type *stream* are represented by values of the type τ given in the implementation. Operations s, *first* and *rest* are implemented by expressions M_1, M_2 and M_3. Since the value of s must be a stream, the expression M_1 must have type τ, the type of values used to represent streams. Similarly, we must have $M_2\colon \tau \to nat$ and $M_3\colon \tau \to \tau$. Using cartesian products, we may put any abstract data type declaration in the form `abstype` t `with` $x\colon\sigma$ `is` $\langle \tau, M \rangle$ `in` N. For example, the *stream* declaration may be put in this form by combining the three operations s, *first* and *rest* into a single operation of type $stream \times (stream \to nat) \times (stream \to stream)$. There is no loss in doing so, since we may recover s, *first* and *rest* using projection functions.

Abstract data type declarations may be added to either predicative or impredicative languages, using the general form described above. While it is possible to formulate a typing rule and equational axioms for `abstype` as described above (as in the original formulation of ML [GMW79]), some useful flexibility is gained by considering abstract data type declarations and data type implementations separately. An implementation for the abstract type *stream* mentioned above consists of a type τ, used to represent *stream*'s, together with expressions for the specified stream s and the stream operations *first* and *rest.* If we want to describe implementations of streams in general, we might say that in any implementation, "there exists a type t with elements of types t, $t \to nat$, and $t \to t$." This description would give just enough information about an arbitrary implementation to determine that an `abstype` declaration makes sense, without giving any information about how streams are represented. This fits the general goals of data abstraction, as discussed in the seminal research paper [Mor73], for example.

We add abstract data type implementations and `abstype` declarations to a language with type variables as follows. The first step is to extend the syntax of type expressions

$$\sigma \ ::= \ \ldots \mid \exists t.\sigma$$

to include *existential types* of the form $\exists t.\sigma$. Since $\exists$ is a binding operator, we have $\exists t.\sigma = \exists s.[s/t]\sigma$, assuming s does not already occur free in σ. In a predicative language, $\exists t_1. \ldots \exists t_k.\tau$ would belong to U_2, assuming $\tau\colon U_1$.

Existential types are used to type implementations of abstract data types. Intuitively, each element of an existential type $\exists t.\sigma$ consists of a type τ and an element of $[\tau/t]\sigma$. Using products to combine s, *first*, and *rest*, an implementation of *stream* would have type $\exists t.[t \times (t \to nat) \times (t \to t)]$, for example. Note that if we read "$\times$" as "and," this type expression may be read, "there exists a type t with elements of type t, $t \to nat$, and $t \to t$," which matches the informal description given above. Existential types, which were part of Girard's System F [Gir71, Gir72] (but not linked to abstract data types), may also be explained using the formulas-as-types analogy. This is considered below.

When we write abstract data type implementations apart from the declarations that use them, it is necessary to include some type information which might at first appear redundant. We will write an implementation in the form $\langle t = \tau, M\colon\sigma\rangle$, where $t = \tau$ binds t in the remainder of the expression. The reader may think of $\langle t = \tau, M\colon\sigma\rangle$ as a "pair" $\langle\tau, M\rangle$ in which access to the representation type τ has been restricted. The bound type variable t and the type expression σ serve to disambiguate the type of the expression. The type of a well-formed expression $\langle t = \tau, M\colon\sigma\rangle$ is $\exists t.\sigma$, according to the following rule.

$$\frac{\Gamma \rhd M\colon [\tau/t]\sigma}{\Gamma \rhd \langle t = \tau, M\colon\sigma\rangle\colon \exists t.\sigma} \qquad (\exists\ \text{Intro})$$

We may read this rule as saying that if $M\colon[\tau/t]\sigma$, then in the "pair" $\langle t = \tau, M\colon\sigma\rangle$, there exists a type t together with a value of type σ. Since t is bound in this expression, we have the equational axiom

$$\Gamma \rhd \langle t = \tau, M\colon\sigma\rangle = \langle s = \tau, M\colon[s/t]\sigma\rangle\colon \exists t.\sigma \quad s \text{ not free in } \sigma \qquad 1$$

allowing renaming of the bound type variable. Exercise 9.4.3 explains why we use the syntactic form $\langle t = \tau, M\colon\sigma\rangle$ instead of simply writing $\langle\tau, M\rangle$.

The following rule for `abstype` declarations allows us to bind names to the type and value components of a data type implementation.

$$\frac{\Gamma \rhd M\colon \exists t.\tau, \quad \Gamma, x\colon\tau \rhd N\colon\sigma}{\Gamma \rhd (\texttt{abstype}\ t\ \texttt{with}\ x\colon\tau\ \texttt{is}\ M\ \texttt{in}\ N)\colon\sigma}\ t \text{ not free in } \Gamma \text{ or } \sigma \qquad (\exists\ \text{Elim})$$

Informally, this rule binds type variable t and ordinary variable x to the type and value part of the implementation M, with scope N. However, there is no syntactic restriction on the form of the implementation. In particular, the data type implementation may be a formal parameter to a function containing this declaration.

As a notational convenience, we treat a declaration with more than on operation as syntactic sugar:

$$\texttt{abstype } t \texttt{ with } x_1\colon\sigma_1, \ldots, x_n\colon\sigma_n \texttt{ is } M \texttt{ in } N$$

$$\stackrel{\text{def}}{\equiv} \texttt{ abstype } t \texttt{ with } y\colon\sigma_1 \times \ldots \times \sigma_n \texttt{ is } M \texttt{ in } [\mathbf{Proj}_1^n y, \ldots, \mathbf{Proj}_n^n y/x_1, \ldots, x_n]N$$

Example 9.4.1 The expression

$$\begin{array}{l} \texttt{abstype } \mathit{cmplx} \texttt{ with} \\ \qquad \mathit{create}\colon \mathit{real} \times \mathit{real} \to \mathit{cmplx}, \\ \qquad \mathit{plus}\colon \mathit{cmplx} \times \mathit{cmplx} \to \mathit{cmplx}, \\ \qquad \mathit{re}\colon \mathit{cmplx} \to \mathit{real} \\ \qquad \mathit{im}\colon \mathit{cmplx} \to \mathit{real} \\ \quad \texttt{is} \\ \qquad \langle t = \mathit{real} \times \mathit{real}, \langle C, P, R, I\rangle\colon (\mathit{real} \times \mathit{real} \to t) \times (t \times t \to t) \times (t \to \mathit{real}) \times \\ \qquad\quad (t \to \mathit{real})\rangle \\ \quad \texttt{in} \\ \qquad N \end{array}$$

declares an abstract data type *cmplx* with operations that create a complex number from two real numbers, add complex numbers, and return the real and imaginary part of a complex number. An implementation $\langle t = \mathit{real} \times \mathit{real}, \langle C, P, R, I\rangle\colon \ldots\rangle$ using rectangular coordinates may be written using

$$C = \lambda p\colon \mathit{real} \times \mathit{real}.\, p$$

$$P = \lambda\langle z\colon \mathit{real} \times \mathit{real},\ w\colon \mathit{real} \times \mathit{real}\rangle.\langle \mathbf{Proj}_1 z + \mathbf{Proj}_1 w,\ \ \mathbf{Proj}_2 z + \mathbf{Proj}_2 w\rangle$$

$$R = \lambda z\colon \mathit{real} \times \mathit{real}.\, \mathbf{Proj}_1 z$$

$$I = \lambda z\colon \mathit{real} \times \mathit{real}.\, \mathbf{Proj}_2 z$$

Exercise 9.4.4 asks you to check the type of the implementation and write a small program using complex numbers. ■

The main equational axiom for `abstype` is

$$\Gamma \triangleright (\texttt{abstype } t \texttt{ with } x\colon\sigma \texttt{ is } \langle t = \tau, M\colon\sigma\rangle \texttt{ in } N) = [M/x][\tau/t]N\colon\rho \qquad (\beta)_\exists$$

which allows us to simplify an `abstype` expression by substituting the two parts of an implementation into the body of the declaration. The main computational reduction rule is obtained by reading this from left to right. In other words, in simplifying expressions involving `abstype`, we generally use this equation to simplify an `abstype` expression to a substitution of the form on the right of this equation. Since `abstype` is a binding operator, we have the renaming equivalence

$$\Gamma \rhd \texttt{abstype } t \texttt{ with } x{:}\sigma \texttt{ is } M \texttt{ in } N \\ = \texttt{abstype } s \texttt{ with } y{:}[s/t]\sigma \texttt{ is } M \texttt{ in } [y/x][s/t]N{:}\rho \qquad (\alpha)_\exists$$

There is also an "extensionality" axiom that is not needed in computation, but can be useful in equational proofs.

$$\Gamma \rhd \texttt{abstype } t \texttt{ with } x{:}\sigma \texttt{ is } y \texttt{ in } \langle t = t, x{:}\sigma\rangle = y{:}\exists t.\sigma \qquad (\eta)_\exists$$

The form of abstract data type declaration presented here is a natural generalization of the constructs used in many programming languages. In addition to capturing the "essence" of abstract data type declarations, this formulation allows data type implementations to be passed as function arguments, returned as function values, or manipulated in any other way provided by the language. The side condition "t not free in σ" in ($\exists$ Elim) has been questioned in the literature [Mac86]. For the languages discussed in this section, it is a necessary scoping condition. However, there are languages with more expressive type systems that allow us to drop this restriction, with some loss of abstraction. If we drop this side condition, we obtain "general" or "strong" sums, used in the next section to characterize the Standard ML module system.

Example 9.4.2 We have regarded values of existential type as implementations of abstract data types. However, there are ways to use these values in a way does not seem to fit the traditional pattern of stacks, queues, trees and the like. We illustrate one possibility, from [MP88], in this example. The main idea is to represent streams as "objects" with a hidden state. The exact method we use is only possible in impredicative systems.

Intuitively, streams are infinite lists. In a functional language, it is convenient to think of a stream as a kind of "process" which has a set of possible internal states and a specific value associated with each state. Since the process implements a list, there is a designated initial state and a deterministic state transition function. Therefore, a stream consists of a type s (of states) with a designated individual (*start* state) of type s, a *next*-state function of type $s \to s$, and a *value* function of type $s \to t$, for some t. An integer stream, for example, will have a value function of type $s \to int$, and so the type of integer streams will be $\exists s(s \times (s \to s) \times (s \to int))$.

The Sieve of Eratosthenes can be used to produce an integer stream enumerating all prime numbers. This stream is constructed using a *sift* operation on streams. Given an integer stream s_1, $sift(s_1)$ is a stream of integers which are not divisible by the first value of s_1. If *num* is the stream 2, 3, 4, . . ., then the sequence formed by taking the first value of each stream *num, sift(num), sift(sift(num)), . . .* will be the sequence of all primes.

With streams represented using existential types, *sift* may be written as the following function over existential types.

$sift = \lambda stream{:}\exists s(s \times (s \to s) \times (s \to int)).$

$$
\begin{array}{l}
\texttt{abstype}\ s\ \texttt{with}\ start\colon s, next\colon s \to s, value\colon s \to int\ \texttt{is}\ stream\ \texttt{in} \\
\quad \texttt{let}\ n = value(start)\ \texttt{in} \\
\quad\quad \texttt{letrec}\ f = \lambda state\colon s.\,\texttt{if} n\ divides\ value(state) \texttt{then}\ f(next(state))\ \texttt{in} \\
\quad\quad\quad \texttt{else}\ state\ \texttt{in} \\
\quad\quad \langle s = s, \langle f(start),\ \lambda x\colon s.\ f(next(x)),\ value\rangle \\
\quad\quad :s \times (s \to s) \times (s \to int)\rangle
\end{array}
$$

Sieve will be the stream with states represented by integer streams, start state the stream of all integers greater than 1, and *sift* the successor function on states. The value associated with each *sieve* state is the first value of the integer stream, so that the values of *sieve* enumerate all primes.

$$
\begin{array}{l}
sieve = \langle t = \exists t\,(t \times (t \to t) \times (t \to int)), \\
\quad\quad\quad \langle\, \langle t' = int, \langle 2, \lambda x\colon int.\, x + 1, \lambda x\colon int.\, x\rangle\rangle\colon t' \times (t' \to t') \times (t' \to int)\rangle, \\
\quad\quad\quad\quad sift, \lambda state\colon \exists t\,(t \times (t \to t) \times (t \to int)). \\
\quad\quad\quad\quad\quad \texttt{abstype}\ r\ \texttt{with}\ r\_start, r\_next, r\_val\ \texttt{is}\ state\ \texttt{in}\ r\_val(r\_start) \\
\quad\quad\quad\quad \rangle\colon t \times (t \to t) \times (t \to int)
\end{array}
$$

Expressed in terms of *sieve*, the i-th prime number is

$$
\begin{array}{l}
\text{abstype } s \text{ with } start\colon s,\ next\colon s \to s,\ value\colon s \to int \\
\quad \text{is } sieve \text{ in } value(next^i start),
\end{array}
$$

where $next^i start$ is the expression $next(next(...(nextstart)...))$ with i occurrences of $next$.

This example is impredicative since the representation type $\exists t\,(t \times (t \to t) \times (t \to int))$ used to define *sieve* is also the type of *sieve* itself. For this reason, *sieve* could not have been written in a predicative system. ∎

Exercise 9.4.3 The reason we use the syntactic form $\langle t = \tau,\ M\colon \sigma\rangle$, instead of the simpler form $\langle \tau,\ M\rangle$, is so that the type of an expression is uniquely determined, given types for all of the free variables.

(a) Find distinct type expressions σ and σ' such that $[\tau/t]\sigma$ and $[\tau/t]\sigma'$ are syntactically identical.

(b) Show that if we use the simpler syntactic form, and typing rule

$$
\frac{\Gamma \rhd M\colon [\tau/t]\sigma}{\Gamma \rhd \langle \tau,\ M\rangle\colon \exists t.\sigma}
$$

there is a single type assignment Γ, type τ and expression M such that $\langle \tau,\ M\rangle$ has two different types (neither an α-variant of the other).

(c) Explain why the rule given in the text guarantees that the type of an expression $\langle t = \tau, M\colon \sigma\rangle$ is unique, assuming that for any specific Γ, there is exactly one type for M.

Exercise 9.4.4 Example 9.4.1 gives the form of an expression declaring an abstract data type of complex numbers and gives an implementation

(a) Show that the implementation $\langle t = \mathit{real} \times \mathit{real}, \langle C, P, R, I\rangle\colon \ldots\rangle$ has the correct type for the `abstype` expression in Example 9.4.1.

(b) Write an expression N that creates two complex numbers, adds them, and returns the real value of the sum. Show that under the assumption $\mathit{create}\colon \mathit{real} \times \mathit{real} \to \mathit{cmplx}$, $\mathit{plus}\colon \mathit{cmplx} \times \mathit{cmplx} \to \mathit{cmplx}$, $\mathit{re}\colon \mathit{cmplx} \to \mathit{real}$, $\mathit{im}\colon \mathit{cmplx} \to \mathit{real}$, your expression N has type *real*. You may also use any variables or constants of type *real*, and assume that $+\colon \mathit{real} \times \mathit{real} \to \mathit{real}$.

(c) Use the equational axioms associated with `abstype`, along with β-reduction and other rules, to simplify your expression

`abstype` *cmplx* `with` *create* ... `is` $\langle t = \mathit{real} \times \mathit{real}, \langle C, P, R, I\rangle\colon \ldots\rangle$ `in` N

to the sum of two real numbers.

(d) Write a different implementation of complex numbers and show by reduction that the value of your expression N, from (b), gives the same result as (c) when your alternative implementation is used, assuming that all of the real-number operations work properly.

9.5 General Products, Sums and Program Modules

9.5.1 The ML Module Language

In this section we briefly review the organization of the Standard ML modules system [Mac85, MTH90, MT91, Ull94]. The basic entities of the Standard ML module system are *structures*, *signatures* and *functors*. Roughly speaking, a structure is a collection of type, value and structure declarations. Signatures are a form of "type" or "interface" for a structure, specifying the kind of declarations as structure must contain. If a structure satisfies the description given in a signature, the structure "matches" the signature. While a structure will, in general, match a number of different signatures, our type-theoretic model of the Standard ML module will impose the simplifying assumption that each structure is declared with a specific signature. Functors are functions from structures to structures. Since ML does not support higher-order functors (*i.e.*, functors taking functors as arguments or yielding functors as results), there is no need for functor signatures.

Structures are defined using structure expressions, which consist of a sequence of declarations between keywords `struct` and end. Structures are not "first-class" in that they may only be bound to structure identifiers or passed as arguments to functors. This is really a universe distinction, a consequence of the predicative nature of the type system rather than an *ad hoc* restriction of the language. (We examine the importance of predicativity in Section 9.5.4.) The following declaration defines a structure with one type and one value component.

```
structure S =
  struct
    type t = int
    val x : t = 3
  end
```

This general declaration form binds an identifier to the value of a structure expression. In this example, the structure expression following the equals sign has type component t equal to int and value component x equal to 3. In Standard ML this structure is "timestamped" when the declaration is elaborated, marking it with a unique name that distinguishes it from all other structures, regardless of their internal structure. Structure expressions are therefore said to be "generative" since each elaboration may be thought of as "generating" a new one. The reason for making structure expressions generative is that the module language provides a form of version control based on specifying that two possibly distinct structures or types must be equal. Since semantic equality of structures is undecidable, timestamps are used as a practical (and efficiently decidable) condition for structure equality. Since this is largely a "pragmatic detail," in comparison with the overall scope and intent of the design, we will not be concerned with generativity in this book.

The components of a structure are accessed by qualified names, written in a form used for record access in many languages. For instance, given the structure declaration for S above, the name S.x refers to the x component of S, and hence has value 3. Similarly, S.t refers to the t component of S, and is equivalent to the type int during type checking. This "transparency" of type definitions distinguishes ML structures from abstract data type declarations.

Signatures are a form of "type" or "interface" for structures, and may be bound to signature identifiers using a signature binding, as follows:

```
signature SIG =
  sig
    type t
    val x : t
  end
```

This signature describes the class of structures having a type component, `t`, and a value component, `x`, whose type is the type bound to `t` in the structure. Since the structure `S` introduced above satisfies these conditions, it is said to *match* the signature `SIG`. The structure S also matches the following signature `SIG'`:

```
signature SIG' =
  sig
    type t
    val x : int
  end
```

This signature is matched by any structure providing a type, `t`, and a value, `x`, of type `int`, such as the structure `S`. Note, however, that there are structures which match `SIG`, but not `SIG'`, namely any structure that provides a type other than `int`, and a value of that type. In addition to ambiguities of this form, there is another, more practically-motivated, reason why a given structure may match a variety of distinct signatures.

In ML signatures may be used to provide distinct "views" of a structure. The main idea is that the signature may specify fewer components than are actually provided. For example, we may introduce the signature

```
signature SIG'' =
  sig
    val x : int
  end
```

and subsequently define a view, `T`, of the structure `S` by declaring

```
structure T : SIG'' = S
```

It should be clear that `S` matches the signature `SIG''` since it provides an `x` component of type `int`. The signature `SIG''` in the declaration of `T` causes the `t` component of `S` to be hidden, so that subsequently only the identifier `T.x` is available. To simplify the development, we do not go into the details of signature matching. Instead, we will assume that each structure is given a unique signature describing each component. In the absence of generativity, we can impose a view on structure `S`, as above, by defining the restricted structure `T` from `S`, and giving the restricted signature in the declaration of `T`. For further discussion of signature matching, we refer the reader to [HMT87, Tof88, MTH90].

Functors, which are functions mapping structures to structures, are introduced using a syntax similar to parameterized forms other programming languages. Here is an example:

```
functor F ( S : SIG ) : SIG =
  struct
    type t = S.t * S.t
    val x : t = (S.x,S.x)
  end
```

This declaration defines a functor F that takes as argument a structure matching the signature SIG, and yields as result a structure matching the same signature. (In Standard ML the parameter signature is mandatory, but the result signature may be omitted.) When applied to a suitable structure S, the functor F yields as result the structure whose type component, t, is bound to the product of S.t with itself, and whose value component, x, is the pair both of whose components evaluate to the value of S.x.

By making use of free structure variables in signatures, certain forms of dependency of functor results on functor arguments may be expressed. For example, the following declaration specifies the type of y in the result signature of G in terms of the type component t of the argument S:

```
functor G ( S : SIG ) : sig val y : S.t * S.t end =
struct
val y = (S.x,S.x)
end
```

This formulation of dependent types is consistent with the account given in [Mac86], and is accounted for similarly in our model of ML.

We will not discuss the "sharing" specifications that are part of the ML module system design.

Example 9.5.1 This example gives signatures, structures and a functor for a simple geometry program. The first three signatures below describe points, circles and rectangles, each signature containing a type name and names of associated operations. The fourth signature, Geom, contains all of the geometric types and operations, plus a bounding box function, bbox, intended to map a circle to the smallest rectangle containing it. Three signatures use the SML include statement to include a previous signature. The effect of include is the same as copying the body of the named signature and placing it within the signature expression containing the include statement.

```
signature Point =
  sig
    type point
    val mk_point : real * real -> point
```

```
    val x_coord : point -> real
    val y_coord : point -> real
    val move_p : point * real * real -> point
  end;

signature Circle =
  sig
    include Point
    type circle
    val mk_circle : point * real -> circle
    val center : circle -> point
    val radius : circle -> real
    val move_c : circle * real * real -> circle
  end;

signature Rect =
  sig
    include Point
  type rect
  (* make rectangle from lower right, upper left corners *)
    val mk_rect : point * point -> rect
    val lleft : rect -> point
    val uright : rect -> point
    val move_r : rect * real * real -> rect
  end;

signature Geom =
  sig
    include Circle
(* include Rect, except Point, by hand *)
    type rect
    val mk_rect : point * point -> rect
    val lleft : rect -> point
    val uright : rect -> point
    val move_r : rect * real * real -> rect
(* Bounding box of circle *)
    val bbox : circle -> rect
  end;
```

For `Point`, `Circle` and `Rect`, we give structures explicitly.

```
structure pt : Point =
  struct
    type point = real*real
    fun mk_point(x,y) = (x,y)
    fun x_coord(x,y) = x
    fun y_coord(x,y) = y
    fun move_p((x,y):point,dx,dy) = (x+dx, y+dy)
  end;

structure cr : Circle =
  struct
    open pt
    type circle = point*real
    fun mk_circle(x,y) = (x,y)
    fun center(x,y) = x
    fun radius(x,y) = y
    fun move_c(((x,y),r):circle,dx,dy) = ((x+dx, y+dy),r)
  end;

structure rc : Rect =
  struct
    open pt
    type rect = point * point
    fun mk_rect(x,y) = (x,y)
    fun lleft(x,y) = x
    fun uright (x,y) = y
    fun move_r(((x1,y1),(x2,y2)):rect,dx,dy) =
                    ((x1+dx,y1+dy),(x2+dx,y2+dy))
  end;
```

The geometry structure is constructed using a functor that takes `Circle` and `Rect` structures as arguments. The signatures `Circle` and `Rect` both name a type called `point`. These two must be implemented in the same way, which is stated explicitly in the "sharing" constraint on the formal parameters. Although we will not include sharing constraints in our type-theoretic account of the SML module system, it is generally possible to eliminate uses of sharing (such as the one here) by adding additional parameters to structures, in this case turning circle and rectangle structures into functors that both require a point structure. However, as pointed out in [Mac86], this may be cumbersome for large programs.

```
functor geom(
    structure c:Circle
    structure r:Rect
    sharing type r.point = c.point) : Geom =
  struct
    type point = c.point
    val mk_point = c.mk_point
    val x_coord = c.x_coord
    val y_coord = c.y_coord
    val move_p = c.move_p
    type circle = c.circle
    val mk_circle = c.mk_circle
    val center = c.center
    val radius = c.radius
    val move_c = c.move_c
    type rect = r.rect
    val mk_rect = r.mk_rect
    val lleft = r.lleft
    val uright = r.uright
    val move_r = r.move_r
(* Bounding box of circle *)
    fun bbox(c) =
        let val x = x_coord(center(c))
            and y = y_coord(center(c))
            and r = radius(c)
        in
            mk_rect(mk_point(x-r,y-r),mk_point(x+r,y+r))
        end
end;
```

■

9.5.2 Predicative Calculus with Products and Sums

Syntax

In this section we extend $\lambda^{\rightarrow,\Pi}$ to a function calculus $\lambda^{\rightarrow,\Pi,\Sigma}$ by adding general general sums and products (from Section 9.1.3). While general sums are closely related to structures, and general cartesian products seem necessary to capture dependently-typed functors, the language $\lambda^{\rightarrow,\Pi,\Sigma}$ is somewhat more general than Standard ML. For example, while an ML structure may contain polymorphic functions, there is no direct way to define a polymorphic structure (*i.e.*, a structure that is parametric in a type) in the implicitly-typed programming language. This is simply because there is no provision for explicit binding of type variables. However, polymorphic structures can be "simulated" in ML by using a functor whose parameter is a structure containing only a type binding. In $\lambda^{\rightarrow,\Pi,\Sigma}$, by virtue of the uniformity of the language definition, there will be no restriction on the types of things that can be made polymorphic. For similar reasons, $\lambda^{\rightarrow,\Pi,\Sigma}$ will have expressions corresponding to higher-order functors and functor signatures. Neither of these were included in the original design of the ML module system [Mac85], but both were added after the type-theoretic analysis given here was developed [Mac86, HM93].

Unfortunately, general products and sums complicate the formalization of $\lambda^{\rightarrow,\Pi,\Sigma}$ considerably. Since a structure may appear in a type expression, for example, it is no longer possible to describe the well-formed type expressions in isolation from the elements of those types. This also makes the well-formed contexts difficult to define. Therefore, we cannot use the simplified presentation of $\lambda^{\rightarrow,\Pi}$ given in Section 9.2.2; we must revert to the general presentation of Section 9.2.1 that uses inference rules for determining the well-formed contexts, types and terms. The un-checked pre-terms of $\lambda^{\rightarrow,\Pi,\Sigma}$ are given by the grammar

$$M ::= U_1 \mid U_2 \mid b \mid M \rightarrow M \mid \Pi x\colon M.M \mid \Sigma x\colon M.M$$

$$\mid x \mid c \mid \lambda x\colon M.M \mid MM$$

$$\mid \langle x\colon M{=}M,\ M\colon M\rangle \mid \mathit{first}(M) \mid \mathit{second}(M)$$

Intuitively, the first row of this grammar gives the form of type expressions, the second row expressions from $\lambda^{\rightarrow,\Pi}$ and the third row the expression forms associated with general sums. However, these three classes of expressions are interdependent; the precise definition of each class is given by the axioms and inference rules below. We will use M, N, P and σ and τ for pre-terms, using σ and τ when the term is intended to be a type. As in our presentation of existential types, we use a syntactic form $\langle x\colon\sigma{=}M, N\colon\sigma'\rangle$, with the variable x bound in σ'. In addition, x is bound in the second component N, so that the "dependent pair" $\langle x\colon\sigma{=}M, N\colon\sigma'\rangle$ is equal to $\langle x\colon\sigma{=}M, [M/x]N\colon\sigma'\rangle$, assuming x is not free in N. Unlike existential types, general sums have unrestricted first and second projection functions that allow us to access either component of a pair directly. In this respect, pairs of general sum type are closer to the ordinary pairs associated with cartesian product types.

Although it is meaningful to extend $\lambda^{\to,\Pi}$ with a polymorphic `let` declaration, `let` is definable in $\lambda^{\to,\Pi,\Sigma}$ using abstraction over polymorphic types in U_2. (See Exercise 9.5.6.)

The typing rules for $\lambda^{\to,\Pi,\Sigma}$ are an extension of the rules for $\lambda^{\to,\Pi}$ given in Section 9.2.1. In addition to general sums, $\lambda^{\to,\Pi,\Sigma}$ allows lambda abstraction over U_2 types, resulting in expressions with Π-types. The associated syntax is characterized by the following three rules, the first giving the form of Π-types in $\lambda^{\to,\Pi,\Sigma}$, and the second and third the associated term forms.

$$\frac{\Gamma \rhd \sigma : U_2 \quad \Gamma, x\!:\!\sigma \rhd \sigma' : U_2}{\Gamma \rhd \Pi x\!:\!\sigma.\sigma' : U_2} \qquad (\Pi\ U_2)$$

$$\frac{\Gamma \rhd \sigma : U_2 \quad \Gamma, x\!:\!\sigma \rhd \sigma' : U_2 \quad \Gamma, x\!:\!\sigma \rhd M : \sigma'}{\Gamma \rhd \lambda x\!:\!\sigma.M : \Pi x\!:\!\sigma.\sigma'} \qquad (\Pi\ \text{Intro})$$

$$\frac{\Gamma \rhd M : \Pi x\!:\!\sigma.\sigma' \quad \Gamma \rhd N : \sigma}{\Gamma \rhd M[N] : [N/x]\sigma'} \qquad (\Pi\ \text{Elim})$$

It is an easy exercise (Exercise 9.5.3) to show that the weaker (Π U_2) rule, in Section 9.2.1, is subsumed by the one given here.

The four rules below give the conditions for forming Σ-types and the associated term forms.

$$\frac{\Gamma \rhd \sigma : U_2 \quad \Gamma, x\!:\!\sigma \rhd \sigma' : U_2}{\Gamma \rhd \Sigma x\!:\!\sigma.\sigma' : U_2} \qquad (\Sigma\ U_2)$$

$$\frac{\Gamma \rhd M : \sigma \quad \Gamma \rhd [M/x]N : [M/x]\sigma' \quad \Gamma, x\!:\!\sigma \rhd \sigma' : U_2}{\Gamma \rhd \langle x\!:\!\sigma{=}M, N\!:\!\sigma'\rangle : \Sigma x\!:\!\sigma.\sigma'} \qquad (\Sigma\ \text{Intro})$$

$$\frac{\Gamma \rhd M : \Sigma x\!:\!\sigma.\sigma'}{\Gamma \rhd \mathit{first}(M) : \sigma} \qquad (\Sigma\ \text{Elim 1})$$

$$\frac{\Gamma \rhd M : \Sigma x\!:\!\sigma.\sigma'}{\Gamma \rhd \mathit{second}(M) : [\mathit{first}(M)/x]\sigma'} \qquad (\Sigma\ \text{Elim 2})$$

These rules require the equational theory below. A simple typing example that does not require equational reasoning is the derivation of

$$x\!:(\Sigma t\!:U_1.t),\;\; y\!:\mathit{first}\,x \to \mathit{first}\,x,\;\; z\!:\mathit{first}\,x \rhd yz\!:\mathit{first}\,x$$

With a "structure" variable $x : \Sigma t\colon U_1.t$ in the context, $\mathit{first}\,x$ is a U_1 type expression and so we may form the U_1 type $\mathit{first}\,x \to \mathit{first}\,x$. The rest of the typing derivation is routine. The following example shows how equational reasoning may be needed in typing derivations. The general form of type equality rule is the same as in Section 9.2.1. However, the rules for deriving equations between types give us a much richer form of equality than the simple syntactic equality (with renaming of bound variables) used in $\lambda^{\to}$ and $\lambda^{\to,\Pi}$.

Example 9.5.2 We can see how equational reasoning is used in type derivations by introducing a "type-transparent" form of `let` declaration,

$$\mathtt{let}_{\Sigma}\ x\colon\sigma = M\ \mathtt{in}\ N \quad \stackrel{\text{def}}{=} \quad \mathit{second}\langle x\colon\sigma{=}M,\, N\rangle$$

The main idea is that in a "dependent pair" $\langle x\colon\sigma{=}M, N\rangle$, occurrences of x in N are bound to M. Moreover, this is incorporated into the (Σ Intro) rule so that N is typed with each occurrence of x replaced by M.

The typing properties of this declaration form are illustrated by the expression

$$\mathtt{let}_{\Sigma}\ x\colon(\Sigma t\colon U_1.t) = \langle t\colon U_1{=}\mathit{int},\, 3\colon t\rangle\ \mathtt{in}\ (\lambda z\colon \mathit{int}.\, z)(\mathit{second}\,x)$$

$$\equiv \quad \mathit{second}\langle\, x\colon(\Sigma t\colon U_1.t){=}\langle t\colon U_1{=}\mathit{int},\, 3\colon t\rangle,\ (\lambda z\colon \mathit{int}.\, z)(\mathit{second}\,x)\,\rangle$$

It is relatively easy to show that the expression, $\langle t\colon U_1{=}\mathit{int}, 3\colon t\rangle$, bound to x has type $\Sigma t\colon U_1.t$, since we assume $\mathit{int}\colon U_1$ and $3\colon \mathit{int}$ are given. The next step is to show that the larger pair

$$\langle\, x\colon(\Sigma t\colon U_1.t){=}\langle t\colon U_1{=}\mathit{int},\, 3\colon t\rangle,\ (\lambda z\colon \mathit{int}.\, z)(\mathit{second}\,x)\,\rangle$$

has type $\Sigma x\colon(\Sigma t\colon U_1.t).\mathit{int}$. Pattern matching against the (Σ Intro) rule, we can see that it suffices to show

$$[M/x](\lambda z\colon \mathit{int}.\, z)(\mathit{second}\,x) : [M/x]\mathit{int} \equiv \mathit{int},$$

where $M \equiv \langle t\colon U_1{=}\mathit{int}, 3\colon t\rangle$. By ($\Sigma$ Elim 2), the type of $\mathit{second}\,M$ is

$$\mathit{second}\langle t\colon U_1{=}\mathit{int},\, 3\colon t\rangle : \mathit{first}\langle t\colon U_1{=}\mathit{int},\, 3\colon t\rangle$$

Using the equational axiom (Σ *first*) below, we may simplify $\mathit{first}\langle t\colon U_1{=}\mathit{int}, 3\colon t\rangle$ to int. This equational step is critical since there is no other way to conclude that the type of $\mathit{second}\,M$ is int. ∎

Equations and Reduction

The equational proof system for $\lambda^{\to,\Pi,\Sigma}$ contains the axioms and rules for $\lambda^{\to,\Pi}$ (with each axiom or rule scheme interpreted as applying to all $\lambda^{\to,\Pi,\Sigma}$ terms), described in Section 9.2.3, plus the rules listed below.

The equational axioms for pairing and projection are similar to the ones for cartesian products in earlier chapters, except for the way the first component is substituted into the second in the (Σ *second*) rule.

$$\Gamma \triangleright \mathit{first}\langle x\colon\sigma{=}M,\ N\colon\sigma'\rangle = M : \sigma \qquad (\Sigma\ \mathit{first})$$

$$\Gamma \triangleright \mathit{second}\langle x\colon\sigma{=}M,\ N\colon\sigma'\rangle = [M/x]N : [M/x]\sigma' \qquad (\Sigma\ \mathit{second})$$

$$\Gamma \triangleright \langle x\colon\sigma{=}\mathit{first}\,M,\ \mathit{second}\,M\colon\sigma'\rangle = M : \Sigma x\colon\sigma.\sigma' \qquad (\Sigma\ \mathit{sp})$$

Note that since σ or σ' may be U_1, axioms (Σ *first*) and (Σ *second*) may yield equations between types. Since type equality is no longer simply syntactic equality, we need the congruence rules for type equality below. Since all types are elements of U_2, we may use the general reflexivity axiom and symmetry and transitivity rules mentioned in Section 9.2.3 for equations between types (see Exercise 9.5.4).

$$\frac{\Gamma \triangleright \tau_1 = \tau_1' : U_1 \quad \Gamma \triangleright \tau_2 = \tau_2' : U_1}{\Gamma \triangleright \tau_1 \to \tau_2 = \tau_1' \to \tau_2' : U_1} \qquad (\to \text{Cong})$$

$$\frac{\Gamma \triangleright \sigma_1 = \sigma_1' : U_2 \quad \Gamma, x\colon\sigma_1 \triangleright \sigma_2 = \sigma_2' : U_2}{\Gamma \triangleright \Pi x\colon\sigma_1.\sigma_2 = \Pi x\colon\sigma_1'.\sigma_2' : U_2} \qquad (\Pi \text{ Cong})$$

$$\frac{\Gamma \triangleright \sigma_1 = \sigma_1' : U_2 \quad \Gamma, x\colon\sigma_1 \triangleright \sigma_2 = \sigma_2' : U_2}{\Gamma \triangleright \Sigma x\colon\sigma_1.\sigma_2 = \Sigma x\colon\sigma_1'.\sigma_2' : U_2} \qquad (\Sigma \text{ Cong})$$

The congruence rules for terms are essentially routine, except that when a term form includes types, we must account for type equations explicitly. To avoid confusion, we list the rules for terms of Π and Σ type here.

$$\frac{\Gamma, x\colon\sigma \triangleright M = M' : \sigma' \quad \Gamma \triangleright \sigma = \sigma'' : U_i}{\Gamma \triangleright \lambda x\colon\sigma.M = \lambda x\colon\sigma''.M' : \Pi x\colon\sigma.\sigma'}$$

$$\frac{\Gamma \triangleright M = M' : \Pi x\colon\sigma.\sigma' \quad \Gamma \triangleright N = N' : \sigma}{\Gamma \triangleright M[N] = M'[N'] : [N/x]\sigma'}$$

$$\frac{\begin{array}{c}\Gamma \triangleright M = M' : \sigma \quad \Gamma \triangleright [M/x]N = [M'/x]N' : [M/x]\sigma' \\ \Gamma \triangleright \sigma = \sigma'' : U_i \quad \Gamma \triangleright [M/x]\sigma' = [M/x]\sigma''' : U_i\end{array}}{\Gamma \triangleright \langle x\colon\sigma{=}M,\ N\colon\sigma'\rangle = \langle x\colon\sigma''{=}M',\ N'\colon\sigma'''\rangle : \Sigma x\colon\sigma.\sigma'}$$

$$\frac{\Gamma \triangleright M = M' : \Sigma x\colon\sigma.\sigma'}{\Gamma \triangleright \mathit{first}(M) = \mathit{first}(M') : \sigma}$$

$$\frac{\Gamma \rhd M = M' : \Sigma x\colon \sigma.\sigma'}{\Gamma \rhd \mathit{second}(M) = \mathit{second}(M') : [\mathit{first}(M)/x]\sigma'}$$

Since $\lambda^{\rightarrow,\Pi,\Sigma}$ contexts are more complicated than in the simplified presentation of $\lambda^{\rightarrow,\Pi}$, the (*add var*) rule should be written

$$\frac{\Gamma \rhd M = N : \sigma \quad \Gamma, x\colon A \text{ context}}{\Gamma, x\colon A \rhd M = N : \sigma} \qquad (\mathit{add\ var})$$

so that only well-formed contexts are used.

If we direct the equational axioms from left to right, we obtain a reduction system of the form familiar from other systems of lambda calculus. Strong normalization for $\lambda^{\rightarrow,\Pi,\Sigma}$ may be proved using a translation into Martin-Löf's 1973 system [Mar73]. It follows that the equational theory of $\lambda^{\rightarrow,\Pi,\Sigma}$ is decidable. It is an interesting open problem to develop a theory of logical relations for full $\lambda^{\rightarrow,\Pi,\Sigma}$, a task that is complicated by the presence of general Σ and Π types.

Exercise 9.5.3 Show that the ($\Pi\ U_2$) rule in Section 9.2.1 is subsumed by the ($\Pi\ U_2$) rule given in this section, in combination with the other rules of $\lambda^{\rightarrow,\Pi,\Sigma}$.

Exercise 9.5.4 A general reflexivity axiom that applies to types as well as terms that have a U_1 or U_2 type is

$$\Gamma \rhd M = M\colon \sigma \qquad (\mathit{refl})$$

assuming that σ may be any well-formed expression of U_2. Write general symmetry and transitivity rules in the same style and write out a proof of the equation

$$s\colon U_1, t\colon U_1 \rhd \mathit{second}\langle r\colon U_1 = s, t\colon U_1\rangle \rightarrow t = t \rightarrow t\colon U_1$$

between U_1 type expressions.

Exercise 9.5.5 Show that if $\Gamma \rhd M\colon \Sigma x\colon \sigma.\sigma'$ is derivable, then the expression $\langle x\colon \sigma = \mathit{first}\,M, \mathit{second}\,M\colon \sigma'\rangle$ used in the (Σ *sp*) axiom has type $\Sigma x\colon \sigma.\sigma'$.

Exercise 9.5.6 Show that if we consider `let` $x\colon \sigma = M$ `in` N as syntactic sugar for $(\lambda x\colon \sigma.\ N)M$, in $\lambda^{\rightarrow,\Pi,\Sigma}$, then typing rule for `let` in Section 9.2.5 is derivable.

Exercise 9.5.7 In some of the congruence rules, it may not be evident that the terms proved equal have the same syntactic type. A representative case is the type congruence rule for lambda abstraction, which assumes that if $\Gamma, x\colon \sigma \rhd M\colon \sigma'$ and $\Gamma \rhd \sigma = \sigma''\colon U_2$ are derivable, then so is $\Gamma \rhd \lambda x\colon \sigma''.\ M\colon \Pi x\colon \sigma.\sigma'$. Prove this by showing that for any M, if $\Gamma \rhd \sigma = \sigma''\colon U_2$ and $\Gamma, x\colon \sigma \rhd M\colon \sigma'$ are derivable, then so is $\Gamma, x\colon \sigma'' \rhd M\colon \sigma'$.

9.5.3 Representing Modules with Products and Sums

General sums allow us to write expressions for structures and signatures, provided we regard environments as tuples whose components are accessed by projection functions. For example, the structure

```
struct type t=int val x:t=3 end
```

may be viewed as the pair $\langle t\colon U_1{=}int,\, 3\colon t\rangle$. In $\lambda^{\to,\Pi,\Sigma}$, the components `t` and `x` are retrieved by projection functions, so that `S.x` is regarded as an abbreviation for $second(S)$. With general sums we can represent the signature

```
sig type t val x:t end
```

as the type $\Sigma t\colon U_1.t$, which has the pair $\langle t\colon U_1{=}int,\, 3\colon int\rangle$ as a member. The representation of structures by unlabeled tuples is adequate in the sense that it is a simple syntactic translation to replace qualified names by expressions involving projection functions. A limitation that may interest ML experts is that this way of viewing structures does not provide any natural interpretation of ML's `open`, which imports declarations from the given structure into the current scope.

Since general products allow us to type functions from any collection to any other collection, we can write functors as elements of product types. For example, the functor `F` from Section 9.5.1 is defined by the expression

$$\lambda S\colon (\Sigma t\colon U_1 t).\langle s\colon U_1{=}first(S) \times first(S),\, \langle second(S),\, second(S)\rangle : s\rangle,$$

which has type

$$\Pi S\colon (\Sigma t\colon U_1.t).\,(\Sigma s\colon U_1.s).$$

An important aspect of Standard ML is that signature and functor declarations may only occur at "top level," which means they cannot be embedded in other constructs, and structures may only be declared inside other structures. Furthermore, recursive declarations are not allowed. Consequently, it is possible to treat signature, structure, and functor declarations by simple macro expansion. An alternative, illustrated in Example 9.5.8 below, is to treat declarations (in $\lambda^{\to,\Pi,\Sigma}$) using the type-transparent $\mathtt{let}_\Sigma$ bindings of Example 9.5.2, which are based on general sums.

The first step in translating a ML program into $\lambda^{\to,\Pi,\Sigma}$ is to replace all occurrences of signature, structure and functor identifiers with the corresponding $\lambda^{\to,\Pi,\Sigma}$ expressions. Then, type expressions may be simplified using the type equality rule of Section 9.2.1, as required. With the exception of "generativity,", which we do not consider, this process models elaboration during the ML type checking phase fairly accurately.

Example 9.5.8 We illustrate the general connection between Standard ML and $\lambda^{\rightarrow,\Pi,\Sigma}$ using the example program

```
structure S =
   struct
      type t = int
      val x : t = 7
   end;
S.x + 3
```

The $\lambda^{\rightarrow,\Pi,\Sigma}$ expression for the structure bound to S is

$$S \stackrel{\text{def}}{=} \langle t{:}\, U_1{=}int, 7{:}\, t\rangle \;:\; \Sigma t{:}\, U_1.t$$

If we treat SML structure declarations by macro expansion, then this program is equivalent to

$$second\, S + 3 \;\equiv\; second\langle t{:}\, U_1{=}int, 7{:}\, t\rangle + 3$$

We may type this program by observing that the type of $second\, S$ is $first(\langle int, 7\rangle)$, which may be simplified to int.

Since structures in Standard ML are transparent, in the sense that the components of a structure are fully visible, structure declarations may be represented in $\lambda^{\rightarrow,\Pi,\Sigma}$ using transparent $\mathtt{let}_\Sigma$ bindings of Example 9.5.2. In this view, the program above is treated as the $\lambda^{\rightarrow,\Pi,\Sigma}$ term

$$\mathtt{let}_\Sigma\;\; S{:}\Sigma t{:}U_1.t = \langle t{:}\, U_1{=}int, 7{:}\, t\rangle \;\;\mathtt{in}\;\; second\, S + 3$$

which has a syntactic structure closer to the original program. As explained in Example 9.5.2, the typing rules for general sums allow us to use the fact that $first(S)$ is equivalent to int.

As mentioned earlier in passing, the $\lambda^{\rightarrow,\Pi,\Sigma}$ calculus is more general than Standard ML in two apparent respects. The first is that since there is no need to require that subexpressions of $\lambda^{\rightarrow,\Pi,\Sigma}$ types be closed, we are able to write explicitly-typed functors with nontrivial dependent types in $\lambda^{\rightarrow,\Pi,\Sigma}$. The second is that due to the uniformity of the language, we have a form of higher-order functors.

9.5.4 Predicativity and the Relationship between Universes

Although each of the constructs of $\lambda^{\rightarrow,\Pi,\Sigma}$ corresponds to a particular part of Standard ML, the lambda calculus allows arbitrary combinations of these constructs, and straightforward extensions like higher-order functor expressions. While generalizing in certain ways that seem syntactically and semantically natural, $\lambda^{\rightarrow,\Pi,\Sigma}$ maintains the ML distinction between monomorphic and polymorphic types by keeping U_1 and U_2 distinct. The restrictions imposed by universes are essential to the completeness of type inference (discussed in Chapter 11) and have the technical advantage of leading to far simpler semantic model constructions, for example. However, it may seem reasonable to generalize ML polymorphism by lifting the universe restrictions (to obtain an impredicative calculus), or alter the design decisions $U_1 \subseteq U_2$ and $U_1 \colon U_2$.

Exercises 9.2.5 and 9.2.11 show that the decision to take $U_1 \subseteq U_2$ is only a syntactic convenience, with no semantic consequence. In this section we show that the decision to take $U_1 : U_2$ is essentially forced by the other constructs of $\lambda^{\rightarrow,\Pi,\Sigma}$, and that in the presence of structures and functors, the universe restrictions are essential if we wish to avoid a type of all types.

Strong Sums and U_1:U_2

In $\lambda^{\rightarrow,\Pi}$, we have $U_1 \subseteq U_2$, but not $U_1 \colon U_2$. However, when we added general product and sum types, we also made the assumption that $U_1 \colon U_2$. The reasons for this are similar to the reasons for taking $U_1 \subseteq U_2$: it makes the syntax more flexible, simplifies the technical presentation, and does not involve any unnecessary semantic assumptions. A precise statement is spelled out in the following proposition.

Proposition 9.5.9 In any fragment of $\lambda^{\rightarrow,\Pi,\Sigma}$ which is closed under the term formation rules for types of the form $\Sigma t \colon U_1.\tau$, with $\tau \colon U_1$, there are contexts

$i[\,] \equiv \langle [\,], * \rangle$ and $j[\,] \equiv \mathit{fst}[\,]$,

where *unit* may be any U_1 type with closed term $* \colon \mathit{unit}$, satisfying the following conditions.

1. If $\Gamma \rhd \tau : U_1$, then $\Gamma \rhd i[\tau] : (\Sigma t \colon U_1.\mathit{unit})$.
2. If $\Gamma \rhd M : (\Sigma t \colon U_1.\mathit{unit})$, then $\Gamma \rhd j[M] : U_1$.
3. $\Gamma \rhd j[i[\tau]] = \tau : U_1$ for all $\Gamma \rhd \tau : U_1$.

In other words, given the hypotheses above, since $(\Sigma t \colon U_1.\mathit{unit}) \colon U_2$, we may assume $U_1 \colon U_2$ without loss of generality.

In words, the proposition says that in any fragment of $\lambda^{\rightarrow,\Pi,\Sigma}$ with sums over U_1 (and some U_1 type *unit* containing a closed term $*$), we can represent U_1 by the type $\Sigma t \colon U_1.\mathit{unit}$. Therefore, even if we drop $U_1 \colon U_2$ from the language definition, we are left with a representation of U_1 inside U_2. For this reason, we might as well simplify matters and take $U_1 \colon U_2$.

Impredicativity and "*type:type*"

In the calculus $\lambda^{\rightarrow,\Pi,\Sigma}$, as in the programming language SML, polymorphic functions are not actually applicable to arguments of all types. For example, the identity function, written $id(x) = x$ in ML and $\lambda t.\, \lambda x{:}\, t.\, x$ in $\lambda^{\rightarrow,\Pi,\Sigma}$, has polymorphic type, but it can only be applied to elements of types from the first universe. One way to eliminate this restriction is to eliminate the distinction between U_1 and U_2. If we replace U_1 and U_2 by a single universe in the definition of $\lambda^{\rightarrow,\Pi}$, then we obtain the impredicative polymorphic calculus. However, if we make the *full* $\lambda^{\rightarrow,\Pi,\Sigma}$ calculus impredicative by eliminating the distinction between U_1 and U_2, we obtain a language with a type of all types. Specifically, since we have general products and $U_1{:}\, U_2$, it is quite easy to see that if we let $U_1 = U_2$, then the *type*: *type* calculus of Section 9.2.2 becomes a sublanguage of $\lambda^{\rightarrow,\Pi,\Sigma}$.

Lemma 9.5.10 Any fragment of $\lambda^{\rightarrow,\Pi,\Sigma}$ with $U_1{:}\, U_2$, $U_1 = U_2$, and closed under the type and term formation rules associated with general products is capable of expressing all terms of the *type*: *type* calculus of Section 9.2.2.

The proof is a straightforward examination of the typing rules of the *type*: *type* calculus of Section 9.2.2.

By Lemma 9.5.9, we know that sums over U_1 give us $U_1{:}\, U_2$. This proves the following theorem.

Theorem 9.5.11 The *type*: *type* calculus of Section 9.2.2 may be interpreted in any fragment of $\lambda^{\rightarrow,\Pi,\Sigma}$ without universe distinctions which is closed under general products, and sums over U_1 of the form $\Sigma t{:}\, U_1.\tau$.

Intuitively, this says that any language without universe distinctions that has general products (ML functors) and general sums restricted to U_1 (ML structures with type and value but not necessarily structure components) also contains the language with a type of all types. Since there are a number of questionable properties of a type of all types, such as nontermination without explicit recursion and undecidable type checking, relaxing the universe restrictions of $\lambda^{\rightarrow,\Pi,\Sigma}$ would alter the language dramatically.

Trade-off between Weak and Strong Sums

Theorem 9.5.11 may be regarded as a "trade-off theorem" in programming language design, when combined with known properties of impredicative polymorphism. The trade-off implied by Theorem 9.5.11 is between impredicative polymorphism and the kind of Σ types used to represent ML structures in $\lambda^{\rightarrow,\Pi,\Sigma}$. Generally speaking, impredicative polymorphism is more flexible than predicative polymorphism, and Σ types allow us to type more terms than the existential types associated with data abstraction.

Either impredicative polymorphism with the "weaker" existential types, or restricted predicative polymorphism with "stronger" general sum types of $\lambda^{\rightarrow,\Pi,\Sigma}$ seems reasonable. By the normalization theorem for the impredicative calculus, we know that impredicative polymorphism with existential types is strongly normalizing (normalization with existential types can be derived by encoding $\exists t.\sigma$ as $\forall r[\forall t(\sigma \rightarrow r) \rightarrow r]$). As noted in Section 9.5.2, a translation into Martin-Löf's 1973 system [Mar73] shows that $\lambda^{\rightarrow,\Pi,\Sigma}$ with predicative polymorphism and "strong" sums is also strongly normalizing. However, by Theorem 9.5.11, we know that if we combine strong sums with impredicative polymorphism by taking $U_1 = U_2$, the most natural way of achieving this end, then we must admit a type of all types, causing strong normalization to fail. In short, assuming we wish to avoid *type*: *type* and non-normalizing recursion-free terms, we have a trade-off between impredicative polymorphism and strong sums.

In formulating $\lambda^{\rightarrow,\Pi,\Sigma}$, it is apparent that there are actually several ways to combine impredicative polymorphism with strong sums. An alternative is that instead of adding impredicative polymorphism by equating the two universes, we may add a form of impredicative polymorphism by adding a new type binding operator with the formation rule

$$\frac{\Gamma, t\colon U_1 \rhd \tau : U_1}{\Gamma \rhd \forall t\colon U_1.\tau : U_1}$$

Intuitively, this rule says that if τ is a U_1 type, then we will also have the polymorphic type $\forall t\colon U_1.\tau$ in U_1. The term formation rules for this sort of polymorphic type would allow us to apply any polymorphic function of type $\forall t\colon U_1.\tau$ to any type in U_1, including a polymorphic type of the form $\forall s\colon U_1.\sigma$. However, we would still have strong sums like $\Sigma t\colon U_1.\tau$ in U_2 instead of U_1. The normalization theorem for this calculus follows from that of the theory of constructions with strong sums at the level of types [Coq86] by considering U_1 to be *prop*, and U_2 to be $type_0$.

10 Subtyping and Related Concepts

10.1 Introduction

This chapter is concerned with subtyping and language concepts that make subtyping useful in programming. In brief, subtyping is a relation on types which implies that values of one type are substitutable for values of another. Some language constructs associated with subtyping are records, objects, and various forms of polymorphism that depend on the subtype relation. The main topics of the chapter are:

- Simply-typed lambda calculus with records and subtyping.
- Equational theories and semantic models.
- Subtyping for recursive types and the recursive-record model of objects.
- Forms of polymorphism appropriate for languages with subtyping.

While the main interest in subtyping stems from the popularity and usefulness of object-oriented programming, many of the basic ideas are illustrated more easily using the simpler example of record structures. Many of the issues discussed in this chapter are topics of current research; some material may be subsumed in coming years. A general reference with research papers representing the current state of the art is [GM94]; other collections representing more pragmatic issues are [SW87, YT87]. An early research/survey paper that proposed a number of influential typing ideas is [CW85].

Subtyping appears in a variety of programming languages. An early form of subtyping appears in the Fortran treatment of "mixed mode" arithmetic: arithmetic expressions may be written using combinations of integer and real (floating point) expressions, with integers converted to real numbers as needed. The conversion of integers to reals has some of the properties that are typical of subtyping. In particular, we generally think of the mathematical integers as a subset of the real numbers. However, conversion in programs involves changing the representation of a number, which is not typical of subtyping with records or objects. Fortran mixed mode arithmetic also goes beyond basic subtyping in two ways. The first is that Fortran provides implicit conversion from reals to integers by truncation, which is different since this operation changes the value of the number that is represented. Fortran also provides overloaded operations, such as $+\colon int \times int \rightarrow int$ and $+\colon real \times real \rightarrow real$. However, if we overlook these two extensions of subtyping, we have a simple example of integers as a subtype of reals that provides some intuition for the general properties of subtyping. Although the evaluation of expressions that involve overloading and truncation is sometimes subtle, the Fortran treatment of arithmetic expressions was generally successful and has been adopted in many later languages.

Another example of subtyping appears in Pascal subranges or the closely related range constraints of Ada (see [Hor84], for example). As discussed again below, the Pascal subrange [1..10] containing the integers between 1 and 10 is subtype of the integers. If x is a variable of type [1..10], and y of type integer, then we can assign y the value of x since every integer between 1 and 10 is an integer.

More powerful examples of subtyping appear in typed object-oriented languages such as Eiffel [Mey92b] and C++ [ES90]. In these languages, a class of objects, which may be regarded for the moment as a form of type, is placed in a subtype hierarchy. An object of a subtype may be used in place of one of any supertype, since the subtype relation guarantees that all required operations are implemented. Moreover, although the representation of objects of one type may differ from the representation of objects of a subtype, the representations are generally compatible in a way that eliminates the need for conversion from one to another.

We may gain some perspective on subtyping by comparing subtyping with type equality in programming languages. In most typed programming languages, some form of type equality is used in type checking. A basic principle of type equality is that when two types are equal, every expression with one type also has the other. With subtyping, we replace this principle with the so-called "subsumption" property of subtyping:

If A is a subtype of B then every expression with type A also has type B.

This is not quite the *definition* of subtyping since it depends on what we mean by having a type, which in turn may be depend on subtyping. However, this is a useful condition for recognizing subtyping when you see it. The main idea is that subtyping is a substitution property: if A is a subtype of B, then we may substitute A's for B's. In principle, if we may meaningfully substitute A's for B's, then it would make sense to consider A a subtype of B.

A simple illustrative example may be given using record types. Consider two record types R and S, where records of type R have an integer a component and boolean b component, and records of type S have only an integer a component. In the type system of Section 10.3, R will be a subtype of S. One way to see why this makes sense is to think about the legal operations on records of each type. Since every $r\colon R$ has a and b components, expressions $r.a$ and $r.b$ are allowed. However, since records of type S have only a components, the only basic operation on a record s of type S is to select the a component by writing $s.a$. Comparing these two types, we can see that every operation that is guaranteed to make sense on elements of type S is also guaranteed to make sense on elements of R. Therefore, in any expression involving a record of type S, we could safely use a record of type R instead, without type error.

We will use the notation $A <: B$ to indicate that A is a subtype of B, since this provides a rough ASCII approximation of the subset symbol "$\subseteq$", and lets us keep $\subseteq$ for the subset relation on sets. There are two general views on the meaning of an assertion $A <: B$. One is that every representation of a value of type A also represents a value of type B. For example, if the subrange type $[1..10]$ is a subtype of *int*, as in Pascal, then we can read this as meaning that every sequence of bits representing an element of $[1..10]$ also is a valid representation of an integer. Another reading of $A <: B$ is that every representation of a value of type A can be converted to a representation of a value of type B in some "standard" or "canonical" way. Looking at $[1..10] <: int$ again, we may read this as saying that we have a way of transforming any representation of an integer between 1 and 10 into a representation of the form used for arbitrary integers. A compiler might actually take advantage of the flexibility provided by the conversion interpretation of subtyping. For example, we might use just one byte for elements of small subranges of integers, and prepend a few bytes to obtain an integer representation. The conversion view of subtyping is more general, but also raises problems. One problem is that there could be many ways to convert subexpressions of an expression so that the whole expression has some type. To be *coherent,* the value of an expression must be independent of the way in which these conversions are done. Another issue is the computational cost of converting values from one representation to another. Pragmatically, the cost of converting among representations must be balanced against the ability to optimize operations for each representation. We generally convert integers to floating-point numbers, since the cost of conversion is relatively small and separate hardware implementations of the standard numeric operations make manipulation of both representations very efficient. We would lose much of the power of a contemporary computer if we tried to use a third "neutral" representation for both integers and real numbers. On the other hand, most implementations of object-oriented languages do not convert arbitrary objects from a subtype to a supertype representation, since this could be expensive and there is no compensating gain in the efficiency of basic operations on objects.

We adopt the general view that a language and its subtyping properties are defined by a set of rules. Any formal semantics or implementation must respect these rules and, in particular, must give provably equal expressions equal values. This allows either a containment interpretation of subtyping, or a conversion view. In developing an understanding of any language, it is both useful to find an interpretation that allows us to think of subtyping as containment, and useful to see whether there is a reasonable interpretation allowing conversion when needed. In principle, both forms of interpretations may be insightful and either form could be useful in practical implementation.

In some research papers and programming language discussions, there is a confusion between subtyping and "inheritance." Although there is no clear, universally accepted definition of inheritance, it is useful to discuss the basic concept and distinguish it from subtyping. In simple terms, subtyping is a relationship between types, while inheritance is a relationship between implementations. In many languages with inheritance, if we ignore type-checking, then inheritance can be viewed as an inessential programming convenience. At least in principle, a definition that uses inheritance could be replaced by an essentially equivalent one that does not use inheritance. (This might make the program much longer, or harder to maintain, but in principle it is generally possible.) Therefore, we would expect that type A could be a subtype of B, regardless of whether inheritance is used to define elements of A from elements of B. However, many programming languages, including Eiffel and C++, only treat A as a subtype of B when objects of type A are defined by inheriting from B. The reason that this is pragmatically convenient is that the form of inheritance that is provided in these languages guarantees a similarity between representation of objects, in a way that makes substitutivity possible without conversion of representations. On the other hand, many object-oriented enthusiasts do not believe that subtyping and inheritance should be linked in this way (*e.g.*, [Sny86]).

10.2 Simply Typed Lambda Calculus with Subtyping

In this section, we extend $\lambda^{\rightarrow}$ with subtyping, resulting in a calculus $\lambda^{\rightarrow}_{<:}$. While most aspects of $\lambda^{\rightarrow}_{<:}$ are routine, we will use this calculus to discuss some essential features of subtyping. Cartesian products, sums, *unit* and *null* may be added to $\lambda^{\rightarrow}_{<:}$ without complication.

Subtyping begins with a set of subtyping assumptions about basic types of the language. Formally, this is incorporated into the definition of signature for the calculus. A $\lambda^{\rightarrow}_{<:}$ *signature* is a triple $\Sigma = \langle B, Sub, C \rangle$ with B a set of type constants, Sub a set of subtyping assertions $b <: b'$ between type constants $b, b' \in B$, and C a set of term constants, each with a specified type written using $\rightarrow$ and type constants from B.

There is a basic, implicit assumption in the form of every $\lambda^{\rightarrow}_{<:}$ signature, namely, all of our basic subtype assumptions are between atomic type names. There will be no provision, in this system, for subtyping between types that have different "functionality." More specifically, as we shall see in Lemma 10.2.1 below, if $\sigma <: \tau$, then the type expressions σ and τ will contain the same number and parenthesization of $\rightarrow$'s. In particular, we will never have $b <: b_1 \rightarrow b_2$, for type constants b, b_1 and b_2. (See Exercise 10.2.7.)

Types

The type expressions of $\lambda^{\rightarrow}_{<:}$ are the same as for $\lambda^{\rightarrow}$:

$\tau \ ::= \ b \mid \tau \to \tau$

The distinguishing feature of $\lambda^{\to}_{<:}$ is the subtype relation, defined by the following axiom and inference rules.

$$\tau <: \tau \qquad (ref\ <:)$$

$$\frac{\rho <: \sigma, \ \sigma <: \tau}{\rho <: \tau} \qquad (trans\ <:)$$

This axiom and rule, which will be part of every system of subtyping we consider, make the subtype relation a preorder. (The definition of *preorder* is that a preorder is a reflexive and transitive relation.)

In each system, we will typically have at least one axiom or inference rule for each type form, identifying the subtyping properties of that type form. For $\lambda^{\to}_{<:}$, we have the following rule for function types:

$$\frac{\rho <: \tau, \ \tau' <: \rho'}{\tau \to \tau' <: \rho \to \rho'} \qquad (\to <:)$$

If we think of subtyping as an ordering, this rule "says" that $\to$ is monotonic in its second argument, but antimonotonic in its first. A simple illustration of this rule is the following arrangement of consequences of $int <: real$:

$$\begin{array}{ccc} & int \to real & \\ int \to int & & real \to real \\ & real \to int & \end{array}$$

For example, if f is a function of one real argument, and integers are a subtype of reals, then f should be applicable to any integer value. The order pictured here has the simple form of a lattice (partial order with least upper bounds and greatest lower bounds; see Exercise 10.2.6.) However, we do not generally have a lattice structure.

We write $\Sigma \vdash \sigma <: \tau$ if the subtype assertion $\sigma <: \tau$ is provable from assertions in *Sub* using the axiom and inference rules given above. It is easy to show that if $\Sigma \vdash \sigma <: \tau$, then the type expressions σ and τ must contain the same number and parenthesization of $\to$'s. To state this precisely, we let the *matching* relation on types be the least relation satisfying the following conditions:

$$b \ \text{ matches } b' \quad \text{for any type constants } b, b'$$

$$\sigma_1 \to \sigma_2 \ \text{ matches } \tau_1 \to \tau_2 \quad \text{whenever } \sigma_i \text{ matches } \tau_i \ \ (i = 1, 2)$$

Lemma 10.2.1 For any $\lambda^{\to}_{<:}$ signature Σ, if $\Sigma \vdash \sigma <: \tau$ then σ matches τ.

The proof and some intuition for the consequences of this lemma are given as Exercise 10.2.7.

Before proceeding with the syntax of terms, we pause to give some thought to the semantic interpretation of subtyping in $\lambda^{\rightarrow}_{<:}$. As mentioned earlier in this chapter, subtyping may be interpreted as either conversion or containment. The conversion interpretation of subtyping, considered in Exercise 10.2.5 and developed more fully in Section 10.4.2, is useful in understanding why subtyping is generally a preorder instead of a partial order. The distinction between pre- and partial orders is that in a preorder, is possible to have $\rho <: \tau$ and $\tau <: \rho$ for distinct $\rho \neq \tau$. If subtyping means that values of one type are convertible to the other, then $\rho <: \tau$ and $\tau <: \rho$ mean that values of these types are interconvertible. However, the natural interpretation of type equality is that values of equal type have the same representation. Clearly, interconvertible sets of values need not have identical representations. In general, this might occur if types A and B are two different representations of the same concept, such as cartesian and polar representations of complex numbers. A compiler could automatically insert conversions from one type to another if required, but would generate incorrect code if the distinction between A and B were eliminated by considering these types equal. An example of this phenomenon appears in the language Modula-3 [CDG$^+$88, CDJ$^+$89, Nel91], where packed and unpacked data are subtypes of each other, but not equal types. Data of the two types are represented differently, with automatic conversion inserted by the compiler. In addition, the compiler must distinguish the two types since composite data structures (such as arrays) of packed data are allocated differently from corresponding structures of unpacked data.

At first glance, a subset interpretation of function types may not seem very intuitive. For example, assuming *nat* <: *real*, we would not expect any function *real* → *nat* to belong to the set of all function from *nat* to *nat*. The reason is that a function *real* → *nat* has a larger domain of definition (the set of all real numbers) than any function from *nat* to *nat*. However, we can think of *real* → *nat* as a subset of *nat* → *nat* if we interpret *nat* → *nat* as the collection of all functions whose domain is *at least* the set of all natural numbers and, for any natural number in their domain, produce a natural number result. The problem with making this intuitive view rigorous is that the "set of all functions whose domain is at least *nat*" is a proper class, in set theory. In less formal terms, this collection is "too big" to be a set; its definition cannot be written in a way that guarantees that this set exists (see Section 1.6). However, this foundational problem can be circumvented by using a "universal domain," or any set containing all the semantic values of all types. (Some examples would be a domain $D \cong D \rightarrow D$ constructed as in Section 7.4 or a partial combinatory algebra, as considered in Section 5.6.2.) Intuitively, the reason we can expect there to be a set containing all the semantic values of interest is that we only need to consider computable values.

Suppose we have a set *Value* containing all the semantic values we need, and some application function **App**: $Value \times Value \rightharpoonup Value$ which, when $f \in Value$ represents a function and $x \in Value$ is an element of the domain of f, gives us the result $\mathbf{App}\ f\ x \in Value$ of applying f to x. (We consider **App** a partial function since we do not need $\mathbf{App}\ f\ x$ to be defined if f does not represent a function or x is not in the domain of f.) Then a natural interpretation of $A \to B$, when A and B are subsets $A, B \subseteq Value$, is the set

$$A \to B = \{f \in Value \mid \forall x \in Value.\ if\ x \in A\ then\ \mathbf{App}\ f\ x \in B\}.$$

With this interpretation of function types, sometimes called the *simple semantics,* it is easy to see that ($\to$ <:) is sound.

Terms

Terms have the same typing rules as in $\lambda^{\to}$, except for the addition of the subsumption rule:

$$\frac{\Gamma \rhd M\colon \sigma,\ \ \Sigma \vdash \sigma <: \tau}{\Gamma \rhd M\colon \tau} \qquad (subsumption)$$

In summary, the typing rules of $\lambda^{\to}_{<:}$, are (*var*),($\to$ Intro), ($\to$ Elim), (*add var*) and (*subsumption*).

Example 10.2.2 Assume the signature has *int* <: *real*, 2: *int*, 2.0: *real* and *div*: $real \to real \to real$. Let M be the term $\lambda x\colon real.(div\ x\ 2.0) : real \to real$. There are two ways to type the application of M to 2: *int*. The first is to use the fact that $real \to real <: int \to real$ to derive $M : int \to real$, since this makes the application $M2$ type-correct. The alternative is to note that since *int* <: *real*, we also have 2: *real*, and so $M2$ is the type-correct application of a real function to a real argument. If we interpret subtyping as conversion, then the conversion of real functions to integer functions should be compatible with the conversion of integers to reals so that we obtain the same answer in both cases. We will see how to achieve this in Exercise 10.2.5 and Section 10.4.2. ■

Equational Rules

The equational proof system consists of exactly the same axioms and proof rules as in $\lambda^{\to}$ without subtyping. Specifically, we have (*ref*), (*sym*) and (*trans*) making provable equality an equivalence relation, the technical rule (*add var*) for adding variables to the type assignment, axioms (α), (β) and (η) for lambda abstraction and application, and (ξ) and (ν) making provable equality a congruence relation. As usual, we consider an equation $\Gamma \rhd M = N\colon \sigma$ well-formed only when both $\Gamma \rhd M\colon \sigma$ and $\Gamma \rhd N\colon \sigma$ are derivable.

There is a common typing confusion associated with the extensionality axiom, (η), that illustrates the importance of writing types as part of equations. (This confusion actually stumped a number of researchers when typed calculi with subtyping were beginning to be studied in the mid-1980's.) The extensionality axiom has the form

$$\Gamma \rhd \lambda x\colon \tau.(Mx) = M, \quad x \text{ not free in } M$$

but it is not clear that the two terms involved necessarily have the same type. For example, suppose M has the form $\lambda y\colon \tau'.N$ with $\tau <: \tau'$. Then M has type $\tau' \to \rho$ but $\lambda x\colon \tau.(Mx)$ does not. Thus, in writing $\lambda x\colon \tau.(Mx) = M$, it could appear that we are equating terms with different types. However, since $\tau' \to \rho <: \tau \to \rho$, both have type $\tau \to \rho$. Our axiom scheme

$$\Gamma \rhd \lambda x\colon \tau.(Mx) = M\colon \tau \to \rho, \quad x \text{ not free in } M,$$

applies whenever $\Gamma \rhd \lambda x\colon \tau.(Mx)\colon \tau \to \rho$ and $\Gamma \rhd M\colon \tau \to \rho$ are both derivable, which will be the case whenever $\Gamma \rhd M\colon \tau \to \rho$ is derivable. Some possibly unexpected interaction between (β) and (η) is described in Example 10.2.4.

Before considering some example derivations, we give some thought to the semantic interpretation of equality. In $\lambda^{\to}$ without subtyping, we write equations in the form $\Gamma \rhd M = N\colon \tau$ simply to indicate the common typing of both terms and to avoid writing ill-typed inference rules. Since the $\lambda^{\to}$ type τ is uniquely determined from Γ and M or N, the type does not have much to do with *how* M and N might be equal. With subtyping, however, terms M and N may have many different types (under the same assumptions about free variables) and so it is *a priori* possible for them to be equal at one type but different at another. A slightly contrived example may be given using the "floor" function $\lfloor \cdot \rfloor$, with $\lfloor x \rfloor$ the greatest integer less than the real number x. (This example is contrived since it does not occur in the pure calculus. However, it is representative of examples that can be defined in more expressive languages we consider later in the chapter.) We have

$$\lambda x\colon real.\, \lfloor x \rfloor \;\neq\; \lambda x\colon real.\, x \;:\; real \to real.$$

since the floor function may change the value of a real argument. However, when considered at type $int \to real$, these two functions are equal, *i.e.*,

$$\lambda x\colon real.\, \lfloor x \rfloor \;=\; \lambda x\colon real.\, x \;:\; int \to real$$

since neither function changes the value of any integral argument. An important property here is that $(real \to real) <: (int \to real)$. In general, if $A <: B$, it is possible for expressions to have distinct values at type A but be equal at type B.

When equality changes with the type of a value, a pure containment interpretation cannot adequately capture typed equality. The reason is simply that two elements x and y

of a set A are equal as elements of A iff they are equal as elements of any superset $B \supseteq A$. However, there are containment-like interpretations that allow equality to vary with type, but do not require conversion of the "computational representation" of any data. Such interpretations, based on partial equivalence relations, are considered in Section 10.4.4. In the remaining sections before 10.4.4, we continue to compare containment and conversion interpretations informally for the useful intuition that this provides.

Example 10.2.3 A general principle about subtyping and equations is given by the inference rule

$$\frac{\Gamma \triangleright M = N\colon \tau,\ \ \Sigma \vdash \tau <: \rho}{\Gamma \triangleright M = N\colon \rho} \qquad (\textit{subsumption eq})$$

which we do *not* need to add to the proof system since it is derivable from reflexivity, application and (β). More specifically, if $\tau <: \rho$, then we have the typing

$$\Gamma \triangleright \lambda x\colon \tau.\, x\colon \tau \to \rho$$

and so by reflexivity, the equation

$$\Gamma \triangleright \lambda x\colon \tau.\, x = \lambda x\colon \tau.\, x\colon \tau \to \rho.$$

If $\Gamma \triangleright M = N\colon \tau$, then by applying the identity to each side, we may prove

$$\Gamma \triangleright (\lambda x\colon \tau.\, x)M = (\lambda x\colon \tau.\, x)N\colon \rho$$

which gives us the conclusion of (*subsumption eq*) by (β) and transitivity. ■

Example 10.2.4 For any $\lambda^{\to}_{<:}$ term $\Gamma \triangleright \lambda x\colon \sigma.\, M\colon \sigma \to \tau$, with $\rho <: \sigma$, we can prove the equation

$$\Gamma \triangleright \lambda x\colon \sigma.\, M = \lambda x\colon \rho.\, M\colon \rho \to \tau$$

One way to develop some intuition for this equation is to suppose that we give the lambda abstraction $\Gamma \triangleright \lambda x\colon \sigma.\, M\colon \sigma \to \tau$ type $\rho \to \tau$ by subsumption. If we then apply this function to an argument $\Gamma \triangleright N\colon \rho$ and β-reduce the resulting term,

$$(\lambda x\colon \sigma.\, M)N \to [N/x]M,$$

we will substitute a term of type ρ for the bound variable of type σ. This suggests that if we change the type of $\lambda x\colon \sigma.\, M$ by subsumption, then we have a term that is "functionally equivalent" to the term $\lambda x\colon \rho.\, M$ with the formal parameter x given type ρ instead of σ. In other words, subsumption effectively changes the types of lambda-bound variables.

We can prove the equation above by applying $\lambda x\colon \sigma.\, M$ to a free variable $x\colon \rho$ and then lambda-abstracting x. We begin with the typing derivation

$$\Gamma \triangleright \lambda x\colon \sigma .\, M\colon \sigma \to \tau \text{ by assumption}$$

$$\Gamma, x\colon \rho \triangleright \lambda x\colon \sigma .\, M\colon \sigma \to \tau \text{ by}(\textit{add var})$$

$$\Gamma, x\colon \rho \triangleright x\colon \sigma \text{ by } (\textit{var}), (\textit{subsumption}), (\textit{add var})$$

$$\Gamma, x\colon \rho \triangleright (\lambda x\colon \sigma .\, M)x\colon \tau \text{ by application}$$

$$\Gamma \triangleright \lambda x\colon \rho .(\lambda x\colon \sigma .\, M)x\colon \rho \to \tau \text{ by } (\to \text{ Intro})$$

At this point, we apply a "trick," using (β) to show

$$\Gamma \triangleright \lambda x\colon \rho .(\lambda x\colon \sigma .\, M)x = \lambda x\colon \rho .\, M\colon \rho \to \tau$$

and (η) to show

$$\Gamma \triangleright \lambda x\colon \rho .(\lambda x\colon \sigma .\, M)x = \lambda x\colon \sigma .\, M\colon \rho \to \tau$$

giving us the desired equation by transitivity. Since both of these terms would be in normal form when M is a normal form, the last few steps also show that confluence fails for β, η-reduction on $\lambda^{\to}_{<:}$ terms. ■

The failure of confluence described in Example 10.2.4 can be repaired by adding the reduction rule

$$\Gamma \triangleright \lambda x\colon \tau .\, M \to \lambda x\colon \sigma .\, M : \sigma \to \rho \quad \text{provided } \Sigma \vdash \sigma <: \tau \qquad (\textit{type label})$$

as shown in [Hoa95].

Exercise 10.2.5 Example 10.2.2 gives two ways to type an application $M2$. The first uses $real \to real <: int \to real$ to give $M\colon real \to real$ type $int \to real$ while the other uses $int <: real$ to give $2\colon int$ type $real$. Suppose that c_{int}^{real} is the conversion function from integers to reals and, given $c_{\sigma'}^{\sigma}$ and $c_{\tau}^{\tau'}$, we define a conversion function from $\sigma \to \tau$ to $\sigma' \to \tau'$ by

$$c_{\sigma\to\tau}^{\sigma'\to\tau'} \stackrel{\text{def}}{=} \lambda f\colon \sigma \to \tau .\, \lambda x\colon \sigma' .\, c_{\tau}^{\tau'}\ (f\ (c_{\sigma'}^{\sigma}\ x))$$

For any type σ, the conversion function c_{σ}^{σ} is just the identity function. Show that

$$(c_{real\to real}^{int\to real}\ M)\, 2 \quad = \quad M\ (c_{int}^{real}\ 2)$$

Exercise 10.2.6 Let $\Sigma = \langle B, Sub, C\rangle$ be a $\lambda^{\to}_{<:}$ signature. Suppose that the subtyping ordering Sub on B is a lattice. This means that any subset $B' \subseteq B$ has a least upper bound $b \in B$ and similarly a greatest lower bound. Is this induced subtype ordering on function types of the form $a \to b$, with $a, b \in B$, necessarily a lattice? Prove or give a counter example.

Exercise 10.2.7 This exercise considers the limitation on $\lambda^{\to}_{<:}$ that subtyping is allowed only between *matching* types.

(a) Prove Lemma 10.2.1 by induction on the length of the proof of $\sigma <: \tau$ from Σ.

(b) Suppose that, instead of limiting our basic subtyping assumptions to relations between type constants, we allow subtyping between arbitrary, non-matching types. Show that there is a signature Σ, type constant b and finite set of subtyping assumptions such that for every pre-term M, we can prove a typing assertion of the form $x_1{:}\, b, \ldots, x_k{:}\, b \rhd M{:}\, b$. (*Hint:* see Exercise 2.6.7.)

Exercise 10.2.8 For any $\lambda^{\to}_{<:}$ signature Σ, type assignment Γ and typable term M, show that there is a "minimum" type τ such that, for all τ', the typing judgement $\Gamma \rhd M{:}\, \tau'$ is derivable iff $\tau <: \tau'$.

Exercise 10.2.9 Prove that if $\Gamma \rhd M{:}\, \tau$ and $M \twoheadrightarrow N$, then $\Gamma \rhd N{:}\, \tau$. Give an example showing that the minimum type of N with respect to Γ (see Exercise 10.2.8) may be a proper subtype of the minimum type of M.

10.3 Records

10.3.1 General Properties of Record Subtyping

Records are a general form of "labeled product" found in Pascal, C (where records are called `struct`'s), ML and other programming languages. In Section 2.5.1, records are treated as syntactic sugar for cartesian products. However, since records have richer subtyping properties than cartesian products, the translation of records to products does not preserve subtyping. Therefore, in this chapter, we will treat records as a basic rather than a derived form. We will not consider so-called "variant records," as in Pascal, since these may be defined using record and union types.

The type of records with components $\ell_1, \ldots, \ell_n$ of types $\tau_1, \ldots, \tau_n$, respectively, is given by the type expression

$$\langle \ell_1{:}\, \tau_1, \ldots, \ell_n{:}\, \tau_n \rangle.$$

For example, the employee records in a simple database might have type

$$employee \stackrel{\text{def}}{=} \langle name{:}\, string, manager{:}\, string, salary{:}\, int \rangle$$

If we want to keep track of the department associated with each manager, we could define a type of manager records by

$$manager \stackrel{\text{def}}{=} \langle name\colon string, manager\colon string, salary\colon int,\ dept\colon department\rangle$$

where *department,* in a more detailed type system, might be an enumerated type of department names or department numbers. As we will see from the subtyping rules below, *manager* is a subtype of *employee*.

The main principle in determining whether one record type is a subtype of another is that all operations must remain sensible and well-defined. In $\lambda^{\rightarrow}$, for example, the type system is defined so that an application MN will be well-typed only if M has a function type $\sigma \rightarrow \tau$ and N is in the domain of the function, *i.e.*, $N\colon\sigma$. With subtyping, this essential agreement between function types and arguments is preserved. For records, the basic operation we must preserve is component selection. The type system must be designed so that if $M.\ell$ is well-typed, M must have a record type that lists component ℓ. (Although records are assignable data structures in many programming languages, it is important to remember that they are not in our function calculus.)

The intuitive reason why *manager* is a subtype of *employee* is that any expression involving an employee record r could contain selections $r.name$, $r.manager$ and $r.salary$. Since each of these would also make sense if r were a manager record, we may safely substitute manager records for employee records, without type error. The opposite would not make sense. If $r\colon manager$, then we could write $r.dept$, but $r.dept$ would not always make sense if we replaced r by an arbitrary employee record.

In general, record subtyping involves both adding components and restricting one or more components to subtypes. Continuing the database example, if we change the type of *manager* salary from *int* to a subtype *large_int*, we may still substitute a manager record for any employee record, since selecting the salary from a manager record will give a *large_int* value that is substitutable for the *int* value that is expected from the *employee* type.

10.3.2 Typed Calculus with Records and Subtyping

Types

A signature for the lambda calculus $\lambda_{<:}^{\rightarrow,\mathtt{record}}$ with records and subtyping is the same as a signature for $\lambda_{<:}^{\rightarrow}$. The type expressions of $\lambda_{<:}^{\rightarrow,\mathtt{record}}$ are type constants, function types and record types.

$$\tau \ ::= \ b \mid \tau \rightarrow \tau \mid \langle \ell_1\colon\tau, \ldots, \ell_n\colon\tau\rangle$$

The ordering of *label*: *type* pairs in a record type is not considered significant. In other words, we consider two record types that differ only in the order of *label*: *type* pairs identical. Since this is a relatively simple idea, we will not take the effort to formalize type equality. Instead, when we write a type expression that contains one or more record types, we implicitly consider this equal to any other type expression that differs only in the order of one or more record-type subexpressions. For example,

$$\langle a\colon int,\ b\colon bool,\ c\colon string\rangle \to \langle a\colon int,\ b\colon bool,\ c\colon string\rangle$$

$$= \quad \langle b\colon bool,\ c\colon string,\ a\colon int\rangle \to \langle c\colon string,\ a\colon int,\ b\colon bool\rangle$$

The subtyping relation is defined by a set of axioms and inference rules that includes (*ref* <:), (*trans* <:) and ($\to$ <:) from $\lambda^{\to}_{<:}$. The only addition is the following axiom for record types:

$$\frac{\tau_1 <: \rho_1, \ldots, \tau_n <: \rho_n}{\langle \ell_1\colon \tau_1, \ldots, \ell_n\colon \tau_n, \ell_{n+1}\colon \sigma_1, \ldots, \ell_{n+m}\colon \sigma_m\rangle <: \langle \ell_1\colon \rho_1, \ldots, \ell_n\colon \rho_n\rangle} \qquad (record\ <:)$$

In words, this rule says that a record subtype is obtained by adding components (labeled $\ell_{n+1}, \ldots, \ell_{n+m}$ in the rule above) or restricting the type ρ_i of a component ℓ_i to a subtype $\tau_1 <: \rho_1$.

As for $\lambda^{\to}_{<:}$, we write $\Sigma \vdash \sigma <: \tau$ if the subtype assertion $\sigma <: \tau$ is provable from the signature using the axiom and inference rules given above. If we extend the definition of matching to record types, by

$$\langle \ell_1\colon \sigma_1, \ldots, \ell_k\colon \sigma_k\rangle \text{ matches } \langle m_1\colon \tau_1, \ldots, m_n\colon \tau_n\rangle \quad \text{if } \sigma_i \text{ matches } \tau_j \text{ whenever } \ell_i = m_j$$

then we can show that subtyping arises only between matching types.

Lemma 10.3.1 For any $\lambda^{\to,\mathtt{record}}_{<:}$ signature Σ, if $\Sigma \vdash \sigma <: \tau$ then σ matches τ.

The proof is the same as the proof of Lemma 10.2.1, with one additional induction step for record types. This is left to the reader as Exercise 10.3.3.

A conversion interpretation of record subtyping is suggested in Exercise 10.3.4. We can also give a containment interpretation of record subtyping by treating a record as a partial function and record type as a set of partial functions satisfying some constraint. This is developed further in Section 10.4.4. The main idea is to consider partial functions as sets of ordered pairs. We begin with a set *Label* of all component labels, and a set *Value* of all possible record component values. Using *Label* and *Value,* we regard a record as a partial function from *Label* to *Value* that has a finite domain. In other words, a record is a finite set of ordered pairs of the form $\langle \ell, v\rangle$, with $\ell \in Label$ and $v \in Value$, such that no label appears in two ordered pairs. For example, the record expression $\langle a = 3, b = true\rangle$ defines the set

$\{\langle a, 3\rangle, \langle b, true\rangle\}$ containing two ordered pairs. In this view, a record type $\langle a\colon int, b\colon bool\rangle$ is the collection of all records which have *at least* one ordered pair $\langle a, x\rangle$ with $x\colon int$, and one ordered pair $\langle b, y\rangle$ with $y\colon bool$. Another way to say this is that $\langle a\colon int, b\colon bool\rangle$ is the set of all partial functions whose domain includes *at least* $\{a, b\}$ such that the function value on a is an integer and on b is a boolean. It is easy to see that a record of type $\langle a\colon int, b\colon bool, c\colon char\rangle$ must map a to an integer and b to a boolean. Therefore, the record type $\langle a\colon int, b\colon bool, c\colon char\rangle$ gives us a subset of the larger collection $\langle a\colon int, b\colon bool\rangle$ of partial functions.

Terms

The preterms of $\lambda_{<:}^{\rightarrow,\texttt{record}}$ are given by the grammar

$$M \ ::= \ c \mid x \mid MM \mid \lambda x\colon \tau.\, M \mid \langle \ell_1 = M, \ldots, \ell_n = M\rangle \mid M.\ell$$

These are the same as $\lambda^{\rightarrow}$ and $\lambda_{<:}^{\rightarrow}$, with the addition of the two record forms, $\langle \ell_1 = M, \ldots, \ell_n = M\rangle$ defining a record and $M.\ell$ selecting a component of a record.

The typing rules for $\lambda_{<:}^{\rightarrow,\texttt{record}}$ are the same as for $\lambda^{\rightarrow}$ and $\lambda_{<:}^{\rightarrow}$, with the addition of the following two rules for record expressions:

$$\frac{\Gamma \rhd M_1\colon \tau_1, \ldots, \Gamma \rhd M_n\colon \tau_n}{\Gamma \rhd \langle \ell_1 = M_1, \ldots, \ell_n = M_n\rangle\colon \langle \ell_1\colon \tau_1, \ldots, \ell_n\colon \tau_n\rangle} \qquad (\textit{Record Intro})$$

$$\frac{\Gamma \rhd M\colon \langle \ell_1\colon \tau_1, \ldots, \ell_n\colon \tau_n\rangle}{\Gamma \rhd M.\ell_i\colon \tau_i} \qquad (\textit{Record Elim})$$

Example 10.3.2 Assume $int <: real$, $2\colon int$, $2.0\colon real$ and $div\colon real \rightarrow real \rightarrow real$, as in Example 10.2.2. Let M be the term $\lambda x\colon \langle \ell_1\colon real\rangle.(div\, x.\ell_1\, 2.0) : \langle \ell_1\colon real\rangle \rightarrow real$ and let R be the record $\langle \ell_1 = 2, \ell_2 = true\rangle$ of type $\langle \ell_1\colon int, \ell_2\colon bool\rangle$. As in Example 10.2.2, there are two ways to type the application MR. The first is to use the fact that

$$\langle \ell_1\colon real\rangle \rightarrow real \quad <: \quad \langle \ell_1\colon int, \ell_2\colon bool\rangle \rightarrow real$$

to derive $M : \langle \ell_1\colon int, \ell_2\colon bool\rangle \rightarrow real$. The alternative is to use $\langle \ell_1\colon int, \ell_2\colon bool\rangle <: \langle \ell_1\colon real\rangle$ directly to deduce that $R\colon \langle \ell_1\colon real\rangle$.

Equational Rules

The equational axioms for records are similar to the equational axioms for pairs. The first pairing axiom, $\mathbf{Proj}_i\langle M_1, M_2\rangle = M_i$, says that the i-th projection function produces the i-th component of a pair (for $i = 1, 2$). The analogous axiom

$$\Gamma \rhd \langle \ell_1 = M_1, \ldots, \ell_n = M_n\rangle.\ell_i = M_i\colon \tau_i \qquad (\textit{record selection})$$

for records gives us component selection.

The second axiom is analogous to the surjective pairing axiom for pairs, which is $\langle \mathbf{Proj}_1 P,\ \mathbf{Proj}_2 P\rangle = P$. For records, the "extensionality" axiom is

$$\Gamma \rhd \langle \ell_1 = M.\ell_1, \ldots, \ell_n = M.\ell_n\rangle = M\colon \langle \ell_1\colon \tau_1, \ldots, \ell_n\colon \tau_n\rangle. \qquad (\textit{record ext})$$

This can be used to prove that any two records which agree on all the components that are listed in their common type are equal at that type.

The (*record ext*) axiom is more powerful than might first appear. Since the numbering $\ell_1, \ldots, \ell_n$ of labels is arbitrary, we obtain the reordering axiom,

$$\Gamma \rhd \langle \ell_1 = M_1, \ldots, \ell_n = M_n\rangle = \langle \ell_{\pi(1)} = M_{\pi(1)}, \ldots, \ell_{\pi(n)} = M_{\pi(n)}\rangle\colon \langle \ell_1\colon \tau_1, \ldots, \ell_n\colon \tau_n\rangle$$

for any permutation π of $\{1, \ldots, n\}$ as a consequence. This may be clearer when illustrated by example. Consider the record

$$M \stackrel{\text{def}}{=} \langle a = 3,\ b = \mathit{true},\ c = \text{“Hello”}\rangle \ :\ \langle a\colon \mathit{int},\ b\colon \mathit{bool},\ c\colon \mathit{string}\rangle$$

Our assumption about type equality means that we can also write the type of this record as $\langle b\colon \mathit{bool},\ a\colon \mathit{int},\ c\colon \mathit{string}\rangle$, for example. The (*record ext*) axiom gives us the equation

$$\langle b = M.b, a = M.a, c = M.c\rangle \ =\ M \ :\ \langle b\colon \mathit{bool},\ a\colon \mathit{int},\ c\colon \mathit{string}\rangle$$

Simplifying $M.b$, $M.a$ and $M.c$, this gives us

$$\begin{aligned}\langle b = \mathit{true}, a = 3, c = \text{“Hello”}\rangle = {} & \langle a = 3,\ b = \mathit{true},\ c = \text{“Hello”}\rangle \\ : {} & \langle b\colon \mathit{bool},\ a\colon \mathit{int},\ c\colon \mathit{string}\rangle\end{aligned}$$

In addition, (*record ext*) gives us some interesting type-dependent equations. Consider another record

$$N \stackrel{\text{def}}{=} \langle a = 3,\ b = \mathit{true},\ c = \text{“Goodbye”}\rangle$$

with the same type as M above. These are not equal as records of type $\langle a\colon \mathit{int},\ b\colon \mathit{bool},\ c\colon \mathit{string}\rangle$, since $M.c \neq N.c$. However, we can prove

$$M = \langle a = 3,\ b = \mathit{true}\rangle : \langle a\colon \mathit{int},\ b\colon \mathit{bool}\rangle$$

and similarly for N using (*record ext*). Therefore, the two records are provably equal at type $\langle a\colon \mathit{int},\ b\colon \mathit{bool}\rangle$. This makes sense since if all we know is that both records have a and b components, we cannot expect to tell M and N apart.

Exercise 10.3.3 Prove the induction step of Lemma 10.3.1 for record types.

Exercise 10.3.4 We can extend the "conversion function interpretation" of Exercise 10.2.5 to record types by defining the conversion function from $\langle \ell_1\colon \tau_1, \ldots, \ell_n\colon \tau_n, \ell_{n+1}\colon \sigma_1, \ldots, \ell_{n+m}\colon \sigma_m\rangle$ to $\langle \ell_1\colon \rho_1, \ldots, \ell_n\colon \rho_n\rangle$, by

$$c^{\langle \ell_1:\rho_1,\ldots,\ell_n:\rho_n \rangle}_{\langle \ell_1:\tau_1,\ldots,\ell_n:\tau_n,\ell_{n+1}:\sigma_1,\ldots,\ell_{n+m}:\sigma_m \rangle} \stackrel{\text{def}}{=} \lambda r\colon \langle \ell_1\colon \tau_1, \ldots, \ell_n\colon \tau_n, \ell_{n+1}\colon \sigma_1, \ldots, \ell_{n+m}\colon \sigma_m \rangle.$$
$$\langle \ell_1 = (c^{\rho_1}_{\tau_1}\ r.\ell_1), \ldots, \ell_n = (c^{\rho_n}_{\tau_n}\ r.\ell_n) \rangle$$

Show that under this interpretation, the two typings of MR in Example 10.3.2 yield equal values.

Exercise 10.3.5 For any Γ and M, show that there is a "minimum" type τ such that, for all τ', the typing judgement $\Gamma \rhd M\colon \tau'$ is derivable iff $\tau <: \tau'$. This is the extension of Exercise 10.2.8 to records.

Exercise 10.3.6 Prove that if $\Gamma \rhd M\colon \tau$ and $M \twoheadrightarrow N$, then $\Gamma \rhd N\colon \tau$.

10.4 Semantic Models of Subtyping

10.4.1 Overview

The most general semantic setting for $\lambda^{\rightarrow}_{<:}$ or any similar language with subtyping consists of a set for each type together with a "conversion" function from A to B whenever $A <: B$. This form of conversion semantics allows subset interpretations as a special case, since we can convert from A to B using the identity function whenever A is a subset of B. The advantage of subset interpretations is that these often seem simpler and they provide more useful intuition since the "conversions" are "no-ops." In particular, a subset interpretation eliminates problems related to coherence and may provide a basis for implementing the language without performing expensive or inconvenient data conversions. Unfortunately, a pure subset interpretation cannot correctly account for typed equality, as described below.

In Section 10.4.2, we examine a simple conversion interpretation, presented in the form of a syntactic translation that replaces subsumption by conversion functions. In the process, we discuss coherence and the way that subtyping enters into the meaning of terms. In Section 10.4.3, we consider the consequences of interpreting subtypes as subset. A "compromise" interpretation based on partial equivalence relations (per's) is developed in Section 10.4.4. In per interpretations, it is possible to model typed equality accurately without introducing coherence problems or requiring conversions between the computational representations of data.

10.4.2 Conversion Interpretation of Subtyping

There are several parts to a conversion interpretation of a language with subtyping. We will use $\lambda^{\rightarrow}_{<:}$ as an illustrative example, with the extension to $\lambda^{\rightarrow,\mathtt{record}}_{<:}$ based on Exercise 10.3.4 left to the reader. An extension to polymorphism appears in [BTCGS91]. Any conversion interpretation must include a conversion function from σ to τ whenever $\sigma <: \tau$

is provable from the signature. If $b_1 <: b_2$ is given directly by the signature, then there is no obvious way to derive the conversion function from b_1 to b_2 from scratch, so this conversion function must be given as part of the interpretation. However, if $\sigma <: \tau$ is provable from the signature using some proof rule, then we can hope to define the corresponding conversion function from the "basic" conversion functions assured by the signature.

Once we have a conversion function for every provable subtyping, we can proceed to give meaning to typed terms. The natural way to define the meaning of a typed term, as usual, is by induction on the typing derivation of the term. With subtyping, we interpret uses of (*subsumption*) as applications of our conversion functions. More specifically, if $\Gamma \triangleright M\colon \tau$ is derived by

$$\frac{\Gamma \triangleright M\colon \sigma \quad \Sigma \vdash \sigma <: \tau}{\Gamma \triangleright M\colon \tau} \qquad (subsumption)$$

then the meaning of the term will be the result of applying the σ-to-τ conversion function to the meaning associated with the typing derivation for $\Gamma \triangleright M\colon \sigma$.

The conversion functions we need for $\lambda^{\rightarrow}_{<:}$ are identity functions, basic conversions, and conversions defined by function composition. Since all of these operations are lambda-definable, given basic conversion functions, we can view our conversion interpretation of $\lambda^{\rightarrow}_{<:}$ as a syntactic translation from $\lambda^{\rightarrow}_{<:}$ to $\lambda^{\rightarrow}$. An advantage of treating the conversion interpretation in this way is that it allows us to use any semantic model of $\lambda^{\rightarrow}$ as a model of $\lambda^{\rightarrow}_{<:}$, provided we can find appropriate interpretations for the basic conversion functions. Coherence requires certain equations between compositions of basic conversion functions, but these can generally be satisfied in any Henkin model for $\lambda^{\rightarrow}$ (or a cartesian closed category). As a result, we may derive equational soundness and completeness theorems for $\lambda^{\rightarrow}_{<:}$ from the corresponding theorems for $\lambda^{\rightarrow}$. This is considered at the end of the section.

Beginning with a $\lambda^{\rightarrow}_{<:}$ signature $\Sigma = \langle B, Sub, C\rangle$, we will translate each $\lambda^{\rightarrow}_{<:}$-term over Σ to a $\lambda^{\rightarrow}$ term over a signature $\langle B, C_{Sub}\rangle$ with the same type constants, no subtype relation, but additional term constants for any necessary type conversions. To be precise, we let C_{Sub} be the union of C and a collection of distinct constant symbols which we will write in the form $c_{b_1}^{b_2}$, with one symbol $c_{b_1}^{b_2}\colon b_1 \rightarrow b_2$ for each subtyping $b_1 <: b_2$ between type constants given by the original signature Σ. For example, if

$$\Sigma = \langle \{int, real\}, \{int <: real\}, \{0\colon int\}\rangle$$

then $C_{Sub} = \{0\colon int,\ c_{int}^{real}\colon int \rightarrow real\}$

As suggested above, the translation from $\lambda^{\rightarrow}_{<:}$ to $\lambda^{\rightarrow}$ will be a translation from typing derivations to typing derivations. In other words, the way we translate a term will depend on its typing derivation, not just the term itself. For example, consider the two ways of typing the application $M\,2$ in Example 10.2.2. If we interpret the application $M\,2$ according to any conversion semantics, then we must either convert M from $real \rightarrow real$

to $int \rightarrow real$ or convert 2 from int to $real$. Each of these choices corresponds to a typing derivation for $M\,2$, with different uses of (*subsumption*). If, instead of interpreting $M\,2$ in a "conversion" model directly, we first translate $M\,2$ to a corresponding $\lambda^{\rightarrow}$ term, then we can see that there will be two corresponding $\lambda^{\rightarrow}$ terms, one for each typing derivation. We must restrict the interpretation of the basic conversion functions so that any two $\lambda^{\rightarrow}$ terms arising in this way are guaranteed to be equal.

The coherence restriction on conversion functions is easily formalized as a $\lambda^{\rightarrow}$ theory. Specifically, if $\Sigma = \langle B, Sub, C\rangle$ is a $\lambda^{\rightarrow}_{<:}$ signature, we let $\mathcal{E}_\Sigma$ be the set of all equations of the form

$$c_b^{a_k} \circ \ldots \circ c_a^{a_1} = c_b^{a'_\ell} \circ \ldots \circ c_a^{a'_1} : a \rightarrow b$$

where $a, b \in B$, the sequences $a_1, \ldots, a_k \in B$ and $a'_1, \ldots, a'_\ell \in B$ are distinct and $a_i <: a_{i+1}, a'_j <: a'_{j+1} \in Sub$ for all $i \leq k$ and $j \leq \ell$. We may also assume that a_i is distinct from a_{i+1} and similarly for a'_j and a'_{j+1}. In words, $\mathcal{E}_\Sigma$ says that if there are two different compositions of basic conversion functions between one type constant and another, the two compositions must give the same function. If we draw the subtype assumptions in *Sub* as a diagram, then $\mathcal{E}_\Sigma$ are the equations stating that this diagram commutes.

Example 10.4.1 Consider a $\lambda^{\rightarrow}_{<:}$ signature $\Sigma = \langle B, Sub, C\rangle$ with

$B = \{number, int, real, complex\}$

$Sub = \{number <: int, number <: real, int <: complex, real <: complex\}$

Then $\mathcal{E}_\Sigma$ contains the single equation

$$c_{real}^{complex} \circ c_{number}^{real} = c_{int}^{complex} \circ c_{number}^{int} : number \rightarrow complex$$ ■

Conversion Functions

We define a conversion function c_σ^τ from σ to τ for every subtype assertion $\Sigma \vdash \sigma <: \tau$ provable from the signature. The definition of c_σ^τ is by induction on the proof of $\sigma <: \tau$. We show below that the actual function is independent of which proof we use.

	Axiom or Rule	Conversion Function
(*ref* <:)	$\sigma <: \sigma$	$c_\sigma^\sigma \stackrel{\text{def}}{=} \lambda x{:}\,\sigma.\, x$
(*trans* <:)	$\dfrac{\rho <: \sigma \quad \sigma <: \tau}{\rho <: \tau}$	$c_\rho^\tau \stackrel{\text{def}}{=} \lambda x{:}\,\rho.\, c_\sigma^\tau(c_\rho^\sigma x)$
($\rightarrow$<:)	$\dfrac{\tau_1 <: \sigma_1 \quad \sigma_2 <: \tau_2}{\sigma_1 \rightarrow \sigma_2 <: \tau_1 \rightarrow \tau_2}$	$c_{\sigma_1\rightarrow\sigma_2}^{\tau_1\rightarrow\tau_2} \stackrel{\text{def}}{=} \lambda f{:}\,\sigma_1 \rightarrow \sigma_2.$ $\lambda x{:}\,\tau_1.\, c_{\sigma_2}^{\tau_2}(f\,(c_{\tau_1}^{\sigma_1} x))$

We show that conversion functions are unique by a series of proof transformations that do not change the associated conversion function. We begin with the elimination of certain uses of (*ref*) and (*trans*).

Lemma 10.4.2 In any proof $\Sigma \vdash \sigma <: \tau$, if an instance of (*ref*) is a hypothesis of (*trans*), then we may eliminate both from the proof. This proof transformation does not change the associated conversion function.

Proof Suppose that the proof $\Sigma \vdash \sigma <: \tau$ ends with a step

$$\frac{\sigma <: \tau \quad \tau <: \tau}{\sigma <: \tau}$$

combining reflexivity and transitivity. Since the hypothesis $\sigma <: \tau$ is the same as the conclusion, we can eliminate this use of (*ref*) and (*trans*) and obtain a shorter proof of $\sigma <: \tau$. To see that the conversion function is unchanged, assume we have a conversion function c_σ^τ defined from the shorter proof of $\sigma \to \tau$. The conversion function $\bar{c}_\sigma^\tau$ for the longer proof is the composition of c_σ^τ with the identity associated with the reflexivity axiom. Since this is equal to c_σ^τ, by the calculation

$$\bar{c}_\sigma^\tau \stackrel{\text{def}}{=} \lambda x\colon \sigma.\, c_\sigma^\tau((\lambda x\colon \sigma.\, x)\, x)$$
$$= c_\sigma^\tau$$

the proof transformation does not change the conversion function. The argument when reflexivity is used for the first, instead of second, hypothesis of transitivity is similar. If a proof of $\Sigma \vdash \sigma' <: \tau'$ contains a similar step in the middle of the proof, then the lemma is proved using an additional induction on the number of steps after the instances of (*ref*) and (*trans*) that are eliminated. ∎

Lemma 10.4.3 We may transform any proof $\Sigma \vdash \sigma <: \tau$ that does not use (*ref*) as a hypothesis for (*trans*) so that (*trans*) is used only for type constants, not function types. This proof transformation does not change the associated conversion function.

In addition to their use for reasoning about conversion functions, Lemmas 10.4.2 and 10.4.3 also shows that if $\Sigma \vdash \sigma_1 \to \sigma_2 <: \tau_1 \to \tau_2$, then $\Sigma \vdash \tau_1 <: \sigma_1$ and $\Sigma \vdash \sigma_2 <: \tau_2$. This follows immediately from the proof transformation described in these lemmas: if the proof $\Sigma \vdash \sigma_1 \to \sigma_2 <: \tau_1 \to \tau_2$ ends with rule (*arrow*), the only possible rule other than (*ref*) or (*trans*), then the hypotheses of the last rule are $\tau_1 <: \sigma_1$ and $\sigma_2 <: \tau_2$.

Proof Suppose that a subtyping proof contains a step

$$\frac{\rho_1 \to \rho_2 <: \sigma_1 \to \sigma_2 \quad \sigma_1 \to \sigma_2 <: \tau_1 \to \tau_2}{\rho_1 \to \rho_2 <: \tau_1 \to \tau_2}$$

using transitivity for function types. Among all such proof steps, let us choose one where transitivity on function types is not used in the proof of either hypothesis. In this case, each hypothesis must be proved using (*arrow*), since a condition of the lemma is that neither can be an instance of (*ref*). Therefore, the proof has the form

$$\dfrac{\dfrac{\sigma_1 <: \rho_1 \quad \rho_2 <: \sigma_2}{\rho_1 \to \rho_2 <: \sigma_1 \to \sigma_2} \quad \dfrac{\tau_1 <: \sigma_1 \quad \sigma_2 <: \tau_2}{\sigma_1 \to \sigma_2 <: \tau_1 \to \tau_2}}{\rho_1 \to \rho_2 <: \tau_1 \to \tau_2}$$

We can replace this sequence of proof steps by uses of (*trans*) before (*arrow*).

$$\dfrac{\dfrac{\tau_1 <: \sigma_1 \quad \sigma_1 <: \rho_1}{\tau_1 <: \rho_1} \quad \dfrac{\rho_2 <: \sigma_2 \quad \sigma_2 <: \tau_2}{\rho_2 <: \tau_2}}{\rho_1 \to \rho_2 <: \tau_1 \to \tau_2}$$

This decreases the total number of $\to$'s that appear in hypotheses of instances of (*trans*) in the proof. Repeating this transformation, we can transform the proof so that (*trans*) is used only on type constants, not function types.

It remains to check that this transformation preserves conversion functions. Both conversion functions are lambda-definable from $c^{\sigma_1}_{\tau_1}$, $c^{\rho_1}_{\sigma_1}$, $c^{\sigma_2}_{\rho_2}$ and $c^{\tau_2}_{\sigma_2}$. In the first case, we have

$$(\lambda f\colon \sigma_1 \to \sigma_2.\, \lambda x\colon \tau_1.\, c^{\tau_2}_{\sigma_2}(f\,(c^{\sigma_1}_{\tau_1}x))) \circ (\lambda f\colon \rho_1 \to \rho_2.\, \lambda x\colon \sigma_1.\, c^{\sigma_2}_{\rho_2}(f\,(c^{\rho_1}_{\sigma_1}x)))$$

while the second conversion function is

$$\lambda f\colon \rho_1 \to \rho_2.\, \lambda x\colon \tau_1.\, c^{\tau_2}_{\sigma_2}(c^{\sigma_2}_{\rho_2}(f\,(c^{\rho_1}_{\sigma_1}(c^{\sigma_1}_{\tau_1}x))))$$

Using the definition $f \circ g \equiv \lambda x\colon \tau.\, f(gx)$ and β-reduction, it is easy to reduce the first conversion function to the second. ■

Proposition 10.4.4 Suppose $\Sigma \vdash \sigma <: \tau$ and c^{τ}_{σ} and $\bar{c}^{\tau}_{\sigma}$ are the conversion functions from σ to τ given by any two proofs of $\sigma <: \tau$. Then $\mathcal{E}_{\Sigma} \vdash c^{\tau}_{\sigma} = \bar{c}^{\tau}_{\sigma}$ using the proof rules of $\lambda^{\to}$.

Proof Suppose we have a proof $\Sigma \vdash \sigma <: \tau$ yielding c^{τ}_{σ} and another such proof yielding $\bar{c}^{\tau}_{\sigma}$. Using the transformations given in Lemmas 10.4.2 and 10.4.3, we may transform both proofs so that all uses of (*trans*) are for type constants. This transformation will not change the associated conversion functions. By Lemma 10.2.1, the type expressions σ and τ must match. This implies that the structure of the two proofs of $\sigma <: \tau$ will now be identical, except for the way that an assertion $b_1 <: b_k$ is proved by transitivity from $b_1 <: b_2 <: \ldots <: b_k$ or $b_1 <: b'_2 <: \ldots <: b_k$. As a consequence, it is an easy induction on the structure of σ (or τ) to show that for any proofs $\sigma <: \tau$ without (*trans*) after (*arrow*) or (*ref*), we must have $\mathcal{E}_{\Sigma} \vdash c^{\tau}_{\sigma} = \bar{c}^{\tau}_{\sigma}$. ■

Translation of Terms

Given any $\lambda^{\rightarrow}_{<:}$ term $\Gamma \triangleright M\colon \sigma$ over a signature $\Sigma = \langle B, Sub, C\rangle$, we define a $\lambda^{\rightarrow}$ term $Trans(\Gamma \triangleright M\colon \sigma)$ over the signature $\langle B, C_{Sub}\rangle$. This translation is defined by induction on the typing derivation of the $\lambda^{\rightarrow}_{<:}$ term, as follows:

(*var*)	$Trans(x\colon \sigma \triangleright x\colon \sigma) = x$
($\rightarrow$ Intro)	$Trans(\Gamma \triangleright \lambda x\colon \sigma.\, M\colon \sigma \rightarrow \tau) = \lambda x\colon \sigma.\, Trans(\Gamma, x\colon \sigma \triangleright M\colon \tau)$
($\rightarrow$ Elim)	$Trans(\Gamma \triangleright MN\colon \sigma) = Trans(\Gamma \triangleright M\colon \tau \rightarrow \sigma) Trans(\Gamma \triangleright N\colon \tau)$
(*add var*)	$Trans(\Gamma, x\colon \sigma \triangleright M\colon \tau) = Trans(\Gamma \triangleright M\colon \tau)$
(*subsumption*)	If $\Gamma \triangleright M\colon \tau$ is derived from $\Gamma \triangleright M\colon \sigma$ using $\Sigma \vdash \sigma <: \tau$, then $Trans(\Gamma \triangleright M\colon \tau) = c_\sigma^\tau Trans(\Gamma \triangleright M\colon \sigma)$

A straightforward induction on the definition of $Trans(\Gamma \triangleright M\colon \sigma)$ shows that the result of translation is well-typed, as stated in the following lemma.

Lemma 10.4.5 If $\Gamma \triangleright M\colon \sigma$ is a derivable typing assertion of $\lambda^{\rightarrow}_{<:}$ over signature $\langle B, Sub, C\rangle$, then $\Gamma \triangleright Trans(\Gamma \triangleright M\colon \sigma)\colon \sigma$ is a derivable typing assertion of $\lambda^{\rightarrow}$ over signature $\langle B, C_{Sub}\rangle$.

We may also show that although the syntactic form of the term depends on the typing derivation, all possible translations of a term are equal. This is proved by transformations on terms that change the $\lambda^{\rightarrow}_{<:}$ typing derivation but preserve the meaning of the resulting $\lambda^{\rightarrow}$ term. Before proceeding, we state a basic lemma that will be used for several purposes.

Lemma 10.4.6 If a $\lambda^{\rightarrow}_{<:}$ typing assertion is proved using two consecutive uses of (*subsumption*, then the two uses of *subsumption*) can be replaced by one. This transformation on typing derivations does not change the meaning of the associated $\lambda^{\rightarrow}$ terms with explicit conversion functions.

The proof is left as Exercise 10.4.11.

There are two ways we might think about transforming typing derivations to a standard form. The first, suggested by β-reduction of the terms resulting from our translation, moves subsumption "down" to the variables. The basic idea is illustrated in the following example.

Example 10.4.7 Example 10.2.4 shows that when we use subsumption, based on $\rho <: \sigma$, to give a lambda term $\Gamma \triangleright \lambda x\colon \sigma.\, M\colon \sigma \rightarrow \tau$ type $\rho \rightarrow \tau$, the result is a term that is provably equal to $\Gamma \triangleright \lambda x\colon \rho.\, M\colon \rho \rightarrow \tau$. We can see that our conversion functions also may change the type of a lambda-bound variable.

If $\rho <: \sigma$, then the conversion function from $\sigma \rightarrow \tau$ to $\rho \rightarrow \tau$ is

$$c_{\sigma\to\tau}^{\rho\to\tau} = \lambda f\colon\sigma\to\tau.\,\lambda x\colon\rho.\,f(c_\rho^\sigma x)$$

Assuming that there is only one use of subsumption in the typing derivation, the translation of $\Gamma \triangleright \lambda x\colon\sigma.\,M\colon\rho\to\tau$ is

$$\begin{aligned}
&\mathit{Trans}(\Gamma \triangleright \lambda x\colon\sigma.\,M\colon\rho\to\tau)\\
&= c_{\sigma\to\tau}^{\rho\to\tau}\mathit{Trans}(\Gamma \triangleright \lambda x\colon\sigma.\,M\colon\sigma\to\tau)\\
&= c_{\sigma\to\tau}^{\rho\to\tau}\ \lambda x\colon\sigma.\,\hat{M}\\
&= (\lambda f\colon\sigma\to\tau.\,\lambda x\colon\rho.\,f(c_\rho^\tau x))\,(\lambda x\colon\sigma.\,\hat{M})\\
&= \lambda x\colon\rho.(\lambda x\colon\sigma.\,\hat{M})(c_\rho^\tau x)\\
&= \lambda x\colon\rho.[c_\rho^\sigma x/x]\hat{M}
\end{aligned}$$

where $\hat{M} = \mathit{Trans}(\Gamma, x\colon\sigma \triangleright M\colon\tau)$. Note that in simplifying $\mathit{Trans}(\Gamma \triangleright \lambda x\colon\sigma.\,M\colon\rho\to\tau)$, we have simplified an expression beginning with a conversion function to one where a conversion function is applied to a variable. ■

The transformation on typing derivations that moves (*subsumption*) to the variables is described in Lemma 10.4.8 below. It is used for several purposes, including the soundness of β-reduction in the conversion semantics and the development of a type inference algorithm in [Mit91b]; see also [LM92, HM95b].

Lemma 10.4.8 Any typing derivation for a $\lambda_{<:}^{\to}$ term $\Gamma \triangleright M\colon\sigma$ may be transformed to a typing derivation of a term $\Gamma \triangleright M'\colon\sigma$ that uses (*subsumption*) only for variables, and uses (*subsumption*) at most once for each variable occurrence in M. The terms M and M' may differ in the types of bound variables but are otherwise identical. Moreover, the equation

$$\Gamma \triangleright \mathit{Trans}(\Gamma \triangleright M\colon\sigma) = \mathit{Trans}(\Gamma \triangleright M'\colon\sigma)\colon\sigma$$

is provable in $\lambda^{\to}$.

The proof is given as Exercise 10.4.12.

For coherence of the conversion semantics, however, we need a transformation that postpones uses of (*subsumption*) as much as possible. The result is a typing derivation in which we first derive the minimum type for the term, then use (*subsumption*) as the final step in deriving any desired type. It may also be necessary to use (*subsumption*) to type an application. However, we can restrict this to (*subsumption*) on the function argument only, as shown in the Lemma 10.4.9. A similar approach to coherence, for a language with polymorphism and subtyping, is given in [CG92].

Lemma 10.4.9 Any typing derivation for a $\lambda^{\rightarrow}_{<:}$ term $\Gamma \triangleright M\colon \sigma$ may be transformed to a typing derivation that uses (*subsumption*) only for the arguments of function applications and one final use of (*subsumption*) on the entire term M. The resulting typing derivation is uniquely determined by M, except for the final conversion, which depends on σ. If $\hat{M}, \ddot{M} = \mathit{Trans}(\Gamma \triangleright M\colon \sigma)$ are the two translations of M given by the original and the final typing derivations, then $\mathcal{E}_\Sigma \vdash \Gamma \triangleright \hat{M} = \ddot{M}\colon \sigma$ in $\lambda^{\rightarrow}$.

Proof Since Lemma 10.4.6 shows that consecutive uses of (*subsumption*) may be collapsed into one, we show only that a use of (*subsumption*) before ($\rightarrow$ Intro) or ($\rightarrow$ Elim) may postponed to after the rule. The analogous property of (*add var*) is straightforward and left to the reader. We begin with the ($\rightarrow$ Elim) case, where we allow the use of (*subsumption*) on the function argument.

Suppose our typing derivation contains steps of the form

$$\dfrac{\dfrac{\Gamma \triangleright M\colon \sigma_1 \rightarrow \tau_1 \quad \sigma_1 \rightarrow \tau_1 <: \sigma \rightarrow \tau}{\Gamma \triangleright M\colon \sigma \rightarrow \tau} \qquad \dfrac{\Gamma \triangleright N\colon \sigma_2 \quad \sigma_2 <: \sigma}{\Gamma \triangleright N\colon \sigma}}{\Gamma \triangleright MN\colon \tau}$$

with (*subsumption*) preceding ($\rightarrow$ Elim). By Lemmas 10.4.2 and 10.4.3, we can see that since $\Sigma \vdash \sigma_1 \rightarrow \tau_1 <: \sigma \rightarrow \tau$, we have $\Sigma \vdash \sigma <: \sigma_1$ and therefore

$$\Sigma \vdash \sigma_2 <: \sigma <: \sigma_1$$

Consequently, we can transform this typing derivation to the form

$$\dfrac{\dfrac{\Gamma \triangleright M\colon \sigma_1 \rightarrow \tau_1 \qquad \dfrac{\Gamma \triangleright N\colon \sigma_2 \quad \sigma_2 <: \sigma_1}{\Gamma \triangleright N\colon \sigma_1}}{\Gamma \triangleright MN\colon \tau_1 \quad \tau_1 <: \tau}}{\Gamma \triangleright MN\colon \tau}$$

with ($\rightarrow$ Elim) before (*subsumption*). This is the form we want, since the use of (*subsumption*) in typing N is a use of (*subsumption*) on a function argument.

We must show that for $\bar{M} = \mathit{Trans}(\Gamma \triangleright M\colon \sigma_1 \rightarrow \tau_1)$ and $\bar{N} = \mathit{Trans}(\Gamma \triangleright N\colon \sigma_2)$, we have

$$(c^{\sigma\rightarrow\tau}_{\sigma_1\rightarrow\tau_1} \bar{M})(c^{\sigma}_{\sigma_2} \bar{N}) \;=\; c^{\tau}_{\tau_1}(\bar{M}(c^{\sigma_1}_{\sigma_2} \bar{N}))$$

This is a routine calculation using

$$c^{\sigma\rightarrow\tau}_{\sigma_1\rightarrow\tau_1} = \lambda f\colon \sigma_1 \rightarrow \tau_1.\, \lambda x\colon \sigma.\, c^{\tau}_{\tau_1}(f(c^{\sigma_1}_{\sigma} x))$$

and $c_{\sigma_2}^{\sigma_1} = c_{\sigma}^{\sigma_1} \circ c_{\sigma_2}^{\sigma}$. This shows that the associated $\lambda^{\rightarrow}$ terms with conversion functions are provably equal.

For the ($\rightarrow$ Intro) case we transform a sequence

$$\dfrac{\dfrac{\Gamma, x\colon\sigma \triangleright M\colon\tau_1 \qquad \tau_1 <: \tau}{\Gamma, x\colon\sigma \triangleright M\colon\tau}}{\Gamma \triangleright \lambda x\colon\sigma.\, M\colon\sigma \rightarrow \tau}$$

with ($\rightarrow$ Intro) after (*subsumption*) to

$$\dfrac{\dfrac{\Gamma, x\colon\sigma \triangleright M\colon\tau_1}{\Gamma \triangleright \lambda x\colon\sigma.\, M\colon\sigma \rightarrow \tau_1} \qquad \sigma \rightarrow \tau_1 <: \sigma \rightarrow \tau}{\Gamma \triangleright \lambda x\colon\sigma.\, M\colon\sigma \rightarrow \tau}$$

with the rules occurring in the opposite order. We show that the associated $\lambda^{\rightarrow}$ terms with conversion functions are provably equal by showing that for $\bar{M} = \mathit{Trans}(\Gamma, x\colon\sigma \triangleright M\colon\tau_1)$ we have

$$\lambda x\colon\sigma.\, c_{\tau_1}^{\tau}\, \bar{M} = c_{\sigma\rightarrow\tau_1}^{\sigma\rightarrow\tau}\, \lambda x\colon\sigma.\, \bar{M}$$

As in the previous case, this is a routine calculation.

The last step of the proof is to show that if a typing derivation uses (*subsumption*) only on arguments to function applications, the typing derivation is uniquely determined by M. This is a straightforward induction on M. The typing derivation with this property gives the minimum typing for M, as described in Exercise 10.2.8. ∎

Proposition 10.4.10 Let $\Sigma = \langle B, \mathit{Sub}, C\rangle$ be a $\lambda_{<:}^{\rightarrow}$ signature and let $\Gamma \triangleright M\colon\sigma$ be a $\lambda_{<:}^{\rightarrow}$ term over Σ. Suppose there are two typing derivations for $\Gamma \triangleright M\colon\sigma$ and let $\hat{M}, \ddot{M} = \mathit{Trans}(\Gamma \triangleright M\colon\sigma)$ be the translations of M taken according to the two typing derivations. Then $\mathcal{E}_\Sigma \vdash \Gamma \triangleright \hat{M} = \ddot{M}\colon\sigma$ using the proof rules of $\lambda^{\rightarrow}$.

Proof The proof is similar in spirit to the proof of Proposition 10.4.10. The main idea is to "normalize" both typing derivations and then use the common structure of the two derivations.

If we have two typing derivations for $\Gamma \triangleright M\colon\sigma$, then by Lemma 10.4.9, we may transform both so that (*subsumption*) is used only on the arguments to function applications and as the last step of the derivation. In both cases, we will obtain the same typing derivation, since all but the last step is determined by M and the final conversion function is determined by the type σ. Since this transformation does not change the associated terms with explicit conversion functions, the terms associated with the original typing derivations must be provably equal (given the equations in $\mathcal{E}_\Sigma$). ∎

Exercise 10.4.11 Prove Lemma 10.4.6.

Exercise 10.4.12 Prove Lemma 10.4.8, using an argument similar to the proof of Lemma 10.4.9.

10.4.3 Subset Interpretation of Types

In this section, we consider models of $\lambda_{<:}^{\rightarrow,\mathtt{record}}$ where subtypes are interpreted semantically as subsets. As mentioned in the informal discussions of containment interpretations in Sections 10.2 and 10.3, this form of semantics usually involves some form of "untyped" value space. Specifically, all types will be subsets of some larger set of semantic values.

With a single "universal" set of all semantic values, we will assign meaning to a term in a way that is independent of any type information that appears in the term. This eliminates the issues and complications associated with coherence in the conversion interpretation of Section 10.4.2. In our subset interpretation, the terms $\lambda x\colon int.\, x$ and $\lambda x\colon bool.\, x$ will have the same meaning. Therefore, types $int \rightarrow int$ and $bool \rightarrow bool$ must have a nonempty intersection. In fact, the meaning of $\lambda x\colon \sigma.\, x$ must belong to all types of the form $\tau \rightarrow \tau$. As a consequence, the subsets we use to interpret types may overlap in interesting and nontrivial ways.

A susbet interpretation of essentially the form we consider here is used in Milner's classic paper on ML type inference to show that the typing rules are sound [Mil78]. Similar interpretations have been used since for other type systems. However, subset semantics do not provide a useful interpretation of the equational theory of typed terms The reason is that equations between terms can only be interpreted in a type-independent way. Two examples illustrating the way equations may depend on types are given in Sections 10.2 and 10.3. Specifically, the two $\lambda_{<:}^{\rightarrow}$ terms

$$\lambda x\colon real.\, \lfloor x \rfloor \qquad \lambda x\colon real.\, x$$

are semantically different at type $real \rightarrow real$, but equal at the supertype $int \rightarrow real$. Since the floor function $\lfloor \cdot \rfloor$ is not definable in $\lambda_{<:}^{\rightarrow}$, the equation at $int \rightarrow real$ is not provable in the equational proof system for $int \rightarrow real$, but it should be semantically sound to axiomatize the floor function in this way. In the record example of Section 10.3, terms

$$\langle a = 3,\ b = true,\ c = \text{“Hello”}\rangle \qquad \langle a = 3,\ b = true,\ c = \text{“Goodbye”}\rangle$$

are unequal at type $\langle a\colon int,\ b\colon bool,\ c\colon string\rangle$ but provably equal at type $\langle a\colon int,\ b\colon bool\rangle$. Therefore, in any reasonable (non-degenerate) semantic model of $\lambda_{<:}^{\rightarrow,\mathtt{record}}$, equality must depend on the type. In short, a subset interpretation of types may provide a useful semantics for type membership, but cannot provide a semantics for typed equality between terms.

In this section, we describe the kind of value space that is required for $\lambda_{<:}^{\rightarrow,\mathtt{record}}$ and give subset interpretation for types and terms. In Section 10.4.4, we modify the semantics to give a sound interpretation of both type membership and the equational rules of the language. In intuitive implementation terms, both interpretations correspond to the form of compiler where code generation does not depend on the types of program expressions. More specifically, a typical complier for a typed language might begin with a parse phase, then invoke a type checker. The output of parsing is usually a parse tree, which the type checker would annotate with type information. If the subsequent code generator uses the type annotations to optimize the generated code, then we could design an implementation along the lines of the conversion interpretation of Section 10.4.2. On the other hand, if code is generated in a type-independent way, the implementation is more likely to corresponds to the form of semantics given here.

Since we will interpret untyped terms, we will use a mapping from the typed $\lambda_{<:}^{\rightarrow,\mathtt{record}}$-terms to untyped λ, `record`-terms. The *erasure function* on $\lambda_{<:}^{\rightarrow,\mathtt{record}}$-terms is defined as follows.

$$
\begin{aligned}
&Erase(c) &&= c\\
&Erase(x) &&= x\\
&Erase(M\,N) &&= Erase(M)\,Erase(N)\\
&Erase(\lambda x\colon \tau.M) &&= \lambda x.Erase(M)\\
&Erase(\langle \ell_1 = M_1, \ldots, \ell_n = M_n\rangle) &&= \langle \ell_1 = Erase(M_1), \ldots, \ell_n = Erase(M_n)\rangle\\
&Erase(M.\ell) &&= Erase(M).\ell
\end{aligned}
$$

Further discussion of erasure functions appears in Section 11.1.

Untyped Value Space

We interpret untyped λ, `record`-terms in a form of partial combinatory algebra with record operations. Intuitively, the structure we use will have a set D of values for terms, a set L of labels, and operations for defining and using functions and records. As in Sections 4.5.7 and 5.6.2, we treat functions using combinators $S, K \in D$ and a binary operation, *app*, on D called application. To be as general as possible, we will allow *app* to be a partial operation. This allows us to construct a partial combinatory algebra with record operations using ordinary partial recursive functions. The other operations we use are a constant *em* for the empty record (the record with no components), an operation that adds a component to a record, and a record selection operation. We allow both of these operations to be partial also since, for example, the result of selecting from the empty record may be considered undefined. When we interpret typed terms, the typing rules will guarantee that every term has a meaning. However, some untyped combinations of functions and record operations may not be defined.

Before defining the appropriate form of partial combinatory structure, we review some notation for partial operations. A *partial applicative structure* is a structure $\mathcal{A} = \langle D, app, c_1^{\mathcal{A}}, c_2^{\mathcal{A}}, \ldots \rangle$ with *app* a partial binary operation on D and distinguished elements $c_1^{\mathcal{A}}, c_2^{\mathcal{A}}, \ldots \in D$ named by term constants $c_1, c_2, \ldots$. If M, N are expressions over the signature of $\mathcal{A}$, then we write $M \downarrow$ to indicate that M has a value and $M \cong N$ for the condition

$$M \cong N \quad \text{iff} \quad (M \downarrow \vee N \downarrow) \supset M = N.$$

In words, $M \cong N$ means that if either expression has a value, then both are defined and have the same value. We will use $\downarrow$ and $\cong$ in describing an appropriate form of partial applicative structure for untyped λ, `record`-terms.

A λ, `record`-combinatory structure is a tuple $\mathcal{D} = \langle D, L, app^{\mathcal{D}}, K^{\mathcal{D}}, S^{\mathcal{D}}, em^{\mathcal{D}}, sel^{\mathcal{D}}, lcond^{\mathcal{D}}, c_1^{\mathcal{D}}, c_2^{\mathcal{D}}, \ldots \rangle$ with

D and L sets,

$app^{\mathcal{D}}\colon D \times D \rightharpoonup D$ a partial function called *application,*

$K^{\mathcal{D}}, S^{\mathcal{D}}, em^{\mathcal{D}} \in D$

$sel^{\mathcal{D}}\colon D \times L \rightharpoonup D$ a partial function called *selection,*

$lcond^{\mathcal{D}}\colon D \times L \times D \rightharpoonup D$ a partial function called *label conditional,*

constants $c_1, c_2, \ldots$ interpreted as elements $c_1^{\mathcal{D}}, c_2^{\mathcal{D}}, \ldots$ of D or L,

satisfying the conditions listed below. In general, we will be interested in λ, `record`-combinatory structures that interpret *label constants* $\ell_1, \ell_2, \ldots$ as distinct elements of L. To simplify notation, we write application and selection as infix binary operations, according to the conventions

$$d \cdot e \stackrel{\text{def}}{=} app\, d\, e$$

$$d.\ell \stackrel{\text{def}}{=} sel\, d\, \ell$$

The remaining conditions of the definition are listed below. The first four lines are the same as the standard definition of partial combinatory algebra (from Section 5.6.2), while the fifth and sixth express natural properties of record formation and selection. Intuitively, if x is a record, then $lcond\; x\; \ell\; y$ defines a record similar to x, but with ℓ component equal to y. (If x is a not a record, then $lcond\; x\; \ell\; y$ need not be defined.)

$$K \cdot x \downarrow$$

$$(S \cdot x) \cdot y \downarrow$$

$$(K \cdot x) \cdot y \cong x$$

$$((S \cdot x) \cdot y) \cdot z \cong (x \cdot z) \cdot (y \cdot z)$$

$$(lcond\, x\, \ell\, y \downarrow) \supset (lcond\, x\, \ell\, y).\ell \cong y$$

$$(lcond\, x\, \ell\, y \downarrow \wedge \ell' \neq \ell) \supset (lcond\, x\, \ell\, y).\ell' \cong x.\ell'$$

We can translate any untyped λ, `record`-term into combinators as follows

$$\bar{x} = x$$

$$\bar{c} = c$$

$$\overline{U \cdot V} = \bar{U} \cdot \bar{V}$$

$$\overline{\lambda x.\, U} = \langle x \rangle \bar{U}$$

$$\overline{U.\ell} = \bar{U}.\ell$$

$$\overline{\langle \ell_1 = U_1, \ldots, \ell_k = U_k \rangle} = lcond\ (lcond(\ldots(lcond\ em\ \ell_k\ \bar{U_k})\ldots)\ \ell_2\ \bar{U_2})\ \ell_1\ \bar{U_1}$$

where untyped "pseudo-abstraction" $\langle x \rangle V$ is defined in the same way as typed pseudo-abstraction, written $\langle x{:}\sigma \rangle M$ in Section 4.5.7, and $\ell_1, \ldots, \ell_k$ are distinct label constants.

A λ, `record`-combinatory structure $\mathcal{D} = \langle D, L, app^{\mathcal{D}}, K^{\mathcal{D}}, S^{\mathcal{D}}, em^{\mathcal{D}}, sel^{\mathcal{D}}, lcond^{\mathcal{D}}, \ell_1^{\mathcal{D}}, \ell_2^{\mathcal{D}}, \ldots \rangle$ with label constants is essentially an algebra for the signature with carriers D, L, function symbols $app : D \to D \to D$, $sel : D \to L \to D$, $lcond : D \to L \to D \to D$ and constants $K, S : D$, $\ell_1, \ell_2, \ldots : L$, except that *app*, *sel* and *lcond* are partial instead of total functions. As a result, the meaning of a term such as $app\, x\, y$ may not be defined. Except for this difference, we interpret any algebraic term over the appropriate signature in a λ, `record`-combinatory structure using the standard definition from algebra, as explained in Section 5.6.2 for partial combinatory algebras. We define the meaning of an untyped λ, `record`-term U in λ, `record`-combinatory structure $\mathcal{D}$ at environment η by translation into combinators:

$$\mathcal{D}[\![U]\!]\eta \cong \mathcal{D}[\![\,\overline{U}\,]\!]\eta$$

Exercise 10.4.19 asks you to verify an equation between record terms. As in Section 4.5.7, the main property of pseudo-abstraction is

$$(\langle x \rangle U) \cdot V \cong [V/x]U$$

as shown in Exercise 10.4.20. The substitution property of λ, record-combinatory structures, and other standard results from algebra, can be proved as in Chapter 3.

Example 10.4.13 Untyped λ, record-structures may be constructed using the general techniques for solving recursive domain equations in Section 7.4. Specifically, any CPO D satisfying the isomorphism

$$D \cong A + [L \to D] + [D \to D]$$

where A is any CPO, L is a countably infinite flat or discrete CPO of labels, $+$ is separated sum and $[C \to D]$ is the collection of all continuous functions from C to D, forms an untyped λ, record-structure. In this case, *app* is given by

$$app\, d\, e \stackrel{\text{def}}{=} \texttt{if}\ d\ in\ [D \to D]\ \texttt{then}\ d(e)\ \texttt{else}\ \bot$$

where the test "d *in* $[D \to D]$" is achieved through case statements and, similarly, *sel* is the function

$$sel\, d\, \ell \stackrel{\text{def}}{=} \texttt{if}\ d\ in\ [L \to D]\ \texttt{then}\ d(\ell)\ \texttt{else}\ \bot$$

Label conditional is defined using ordinary continuous conditional and equality test, by

$$lcond\, d \ell e \stackrel{\text{def}}{=} \texttt{if}\ d\ in\ [L \to D]\ \texttt{then}\ (\lambda \ell' \in L.$$

$$\texttt{if}\ \ell' = \ell\ \texttt{then}\ e\ \texttt{else}\ seld\ell')\ \texttt{else}\ \bot \blacksquare$$

Example 10.4.14 We may construct an untyped λ, record-structure from any partial combinatory algebra (defined in Section 5.6.2). In particular, the recursive structure with $D = \mathcal{N}$ the set of natural numbers and $app\, n\, m = \phi_n(m)$ the result of applying the n-th partial recursive function to m may be extended to an untyped λ, record-structure. For an arbitrary partial combinatory algebra, we could use the Church numerals, combinatory terms representing functions of the form $\lambda f.\, \lambda x.\, f^n x$, as labels, since equality test and conditional are definable on these terms. However, for the recursive structure with $D = \mathcal{N}$, it is simpler to let $L = \mathcal{N}$ and let record selection $sel\, n\, m = \phi_n(m)$ be recursive function application. This is possible since equality test and conditional are computable functions on the natural numbers, giving us a computable label conditional

$$(lcond\, d\, \ell\, e) \cdot \ell' \cong \begin{cases} e & \text{if } \ell' = \ell \\ d \cdot \ell' & \text{otherwise} \end{cases} \qquad \blacksquare$$

Example 10.4.15 We may construct a "term" untyped λ, record-structure using algebraic terms over *app*, K, S, *em*, *sel* and *lcond*. In this structure, it is simpler to make all operations total. To be more specific, we take algebraic terms over the two-sorted signature with sorts D and L and function symbols

$$\begin{aligned} \ell_0, \ell_1, \ell_2, \ldots &: L \\ K, S, em &: D \\ app &: D \times D \to D \\ sel &: D \times L \to D \\ lcond &: D \times L \times D \to D \end{aligned}$$

modulo the equations provable from

$$\begin{array}{lll} K \cdot x \cdot y & = x & \\ S \cdot x \cdot y \cdot z & = (x \cdot z) \cdot (y \cdot z) & \\ (lcond\; d\; \ell\; e).\ell & = e & \ell \text{ any label constant} \\ (lcond\; d\; \ell\; e).\ell' & = d.\ell' & \ell, \ell' \text{ distinct label constants} \end{array}$$

The reason for using infinitely many label constants is that this makes it possible to give a completely equational axiomatization. (Otherwise, we would need an inequational hypothesis $\ell \neq \ell'$ for label variables in the last line above.) This is an extension of the term combinatory algebra described in Example 5.6.6. As in Example 5.6.6, this equational theory gives rise to a confluent rewrite system, allowing us to analyze provability using reduction. ■

Subset Interpretation of Types

We interpret types as *subsets* of D. A *subset interpretation* for signature $\Sigma = \langle B, Sub, C\rangle$ consists of a λ, `record`-combinatory structure $\mathcal{D} = \langle D, L, app^{\mathcal{D}}, K^{\mathcal{D}}, S^{\mathcal{D}}, em^{\mathcal{D}}, sel^{\mathcal{D}}, lcond^{\mathcal{D}}, \ell_1^{\mathcal{D}}, \ell_2^{\mathcal{D}}, \ldots\rangle$ and a family of subsets $\mathcal{S} = \{S^{\tau} \subseteq D \mid \tau \text{ a type}\}$ satisfying the conditions:

$$S^{b_1} \subseteq S^{b_2} \text{ whenever } (b_1 <: b_2) \in Sub$$

$$S^{A \to B} = \{d \in D \mid \forall e \in D.\ \text{if } e \in S^A \text{ then } d \cdot e \in S^B\}$$

$$S^{\langle \ell_1 : A_1, \ldots, \ell_k : A_k\rangle} = \{d \in D \mid \forall i \in \{1, \ldots, k\}.\ d.\ell_i \in S_i^A\}$$

Example 10.4.16 We can get some feel for this definition by looking at the recursive function interpretation of records described in Example 10.4.14. Some natural interpretations of types are $S^{nat} = \mathcal{N}$, $S^{bool} = \{0, 1\}$ and $S^{char} = \{n \mid 0 \leq n \leq 256\}$, the last based on an 8-bit byte per character. We then have $S^{nat \to nat} = \{n \mid \forall m \in \mathcal{N}.\, n \cdot m \downarrow\}$, *i.e.*, $nat \to nat$ is the set of indices (or Gödel numbers) of total recursive functions. Two illustrative record examples are $\langle a\colon nat, b\colon bool\rangle$ and $\langle a\colon nat, b\colon bool, c\colon char\rangle$, since one is a subtype of the other.

In our untyped λ, `record`-structure, a record is a partial function from natural numbers, regarded as labels, to natural numbers, regarded as values. For concreteness, let us use natural numbers 0,1,2 for labels a, b and c. Then $S^{\langle a:nat,b:bool\rangle}$ is the set of all elements $d \in \mathcal{N}$ such that $d.0 \in S^{nat}$, and $d.1 \in S^{bool}$. It is easy to see that $S^{\langle a:nat,b:bool,c:char\rangle}$ is the subset of all $d \in S^{\langle a:nat,b:bool\rangle}$ with $d.2 \in S^{char}$. Thus $S^{\langle a:nat,b:bool,c:char\rangle} \subseteq S^{\langle a:nat,b:bool\rangle}$. ■

It is easy to prove that the subtyping rules are sound.

Lemma 10.4.17 Let ρ and τ be two type expressions over signature Σ. If $\rho <: \tau$ is provable from Σ, then $S^{\rho} \subseteq S^{\tau}$ in any subset interpretation $\mathcal{S}$ for Σ.

The proof is an easy induction on types, left as an exercise for the reader. (See Exercise 10.4.28 for a related exercise on relational interpretations of types.)

Type Soundness

We prove that typing rules for terms are sound. In the process, we show that although the basic operations of a λ, `record`-structure may be partial, the meaning of a typed term is always defined. If $\mathcal{S}$ is a subset interpretation over $\mathcal{D}$, and η is an environment for $\mathcal{D}$, we write $\eta \models \Gamma$ if $\eta(x) \in S^{\tau}$ for every $x\colon \tau \in \Gamma$.

Lemma 10.4.18 Suppose $\Gamma \triangleright M\colon \tau$ is a well-typed $\lambda_{<:}^{\rightarrow,\mathtt{record}}$-term over some signature Σ. If $\eta \models \Gamma$, then

$$[\![Erase(M)]\!]\eta \in S^{\tau}$$

in any subset interpretation for Σ.

Proof The proof is by induction on the typing derivation for $\Gamma \triangleright M\colon \tau$. For a variable, $x\colon \tau \triangleright x\colon \tau$, we assume that $\eta \models x\colon \tau$, which means that $\eta(x) \in S^{\tau}$. The base case for a constant is similarly straightforward.

The induction step for (*add var*) is straightforward; for (*subsum*), we use Lemma 10.4.17.

The induction steps for lambda abstraction and application are similar to logical predicate (unary logical relation) arguments in Chapter 8, using Exercise 10.4.20. Therefore, we show only the record cases. Suppose typing $\Gamma \triangleright \langle \ell_1 = M_1, \ldots, \ell_k = M_k\rangle\colon \langle \ell_1\colon \tau_1, \ldots, \ell_k\colon \tau_k\rangle$ follows from typings $\Gamma \triangleright M_i\colon \tau_i$ for $1 \le i \le k$. Our inductive hypothesis is that for each i, we have

$$[\![Erase(M_i)]\!]\eta \in S^{\tau_i}$$

By Exercise 10.4.19, we have

$$([\![Erase(\langle \ell_1 = M_1, \ldots, \ell_k = M_k \rangle)]\!]\eta).\ell_i \cong [\![Erase(M_i)]\!]\eta$$

for $1 \leq i \leq k$ and this case of the lemma follows by definition of $S^{\langle \ell_1:\tau_1,\ldots,\ell_k:\tau_k \rangle}$. The case for record selection is proved similarly. ∎

Exercise 10.4.19 Show that in any λ, record-combinatory structure, we have

$$\langle \ell_1 = U_1, \ldots, \ell_k = U_k \rangle.\ell_i \cong U_i$$

In particular, the equation

$$\langle \ell_1 = x_1, \ldots, \ell_k = x_k \rangle.\ell_i = x_i$$

is valid in λ, record-combinatory structures.

Exercise 10.4.20 Show that in any λ, record-combinatory structure, we have

$$(\langle x \rangle U) \cdot V \cong [V/x]U$$

This is the analog of Lemma 4.5.30 for partial combinatory algebras. Use induction on the definition of $\langle x \rangle U$ from Section 4.5.7.

10.4.4 Partial Equivalence Relations as Types

The main reason that subset models do not form models of typed lambda calculus is that equality is untyped, or independent of type. However, we can construct models in much the same spirit if, in addition to a membership predicate, we also associate an equivalence relation with each type. The combination of a membership predicate and an equivalence relation results in a *partial equivalence relation (per),* as explained in Section 5.6.1. One intuitive explanation for using pers is based on computer implementation. In compiling a typed language, we might choose to represent characters or boolean values as single bytes. Any byte would be accepted as a valid representation of either a boolean or a character. However, since we are likely to regard any byte with least significant bit 1 as a representation of *true*, any two bytes ending with 1 will be regarded as equal booleans. However, two bytes with the same least significant bit will not be considered equal characters. Thus, although characters and booleans may have the same membership predicate on machine-level representations, the equality relations are different.

The intuitive formulation of a partial equivalence relation on a set D is as a pair $\langle S, =_S \rangle$ with $S \subseteq D$ a set and $=_S$ an equivalence relation on S. We will simplify this definition below by dropping the subset. This makes many definitions and constructions mathematically simpler. However, the explanation of subtyping with pers is more intuitive using pairs $\langle S, =_S \rangle$.

When we represent a type by a pair $\langle S, =_S \rangle$, there are two conditions involved in subtyping. The first is that when $\langle S, =_S \rangle <: \langle R, =_R \rangle$, we must have $S \subseteq R$. The second condition may be explained by saying that if two values are equal at type A, and $A <: B$, then the values are also equal at type B. This very plausible property of subtyping is discussed in Section 10.2 (Example 10.2.3 in particular) in connection with the equational inference rule (*subsumption eq*). Put in terms of equivalence relations, the second condition is that for $\langle S, =_S \rangle <: \langle R, =_R \rangle$, we must have the relation $=_S$, regarded as a set of ordered pairs, contained in the relation $=_R$. The reader may recall from Section 10.2 that (*subsumption eq*) is not an additional condition imposed on the calculus with subtyping, but a consequence of subsumption and ordinary equational properties of typed lambda calculus. Therefore, this is really an essential condition on subtyping.

Although two-part partial equivalence relations are intuitively reasonable, it is technically convenient to combine the membership predicate and the equivalence relation. If we have a pair $\langle S, =_S \rangle$ with $S \subseteq D$ and $=_S$ an equivalence relation on S, then it is easy to see that S is determined by $=_S$. This is discussed in Section 5.6.1. Therefore, we say a binary relation R on a set D is a *partial equivalence relation* if R is symmetric and transitive.

With types interpreted as partial equivalence relations, subtyping is defined to be subset of relations. This implies both subset of elements and preservation of equality. More specifically, if R and S are partial equivalence relations on D, then $R \subseteq S$ implies first that if $d\ R\ d$ then $d\ S\ d$, so every element of type R is an element of type S, and secondly that if $d\ R\ e$, meaning d and e are equivalent at type R, then $d\ S\ e$. This agrees with our earlier discussion of subtyping for types represented as sets and equivalence relations. For a general discussion of partial equivalence relations, and a connection with so-called modest sets, see Section 5.6.

PER Interpretation of Type Expressions

A *per interpretation* for signature $\Sigma = \langle B, Sub, C \rangle$ consists of a λ, `record`-combinatory structure $\mathcal{D} = \langle D, L, app^{\mathcal{D}}, K^{\mathcal{D}}, S^{\mathcal{D}}, em^{\mathcal{D}}, sel^{\mathcal{D}}, lcond^{\mathcal{D}}, \ell_1^{\mathcal{D}}, \ell_2^{\mathcal{D}}, \ldots \rangle$ and a family of symmetric transitive relations $\mathcal{R} = \{R^\tau \subseteq D \times D \mid \tau \text{ a type}\}$ satisfying the conditions:

$$R^{b_1} \subseteq R^{b_2} \text{ whenever } (b_1 <: b_2) \in Sub$$

$$d\ R^{\sigma\to\tau}\ e \text{ iff } \forall d', e' \in D.\ \text{if } d'\ R^\sigma\ e' \text{ then } d \cdot d'\ R^\tau\ e \cdot e'$$

$$d\ R^{\langle \ell_1:\sigma_1,\ldots,\ell_k:\sigma_k \rangle}\ e \text{ iff } \forall i \in \{1,\ldots,k\}.\ d.\ell_i\ R^{\sigma_i}\ e.\ell_i$$

Example 10.4.21 A number of examples of pers over the natural numbers appear in Section 5.6, including $R^{nat} = \{\langle n, n \rangle \mid n \in \mathcal{N}\}$, $R^{bool} = \{\langle 0, 0 \rangle, \langle 1, 1 \rangle\}$, $R^{char} = \{\langle n, m \rangle \mid n, m$

< 256 and $n = m\}$ and $R^{nat \to nat} = \{\langle n, m\rangle \mid \forall k \in \mathcal{N}. n \cdot k = m \cdot k\}$. Note that these are all equivalence relations on the subsets given in Example 10.4.16, *i.e.*, if $\langle n, m\rangle \in R^{\tau}$, then $n, m \in S^{\tau}$.

Two illustrative record examples are $\langle a\colon nat,\, b\colon bool\rangle$ and $\langle a\colon nat,\, b\colon bool,\, c\colon char\rangle$, since one is a subtype of the other. These also turn out to be equivalence relations on the subsets given in Example 10.4.16.

In the recursive function interpretation of records, a record is a partial function from natural numbers, regarded as labels, to natural numbers, regarded as values. As in Example 10.4.16, we use natural numbers 0,1,2 for labels a, b and c. Then $R^{\langle a:nat, b:bool\rangle}$ is the set of all pairs $\langle d_1, d_2\rangle \in \mathcal{N} \times \mathcal{N}$ such that $\langle d_1 \cdot 0, d_2 \cdot 0\rangle \in R^{nat}$, and $\langle d_1 \cdot 1, d_2 \cdot 1\rangle \in R^{bool}$. It is easy to see that $R^{\langle a:nat, b:bool, c:char\rangle}$ is the subset of all $d \in R^{\langle a:nat, b:bool\rangle}$ with $\langle d_1 \cdot 2, d_2 \cdot 2\rangle \in R^{char}$. Thus $R^{\langle a:nat, b:bool, c:char\rangle} \subseteq R^{\langle a:nat, b:bool\rangle}$ as sets of ordered pairs. Moreover, records $\langle a = 1, b = true, c = \text{"hot"}\rangle$ and $\langle a = 1, b = true, c = \text{"cold"}\rangle$ are related by $R^{\langle a:nat, b:bool\rangle}$ since the two partial recursive functions agree on a and b. However, they are not related by $R^{\langle a:nat, b:bool, c:char\rangle}$ since they are different on c.

The subtyping rules are proved sound using essentially the same induction as in the proof of Lemma 10.4.17 (which is left to the reader).

Lemma 10.4.22 Let ρ and τ be two type expressions over signature Σ. If $\rho <: \tau$ is provable from Σ, then $R^{\rho} \subseteq R^{\tau}$ in any per interpretation $\mathcal{R}$ for Σ.

Exercise 10.4.28 asks you to check the induction step for record types, which resembles the particular record subtype instance considered in Example 10.4.21.

Type Soundness

Type soundness for a semantic model is the property that for every typed term $\Gamma \triangleright M\colon \sigma$, if every variable x in Γ is given a value of the correct semantic type, then the meaning of M is an element of type σ (see Lemma 4.5.13). For per models, the elements of a per R are the equivalence classes of values a such that $R(a, a)$. Type soundnessis therefore the property that, for any $\Gamma \triangleright M\colon \sigma$, if $R^{\tau}(\eta(x), \eta(x))$ for each $x\colon \tau \in \Gamma$, then $R^{\sigma}([\![Erase(M)]\!]\eta,\ [\![Erase(M)]\!]\eta)$. We prove type soundness by showing a slightly stronger property involving pairs of environments. We say environments η_1 and η_2 to are *related by* $\mathcal{R}$ *with respect to* Γ, written $\mathcal{R}^{\Gamma}(\eta_1, \eta_2)$, if $R^{\sigma}(\eta_1(x), \eta_2(x))$ for every $x\colon \sigma \in \Gamma$. Note that if $\mathcal{R}^{\Gamma}(\eta_1, \eta_2)$ then $\eta_1 \models \Gamma$ and $\eta_2 \models \Gamma$.

Lemma 10.4.23 Suppose $\Gamma \triangleright M\colon \tau$ is well-typed with respect to some signature. If η_1 and η_2 are environments for a *per* interpretation $\mathcal{R}$ with $\mathcal{R}^{\Gamma}(\eta_1, \eta_2)$, then

$R^{\tau}([\![Erase(M)]\!]\eta_1,\ [\![Erase(M)]\!]\eta_2)$

Proof The proof is a straightforward induction on typing derivations, as in the proof of Lemma 10.4.18. ∎

Equational Soundness

We prove equational soundness by showing the following stronger property. Although type soundness follows from this theorem, we must prove type soundness separately since we need Lemma 10.4.23 to show soundness of the equational axiom for reflexivity.

We say a relational interpretation $\mathcal{R}$ over $\mathcal{D}$ *satisfies* an equation $\Gamma \rhd M = N : \tau$ if we have $R^{\tau}([\![Erase(M)]\!]\eta_1, [\![Erase(N)]\!]\eta_2)$ for all environments η_1 and η_2 with $\mathcal{R}^{\Gamma}(\eta_1, \eta_2)$.

Theorem 10.4.24 Let $\mathcal{R}$ be a relational interpretation over λ, $\texttt{record}$-combinatory structure $\mathcal{D}$ and suppose $\Gamma \rhd M = N : \tau$ is provable from the set $\mathcal{E}$ of equations. If $\mathcal{R}$ satisfies every equation in $\mathcal{E}$, then $\mathcal{R}$ satisfies $\Gamma \rhd M = N : \tau$.

Proof We proceed by induction on the proof of $\Gamma \rhd M = N : \tau$ from $\mathcal{E}$. The theorem clearly holds if the equation is in the set $\mathcal{E}$, and by Lemma 10.4.23 if the equation is an instance of the reflexivity axiom. Axiom (α) is immediate, since this holds in the λ, $\texttt{record}$-combinatory structure $\mathcal{D}$, axiom (β) by Exercise 10.4.20 and the substitution lemma, and (*record selection*) similarly using Exercise 10.4.19. Congruence rules such as symmetry, transitivity and (ν) are also straightforward.

The remaining cases are the extensionality axioms (η) for functions and (*record ext*) for records, and rule (ξ) for functions. Since these are all similar, we show the case for (*record ext*). If $\Gamma \rhd \langle \ell_1 = M.\ell_1, \ldots, \ell_n = M.\ell_n \rangle = M : \langle \ell_1 : \tau_1, \ldots, \ell_n : \tau_n \rangle$ is an instance of this axiom, then for any environments η_1 and η_2 with $\mathcal{R}^{\Gamma}(\eta_1, \eta_2)$ we have

$$R^{\langle \ell_1:\tau_1,\ldots,\ell_n:\tau_n\rangle}([\![Erase(\langle \ell_1 = M.\ell_1, \ldots, \ell_n = M.\ell_n \rangle)]\!]\eta_1, [\![Erase(M)]\!]\eta_2)$$

$$\text{iff} \quad R^{\langle \ell_1:\tau_1,\ldots,\ell_n:\tau_n\rangle}([\![\langle \ell_1 = Erase(M).\ell_1, \ldots, \ell_n = Erase(M).\ell_n \rangle]\!]\eta_1, [\![Erase(M)]\!]\eta_2)$$

$$\text{iff} \quad \forall i \in \{1 \ldots n\},\ R^{\tau_i}([\![\langle \ell_1 = Erase(M).\ell_1, \ldots, \ell_n = Erase(M).\ell_n \rangle]\!]\eta_1.\ell_i, [\![Erase(M)]\!]\eta_2.\ell_i)$$

$$\text{iff} \quad \forall i \in \{1 \ldots n\},\ R^{\tau_i}([\![Erase(M).\ell_i]\!]\eta_1, [\![Erase(M)]\!]\eta_2.\ell_i)$$

$$\text{iff} \quad \forall i \in \{1 \ldots n\},\ R^{\tau_i}([\![Erase(M)]\!]\eta_1.\ell_i, [\![Erase(M)]\!]\eta_2.\ell_i))$$

Since the final condition follows from the soundness of the typing rules and the typing assumptions $\Gamma \rhd M_i.\ell_i : \tau_i$ for $i \in \{1 \ldots n\}$, this completes the proof. ∎

Equational Completeness without Empty Types

It is easy to see, from the way terms are interpreted, that if $Erase(M)$ and $Erase(N)$ are equal in the underlying λ, $\texttt{record}$-combinatory structure $\mathcal{D}$, then $\Gamma \rhd M = N : \tau$ will hold in every relational interpretation over $\mathcal{D}$. (This is essentially the same phenomenon as observed in Lemma 8.2.26 and Theorem 9.3.46.) We can prove a completeness theorem, showing that these are the only equations that hold in all per interpretations. This is analogous to the completeness Theorem 9.3.47 for polymorphic $\lambda^{\rightarrow,\forall}$-terms in per models. For simplicity, we prove the theorem under the assumption that no types are empty. Recall that under this assumption, the following equational proof rule from Section 4.5.5 is sound.

$$\frac{\Gamma, x\colon\sigma \rhd M = N\colon\tau}{\Gamma \rhd M = N\colon\tau}\; x \text{ not free in } M, N. \qquad (\textit{nonempty})$$

For the purposes of this theorem, we say a set $\mathcal{E}$ of equations between λ, `record`-terms is *coherent* if $\mathcal{E} \vdash \Gamma \rhd M = N\colon\tau$ whenever $\textit{Erase}(M) = \textit{Erase}(N)$ is provable from the equational axioms given in Example 10.4.15, using the standard proof rules of algebra (given in Chapter 3).

Theorem 10.4.25 Let $\mathcal{E}$ be a coherent set of equations between $\lambda_{<:}^{\rightarrow,\mathtt{record}}$-terms, containing all equations provable from $\mathcal{E}$ using the equational inference rule (*nonempty*) and other axioms and proof rules of $\lambda_{<:}^{\rightarrow,\mathtt{record}}$. Then there is a λ, `record`-combinatory structure $\mathcal{D}$, and relational interpretation $\mathcal{R}$ over $\mathcal{D}$ satisfying precisely the equations in $\mathcal{E}$.

Proof Let Σ be an algebraic signature as in Example 10.4.15, containing constants for combinators K and S and record operations *em*, *lcond* and *sel*, so that if M is a λ, `record`-term, then $\textit{Erase}(M)$ is an algebraic term over Σ. Let $\mathcal{D}$ be the Σ-term algebra over the infinite collection of variables (considered of sort D) that may appear in λ, `record`-terms, modulo the algebraic theory given in Example 10.4.15. We write $[U]$ for the equivalence class of algebraic term U. It is helpful to keep in mind that for any typed term $\Gamma \rhd M\colon\tau$, there will be algebraic terms in $[\textit{Erase}(M)]$ that are not the erasure of any typable $\lambda_{<:}^{\rightarrow,\mathtt{record}}$-term.

We construct a family of relations over $\mathcal{D}$ in the same manner as the logical relations completeness proof for $\lambda^{\rightarrow}$ given in Section 8.3.1. Let $\mathcal{H}$ be a set of *variable*: *type* pairs, providing infinitely many variables of each type, and let η be the environment that maps each variable x to its equivalence class $[x]$. We define $\mathcal{R} = \{R^{\tau_i}\}$ by

$R^{\tau}([U], [V])$ if there exist$\Gamma \rhd M\colon\tau,\ \Gamma \rhd N\colon\tau$ with

$$\Gamma \subseteq \mathcal{H},\ \textit{Erase}(M) \in [U],\ \textit{Erase}(N) \in [V] \text{ and}$$

$$\mathcal{E} \vdash \Gamma \rhd M = N\colon\tau$$

Note that $R^{\tau}([x], [x])$ if $x\colon\tau \in \mathcal{H}$ and therefore no R^{τ} is the empty relation.

It is easy to see that each R^{τ} is symmetric, but transitivity is slightly more complicated. Suppose $R^{\tau}([U], [V])$ and $R^{\tau}([V], [W])$. Then there are terms $\Gamma_1 \rhd M\colon\tau$, $\Gamma_1 \rhd N_1\colon\tau$,

$\Gamma_2 \triangleright N_2\colon \tau$ and $\Gamma_2 \triangleright P\colon \tau$ with $Erase(M) \in [U]$, $Erase(N_1)$, $Erase(N_1) \in [V]$, $Erase(P) \in [W]$ and

$$\mathcal{E} \vdash \Gamma_1 \triangleright M = N_1\colon \tau \qquad \mathcal{E} \vdash \Gamma_2 \triangleright N_2 = P\colon \tau$$

We must show that $\mathcal{E} \vdash \Gamma_3 \triangleright M = P\colon \tau$, where by (*add var*) we may take $\Gamma_3 = \Gamma_1 \cup \Gamma_2 \subseteq \mathcal{H}$. By (*trans*), it suffices to show $\mathcal{E} \vdash \Gamma_1 \triangleright N_1 = N_2\colon \tau$, but this follows from the assumption that $\mathcal{E}$ is coherent.

There are two remaining parts of the proof. The first is to show that $\mathcal{R} = \{R^{\tau_i}\}$ satisfies the conditions

$R^{b_1} \subseteq R^{b_2}$ for every $(b_1 <: b_2) \in Sub$

$d\ R^{\sigma \to \tau}\ e$ iff $\forall d', e' \in D.$ if $d'\ R^{\sigma}\ e'$ then $d \cdot d'\ R^{\tau}\ e \cdot e'$

$d\ R^{\langle \ell_1:\sigma_1,\ldots,\ell_k:\sigma_k\rangle}\ e$ iff $\forall i \in \{1, \ldots, k\}.\ d.\ell_i\ R^{\sigma_i}\ e.\ell_i$

The second part is to show that exactly the equations provable from $\mathcal{E}$ are satisfied.

Suppose $(b_1 <: b_2) \in Sub$ and $R^{b_1}([Erase(M)], [Erase(N)])$ with $\mathcal{E} \vdash \Gamma \triangleright M = N\colon b_1$. Then as shown in Example 10.2.3, we have $\mathcal{E} \vdash \Gamma \triangleright M = N\colon b_2$ and therefore $R^{b_2}([Erase(M)], [Erase(N)])$. The conditions on $R^{\sigma \to \tau}$ and $R^{\langle \ell_1:\sigma_1,\ldots,\ell_k:\sigma_k\rangle}$ are left as Exercise 10.4.29.

We show that exactly the equations provable from $\mathcal{E}$ are satisfied using the same argument as in the proof of Theorem 8.3.2. This completes the proof. ∎

Exercise 10.4.26 Show that if $A \cong C$ and $B \cong D$ then $\langle \ell\colon A, \ell'\colon B\rangle \cong \langle \ell\colon C, \ell'\colon D\rangle$.

Exercise 10.4.27 In Example 10.4.21, we have $bool <: nat$, essentially by accident. Give an alternative per, $bool'$, for booleans such that $bool' \cong bool$ but $bool' \not<: nat$. Can you find such a $bool'$ with only one proper supertype?

Exercise 10.4.28 Prove the record type case of Lemma 10.4.22

Exercise 10.4.29 Prove the conditions on $R^{\sigma \to \tau}$ and $R^{\langle \ell_1:\sigma_1,\ldots,\ell_k:\sigma_k\rangle}$ required in the proof of Theorem 10.4.25.

10.5 Recursive Types and a Record Model of Objects

While subtyping adds some useful flexibility to type systems for records and functions, object-oriented styles of programming require more expressive type systems. In this section, we begin the study of objects using records with function components. The main idea is that we represent an object by a record of "method results," in such a way that selecting a component of a record returns the same value as sending the corresponding message to an object. For methods with parameters, record selection will return a function. Since we use a function calculus without side-effects, object identity and manipulation of "instance variables" are simpler than they might be in imperative programming languages. This relatively simple model is a not as comprehensive as some more recent proposals [AC94b, AC94a, Bru94, FHM94], but it does provide some feel for the way that object-oriented concepts may be studied using typed lambda calculus.

In object-oriented programming, the types of objects are often recursively defined. A simple example is the type *point* of points with integer x and y coordinates and a *move* function. Written as a record type, *point* could be given by the recursive declaration

$$\texttt{type}\ point\ =\ \langle x\colon int,\ y\colon int,\ move\colon int \to int \to point\rangle$$

One motivation for object-oriented programming is that point objects may each contain specialized methods that behave in different manners. For example, if we have "oriented" points with x, y coordinates and a direction, each oriented point could have a *move* method that preserves its orientation. A function intended to manipulate ordinary points with only x and y coordinates would then have a reasonable effect on directed points, since each directed point would be moved by its own specialized *move* function. We will see that this phenomenon, sometimes called *late binding* or *dynamic lookup* of methods, can be simulated using recursively-defined records. For further information on this feature, and other pragmatic aspects of object-oriented programming, the reader may consult books such as [Boo91, GR83, Str86].

We can write the type *point* in $\lambda_{<:}^{\to,\texttt{record}}$ if we extend the type expressions with type variables and the recursive form $\mu t.\tau$. The resulting language, $\lambda_{<:}^{\to,\texttt{record},\mu}$, has type expressions of the form

$$\tau\ ::=\ t \mid b \mid \tau \to \tau \mid \langle \ell_1\colon \tau_1, \ldots, \ell_k\colon \tau_k\rangle \mid \mu t.\tau$$

Intuitively, as discussed in Section 2.6.3, $\mu t.\tau$ is the type t defined by the recursive condition $t = \tau$, where typically t will occur in τ. With this syntax, we may regard *point* above as syntactic sugar for the type

$$point\ \stackrel{\text{def}}{=}\ \mu t.\,\langle x\colon int,\ y\colon int,\ move\colon int \to int \to t\rangle$$

For readability, we will often define recursive types by writing a declaration of the form $\texttt{type}\ t = \tau$, with the understanding that t will then be regarded as syntactic sugar for $\mu t.\tau$. Since μ is a binding operator, we have the equational axiom

$$\mu t.\tau\ =\ \mu s.\,[s/t]\tau \quad s \text{ not free in } \tau \qquad (\alpha)_\mu$$

where substitution involves renaming of bound variables as usual.

As discussed in Section 2.6.3, there are two basic approaches to recursive types, one using the type equation

$$\mu t.\,\tau \;=\; [\mu t.\,\tau/t]\tau \qquad \textit{(unfold)}$$

and the second an isomorphism between $\mu t.\,\tau$ and $[\mu t.\,\tau/t]\tau$ given by term operations up and dn. The term-formation rules associated with the second approach are

$$\frac{\Gamma \rhd M\colon [\mu t.\tau/t]\tau}{\Gamma \rhd \mathrm{up}\, M\colon \mu t.\tau} \qquad (\mu\ \textit{Intro})$$

$$\frac{\Gamma \rhd M\colon \mu t.\tau}{\Gamma \rhd \mathrm{dn}\, M\colon [\mu t.\tau/t]\tau} \qquad (\mu\ \textit{Elim})$$

These allow us to map any term of type $\mu t.\tau$ to a term with type $[\mu t.\tau/t]\tau$, and vice versa. The equations (up/dn) associated with up and dn are discussed in Section 2.6.3. With the type equation (*unfold*), the operators up and dn and therefore typing rules (μ *Intro*) and (μ *Elim*) are superfluous.

In both approaches to recursive types, we can select components of a value of type *point*. Specifically, if $pt : point \equiv \mu t.\,\langle x\colon int,\ y\colon int,\ move\colon int \to int \to t\rangle$, then using the type equation (*unfold*) we have

$$pt : \langle x\colon int,\ y\colon int,\ move\colon int \to int \to point\rangle$$

and therefore $pt.move : int \to int \to point$. Alternatively, we could use $pt : point$ and (μ *Elim*) to derive

$$(\mathrm{dn}\, pt) : \langle x\colon int,\ y\colon int,\ move\colon int \to int \to point\rangle$$

and therefore $(\mathrm{dn}\, pt).move : int \to int \to point$.

For simplicity, we will adopt the first view of recursive types in the rest of this section. More specifically, we assume that there is some theory of type equality, including at least α-conversion and (*unfold*), and that if a term may be assigned one type, it may be assigned any equal type. In some cases, it is possible to also adopt the second explicit-isomorphism view that is used in Chapter 2, regarding example terms with recursive types as abbreviations for expressions with missing up's and dn's inserted. For $pt.move$ and other record selections, it is generally a straightforward process to add up and dn according to the typing derivation of the term. On the other hand, a significant difference between axiom (*unfold*) and explicit term operations up and dn arises in connection with subtyping, as discussed below. In particular, the use of F-bounded polymorphism for object polymorphism and inheritance, discussed in Section 10.6, relies on (*unfold*).

Intuitively, *pt*.*move* 2 3 is a point similar to *pt*, except that the x and y coordinates have been incremented by 2 and 3, respectively. In the following example, we show how to define a point with this behavior, using the language $\lambda_{<:}^{\to,\mathtt{record},\mu}$ with recursive types.

Example 10.5.1 Using a generic syntax intended to suggest existing object-oriented programming languages (with Curried functions for easy translation into lambda calculus), we might define a point "class" by writing

```
class point
  instance variables
           xval:int, yval:int
  constructor point(xv:int)(yv:int)
           xval=xv, yval=yv
  method x : int
           return xval
  method y : int
           return yval
  method move(dx:int)(dy:int) : point
           return point(self.x + dx)(self.y + dy)
  end
```

In typed object-oriented languages such as C++ [ES90] and Eiffel [Mey92b], a class defines both a type and a function for creating objects. In our treatment of object-oriented languages, we will separate these two notions, writing the types of objects as record types, and the functions that create objects as functions returning records. The way we represent objects by records is sometimes called the "record model of objects." The main idea was first explored mathematically in [Car84], with a number of important advances pioneered in [Coo89].

When we represent objects by records, the type of point objects is the recursive record type

$$\mathtt{type}\ point\ =\ \langle x\colon int,\ y\colon int,\ move\colon int \to int \to point\rangle$$

We may define a function creating points of this type using recursion as follows:

$$\mathtt{letrec}\ mk\_point(xv\colon int)(yv\colon int)\ =$$

$$\langle x = xv,\ y = yv,\ move = \lambda dx\colon int.\,\lambda dy\colon int.\, mk\_point(xv + dx)(yv + dy)\rangle$$

Although this declaration is relatively easy to read, it may not be immediately clear that we can write the function *mk_point* in $\lambda_{<:}^{\to,\mathtt{record},\mu}$. However, as shown in Section 2.6.3, we may define a fixed point operator of each type using recursive types. Therefore, we may write a term

$$\mathit{fix}\colon ((\mathit{int} \to \mathit{int} \to \mathit{point}) \to (\mathit{int} \to \mathit{int} \to \mathit{point})) \to (\mathit{int} \to \mathit{int} \to \mathit{point})$$

of the type needed to define *mk_point*, and rewrite *mk_point* as

$$\begin{aligned} \mathit{mk\_point} \stackrel{\text{def}}{=}\ & \mathit{fix}(\,\lambda f\colon \mathit{int} \to \mathit{int} \to \mathit{point}.\,\lambda xv\colon \mathit{int}.\,\lambda yv\colon \mathit{int}. \\ & \quad \langle x = xv,\ y = yv,\ \mathit{move} = \lambda dx\colon \mathit{int}.\,\lambda dy\colon \mathit{int}.\ f(xv + dx)(yv + dy)\rangle\,) \end{aligned}$$

Since the argument of *fix* is a straightforward lambda expression of $\lambda_{<:}^{\to,\mathtt{record}}$, it should be easy to see that *mk_point* is definable in $\lambda_{<:}^{\to,\mathtt{record},\mu}$.

We complete the example by showing how to find the result of "sending a message" to a point object. In the record model of objects, we send a message to an object simply by selecting a component of the recursively-defined record. The most interesting case for points is *move*, which works as follows.

$$\begin{aligned} & (\mathit{mk\_point}\ 3\ 2).\mathit{move}\ 4\ 6 \\ =\ & \mathit{fix}(\lambda f\colon (\mathit{int} \to \mathit{int} \to \mathit{point}.\,\lambda xv\colon \mathit{int}.\,\lambda yv\colon \mathit{int}. \\ & \quad \langle x = xv,\ y = yv,\ \mathit{move} = \lambda dx\colon \mathit{int}.\,\lambda dy\colon \mathit{int}.\ f(xv + dx)(yv + dy)\rangle)\ 3\ 2).\mathit{move}\ 4\ 6 \\ =\ & ((\lambda xv\colon \mathit{int}.\,\lambda yv\colon \mathit{int}.\langle x = xv,\ y = yv, \\ & \quad \mathit{move} = \lambda dx\colon \mathit{int}.\,\lambda dy\colon \mathit{int}.(\mathit{fix}(\ldots))(xv + dx)(yv + dy)\rangle)\ 3\ 2).\mathit{move}\ 4\ 6 \\ =\ & \langle x = 3,\ y = 2,\ \mathit{move} = \lambda dx\colon \mathit{int}.\,\lambda dy\colon \mathit{int}.(\mathit{fix}(\ldots))(3 + dx)(2 + dy)\rangle.\mathit{move}\ 4\ 6 \\ =\ & (\lambda dx\colon \mathit{int}.\,\lambda dy\colon \mathit{int}.(\mathit{fix}(\ldots))(3 + dx)(2 + dy))\ 4\ 6 \\ =\ & (\mathit{fix}(\ldots))(3 + 4)(2 + 6) \\ =\ & \langle x = 7,\ y = 8,\ \mathit{move} = \lambda dx\colon \mathit{int}.\,\lambda dy\colon \mathit{int}.(\mathit{fix}(\ldots))(7 + dx)(8 + dy)\rangle \end{aligned}$$

In words, we evaluate (*mk_point* 3 2)*.move* 4 6 by first "unfolding" the recursive definition of *mk_point* 3 2 to get the record with $x = 3$ and $y = 2$ that appears in the third step of the calculation. Selecting the *move* component gives a function that is applied to 4 and 6. The result of this function application is the record with $x = 7$ and $y = 8$ given in the last line. ■

Subtyping for Recursive Types

Before giving the subtyping rules for recursive types, we consider some intuitive examples. The first concerns the type *point* defined above, and the following type of colored points:

type $col\_point = \langle x\colon int,\ y\colon int,\ c\colon color,\ move\colon int \to int \to col\_point\rangle$

There are two differences between points and colored points. The first is that each colored point has a c component of type *color*, intended to give the color of the point. The second is that when we move a colored point, as in the expression

$c\_pt.move\ 2\ 3$

where $c\_pt\colon col\_point$, we obtain a colored point instead of a point. This is reflected in the type of *move* in *col_point*. In spite of the change in the type of *move*, we expect *col_point* to be a subtype of *point*. An intuitive argument may be based on substitutivity; we will later justify this by formal semantics. If we have an expression containing *pt* with $pt\colon point$, this expression might involve $pt.x$, $pt.y$ and $pt.move$. In each of these cases, we would get a "type compatible" expression if we replace *pt* with *c_pt* of type *col_point*. This is clear for $pt.x$ and $pt.y$, since the types are the same in both cases. The "compatibility" of $pt.move$ and $c\_pt.move$ may be understood by considering sequences of operations. We cannot get an immediate type error from $c\_pt.move$, since this function has the same argument types as $pt.move$. So the only way to eventually get a type error would be to select the x or y component of the result of applying $c\_pt.move$ to two integer arguments. But since points and colored points have the same type of x and y components, this cannot produce a type error.

A second example illustrates the subtlety of subtyping, showing that subtyping may fail between apparently similar recursive record types. The basic phenomenon can be illustrated by adding equality components (or methods) to points and colored points, as shown below in Example 10.5.3. For variety, we will also describe this using two kinds of set objects. The first has membership test, an insert operation and an intersection operation. The second also has an operation returning the number of elements in the set. In more detail, we consider the two recursive record types

$$\begin{aligned}
\texttt{type}\ simple_set = \langle & member?\colon elt \to bool,\\
& insert\colon elt \to simple_set,\\
& intersect\colon simple_set \to simple_set\rangle\\
\texttt{type}\ sized_set = \langle & member?\colon elt \to bool,\\
& insert\colon elt \to sized_set,\\
& intersect\colon sized_set \to sized_set,\\
& size\colon int\rangle
\end{aligned}$$

whose elements are "sets" with various operations. Although it is possible to define records with these types that do not behave at all like sets, we give some intuition for these types by explaining the intended meaning of each operation. If s: *simple_set* or s: *sized_set* and x: *elt* is a potential member of s, then s.*member*? x will be *true* if x is an element of s, and *false* otherwise. The operation s.*insert* x will produce a set of the same type, with x as a member. If s, t: *simple_set* are two simple sets, then s.*intersect* t would be a simple set representing the intersection of s and t. Similarly, if s, t: *sized_set* are two sized sets, then s.*intersect* t would be a sized set representing the intersection of s and t. An important part of this example is that the domain of function s.*intersect* is *simple_set* if s: *simple_set* and *sized_set* if s: *sized_set*. A sized set also has a *size* component, intended to return the number of elements in the set.

By analogy with points and colored points, we might expect *sized_set* to be a subtype of *simple_set*. More specifically, the main difference between *sized_set* and *simple_set* is that *sized_set*'s have an additional *size* operation. Therefore, we might at first expect *sized_set*'s to be substitutable for *simple_set*'s. However, the important difference between this example and points and colored points (discussed above) is that the argument type for *intersect* is different, whereas with points and colored points, the only difference is in the result type of a function component.

We will give an intuitive explanation of the failure of subtyping using substitutivity. Suppose that s, t: *simple_set* and let r: *sized_set* be a sized set. If we have an expression

s.*intersect* t

computing the intersection of two simple sets and replace s by a sized set r, then we have the expression

r.*intersect* t

However, this expression intersecting a *sized_set* with a simple set could produce a run-time type error by selecting a record component that does not exist. We can see how this might happen by considering an implementation for set intersection.

In a reasonable implementation of intersection for sized sets, the *intersect* function of r might apply t.*member*? to each element of r, collecting together the elements that appear in both sets. A problem arises, however, if the implementation of r.*intersect* uses the operation t.*size* to find the number of elements of t. (This would be useful if, for example, r had many elements but t turned out to have very few. In this case, the algorithm implementing intersection could stop after t.*size* elements of the intersection were found.) Since the type of r.*intersect* is *sized_set* $\rightarrow$ *sized_set*, it would be reasonable for the code for r.*intersect* to assume it is passed a sized set t as an actual parameter, making t.*size* a legal operation. However, in the expression $r.intersect\, t$ above, the type of t is only *simple_set*, and therefore $t.size$ could produce a run-time type error. In summary, the type declaration for *sized_set* allows $r.intersect$ to ask the size of its argument, and this prevents *sized_set*'s from being substitutable for *simple_set*'s. Therefore, we could *not* safely have *sized_set* <: *simple_set*.

A pragmatic solution to the incompatibility between *sized_set* and *simple_set* would be to define sized sets by

$$\texttt{type}\ sized\_set' = \langle member?\colon elt \to bool,\quad insert\colon elt \to sized\_set',\quad intersect\colon simple\_set \to sized\_set',\quad size\colon int\rangle$$

with *intersect* operation only requiring a simple set. Intuitively, this change in the type of *intersect* means that the *intersect* function component of a *sized_set* only requires an argument with *member?*, *insert* and *intersect* operations. With this change, we have $sized\_set' <: simple\_set$, as shown in Exercise 10.5.6.

Formally, the simplest way to characterize subtyping with recursive types is through a combination of equational rules and subtyping rules. In any use of recursive types, we have an equational axiom $(\alpha)_\mu$, mentioned above, for renaming bound type variables. In some circumstances, we may adopt the type equation (*unfold*); for algorithmic reasons we might also prefer to omit this rule and obtain a simpler typing theory. Some additional equational principles for recursive types are discussed in Exercise 10.5.7.

Given an equational theory for types, we need one inference rule for introducing equations into subtyping assertions and one rule for recursive types. For $\lambda_{<:}^{\to,\mathtt{record},\mu}$, these are combined with the (*trans* <:) and (→ <:) rules of Section 10.2 and the (*record* <:) rule in Section 10.3. The equality rule is

$$\frac{\sigma = \tau}{\sigma <: \tau} \qquad (= <:)$$

The subtyping rule for recursive types is written using a set Δ of subtyping hypotheses of the form $t <: \tau$, where t is a type variable. We write $\Delta \vdash \tau <: \tau'$ to indicate that $\tau <: \tau'$ is provable from hypotheses in Δ, combined with subtyping hypothesis about type constants given in the signature of the language. The subtyping rule

$$\frac{\Delta, s <: t \vdash \sigma <: \tau}{\Delta \vdash \mu s.\sigma <: \mu t.\tau}\ t \text{ not free in } \sigma,\ s \text{ not free in } \tau \qquad (\mu\ <:)$$

for recursive types requires that $\sigma <: \tau$ follows from the assumption $s <: t$ about type variables. This rule was first proposed in [Car86] for the experimental programming language Amber. A comprehensive study of subtyping in the presence of a strong form of type equality appears in [AC91]. A simpler-looking unsound rule is shown in Exercise 10.5.5 for comparison.

Example 10.5.2 We can prove $col\_point <: point$ using the subtyping rules for records and recursive types. As an aid to readability, we use suggestive names *point* and *col_point* for type variables. Looking at the $(\mu\ <:)$ rule, we can see that the last step must have the form

$$\frac{col\_point <: point \vdash \begin{array}{l}\langle x\colon int,\ y\colon int,\ move\colon int \to int \to col\_point,\ c\colon color\rangle \\ <: \quad \langle x\colon int,\ y\colon int,\ move\colon int \to int \to point\rangle\end{array}}{\mu\, col\_point.\, \langle \ldots \rangle <: \mu\, point.\, \langle \ldots \rangle}$$

By the record subtyping rule, it suffices to show that $int <: int$, which is immediate by reflexivity of subtyping, and

$$col\_point <: point \vdash int \to (int \to col\_point) <: int \to (int \to point)$$

which is easily proved using reflexivity, and the hypothesis $col\_point <: point$, by two applications of the $(\to\ <:)$ rule. ∎

Example 10.5.3 If we add an equality component (method) to points and colored points, then subtyping fails. For simplicity, we define these recursive record types without *move* as follows:

`type` $eq\_point \quad = \langle x\colon int,\ y\colon int,\ eq\colon eq\_point \to bool\rangle$

`type` $eq\_col\_point = \langle x\colon int,\ y\colon int,\ eq\colon eq\_col\_point \to bool,\ c\colon color\rangle$

We can see why $eq\_col\_point <: eq\_point$ is not provable by considering the way we might try to prove $eq\_col\_point <: eq\_point$ using the subtyping rules for records and recursive types. Looking at the $(\mu\ <:)$ rule, we can see that *if* this were provable, the last step would have the form

$$\frac{eq\_col\_point <: eq\_point \vdash \begin{array}{l}\langle x\colon int,\ y\colon int,\ eq\colon eq\_col\_point \to bool,\ c\colon color\rangle \\ <: \quad \langle x\colon int,\ y\colon int,\ eq\colon eq\_point \to bool\rangle\end{array}}{\mu\, eq\_col\_point.\, \langle \ldots \rangle <: \mu\, eq\_point.\, \langle \ldots \rangle}$$

By the record subtyping rule, we would have to show that $int <: int$, which is immediate by reflexivity of subtyping, and

$$eq\_col\_point <: eq\_point \vdash (eq\_col\_point \to bool) <: (eq\_point \to bool)$$

which requires showing

$$eq\_col\_point <: eq\_point \vdash eq\_point <: eq\_col\_point$$

In other words, we can only show that $eq\_col\_point <: eq\_point$ if we can in the process show that each type is a subtype of the other. However, these types cannot be subtyped of each other since one has a *color* component and the other does not.

Inheritance

Inheritance is a mechanism for reusing the implementation of objects. Typically, we would like to define one kind of object from another by adding new methods and/or redefining existing methods. A very simple example is that once we have implemented point objects by defining the *mk_point* function of Example 10.5.1, we have implemented x, y-coordinates and a *move* function in a way that could also be useful for colored points. However, the *mk_point* function is not written in a way that makes it possible to reuse parts of it in the definition of a related *mk_col_point* function for colored points. Ideally, we would like to define *mk_col_point* by specifying only the additional components required for colored points. Although we will see that some of the type constraints of $\lambda_{<:}^{\rightarrow,\mathtt{record},\mu}$ intrude, we can clarify the issues and motivate a polymorphic extension of $\lambda_{<:}^{\rightarrow,\mathtt{record},\mu}$ by setting out the framework for implementing colored points from points in a systematic way. The sketch given here is completed in Section 10.6.

A crucial issue in modeling inheritance is the way that inheritance interacts with dynamic method lookup (also called late binding). Suppose we have objects of some type, with methods f and g that are implemented as mutually-recursive functions; invoking method f may cause g to be invoked, and conversely. If we define another type of object using inheritance, and redefine method g, say, then in the new objects, the "old" method f (obtained via inheritance) will be mutually recursive with the "new" method g. As a result, the behavior of the new objects (the ones defined via inheritance) will depend on the *way* that f and g depend on each other.

A general approach that allows interaction between inheritance and dynamic lookup involves defining each constructor function (such as *mk_point*) as the application of *fix* to a function called a *generator*. The purpose of doing so is that the generator explicitly represents the way that different methods of the object may depend on each other. For points, we therefore re-define *mk_point* as follows:

$$mk\_point \stackrel{\mathrm{def}}{=} fix(point\_gen)$$

$$point\_gen \stackrel{\mathrm{def}}{=} \lambda f\colon int \rightarrow int \rightarrow point.\, \lambda xv\colon int.\, \lambda yv\colon int.$$

$$\langle x = xv,\ y = yv,\ move = \lambda dx\colon int.\, \lambda dy\colon int.\, f\,(xv + dx)(yv + dy)\rangle$$

For colored points, we can write similar definitions.

$$mk\_col\_point \stackrel{\text{def}}{=} fix(col\_point\_gen)$$

$$col\_point\_gen \stackrel{\text{def}}{=} \lambda f\colon int \to int \to color \to point.\ \lambda xv\colon int.\ \lambda yv\colon int.\ \lambda cv\colon color.$$
$$\langle x = xv,\ y = yv,\ c = cv,\ move = \lambda dx\colon int.\ \lambda dy\colon int.\ f(xv + dx)(yv + dy)(cv)\rangle$$

This shows how we can implement colored points according to the same general pattern, but without inheritance. In the record model of objects, inheritance is formulated as a way of defining one "generator" from another. In particular, we will see how to define *col_point_gen* from *point_gen* in Section 10.6, using a sophisticated form of polymorphism and a record-extension primitive.

Exercise 10.5.4 Show that the following type of "movable records,"

$$\texttt{type}\ movable = \langle move\colon int \to int \to movable\rangle$$

is a supertype of *point*, given at the beginning of this section.

Exercise 10.5.5 Explain why the alternative subtyping rule

$$\frac{\Delta \vdash \sigma <: \tau}{\Delta \vdash \mu t.\sigma <: \mu t.\tau}\ t \text{ not in } \Delta \qquad (\mu\ <:)_{unsound}$$

is not semantically sound. (*Hint:* Consider $\tau \equiv t \to int$.)

Exercise 10.5.6 Show that $sized\_set' <: simple\_set$ using the proof rule for recursive record types.

Exercise 10.5.7 A natural equivalence is that two recursive types are equal if they have the same infinite unfolding. For example, $\mu t.\, nat \to t$ has the infinite unfolding

$$\mu t.\, nat \to t = nat \to (\mu t.\, nat \to t) = nat \to nat \to nat \to \ldots$$

This is the same as the infinite unfolding of $\mu t.\, nat \to (nat \to t)$, this view leads to the equation $\mu t.\, nat \to t = \mu t.\, nat \to (nat \to t)$.

A complete axiom system for infinite-expansion-equality can be formulated using the (*unfold*) rule, axiom for a least type $\bot$

$$\mu t.t = \bot \qquad (\mu\ \bot)$$

and a rule

$$\frac{\sigma = [\sigma/t]\tau}{\sigma = \mu t.\,\tau}\quad \tau \text{ "contractive" in } t \qquad (\mu\ unique)$$

based on the idea that $\mu t.\tau$ is the unique type satisfying $\mu t.\tau = [\mu t.\tau/t]\tau$. The side condition is that we must be able to unfold τ to a form which is not the type variable t and does not begin with μ. More specifically, we say τ *is contractive in t* if either t is not free in τ or $(unfold) \vdash \tau = \tau_1 \to \tau_2$ or $(unfold) \vdash \tau = \langle \ell_1 \colon \tau_1, \ldots, \ell_k \colon \tau_k \rangle$. (The name "contractive" comes from a metric-space interpretation of types.) For subtyping with $\bot$, we also have the axiom

$$\bot <: \tau \qquad (\bot <:)$$

Prove the following assertions using the axioms and rules here, together with subtyping rules for function, record and recursive types discussed in this section:

(a) $\mu s.\,\mu t.\, s \to t = \mu t.\, t \to t$

(b) $\mu s.\,\mu t.\, t \to t = \mu t.\,\mu s.\, t \to t$

(c) $\mu t.\, nat \to t = \mu t.\, nat \to (nat \to t)$

(d) $\mu t.(t- > t)- > t = \mu t.t- > (t- > t)$.

(e) $\mu t.\, int \to t <: \mu t.\, nat \to (nat \to t)$, assuming $nat <: int$

(f) $\mu t.\, t \to t <: (\mu t.t) \to (\mu t.\, t \to (t \to t))$

10.6 Polymorphism with Subtype Constraints

The polymorphic functions described in Chapter 9 are functions whose domain is the collection of all types, or all types from some universe. Using subtyping, we may define more specific polymorphic functions, each applicable to all subtypes of a given type. The reason for considering this form of polymorphism is that since subtypes generally share some structural properties, polymorphic functions with restricted type domains may take advantage of known properties of their type arguments. This is illustrated below by a series of examples.

The first example illustrates the general idea in an essentially trivial way. If t is a subtype of the record type $\langle print \colon string \rangle$, then every element of type t must be a record that has a *print* component of type *string*. Therefore, if $x \colon t$ and $t <: \langle print \colon string \rangle$, the expression $x.print$ has type *string*. The term

$$P \stackrel{\text{def}}{=} \lambda t <: \langle print \colon string \rangle.\, \lambda x \colon t.\, x.print$$

defines a function whose domain is the collection of subtypes of $\langle print \colon string \rangle$. The type of this function is written

$$\Pi t <: \langle print \colon string \rangle.\, t \to string$$

using a subtype restriction on the bound type variable. This is called a "subtype-bounded polymorphic type," or "bounded polymorphic type" for short. We may apply P to any subtype of $\langle print\colon string\rangle$, such as $\langle x\colon int, print\colon string\rangle$. The type of an application is determined using substitution, as usual:

$$\begin{aligned} P\ \langle x\colon int, print\colon string\rangle &: [\langle x\colon int, print\colon string\rangle / t](t \rightarrow string) \\ &: \langle x\colon int, print\colon string\rangle \rightarrow string \end{aligned}$$

and the value of an application may be computed using β-reduction as for other types of polymorphic functions. In particular, the application above gives $\lambda x\colon \langle x\colon int, print\colon string\rangle.\ x.print$.

This example does not really illustrate the expressiveness of bounded polymorphism since the function P is no more useful than the simpler function $\lambda x\colon \langle print\colon string\rangle.\ x.print$. By (*subsumption*), we could use the second function in any context we could apply the first, without the added necessity of applying to a type argument. One might wonder whether we could use bounded polymorphism in place of subsumption. However, this does not appear possible since we cannot type the expression P without using subsumption to show that if $x\colon t$ then $x.print$ is well-typed.

The reason why bounded polymorphism actually allows more expressive typing of expressions is that by using type variables, we can give a more explicit connection between the types of function arguments and the types of results. An example illustrating this is given after the formal typing rules. Bounded polymorphism may be considered in either a predicative or impredicative context, by essentially the same typing rules for terms. Since the impredicative case arises from the predicative one by adding a rule relating universes, we give the context rules appropriate to the predicative case here.

The syntactic typing rules for bounded polymorphism are similar to ordinary polymorphism, but require subtyping hypotheses in contexts. If we begin with the original, full formalization of $\lambda^{\rightarrow,\Pi}$ given in Section 9.2, we need the context rule

$$\frac{\Gamma \rhd \tau\colon U_1}{\Gamma, t <: \tau \text{ context}}\ t \text{ not in } \Gamma \qquad (<:\ context)$$

for adding subtyping hypotheses to contexts, and the converse rule

$$\frac{\Gamma, t <: \tau \text{ context}}{\Gamma, t <: \tau \rhd t <: \tau}$$

for extracting assertions from the context. Note that the side condition in ($<:$ *context*) allows only one subtype assumption for each type variable. It is possible to generalize this and allow more than one subtyping assumption, with the type-binding forms generalized appropriately. For simplicity, however, we will stick with the simpler case illustrated here.

The typing rules for terms provide lambda abstraction of type variables and application to type arguments that satisfy the subtype conditions.

$$\frac{\Gamma, t <: \tau \triangleright M\colon \sigma}{\Gamma \triangleright \lambda t <: \tau .\, M\colon \Pi t <: \tau .\, \sigma} \qquad (\Pi <:\ \mathit{Intro})$$

$$\frac{\Gamma \triangleright M\colon \Pi t <: \tau .\, \sigma \qquad \Gamma \vdash \rho <: \tau}{\Gamma \triangleright M\rho\colon [\rho/t]\sigma} \qquad (\Pi <:\ \mathit{Elim})$$

The standard equational rules are (α), (β) and (η), as for other types of polymorphic functions. There are also a variety of additional equational principles that could be adopted, some related to parametricity (see Section 9.3.2). However, we leave it to the interested reader to consult the literature on this topic (*e.g.*, [CMMS94, LMS93]).

Example 10.6.1 This example shows a form of conditional function that could not be written in without bounded polymorphism. The type

$$\mathit{testable} \stackrel{\text{def}}{=} \langle \mathit{test}\colon \mathit{bool} \rangle$$

of "testable records" would not be very useful by itself, since records of this type have only one boolean component. However, type *testable* will be useful in the subtype constraint. Let F be the function

$$F \stackrel{\text{def}}{=} \lambda t <: \mathit{testable}.\, \lambda x\colon t.\, \lambda y\colon t.\, \texttt{if}\ x.\mathit{test}\ \texttt{then}\ x\ \texttt{else}\ y$$

$$:\quad \Pi t <: \mathit{testable}.\, t \to t \to t$$

with a bounded polymorphic type. The reader may wish to verify the typing of F using the rules above. We can see the effect of subtype-bounded polymorphism by comparing F with the similar function

$$G \stackrel{\text{def}}{=} \lambda x\colon \mathit{testable}.\, \lambda y\colon \mathit{testable}.\, \texttt{if}\ x.\mathit{test}\ \texttt{then}\ x\ \texttt{else}\ y$$

$$:\quad \mathit{testable} \to \mathit{testable} \to \mathit{testable}$$

which may be applied to the same types of arguments, by subsumption. Suppose x and y belong to a subtype

$$\texttt{type}\ \mathit{testable\_point} = \langle \mathit{test}\colon \mathit{bool}, x\colon \mathit{int}, y\colon \mathit{int}, \mathit{move}\colon \mathit{int} \to \mathit{int} \to \mathit{testable\_point} \rangle$$

The difference between F and G is that in the bounded polymorphic case, the result of the function application will have type *testable_point*, and so we may write

$$(F\ \mathit{testable\_point}\ x\ y).\mathit{move}\ 2\ 3$$

The reader may wish to verify this using the rules above. In contrast, if we apply G to x and y, the result

$$G\,x\,y : \mathit{testable}$$

will only have type *testable*. Therefore, $(G\,x\,y)\mathbf{.}\mathit{move}\,2\,3$ is not well-typed, even though it seems semantically sensible if we ignore typing constraints. In summary, the reason the bounded polymorphic typing of F is useful is that it allows us to apply F to records of subtypes of *testable*, without leading to any loss of type information. The result has the same static type as both arguments, whereas the related function G using subsumption results in loss of type information. ■

Two additional examples illustrate limitations of subtype-bounded polymorphism and motivate two possible extensions.

Example 10.6.2 Since elements of any subtype of *point* have a *move* component, we might want to write a general function that moves points (from any subtype) in a particular way. To give a simple example, we will move points two units in each direction. Intuitively, we might expect to write a *move2* function using the expression

$$\mathit{move2} \stackrel{\text{def}}{=} \lambda t <: \mathit{point}.\,\lambda x\!: t.\,x\mathbf{.}\mathit{move}\,2\,2$$

and give this function type

$$\Pi t <: \mathit{point}.\, t \to t.$$

This seems reasonable since any subtype of *point* must provide a move function. However, this type is not correct. We can see why *move2* does not have type $\Pi t <: \mathit{point}.\, t \to t$ by attempting to type the expression. (The definition of *point* appears on page 740.)

Suppose $t <: \mathit{point}$ and $x\!: t$. By subsumption, we have $x\!: \mathit{point}$ and therefore

$$x\mathbf{.}\mathit{move} : \mathit{int} \to \mathit{int} \to \mathit{point}$$

Consequently, $x\mathbf{.}\mathit{move}\,2\,2 : \mathit{point}$ and the best subtype-bounded type we can give for *move2* is

$$\mathit{move2} : \Pi t <: \mathit{point}.\, t \to \mathit{point}$$

An informal semantic argument suggests that it would be unsound to strengthen the typing rules so that *move2* would have $\Pi t <: \mathit{point}.\, t \to t$. In a containment interpretation of subtyping, any subset of *point* would be a subtype. This includes singleton subsets. If x is an element of type *point,* and $t_x <: \mathit{point}$ is the type containing only x, then the result of applying any function f with type $\Pi t <: \mathit{point}.\, t \to t$ to t_x and x would have to have type

t_x. However, since the only element of t_x is x, this means that if $f : \Pi t <: point.\, t \to t$, then $f\ t_x\ x = x$. But since *move2* is not the identity function, *move2* therefore cannot have type $\Pi t <: point.\, t \to t$. ∎

Example 10.6.3 With subtype-bounded polymorphism, we might hope to write a form of sorting function that is applicable to any list of records, as long as each record contains a less-than-or-equal-to function for comparing itself to other records in the list. Unfortunately, this is not quite possible. However, either of two extensions considered later in this section allow us to complete this example.

By analogy with the type of "testable" records in Example 10.6.1, we begin with a type whose elements are records with a comparison function, called *less*:

$$\texttt{type}\ ordered = \langle less\colon ordered \to bool\rangle$$

Note that *ordered* is defined recursively. This is an important difference from Example 10.6.1.

We may attempt to write a sorting function with the type

$$sort : \Pi t <: ordered.\, list(t) \to list(t)$$

where $list(t)$ is the type of lists of elements of type t. It is possible to define a sort function with this type, assuming a polymorphic fixed-point operator (for recursion) and polymorphic list operations. However, this function is not as useful as might be expected. The reason is that since *ordered* occurs to the left of the $\to$ in the type of *less*, the type *ordered* does not have the subtypes we would like. For example, consider the type

$$\texttt{type}\ string = \langle less\colon string \to bool,\ concat\colon string \to string,\ first\colon letter,\ rest\colon string\rangle$$

of strings with a *less* function. We would like to sort lists of strings using a polymorphic sorting function, but *string* is not a subtype of *ordered*. (The intuitive reason is essentially the same as for *simple_set* and *sized_set*, as described on page 745; see also Example 10.5.3.) If we try to derive $string <: ordered$ using the subtyping rule, we would need to show that

$$\begin{array}{ll} & \langle less\colon string \to bool,\ concat\colon string \to string,\ first\colon letter,\ rest\colon string\rangle \\ string <: ordered \vdash & \\ & <:\quad \langle less\colon ordered \to bool\rangle \end{array}$$

However, the hypothesis $string <: ordered$ gives us $ordered \to bool <: string \to bool$, which is the opposite of what we need. Therefore, we cannot use a polymorphic sorting function, of the type above, on lists of strings. ∎

F-bounded Subtype Polymorphism

In the remainder of this section, we consider two extensions of subtype-bounded polymorphism that allow us to solve the problem raised in Example 10.6.3. Using the first, we show how to express inheritance in the recursive record model of objects, completing the sketch given at the end of Section 10.5. The first form of polymorphism is called "F-bounded polymorphism" since it is an extension of subtype-bounded polymorphism that allows a type to be constrained using a function F from types to types. (This is not a particularly good name, but it seems to be used more commonly used than any other.) The second extension, *higher-order subtype bounded polymorphism* also involves functions from types to types. Although not formally equivalent, higher-order bounded polymorphism seems approximately as expressive as F-bounded polymorphism; for many examples, the two seem to work equally well. Moreover, higher-order bounded polymorphism seems to have some nicer properties, such as transitivity (see Exercise 10.6.5) and less dependence on equational principles such as (*unfold*).

F-bounded polymorphism is a natural extension of subtype-bounded quantification that seems particularly useful in connection with recursive types. The essential idea may be illustrated by comparison with subtype bounded quantification. Recall from Example 10.6.3 that the recursive types

$\texttt{type}\ ordered = \langle less\colon ordered \rightarrow bool\rangle$

$\texttt{type}\ string = \langle less\colon string \rightarrow bool,\ concat\colon string \rightarrow string,\ first\colon letter,\ rest\colon string\rangle$

appear structurally similar, since both have *less* functions that allow us to compare two records of the same type. However, a sorting function with type

$sort : \Pi t <: ordered.\ list(t) \rightarrow list(t)$

cannot be applied to lists of strings since *string* fails to be a subtype of *ordered.* This is a practical problem, since the reason for incorporating polymorphism into programming languages is to allow a single function to be applied to many types of data, without giving up static type checking.

We can solve this problem by giving *sort* a more informative type. Instead of constraining the type argument using the type *ordered,* we use the function F from types to types given by

$F(t) = \langle less\colon t \rightarrow bool\rangle.$

Another way to write this is

$F \stackrel{\text{def}}{=} \lambda t.\langle less\colon t \rightarrow bool\rangle.$

This involves lambda abstraction over types, which we have not used previously in type expressions. However, this is essentially straightforward, as described below. We may write a polymorphic sorting function of type

$sort : \Pi t <: F(t).\, list(t) \to list(t)$

as elaborated in Exercise 10.6.4. Intuitively, this F-bounded polymorphic type means that *sort* is defined on any type t satisfying the condition $t <: F(t)$. We check that $string <: F(string)$ by first computing $F(string)$ by β-reduction. This gives us

$F(string) = \langle less\colon string \to bool\rangle.$

Then it is easy to see that $string <: F(string)$, using (*unfold*) and other subtyping rules. Since we may apply *sort* to the type *string* and a list of strings, F-bounded polymorphism solves the typing problem described in Example 10.6.3.

The formal typing rules for F-bounded polymorphism are a straightforward extension of those for subtype-bounded polymorphism, but require an extension of the language with functions from types to types. Since we already have type variables, we can add type-function expressions by adding a grammar for functions and extending the grammar for type expression to include type-function applications:

$F \ ::= \ \lambda t.\tau$

$\tau \ ::= \ t \mid \ \ldots \ \mid F(\tau)$

In a predicative language, for example, where we have a syntactic convention that t indicates a type in U_i, then the type of F would be $U_i \to U_i$, which would presumably be an element of U_{i+1}. In an impredicative setting, we would treat type functions similarly, giving F "kind" $T \to T$, sometimes written $T \Rightarrow T$ to make clear that we are not treating the collection T of all types as a type itself. For type-functions, we have the usual equational rules for lambda abstraction and application, (α), (β) and (η). As suggested by the example above, we generally need (*unfold*) to use F-bounded polymorphism effectively.

Formally, F-bounded polymorphism is presented by generalizing rule ($<:$ *context*) to allow $t <: \tau$ to be added to a context when t occurs free in τ, together with the following introduction and elimination rules.

$$\frac{\Gamma, t <: F(t) \rhd M\colon \tau}{\Gamma \rhd \lambda t <: F(t).\, M\colon \Pi t <: F(t).\, \tau} \qquad (\Pi <: F\mathit{Intro})$$

$$\frac{\Gamma \rhd M\colon \Pi t <: F(t).\, \sigma \qquad \Gamma \vdash \rho <: F(\rho)}{\Gamma \rhd M\rho\colon [\rho/t]\sigma} \qquad (\Pi <: F\mathit{Elim})$$

Note that in the term $\lambda t <: F(t).\, M$ and type $\Pi t <: F(t).\, \tau$, the type variable t is bound in $F(t)$, whereas in ordinary subtype-bounded polymorphism, a free occurrence of t in τ would remain free in $\lambda t <: \tau.\, M$, and similarly for $\Pi t <: \tau.\, \rho$.

With definitions

$$\texttt{type function}\ ord(t) = \langle less\colon t \to bool \rangle$$

$$\texttt{type}\ \ string = \langle less\colon string \to bool,\ \ concat\colon string \to string,\ \ first\colon letter,\ \ rest\colon string \rangle$$

it is easy to check that $string <: ord(string) = \langle less\colon string \to bool \rangle$ and therefore a sorting function with type

$$sort\ :\ \Pi t <: ord(t).\ list(t) \to list(t)$$

may be used to sort a list of strings.

F-bounded Polymorphism and Inheritance

Using F-bounded polymorphism, we can complete the sketch of inheritance given at the end of Section 10.5. The typing of inheritance in the record model is relatively subtle. However, the translation of object inheritance into our record calculus does provide some useful conclusions. For example, we can base optimizations or equational proofs on this translation, since we have sound equational rules for $\lambda_{<:}^{\to,\mathtt{record},\mu}$. We illustrate the approach, which is difficult to follow if presented in full generality, using the example of points and colored points.

Our use of F-bounded polymorphism for inheritance relies on the type equation $\mu t.\sigma = [\mu t.\sigma/t]\sigma$ discussed in Section 10.5.

In an object-oriented programming language, we might have declarations of *point* and *col_point* of the form

```
class point
      instance variables
               xval:int, yval:int
      constructor point(xv:int)(yv:int)
                    . . .
      method x : int
                    . . .
       . . .
      end

class col_point
      inherits from
               point
```

```
instance variables
        cval:color
constructor col_point(xv:int)(yv:int)(cv:color)
        extend point(xv)(yv) with cval=cv
method c : color
        return cval
end
```

where the elided portions of `point` are given in full in Section 10.5. In Section 10.5, we saw how to define types *point* and *col_point*, corresponding to the types of object defined in the pseudo-code above, together with functions *point_gen*, *mk_point*, *col_point_gen* and *mk_col_point*, where *mk_point* and *mk_col_point* correspond to the constructors defined in the code above and "generators" *point_gen* and *col_point_gen* are functions whose fixed points are the constructors. However, each of the constructors was defined independently; the definition of *mk_col_point* does not depend on any part of the definition of the point constructor. Therefore, the only systematic correspondence we can claim between the constructor definitions in Section 10.5 and the code above is that if we eliminate inheritance by a program transformation, then we can produce the definitions of *point_gen* and *col_point_gen* from the resulting code.

In this section, we give the essential parts of a better translation of the object-oriented pseudo-code into typed lambda calculus. The sense in which it is "better" is that we show how each class declaration above determines a constructor function, obtained as the fixed point of a "generator." Moreover, the relationship between the generators explicitly reflects the relationship between the classes above. Specifically, the colored point generator, *col_point_gen*, is written using the point generator, *point_gen*, without duplicating the definitions of x, y or *move*. As a result, if a programmer were to change the implementation of the point class, this would also change the implementation of colored points. This partly "syntactic" property, concerning the organization of code, is an important part of object-oriented programming.

The first step in representing inheritance with this particular object model is to add a type parameter to each generator function. This parameter represents the type of object that will contain the method definitions. The reason we use a type parameter is that the type of object containing these methods will change as we add or redefine methods via inheritance. This type parameter cannot be an unconstrained type variable, since typing the methods requires some information about the type of objects we will create. In particular, we need to know that the object will contain at least the methods we are defining, and that these methods have the appropriate types. Therefore, we use an F-bounded type parameter.

For points, we use the type function

$$P(t) = \langle x\colon int,\ y\colon int,\ move\colon int \to int \to t\rangle,$$

obtained by lambda-abstracting the body of the recursive definition of *point* with respect to *point*. The polymorphic generator for points is

$$\begin{aligned} point\_gen &\stackrel{\text{def}}{=} \lambda t <: P(t).\, \lambda f\colon int \to int \to t.\, \lambda xv\colon int.\, \lambda yv\colon int.\\ &\qquad \langle x = xv,\ y = yv,\ move = \lambda dx\colon int.\, \lambda dy\colon int.\, f\ (x + dx)\ (y + dy)\rangle\\ &:\ \ \forall t <: P(t).\, (int \to int \to t) \to (int \to int \to P(t))\end{aligned}$$

We wish to define the point constructor *mk_point* as a fixed point of *point_gen*. However, it may not be immediately clear how to do so because of the type of *point_gen*. The solution is to notice that by the type equation $point = \mu t.P(t) = P(\mu t.P(t))$, we can define *mk_point* as

$$mk\_point \stackrel{\text{def}}{=} fix_{int \to int \to \mu t.P(t)}(point\_gen\ \mu t.P(t))$$

We will see the purpose for introducing the type parameter in *point_gen* when we define *colpoint_gen*.

For inheritance in the record model of objects, we need some form of record concatenation. Specifically, in the generator for the derived class of objects, the record of methods from the base class is concatenated with the record of methods to be added. This concatenation may be accomplished using the *with* record combination operator, which is typed using the following rule:

$$\frac{\begin{array}{l} M\colon \langle \ell_1\colon \sigma_1, \ldots, \ell_j\colon \sigma_j\rangle\\ N\colon \langle \ell_{j+1}\colon \sigma_{j+1}, \ldots, \ell_n\colon \sigma_n\rangle \end{array}}{M\ with\ N\colon \langle \ell_1\colon \sigma_1, \ldots, \ell_n\colon \sigma_n\rangle\ (n \geq k)} \qquad (with)$$

Note that because of subtyping, the two records in this rule may have one or more fields in common. However, if

$$M\colon \langle \ell_1\colon \sigma_1, \ldots, \ell_j\colon \sigma_j, \ell_{j+1}\colon \tau_1, \ldots \ell_k\colon \tau_{k-j}\rangle <: \langle \ell_1\colon \sigma_1, \ldots, \ell_j\colon \sigma_j\rangle$$

and $N\colon \langle \ell_{j+1}\colon \sigma_{j+1}, \ldots, \ell_n\colon \sigma_n\rangle$, then fields $\ell_{j+1}\colon \tau_1, \ldots \ell_k$ of M will be subsumed by fields of N in M *with* N. In other words, if two records M and N have common fields, the conflict in M *with* N is resolved according to the way that M *with* N is typed. Therefore, if we want the meaning of a term to be independent of ists typing derivation, we should subscript the *with* operator with the field names assumed for its two arguments, as in $M\ with_{\ell_1,\ldots,\ell_j \| \ell_{j+1},\ldots,\ell_n}\ N$. However, since this subscripted notation is syntactically awkward, we will omit the subscripts.

Using the *with* operator, we can define a generator for colored points from *point_gen* as follows:

$$\begin{aligned} col\_point\_gen \stackrel{\text{def}}{=}\ & \lambda t <: C(t).\, \lambda g\colon int \to int \to color \to t.\, \lambda xv\colon int.\, \lambda yv\colon int.\, \lambda cv\colon color. \\ & \quad point\_gen\, t\ (\lambda x\colon int.\, \lambda y\colon int.\, g\ x\ y\ cv)\ xv\ yv \\ & \quad with\ \langle c = cv \rangle \\ :\ & \forall t <: C(t).\, (int \to int \to color \to t) \to (int \to int \to color \to C(t)) \end{aligned}$$

where

$$C(t) \stackrel{\text{def}}{=} \langle x\colon int,\ y\colon int,\ c\colon color,\ move\colon int \to int \to t \rangle$$

Intuitively, *col_point_gen* is a function which, given a type of record, returns a function shows fixed point is a colored point constructor. The main constructor function, which begins with $\lambda xv\colon int.\, \lambda yv\colon int.\, \lambda cv\colon color.$ and runs through the end of the function body, takes initial values for x, y and c, and constructs a record with this values. This is accomplished by calling *point_gen*, instantiated to the correct type, with a point constructor and x value and y value, and adding a c value using the *with* operator. A subtle aspect of this function is the way the first argument to *point_gen* is defined. One way to understand this is to recall that we will take the fixed-point of *col_point_gen*. In this case, the argument g will effectively denot the colored point constructor. If g is a colored point constructor, then $\lambda x\colon int.\, \lambda y\colon int.\, g\ x\ y\ cv$ is a function which takes x and y values and produces a colored point with c value passed to the surrounding colored point generator. The easiest and most effective way to see how this function works is to work Exercises 10.6.6–10.6.8 summarized below.

Using *col_point_gen*, we can define the colored point constructor as follows:

$$mk\_col\_point \stackrel{\text{def}}{=} fix_{int \to int \to color \to \mu t.C(t)}(col\_point\_gen\ \mu t.C(t))$$

using the convention explained for points above.

Since *col_point_gen* depends on *point_gen*, these definitions of *point_gen*, *mk_point*, *col_point_gen* and *mk_col_point* capture the object-oriented pseudo-code above more faithfully than the simpler translation in Section 10.5. Exercise 10.6.6 shows that the definition of *mk_col_point* here give the same objects as the definition in Section 10.5, Exercise 10.6.7 shows how to model the pseudo-variable `self` found in object-oriented languages (called `this` in C++), and Exercise 10.6.8 asks you to extend *col_point* with a method that changes the color of an object.

Higher-order Subtype Polymorphism

An alternative to F-bounded polymorphism involves a point-wise subtype ordering on type functions. This is given by the rule

$$\frac{\Gamma, t\colon T \vdash \sigma <: \tau}{\Gamma \vdash \lambda t.\,\sigma <: \lambda t.\,\tau} \qquad (\mathit{Type} \rightarrow \mathit{Type}_{<:})$$

Typing rules for terms.

$$\frac{\Gamma, (F <: G) \rhd M\colon \sigma}{\Gamma \rhd \lambda F <: G.\, M\colon \Pi F <: G.\, \sigma} \qquad (\Pi F <: \mathit{Intro})$$

$$\frac{\Gamma \rhd M\colon \Pi F <: G.\, \sigma, \;\; \Gamma \vdash H <: G}{\Gamma \rhd M(H)\colon [H/F]\sigma} \qquad (\Pi F <: \mathit{Elim})$$

In the term $\lambda F <: G.\, M$ and type $\Pi F <: G.\, \tau$, any occurrence of the type-function variable F would remain free in G. Note that here F is a type-function variable while G and H may be any type-function expressions.

It is interesting to see how higher-order bounded quantification gives us a polymorphically-typed sort function that can be used in much the same ways as the F-bounded polymorphic sort function discussed above. We begin with two type functions,

`type function` $ord(t) = \langle less\colon t \rightarrow bool \rangle$

`type function` $str(t) = \langle less\colon t \rightarrow bool,\ concat\colon t \rightarrow t,\ first\colon letter,\ rest\colon t \rangle$

with the properties

$string \stackrel{\text{def}}{=} \mu t.str(t)$

$ord(t) <: str(t)$

A sorting function with type

$sort : \Pi F <: ord.\ list(\mu t.F(t)) \rightarrow list(\mu t.F(t))$

may be applied to a list of strings since

$sort\ str : list(string) \rightarrow list(string)$

It is a useful exercise to translate the inheritance example using points and colored points from F-bounded to hinger-order bounded polymorphism.

Exercise 10.6.4 This exercise asks you to write parts of a polymorphic sorting function using F-bounded polymorphism. In a prototypical polymorphic programming language, we might write merge sort in the form

```
function sort(type t <: ord(t))(a : list(t))
        if (length t a) < 1 then a
           else let p = split t a
                in merge t (sort t (fst p), sort t (snd p))
```

where we assume that `length`, `split` and `merge` are polymorphic functions that split a list into two parts and merge two sorted lists into one, respectively. Assume that `length`, `split` and `merge` have types

`length`: $\forall t.\, list(t) \rightarrow int$

`split`: $\forall t.\, list(t) \rightarrow list(t) \times list(t)$

`merge`: $\forall t <: \mathtt{ord}(t).\, list(t) \times list(t) \rightarrow list(t)$

(a) Assuming `merge` has the form

```
function merge(type t <: ord(t))(a : list(t), b: list(t))
        if (length t a) = 0 then b
           else if (length t b) = 0 then a
                  else if (hd t a)less (hd t b)
                         then (hd t a)::merge(tl t a, b)
                         else (hd t b)::merge(a, tl t b)
```

explain why `merge` should typecheck.

(b) Using the types of `length`, `split` and `merge`, explain why `sort` has the type given in this section.

Exercise 10.6.5 [AC95] Higher-order subtyping is transitive, in the sense that if F, G and H are type functions then $F <: G <: H$ implies $F <: H$. However, a natural form of transitivity for F-bounded polymorphism fails. Specifically, find type functions F, G and H such that $\mu t.F(t) <: G(\mu t.F(t))$ and $\mu t.G(t) <: H(\mu t.G(t))$ but *not* $\mu t.F(t) <: H(\mu t.F(t))$.

Exercise 10.6.6 Definitions of *mk_point* and *mk_col_point* are given at the end of Section 10.5 and again in this section. The difference is that in Section 10.5, no inheritance is used. Show that the two definitions of *mk_point* give equal functions, and similarly for *mk_col_point*.

Exercise 10.6.7 The pseudo-variable `self`, called `this` in C++, occurs in a number of object-oriented languages. In the pseudo-code for `point` on page 742, for example, the move function refers to `self.x` and `self.y`. However, in writing a lambda-term *mk_point*, we replaced these expressions by x and y values *xv* and *yv*. We can rewrite the definition of *mk_point* using explicit *self* as follows:

$\texttt{letrec}\ mk\_point(xv\colon int)(yv\colon int)\ =$

$\quad fix(\lambda self\colon point.$

$\quad \langle x = xv,\ y = yv,\ move = \lambda dx\colon int.\ \lambda dy\colon int.\ mk\_point(self.x + dx)(self.y + dy)\rangle)$

Explain why this is equivalent to the definition of *mk_point* on page 742.

Exercise 10.6.8 Add a *new_color* method to colored points by modifying the definition of *col_point_gen*. Intuitively, *new_color* takes a color argument and changes the color of the colored point to the "new" color given. Modify the definition of *col_point_gen* in this section that uses F-bounded polymorphism.

11 Type Inference

11.1 Introduction to Type Inference

Type inference is the general problem of transforming untyped or "partially-typed" expressions into well-typed terms by inferring missing type information. Although there are interesting theoretical questions surrounding type inference, this is also a pragmatic issue. If we wish to program in a typed language, with type errors detected at compile time, but find the process of declaring and manipulating types tedious, then we may use type inference to insert some or all of the type information automatically. In other words, type inference can provide the best of two worlds: compile-time type checking without excessive type information in programs. For the known examples, a programmer may include type information, either for documentation purposes or to constrain the behavior of the type inference algorithm, without complicating the process of type inference.

In outline, the main topics of the chapter are:

- General framework for type inference problems, based on "erasure" functions from typed to untyped languages.
- Type inference for $\lambda^{\rightarrow}$, with type variables added, including discussion of principal typings, unification and algorithmic issues.
- Type inference algorithm for $\lambda^{\rightarrow,\Pi,\mathtt{let}}$, with polymorphic declarations.
- Overview of additional systems: polymorphic record operations, subtyping, and impredicative polymorphism.

A number of other type inference problems, such as imperative constructs [Tof88, Tof90, MV95] and intersection types [BCDC83, Ron], are not covered.

A simple example can be given using PCF. We may declare a "doubling" function and apply it to two arguments by writing

$$\bar{D} \stackrel{\text{def}}{=} \mathtt{let}\ dbl\colon (nat \rightarrow nat) \rightarrow nat \rightarrow nat = \lambda f\colon nat \rightarrow nat.\, \lambda x\colon nat.\, f(fx)$$
$$\mathtt{in}\ dbl\,(\lambda x\colon nat.\, x + 2)\, 4$$

Since all the type information in this term is determined by context, we might prefer to write

$$D \stackrel{\text{def}}{=} \mathtt{let}\ dbl = \lambda f.\, \lambda x.\, f(fx)\ \mathtt{in}\ dbl\,(\lambda x.\, x + 2)\, 4$$

and let a smart editor or compiler use a type inference algorithm to fill in the missing types. Type inference is particularly useful in polymorphic languages since polymorphic terms involve types for lambda-bound variables, type abstraction and type application. When one or more of these cases are handled automatically by a programming tool or compiler, polymorphism becomes more convenient. The is the approach used in the programming languages ML [GMW79, Mil85a], Haskell [HF92, H^+92] and Miranda [Tur85]. Historically, the main principles were identified in a mathematical context by Curry, Feys and Hindley [CF58, Hin69] and developed independently for programming language applications by Milner [Mil78].

Type Inference and Erasure Functions

Since type inference may be studied for a variety of languages, it seems useful to present the problem in a general way. One view is that a type inference problem is determined by choosing an *erasure function Erase* from a typed language $\mathcal{L}$ to some other language $\mathcal{L}'$. Usually, $\mathcal{L}'$ will be a related "untyped" language, or perhaps a version of $\mathcal{L}$ with some of the type information or type operations omitted. Before discussing the type inference problem, we consider two illustrative examples.

Example 11.1.1 The erasure function from $\lambda^{\rightarrow}$ to untyped lambda terms removes the type designations from lambda bindings. Recall that untyped lambda terms have the form

$$U \quad ::= \quad c \mid x \mid \lambda x.\, U \mid U U$$

where we assume that the same term constants are used in typed and untyped terms. We define *Erase* as follows:

$$
\begin{aligned}
Erase(c) &= c\\
Erase(x) &= x\\
Erase(\lambda x\colon \tau.\, M) &= \lambda x.\, Erase(M)\\
Erase(M N) &= Erase(M) Erase(N)
\end{aligned}
$$

This function simply erases the type designations from lambda bindings, producing an untyped lambda term from any $\lambda^{\rightarrow}$ term. ∎

Example 11.1.2 For extensions or variants of $\lambda^{\rightarrow}$, there may be one or more analogous *Erase* functions. We will illustrate this using an erasure function for $\lambda^{\rightarrow,\Pi}$ that keeps type abstractions and type specifications for lambda-bound term variables, but eliminates type applications. The resulting input syntax for $\lambda^{\rightarrow,\Pi}$ programs is given by the grammar

$$M \quad ::= \quad c \mid x \mid \lambda x\colon \tau.\, M \mid \lambda t.\, M$$

where τ may be any U_1 type of $\lambda^{\rightarrow,\Pi}$. Since we consider type applications implicit, a program written using this syntax could contain complete $\lambda^{\rightarrow,\Pi}$ expressions for every function, but allow polymorphic functions to be applied to non-polymorphic arguments without intermediate type applications. The *Erase* function giving this effect is defined by

$$
\begin{aligned}
Erase(c) &= c \\
Erase(x) &= x \\
Erase(\lambda x\colon \tau .\, M) &= \lambda x\colon \tau .\, Erase(M) \\
Erase(M N) &= Erase(M) Erase(N) \\
Erase(\lambda t .\, M) &= \lambda t .\, Erase(M) \\
Erase(M \tau) &= Erase(M)
\end{aligned}
$$

For languages with several kinds of type designations, we may make the type inference problem easier or harder by varying the definition of *Erase*. In particular, it is likely to be harder to infer types if we also erase type abstractions or the types of lambda-bound term variables. Another consideration, of course, is program readability. Some programmers might find that complete type information in function declarations makes programs easier to read and understand, while others may consider this an unnecessary annoyance. ■

Given a language and erasure function, type inference is the problem of recovering a term from its erasure. More precisely, the *type inference problem* for language $\mathcal{L}$ and erasure function $Erase : \mathcal{L} \to \mathcal{L}'$ is,

Type Inference Problem: Given an expression $U \in \mathcal{L}'$, find a typed term $\Gamma \triangleright M\colon \tau$ of $\mathcal{L}$ with $Erase(M) = U$.

Example 11.1.3 One example of type inference is computing the typed expression, $\bar{D}$, at the beginning of this chapter from the untyped term, D. It is easy to check that the *Erase* function from Example 11.1.1 maps $\bar{D}$ to D, regarding `let` as syntactic sugar for λ-abstraction and application as described in Chapter 2. In this specific example, there is only one typed expression whose erasure is D. The reason is that 2 and 4 only have type *nat* in PCF, and $+$ similarly has a fixed type. This determines the types of the arguments of *dbl*, and therefore the return type. ■

In general, there may be infinitely-many ways of inserting type information into terms. For example, we could give $\lambda f .\, \lambda x .\, f(f x)$ any type of the form $(\tau \to \tau) \to \tau \to \tau$. If we use the result of type inference in code generation, or in giving formal semantics to expressions, this raises a coherence problem similar to the coherence problem associated with subtyping. Specifically, if there are many ways to insert type information, then we should make sure that arbitrary decisions in type inference do not affect the overall meaning of an expression. Since coherence is considered in some detail in Chapter 10 (and Section 10.4.2 in particular), however, we will not go into detail on this subject here.

Example 11.1.4 An inference example using the erase function of Example 11.1.2 begins with

$$(\lambda t.\, \lambda x{:}\, t.\, x)\; (\lambda t.\, \lambda x{:}\, t.\, x)$$

Since we can only apply non-polymorphic functions to non-polymorphic arguments in $\lambda^{\rightarrow,\Pi}$, both function expressions must be applied to some type argument. Therefore, any well-typed $\lambda^{\rightarrow,\Pi}$-term with this erasure must have the form

$$((\lambda t.\, \lambda x{:}\, t.\, x)\, \tau_1)\;\; ((\lambda t.\, \lambda x{:}\, t.\, x)\, \tau_2)$$

Any pair of types with $\tau_1 \equiv \tau_2 \rightarrow \tau_2$ will suffice. In particular, the reader may verify that

$$((\lambda t.\, \lambda x{:}\, t.\, x)\, t \rightarrow t)\;\; ((\lambda t.\, \lambda x{:}\, t.\, x)\, t)$$

is a well-typed $\lambda^{\rightarrow,\Pi}$-term whose erasure is the original term above. ∎

A variant of type inference is the simpler-looking recognition problem.

Type Recognition Problem: Given an expression $U \in \mathcal{L}'$, determine whether there exists a typed term $\Gamma \triangleright M{:}\, \tau$ of $\mathcal{L}$ with $Erase(M) = U$.

The difference between type inference and type recognition is that a type inference algorithm must construct a typed term, while a type recognition algorithm returns only a yes or no answer. One reason we may be interested in finding a fully-typed term is that types of subterms may be useful in compilation or optimization. In studying complexity, however, it is common to consider recognition problems (problems with a yes/no answer) since this eliminates the often dominant cost of writing the output. This is also all that may be needed in a compiler if code generation does not use the types of expressions.

An alternate view of type inference is that typing is given by some set of inference rules, and a type inference algorithm is just a decision procedure for an axiomatic theory. More generally, if we define some logical system by a syntax of formulas and a set of proof rules for proving formulas, the decision problem is the problem of deciding whether a given well-formed formula is provable. This general concept from logic may be applied to proof systems for typing assertions, where we traditionally call a decision procedure a type inference algorithm.

In either view, it may be useful to distinguish between type inference and type checking. Although it is difficult to make this distinction precise, we generally regard *type checking* as a routine check of some context-sensitive typing conditions in a syntax-directed manner. For example, we can decide whether a $\lambda^{\rightarrow,\Pi}$ term is well-typed by type checking, since any derivation of $\Gamma \triangleright M{:}\, \sigma$ in $\lambda^{\rightarrow,\Pi}$ must follow the structure of M. There is not enough flexibility in the proof rules for it to be difficult to determine whether a given typing assertion is derivable. In particular, a lambda abstraction of the form $\lambda x\colon \tau.\, M$ specifies the type that must be given to x when type-checking M. On the other hand, if we omit the type and write a lambda abstraction in the form $\lambda x.\, M$, it is not clear what type to use for x; a more complicated analysis of M may needed. We would therefore call the decision problem for typing with untyped λ's a *type inference* problem.

To avoid confusion, we use the erasure-function view of type inference until Section 11.2.4, where we show that the erasure-function formulation is equivalent to a decision-procedure formulation.

Generally, if typing is decidable, then typing must be a syntactic property of terms, not a semantic one. This is shown for $\lambda_t^{\rightarrow}$ in Exercise 11.2.2, using an argument that applies to virtually any decidable type system.

11.2 Type Inference for $\lambda^{\rightarrow}$ with Type Variables

11.2.1 The Language $\lambda_t^{\rightarrow}$

In this section, we consider type inference for the language $\lambda_t^{\rightarrow}$, which is the result of adding type variables to $\lambda^{\rightarrow}$. The type inference algorithm for $\lambda_t^{\rightarrow}$ is essentially due to Hindley [Hin69], with the extension to polymorphic declarations due to Milner, independently [Mil78].

The types of $\lambda_t^{\rightarrow}$ are defined by the grammar

$$\tau \quad ::= \quad b \mid t \mid \tau \rightarrow \tau$$

where b may be any type constant and t may be any type variable. The terms of $\lambda_t^{\rightarrow}$ have the context-free forms

$$M \quad ::= \quad c \mid x \mid \lambda x\colon \tau.\, M \mid MM$$

The typing axioms and inference rules for $\lambda_t^{\rightarrow}$ are the same as for $\lambda^{\rightarrow}$, but with type expressions in terms and type assignments allowed to contain type variables. We may also think of $\lambda_t^{\rightarrow}$ as the Π-free fragment of $\lambda^{\rightarrow,\Pi}$, with typing assertions $\Gamma \triangleright M\colon \tau$ restricted so that Γ does not contain any U_2 types. A restriction on $\lambda_t^{\rightarrow}$ signatures is that the type of a term constant must not contain type variables. Semantically, this is sensible since it makes the value of a constant really "constant," as opposed to some value that depends implicitly on the values of type variables. Syntactically, it is convenient since it guarantees a substitution property of derivable typing assertions.

We are interested in the type inference problem determined by the *Erase* function of Example 11.1.1, regarded as a function from $\lambda_t^{\rightarrow}$ terms to untyped lambda terms. This is called the *Curry type inference problem*, after H.B. Curry, since the main ideas appeared first in [CF58].

Since we have seen some examples of Curry typing in Example 11.1.3, we now consider some methods for showing that certain terms do not have types.

The strong normalization property of $\lambda_t^{\rightarrow}$, which follows from strong normalization for $\lambda^{\rightarrow}$, may be used to show that certain typing judgements are not derivable. Specifically, it is easy to check that any reduction applicable to a typed $\lambda^{\rightarrow}$ term M corresponds to a reduction in the untyped term $Erase(M)$, and conversely. This is because the reduction rules of $\lambda^{\rightarrow}$ do not depend on the type of the term, or the presence of any type information. We state this more precisely in the following proposition.

Proposition 11.2.1 Let $\Gamma \triangleright M{:}\,\tau$ be any well-typed $\lambda^{\rightarrow}$ term. If $M \twoheadrightarrow N$ by β, η-reduction on typed terms, then $Erase(M) \twoheadrightarrow Erase(N)$ by the same reduction steps on untyped terms. Conversely, if $Erase(M) \twoheadrightarrow V$ by untyped reduction, then there is a typed $\lambda^{\rightarrow}$ term $\Gamma \triangleright N{:}\,\tau$ with $M \twoheadrightarrow N$ and $Erase(N) = V$.

It follows from Theorem 8.3.6 that an untyped term U can be typed only if there is no infinite sequence of untyped reductions from U. This means that if U is not strongly normalizing, there is no derivable typing of the form $\Gamma \triangleright M{:}\,\tau$ with $Erase(M) = U$. A specific example of a non-normalizing term which, by Proposition 11.2.1, cannot be typed, is

$$\Omega \stackrel{\text{def}}{=} (\lambda x.xx)(\lambda x.xx)$$

A second consequence is that if U is not typable, then by the subject reduction property of $\lambda_t^{\rightarrow}$ (see Lemma 4.4.16), no untyped term reducing to U is typable. For example, it is a bit difficult to show by direct analysis that no term of the form

$$\lambda x.((\lambda y.yx)\,\lambda z.z)\,((\lambda u.\lambda v.uvx)\,(\lambda z.\lambda w.z)U),$$

can be typed. However, if we notice that any such term reduces to $\lambda x.xx$, then we need only analyze possible typings for $\lambda x.xx$ to show that there is no Curry typing.

It is important to understand that while types are closed under reduction, the converse fails. The term $(\lambda x.\lambda y.y)\Omega$ is not typable since it has a non-normalizing subterm, even though it reduces to a typable term in one step. (See Exercise 11.2.2.)

Exercise 11.2.2 Scott's version of Rice's theorem for untyped lambda calculus is that if any set S of untyped lambda terms is nontrivial (*i.e.*, S is neither empty nor the set of all untyped lambda terms) and closed under conversion (if $U \in S$ and $U \leftrightarrow V$ then $V \in S$), then membership in S is undecidable [Bar84, Theorem 6.6.2]. Use this to show that there is no algorithm which, given an untyped term U, decides whether there exists a typed term $\Gamma \triangleright M\colon \tau$ with $Erase(M) \leftrightarrow U$.

11.2.2 Substitution, Instances and Unification

In the type inference algorithm for $\lambda_t^{\rightarrow}$, we will use the fact that the derivable typing assertions are closed under substitution. For completeness, we review substitution briefly before defining the "instance" relation on typing assertions. This subsection concludes with a brief summary of unification.

A *type substitution*, or *substitution* for short, is a function from type variables to type expressions. If τ is a type expression and S is a substitution, then $S\tau$ is the type expression obtained by replacing each variable t in τ with $S(t)$. A substitution S may be applied to a type assignment Γ, with the result given by

$$S\Gamma = \{x\colon S\tau \mid x\colon \tau \in \Gamma\}.$$

If we apply a type substitution S to a $\lambda_t^{\rightarrow}$ term M, the result SM differs from M only in the types of lambda bound variables. It is probably not surprising that if $\Gamma \triangleright M\colon \tau$ is derivable, so is any substitution instance $S\Gamma \triangleright SM\colon S\tau$. This is proved as part of Lemma 11.2.3 below. The simple reason is that all of the typing axioms and inference rules are preserved by substitution.

For technical convenience, we will use "instance" to refer to a slightly more general relation than substitution. Because of rule (*add hyp*), typings are preserved by adding hypotheses to type assignments. Combining (*add hyp*) with substitution leads to the following definition. A typing assertion $\Gamma' \triangleright M'\colon \tau'$ *is an instance of* $\Gamma \triangleright M\colon \tau$ if there is a type substitution S with

$$\Gamma' \supseteq S\Gamma,\ \ M' = SM \text{ and } \tau' = S\tau.$$

In this case we say $\Gamma' \triangleright M'\colon \tau'$ is an instance of $\Gamma \triangleright M\colon \tau$ by substitution S.

One important property of this relation is that every instance of a provable typing statement is also provable.

Lemma 11.2.3 If $\lambda_t^{\rightarrow}$ typing assertion $\Gamma \triangleright M\colon \tau$ is derivable, then so is any instance $S\Gamma \cup \Gamma' \triangleright SM\colon S\tau$.

Proof The proof is an easy induction on the derivation of $\Gamma \triangleright M\colon \tau$. The two base cases are the typing axiom $x\colon \tau \triangleright x\colon \tau$ for variables and the axiom $\emptyset \triangleright c\colon \tau$ for a term constant c. In the variable case, if S is any substitution, then we can prove any typing judgement

$$x\colon S\tau,\ y_1\colon \tau_1, \ldots, y_k\colon \tau_k \triangleright x\colon S\tau$$

beginning with the typing axiom $x\colon S\tau \rhd x\colon S\tau$ and continuing with k uses of the (*add hyp*) rule, each adding some $y_i\colon \tau_i$ to the typing context. In the case of a constant c, the argument is similar but simpler since we assume that each constant has a variable-free type, and therefore $S\tau = \tau$.

The inductive steps are all essentially straightforward. We show the ($\rightarrow$ Intro) case as an example, since this is the most complicated. Suppose $\Gamma \rhd \lambda x\colon \tau..M\colon \tau \rightarrow \tau'$ is derivable from $\Gamma, x\colon \tau \rhd M\colon \tau'$ by ($\rightarrow$ Intro). Any instance of $\Gamma \rhd \lambda x\colon \tau..M\colon \tau \rightarrow \tau'$ will have the form

$$S\Gamma, y_1\colon \tau_1, \ldots, y_k\colon \tau_k \rhd \lambda x\colon S\tau..SM\colon S\tau \rightarrow S\tau'$$

for some type substitution S. By the inductive hypothesis, we know that $S\Gamma, x\colon S\tau \rhd SM\colon S\tau'$ is derivable. This gives us

$$S\Gamma \rhd \lambda x\colon S\tau..SM\colon S\tau \rightarrow S\tau'$$

by rule ($\rightarrow$ Intro). We may now derive the desired judgement by k uses of the (*add hyp*) rule, each adding some $y_i\colon \tau_i$ to the typing context. Note that we do not assume all the y_i's are different from x. ■

An important part of the type inference algorithm is the way that unification is used to combine typing assertions about subterms. If E is a set of equations between type expressions, then a type substitution S *unifies* E if $S\tau \equiv S\rho$ for every equation $\tau = \rho \in E$. In other words, unification finds a substitution making each equation syntactically true. For example, a unifier of the set $\{s = t \rightarrow v,\ t = v \rightarrow w\}$ is the substitution replacing t by $v \rightarrow w$ and s by $(v \rightarrow w) \rightarrow v$.

The unification algorithm computes a most general unifying substitution, where S *is more general than* R if there is a substitution T with $R = T \circ S$. Intuitively, the most general substitution unifying a set E of equations is the simplest way of making each equation syntactically true. For example, the substitution replacing s by $((w \rightarrow w) \rightarrow w) \rightarrow (w \rightarrow w)$, t by $(w \rightarrow w) \rightarrow w$ and v by $w \rightarrow w$ also unifies $\{s = t \rightarrow v,\ t = v \rightarrow w\}$, but the simpler substitution above is more general. In fact, the simpler substitution above is the most general unifier.

Lemma 11.2.4 [Rob65] Let E be any set of equations between type expressions. There is an algorithm *Unify* such that if E is unifiable, then *Unify*(E) computes a most general unifier. If E is not unifiable, then *Unify*(E) *fails.*

The traditional blackboard explanation of unification uses a graph representation of expressions, as in Section 3.7. (These are similar but not exactly the same as the parse trees described in Section 1.7.2.) We illustrate this briefly by example and then give a more

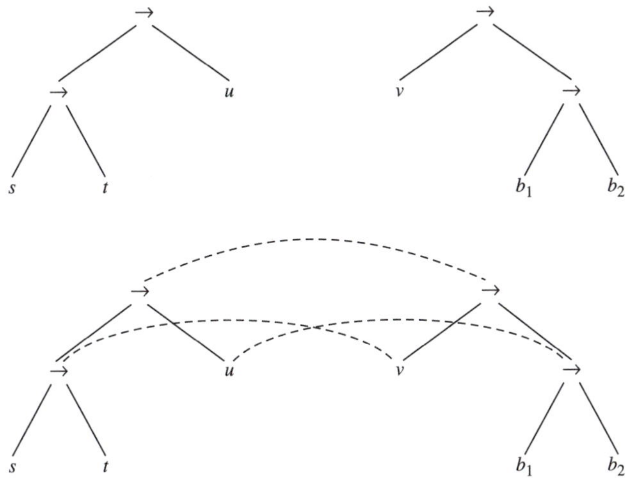

Figure 11.1
Unification on expression graphs

precise "pseudo-code" description of unification below. A simple example is to unify the two type expressions $(s \rightarrow t) \rightarrow u$ and $v \rightarrow (b_1 \rightarrow b_2)$, where s, t, u, v are type variables and b_1 and b_2 are type constants. Trees for these expressions are drawn at the top of Figure 11.1. To find a substitution making these two expressions syntactically equal, we begin by drawing a dotted line between the tops (roots) of the two graphs. This indicates that the expressions below these two nodes must be made syntactically equal. Then, for each horizontal dotted edge, we draw an edge from the first child on the left to the first child on the right, and similarly for the second child. If we had some type constructor with additional arguments, we would draw a horizontal dotted edge for each pair of corresponding subexpressions. The next step, which does not arise in our example but is considered in Exercise 11.2.7, is to add a horizontal dotted edge for each path of horizontal dotted edges (keeping the graph of dotted edges transitively closed). These two steps are repeated until no further dotted edges can be drawn. At this point, the dotted edges give all the equations that must be satisfied. We can satisfy each equation if, for any path of dotted edges, there is at most one constant symbol or type connective (in this case $\rightarrow$) and there are no "induced cycles" that involve at least one directed expression-tree edge. Since there are no cycles in the trees above, we can read off a unifying substitution by choosing, for each path of dotted edges containing a variable, one subtree that will be the result of substitution. In this example, we must make u equal to $b_1 \rightarrow b_2$, the expression represented by the subtree connected to u, and similarly v equal to $s \rightarrow t$. An "induced cycles" would occur if we

Table 11.1
Recursive algorithm *Unify*.

$Unify(\emptyset) = \emptyset$

$Unify(E \cup \{b_1 = b_2\}) =$
  if $b_1 \not\equiv b_2$ then *fail*
    else $Unify(E)$

$Unify(E \cup \{t = \tau\}) =$
  if $t \equiv \tau$ then $Unify(E)$
    else if t occurs in τ then *fail*
      else $Unify([\tau/t]E) \circ [\tau/t]$

$Unify(E \cup \{\sigma_1 \to \sigma_2 = \tau_1 \to \tau_2\}) =$
  $Unify(E \cup \{\sigma_1 = \tau_1,\ \sigma_2 = \tau_2\})$

had to make some variable equal to an expression containing itself. (This is considered in more detail below.) This algorithm, which is explained more fully in Exercise 11.2.7, is essentially the algorithm used in practice, with expression graphs represented as linked data structures and undirected dotted edges represented using a set data structure with *union* and *find* operations (see [ASU86, Section 6.7]).

Another presentation of essentially the same idea is given in Table 11.1, using different data structures. Essentially, the idea is to recursively decompose equations between compound types of the same "shape," substituting types for type variables when necessary. The algorithm "fails" if it is necessary to unify two distinct type constants or if the "occurs check" fails. More specifically, since we do not have recursive types, an equation like $t = t \to t$ will never have a solution. No matter what we substitute for t, the right-hand-side will always be a larger expression than the left-hand-side. Therefore, prior to replacing a type variable by a type, the algorithm checks that the type variable does not occur in the type. The set of equations generated in the execution of *Unify* correspond to the set of horizontal dotted lines drawn in the blackboard algorithm above. The algorithm *Unify* is nondeterministic, in that a set of equations could match more than one clause. For example, the set $\{s \to r = t \to r,\ t = b\}$ could be written in the form $E \cup \{s \to r = t \to r\}$ or $E \cup \{t = b\}$, allowing either the second or third clause of *Unify* to be applied. However, it follows from the proof of correctness that the result of the algorithm is deterministic. In other words, although the order of execution is not specified, the final result is uniquely determined for any input set of equations.

Proof of Lemma 11.2.4 We prove Lemma 11.2.4 by showing three properties of *Unify*:

1. *Unify*(E) halts, for any set E.
2. If *Unify*(E) succeeds, then *Unify*(E) returns a substitution that unifies E.
3. If there is a substitution T that unifies E, then *Unify*(E) succeeds and produces a substitution S that unifies E. Furthermore, there exists a substitution U such that $T = U \circ S$.

In order to prove (1), we let the *degree* of a set E to be the pair $\langle m, n \rangle$, where m is the number of distinct type variables in E, and n is the total number of occurrences of $\rightarrow$, type variables and type constants in E. We say that $\langle m, n \rangle$ is smaller than $\langle m', n' \rangle$ if either $m < m'$, or $m = m'$ and $n < n'$. It is easy to check that each clause of the algorithm reduces the degree of the set E, which shows that the algorithm terminates on any input.

Properties (2) and (3) are both proved induction on the number of recursive calls in the computation of *Unify*(E). For (2), the only non-trivial step is to note that if S unifies $[\tau/t]E$, then $S \circ [\tau/t]$ unifies $E \cup \{t = \tau\}$.

For (3), the base case is straightforward. For the induction step, there are three cases, one for each nontrivial clause in the definition of the algorithm. The first, $E \cup \{b_1 = b_2\}$, is straightforward. For the second case, suppose T unifies $E \cup \{t = \tau\}$. Then $T(t) = T\tau$ and T must unify $[\tau/t]E$. It is easy to see that t must not occur in τ. By the induction hypothesis, *Unify*$([\tau/t]E) = S$ with $T = U \circ S$. Therefore *Unify*$(E \cup \{t = \tau\}) = S \circ [\tau/t]$ succeeds with a substitution unifying $E \cup \{t = \tau\}$. We now argue that $T = U \circ (S \circ [\tau/t])$. For any variable t' different from t, we have $(U \circ (S \circ [\tau/t]))t' = Tt'$ since $U \circ S = T$. For the variable t, we have $(U \circ (S \circ [\tau/t]))t = (U \circ S)\tau = T\tau$. But since we have already seen that $Tt = T\tau$, we have $(U \circ (S \circ [\tau/t]))t = Tt$ and therefore $T = U \circ (S \circ [\tau/t])$. The argument for $E \cup \{\sigma_1 \rightarrow \sigma_2 = \tau_1 \rightarrow \tau_2\}$ is straightforward. ∎

If Γ and Γ' are type assignments, then unification can be used to find a most general substitution S such that $S\Gamma \cup S\Gamma'$ is well-formed, which means that no variable x is assigned two types by $S\Gamma \cup S\Gamma'$. To find such a substitution, we simply unify the set of all equations $\tau = \rho$ with $x{:}\,\tau \in \Gamma$ and $x{:}\,\rho \in \Gamma'$.

Exercise 11.2.5 Show, by counterexample, that Lemma 11.2.3 fails if the type of a term constant may contain type variables.

Exercise 11.2.6 Unlike the simple example in Figure 11.1, most of the graphs used in unification are not trees. The reason is that when a variable occurs more than once in either or both expressions, it must be drawn only once in the graph representing both expressions. For example, the graph for $s \rightarrow t = t \rightarrow u$ will look like two trees, sharing a common leaf (for t). In general, the graph representation of an expression will be a *directed acyclic graph*, or *dag* for short.

(a) Draw a dag representing $t \to t$. Your graph should have two nodes and two directed arcs.

(b) Draw two dags representing $((r \to r) \to (r \to r))$, one with three nodes and the other with more than three. Can this expression be represented using fewer than three nodes? Give an example or explain why not.

(c) Show that for any $n > 0$, there is a type expression τ_n which can be represented by a dag with at most $n + 1$ nodes, but which requires more than 2^n symbols to write out in the usual way.

(d) Show that if dag d with n nodes represents a type expression τ, then τ can be written out as an expression that is at most 2^n symbols long, not counting parentheses.

Exercise 11.2.7 For each of the following equations, find the most general unifier using the "blackboard" algorithm on expression graphs. As described in Exercise 11.2.6, most of the graphs you use will not be trees. Instead, the expression graphs will be dag's, with each arc assumed to be drawn directed downward. Begin the algorithm by connecting the two nodes representing expressions to be unified with an undirected, dotted edge. Then repeat the following two steps until the first step cannot be applied to any remaining undirected edges.

1. Choose an undirected dotted edge between two nodes that are not leaves. Then draw an undirected dotted edge between each pair of corresponding children of these nodes.

2. Connect by a single undirected edge any pair of nodes already connected by a path of undirected edges.

The "occurs check" mentioned informally in the text is that unification must fail when there is a cycle consisting of some combination of expression-graph arcs (traversed in the correct downward direction) and undirected dotted edges (traversed in either direction) that contains at least one expression-graph arc. For example, the expression graph for $s \to t = u \to (t \to t)$ will have three leaves, for s, t and u. After drawing undirected dotted edges, there will be a cycle involving t and $t \to t$. (Draw this out to make sure you understand.)

(a) $r \to r = (t \to u) \to (v \to w)$ (Your graph should have six horizontal dotted edges.)

(b) $(r \to r) \to (s \to t) = (b_1 \to b_2) \to (b_1 \to b_2)$.

(c) $r \to s = (s \to s) \to (s \to s)$.

(d) $((r \to r) \to (r \to r)) \to (s \to s) = (s \to s) \to ((r \to r) \to (r \to r))$. (You may draw $((r \to r) \to (r \to r))$ as a graph with shared subexpressions, *i.e.*, with the two arcs from the root both going to the same node labeled $\to$.)

Exercise 11.2.8 For parts (a)–(d) of this question, unify the pairs given in Exercise 11.2.7 using the set-based *Unify* pseudo-code of Table 11.1.

Exercise 11.2.9 This exercise asks you to write out missing cases in the proof of Lemma 11.2.4.

(a) Write out the proof of property (2). You should write one or two sentences per case.

(b) Write out the omitted case for $E \cup \{\sigma_1 \rightarrow \sigma_2 = \tau_1 \rightarrow \tau_2\}$ in the proof of property (3).

11.2.3 An Algorithm for Principal Curry Typings

If U is any untyped lambda term, then an *explicit typing for* U is a well-formed typed term $\Gamma \triangleright M\colon \tau$ with $Erase(M) = U$. As illustrated by example earlier in this section, an untyped term may have many explicit typings. We show that in $\lambda_t^{\rightarrow}$, every typable term has a *principal* explicit typing. This is a single explicit typing that that may be regarded as a description of all possible typings for the term. More precisely, we say that an untyped term U is *typable* if there is a well-formed typed term $\Gamma \triangleright M\colon \tau$ with $Erase(M) = U$ and that an explicit typing $\Gamma \triangleright M\colon \tau$ for U is *principle* if every explicit typing for U is an instance of $\Gamma \triangleright M\colon \tau$. The main result in this section is that there is an algorithm computing the principal explicit typing for every typable term and rejecting any untypable term.

Given any untyped term U, the algorithm PT Table 11.2 either produces an explicit typing $\Gamma \triangleright M\colon \tau$ for U or *fails.* The algorithm is written using an applicative, pattern-matching notation resembling the programming language Standard ML.

We give an informal description of the algorithm before stating and proving the main theorems. The constant case is straightforward since a constant can have only one type (without type variables). The most general statement we can make about a variable x is that if our assumptions include $x\colon \tau$, then the variable x has type τ. We represent all such statements about x using the typing $x\colon t \triangleright x\colon t$, since this has every assertion of the form $\Gamma, x\colon \tau \triangleright x\colon \tau$ as an instance. The lambda abstraction case is relatively simple. If we know that the body U of a lambda abstraction has typing $\Gamma \triangleright M\colon \rho$, then we would expect to give $\lambda x.U$ the typing $\Gamma' \triangleright \lambda x\colon \tau.M\colon \tau \rightarrow \rho$, where $\Gamma = \Gamma', x\colon \tau$. The test in the algorithm takes care of the possibility that Γ might not have the form $\Gamma', x\colon \tau$. An easy inductive argument shows that if x does not appear in Γ, then x must not occur free in U. In this case, the function may be applied to an argument of any type.

The application case is the most complicated one. It will succeed in producing a typing only if unification succeeds, and *fail* otherwise. Given typings $\Gamma \triangleright M\colon \tau$ for U and $\Gamma' \triangleright N\colon \rho$ for V, we must find instances which match the antecedent of the ($\rightarrow$ Elim) typing rule. In general, we must find a substitution that allows us to combine type assignments

Table 11.2
Algorithm PT for principal $\lambda_t^{\rightarrow}$ (Curry) typing.

$PT(c) \;=\; \emptyset \rhd c\colon \tau$, where τ is the variable-free type of c

$PT(x) \;=\; \{x\colon t\} \rhd x\colon t$

$PT(UV) \;=$ **let**
  $\Gamma \rhd M\colon \tau = PT(U)$
  $\Gamma' \rhd N\colon \rho = PT(V)$,
    with type variables renamed to be disjoint from those in $PT(U)$
  $S = \mathit{Unify}(\{\alpha = \beta \mid x\colon\alpha \in \Gamma \text{ and } x\colon\beta \in \Gamma'\} \cup \{\tau = \rho \to t\})$
    where t is a fresh type variable
 in
  $S\Gamma \cup S\Gamma' \rhd S(MN)\colon St$

$PT(\lambda x.U) =$
 let $\Gamma \rhd M\colon \rho = PT(U)$
 in
  if $x\colon\tau \in \Gamma$ for some τ
   then $\Gamma - \{x\colon\tau\} \rhd \lambda x\colon\tau.\, M\colon \tau \to \rho$
   else $\Gamma \rhd \lambda x\colon s.\, M\colon s \to \rho$
    where s is a fresh type variable

(after renaming of type variables to avoid accidental coincidences), and which gives the terms appropriate types. The type assignments may be combined by finding a substitution S such that $S\Gamma \cup S\Gamma'$ gives each variable at most one type. We must also make $S\tau$ a function type of the form $S\rho \to \sigma$. These constraints may be satisfied simultaneously iff there exists a substitution

$$S = \mathit{Unify}(\{\alpha = \beta \mid x\colon\alpha \in \Gamma \text{ and } x\colon\beta \in \Gamma'\} \cup \{\tau = \rho \to t\})$$

for some fresh type variable t not occurring in either typing. It is implicit in our notation (as in Standard ML) that if there is no unifier, the result of unification is undefined (or results in raising an exception) and the entire algorithm *fails*. In the case of failure, the term does not have a Curry typing, as demonstrated in Theorem 11.2.13 below.

Although the running time of $PT(U)$ is not immediately clear, we may give another algorithm that runs in linear time in the worst case, using the linear-time unification algorithm given in [PW78]. This is discussed in Section 11.2.5.

Example 11.2.10 We can see how unification is used by computing the principal typing for $\lambda x.\lambda y.xy$. Tracing the recursive calls, we can see that $PT(xy)$ involves the following steps:

$$
\begin{aligned}
PT(xy) \ = \ & \textbf{let} \\
& \quad x\colon r \rhd x\colon r = PT(x) \\
& \quad y\colon s \rhd y\colon s = PT(y) \\
& \quad S = \mathit{Unify}(\{r = s \to t\}) \\
& \textbf{in} \\
& \quad \{x\colon Sr\} \cup \{y\colon Ss\} \rhd xy\colon St
\end{aligned}
$$

Since S will simply replace r by $s \to t$, we have

$$PT(xy) = \{x\colon s \to t,\ y\colon s\} \rhd xy\colon t$$

and therefore

$$PT(\lambda x.\lambda y.xy) = \emptyset \rhd \lambda x\colon s \to t.\,\lambda y\colon s.\,xy\colon (s \to t) \to s \to t$$ ■

Example 11.2.11 It is also instructive to see how Algorithm PT fails on $\lambda x.xx$. Tracing the recursive calls, we can see that $PT(xx)$ involves the following steps:

$$
\begin{aligned}
PT(xx) \ = \ & \textbf{let} \\
& \quad x\colon r \rhd x\colon r = PT(x) \\
& \quad x\colon s \rhd x\colon s = PT(x) \\
& \quad S = \mathit{Unify}(\{r = s\} \cup \{r = s \to t\}) \\
& \textbf{in} \\
& \quad \{x\colon Sr\} \cup \{x\colon Ss\} \rhd xx\colon St
\end{aligned}
$$

However, unlike Example 11.2.10, the call to *Unify* will *fail* and therefore $PT(\lambda x.xx)$ will fail on the recursive call to $PT(xx)$. By Theorem 11.2.13, it follows that the untyped lambda term $\lambda x.xx$ cannot be typed. ■

The next two theorems establish that whenever $PT(U)$ succeeds, the algorithm produces a provable typing and, conversely, if there is a typing for U, the algorithm finds a principal typing. Before reading these proofs, the reader may wish to work out some of the examples given in Exercise 11.2.14.

Theorem 11.2.12 If $PT(U) = \Gamma \rhd M\colon \rho$, then $\mathit{Erase}(M) = U$ and every instance of $\Gamma \rhd M\colon \rho$ is provable.

Proof It follows from Lemma 11.2.3 that if $\Gamma \rhd M\colon \rho$ is provable, then so are all of its instances. Therefore, we need only establish that if $PT(U) = \Gamma \rhd M\colon \rho$ then $\Gamma \rhd M\colon \rho$ is provable and $\mathit{Erase}(M) = U$. The proof proceeds by induction on the structure of terms. Since it is easy to see that $\mathit{Erase}(M) = U$ in each case, we only show that if $PT(U) = \Gamma \rhd M\colon \rho$ then $\Gamma \rhd M\colon \rho$ is provable.

It is easy to see that for any variable x, $PT(x) = \{x\colon t\} \triangleright x\colon t$ is derivable. Since the constant symbol case is also immediate, we move on to application and abstraction.

Suppose $PT(UV) = S\Gamma \cup S\Gamma' \triangleright S(MN)\colon St$. By the inductive hypothesis, both

$PT(U) = \Gamma \triangleright M\colon \tau$ and $PT(V) = \Gamma' \triangleright N\colon \rho$

are derivable. Since S must unify $\{\alpha = \beta \mid x\colon\alpha \in \Gamma$ and $x\colon\beta \in \Gamma'\}$ and $\{\tau = \rho \to t\}$, it follows that $S\Gamma \cup S\Gamma'$ is a well-formed type assignment. By Lemma 11.2.3, the two typing assertions

$S\Gamma \cup S\Gamma' \triangleright SM\colon S\tau$

$S\Gamma \cup S\Gamma' \triangleright SN\colon S\rho$

are both derivable. Since $S\tau \equiv S(\rho \to t)$, it follows that $S\Gamma \cup S\Gamma' \triangleright S(MN)\colon St$ is derivable by ($\to$ Elim).

The final case is a λ-abstraction $\lambda x.U$. By the inductive hypothesis,

$PT(U) = \Gamma \triangleright M\colon \rho$

is derivable. If $x\colon\tau \in \Gamma$ for some τ, then $\Gamma = \Gamma', x\colon\tau$ and $\Gamma' \triangleright \lambda x\colon\tau.\, M\colon \tau \to \rho$ is derivable by rule ($\to$ Intro). If x does not occur in Γ, then $\Gamma, x\colon s \triangleright M\colon\rho$ is derivable by rule (*add var*). This gives us $\Gamma \triangleright \lambda x\colon s.\, M\colon s \to \rho$, again by rule ($\to$ Intro). This proves the theorem. ■

Theorem 11.2.13 If $\Gamma \triangleright M\colon\rho$ is a provable typing assertion and $Erase(M) = U$, then $PT(U)$ succeeds and produces a typing with $\Gamma \triangleright M\colon\rho$ as an instance.

Proof An easy induction shows that when $PT(U) = \Gamma \triangleright M\colon\rho$ succeeds, it produces a typing with $x \in \Gamma$ iff x occurs free in U. The main argument proceeds by induction on the structure of terms.

For a variable x, suppose $\Gamma \triangleright x\colon\tau$ is derivable. Since the derivation must use axiom (*var*), followed by zero or more uses of (*add var*), the type assignment must have the form $\Gamma = \{x\colon\tau, y_1\colon\sigma_1, \ldots, y_k\colon\sigma_k\}$. It is easy to see that $\Gamma \triangleright x\colon\tau$ must therefore be an instance of $PT(x) = \{x\colon t\} \triangleright x\colon t$ by the substitution mapping t to τ. The case for a constant symbol is similar.

Suppose $\Gamma \triangleright MN\colon\sigma$ is derivable with $Erase(M) = U$ and $Erase(N) = V$. Then for some $k \geq 0$, we can write $\Gamma = \Gamma_0, y_1\colon\sigma_1, \ldots, y_k\colon\sigma_k$ such that the derivation concludes with

$$\frac{\Gamma_0 \triangleright M\colon\sigma' \to \sigma \qquad \Gamma_0 \triangleright N\colon\sigma'}{\Gamma_0 \triangleright MN\colon\sigma}$$

by ($\to$ Elim), followed by k uses of (*add var*). By the inductive hypothesis,

$$\Gamma_1 \rhd M' : \tau = PT(U) \text{ and } \Gamma_2 \rhd N' : \rho = PT(V)$$

are most general typings for U and V. This means that there exist substitutions T_1 and T_2 such that

$$T_1\Gamma_1 \subseteq \Gamma_0, \quad M = T_1M' \text{ and } T_1\tau = \sigma' \rightarrow \sigma$$

$$T_2\Gamma_2 \subseteq \Gamma_0, \quad N = T_2N' \text{ and } T_2\rho = \sigma'$$

Since the type variables in $PT(V)$ are renamed to be distinct from any type variables in $PT(V)$, the substitutions T_1 and T_2 may be chosen so that any type variable changed by one is not affected by the other. Anticipating the need for a substitution that behaves properly on the fresh variable t introduced in the algorithm, we let T be the substitution with

$$Ts = T_1 s \text{if } s \text{ appears in } PT(U),$$

$$Ts = T_2 s \text{if } s \text{ appears in } PT(V),$$

$$Tt = \sigma$$

Since the type assignments Γ_1 and Γ_2 must contain exactly the term variables that occur free in U and V, and $T\Gamma_i \subseteq \Gamma_0$ for $i = 1, 2$, the substitution T must unify $\{\alpha = \beta \mid x{:}\alpha \in \Gamma_1 \text{ and } x{:}\beta \in \Gamma_2\}$. In addition, since $T\tau = \sigma' \rightarrow \sigma = T\rho \rightarrow Tt$, the substitution T unifies $\tau = \rho \rightarrow t$. It follows that there is a most general unifier

$$S = \mathit{Unify}(\{\alpha = \beta \mid x{:}\alpha \in \Gamma_1 \text{ and } x{:}\beta \in \Gamma_2\} \cup \{\tau = \rho \rightarrow t\})$$

and the call to $PT(UV)$ must succeed. Since S is a most general unifier for these equations, there is a substitution R with $T = R \circ S$. It is easy to see that $\Gamma \rhd MN{:}\sigma$ is an instance of $PT(UV)$ by substitution R.

The final case is a derivable typing assertion $\Gamma \rhd \lambda x{:}\sigma'.\, M{:}\sigma' \rightarrow \sigma$ with *Erase* $(\lambda x{:}\sigma'.\, M) = \lambda x.\, U$. For some $k \geq 0$, we can write $\Gamma = \Gamma_0, y_1{:}\sigma_1, \ldots, y_k{:}\sigma_k$ such that the derivation concludes with

$$\frac{\Gamma_0, x{:}\sigma' \rhd M{:}\sigma}{\Gamma_0 \rhd \lambda x{:}\sigma'.\, M{:}\sigma' \rightarrow \sigma}$$

by ($\rightarrow$ Intro), followed by k uses of (*add var*). By the inductive hypothesis,

$$\Gamma_1 \rhd M'{:}\rho = PT(U)$$

is a most general typing for U, which means that there is a substitution T with

$$T\Gamma_1 \subseteq \Gamma_0, \quad M = TM' \text{ and } T\rho = \sigma$$

If $x{:}\,\tau \in \Gamma_1$ for some τ, then $T\tau$ must be σ', and $\Gamma \rhd \lambda x{:}\,\sigma'.\, M{:}\,\sigma' \to \sigma$ is an instance of $\Gamma - \{x{:}\,\tau\} \rhd \lambda x{:}\,\tau.\, M'{:}\,\tau \to \rho$ by substitution T. If x does not occur in Γ, then we may further assume without loss of generality that $Ts = \sigma'$, where s is the fresh type variable introduced in Algorithm PT. In this case, it is easy to verify that $\Gamma \rhd \lambda x{:}\,\sigma'.\, M{:}\,\sigma' \to \sigma$ must be an instance of $\Gamma \rhd \lambda x{:}\,s.\, M{:}\,s \to \rho$ by substitution T. This proves the theorem. ■

Exercise 11.2.14 Execute the principal typing algorithm "by hand" on the following terms.

(a) $K \equiv \lambda x.\, \lambda y.\, x$.

(b) $S \equiv \lambda x.\, \lambda y.\, \lambda z.\, (xz)(yz)$.

(c) $\lambda f.\, \lambda x.\, f(fx)$

(d) SKK, where K and S are given in parts (a) and (b).

(e) $\lambda f.\, (\lambda x.\, f(xx))(\lambda x.\, f(xx))$. This is the untyped "fixed-point combinator" Y. It has the property that for any untyped lambda term U, $YU = U(YU)$.

11.2.4 Implicit Typing

Historically, many type inference problems have been formulated using proof rules for untyped terms. These proof systems are often referred to as systems for *implicit typing*, since the type of a term is not explicitly given by the syntax of terms. In this context, type inference is essentially the decision problem for an axiomatic theory: given a formula asserting the type of an untyped term, determine whether the formula is provable. In this section, we show how $\lambda_t^{\to}$ type inference may be presented using "implicit" typing rules that correspond, via *Erase*, to the standard "explicit" typing rules of $\lambda_t^{\to}$.

The following proof system may be used to derive typing assertions of the form $\Gamma \rhd U{:}\,\tau$, where U is any *untyped* lambda term, τ is a $\lambda_t^{\to}$ type expression, and Γ is a $\lambda_t^{\to}$ type assignment.

$$\emptyset \rhd c{:}\,\tau, \quad c \text{ a constant of type } \tau \text{ without type variables} \qquad (cst)$$

$$x{:}\,\tau \rhd x{:}\,\tau \qquad (var)$$

$$\frac{\Gamma, x{:}\,\tau \rhd U{:}\,\rho}{\Gamma \rhd (\lambda x.U){:}\,\tau \to \rho} \qquad (abs)$$

$$\frac{\Gamma \rhd U{:}\,\tau \to \rho, \quad \Gamma \rhd V{:}\,\tau}{\Gamma \rhd UV{:}\,\rho} \qquad (app)$$

$$\frac{\Gamma \rhd U{:}\,\tau}{\Gamma, x{:}\,\rho \rhd U{:}\,\tau}, \; x \text{ not in } \Gamma \qquad (add\ hyp)$$

These rules are often called the *Curry typing rules.* Using C as an abbreviation for Curry, we will write $\vdash_C \Gamma \triangleright U\colon \tau$ if this assertion is provable using the axiom and rules above.

There is a recipe for obtaining the proof system above from the definition of $\lambda_t^{\rightarrow}$: we simply apply *Erase* to all of the terms appearing in the antecedent and consequent of every rule. Given this characterization of the inference rules, the following lemma should not be too surprising.

Lemma 11.2.15 If $\Gamma \triangleright M\colon \tau$ is a well-typed term of $\lambda_t^{\rightarrow}$, then $\vdash_C \Gamma \triangleright \mathit{Erase}(M)\colon \tau$. Conversely, if $\vdash_C \Gamma \triangleright U\colon \tau$, then there is a typed term $\Gamma \triangleright M\colon \tau$ of $\lambda_t^{\rightarrow}$ with $\mathit{Erase}(M) = U$.

The proof (below) is a straightforward induction on typing derivations. It may be surprising that this lemma fails for certain (much more complicated) type systems, as shown in [Sal89].

Proof If $\Gamma \triangleright M\colon \tau$ is a well-typed term of $\lambda_t^{\rightarrow}$, then it is easy to show $\vdash_C \Gamma \triangleright \mathit{Erase}(M)\colon \tau$ by induction on the typing derivation of $\Gamma \triangleright M\colon \tau$. For the converse, assume we have a proof of $\Gamma \triangleright U\colon \tau$. We must construct a $\lambda_t^{\rightarrow}$ term M with $\Gamma \triangleright M\colon \tau$ and $\mathit{Erase}(M) = U$, by induction on the proof of $\Gamma \triangleright U\colon \tau$. Since this is essentially straightforward, we simply illustrate the ideas involved using the lambda-abstraction case.

Suppose $\Gamma \triangleright \lambda x.U\colon \tau \rightarrow \tau'$ follows from $\Gamma, x\colon \tau \triangleright U\colon \tau'$ and we have a well-typed term $\Gamma, x\colon \tau \triangleright M\colon \tau'$ with $\mathit{Erase}(M) = U$. Then clearly $\Gamma \triangleright \lambda x\colon \tau.M\colon \tau \rightarrow \tau'$ and $\mathit{Erase}(\lambda x\colon \tau.M) = \lambda x.U$. ■

In the proof of Lemma 11.2.15, it is worth noting that in constructing a well-typed term from a typable untyped term, the term we construct depends on the proof of the untyped judgement. In particular, if there are two proofs of $\Gamma \triangleright U\colon \tau$, we might obtain two different explicitly typed terms with erasure U from these two proofs.

When we work with typing assertions about untyped terms, some terminology and definitions change slightly. We say untyped term U has *typing* $\Gamma \triangleright U\colon \tau$ if this typing assertion is derivable using the Curry rules of Section 11.2.4 or, equivalently, if there is a well-typed $\lambda_t^{\rightarrow}$ term $\Gamma \triangleright M\colon \tau$ with $\mathit{Erase}(M) = U$. We say $\Gamma' \triangleright U\colon \tau'$ is an *instance* of $\Gamma \triangleright U\colon \tau$ if there is a substitution S with $S\Gamma \subseteq \Gamma'$ and $S\tau = \tau'$. A typing $\Gamma \triangleright U\colon \tau$ is *principal* for U if it is a typing for U and every other typing for U is an instance of $\Gamma \triangleright U\colon \tau$. It is easy to use Theorems 11.2.12 and 11.2.13 to show that any typable untyped term has a principal typing, and that this may be computed using algorithm PT.

It is possible to study the Curry typing rules, and similar systems, by interpreting them semantically. As in other logical systems, a semantic model may make it easy to see that certain typing assertions are not provable. To interpret $\Gamma \triangleright U\colon \tau$ as an assertion about U, we need an untyped lambda model to make sense of U and additional machinery to interpret type expressions as subsets of the lambda model. One straightforward interpretation of type expressions is to map type variables to arbitrary subsets and interpret $\tau \to \rho$ as all elements of the lambda model which map elements of τ to elements of ρ (via application). This is the so-called *simple semantics of types,* also discussed in Section 10.4.3 in connection with subtyping. It is easy to prove soundness of the rules in this framework, showing that if $\vdash_C \Gamma \triangleright U : \tau$, then the meaning of U belongs to the collection designated by τ. With an additional inference rule

$$\frac{\Gamma \triangleright U : \tau, \quad U = V}{\Gamma \triangleright V : \tau} \qquad (term\ eq)$$

for giving equal untyped terms the same types, we also have semantic completeness. Proofs of this are given in [BCDC83, Hin83]. Some generalizations and related studies may be found in [BCDC83, CDCV80, CZ86, CDCZ87, MPS86, Mit88], for example. It is easy to show using a semantic model that the only terms of type $t \to t$, for example, are those equal to $\lambda x.x$. However, since semantically equal untyped terms must have the same types in any model, no decidable type system can be semantically complete, by Exercise 11.2.2.

11.2.5 Equivalence of Typing and Unification

While algorithm PT uses unification, the connection between $\lambda_t^{\to}$ type inference and unification is stronger than the text of algorithm PT might suggest. A general theme in this section is that type inference and unification are algorithmically equivalent, in the sense that every type inference problem generates a unification problem, and every unification problem arises in type inference for some term.

We begin this section with an alternative type inference algorithm whose complexity is easier to analyze than PT. This algorithm is essentially a reduction (in the sense of recursion theory or complexity theory) from typing to unification. When combined with the linear-time unification algorithm given in [PW78], this reduction gives a linear-time algorithm for $\lambda_t^{\to}$ typing.

The remainder of this section develops the converse reduction, from unification to type inference, with some consequences of independent interest noted along the way. To establish intuition, we give some examples of terms with large types, showing that in the worst case a term may have a type whose string representation is exponential in the length of the term. Next, we show that if τ is the type of some closed term, then τ must be the principal type of some term. This fact, which was originally proved by Hindley for combinatory terms [Hin69], is used in our reduction from unification to type

Table 11.3
Algorithm reducing $\lambda_t^{\rightarrow}$ (Curry) typing to unification.

$TE(c, t) \ = \{t = \tau\}$, where τ is the variable-free type of c
$TE(x, t) \ = \{t = t_x\}$, where t_x is the type variable for x
$TE(UV, t) = TE(U, r) \cup TE(V, s) \cup \{r = s \rightarrow t\}$, where r, s are fresh type variables
$TE(\lambda x.U, t) = TE(U, s) \cup \{t = t_x \rightarrow s\}$, where s is a fresh type variable

inference. The reduction from first-order unification to type inference and the examples of terms with large types provide useful background for analyzing ML typing in Section 11.3.5.

We will work with typing assertions about untyped terms, as in Section 11.2.4.

Given an untyped term, algorithm TE in Table 11.3 produces a set of equations between type expressions. These equations are solvable by unification iff the given untyped term has a typing. The input to TE must be an untyped term with all bound variables distinct, and no variable occurring both free and bound. The reason for this restriction, which is easily satisfied by renaming bound variables, is that it allows us to simplify the association between term variables to type variables. Specifically, since each term variable is used in only one way, we can choose a specific type variable t_x for each term variable x. For any untyped term U, let Γ_U be the type assignment

$$\Gamma_U = \{x\colon t_x \mid x \text{ free in } U\}$$

If U is an untyped term, t is a type variable, and $E = TE(U, t)$, then every typing for U is an instance of $S\Gamma_U \triangleright U\colon St$ for some S unifying E. In particular, the principal typing for U is given by the most general unifier for E. This is illustrated by example below.

Example 11.2.16 We can see how algorithm TE works using the example term $S \equiv \lambda x.\,\lambda y.\,\lambda z.(xz)(yz)$. Note first that all bound variables are distinct. Tracing the calls to TE, we have

$$\begin{aligned}
&TE(\lambda x.\,\lambda y.\,\lambda z.(xz)(yz), r)\\
&= \quad TE(\lambda y.\,\lambda z.(xz)(yz), s) \cup \{r = t_x \rightarrow s\}\\
&= \quad TE(\lambda z.(xz)(yz), t) \cup \{s = t_y \rightarrow t, r = t_x \rightarrow s\}\\
&= \quad TE((xz)(yz), u) \cup \{t = t_z \rightarrow u, s = t_y \rightarrow t, r = t_x \rightarrow s\}\\
&= \quad TE(xz, v) \cup TE(yz, w) \cup \{v = w \rightarrow u, t = t_z \rightarrow u, s = t_y \rightarrow t, r = t_x \rightarrow s\}\\
&= \quad TE(x, v_1) \cup TE(z, v_2) \cup \{v_1 = v_2 \rightarrow v\}
\end{aligned}$$

$$\cup \; TE(y, w_1) \cup TE(z, w_2) \cup \{w_1 = w_2 \to w\}$$

$$\cup \; \{v = w \to u, t = t_z \to u, s = t_y \to t, r = t_x \to s\}$$

$$= \; \{v_1 = t_x, v_2 = t_z, v_1 = v_2 \to v\}$$

$$\cup \; \{w_1 = t_y, w_2 = t_z, w_1 = w_2 \to w\}$$

$$\cup \; \{v = w \to u, t = t_z \to u, s = t_y \to t, r = t_x \to s\}$$

Eliminating v_1, v_2, w_1 and w_2, since each must be equal to the type of some term variable, we have the unification problem

$$\{t_x = t_z \to v, t_y = t_z \to w, v = w \to u, t = t_z \to u, s = t_y \to t, r = t_x \to s\}$$

We can solve this set of equations by repeatedly using substitution to eliminate variables, working from left to right. If we stop with the equation for r, we find that the type of S is

$$r = (t_z \to (w \to u)) \to (t_z \to w) \to (t_z \to u)$$ ■

Since the main ideas are similar to the correctness proof for PT in Section 11.2.3, we will not prove correctness of Algorithm TE. (A correctness proof for this algorithm may be found in [Wan87].) In analyzing the complexity, we assume the input term is given by a parse tree (Section 1.7) so that the length of UV is the length of U plus the length of V plus some constant factor (for the symbols indicating that this is an application of one term to another). Given this, it is an easy induction on terms to show that the running time of $TE(U, t)$ on parsed term U is linear in the length of U. If the output of TE is presented using the dag representation of type expressions discussed in Section 11.2.2 and Exercise 11.2.6, then we may apply the linear time unification algorithm of [PW78]. This gives a linear time typing algorithm. The output of the linear time typing algorithm is a typing in which all of the type expressions are again represented by directed acyclic graphs. This is necessary, since the examples we consider below show that representing the types as strings could require exponential time. (As shown in Exercise 11.2.6, a dag of size n may represent a type expression of length 2^n.)

In the following theorem, we use the standard "big-oh" notation from algorithm analysis. Specifically, we say a function f is $O(g(n))$ if there is some positive real number $c > 0$ such that $f(n) \leq cg(n)$ for all sufficiently large n. We similarly write $f(n) = g(O(h(n)))$ if there is a positive real number $c > 0$ with $f(n) \leq g(ch(n))$ for all sufficiently large n. In particular, a function f is $2^{O}(n)$ if there is some positive real number $c > 0$ with $f(n) \leq 2^{cn}$ for all sufficiently large n.

Theorem 11.2.17 Given an untyped lambda term U of length n with all bound variables distinct, there is a linear time algorithm which computes a dag representing the principal typing of U if it exists, and *fails* otherwise. If it exists, the principal typing of U has length at most $2^{O(n)}$ and dag size $O(n)$.

Before proving the converse of Theorem 11.2.17, we develop some intuition for the difficulty of type inference by looking at some example terms with large types. Product types and pairing and projection functions are not essential, but do make it easier to construct expressions with specific principal types. An alternative to adding product types and associated operations is to introduce syntactic sugar that is equivalent for the purpose of typing. To be specific, we will adopt the abbreviation

$$\langle U_1, \ldots, U_k \rangle \stackrel{\text{def}}{=} \lambda z.zU_1 \ldots U_k$$

where z is a fresh variable not occurring in any of the U_i. This abbreviation is based on a common encoding of sequences in untyped lambda calculus that does not quite work for typed lambda calculus (see Exercise 11.2.24). It is easy to verify that if U_i has principal type σ_i, then the principal type of the sequence is

$$\langle U_1, \ldots, U_k \rangle : (\sigma_1 \rightarrow \ldots \rightarrow \sigma_k \rightarrow t) \rightarrow t$$

where t is a fresh type variable not occurring in any of the σ_i. We will write $\sigma_1 \times \ldots \times \sigma_k$ as an abbreviation for any type expression $(\sigma_1 \rightarrow \ldots \rightarrow \sigma_k \rightarrow t) \rightarrow t$ with t not occurring in any σ_i.

Example 11.2.18 The closed term

$$P \stackrel{\text{def}}{=} \lambda x.\, \langle x, x \rangle$$

has principal type $s \rightarrow (s \times s)$. If we apply P to an expression M with principal type σ, then the application PM will be typed by unifying s with σ, resulting in the typing $PM : \sigma \times \sigma$. Thus applying P to a typable expression doubles the length of its principal type. ■

By iterating the application of P from Example 11.2.18 to any typable expression M it is easy to prove the following lemma.

Proposition 11.2.19 For arbitrarily large n, there exist closed lambda terms of length n whose principal types have length $2^{\Omega(n)}$.

Another useful observation about principal types involves terms of the form

$$V \stackrel{\text{def}}{=} \lambda w.Kw\langle U_1, \ldots, U_n \rangle,$$

where K is the untyped term $\lambda x.\lambda y.x$. If w does not occur free in any of the U_i's, then V is typable, with the same principal type, $t \to t$, as the I combinator $\lambda x.x$. However, a term of form V might be untypable if the type constraints introduced by the U_i's cannot be satisfied. This gives us a way of imposing constraints on the types of terms, as illustrated in the following example.

Example 11.2.20 The term

$$EQ \stackrel{\text{def}}{=} \lambda u.\, \lambda v.\, \lambda w.\, K\, w\, (\lambda z.\, \lambda w.\, w\, (zu)\, (zv)).$$

has principal type

$$t \to t \to s \to s.$$

Therefore $EQ\, U\, V$ is typable iff the principal types of U and V are unifiable. ∎

An interesting and useful property of Curry typing is that if $\Gamma \rhd U : \tau$ is a typing for some Γ, τ not containing type constants, then $\Gamma \rhd V : \tau$ is a principal typing for some term V [Hin69]. Our proof uses the following lemma.

Lemma 11.2.21 If τ is any type expression without type constants and $t_1, \ldots, t_k$ is a list containing all the type variables in τ, then there is a closed untyped lambda term with principal type $t_1 \to \ldots \to t_k \to \tau \to s \to s$ for some (arbitrary) type variable s not among $t_1, \ldots, t_k$.

Proof The proof is by induction on the structure of τ, with $t_1, \ldots, t_k$ fixed. If τ is one of the type variables t_i, then $t_1 \to \ldots \to t_k \to t_i \to s \to s$ is a principal type of the term

$$\lambda x_1.\, \ldots \lambda x_k.\lambda y.\, \lambda z.\, K\, z\, (EQ\, x_i\, y)$$

where $K \equiv \lambda u.\, \lambda v.\, u$ and EQ is the term given in Example 11.2.20.

If τ has the form $\tau_1 \to \tau_2$, then by the inductive hypothesis we assume we have untyped lambda terms U_1 and U_2 with principal types $t_1 \to \ldots \to t_k \to \tau_1 \to s \to s$ and $t_1 \to \ldots \to t_k \to \tau_2 \to s \to s$, respectively. It is not hard to see that the untyped term

$$\lambda x_1.\, \ldots \lambda x_k.\lambda y.\, \lambda z.\, K\, z\, (\lambda u_1.\lambda u_2.\lambda w.\, w\, (U_1 x_1 \ldots x_k u_1)\, (U_2 x_1 \ldots x_k u_2)\, (EQ\, (y u_1)\, u_2))$$

has principal typing

$$t_1 \to \ldots \to t_k \to (\tau_1 \to \tau_2) \to s \to s.$$

This proves the lemma. ∎

For simplicity, we state and prove the following theorem for closed terms. The more general statement for open terms follows as a corollary. This is left to the reader as Exercise 11.2.25.

Theorem 11.2.22 If U is a closed untyped lambda term with type τ, not necessarily principal, and τ does not contain type constants, then there is a closed V with principal type τ and $V \twoheadrightarrow U$.

Proof By Lemma 11.2.21, there is a closed term W with principal type $t_1 \rightarrow \ldots \rightarrow t_k \rightarrow \tau \rightarrow s \rightarrow s$, where $t_1, \ldots, t_k$ lists all the type variables in τ. Let V be the term $(\lambda y.\, K\, y\, W')\, U$, where W' is the term

$$\lambda x_1. \ldots \lambda x_k.\lambda z.\, z\, (W x_1 \ldots x_k y).$$

Note that y occurs free in W'. The occurrence of y in W' forces y to have type τ. Therefore, the principal type of $\lambda y.\, K\, y\, W'$ is $\tau \rightarrow \tau$. Since U has type τ by hypothesis, the principal type of the entire term must be τ. ■

Recall from Proposition 4.3.13 that there is a closed $\lambda^{\rightarrow}$ term of type τ iff τ is a valid formula of intuitionistic propositional logic, with $\rightarrow$ read as implication. This means that $\emptyset, \tau$ is a typing for some closed term iff τ is a valid formula of intuitionistic propositional logic. It follows from the PSPACE complexity of propositional intuitionistic logic [Sta79] that it is PSPACE-complete to determine whether a given pair Γ, τ is a typing for some (untyped) lambda term.

From Theorem 11.2.22 and Proposition 4.3.13, it is relatively easy to prove that for any type expressions τ and τ', there is a closed term that is typable iff τ and τ' are unifiable.

Theorem 11.2.23 Let τ and τ' be type expressions without type constants. There is a closed, untyped lambda term that is $\lambda_t^{\rightarrow}$ typable iff τ and τ' are unifiable.

Proof Read as an implication, $\tau \rightarrow \tau' \rightarrow s \rightarrow s$ says that τ and τ' imply *true*. This is an intuitionistically valid implication. By Proposition 4.3.13, there is a term with this type, and by Theorem 11.2.22 there is a term U which has $\tau \rightarrow \tau' \rightarrow s \rightarrow s$ as a principal type. Therefore, $\lambda x.\, U x x$ is typable iff τ and τ' are unifiable. ■

It follows from the P-completeness of unification [DKM84] that deciding $\lambda^{\rightarrow}$ typability is complete for polynomial time with respect to log-space reduction. This means that unless certain conjectures about parallel computation and polynomial time fail (specifically, the class NC contains all of P), it is unlikely that a parallel algorithm for $\lambda^{\rightarrow}$ typing could be made to run any faster in the asymptotic worst case than the best sequential algorithm.

As shown in Exercise 11.2.26, Theorem 11.2.23 may be proved directly from Lemma

11.2.21. However, the proof using Proposition 4.3.13 seems easier to remember. An alternate direct proof is given in [Tys88].

Exercise 11.2.24 Consider $\langle U, V\rangle \equiv \lambda x.\, xUV : (\sigma \to \tau \to t) \to t$ for $U{:}\sigma$ and $V{:}\tau$. Write untyped terms P_1 and P_2 such that $\langle U, V\rangle P_1 = U$ and $\langle U, V\rangle P_2 = V$. Show that typing $\langle U, V\rangle P_1{:}\,\sigma$ and $\langle U, V\rangle P_2{:}\,\tau$ require different typings for $\langle U, V\rangle$.

Exercise 11.2.25 Use Theorem 11.2.22 to show that if $\Gamma \rhd U{:}\,\tau$ is a typing for some open term U, then there is a term $V \twoheadrightarrow U$ with principal typing $\Gamma \rhd V{:}\,\tau$.

Exercise 11.2.26 Prove Theorem 11.2.23 directly from Lemma 11.2.21, without using Proposition 4.3.13.

11.3 Type Inference with Polymorphic Declarations

11.3.1 ML Type Inference and Polymorphic Variables

In this section, we consider type inference for the language $\lambda^{\to,\Pi,\mathtt{let}}$ from Section 9.2.5. Recall that this language is the extension of $\lambda_t^{\to}$ with type abstraction, type application, and polymorphic `let` declarations. The type expressions of $\lambda^{\to,\Pi,\mathtt{let}}$ may contain the binding operator Π, giving us polymorphic types of a second universe U_2. The typing contexts may include both U_1 and U_2 type expressions, and the type of a constant symbol may be any U_2 type expression without free type variables (*i.e.*, all type variables must be bound by Π). Since this language exhibits the kind of polymorphism provided by the programming language ML, we may call the resulting type inference problem *ML type inference.*

The main feature of $\lambda^{\to,\Pi,\mathtt{let}}$ that we use in type inference is that all polymorphic types have the form $\Pi t_1 \ldots . \Pi t_k.\tau$, with τ a simple non-polymorphic type. As a result, the general techniques used for $\lambda^{\to,\Pi,\mathtt{let}}$ type inference apply to extensions of the language with cartesian product types, recursion operators, and other features that do not change the way that type binding occurs in type expressions. If we extend the language to include function types of the form $\Pi t.\tau \to \Pi t'.\tau'$, however, then the type inference problem appears to be harder. With full impredicative typing, type inference becomes algorithmically unsolvable [Wel94].

The ML type inference problem is defined precisely below by extending the *Erase* function of Section 11.1 to type abstraction, type application and `let` as follows:

$$Erase(\lambda t.M) = Erase(M)$$

$$Erase(M\tau) = Erase(M)$$

$$Erase(\mathtt{let}\ x{:}\sigma = M\ \mathtt{in}\ N) = \mathtt{let}\ x = Erase(M)\ \mathtt{in}\ Erase(N)$$

Given any $\lambda^{\rightarrow,\Pi,\texttt{let}}$ pre-term, *Erase* produces a term of an untyped lambda calculus extended with untyped `let` declarations of the form $\texttt{let}\ \ x = U\ \ \texttt{in}\ \ V$. Note that this is not the same as the *Erase* function in Example 11.1.2.

A property of $\lambda^{\rightarrow,\Pi,\texttt{let}}$ that complicates type inference for terms with free variables is that there are two distinct type universes. This means that there are two kinds of types that may be assigned to free variables. If we attempt to infer ML typings "bottom-up," as in the typing algorithm PT of Section 11.2.3, then there is no way to tell whether we should assume that a term variable has a U_1 type or a U_2 type. Furthermore, if we wanted to choose a "most general" U_2 type, it is not clear how to do this without extending the type language with U_2 type variables. However, this problem does not arise for closed terms. The reason is that each variable in a closed term must either be lambda bound or `let` bound. The lambda-bound variables must have U_1 types, while the type of each `let`-bound variable may be determined from the declaration. For example, in $\texttt{let}\ \ I = \lambda x.x\ \ \texttt{in}\ \ II$, the type of the `let`-bound variable I can be determined by typing the term $\lambda x.x$; there is no need to find an arbitrary type for I that makes II well-typed. More generally, we can type an expression of the form $\texttt{let}\ \ x = U\ \ \texttt{in}\ \ V$ by first finding the principal typing for U, then using instances of this type for each occurrence of x in V. Since this eliminates the need to work with U_2 types, we can infer types for closed $\lambda^{\rightarrow,\Pi,\texttt{let}}$-terms using essentially the same unification-based approach as for $\lambda_t^{\rightarrow}$-terms.

We consider three algorithms for ML type inference. Since the first two involve substitution on terms, it is easier to describe these algorithms if we do not try to compute the corresponding explicitly-typed $\lambda^{\rightarrow,\Pi,\texttt{let}}$ term. This leads us to consider the following *ML type inference problem*:

ML Type Inference Problem: Given a closed, untyped λ-term V, possibly containing untyped `let`'s and term constants with closed U_2 types, find a U_1 type τ such that there exists a well-typed $\lambda^{\rightarrow,\Pi,\texttt{let}}$ term $\emptyset \triangleright M\colon \tau$ with $\mathit{Erase}(M) = V$.

It is possible to modify each of the algorithms we develop so that the explicitly-typed term $\emptyset \triangleright M\colon \tau$ is actually computed. It is easy to see that there is no loss of generality in only considering U_1 types for terms, since $\emptyset \triangleright M\colon \Pi t_1.\ldots \Pi t_k.\tau$ is well-typed iff $\emptyset \triangleright M t_1 \ldots t_k\colon \tau$ is.

11.3.2 Two Sets of Implicit Typing Rules

We consider two sets of implicit typing rules and prove that they are equivalent for deriving non-polymorphic typings. The first set matches the typing rules of $\lambda^{\rightarrow,\Pi,\texttt{let}}$ while the second gives us a useful correspondence between ML type inference and $\lambda_t^{\rightarrow}$ type inference. The first set of rules is obtained by erasing types from the antecedent and consequent of each typing rule of $\lambda^{\rightarrow,\Pi,\mathtt{let}}$. This gives us rules (*cst*), (*var*), (*abs*), (*app*) and (*add hyp*) of Section 11.2.4, together with the following rules for type abstraction, type application and `let`. The names (*gen*) and (*inst*) are short for "generalization" and "instantiation."

$$\frac{\Gamma \triangleright V\colon \sigma}{\Gamma \triangleright V\colon \Pi t.\sigma}\ t \text{ not free in } \Gamma \qquad (gen)$$

$$\frac{\Gamma \triangleright V\colon \Pi t.\sigma}{\Gamma \triangleright V\colon [\tau/t]\sigma} \qquad (inst)$$

$$\frac{\Gamma \triangleright U\colon \sigma,\ \Gamma, x\colon \sigma \triangleright V\colon \sigma'}{\Gamma \triangleright (\mathtt{let}\ x = U\ \mathtt{in}\ V)\colon \sigma'} \qquad (\mathtt{let})_2$$

Since we often want `let`-bound variables to have polymorphic types, this `let` rule requires U_2 types, hence the subscript "2" in the name $(\mathtt{let})_2$. We will write $\vdash_{ML2} \Gamma \triangleright V\colon \sigma$ if the typing assertion $\Gamma \triangleright V\colon \sigma$ is provable using (*cst*), (*var*), (*abs*), (*app*), (*add hyp*), (*gen*), (*inst*) and $(\mathtt{let})_2$. With these rules, we have the straightforward analog of Lemma 11.2.15 for $\lambda^{\rightarrow,\Pi,\mathtt{let}}$.

Lemma 11.3.1 If $\Gamma \triangleright M\colon \sigma$ is a well-typed term of $\lambda^{\rightarrow,\Pi,\mathtt{let}}$, then $\vdash_{ML2} \Gamma \triangleright Erase(M)\colon \sigma$. Conversely, if $\vdash_{ML2} \Gamma \triangleright V\colon \sigma$, then there is a typed term $\Gamma \triangleright M\colon \sigma$ of $\lambda^{\rightarrow,\Pi,\mathtt{let}}$ with $Erase(M) = V$.

Proof The proof follows the same induction as the proof of Lemma 11.2.15, but with additional cases for (*gen*), (*inst*) and $(\mathtt{let})_2$. Each of these is straightforward, and essentially similar to the cases considered in the proof of Lemma 11.2.15. ■

As a step towards an algorithm that solves the ML type inference problem without using polymorphic U_2 types, we reformulate the type inference rules so that no polymorphic types are required. Essentially, the alternative rule for `let` uses substitution on terms in place of the kind of substitution on types that results from rules (*gen*) and (*inst*). More specifically, $\mathtt{let}\ x = U\ \mathtt{in}\ V$ has precisely the same ML typings as $[U/x]V$, provided $\Gamma \triangleright U\colon \rho$ for some non-polymorphic type ρ. This suggests the following rule:

$$\frac{\Gamma \triangleright U\colon \rho,\ \Gamma \triangleright [U/x]V\colon \tau}{\Gamma \triangleright \mathtt{let}\ x = U\ \mathtt{in}\ V\colon \tau} \qquad (\mathtt{let})_1$$

If we ignore the hypothesis about U, then this rule allows us to type $\mathtt{let}\ x = U\ \mathtt{in}\ V$ by typing the result $[U/x]V$ of `let` reduction. It is not hard to show that if x occurs in V, and $\Gamma \triangleright [U/x]V\colon \tau$ is an ML typing, then we must have $\Gamma \triangleright U\colon \sigma$ for some σ. Therefore, the assumption about U only prevents us from typing $\mathtt{let}\ x = U\ \mathtt{in}\ V$ when x does not occur in V and U is untypable.

A comparison of the two `let` rules appears in Example 11.3.2 below.

Since we wish to eliminate the typing rules that involve polymorphic types, we reformulate the rule for constants to incorporate (*inst*).

$$\emptyset \rhd c\colon [\tau_1, \ldots, \tau_k/t_1, \ldots, t_k]\tau, \text{ if } \Pi t_1.\ldots\Pi t_k.\,\tau \text{ is the type of } c \qquad (cst)_1$$

We will write $\vdash_{ML1} \Gamma \rhd U\colon \tau$ if the typing assertion $\Gamma \rhd U\colon \tau$ is provable from (*var*), (*abs*), (*app*) and (*add hyp*) of Section 11.2.4, together with $(cst)_1$ and $(\mathtt{let})_1$. It follows from the proof that the two inference systems are equivalent that with $(cst)_1$ and $(\mathtt{let})_1$, we do not need (*inst*) or (*gen*).

Example 11.3.2 Consider the term

$$\mathtt{let}\ y = \lambda x.\lambda f.\,fx\ \mathtt{in}\ \mathtt{if}\ z\ \mathtt{then}\ y\ \mathit{true}\ \lambda x.5\ \mathtt{else}\ y\ 3\ \lambda x.7$$

where we assume that $\mathit{true}\colon \mathit{bool}$ and $3\colon \mathit{nat}$ as usual. Using rules common to ML_1 and ML_2, we may derive the typing assertion

$$\emptyset \rhd \lambda f.\lambda x.\,fx\colon s \to (s \to s) \to s$$

In the ML_2 system, we can then generalize s by rule (*gen*) to obtain

$$\emptyset \rhd \lambda f.\lambda x.\,fx\colon \Pi s.\,s \to (s \to s) \to s$$

and use (*inst*) to derive

$$y\colon \Pi s.\,s \to (s \to s) \to s \rhd y\colon \mathit{nat} \to (\mathit{nat} \to \mathit{nat}) \to \mathit{nat}$$

and similarly for *bool*. This allows us to prove

$$y\colon \Pi s.\,s \to (s \to s) \to s \rhd (\mathtt{if}\ z\ \mathtt{then}\ y\ \mathit{true}\ \lambda x.5\ \mathtt{else}\ y\ 3\ \lambda x.7)\colon \mathit{nat}$$

which makes it possible to type the original term by the $(\mathtt{let})_2$ rule.

We can also derive

$$\emptyset \rhd \mathtt{let}\ y = \lambda x.\lambda f.\,fx\ \mathtt{in}\ \mathtt{if}\ z\ \mathtt{then}\ y\ \mathit{true}\ \lambda x.5\ \mathtt{else}\ y\ 3\ \lambda x.7\colon \mathit{nat}$$

using $(\mathtt{let})_1$. Working backwards, it suffices to show

$$\emptyset \rhd \mathtt{if}\ z\ \mathtt{then}\ (\lambda x.\lambda f.\,fx)\,\mathit{true}\ \lambda x.5\ \mathtt{else}\ (\lambda x.\lambda f.\,fx)\,3\ \lambda x.7\colon \mathit{nat}$$

which can be done by showing that both $(\lambda x.\lambda f.\,fx)\,\mathit{true}\ \lambda x.5$ and $(\lambda x.\lambda f.\,fx)\,3\ \lambda x.7$ have type *nat*. These typings can be shown in the $\lambda_t^{\to}$-fragment of ML_1 in the usual way. The difference between the ML_1 and ML_2 derivations is that in ML_1, we type each occurrence of $\lambda x.\,\lambda f.\,f x$ in a different way, while in ML_2 we give one polymorphic typing for this term, and instantiate the bound type variable differently for each occurrence. ■

Since ML_1 typings use the same form of typing assertions as Curry typing, we may adopt the definition of instance given in Section 11.2.4. It is not hard to see that Lemma 11.2.3 extends immediately to $\vdash_{ML1}$.

Lemma 11.3.3 Let $\Gamma' \triangleright U\colon \tau'$ be an instance of the typing $\Gamma \triangleright U\colon \tau$. If $\vdash_{ML1} \Gamma \triangleright U\colon \tau$, then $\vdash_{ML1} \Gamma' \triangleright U\colon \tau'$.

Proof This proof by induction on typing derivations is identical to the proof of Lemma 11.2.3 except for an additional case for $(\texttt{let})_1$. ■

We also have a similar property for ML_2 typings, where we define instance exactly as before. Specifically, $\Gamma' \triangleright U\colon \tau'$ is an instance of $\Gamma \triangleright U\colon \tau$ if there is a substitution S with $S\Gamma \subseteq \Gamma'$ and $S\tau = \tau'$. As usual, a substitution only effects free type variables, not those bound by Π.

Lemma 11.3.4 Let $\Gamma' \triangleright U\colon \tau'$ be an instance of the typing $\Gamma \triangleright U\colon \tau$, where Γ and τ may contain polymorphic types. If $\vdash_{ML2} \Gamma \triangleright U\colon \tau$, then $\vdash_{ML2} \Gamma' \triangleright U\colon \tau'$.

This lemma will be used in proving that ML_1 and ML_2 are equivalent. The proof is again by induction on typing derivations.

We can prove that the two inference systems are equivalent for typing judgements without polymorphic types.

Theorem 11.3.5 Let Γ be a type assignment with no polymorphic types, and let τ be any nonpolymorphic type. Then $\vdash_{ML2} \Gamma \triangleright U\colon \tau$ iff $\vdash_{ML1} \Gamma \triangleright U\colon \tau$.

Although the details are involved, the main idea behind this equivalence is relatively simple. We give a short sketch here and postpone the full proof to Section 11.3.4.

The proof of Theorem 11.3.5 has two parts, the first showing that ML_1 is as powerful as ML_2 and the second showing the converse. The first part is easier. To show that ML_1 is as powerful as ML_2, we first show that adding the ML_2 rules (*gen*) and (*inst*) would not change the ML_1. The essential reason is that if $\Gamma \triangleright U\colon \tau'$ is proved from $\Gamma \triangleright U\colon \tau$ by some sequence of steps involving only (*gen*) and (*inst*), then $\Gamma \triangleright U\colon \tau'$ is an instance of $\Gamma \triangleright U\colon \tau$. But since any instance of an ML_1 typing is already ML_1-provable, rules (*gen*) and (*inst*) are unnecessary. The second step in showing ML_1 is as powerful as ML_2 is to show that $(\texttt{let})_2$ can only be used to derive typing assertion that could already be proved using ML_1 rules. If we prove a typing by $(\texttt{let})_2$,

$$\frac{\Gamma \triangleright U\colon \Pi t_1.\ldots\Pi t_k.\tau,\ \ \Gamma, x\colon \Pi t_1.\ldots\Pi t_k.\tau \triangleright V\colon \tau'}{\Gamma \triangleright \texttt{let}\ x = U\ \texttt{in}\ V\colon \tau'}$$

then every occurrence of x in V is given a substitution instance of τ by applying some combination of (*inst*) and (*gen*) steps. Therefore, we could prove $\Gamma \triangleright [U/x]V\colon \tau'$ using the ML_1 rules. This is the outline of the proof that ML_1 is as powerful as ML_2.

The converse, however, requires principal typing. The main problem is to show that if x occurs in V and $\Gamma \triangleright [U/x]V\colon \tau'$ is ML_1-provable, then there is some type τ such that $\Gamma \triangleright U\colon \Pi t_1.\ldots\Pi t_k.\tau$ and $\Gamma, x\colon \Pi t_1.\ldots\Pi t_k.\tau \triangleright V\colon \tau'$ are both ML_2-provable. The only reasonable choice for τ is the principal type for U. If we set up the inductive proof of equivalence properly, then it suffices to show that ML_1 has principal types. Therefore, we proceed with the typing algorithms based on ML_1. These give us the existence of principal typings as a corollary, allowing use to prove the equivalence of ML_1 and ML_2 in Section 11.3.4.

Theorem 11.3.5 gives us the following correspondence between $\vdash_{ML1}$ and the explicitly typed language $\lambda^{\rightarrow,\Pi,\texttt{let}}$.

Corollary 11.3.6 Let τ be any U_1 type of $\lambda^{\rightarrow,\Pi,\texttt{let}}$ and Γ any type assignment containing only U_1 types. If $\Gamma \triangleright M\colon \tau$ is a well-typed term of $\lambda^{\rightarrow,\Pi,\texttt{let}}$, then $\vdash_{ML1} \Gamma \triangleright$ *Erase*$(M)\colon \tau$. Conversely, if $\vdash_{ML1} \Gamma \triangleright V\colon \tau$, then there is a typed term $\Gamma \triangleright M\colon \tau$ of $\lambda^{\rightarrow,\Pi,\texttt{let}}$ with *Erase*$(M) = V$.

Proof This follows immediately from Lemma 11.3.1 and Theorem 11.3.5. ∎

11.3.3 Type Inference Algorithms

We consider three algorithms for computing principal ML_1 typings of untyped λ, `let`-terms. The first eliminates `let`'s and applies algorithm *PT* of Section 11.2.3. This takes exponential time in the worst case, since eliminating `let`'s may lead to an exponential increase in the size of the term. However, as we shall see in Section 11.3.5, exponential time is the asymptotic lower bound on the running time of any correct typing algorithm. The second algorithm is based on the same idea, but is formulated as an extension to algorithm *PT*. This serves as an intermediate step towards the third algorithm, which uses a separate "environment" to store the types of `let`-bound variables, eliminating the need for substitution on terms. This algorithm more closely resembles the algorithms actually used in ML and related compilers. Although the third algorithm has the same asymptotic worst-case running time as the first, it has a simple recursive form and may be substantially more efficient in practice since it does not perform any operations on terms. All three algorithms are explained and proved correct for ML_1 typing. It follows by Theorem 11.3.5 that the algorithms are also correct for and produce principal typings for ML_2 typing.

First Algorithm

The main idea behind the first algorithm is that when x occurs in V, the term $\texttt{let}\ x = U\ \texttt{in}\ V$ has exactly the same typings as $[U/x]V$. We can treat the special case where x does not occur in V by the following general transformation on terms.

Lemma 11.3.7 An untyped λ, let-term of the form $\texttt{let}\ x = U\ \texttt{in}\ V$ has precisely the same ML_1 typings as $\texttt{let}\ x = U\ \texttt{in}\ (\lambda y.V)x$, provided y not free in V, and precisely the same ML_1 typings as the result $[U/x]((\lambda y.V)x)$ of let-reducing the latter term.

The proof is straightforward, by inspection of the ML_1 inference rules. A second induction shows that we may repeat this transformation anywhere inside a term, any number of times.

Lemma 11.3.8 Let W_1 be any untyped λ, let-term and let W_2 be the result of repeatedly replacing any subterm of the form $\texttt{let}\ x = U\ \texttt{in}\ V$ by either $\texttt{let}\ x = U\ \texttt{in}\ (\lambda y.V)x$ or $[U/x]((\lambda y.V)x)$. Then W_1 and W_2 have precisely the same ML_1 typings.

Lemma 11.3.8 gives a transformation of untyped λ, let-terms that preserves typability. Since this transformation can be used to eliminate all let's from a term, we may compute ML_1 typings using the algorithm PT for $\lambda_t^{\rightarrow}$ typings. Given an untyped λ, let-term, algorithm PTL_1 eliminates all let's according to Lemma 11.3.8 and applies algorithm PT to the resulting untyped lambda term. If we write let-expand(U) for the result of removing all let's according to Lemma 11.3.8, then we may define algorithm PTL_1 as follows:

$$
\begin{aligned}
PTL_1(U) &= \textbf{let} \\
&\qquad \Gamma \rhd M\colon \tau = PT(\texttt{let-expand}(U)) \\
&\quad\ \textbf{in} \\
&\qquad \Gamma \rhd U\colon \tau
\end{aligned}
$$

Termination follows from Proposition 9.2.15. Specifically, we can compute the let-expansion of a term in two-phases. We begin by replacing each subterm of the form $\texttt{let}\ x = U\ \texttt{in}\ V$ by $\texttt{let}\ x = U\ \texttt{in}\ (\lambda y.V)x$, where y is not free in V. This is clearly a terminating process. Then, by Proposition 9.2.15, we can let-reduce each $\texttt{let}\ x = U\ \texttt{in}\ (\lambda y.V)x$ to $[U/x]((\lambda y.V)x)$. The theorems below follow immediately from Lemmas 11.3.3 and 11.3.8 and Theorems 11.2.12 and 11.2.13.

Theorem 11.3.9 If $PTL_1(U) = \Gamma \rhd U\colon \tau$, then every instance of $\Gamma \rhd U\colon \tau$ is ML_1-provable.

Theorem 11.3.10 Suppose $\vdash_{ML1} \Gamma \triangleright U : \tau$ is an ML_1 typing for U. Then $PTL_1(U)$ succeeds and produces a typing assertion with $\Gamma \triangleright U : \tau$ as an instance.

Corollary 11.3.11 Let U be an untyped λ, `let`-term. If U has an ML_1 typing, then U has a principal ML_1 typing.

Second Algorithm

We can reformulate algorithm PTL_1 as an extension of *PT*, rather than a two phase algorithm with a preprocessing step. If we read typing rule $(\mathtt{let})_1$ from the bottom up, this rule suggests that we extend algorithm *PT* to `let` by adding the following clause:

$$\begin{aligned} PT(\mathtt{let}\ x = U\ \mathtt{in}\ V) = & \ \mathbf{let} \\ & \quad \Gamma \triangleright U : \tau = PT(U) \\ & \mathbf{in} \\ & \quad PT([U/x]V) \end{aligned}$$

We write PTL_2 for the algorithm given by this extension to PT.

It is intuitively clear from the $(\mathtt{let})_1$ rule that this algorithm is correct. We state and prove this precisely using `let`-expansion of terms. For any terms U and V, we write $PTL_i(U) \cong PTL_j(V)$ if either both $PTL_i(U)$ and $PTL_j(V)$ fail, or $PTL_i(U) = \Gamma_1 \triangleright U : \tau_1$ and $PTL_j(V) = \Gamma_2 \triangleright V : \tau_2$ both succeed with $\Gamma_1 = \Gamma_2$ and $\tau_1 = \tau_2$.

Lemma 11.3.12 For any untyped λ, `let`-term U, we have $PTL_2(U) \cong PTL_2(\mathtt{let}\text{-}\mathrm{expand}(U))$.

Proof The proof uses induction on an ordering of untyped terms by "degree." Recall from Proposition 9.2.15 that there are no untyped λ, `let`-terms with an infinite sequence of `let` reductions. If V is an untyped λ, `let`-term, then the *degree of V* is the pair $dg(V) = \langle \ell, m \rangle$ of natural numbers with ℓ the length of the longest `let`-reduction sequence from V and $m = |V|$ the length of V. We order degrees *lexicographically*, so that $\langle \ell, m \rangle < \langle \ell', m' \rangle$ iff either $\ell < \ell'$ or both $\ell = \ell'$ and $m < m'$. Induction on this well-founded ordering lets us prove the theorem for V from the inductive assumption that the theorem holds for all U with $dg(U) < dg(V)$. In other words, we assume that the theorem holds for every term that either does not have as long a maximal `let` reduction sequence, or has the same number of `let` reductions but is a shorter term. The reason that this form of induction works is that for terms that are not `let`'s, we can use ordinary induction, and for a term of the form $\mathtt{let}\ x = U\ \mathtt{in}\ V$, we may assume inductively that the lemma holds for $[U/x]V$ since this cannot have as long a sequence of `let` reductions.

We show the cases for application and `let`, since these are representative. $PTL_2(UV)$ is computed using $PTL_2(U)$ and $PTL_2(V)$. By the inductive hypothesis, we have

$PTL_2(U) \cong PTL_2(\texttt{let}\text{-expand}(U))$ and $PTL_2(V) \cong PTL_2(\texttt{let}\text{-expand}(V))$. If either of these fails, then the lemma holds in this case. Otherwise, we can see by inspection of the application case of the algorithm that the result only depends on the type assignments and types involved, not the terms. Therefore, $PTL_2(UV) \cong PTL_2(\texttt{let}\text{-expand}(UV))$.

For $\texttt{let}\ x = U\ \texttt{in}\ V$, we have

$$PTL_2(\texttt{let}\ x = U\ \texttt{in}\ V) = \textbf{let}\ \ \Gamma \rhd U : \tau = PTL_2(U)\ \ \textbf{in}\ \ PTL_2([U/x]V)$$

where by the inductive hypothesis $PTL_2(U) \cong PTL_2(\texttt{let}\text{-expand}(U))$ and $PTL_2([U/x]V) \cong PTL_2(\texttt{let}\text{-expand}([U/x]V))$, since both terms have lower degree. If $PTL_2(U)$ fails, then we are done. Otherwise, since $\texttt{let}\text{-expand}(\texttt{let}\ x = U\ \texttt{in}\ V) = \texttt{let}\text{-expand}([U/x]V)$, it follows that

$$\begin{aligned} & PTL_2(\texttt{let}\ x = U\ \texttt{in}\ V) \\ = \quad & PTL_2([U/x]V) \\ = \quad & PTL_2(\texttt{let}\text{-expand}([U/x]V)) \\ = \quad & PTL_2(\texttt{let}\text{-expand}(\texttt{let}\ x = U\ \texttt{in}\ V)). \end{aligned}$$

This proves the lemma. ■

Using the fact that for let-free U, $PTL_2(U) = PT(U)$, we have the following theorem relating the typing algorithms.

Theorem 11.3.13 For any untyped λ, let-term U, $PTL_2(U) \cong PTL_1(U) \cong PT(\texttt{let}\text{-expand}(U))$.

Third Algorithm

Algorithm *PTL* given in Table 11.4 has two arguments, a term to be typed and an environment mapping variables to typings. The purpose of the environment is to handle let-bound variables. Therefore, in a "top-level" function call, with a closed expression, this environment would be empty. It is assumed that the input to *PTL* is an untyped expression with all bound variables renamed to be distinct. This guarantees that if a variable is let-bound, it is not also λ-bound (see Exercise 11.3.18).

Algorithm *PTL* works just like algorithm *PT*, except in the let case. In the inefficient extension PTL_2 of *PT* to let above, we compute the most general type of $\texttt{let}\ x = U\ \texttt{in}\ V$ by typing U to make sure it is typable, then invoking the algorithm on $[U/x]V$. Essentially, *PTL* simulates this inefficient algorithm by storing the most general typing

Table 11.4
Algorithm *PTL* for principal typing with `let`.

$PTL(c, A) = \emptyset \triangleright c\!: \tau$, where $\Pi t_1. \ldots \Pi t_k. \tau$ is the type of c

$PTL(x, A) =$ **if** $A(x) = \langle \Gamma,\ \tau \rangle$ **then** $\Gamma \triangleright x\!: \tau$
else $\{x\!: t\} \triangleright x\!: t$

$PTL(UV, A) =$
let =
$\Gamma \triangleright U\!: \tau = PTL(U, A)$
$\Gamma' \triangleright V\!: \rho = PTL(V, A)$,
with type variables renamed to be disjoint from those in $PTL(U, A)$
$S = Unify(\{\alpha = \beta \mid x\!:\alpha \in \Gamma \text{ and } x\!:\beta \in \Gamma'\} \cup \{\tau = \rho \to t\})$
where t is a fresh type variable
in
$S\Gamma \cup S\Gamma' \triangleright UV\!: St$

$PTL(\lambda x.U, A) =$
let $\Gamma \triangleright U\!: \rho = PTL(U, A)$
in
if $x\!: \tau \in \Gamma$ for some τ
then $\Gamma - \{x\!: \tau\} \triangleright \lambda x.U\!: \tau \to \rho$
else $\Gamma \triangleright \lambda x.U\!: s \to \rho$
where s is a fresh type variable

$PTL($`let` $x = U$ `in` $V, A) =$
let $\Gamma \triangleright U\!: \tau = PTL(U, A)$
$A' = A \cup \{x \mapsto \langle \Gamma,\ \tau \rangle\}$
$\Gamma' \triangleright V\!: \rho = PTL(V, A')$
in $\Gamma' \triangleright$ `let` $x = U$ `in` $V\!: \rho$

for U in the environment A. Then, whenever x is encountered in typing the declaration body V, the typing for x may be retrieved from the environment. This eliminates the cost of computing the typing for V for each occurrence of x, but gives the same result as substituting U for x in V. Like *PT*, algorithm *PTL* may *fail* in the application case if the call to *Unify* fails. The following examples show how this algorithm may succeed or fail on `let`-declarations.

Example 11.3.14 An easy example is `let` $I = \lambda x.x$ `in` II. By Lemma 11.3.7, this untyped term has exactly the same typings as $(\lambda x.x)(\lambda x.x)$. Therefore, we may determine the principal typing by applying algorithm *PT* to this `let`-reduced term. It is easy to see that $PT(\lambda x.x) = \emptyset \triangleright \lambda x.x\!: r \to r$, and therefore

$$PT(\,(\lambda x.x)(\lambda x.x)\,) = \emptyset \triangleright (\lambda x.x)(\lambda x.x)\!: s \to s$$

by unifying $r \to r$ with $(s \to s) \to t$ and applying the resulting substitution to t.

If we apply *PTL* directly, we should get the same answer. In fact, we do essentially the same computation, except that we only compute the principal typing of $\lambda x.x$ once. The first step of the algorithm is to compute $PTL(\lambda x.x, \emptyset)$, which gives the same result as $PT(\lambda x.x)$. Then, we "store" the pair $\langle \emptyset,\ r \to r\rangle$ as $A(I)$ and type the application II. Here we look up $\emptyset \rhd \lambda x.x\colon r \to r$ twice, rename all type variables in one copy, and compute the type of the application. This involves exactly the same unification as in the final application step for $PT(\,(\lambda x.x)(\lambda x.x)\,)$ and so we obtain the same typing. ■

Example 11.3.15 A subtle point in algorithm *PTL* is the treatment of free variables in `let`-declarations. To give a relatively simple example, consider the term

$\lambda x.\mathtt{let}\ f = \lambda y.yx\ \mathtt{in}\ (f\ \lambda z.z)\,(f\ \lambda u.\lambda v.u).$

Here we have a function f whose body contains a free variable x. Since x is λ-bound in the larger expression containing the `let`, x cannot be polymorphic. This makes f "partly" polymorphic and partly not. We can see this by examining the way that the type assumption about x is handled in the application of *PTL* to this term.

The execution of *PTL* begins by typing the body of f. The result is

$PTL(\lambda y.yx,\ \emptyset) = x\colon t \rhd \lambda y.yx\colon (t \to s) \to s.$

The pair $\langle x\colon t,\ (t \to s) \to s\rangle$ is then "stored" in A and we proceed to type the application $(f\ \lambda z.z)\,(f\ \lambda u.\lambda v.u)$ by typing function and argument separately. We type $f\ \lambda z.z$ by combining the typing

$x\colon t \rhd f\colon (t \to s) \to s$

for f with the type of the identity $\lambda z.z : r \to r$. Unifying $t \to s$ with $r \to r$, this gives us the most general typing

$PTL(\,(f\ \lambda z.z),\ \{f \mapsto \langle x\colon t,\ \ (t \to s) \to s\rangle\}\,) = x\colon t \rhd (f\ \lambda z.z)\colon t.$

By similar steps, we also obtain

$PTL(\,(f\ \lambda u.\lambda v.u),\ \{f \mapsto \langle x\colon t,\ \ (t \to s) \to s\rangle\}\,) = x\colon s \rhd (f\ \lambda u.\lambda v.u)\colon r \to s,$

where to avoid confusion we have written the typing with all type variables already renamed, as specified in the algorithm. We can see now that the algorithm fails on $(f\ \lambda z.z)\,(f\ \lambda u.\lambda v.u)$ since this involves unifying the set $\{s = t, t = (r \to s) \to t'\}$. The equation $s = t$ arises from the two assumptions about the type of x. However, if we were to incorrectly drop the assumptions about x in both of the typings, the algorithm would succeed.

We may verify that *PTL* should fail by reducing the original expression:

$\lambda x.\texttt{let}\ f = \lambda y.yx\ \texttt{in}\ (f\ \lambda z.z)\,(f\ \lambda u.\lambda v.u)$

$\rightarrow\quad \lambda x.((\lambda y.yx)\ \lambda z.z)\,((\lambda y.yx)\ \lambda u.\lambda v.u)$

$\rightarrow\quad \lambda x.x\,(\lambda v.x)$

Since $\lambda x.x\,(\lambda v.x)$ is not $\lambda_t^{\rightarrow}$ typable, no term reducing to $\lambda x.x\,(\lambda v.x)$ can be $\lambda^{\rightarrow,\Pi,\texttt{let}}$ typable. A variant of this term that is typable is given in Exercise 11.3.17. ■

The correctness of PTL is stated in the following theorem, which gives $PTL(V, \emptyset) \cong PTL_2(V)$ as a special case.

Theorem 11.3.16 Let A be an environment mapping x_i to $\langle \Gamma_i, \tau_i \rangle$ for $1 \leq i \leq n$ and undefined on any variable other than $x_1, \ldots, x_n$. Suppose there are untyped λ-terms $U_1, \ldots, U_n$ with $PT(U_i) = \Gamma_i \triangleright U_i : \tau_i$ for $1 \leq i \leq n$. Then, writing $[A]V$ for $[U_1, \ldots, U_n / x_1, \ldots, x_n]V$, we have $PTL(V, A) \cong PTL_2([A]V)$ for any untyped λ, `let`-term V whose bound variables are all distinct from $x_1, \ldots, x_n$.

Proof The proof uses induction on the degree of untyped λ, `let`-terms, as in the proof of Lemma 11.3.12. Specifically, we check each case of the algorithm, assuming that the theorem holds for all terms of lower degree.

For a variable, constant or application, the theorem is straightforward. For a lambda abstraction $\lambda x.V$, we use the fact that since all of the variables are distinct, $[A]\,\lambda x.V = \lambda x.([A]V)$.

For $\texttt{let}\ x = U\ \texttt{in}\ V$, we assume that $PTL(U, A) \cong PTL_2([A']U) = \Gamma \triangleright [A']U : \tau$ succeeds, since the theorem clearly holds otherwise. By the inductive hypothesis, we have $PTL(V, A') \cong PTL_2([A']V)$ for any A', in particular $A' = A \cup \{x \mapsto \langle \Gamma, \tau \rangle\}$ as in algorithm PTL. The theorem holds since

$$PTL(\texttt{let}\ x = U\ \texttt{in}\ V, A) \cong PTL(V, A') \cong PTL_2([A][U/x]V)$$

$$\cong PTL_2([A](\texttt{let}\ x = U\ \texttt{in}\ V)).$$

This concludes the proof. ■

Exercise 11.3.17 Example 11.3.15, shows that the term

$\lambda x.\texttt{let}\ f = \lambda y.yx\ \texttt{in}\ (f\ \lambda z.z)\,(f\ \lambda u.\lambda v.u)$

is not typable. Find an untyped λ-term U such that the similar expression

$\texttt{let}\ x = U\ \texttt{in}\ \texttt{let}\ f = \lambda y.yx\ \texttt{in}\ (f\ \lambda z.z)\,(f\ \lambda u.\lambda v.u)$

is typable. Describe the application of *PTL* to this term, in approximately the same detail as Example 11.3.15. Check your calculation by `let`-reducing twice and applying algorithm PT.

Exercise 11.3.18 It is assumed that the input to *PTL* is an expression with all bound variables renamed to be distinct, so that if a variable is `let`-bound, it is not also λ-bound. Demonstrate the importance of this restriction by finding a term U such that the typing obtained by `let`-reducing U and then applying algorithm *PT* is different from naive application of *PTL* without renaming bound variables in U. Then rename bound variables in U so that they are distinct and show that *PTL* now gives the same result as *PT*.

11.3.4 Equivalence of ML_1 and ML_2

This section is devoted to showing that the two type inference systems, ML_1 and ML_2, are equivalent for proving typing assertions of the form $\Gamma \rhd V\colon \tau$, where Γ contains no polymorphic types and τ is not polymorphic (*i.e.*, Γ and τ are Π-free). An informal overview of the main ideas in the equivalence proof is given in Section 11.3.2 immediately following the statement of Theorem 11.3.5. Although the typing rules are slightly different, the proof here is essentially the same as the one given in the Appendix of [KMM91].

When we compare two proofs of the same typing judgement, the possibility that either proof might end in rule (*add hyp*) leads to unnecessary and uninteresting complications. Therefore, we will restrict the use of (*add hyp*). It is easy to establish the following property.

Lemma 11.3.19 Let Γ be any typing context and let Γ' be the subset of Γ only mentioning term variables that occur free in U. Then $\Gamma \rhd U\colon \sigma$ is derivable, in either the ML_1 or ML_2 proof system, iff $\Gamma' \rhd U\colon \sigma$ is derivable in the same proof system.

The proof is an easy induction on typing derivations. The value of the lemma is that we only need to prove that ML_1 and ML_2 are equivalent for judgements $\Gamma \rhd U\colon \sigma$ with Γ containing exactly the free variables of U. This lets us dispense with (*add hyp*) in certain critical cases, as the reader will see in the proof of Lemma 11.3.20 below.

We will need two technical properties of the ML_2 typing system. The first lemma gives a "normal form" property for typing derivations.

Lemma 11.3.20 Let Γ be a type assignment only containing free variables of V and let τ be any non-polymorphic type. Suppose that either Γ contains no polymorphic types or the untyped term V is not a variable. If $\vdash_{ML2} \Gamma \rhd V\colon \Pi t_1 \ldots \Pi t_k.\, \tau$, then $\vdash_{ML2} \Gamma \rhd V\colon \tau$ by a proof whose last step is either the axiom (*var*) or an application of one of the proof rules (*abs*), (*app*), or $(\mathtt{let})_2$, depending on the syntactic form of V.

Proof The proof is by cases (not induction), depending on the structure of terms. For a variable x, every proof must begin with the axiom $\{x\colon \tau\} \rhd x\colon \tau$. But this is all we can prove, since every type in the type assignment is assumed Π-free, and we cannot add extraneous variables to the typing context. In particular, we cannot apply (*gen*) nontrivially since every type variable free in τ obviously appears in the type assignment $x\colon \tau$. The remaining cases all resemble each other. We show only the application case and leave the remaining details to the reader.

Consider a provable typing assertion $\Gamma \rhd U V\colon \tau$. The proof of this assertion must involve some application of the rule

$$\frac{\Gamma \rhd U\colon \tau_1 \rightarrow \tau_2, \quad \Gamma \rhd V\colon \tau_1}{\Gamma \rhd U V\colon \tau_2} \qquad (app)$$

possibly followed by rules (*add hyp*), (*gen*) and (*inst*). However, since Γ must contain exactly the free variables of $U V$, we may disregard (*add hyp*). Since (*gen*) and (*inst*) may only lead to the substitution of type expressions for type variables in τ_2, we have $\tau = S\tau_2$ for some substitution S. By Lemma 11.3.4, the provable typings are closed under substitution. Therefore, both $\Gamma \rhd U\colon S(\tau_1 \rightarrow \tau_2)$ and $\Gamma \rhd V\colon S\tau_1$ must be provable. This shows that there must be a proof of $\Gamma \rhd U V\colon \tau$ by rule (*app*). ■

It follows from Corollary11.3.11 that every typable λ, `let`-term has a principal typing. In proving the equivalence of the ML_1 and ML_2 typing rules, it will be useful to have an additional form of principal typing. We will say that a provable typing assertion $\Gamma \rhd U\colon \tau$ is Γ-*principal* if for every other provable typing assertion $\Gamma \rhd U\colon \tau'$ there is a substitution S affecting only type variables not in Γ such that $\tau' = S\tau$. Using simple properties of first-order substitution and unification, it is easy to see that principal typings give us Γ-principal typings.

Lemma 11.3.21 Suppose $\Gamma \rhd V\colon \tau$ is a principal typing for V and $\Gamma' \rhd V\colon \tau'$ is provable. Then $\Gamma' = S\Gamma \cup \Gamma''$ for some substitution S which only affects type variables in Γ, and $\Gamma' \rhd V\colon S\tau$ is a Γ'-principal typing for V.

We use the idea of Γ-principal typing in the final lemma, which involves substitution and polymorphically-typed variables.

Lemma 11.3.22 Let Γ be any type assignment, possibly containing polymorphic types but not containing the term variable x. Assume $\vdash_{ML2} \Gamma \rhd U\colon \Pi t_1 \ldots \Pi t_k.\, \tau$ and that for every provable typing assertion $\Gamma \rhd U\colon \tau'$, the type τ' is a substitution instance of τ. Then $\vdash_{ML2} \Gamma \rhd [U/x]V\colon \tau''$ iff $\vdash_{ML2} \Gamma, x\colon (\Pi t_1 \ldots \Pi t_k.\, \tau) \rhd V\colon \tau''$.

Proof The proof is by induction on the structure of V. The variable case involves reasoning about sequences of (*inst*) and (*gen*) proof steps. The main idea is that $\vdash_{ML2}$ $\Gamma \triangleright U : \tau''$ iff $\tau'' = [\tau_1, \ldots, \tau_k/t_1, \ldots, t_k]\tau$ iff the typing assertion $\Gamma \triangleright U : \tau''$ may be obtained from $\Gamma \triangleright U : \Pi t_1 \ldots \Pi t_k.\, \tau$ by a series of applications of (*inst*) and (*gen*). But then this same series of proof steps may be used to obtain $\Gamma, x : (\Pi t_1 \ldots \Pi t_k.\, \tau) \triangleright x : \tau''$ from $\Gamma, x : (\Pi t_1 \ldots \Pi t_k.\, \tau) \triangleright x : \Pi t_1 \ldots \Pi t_k.\, \tau$, and conversely.

The remaining cases are essentially alike. We will illustrate the argument using the `let` case, since this is slightly more involved than the others. By Lemma 11.3.20, we need only consider proofs that end with rule $(\mathtt{let})_2$. Therefore, we have $\vdash_{ML2} \Gamma \triangleright [U/x](\mathtt{let}\ y = V_1\ \mathtt{in}\ V_2) : \tau''$ iff $\vdash_{ML2} \Gamma \triangleright (\mathtt{let}\ y = [U/x]V_1\ \mathtt{in}\ [U/x]V_2) : \tau''$ iff by the last proof rule both $\vdash_{ML2} \Gamma \triangleright [U/x]V_1 : \sigma'$ and $\vdash_{ML2} \Gamma, y : \sigma' \triangleright [U/x]V_2 : \tau''$. Since τ'' is not a polymorphic type, the inductive hypothesis implies that the second condition is equivalent to $\vdash_{ML2} \Gamma, x : \sigma, y : \sigma' \triangleright V_2 : \tau''$, where $\sigma = (\Pi t_1 \ldots \Pi t_k.\, \tau)$.

To apply the inductive hypothesis to $\Gamma \triangleright [U/x]V_1 : \sigma'$, we note that σ' must have the form $\sigma' = \Pi s_1 \ldots \Pi s_\ell.\, \tau'$. We assume without loss of generality that $s_1, \ldots, s_\ell$ do not occur free in Γ and remove the quantifiers by rule (*inst*). Using the inductive hypothesis on the typing assertion obtained in this way, we observe:

$$\begin{aligned} \vdash_{ML2} \Gamma \triangleright [U/x]V_1 : \Pi s_1 \ldots \Pi s_\ell.\, \tau' &\text{iff } \vdash_{ML2} \Gamma \triangleright [U/x]V_1 : \tau' \\ &\text{iff } \vdash_{ML2} \Gamma, x : \sigma \triangleright V_1 : \tau' \\ &\text{iff } \vdash_{ML2} \Gamma, x : \sigma \triangleright V_1 : \Pi s_1 \ldots \Pi s_\ell.\, \tau' \blacksquare \end{aligned}$$

Proof of Theorem 11.3.5 The proof uses induction on an ordering of untyped terms by degree, as described in the proof of Lemma 11.3.12. Specifically, the degree of V is the pair $dg(V) = \langle \ell, m \rangle$ of natural numbers with ℓ the length of the longest `let`-reduction sequence from V and $m = |V|$ the length of V.

We show that the two systems are equivalent for terms of each syntactic form. The cases for variable, application and abstraction are essentially straightforward, using Lemma 11.3.20. To give an example, we will prove the theorem for abstractions. By Lemma 11.3.20, we have $\vdash_{ML2} \Gamma \triangleright \lambda x.U : \tau \to \tau'$ iff $\vdash_{ML2} \Gamma, x : \tau \triangleright U : \tau'$, where by Lemma 11.3.19 we assume that x does not occur in Γ. By the inductive hypothesis, $\vdash_{ML2} \Gamma, x : \tau \triangleright U : \tau'$ iff $\vdash_{ML1} \Gamma, x : \tau \triangleright U : \tau'$. By inspection of the ML_1 rules, we can see that since x does not occur in Γ, $\vdash_{ML1} \Gamma, x : \tau \triangleright U : \tau'$ iff $\vdash_{ML1} \Gamma \triangleright \lambda x.U : \tau \to \tau'$.

Since the primary difference between the two systems is in the `let` rules, this is the main case of the proof. We prove each direction of the equivalence separately. If $\vdash_{ML1}$ $\Gamma \triangleright \mathtt{let}\ x = U\ \mathtt{in}\ V : \tau$, then the derivation concludes with the rule

$$\frac{\Gamma \triangleright U : \tau', \quad \Gamma \triangleright [U/x]V : \tau}{\Gamma \triangleright \mathtt{let}\ x = U\ \mathtt{in}\ V : \tau}$$

There are two cases to consider. If x does not occur free in V, then by the inductive hypothesis, we know that both hypotheses of this proof rule are ML_2-provable. From $\Gamma \triangleright V\colon \tau$ we obtain $\Gamma, x\colon \tau' \triangleright V\colon \tau$ and so we complete the ML_2 proof by

$$\frac{\Gamma \triangleright U\colon \tau', \quad \Gamma, x\colon \tau' \triangleright V\colon \tau}{\Gamma \triangleright \mathtt{let}\ x = U\ \mathtt{in}\ V\colon \tau}$$

using rule $(\mathtt{let})_2$.

The more difficult case is when x occurs free in V. Since we have shown that $\vdash_{ML1}$ has principal typings, in Corollary 11.3.11, we may assume by Lemma 11.3.21 that $\Gamma \triangleright U\colon \tau'$ is the Γ-principal typing of U. This means that every ML_1-provable typing assertion of the form $\Gamma \triangleright U\colon \tau''$ has $\tau'' = S\tau'$ for some substitution S which only affects type variables $t_1, \ldots, t_k$ that are free in τ' but not in Γ. The Γ-principality of $\Gamma \triangleright U\colon \tau'$ carries over to ML_2 by the induction hypothesis. By the inductive hypotheses, we also have $\vdash_{ML2}$ $\Gamma \triangleright U\colon \tau'$ and $\vdash_{ML2} \Gamma \triangleright [U/x]V\colon \tau$. By rule (*gen*), we have $\vdash_{ML2} \Gamma \triangleright U\colon \Pi t_1 \ldots \Pi t_k.\, \tau'$ and by Lemma 11.3.22 $\vdash_{ML2} \Gamma, x\colon (\Pi t_1 \ldots \Pi t_k.\, \tau') \triangleright V\colon \tau$. This allows us to apply rule $(\mathtt{let})_2$, concluding this direction of the proof.

For the converse, we assume $\vdash_{ML2} \Gamma \triangleright \mathtt{let}\ x = U\ \mathtt{in}\ V\colon \tau$. By Lemma 11.3.20, we may assume that the proof ends with the proof step

$$\frac{\Gamma \triangleright U\colon \sigma, \quad \Gamma, x\colon \sigma \triangleright V\colon \tau}{\Gamma \triangleright \mathtt{let}\ x = U\ \mathtt{in}\ V\colon \tau} \qquad (\mathtt{let})_2$$

where $\sigma = \Pi t_1 \ldots \Pi t_k.\, \tau'$ for some sequence $t_1, \ldots, t_k$ of type variables and nonpolymorphic type τ'. Without loss of generality, we may assume that $t_1, \ldots, t_k$ do not appear free in Γ. By (*inst*), we have $\vdash_{ML2} \Gamma \triangleright U\colon \tau'$, and hence this assertion is ML_1-provable by the induction hypothesis. There is no loss of generality in assuming that $\Gamma \triangleright U\colon \tau'$ is a Γ-principal typing for U. This does not affect the provability of $\Gamma, x\colon \sigma \triangleright V\colon \tau$; since we may use (*inst*) on the variable x to obtain any substitution instance of τ in the typing for V. This gives us $\vdash_{ML2} \Gamma \triangleright [U/x]V\colon \tau$ by Lemma 11.3.22 and therefore $\vdash_{ML1} \Gamma \triangleright [U/x]V\colon \tau$ by the inductive hypothesis. We now use rule $(\mathtt{let})_1$ to finish the proof. ∎

11.3.5 Complexity of ML Type Inference

In this section, we show that the recognition problem for ML-typing is exponential-time complete. In other words, any algorithm that decides whether untyped λ, `let`-terms are ML-typable requires exponential time, in the worst case. All of the algorithms given in Section 11.3.3 run in at most exponential time, and are therefore optimal in principle. This stands in contrast to the complexity of Curry type inference, which may be decided in linear time, as shown in Theorem 11.2.17.

In discussing size and running time, we use standard "big-oh" notation as in Section 11.2.5, writing $f(n) = g(O(h(n))$ if there is a positive real number $c > 0$ with $f(n) \leq g(ch(n))$ for all sufficiently large n. For lower bounds, we write $f(n) = g(\Omega(h(n))$ if there is a positive real number $c > 0$ with $f(n) \geq g(ch(n))$ for infinitely many n.

A more detailed analysis of any of the ML typing algorithms shows that the running time is exponential in the `let`-depth of a term, and otherwise linear. (To be precise, the running time on input U is $2^{O(\ell d(U) log_2 |U|)}$, where $|U|$ is the length of U and $\ell d(U)$ is its `let`-depth.) This is also true of the lower bound. Intuitively, the `let`-depth of a term, defined in Section 9.2.5, is the depth of nesting of `let`-declarations. In the worst case, the `let`-depth of U may be proportional to the length of U. However, for many practical kinds of programs, the depth of non-trivial nesting appears bounded.

There are two main proofs of the exponential-time lower bound for ML typing. One is a direct encoding of exponential-time Turing machines as typing problems. The other uses a variant of unification called *semi-unification.* The first style of proof was developed and refined in a series of papers by several closely-communicating authors [KM89, Mai90, KMM91, HM94]. The semi-unification proof of [KTU90b] is related to a larger investigation of polymorphic type inference carried out in a separate series of papers [KTU88, KTU89, KTU90a].

One intriguing aspect of the algorithmic lower bound for ML typing is that it does not seem to effect the practical use of the ML type inference algorithm. The lower bound shows that for arbitrarily large n, there exist terms of length n that require on the order of 2^n steps to decide whether they are typable. Like any other algorithmic lower bound, the lower bound for ML type inference relies on the construction of an infinite family of "hard instances" of the typing problem. However, the empirical evidence is that these hard instances do not often arise in practice. In spite of twenty years of ML programming, the lower bounds were a complete surprise to most ML programmers. An interesting direction for future research would be to characterize the form of most "practical" ML programs in a way that explains the apparent efficiency of the algorithm in practice. We do have some explanation, in the way that the complexity depends on the `let`-depth of an expression, but there is likely to be more to the story.

A few example terms with large types will give us some useful intuition for the difficulties of ML typing. Before proceeding, it may be helpful to recall that in algorithm PTL, type variables in the types of `let`-bound expression are renamed at each occurrence. For example, consider a term of the form `let` $f = M$ `in` N with M closed. The first step in typing this term is to compute the principal type of M. Then, for each occurrence of f in N, the algorithm uses a copy of this principal type of M *with all type variables renamed to be different from those used in every other type.* (Something similar but slightly more complicated is done when M is not closed.) Because of variable renaming, the number of type variables in the principal type of a term may be exponential in the length of the term. The following example illustrating this exponential growth is due to Mitchell Wand and, independently, Peter Buneman.

Example 11.3.23 Consider the expression

$$\texttt{let } x = M \texttt{ in } \langle x, x\rangle$$

where M is closed with principal type σ. The principal type of this expression is $\sigma' \times \sigma''$, where σ' and σ'' are copies of σ with type variables renamed differently in each case. Unlike the expression $(\lambda x.\langle x, x\rangle)M$ in Example 11.2.18, not only is the type twice as long as σ, but the type has twice as many type variables. For this reason, even the dag representation (see Exercise 11.2.6) for the type of the expression with `let` is twice as large as the dag representation for the type of M. We can iterate this doubling of type variables using terms of the following form:

$$\begin{aligned} W_n \stackrel{\text{def}}{=} \; & \texttt{let } x_0 = M \texttt{ in} \\ & \texttt{let } x_1 = \langle x_0, x_0\rangle \texttt{ in} \\ & \quad \ldots \\ & \quad \texttt{let } x_n = \langle x_{n-1}, x_{n-1}\rangle \texttt{ in } x_n \end{aligned}$$

It is not hard to check that for each n, the principal type of W_n has $2^{\Omega(n)}$ type variables. Consequently, the dag representation of this type will have $2^{\Omega(n)}$ nodes. ■

Although the dag representation of the principal type for the expression in Example 11.3.23 has exponential size, other types for this expression have smaller dag representations. In particular, consider the instance obtained by applying a substitution which replaces all type variables with a single variable t. Since all subexpressions of the resulting type share the same type variable, this produces a typing with linear size dag representation. In the following example, we construct expressions such that the principal types have doubly-exponential size when written out as strings, and the dag representations of *every* typing must have at least exponential size.

Example 11.3.24 Recall that the expression $P \equiv \lambda x.\langle x, x\rangle$ from Example 11.2.18 doubles the length of the principal type of its argument. Consequently, the n-fold composition of P (with itself) increases the length of the principal type by a factor of 2^n. Using nested `let`s, we can define the 2^n-fold composition of P using an expression of length n. This gives us an expression whose principal type has doubly-exponential length and exponential dag size. Since the dag must contain an exponential-length path, any substitution instance of the principal type also has exponential dag size. Such an expression V_n is defined as follows:

$V_n \stackrel{\text{def}}{=}$ `let` $x_0 = P$ `in`

  `let` $x_1 = \lambda y.x_0(x_0 y)$ `in`

  ...

  `let` $x_n = \lambda y.x_{n-1}(x_{n-1} y)$ `in` $x_n\ Q$

where for simplicity we may let Q be $\lambda z.\, z$. To write the principal type of this expression simply, let us use the notation $\tau^{[k]}$ for the n-ary product, defined inductively by $\tau^{[1]} \stackrel{\text{def}}{=} \tau$ and $\tau^{[k+1]} \stackrel{\text{def}}{=} (\tau^{[k]}) \times (\tau^{[k]})$. It is easy to see that $\tau^{[n]}$ has $2^{\Omega(n)}$ symbols. By examining the expression V_n and tracing the behavior of PTL, we see that x_0 has principal type $t \to t^{[2]}$, and for each $k > 0$ the principal type of x_k is $t \to t^{[2^k+1]}$. Consequently, the principal type of the entire expression V_n is $(t \to t)^{[2^n+1]}$, which has length $2^{2^{\Omega(n)}}$. Since a dag representation can reduce this by at most one exponential (see Exercise 11.2.6), the dag size of the principal type is $2^{\Omega(n)}$. ∎

Proposition 11.3.25 For arbitrarily large n, there exist closed expressions of length $O(n)$ whose principal types have length $2^{2^{\Omega(n)}}$, dag size $2^{\Omega(n)}$, and $2^{\Omega(n)}$ distinct type variables. Furthermore, every instance of the principal type must have dag size $2^{\Omega(n)}$.

Proof For any $n \geq 1$, we may construct an expression W_n as in Example 11.3.23 whose principal type has exponentially many type variables, and an expression V_n as in Example 11.3.24 satisfying the remaining conditions. The expression $\langle W_n, V_n \rangle$ proves the proposition. ∎

The exponential-time lower bound for ML typing is proved using an adaptation of Example 11.3.24. By Lemma 11.3.7, `let` $x = M$ `in` N has the same types as $[M/x]N$ when x occurs in N. It follows that the principal type of V_n is the same as the type of the term obtained by `let`-reduction,

$$V_n = P^{2^n} Q$$

Therefore, we may compute the type of V_n by working across the term $P^{2^n} Q$ from right to left. This process begins with the principal type of Q and, for each of the 2^n occurrences of P, finds a type that makes the application well-formed. Since there are 2^n occurrences of P, we unify the type giving the domain of P a total of 2^n times, even though the term V_n has length $O(n)$. We may see the general pattern a little more clearly if we introduce some notation. Let ρ_0 be the principal type of Q and $\sigma \to \tau$ the principal type of P. Then we type V_n by computing a sequence of types $\rho_1, \ldots, \rho_{2^n}$, with ρ_{i+1} determined from ρ_i and $\sigma \to \tau$ by letting $S = \mathit{Unify}(\rho_i, \sigma)$ and $\rho_{i+1} = S\tau$. We may think of the type $\sigma \to \tau$ as an "instruction" for computing ρ_{i+1} from ρ_i by unification, with this instruction executed 2^n times in the typing of V_n.

In the lower bound proof, we replace the "initial" term Q and the "instruction" P in V_n by terms whose types code parts of a Turing machine computation. More specifically, suppose ρ_0 codes the initial configuration of a Turing machine in some way, and the type $\sigma \to \tau$ has the property that if $S\sigma$ codes the i-th configuration in some computation, then $S\tau$ codes the $(i+1)$-st configuration. Then ρ_{2^n} computed as above will be the configuration of the Turing machine after 2^n computation steps. Consequently, we can represent an exponential-time computation by an appropriate adaptation of V_n, provided we have some way to code an initial configuration and the one-step function of the Turing machine. Given the results in Section 11.2.5, which show that we can represent any unification problem, combined with the idea in [DKM84] that boolean circuit evaluation can be represented by unification, it should not be difficult to imagine that we can encode Turing machine computation in this way. Note that the number of steps we can encode depends on the `let`-depth of the term. This leads us to the following theorem.

Theorem 11.3.26 Any algorithm that decides whether any given untyped λ, `let`-term is ML typable requires time $2^{\Omega(\ell d(U) log_2 |U|)}$ on input U, where $|U|$ is the length of U and $\ell d(U)$ is its `let`-depth.

We first look at an outline of the proof, then fill in the details.

Proof Sketch Let T be any deterministic, single-tape Turing machine and let a be an input string of length n. We assume without loss of generality that T has exactly one accepting state and that once T enters this state, no subsequent computation step leads to a different state. This assumption, which may be justified by standard manipulation of Turing machines [HU79], makes it easy to see whether T accepts its input. There are also some minor details associated with the way we represent an infinite tape by a type expression. This leads us to modify the standard Turing machine model slightly. Specifically, we represent the tape by a list of symbols to the left of the input head and list of symbols to the right of the input head. The list of symbols to the left of a Turing machine tape head is always finite. On the right, there will always be a finite list of symbols after which all symbols will be blank. Therefore, we can also represent the infinite tape to the right of the head by a finite list. The only complication comes when executing a move to the right, onto a blank tape square that is not in our finite list. To handle this case, we assume that the Turing machine is started with a special end marker symbol, \$, at the end of the input. We also assume that the Turing machine moves the end marker to the right as needed, so that it always marks the right-most tape position scanned in the computation. To make this possible, we augment the standard "left" and "right" moves of the Turing machine with a special "insert" move that simultaneously writes a symbol on the tape and moves all symbols currently to the right of the tape head one additional tape square to the right. This allows the machine to insert as many blanks (or other symbols) on the tape as needed, without running over the end marker. An essentially equivalent approach would be to work with 2-stack machines instead of Turing machines. However, since Turing machines are more familiar, we will stick to Turing machines.

We will construct a term that is ML-typable iff T accepts input a in 2^n or fewer steps.

A configuration of T will be represented by a triple $\langle q, L, R\rangle$, where q is the state of the machine, L is the list of symbols appearing to the left of the tape head, and R is the list of symbols appearing to the right of the tape head.

Let *Init* be an untyped lambda term whose principal type represents the initial configuration of T on input a. (This configuration is $\langle q_1, \epsilon, a\$\rangle$, where ϵ is the empty string, q_1 is the starting state of T and the input a sits to the right of the tape head, terminated by the end marker \$.) Let *Next* be an untyped lambda term whose principal type represents the transition function of T. Specifically, the principal type of *Next* must have the form $\sigma \to \tau$, with the property that if $S\sigma$ represents a configuration of T, for some substitution S, then $S\tau$ represents the configuration of T after one move of the Turing machine. We choose two distinct types representing boolean values "true" and "false" and assume there are untyped lambda terms with these principal types.

Let *Accept* be an untyped lambda term whose principal type has the form $\alpha \to \beta$ with the property that if $S\alpha$ represents an accepting configuration, then $S\beta$ represents "true," while if $S\alpha$ represents a non-accepting configuration, $S\beta$ represents *false*.

These lambda terms are constructed so that if T accepts input a in 2^n or fewer steps, then the type of $Run = Accept(Next^{2^n} Init)$ represents "true," and "false" otherwise. Choosing "true" and "false" appropriately, we may apply *Run* to arguments so that the resulting term is typable only if the type represents "true." This allows us to decide whether T accepts input a by deciding whether a term involving *Run* has an ML type. Since we can write *Run* as a term of length linear in a and the description of T, using the pattern of V_n from Example 11.3.24, it requires exponential time to decide whether a given term is ML-typable. ■

In the remainder of the section, we describe the construction of untyped lambda terms *Init*, *Next* and *Accept* for a Turing machine T satisfying the assumptions given in the proof sketch for Theorem 11.3.26. An important insight in [Hen90a, HM94] is that these terms can be motivated by considering a particular coding of Turing machines by lambda terms, then showing that the computation is also coded by the types of these terms. A consequence of this approach is that the lower bound may be extended to impredicative systems that only give types to terms with normal forms.

We begin with terms for booleans,

$$tt \stackrel{\text{def}}{=} \lambda x.\,\lambda y.\,x$$
$$:t \to s \to t$$
$$ff \stackrel{\text{def}}{=} \lambda x.\,\lambda y.\,y$$
$$:t \to s \to s$$

and consider the types as well as the terms as representing "true" and "false." This coding for booleans is a special case of a general idea. Specifically, if we wish to code elements of some finite set of size k, we can use the Curried projection function

$$\pi_i^k \stackrel{\text{def}}{=} \lambda x_1.\,\lambda x_2.\,\ldots\,\lambda x_k.\,x_i$$
$$:t_1 \to t_2 \to \ldots \to t_k \to t_i$$

or its type to represent the ith element of the set. We therefore represent the states $q_1, \ldots, q_k \in Q$ of T by $\pi_1^k, \ldots, \pi_k^k$, tape symbols $c_1, \ldots, c_m \in C$ by $\pi_1^m, \ldots, \pi_m^m$ and the tape head directions *left*, *right* and *insert* by π_1^3, π_2^3 and π_3^3. (The end marker $\$ \in C$ is one of the tape symbols.) An *insert* move is our special move that allows the machine to insert a tape symbol in front of the end marker in a single move.

We may represent a tuple $\langle V_1, V_2, \ldots, V_k\rangle$ by the function $\lambda x.\,x V_1 \ldots V_k$ and a list $[V_1, \ldots, V_k]$ by the nested sequence of pairs

$$[V_1, \ldots, V_k] \stackrel{\text{def}}{=} \langle V_1, \langle V_2, \ldots, \langle V_k, nil\rangle \ldots\rangle\rangle$$

where $nil \stackrel{\text{def}}{=} \lambda z.\,z$.

Exercise 11.3.29 illustrates some typing difficulties associated with projection functions. We circumvent these problems using the following syntactic form

$$\texttt{match}\ \langle x, y\rangle = U\ \texttt{in}\ V \quad \stackrel{\text{def}}{=} \quad U\,(\lambda x.\,\lambda y.\,V)$$

and similarly for $\texttt{match}\ \langle x, y, z\rangle = U\ \texttt{in}\ V$. For untyped terms, $\texttt{match}\ \langle x, y\rangle = U\ \texttt{in}\ V$ is equivalent to the pattern-matching form $\texttt{let}\ \langle x, y\rangle = U\ \texttt{in}\ V$ as in Section 2.2.6. However, the typing properties are different, as explained in Exercise 11.3.29.

Using these general coding ideas, we can represent the initial Turing machine configuration of T on input a by a triple

$$Init \stackrel{\text{def}}{=} \langle \pi_1^k, nil, [a_1, a_2, \ldots, a_n, \$]\rangle$$

where we assume q_1 is the start state of T, *nil* represents the empty list of symbols to the left of the tape and $[a_1, a_2, \ldots, a_n, \$]$ represents the list of input symbols to the right of the tape, followed by the end marker symbol *i.e.*, if the ith symbol of input a is the jth tape symbol c_j, then $a_i = \pi_j^m$. The transition function of the Turing machine is represented by

$$
\begin{aligned}
\mathit{Next} \;&\stackrel{\text{def}}{=}\; \lambda \mathit{config}.\\
&\quad \texttt{match}\ \langle q, \mathit{Left}, \mathit{Right}\rangle = \mathit{config}\ \texttt{in}\\
&\quad\quad \texttt{match}\ \langle \ell, L\rangle = \mathit{Left}\ \texttt{in}\\
&\quad\quad\quad \texttt{match}\ \langle r, R\rangle = \mathit{Right}\ \texttt{in}\\
&\quad\quad\quad\quad \texttt{match}\ \langle q', c', d'\rangle = \mathit{delta}\, q\, r\ \texttt{in}\\
&\quad\quad\quad\quad\quad d'\ \mathit{MoveL}\ \mathit{MoveR}\ \mathit{Insert}
\end{aligned}
$$

$$\mathit{MoveL} \stackrel{\text{def}}{=} \langle q',\ L,\ \langle \ell, \langle c', R\rangle\rangle\rangle$$

$$\mathit{MoveR} \stackrel{\text{def}}{=} \langle q',\ \langle c', \langle \ell, L\rangle\rangle,\ R\rangle$$

$$\mathit{Insert} \stackrel{\text{def}}{=} \langle q',\ \langle c', \langle \ell, L\rangle\rangle,\ \langle r, R\rangle\rangle$$

where configurations *MoveL*, *MoveR* and *Insert* correspond to moving the tape head left, right or inserting a new tape symbol, and *delta* is a function returning the next state, tape symbol, and direction for the tape head move. In words, *Next* assumes its argument is a triple $\langle q, \langle \ell, L\rangle, \langle r, R\rangle\rangle$ representing a configuration of T. The function *delta* is applied to the state q and symbol r under the tape head, returning a tuple $\langle q', c', d'\rangle$ containing the next state, tape symbol to be written and direction for the tape head to move. Since the direction d will be either π_1^3, π_2^3 or π_3^3, we can apply d to terms that represent the next configuration if the machine moves left, the next configuration if the machine moves right, and the next configuration if the machine inserts a symbol. The function *delta* depends on the transition function of T. It is straightforward, although potentially tedious, to write this function out completely. If there are three states and two tape symbols, for example, then the state will be represented by a projection function on triples and the tape symbol by a projection function on pairs. In this case, *delta* could be written in the form

$$
\begin{aligned}
\mathit{delta} \stackrel{\text{def}}{=} \langle\ & \langle\langle q_1', c_1', d_1'\rangle,\ \langle q_2', c_2', d_2'\rangle\rangle,\\
& \langle\langle q_3', c_3', d_3'\rangle,\ \langle q_4', c_4', d_4'\rangle\rangle,\\
& \langle\langle q_5', c_5', d_5'\rangle,\ \langle q_6', c_6', d_6'\rangle\rangle\\
\rangle &
\end{aligned}
$$

where $\langle q'_{2i+j-2}, c'_{2i+j-2}, d'_{2i+j-2}\rangle$ represents the move from state q_i and tape symbol c_j.

It is not hard to verify that *Next* works properly. What is slightly more surprising is that we can read the computation of T from the types of *Init* and *Next*. More specifically, consider the types of *tt* and *ff* as representing "true" and "false", and similarly for the types of projection functions. Abusing notation slightly, let us write

$$\langle \sigma_1, \ldots, \sigma_k \rangle \stackrel{\text{def}}{=} \sigma_1 \to \ldots \to \sigma_k \to (t \to t)$$

for the principal type of $\langle U_1, \ldots, U_k \rangle$, assuming U_i has principal type σ_i and t is not in $\sigma_1, \ldots, \sigma_k$, and similarly

$$[\sigma_1, \ldots, \sigma_k] \stackrel{\text{def}}{=} \langle \sigma_1, \ldots, \langle \sigma_k, nil \rangle \ldots \rangle$$

Then the type if *Init* also codes the initial configuration of T and the type of *Next* codes the transition function of T. This gives us the following lemma.

Lemma 11.3.27 Let $C\colon \sigma$ be a term and its principal type, both representing a configuration of Turing machine T and let C', σ' similarly represent the configuration after one computation step of T. Then $(Next\ C) \twoheadrightarrow C'$ and $Next\ C : \sigma'$.

This essentially completes proof of Theorem 11.3.26. If $Next^k Init$ gives us the machine configuration after k steps, it is easy to use `match` or application to projection functions to obtain the machine state after k steps. This lets us write the term *Accept* as required in the proof sketch. Exercise 11.3.28 asks you to find terms so that *Run* is typable iff the Turing machine accepts. An interesting way to "check" the proof is to convert the lambda terms *Init* and *Next* into ML syntax and use the ML type checker. A simple, illustrative example appears in Exercise 11.3.30.

Exercise 11.3.28 Suppose untyped λ, `let`-term *Run* has type $s \to t \to s$ if a Turing machine T accepts and $s \to t \to t$ otherwise. Write a term using *Run* that is ML-typable iff the Turing machine accepts.

Exercise 11.3.29 We may define untyped projection functions by

$$fst \stackrel{\text{def}}{=} \lambda p.\, p(\lambda x.\, \lambda y.\, x)$$

$$snd \stackrel{\text{def}}{=} \lambda p.\, p(\lambda x.\, \lambda y.\, y)$$

It is easy to check that for the coding of pairs by $\langle U, V \rangle = \lambda z.\, zUV$, we have $fst\langle U, V \rangle = U$ and $snd\langle U, V \rangle = V$ by untyped β-reduction. However, there is a typing problem with these projection functions in ML. This may be illustrated by considering an alternate definition

$$\texttt{match}\ \langle x, y \rangle = U\ \texttt{in}\ V \quad \stackrel{\text{def}}{=} \quad (\lambda x.\, \lambda y.\, V)(fst\ U)(snd\ U)$$

(a) Show that for both versions of `match`, we have `match` $\langle x, y \rangle = \langle U_1, U_2 \rangle$ `in` $V = (\lambda x.\, \lambda x.\, V)U_1 U_2$ in untyped lambda calculus.

(b) Show that the type of $(\lambda z.\mathtt{match}\ \langle x, y\rangle = z\ \mathtt{in}\ \langle x, y\rangle)\,\langle tt, ff\rangle$ depends on which definition of `match` we use. Why is the first definition given in this section better than the alternative given in this exercise?

Exercise 11.3.30 The following Standard ML code gives the representation of a simple Turing machine with three states, $q_1, q_2, q_3 \in Q$ and two tape symbols, $c_1, c_2 \in C$. For simplicity, the special "insert" move is omitted. The machine moves right until the second occurrence of c_2, then moves back and forth indefinitely over the second occurrence of c_2. Type this program in and "run" the simulation for enough steps to verify that the machine enters state q_3 when passing over the second c_2. Then modify the machine so that instead of leaving the input tape alone, it changes all of the symbols to c_1, up to and including the second c_2, before looping back and forth over the square containing the second c_2. Test your encoding by computing enough steps to verify that you have made the modification correctly.

```
fun pi_1_2(x_1)(x_2) = x_1;              val tt = pi_1_2;
fun pi_2_2(x_1)(x_2) = x_2;              val ff = pi_1_2;

fun pi_1_3(x_1)(x_2)(x_3) = x_1;         val q1 = pi_1_3;
fun pi_2_3(x_1)(x_2)(x_3) = x_2;         val q2 = pi_2_3;
fun pi_3_3(x_1)(x_2)(x_3) = x_3;         val q3 = pi_3_3;

val c1 = pi_1_2;                          val left = pi_1_2;
val c2 = pi_2_2;                          val right = pi_2_2;

fun pair(x)(y) = fn w => w x y ;  fun nil(x) = x;
fun triple(x)(y)(z) = fn w => w x y z;  val cons = pair;

val t1 = triple q1 c1 right; (* move from state q1 on symbol c1 *)
val t2 = triple q2 c2 right; (* move from state q1 on symbol c2 *)
val t3 = triple q2 c1 right; (* move from state q2 on symbol c1 *)
val t4 = triple q3 c2 left; (* move from state q2 on symbol c2 *)
val t5 = triple q2 c1 left; (* move from state q3 on symbol c1 *)
val t6 = triple q2 c1 left ; (* move from state q3 on symbol c2 *)

val delta = (triple (pair t1 t2) (pair t3 t4) (pair t5 t6));

val a = cons c1 (cons c2 (cons c1 (cons c2 (cons c1 nil))));
```

```
val init = triple q1 (cons c1 nil) a;

fun next(config) =
  config
  (fn q => fn Left => fn Right =>
    (Left (fn l => fn L =>
      (Right (fn r => fn R =>
        (delta q r)
          (fn q' => fn c' => fn d' =>
            d' (triple q' L (cons l (cons c' R)))
              (triple q' (cons c' (cons l L)) R)
  ))))));
```

Bibliography

[ABL86] R.M. Amadio, K. Bruce, and G. Longo. The finitary projection model for second order lambda calculus and solutions to higher order domain equations. In *Proc. IEEE Symp. on Logic in Computer Science*, pages 122–130, 1986.

[Abr90] S. Abramsky. Abstract interpretation, logical relations and Kan extensions. *J. of Logic and Computation*, 1(1):5–40, 1990.

[AC80] E. Astesiano and G. Costa. Nondeterminism and fully abstract models. *RAIRO*, 14(4):323–347, 1980.

[AC91] R.M. Amadio and L. Cardelli. Subtyping recursive types. In *Proc. ACM Symp. Principles of Programming Languages*, pages 104–118, 1991.

[AC94a] M. Abadi and L. Cardelli. A theory of primitive objects: second-order systems. In *Proc. European Symposium on Programming*, pages 1–24. Springer-Verlag, 1994.

[AC94b] M. Abadi and L. Cardelli. A theory of primitive objects: untyped and first-order systems. In *Proc. Theor. Aspects of Computer Software*, pages 296–320. Springer-Verlag LNCS 789, 1994.

[AC95] M. Abadi and L. Cardelli. On subtyping and matching. In *Proc. European Conf. on Object-Oriented Programming*, Springer LNCS 952 page145–167, 1995.

[ACP+92] M. Abadi, L. Cardelli, B. Pierce, G. Plotkin, and D. Rèmy. Dynamic typing in polymorphic languages. In *Proceedings of the ACM SIGPLAN Workshop on ML and its Applications*, San Francisco, June 1992. ACM.

[ACPP91] M. Abadi, L. Cardelli, B. Pierce, and G. Plotkin. Dynamic typing in a statically typed language. *ACM Transactions on Programming Languages and Systems*, 13(2):237–268, April 1991.

[Acz77] P. Aczel. An introduction to inductive definitions. In *Handbook of Mathematical Logic*, pages 739–782. North-Holland, Amsterdam, 1977.

[AHU83] A.V. Aho, J.E. Hopcroft, and J.D. Ullman. *Data Structures and Algorithms*. Addison-Wesley, 1983.

[AJ91] S. Abramsky and T.P. Jensen. A relational approach to strictness analysis for higher-order polymorphic functions. In *Proc. ACM Symp. Principles of Programming Languages*, pages 49–54, 1991.

[AL91] A. Asperti and G. Longo. *Categories, Types and Structures*. MIT Press, 1991.

[All86] L. Allison. *A practical introduction to denotational semantics*. Cambridge Computer Science Texts 23. Cambridge Univ Press, 1986.

[AM75] M.A. Arbib and E.G. Manes. *Arrows, Structures, and Functors: The Categorical Imperative*. Academic Press, 1975.

[Ama91] R.M. Amadio. Recursion over realizability structures. *Information and Computation*, 91(1):55–86, 1991.

[And86] P.B. Andrews. *An introduction to mathematical logic and type theory: to truth through proof*. Academic Press, 1986.

[AO91] K.R. Apt and E.-R. Olderog. *Verification of sequential and concurrent programs*. Springer-Verlag, New York, Berlin, 1991.

[CF58] H.B Curry and R. Feys. *Combinatory Logic I*. North-Holland, Amsterdam, 1958.

[CG92] P.-L. Curien and G. Ghelli. Coherence of subsumption, minimum typing and type-checking in $f_{\leq}$. *Math. Struct. in Comp. Sci.*, 2:55–91, 1992. Reprinted in [GM94].

[CGW89] T. Coquand, C.A. Gunter, and G. Winskel. Domain-theoretic models of polymorphism. *Information and Computation*, 81(2):123–167, 1989.

[CH88] T. Coquand and G. Huet. The calculus of constructions. *Information and Computation*, 76(2/3):95–120, 1988.

[CH94a] T. Coquand and H. Herbelin. A-translation and looping combinators in pure type systems. *J. Functional Programming*, 4(1):77–88, 1994.

[CH94b] P.-L. Curien and T. Hardin. Theoretical Pearl: Yet yet a counterexample for $\lambda + sp$. *J. Functional Prog.*, 4(1):113–115, 1994.

[Chu32] A. Church. A set of postulates for the foundation of logic. *Ann. of Math.*, 33:346–366, 1932. Second paper with same title in Vol. 33, pages 839–864, of same journal.

[Chu36] A. Church. An unsolvable problem of elementary number theory. *Amer. J. Math.*, 58:345–363, 1936.

[Chu40] A. Church. A formulation of the simple theory of types. *J. Symbolic Logic*, 5:56–68, 1940.

[Chu41] A. Church. *The Calculi of Lambda Conversion*. Princeton Univ. Press, 1941. Reprinted 1963 by University Microfilms Inc., Ann Arbor, MI.

[CMMS94] L. Cardelli, S. Martini, J. Mitchell, and A. Scedrov. An extension of System F with subtyping. *Information and Computation*, 109:4–56, 1994. Preliminary version appeared *Proc. Theor. Aspects of Computer Software,* Springer LNCS 526, September 1991, pages 750–770.

[Coo78] S.A. Cook. Soundness and completeness of an axiom system for program verification. *SIAM J. Computing*, 7:129–147, 1978.

[Coo89] W.R. Cook. *A Denotational Semantics of Inheritance*. PhD thesis, Brown University, 1989.

[Coq86] T. Coquand. An analysis of Girard's paradox. In *Proc. IEEE Symp. on Logic in Computer Science*, pages 227–236, June 1986.

[CP92] R.L. Crole and A.M. Pitts. New foundations for fixpoint computations: FIX-hyperdoctrines and the FIX-logic. *Information and Computation*, 98(2):171–210, 1992.

[CR36] A. Church and J.B. Rosser. Some properties of conversion. *Trans. Amer. Math. Soc.*, 39:472–482, 1936.

[Cur86] P.-L. Curien. *Categorical combinators, sequential algorithms, and functional programming*. Birkhauser, Boston, 1993. Second edition.

[Cut80] N.J. Cutland. *Computability: An introduction to recursive function theory*. Cambridge Univ. Press, Cambridge, 1980.

[CW85] L. Cardelli and P. Wegner. On understanding types, data abstraction, and polymorphism. *Computing Surveys*, 17(4):471–522, 1985.

[CZ86] M. Coppo and M. Zacchi. Type inference and logical relations. In *Proc. IEEE Symp. on Logic in Computer Science*, pages 218–226, June 1986.

[DB80] N.G. De Bruijn. A survey of the project Automath. In *To H.B. Curry: Essays on Combinatory Logic, Lambda Calculus and Formalism*, pages 579–607. Academic Press, 1980.

[Dij75] E.W. Dijkstra. Guarded commands, nondeterminacy and formal derivation of programs. *CACM*, 18(8):453–457, 1975.

[Dij76] E.W. Dijkstra. *A Discipline of Programming*. Prentice-Hall, 1976.

[DJ90] N. Dershowitz and J.-P. Jouannaud. Rewrite systems. In J. van Leeuwen, editor, *Handbook of Theoretical Computer Science, Volume B*, pages 243–320. North-Holland, Amsterdam, 1990.

[DKM84] C. Dwork, P. Kanellakis, and J.C. Mitchell. On the sequential nature of unification. *J. Logic Programming*, 1:35–50, 1984.

[DM82] L. Damas and R. Milner. Principal type schemes for functional programs. In *Proc. 9th ACM Symposium on Principles of Programming Languages*, pages 207–212, 1982.

[Don79] J. Donahue. On the semantics of data type. *SIAM J. Computing*, 8:546–560, 1979.

[EM85] H. Ehrig and B. Mahr. *Fundamentals of Algebraic Specification 1*. Springer-Verlag, Berlin, 1985.

[End72] H.B. Enderton. *A Mathematical Introduction to Logic*. Academic Press, 1972.

[Ers71] Yu. L. Ershov. Computable numerations of morphisms. *Algebra i Logika*, 10(3): 247–308, 1971.

[Ers72] Yu. L. Ershov. Computable functions of finite types. *Algebra i Logika*, 11(4):367–437, 1972.

[Ers76] Yu. L. Ershov. Hereditarily effective operations. *Algebra i Logika*, 15(6):642–654, 1976.

[ES90] M. Ellis and B. Stroustrop. *The Annotated* C^{++} *Reference Manual*. Addison-Wesley, 1990.

[Fef79] S. Feferman. Constructive theories of functions and classes. In *Logic Colloquium '78*, pages 159–224, Amsterdam, 1979. North-Holland.

[FGSS88] P. Freyd, J.-Y. Girard, A. Scedrov, and P.J. Scott. Semantic parametricity in polymorphic lambda calculus. In *Proc. IEEE Symp. on Logic in Computer Science*, pages 274–279, July 1988.

[FHM94] K. Fisher, F. Honsell, and J.C. Mitchell. A lambda calculus of objects and method specialization. *Nordic J. Computing* (formerly *BIT*), 1:3–37, 1994. Preliminary version appeared in *Proc. IEEE Symp. on Logic in Computer Science,* 1993, 26–38.

[Fit69] M.C. Fitting. *Intuitionistic Logic, Model Theory and Forcing*. North-Holland, Amsterdam, 1969.

[Flo67] R.W. Floyd. Assigning meaning to programs. In J.T. Schwartz, editor, *Proc. Symp. in Applied Mathematics*, pages 19–32. AMS, 1967.

[FLO83] S. Fortune, D. Leivant, and M. O'Donnell. The expressiveness of simple and second order type structures. *JACM*, 30(1):151–185, 1983.

[Fre88] P. Freyd. Polynat in PER, 1988.

[Fri75] H. Friedman. Equality between functionals. In R. Parikh, editor, *Logic Colloquium*, pages 22–37. Springer-Verlag, Berlin, 1975.

[FRMS92] P. Freyd, G. Rosolini, P. Mulry, and D.S. Scott. Extensional PER's. *Information and Computation*, 98(2):211–227, 1992. Preliminary version appeared in *Proc. IEEE Symp. on Logic in Computer Science,* IEEE, 1990, 346–354.

[FS87] P. Freyd and A. Scedrov. Some semantic aspects of polymorphic lambda calculus. In *Proc. IEEE Symp. on Logic in Computer Science*, pages 315–319, June 1987.

[FS90] P. Freyd and A. Scedrov. *Categories, Allegories*. Mathematical Library, North-Holland, 1990.

[Gab81] D.M. Gabbay. *Semantical Investigations in Heyting's Intuitionistic Logic*. D. Reidel, 1981.

[Gan56] R.O. Gandy. On the axiom of extensionality – part i. *J. Symbolic Logic*, 21:??–??, 1956.

[Gan80] R.O. Gandy. An early proof of normalization by A.M. Turing. In *To H.B. Curry: Essays on Combinatory Logic, Lambda Calculus and Formalism*, pages 453–455. Academic Press, 1980.

[GHM78] J.V. Guttag, E. Horowitz, and D.R. Musser. Abstract data types and software validation. *Comm. ACM*, 21(12):1048–1064, 1978.

[Gir71] J.-Y. Girard. Une extension de l'interpretation de Gödel à l'analyse, et son application à l'élimination des coupures dans l'analyse et la théorie des types. In J.E. Fenstad, editor, *2nd Scandinavian Logic Symposium*, pages 63–92. North-Holland, Amsterdam, 1971.

[Gir72] J.-Y. Girard. Interpretation fonctionelle et elimination des coupures de l'arithmetique d'ordre superieur. These D'Etat, Universite Paris VII, 1972.

[Gir86] J.-Y. Girard. The system F of variable types, fifteen years later. *Theor. Comp. Sci.*, 45(2):159–192, 1986.

[GLT89] J.-Y. Girard, Y. Lafont, and P. Taylor. *Proofs and Types*. Cambridge Tracts in Theoretical Computer Science. Cambridge University Press, 1989.

[GM94] C.A. Gunter and J.C. Mitchell, editors. *Theoretical aspects of object-oriented programming*. MIT Press, Cambridge, MA, 1994.

[GMW79] M.J. Gordon, R. Milner, and C.P. Wadsworth. *Edinburgh LCF*. Springer LNCS 78, Berlin, 1979.

[Göd58] K. Gödel. Über eine bisher noch nicht benützte Erweiterung des finiten Standpunktes. *Dialectica*, 12:280–287, 1958.

[Gog78] J.A. Goguen. Order-sorted algebras. Technical Report 14, Computer Science Dept., UCLA, 1978.

[Gol79] R. Goldblatt. *Topoi: The categorical analysis of logic*. North-Holland, 1979.

[Gor79] M.J.C. Gordon. *The Denotational Description of Programming Languages*. Springer- Verlag, Berlin, 1979.

[Gor93] M.J.C. Gordon. *Introduction to HOL: A Theorem Proving Environment*. Cambridge University Press, 1993.

[GR83] A. Goldberg and D. Robson. *Smalltalk–80: The language and its implementation*. Addison Wesley, 1983.

[Grä68] G. Grätzer. *Universal Algebra*. Van Nostrand, 1968.

[GS90] C.A. Gunter and D.S. Scott. Semantic domains. In J. van Leeuwen, editor, *Handbook of Theoretical Computer Science, Volume B*, pages 633–674. North-Holland, Amsterdam, 1990.

[GTW78] J.A. Goguen, J.W. Thatcher, and E.G. Wagner. An initial algebra approach to the specification, correctness, and implementation of abstract data types. In R.T. Yeh, editor, *Current Trends in Programming Methodology*, volume 4. Prentice-Hall, 1978.

[Gun92] C.A. Gunter. *Semantics of Programming Languages: Structures and Techniques*. MIT Press, Cambridge, MA, 1992.

[Gut77] J.V. Guttag. Abstract data types and the development of data structures. *Comm. ACM*, 20(6):396–404, 1977.

[H$^+$92] P. Hudak et al. Report on the programming language Haskell. *SIGPLAN Notices*, 27(5):Section R, 1992.

[Hal60] P.R. Halmos. *Naive Set Theory*. D. Van Nostrand, 1960.

[Har84] D. Harel. Dynamic logic. In D.M. Gabbay and F. Guenthner, editors, *Handbook of Philosophical Logic, II: Extensions of Classical Logic*, pages 497–604. Reidel, Boston, 1984.

[Hay84] C.T. Haynes. A theory of data type representation independence. In *Proc. Int. Symp. on Semantics of Data Types, Sophia-Antipolis (France)*, pages 157–176, Berlin, 1984.

[Hen50] L. Henkin. Completeness in the theory of types. *Journal of Symbolic Logic*, 15(2):81–91, June 1950.

[Hen63] L. Henkin. A propositional theory of types. *Fund. Math.*, 52:323–344, 1963.

[Hen90a] F. Henglein. A lower bound for full polymorphic type inference: Girard/Reynolds typability is DEXPTIME-hard. Technical Report RUU-CS-90-14, Univerity of Utrecht, 1990.

[Hen90b] M. Hennessy. *The Semantics of Programming Languages: An elementary introduction using Structured Operational Semantics*. Wiley, 1990.

[HF92] P. Hudak and J. Fasel. A gentle introduction to Haskell. *SIGPLAN Notices*, 27(5): Section T, 1992.

[HHP87] R. Harper, F. Honsell, and G. Plotkin. A framework for defining logics. In *Proc. IEEE Symp. on Logic in Computer Science*, pages 194–204, June 1987. To appear in *J. Assoc. Comput. Machinery.*

[Hin69] J.R. Hindley. The principal type-scheme of an object in combinatory logic. *Trans. AMS*, 146:29–60, 1969.

[Hin83] J.R. Hindley. The completeness theorem for typing lambda terms. *Theor. Comp. Sci.*, 22:1–17, 1983.

[HL80] J.R. Hindley and G. Longo. Lambda calculus models and extensionality. *Z. Math. Logik Grundlag Math*, 26:289–310, 1980.

[HM90] B.T. Howard and J.C. Mitchell. Operational and axiomatic semantics of PCF. In *ACM Conference on LISP and Functional Programming*, pages 298–306, 1990.

[HM93] R. Harper and J.C. Mitchell. On the type structure of Standard ML. *ACM Trans. Programming Lang. and Systems*, 15(2):211–252, 1993. Earlier version appears as "The Essence of ML" in *Proc. 15th ACM Symp. on Principles of Programming Languages,* 1988, pp. 28–46.

[HM94] F. Henglein and H. Mairson. The complexity of type inference for higher-order typed lambda calculi. *J. Functional Programming*, 4(4):435–478, 1994.

[HM95a] R. Harper and G. Morrisett. Compiling polymorphism using intensional type analysis. In *Proc. 22nd ACM Symp. on Principles of Programming Languages*, pages 130–141, January 1995.

[HM95b] M. Hoang and J.C. Mitchell. Lower bounds for type inference with subtyping. In *ACM Symp. Principles of Programming Languages*, pages 176–185, 1995.

[HMT87] R. Harper, R. Milner, and M. Tofte. A type discipline for program modules. In *TAPSOFT '87*, Berlin, 1987. Springer LNCS 250.

[HN88] S. Hayashi and H. Nakano. *PX – A Computational Logic*. MIT Press, 1988.

[HO80] G. Huet and D.C. Oppen. Equations and rewrite rules: a survey. In R. Book, editor, *Formal Languages: Perspectives and Open Problems*. Academic Press, 1980. Revised version appears as SRI International Tech. Report CSL-111, 1980.

[Hoa69] C.A.R. Hoare. An axiomatic basis for computer programming. *CACM*, 12(10):576–580, 1969.

[Hoa72] C.A.R. Hoare. Proof of correctness of data representations. *Acta Informatica*, 1:271–281, 1972.

[Hoa95] M. Hoang. *Type Inference and Program Evaluation in the Presence of Subtyping*. PhD thesis, Stanford University, 1995.

[Hor84] E. Horowitz. *Fundamentals of Programming Languages*. Computer Science Press, 1984.

[How73] W. Howard. Hereditarily majorizable functionals. In *Mathematical Investigation of Intuitionistic Arithmetic and Analysis*, pages 454–461. Springer LNM 344, Berlin, 1973.

[How80] W. Howard. The formulas-as-types notion of construction. In *To H.B. Curry: Essays on Combinatory Logic, Lambda-Calculus and Formalism*, pages 479–490. Academic Press, 1980.

[How87] D.J. Howe. The computational behavior of Girard's paradox. In *Proc. IEEE Symp. on Logic in Computer Science*, pages 205–214, June 1987.

[How92] B.T. Howard. *Fixed points and extensionality in typed functional programming languages*. PhD thesis, Stanford University, 1992.

[HS86] J.R. Hindley and J.P. Seldin. *Introduction or Combinators and Lambda Calculus*. London Mathematical Society Student Texts 1, Cambridge University Press, 1986.

[HU79] J.E. Hopcroft and J.D. Ullman. *Introduction to Automata Theory, Languages and Computation*. Addison-Wesley, 1979.

[Hue80] G. Huet. Confluent reductions: abstract properties and applications to term rewriting systems. *J. Assoc. Comput. Mach.*, 27(4):797–821, 1980.

[Hyl76] J.M.E. Hyland. A syntactic characterization of the equality in some models of the lambda calculus. *J. London Math. Society*, 2(12):361–370, 1976.

[Hyl82] J.M.E. Hyland. The effective topos. In *The L.E.J. Brouwer Centenary Symposium*, pages 165–216. North-Holland, Amsterdam, 1982.

[Hyl88] J.M.E. Hyland. A small complete category. *Ann. Pure and Applied Logic*, 40, 1988. Lecture delivered at the conference Church's Thesis: Fifty Years Later, Zeiss(NL), June 1986.

[Jac75] G. Jacopini. A condition for identifying two elements of whatever model of combinatory logic. In C. Böhm, editor, *Proc. Lambda calculus and computer science theory*, pages 213–219. Springer LNCS 37, 1975.

[Joh77] P. Johnstone. *Topos Theory*. Academic Press, 1977.

[Kam83] S. Kamin. Final datatypes and their specification. *ACM Trans. Prog. Languages and Systems*, 5:97–121, 1983.

[KB70] D.E. Knuth and P.B. Bendix. Simple word problems in universal algebra. In J. Leech, editor, *Computational problems in abstract algebra*, pages 263–297. Pergamon Press, Elmsford, N.Y, 1970.

[KJ35] S.C. Kleene and Rosser J.B. The inconsistency of certain formal logics. *Ann. of Math.*, 36:630–636, 1935.

[Kle36] S.C. Kleene. Lambda definability and recursiveness. *Duke Math. J.*, 2:340–353, 1936.

[Kle45] S.C. Kleene. On the interpretation of intuitionistic number theory. *J. Symbolic Logic*, 10:109–124, 1945.

[Kle71] S.C. Kleene. Realizability: A retrospective survey. In *Cambridge Summer School in Mathematical Logic*, pages 95–112. Springer LNM 337, Berlin, 1971.

[Klo80] J.W. Klop. *Combinatory Reduction Systems*. PhD thesis, University of Utrecht, 1980. Published as Mathematical Center Tract 129.

[Klo87] J.W. Klop. Term rewriting: a tutorial. *EATCS Bulletin*, 32:143–182, 1987.

[KM89] P.C. Kanellakis and J.C. Mitchell. Polymorphic unification and ML typing. In *16th ACM Symposium on Principles of Programming Languages*, pages 105–115, 1989.

[KMM91] P.C. Kanellakis, H.G. Mairson, and J.C. Mitchell. Unification and ML type reconstruction. In *Computational Logic, Essays in Honor of Alan Robinson*, pages 444–478. MIT Press, 1991.

[Koy82] C.P.J. Koymans. Models of the lambda calculus. *Information and Control*, 52(3): 306–323, 1982.

[KR77] A. Kock and G.E. Reyes. Doctrines in categorical logic. In *Handbook of Mathematical Logic*, pages 283–316. North-Holland, Amsterdam, 1977.

[KR78] B.W. Kernighan and D.M. Ritchie. *The C programming language*. Prentice-Hall Software Series, 1978.

[Kre59] G. Kreisel. Interpretation of analysis by means of constructive functionals of finite types. In A. Heyting, editor, *Constructivity in Mathematics*, pages 101–128. North-Holland, Amsterdam, 1959.

[Kri65] S.A. Kripke. Semantical analysis of intuitionistic logic i. In *Formal Systems and Recursive Functions*, pages 92–130. (Proc. 8th Logic Colloq. Oxford 1963) North-Holland, Amsterdam, 1965.

[KT90] D. Kozen and J. Tiuryn. Logics of programs. In J. van Leeuwen, editor, *Handbook of Theoretical Computer Science, Volume B*, pages 789–840. North-Holland, Amsterdam, 1990.

[KTU88] A.J. Kfoury, J. Tiuryn, and P. Urzyczyn. A proper extension of ML with effective type assignment. In *Proc. 15th ACM Symp. Principles of Programming Languages*, pages 58–69, 1988.

[KTU89] A.J. Kfoury, J. Tiuryn, and P. Urzyczyn. Computational consequences and partial solutions of a generalized unification problem. In *Proc. IEEE Symp. on Logic in Computer Science*, June 1989.

[KTU90a] A.J. Kfoury, J. Tiuryn, and P. Urzyczyn. The undecidability of the semi-unification problem. In *Proc. 22nd Annual ACM Symp. on Theory of Computation (STOC), Baltimore, Maryland*, pages 468–476, May 1990.

[KTU90b] A.J. Kfoury, J. Tiuryn, and P. Urzyczyn. ML typability is Dexptime-complete. In *Proc. 15th Colloq. on Trees in Algebra and Programming*, pages 206–220. Springer LNCS 431, 1990. Revised version 41(2):368–398, 1994 in *J. Assoc. Comput. Machinery* under title, "An Analysis of ML Typability".

[L^+81] B. Liskov et al. *CLU Reference Manual*. Springer LNCS 114, Berlin, 1981.

[Lam80] J. Lambek. From lambda calculus to cartesian closed categories. In *To H.B. Curry: Essays on Combinatory Logic, Lambda Calculus and Formalism*, pages 375–402. Academic Press, 1980.

[Lan63] P.J. Landin. The mechanical evaluation of expressions. *Comput. J.*, 6:308–320, 1963.

[Lan65] P.J. Landin. A correspondence between Algol 60 and Church's lambda notation. *CACM*, 8:89–101; 158–165, 1965.

[Lan66] P.J. Landin. The next 700 programming languages. *CACM*, 9:157–166, 1966.

[Lau65] H. Lauchli. Intuitionistic propositional calculus and definably non-empty terms. *Journal of Symbolic Logic*, 30:263, 1965.

[Lau70] H. Lauchli. An abstract notion of realizability for which intuitionistic predicate calculus is complete. In *Intuitionism and Proof Theory: Proc. of the Summer Conference at Buffalo N.Y.*, pages 227–234, 1970.

[Law69] F.W. Lawvere. Diagonal arguments and cartesian closed categories. In *Category Theory, Homology Theory and their Applications II*, pages 143–145. Springer LNM 92, 1969.

[Les92] P. Lescanne. Termination of rewrite systems by elementary interpretations. In H. Kirchner and G. Levi, editors, *Proceeding 3rd Conference on Algebraic and Logic Programming, Volterra (Italy)*, number 632 in Lecture Notes in Computer Science, pages 21–36. Springer-Verlag, September 1992.

[Lév75] J.-J. Lévy. An algebraic interpretation of the λ-β-k-calculus and a labeled λ-calculus. In C. Böhm, editor, *Proc. Lambda calculus and computer science theory*, pages 147–165. Springer LNCS 37, 1975.

[LG86] B. Liskov and J. Guttag. *Abstraction and Specification in Software Development*. MIT Press, 1986.

[Lip77] R. Lipton. A necessary and sufficient condition for the existence of hoare logics. In *Proc. 18th IEEE Symp. on Foundations of Computer Science*, pages 1–6, 1977.

[LM92] P.D. Lincoln and J.C. Mitchell. Algorithmic aspects of type inference with subtypes. In *Proc. 19th ACM Symp. on Principles of Programming Languages*, pages 293–304, January 1992.

[LMS93] G. Longo, K. Milstead, and S. Soloviev. The genericity theorem and the notion of parametricity in the polymorphic lambda calculus. In *Proc. IEEE Symp. Logic in Computer Science*, pages 6–14, 1993.

[Löb75] M.H. Löb. Embedding first-order predicate logic in fragments of intuitionistic logic. *J. Symbolic Logic* 41, pages 705–718, 1976.

[LS86] J. Lambek and P.J. Scott. *Introduction to Higher-Order Categorical Logic*. Cambridge University Press, Cambridge, U.K, 1986.

[LSAS77] B. Liskov, A. Snyder, R. Atkinson, and C. Schaffert. Abstraction mechanisms in clu. *Comm. ACM*, 20:564–576, 1977.

[LZ74] B. Liskov and S. Zilles. Programming with abstract data types. *ACM Sigplan Notices*, 9:50–59, 1974.

[Mac71] S. MacLane. *Categories for the Working Mathematician*, volume 5 of *Graduate Texts in Mathematics*. Springer-Verlag, Berlin, 1971.

[Mac85] D.B. MacQueen. Modules for Standard ML. *Polymorphism*, 2(2), 1985. 35 pages. An earlier version appeared in Proc. 1984 ACM Symp. on Lisp and Functional Programming.

[Mac86] D.B. MacQueen. Using dependent types to express modular structure. In *Proc. 13th ACM Symp. on Principles of Programming Languages*, pages 277–286, 1986.

[Mai90] H.G. Mairson. Deciding ML typability is complete for deterministic exponential time. In *Proc. 17th ACM Symp. Principles of Programming Languages*, pages 382–401, January 1990.

[Mal70] A Malcev. Algorithms and recursive functions. Technical report, 1970. Translation Woolters, Ne, 1970.

[Mar73] P. Martin-Löf. An intuitionistic theory of types: Predicative part. In H. E. Rose and J. C. Shepherdson, editors, *Logic Colloquium, '73*, pages 73–118, Amsterdam, 1973. North-Holland.

[Mar76] G. Markowsky. Chain-complete posets and directed sets with applications. *Algebra Universalis*, 6:53–68, 1976.

[Mar82] P. Martin-Löf. Constructive mathematics and computer programming. In *Sixth International Congress for Logic, Methodology, and Philosophy of Science*, pages 153–175, Amsterdam, 1982. North-Holland.

[Mar84] P. Martin-Löf. *Intuitionistic Type Theory*. Bibliopolis, Napoli, 1984.

[McC60] J. McCarthy. Recursive functions of symbolic expressions and their computation by machine. *Comm. Assoc. Comput. Mach.*, 3(3):184–195, 1960.

[McC61] J. McCarthy. A basis for mathematical theory of computation. In *Proc. Western Joint Computer Conf*, pages 225–238, May 1961. Later version in P. Braffort and D. Hirschberg (eds.), *Computer Programming and Formal Systems*, North-Holland, Amsterdam, pages 33–70, 1963.

[McC63] J. McCarthy. Towards a mathematical theory of computation. In *Proc. IFIP Congress 62*, pages 21–28, Amsterdam, 1963. North-Holland.

[McC78] J. McCarthy. History of LISP. *ACM Sigplan Notices*, 13(8):217–223, 1978.

[McC79] N. McCracken. *An Investigation of a Programming Language with a Polymorphic Type Structure*. PhD thesis, Syracuse Univ., 1979.

[McC84] N. McCracken. A finitary retract model for the polymorphic lambda calculus. Manuscript, 1984.

[Men64] E. Mendelson. *Introduction to Mathematical Logic*. D. Van Nostrand Co., Princeton, 1964.

[Mes89] J. Meseguer. Relating models of polymorphism. In *Proc. 16th ACM Symp. on Principles of Programming Languages*, pages 228–241, January 1989.

[Mey82] A.R. Meyer. What is a model of the lambda calculus ? *Information and Control*, 52(1):87–122, 1982.

[Mey88] B. Meyer. *Object-Oriented Software Construction*. Prentice-Hall, 1988.

[Mey92a] A.R. Meyer. MIT 6.830 course notes. Unpublished, 1992.

[Mey92b] B. Meyer. *Eiffel: The Language*. Prentice-Hall, 1992.

[MH88] J.C. Mitchell and R. Harper. The essence of ML. In *Proc. 15th ACM Symp. on Principles of Programming Languages*, pages 28–46, January 1988.

[Mil77] R. Milner. Fully abstract models of typed lambda calculi. *Theoretical Computer Science*, 4(1):1–22, 1977.

[Mil78] R. Milner. A theory of type polymorphism in programming. *JCSS*, 17:348–375, 1978.

[Mil85a] R. Milner. The Standard ML core language. *Polymorphism*, 2(2), 1985. 28 pages. An earlier version appeared in Proc. 1984 ACM Symp. on Lisp and Functional Programming.

[Mit86a] J.C. Mitchell. Abstract realizability for intuitionistic and relevant implication (abstract). *Journal Symbolic Logic*, 51(3):851–852, 1986.

[Mit86b] J.C. Mitchell. Representation independence and data abstraction. In *Proc. 13th ACM Symp. on Principles of Programming Languages*, pages 263–276, January 1986.

[Mit86c] J.C. Mitchell. A type-inference approach to reduction properties and semantics of polymorphic expressions. In *ACM Conference on LISP and Functional Programming*, pages 308–319, August 1986. Reprinted with minor revisions in *Logical Foundations of Functional Programming,* ed. G. Huet, Addison-Wesley (1990) 195–212.

[Mit88] J.C. Mitchell. Polymorphic type inference and containment. *Information and Computation*, 76(2/3):211–249, 1988. Reprinted in *Logical Foundations of Functional Programming,* ed. G. Huet, Addison-Wesley (1990) 153–194.

[Mit91a] J.C. Mitchell. On the equivalence of data representations. In V. Lifschitz, editor, *Artificial Intelligence and Mathematical Theory of Computation: Papers in Honor of John McCarthy*, pages 305–330. Academic Press, 1991.

[Mit91b] J.C. Mitchell. Type inference with simple subtypes. *J. Functional Programming*, 1(3):245–286, 1991.

[MM85] J.C. Mitchell and A.R. Meyer. Second-order logical relations. In *Logics of Programs*, pages 225–236, Berlin, June 1985. Springer-Verlag LNCS 193.

[MM91] J.C. Mitchell and E. Moggi. Kripke-style models for typed lambda calculus. *Ann. Pure and Applied Logic*, 51:99–124, 1991. Preliminary version in *Proc. IEEE Symp. on Logic in Computer Science,* 1987, pages 303–314.

[MMMS87] A. R. Meyer, J. C. Mitchell, E. Moggi, and R. Statman. Empty types in polymorphic lambda calculus. In *Proc. 14th ACM Symp. on Principles of Programming Languages*, pages 253–262, January 1987. Reprinted with minor revisions in *Logical Foundations of Functional Programming,* ed. G. Huet, Addison-Wesley (1990) 273–284.

[MO86] J.C. Mitchell and M.J. O'Donnell. Realizability semantics for error-tolerant logics.

In *Theoretical Aspects of Reasoning About Knowledge*, pages 362–382. Morgan Kaufman, 1986.

[Mon76] J. D. Monk. *Mathematical Logic*, volume 37 of *Graduate Texts in Mathematics*. Springer-Verlag, Berlin, 1976.

[Mor73] J.H. Morris. Types are not sets. In 1st *ACM Symp. on Principles of Programming Languages*, pages 120–124, 1973.

[Mor90] C. Morgan. *Programming from Specifications*. Prentice–Hall, 1990.

[Mos74] Y.N. Moschovakis. *Elementary induction on abstract structures*. North-Holland, Amsterdam, 1974.

[MP88] J.C. Mitchell and G.D. Plotkin. Abstract types have existential types. *ACM Trans. on Programming Languages and Systems*, 10(3):470–502, 1988. Preliminary version appeared in *Proc. 12th ACM Symp. on Principles of Programming Languages,* 1985.

[MPS86] D. MacQueen, G Plotkin, and R. Sethi. An ideal model for recursive polymorphic types. *Information and Control*, 71(1/2):95–130, 1986.

[MR77] M. Makkai and G.E. Reyes. *First-order categorical logic*. Springer LNM 611, Berlin, 1977.

[MR86] A.R. Meyer and M.B. Reinhold. Type is not a type. In *Proc. 13th ACM Symp. on Principles of Programming Languages*, pages 287–295, January 1986.

[MR92] Q. Ma and J.C. Reynolds. Types, abstraction, and parametric polymorphism, part 2. In *Mathematical Foundations of Programming Semantics, Proceedings 1991*, pages 1–40. Springer-Verlag LNCS 598, 1992.

[MS55] J.R. Myhill and J.C. Shepherdson. Effective operations on partial recursive functions. *Zeitschrift fur mathematische Logik und Grundlagen der Mathematik*, 1, 1955.

[MS76] R.E. Milne and C. Strachey. *A theory of programming language semantics*. Chapman and Hall, London, and Wiley, New York, 1976.

[MS88] A.R. Meyer and K. Sieber. Towards fully abstract semantics for local variables: preliminary report. In *Proc. 15th ACM Symp. on Principles of Programming Languages*, pages 191–203, January 1988.

[MS89] J.C. Mitchell and P.J. Scott. Typed lambda calculus and cartesian closed categories. In *Categories in Computer Science and Logic, Proc. Summer Research Conference, Boulder, Colorado, June, 1987*, volume 92 of *Contemporary Mathematics*, pages 301–316. Amer. Math. Society, 1989.

[MS93] J.C. Mitchell and A. Scedrov. Notes on sconing and relators. In E. Boerger et al., editor, *Computer Science Logic '92, Selected Papers*, pages 352–378. Springer LNCS 702, 1993.

[MT91] R. Milner and M. Tofte. *Commentary on Standard ML*. MIT Press, 1991.

[MTH90] R. Milner, M. Tofte, and R. Harper. *The Definition of Standard ML*. MIT Press, 1990.

[Mul87] K. Mulmuley. *Full abstraction and semantic equivalence*. The MIT Press, 1987.

[MV95] J.C. Mitchell and R. Viswanathan. Standard ML-NJ weak polymorphism and imperative constructs. *Information and Computation*, 1995. A preliminary version appeared as M. Hoang, J.C. Mitchell and R. Viswanathan, Standard ML-NJ weak polymorphism and imperative constructs, in *Proc. IEEE Symp. on Logic in Computer Science,* 1993, 15–25.

[MW90] Z. Manna and R. Waldinger. *The logical basis for computer programming (Vol. 1 and 2).* Addison-Wesley, 1985,1990.

[Ned73] R.P. Nederpelt. *Strong Normalization in a typed lambda calculus with lambda structured types*. PhD thesis, Technological Univ. Eindhoven, 1973.

[Nel91] G. Nelson, editor. *Systems programming with Modula-3*. Prentice-Hall, 1991.

[New42] M.H.A. Newman. On theories with a combinatorial definition of 'equivalence'. *Ann. Math.*, 43(2):223–243, 1942.

[O'H90] P.W. O'Hearn. *The semantics of non-interference: a natural approach.* PhD thesis, Queen's University, Kingston, Canada, 1990.

[Ole82] F.J- Oles. *A category-theoretic approach to the semantics of programming languages*. PhD thesis, Syracuse University, Syracuse, N.Y, 1982.

[Ole85] F.J- Oles. Type algebras, functor categories and block structure. In *Algebraic Methods in Semantics*, pages 543–573. Cambridge Univ. Press, 1985.

[OT92] P.W. O'Hearn and R.D. Tennent. Semantics of local variables. In M.P. Fourman, P.T. Johnstone, and A.M. Pitts, editors, *Applications of Categories in Computer Science*, volume 177 of *London Mathematical Society Lecture Note Series*, pages 217–238. Cambridge University Press, Cambridge, England, 1992.

[OT93] P.W. O'Hearn and R.D. Tennent. Relational parametricity and local variables. In *Proc. 20th ACM Symp. Principles of Programming Languages*, pages 171–184, 1993.

[Par72] D. Parnas. On the criteria to be used in decomposing systems into modules. *Communications of the ACM*, 5(12):1053–1058, December 1972.

[Pau87] L.C. Paulson. *Logic and computation: interactive proof with Cambridge LCF*. Cambridge Univ. Press, 1987.

[Pey87] S.L. Peyton Jones. *The Implementation of Functional Programming Languages*. Prentice–Hall, 1987.

[Pho90a] W. Phoa. *Domain theory in realizability toposes*. PhD thesis, Cambridge, 1990. Available as University of Edinburgh Dept. of Computer Science report CST-82-91 and ECS-LFCS-91-171.

[Pho90b] W. Phoa. Effective domains and intrinsic structure. In *Proc. IEEE Symp. on Logic in Computer Science*, pages 366–377, 1990.

[Pie91] B. Pierce. *Basic category theory for computer scientists*. MIT Press, 1991.

[Pit87] A.M. Pitts. Polymorphism is set-theoretic, constructively. In *Proceedings Summer Conf. on Category Theory and Computer Science*, pages 12–39, Berlin, 1987. Springer LNCS 283.

[Pit89] A.M. Pitts. Non-trivial power types can't be subtypes of polymorphic types. In *Proc. IEEE Symp. on Logic in Computer Science*, pages 6–13, 1989.

[Pit99] A.M. Pitts. Categorical logic. In *Handbook of Logic in Computer Science, Volume VI - Logical Methods in Computer Science*. Oxford University Press, 199? To appear.

[Plo73] G.D. Plotkin. Lambda-definability and logical relations. Technical Report (Memo.) SAI-RM-4, University of Edinburgh, School of Artificial Intelligence, 1973.

[Plo75] G.D. Plotkin. Call-by-name, call-by-value and the lambda calculus. *Theoretical Computer Science*, 1:125–159, 1975.

[Plo77] G.D. Plotkin. LCF considered as a programming language. *Theoretical Computer Science*, 5:223–255, 1977.

[Plo80] G.D. Plotkin. Lambda definability in the full type hierarchy. In *To H.B. Curry: Essays on Combinatory Logic, Lambda Calculus and Formalism*, pages 363–373. Academic Press, 1980.

[Plo81] G.D. Plotkin. A structural approach to operational semantics. Technical Report DAIMI FN-19, Aarhus University Computer Science Department, 1981.

[Plo82] G.D. Plotkin. Notes on completeness of the full continuous hierarchy. Unpublished manuscript, 1982.

[Plo85] G.D. Plotkin. Denotational semantics with partial functions. Lecture notes, C.S.L.I. Summer School, Stanford, 1985.

[Pra65] D. Prawitz. *Natural Deduction*. Almquist and Wiksell, Stockholm, 1965.

[PW78] M.S. Paterson and M.N. Wegman. Linear unification. *JCSS*, 16:158–167, 1978.

[Rey74a] J.C. Reynolds. On the relation between direct and continuation semantics. In *Second Colloq. Automata, Languages and Programming*, pages 141–156, Berlin, 1974. Springer-Verlag LNCS.

[Rey74b] J.C. Reynolds. Towards a theory of type structure. In *Paris Colloq. on Programming*, pages 408–425, Berlin, 1974. Springer-Verlag LNCS 19.

[Rey81] J.C. Reynolds. The essence of Algol. In de Bakker and van Vliet, editors, *Algorithmic Languages*, pages 345–372, Amsterdam, 1981. IFIP, North-Holland.

[Rey83] J.C. Reynolds. Types, abstraction, and parametric polymorphism. In *Information Processing '83*, pages 513–523. North-Holland, Amsterdam, 1983.

[Rey84] J.C. Reynolds. Polymorphism is not set-theoretic. In *Proc. Int. Symp. on Semantics of Data Types, Sophia-Antipolis (France)*, pages 145–156, Berlin, 1984. Springer LNCS 173.

[Rie94] J.G. Riecke. Statman's 1-section theorem. *Information and Computation*, 116(2): 294–303, 1995.

[Rob65] J.A. Robinson. A machine oriented logic based on the resolution principle. *JACM*, 12(1):23–41, 1965.

[Rog67] H. Rogers. *Theory of Recursive Functions and Effective Computability*. McGraw-Hill, 1967.

[Ron] S. Ronchi Della Rocca. An unification semi-algorithm for intersection type schemes Manuscript.

[Ros92] G. Rosolini. An exper model for quest. In S. Brookes, M. Main, A. Melton, M. Mislove, and D.Schmidt, editors, *Mathematical Foundations of Programming Semantics*, volume 598 of *Lecture Notes in Computer Science*, pages 436–445. Springer-Verlag, 1992.

[RP93] J.C. Reynolds and G.D. Plotkin. On functors expressible in the polymorphic lambda calculus. *Information and Computation*, 105:1–29, 1993. Reprinted in *Logical Foundations of Functional Programming,* ed. G. Huet, Addison-Wesley (1990) 127–152.

[Rus03] B. Russell. *The Principles of Mathematics*. Cambridge, 1903.

[Sal89] A. Salveson. *Polymorphism and Monomorphism in Martin-Löf's Type Theory*. PhD thesis, Institutt for Informatikk, University of Oslo, March 1989.

[Saz76] V.Y. Sazonov. Expressibility of functions in D. Scott's LCF language. *Algebra i Logika*, 15(3):308–330, 1976. Translation.

[Sce88] A. Scedrov. Kleene computable functionals and the higher-order existence property. *J. Pure Appl. Algebra*, 52:313–320, 1988.

[Sch86] D.A. Schmidt. *Denotational Semantics*. Allyn and Bacon, 1986.

[Sco69] D.S. Scott. A type–theoretic alternative to CUCH, ISWIM, OWHY. Manuscript, 1969. Later published in *Theor. Comp. Sci.* 121:411–440, 1993.

[Sco76] D.S. Scott. Data types as lattices. *Siam J. Computing*, 5(3):522–587, 1976.

[Sco80a] D.S. Scott. Relating theories of the lambda calculus. In *To H.B. Curry: Essays on Combinatory Logic, Lambda Calculus and Formalism*, pages 403–450. Academic Press, 1980.

[Sco80b] D.S. Scott. A space of retracts. Manuscript, Merton College, Oxford., 1980.

[See84] R.A.G. Seely. Locally cartesian closed categories and type theory. *Math. Proc. Camb. Phil. Soc.*, 95:33–48, 1984.

[See87] R.A.G. Seely. Categorical semantics for higher-order polymorphic lambda calculus. *J. Symbolic Logic*, 52:969–989, 1987.

[Set89] R. Sethi. *Programming Languages: Concepts and Constructs*. Addison-Wesley, 1989.

[Sie92] Kurt Sieber. Reasoning about sequential functions via logical relations. In M. P. Fourman, P. T. Johnstone, and A. M. Pitts, editors, *Proc. LMS Symposium on Applications of Categories in Computer Science, Durham 1991*, volume 177 of *LMS Lecture Note Series*, pages 258–269. Cambridge University Press, 1992.

[SNGM89] G. Smolka, W. Nutt, J.A. Goguen, and J. Meseguer. Order-sorted equational computation. In *Resolution of equations in algebraic structures, Vol. 2*, pages 299–367. Academic Press, New York, 1989.

[Sny86] A. Snyder. Encapsulation and inheritance in object-oriented programming languages. In *Proc. ACM Symp. on Object-Oriented Programming Systems, Languages, and Applications*, pages 38–46, October 1986.

[SP82] M. Smyth and G.D. Plotkin. The category-theoretic solution of recursive domain equations. *SIAM J. Computing*, 11:761–783, 1982.

[Spi88] J.M. Spivey. *Understanding Z*. Cambridge University Press, 1988.

[SS71] D.S. Scott and C. Strachey. Toward a mathematical semantics for computer languages. In J. Fox, editor, *Proc. Symp. Computers and Automata*. Polytechnic Inst. of Brooklyn Press, 1971. Also Technical Monograph PRG-6, Programming Research Group, Oxford University.

[SS75] G.L. Steele and G.J. Sussman. Scheme: an interpreter for the extended lambda calculus. Technical Report 349, MIT Artificial Intelligence Laboratory, 1975.

[SS82] A. Scedrov and P.J. Scott. A note on the Friedman slash and Freyd covers. In *The L. E. J. Brouwer Centenary Symposium*, pages 443–452. North-Holland, Amsterdam, 1982.

[Sta79] R. Statman. Intuitionistic propositional logic is polynomial-space complete. *Theoretical Computer Science*, 9:67–72, 1979.

[Sta81] R. Statman. Number theoretic functions computable by polymorphic programs. In 22nd *IEEE Symp. on Foundations of Computer Science*, pages 279–282, 1981.

[Sta82] R. Statman. Completeness, invariance and λ-definability. *J. Symbolic Logic*, 47(1): 17–26, 1982.

[Sta85a] R. Statman. Equality between functionals, revisited. In *Harvey Friedman's Research on the Foundations of Mathematics*, pages 331–338. North-Holland, Amsterdam, 1985.

[Sta85b] R. Statman. Logical relations and the typed lambda calculus. *Information and Control*, 65:85–97, 1985.

[Ste72] S. Stenlund. *Combinators, λ-terms and Proof Theory*. Reidel, Dordrecht-Holland, 1972.

[Ste84] G.L. Steele. *Common Lisp: The language*. Digital Press, 1984.

[Sto77] J.E. Stoy. *Denotational Semantics: The Scott-Strachey Approach to Programming Language Theory*. MIT Press, 1977.

[Sto88] A. Stoughton. *Fully Abstract Models of Programming Languages*. Pitman, London, and John Wiley and Sons, New York, 1988.

[Sto91a] A. Stoughton. Interdefinability of parallel operations in pcf. *Theoretical Computer Science*, 79:357–358, 1991.

[Sto91b] H. Stoyan. The influence of the designer on the design—John McCarthy and LISP. In V. Lifschitz, editor, *Artificial Intelligence and Mathematical Theory of Computation: Papers in Honor of John McCarthy*, pages 409–426. Academic Press, 1991.

[Str66] C. Strachey. Towards a formal semantics. In T.B. Steel, editor, *Formal Lan-*

guage Description Languages for Computer Programming, pages 198–220. North-Holland, 1966.

[Str67] C. Strachey. Fundamental concepts in programming languages. Lecture Notes, International Summer School in Computer Programming, Copenhagen, August 1967.

[Str86] B. Stroustrop. *The C^{++} Programming Language*. Addison-Wesley, 1986.

[SW87] B. Shriver and P. Wegner, editors. *Research Directions in Object-oriented Programming*. MIT Press, 1987.

[Tai67] W.W. Tait. Intensional interpretation of functionals of finite type. *J. Symbolic Logic*, 32:198–212, 1967.

[Tay87] P. Taylor. *Recursive Domains, Indexed Category Theory and Polymorphism*. PhD thesis, Mathematics Dept., Cambridge University, 1987.

[Ten81] R.D. Tennent. *Principles of Programming Languages*. Prentice-Hall International, 1981.

[Ten86] R.D. Tennent. Functor-category semantics of programming languages and logics. In *Category Theory and Computer Science*, pages 206–224, Berlin, 1986. Springer LNCS 240.

[Ten91] R.D. Tennent. *Semantics of Programming Languages*. Prentice-Hall International, 1991.

[Tof88] M. Tofte. *Operational Semantics and Polymorphic Type Inference*. PhD thesis, Edinburgh University, 1988. Available as Edinburgh University Laboratory for Foundations of Computer Science Technical Report ECS–LFCS–88–54.

[Tof90] M. Tofte. Type inference for polymorphic references. *Information and Computation*, 89(1):1–34, 1990.

[Toy87] Y. Toyama. On the Church-Rosser property for the direct sum of term rewriting systems. *J. Assoc. Computing Machinery*, 34:128–143, 1987.

[Tro73] A.S. Troelstra. *Mathematical Investigation of Intuitionistic Arithmetic and Analysis*. Springer LNM 344, Berlin, 1973.

[Tur37] A.M. Turing. Computability and lambda definability. *J. Symbolic Logic*, 2:153–163, 1937.

[Tur85] D.A. Turner. Miranda: a non-strict functional language with polymorphic types. In *IFIP Int'l Conf. on Functional Programming and Computer Architecture, Nancy*, pages 1–16, Berlin, 1985. Springer LNCS 201.

[Tys88] J. Tyszkiewicz. Complexity of type inference in finitely typed lambda calculus. Master's thesis, University of Warsaw, 1988.

[Ull94] J.D. Ullman. *Elements of ML programming*. Prentice Hall, 1994.

[US 80] US Dept. of Defense. *Reference Manual for the Ada Programming Language*. GPO 008-000-00354-8, 1980.

[vD80] D.T. van Dalen. *The language theory of Automath*. PhD thesis, Technological Univ. Eindhoven, 1980.

[Wad76] C. Wadsworth. The relation between computational and denotational properties for Scott's D^∞ models. *Siam J. Comput.*, 5(3):488–521, 1976.

[Wad89] P. Wadler. Theorems for free! In *Proc. ACM Conf. Functional Programming and Computer Architecture*, pages 347–359, 1989.

[Wan79] M. Wand. Final algebra semantics and datatype extensions. *J. Comput. System Sci.*, 19:27–44, 1979.

[Wan87] M. Wand. A simple algorithm and proof for type inference. *Fundamenta Informaticae*, 10:115–122, 1987.

[Wel94] J. Wells. Typability and type checking in the second-order lambda-calculus are equivalent and undecidable. In *Proc. IEEE Symp. on Logic in Computer Science*, pages 176–185, 1994.

[Win93] G. Winskel. *The formal semantics of programming languages*. MIT Press, 1993.

[Wir90] M. Wirsing. Algebraic specification. In J. van Leeuwen, editor, *Handbook of Theoretical Computer Science, Volume B*, pages 675–788. North-Holland, Amsterdam, 1990.

[WSH77] J. Welsh, W. Sneeringer, and C.A.R Hoare. Ambiguities and insecurities in pascal. *Software – Practice and Experience*, 7(6):685–696, 1977.

[YT87] A. Yonezawa and M. Tokoro, editors. *Object-oriented Concurrent Programming*. MIT Press, 1987.

Index

$\in$ (element of), 13
$\cap$ (intersect), 13
$\cup$ (union), 13
$\subseteq$ (subset), 13
$\times$ (ordered pairs), 13
$\exists$ (there exists), 12
$\forall$ (for all), 12
$\supset$ (implies), 12
$\wedge$ (and), 12
$\neg$ (not), 12
iff (if and only if), 12
$[\![e]\!]$ (meaning of e), 25
$\mathcal{A}[\![M]\!]\eta$, 152, 283, 369
$\models$ (satisfies, implies), 158, 283, 290, 414
$\vdash$ (provable), 35, 38, 162, 259
$\vdash^{(emptyI,E)}$, 296

$=$ (equal), 12
$=_{ax}$, 77, 339
$=_{den}$, 77, 339
$=_{op}$, 77, 339
$\stackrel{\text{def}}{=}$ (defined to be), 12, 58, 65
$\equiv$ (syntactic equality), 12, 47
$::=$ (production in grammar), 12, 22
$\simeq$ (equal if either defined), 77, 368
$\cong$ (isomorphic) *See* isomorphism.
$\sim_{\mathcal{E},\Gamma}$, 175
$[a]_{\sim}$, 173
$\mathcal{A}/\sim$, 173

$\to$ (function), 8, 18
$\rightharpoonup$ (partial function), 19
$\to$ (reduction), 7, 75, 79
$\twoheadrightarrow$, 7, 79
$\twoheadleftarrow$, 205
$\twoheadrightarrow \circ \twoheadleftarrow$, 205
$\stackrel{eager}{\to}$, 93
$\stackrel{lazy}{\to}$, 89
$\stackrel{left}{\twoheadrightarrow}$, 87
$\Rightarrow$, 91
$\Rightarrow\!\!\!\!\Rightarrow$, 92
$\to_{\mathcal{R}}$, 204
$\stackrel{\mathcal{R},\beta,p,lab_{+}}{\twoheadrightarrow}$, 564
$\stackrel{eval}{\rightsquigarrow}$, 394
$\stackrel{exec}{\rightsquigarrow}$, 395
$\stackrel{exec}{\mapsto}$, 399
$M\downarrow$ (defined), 359, 368
$M\uparrow$ (undefined), 368
$d \uparrow d'$ (consistent), 348

$\leq_{D\to E}$, 314
$\leq_{D\times E}$, 310
$\leq_{den}$, 354
$\leq_{op}$, 354

$\bot_D$ (least element), 309
$\bigvee S$ (least upper bound), 309

$f \circ g$ (function compostion; $\lambda x.\, f(g(x))$), 20
$f;\, g$ (composition in diagrammatic order; $\lambda x.\, g(f(x))$), 449
$f_{i,j}$ (composition along ω-chain), 514
$f(S)$ (function applied to set of arguments), 312
$S(d)$ (set of functions applied to argument), 314
$\lambda x\colon \sigma.\, M$ (lambda notation for function), 3
MN (application of function expression to argument), 4,5
$M^n N$ (iterated application), 66
$M \cdot N$ (strict application), 402
$M \diamond N$ (strict composition), 402
$M|_{\vec{n}}$ (subterm at a position), 206
$[N/x]M$ (substitution) , 150
$\langle M_1, \ldots, M_n\rangle$ (tupling on terms), 97
$\langle h_1, \ldots, h_n\rangle$ (tupling on arrows of category), 470
$\sigma_1 \times \ldots \times \sigma_n$ (iterated product type), 97
σ^k (iterated product of single type), 97
$\lceil n \rceil$ (numeral for number n), 50

($\to$ Intro) typing rule, 243, 622, 628
($\to$ Elim) typing rule, 244, 622, 628
($\to$ U_1) type formation, 620
($\to$ Cong) type equation, 695
($\to$ <:) subtyping, 707, 720
($\times$ Intro) typing rule, 248
($\times$ Elim) typing rule, 248
($+$ Intro) typing rule, 249
($+$ Elim) typing rule, 249
($\lfloor\ \rfloor$ Intro) typing rule for lifted type $\sigma_\bot$, 135, 402
($\lfloor\ \rfloor$ Elim) typing rule for lifted type $\sigma_\bot$, 135
($\forall$ Intro), 639; *See* (Π Intro).
($\forall$ Elim), 639, 658; *See* (Π Elim).
($\exists$ Intro) typing rule, 681
($\exists$ Elim) typing rule, 681
($=$ <:) subtyping, 746
($\bot$ <:) subtyping, 750
(<: *context*) structural rule, 751
(*abs*) type inference, 782
(*acong*) for approximations, 335
(*add hyp*) type inference, 782
(*add var*) equational rule, 162, 258
(*add var*) typing rule, 243, 469, 620, 696
(*app*) type inference, 782, 803
(*asg*) for Hoare logic, 416
(*asym*) for approximations, 335
(α) equation, 6, 53, 259
$(\alpha)_\Pi$ equation, 628
$(\alpha)_\exists$ equation, 683
(*bot*) for approximations, 335
(*botf*) for approximations, 335

(β) equation, 6, 7, 53, 259, 268
$(\beta)_{\Pi}$ equation, 628
$(\beta)_{\exists}$ equation, 682
$(case)_1$ equation, 123, 264
$(case)_2$ equation, 123, 264
$(case)_3$ equation, 123, 125, 264
(*cond*) for Hoare logic, 416
(*cong*) equational rule, 164
(*conseq*) for Hoare logic, 415
(*cst*) typing axiom, 242, 621, 628, 782, 793
(*cst* U_1) type formation, 620
(*empty I*) equation, 296
(*empty E*) equational rule, 296
(*empty context*) structural rule, 619
(*eq*) for approximations, 335
(η) equation, 54, 81, 259, 268
$(\eta)_{\Pi}$ equation, 629
$(\eta)_{\exists}$ equation, 683
(*fcong*) for approximations, 335
(*fix*) equation, 62
$(fix)_{alt}$ alternate axiom, 84
(*fpind*) for approximations, 336
(*gen*) type inference, 792
(*inst*) type inference, 792
(*let*) equation, 636
(*let*) typing rule, 635, 792
(*let* $\lfloor\ \rfloor$) equation, 135
(*lookup*) equation, 393
(μ *Intro*) typing rule, 127, 741
(μ *Elim*) typing rule, 127, 741
(μ $<:$) subtyping, 746, 749
(μ $\perp$) type equation, 749
(μ *unique*) type equation, 749
(*nonempty*) equational rule, 177, 293
(*null*) equation, 265, 270
(*null* Elim) typing axiom, 250
(ν) equational rule, 259
$(\nu)_{\Pi}$ equational rule, 629
(*proj*) equation, 51, 264, 270
(Π Intro) typing rule, 615, 622, 628, 693
(Π Elim) typing rule, 616, 622, 628, 693
(Π U_2) type formation, 620, 693
(Π $<:$ *Intro*) typing rule, 752
(Π $<:$ *Elim*) typing rule, 752
(Π $<:$ F Intro) typing rule, 756
(Π $<:$ F Elim) typing rule, 756
(Π Cong) type equation, 695
(ΠF $<:$ *Intro*) typing rule, 761
(ΠF $<:$ *Elim*) typing rule, 761
(*rec ind*) equational rule, 72
(*record Intro*) typing rule, 716
(*record Elim*) typing rule, 716
(*record ext*) equation, 717
(*record selection*) equation, 96, 716
(*record* $<:$) subtyping, 715
(*ref*) equation, 35, 53, 162, 258
(*ref* $<:$) subtyping, 707, 720
(*seq*) for Hoare logic, 415
(*sp*) equation, 52, 81, 264, 270
($store_{\perp}$ Elim) typing rule, 402
(*subst*) equational rule, 162, 260
(*subsumption*) typing rule, 709, 719
(*subsumption eq*) equational rule, 711
(*sym*) equational rule, 71, 162, 258
(Σ Intro) typing rule, 693
(Σ Elim) typing rule, 693
(Σ U_2) type formation, 693
(Σ Cong) type equation, 695
(Σ *first*) equation, 695
(Σ *second*) equation, 695
(Σ *sp*) equation, 695
(*term eq*) type inference, 784
(*trans*) equational rule, 35, 53, 162, 258, 335
(*trans* $<:$) subtyping, 707, 720
(*type eq*) typing rule, 622
(*type label*) equation, 712
(*TypeCond*) typing rule, 645
(*Type* $\to$ *Type* $<:$) subtyping, 761
(U_1 *context*) structural rule, 619
(U_i *type context*) structural rule, 619
($U_1 \subseteq U_2$) typing rule, 620, 623
($U_2 \subseteq U_1$) typing rule, 625
($U_1\colon U_2$) typing rule, 623, 625, 699
($U_1 = U_2$) typing rule, 625, 700
(*unfold*) type equation, 126, 741
(*unit*) equation, 122, 264, 270
(*unit* Intro) typing axiom, 250
(*update*) equation, 393
(*up*/*dn*) equation, 127
(*while*) for Hoare logic, 418
(*with*) typing rule, 759
(ξ) equational rule, 258, 301
$(\xi)_{\Pi}$ equational rule, 629
(*var*) typing axiom, 243, 620, 628, 782
$(var)_{alt}$ typing axiom, 624

1-section theorem, 574

anf(M), 340
$A_{\perp}$, 310
$\mathcal{A}_0$-valid, 421
$\mathcal{A}_{pcf}$, 148
abstract syntax, 21
acceptable enumeration of p.r. functions, 356
acceptable meaning function, 539
Ada programming language, 607
adequacy of semantics, 77, 344
ad hoc polymorphism, 613

adjoint situation, 467
admissible (inclusive) predicate, 337, 339
admissible logical relation, 540
with product types, 560
Alg_{Σ}, 449
$Alg_{\Sigma,\mathcal{E}}$, 449
algebra, 145, 151
algebraic
CPO, 348
datatype, 145
function, 148
function type, 149
specification, 147, 157, 161, 188
term, 150
alias, 392
ambiguous grammar, 23
antecedent, 163
antisymmetry, 18
application in lambda notation, 3
applicative structure, 280
in a category, 493
extensional, 281
impredicative, 633, 663
polymorphic, 631, 663
type:type, 633
appropriate (environment and store), 435
approximate normal form, 340
approximation theorem, 340
arrow of a category, 447
associativity
left- or right-, 24
associativity of composition, 21
axiom, 35
axiomatic semantics, 6

$\mathcal{B}_{\perp}$, 310
base case of induction, 27
base type (in $\lambda^{\rightarrow}$), 241
BCPO, 353
beta-reduction, 7
bijective function, 20
binary tree, 30
Böhm tree, 276, 341
bool
as sum type, 124
in $\lambda^{\rightarrow,\forall}$, 642
in PCF, 47, 49, 71
bound variable, 4, 243
bounded complete CPO, 353
bounded polymorphism, 751

$\mathcal{C}[\cdot, \ldots, \cdot]$, 116
$\mathcal{C}[\,]$, 77
$\mathcal{C}^{\mathcal{E}}$, 520
$\mathcal{C}^{op}$, 451
$\mathcal{C}_{\Sigma}(\mathcal{E})$, 462
$\mathcal{C}_{\rightarrow,\forall}$, 653
C programming language, 584
C++ programming language, 607
call-by-value reduction, 93
canonical rewrite system, 205
carrier of multi-sorted algebra, 148, 151
cartesian
closed category, 280, 293, 458, 459, 460, 461
closed functor, 464
product, 14
of CPOs, 310
of modest sets, 359
$\mathcal{C}at$, 453
categorical
combinator, 474
duality, 457
function space (exponential), 454
product, 454
sum (coproduct), 457
category, 447
formal (in a typed language), 652
generated by a theory, 462
of embeddings, 520
of projections, 520
of types and terms, 653
cc-functors, 464
CCC; *see* cartesian closed category.
CCC (category of cartesian closed categories), 464
Church's theory of simple types, 262
Church's thesis, 105
Church-Rosser property, 8, 80, 556
Church numeral, 642
$CL(\Sigma)$, 297
closed expression, 4
closure, 667
coalesced sum, 326
cocone in a category, 511
codomain of function, 19
codomain of morphism, 447
coherence, 286, 475, 705
combinator, 298
combinatory
algebra, 227
algebra, partial, 368
logic, 222, 226, 297
model condition, 297, 298
structure for λ, `record`, 729
term, 297
comma category, 466, 596
commuting diagram, 448, 510
compact element of CPO, 347

complete
induction, 29
partial order (CPO), 239, 305, 309
bounded complete, 353
pairwise consistent complete, 348
pointed, 309
predicate, 588
proof system; *see* completeness.
completeness, 157
deductive, 172
least model form, 172
for $\lambda^{\rightarrow}$
with empty types, 295
without empty types, 293
for multi-sorted algebra, 161, 172
completion, 228
composite number, 29
composition, 17, 19
diagrammatic order $(f; g)$, 449
function and relation, 20
in a category, 447
set closed under, 106, 110
compositionality, 74, 388
computable
function on numbers, 105
function on modest sets, 359
increasing sequence, 378
test, 377
computational adequacy, 76, 77, 344
cone in a category, 510
confluence, 8, 80, 205, 556
from a term, 227
congruence proof rule
in algebra, 164
congruence relation, 70, 173
partial, 177
consequent, 35, 163
conservativity, 260, 265, 266
consistent, 193, 199, 200
elements of CPO, 348
lifted types and fixed-points, 133
proof system, 72, 78
set of equations, 163
sums and fixed-points, 125
constant symbol
in algebra, 149
in $\lambda^{\rightarrow}$, 241
constructor
of a datatype, 190
of an algebra, 192
context (term with hole), 77
evaluation, 114
multiple holes, 116
σ, τ-context, 560
typing; *see* typing context
contextual theory, 649
continuous function, 239
on CPO, 312
hierarchy, 238, 318
on lifted CPO, 313
of several arguments, 316, 317
contractive, 750
contravariant functor, 455
conversion, 205
covariant functor, 455
CPO, 239, 305, 309
bounded complete, 353
pairwise consistent complete, 348
pointed, 309
Cpo, 449, 463
$Cpo_{\perp}$, 452, 463
$Cpo_{\rightharpoonup}$, 520
Cppo, 464, 520
critical pair, 216, 221
trivial, 221
Curry-Howard isomorphism, 252, 615
currying, 55, 321
Curry type inference rules, 782
Curry typing, 770

$\mathcal{D}^{\mathcal{C}}$, 456
$\mathcal{D}_{\perp}$, 310
Δ^{prj}, 519, 523
dag (directed acyclic graph), 775
datatype, in ML, 131, 194
datatype induction, 192
deductive completeness, 172
definable function
implicitly, 50
partial function, 110
in PCF, 106
denotation, 50, 73
denotational
equivalence, 77
semantics, 6, 73, 388
dependent types, 614
derivation tree, 22
derived inference rule, 56, 163
Diaconescu cover, 503
$diag(A)$, 367
diagonal functor, 468
diagram in category, 448, 510
directed-complete predicate, 588
directed subset of a CPO, 239, 309
discrete order, 308
disjoint union (sum) type, 122, 239, 303
domain
of definition, 19

of function, 19
of morphism, 447
ordered set of values, 305, 308
dynamic lookup, 740, 748
dynamic scope, 60

e_n, 666
$\eta[x \mapsto a]$, 156
$\eta_\sim$, 174
eager evaluation, 46, 86
eager reduction, 93
effective CPO, 378
elimination context, 354, 559
embedding, 519
embedding-projection pair, 519
empty set, 14
empty types, 295, 664
enumeration types, 124, 125
environment, 73, 152, 283
satisfying sort assignment, 152
satisfying type assignment, 283
model condition, 283
equalizer in a category, 457, 511
equation
between algebraic terms, 158
between typed lambda terms, 258
equational logic, 145
equivalence class, 173, 546
equivalence relation, 18, 161, 173
erasure function (*Erase*), 658, 673, 728, 766, 767, 790
evaluation context, 114
evaluation partial function (*eval*), 75, 84
existential type, 614, 680
explicit typing for untyped term, 777
exponential (function) object, 454
expressive (in Hoare logic), 424
extended equation, 295
extensional
applicative structure, 281
Kripke, 494
impredicative, 664
polymorphic, 632
collapse, 547
extensionality, 76, 302
for sets, 14

F-algebra, 512
F-bounded polymorphism, 755
final algebra, 147, 195
finitary retraction, 669
finite (compact) element of CPO, 348
first-order
dependent products, 614
function, 148
function type, 149
$fix^{[n]}\ F$, 307
fixed-point
induction, 336
of function, 61
of functor, 513
operator, 61, 306, 318, 381
untyped, 96
untyped eager, 96
flat CPO, 310
floor function, 710
formulas-as-types, 252, 614, 640, 649
free variable, 4
full abstraction, 78, 345
full set-theoretic function hierarchy, 284
full subcategory, 449
function, 18
composition, 17
object (in category), 454
space functor, 452
symbol (in algebra), 149
functor, 452
category, 456
definable, 653
$FV(M)$, 4, 53

Γ (sort/type assignment), 149, 240
$\Gamma, x{:}s$, 150, 240–241
$\Gamma \triangleright M{:}\tau$, 240
$\Gamma \triangleright M = N{:}\tau$, 258
$M \leftrightarrow_{\mathcal{R}} N\ [\Gamma]$, 205
$\Gamma \triangleright \tau$, 649
$\Gamma \vdash M{:}\sigma$, 241
Γ_f, 470
Γ_M, 245
Gandy hull, 547
general product (Π) type, 613
general sum (Σ) type, 613
generated algebra, 195
generated semantics, 195
global element
functor into $\mathcal{S}et$, 595
of category, 486
of Kripke model, 492
Gödel's $\mathcal{T}$, 571
Gödel numbering, 358
graph of function, 18
ground
instance of equation, 186
instance of term, 186
substitution, 186
term, 186

halting problem, 112, 113
Haskell programming language, 607
head normal form, 110
height of a tree, 30
Henkin model, 280
  for higher-order logic, 292
  impredicative, 633, 663, 664
  polymorphic, 633
  type:type, 633
hereditary permutation, 538, 544
higher-order logic, 292, 295
higher-order subtype bounded polymorphism, 755
holds (formula . . . in model), 158
hom-set *Hom*(a, b), 449
homomorphism
  between algebras, 179
  between applicative structures, 281

imperative programs, 387
implementation (model with standard observables), 581
implication, semantic, 161
implicit typing, 782
impredicative polymorphism, 611, 625, 639, 700
inclusion, 458
inclusive predicate, 337, 339
inconsistent; *see* consistent.
  proof system, 72
  sums and fixed-points, 125, 133, 463
index of p.r. function, 356
induction, 27
  fixed-point, 336
  hypothesis, 27, 29, 150
  on natural numbers, 27
  on proofs, 34
  on terms, 32, 150
  recursion, 73
  well-founded, 38
inequational full abstraction, 354
inference rule, 35
  derived, 56, 163
inheritance, 706, 748
initial
  algebra, 147
    for class $\mathcal{C}$, 181
    for equations $\mathcal{E}$, 183
    semantics, 191
  F-algebra, 512
  weak, 652, 654
  object, 456
  type, 297
injective function, 20
instance relation on typings, 771
intended model, 183
intersection, 15
intrinsic preorder, 377
invariant
  of while loop, 418
isomorphism ($\cong$), 12, 17
  and recursive types, 127
  between algebras, 181
  between applicative structures, 281
  in a category, 450
  of modest sets, 360
  of partial equivalence relations, 366
  recursive, 360

K combinator , 297, 788
$K(\mathcal{D})$, 348
Kleene normal form, 112
Knuth-Bendix completion, 228
Knuth-Bendix test, 228
Kripke
  applicative structure, 491
  lambda model, 494
  logical relation, 590
k-tuple, 16

L–value, 389
$\lambda^{\rightarrow}$, 237
$\lambda_t^{\rightarrow}$, 769
$\lambda^{\rightarrow,\times}$, 237
$\lambda^{\rightarrow,\times,+}$, 237
$\lambda^{\rightarrow,\Pi}$, 620, 627
$\lambda^{\rightarrow,\forall}$, 639
$\lambda^{\rightarrow,\Pi,\Sigma}$, 692
$\lambda_{<:}^{\rightarrow}$, 706
$\lambda_{<:}^{\rightarrow,\mathtt{record}}$, 714
$\lambda_{<:}^{\rightarrow,\mathtt{record},\mu}$, 740
$\lambda\langle x{:}\sigma, y{:}\tau\rangle.\, M$, 59, 66
lab(M), 342
$lab_{+(0)}$, 563
$lab_{+,0}$, 563
lab_{+}, 563
lab_{0}, 563
label constants, 729
labeled
  fixed-point operator, 342, 563
  reduction, 563
    positive, 563
  term, 342, 563
lambda–
  abstraction, 3
  algebra, typed, 301
  calculus, 5
  definable, 543
  expression, 3
  interpretation, 658

term, 3
late binding, 740, 748
lazy evaluation, 46, 86
lazy normal form, 89
LCF, 334
least
fixed point, 318
model completeness, 172
model property, 172
upper bound, 309
left–
linear rewrite rule, 222
most evaluation, 46, 85, 86
normal rewrite rules, 272, 570
adjoint, 467
inverse, 519
Leibniz equality, 262
length of a lambda term, 637
let-depth of term, 637
let-reduction, 636
lexicographic order, 40, 210, 797
lifted
function, 313
set, 309
type, 122, 132, 401
lifting functor, 452, 514
limit in a category, 510
linear rewrite rule, 222
list datatype, 196
locally
confluent, 216, 559
continuous, 526
determined ω-colimits, 524
monotonic, 526
logical
partial equivalence relation, 545
partial function, 544
relation, 536
on environments ($\mathcal{R}^{\Gamma}(\eta_1, \eta_2)$), 538, 736
satisfies (β), 547
logic for computable functions (LCF), 334
loose semantics, 191, 195

$\mu: c \to \Delta$, 511
$\mu: \Delta \to c$, 511
$\mu t.\sigma$, 126
m, n-function, 470
many-sorted algebra, 152
meta-language, 21, 47, 389
minimal element, 39
minimization, 98, 106, 110
Miranda programming language, 607
ML programming language, 11, 390, 607, 635, 766
datatype, 131, 194
`let` declaration, 635
type inference problem, 791
model; *see also* Henkin model
of a logic, 279
of $\lambda^{\to}$, 279
untyped lambda calculus, 659, 666
modest set, 238, 355, 357
category of (M*od*), 449
monotonic function on partial order, 312
morphism (arrow) of a category, 447
most general substitution, 220
multi-sorted algebra, 152
mutual recursion, 63

$\mathcal{N}_{\perp}$, 310
natural deduction, 251
nat
as recursive type, 128
in $\lambda^{\to,\forall}$, 642
in PCF, 47, 49, 71
Newman's lemma, 227
non-overlapping rewrite system, 222
nonempty types, 293, 664
noninformative, 134
nonlogical axioms, 37
nonterminals, 22
nontrivial model, 294
nonvoid sort in algebraic signature, 178
normal form, 8, 80, 205, 268
normalization, 8, 553
n-tuple, 16
numerals, 47, 50
numeric function, 106
numeric partial function, 110

O (order of); $O(f(n))$, 786, 806
O-category, 518
O-colimit, 521
ω-category, 515
ω-chain, 514
ω-chain CPO, 312
ω-chain in a CPO, 312
ω-complete pointed category, 515
ω-continuous, 515
ω^{op}-chain, 517
object-oriented programming, 740
object language, 21, 47
object of a category, 447
observable type, 68, 78
observable value, 68
observational congruence, 77
observational equivalence, 77
observationally equivalent models, 582
observer of a datatype, 190

one-step reduction, 79
one-to-one function, 20
operational equivalence, 77
operational semantics, 6, 387, 388
operator of a datatype, 190
opposite category, 451
order (collection of types), 9
ordered pair, 14, 15
orthogonal rewrite systems, 568

ϕ_i (*i*th partial recursive function), 356
pairwise consistent complete, 348
pairwise consistent subset of CPO, 348
parallel-or, 113, 345, 574
parallel reduction, 223
parametric polymorphism, 613, 645
parse tree, 22
partial
  applicative structure, 729
  combinatory algebra (pca), 305, 368, 734
  correctness assertion, 389, 413
  enumeration function, 357
  equivalence relation (per), 355, 364, 365, 545, 718, 734
    interpretation, 735
    model, 663, 672
    notation n: R for per R, 367
  function, 19, 311
  order, 18, 308
  recursive function, 111
  surjection, 575
    recursive, 576
pass-by-reference, 440
pass-by-value, 440
PCF, 45
$pcf_{+,0}$-reduction, 566
pcf_{+}-reduction, 566
PCPO, 348
per; *see* partial equivalence relation
permutation invariant, 544
P*fn*, 525
pointed
  CPO, 309
  effective CPO, 381
  predicate, 588
point of a category, 486
polymorphic
  composition, 609
  function, 609
  identity, 610
  lambda calculus, 611
position in a term, 205
positive labeled reduction, 563
powerset, 16

pre-fixed-point, 325
pre-term
  of $\lambda^{\rightarrow}$, 255, 269
  of $\lambda^{\rightarrow,\Pi}$, 621, 657
  of $\lambda^{\rightarrow,\Pi,\Sigma}$, 692
precedence, 24, 25
  in type expressions, 237
predecessor, 100
predicate, 18
predicative polymorphism, 611
prefix order, 308
preorder, 707
prime number, 29
primitive recursion, 101, 106, 110, 571
primitive recursive function, 112
principal function symbol, 206
principal typing, 777, 783
product category, 450
product functor, 452
program (closed term of observable type), 68, 581
$\mathcal{PR}$, 356
$\mathbf{Proj}_i^{a_1 \times \ldots \times a_n}$, 470
$\mathbf{Proj}_i S$, 310, 312
projection, 519
proof, 35, 162
  from assumptions, 38
  from nonlogical axioms, 38
proper function symbol, 149
provable equation, 162
provably total functions of a theory, 641
$\mathcal{P}\omega$, 666

queue, 200
quotient
  algebra, 173
  applicative structure, 546
  Henkin model, 548

R–value, 389
$\mathcal{R}, \beta, proj, lab_{+}$, 564
range of function, 19
reachable algebra, 195
reachable semantics, 195
records
  combination, 759
  concatenation, 759
  in $\lambda^{\rightarrow}$ or PCF, 96
  with subtyping, 713
recursion theorem, 375
recursive
  embedding, 576
  function, 105
    hierarchy, 238
    hierarchy over modest sets, 361

on modest sets, 238, 359
in PCF, 105
isomorphism, 360
types, 122, 126, 739
redex, 49, 268
reduction, 6, 79, 268, 629
axiom, 49, 75
call-by-name, 85
eager (call-by-value), 86
lazy, 86, 89
left-most outer-most, 85, 87
one-step, 204, 268
parallel, 223
strategy, 84
reflexivity, 18
related environments, 736
relation, 17
relative completeness, 423
representation of CCC, 464
result (closed term of . . .), 69
retract, 578, 665
retraction, 665
rewrite rules, 145, 203
right adjoint, 467
rule of consequence
for Hoare logic, 415
Russell's paradox, 14, 236

S combinator , 297
Σ (signature), 149, 241
$\Sigma_{\to}$, 242, 247
Σ-CCC, 468
satisfaction
in CCC, 480
equation by lambda model, 290
equation by per interpretation, 737
formula by model, 158, 290
Hoare logic, 414
partial correctness assertion, 414
by a set of algebras, 158
of set of formulas, 158
of sort assignment, 152
of type assignment, 283
scone of a category, 587, 595
scope
dynamic, 60
static, 7, 54, 59
search, 99
second-order lambda calculus, 611
semantic functions, 405
semantics of programs, 69
semantic theory, 176
semi-unification, 806
separated sum of CPOs, 326
sequences
finite sequences (S^+), 311
finite and infinite (S^*), 311
infinite sequences (S^∞), 311
sequential-or, 113
set, 13
Set (category of sets), 449
set-theoretic function hierarchy, 238, 282
set union, 15
signature
for $\lambda^{\to}$, 241
for $\lambda^{\to}_{<:}$, 706
for multi-sorted algebra, 149
polymorphic, 620
simple semantics (of types), 709, 784
simply-typed lambda calculus, 237
simultaneous substitution (exercise), 160
single-sorted algebra, 152
singleton set, 14
small category, 451
smash product, 326
sort (in algebra), 145, 149
sort assignment for algebraic terms, 149
soundness, 37, 74, 157
for CCC's, 480
for $\lambda^{\to}$, 290
for multi-sorted algebra, 161, 165
of typing rules, 288
specification of algebraic datatype, 161, 188
start symbol, 22
static scope, 7, 54, 59
step function, 349
store ("memory state"), 387, 388, 392
strict function application, 402
strict function on CPO, 313
string, 42
strong induction, 29
strong normalization, 8, 268, 553, 770
strongly confluent reduction, 224
structured operational semantics, 87
subcategory, 449
subject reduction property, 268, 629
subquotient of a set, 366
subscone, 596
subset, 16
subset interpretation, 732
substitution, 6, 53
as environment, 159
identities, 54
inference rule, 162, 169, 260
lemma, for algebra, 156
lemma, for CCC's, 478
lemma, for Henkin models, 290
on algebraic terms, 150
on lambda terms, 6, 53

substitution *(cont.)*
  on PCF terms, 54
  on type assignment, 771
  on types, 771
subtype, 703
subtype-bounded polymorphism, 751
sum types, 122, 123
surjective function, 20
surjective pairing, 52, 76, 272
symmetry, 18
syntactic sugar, 57, 58, 65
syntactic theory, 176
System F, 611; *see* impredicative polymorphism.

tail-recursive function, 102
term, 3
  algebra, 159
  category, 462, 483
  constant (in $\lambda^{\rightarrow}$), 241
  generated algebra, 195
  model (for $\lambda^{\rightarrow}$), 294, 550
$Terms^{s}(\Sigma, \Gamma)$, 150
terminal object, 264, 265, 456
terminals, 22
termination assertion, 389
termination property, 8, 205
theory, 176
  of an algebra ($Th(\mathcal{A})$), 161, 163
  determined by set of equations, 259
  semantic, 161
  syntactic, 163
total order, 18
total recursive function, 106
transitivity, 18
trivial algebra, 159
tuples, 16
Turing machine, 108
type, 9, 46, 145
  abstraction, 609
  application, 610
  assignment, 240
    as ordered sequence, 469, 618
  checking, 255, 768
  constant (in $\lambda^{\rightarrow}$), 241
  error, 288
  expression
    $\lambda^{\rightarrow}$, 237
    $\lambda_t^{\rightarrow}$, 769
    $\lambda^{\times,\rightarrow}$, 237
    $\lambda^{\rightarrow,\Pi}$, 620, 627
    $\lambda^{\rightarrow,\forall}$, 639
    $\lambda_{<:}^{\rightarrow}$, 706
    $\lambda_{<:}^{\rightarrow,\mathtt{record}}$, 714
  frame for $\lambda^{\rightarrow}$, 282
  inference, 765, 767, 769
  of untyped term, 777
  set relative to S, 661
  soundness, 288
  system, 9
  theory, 262
  universe, 9, 618
type-closed property of terms, 556
  for $\lambda^{\times,\rightarrow}$, 560
  for $\lambda^{\rightarrow,\forall}$, 661
$\mathtt{type}\ t = \tau$, 740
typed
  applicative structure, 280
  function symbol (in algebra), 149
  lambda term, 244
  lambda theory, 259
typing
  axiom, 240
  context (type assignment), 240, 618
    as ordered sequence, 469
  derivation, 244
  judgement, 241
    for untyped term, 783
type: *type*, 612, 625, 665

unambiguous grammar, 23
undefined, 19
unification, 772
union, 15
unit and $*$: *unit*, 122
universal algebra, 145
universe of types, 9, 618
untyped lambda calculus, 96, 131, 227, 236, 267, 295, 369, 657
  model, 292
upper bound, 309

valid formula, 158, 421
value (in eager reduction), 92
value-result parameters, 444
Var(M), 150
variable (in algebra), 149
variant types, 124

weak Church-Rosser, 559
weakest liberal precondition (wlp), 424
weakest precondition, 424
weakly initial, 652, 654
weak normalization, 268
well-founded relation, 38, 210
well-pointed category, 486
while programs, 387
with (record combination), 759

Yoneda embedding, 486, 503
Yoneda lemma, 504